REMEDIES IN AUSTRALIAN PRIVATE LAW

Second edition

Remedies in Australian Private Law offers readers a clear and detailed introduction to remedies and their functions under Australian law. Clearly structured, with a strong black-letter law focus, the text provides a complete treatment of remedies in common law, equity and statute, and develops a framework for understanding the principles of private law remedies and their practical application.

The second edition has been significantly revised and offers up-to-date coverage of case law and legislation, including the Australian Consumer Law. It builds on the detailed treatment of remedies and their broad functions across a range of private law categories, including torts, contract, equity, trusts and property law. It also offers expanded coverage of vindicatory damages, debt, specific restitution and coercive remedies. Theoretical perspectives on issues such as equitable obligations, the fusion of common law and equity, the nature of reasonable fee awards and the concept of unjust enrichment are also discussed.

With its systematic and accessible approach, *Remedies in Australian Private Law* enables students and practitioners to develop a coherent understanding of remedial law and to analyse legal problems and identify appropriate remedial solutions.

Katy Barnett is Associate Professor in the Melbourne Law School at the University of Melbourne.

Sirko Harder is Reader in Law in the Sussex Law School at the University of Sussex.

REMEDIES IN AUSTRALIAN PRIVATE LAW

Second edition

Katy Barnett
Sirko Harder

CAMBRIDGE
UNIVERSITY PRESS

CAMBRIDGE
UNIVERSITY PRESS

University Printing House, Cambridge CB2 8BS, United Kingdom

One Liberty Plaza, 20th Floor, New York, NY 10006, USA

477 Williamstown Road, Port Melbourne, VIC 3207, Australia

314–321, 3rd Floor, Plot 3, Splendor Forum, Jasola District Centre, New Delhi – 110025, India

79 Anson Road, #06–04/06, Singapore 079906

Cambridge University Press is part of the University of Cambridge.

It furthers the University's mission by disseminating knowledge in the pursuit of education, learning and research at the highest international levels of excellence.

www.cambridge.org
Information on this title: www.cambridge.org/9781108404754

First published 2014
Second edition 2018

Cover designed by Fiona Byrne
Typeset by SPi Global
Printed in China by C & C Offset Printing Co. Ltd, June 2018

A catalogue record for this publication is available from the British Library

A catalogue record for this book is available from the National Library of Australia

ISBN 978-1-108-40475-4 Paperback

CONTENTS

PREFACE

The second edition of this text seeks to build on the strengths of the first edition in presenting a detailed, scholarly map of remedies in Australian private law, which is intended to be helpful to judges, professionals, scholars and students.

Since the last edition, there have been several Australian cases which have required consideration. They include *Badenach v Calvert* [2016] HCA 18, (2016) 257 CLR 440 (on the availability of damages for loss of a chance in negligence), *Westpac Banking Corporation v Jamieson* [2015] QCA 50, [2016] 1 Qd R 495 (on alternative investments and calculation of damages for misrepresentation), *Stone v Chappell* [2017] SASCFC 72, (2017) 128 SASR 165 (on damages for rectification costs in excess of diminution in value), *Gray v Richards* [2014] HCA 40, (2014) 253 CLR 660 (on damages for fund management costs in personal injury cases), *Paciocco v Australia and New Zealand Banking Group Ltd* [2016] HCA 28, (2016) 258 CLR 525 (on penalty clauses in contracts), *Cheng v Farjudi* [2016] NSWCA 316, (2016) 93 NSWLR 95 (on the availability of exemplary damages) and *Australian Financial Services and Leasing Pty Ltd v Hills Industries Ltd* [2014] HCA 14, (2014) 253 CLR 560, (on unjust enrichment law and its relationship with equity).

We also consider several new overseas cases, mainly from the United Kingdom, in particular *AIB Group (UK) plc v Mark Redler & Co Solicitors* [2014] UKSC 58, [2015] AC 1503 (on equitable compensation for breach of trust), *Lawrence v Fen Tigers Ltd* [2014] AC 822, [2014] UKSC 13 (on nuisance, injunctions and Lord Cairns' Act damages), *Cavendish Square Holding BV v Makdessi* [2015] UKSC 67, [2016] AC 1172 (on penalty clauses in contracts), *One Step (Support) Ltd v Morris-Garner* [2016] EWCA Civ 180, [2017] QB 1 (on gain-based relief in contract) and *FHR European Ventures LLP v Mankarious* [2014] UKSC 45, [2015] AC 250 (on proprietary remedies for bribes taken in breach of fiduciary duty).

In addition to incorporating new material, we have made changes to some of the existing material. In Chapter 2, we have extended the discussion of *British Westinghouse Electric and Manufacturing Co Ltd v Underground Electric Railways Company of London Ltd* [1912] AC 673 and the avoided loss rule, and we have reorganised the discussion of certainty of loss and recovery for the loss of a chance in order to make the various categories of case clearer. In Chapter 5, we have added a more detailed discussion of *Clark v Macourt* [2013] HCA 56, (2013) 253 CLR 1. In Chapter 14, we have added a section on vindicatory damages. The sections on debt and specific restitution are now integrated into the discussion of specific relief in Chapter 11. We have also reorganised some of the material in Chapters 3 and 12.

As in the first edition, the primary responsibility for Chapters 2 to 9 lay with Sirko and the primary responsibility for the other chapters lay with Katy, but the text is very much a joint work. We have considered material available to us before 1 December 2017.

Katy would like to thank her family (Scott, Eloise, Josh and Hamish) for supporting her through the book revision process. She would also like to thank her JD and Masters students at Melbourne Law School for making her constantly think about how to present the law of remedies more clearly. Special thanks to Stephanie McHugh for providing research assistance to Katy.

Sirko would like to thank his family (Huan, Oliver and Alina) for their constant support. He would also like to thank Professor Harold Luntz for insightful conversations about various issues relating to damages for personal injury or death.

We both would like to thank the anonymous reviewers for their helpful comments. We would also like to thank Tanya Bastrakova, Lucy Russell, Shelley Barons and the other staff at Cambridge University Press for their professionalism and patience during the revision process.

Katy Barnett
Sirko Harder
January 2018

ACKNOWLEDGEMENTS

The authors and Cambridge University Press would like to thank the following for permission to reproduce material in this book.

Text extracts on pages 12–13 from *Roxborough v Rothmans of Pall Mall Australia Ltd* [2001] HCA 68, (2001) 208 CLR 516; **136** and **154** from *Commonwealth v Amann Aviation Pty Ltd* (1991) 174 CLR 64; **514**, **519** and **526** from *Muschinski v Dodds* (1985) 160 CLR 583, reproduced with permission of Thomson Reuters (Professional) Australia Limited, legal.thomsonreuters.com.au. **Text extracts on page 555** from *Choice Investments Ltd v Jeromnimon Midland Bank Ltd, Garnishee* [1981] QB 149 reproduced with permission of the Incorporated Council of Law Reporting (ICLR) for England and Wales.

Every effort has been made to trace and acknowledge copyright. The publisher apologises for any accidental infringement and welcomes information that would redress this situation.

TABLE OF CASES

Australian Paper Ltd v Communications, Electrical, Electronic, Energy, Information, Postal, Plumbing and Allied Services Union (1998) 81 IR 15, **545**

Australian Safeway Stores Pty Ltd v Zaluzna (1987) 162 CLR 479, **374**

Australian Securities and Investments Commission v Australian Property Custodian Holdings Ltd (2014) 322 ALR 45, **275**

Australian Securities and Investments Commission v Drake (No 2) (2016) 340 ALR 75, **287**

Australian Securities and Investments Commission v Mauer-Swisse Securities Ltd (2002) 42 ACSR 605, **547**

Australian Securities and Investments Commission v Parkes (2001) 38 ACSR 355, **547**

Australian Securities and Investments Commission v Pegasus Leveraged Options Group Pty Ltd (2002) 41 ACSR 561, **547**

Australian Securities and Investments Commission v Rich (2009) 236 FLR 1, **286**

Australian Securities and Investments Commission v Triton Underwriting Insurance Agency (2008) 48 ACSR 249, **547**

Australian Telecommunications Commission v Parsons (1985) 59 ALR 535, **241–2**

Australian Winch and Haulage Co Pty Ltd v Collins [2013] NSWCA 327, **42, 55**

Autodesk Inc v Yee (1996) 68 FCR 391, **398**

Automotive, Food, Metals, Engineering, Printing and Kindred Industries Union v McCain Foods (Australia) Pty Ltd [2012] FCA 1126, **306**

Avram v Gusakoski (2006) 31 WAR 400, **201**

A W v New South Wales [2005] NSWSC 543, **396**

Awad v Twin Creeks Properties Pty Ltd [2012] NSWCA 200, **490–1**

Axiak v Ingram (2012) 82 NSWLR 36, **205**

Aynsley v Glover (1874) LR 18 Eq 544, **351, 355**

Aynsley v Glover [1875] LR 10 Ch App 283, **355**

B v Reineker [2015] NSWSC 949, **67**

B J McAdam Pty Ltd v Jax Tyres Pty Ltd (No 3) [2012] FCA 1438, **162**

Babanaft International Co SA v Bassatne [1990] Ch 13, **551**

Bacchus Marsh Concentrated Milk Co Ltd (in liq) v Joseph Nathan & Co Ltd (1919) 26 CLR 410, **338**

Backwell v AAA [1997] 1 VR 182, **396, 409–10**

Badenach v Calvert (2016) 257 CLR 440, **41, 43, 53–4**

Badman v Drake [2008] NSWSC 1366, **489, 501, 523, 525, 531**

Baghdadi v Quality P & M Smallgoods Pty Ltd [2008] NSWSC 406, **215**

Baguley v Lifestyle Homes Mackay Pty Ltd [2015] QCA 75, **62**

Bahr v Nicolay (No 2) (1988) 164 CLR 604, **305, 321**

Baig v Baig [1970] VR 833, **303**

Bailey v Namol Pty Ltd (1994) 53 FCR 102, **398–9, 411**

Bailey v Nominal Defendant [2004] QCA 344, **97**

Bailey v Truth and Sportsman Ltd (1938) 60 CLR 700, **426**

Baily v Taylor (1829) 39 ER 28, **439**

Bain v Fothergill (1874) LR 7 HL 158, **141**

Baird v BCE Holdings Pty Ltd (1996) 40 NSWLR 374, **507**

Baird v Roberts [1977] 2 NSWLR 389, **222**

Baird Textile Holdings Ltd v Marks & Spencer plc [2001] CLC 999, 1017, **135**

Bak v Glenleigh Homes Pty Ltd [2006] NSWCA 10, **107**

Baker v Bolton (1808) 170 ER 1033, **239**

Davis v Foreman [1894] 3 Ch 654, **339**
Davis v Nationwide News Pty Ltd [2008] NSWSC 693, **174**
Day v Mead [1987] 2 NZLR 443, **283**
De Beer v Kanaar & Co (No 2) [2002] EWHC 688 (Ch), **284**
De Brassac v Martyn (1863) 9 LT 287, **312**
De Cesare v Deluxe Motors Pty Ltd (1996) 67 SASR 28, **148**
De Reus v Gray (2003) 9 VR 432, **119**, **395**, **408–9**
De Sales v Ingrilli (2002) 212 CLR 338, **239**, **242–3**, **245**
De Vitre v Betts (1873) LR 6 HL 319, **439**
Deabel v V'Landys [2002] NSWSC 438, **513**
Deane v Clayton (1817) 129 ER 196, **374**
Deane v Lloyd [1991] ANZ ConvR 103, **307**
Dein v Wentworth Gold Field Pty Co (1899) 15 WN (NSW) 280, **140**
Del Ponte v Del Ponte (1987) 11 NSWLR 498, **227**
Dell v Beasley [1959] NZLR 89, **352**
Delphic Wholesalers Pty Ltd v Elco Food Co Pty Ltd (1987) 8 IPR 545, **333**
Delphin v Martin [2012] TASSC 13, **225**
Delta Corporation v Davies [2002] WASCA 125, **410**
Demagogue Pty Ltd v Ramensky (1992) 39 FCR 31, **314**
Demetrios v Gikas Dry Cleaning Industries Pty Ltd (1991) 22 NSWLR 561, **265**
Dempster v Mallina Holdings Ltd (1994) 13 WAR 124, **267**
Denkewitz v Hodgson (QSC, Ambrose J, 6 November 1998), **158**
Denne v Light (1857) 44 ER 58, **313**
Derby & Co Ltd v Weldon [1990] Ch 48, **551**
Derbyshire Building Co Pty Ltd v Becker (1962) 107 CLR 633, **93**
Dering v Uris [1964] 2 QB 669, **426**
Derry v Peek (1889) 14 App Cas 337, **187**, **265**
Design Joinery & Doors Pty Ltd v iPower Pty Ltd [2015] SASC 93, **479**
Dessent v Commonwealth (1977) 13 ALR 437, **223**
Devenish Nutrition Ltd v Sanofi-Aventis SA (France) [2009] Ch 390, **458**
Devine v Colvilles Ltd 1969 SC (HL) 67, **94**
Di Napoli v New Beach Apartments Pty Ltd (2004) 11 BPR 21,493, **331**
Diagnostic X-Ray Services Pty Ltd v Jewel Food Stores Pty Ltd (2001) 4 VR 632, **320**
Diakos v Mason (2010) 272 LSJS 185, **381**
Diamond v Campbell-Jones [1961] Ch 22, **142**
Diesen v Samson [1971] SLT 49, **158**
Digital Pulse Pty Ltd v Harris (2002) 166 FLR 421, **267**, **403–4**
Dillingham Constructions Pty Ltd v Steel Mains Pty Ltd (1975) 132 CLR 323, **85**
Dimond v Lovell [2002] 1 AC 384, **85**
Dimskal Shipping Co SA v International Transport Workers Federation [1992] 2 AC 152, **488**
Dionisatos v Acrow Formwork & Scaffolding Pty Ltd (2015) 91 NSWLR 34, **172**
Director of Consumer Affairs Victoria v Dimmeys Stores Pty Ltd (2013) 213 FCR 559, **345**
Director of Consumer Affairs Victoria v Gibson (No 3) [2017] FCA 1148, **427**, **448**
Director of War Service Homes v Harris [1968] Qd R 275, **148**
Disctronics Ltd v Edmonds [2002] VSC 454, **267**
Dixon v Deveridge (1825) 172 ER 50, **426**
Dixson v Tange (1891) 12 LR (NSW) Eq 204, **352**
Djordjevic v Australian Iron & Steel Ltd (1964) 82 WN (Pt 1) (NSW) 218, **59**

Fothergill v Rowland (1873) LR 17 Eq 132, **302**
Francis v Lyon (1907) 4 CLR 1023, **139**
Francis v Municipal Councillors of Kuala Lumpur [1962] 3 All ER 633, **305, 338**
Francis v Nash (1734) 95 ER 32, **554**
Frankipile Pty Ltd v Acsas Pty Ltd (NSWCA, 7 November 1988), **35**
Fraser v Booth (1949) 50 SR (NSW) 113, **332**
Fraser v Judicial and Legal Services Commission [2008] UKPC 25, **413**
Fraser v State Transport Authority (1985) 39 SASR 57, **96**
Free v Thomas [2009] NSWSC 642, **157**
Freemantle's Pastoral Pty Ltd v Hyett [1999] VSC 129, **110**
Freese v Collins [1948] St R Qd 18, **180**
French v Macale [1835–42] All ER Rep 6, **382**
French v QBE Insurance (Australia) Ltd (2011) 58 MVR 214, **169**
Friend v Brooker (2009) 239 CLR 129, **116, 474**
Frigo v Culhaci (NSWCA, 17 July 1998), **550–1**
Fritz v Hobson (1880) 14 Ch D 542, **355, 362**
Froom v Butcher [1976] QB 286, **204**
Fu v Winstar Group Pty Ltd [2014] WASC 496, **334**
Fudlovski v JGC Accounting and Financial Services Pty Ltd (No 2) [2013] WASC 301, **126**
Fulton Hogan Construction Pty Ltd v Grenadier Manufacturing Pty Ltd [2012] VSC 358, **123**
Furness v Adrium Industries Pty Ltd [1996] 1 VR 668, **40, 182**
Futuretronics International Pty Ltd v Gadzhis [1990] 2 VR 217, **321–2**

G & A Lanteri Nominees Pty Ltd v Fishers Stores Consolidated Pty Ltd [2007] VSCA 4, **65**
Gaba Formwork Contractors Pty Ltd v Turner Corporation Ltd (1991) 32 NSWLR 175,
    62, 183–4, 451, 457–8
Gaca v Pirelli General plc [2004] 1 WLR 2683, **232**
Gacic v John Fairfax Publications Pty Ltd [2005] NSWSC 1210, **188**
Gadens Lawyers Sydney Pty Ltd v Symond (2015) 89 NSWLR 60, **188**
Gafford v Graham (1999) 77 P & CR 73, **355, 449, 467**
Gaggin v Moss [1983] 2 Qd R 486, **180**
Gagner Pty Ltd v Canturi Corporation Pty Ltd (2009) 262 ALR 691, **29, 31, 40, 176–8**
Galafassi v Kelly (2014) 87 NSWLR 119, **109**
Gales Holdings Pty Ltd v Tweed Shire Council [2011] NSWSC 1128, **332**
Gales Holdings Pty Ltd v Tweed Shire Council (2013) 85 NSWLR 514, **190**
Gall v Mitchell (1924) 35 CLR 222, **314**
Gander v Murray (1907) 5 CLR 575, **308**
Garden Cottage Foods Ltd v Milk Marketing Board [1984] AC 130, **537**
Gas & Fuel Corporation (Vic) v Barba [1976] VR 755, **353**
Gates v City Mutual Life Assurance Society Ltd (1986) 160 CLR 1, **27, 63, 187–9, 250–3, 322**
Gazzard v Hutchesson (1995) Aust Torts Reports 81–337, **178**
GE Commercial Corporation (Australia) Pty Ltd v Nichols [2012] NSWSC 562, **303**
GEC Marconi Systems Pty Ltd v BHP Information Technology Pty Ltd (2003) 128 FCR 1, **149**
Gedbury Pty Ltd v Michael David Kennedy Autos [1986] 1 Qd R 103, **342**
GEJ & MA Geldard Pty Ltd v Mobbs (No 2) [2012] 1 Qd R 120, **124**
Geldard Pty Ltd v Mobbs (No 2) [2012] 1 Qd R 120, **126**
Gemstone Corporation of Australia Ltd v Grasso (1994) 62 SASR 239, **278**
General Tire and Rubber Co v Firestone Tyre and Rubber Co Ltd [1975] 1 WLR 819, **454**

Hausmann v Smith (2006) 24 ACLC 688, **542–3**

Havenaar v Havenaar [1982] 1 NSWLR 626, **97**

Haviv Holdings Pty Ltd v Howards Storage World Pty Ltd (2009) 254 ALR 273, **162, 167**

Havyn Pty Ltd v Webster (2005) 12 BPR 22,837, **253**

Hawker Pacific Pty Ltd v Helicopter Charter Pty Ltd (1991) 22 NSWLR 298, **503**

Hawthorn Football Club Ltd v Harding [1988] VR 49, **306, 339**

Hay v Hughes [1975] QB 790, **245**

Hay Properties Consultants Pty Ltd v Victorian Securities Corporation Ltd (2010) 29 VR 503, **96**

Hayle Holdings Pty Ltd v Australian Technology Group Ltd [2000] FCA 1242, **52**

Haynes v Top Slice Deli Pty Ltd (1995) ATPR (Digest) 46–147, **261**

Healing (Sales) Pty Ltd v Inglis Electrix Pty Ltd (1968) 121 CLR 584, **183, 396**

Hearne v Smith (2008) 235 CLR 125, **558**

Heavener v Loomes (1924) 34 CLR 306, **328, 331, 333, 536, 542**

Hedley Byrne & Co Ltd v Heller & Partners Ltd [1964] AC 465, **187**

Heenan v Di Sisto (2008) Aust Torts Reports 81–941, **49–51**

Heid v Reliance Finance Corporation Pty Ltd (1983) 154 CLR 326, **518**

Heine Bros (Australia) Pty Ltd v Forrest [1963] VR 383, **339–40**

Hemmings v Stoke Poges Golf Club [1920] 1 KB 820, **371–2**

Henderson v Campbell [2002] NSWSC 1202, **218**

Hendriks v McGeoch (2008) Aust Torts Reports 81–942, **53–4**

Henjo Investments Pty Ltd v Collins Marrickville Pty Ltd (1988) 39 FCR 546, **490**

Henjo Investments Pty Ltd v Collins Marrickville Pty Ltd (No 2) (1989) 40 FCR 76, **262**

Henley v Commane [1971] Tas SR 180, **230–1**

Henry v Birch (1804) 32 ER 640, **311**

Henry v Perry [1964] VR 174, **242**

Henry v Thompson [1989] 2 Qd R 412, **114, 396, 409**

Henville v Walker (2001) 206 CLR 459, **99, 250–1, 253–4, 256–60, 322**

Heperu Pty Ltd v Morgan Brooks Pty Ltd (No 2) [2007] NSWSC 1438, **199**

Herbert v American Express Australia Ltd [2016] NSWCATAP 47, **248**

Herbert Clayton & Jack Waller Ltd v Oliver [1930] AC 209, **156, 159**

Hercy v Birch (1804) 32 ER 640, **311**

Hermann v Hodges (1873) LR 16 Eq 18, **303**

Hewett v Court (1983) 149 CLR 639, **521**

Heydon v NRMA Ltd (No 2) (2001) 53 NSWLR 600, **68**

Hickey & Co Ltd v Roche Stores (Dublin) Ltd [1993] RLR 196, **445**

Higgins v Betts [1905] 2 Ch 210, **358**

Higgins v Statewide Developments Pty Ltd (2010) 14 BPR 27,293, **65**

Highland and Universal Properties Ltd v Safeway Properties Ltd 2000 SC 297, **294**

Highway Hauliers Pty Ltd v Maxwell [2012] WASC 53, **198**

HIH Casualty and General Insurance Ltd v Chase Manhattan Bank [2003] 1 All ER (Comm) 349, **488**

HIH Claims Support Ltd v Insurance Australia Ltd (2011) 244 CLR 72, **116–17**

Hill v Barclay (1810) 33 ER 1037, **318**

Hill v Forrester (2010) 79 NSWLR 470, **217**

Hill v Rose [1990] VR 129, **267, 281**

Hinde v Liddell (1875) LR 10 QB 265, **139**

Re Pile's Caveat [1981] Qd R 81, **517**

Re Polemis v Furness, Withy & Co Ltd [1921] 3 KB 560, **191**

Re Rose [1952] Ch 499, **522**

Re Schwabacher (1907) 98 LT 127, **302**

Re Vandervell's Trusts (No 2) [1974] Ch 269, **527**

Re Wait [1927] 1 Ch 606, **302**

Re Wan Ze Property Development (Australia) Pty Ltd (2012) 90 ACSR 593, **526**

Re York Street Mezzanine Pty Ltd (in liq) (2007) 162 FCR 358, **517**

Reader's Digest Services Pty Ltd v Lamb (1982) 150 CLR 500, **173**

Reardon Smith Line Ltd v Australian Wheat Board (1956) 93 CLR 577, **167**

Redding v Lee (1982) 151 CLR 117, **232**

Redgrave v Hurd (1881) 20 Ch D 1, **489**

Redland Bricks Ltd v Morris [1970] AC 652, **319, 329, 351, 559**

Redwood Music Ltd v Chappell & Co Ltd [1982] RPC 109, **463**

Reed International Books Australia Pty Ltd (t/as Butterworths) v King & Prior Pty Ltd (1993) 44 FCR 587, **474**

Rees v Marquis of Bute [1916] 2 Ch 64, **310**

Reeves v Commissioner of Police of the Metropolis [2000] 1 AC 360, **240**

Reeves v Reeves (2002) 36 MVR 488, **203**

Regal (Hastings) Ltd v Gulliver [1967] 2 AC 134, **435, 437, 461**

Regan v Paul Properties DPF No 1 Ltd [2007] Ch 135, **348**

Regent v Millett (1976) 133 CLR 679, **307**

Reibl v Hughes (1981) 114 DLR (3d) 1, **80**

Reid v Brown (1952) 69 WN (NSW) 131, **181**

Reid v Graybriar Industries Ltd (2006) 61 Alta LR (4th) 264, **284**

Reid v Reid (NSWSC, 30 November 1998), **489, 523, 525**

Reindel v James Hardie & Co Pty Ltd [1994] 1 VR 619, **396**

Reinhold v New South Wales Lotteries Corporation (No 2) (2008) 82 NSWLR 762, **120, 123–4, 128**

Reinhold v New South Wales Lotteries Corporation [2008] NSWSC 5, **162**

Reliance Finance Corporation Pty Ltd v Heid [1982] 1 NSWLR 446, **518**

Rely-A-Bell Burglar and Fire Alarm Company Ltd v Eisler [1926] 1 Ch 609, **339–40**

Renard Constructions (ME) Pty Ltd v Minister of Public Works (1992) 26 NSWLR 234, **481**

Rendell v Associated Finance Pty Ltd [1957] VR 604, **189**

Renehan v Leeuwin Ocean Adventure Foundation Ltd (2006) 17 NTLR 83, **225**

Rennie Golledge Pty Ltd v Ballard (2012) 82 NSWLR 231, **124–5, 261**

Rentokil Pty Ltd v Channon (1990) 19 NSWLR 417, **63–4, 186**

Rentokil Pty Ltd v Lee (1995) 66 SASR 301, **338**

Restifa v Pallotta [2009] NSWSC 958, **174**

Retail Parks Investments Ltd v Royal Bank of Scotland plc (No 2) 1996 SC 227, **294**

Revill v Newbery [1996] QB 567, **374**

REW08 Projects Pty Ltd v PNC Lifestyle Investments Pty Ltd [2017] NSWCA 269, **310, 315**

Reynolds v Times Newspapers Ltd [1998] 3 WLR 862, **426**

Richard West & Partners (Inverness) Ltd v Dick [1969] 2 Ch 424, **307**

Richard West & Partners (Inverness) Ltd v Dick [1969] 2 WLR 383, **307**

Richards v Mills (2003) 27 WAR 200, **202–4**

Richards v Victoria [1969] VR 136, **195**

Richardson v Schultz (1980) 25 SASR 1, **215**

Royal v Smurthwaite (2007) 47 MVR 401, **215**
Royal Bank of Canada v W Got & Associates Electric Ltd [1999] 3 SCR 408, **10**, **399**
Royal Bristol Permanent Building Society v Bomash (1887) 35 Ch D 390, **142**
Royal Brompton Hospital NHS Trust v Hammond [2002] 1 WLR 1397, **114**
Rozsa v Samuals [1969] SASR 205, **375**
Ruby v Marsh (1975) 132 CLR 642, **68**
Ruddy v Chief Constable of Strathclyde [2003] SC (UKSC) 126, **114**
Ruffy Investments Pty Ltd v Payless Superbarn (Vic) Pty Ltd (2000) V Conv R 54–617,
    320
Rufo v Hosking (2004) 61 NSWLR 678, **43**, **46**
Rural Press Ltd v Australian Competition and Consumer Commission (2003) 216
    CLR 53, **422**
Russell v Commissioner of Police, New South Wales Police Service (2001) 6 AILR 75, **418**
Russell v Rail Infrastructure Corporation [2007] NSWSC 402, **201**
Russell v Trustees of the Roman Catholic Church for the Archdiocese of Sydney (2008)
    72 NSWLR 559, **158–9**, **166**
Ruthol Pty Ltd v Mills (2003) 11 BPR 20,793, **516**
Ruthol Pty Ltd v Tricon (Australia) Pty Ltd (2005) 12 BPR 23,923, **33**, **35–7**, **71**, **142**
Ruxley Electronics & Construction Ltd v Forsyth [1996] AC 344, **143**, **145–6**, **148**, **157**
Ryan v AF Concrete Pumping Pty Ltd [2013] NSWSC 113, **224**
Ryan v Mutual Tontine Westminster Chambers Association [1893] 1 Ch 116, **318–19**, **339**, **350**,
    355, **363**
Ryan v Urban Construct (SA) Pty Ltd [2012] SASC 128, **110**
Ryder v Hall (1904) 27 NZLR 385, **355**

Saccardo Constructions Pty Ltd v Gammon (No 2) (1994) 63 SASR, **120**
Sacher Investments Pty Ltd v Forma Stereo Consultants Pty Ltd [1976] 1 NSWLR 5, **110–11**
Sainsbury v Great Southern Energy Pty Ltd [2000] NSWSC 479, **201**
Saler v Klingbiel [1945] SASR 171, **375**
Saleslease Ltd v Davis [1999] 1 WLR 1664, **195**
Salway v Salway (1831) 39 ER 376, **271**
Sam (aka Al-Sam) v Atkins [2006] RTR 14, **27**
Sampson v Murray, 415 US 61 (1974), **305**, **338**
Samsung Electronics Co Ltd v Apple Inc (2011) 286 ALR 257, **540**
Sandeman Coprimar SA v Transitos y Transportes Integrales SL [2003] QB 1270, **195**
Sanders v Snell (1997) 73 FCR 569, **396**
Sanders v Snell (1998) 196 CLR 329, **396**
Sanderson Motors (Sales) Pty Ltd v Yorkstar Motors Pty Ltd [1983] 1 NSWLR 513, **330**
Sargent v ASL Developments Ltd (1974) 131 CLR 634, **494–5**, **503**
Sarkis v Summitt Broadway Pty Ltd (2006) Aust Torts Reports 81–868, **240**
Satnam Investments Ltd v Dunlop Heywood & Co Ltd [1999] 3 All ER 652, **279**
Saunby v London (Ontario) Water Commissioners [1906] AC 110, **355**
Saunders v Smith (1838) 40 ER 1100, **540**
Saunders v Vautier (1841) 49 ER 282, **513**
Say-Dee Pty Ltd v Farah Constructions Pty Ltd [2005] NSWCA 309, **280**
Sayers v Collyer (1884) 28 Ch D 103, **352**, **357**, **364–5**
Sayers v Harlow UDC [1958] 1 WLR 623, **94**

Stocker v Wedderburn (1857) 69 ER 1163, **305**

Stocks v Retirement Benefits Fund Board [2007] ANZ ConvR 254, **188**

Stockwell v Victoria [2001] VSC 497, **179**

Stocovaz v Fung [2007] NSWCA 199, **29**

Stocznia Gdanksa SA v Latvian Shipping Co [1998] 1 WLR 574, **386**

Stoke-on-Trent City Council v W and J Wass Ltd [1988] 1 WLR 1406, **362, 456, 458**

Stone v Chappel (2017) 128 SASR 165, **146, 257**

Strand Electric & Engineering Co Ltd v Brisford Entertainments Ltd [1952] 2 QB 246, **184, 401, 451, 457–8**

Strong v Woolworths Ltd (t/as Big W) (2012) 246 CLR 182, **79, 82, 88, 91**

Stuart Pty Ltd v Condor Commercial Insulation Pty Ltd (2006) Aust Contract R 90–245, **162, 164, 167**

Stubing v Halling (2012) 115 SASR 1, **72**

Stump v Gaby (1852) 42 ER 1015, **516**

Sturch v Willmott [1997] 2 Qd R 310, **226**

Subiah v Attorney-General of Trinidad and Tobago [2008] UKPC 47, **413**

Sudbrook Trading Estate Ltd v Eggleton [1983] 1 AC 444, **300**

Sullivan v Gordon (1999) 47 NSWLR 319, **223, 226**

Sullivan Nicolaides Pty Ltd v Papa [2012] 2 Qd R 48, **48**

Summers v Cocks (1927) 40 CLR 321, **299, 314–15**

Summertime Holdings Pty Ltd v Environmental Defender's Office Ltd (1998) 45 NSWLR 291, **159, 419**

Sunbird Plaza Pty Ltd v Maloney (1988) 166 CLR 245, **134**

Sunderland v Macco-Palmer (1972) 3 SASR 314, **230**

Sungravure Pty Ltd v Meani (1964) 110 CLR 24, **202**

Sunland Waterfront (BVI) Ltd v Prudentia Investments Pty Ltd (No 2) (2012) 266 FLR 243, **253**

Sunrock Aircraft Corporation Ltd v Scandinavian Airlines System Denmark-Norway-Sweden [2007] 2 Lloyd's Rep 612, **145, 425**

Supershield Ltd v Siemens Building Technologies FE Ltd [2010] 2 All ER (Comm) 1185, **165**

Surf Coast Shire Council v Webb [2003] VSCA 162, **220**

Surrey County Council v Bredero Homes Ltd [1993] 1 WLR 1361, **449, 467**

Sutherland Shire Council v Becker (2006) 150 LGERA 184, **190**

Sutton v AJ Thompson Pty Ltd (in liq) (1987) 73 ALR 233, **258**

Sutton v Sutton [1984] Ch 184, **310**

Suttor v Gundowda Pty Ltd (1950) 81 CLR 418, **387**

Svanosio v McNamara (1956) 96 CLR 186, **141–2, 506**

Sved v Woollahra Municipal Council (1995) 86 LGERA 222, **186**

Sved v Woollahra Municipal Council (1998) NSW ConvR 55–842, **185**

Swan v Williams (Demolition) Pty Ltd (1987) 9 NSWLR 172, **242**

Swanston Mortgage Pty Ltd v Trepan Investments Pty Ltd [1994] 1 VR 672, **516**

Swimsure (Laboratories) Pty Ltd v McDonald [1979] 2 NSWLR 796, **333–4**

Swindle v Harrison [1997] 4 All ER 705, **279–80**

Swordheath Properties Ltd v Tabet [1979] 1 WLR 285, **455**

Sydney Refractive Surgery Centre Pty Ltd v Commissioner of Taxation (2008) 247 ALR 313, **38**

Sykes v Beadon (1879) 11 Ch D 170, **310**

Symons v Stacey (1922) 30 CLR 169, **199**

Szarfer v Chodos (1986) 27 DLR (4th) 388, **268**

TABLE OF
STATUTES

INTRODUCTION

I   Why have a book on remedies?

[1.1]   The first question a client often has when consulting her solicitor is 'what can I get?' rather than 'what cause of action do I have?' Thus it has been said, 'we must always remember that legal advice is, at bottom, simply advice as to the remedy likely to be available (or unavailable) to the client'.[1] Similarly, in *Letang v Cooper*, Diplock LJ said that 'a cause of action is simply a factual situation the existence of which entitles one person to obtain from the court a remedy against another person'.[2] Indeed, as Diplock LJ goes on to note, historically, remedies have come before analysis of primary rights and obligations in English law because as long as a plaintiff could make out a particular 'form of action' she could then obtain a remedy.[3] The remedy was the starting point, and lawyers worked backwards to fit within the form of action.

[1.2]   The law of civil remedies has frequently been described as a 'capstone' private law subject.[4] In other words, it is the culmination of a student's knowledge of private law, and it is intended to assist all the disparate strands from previously studied private law subjects to come together. It is 'horizontal' rather than 'vertical', as it cuts across all private law categories, and integrates material from torts, contract, equity, trusts, property law and other private law causes of action. Waddams has aptly noted:

> The subject [of remedies] is worthy of study because it enables illuminating parallels to be drawn that cross the boundaries between contract and tort, and between law and equity.[5]

It is for this reason (as will be explained in the last section of this chapter) that we will take a generally 'functional' approach to the organisation of this book, grouping remedies from across different areas according to the broad functions they perform so that parallels and contrasts can be made.

[1.3]   The law of remedies has been growing in popularity in Australian law schools in recent decades. It is an important and deeply practical subject, as it attempts to answer the question of the redress a plaintiff may obtain in a legal action. It 'nurture[s] and foster[s] students' professional judgment to choose wisely between alternative remedial solutions within the range permitted by the wrongdoer's substantive violation and the victim's injury'.[6] Often the preferred cause of action for the plaintiff will depend upon the remedies available for that cause of action. It is essential for any person who practises law to have some knowledge of this. The aim of this book is to provide a road map whereby the alternative remedial solutions are set out in a clear and logical fashion. Our primary aim is to describe the law as it is, not the law as it should be, although we will make suggestions as to reform from time to time. We will consider private law remedies, including remedies for tort, breach of contract, equitable wrongdoing, and a variety of statutory remedies with a private law flavour, including remedies

---

1   A Tettenborn, 'Remedies: A Neglected Contribution' [1999] Denning LJ 41, 41.
2   [1965] 1 QB 232, 242–43.
3   [1965] 1 QB 232, 243.
4   See, eg, JM Fischer, 'Teaching Remedies Versus Learning Remedies' (2000) 39 Brandeis LJ 575, 576; MP Allen, 'Remedies as a Capstone Experience: How the Remedies Course Can Help Address the Challenges Facing Legal Education' (2013) 57 Saint Louis University LJ 547.
5   SM Waddams, 'Remedies as a Legal Subject' (1983) 3 OJLS 113, 121.
6   D Rendleman, 'Remedies – The Law School Course' (2000) 39 Brandeis LJ 535, 536.

for breach of Schedule 2 of the *Competition and Consumer Act 2010* (Cth), otherwise known as the 'Australian Consumer Law'. However, it should be emphasised that this book is aimed not solely at undergraduate students. It is also intended for postgraduate students, practitioners and the judiciary.

II   What is a remedy?

It has been observed that 'remedies' are notoriously difficult to define, leaving some writers to avoid the definition altogether because of disagreements as to an appropriate definition.[7] Zakrzewski has observed that the word 'remedy' is often used in multiple senses which overlap to different degrees.[8] In common parlance it is often used in the sense of healing and alleviation of pain.[9] In legal parlance, it is often used variously to describe an action or cause of action, a substantive right, a court order, a means of enforcing a court order and a final outcome of litigation.[10] Ultimately Zakrzewski defines remedies as 'the rights immediately arising from certain judicial commands and statements which aim to redress a pre-suit grievance, usually an actual or threatened infringement of a substantive right'.[11] [1.4]

In one sense, remedies could be said to arise primarily because defendants commit civil wrongs against plaintiffs.[12] In other words, the defendant contravenes some legally recognised duty that he owes to the plaintiff, causing damage to the plaintiff. Thus, we could say simply that a remedy is a legal response to civil wrongdoing, although, as we will see, the way in which we will ultimately define 'remedy' in this book is broader than this. [1.5]

A remedy confers a 'right' in that the plaintiff has an ability to enforce a correlative 'duty'. For example, my right as a plaintiff to receive compensatory damages for your breach of contract arises because you have a pre-existing duty to perform the contract which you have failed to meet, which has injured me. Thus, the remedy arises because of the defendant's pre-existing duty to the plaintiff which has been breached. [1.6]

On the view of John Austin, remedies can be regarded as 'secondary rights', which spring from injuries or violations of 'primary rights' granted by law.[13] He said that primary rights serve the purposes of law, whereas secondary rights are conferred for the better protection and enforcement of primary rights and duties. Primary rights do not arise from wrongdoing or from violation of other rights, whereas secondary rights do. Secondary rights suppose that obedience to the law is not perfect, because otherwise there would be no injuries [1.7]

---

7   J Berryman, 'The Law of Remedies: A Prospectus for Teaching and Scholarship' (2010) 10 OUCLJ 123, 124, citing J Berryman, V Black, J Cassels, M Pratt, K Roach and S Waddams (eds), *Remedies: Cases and Materials* (5th edn, Edmond Montgomery 2006).

8   R Zakrzewski, *Remedies Reclassified* (OUP 2005) 7–22.

9   Ibid, 8–9.

10   Ibid, 10–22.

11   Ibid, 2. See also S Smith, 'Why Courts Make Orders (And What This Tells Us About Damages)' (2011) 64 CLP 51; S Smith, 'Duties, Liabilities and Damages' (2012) 125 Harvard LR 1727.

12   For judicial expressions of this view see *Attorney-General v Blake* [2001] 1 AC 268, 284 (Lord Nicholls); *Australian Broadcasting Corporation v Lenah Game Meats Pty Ltd* [2001] HCA 63, (2001) 208 CLR 199 [60] (Gaudron J).

13   J Austin, *Lectures on Jurisprudence*, 5th edn, Robert Campbell and John Murray (eds), 1885, Lecture XLV, Vol 2, 760.

or violations of the law. On this view, remedies are simply a response to wrongdoing or violation of rights.

[1.8]   An example of the distinction between a primary right and a secondary right can be seen in contract. The primary right arising from a contract is the right for the plaintiff to obtain performance of the contract from the defendant. It exists independently of any wrong. Suppose, however, that the defendant does not perform the contract. If the plaintiff did not have a secondary right to expectation damages, just to take an example, the plaintiff's primary right would be useless. Thus, expectation damages represent a secondary right which protects and enforces the plaintiff's contractual right. Specific performance on the other hand is a remedy that provides the plaintiff with an effective substitute for the primary right. In fact, this distinction has been accepted in contract by Lord Diplock in the celebrated case of *Photo Production Ltd v Securicor Transport Ltd.*[14]

[1.9]   As Austin notes, there is a symbiotic relationship between the two: primary rights are of no use without the 'teeth' provided by secondary rights, and secondary rights cannot exist without a primary right giving rise to them. Thus, he argues, in this sense there is truth in the old maxim *ubi jus ibi remedium* ('where there is a right there is a remedy').

[1.10]   Austin concedes that the distinction between primary rights and secondary rights could be criticised, noting:

> In strictness, my own terms, 'primary and secondary rights and duties', do not represent a logical distinction. For a primary right or duty is not of itself a right or duty, without the secondary right or duty by which it is sustained; and *e converso*.[15]

Nonetheless, Austin argues that it is worthwhile to draw this distinction because it gives rise to 'clearness and compactness'.

[1.11]   Austin also concedes that some primary duties cannot be described without looking at the description of the corresponding injury. An example is those torts where damage is the gist of the cause of action, for example malicious falsehood, passing off and negligence. The primary duty is defined in terms of a duty not to cause harm.

[1.12]   A second example is of a transfer made by mistake: Alan transfers money to Bertha under a mistake. Alan can generally recover the money from Bertha. Bertha commits no wrong, but Bertha is obliged to return the money to Alan, lest she be unjustly enriched. The remedial response ('restitution') is a primary right because it does not respond to a breach of duty.[16]

[1.13]   Another remedy that does not respond to a legal wrong arises where a contracting party is aggrieved because the other party insists that the contract has not come to an end. While there is no breach of duty, the first party can obtain a legal remedy.[17] Similarly, there is

---

14   [1980] AC 827, 848–50. For a more detailed history of other cases where Lord Diplock advanced this view, see B Dickson, 'The Contribution of Lord Diplock to the Law of Contract' (1989) 9 OJLS 441.

15   J Austin, *Lectures on Jurisprudence*, 5th edn, Robert Campbell and John Murray (eds), 1885, Lecture XLV, Vol 2, 760.

16   N Witzleb, E Bant, S Degeling and K Barker, *Remedies: Commentary and Materials* (6th edn, LBC 2015) [1.20]. Cf K Barker, 'Rescuing Remedialism in Unjust Enrichment: Why Remedies Are Right' (1998) 57 Camb LJ 301, 320–22, who argues that the rights–remedy distinction still holds in the context of mistaken payments.

17   *Guaranty Trust Co of New York v Hannay & Co* [1915] 2 KB 536. See R Zakrzewski, *Remedies Reclassified* (OUP 2005) 11.

no breach of duty in testator family maintenance claims, but it is generally thought that the dependant who seeks maintenance obtains a legal remedy in response.[18]

Thus, Austin's definition is too narrow, as it does not cover certain court-ordered responses to events that are not based on wrongdoing but nonetheless give rise to a remedial response, such as unjust enrichment. [1.14]

For Birks, 'wrongs' referred to breaches of duty including tort, breach of contract, breach of fiduciary duty and breach of confidence, which were to be contrasted with causes of action such as unjust enrichment which were 'not-wrongs'.[19] He argued that courts have a wider range of remedial response available for wrongs, but the remedial response for a not-wrong (such as restitution of a mistaken payment) was very limited, and courts were justified only in returning the value of the unjust enrichment.[20] [1.15]

Many, if not most, of the remedies discussed in this book generally fall within Zakrzewski's core definition of 'remedy' as a court order replicating pre-existing rights.[21] However, we will also consider some remedies which do not fit within this definition, namely pre- and post-judgment remedies, which are a matter of civil procedure, and self-help remedies.[22] Self-help 'remedies' may not be remedies at all, but effectively involve permission from the court for a plaintiff to act in a particular way. Nevertheless, in a broader sense, they provide a means for a plaintiff to redress a grievance by allowing her to vindicate her own right, and accordingly we cover them in this book. We also cover pre- and post-judgment orders in this book, for three reasons. First, many of the cases involving interlocutory injunctions are relevant to the law on final injunctions. Secondly, it is necessary to know about the procedural means the courts have at their disposal to ensure that remedies in the narrow sense are effective, Thirdly, many Australian lawyers would expect to see at least some discussion of these topics in a book of this kind. [1.16]

A   Monism and dualism

There are further questions which flow from the discussion above regarding the right giving rise to the remedy. As Birks notes, the range of remedial response to unjust enrichment (that is, restitution) is generally more limited than the range of remedial response to breaches of duty such as breach of contract or equitable wrongdoing. The question is then whether the remedy inevitably flows from the right in question, or whether the court can choose from a range of remedies for that particular cause of action. [1.17]

The traditional view, which is still the dominant English view, is the monist view. The remedy is simply a mirror of the plaintiff's cause of action and is set by the law as appropriate to the specific primary right in question. This view has been adopted by several theoretical strands of thought, including corrective justice theories such as Ernest Weinrib's (see [1.55]), unjust enrichment theories such as Peter Birks's (see [1.27]–[1.29]), and rights based theories such as Robert Stevens's (see [1.58]–[1.59], [1.61], [1.64]). [1.18]

---

18   Zakrzewski, ibid.
19   P Birks, 'Rights, Wrongs and Remedies' (2000) 20 OJLS 1, 25–36.
20   Ibid, 28.
21   R Zakrzewski, *Remedies Reclassified* (OUP 2005).
22   Ibid, 18–21, 44–45, 47–48.

[1.19]   The other extreme is a dualist view, which maintains that once liability has been deter-mined, the court can exercise its discretion to choose the most appropriate remedy in the case at hand. For example, once the plaintiff has proved a breach of contract, under a dualist view the court should have a discretion as to what remedy is granted, and the court can choose from a large range of potential remedies.

[1.20]   There is a moderate approach which involves a compromise of the monist and dualist positions.[23] Under this theory, there is a strong but not absolute link between the primary right and the secondary right.[24] Thus, there is a 'default' remedy for many causes of action, but if circumstances require it the court can depart from that remedy. As will become evident, this approach is favoured by the authors of this book. This is because it better reflects the reality of what occurs in case law. Moreover, the authors do not subscribe to an overarching theory: in Isaiah Berlin's terms, we are 'foxes' who draw ideas and research from many streams rather than 'hedgehogs' who follow one big idea.[25]

B   Sources of remedies in Australia

[1.21]   Even if one is a monist (see [1.18]), one's view of which remedy is appropriate for a particular cause of action depends on one's view of the broader scheme of how causes of action should be organised. Traditionally, private law has been viewed as being divided into categories such as 'contract', 'tort', 'breach of trust', 'breach of confidence' and so forth, and the appropriate remedies are seen to flow from that categorisation. As will be discussed below, if one chooses to categorise causes of action in a different way, then the appropriate remedies will change accordingly.

[1.22]   The three sources of legal remedies in Australia are common law, equity and statute. There is a division between the remedies available for common law and equitable causes of action. Common law and equity start from different 'default' positions. The 'default' remedy for a common law breach of duty is generally compensatory damages. If compensatory damages are inappropriate, the court may award specific relief, but other remedies such as gain-based relief and punitive damages are available only, if at all, in limited circumstances when compen-satory damages are inadequate and specific relief is no longer available. Common law wrongs include breach of contract and torts such as negligence, trespass to land, trespass to goods, conversion, and deceit.

[1.23]   By contrast, the 'default' remedy for equitable wrongdoing is generally either specific relief or gain-based relief. Although compensatory relief is now available in equity, the rules regarding the attribution of responsibility are said to differ from those applying at common law.

---

23   D Wright, *Remedies* (2nd edn, Federation Press 2014) 8–9; D Wright, 'Wrong and Remedy: A Sticky Relationship' [2001] Sing J Leg Stud 1.

24   See, eg, P Gewirtz, 'Remedies and Resistance' (1983) 92 Yale LJ 585; K Cooper-Stephenson, 'Principle and Pragmatism in the Law of Remedies' in J Berryman (ed), *Remedies: Issues and Perspectives* (Carswell 1991) 1; K Barker, 'Rescuing Remedialism in Unjust Enrichment: Why Remedies Are Right' (1998) 57 Camb LJ 301, 323.

25   I Berlin, *The Hedgehog and the Fox: An Essay on Tolstoy's View of History* (Weidenfeld & Nicolson 1953). Berlin took his title from the Ancient Greek poet Archilochus who said that 'a fox knows many things, but a hedgehog one important thing'. See also PE Tetlock, *Expert Political Judgment: How Good Is It? How Can We Know?* (Princeton University Press 2005), discussing this division in relation to political academics.

Equitable wrongs include breach of trust, breach of fiduciary duty and breach of confidence. Equitable remedies are always subject to discretionary considerations and thus, in that sense, equitable remedies are more 'dualist' in nature than common law remedies because the court has more choice of what remedy to award and upon what conditions to do so.

Although the common law and equity have differences in the way in which they operate, they are also similar because the causes of action and the remedies arise from 'judge-made law'. Another source of law which cannot be ignored by lawyers is statute, which is enacted by Parliament rather than developed by judges. Statute law has had a massive impact on private law,[26] including remedies.   [1.24]

Statute has now been enacted to deal with a variety of wrongs and remedies in Australia. Pivotally, the *Competition and Consumer Act 2010* (Cth) ('CCA') has been enacted to cover, inter alia, misleading and deceptive conduct. The remedial structure of this regime is quite different to that of the common law. Mason P described the remedial scheme under the predecessor to the CCA (the *Trade Practices Act 1974* (Cth)) as a 'remedial smorgasbord' according to which a judge could look at the variety of remedies on offer and choose which was best for the particular case.[27] This 'smorgasbord' approach is quite different to the approach traditionally taken in common law and equity. It remains unclear to what extent statutory remedies should be developed by analogy with common law remedies or, conversely, the extent to which common law remedies should be developed by analogy with statute.[28] Clearly statutory remedies are highly 'dualist' in nature (even more so than equitable remedies).   [1.25]

Statute has also been used by courts to traverse the common law/equitable remedy divide. The *Chancery Amendment Act 1858* (UK) (Lord Cairns' Act) allows damages in lieu of specific relief to be used by courts as a means of awarding arguably gain-based remedies for common law wrongs,[29] and compensatory damages in equity.[30]   [1.26]

C   The unjust enrichment school of thought

There are other ways of analysing private law causes of action. One important school of thought is that of unjust enrichment. Birks, a prominent unjust enrichment scholar, was a monist because he considered that certain causative events triggered a particular remedy. He famously said, '[t]he secondary obligation to pay compensatory damages is . . . the same thing as the right looked at from the other end'.[31] In other words, the remedy reflects the right, and the right reflects the remedy. However, he suggested that private law causes of action should   [1.27]

---

26   A Burrows, 'The Relationship between Common Law and Statute in the Law of Obligations' (2012) 128 LQR 232.

27   *Akron Securities Ltd v Iliffe* (1997) 143 ALR 457, 469.

28   E Bant and J Paterson, 'Limitations on Defendant Liability for Misleading or Deceptive Conduct under Statute: Some Insights from Negligent Misstatement' in K Barker, R Grantham and W Swain (eds), *The Law of Misstatements: 50 Years on from Hedley Byrne v Heller* (Hart 2015) 159.

29   *Wrotham Park Estate Co Ltd v Parkside Homes Ltd* [1974] 1 WLR 798. Some have argued that the 'reasonable fee award' in *Wrotham Park* is compensatory, not gain-based; see [16.64]–[16.66], [16.70]–[16.72].

30   *Giller v Procopets* [2008] VSCA 236, (2008) 24 VR 1.

31   P Birks, 'Definition and Division: A Meditation on *Institutes* 3.13' in P Birks (ed), *The Classification of Obligations* (Clarendon 1997) 24.

be conceived of in a different fashion to the traditional categorisation of private law into 'contract', 'tort', and so on. He and other scholars drew on Roman law and English law to devise a taxonomy which sought to link the 'trigger' for the cause of action with the appropriate remedy. Birks distinguished four different categories:

1. wrongs;
2. consent;
3. unjust enrichment; and
4. other.

He placed tort and equitable wrongs in the category of 'wrongs' and contract and trusts in the category of 'consent'. This taxonomy cuts across common law and equity.

[1.28]   Birks argued that 'like cases should be treated alike'. It follows from Birks's analysis that wrongs in tort and equity should be analogised rather than distinguished because they have the same 'trigger' (namely wrongdoing), and the different historical origins between tort and equity should be de-emphasised. For example, if exemplary damages are awarded for a tortious wrong, it follows that exemplary damages should also be available for equitable wrongdoing because the two have the same trigger (wrongdoing). To take another example, if an account of profits is available for breach of trust, it should also be available for breach of contract because each arises by consent. Indeed, Burrows has argued for a greater coherence between common law and equitable remedies on this basis.[32] As will be discussed in greater detail at [1.35]–[1.38], this argument has not found favour with some Australian judges and academics because of their emphasis on the historical divide between common law and equity.[33]

[1.29]   Birks and other unjust enrichment scholars tend to be chary of the notion of discretion in the award of remedies. They favour monist certainty over a dualist approach. The fear with a dualist view is that if wrong is not intrinsically linked to remedy, then it will be difficult for parties to predict what remedy they will get, because it is up to the judge's discretion. If discretion is unbounded, it undermines the rule of law because it means that like cases are not treated alike (Birks's notion of 'palm tree justice').[34]

[1.30]   Indeed, even in equity, there is an awareness of the ills of unbounded discretion. Lord Mansfield said:

> Discretion, when applied to a court of justice, means sound discretion guided by law. It must be governed by rule not by humour; it must not be arbitrary, vague and fanciful, but legal and regular.[35]

[1.31]   Grant Hammond argues that a dualist approach is preferable because courts are given a greater ability to choose a just remedy, and he outlines a series of factors courts should consider when making a choice between remedies:

- relative severity of the impact of the claimed remedies on the parties;
- economic efficiency;

---

32   A Burrows, 'We Do This at Common Law but That in Equity' (2002) 22 OJLS 1.
33   See, eg, *Harris v Digital Pulse Pty Ltd* [2003] NSWCA 10, (2003) 56 NSWLR 298.
34   P Birks, 'Three Kinds of Objection to Discretionary Remedialism' (2000) 29 UWALR 1.
35   *R v Wilkes* (1770) 4 Burr Rep 2527, 2539; 98 ER 327, 334.

- the 'weight' or moral value to be attached to the interest at stake;
- the effect of a remedy on third parties or the public;
- the conduct of the parties;
- the difficulty of calculating loss; and
- the practicability of enforcement.[36]

He argues that flexibility is necessary to give judicial actors the choice to tailor remedial solutions to the circumstances. Other scholars agree that discretion in the granting of remedies is not necessarily problematic, and question the resistance of unjust enrichment scholars towards the notion.[37]

Undue rigidity in remedial options could produce injustice because the remedy mandated for a particular cause of action may be inappropriate for the specific case at hand, but, similarly, unbounded flexibility could also produce injustice, because cases may not be treated alike. Consequently, the best solution is a moderate compromise between the monist and the dualist approach: to acknowledge that for many causes of action (even statutory causes of action) there is a 'default' remedy which is often the first remedy of choice, but to acknowledge that courts may depart from this remedy and award other remedies if certain specified conditions are made out and it is more appropriate in the circumstances. [1.32]

III The common law and equity divide in Australia

Before discussing the taxonomical approach this book takes towards remedies, it is necessary to discuss the historical division between common law and equity, because it has shaped the Australian law of remedies. Although equitable remedies are available for both breach of equitable obligations (the 'exclusive' jurisdiction of equity) and for breach of common law obligations (the 'auxiliary' jurisdiction of equity), they are usually available in the latter case only where the default remedy (usually compensatory damages) is 'inadequate'. The equitable remedy which is usually awarded instead of common law compensatory damages is specific relief. Australian courts have become more willing to award specific relief in the form of specific performance or an injunction in support of a common law right.[38] While specific relief is still said to be exceptional in common law contexts, for some common law wrongs such as the tort of trespass, courts award an [1.33]

---

36   G Hammond, 'Rethinking Remedies: The Changing Nature of the Conception of the Relationship between Legal and Equitable Remedies' in J Berryman (ed), *Remedies: Issues and Perspectives* (Carswell 1991) ch 4.

37   S Evans, 'Defending Discretionary Remedialism' (2001) 23 Syd L Rev 463; P Loughlan, 'No Right to the Remedy? An Analysis of Judicial Discretion in the Imposition of Equitable Remedies' (1990) 17 MULR 132; D Jensen, 'The Rights and Wrongs of Discretionary Remedialism' [2003] Sing J Leg Stud 178; K Barker, 'Rescuing Remedialism in Unjust Enrichment Law: Why Remedies Are Right' (1998) 57 Camb LJ 301.

38   See Chs 10 and 11.

injunction in preference to damages because it is easier and better to prevent the wrongdoing than to measure the damage arising from it. Moreover, there is an increasing tendency to award specific relief simply where justice requires it.[39]

[1.34]   Restitution, disgorgement, and punitive remedies have become increasingly available for common law wrongs in other common law jurisdictions such as England and Wales,[40] Canada[41] and the United States.[42] Australian law has been less enthusiastic in doing so for reasons relating to the continued adherence to the historical division between common law and equity.

A   Fusion fallacy

[1.35]   The resistance of the Australian judiciary towards unjust enrichment scholarship comes from a perception that unjust enrichment scholarship commits the sin of 'fusion fallacy', or a failure to pay attention to the historical origins of remedies.[43] Historically, equity and common law were entirely different jurisdictions administered by different courts. The UK Judicature Acts (*Judicature Act 1873* and *Judicature Act 1875*) 'fused' common law and equity such that a single judge could administer both. The Judicature Acts were mirrored in Australia. In most Australian jurisdictions this occurred shortly after the UK Acts, but in New South Wales it did not occur before the 1970s.[44] It is no surprise that the staunchest supporters of the historical divide between common law and equity emanate from the New South Wales Equity Bar where fusion is a comparatively recent phenomenon.

[1.36]   Fusion fallacy is described as involving:

> the administration of a remedy, for example common law damages for breach of fiduciary duty, not previously available at law or in equity, or in the modification of principles in one branch of the jurisdiction by concepts that are imported from the other and thus are foreign, for example by holding that the existence of a duty in tort may be tested by asking whether the parties concerned were in fiduciary relationships.[45]

---

39   Ibid.

40   See, eg, account of profits for breach of contract: *Attorney-General v Blake* [2001] 1 AC 268.

41   See, eg, account of profits for breach of contract: *Bank of America Canada v Mutual Trust Co* [2002] SCC 43, [2002] 2 SCR 601 [25]; *Amertek Inc v Canadian Commercial Corporation* (2003) 229 DLR (4th) 419, 467 (O'Driscoll J) (on appeal held that there was no collateral contract: (2005) 256 DLR (4th) 287). See, eg, punitive damages for breach of contract: *Vorvis v Insurance Corporation of British Columbia* [1989] 1 SCR 1085; *Royal Bank of Canada v W Got & Associates Electric Ltd* [1999] 3 SCR 408; *Whiten v Pilot Insurance Co* [2002] SCC 18, [2002] 1 SCR 595.

42   See, eg, account of profits for breach of contract: American Law Institute, *Restatement (Third) of Restitution and Unjust Enrichment* (2011) §39; account of profits for tort: *Edwards v Lee's Administrator*, 96 SW 2d 1028 (Ky Ct App, 1936) and perhaps *Olwell v Nye & Nissen*, 173 P 2d 652 (1946).

43   Principally JD Heydon, MJ Leeming and PG Turner, *Meagher, Gummow and Lehane's Equity: Doctrines and Remedies* (5th edn, Lexis Nexis 2015) ch 2.

44   *Supreme Court Act 1933* (ACT), ss 25–32; *Supreme Court Act 1970* (NSW), ss 57–63; *Law Reform (Law and Equity) Act 1972* (NSW), s 5; *Civil Proceedings Act 2011* (Qld), s 7; *Supreme Court Act 1935* (SA), ss 20–28; *Supreme Court Civil Procedure Act 1932* (Tas), ss 10–11; *Supreme Court Act 1986* (Vic), s 29; *Supreme Court Act 1935* (WA), ss 24–25.

45   JD Heydon, MJ Leeming and PG Turner, *Meagher, Gummow and Lehane's Equity: Doctrines and Remedies* (5th edn, Lexis Nexis 2015) [2–140].

The previous authors of *Meagher, Gummow and Lehane's Equity* trenchantly condemned fusion fallacy as 'evil' because judges who committed it did not take account of the historical background of equity and common law.[46] In the fifth edition, while the previous views are still quoted within the text, the new authors appear to take a more conciliatory approach.[47]

There are two limbs to the fusion fallacy. The first limb 'asserts only that remedies from the one jurisdiction cannot go in support of rights in the other jurisdiction where that was impossible before the fusion of the administration of law and equity'.[48] This might include, for example, an award of common law damages for an equitable cause of action such as breach of confidence.[49] It is less problematic when equitable remedies are for common law causes of action, as equity has always had an auxiliary aspect.   [1.37]

The second limb is more general, and involves the alteration of principles in common law by equity or vice versa. This question was canvassed in *Harris v Digital Pulse Pty Ltd*[50] in respect of the availability of exemplary damages in equity. Exemplary damages are discussed in Ch 14. For now it suffices to note that courts sometimes award damages to punish a defendant for contumelious disregard of the plaintiff's right, often where an egregious tort has been committed.[51] However, they have not been awarded in equity. The availability of exemplary damages is not a simple 'crossover of remedies' question because exemplary damages are generally seen as parasitic on other awards – thus the question is really whether the common law *concept* of exemplary damages is appropriate to equitable money awards. In *Harris v Digital Pulse*, a majority of the NSW Court of Appeal decided that exemplary damages should not be available for breach of fiduciary duty; see [14.41]–[14.48].   [1.38]

B Unjust enrichment scholars breaking down the common law and equitable divide

As noted earlier, unjust enrichment scholarship organises private law remedies in a different manner to the way in which they have traditionally been organised. One of the consequences of this reorganisation is that common law and equitable remedies are placed in the same category (for example, on some analyses, both the action for money had and received and the resulting trust arise to prevent unjust enrichment).   [1.39]

Andrew Burrows argues that common law and equity should not operate side by side in an inconsistent manner, and that there *should* be some fusion between common law and equity in order to make it more coherent (notwithstanding that this was not the historical intention of the Judicature Acts).[52] Burrows posits that it is legitimate for courts to reason from common law to equity or vice versa, and that the law should develop in this way. He identifies three categories where common law and equity mix: [1.40]

---

46   Ibid.
47   Ibid, [2–145], [2–330]–[2–400].
48   M Tilbury, 'Fallacy or Furphy? Fusion in a Judicature World' (2003) 26 UNSWLJ 357, 358–59.
49   *Seager v Copydex (No 1)* [1967] 1 WLR 923.
50   [2003] NSWCA 10, (2003) 56 NSWLR 298.
51   See, eg, *Gray v Motor Accident Commission* (1998) 196 CLR 1.
52   A Burrows, 'We Do This at Common Law but That in Equity' (2002) 22 OJLS 1.

1. where common law and equity labels are useful;

2. where common law and equity coexist coherently, but there is nothing to be gained by adherence to the common law and equitable labels for different doctrines; and

3. where common law and equity do not coexist coherently.

Burrows argues that in these instances, a change in the law is needed to make equitable and common law doctrines coherent.

[1.41]   Burrows focuses on monetary remedies for civil causes of action, and the differences between the common law and equity. He argues that (1) common law and equitable wrongs (such as breach of fiduciary duty) should all be treated as wrongs; (2) the rules on attributing responsibility (factual causation and scope of liability) should generally be the same in common law and equity; (3) it should be recognised that the common law also allows for restitution for wrongs; (4) punitive damages should be available across the board for contumelious common law and equitable wrongs; (5) in exceptional circumstances, damages should be available across common law and equity for anticipated wrongs; and (6) the discretionary equitable defences and the common law defences should be rationalised.

C   Australian reception of unjust enrichment scholarship

[1.42]   In an Australian context, restitutionary theory has not been embraced by many judges.[53] For example, in *Roxborough v Rothmans of Pall Mall Australia Ltd*, Gummow J said:

> Considerations such as these, together with practical experience, suggest caution in judicial acceptance of any all-embracing theory of restitutionary rights and remedies founded upon a notion of 'unjust enrichment'. To the lawyer whose mind has been moulded by civilian influences, the theory may come first, and the source of the theory may be the writing of jurists not the decisions of judges. However, that is not the way in which a system based on case law develops; over time, general principle is derived from judicial decisions upon particular instances, not the other way around.
>
> In *McGinty v Western Australia*, McHugh J referred to Judge Posner's description of 'top-down reasoning' by which a theory about an area of law is invented or adopted and then applied to existing decisions to make them conform to the theory and to dictate the outcome in new cases. Judge Posner spoke of the use of the theory by its adherents:
>
> 'to organize, criticize, accept or reject, explain or explain away, distinguish or amplify the existing decisions to make them conform to the theory and generate an outcome in each new case as it arises that will be consistent with the theory and with the canonical cases, that is, the cases accepted as authoritative within the theory'.
>
> As it happens, Lord Mansfield favoured the development of legal principle by a journey in the opposite direction. . . .
>
> Unless ... unjust enrichment is seen as a concept rather than a definitive legal principle, substance and dynamism may be restricted by dogma. In turn, the dogma will

---

53   However, cf Edelman J, formerly of the Western Australian Supreme Court and the Federal Court of Australia, but now of the High Court, and co-author of J Edelman and E Bant, *Unjust Enrichment* (2nd edn, Hart 2016) and Keith Mason, former President of the NSW Court of Appeal, one of the authors of K Mason, JW Carter and G Tolhurst, *Restitution Law in Australia* (3rd edn, LexisNexis 2016).

tend to generate new fictions in order to retain support for its thesis. It also may distort well settled principles in other fields, including those respecting equitable doctrines and remedies, so that they answer the newly mandated order of things. Then various theories will compete, each to deny the others. There is support in Australasian legal scholarship for considerable scepticism respecting any all-embracing theory in this field, with the treatment of the disparate as no more than species of the one newly discovered genus.[54]

We must be mindful of the historical and practical ways in which the law has developed, and to pay regard to the reasons courts give for their decisions. There are often good reasons why judges and lawyers have chosen to do things in the way that they have. Insofar as this represents Gummow J's point, it is worth remembering that our legal system works by interpreting what the judges have said and applying it to new fact situations. However, this does not mean that theory is irrelevant. Theory assists in understanding the law and makes us appreciate the law in different ways. There should always be some place for top-down reasoning in the law.   [1.43]

Bottom-up reasoning is explained by Richard Posner as encompassing 'such familiar lawyers' techniques as "plain meaning" and "reasoning by analogy," [where] one starts with the words of a statute or other enactment, or with a case or a mass of cases, and moves from there. . .'.[55] By contrast, Posner explains top-down reasoning as occurring when 'the judge or other legal analyst invents or adopts a theory about an area of law – perhaps about all law – and uses it to organize, criticize, accept or reject, explain or explain away, distinguish or amplify the existing decisions to make them conform to the theory and generate an outcome in each new case as it arises that will be consistent with the theory and with the canonical cases, that is, the cases accepted as authoritative within the theory.'[56] Posner then argues that the two cannot coexist.[57] However, courts cannot avoid making decisions according to a broader theoretical structure. By choosing which cases are analogous and which are not, courts necessarily engage in 'top-down reasoning'. Indeed, courts *must* explain and organise existing case law for the common law to work.[58] Accordingly, the dichotomy between 'top-down reasoning' and 'bottom-up reasoning' is incoherent: courts necessarily do both simultaneously when making a decision. Consequently, the observations of restitutionary scholars are worth considering with a critical and open mind, but with the caveat that the theory does not reflect the way in which Australian courts presently approach these issues.   [1.44]

D   The position of the authors

We are open-minded towards the idea of categorising private law according to broad thematic principles. On the other hand, the historical context in which common law and equitable   [1.45]

---

54   [2001] HCA 68, (2001) 208 CLR 516 [72]–[74].
55   RA Posner, 'Legal Reasoning from the Top Down and from the Bottom Up: The Question of Unenumerated Constitutional Rights' (1992) 59 U Chi L Rev 433, 433.
56   Ibid.
57   Ibid.
58   D Jensen, 'Theories, Principles, Policies and Common Law Adjudication' (2011) 36 AJLP 34.

remedies arose cannot be ignored, and our aim is to provide an accurate description of Australian law rather than a scheme as to how the law should be organised. Where necessary, we describe the important and significant differences between common law and equity. But we are not averse to common law principles informing the development of equity, or equitable principles informing the development of the common law as long as this exercise is undertaken with care.

[1.46]   Courts, whether in common law or equity, tend towards similar solutions to the same problem. If a remedy is more commonly awarded at common law (as, for example, with compensatory damages) there is no sense in requiring equity to 'reinvent the wheel' and develop its own distinct doctrine. The common law has a greater level of experience with compensatory causes of action, and it makes sense to learn from the common law rather than to develop a parallel jurisprudence in equity. By contrast, if a remedy is more commonly awarded in equity (for example, an account of profits) but a court wishes to award it at common law, it is well to learn from the equitable jurisprudence as to the proper bases and limits of such an award. Any 'fusion' should be undertaken with careful consideration of the history and rationales behind the cause of action and the remedy. With careful development, remedies can be extended without fracturing 'the skeleton of principle which gives the body of our law its shape and internal consistency'.[59]

[1.47]   It is also worth observing that the Australian statutory 'remedial smorgasbord' ignores the distinction between common law and equity, and allows a court to award an array of remedies as equal options.[60] In addition, the Lord Cairns' Act provisions have arguably allowed courts to traverse the barriers between common law and equity. In the face of statute, it may be that the divisions between common law and equity will be increasingly broken down, history notwithstanding.

IV   A functional approach to remedies

[1.48]   Remedies may be categorised according to the *goals* that are sought to be achieved (a functional approach). Under this approach, the general goal is ascertained and individual remedies are correlated against that aim.[61] This book, like some other books on this topic,[62] is arranged in a broadly functionalist way, rather than by cause of action.[63] This is because it is useful and instructive to take remedies which perform a particular function (say, compensation) from across private law and to consider them side by side to ascertain their similarities and differences.

---

59   *Mabo v Queensland (No 2)* (1992) 175 CLR 1, 29 (Brennan J).

60   For example, courts may choose equally from the following possible remedies for misleading or deceptive conduct: compensatory damages, injunctions, rescission, and a variety of other awards. The remedies which are not available are the account of profits and punitive damages, although there are civil penalty provisions.

61   M Tilbury, 'Teaching Remedies in Australia' (2000) 39 Brandeis LJ 587, 588–89; J Berryman, 'The Law of Remedies: A Prospectus for Teaching and Scholarship' (2010) 10 OUCLJ 123, 125.

62   See, eg, N Witzleb, E Bant, S Degeling and K Barker, *Remedies: Commentary and Materials* (6th edn, LBC 2015); A Burrows, *Remedies for Torts and Breach of Contract* (3rd edn, OUP 2004).

63   Cf W Covell, K Lupton and J Forder, *Principles of Remedies* (6th edn, LexisNexis 2015); D Wright, *Remedies* (2nd edn, Federation Press 2014).

Our book divides remedies according to the following general functions:

1. compensation;
2. compulsion;
3. deterrence;
4. vindication (including punishment);[64] and
5. restitution.

Zakrzewski has criticised functional approaches, suggesting that the use of 'compulsion' or   [1.49]
similar as a goal should not be included in a series including 'compensation', 'restitution' and
'punishment' because it is taxonomically incoherent.[65] He suggests instead that there should be
a distinction between 'replicative remedies' (which replicate primary rights or secondary
rights) and 'transformative remedies' (which create a new legal relationship different to that
which existed before trial). Thus, payment of a debt or specific performance would be a
replication of a primary right arising from the primary obligation; an award of compensatory
damages for tort or an award of an account of profits for breach of contract would be a
replication of a secondary right arising from the breach.[66] A remedial constructive trust would
be a transformative remedy which creates a new right altogether.[67]

Despite any taxonomical challenges, we persist with a functional scheme. It is pragmatic   [1.50]
and has a certain logical flow because it generally maps the way in which the law operates.
Compensatory awards are a common award in private law, and we consider them first. Where
damages are inadequate the court often attempts to compel the defendant to perform, which is
why remedies which attempt to compel behaviour are considered directly after compensation.
The book then moves to remedies that seek to deter, such as the account of profits, which is
only exceptionally available at common law. Of course, the equitable hierarchical structure is
the inverse to this, but it is helpful with a practical book to present the areas of law in a way that
maps practice to a degree and gives a clear shape to the law.

In what follows, the structure of this book is outlined, along with an interleaving of   [1.51]
some theoretical approaches which may be relevant to the remedy or area in question. We
have not been able to divide remedies perfectly between these categories. Lord Cairns' Act
damages present particular difficulties, as they have been argued to perform multiple functions
(including compensation and prevention of unjust enrichment). They can also be seen as a
monetarised version of specific relief and are therefore placed with specific performance and
injunctions in this book.

Two parts of this book do not fit neatly within a functional scheme. First, proprietary   [1.52]
remedies fulfil more than one function, and there is no general rule for when they will be
awarded, so they are considered in a separate part. Secondly, enforcement of remedies
(including interlocutory injunctions) is also considered in a separate part because these orders

---

64   We concede that vindication and punishment are separate goals, but they are intertwined. We use the
       term vindication in the sense suggested in JNE Varuhas, 'The Concept of "Vindication" in the Law of
       Torts: Rights, Interests and Damages' (2014) 34 OJLS 253, 258.
65   R Zakrzewski, *Remedies Reclassified* (OUP 2005) 68–75.
66   Ibid, 75–84.
67   Ibid, 214–15.

do not usually finally determine a matter; they are procedural in nature, ensuring that the court's process is upheld and that a plaintiff can obtain the remedy she seeks.

A   Parts 1 and 2: Compensation

[1.53]   Parts 1 and 2 consider remedies which seek to compensate for loss. Compensation is the primary remedy which parties seek in private law disputes and thus necessitates consideration at the outset because of its prevalence and importance in private law. Part 1 explores general rules that are not unique to one area of law. Part 2 explores the specific rules for breach of contract, tort, contraventions of the Australian Consumer Law, and equitable obligations. Part 2 contains a separate chapter on personal injury because the rules laid down by courts and legislatures in that area are unique and require detailed consideration.

[1.54]   Compensatory awards are an extremely important part of the private law remedial landscape. Often a plaintiff's central concern is that she has lost something because the defendant has injured her in some way through his actions, and that the defendant should compensate her for that loss.

[1.55]   Some scholars, such as Ernest Weinrib, argue that the only legitimate situation when a court can intervene in a private law dispute is when there has been a gain on behalf of one person, and a loss at the expense of the other.[68] Weinrib draws on Aristotle and Kant to define 'loss' and 'gain' in normative terms. Corrective justice exercised by the court returns the parties to equality, and ensures that the dispute is a bilateral *private* transaction. According to this theory there is no room in the law for remedies that have concerns 'extrinsic' to correcting the plaintiff's loss at the defendant's hands. Remedies which are granted to deter other defendants or to punish the defendant are considered to be illegitimate. Weinrib's theories have proved influential in his home jurisdiction of Canada, but are not influential in Australia.

[1.56]   Some law-and-economics scholars argue that the primary remedy for breach of contract should be compensatory damages, but for very different reasons to the corrective justice scholars. Richard Posner, an academic and former judge, argues that we wish to allow a defendant to efficiently breach his contract where he could contract more profitably with a third party other than the plaintiff, as this maximises efficiency in society.[69] This theory has proved highly influential in the United States. By contrast, in a series of cases Australian and New Zealand courts have unequivocally rejected efficient breach theory.[70]

[1.57]   Several scholars have advanced theories regarding substitutionary (or substitutive) money awards for various kinds of civil wrong, which are said to be distinguishable from normal compensatory damages for pecuniary loss. It is necessary to canvass those theories in some

---

68   See, eg, E Weinrib, 'The Gains and Losses of Corrective Justice' (1994) 44 Duke LJ 277; E Weinrib, 'Restitutionary Damages as Corrective Justice' (2001) 1 *Theoretical Inquiries in Law* 1; E Weinrib, 'Corrective Justice in a Nutshell' (2002) 52 *University of Toronto Law Journal* 349; E Weinrib, 'Punishment and Disgorgement as Contract Remedies' (2003) 78 Chi-Kent L Rev 55; E Weinrib, *The Idea of Private Law* (2nd edn, OUP 2012); E Weinrib, *Corrective Justice* (OUP 2012).
69   R Posner, *Economic Analysis of Law* (9th edn, Aspen 2014) §4.10.
70   *Butler v Countrywide Finance Ltd* [1993] 3 NZLR 623, 635; *Zhu v Treasurer of the State of New South Wales* [2004] HCA 56, (2004) 218 CLR 530 [129]; *Tabcorp Holdings Ltd v Bowen Investments Pty Ltd* [2009] HCA 8, (2009) 236 CLR 272 [13].

detail because there has been some explicit judicial acceptance of them,[71] and arguably some implicit acceptance.[72] While there are differences between the theories, both semantic and substantial, the common core is the distinction between a compensatory money award, which compensates for consequential loss caused by a civil wrong, and another type of award, which is a substitute for the fulfilment of the wrongdoer's primary obligation and is not concerned with the compensation of loss (although it may effectively compensate loss). The latter type of award is often called a substitutionary award. Both types of award are cumulative, subject to the rule against double recovery. Crucially, a substitutionary money award is available even if the wrong has caused no actual loss, and is not subject to the rules of remoteness and mitigation.

In the context of breach of contract, the theories of three scholars will be mentioned. **[1.58]**
Stephen Smith argues that damages in the amount of cost of cure, as opposed to diminution in value, do not compensate for loss suffered but constitute a form of substitute specific performance. They should be available for every breach of contract unless rectification will not be done, or the cost of repair is wholly disproportionate to the value of the loss, or the plaintiff is seeking the award in bad faith.[73] Robert Stevens argues that substitutionary damages represent the value of the infringed right to performance. Their measure is the difference in value between the performance contracted for and that provided.[74] David Winterton argues that substitutionary damages substitute not for the right to performance but for performance itself. Their measure is generally the minimum cost of substitute performance (repair or replacement) whether or not the plaintiff intends to cure the breach, but where that cost is unquantifiable or unreasonable, the price of release from further performance is the next-best substitute for performance.[75]

In the context of tort, Robert Stevens argues that substitutionary damages as the next-best **[1.59]**
substitute for the primary right infringed are assessed objectively as at the time of the infringement and are available even if there is no loss to the plaintiff or gain to the defendant. By contrast, consequential loss is assessed subjectively as at the time of the judgment, and its recovery is subject to limitations that do not apply to the substitutive award, such as remoteness of loss.[76]

In the context of the misapplication of trust property by a trustee, Steven Elliott and others **[1.60]**
distinguish two types of money award. One is an award of 'reparative compensation' for loss caused by the breach of trust. Its measure is the difference between the beneficiary's actual position and the position the beneficiary would have occupied but for the wrong. The other type of award is 'substitutive compensation', which requires the balancing of the account with

---

71   *Agricultural Land Management Ltd v Jackson (No 2)* [2014] WASC 102, (2014) 48 WAR 1 (Edelman J cites Stephen Elliott at [348]–[349]); *Hampton v BHP Billiton Minerals Pty Ltd (No 2)* [2012] WASC 285 (Edelman J cites Robert Stevens at [342]).
72   *Clark v Macourt* [2013] HCA 56, (2013) 253 CLR 1; see [5.51]–[5.56].
73   SA Smith, *Contract Theory* (OUP 2004) 420–23; SA Smith, 'Substitutionary Damages' in CEF Rickett (ed), *Justifying Private Law Remedies* (Hart 2008) 100–05 (where the theory is advanced for the loss of property or services in general).
74   R Stevens, 'Damages and the Right to Performance: A *Golden Victory* or Not?' in JW Neyers, R Bronaugh and SGA Pitel (eds), *Exploring Contract Law* (Hart 2009) 171–74.
75   D Winterton, 'Money Awards Substituting for Performance' [2012] LMCLQ 446, 450–51; D Winterton, *Money Awards in Contract Law* (Hart 2015).
76   R Stevens, *Torts and Rights* (OUP 2007) 60.

the trustee's own money where the property cannot be returned in specie. This award is measured by the property's objective value, and is available regardless of whether the beneficiary's overall financial position is diminished or improved by the deprivation of the property.[77]

[1.61]   Each of the substitutionary theories relies on (mostly English) cases in which a purportedly compensatory award was made in excess of the actual loss suffered by the plaintiff. However, none of the theories has received express judicial approval in either Australia or England. Moreover, the theories have faced criticism. Robert Stevens's theory in particular has been said to conflict with the conventional understanding of damages and the law on mitigation.[78] More fundamentally, the substitutionary theories fail to justify the award of money in response to the occurrence of a civil wrong as such, irrespective of the consequences of the wrong.[79] They fail to explain why it is not sufficient to address the consequences of a wrong (where an enforcement of the primary obligation is impossible or inappropriate) by, for example, compensating loss caused by the wrong or stripping the wrongdoer of profit made through the wrong. Where a civil wrong has not generated any consequences to be addressed and it is for some reason necessary to put on record that a wrong has occurred, this can be done through a declaration by the court or, where available, an award of nominal damages. Indeed, the substitutionary theories cannot account for the availability of nominal damages.[80]

[1.62]   Before moving on from compensation, one further important point should be made. While compensation is pivotal to the private law remedial landscape, Birks argued that one should not be misled into thinking that compensatory remedies are the *only* remedies available for private law wrongs, and decried the 'false monopoly of compensation' in private law.[81] The sheer variety of remedies shows that there is a multiplicity of concerns behind the award of remedies in private law.

B   Part 3: Remedies compelling performance and related remedies

[1.63]   Part 3 considers specific performance, injunctions and other remedies which compel performance of the primary obligation. Of course, within the general category of compulsion, a defendant may be either compelled to do a positive act, or compelled not to do a specific act. In common law causes of action such as tort and contract, typically specific relief is awarded

---

77   SB Elliott, 'Remoteness Criteria in Equity' (2002) 65 Mod LR 588, 590; SB Elliott and C Mitchell, 'Remedies for Dishonest Assistance' (2004) 67 Mod LR 16, 23–34; J Edelman and SB Elliott, 'Money Remedies against Trustees' (2004) 18 TLI 116, 116–25; D Hayton, P Matthews and C Mitchell, *Underhill and Hayton Law Relating to Trusts and Trustees* (19th edn, LexisNexis 2016) [87.7]–[87.11].

78   A Burrows, 'Are "Damages on the *Wrotham Park* Basis" Compensatory, Restitutionary or Neither?' in D Saidov and R Cunnington (eds), *Contract Damages: Domestic and International Perspectives* (Hart 2008) 181–83.

79   See C Webb, 'Justifying Damages' in JW Neyers, R Bronaugh and SGA Pitel (eds), *Exploring Contract Law* (Hart 2009) 167–68.

80   A Burrows, 'Are "Damages on the *Wrotham Park* Basis" Compensatory, Restitutionary or Neither?' in D Saidov and R Cunnington (eds), *Contract Damages: Domestic and International Perspectives* (Hart 2008) 184–85.

81   P Birks, 'The Law of Restitution at the End of an Epoch' (1999) 28 UWALR 52, 54.

where compensatory damages are 'inadequate' and it makes logical sense to consider this category of remedy after considering compensatory damages. Part 3 also considers monetary awards made in lieu of an injunction pursuant to Lord Cairns' Act as they represent a monetarised form of specific relief.

In some senses, compelling a defendant to do what he ought to do (or to desist from doing what he ought not to do) is the ultimate vindication of the plaintiff's primary right. Some scholars, such as Robert Stevens (see above [1.58]–[1.59], [1.61]), argue that tort law more generally can be understood as a vindication of the plaintiff's rights infringed by the defendant, rather than as compensation for foreseeable loss.[82] Other scholars have extended this theory to other areas of law.[83]   [1.64]

It is helpful to consider private law as a mechanism for vindicating rights. It will be seen that courts are often concerned to award the 'next-best' remedy to the primary right itself. However, this must not be overemphasised, and courts balance awarding a 'next-best' remedy against other considerations. For example, even though compensatory damages for breach of contract are less perfect than specific relief, they are the preferred remedy (where they provide an adequate substitute for performance) because they are less intrusive to the defendant. There is a balancing of the rights of the parties. Lord Cairns' Act damages are sometimes awarded in lieu of an injunction or specific performance precisely because it is not appropriate to compel the defendant to do a particular thing but it is still appropriate that the plaintiff receive some monetary sum in lieu of the specific relief. However, Lord Cairns' Act damages also have other functions (including, arguably, a restitutionary aspect), which make them difficult to categorise.   [1.65]

C   Part 4: Remedies as vindication

Part 4 considers remedies with a vindicatory function, such as self-help remedies, exemplary damages, aggravated damages, apologies, declarations and nominal damages, and miscellaneous awards under the Australian Consumer Law.   [1.66]

Vindication of rights in the broad sense is the overarching aim of all remedies if we take vindication to mean a making good of, and recognition of, the plaintiff's rights.[84] For a plaintiff's rights to be recognised, she must have an adequate remedy. For example, in *Ashby v White*, Holt CJ said: [1.67]

> If the plaintiff has a right, he must of necessity have a means to vindicate and maintain it, and a remedy if he is injured in the exercise or enjoyment to it; and, indeed, it is a vain thing to imagine a right without a remedy; for want of right and want of remedy are reciprocal.[85]

---

82   R Stevens, *Torts and Rights* (OUP 2007).
83   See, eg, B McFarlane, *The Structure of Property Law* (Hart 2008).
84   Stephen Smith has argued that this is the only function of damages awards: SA Smith, 'Duties, Liabilities and Damages' (2012) 125 Harvard LR 1727, 1728. See also JNE Varuhas, 'The Concept of "Vindication" in the Law of Torts: Rights, Interests and Damages' (2014) 34 OJLS 253, 258.
85   *Ashby v White* (1703) 2 Ld Raym 938; 92 ER 126, 136. For a more recent expression of a similar sentiment, see *Chester v Afshar* [2004] UKHL 41, [2005] 1 AC 134 [87] (Lord Hope): 'The function of the law is to enable rights to be vindicated and to provide remedies when duties have been breached'.

[1.68]   However, vindication theory has been criticised on the basis that it is not clear what precisely is meant by 'vindication'.[86] Varuhas identifies a more specific sense of vindication, where the law attests to, affirms, and reinforces the importance and inherent value of particular interests.[87] He argues that vindication is particularly evident in the torts actionable *per se*, which protect interests such as bodily integrity,[88] property rights,[89] reputation,[90] economic interests[91] and fair process.[92] It is argued here that vindicatory remedies include remedies which allow one to make one's own rights good,[93] remedies which seek to punish the defendant,[94] and remedies which seek to assuage the plaintiff or to recognise the distressing impact of the defendant's conduct on the plaintiff.[95] All of these remedies involve the legal affirmation of the importance and value of certain interests, which is why we group these remedies together.

[1.69]   Exemplary damages have a clear punitive aspect as well. In general, punishment is a matter of criminal law and not a rationale that enters private law remedies. Some scholars have argued that punishment should not enter private law at all.[96] Ultimately, it seems that exemplary damages are here to stay; the main issues are first, whether they can be awarded for causes of action other than tort, and secondly, the extent to which they are available in tort itself.

D   Part 5: Account of profits and other gain-based relief for wrongs

[1.70]   Part 5 considers accounts of profit, disgorgement, and other forms of gain-based relief. In equity, the account of profit is the remedy of choice where a defaulting fiduciary has made a profit as a result of his breach, and it is available subject to discretionary considerations. By contrast, gain-based awards have not been openly available for common law wrongs, and are generally available only if compensatory damages are inadequate and specific relief is unavailable. Part 5 also explores 'reasonable fee' damages, as both authors of this book have argued

---

86   K Barker, 'Private and Public: The Mixed Concept of Vindication in Torts and Private Law' in S Pitel, J Neyers and E Chamberlain (eds), *Tort Law: Challenging Orthodoxy* (Hart 2013) 59.

87   JNE Varuhas, 'The Concept of "Vindication" in the Law of Torts: Rights, Interests and Damages' (2014) 34 OJLS 253, 258.

88   Assault, battery, false imprisonment.

89   Nuisance, trespass to land, wrongful interference with goods.

90   Defamation.

91   Eg interference with contractual relations, intimidation, conspiracy, deceit, injurious falsehood, passing off.

92   Misfeasance in public office, malicious prosecution, maintenance and champerty.

93   JNE Varuhas, 'The Concept of "Vindication" in the Law of Torts: Rights, Interests and Damages' (2014) 34 OJLS 253, 290 (nominal damages).

94   Ibid (exemplary damages).

95   Ibid, 284 (aggravated damages).

96   E Weinrib, 'Punishment and Disgorgement as Contract Remedies' (2003) 78 Chi-Kent L Rev 55, 86–87; A Beever, 'The Structure of Aggravated and Exemplary Damages' (2003) 23 OJLS 87; S Todd, 'A New Zealand Perspective on Exemplary Damages' (2004) 33 *Common Law World Review* 255. Cf, however, R Stevens, *Torts and Rights* (OUP 2007) 85; J Edelman, *Gain-Based Damages – Contract, Tort, Equity and Intellectual Property* (Hart 2002) 19; R Cunnington, 'Should punitive damages be part of the judicial arsenal in contract cases?' (2006) 26 LS 369.

elsewhere that these awards are gain-based.[97] Finally, we consider the availability of allowances for work and skill, and the operation of discretionary factors and bars to relief.

[1.71]

The primary rationale of gain-based remedies has been identified as deterrence and prophylaxis of breach by a range of scholars.[98] Deterrence looks not to the dispute in question, but to the future conduct of the specific defendant (specific deterrence) and the future conduct of other potential defendants (general deterrence). By stripping the defendant of his gain (or part of his gain), the defendant (and other potential wrongdoers) will be deterred from engaging in similar conduct in the future. Deterrence and encouraging people to adhere to the law in the most efficient way appeals to law-and-economics scholars.

E   Part 6: Restitution and giving back

Part 6 considers personal remedies for unjust enrichment such as the action for money had and received, the *quantum meruit* and the *quantum valebat*. It also considers the defences to a claim for restitutionary remedies, and the overlap between unjust enrichment law and contract law.

[1.72]

These remedies have at their heart the rationale of prevention of unjust enrichment. Unjust enrichment has come to prominence in recent years with a blossoming of restitutionary scholars in England and Wales. These scholars have identified the action for unjust enrichment as an important cause of action in private law concealed by notions such as 'quasi-contract'. They see its proper recognition as reshaping private law generally. In Australia, as will be discussed in greater detail in Part 6, the High Court has not been receptive towards unjust enrichment scholarship and has been deeply sceptical of the restitutionary reshaping of private law generally.

[1.73]

Another issue worth noting is the difficulty in distinguishing between the cause of action and the remedy. Part 6 briefly examines the nature of the restitutionary causes of action in order to explain the remedies available, because the cause of action (such as an action for money had and received) is simultaneously the restitutionary remedy.

[1.74]

Part 6 also considers rescission of contracts and other transfers. It considers common law, equitable and statutory rescission, the requirement of *restitutio in integrum*, election, partial rescission, bars to rescission and the possible proprietary consequences of rescission. This topic follows unjust enrichment because there is a certain synergy between notions of unjust enrichment and the way in which rescission operates to unwind transfers. An understanding of unjust enrichment is helpful and informs an understanding of rescission. Even though rescission is placed under the broader rationale of restitution and giving back, some aspects of rescission arguably have a self-help aspect.

[1.75]

---

97   K Barnett, *Accounting for Profit for Breach of Contract: Theory and Practice* (Hart 2012) 18–22, 164–65; S Harder, *Measuring Damages in the Law of Obligations: The Search for Harmonised Principles* (Hart 2010) 179–81.

 98   J Edelman, *Gain-Based Damages: Contract, Tort, Equity and Intellectual Property* (Hart 2002) 83–86; I Samet, 'Guarding the Fiduciary's Conscience – A Justification of a Stringent Profit-Stripping Rule' (2008) 28 OJLS 763; S Worthington, 'Reconsidering Disgorgement for Wrongs' (1999) 62 Mod LR 218; M Conaglen, *Fiduciary Loyalty: Protecting the Due Performance of Non-Fiduciary Duties* (Hart 2010); R Cooter and B Freedman, 'The Fiduciary Relationship: Its Economic Character and Legal Consequences' (1991) 66 NYULR 1045; P Devonshire, *Account of Profits* (Thomson Reuters 2013) 58–59.

F   Part 7: Proprietary remedies

[1.76]   Part 7 considers proprietary remedies. There are several forms of proprietary remedy (the constructive trust, the proprietary power, and the lien), but courts have not traditionally exercised the choice between these remedies in a principled manner. We consider the award of proprietary remedies in the context of equitable wrongdoing, in the context of unjust enrichment, and in the context of rescission (linking to the discussion in Part 6). Part 7 notes the operation of discretionary factors and bars to relief in this area because proprietary remedies are by and large creatures of equity. Finally, Part 7 discusses the need for more defined and certain criteria for the award of proprietary remedies.

G   Part 8: Enforcement of remedies

[1.77]   Part 8 considers enforcement of remedies, including interlocutory injunctions, other pre-judgment remedies and the ways in which remedies are enforced post-judgment. This section is concerned with those orders of the court which allow the court to enforce final remedies effectively.

H   Conclusion

[1.78]   In writing this book, we have attempted to ensure that our discussion of private law remedies flows in a logical fashion, and that recurring issues (such as the role of remoteness in various species of compensatory damages) are dealt with clearly in each chapter. Our intention is to create a coherent functional narrative of remedies which is accessible to a variety of audiences ranging from the newcomer to the specialist.

PART 1

GENERAL PRINCIPLES OF COMPENSATION

2

ASSESSMENT OF COMPENSATION

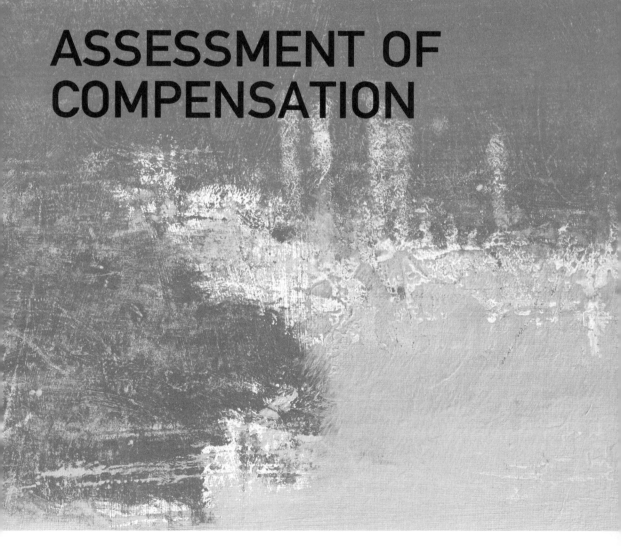

I   Introduction

[2.1]   This chapter discusses the general principles relating to the assessment of compensation for a civil wrong. Since courts and legislatures often lay down legal rules for a certain area of law, the assessment of compensation differs between areas. This is why Part 2 contains separate chapters for contract, tort, the Australian Consumer Law and equity. However, there are several commonalities between the areas, in particular contract and tort. This chapter discusses the rules that are common to at least contract and tort. Most of them also apply in equity and under the Australian Consumer Law. Deviations from those rules in equity or under the Australian Consumer Law are discussed in the relevant chapters. This chapter also provides a brief introduction to those matters that differ between contract and tort. Comprehensive treatment is given to the date of assessment; even though there are significant differences between the causes of actions, there has been considerable convergence.

II   The compensatory principle and the identification of the wrong

[2.2]   Compensation for civil wrongdoing aims to place the plaintiff in the same position financially as if the wrong had not occurred.[1] In general, the court awards compensation for all losses that the plaintiff would not have suffered but for the wrong. The amount of compensation is not proportionate to the defendant's degree of culpability. However, compensation for losses factually caused by a civil wrong may be denied on the ground that they fall outside the scope of the defendant's liability; see [3.69]–[3.119].

[2.3]   Conversely, an award of compensation must not place the plaintiff in a better position than if the wrong had not occurred.[2] It follows that account must generally be taken of benefits that the plaintiff has obtained because of the wrong,[3] and of detriments that the plaintiff would have incurred but for the wrong. In *Butler v Egg and Egg Pulp Marketing Board*,[4] statute provided that property in eggs, when they came into existence, was divested from the producer and vested in a marketing board. The producer was entitled to a share of the proceeds obtained by the board from a sale of the eggs. A producer failed to deliver eggs to the board and sold them to a third party. This constituted a conversion of the eggs. The trial judge calculated damages by reference to the market value of the eggs at the time of the conversion. The High Court of Australia overturned that judgment, holding that the board's loss was the difference between the amount that the board would have obtained from a sale of the eggs and the amount that the board in that event would have had to pay to the producer.

[2.4]   Since compensation aims to place the plaintiff in the same position as if the wrong had not occurred, it is necessary to determine exactly what would have happened had the wrong not occurred. This requires precision in determining what the wrong is. For example, suppose that the plaintiff, a pedestrian, suffered injuries as a result of being hit by a car driven by the

---

1   Eg *Haines v Bendall* (1991) 172 CLR 60, 63; *McCrohon v Harith* [2010] NSWCA 67 [52], [60].
2   Eg *Haines v Bendall* (1991) 172 CLR 60, 63; *McCrohon v Harith* [2010] NSWCA 67 [53].
3   However, there are significant exceptions; see [2.39]–[2.43], [7.72]–[7.79].
4   (1966) 114 CLR 185.

defendant at an excessive speed. The (putative) wrong is not the fact that the defendant happened to drive his car at that place and time. It is the fact that the defendant drove faster than was permitted or prudent. In order to calculate the loss (if any) caused by the (putative) wrong, it is therefore necessary to determine what would have happened had the defendant adhered to a reasonable speed while still driving at the same place at the same time. If the plaintiff would still have been hit, the loss to be compensated is only that part of the plaintiff's actual loss that the plaintiff would not have suffered had the defendant driven reasonably. If the plaintiff would still have suffered exactly the same injuries, the defendant is not liable to compensate any loss.[5]

The identification of the wrong is particularly important where an incorrect statement of fact by the defendant induced the plaintiff to take, or refrain from taking, a certain action, for example to enter into a contract. In those circumstances, there are two possible wrongs.   **[2.5]**

First, the wrong can be the fact that the state of affairs is not as represented by the defendant. Shortly, the wrong is the non-existence of the represented facts. At least at common law, the discrepancy between the actual state of affairs and the state of affairs as represented can be a wrong only if the defendant gave a contractual guarantee that the state of affairs is as represented. Compensation for that wrong aims to place the plaintiff in the position as if the represented state of affairs existed.[6] For example, suppose that a vendor of land gives the purchaser, a developer, a contractual guarantee that the land is zoned in such a way as to permit development.[7] If the land is not so zoned, the loss resulting from the breach of guarantee is the loss of the profit that the purchaser would have made from developing the land. This is called expectation loss.[8]   **[2.6]**

Secondly, the wrong can be the defendant's failure to represent the true state of affairs. The defendant may be liable for deceit, negligent misrepresentation or breach of s 18 of the Australian Consumer Law. Compensation for that wrong aims to place the plaintiff in the position as if the defendant had stated the true facts.[9] This is called reliance loss.[10] In the example given in the preceding paragraph, compensation for misrepresentation aims to place the purchaser in the position as if she had not purchased the land. Compensable loss may include the cost of entering into the contract, the cost of exploring the land, and so on. But it does not include the loss of the profit the purchaser would have made from developing *that* land.[11] It is possible that the purchaser, had the vendor stated the true facts, would have bought another plot of land and made a profit from its development. This is part of the plaintiff's reliance loss. Reliance loss may thus be of the same amount as expectation loss. But the calculation involves different factors.   **[2.7]**

---

5   *Sam (aka Al-Sam) v Atkins* [2005] EWCA Civ 1452, [2006] RTR 14; T Honoré, 'Necessary and Sufficient Conditions in Tort Law' in DG Owen (ed), *Philosophical Foundations of Tort Law* (Clarendon 1995) 367–74.

6   *Gates v City Mutual Life Assurance Society Ltd* (1986) 160 CLR 1, 11–12.

7   Facts of *Kyogle Shire Council v Francis* (1988) 13 NSWLR 396.

8   *Gates v City Mutual Life Assurance Society Ltd* (1986) 160 CLR 1, 11–12.

9   *South Australia v Johnson* (1982) 42 ALR 161, 170; *Gates v City Mutual Life Assurance Society Ltd* (1986) 160 CLR 1, 12.

10   *Gates v City Mutual Life Assurance Society Ltd* (1986) 160 CLR 1, 11–12.

11   *Kyogle Shire Council v Francis* (1988) 13 NSWLR 396, 411–14, 417–18.

III Losses and benefits

A Non-pecuniary loss

[2.8]   A civil wrong may adversely affect the plaintiff's financial situation. It may cause the plaintiff to incur medical expenses, to incur the cost of repairing property, to lose assets, and so on. Such loss is called pecuniary loss. A civil wrong may also adversely affect the plaintiff without affecting the plaintiff's financial situation. For example, the plaintiff's reputation may be affected or the plaintiff may suffer anxiety, distress, pain, and so on. Those detriments constitute loss because people are willing to spend money to avoid them. Such loss is called non-pecuniary loss.

[2.9]   Since non-pecuniary loss constitutes a form of loss, the compensatory principle calls for its compensation. Two objections might be made. First, awarding money as compensation for non-pecuniary loss may be considered inappropriate since no amount of money can place the plaintiff in the same position as if the loss had not been suffered. However, an award of money is the next-best thing the law can provide.[12] Secondly, placing a money figure on non-pecuniary loss may be considered impossible. It is indeed difficult. But problems of quantification must not deprive the plaintiff of compensation for loss suffered.

[2.10]   In Australian law, the availability and amount of compensation for non-pecuniary loss depends upon the cause of action. In contract, compensation for non-pecuniary loss is generally barred at common law, but there are significant exceptions; see [5.73]–[5.80]. Non-pecuniary loss is generally compensable in tort and under the Australian Consumer Law. However, legislation imposes a maximum amount that may be awarded in defamation actions (see [6.9]), and, with the exception of the Australian Capital Territory, regulates the availability and/or amount of compensation for non-pecuniary loss resulting from personal injury; see [7.63]–[7.68]. The latter restriction is significant because some types of non-pecuniary loss have themselves been held to constitute 'personal injury' for the purpose of some of the statutes; see [7.16]–[7.20]. In equity, non-pecuniary loss is not generally compensable, but breach of confidence constitutes an exception; see [9.11]–[9.13]. The details of all these rules are discussed in the relevant chapters.

B Cost of repair and diminution in value

[2.11]   Where the defendant has wrongfully damaged or destroyed the plaintiff's property (a building or goods) or has breached a contractual promise to do certain work on the plaintiff's property (for example, to construct a building or repair goods), there are usually two methods by which the plaintiff's loss can be calculated. One method is to take the amount of money that the plaintiff needs to spend to have the property brought into the state in which it would be without the defendant's wrong. This will be called cost of repair. It includes, for example, the cost of having damaged property repaired and the cost of employing another builder to construct the building that the defendant should have constructed. The other method of calculating the plaintiff's loss is to take the difference between the plaintiff's actual financial

---

12   Sometimes, an apology by the defendant may be an effective remedy. But an apology cannot be ordered by a court. Apologies are discussed at [15.2]–[15.13].

position and the financial position the plaintiff would be in without the defendant's wrong. This will be called diminution in value. For example, where the defendant has damaged the plaintiff's property, diminution in value is the difference between the value of the property with the damage and its value without the damage.

Since the two methods can yield significantly different figures, it must be determined which of the two methods is used. This depends upon a number of factors. Very broadly, cost of repair is awarded unless repair is unreasonable. The details are complex and differ between claims in contract and claims in tort, and may differ within tort between land and goods, and between commercial and private property. The rules are discussed separately in the relevant contexts; see [5.26]–[5.48], [6.12]–[6.20], [6.26]–[6.30]. [2.12]

A few general points on the cost of repair will be made here. Loss may be calculated by the cost of repair even though repair has not been carried out. But the plaintiff is not then obliged to spend the compensation on repair. A court is not concerned with the manner in which the plaintiff uses the compensation. The plaintiff has absolute freedom in that respect.[13] It does not necessarily follow, however, that an intention by the plaintiff to carry out repair is always irrelevant. Such an intention may constitute a prerequisite for an award of cost of repair. This will be discussed in the relevant context. [2.13]

Where no repair has been carried out before trial, the court will use expert evidence or quotes or tenders by contractors to determine the cost of repair. Goods and services tax payable by the plaintiff in relation to the repair work must be taken into account,[14] unless the plaintiff is entitled to an input tax credit;[15] see [2.55]. Where the repair has been carried out before trial at a cost lower than that estimated by experts, the court cannot award more than the actual cost of repair.[16] Where the repair has been carried out before trial at a cost higher than the reasonable cost estimated by experts, a court may award only that reasonable cost.[17] [2.14]

For some scholars, an award of damages measured by reference to the cost of repair is not of compensatory nature (although it may have the effect of compensating loss) but constitutes an award of what they call substitutionary damages.[18] The theories of substitutionary damages, which are relevant in various contexts, are considered at [1.57]–[1.61]. [2.15]

The repair of damaged property or replacement of destroyed property may place the plaintiff in a better position than without the defendant's wrong, the plaintiff having a new item rather than an old one. The question arises whether a deduction from the cost of repair or replacement must be made to reflect this betterment. This is discussed in the next section. [2.16]

---

13   *O'Brien v McKean* (1968) 118 CLR 540, 559–60; *Cullen v Trappell* (1980) 146 CLR 1, 15; *Todorovic v Waller* (1981) 150 CLR 402, 412.

14   *Nemeth v Prynew Pty Ltd* [2009] NSWSC 511 [3].

15   *Gagner Pty Ltd v Canturi Corporation Pty Ltd* [2009] NSWCA 413, (2009) 262 ALR 691 [147], [151].

16   *Hyder Consulting (Australia) Pty Ltd v Wilh Wilhelmsen Agency Pty Ltd* [2001] NSWCA 313, (2001) 18 BCL 122 [18]–[20], [91]–[103]; *Stocovaz v Fung* [2007] NSWCA 199 [39].

17   *Stocovaz v Fung* [2007] NSWCA 199 [39]; *Piling Contractors (Qld) Pty Ltd v Prynew Pty Ltd* [2008] NSWSC 118 [26].

18   Eg SA Smith, 'Substitutionary Damages' in CEF Rickett (ed), *Justifying Private Law Remedies* (Hart 2008) 93–100; D Winterton, 'Money Awards Substituting for Performance' [2012] LMCLQ 446, 450–51; D Winterton, *Money Awards in Contract Law* (Hart 2015).

C   Betterment discount

[2.17]   The repair or replacement of damaged or destroyed property may place the plaintiff in a better position than she would have been in without the defendant's wrong if the defendant is obliged to compensate for the full cost of repair or replacement. Suppose that the defendant has wrongfully destroyed the plaintiff's 10-year-old tractor. The plaintiff, who needs a tractor to work his farm, buys a brand new tractor of the same make and model as the one destroyed by the defendant. Since the new tractor will last longer than the old one would have, the plaintiff will be better off than without the defendant's wrong if the defendant is obliged to compensate the full purchase price of the new tractor.

[2.18]   The question arises how the plaintiff's compensation is to be calculated in those circumstances. In *Tyco Australia Pty Ltd v Optus Networks Pty Ltd*, Hodgson JA pronounced two rules:

> First, if a plaintiff choses [sic] to acquire a more valuable asset than that which had to be replaced, where the plaintiff could for a lesser expenditure have acquired an asset that would have been as satisfactory as that replaced, the plaintiff cannot recover more than that lesser expenditure ...
>
> Second, even if there is no alternative available to a plaintiff other than to acquire a more valuable asset, a plaintiff may have to give credit reflecting the greater value of this asset to the plaintiff, if there is a benefit to the plaintiff which is not remote in time or speculative, and which can be quantified.[19]

[2.19]   In line with this exposition of the law, it is necessary to distinguish three categories of case, although the demarcation lines between them may be blurred. The first category of case is where the plaintiff could have chosen a non-improving remedial measure. The second category of case is where a non-improving remedial measure was not available and the plaintiff has derived concrete benefits from the improvement. The third and most difficult category of case is where a non-improving remedial measure was not available and the plaintiff has not derived concrete benefits from the improvement, but enjoys the abstract advantage of having a new rather than an old item. These three categories of case will now be considered.

[2.20]   It must first be asked whether there was available a remedial measure that would have placed the plaintiff in exactly the position (and no more) that the plaintiff would have been in but for the defendant's wrong. Where such a remedial measure was practically available to the plaintiff, the plaintiff's decision to undertake a more expensive improvement or upgrading of the property instead constitutes an intervening act.[20] Neither the costs nor the benefits of the upgrading are the defendant's concern. The plaintiff can claim no less and no more than the cost of the basic, non-improving remedial measure. In *State Transport Authority v Twiteco Pty Ltd*,[21] a 70-year-old railway bridge was substantially damaged. Its owner decided to install a new model capable of bearing heavier trains and requiring less maintenance. The owner was

---

19   [2004] NSWCA 333 [261]–[262]; approvingly cited in *Walker Group Constructions Pty Ltd v Tzaneros Investments Pty Ltd* [2017] NSWCA 27, (2017) 94 NSWLR 108 [203], [205].

20   Where, prior to the defendant's wrong, the plaintiff had already planned to undertake the upgrading at the time it did take place, the defendant is not liable at all for lack of factual causation.

21   (1984) Aust Torts Reports 80–596.

awarded the cost of reconstructing the old bridge. In *Gagner Pty Ltd v Canturi Corporation Pty Ltd*,[22] water escaping from the defendant's restaurant damaged 10% of the floor in the plaintiff's jewellery store on the floor below. A repair of the damaged part of the floor would have taken 10 days. The plaintiff decided to refurbish the whole floor, which required the jewellery store to be closed for 29 days. The plaintiff was awarded the cost of repairing only the damaged part of the floor and loss of business for 10 days.

Things are different where a basic, non-improving remedial measure was not available to the plaintiff or where, while it was strictly available, the improving remedial measure can still be regarded as nothing more than a response to the defendant's wrong. In those circumstances, the improving remedial measure can be attributed to the defendant's wrong, and its cost is the starting point in calculating the compensation to be awarded. The question arises whether a deduction must be made to reflect the fact that the plaintiff is better off than without the defendant's wrong. [2.21]

Concrete benefits actually derived from the superior position must be deducted unless they are collateral. This is a consequence of the more general rule that benefits flowing from a mitigating action of the plaintiff must be deducted unless they are collateral; see [2.28]. That rule is discussed in the next section. The rule was applied in the context of property improvement in *Tyco Australia Pty Ltd v Optus Networks Pty Ltd*,[23] where the defendant's negligence caused significant damage to a first-class data centre of the plaintiff. In mitigating its loss, the plaintiff upgraded another data centre to a first-class data centre. The plaintiff's benefit of having obtained an additional first-class data centre was taken into account in assessing damages. [2.22]

Where the plaintiff has not derived concrete benefits from the improving remedial measure, it is not settled whether a deduction from its cost must be made to reflect the abstract advantage that the plaintiff enjoys by having a new rather than an old item,[24] the quantum to be proved by the defendant.[25] A deduction has been approved in some cases[26] and rejected in others.[27] The division is illustrated by split decisions of the NSW Court of Appeal in two cases with different outcomes. [2.23]

The first case is *Hoad v Scone Motors Pty Ltd*.[28] The defendants negligently caused the destruction of the plaintiffs' seven-year-old tractor and three-year-old mower. The plaintiffs urgently needed a tractor and a mower to crop lucerne on their farm. Being unable to find suitable second-hand equipment, the plaintiffs purchased a new tractor and a new mower. The plaintiffs normally replaced their tractor every five years, but they had not replaced the [2.24]

22   [2009] NSWCA 413, (2009) 262 ALR 691.
23   [2004] NSWCA 333.
24   In *Tabcorp Holdings Ltd v Bowen Investments Pty Ltd* [2009] HCA 8, (2009) 236 CLR 272 [24]–[25], the issue was left open since the defendant tenant had not argued for a betterment discount.
25   *Paper Australia Pty Ltd v Ansell Ltd* [2007] VSC 484 [364].
26   *Bushells Pty Ltd v Commonwealth* [1948] St R Qd 79, 92; *Eastern Construction Co Pty Ltd v Southern Portland Cement Ltd* [1960] NSWR 505, 506; *Westwood v Cordwell* [1983] 1 Qd R 276, 277–78; *Nationwide News Ltd v Power and Water Authority* [2006] NTSC 32 [121]–[122].
27   *Bland Shire Council v Anthoness* [1960] NSWR 254, 260–61; *South Parklands Hockey & Tennis Centre Inc v Brown Falconer Group Pty Ltd* [2004] SASC 81, (2004) 88 SASR 65 [126]; *Port Kembla Coal Terminal Ltd v Braverus Maritime Inc* [2004] FCA 1211, (2004) 140 FCR 445 [488]; *Clifford v Dove* [2006] NSWSC 314 [27]; *Paper Australia Pty Ltd v Ansell Ltd* [2007] VSC 484 [363].
28   [1977] 1 NSWLR 88.

tractor destroyed by the defendants because they were about to give up the lease of the farm. In the New South Wales Court of Appeal, Moffitt P and Hutley JA held that the plaintiffs could not claim compensation for the full cost of buying the replacement equipment because they were better off with the new equipment. Samuels JA, dissenting, opined that the plaintiffs were entitled to compensation for the full cost of buying the new equipment (without betterment discount) because they had made a reasonable attempt to mitigate their loss.[29]

[2.25] The second case is *Hyder Consulting (Australia) Pty Ltd v Wilh Wilhelmsen Agency Pty Ltd*.[30] The defendants were negligent in designing the premises of the plaintiff's container terminal. The pavement was supposed to last 20 years. However, soon after business commenced, the pavement began to fail under the heavy loads transported on the premises. After using the inadequate pavement for four years, the plaintiffs had it replaced with a sufficiently strong pavement, which was to last for 20 years. The plaintiffs claimed the cost of replacing the pavement, and the defendants argued that a deduction of 20% ought to be made from that cost because the new pavement would last for four years longer than the old pavement (even if sound) would have done. In the NSW Court of Appeal, Sheller JA and Giles JA rejected a betterment discount on the ground that the defective pavement could not have been replaced with a four-year-old sound pavement and that a percentage discount was too crude a method.[31] Meagher JA, dissenting, said, without further explanation, that a betterment discount of 20% ought to be made.[32]

[2.26] It is difficult to reconcile the two decisions considered at [2.24]–[2.25]. It might be thought that the difference lies in the nature of the property damaged. Goods such as tractors need regular replacement whereas pavements and other structures do not.[33] However, a general distinction between goods and structures would be unconvincing. Few structures last forever, and some goods last even longer than some structures. So the real criterion would be the frequency of replacement, but any demarcation line (such as five years or 10 years) would be arbitrary.

[2.27] The problem in the circumstances under discussion is that the plaintiff has made a capital investment (undertaking the improving remedial measure) but has yet to reap concrete benefits from it. If the plaintiff is compensated for the full cost of the improving remedial measure, the plaintiff will, in some sense, be better off than without the defendant's wrong. However, making a betterment discount (without more) will not reflect the fact that the plaintiff would not have made the capital investment but for the defendant's wrong. As a middle course between the two extremes, it has been suggested that a betterment discount should be made

29   Samuels JA relied on *Harbutt's 'Plasticine' Ltd v Wayne Tank and Pump Co Ltd* [1970] 1 QB 447, where the owner of a factory that had been wrongfully destroyed recovered the full cost of rebuilding the factory, without betterment discount.

30   [2001] NSWCA 313, (2001) 18 BCL 122.

31   Ibid, [55] (Sheller JA), [107] (Giles JA). The reasoning was adopted, on very similar facts, in *Walker Group Constructions Pty Ltd v Tzaneros Investments Pty Ltd* [2017] NSWCA 27, (2017) 94 NSWLR 108 [206], [208].

32   [2001] NSWCA 313, (2001) 18 BCL 122 [22].

33   C Penhallurick, 'The Principle of "Betterment" in Damages for Contract and Tort' (2002) 22 Aust Bar Rev 109, 115; A Sidhu, 'The Issue of Betterment in Claims for Reinstatement Costs' (2016) 16 Macquarie LJ 127, 151–52.

but the plaintiff should be compensated for the cost of the capital investment – that is, the value of the use of the capital or the cost of borrowing it.[34]

D   Benefits flowing from mitigating actions of the plaintiff

The third rule of the doctrine of mitigation (discussed at [3.132]–[3.138]), as identified in [2.28] *McGregor on Damages*[35] and adopted by Australian courts,[36] is that the defendant is entitled to the benefit accruing from mitigating steps taken by the plaintiff unless the benefit is regarded as collateral; this applies even where it would have been reasonable for the plaintiff not to take the mitigating steps. The defendant bears the onus of proving that benefits have flowed from a mitigating action,[37] but the evidential onus may shift to the plaintiff in respect of matters that are solely within the plaintiff's knowledge.[38] It has been said that uncertainty in respect of whether the plaintiff has obtained benefits is to be resolved on the balance of probabilities rather than by making a proportionate discount according to the degree of probability.[39]

The avoided loss rule is unexceptional where certain loss that could have occurred did not [2.29] in fact occur because the plaintiff took protective measures. In *Haines v Bendall*,[40] an injured worker received statutory workers' compensation, of which about $50 000 was for non-pecuniary loss. The worker subsequently received common law damages, of which $75 000 was for past non-pecuniary loss. On receipt of the damages, the workers' compensation was to be paid back. The High Court of Australia held, by majority, that pre-judgment interest on damages for past non-pecuniary loss could be awarded on only $25 000 because the plaintiff had not lost the use of the money in the amount of $50 000. Similarly, there can be no compensation for the cost of repair (or diminution in value) of property that was not in fact damaged because the plaintiff responded to the defendant's wrong by successfully protecting the property.[41]

The concept of avoided loss has also been extended to cover loss that is set-off by [2.30] benefits flowing from mitigating steps by the plaintiff. This wide concept of avoided loss has been derived from *British Westinghouse Electric and Manufacturing Co Ltd v Underground Electric Railways Company of London Ltd*.[42] The defendant supplied steam turbines

---

34   *James Street Hardware and Furniture Co Ltd v Spizziri* (1987) 62 OR (2d) 385, 404; *J & B Caldwell Ltd v Logan House Retirement Home Ltd* [1999] 2 NZLR 99, 107; Penhallurick, ibid, 117–18; SM Waddams, *The Law of Damages* (5th edn, Canada Law Book 2012) [1.2790].

35   J Edelman, *McGregor on Damages* (20th edn, Sweet & Maxwell 2018) [9–006].

36   Eg *Monroe Schneiders Associates (Inc) v No 1 Raberem Pty Ltd* (1991) 33 FCR 1, 27; *Ruthol Pty Ltd v Tricon (Australia) Pty Ltd* [2005] NSWCA 443, (2005) 12 BPR 23,923 [40].

37   *Tyco Australia Pty Ltd v Optus Networks Pty Ltd* [2004] NSWCA 333 [264] (Hodgson JA); *Ruthol Pty Ltd v Tricon (Australia) Pty Ltd* [2005] NSWCA 443, (2005) 12 BPR 23,923 [44]; *Tasman Capital Pty Ltd v Sinclair* [2008] NSWCA 248, (2008) 75 NSWLR 1 [72], [93]–[95].

38   *Harold R Finger & Co Pty Ltd v Karellas Investments Pty Ltd* [2015] NSWSC 354 [563].

39   *Tyco Australia Pty Ltd v Optus Networks Pty Ltd* [2004] NSWCA 333 [197] (Handley JA).

40   (1991) 172 CLR 60. The case was applied, eg, in *Screenco Pty Ltd v R L Dew Pty Ltd* [2003] NSWCA 319, (2003) 58 NSWLR 720.

41   The plaintiff may be able to recover the cost of the protecting measures under the second rule of mitigation unless the measures prevented the wrong from occurring; see [3.138]. Where the property was damaged and the plaintiff repaired it personally, damages for the commercial cost of repair may be awarded: *Powercor Australia Ltd v Thomas* [2012] VSCA 87, (2012) 43 VR 220 [46]–[73].

42   [1912] AC 673.

to the plaintiff railway company and guaranteed that they would consume a certain amount of coal. The turbines consumed much more coal than guaranteed. The plaintiff used the turbines for a few years but then replaced them with different turbines which, because of technological advances, were much more efficient than the defendant's turbines, even if the latter had conformed to the contract. The House of Lords held that, in calculating the plaintiff's damages, the benefits derived by the plaintiff from the superiority of the substitute turbines had to be deducted from the cost of installing them. Viscount Haldane LC, speaking for the House, said that 'when in the course of his business [the plaintiff] has taken action arising out of the transaction, which action has diminished his loss, the effect in actual diminution of the loss he has suffered may be taken into account even though there was no duty on him to act'.[43]

[2.31]   Viscount Haldane LC seems to have taken the view that by purchasing more efficient turbines the plaintiff had done more than required by the avoidable loss rule. This is why *British Westinghouse* is often seen as an example of a case in which avoided loss was held irrecoverable even though it would have been reasonable to incur the loss.[44] However, it is difficult to accept that the plaintiff would not have failed to mitigate its loss if it had continued to use the defendant's turbines while much more efficient turbines were coming onto the market.[45] It would have been in the plaintiff's interest to buy the more efficient turbines even if the defendant's turbines had conformed to the contract.

[2.32]   Nevertheless, in reliance on *British Westinghouse*, benefits flowing from a mitigating action of the plaintiff have been taken into account in a number of Australian cases, without consideration of whether it would have been unreasonable not to take the action. One example is *Cardno BSD Pty Ltd v Water Corporation (No 2)*,[46] where the defendant negligently specified Class 2 pipes rather than Class 4 pipes for the plaintiff's sewerage project. When the Class 2 pipes cracked, the plaintiff replaced them with Class 4 pipes. The plaintiff refurbished the Class 2 pipes and used them in other projects, for which it would otherwise have purchased new Class 2 pipes. The difference between the cost of purchasing new Class 2 pipes and the cost of refurbishing the old Class 2 pipes was deducted from the cost of purchasing Class 4 pipes.[47]

[2.33]   Another example is *Jenkinson v Young*,[48] where the plaintiffs and the defendant entered into a joint venture agreement relating to a business largely concerned with the acquisition, refurbishment and sale of antique furniture. The defendant repudiated the agreement, which forced the plaintiffs to relocate the business to premises less suited to a retail business. The plaintiffs put more time and effort into other aspects of the business, in particular eBay sales, and made a significant profit from those activities. It was held that the extra profit made from the other activities had to be set off against the profit lost in the antique furniture side of the

---

43   Ibid, 689.
44   Eg H McGregor, 'The Role of Mitigation in the Assessment of Damages' in D Saidov and R Cunnington (eds), *Contract Damages: Domestic and International Perspectives* (Hart 2008) 338.
45   A Dyson, 'British Westinghouse Revisited' [2012] LMCLQ 412, 422–23; D Winterton, '*Clark v Macourt*: Defective Sperm and Performance Substitutes in the High Court of Australia' (2014) 38 MULR 755, 788–89.
46   [2011] WASCA 161, (2011) 27 BCL 413.
47   Ibid, [156]–[157].
48   [2004] SADC 30.

business, without regard to whether it would have been unreasonable for the plaintiff not to put more time and effort into the other aspects of the business.[49]

However, benefits flowing from an action taken by the plaintiff in the knowledge of the defendant's wrong are not always taken into account. Viscount Haldane LC in *British Westinghouse* said that benefits flowing from the plaintiff's action will be ignored where the action is *res inter alios acta*.[50] Other terms used include 'collateral' and 'indirect'.[51] Some commentators suggest that benefits will not be taken into account unless they derive from actions taken by the plaintiff to avoid the consequences of the wrong.[52] This gains support from *Frankipile Pty Ltd v Acsas Pty Ltd*,[53] where the lessee of a crane repudiated the contract of lease 10 weeks before it was due to expire. The lessor, who sold the crane nine weeks later, recovered damages for the loss of rent for 10 weeks. The NSW Court of Appeal refused to take the proceeds of the sale of the crane (or part of it) into account in reducing the lessor's loss, on the ground that the sale of the crane had not aimed to mitigate the loss flowing from the lessee's breach.

[2.34]

In more recent cases, it has been observed that the deductibility of benefits flowing from the plaintiff's actions requires a value judgement, often by reference to policy considerations.[54] This is the best approach as it aligns the determination of whether benefits flowing from the plaintiff's actions are deductible with the determination of responsibility for loss, which involves an inquiry into factual causation as well as a value judgement; see Ch 3. It must be asked whether there is a sufficient connection between the benefit and the loss to make a set-off appropriate.

[2.35]

In *British Westinghouse*, it was appropriate to deduct the benefit of using more efficient turbines (saved cost of coal) from the cost of purchasing them, for which compensation was claimed. Benefit and loss were closely connected. It has been argued that the benefit of using more efficient turbines should have been deducted also from the loss suffered as a result of using the defendant's turbines for a few years (cost of extra coal), for which compensation was also claimed.[55] The question did not arise as the plaintiff's entitlement to compensation for the latter loss, without deduction, was not contested. By contrast, if the plaintiff had claimed compensation only in the amount of the difference between the actual value of the turbines delivered and the value of compliant turbines at the time of delivery, the benefit of using more efficient turbines should not have been deducted.[56]

[2.36]

---

49   Ibid, [288]–[290].

50   [1912] AC 673, 691. The Latin phrase *res inter alios acta* means 'a thing done between others' and denotes that the transaction does not concern the defendant.

51   Eg *Harold R Finger & Co Pty Ltd v Karellas Investments Pty Ltd* [2015] NSWSC 354 [500].

52   A Burrows, *Remedies for Torts and Breach of Contract* (3rd edn, OUP 2004) 158; J Edelman, *McGregor on Damages* (20th edn, Sweet & Maxwell 2018) [9–120].

53   (NSWCA, 7 November 1988). See also *Monroe Schneiders Associates (Inc) v No 1 Raberem Pty Ltd* (1991) 33 FCR 1, 27.

54   *Tyco Australia Pty Ltd v Optus Networks Pty Ltd* [2004] NSWCA 333 [253] (Giles JA); *Ruthol Pty Ltd v Tricon (Australia) Pty Ltd* [2005] NSWCA 443, (2005) 12 BPR 23,923 [51]; *Harold R Finger & Co Pty Ltd v Karellas Investments Pty Ltd* [2015] NSWSC 354 [498]–[500].

55   A Dyson, 'British Westinghouse Revisited' [2012] LMCLQ 412, 424–25.

56   *Clark v Macourt* [2013] HCA 56, (2013) 253 CLR 1 [143] (Keane J). The same view is taken by R Stevens, 'Damages and the Right to Performance: A *Golden Victory* or Not?' in JW Neyers, R Bronaugh and SGA Pitel (eds), *Exploring Contract Law* (Hart 2009) 181, who regards an award of diminution in value as substitutionary damages not subject to the avoided loss rule; see [1.58].

[2.37]   A case in which benefits flowing from a mitigating action of the plaintiff were not deducted is *Origin Energy LPG Ltd v Bestcare Foods Ltd*.[57] The defendant's negligence caused the destruction of the plaintiff's pet food factory. Instead of repairing the factory, the plaintiff bought another factory and equipped it for its purposes. It was common ground that this was reasonable. After two years' operation of the new factory, the plaintiff sold the new factory. The NSW Court of Appeal held that neither the goodwill nor any other part of the proceeds of the sale of the new factory were to be taken into account in assessing the plaintiff's loss.[58]

[2.38]   The question of whether benefits flowing from a mitigating action of the plaintiff are deductible has also arisen in cases in which the plaintiff bought certain land in reliance on a misrepresentation by the defendant and at some later point sold the land at a profit. Where the profit was due purely to an increase in the value of the land, it was held that the increase in value must be taken into account in reducing the plaintiff's loss, but that account must also be taken of the increase in value of the alternative property the plaintiff would have bought in the absence of the defendant's wrong.[59] Where the plaintiff bought the land in order to develop it and then developed it in a different way (because the initial plan turned out to be impossible), the profit made from the actual development was deducted from the loss of the profit that would have been made from the intended development,[60] but it is not settled whether the actual profit must also be deducted from the diminution in value (the difference between the price paid for the land and the land's actual value) at the time the plaintiff bought the land.[61]

E   Other benefits arising from the wrong

[2.39]   The victim of a civil wrong may obtain a benefit (from the wrongdoer or a third party) that the victim would not have obtained but for the wrong. Such benefits do not necessarily reduce the defendant's liability. In the same way in which factual causation of loss is necessary but not sufficient for an imposition of liability, factual causation of benefits is necessary but not sufficient for a reduction of liability.[62]

[2.40]   Benefits are deducted where they are a direct result of the wrong, and are not deducted where they are indirect or collateral.[63] The determination of whether a benefit is collateral involves a value judgement, often based on policy considerations.[64] The application of this principle to benefits flowing from mitigating actions of the plaintiff is discussed at [2.28]–[2.38]. The principle applies to other benefits too. For example, it has been held that where a

---

57   [2013] NSWCA 90.

58   Ibid, [197]–[225]. The court relied, among others, on *Dominion Mosaics and Tile Co Ltd v Trafalgar Trucking Co Ltd* [1990] 2 All ER 246.

59   *Brown v Dream Homes South Australia Pty Ltd* [2008] SASC 295, (2008) 102 SASR 93 [199]–[201].

60   See *Fenridge Pty Ltd v Retirement Care Australia (Preston) Pty Ltd* [2013] VSC 464 [335]; *Harold R Finger & Co Pty Ltd v Karellas Investments Pty Ltd* [2015] NSWSC 354 [550]–[561].

61   Compare *Tay v Koh* (Full Court of the Supreme Court of WA, 28 May 1998) (profit ignored) and *Manwelland Pty Ltd v Dames & Moore Pty Ltd* [2001] QCA 436, (2002) ASAL 55–074 (profit taken into account).

62   *Ruthol Pty Ltd v Tricon (Australia) Pty Ltd* [2005] NSWCA 443, (2005) 12 BPR 23,923 [51].

63   *Johns v Prunell* [1960] VR 208, 210; *Ruthol Pty Ltd v Tricon (Australia) Pty Ltd* [2005] NSWCA 443, (2005) 12 BPR 23,923 [45]–[51].

64   *Johns v Prunell* [1960] VR 208, 210; *Ruthol Pty Ltd v Tricon (Australia) Pty Ltd* [2005] NSWCA 443, (2005) 12 BPR 23,923 [51].

contracting party is entitled to, and does, pay the contractual fee or price later because of the other party's breach of contract (for example, delayed delivery of goods), the advantage of having the use of the money in the intervening period is not brought into account because the assessment of the advantage would be complex and unduly burden wronged parties.[65]

Where a third party has given money to the plaintiff in order to provide assistance, it must be asked whether the third party intended to reduce the defendant's liability: [2.41]

> There is a broad principle, applicable at least in insurance law and torts law, that credit need not be given by an injured party for moneys received by it which are not to be characterised as extinguishing or reducing that party's loss, but are rather to be character-ised as having been received independently of right of redress.[66]

On this principle, charitable actions by a third party will not reduce the defendant's liability unless the third party exceptionally intended such an effect. Thus, the plaintiff can claim the commercial cost of repairing property damaged by the defendant even though a third party has gratuitously carried out the repair,[67] or paid for the repair,[68] or provided some general assistance to the plaintiff because of the damage.[69] The application of these principles in cases of personal injury is discussed at [7.72]–[7.79]. [2.42]

A deduction of payments made by a third party may be rejected even though the third party had no charitable motive. For example, in *Monroe Schneiders Associates (Inc) v No 1 Raberem Pty Ltd*,[70] the plaintiff, a carpet wholesaler, delivered carpet to the defendant for a significantly lower price than it had cost the plaintiff to acquire. The plaintiff did so because the defendant had fraudulently represented to the plaintiff that the defendant had already sold-on the carpet to third parties at a low margin in reliance on a quote of the lower price by an executive of the plaintiff. The transaction put the plaintiff in financial difficulty. In order to maintain a good commercial relationship with the plaintiff, the company that had delivered the carpet to the plaintiff contributed to the cost of an advertising campaign by the plaintiff. When the defendant's fraud was discovered and the plaintiff claimed damages for its loss from the defendant, the defendant argued that the payment that the plaintiff had received from the supplier of the carpet ought to be deducted. The Full Federal Court rejected such deduction on the ground that the supplier's payment had not been intended to reduce the defendant's liability. [2.43]

F The impact of tax law

The assessment of loss caused by a civil wrong may involve the consideration of tax law, which can be a complex matter. Some general principles relating to the impact of income tax (including capital gains tax) and goods and services tax will be set out. [2.44]

---

65   *Ruthol Pty Ltd v Tricon (Australia) Pty Ltd* [2005] NSWCA 443, (2005) 12 BPR 23,923 [67]–[68].
66   *Insurance Australia Ltd v HIH Casualty & General Insurance Ltd (in liq)* [2007] VSCA 223, (2007) 18 VR 528 [160] (Ashley JA, with whom Chernov and Redlich JJA agreed).
67   *Powercor Australia Ltd v Thomas* [2012] VSCA 87, (2012) 43 VR 220 [74]–[91].
68   *Cusack v Heath* (1950) 44 QJPR 88; [1950] QWN 16; *Jones v Stroud DC* [1986] 1 WLR 1141, 1150–51, approved in *Powercor Australia Ltd v Thomas*, ibid, [42].
69   *Wollington v State Electricity Commission of Victoria (No 2)* [1980] VR 91.
70   (1991) 33 FCR 1.

[2.45]   Income tax and capital gains tax can be relevant in two respects: the calculation of lost income may involve the consideration of tax that would have been payable had the income been earned, and income tax or capital gains tax may be payable on the compensation itself.

[2.46]   Compensation for lost income must generally be assessed by reference to the net income that the plaintiff would have been left with after paying income tax on the gross income. This applies whether the loss of income is due to personal injury,[71] property damage,[72] injury to business reputation,[73] damage to other economic interests,[74] or otherwise.[75] An assessment of compensation by reference to lost pre-tax income cannot generally be justified on the ground that the compensation award itself will be liable to income tax. Even where this is the case, the tax rate that applies to the compensation may differ from the tax rate that would have applied to the income lost.[76] However, difficulties in calculating the tax liability of the compensation award may justify an assessment of compensation by reference to lost pre-tax income in an appropriate case.[77]

[2.47]   A plaintiff may be liable to pay capital gains tax or income tax on compensation received. The details are complex.[78] Only a few brief comments will be made. For tax purposes, compensation for a wrong generally acquires the character of that which it substitutes.[79] Compensation that constitutes a substitute for lost income is thus subject to income tax, even if received as a lump sum.[80]

[2.48]   Where personal injury impairs the plaintiff's ability to work, the ensuing loss is conceptualised as the loss of earning capacity rather than the loss of income. Even though the value of the lost earning capacity is usually assessed by reference to the amount of lost income (see [7.39]), the compensation is conceptualised as being of a capital nature and thus not subject to income tax.[81] The same concept has been applied to compensation for an injury to business reputation. Even though the compensation is assessed by reference to the income lost as a result of the defamation, it is conceptualised as compensation for a diminution in earning capacity and thus not subject to income tax.[82]

---

71   *Cullen v Trappell* (1980) 146 CLR 1; *Mitchell Erectors Pty Ltd v Hinnen* [2002] WASCA 169 [24]; *Civil Proceedings Act 2011* (Qld), s 60; *Wrongs Act 1958* (Vic), s 28A.

72   *Gill v Australian Wheat Board* [1980] 2 NSWLR 795, 807.

73   *Sydney Refractive Surgery Centre Pty Ltd v Commissioner of Taxation* [2008] FCA 454, (2008) 247 ALR 313 [71].

74   *Daniels v Anderson* (1995) 37 NSWLR 438, 585; *Davinski Nominees Pty Ltd v I & A Bowler Holdings Pty Ltd* [2011] VSC 220 [61].

75   Conflicting decisions have been made in wrongful dismissal cases, as discussed in *Davinski Nominees Pty Ltd v I & A Bowler Holdings Pty Ltd* [2011] VSC 220 [39]–[43].

76   *Cullen v Trappell* (1980) 146 CLR 1, 16; *Gill v Australian Wheat Board* [1980] 2 NSWLR 795, 806.

77   *Davinski Nominees Pty Ltd v I & A Bowler Holdings Pty Ltd* [2011] VSC 220 [75].

78   See R Krever, 'The Capital Gains Tax Consequences of Litigation' (1997) 71 Aust LJ 699; CW Pincus and S White, 'Taxation of Compensatory Payments and Judgments' (2001) 75 Aust LJ 378.

79   *Federal Commissioner of Taxation v Dixon* (1952) 86 CLR 540.

80   Australian Taxation Office Taxation Determination 93/58; *Re Cooper v Federal Commissioner of Taxation* (2003) 52 ATR 1199; *Construction, Forestry, Mining and Energy Union v Hail Creek Coal Pty Ltd* [2016] FCA 1032 [59].

81   *Groves v United Pacific Transport Pty Ltd* [1965] Qd R 62, 65; *Commissioner of Taxation v Sydney Refractive Surgery Centre Pty Ltd* [2008] FCAFC 190, (2008) 172 FCR 557 [10]; *Davinski Nominees Pty Ltd v I & A Bowler Holdings Pty Ltd* [2011] VSC 220 [64].

82   *Commissioner of Taxation v Sydney Refractive Surgery Centre Pty Ltd* [2008] FCAFC 190, (2008) 172 FCR 557.

It has further been held that pre-judgment interest on compensation for personal injury is also of a capital nature and thus not subject to income tax, whereas post-judgment interest is of an income nature.[83] However, statute now exempts plaintiffs from income tax for interest on compensation for personal injury between the date judgment is given and the date the judgment takes effect.[84] Furthermore, compensation for a wrong or injury suffered in one's 'occupation' is exempt from capital gains tax.[85] This does not include injury suffered by a company or trust.[86] Compensation for personal injury is also exempt from capital gains tax.[87]

[2.49]

Where the plaintiff must pay capital gains tax or income tax on the compensation received, the amount awarded must in general be such that a deduction of the tax rate leads to the amount that would be awarded were no tax payable.[88] An exception has been made in relation to interest. In *Mulvaney Holdings Pty Ltd v Thorne (No 2)*,[89] an increase in the award of interest in order to take account of income tax payable on the award was rejected on the ground that an award of interest aims to compensate the plaintiff for being kept out of money and that the plaintiff had saved income tax by being kept out of money. It may be true that a plaintiff has saved income tax by being kept out of money. But it cannot simply be assumed that that saving is of the same amount as the income tax payable on the award of interest. It is preferable to consider the two issues separately.

[2.50]

A special method of taking account of income tax payable on compensation has been devised in relation to compensation for future loss, which constitutes the present value of future loss. It provides the plaintiff with a lump sum which, if invested, provides the plaintiff with a continuous income stream. If that income is subject to income tax, the lump sum awarded to the plaintiff must in principle be increased by the relevant proportion. While the courts refuse to engage in speculating about future tax law, they do not ignore the potential tax to be paid on the compensation. Where the plaintiff receives a lump sum as compensation for future loss, the compensation must be reduced to reflect the advantage of obtaining compensation for loss earlier than the loss is suffered. That reduction is itself reduced to take account of the tax likely to be paid on the income obtained from investing the lump sum; see [2.151].

[2.51]

In some cases in which it was too difficult for the court to determine whether and to what extent the compensation will be subject to income tax or capital gains tax, the court awarded an amount calculated on the assumption that no tax was payable and gave the plaintiff leave to apply for additional compensation should the original award be assessed as

[2.52]

---

83   *Whitaker v Federal Commissioner of Taxation* (1998) 82 FCR 261.
84   *Income Tax Assessment Act 1997* (Cth), s 51.57.
85   Ibid, s 118.37(1)(a).
86   Australian Taxation Office Ruling TR 95/35 Income tax: capital gains: treatment of compensation receipts [22].
87   *Income Tax Assessment Act 1997* (Cth), s 118.37(1)(b).
88   *Provan v HCL Real Estate Ltd* (1992) 24 ATR 238, 248; *Construction, Forestry, Mining and Energy Union v Hail Creek Coal Pty Ltd* [2016] FCA 1032 [60]–[64]. Cf *Daniels v Anderson* (1995) 37 NSWLR 438, 586. The additional amount awarded is not itself liable to income tax and thus does not need to be 'grossed up' again: *Westpac Banking Corporation v Jamieson* [2015] QCA 50, [2016] 1 Qd R 495 [204]–[209].
89   [2012] QSC 146 [52]–[56].

liable to tax.[90] This is an exception to the 'once and for all' rule in assessing compensation for a civil wrong; see [2.122].

[2.53]   Goods and services tax ('GST') can be relevant in two respects: GST may affect the price or value of certain goods or services in relation to which compensation is awarded, and GST may be payable on the compensation itself.

[2.54]   Compensation is often assessed by reference to the price or value of certain goods or services. GST payable under the transaction in question must be taken into account. For example, the value of converted goods is usually determined by reference to the price that can be obtained by selling them on the market or otherwise.[91] Since the price paid by a buyer includes GST, compensation for the loss of the goods must be assessed by reference to the market price including GST.[92]

[2.55]   Furthermore, compensation for the cost of reinstating or repairing damaged or destroyed property is assessed by reference to the price that a commercial contractor charges for the work in question; see [2.14]. A contractor charges GST on top of the net price. In general, therefore, the compensation must include the GST component.[93] Things are different where the damage relates to the plaintiff's business and the plaintiff is registered for GST purposes. A person registered for GST purposes is entitled to an input tax credit for GST paid for goods and services supplied to him in connection with his business. Thus, where the damage caused by the defendant relates to the plaintiff's business, the GST paid by the plaintiff to the contractor doing the repair work either reduces the GST payable by the plaintiff (for supplies to the plaintiff's customers) or entitles the plaintiff to a refund.[94] In those circumstances, the compensation for the damage must be assessed by reference to the net price (exclusive of GST) charged by the contractor for the repair work.[95]

[2.56]   A plaintiff must pay GST on the compensation received if it constitutes a 'supply for consideration',[96] for example where the defendant pays the outstanding price for goods or services delivered by the plaintiff. The details are complex.[97] Suffice it to say that if the plaintiff is obliged to pay GST on the compensation and is not entitled to an input tax credit for that payment (because, for example, the plaintiff is not registered for GST purposes), the amount awarded must be such that a deduction of the GST rate (currently 10%) leads to the amount that would be awarded were no GST payable. Where the matter is too complex to be determined by the court, the court ought to award an amount calculated on the assumption

---

90   *Rabelais Pty Ltd v Cameron* (1995) 95 ATC 4552, 4553; *Turner v TR Nominees Pty Ltd* (1995) 31 ATR 578, 596; *PM Sulcs & Associates Pty Ltd v Daihatsu Australia Pty Ltd* [2001] NSWSC 798 [119]; *Guy v Commonwealth* [2013] ACTSC 128 [95].

91   *Bilambil-Terranora Pty Ltd v Tweed Shire Council* [1980] 1 NSWLR 465, 477, 489; *Furness v Adrium Industries Pty Ltd* [1996] 1 VR 668, 669; *Jiwira Pty Ltd v Primary Industry Bank of Australia Ltd* [2000] NSWSC 1094 [256]. See [6.34].

92   *Bennett v Goodwin* [2005] NSWSC 930, (2005) 62 ATR 515 [17].

93   *Glenmont Investments Pty Ltd v O'Loughlin* [2000] SASC 429, (2000) 79 SASR 185 [426]; *Nemeth v Prynew Pty Ltd* [2009] NSWSC 511 [3].

94   *Gagner Pty Ltd v Canturi Corporation Pty Ltd* [2009] NSWCA 413, (2009) 262 ALR 691 [142]–[145].

95   Ibid, [147], [151].

96   *A New Tax System (Good and Services Tax) Act 1999* (Cth), s 9.5.

97   Guidance is given in the Australian Taxation Office's Ruling GSTR 2001/4 Goods and Services Tax: GST consequences of court orders and out-of-court settlements.

that no GST is payable and give the plaintiff leave to apply for additional compensation should the original award be assessed as liable to GST.

IV Certainty of loss and recovery for the loss of a chance

The assessment of loss resulting from a wrong involves a consideration of actual events (for example, the defendant driving his car into the plaintiff) and hypothetical events (for example, the plaintiff making a profit had the defendant not injured her). Where the court is neither wholly convinced of the occurrence of the event nor wholly convinced of the non-occurrence of the event, a legal system has the choice between two basic approaches. One possibility is to determine the event's occurrence on the balance of probabilities and to award the amount of loss generated by the event's occurrence where the probability of the event's occurrence is more than 50%, and to award nothing otherwise. The other possibility is to assess loss on a 'sliding scale' according to the degree of probability of the event's occurrence, and to award a sum calculated by multiplying the probability of the event's occurrence with the amount of loss generated by the event's occurrence.

[2.57]

For example, suppose that the event's occurrence generates a loss of $100 000 for the plaintiff. If the probability of the event's occurrence is 40%, the plaintiff will receive nothing under the first approach (balance of probabilities) and $40 000 under the second approach (degree of probability). If the probability of the event's occurrence is 60%, the plaintiff will receive $100 000 under the first approach and $60 000 under the second approach.

[2.58]

In circumstances in which the probability of the initial harm being avoided in the absence of the defendant's wrong is 50% or less (so that the plaintiff recovers nothing under the balance-of-probabilities approach), plaintiffs have claimed compensation for the loss of the chance of avoiding the harm. It is now common to ask whether the loss of a chance is recoverable in particular circumstances. The issue is seen as whether there is actionable loss, rather than as one of resolving uncertainty. There is thus a distinction between a claim in respect of the loss of a chance and a claim in respect of what may be called the ultimate loss, that is, the loss resulting from the defendant's wrong if all uncertainties are resolved in the plaintiff's favour.

[2.59]

The reference to 'loss of a chance' is problematic in at least two respects. First, it implies that the plaintiff has a choice between claiming compensation for the ultimate loss and claiming compensation for the loss of a chance. But it is difficult to justify that one party alone should be entitled to choose the court's approach to resolving uncertainty. Secondly, the distinction between ultimate loss and loss of a chance has led to suggestions that a claim for the loss of a chance must be specifically pleaded.[98] However, the Victorian Court of Appeal has now held that pleadings and particulars which allege a loss dependent upon a hypothetical event do not need to use the terms 'loss of a chance' or 'loss of opportunity'.[99]

[2.60]

98 Eg *Rogers v Roche* [2015] QSC 272, (2017) 105 ATR 114 [13]; *Ralston v Jurisich* [2017] NSWCA 63 [101].
99 *Bennett v Estate of Talacko (dec'd)* [2017] VSCA 163 [106]. The same view was expressed in *Calvert v Badenach* [2015] TASFC 8 [140] (Estcourt J); rev'd on other grounds [2016] HCA 18, (2016) 257 CLR 440. The specific hypothetical chain of events leading to the loss must be pleaded: *Barnes v Forty Two International Pty Ltd* [2014] FCAFC 152, (2014) 316 ALR 408.

[2.61]   Australian courts do not apply the same approach to resolving uncertainty in every case. Several categories of case must be distinguished. The following starts with a brief outline of the key milestones in the development of the current rules, and then looks more closely at each category of case.

A   Overview of the current law

[2.62]   The development of the current rules started in *Malec v JC Hutton Pty Ltd*,[100] considered at [2.71]–[2.73]. The case involved personal injury. It was more likely than not (but not certain) that some of the consequences of the injury would have occurred as a result of an unrelated condition even in the absence of the defendant's wrong. The High Court of Australia over-turned the denial of liability for those consequences, requiring an assessment by reference to the degree of probability. Deane, Gaudron and McHugh JJ explained:

> When liability has been established and a common law court has to assess damages, its approach to events that allegedly would have occurred, but cannot now occur, or that allegedly might occur, is different from its approach to events which allegedly have occurred. A common law court determines on the balance of probabilities whether an event has occurred ... But in the case of an event which it is alleged would or would not have occurred, or might or might not yet occur, the approach of the court is different. The future may be predicted and the hypothetical may be conjectured. But questions as to the future or hypothetical effect of physical injury or degeneration are not commonly suscep-tible of scientific demonstration or proof. If the law is to take account of future or hypothetical events in assessing damages, it can only do so in terms of the degree of probability of those events occurring ... Thus, the court assesses the degree of probability that an event would have occurred, or might occur, and adjusts its award of damages to reflect the degree of probability.[101]

[2.63]   This passage distinguishes between two groups of events. Actual past events (events that are alleged to have actually occurred before trial) are determined on the balance of probabil-ities, whereas an assessment by evaluating chances is made for all other events, namely hypothetical past events (events that allegedly would have occurred before trial but for the defendant's wrong) and future events, whether actual or hypothetical.

[2.64]   In *Malec*, it was clear that the defendant was liable for some loss, and the three rules laid down were expressed as rules of assessment to be applied once liability has been established. But actual and hypothetical past events are also relevant to determining whether the initial harm (without which the defendant would not be liable to pay any compensation) would have occurred but for the defendant's wrong. It is uncontroversial in that context that actual past events must always be assessed on the balance of probabilities.[102] The way of resolving uncertainty in respect of hypothetical past events upon which the initial harm depends has been considered in some key cases.

---

100   (1990) 169 CLR 638.
101   Ibid, 643–44. Brennan and Dawson JJ (at 641) generally agreed, but rejected the idea of using a percentage figure in assessing damages.
102   Eg *Australian Winch and Haulage Co Pty Ltd v Collins* [2013] NSWCA 327 [11], [66], [109]; *Geyer v Redeland Pty Ltd* [2013] NSWCA 338 [51], [70].

The key case involving pure economic loss is *Sellars v Adelaide Petroleum NL*,[103] con- **[2.65]**
sidered at [2.92]–[2.94]. The only loss that the defendant's misleading or deceptive conduct
could have caused to the plaintiff was the loss of profit from a contract between the plaintiff
and a third party. Even though the chance of the plaintiff making that profit in the absence of
the defendant's wrong was less than 50%, the High Court confirmed an award of damages in
the amount of a proportion of the potential profit. Mason CJ, Dawson, Toohey and Gaudron
JJ said:

> [T]he applicant must prove on the balance of probabilities that he or she has sustained
> *some* loss or damage. However, in a case such as the present, the applicant shows *some*
> loss or damage was sustained by demonstrating that the contravening conduct caused the
> loss of a commercial opportunity which had *some* value (not being a negligible value), the
> value being ascertained by reference to the degree of probabilities or possibilities.[104]

Thus, the High Court distinguished between the existence of an opportunity in the absence **[2.66]**
of the defendant's wrong, which must be established on the balance of probabilities, and the
value of that opportunity, which is assessed by reference to the degree of probability of the
relevant events occurring.[105] This distinction reconciled the applicability of the degree-of-
probability approach with the plaintiff's onus of proving factual causation, and permitted the
Sellars approach to survive the enactment of the civil liability statutes, which provide that the
plaintiff bears the onus of proving, on the balance of probabilities, any fact relevant to
causation; see [3.25].

After *Sellars*, it was unclear whether the *Sellars* approach applies where the initial harm is **[2.67]**
personal injury. More precisely, it was unclear whether a plaintiff can recover damages for
personal injury where it is more likely than not (but not certain) that the initial injury would
have occurred even in the absence of the defendant's wrong. This was settled in *Tabet v
Gett*,[106] considered at [2.78]–[2.80]. Medical negligence deprived the plaintiff of a 40% chance
of avoiding an injury. The High Court rejected the plaintiff's claim, and thus rejected an
application of the degree-of-probability approach to personal injury as initial harm. This does
not affect *Malec*. The degree-of-probability approach still applies to consequential loss
resulting from personal injury.

Even though *Tabet v Gett* involved personal injury, the rejection of recovery for loss of a **[2.68]**
chance in that case has had some impact on the approach taken in cases of pure economic
loss. It has recently been held that *Sellars* does not permit an award of damages for pure
economic loss on the mere basis that the defendant's wrong deprived the plaintiff of a chance
of avoiding certain loss, but that an assessment of the loss by valuing chances is possible only
once it has been proved, on the balance of probabilities, that the defendant's wrong deprived
the plaintiff of a valuable opportunity.[107]

---

103 (1994) 179 CLR 332.
104 Ibid, 355 (emphasis in original).
105 See *Masters Home Improvement Pty Ltd v North East Solution Pty Ltd* [2017] VSCA 88 [411].
106 [2010] HCA 12, (2010) 240 CLR 537, disapproving *Rufo v Hosking* [2004] NSWCA 391, (2004) 61 NSWLR
     678, and following *Laferrière v Lawson* [1991] 1 SCR 541 and *Gregg v Scott* [2005] UKHL 2, [2005] 2
     AC 176.
107 *Badenach v Calvert* [2016] HCA 18, (2016) 257 CLR 440; discussed at [2.103]–[2.106].

[2.69]   Four further remarks will be made. First, in resolving uncertainty in respect of the initial harm, hypothetical conduct of the plaintiff is always assessed on the balance of probabilities.[108] Secondly, apart from the rule just mentioned, it is unclear how uncertainty in respect of property damage as initial harm is resolved.[109] Thirdly, where chances have to be evaluated but it is not possible to precisely determine the amount of loss flowing from the occurrence of an event or the degree of probability of its occurrence (which is often the case), the loss needs to be estimated as best as possible.[110] Finally, while the vast majority of cases establishing the rules discussed here involved claims in contract, in tort or under statute, the rules have also been applied in cases involving breach of fiduciary duty.[111]

[2.70]   To summarise, loss dependent upon an actual past event is always assessed on the balance of probabilities,[112] and loss dependent upon a future event is always assessed by reference to the degree of probability of the event occurring. With regard to hypothetical events, it is necessary to distinguish between consequential loss, which is always assessed by valuing chances, and the initial harm. With regard to the initial harm, leaving aside property damage, it is necessary to distinguish between personal injury, where uncertainty is always resolved on the balance of probabilities, and pure economic loss, where further distinctions must be made. The various categories of case relating to hypothetical events will now be looked at in more detail.

B   Consequential loss

[2.71]   Once liability for the initial harm has been established, consequential loss dependent upon hypothetical past events will be assessed by evaluating the chances of each event occurring. The leading case is *Malec v JC Hutton Pty Ltd*.[113] The plaintiff, a labourer in the defendant's meatworks, contracted brucellosis, a disease acquired from animals, as a result of the defendant's negligence. One possible effect of brucellosis is the development of depressive illness. The plaintiff subsequently developed a neurotic illness and was unable to work. Soon afterwards, he developed a back condition, which alone would have rendered him unemployable. He claimed damages for the loss (financial and otherwise) resulting from the neurotic illness.

[2.72]   A majority in the Full Court of the Supreme Court of Queensland found it more likely than not that, even if he had not contracted brucellosis, the plaintiff would have developed the back condition and that condition coupled with the resulting unemployment would have caused the

---

108   *Sellars v Adelaide Petroleum NL* (1994) 179 CLR 332, 353. See [2.77], [2.89]–[2.90]. The justification of that rule is discussed at [2.117].

109   The resolution of uncertainty on the balance of probabilities seems to have been favoured in *Tabet v Gett* [2010] HCA 12, (2010) 240 CLR 537 [52] (Gummow ACJ).

110   *Rockdale City Council v Micro Developments Pty Ltd* [2008] NSWCA 128, (2008) Aust Torts Reports 81–954 [66]. This rule may not apply to an alleged chance that the plaintiff derived a benefit from the defendant's wrong: *Tyco Australia Pty Ltd v Optus Networks Pty Ltd* [2004] NSWCA 333 [197] (Handley JA).

111   *BigTinCan Pty Ltd v Ramsay* [2013] NSWSC 1248 [94]–[101]; *Hart Security Australia Pty Ltd v Boucousis* [2016] NSWCA 307, (2016) 339 ALR 659.

112   This includes, eg, the presence of latent defects in a building: *Dunn v Hanson Australasia Pty Ltd* [2017] ACTSC 169, (2017) 12 ACTLR 138 [30].

113   (1990) 169 CLR 638.

plaintiff to develop a neurotic illness. Assessing the matter on the balance of probabilities, the majority in the Full Court denied damages for the time after the onset of the back condition. The High Court of Australia overturned the judgment.

While the High Court accepted the factual finding by the majority in the Full Court, the High Court held that the plaintiff's loss was to be assessed by reference to the degree of probability rather than the balance of probabilities. Damages for the period after the onset of the back condition could be completely denied only if it was 100% certain (which it was not) that the plaintiff would have developed the neurotic condition even without the defendant's negligence. A probability of less than 100% (even if more than 50%) led only to a proportionate reduction in the compensable loss. In a passage quoted at [2.62], Deane, Gaudron and McHugh JJ set out the distinction between actual past events, which are assessed on the balance of probabilities, and hypothetical and future events, which are assessed by evaluating chances.[114]   [2.73]

Malec is routinely applied to loss resulting from personal injury. For example, in assessing loss of earning capacity, the court considers the probabilities of what employment (if any) the plaintiff will have in the future and what employment she would have had but for the injury, the probability of (actual and hypothetical) promotion, the probability of unemployment even without the injury (for example, as a result of illness or redundancy), and so on.[115]   [2.74]

Malec was applied in the context of property damage in *Glenmont Investments Pty Ltd v O'Loughlin*.[116] A large mechanical dinosaur was destroyed in a fire for which the defendants were held liable. Damages were awarded for the cost of rebuilding the dinosaur, and for the loss of the opportunity to exploit the dinosaur commercially in the United States, through exhibitions, a film and other means. The South Australian Full Court took the view that the plaintiff might have made a profit of up to $50 million, but that there would have been significant obstacles to overcome. The court awarded $5 million for loss of profit.[117]   [2.75]

Malec also applies in the context of pure economic loss, where it has been absorbed into the rules laid down in *Sellars* and subsequent cases, discussed at [2.92]–[2.106]. Once the hypothetical existence and exercise of an opportunity has been proved on the balance of probabilities, all subsequent hypothetical events, including actions of the plaintiff,[118] are assessed by evaluating chances, whether they relate to the initial harm or consequential loss. Reference is usually made to both *Sellars* and *Malec*.[119]   [2.76]

C   Personal injury as initial harm

Where the initial harm is personal injury, uncertainty in respect of hypothetical past events upon which the initial harm depends is resolved on the balance of probabilities. This has long   [2.77]

---

114   Ibid, 643–44.
115   Eg *Norris v Blake (No 2)* (1997) 41 NSWLR 49, 64. See [7.45]–[7.46].
116   [2000] SASC 429, (2000) 79 SASR 185.
117   Ibid, [441]–[443]. See also *Hobbs v Oildrive Pty Ltd* [2008] QSC 45 [122]; *Tre Cavalli Pty Ltd v Berry Rural Co Operative Society Ltd* [2013] NSWCA 235 [118], [125].
118   *Falkingham v Hoffmans (a firm)* [2014] WASCA 140, (2014) 46 WAR 510 [242] (Buss JA); *Oneflare Pty Ltd v Chernih* [2017] NSWCA 195 [92]–[93].
119   Eg *Rockdale City Council v Micro Developments Pty Ltd* [2008] NSWCA 128, (2008) Aust Torts Reports 81-954 [66]; *Falkingham v Hoffmans (a firm)* (2014) 46 WAR 510 [220]–[221].

been established for hypothetical past conduct of the plaintiff. For example, where an employer negligently failed to provide the employee with safety equipment, uncertainty as to whether the employee would have used that equipment is resolved on the balance of probabilities.[120] Furthermore, where a doctor negligently failed to warn the patient of a risk inherent in a proposed operation, uncertainty as to what the plaintiff would have done if advised of the risk is resolved on the balance of probabilities.[121] It is asked what the individual plaintiff, not a reasonable person in the plaintiff's position, would have done in the absence of the defendant's wrong; see [3.26].

[2.78]   For some time, it was unclear how uncertainty in respect of hypothetical past natural events (in particular the hypothetical development of a medical condition) is to be assessed. More precisely, it was unclear whether a patient who as a result of medical malpractice lost a less than even chance of avoiding a condition can recover damages for a proportion of the loss resulting from the condition. The High Court of Australia rejected such a claim in *Tabet v Gett*.[122]

[2.79]   The plaintiff was admitted to hospital with headaches, nausea and vomiting. After three days in hospital, the plaintiff suffered a seizure. A CT scan was performed and a brain tumour was diagnosed. Despite immediate treatment, the plaintiff suffered irreversible brain damage, causing loss of some $6 million. The plaintiff brought an action in negligence against the doctors who had treated her, alleging that a CT scan should have been performed earlier and that if it had, she would have had a better medical outcome. The trial judge found that the seizure contributed to 25% of the plaintiff's loss (some $1.5 million), and that there was a 40% chance that the loss referable to the seizure would have been avoided had a CT scan been performed earlier. Assessing damages by reference to the degree of probability, he awarded damages of approximately $600 000. The NSW Court of Appeal overturned that judgment and dismissed the plaintiff's claim.

[2.80]   The High Court dismissed the plaintiff's appeal. The decision was unanimous but very different reasons were given. Gummow ACJ said that while an assessment by reference to the degree of probability can be used where liability is otherwise established (for example, in cases involving breach of contract), it cannot be used to establish liability except in cases of pure economic loss.[123] Heydon J based his decision solely on what he regarded as a lack of evidence that the plaintiff had lost even a chance of a better medical outcome.[124] Kiefel J said that while a commercial opportunity lost may be seen to be of value itself, the same cannot be said of the chance of a better medical outcome.[125] Hayne and Bell JJ agreed with Kiefel J.[126] So did Crennan J, who added that to allow recovery for the lost chance of a better medical

---

120   *Duyvelshaff v Cathcart & Ritchie Ltd* (1973) 1 ALR 125, 138 (Gibbs J), 142–43 (Mason J); *Anyco Pty Ltd v Kleeman* [2008] WASCA 30, (2008) Aust Torts Reports 81–933 [48].

121   *Wallace v Kam* [2013] HCA 19, (2013) 250 CLR 375 [20].

122   [2010] HCA 12, (2010) 240 CLR 537, disapproving *Rufo v Hosking* [2004] NSWCA 391, (2004) 61 NSWLR 678, and following *Laferrière v Lawson* [1991] 1 SCR 541 and *Gregg v Scott* [2005] UKHL 2, [2005] 2 AC 176.

123   [2010] HCA 12, (2010) 240 CLR 537 [46]–[62].

124   Ibid, [96].

125   Ibid, [124].

126   Ibid, [65]–[69].

outcome could encourage defensive medicine and would place a burden upon public and private health insurance schemes and medical professional liability insurance schemes.[127]

Kiefel J's distinction between a commercial opportunity and the chance of a better medical outcome is not convincing. Unless the commercial opportunity was marketable, which is rarely the case, a plaintiff losing a commercial opportunity has simply lost the chance of avoiding the ultimate loss suffered, which is not different from the chance of a better medical outcome.[128] Be that as it may, it is necessary to determine the precise scope of the rule laid down in *Tabet v Gett* by reference to five particular features of the facts. **[2.81]**

First, in *Tabet v Gett*, the adverse medical condition had already occurred by the time of the trial. But this was not crucial to the High Court's decision. On the contrary, the arguments that damage is the gist of an action in negligence and that plaintiffs must not unduly be advantaged have even greater force in a case where the condition has not occurred by the time of the trial and the plaintiff may still be healed.[129] **[2.82]**

Secondly, the fact that *Tabet v Gett* involved medical malpractice was not crucial to the High Court's decision. Crennan J did refer to policy arguments that apply only to defendants who are medical practitioners, but none of the other judges did so and Crennan J expressly agreed with Kiefel J's reasons. Moreover, the High Court has since described the rule in *Tabet v Gett* as one 'relating to personal injuries'[130] without restricting it to cases of medical malpractice, and the rule was applied outside the context of medical malpractice in *Carangelo v New South Wales*.[131] A police officer suffered psychiatric injury as a result of stress at work. He claimed that his employer had been negligent in failing to take reasonable precautions against the risk of psychiatric injury. But he could not prove that it was more likely than not that he would not have suffered psychiatric injury had the precautions been taken. The NSW Court of Appeal, relying on *Tabet v Gett*, upheld a dismissal of the claim.[132] **[2.83]**

Thirdly, the fact that the uncertain hypothetical event in *Tabet v Gett* was a natural event, as opposed to human conduct, was not crucial to the High Court's decision. The arguments that damage is the gist of an action in negligence and that plaintiffs must not unduly be advantaged apply equally to human conduct. The applicability of the rule in *Tabet v Gett* to hypothetical actions of third parties was confirmed by the High Court in *Robinson Helicopter Co Inc v McDermott*.[133] A helicopter crashed, resulting in the plaintiff suffering serious injury. The crash was caused by the incorrect installation of a certain part, contrary to instructions given in the manufacturer's manual. The High Court considered the possible argument that the failure to recommend a more sophisticated procedure in the manual deprived the plaintiff of the chance that such a recommendation would have led to the correct installation of the part. Citing *Tabet* **[2.84]**

---

127   Ibid, [100]–[102].
128   For a discussion of the arguments pro and con, see, eg, D Birch, '*Tabet v Gett*: The High Court's Own Lost Chance of a Better Outcome' (2011) 19 Tort L Rev 76; J Edelman, 'Loss of a Chance' (2013) 21 Torts LJ 1; SA Holloway, 'The Legal Labyrinth of Lost Chances: Can a Plaintiff Recover for Loss of a Less than Even Chance in Medical Negligence Cases after *Tabet v Gett*?' (2013) 21 Tort L Rev 96; C McKay, 'Concurrent Liability in Claims for Loss of Chance of a Better Medical Outcome' (2012) 20 Torts LJ 29, 38–46.
129   See [2010] HCA 12, (2010) 240 CLR 537 [130] (Kiefel J).
130   *Robinson Helicopter Co Inc v McDermott* [2016] HCA 22, (2016) 331 ALR 550 [86].
131   [2016] NSWCA 126.
132   [2016] NSWCA 126 [70].
133   [2016] HCA 22, (2016) 331 ALR 550 ('*McDermott*').

v Gett, the court said that the argument would fail because 'this Court has set its face against recovery of loss of a chance in the law of negligence relating to personal injuries'[134] It follows that the rule in *Tabet v Gett* must also apply, for example, where the defendant negligently failed to refer the plaintiff to a doctor and it is uncertain whether a doctor, acting with reasonable care, would have administered the treatment necessary for recovery.[135]

[2.85]   Fourthly, *Tabet v Gett* involved an action in negligence. Both Kiefel J, with whom Hayne, Bell and Crennan JJ agreed, and Gummow ACJ placed emphasis on the fact that damage is the gist of an action in negligence, and Gummow ACJ contrasted this with breach of contract, which is actionable per se.[136] In *McDermott*,[137] as mentioned at [2.84], the High Court referred to the law of negligence in the context of describing the rule in *Tabet v Gett*. However, the fact that a wrong is actionable per se simply means that the plaintiff may obtain nominal damages (and exemplary damages where warranted) without having to prove loss. This should not affect the rules relating to substantive damages. Furthermore, where a claim is concurrently brought in contract and negligence, it would be odd if the rules as to the resolution of uncertainty differed between the two causes of action. The rule in *Tabet v Gett* must also apply where the claim is brought in contract unless the contract provides otherwise.[138]

[2.86]   Finally, in *Tabet v Gett*, the probability of the plaintiff avoiding the injury in the absence of the defendant's negligence was less than 50%, and the High Court focused on the question of whether the loss of the chance of a better medical outcome is actionable loss. It might be thought that the approach of evaluating chances applies where the probability of the plaintiff avoiding the injury in the absence of the defendant's wrong is more than 50%. However, this would be illogical,[139] and Kiefel J in *Tabet v Gett* said that 'proportionate recovery cuts both ways'.[140] The balance-of-probabilities approach has been applied in cases in which it was more likely than not (but not certain) that the plaintiff would have avoided the injury but for the defendant's wrong.[141]

[2.87]   In conclusion, where the initial harm is personal injury, uncertainty in respect of a hypothetical past event upon which the initial harm depends is always resolved on the balance of probabilities.

---

134   [2016] HCA 22, (2016) 331 ALR 550 at [86].
135   See *Sullivan Nicolaides Pty Ltd v Papa* [2011] QCA 257, [2012] 2 Qd R 48. The contrary decision in *Jang v Australia Meat Holdings Pty Ltd* [2001] QCA 51 [28] must now be regarded as wrongly decided.
136   [2010] HCA 12, (2010) 240 CLR 537 [47].
137   [2016] HCA 22, (2016) 331 ALR 550 at [86].
138   A Burrows, 'Comparing Compensatory Damages in Tort and Contract: Some Problematic Issues' in S Degeling, J Edelman and J Goudcamp (eds), *Torts in Commercial Law* (LBC 2011) 383; C McKay, 'Concurrent Liability in Claims for Loss of Chance of a Better Medical Outcome' (2012) 20 Torts LJ 29, 48–59.
139   *Naxakis v Western General Hospital* [1999] HCA 22, (1999) 197 CLR 269 [33] (Gaudron J). However, Callinan J (at [129]–[130]) seems to suggest an application of the degree-of-probability approach to less-than-even chances and of the balance-of-probabilities approach to more-than-even chances.
140   [2010] HCA 12, (2010) 240 CLR 537 [150], citing *Gregg v Scott* [2005] UKHL 2, [2005] 2 AC 176 [225] (Baroness Hale).
141   *Flinders Medical Centre v Waller* [2005] SASC 155, (2005) 91 SASR 378 [209]–[211]; *Martin v Minister for Health* [2016] WADC 15 at [299]–[300] (the decision on causation was affirmed on appeal: *East Metropolitan Health Service v Martin* [2017] WASCA 7 at [48]–[56]); *Panagoulias v East Metropolitan Health Service (No 4)* [2017] WADC 118 [455].

D Pure economic loss as initial harm

Where the initial harm is pure economic loss, four types of hypothetical past event must be distinguished. One is conduct of the defendant, which raises specific issues and is considered separately at [2.108]–[2.117]. Another type of event is what may be called a natural event, which encompasses everything other than voluntary human conduct. Natural events do not often feature in the cases, but it seems clear that they are treated in the same way as conduct of a third party. The two types of event that regularly come up in the cases are conduct of the plaintiff and conduct of a third party. In short, the hypothetical existence and exercise of an opportunity to benefit the plaintiff must be proved on the balance of probabilities, and subsequent hypothetical events are assessed by reference to the degree of probability of their occurrence. This will now be explained in more detail.

[2.88]

In most cases of pure economic loss, the chain of hypothetical events includes a key action of the plaintiff, such as the entry into a contract or the engagement in a business venture. Uncertainty as to whether the plaintiff would have taken that action is resolved on the balance of probabilities.[142] Thus, where the realisation of a commercial opportunity depends upon the plaintiff's decision to take it up, the question of whether the plaintiff would have taken it up will be determined on the balance of probabilities.[143] Where an overvaluation of property induces a lender to loan money on the security of that property, it will be determined on the balance of probabilities whether the lender, if aware of the property's true value, would still have granted a loan (possibly in a lesser amount) to the same borrower or would have sought to lend the money to someone else.[144]

[2.89]

Another example is *Crown Insurance Services Pty Ltd v National Mutual Life Association of Australasia Ltd*,[145] where an insurer issued a policy of disability insurance to a person who, unknown to the insurer, had had a CT scan and X-ray of his spine. The insurer's agent had failed to ask the insured about medical conditions. The insured claimed the insurance payout, alleging that he had become disabled two weeks after the policy was issued. The insurer settled with the insured and claimed reimbursement from the agent. It was found that the agent had breached duties in contract and tort towards the insurer by failing to ask the insured about medical conditions, and that the insured, if asked, would have revealed the CT scan and X-ray. But it was also found that there was an 80% chance that the insurer, if advised of the CT scan and X-ray, would still have issued an insurance policy without excluding liability for back

[2.90]

---

142   *Sellars v Adelaide Petroleum NL* (1994) 179 CLR 332, 353; *Daniels v Anderson* (1995) 37 NSWLR 438, 529, 539; *Price Higgins & Fidge (a firm) v Drysdale* [1996] 1 VR 346, 355; *Falkingham v Hoffmans (a firm)* [2014] WASCA 140, (2014) 46 WAR 510 [40], [242].

143   *Hanflex Pty Ltd v NS Hope & Associates* [1990] 2 Qd R 218, 228; *Hall v Foong* (1995) 65 SASR 281, 301; *Heenan v Di Sisto* [2008] NSWCA 25, (2008) Aust Torts Reports 81–941 [32]; *Fabcot Pty Ltd v Port Macquarie-Hastings Council* [2010] NSWSC 726 [140]; *Doolan v Renkon Pty Ltd* [2011] TASFC 4, (2011) 21 Tas R 156 [60]; *Principal Properties Pty Ltd v Brisbane Broncos Leagues Club Ltd (No 2)* [2016] QSC 252 [153]. Cf *Berryman v Hames Sharley (WA) Pty Ltd* [2008] WASC 59, (2008) 38 WAR 1 [802].

144   *St George Bank Ltd v Quinerts Pty Ltd* [2009] VSCA 245, (2009) 25 VR 666 [22]; *La Trobe Capital & Mortgage Corporation Ltd v Hay Property Consultants Pty Ltd* [2011] FCAFC 4, (2011) 190 FCR 299 [89]. See also *Richtoll Pty Ltd v WW Lawyers Pty Ltd (in liq)* [2016] NSWCA 308 [52]: where a solicitor failed to advise a lender of the appointment of receivers to the borrower, the lender must prove on the balance of probabilities that it would not have advanced the loan if advised of the receivership.

145   [2005] VSCA 218, (2005) 13 ANZ Ins Cas 61–659.

injury. The trial judge awarded the insurer damages in the amount of 20% of the settlement sum. The Victorian Court of Appeal reduced the award to a nominal sum on the ground that since it was relevant what the insurer would have done but for the agent's breach, the case was to be determined on the balance of probabilities.[146]

[2.91]   Once it is established, on the balance of probabilities, that the plaintiff would have taken a particular key action in the absence of the defendant's wrong, the degree-of-probability approach applies to all subsequent hypothetical events of any type.[147] For example, where a solicitor's negligence deprived the client of the opportunity to sue a third party, the hypothetical litigation between the client and the third party would have involved actions of the client, the solicitor and third parties. Once it is established, on the balance of probabilities,[148] that the client would have sued the third party in the absence of the solicitor's negligence, damages are assessed by first determining the likely amount that would have been awarded had the plaintiff won the action, and by then discounting this amount by the chance that the action might have been unsuccessful.[149] Similarly, where the plaintiff asserts that, in the absence of the defendant's wrong, the plaintiff would have entered into a contract containing particular terms, it must first be established on the balance of probabilities that the plaintiff would have sought to enter into such a contract, and damages will then be calculated by reference to the degree of probability of a third party being willing to enter into such a contract with the plaintiff.[150]

[2.92]   The same rules apply to uncertainty as to whether the plaintiff would have made a profit from a hypothetical contract. The leading case is *Sellars v Adelaide Petroleum NL*.[151] Adelaide Petroleum NL ('Adelaide') entered into parallel negotiations about the sale of some of its shares with Poseidon Ltd ('Poseidon') and Pagini Resources NL ('Pagini'). When Adelaide and Pagini produced a draft agreement (but not yet a concluded contract), Adelaide discontinued the negotiations with Pagini in reliance on a misleading statement by Poseidon. When Adelaide discovered the truth, it resumed negotiations with Pagini, and an agreement was reached. Adelaide asserted that, if it had continued the initial negotiations with Pagini, it would have reached a more favourable agreement, and claimed damages for that difference from Poseidon.

[2.93]   The trial judge found that it was more likely than not that, had the initial negotiations between Adelaide and Pagini not been discontinued, they would have entered into a contract on the terms set out in the draft agreement. Those terms included a number of conditions precedent for the contractual obligations to arise, including the absence of material breaches of contract by either party. The trial judge found that there was a less than even chance that all

---

146   Ibid, [14].

147   For actions of third parties, see, eg, *Heenan v Di Sisto* [2008] NSWCA 25, (2008) Aust Torts Reports 81–941 [28]–[34]; *Thompson v Schacht* [2014] NSWCA 247, (2014) 53 Fam LR 133 [39], [122].

148   *Falkingham v Hoffmans (a firm)* [2014] WASCA 140, (2014) 46 WAR 510 [40], [216], [219].

149   Eg *Leitch v Reynolds* [2005] NSWCA 259, (2005) Aust Torts Reports 81–806 [85]–[86]; *Worthington v Da Silva* [2006] WASCA 180 [125]–[130]; *Firth v Sutton* [2010] NSWCA 90 [160]; *Nigam v Harm (No 2)* [2011] WASCA 221 [258]–[266]; *Falkingham v Hoffmans (a firm)* [2014] WASCA 140, (2014) 46 WAR 510 [44], [237]. For a discussion of the complex details, see S Harder, 'Evaluating a Lost Opportunity to Sue' (2016) 28 Bond LR 1.

150   *Kronenberg v Bridge* [2014] TASFC 10 [61]–[64].

151   (1994) 179 CLR 332.

conditions would have been satisfied. In other words, there was a less than even chance that Adelaide would have obtained anything from Pagini had Poseidon's misleading statement not been made. Nevertheless, the trial judge awarded damages. He started with the amount Adelaide would have obtained from the hypothetical contract with Pagini if all conditions precedent had been satisfied, deducted the amount Adelaide obtained from the actual contract with Pagini, and deducted 60% to reflect the possibility that the conditions precedent in the hypothetical agreement would not have been satisfied (and made further deductions in respect of some of the conditions).

The High Court of Australia upheld the award, saying that once the loss of a commercial opportunity of some value has been proved on the balance on probabilities,[152] the lost opportunity must be valued by reference to the degree of probability and not on the balance of probabilities.[153] The High Court emphasised that this two-step approach applies not only to actions for misleading or deceptive conduct under statute, but also to actions for breach of contract or tort.[154]   **[2.94]**

Three matters should be noted about the rule laid down in *Sellars*. First, *Sellars* involved a less than even chance that the plaintiff would have made a certain profit but for the defendant's wrong, and the plaintiff recovered a proportion of that profit. Where there is a more than even chance (but no certainty) that the plaintiff would have made a profit but for the defendant's wrong, the plaintiff will still recover a proportion of that profit and not the whole profit. In other words, the plaintiff cannot choose between an assessment on the balance of probabilities and an assessment by evaluating chances.[155]   **[2.95]**

Secondly, in *Sellars*, the hypothetical contract would have been beneficial to the plaintiff or neutral, but not detrimental. Contingencies adverse to the plaintiff, where they exist, must be taken into account. Thus, where the hypothetical contract or business venture might have resulted in a loss or a profit, compensation may not be awarded unless it is established on the balance of probabilities that the opportunity had some value, either because the opportunity was marketable or because the plaintiff would have been more likely to make a profit than a loss.[156] Finally, in *Sellars*, the hypothetical events following the key action of the plaintiff were actions of the plaintiff and of third parties. The degree-of-probability approach also applies to hypothetical events other than human conduct. In *Howe v Teefy*,[157] a racehorse trainer who had been wrongfully deprived of the possession of a horse recovered for the loss of the chance of winning prizes with the horse.   **[2.96]**

Sometimes, in order for the plaintiff to have had an opportunity to take a beneficial action, a third party must first have acted in a particular way. *Sellars* might be understood as laying   **[2.97]**

---

152   This onus was not discharged, eg, in *Cosbott v Barry* [2009] NSWCA 34; *Prosperity Advisers Pty Ltd v Secure Enterprises Pty Ltd* [2012] NSWCA 192; *Origin Energy LPG Ltd v Bestcare Foods Ltd* [2013] NSWCA 90.
153   (1994) 179 CLR 332, 355, 368.
154   Ibid, 355.
155   *Heenan v Di Sisto* [2008] NSWCA 25, (2008) Aust Torts Reports 81–941 [41]–[50]; *University of Western Australia v Gray (No 28)* [2010] FCA 586, (2010) 185 FCR 335 [60]. See also *La Trobe Capital & Mortgage Corporation Ltd v Hay Property Consultants Pty Ltd* [2011] FCAFC 4, (2011) 190 FCR 299 [97]–[102].
156   *Principal Properties Pty Ltd v Brisbane Broncos Leagues Club Ltd (No 2)* [2016] QSC 252 [149], [325]–[326].
157   (1927) 27 SR (NSW) 301.

down that the degree-of-probability approach applies to all hypothetical past events other than the key action of the plaintiff, whether they would have occurred before or after that action. However, emphasis has been placed on the High Court's reference to the loss of an opportunity, as opposed to the loss of a chance, and it has been held that the plaintiff must establish, on the balance of probabilities, that an opportunity would have existed in the absence of the defendant's wrong.

[2.98]   In particular, plaintiffs who claimed to have lost the opportunity to enter into a beneficial contract with a third party have been required to prove, on the balance of probabilities, that the third party would have entered into the contract. Two cases illustrate this proposition.[158] In *Hayle Holdings Pty Ltd v Australian Technology Group Ltd*,[159] the plaintiff asserted that in the absence of the defendant's misleading conduct the plaintiff would have closed down its operations in Sydney, sought and obtained venture capital in the United States and pursued its business there. Compensation was denied on the ground that there was a less than even chance that the plaintiff would have obtained venture capital in the United States.[160]

[2.99]   In *Hart Security Australia Pty Ltd v Boucousis*,[161] the defendant's breach of fiduciary duty caused a third party to discontinue contractual negotiations with the plaintiff. The plaintiff asserted that those negotiations would have led to a contract lucrative to the plaintiff. Before the negotiations were discontinued, the third party demanded that the proposed contract include an obligation of the plaintiff to provide a bank guarantee of $1 million, and the plaintiff refused that demand. The trial judge was not persuaded that either the plaintiff would have agreed to provide the bank guarantee or that the third party would have relaxed the bank guarantee requirement, and denied compensation on that ground. The NSW Court of Appeal held that the trial judge had been correct to determine these matters on the balance of probabilities, and that compensation could not be awarded on the mere basis that there had been some reduction in the plaintiff's chances of a favourable outcome to its negotiations with the third party.[162]

[2.100]   Thus, the plaintiff must establish that it is more likely than not that the events whose occurrence would have given the plaintiff an opportunity would have occurred. In other words, the balance-of-probabilities approach applies to the key action of the plaintiff and all prior hypothetical past events. This is also demonstrated by *Crown Insurance Services Pty Ltd v National Mutual Life Association of Australasia Ltd*,[163] considered at [2.90], where the balance-of-probabilities approach was applied not only to the hypothetical action of the plaintiff insurer but also to the prior hypothetical action of the insured, a third party.

[2.101]   Sometimes, the defendant's wrong did not deprive the plaintiff of an opportunity to take a beneficial action, but deprived a third party of the opportunity to act to the benefit of the plaintiff, who would have been a passive recipient of the benefit. *Sellars* used to be understood as prescribing the application of the degree-of-probability approach in those circumstances.

---

158   See also *Castel Electronics Pty Ltd v Toshiba Singapore Pte Ltd* [2011] FCAFC 55, (2011) 192 FCR 445 [166].
159   [2000] FCA 1242.
160   Ibid, [455]–[459].
161   [2016] NSWCA 307, (2016) 339 ALR 659.
162   Ibid, [166]–[171].
163   [2005] VSCA 218, (2005) 13 ANZ Ins Cas 61–659.

An example is *Hendriks v McGeoch*,[164] where a solicitor was instructed to draw up a will [2.102] but failed to do so before the testatrix died. The beneficiary under the intended will sought to recover from the solicitor the value of what he would have received under the intended will. Having found the solicitor liable, the trial judge awarded damages in the full amount of the lost inheritance, without determining whether the degree of probability of the testatrix actually executing the will had it been drawn up was 51% or 100% or something in between. The NSW Court of Appeal reduced the award to 80% of the lost inheritance, finding a 20% chance that the testatrix would not have executed the will even if it had been drawn up. The court said that once the fact that a chance had been lost was established on the balance of probabilities, the loss must be assessed by reference to degrees of probabilities.[165] This implies that the beneficiary would have recovered damages for a proportion of the inheritance even if the probability of the testatrix executing the will had been less than 50% (but more than negligible).

However, the High Court of Australia laid down a different approach in *Badenach v* [2.103] *Calvert*.[166] The defendant solicitor was instructed by a client to prepare a will leaving the entirety of his estate to the plaintiff (the son of the client's de facto partner). The client executed a will drawn according to his instructions. After the client's death, the client's daughter (of whose existence the defendant had been unaware) brought a successful maintenance claim against the estate, depleting the estate. The plaintiff sued the defendant, claiming that the defendant had been negligent in failing to advise the testator of the possibility that his children could have a maintenance claim against the estate, and of the steps that could be taken to avoid such a claim (for example, the creation of joint tenancies between the testator and the plaintiff).

The trial judge left open whether the defendant had owed the plaintiff a duty of care to [2.104] advise the testator of the risk of a maintenance claim,[167] and dismissed the action on the ground that he was 'not satisfied, on the balance of probabilities, that a conversation about the daughter and a possible [maintenance] claim by her would have triggered an enquiry by the testator about ways of protecting the plaintiff's position'.[168] The Tasmanian Full Court held that the defendant had owed the plaintiff the relevant duty of care, and that the plaintiff was entitled to damages because he had lost a more than negligible chance that the testator would have taken action to protect his estate from a maintenance claim by his daughter.[169]

The High Court of Australia reinstated the trial judge's decision. The High Court unani- [2.105] mously held that the defendant had not owed the plaintiff a duty of care to advise the testator of the risk of a maintenance claim. Four of the five judges added that, even if a duty of care had existed, the claim would have been dismissed on the ground that the plaintiff had not established causation because he had not proved, on the balance of probabilities, that the testator, if properly advised, would have taken steps to protect the estate from a maintenance claim; damages cannot be awarded on the mere basis that the plaintiff has lost a chance, even a substantial chance, of a beneficial outcome.[170]

---

164   [2008] NSWCA 53, (2008) Aust Torts Reports 81–942.
165   [2008] NSWCA 53, (2008) Aust Torts Reports 81–942 [88].
166   [2016] HCA 18, (2016) 257 CLR 440.
167   *Calvert v Badenach* [2014] TASSC 61, (2014) 11 ASTLR 536 [33].
168   *Calvert v Badenach* [2014] TASSC 61, (2014) 11 ASTLR 536 [25] (Blow CJ).
169   *Calvert v Badenach* [2015] TASFC 8.
170   [2016] HCA 18, (2016) 257 CLR 440, [36]–[41] (French CJ, Kiefel and Keane JJ), [94]–[99] (Gordon J).

[2.106]   In *Badenach v Calvert*, the High Court thus laid down that where the defendant's wrong deprived a third party of an opportunity to act to the benefit of the plaintiff, the plaintiff recovers nothing unless it is more likely than not that the third party would have so acted. What is not entirely clear is how damages are to be assessed where a plaintiff has discharged that onus of proof. A complete application of the balance-of-probabilities approach would lead to recovery for the whole loss. However, the four judges who addressed the issue focused on the requirement to prove factual causation and did not disapprove *Sellars* or the distinction between causation and assessment derived from that case. Thus, unless it is certain that the third party would have acted to the plaintiff's benefit, a deduction should be made to reflect the possibility of the third party not so acting. The outcome in *Hendriks v McGeoch*, considered at [2.102], should be the same today.

[2.107]   To summarise, in cases of pure economic loss, where the chain of hypothetical events contains a key action of the plaintiff, the balance-of-probabilities approach applies to that action and any prior event, while the degree-of-probability approach applies to any subsequent event. Where the defendant's wrong deprived a third party of an opportunity to act to the benefit of the plaintiff (without an active involvement of the plaintiff), no compensation can be awarded unless the plaintiff proves, on the balance of probabilities, that the third party would have so acted. If the plaintiff discharges that onus of proof, damages are probably assessed by reference to the degree of probability of the third party acting to the plaintiff's benefit.

E   Hypothetical conduct of the defendant

[2.108]   In the context of pure economic loss, it is unclear how uncertainty in respect of hypothetical conduct of the defendant is to be resolved. The question may arise where the defendant would have had a choice between two or more non-wrongful courses of action. For example, where a party to a contract terminable by giving notice repudiates the contract, the question may arise whether that party, if not repudiating, would have given notice or continued with the contract. Sometimes, as the example shows, at least one of the courses of action would have inflicted loss upon the plaintiff, possibly in the same amount as the loss actually suffered. In those circumstances, the question arises whether it should be irrebuttably assumed that the defendant would have taken the course of action most detrimental to the plaintiff, or whether it should be determined which course of action is the most probable to have been taken. If the latter, the question arises whether the plaintiff's loss should be assessed by reference to the balance of probabilities or the degree of probability. All these approaches have found judicial support.

[2.109]   In some cases, it was simply assumed that the defendant would have taken the course of action most detrimental to the plaintiff.[171] A facet of that principle is the 'least burdensome' rule in contract law:

---

171   *Lavarack v Woods of Colchester Ltd* [1967] 1 QB 278; *Gunton v Richmond-upon-Thames LBC* [1981] Ch 448, 469 (Buckley LJ); *Hamilton v Open Window Bakery Ltd* [2004] SCC 9, [2004] 1 SCR 303; *Paper Reclaim Ltd v Aotearoa International Ltd* [2007] NZSC 26, [2007] 3 NZLR 169 [25].

The principle is that where a contract-breaker has a choice of methods of performance, damages will be assessed on the basis of the contract-breaker's minimum legal obligation – the method which would have been least onerous to the contract-breaker in the sense that non-compliance with it attracts the lowest measure of damages.[172]

In a second line of cases, the court determined what the defendant would in fact have done in the absence of the wrong, and resolved uncertainty in that respect on the balance of probabilities.[173] In *Commonwealth v Amann Aviation Pty Ltd*,[174] considered at [5.66], the Commonwealth repudiated a contract but would otherwise have become entitled to terminate the contract because of a breach by the other party. The probability of lawful termination was assessed at 20%. The High Court of Australia did not simply assume that the Commonwealth would have lawfully terminated the contract, but regarded the actual probability of lawful termination as significant. The majority made a decision on the balance of probabilities, awarding the plaintiff compensation for its whole reliance loss.[175]   [2.110]

In a third line of cases, the court determined which course of action was the most probable to have occurred, and assessed loss by reference to the degree of probability.[176] In *Chaplin v Hicks*,[177] the defendant, in breach of contract, failed to see the plaintiff to decide whether, in his opinion, she was one of the 12 most beautiful women out of a group of 50 women, those 12 obtaining employment as actresses. The English Court of Appeal upheld a jury award of substantial damages. Only nominal damages could have been awarded had it been irrebuttably assumed that the defendant, had he seen the plaintiff, would not have selected her, which he would have been free to do. Furthermore, only nominal damages could have been awarded had the plaintiff's loss been determined on the balance of probabilities, as her chance of being selected was only about 25%.   [2.111]

The degree-of-probability approach was also applied in *Port Macquarie-Hastings Council v Diveva Pty Ltd*.[178] In 2005, 2008 and 2011, the plaintiff was the successful tenderer for the supply and laying of asphalt for the defendant local authority. The 2011 contract was for a two-year period with an option for the plaintiff to extend the contract by one year. When the plaintiff gave notice that it intended to exercise that option, the defendant repudiated the contract, based on its incorrect view that the plaintiff's work was defective.   [2.112]

In addition to damages for the loss of profits in the additional one-year period, the trial judge awarded damages for the loss of profit that the plaintiff would have made under two   [2.113]

---

172 *Gumland Property Holdings Pty Ltd v Duffy Bros Fruit Market (Campbelltown) Pty Ltd* [2008] HCA 10, (2008) 234 CLR 237 [89] (Gleeson CJ, Kirby, Heydon, Crennan and Kiefel JJ). The rule goes back to *Cockburn v Alexander* (1848) 6 CB 791, 814 (Maule J): 'where there are several ways in which the contract might be performed, that mode is adopted which is the least profitable to the plaintiff, and the least burthensome to the defendant'.

173 *TCN Channel Nine Pty Ltd v Hayden Enterprises Pty Ltd* (1989) 16 NSWLR 130, 154–56; *Horkulak v Cantor Fitzgerald International* [2004] EWCA Civ 1287, [2005] ICR 402 [51]; *Australian Winch and Haulage Co Pty Ltd v Collins* [2013] NSWCA 327 [17], [112]–[122].

174 (1991) 174 CLR 64.

175 Three of the seven judges preferred a reduction to reflect the possibility of lawful termination: (1991) 174 CLR 64, 131–32 (Deane J), 147 (Toohey J), 176–77 (McHugh J).

176 *Lavarack v Woods of Colchester Ltd* [1967] 1 QB 278, 289 (Lord Denning MR, dissenting); *Kooee Communications Pty Ltd v Primus Telecommunications Pty Ltd* [2011] FCAFC 119 [133].

177 [1911] 2 KB 786.

178 [2017] NSWCA 97.

future contracts with the defendant, which would have been awarded through new tender processes. Based on the plaintiff's advantages over its competitors (because of its intimate knowledge of the defendant's requirements), the judge assessed the probability of the plaintiff being successful in the first tender process as 80% and the probability of the plaintiff being successful in the second tender process as 60%, and held the plaintiff entitled to the respective proportion of lost profits as damages.

[2.114]   The NSW Court of Appeal dismissed the defendant's appeal. With regard to the award of damages for the loss of profit under future contracts, the court said that it would be wrong to apply the 'least burdensome' rule (see [2.109]) and assume that the defendant would have acted against its own interests by rejecting the best tender.[179] The court cited *Sellars* (see [2.65]) as authority for the applicability of the degree-of-probability approach.[180] The court also cited *Commonwealth v Amann Aviation Pty Ltd* (see [2.110]),[181] but failed to explain how it reconciled its own endorsement of the degree-of-probability approach with the application of the balance-of-probabilities approach by the majority of the High Court in *Commonwealth v Amann Aviation Pty Ltd*.

[2.115]   On principle, it is defensible to start with a presumption that the defendant would have taken the course of action most detrimental to the plaintiff. After all, the plaintiff could not have complained if the defendant had in fact taken that course of action instead of committing the wrong.[182] But this presumption should be rebuttable. It should be open to the plaintiff to establish that the defendant would, or might, have taken a course of action less detrimental to the plaintiff. Commentators have supported an irrebuttable presumption with the arguments that it would be odd to consider evidence from the plaintiff on what the defendant would have done,[183] and that evidence from the defendant on that matter would be a self-serving action.[184] These arguments are not convincing, as the courts routinely consider evidence from either party on what a third party would have done, and – unless excluded by statute (see [3.26]) – the courts consider evidence from the plaintiff on what the plaintiff would have done.

[2.116]   Furthermore, it would be odd to have an irrebuttable presumption that the defendant would have acted arbitrarily or neglected his own interests.[185] As Deane J said in *Commonwealth v Amann Aviation Pty Ltd*:

> The 'rule' [that a party in default should be assumed not to act so as to increase its liability] does not require an assumption that, after full performance of a contract, the defaulting party would have acted against his own interests and obligations by, for example, declining to accept the most favourable tender for a further contract. It is no more an answer to Amann's claim to say that the Commonwealth might, at the end of the day, have arbitrarily refused to deal with Amann than was the possibility that the defendant might have arbitrarily refused to give the plaintiff a prize an answer to the claim in *Chaplin v. Hicks* ...[186]

---

179   Ibid, [88].
180   Ibid, [81].
181   Ibid, [79], [82].
182   A Burrows, *Remedies for Torts and Breach of Contract* (3rd edn, OUP 2004) 151.
183   Ibid, 151–52.
184   J Poole, 'Loss of Chance and the Evaluation of Hypotheticals in Contractual Claims' [2007] LMCLQ 63, 68.
185   *TCN Channel Nine Pty Ltd v Hayden Enterprises Pty Ltd* (1989) 16 NSWLR 130, 154.
186   (1991) 174 CLR 64, 133. Approvingly quoted in *Port Macquarie-Hastings Council v Diveva Pty Ltd* [2017] NSWCA 97 [82].

If an irrebuttable presumption as to the defendant's hypothetical conduct is rejected, it must be decided whether uncertainty as to what the defendant would have done ought to be resolved on the balance of probabilities or by making an award proportionate to the degree of probability. In general, the balance-of-probabilities approach applies to hypothetical conduct of the plaintiff and the degree-of-probability approach to hypothetical conduct of third parties; see [2.89]–[2.91]. The justification provided for this difference is that the plaintiff can be expected to adduce persuasive evidence as to her own hypothetical conduct, but not the hypothetical conduct of third parties.[187] If this justification is accepted, uncertainty as to what the defendant would have done should be resolved on the balance of probabilities. However, the justification is weak, as the third party may appear as a witness and evidence from the plaintiff may be unavailable or excluded by statute; see [3.26]. There is much to be said for an application of the degree-of-probability approach to hypothetical conduct of any person including the plaintiff and the defendant. [2.117]

V   Temporal considerations

An award of money is calculated by reference to the value of money at a certain date. But a court does not assess loss exactly at the time the loss occurs. The assessment takes place some time, possibly years, after the wrong occurred. Some loss is usually suffered at a date before trial. Different items of loss may have been suffered at different dates. Moreover, the wrong may cause the plaintiff to suffer loss at some date after judgment. For example, a permanent personal injury may require the plaintiff to buy medicine, or undergo medical treatment, for some period into the future. [2.118]

In the period between the date of the loss (past or future) and the date of judgment, the purchasing power of money and the prices of goods and services change. The date as at which loss is assessed is therefore significant. It must also be asked whether future loss is assessed at the same time as past loss or later. Furthermore, the plaintiff obtains compensation (once it is paid) some time after past loss occurred and some time before future loss will occur. The question arises whether the plaintiff must be compensated for being kept out of money in relation to past loss, and whether the calculation of compensation for future loss must reflect the fact that the plaintiff obtains the compensation before the loss occurs. The rules on all these matters will be discussed now. [2.119]

A   The lump sum rule and the 'once and for all' rule

The lump sum rule and the 'once and for all' rule are usually mentioned together but are in fact two distinct rules. Each rule could exist without the other. [2.120]

The lump sum rule is straightforward. In the absence of legislation providing otherwise,[188] compensation must be awarded as a lump sum; the court cannot order a defendant to make [2.121]

---

187   *Gregg v Scott* [2002] EWCA Civ 1471, (2003) 71 BMLR 16 [71]; A Burrows, 'Uncertainty about Uncertainty: Damages for Loss of a Chance' [2008] JPIL 31, 36–37.

188   *Motor Vehicle (Third Party Insurance) Act 1943* (WA), s 16; discussed by H Luntz, *Assessment of Damages for Personal Injury and Death: General Principles* (LexisNexis Butterworths 2006) [3.2]–[3.4].

periodic payments to the plaintiff.[189] Legislation in some jurisdictions permits an order of interim payments in certain circumstances.[190] In cases involving personal injury or death, statutes in all jurisdictions (including the Commonwealth) other than the Australian Capital Territory permit courts to approve settlements that provide for the payment of all or part of compensation in the form of periodic payments funded by an annuity or otherwise (structured settlements).[191]

[2.122]   Turning to the 'once and for all' rule, loss resulting from a civil wrong is generally assessed once and for all.[192] That applies to future loss as well as past loss. Loss dependent upon future contingencies must be assessed by reference to the degree of probability of the contingencies materialising.[193] In dust disease cases, statutes in some jurisdictions permit an award of provisional damages for the initial condition and a further award of damages for a different condition in the future.[194] At common law, a court can neither defer the assessment of future loss to a later date nor make an award conditional upon the occurrence or non-occurrence of a certain event.[195] However, where it is very difficult to determine whether the plaintiff will have to pay tax on the compensation received, the court may award an amount calculated on the assumption that no tax is payable and give the plaintiff leave to apply for additional compensation should the original award be assessed as liable to tax.[196]

[2.123]   In the absence of special leave, a plaintiff cannot return to court and claim compensation for unanticipated additional loss (for example, a deterioration of personal injury) suffered after judgment as a result of the same wrong.[197] This rule has been justified on two policy grounds often expressed in Latin terms: the public interest in finality of litigation (*interest reipublicae ut sit finis litium*), and the defendant's interest in not being sued twice for the same wrong (*nemo debet bis vexari pro eadem causa*).[198]

[2.124]   The 'once and for all' rule applies only to loss resulting from the same wrong. Losses resulting from different wrongs can be claimed in separate actions, even if the same general

---

189   *O'Brien v McKean* (1968) 118 CLR 540, 559; *Cullen v Trappell* (1980) 146 CLR 1, 37; *Todorovic v Waller* (1981) 150 CLR 402, 412.

190   *Civil Procedure Act 2005* (NSW), ss 81–84; *Dust Diseases Tribunal Act 1989* (NSW), pt 6; *Supreme Court Act 1935* (SA), s 30B. These and other provisions are discussed by H Luntz, *Assessment of Damages for Personal Injury and Death: General Principles* (LexisNexis Butterworths 2006) [3.5]–[3.16].

191   *Competition and Consumer Act 2010* (Cth), s 87ZC; *Civil Liability Act 2002* (NSW), ss 22–26; *Personal Injuries (Civil Claims) Act* (NT), s 12; *Personal Injuries (Liabilities and Damages) Act 2003* (NT), ss 31, 32; *Civil Liability Act 2003* (Qld), s 65; *Supreme Court Act 1935* (SA), s 30BA; *Civil Liability Act 2002* (Tas), s 8; *Wrongs Act 1958* (Vic), s 28N; *Civil Liability Act 2002* (WA), s 15.

192   *Cullen v Trappell* (1980) 146 CLR 1, 37; *Todorovic v Waller* (1981) 150 CLR 402, 412.

193   *Malec v JC Hutton Pty Ltd* (1990) 169 CLR 638, 643–44.

194   *Dust Diseases Tribunal Act 1989* (NSW), s 11A; *Dust Diseases Act 2005* (SA), s 9(1); *Civil Liability Act 2002* (Tas), s 8B; *Asbestos Diseases Compensation Act 2008* (Vic), s 4. The introduction of provisional damages for all cases of personal injury has been recommended by the Law Reform Commission of Western Australia, *Provisional Damages and Damages for Gratuitous Services*, Report No 106 (2016) ch 4.

195   *Namol Pty Ltd v AW Baulderstone Pty Ltd (No 2)* (1993) 47 FCR 388, 391.

196   *Rabelais Pty Ltd v Cameron* (1995) 95 ATC 4552, 4553; *Turner v TR Nominees Pty Ltd* (1995) 31 ATR 578, 596; *PM Sulcs & Associates Pty Ltd v Daihatsu Australia Pty Ltd* [2001] NSWSC 798 [119]; *Guy v Commonwealth* [2013] ACTSC 128 [95].

197   The classic illustration is *Fitter v Veal* (1701) 12 Mod Rep 542, 88 ER 1506.

198   *Jackson v Goldsmith* (1950) 81 CLR 446, 467 (Fullagar J).

facts underlie all actions. For example, a plaintiff who has been assaulted on several separate occasions by the same defendant has a separate cause of action in relation to each assault.[199] Furthermore, a plaintiff who had received damages in relation to the publication of a defamatory book was allowed to bring a fresh action in relation to the republication of the same book.[200]

A distinction must be made in cases of a truly continuing wrong such as a continuing nuisance. If specific relief is sought and denied, the plaintiff's future as well as past losses will be assessed once and for all since the defendant now has a 'permission' to continue the conduct.[201] If specific relief is either granted or not sought, only past losses will be compensated, and the plaintiff is free to bring a fresh action in relation to the continuation of the wrongful conduct after judgment.[202]

[2.125]

Continuing wrongs must be distinguished from repeated breaches of recurring obligations, particularly in a contractual context. A continuing breach exists where there is one continuous conduct breaching one obligation, for example an employer's failure to provide work to the employee as promised[203] or an employee's operation of a business competing with his employer's business in breach of a restraint-of-trade covenant.[204] By contrast, breaches of recurring obligations constitute separate breaches of contract. Two separate breaches exist, for example, where neither an instalment due on 1 January nor an instalment due on 1 February is paid,[205] and where an employee obliged to work on Saturdays fails to work on two Saturdays.[206]

[2.126]

The 'once and for all' rule prevents the victim of a wrong from splitting the claim for compensation in terms of heads of loss or periods of time.[207] However, plaintiffs have been allowed to bring separate actions for personal injury and property damage caused by the same negligent act of the same defendant.[208] This rule may be regarded as an exception to the 'once and for all' rule, or it may be said that personal injury and property damage constitute separate wrongs. Either way, a plaintiff who has obtained compensation for certain personal injury caused by a certain act cannot bring an action in respect of other personal injury caused by the same act,[209] and a plaintiff who has obtained compensation for damage to certain property caused by a certain act cannot bring an action in respect of damage to another property caused

[2.127]

---

199 *Tusyn v State of Tasmania (No 2)* [2008] TASSC 76, (2008) 18 Tas R 313 [25].
200 *Harris v 718932 Pty Ltd (formerly Globe Press Pty Ltd)* [2003] NSWCA 38, (2003) 56 NSWLR 276.
201 *Miller v Jackson* [1977] QB 966, 982.
202 *Mann v Capital Territory Health Commission* (1982) 148 CLR 97, 101. Lord Cairns' Act damages may be awarded for future wrongs; see [12.58].
203 *Mann v Capital Territory Health Commission* (1982) 148 CLR 97, 101.
204 *National Coal Board v Galley* [1958] 1 WLR 16, 26.
205 Ibid, 26.
206 Ibid, 27.
207 *Djordjevic v Australian Iron & Steel Ltd* (1964) 82 WN (Pt 1) (NSW) 218, 220; *Tusyn v State of Tasmania (No 2)* [2008] TASSC 76, (2008) 18 Tas R 313 [13].
208 *Brunsden v Humphrey* (1884) 14 QBD 141; *Jackson v Goldsmith* (1950) 81 CLR 446, 467 (Fullagar J); *Port of Melbourne Authority v Anshun Pty Ltd* (1981) 147 CLR 589, 611 (Brennan J); *Marlborough Harbour Board v Charter Travel Co Ltd* (1989) 18 NSWLR 223, 230–31; *Linsley v Petrie* [1998] 1 VR 427, 431–37, 448. A different view was taken in *Cahoon v Franks* [1967] SCR 455.
209 *Cartledge v E Jopling & Sons Ltd* [1963] AC 758, 780.

by the same act.[210] A plaintiff who has claimed compensation for certain loss based on a certain cause of action (for example, a breach of contract) cannot generally claim compensation for the same loss based on a different cause of action (for example, negligence).[211]

B   Date of assessment

[2.128]   Since the purchasing power of money and the price of goods and services change over time, the date as at which the court assesses loss ('date of assessment') is significant. Non-pecuniary loss, both past and future, is assessed as at the date of judgment.[212] The same is true for future pecuniary loss.[213] The date of assessment of past pecuniary loss used to differ considerably between the causes of action. While those differences have not disappeared completely, there has been a significant convergence. There is now a great deal of flexibility in 'tailoring' the date of assessment to the circumstances of the individual case.[214]

[2.129]   In equity, the general rule is that 'the losses are to be assessed as at the time of trial, using the full benefit of hindsight'.[215] Loss is generally assessed as at the latest possible time, which may be the date of judgment.[216] Loss is not generally assessed as at the date of breach. For example, in *Re Dawson*,[217] a trustee improperly paid away NZ£4700 of the trust moneys. At that time there was parity between Australian and New Zealand currency, but at the time of proceedings in Australia to enforce restoration NZ£4700 was worth AU£5829 8s 3d. Street J ordered the trustee to pay AU£5829 8s 3d into the trust, on the basis that a trust is entitled to receive any increase in market value of a misappropriated asset between the date of breach and the date of recoupment.[218]

[2.130]   However, courts are willing to assess equitable compensation as at a date earlier than the date of trial (or judgment), even as at the date of breach, where this is more appropriate. This is particularly relevant in relation to assets (such as shares) whose value fluctuates rapidly. In *Cassegrain v Gerard Cassegrain & Co Pty Ltd*,[219] shares were sold in breach of fiduciary duty, and the hearing took place 10 years later. Equitable compensation was assessed by reference to the value of the shares at the date of breach.[220]

---

210   *Marlborough Harbour Board v Charter Travel Co Ltd* (1989) 18 NSWLR 223, 231.

211   *Port of Melbourne Authority v Anshun Pty Ltd* (1981) 147 CLR 589.

212   *Andjelic v Marsland* (1996) 186 CLR 20, 28.

213   *Cullen v Trappell* (1980) 146 CLR 1, 12.

214   The date of assessment of Lord Cairns' Act damages is discussed at [12.47]–[12.51].

215   *Canson Enterprises Ltd v Boughton & Co* [1991] 3 SCR 534, 555 (McLachlin J), approvingly quoted in *Youyang Pty Ltd v Minter Ellison Morris Fletcher* [2003] HCA 15, (2003) 212 CLR 484 [35]; *McCrohon v Harith* [2010] NSWCA 67 [61]. See also *ABN AMRO Bank NV v Bathurst Regional Council* [2014] FCAFC 65, (2014) 224 FCR 1 [1092]; *AIB Group (UK) plc v Mark Redler & Co Solicitors* [2014] UKSC 58, [2015] AC 1503 [135]. It has been argued that there should be no prima facie rule, the assessment being made as at the date required by justice in the individual case: M Tilbury and G Davis, 'Equitable Compensation' in P Parkinson (ed), *The Principles of Equity* (2nd edn, LBC 2003) [2217].

216   *Greater Pacific Investments Pty Ltd (in liq) v Australian National Industries Pty Ltd* (1996) 39 NSWLR 143, 154; *Duke Group Ltd (in liq) v Pilmer* [1999] SASC 97, (1999) 73 SASR 64 [826]–[827].

217   [1966] 2 NSWR 211.

218   Ibid, 216.

219   [2015] NSWSC 851.

220   Ibid, [78].

In *McNally v Harris (No 3)*,[221] shares held on trust were misappropriated by the trustees. **[2.131]**
New trustees were appointed, and they sought equitable compensation from the former
trustees. The share price was $1.33 when the proceedings were instituted, $4 on the first day
of the hearing on liability, $2.60 when judgment on liability was delivered, and $1.78 on the
day the court heard argument on the assessment of equitable compensation. The plaintiffs
contended that the figure of $4 be used, arguing that the defendants' failure to restore the
shares to the trust fund as soon as proceedings commenced deprived the plaintiffs of the
opportunity to sell the shares in a rising market. It was held that if the plaintiffs could prove that
they would have sold the shares at some favourable time had the defendants restored the
shares when proceedings commenced, equitable compensation would be assessed by reference to the share price on the date of the hypothetical sale.[222] But the plaintiffs offered no
evidence to that effect, and the latest share price ($1.78) was used in assessing
compensation.[223]

Compensation for personal injury and wrongful death is assessed as at the 'date of **[2.132]**
verdict'.[224] This rule has been laid down in cases involving claims in tort, but the same rule
must apply to other causes of action. The rule favours plaintiffs since over time the value of
money usually depreciates and the costs of goods and services rise. Where the plaintiff
unreasonably delays bringing or prosecuting her claim, compensation may be assessed as
at the date at which a diligent plaintiff would have obtained judgment.[225] The phrase 'date
of verdict' stems from the time when juries were involved and when the date of assessment
was probably the last day of the trial.[226] Today, where a judge decides alone, the date of
assessment is the date of judgment or the most practical date between the conclusion of the
trial and the judgment.[227] If there is an appeal and the appellate court reassesses the
compensation, such reassessment will be made as at the date of the appellate judgment.[228]
Thus, if a statutory cap on a head of loss changes between the date of the judgment
appealed and the date of the appellate judgment, the appellate court will use the new
figure.[229]

The rules established for personal injury also apply to the violation of other personal **[2.133]**
interests of the plaintiff, such as reputation or freedom of movement. Thus, pecuniary loss
resulting from defamation or false imprisonment is also assessed as at the date of the judgment
(or hearing).[230]

---

221   [2008] NSWSC 861.
222   Ibid, [25].
223   Ibid, [17], [45].
224   *O'Brien v McKean* (1968) 118 CLR 540, 545 (Barwick CJ); *Richardson v Whymark Nominees Pty Ltd*
       [2004] WASCA 208 [289] (Jenkins J); *Goodman v Impact Hire Australia Pty Ltd* [2009] NSWSC 941 [6]–[7]
       (Patten AJ). See also *Monie v Commonwealth* [2007] NSWCA 230 [121].
225   *O'Brien v McKean* (1968) 118 CLR 540, 545 (Barwick CJ).
226   *Richardson v Whymark Nominees Pty Ltd* [2004] WASCA 208 [289] (Jenkins J). See *O'Brien v McKean*
       (1968) 118 CLR 540, 554–55 (Windeyer J): 'date of the hearing'.
227   *Harvey v Electrolytic Zinc Co of Australasia Ltd* [1980] Tas R 167, 171; *Richardson v Whymark Nominees
       Pty Ltd* [2004] WASCA 208 [289]–[290] (Jenkins J); *Warrick v Bryan* [2005] WASCA 70 [91]–[93]; *Goodman
       v Impact Hire Australia Pty Ltd* [2009] NSWSC 941 [6]–[7].
228   *Monie v Commonwealth* [2007] NSWCA 230 [122]–[124].
229   *Marsland v Andjelic* (1993) 31 NSWLR 162, 168; *Nicholson v Nicholson* (1994) 35 NSWLR 308, 319;
       Monie v Commonwealth [2007] NSWCA 230 [123]. Cf *Hughes v Cornwall* [2001] WASCA 157 [65].
230   This is implicit in *Webster v Coles Myer Ltd* [2009] NSWDC 4 [343]–[349].

[2.134]   Leaving aside violations of personal interests, the general rule at common law is that 'damages for tort or for breach of contract are assessed as at the date of the breach'.[231] But this rule is not rigid and 'will yield if, in the particular circumstances, some other date is necessary to provide adequate compensation'.[232] It has been recognised that rules governing the date of assessment are second-order rules that must yield to the first-order principle that the plaintiff must be fairly compensated for the wrong suffered.[233] What is 'fair' compensation has to take into account what is fair to the defendant as well as the plaintiff.[234] The party who wishes to have damages assessed as at a date other than the date of the breach must demonstrate why an assessment as at the date of the breach would be unjust.[235] While the refusal to adhere to a rigid rule may be welcomed, the increasing willingness of the courts to depart from the 'date of breach' rule has created uncertainty. The date as at which a court will assess common law damages for property damage or pure economic loss can no longer be predicted with confidence. Nevertheless, certain broad principles may be identified.

[2.135]   The rule that damages for conversion are assessed as at the date of the conversion[236] has become a 'rebuttable presumption',[237] since 'it has been recognised that the assessment of damages for conversion should be carried out in a flexible manner so as to achieve the true compensatory purpose of damages'.[238] Similarly, the rule that damages for detinue are assessed as at the date of judgment[239] (because the tort is not complete until the defendant fails to deliver up the goods at the time of judgment[240]) is no longer rigidly applied.[241] 'For example, if the plaintiff would have sold the goods had they been delivered to him when they should have been, his basic measure of loss will be the market price at that date plus interest.'[242]

[2.136]   Under the 'date of breach' rule, the cost of having damaged property repaired or rebuilt would be assessed as at the date of the damage. However, it is not always possible for the

---

231   *Miliangos v George Frank (Textiles) Ltd* [1976] AC 443, 468 (Lord Wilberforce), approvingly quoted in *Johnson v Perez* (1988) 166 CLR 351, 368 (Wilson, Toohey and Gaudron JJ); *McCrohon v Harith* [2010] NSWCA 67 [54]. In cases of an accepted repudiation of a contract, it is not clear whether the date of assessment under the general rule is the date of the repudiation or the date of its acceptance; see *C & P Syndicate Pty Ltd v Reddy* [2013] NSWSC 643 [197].

232   *Johnson v Perez* (1988) 166 CLR 351, 368 (Wilson, Toohey and Gaudron JJ); *McCrohon v Harith* [2010] NSWCA 67 [54].

233   *Johnson v Perez* (1988) 166 CLR 351, 356–57 (Mason CJ); *Narni Pty Ltd v National Australia Bank Ltd* [2001] VSCA 31 [29]; *McCrohon v Harith* [2010] NSWCA 67 [55]; *CHEP Australia Ltd v Bunnings Group Ltd* [2010] NSWSC 301 [227].

234   *Narni Pty Ltd v National Australia Bank Ltd* [2001] VSCA 31 [29]; *McCrohon v Harith* [2010] NSWCA 67 [55].

235   *Ng v Filmlock Pty Ltd* [2014] NSWCA 389, (2014) 88 NSWLR 146 [59]; *Baguley v Lifestyle Homes Mackay Pty Ltd* [2015] QCA 75 [53]; *Broughton v B & B Group Investments Pty Ltd* [2017] VSCA 227 [157].

236   *Ley v Lewis* [1952] VLR 119, 121–22; *Pratten v Pratten* [2005] QCA 213 [61].

237   *Semenov v Pirvu* [2011] VSC 605 [19] (Dixon J).

238   *CHEP Australia Ltd v Bunnings Group Ltd* [2010] NSWSC 301 [229] (McDougall J), citing *IBL Ltd v Coussens* [1991] 2 All ER 133.

239   *Ley v Lewis* [1952] VLR 119, 120–21; *Egan v State Transport Authority* (1982) 31 SASR 481, 529; *Gaba Formwork Contractors Pty Ltd v Turner Corporation Ltd* (1991) 32 NSWLR 175, 178; *Pratten v Pratten* [2005] QCA 213 [61].

240   *Egan v State Transport Authority* (1982) 31 SASR 481, 529.

241   *Brandeis Goldschmidt & Co Ltd v Western Transport Ltd* [1981] QB 864, 870 (Brandon LJ, with whom Ackner and Donaldson LJJ agreed): 'I cannot see why there should be any universally applicable rule for assessing damages for wrongful detention of goods'.

242   *IBL Ltd v Coussens* [1991] 2 All ER 133, 143 (Nicholls LJ).

plaintiff to arrange for repair work immediately. Sometimes, the plaintiff may delay repair for good reason. Since the cost of goods and services rises over time, an application of the 'date of breach' rule would disadvantage the plaintiff. It has therefore been established that the cost of repair is usually assessed as at the date by which repair could reasonably have occurred.[243]

In the English case *Dodd Properties Ltd v Canterbury City Council*,[244] the cost of repairing a damaged building was assessed as at the date of trial because the defendant had denied liability until shortly before trial and the plaintiff had not wanted to spend a significant amount of money on repair before the defendant's liability was established. This case has been followed in Australia, for example in *Glenmont Investments Pty Ltd v O'Loughlin*,[245] where the cost of rebuilding a large mechanical dinosaur that had been destroyed by fire was assessed as at the date of trial because the owner of the dinosaur could not afford to rebuild the dinosaur until it recovered damages.[246]

[2.137]

The basic loss suffered by a plaintiff who was wrongfully (through deceit, negligence, breach of contract or breach of s 18 of the Australian Consumer Law) induced to purchase an asset from the defendant or a third party is in general the difference between the price paid and the value of the asset *at the time of purchase*.[247] The date of the transaction is in general also the date of assessment where the plaintiff was induced to sell an asset. An assessment as at the date of the transaction can be problematic where the plaintiff discovers the defendant's wrong only after some time or is practically unable to take remedial action immediately after discovery. In the intervening period, the value of the asset may have changed to the plaintiff's detriment. The courts have often assisted plaintiffs in two ways. In some cases of induced purchase, while still applying the 'date of purchase' rule, the courts considered events occurring after the purchase in determining the 'real value' of the asset at the time of purchase.[248]

[2.138]

In other cases, the courts assessed the value of the asset as at a date later than the date of the induced transaction.[249] In *Rentokil Pty Ltd v Channon*,[250] the plaintiff purchased a house in reliance on the defendant's pest report that the house was free of termites. In fact, the house was so infested with termites as to require demolition. The plaintiff could not afford to purchase another property and could not be confident that the defendant would reimburse her since the defendant denied liability until the morning of the trial. The trial judge calculated

[2.139]

---

243   *Westwood v Cordwell* [1983] 1 Qd R 276, 277; *Warragamba Winery Pty Ltd v New South Wales (No 9)* [2012] NSWSC 701 [1294].
244   [1980] 1 WLR 433.
245   [2000] SASC 429, (2000) 79 SASR 195.
246   Ibid, [404], [417].
247   *Holmes v Jones* (1907) 4 CLR 1692, 1702–03; *Potts v Miller* (1940) 64 CLR 282, 289, 297; *Toteff v Antonas* (1952) 87 CLR 647, 650, 654; *South Australia v Johnson* (1982) 42 ALR 161, 170; *Gould v Vaggelas* (1985) 157 CLR 215, 220, 255, 265; *Gates v City Mutual Life Assurance Society Ltd* (1986) 160 CLR 1, 12; *Kizbeau Pty Ltd v WG & B Pty Ltd* (1995) 184 CLR 281, 291; *HTW Valuers (Central Qld) Pty Ltd v Astonland Pty Ltd* [2004] HCA 54, (2004) 217 CLR 640 [34]–[35].
248   *Kizbeau Pty Ltd v WG & B Pty Ltd* (1995) 184 CLR 281, 291–96; *HTW Valuers (Central Qld) Pty Ltd v Astonland Pty Ltd* [2004] HCA 54, (2004) 217 CLR 640 [40]–[43]. See also *Potts v Miller* (1940) 64 CLR 282, 298 (Dixon J); *Gould v Vaggelas* (1985) 157 CLR 215, 220 (Gibbs CJ).
249   *Koutsonicolis v Principle (No 2)* (1987) 48 SASR 328. See also *North East Equity Pty Ltd v Proud Nominees Pty Ltd* [2010] FCAFC 60, (2010) 269 ALR 262 [176]. Cf *Bamford v Albert Shire Council* [1998] 2 Qd R 125, 135.
250   (1990) 19 NSWLR 417.

damages by reference to diminution in value (the difference between the value of the land alone and the value of the land with a house free of termites) and used the value at the date of trial, which was significantly higher than the value at the date of purchase. A majority in the NSW Court of Appeal upheld the award.

[2.140]   In *Hocking Stuart (Hawthorn) Pty Ltd v Vernea*,[251] the plaintiffs employed the defendant real estate agent to sell the plaintiffs' property for not less than $850 000. The defendant, acting on behalf of the plaintiffs, signed a contract for a sale of the property to a purchaser for $750 000. The plaintiffs initially denied being bound by that contract but, after being sued by the purchaser, they acknowledged that they were bound and sought damages for the loss of the property from the defendant. The market value of the property rose during that period. The Victorian Court of Appeal rejected an assessment of the damages by reference to the value of the property at the time of the defendant's breach or any other date before the plaintiffs settled with the purchaser, on the ground that the plaintiffs could not have been expected to purchase an alternative property while it was still unclear whether they were bound by the contract.[252]

[2.141]   In *Vieira v O'Shea*,[253] the plaintiff bought an interest in a racehorse in reliance on the defendant's advice that the horse was free of any health problems that would inhibit its capacity to race. The horse had an illness at the time of the advice and later required surgery. Damages for breach of contract were assessed in the amount of the difference, not between the price the plaintiff had paid for his interest in the horse and the actual value of that interest at the time the plaintiff acquired the interest, but between the price paid by the plaintiff and the actual value of the interest at the earliest date at which the plaintiff could reasonably have been expected to sell the interest, which was more than two years after the acquisition. The NSW Court of Appeal upheld that assessment, observing that the interests of justice require a deviation from the 'date of the breach' rule where the plaintiff was induced to acquire an asset and the asset is not readily marketable at the time of the acquisition, or the plaintiff does not discover the defendant's wrong until some time after the acquisition, or if for some other reason the plaintiff is 'locked in' to holding the asset.[254] The plaintiff in that case was effectively 'locked in' until the horse's condition settled down, which was two years after the acquisition.[255]

[2.142]   By contrast, the courts have usually adhered to the 'date of breach' rule where the plaintiff's exposure to the fluctuation of property prices was a result of a free decision by the plaintiff. Vendors of land who accepted the purchaser's repudiation of the contract have been awarded damages in the amount of the difference between the contract price and the property's market value *at the date of the breach*,[256] both where the vendor kept the

---

251   [2005] VSCA 129, (2005) V ConvR 54–706.
252   Ibid, [18]. The court upheld the trial judge's award based upon the value of the property at the date of trial, on the ground that the date of the trial was sufficiently close to the earlier date that, on principle, should have been chosen.
253   [2012] NSWCA 21.
254   Ibid, [45].
255   Ibid, [46].
256   It is not settled whether the date of the breach in this context is the date of completion or the date of the acceptance of the repudiation; see *C & P Syndicate Pty Ltd v Reddy* [2013] NSWSC 643, (2013) 16 BPR 31,771 [197], where the issue was left open. It was also left open in *Ng v Filmlock Pty Ltd* [2014] NSWCA 389, (2014) 88 NSWLR 146 [45].

property[257] and where the vendor sold the property to a third party more than a year later in a falling market.[258] In one of the latter cases it was said that the vendor could have obtained protection against the consequences of a falling market by seeking specific performance rather than terminating the contract.[259] However, damages in the amount of the difference between the contract price and the resale price were awarded in a case in which the seller immediately re-advertised the property but was not able to sell it in a falling market until more than two years later.[260]

More generally, damages are not assessed as at the date of trial where this would provide a windfall for the plaintiff. In *Johnson v Perez*,[261] the plaintiff engaged the defendants to act as his solicitors in two personal injury actions against his employer. Although each claim was filed in time, each was dismissed for want of prosecution several years later. In that period, mainly due to inflation, there was a general increase in the amount of damages awarded for personal injury. The plaintiff brought an action against the defendants for negligence and breach of contract. It was held that the defendants had breached their duty of care towards the plaintiff and that the plaintiff would have succeeded in the action against his employer. The trial judge assessed the value of the lost claim against the plaintiff's employer by reference to the most recent amounts awarded for personal injury. A majority in the High Court of Australia overturned that decision, holding that damages ought to be assessed as at the date when the personal injury action would ordinarily have been determined.

[2.143]

Where the date of assessment is prior to trial, the court may consider developments after the date of assessment insofar as they assist in determining the loss at the date of assessment.[262] As mentioned earlier, where the loss suffered at the date of breach depends upon the market value of a certain asset at that time, events occurring after the date of breach may be considered in determining the value of the asset at the date of breach. Furthermore, in *Johnson v Perez*,[263] it was said that evidence emerging after the date at which the personal injury action would have been decided may be considered for the purpose of evaluating the case that the plaintiff would have made in that action. By contrast, in *Nikolaou v Papasavas, Phillips & Co*,[264] which involved facts relevantly identical to those in *Johnson v Perez*, it was held that a worsening of the plaintiff's injury occurring after the date at which the personal injury action would have been decided was irrelevant to the determination of the plaintiff's loss, since such evidence would not have been known to the court in the personal injury action and thus cannot assist in determining what that court would have decided.

[2.144]

---

257   *Higgins v Statewide Developments Pty Ltd* [2010] NSWSC 183, (2010) 14 BPR 27,293 [97].

258   *Ng v Filmlock Pty Ltd* [2014] NSWCA 389, (2014) 88 NSWLR 146 (where the possibility of deviating from the breach date rule 'in an appropriate case' was recognised; see [56]); *C & P Syndicate Pty Ltd v Reddy* [2013] NSWSC 643, (2013) 16 BPR 31,771.

259   *C & P Syndicate Pty Ltd v Reddy* [2013] NSWSC 643, (2013) 16 BPR 31,771 [192]–[194].

260   *Lords v Von Thomann (No 2)* [2014] WASC 320, (2014) 47 WAR 473 [161]–[172]. See also *Hooper v Oates* [2013] EWCA Civ 91, [2014] Ch 287.

261   (1988) 166 CLR 351.

262   *G & A Lanteri Nominees Pty Ltd v Fishers Stores Consolidated Pty Ltd* [2007] VSCA 4 [11]; *Luxer Holdings Pty Ltd v Glentham Pty Ltd* [2007] WASCA 209, (2007) 35 WAR 254 [35]; *Tebb v Filsee Pty Ltd* [2010] VSCA 311, (2010) 30 VR 473 [9]–[13].

263   (1988) 166 CLR 351, 369–70. See also *Nikolaou v Papasavas, Phillips & Co* (1989) 166 CLR 394, 399 (Mason CJ).

264   (1989) 166 CLR 394.

C   Relevance of inflation

[2.145]   In Australia, as in most countries, the purchasing power of money declines continuously. While the decline may be small in a single year, it is often considerable over a longer period of time. Thus, the amount of compensation for loss may vary significantly depending upon whether or not the assessment of compensation takes inflation into account. It is necessary to distinguish between loss occurring before judgment and loss occurring after judgment.

[2.146]   With regard to loss occurring before judgment, the courts often take account of inflation, in one of two ways. One way is to assess past loss as at the date of the judgment, which is the rule in equity and in cases of personal injury; see [2.129], [2.132]. The other way is to assess past loss as at the day it occurred (or some other day prior to trial) and then to increase the amount in line with the rate of inflation between the date of assessment and the date of judgment.[265] Where neither of these approaches is taken, the plaintiff will bear the effect of past inflation.

[2.147]   With regard to loss occurring after judgment (for example future medical expenses), the High Court of Australia has refused to increase awards by the estimated rate of future infla-tion,[266] arguing that such estimation would be nothing more than speculation,[267] and that the plaintiff can obtain protection against inflation by investing the money.[268] A probable rise in the price of goods and services in the future is also disregarded because the rate of price increase would be a matter of speculation.[269] However, future inflation and price increase is taken into account in determining whether and to what extent a reduction ought to be made to reflect the advantage of obtaining compensation for future loss before that loss is suffered. This is discussed in the following section.

D   Determining the present equivalent of future pecuniary loss

[2.148]   Where, as usual, the plaintiff receives a lump sum rather than periodic payments as compen-sation for future pecuniary loss (see [2.121]), the plaintiff receives the compensation before that loss is actually suffered. In the meantime, the plaintiff can invest the money awarded as compensation. This must be considered in assessing compensation for future loss. In other words, the court must find 'a present equivalent for all future pecuniary loss'.[270] This is usually done through actuarial calculations.

---

265   *Egan v State Transport Authority* (1982) 31 SASR 481, 528–31.
266   *O'Brien v McKean* (1968) 118 CLR 540; *Todorovic v Waller* (1981) 150 CLR 402. The House of Lords has taken the same approach: *Cookson v Knowles* [1979] AC 556; *Lim Poh Choo v Camden & Islington Area Health Authority* [1980] AC 174, 193–94.
267   *O'Brien v McKean* (1968) 118 CLR 540, 552, 553, 560.
268   Ibid, 547 (Barwick CJ).
269   Ibid, 549–51.
270   *McDade v Hoskins* (1892) 18 VLR 417, 421 (Higinbotham CJ), quoted in *Todorovic v Waller* (1981) 150 CLR 402, 414 (Gibbs CJ and Wilson J).

The advantage of obtaining a lump sum for loss spread over future years may be dimin-   **[2.149]**
ished by three factors: inflation, a rise in the price of goods and services, and tax payable on the
income earned from investing the lump sum. In times of low interest rates, as at present, these
factors may completely eradicate the advantage of obtaining a lump sum in relation to future
pecuniary loss. In times of higher interest rates, a net advantage will remain.

In order to precisely assess the net advantage (if any), it would be necessary to determine   **[2.150]**
the future rate of return from investing the money, the future rate of inflation, the future rise in
the price of goods and services, and the future impact of tax. However, this would be a
complicated exercise and, at least with regard to inflation and price increase, a matter of pure
speculation, which courts do not engage in; see [2.147]. In the context of personal injury,
where this issue often arises, both the common law and statute have therefore adopted the
approach of a discount rate that deals with all factors at once.

In *Todorovic v Waller*,[271] a majority in the High Court of Australia held that at common law   **[2.151]**
account must be taken of the advantage of receiving an investable lump sum, and that this is to
be done by way of a discount rate (uniform across Australia) that takes account also of future
inflation, future rise in the price of goods and services, and tax. The rate was set at 3% per
annum.[272] *Todorovic v Waller* involved personal injury. The 3% discount rate laid down in that
case has also been applied (in the absence of statutory modification) in actions for wrongful
death under the equivalent to Lord Campbell's Act, discussed at [7.93]ff.[273] In cases not
involving personal injury or death, discount rates between 3% and 6% have been applied at
common law.[274]

The Commonwealth, all states and the Northern Territory now have statutes that prescribe   **[2.152]**
a discount rate in certain cases of personal injury and death. The rate is 5% under most
statutes,[275] and 6% otherwise.[276] It is thus higher than the rate that applies at common law,
which leads to lower awards to plaintiffs. The common law rate of 3% continues to apply in
personal injury cases not governed by legislation.[277]

---

271   (1981) 150 CLR 402.

272   Gibbs CJ and Wilson J (at 424) would have preferred 4%, and Mason J (at 449–51) would have preferred
        2%, but all of them expressly joined in a declaration that the rate is 3%.

273   Eg *Roads and Traffic Authority v Jelfs* [1999] NSWCA 179, (2000) Aust Torts Reports 81–583 [30], [46];
        Roads and Traffic Authority v Cremona [2001] NSWCA 338, (2001) 35 MVR 190 [95]; *Hanlon v Hanlon*
        [2006] TASSC 1 [140]–[142], [146].

274   Eg *Commonwealth v Silverton Ltd* (1997) 130 ACTR 1, 30 (4%); *Environmental Systems Pty Ltd v Peerless
        Holdings Pty Ltd* [2008] VSCA 26, (2008) 19 VR 358 [76] (6%); *Bovaird v Frost* [2009] NSWSC 337, (2009)
        3 ASTLR 155 [73] (3%); *Construction, Forestry, Mining and Energy Union v Hail Creek Coal Pty Ltd*
        [2016] FCA 1032 [89] (3%).

275   *Competition and Consumer Act 2010* (Cth), s 87Y; *Civil Liability Act 2002* (NSW), s 14; *Motor Accident
        Injuries Act 2017* (NSW), s 4.9; *Workers Compensation Act 1987* (NSW), s 151J; *Personal Injuries
        (Liabilities and Damages) Act 2003* (NT), s 22; *Civil Liability Act 2003* (Qld), s 57; *Civil Proceedings Act
        2011* (Qld) s 61; *Civil Liability Act 1936* (SA), s 55; *Civil Liability Act 2002* (Tas), s 28A; *Wrongs Act 1958*
        (Vic), s 28I.

276   *Transport Accident Act 1986* (Vic), s 93(13); *Workplace Injury Rehabilitation and Compensation Act
        2013* (Vic), s 345; *Law Reform (Miscellaneous Provisions) Act 1941* (WA), s 5.

277   Eg *Mercer v Allianz Australia Insurance Ltd (No 2)* [2013] TASSC 35 [68]; *B v Reineker* [2015]
        NSWSC 949 [58]–[61], [72]; *New South Wales v McMaster* [2015] NSWCA 228, (2015) 91 NSWLR 666
        [295]–[297]; *Raper v Bowden* [2016] TASSC 35, (2016) 76 MVR 369 [103]–[106]; *Cooper v Neubert* [2017]
        TASSC 33 [72].

[2.153]   Even a rate of 3% is too high in the current period of low inflation and low interest rates. Plaintiffs are not receiving sufficient compensation for future economic loss. Legislation in the United Kingdom currently prescribes a discount rate of *minus* 0.75%.[278]

E   Interest on compensation awards and compensation for the loss of the use of money

[2.154]   A plaintiff often receives compensation for loss several years after the cause of action accrued. On principle, the defendant ought to pay interest on the compensation to reflect the fact that the plaintiff did not receive the compensation as soon as the cause of action accrued. An award of interest also discourages wrongdoers from delaying settlement of the claim or an early conclusion of proceedings.[279]

[2.155]   Nevertheless, traditionally, the common law prohibited an award of interest in the absence of an agreement.[280] This rule developed in a time when currency was stable and the payment of interest was stigmatised as usury.[281] Some exceptions emerged.[282] For example, interest can be awarded in an action for money had and received.[283] Courts of equity have taken a different approach. In equity's inherent jurisdiction, a court may award compound interest or simple interest,[284] depending upon discretionary factors such as the culpability of the defendant.[285] Where an account of profit is ordered, the order to pay interest reflects the profit that the defendant has, or could have, made by investing the money.[286] Where equitable compensation is ordered, the order to pay interest reflects the profit that the plaintiff could have made by investing the money.[287]

[2.156]   Statutes in all Australian jurisdictions including the Commonwealth now provide for an award of interest in certain circumstances. These statutes do not prevent a court from awarding interest pursuant to a rule of the common law or equity.[288] There are considerable differences

---

278   *Damages Act 1996* (UK), s 1; *Damages (Personal Injury) Order 2017* (UK), s 2; *Damages (Personal Injury) (Scotland) Order 2017* (UK), s 2.
279   *Ruby v Marsh* (1975) 132 CLR 642, 652–53 (Barwick CJ).
280   *Hungerfords v Walker* (1989) 171 CLR 125, 137–38.
281   *Tehno-Impex v Gebr van Weelde Scheepvaartkantoor BV* [1981] QB 648, 660 (Lord Denning MR); *Government Insurance Office of NSW v Healey (No 2)* (1991) 22 NSWLR 380, 385.
282   See *Heydon v NRMA Ltd (No 2)* [2001] NSWCA 445, (2001) 53 NSWLR 600 [15].
283   *Bayne v Stephens* (1908) 8 CLR 1; *Lexane Pty Ltd v Highfern Pty Ltd* [1985] 1 Qd R 446, 461–62; *State Bank of New South Wales Ltd v Commissioner of Taxation* (1995) 62 FCR 371, 380; *Chow v Yang* [2010] SASC 96 [35]. It is unclear whether compound interest, rather than simple interest, can be awarded; see *Peet Ltd v Richmond* [2011] VSCA 343, (2011) 33 VR 465 [125].
284   *Hungerfords v Walker* (1989) 171 CLR 125, 149; *Maguire v Makaronis* (1997) 188 CLR 449, 475–77; *Commonwealth v SCI Operations Pty Ltd* [1998] HCA 20, (1998) 192 CLR 285 [74]–[75]; *Victorian WorkCover Authority v Esso Australia Ltd* [2001] HCA 53, (2001) 207 CLR 520 [24].
285   *Duke Group Ltd (in liq) v Pilmer* [1999] SASC 97, (1999) 73 SASR 64 [806]–[808].
286   Ibid, [806]; *Grimaldi v Chameleon Mining NL (No 2)* [2012] FCAFC 6, (2012) 200 FCR 296 [551], [753].
287   *Duke Group Ltd (in liq) v Pilmer* [1999] SASC 97, (1999) 73 SASR 64 [809]–[811].
288   *Hungerfords v Walker* (1989) 171 CLR 125, 148–49; *Federal Court of Australia Act 1976* (Cth), s 51A(2)(d); *Supreme Court Act 1935* (SA), s 30C(4)(e); *Supreme Court Civil Procedure Act 1932* (Tas), s 35(2); *Supreme Court Act 1986* (Vic), s 60(2)(f).

between the statutes, and only a general outline will be given. No goods and services tax is payable on either post-judgment or pre-judgment interest.[289]

Post-judgment interest on the whole amount is generally to be awarded,[290] although some statutes allow the court to exclude a period of 21 days[291] or 28 days[292] from the day the judgment takes effect. Some statutes prescribe the rate of interest,[293] the federal statute prescribes a maximum rate,[294] and some statutes prescribe a default rate from which the court can deviate in either direction.[295] The statutes of the Australian Capital Territory and New South Wales allow the award of simple interest only, not compound interest.[296]   **[2.157]**

Pre-judgment interest is more complex. In Tasmania, a power to award pre-judgment interest exists only in actions for 'debts or sums certain',[297] for trespass to goods,[298] or on a policy of insurance,[299] but not for damages in general. The rate of interest is prescribed for 'debts and sums certain',[300] but not otherwise. There is no prohibition of compound interest. In Victoria, a power to award interest for the period prior to the commencement of the proceedings exists only in those types of action in which pre-judgment interest can be awarded in Tasmania.[301] A maximum rate of interest is prescribed for 'a debt or sum certain',[302] but not otherwise. Interest for the period between the commencement of the proceedings and the judgment may be awarded on any 'debt or damages' excluding compensation for future loss and exemplary or punitive damages.[303] A maximum rate of interest is prescribed,[304] and compound interest is prohibited.[305]   **[2.158]**

In the remaining jurisdictions, including the Commonwealth, pre-judgment interest may generally be awarded in any proceedings for the recovery of money including debt and damages, with a power to award interest for all or part of the amount and for all or part of the period between the date when the cause of action arose and the date of judgment.[306] The   **[2.159]**

---

289   Australian Taxation Office, *Goods and Services Tax: is the payment of judgment interest consideration for a supply?*, GSTD 2003/1.

290   *Federal Court of Australia Act 1976* (Cth), s 52(1); *Court Procedures Rules 2006* (ACT), r 1617; *Civil Procedure Act 2005* (NSW), s 101(1); *Supreme Court Act* (NT), s 85; *Civil Proceedings Act 2011* (Qld), s 59(2); *Supreme Court Act 1935* (SA), s 114(1); *Supreme Court Civil Procedure Act 1932* (Tas), s 165; *Supreme Court Act 1986* (Vic), s 101(1); *Civil Judgments Enforcement Act 2004* (WA), s 8(1).

291   *Civil Proceedings Act 2011* (Qld), s 59(4).

292   *Court Procedures Rules 2006* (ACT), r 1617(2); *Civil Procedure Act 2005* (NSW), s 101(3).

293   *Supreme Court Act* (NT), s 85; *Supreme Court Act 1935* (SA), s 114(1); *Supreme Court Civil Procedure Act 1932* (Tas), s 165; *Supreme Court Act 1986* (Vic), s 101(1).

294   *Federal Court of Australia Act 1976* (Cth), s 52(2).

295   *Court Procedures Rules 2006* (ACT), r 1617(1), (4)(a); *Civil Procedure Act 2005* (NSW), s 101(2), (5); *Civil Proceedings Act 2011* (Qld), s 59(3); *Civil Judgments Enforcement Act 2004* (WA), s 8(1).

296   *Court Procedures Rules 2006* (ACT), r 1617(5); *Civil Procedure Act 2005* (NSW), s 101(6).

297   *Supreme Court Civil Procedure Act 1932* (Tas), s 34(1).

298   Ibid, s 35(1)(a).

299   Ibid, s 35(1)(b).

300   Ibid, s 34.

301   *Supreme Court Act 1986* (Vic), ss 58 and 59.

302   Ibid, s 58(1).

303   Ibid, s 60(1), (3).

304   Ibid, s 60(1).

305   Ibid, s 60(2)(a).

306   *Federal Court of Australia Act 1976* (Cth), s 51A; *Court Procedures Rules 2006* (ACT), r 1616; *Civil Procedure Act 2005* (NSW), s 100(1), (2); *Supreme Court Act* (NT), s 84(1); *Civil Proceedings Act 2011* (Qld), s 58(3); *Supreme Court Act 1935* (SA), s 30C; *Supreme Court Act 1935* (WA), s 32(1).

rate of interest is generally in the court's discretion,[307] but compound interest is prohibited.[308] In all these jurisdictions except the Australian Capital Territory, the civil liability reform brought changes in relation to personal injury and death. The changes include a prohibition of pre-judgment interest for non-pecuniary loss[309] and sometimes also for gratuitous attendant care services and/or the lost capacity to provide domestic services,[310] as well as a prescription of the interest rate,[311] or a maximum rate,[312] for other loss resulting from personal injury.

[2.160]   A court's discretion to set the interest rate under statute must be exercised in conformity with the general principle that compensation aims to do no more than place the plaintiff in the position as if the wrong had not occurred.[313] Interest on compensation running from the time when the cause of action arose may be awarded only if all the losses for which the compensation is awarded were suffered when the cause of action arose. Where at least some of the losses were suffered at a later time, this must be taken account of by setting a lower rate of interest or a later date from which interest starts to run.[314] Interest on common law damages may not be awarded insofar as the plaintiff has received compensation under a statutory compensation scheme, since the plaintiff has not been out of pocket to that extent.[315] The time at which the statutory compensation was received must be taken into account.[316]

[2.161]   The High Court of Australia has held that when setting the interest rate under statute, common law damages for non-pecuniary loss suffered prior to judgment should normally attract a rate of interest of only 4% rather than the higher commercial rate, on the ground that the detriment that a plaintiff suffers by being kept out of damages for pre-judgment non-pecuniary loss cannot be equated with the amount which those damages, invested at the commercial rate of interest, would have earned during that period.[317] Whatever the merits of this rule, its significance is diminished because interest on compensation for non-pecuniary loss suffered before the commencement of proceedings cannot be awarded in Tasmania or Victoria and, in cases of personal injury, cannot be awarded in the other jurisdictions except the Australian Capital Territory.

---

307   *Federal Court of Australia Act 1976* (Cth), s 51A(1)(a); *Court Procedures Rules 2006* (ACT), r 1616(1)(a)(i); *Civil Procedure Act 2005* (NSW), s 100(1), (2); *Supreme Court Act* (NT), s 85(1); *Civil Proceedings Act 2011* (Qld), s 58(3); *Supreme Court Act 1935* (SA), s 30C(2)(a); *Supreme Court Act 1935* (WA), s 32(1).

308   *Federal Court of Australia Act 1976* (Cth), s 51A(2)(a); *Court Procedures Rules 2006* (ACT), r 1616(6)(a); *Civil Procedure Act 2005* (NSW), s 100(3)(a); *Supreme Court Act* (NT), s 85(2)(a); *Civil Proceedings Act 2011* (Qld), s 58(4)(a); *Supreme Court Act 1935* (SA), s 30C(4)(a); *Supreme Court Act 1935* (WA), s 32(2)(a).

309   *Civil Liability Act 1936* (SA), s 56; *Supreme Court Act 1935* (WA), s 32(2)(aa).

310   *Competition and Consumer Act 2010* (Cth), s 87ZA(1); *Civil Liability Act 2002* (NSW), s 18(1); *Personal Injuries (Liabilities and Damages) Act 2003* (NT), s 29; *Civil Liability Act 2003* (Qld), s 60(1).

311   *Competition and Consumer Act 2010* (Cth), s 87ZA(2) and (4); *Civil Liability Act 2002* (NSW), s 18(3) and (4); *Personal Injuries (Liabilities and Damages) Act 2003* (NT), s 30.

312   *Civil Liability Act 2003* (Qld), s 60(2) and (3).

313   *Haines v Bendall* (1991) 172 CLR 60, 66–67.

314   *Cullen v Trappell* (1980) 146 CLR 1, 19.

315   *Batchelor v Burke* (1981) 148 CLR 448; *Haines v Bendall* (1991) 172 CLR 60.

316   *Firth v Sutton (No 2)* [2010] NSWCA 109.

317   *MBP (SA) Pty Ltd v Gogic* (1991) 171 CLR 657, 663, disapproving *Cullen v Trappell* (1980) 146 CLR 1, 21. However, interest at the commercial rate may be awarded on compensation for non-pecuniary loss under a statutory compensation scheme that imposes a ceiling and a threshold in respect of such loss: *Andjelic v Marsland* (1996) 186 CLR 20, 27–28.

An award of pre-judgment interest goes some way towards compensating plaintiffs for [2.162] being kept out of money prior to judgment. But it does not provide full compensation, since compound interest is prohibited in all jurisdictions except Tasmania. In *Hungerfords v Walker*,[318] the High Court of Australia responded to this problem by holding that the loss of the use of money may sometimes be compensated at common law. Carelessness on the part of accountants caused their client to pay too much tax for several years. When this was eventually discovered, the claim for the return of the tax overpaid in the early years had become statute-barred. The client, who had operated its business by using borrowed money, sued the accountants for breach of contract and negligence, and claimed compensation including compensation for the loss of the use of the money in the intervening period.

The High Court upheld an award of damages assessed by reference to an annual com- [2.163] pound interest rate of 20%.[319] The court held that the statutory power to award simple interest for the period before judgment is meant to complement any power to award interest at common law or in equity, and does not prevent the award of compound interest at common law.[320] Expenses incurred and opportunity costs arising from money being paid away or withheld as a result of a breach of contract or negligence are pecuniary losses suffered by the plaintiff as a result of the defendant's wrong and should therefore be compensated subject to the rules on remoteness and mitigation.[321]

The recognition of the loss of the use of money as a head of loss compensable at common [2.164] law is to be welcomed. But it is important to determine the precise scope and effect of the rule laid down in *Hungerfords v Walker*. First, as a matter of form, the rule in *Hungerfords v Walker* does not allow an award of interest as such. It allows an award of a lump sum for the loss of the use of the money.[322] It should be noted that the interest statutes also allow an award of a lump sum for the period before judgment. Secondly, and as a consequence of the first point, the rule in *Hungerfords v Walker* is concerned only with the loss of the use of money before judgment, not after judgment. This has significance in the Australian Capital Territory and New South Wales where the interest statutes prohibit compound interest for the period after judgment.

Thirdly, the High Court's reference to opportunity costs (in addition to expenses incurred) [2.165] made clear that damages for the loss of the use of money are available not only where the defendant's wrong forced the plaintiff to borrow (more) money but also where the defendant's wrong deprived the plaintiff of the opportunity to profitably invest (more) money.[323] Fourthly, the plaintiff bears the onus of proving the loss of the use of money.[324] A plaintiff who has not

---

318   (1989) 171 CLR 125. A similar decision was made in *Sempra Metals Ltd v Inland Revenue Commissioners* [2007] UKHL 34, [2008] 1 AC 561.

319   The award contained some $47,500 for tax overpaid and not recoverable, and $270,000 for the loss of the use of the first amount: (1987) 49 SASR 93, 105.

320   (1989) 171 CLR 125, 148–49.

321   Ibid, 144.

322   Ibid, 153 (Brennan and Deane JJ); *Doolan v Renkon Pty Ltd* [2011] TASFC 4, (2011) 21 Tas R 156 [97].

323   *Hungerfords v Walker* (1989) 171 CLR 125, 144; *Hardie v Shadbolt* [2004] WASCA 175 [57]–[64]; *Doolan v Renkon Pty Ltd* [2011] TASFC 4, (2011) 21 Tas R 156 [96]. Cf *Commonwealth v Chessell* (1991) 30 FCR 154, 164–65 (Wilcox J).

324   *Commonwealth v Chessell* (1991) 30 FCR 154, 162 (Sheppard J); *Ruthol Pty Ltd v Tricon (Australia) Pty Ltd* [2005] NSWCA 443, (2005) 12 BPR 23,923 [62]; *Doolan v Renkon Pty Ltd* [2011] TASFC 4, (2011) 21 Tas R 156 [101].

borrowed money must prove that the money would have been invested, and must prove the rate at which it would have been invested.[325] That applies even to banks.[326]

[2.166]   Fifthly, the High Court's reference to breach of contract and negligence in *Hungerfords v Walker* might be taken as limiting the rule laid down in that case to those two causes of action. However, such limitation could not be justified on principle and is in fact at odds with the High Court's rejection of a distinction between debt and unliquidated damages.[327] The High Court's reference to breach of contract and negligence simply reflects the fact that these were the causes of action pleaded in that case. Damages for the loss of the use of money have since been awarded in a case involving trespass to land.[328]

[2.167]   Sixthly, the High Court's repeated reference to 'money being paid away or withheld' in *Hungerfords v Walker* seems to have been intended as imposing a limit on the rule laid down in that case. Nevertheless, damages for the loss of the use of money were awarded when a defendant withheld an asset which the plaintiff would have sold immediately after receipt.[329] But even that wide interpretation of the phrase 'money being paid away or withheld' excludes instances where the use of money is lost because, for example, the plaintiff loses custom or income, or needs to pay for medical treatment or the repair of property, as a result of the defendant's wrong. This distinction cannot be justified on principle.

[2.168]   Finally, where the requirements of the rule in *Hungerfords v Walker* are satisfied, the plaintiff is entitled to an award of damages for the loss of the use of money, subject to the rules on remoteness and mitigation. While the court, in assessing those damages, may have regard to contingencies affecting the return from the hypothetical investment of the money,[330] the court cannot reduce the amount on discretionary grounds (such as delay) by invoking a statute that confers discretion in awarding pre-judgment interest under that statute.[331] However, in calculating the loss of the use of money, courts may have regard to the interest rate prescribed (as a default or fixed rate) by such a statute.[332]

---

325   *Duke Group Ltd (in liq) v Pilmer* [1999] SASC 97, (1999) 73 SASR 64 [499]. See also *Pooraka Holdings Pty Ltd v Participation Nominees Pty Ltd* (1991) 58 SASR 184, 196 (King CJ). Cf *Commonwealth v Chessell* (1991) 30 FCR 154, 170–72 (Einfeld J).
326   *St George Bank Ltd v Quinerts Pty Ltd* [2009] VSCA 245, (2009) 25 VR 666 [25].
327   *Hungerfords v Walker* (1989) 171 CLR 125, 147. See also *Commonwealth v Chessell* (1991) 30 FCR 154, 163 (Wilcox J); *CIC Insurance Ltd v Bankstown Football Club Ltd* (1995) 8 ANZ Ins Cas 61–232, 75,598 (Powell JA).
328   *Balanced Securities Ltd v Bianco (No 2)* [2010] VSC 201, (2010) 27 VR 599 [16].
329   Ibid.
330   Ibid, [37].
331   *Stubing v Halling* [2012] SASCFC 123, (2012) 115 SASR 1 [85]–[88].
332   *Palasty v Parlby* [2007] NSWCA 345, (2007) 13 BPR 25,311 [35].

3

ATTRIBUTION OF RESPONSIBILITY

I   Introduction

[3.1]   Every civil wrong has a number of requirements that must be satisfied before the plaintiff may obtain compensation for harm suffered. One requirement common to all wrongs is that the harm must be attributable to the defendant's wrongful conduct. It may broadly be said that the defendant's wrongful conduct must constitute a cause of the harm. This always involves an inquiry into whether there is a historical link in fact between the wrong and the harm, and usually also a value judgement on whether liability for the harm ought to be imposed upon the defendant.[1]

[3.2]   With regard to wrongs actionable only on proof of damage (for example, negligence), the attribution of responsibility for harm is part of establishing liability rather than a matter of remedy. With regard to wrongs actionable per se, the attribution of responsibility for harm is a matter of remedy since nominal damages can be awarded in the absence of loss. In any event, it is customary to discuss attribution of responsibility in books on remedies, and this book follows that custom.

[3.3]   The rules on attribution of responsibility are not the same for every wrong, but there are significant commonalities, in particular between contract and tort. This chapter discusses those rules that are common to all or a large number of wrongs, and provides a brief introduction to those rules that differ between wrongs. The details of the latter rules are discussed in the chapters on the individual wrongs.

II   The legal concept of causation

[3.4]   The legal concept of causation differs from philosophical and scientific notions of causation. Philosophy and science search for explanations, whereas law is concerned with the attribution of legal responsibility.[2] The legal concept of causation has plagued judges and scholars in many countries and has generated a vast amount of literature. It is not possible here to review every aspect of the discourse. The focus is on the current law of Australia and the major influential theories.

[3.5]   A brief look at English law sets the scene for discussing Australian law. English courts have broken down the causal inquiry into two distinct phases.[3] In the first phase, it will be determined whether the plaintiff's harm would have occurred but for the defendant's wrongful conduct (the 'but for' test). If the harm would have occurred in any event, the defendant's conduct cannot generally be regarded as a cause of the harm.

[3.6]   In *Barnett v Chelsea and Kensington Hospital Management Committee*,[4] a hospital breached its duty of care by sending home a man who had complained about having vomited for three hours after drinking tea. Five hours later, the man died of arsenic poisoning. An action

---

1   The distinction between historical involvement and policy considerations is explained by J Stapleton, 'Cause-in-Fact and the Scope of Liability for Consequences' (2003) 119 LQR 388.

2   *March v E & MH Stramare Pty Ltd* (1991) 171 CLR 506, 509 (Mason CJ).

3   *Kuwait Airways Corporation v Iraqi Airways Co (Nos 4 and 5)* [2002] UKHL 19, [2002] 2 AC 883 [69]–[70]; *Essa v Laing Ltd* [2004] EWCA Civ 2, [2004] ICR 746 [90]–[91] (Rix LJ); *Wright v Cambridge Medical Group (a partnership)* [2011] EWCA Civ 669, [2013] QB 312 [96] (Elias LJ).

4   [1969] 1 QB 428.

in negligence against the hospital was unsuccessful because the man would still have died had the hospital admitted and treated him. In *Bank of Credit and Commerce International SA v Ali (No 2)*,[5] a bank engaged in large-scale fraudulent activities for a number of years. When the scandal broke, the bank was wound up. Five of its former employees, who had been unable to find employment with another bank, brought an action for breach of an implied term in their employment contract not to carry on a dishonest business, and alleged that their inability to find new employment was due to the stigma attached to them as former employees of a dishonest bank. The action failed since the plaintiffs could not prove that they would have found new employment had the defendant not engaged in fraud.

[3.7] The inquiry in the first phase is in general purely 'scientific' in the sense that normative questions are not raised. However, in exceptional circumstances, English courts have, on policy grounds, regarded conduct as a cause of the harm even though the 'but for' test was not satisfied.[6]

[3.8] If the 'but for' test is satisfied, English courts may, in the second phase, still exonerate the defendant on the ground that an intervening act (*novus actus interveniens*) broke the chain of causation between the defendant's conduct and the plaintiff's harm, or that the harm was too remote from the wrong, or that the harm fell outside the scope of the duty breached by the defendant, or that the plaintiff failed to mitigate loss. The second phase involves a value judgement. The two phases of inquiry in English law have sometimes been described as causation in fact (or factual causation) and causation in law (or legal causation).[7]

[3.9] At common law, Australian courts, like English courts, have used the 'but for' test and concepts such as *novus actus interveniens*, remoteness and mitigation in attributing responsibility for loss. But Australian courts have refused to conduct the inquiry in two distinct phases as is done in England. Instead, they have adopted a single test involving factual and normative issues, by asking whether, *as a matter of common sense*, the defendant's conduct constitutes a cause of the plaintiff's harm. This test was laid down in relation to breach of contract by the NSW Court of Appeal in *Alexander v Cambridge Credit Corporation Ltd*,[8] and in relation to negligence by the High Court of Australia in *March v E & MH Stramare Pty Ltd*.[9] It has been applied on numerous occasions.[10] While the 'but for' test is an integral part of the causal inquiry, common sense may classify an event as causative when it would not be under the 'but for' test, and vice versa.[11] The test of common sense involves an examination of the nature and scope of the defendant's obligations in the particular circumstances.[12]

5   [2002] EWCA Civ 82, [2002] 3 All ER 750.
6   The main example is *Fairchild v Glenhaven Funeral Services Ltd* [2002] UKHL 22, [2003] 1 AC 32, discussed at [3.63].
7   Eg *McLoughlin v O'Brian* [1983] 1 AC 410, 432 (Lord Bridge); *Essa v Laing Ltd* [2004] EWCA Civ 2, [2004] ICR 746 [92], [105].
8   (1987) 9 NSWLR 310.
9   (1991) 171 CLR 506. In the context of how a jury should be instructed, the test of common sense had already been laid down in *Fitzgerald v Penn* (1954) 91 CLR 268, 277.
10   Eg *Roads and Traffic Authority v Royal* [2008] HCA 19, (2008) 245 ALR 653 [32], [135]; *Davies v Nilsen* [2017] VSCA 202, (2017) 81 MVR 75 [55]–[56].
11   *March v E & MH Stramare Pty Ltd* (1991) 171 CLR 506, 515–16 (Mason CJ), 522–23 (Deane J).
12   *Chappel v Hart* [1998] HCA 55, (1998) 195 CLR 232 [63]–[64] (Gummow J), [122] (Hayne J); *Allianz Australia Insurance Ltd v GSF Australia Pty Ltd* [2005] HCA 26, (2005) 221 CLR 568 [96]–[98]; *Travel Compensation Fund v Tambree* [2005] HCA 69, (2005) 224 CLR 627 [45] (Gummow and Hayne JJ).

[3.10]   In *Alexander* and *March*, various reasons were given for the perceived superiority of the test of common sense over the 'but for' test. First, certain essential conditions (in the 'but for' sense) of harm cannot properly be described as a 'cause' of the harm, for example the manufacture and sale of a revolver that was used to inflict harm,[13] or the having of a head that was decapitated by a negligently wielded sword.[14] Secondly, the 'but for' test produces absurd results in cases of multiple sufficient causes.[15] Thirdly, the 'but for' test does not provide a satisfactory answer in cases of an intervening act.[16]

[3.11]   McHugh J, who participated in the unanimous decision in *Alexander*, subsequently changed his view and dissented in *March*, saying that the common sense test is too vague[17] and 'gives the tribunal an unfettered discretion to ignore a condition or relation which was in fact a precondition of the occurrence of the damage'.[18] Causation, he said, ought to be determined exclusively under the 'but for' test, modified in cases of multiple sufficient causes.[19] Any denial of legal responsibility on policy and value grounds ought to be regarded as being concerned with remoteness of damage rather than causation.[20] Remoteness of damage ought to be determined by reference to the scope of the risk created by the defendant.[21]

[3.12]   The civil liability statutes of the Australian Capital Territory and the states lay down rules for the determination of 'causation' in respect of the types of wrong to which the relevant statute applies.[22] Adopting the English approach, the statutes prescribe a two-step inquiry into factual causation and the scope of liability. The substance of the provisions is the same in all statutes, but the wording varies because the provisions apply to different types of wrong. By way of example, s 5D(1) and (4) of the *Civil Liability Act 2002* (NSW) provide:

(1)   A determination that negligence caused particular harm comprises the following elements:

(a)   that the negligence was a necessary condition of the occurrence of the harm (*'factual causation '*), and

(b)   that it is appropriate for the scope of the negligent person's liability to extend to the harm so caused (*'scope of liability '*).

. . .

(4)   For the purpose of determining the scope of liability, the court is to consider (amongst other relevant things) whether or not and why responsibility for the harm should be imposed on the negligent party.

---

13   *Alexander v Cambridge Credit Corporation Ltd* (1987) 9 NSWLR 310, 335–36 (Mahoney JA).

14   *March v E & MH Stramare Pty Ltd* (1991) 171 CLR 506, 523 (Deane J).

15   Ibid, 516 (Mason CJ), 523 (Deane J), 524 (Toohey J).

16   Ibid, 517 (Mason CJ), 524 (Toohey J).

17   Ibid, 532–33. Minds may reasonably differ as to what is common sense in certain circumstances, as illustrated by *Chappel v Hart* [1998] HCA 55, (1998) 195 CLR 232.

18   (1991) 171 CLR 506, 532.

19   Ibid, 533–34.

20   Ibid, 534.

21   Ibid, 535–36.

22   *Civil Law (Wrongs) Act 2002* (ACT), s 45(1); *Civil Liability Act 2002* (NSW), s 5D(1); *Civil Liability Act 2003* (Qld), s 11(1); *Civil Liability Act 1936* (SA), s 34(1); *Civil Liability Act 2002* (Tas), s 13(1); *Wrongs Act 1958* (Vic), s 51(1); *Civil Liability Act 2002* (WA), s 5C(1).

Under s 5D and its equivalents in other jurisdictions, it must first be determined whether the [3.13] defendant's conduct is a factual cause of the plaintiff's harm. If it is not, it cannot have caused the harm for the purpose of attributing responsibility. If the conduct is a factual cause of the harm, it must then be determined whether considerations relating to the scope of liability nonetheless lead to the conclusion that the conduct did not cause the harm for the purpose of attributing responsibility. The High Court of Australia has said that the exercise undertaken under s 5D(1)(a) is 'entirely factual' whereas the exercise undertaken under s 5D(1)(b) and (4) is 'entirely normative'.[23] While the use of the word 'cause' in two different meanings in the same provision is not the best drafting technique, it is clear that s 5D and its equivalents in other jurisdictions leave no room for a mixture of factual and normative issues in a one-step test of common sense.[24]

This does not mean that the conclusion reached under statute needs to differ from the [3.14] conclusion that would be reached at common law. The High Court of Australia has said that policy choices made at common law will be maintained under statute unless confronted and overruled.[25] In novel cases decided under statute, the scope of liability must be determined by reference to the purposes and policy of the relevant part of the law, and not by reference to common sense 'unless the perceptions or experience informing the sense that is common can be unpacked and explained'.[26]

The civil liability statutes' provisions on causation do not apply to every civil wrong. The [3.15] Western Australian provision has the largest scope, applying to 'any claim for damages for harm caused by the fault of a person',[27] regardless of the cause of action.[28] The term 'fault' is not defined and must therefore have its usual meaning, namely culpable conduct. Thus, the provision applies to any wrong that requires culpable conduct (including, for example, intentional torts), and applies in cases of strict liability where the defendant was in fact at fault, since it involves 'harm caused by the fault of a person'. The provisions in Queensland and Tasmania have the narrowest scope, applying only to the breach of a tortious duty of care, of a contractual duty of care that is coextensive with a tortious duty of care, and of any other duty (under statute or otherwise) that is concurrent with one of the duties mentioned before.[29] This excludes misleading or deceptive conduct prohibited by s 18 of the Australian Consumer Law (see [8.5]).[30]

The provisions in the Australian Capital Territory, New South Wales, South [3.16] Australia and Victoria apply to 'negligence',[31] defined as 'failure to exercise reasonable

---

23   *Wallace v Kam* [2013] HCA 19, (2013) 250 CLR 375 [14] (French CJ, Crennan, Kiefel, Gageler and Keane JJ). Both propositions are rejected by D Hamer, '"Factual Causation" and "Scope of Liability": What's the Difference?' (2014) 77 Mod LR 155.

24   *Wallace v Kam* [2013] HCA 19, (2013) 250 CLR 375 [12]–[16].

25   Ibid, [22].

26   Ibid, [23] (French CJ, Crennan, Kiefel, Gageler and Keane JJ).

27   *Civil Liability Act 2002* (WA), s 5A(1).

28   Ibid, s 5A(2).

29   *Civil Liability Act 2003* (Qld), s 11 and sch 2 (definition of 'duty'); *Civil Liability Act 2002* (Tas), ss 3 (definition of 'duty') and 13.

30   *Mineralogy Pty Ltd v BGP Geoexplorer Pte Ltd* [2017] QSC 219 [173], decided under the former *Trade Practices Act 1974* (Cth).

31   *Civil Law (Wrongs) Act 2002* (ACT), s 45; *Civil Liability Act 2002* (NSW), s 5D; *Civil Liability Act 1936* (SA), s 34; *Wrongs Act 1958* (Vic), s 51.

care',[32] whether the claim is brought in tort, in contract, under statute or otherwise.[33] This includes breach of a contractual or equitable duty of care, whether or not the duty is coextensive with a tortious duty of care. It also includes the breach of a consumer guarantee to provide services with due care and skill pursuant to s 60 of the Australian Consumer Law, even where the Australian Consumer Law applies as a law of the Commonwealth (see [8.1]–[8.2]).[34] Each of the statutes mentioned in this paragraph and the preceding paragraph excludes certain cases (such as intentional acts, dust diseases, injuries resulting from smoking, motor accidents, workplace injuries) from the scope of the provisions on causation, but those exclusions differ between the jurisdictions.

[3.17]   So far, the test of common sense has still been used at common law.[35] However, in *Wallace v Kam*, where statute applied, the High Court of Australia said that the determination of causation at common law 'inevitably involves two questions: a question of historical fact as to how particular harm occurred; and a normative question as to whether legal responsibility for that particular harm occurring in that way should be attributed to a particular person'.[36] This may indicate that the statutory two-step test will eventually be adopted at common law. This would be welcome since the common sense test lacks clarity,[37] and it is undesirable to have two different tests of causation in Australian private law, particularly because the scope of the civil liability statutes differs between jurisdictions. These differences may require a choice-of-law exercise for the mere purpose of attributing responsibility.

[3.18]   This chapter makes no separation in discussing the common law rules and the statutory provisions. While the civil liability statutes prescribe a two-step inquiry in attributing responsibility, they do not abolish the refined rules used at common law. These rules will inform the application of the civil liability statutes' provisions on causation unless those provisions or other legislation require otherwise; see [3.14]. This chapter does separate factual causation and scope of liability, which is necessary under the civil liability statutes and also assists in analysing the common law doctrines.

III   Factual causation

A   Overview

[3.19]   The establishment of factual causation is necessary (but not sufficient) for the attribution of responsibility for certain harm, both at common law and under the civil liability statutes. The statutes require that the defendant's wrongful conduct was 'a necessary condition of the

---

32   *Civil Law (Wrongs) Act 2002* (ACT), s 40; *Civil Liability Act 2002* (NSW), s 5; *Civil Liability Act 1936* (SA), s 3 (definition of 'negligence'); *Wrongs Act 1958* (Vic), s 43 (definition of 'negligence').

33   *Civil Law (Wrongs) Act 2002* (ACT), s 41(1); *Civil Liability Act 2002* (NSW), s 5A(1); *Civil Liability Act 1936* (SA), s 3 (definition of 'negligence'); *Wrongs Act 1958* (Vic), s 44.

34   *Barrett v Lets Go Adventures Pty Ltd* [2016] NSWDC 345, (2016) 23 DCLR (NSW) 329 [21]–[28]; *JC Automotive Repairs Pty Ltd v Hardy* [2017] NSWSC 1218 [48].

35   *Travel Compensation Fund v Tambree* [2005] HCA 69, (2005) 224 CLR 627 [55]–[56], [63], [78]–[80]; *Tabet v Gett* [2010] HCA 12, (2010) 240 CLR 537 [112], [150].

36   [2013] HCA 19, (2013) 250 CLR 375 [11] (French CJ, Crennan, Kiefel, Gageler and Keane JJ).

37   J Stapleton, 'Reflections on Common Sense Causation in Australia' in S Degeling, J Edelman and J Goudkamp (eds), *Torts in Commercial Law* (LBC 2011) 349–50.

occurrence of the harm'. An application of the 'but for' test, discussed at [3.24]–[3.26], can resolve that question in the vast majority of cases.

However, it is recognised at common law that wrongful conduct may constitute a cause of certain harm even though it cannot be shown that the harm would not have occurred but for the conduct. Similarly, the civil liability statutes provide that wrongful conduct that is not a necessary condition of the occurrence of the harm can sometimes be regarded as a factual cause of the harm. Section 5D(2) of the *Civil Liability Act 2002* (NSW) provides: [3.20]

> In determining in an exceptional case, in accordance with established principles, whether negligence that cannot be established as a necessary condition of the occurrence of the harm should be accepted as establishing factual causation, the court is to consider (amongst other relevant things) whether or not and why responsibility for the harm should be imposed on the negligent party.

Queensland and Tasmania have similar provisions.[38] The same is true for Victoria and Western Australia except that their provisions refer to an 'appropriate case' instead of an 'exceptional case'.[39] The Australian Capital Territory and South Australia have provisions with a more limited scope; see [3.65]–[3.66]. [3.21]

Section 5D(2) of the *Civil Liability Act 2002* (NSW) and its equivalents in other jurisdictions are not engaged simply because the plaintiff is unable to prove factual causation. The case must be out of the ordinary. This is true even for those provisions that refer to an 'appropriate case' instead of an 'exceptional case'.[40] [3.22]

There are two broad categories of case in which it may be appropriate to regard the defendant's wrongful conduct as a factual cause of certain harm even though the plaintiff cannot establish that the harm would not have occurred but for the wrong. The first category of case involves what is often called overdetermination, which means that both the defendant's wrong and some other event for which the defendant is not responsible were each sufficient to bring about the harm in question. This is discussed at [3.28]–[3.48]. The second category of case is where there is evidential uncertainty as to whether the harm was brought about by the defendant's wrong or by some other event for which the defendant is not responsible. This is discussed at [3.53]–[3.68]. [3.23]

B   The 'but for' test and its application

The 'but for' test informs the common sense view of causation at common law,[41] and generally applies under the civil liability statutes in determining whether the defendant's wrongful conduct was 'a necessary condition of the occurrence of the harm'.[42] It is asked whether the harm would have occurred but for the event that is alleged to trigger liability. If the harm would not have occurred, the event is a factual cause of the harm. If the harm would still have occurred, the event is not generally a factual cause of the harm. [3.24]

---

38   *Civil Liability Act 2003* (Qld), s 11(2); *Civil Liability Act 2002* (Tas), s 13(2).
39   *Wrongs Act 1958* (Vic), s 51(2); *Civil Liability Act 2002* (WA), s 5C(2).
40   *Powney v Kerang and District Health* [2014] VSCA 221, (2014) 43 VR 506 [96]–[97].
41   *March v E & MH Stramare Pty Ltd* (1991) 171 CLR 506, 515–16, 522, 530.
42   *Adeels Palace Pty Ltd v Moubarak* [2009] HCA 48, (2009) 239 CLR 420 [55]; *Strong v Woolworths Ltd (t/as Big W)* [2012] HCA 5, (2012) 246 CLR 182 [18].

[3.25]   With regard to the question of what would have occurred but for the event, the standard of proof is the balance of probabilities, and the plaintiff bears the legal onus of proof, both at common law[43] and under the civil liability statutes.[44] In *Adeels Palace Pty Ltd v Moubarak*,[45] the plaintiffs were shot by a gunman during a New Year celebration on the defendant's licensed premises. The plaintiffs alleged that the defendant had breached its duty of care towards its patrons by failing to provide sufficient security personnel. Without determining that issue, the High Court of Australia rejected the plaintiffs' claim in negligence on the ground that they had failed to prove that the provision of more security personnel would have prevented the shooting.[46]

[3.26]   It is sometimes necessary to determine what the plaintiff would have done had the defendant not engaged in the allegedly wrongful conduct. This is relevant, for example, where the defendant failed to disclose certain information to the plaintiff. In the context of whether the initial harm would have occurred but for the defendant's wrong, uncertainty as to what the plaintiff would have done is determined on the balance of probabilities (see [2.69]), the plaintiff bearing the onus of proof. In determining that issue, the choice is between an objective test (asking what a reasonable person in the plaintiff's position would have done) and a subjective test (asking what the individual plaintiff would have done). The subjective test applies at common law,[47] and is prescribed by the civil liability statutes of most jurisdictions.[48] However, most of the statutes also provide that a statement by the plaintiff about what she would have done is either always inadmissible,[49] or is inadmissible to the extent (if any) that the statement is against the plaintiff's interests.[50] It is not settled whether these provisions preclude a statement by a director of a corporate plaintiff.[51]

[3.27]   Uncertainty with regard to hypothetical events other than conduct of the plaintiff is not always resolved on the balance of probabilities. In certain circumstances, loss dependent upon the occurrence of such an event is assessed on a 'sliding scale' by reference to the degree of probability that the event would have occurred but for the defendant's wrong. Loss dependent upon an event in the future is always assessed in this way. The complex details are discussed at [2.57]ff.

---

43   *Chappel v Hart* (1998) 195 CLR 232, 247, 270.
44   *Civil Law (Wrongs) Act 2002* (ACT), s 46; *Civil Liability Act 2002* (NSW), s 5E; *Civil Liability Act 2003* (Qld), s 12; *Civil Liability Act 1936* (SA), s 35; *Civil Liability Act 2002* (Tas), s 14; *Wrongs Act 1958* (Vic), s 52; *Civil Liability Act 2002* (WA), s 5D.
45   [2009] HCA 48, (2009) 239 CLR 420.
46   Ibid, [47]–[53].
47   *Chappel v Hart* (1998) 195 CLR 232, 246, 272; *Rosenberg v Percival* [2001] HCA 18, (2001) 205 CLR 434 [24], [44], [87], [154]. The Supreme Court of Canada has adopted the objective test: *Reibl v Hughes* (1981) 114 DLR (3d) 1, 16–17; *Arndt v Smith* [1997] 2 SCR 539, 544–54.
48   *Civil Liability Act 2002* (NSW), s 5D(3)(a); *Civil Liability Act 2003* (Qld), s 11(3)(a); *Civil Liability Act 2002* (Tas), s 13(3)(a); *Wrongs Act 1958* (Vic), s 51(3); *Civil Liability Act 2002* (WA), s 5C(3)(a).
49   *Civil Liability Act 2002* (WA), s 5C(3)(b).
50   *Civil Liability Act 2002* (NSW), s 5D(3)(b); *Civil Liability Act 2003* (Qld), s 11(3)(b); *Civil Liability Act 2002* (Tas), s 13(3)(b).
51   The view that they do was taken in *AI McLean Pty Ltd v Hayson* [2008] NSWSC 927 [245]. The correctness of that view was doubted in *UGL Rail Pty Ltd v Wilkinson Murray Pty Ltd* [2014] NSWSC 1959 [191].

C   Causal overdetermination (multiple sufficient causes)

Sometimes, the defendant's wrongful conduct and another event, which may be a wrong   [3.28]
committed by a third party or a non-wrongful event, were each sufficient to bring about the
plaintiff's harm, or would each have been sufficient if the other event had not occurred. This
situation has been described as one of causal overdetermination,[52] or as involving multiple
sufficient causes.[53]

Two categories of overdetermination must be distinguished.[54] One is where each event   [3.29]
duplicates or reinforces the effects of the other event (duplicative causation). For example,
suppose that D and T independently start separate fires, each of which would have been
sufficient to destroy P's house. The fires converge and together burn down the house. The
other category of overdetermination is where one event pre-empts the effects of the other
event (pre-emptive causation). The pre-empted condition may be an actual event or a
hypothetical event (it would have occurred in the absence of the defendant's wrong). An
example of an actual pre-empted condition is where P drinks a cup of tea poisoned by T, but
before the poison takes effect, D shoots and kills P instantly. An example of a hypothetical pre-
empted condition is where D shoots and kills P just as P was about to drink a cup of tea
poisoned by T.

Under the 'but for' test, D's conduct in those examples would not be a factual cause of P's   [3.30]
harm as it cannot be said that the harm would not have occurred but for D's conduct.[55] It is
commonly accepted that this is an absurd outcome. In order to solve the problem, Richard
Wright has developed the NESS (Necessary Element of a Sufficient Set) test, under which a
factual cause of harm is every element necessary for the sufficiency of a set of conditions that
are jointly sufficient to bring about the harm.[56]

Wright gives the following example.[57] Five units of pollution were necessary and sufficient   [3.31]
for certain environmental damage to occur. Each of seven wrongdoers, acting independently

---

52   RW Wright, 'Causation in Tort Law' (1985) 73 Cal L Rev 1735, 1740; S Ferey and P Dehez,
      'Overdetermined Causation Cases, Contribution and the Shapley Value' (2016) 91 Chi-Kent L Rev 637;
      Zanner v Zanner [2010] NSWCA 343, (2010) 79 NSWLR 702 [6] (Allsop P).
53   American Law Institute, *Restatement (Third) of Torts: Liability for Physical and Emotional Harm* (2010)
      §27.
54   The terminology and the examples are taken from RW Wright, 'Causation in Tort Law' (1985) 73 Cal
      L Rev 1735, 1775–76, 1795–96.
55   Where D's conduct brought forward the time at which the harm occurred, D's conduct is a factual cause
      of any loss resulting from that acceleration of the harm.
56   RW Wright, 'Causation in Tort Law' (1985) 73 Cal L Rev 1735, 1788–1803; RW Wright, 'The NESS Account
      of Natural Causation: A Response to Criticisms' in R Goldberg (ed), *Perspectives on Causation* (Hart
      2011) 285. See also *Nader v Urban Transit Authority of New South Wales* (1985) 2 NSWLR 501, 531
      (McHugh JA): 'every necessary member of the group of conditions jointly sufficient to produce the injury
      or damage is a cause of that injury or damage'.
57   RW Wright, 'Causation in Tort Law' (1985) 73 Cal L Rev 1735, 1793. See also *Thorpe v Brumfitt* (1873)
      LR 8 Ch App 650, 656–57 (James LJ): 'Suppose one person leaves a wheelbarrow standing on a way,
      that may cause no appreciable inconvenience, but if a hundred do so, that may cause a serious
      inconvenience, which a person entitled to the use of the way has a right to prevent, and it is no defence
      to any one person among the hundred to say that what he does causes of itself no damage to the
      complainant'. Assuming that 99 wheelbarrows would still have created serious inconvenience, the
      contribution of the one wheelbarrow does not satisfy the 'but for' test, but does satisfy the NESS test:
      J Stapleton, 'Unnecessary Causes' (2013) 129 LQR 39, 44.

of each other, discharged one unit of pollution. Each wrongdoer can say that its own unit of pollution was neither necessary nor itself sufficient to inflict the damage. But under the NESS test, each wrongdoer's unit of pollution is a factual cause of the damage because every set of five units was sufficient to inflict the damage, and in every set of five units, each unit was necessary for the sufficiency of that set of units.

[3.32]   We will now consider the courts' approach in cases of duplicative and pre-emptive causation.

1   Duplicative causation

[3.33]   A case of duplicative causation is present where both the defendant's conduct and another event (for which the defendant is not responsible) were each sufficient to bring about the harm suffered by the plaintiff, and each event duplicated or reinforced the effects of the other. The attribution of responsibility in those circumstances depends upon whether the event 'competing' with the defendant's wrong is a wrong committed by a third party or a non-wrongful event.

[3.34]   Where the event 'competing' with the defendant's wrong is a wrong committed by a third party, each wrong is regarded as a factual cause of the harm. For example, suppose that A and B, acting independently of each other, simultaneously shoot at and hit C, each bullet alone being sufficient to kill C instantly. It is commonly accepted that it would be absurd if A and B were exonerated on the ground that the conduct of neither satisfies the 'but for' test.[58] At common law, a finding of factual causation has been made either by applying the NESS test (see [3.30]–[3.31])[59] or by making an exception to the 'but for' test as a matter of common sense.[60]

[3.35]   Under the civil liability statutes' provisions on causation, conduct necessary to complete a set of conditions jointly sufficient to produce the plaintiff's harm should be regarded as 'a necessary condition for the occurrence of the harm'.[61] It has been said obiter that an instance of duplicative causation does not satisfy s 5D(1) of the *Civil Liability Act 2002* (NSW) (see [3.12]) and that the exception in s 5D(2) (see [3.20]) needs to be invoked to establish factual causation.[62] While this approach would work in New South Wales and the jurisdictions that have an equivalent to s 5D(2) (see [3.21]), it would not work in the Australian Capital Territory and South Australia, where the exception to the general requirement of factual causation is confined to (certain) circumstances of an evidentiary gap; see [3.65]–[3.66].

[3.36]   Where the event 'competing' with the defendant's wrong is not a wrong, the defendant will not be liable.[63] This follows from the fact that the person responsible for a pre-empting

---

58   Eg *Elayoubi v Zipser* [2008] NSWCA 335 [57]; quoted at [3.42].

59   *Amaca Pty Ltd v Booth* [2011] HCA 53, (2011) 246 CLR 36 [48] (French CJ).

60   *March v E & MH Stramare Pty Ltd* (1991) 171 CLR 506, 516, 524; *City of Stirling v Tremeer* [2006] WASCA 73, (2006) 32 WAR 155 [74]; *South Australia v Ellis* [2008] WASCA 200, (2008) 37 WAR 1 [309]; *Nominal Defendant v Bacon* [2014] NSWCA 275, (2014) 67 MVR 425 [31] (Macfarlan JA).

61   *Strong v Woolworths Ltd (t/as Big W)* [2012] HCA 5, (2012) 246 CLR 182 [20].

62   *Nominal Defendant v Bacon* [2014] NSWCA 275, (2014) 67 MVR 425 [31] (Macfarlan JA) [33]–[42]. By contrast, in *Jovanovski v Billbergia Pty Ltd* [2010] NSWSC 211 at [71], it was said that s 5D(2) covers only cases where the plaintiff's inability to prove that the 'but for' or NESS test is satisfied is due to inadequacy of the state of scientific knowledge. This was not challenged on appeal: [2011] NSWCA 135 [16].

63   G Williams, 'Causation in the Law' [1961] Camb LJ 62, 75–76.

condition is not liable where the pre-empted condition is not a wrong; see [3.101]–[3.102]. If a non-wrongful event exonerates the defendant even though its effects were pre-empted by the defendant's wrong, it must do the same if it duplicated or reinforced the defendant's wrong. However, the exoneration of the defendant should be seen as a matter relating to the scope of liability. The defendant's wrong should be regarded as a factual cause of the harm even if the 'competing' event is non-wrongful.[64]

So far, it has been assumed that the conduct of the defendant and any third party is a positive action. But it may be an omission. It is controversial whether the same rules apply to a case of dependent double omissions.[65] These circumstances arise where each of two persons (acting independently of each other) fails to perform a certain act, and harm ensues because the harm could have been prevented only by both persons performing the required act.[66] Under the 'but for' test, neither omission is a factual cause of the harm because the other omission would have inflicted the harm in any event.   [3.37]

For example, suppose that an employer acquires a tool and gives it to an employee to use. The manufacturer fails to include a warning against a certain use of the tool on the warning sheet, and the employer fails to read the warning sheet before handing the tool to the employee. The employee is injured by using the tool in the manner against which the manufacturer failed to warn. In those circumstances, the 'but for' test is not satisfied for either the manufacturer's omission (the employee would still have been injured because the employer would not have read the warning) or the employer's omission (the employee would still have been injured because the particular warning was not on the warning sheet).   [3.38]

Richard Wright argues that the chronologically later omission pre-empted the effects of the chronologically earlier omission.[67] But it could equally be argued that the chronologically earlier omission pre-empted the effects of the chronologically later omission. A case of dependent double omissions ought to be classified as an instance of duplicative causation, and each omission ought to be regarded as a factual cause of the harm.[68] Consistently with the rules governing multiple sufficient positive actions, where one of the omissions was non-wrongful, the harm should be attributed solely to that omission, but this should be seen as a matter of the scope of liability and not factual causation.   [3.39]

In *Elayoubi v Zipser*,[69] decided under the common law rules on causation, the NSW Court of Appeal said in obiter that where both omissions were wrongful, both are a factual cause of the harm, and left open the outcome where one omission was non-wrongful. A woman gave birth to a child in Preston Hospital. The child was delivered by caesarean section, which involved an incision encroaching into the upper uterine segment. Preston Hospital negligently failed to advise the mother that the procedure undertaken caused certain risks in a subsequent   [3.40]

---

64   RW Wright, 'Causation in Tort Law' (1985) 73 Cal L Rev 1735, 1775–76, 1798; American Law Institute, *Restatement (Third) of Torts: Liability for Physical and Emotional Harm* (2010) §27 cmt (d).
65   The terminology is taken from J Stapleton, 'Choosing What We Mean by "Causation" in the Law' (2008) 73 Missouri L Rev 433, 477.
66   If performance by either party would have been sufficient to avoid the harm, the 'but for' test is satisfied for both omissions.
67   R Wright, 'Acts and Omissions as Positive and Negative Causes' in JW Neyers, E Chamberlain and SGA Pitel (eds), *Emerging Issues in Tort Law* (Hart 2007) 303–05.
68   J Stapleton, 'Choosing What We Mean by "Causation" in the Law' (2008) 73 Missouri L Rev 433, 477–79.
69   [2008] NSWCA 335.

pregnancy. A few years later, the woman fell pregnant again. Antenatal care was provided by Bankstown Hospital, which negligently failed to make inquiries with Preston Hospital about the previous pregnancy. During the birth process, the child was deprived of oxygen and became disabled. This would have been prevented had Bankstown Hospital been aware of the previous upper uterine incision.

[3.41]   The child's disability could have been prevented only by Preston Hospital mentioning the upper uterine incision in the woman's medical records *and* by Bankstown Hospital obtaining those records. Bankstown Hospital alleged that Preston Hospital had failed to mention the upper uterine incision in the woman's medical records, and denied causing the harm on the basis that it would not have become aware of the upper uterine incision even if it had obtained the medical records from Preston Hospital. The records were destroyed before trial (but after the birth of the second child) but it was found, on the balance of probabilities, that they had mentioned the upper uterine incision. Thus, the case was not one of dependent double omissions.

[3.42]   However, the NSW Court of Appeal observed that Bankstown Hospital's failure to request the medical records would have been a factual cause of the second child's disability even if Preston Hospital had wrongfully failed to mention the upper uterine incision in the records. Basten JA, speaking for the court, said:

> If the negligence of two tortfeasors each contributes to the indivisible harm suffered by the victim, each is liable for the harm suffered. If neither were negligent, no harm would have been caused. If either one were negligent and the other not, in each case the negligence would have caused the harm. But a conclusion that if both were negligent and the harm eventuated, neither was responsible for that harm, invites a question as to whether the reasoning process has gone awry.[70]

[3.43]   The court left open whether there would have been a 'break in the causal link' between Bankstown Hospital's failure to obtain the medical records from Preston Hospital and the second child's disability if Preston Hospital had *innocently* failed to mention the upper uterine incision in the records.[71] In a different context, it is recognised that where one of dependent double omissions is not wrongful, the harm will be attributed to that omission. An employer who failed to provide an employee with safety equipment is not liable for the employee's injury resulting from the failure to use the equipment if the employee would not have used the equipment had it been provided.[72]

2   Pre-emptive causation

[3.44]   A case of pre-emptive causation exists where each of two factors was sufficient to bring about certain harm (or would have been sufficient if the other factor had not been present), but one factor pre-empts the effects of the other factor. The pre-empted factor may be an actual event or an event that would have occurred in the absence of the pre-empting factor; see [3.29].

70   Ibid, [57].
71   Ibid, [52]–[54].
72   *Duyvelshaff v Cathcart & Ritchie Ltd* (1973) 1 ALR 125, 138 (Gibbs J), 142–43 (Mason J); *Anyco Pty Ltd v Kleeman* [2008] WASCA 30, (2008) Aust Torts Reports 81–933 [48].

The pre-empted factor is not a factual cause of the harm, whether or not the pre-empting [3.45] factor is a wrong.[73] A factor is not a factual cause of harm only because it would have brought about the harm had things been different. In *Performance Cars Ltd v Abraham*,[74] the plaintiff's Rolls Royce was involved in two minor collisions a fortnight apart, each of which alone would have necessitated a respray of the lower part of the car. The car was still unrepaired at the time of the second collision. The plaintiff's action against the driver responsible for the second collision was rejected because the second driver caused no (additional) loss to the plaintiff.

Similarly, in *Cambridge v Anastasopolous*,[75] the plaintiff's motorboat sustained significant [3.46] damage to its engine while in the first and second defendants' custody. Before the motorboat was repaired, it was destroyed in an accident for which all three defendants were responsible. The trial judge assessed the loss caused by that accident at $46 500, being the difference between the value of the motorboat in an undamaged condition and the salvage value after the accident. No allowance was made for the pre-existing damage to the boat, assessed at $24 681. The NSW Court of Appeal held that the third defendant was liable only for the additional loss inflicted by the accident ($21 819).[76]

Where both factors are wrongs (committed by different persons), the pre-empting factor [3.47] has usually been regarded as a factual cause of the harm.[77] Lord Hobhouse has said that if a car is negligently damaged by one tortfeasor and destroyed by fire the next day by the negligence of another, the first tortfeasor remains liable for the cost of repairing the damage he caused.[78]

By contrast, where the pre-empted factor is not a wrong, the person responsible for the [3.48] pre-empting factor has not been held liable for the harm.[79] It is not clear whether this results from a denial of factual causation or from a value judgement that the harm is outside the scope of liability. On principle, it should be the latter.[80] The pre-empting factor satisfies the NESS test (see [3.30]–[3.31]) and should be regarded as a factual cause of the harm even if the pre-empted factor is not a wrong. The relevant cases are therefore discussed under scope of liability at [3.99]–[3.108].

D   Evidential uncertainty

Sometimes, there is an evidential uncertainty as to whether or not the plaintiff's harm would [3.49] have occurred without the defendant's conduct. In those circumstances, the plaintiff, who bears the onus of proof, may not be able to establish factual causation under the 'but for' test.

---

73   *Dillingham Constructions Pty Ltd v Steel Mains Pty Ltd* (1975) 132 CLR 323, 327 (Barwick CJ); *Davidson v J S Gilbert Fabrications Pty Ltd* [1986] 1 Qd R 1, 4; *Nilon v Bezzina* [1988] 2 Qd R 420, 426; *Dimond v Lovell* [2002] 1 AC 384, 406 (Lord Hobhouse).
74   [1962] 1 QB 33.
75   [2012] NSWCA 405.
76   Ibid, [49]–[50]. See also *Brand v Monks* [2009] NSWSC 1454 [493]: the defendant's breach of confidence by informing the local council of certain facts was not a cause of the council's investigation against the plaintiff which had started before the defendant contacted the council.
77   Eg *Baker v Willoughby* [1970] AC 467; *Davidson v J S Gilbert Fabrications Pty Ltd* [1986] 1 Qd R 1, 4.
78   *Dimond v Lovell* [2002] 1 AC 384, 406.
79   Eg *K-Mart Australia Ltd v McCann* [2004] NSWCA 283, considered at [3.101].
80   RW Wright, 'Causation in Tort Law' (1985) 73 Cal L Rev 1735, 1775–76, 1798.

However, the courts have assisted plaintiffs by inferring factual causation from the established facts or, in certain circumstances, by replacing the 'but for' test with a different test. These methods will now be discussed.

1   Inference of factual causation

[3.50]   A court may infer from the established facts that the defendant's conduct caused or materially contributed to the plaintiff's harm.[81] As French CJ has said:

> An after-the-event inference of causal connection may be reached on the civil standard of proof, namely, balance of probabilities, notwithstanding that the statistical correlation between the first event and the second event indicated, prospectively, no more than a 'mere possibility' or 'real chance' that the second event would occur given the first event.[82]

[3.51]   In *Tubemakers of Australia Ltd v Fernandez*,[83] the plaintiff received a blow to his right hand while working on a machine. His hand, which had not shown any problems before, became increasingly painful. The condition was diagnosed as Dupuytren's contracture, involving a contraction of the fingers towards the palm. His treating doctor testified that the blow 'could have' played a part in the condition. The defendant's medical witnesses deposed that the two were not related, but they suggested no alternative cause. A majority of the High Court of Australia held that the evidence was sufficient for a reasonable jury to find that the blow caused the condition.

[3.52]   In *Amaca Pty Ltd v King*,[84] the plaintiff, who suffered from mesothelioma, had been exposed to asbestos 38 years earlier while in the defendant's factory for a period of six hours. The only other possible source of exposure was the background level of atmospheric asbestos dust. The Victorian Court of Appeal held that the jury had been entitled to find that the exposure in the defendant's factory caused or materially contributed to the plaintiff's disease:

> [T]he jury was authorised, having considered all the evidence, to return a verdict for the respondent so long as – (1) the present state of medical knowledge admitted of an affirmative answer in his favour, or (2), 'competent and trustworthy expert opinion' regarded an affirmative answer as not lacking justification as a probable inference, or at least as 'an accepted hypothesis'.[85]

2   Material contribution to the harm

[3.53]   Sometimes, the cumulative operation of two or more factors, one of which is the defendant's responsibility, operated in the occurrence of an indivisible harm, and the extent to which each factor contributed to the harm cannot be ascertained. In other words, there is a wrongful factor and a non-wrongful factor, and it cannot be ascertained to what extent each factor contributed

---

81   Material contribution to the harm is discussed at [3.53]–[3.59].
82   *Amaca Pty Ltd v Booth* [2011] HCA 53, (2011) 246 CLR 36 [43].
83   (1976) 10 ALR 303.
84   [2011] VSCA 447, (2011) 35 VR 280.
85   Ibid, [87] (Nettle, Ashley and Redlich JJA). The quoted phrases were taken from *Adelaide Stevedoring Co Ltd v Forst* (1940) 64 CLR 538, 569 (Dixon J).

to the harm. This may make it impossible for the plaintiff to prove causation under the 'but for' test. In order to assist plaintiffs in those circumstances, the common law has developed the principle that an event that materially contributed to the harm constitutes a factual cause of the harm. This principle has been applied in cases in which the plaintiff contracted a disease as a result of being exposed to a certain noxious substance over time, and the likelihood of contracting the disease rose with the length of exposure or the amount of substance to which the plaintiff was exposed (or both).

In *Bonnington Castings Ltd v Wardlaw*,[86] the employment of the respondent steel dresser exposed him to silica dust emanating from two sources: pneumatic hammers and swing grinders. His employer breached its duty of care because it failed to use available methods of protecting workers against the dust from the swing grinders. It was not possible to protect workers against the dust from the hammers, and the employer was not in breach of duty in that respect. The respondent contracted pneumoconiosis, a disease caused by gradual inhalation and subsequent accumulation of silica particles in the lungs. The respondent could not prove that he would have avoided contracting the disease if he had been protected against the dust from the swing grinders, because the dust from the hammers alone might have been sufficient to cause the disease. The House of Lords held the employer liable on the ground that the dust from the swing grinders had materially contributed to the development of the disease.[87]

[3.54]

The concept of material contribution to the risk was applied at common law by the High Court of Australia in *Amaca Pty Ltd v Booth*.[88] The plaintiff, a retired motor mechanic, was diagnosed with mesothelioma, a disease caused by the inhalation of asbestos fibres. In his former job as a mechanic, which he had for almost 30 years, he worked with brake linings which contained asbestos. They were manufactured by the defendants. Prior to working as a mechanic, the plaintiff had had three further exposures to asbestos. Although these exposures were brief, it could not be established that the plaintiff would not have developed mesothelioma without the exposure to asbestos while working as a mechanic. The accepted expert evidence stated that the likelihood of developing mesothelioma increases with the number of asbestos fibres inhaled.[89] The High Court of Australia (Heydon J dissenting) held the defendants liable because the plaintiff's exposure to products manufactured by the defendants had materially contributed to the plaintiff's mesothelioma.[90]

[3.55]

In the two cases considered at [3.54]–[3.55], the substance to which the plaintiff was exposed by virtue of the defendant's breach of duty was the same as the substance to which the plaintiff was exposed through other means: silica dust in *Wardlaw* and asbestos in *Booth*. On principle, the concept of material contribution to the harm should equally apply where the

[3.56]

---

86   [1956] AC 613.
87   Pneumoconiosis has since been regarded as a divisible disease and the imposition of liability in principle in *Wardlaw* as orthodox: *Sienkiewicz v Greif (UK) Ltd* [2011] UKSC 10, [2011] 2 AC 229 [17] (Lord Phillips), [176] (Lord Brown); J Stapleton, 'Unnecessary Causes' (2013) 129 LQR 39, 51–53.
88   [2011] HCA 53, (2011) 246 CLR 36. See also *March v E & MH Stramare Pty Ltd* (1991) 171 CLR 506, 514 (Mason CJ); *Chappel v Hart* (1998) 195 CLR 232, 239 (Gaudron J), 244 (McHugh J); *Insurance Commission of Western Australia v Container Handlers Pty Ltd* [2004] HCA 24, (2004) 218 CLR 89 [133] fn 151 (Callinan J).
89   Different expert evidence was accepted in *Fairchild v Glenhaven Funeral Services Ltd* [2002] UKHL 22, [2003] 1 AC 32, considered at [3.63].
90   On similar facts, liability was also imposed in *Allianz Australia Ltd v Sim* [2012] NSWCA 68, (2012) 10 DDCR 325.

two substances are different. However, in *Amaca Pty Ltd v Ellis*,[91] the High Court of Australia held that the concept applies only where it is established, on the balance of probabilities, that the plaintiff's disease was caused by the substance to which the plaintiff was exposed by virtue of the defendant's breach of duty.

[3.57]   In *Ellis*, Paul Cotton died from lung cancer. During his working life, he had been exposed to asbestos fibres by two separate employers. However, he had also smoked on average 15 to 20 cigarettes a day for 26 years before he was diagnosed with lung cancer. His estate brought an action against the persons responsible for exposing him to asbestos. The expert evidence showed that lung cancer can be caused by smoking and by inhaling asbestos fibres. It could not be proved that Mr Cotton would not have developed lung cancer had he not been exposed to asbestos. The High Court of Australia denied the employer's liability, rejecting an application of the concept of material contribution to the harm:

> Questions of material contribution arise only if a connection between Mr Cotton's inhaling asbestos and his developing cancer was established. Knowing that inhaling asbestos *can* cause cancer does not entail that in this case it probably *did*.[92]

[3.58]   The civil liability statutes' provisions on causation generally require for factual causation that the defendant's conduct was 'a necessary condition of the occurrence of the harm'; see [3.12]. A material contribution to the harm that does not satisfy the 'but for' test is not a 'necessary condition'.[93] However, the statutes of most states provide that in an 'appropriate' or 'exceptional' case, 'in accordance with established principles', conduct that cannot be established as a necessary condition of the occurrence of the harm may nonetheless be accepted as establishing factual causation; see [3.20]–[3.21]. The 'established principles' include the concept of material contribution to the harm.[94]

[3.59]   However, the statutes of the Australian Capital Territory and South Australia do not provide for 'appropriate' or 'exceptional' cases or for material contribution to the harm. The statutes provide only for a material increase in risk, discussed immediately below. This is surprising since liability on the basis of material increase of risk is more controversial than liability on the basis of material contribution to the harm. It remains to be seen whether the courts find a way to interpret those two statutes in a way that allows factual causation to be established on the basis of material contribution to the harm.

3   Material increase in risk

[3.60]   At least under the civil liability statutes of the Australian Capital Territory and South Australia, factual causation may be established by proving that the defendant's conduct materially increased the risk of the occurrence of the harm suffered by the plaintiff, even though it cannot be proved that the harm would not have occurred but for the defendant's conduct or even that the conduct materially contributed to the harm.

---

91   [2010] HCA 5, (2010) 240 CLR 111.
92   Ibid, [68] (French CJ, Gummow, Hayne, Heydon, Crennan, Kiefel and Bell JJ). Emphasis in original.
93   *Zanner v Zanner* [2010] NSWCA 343, (2010) 79 NSWLR 702 [11] (Allsop P); *Strong v Woolworths Ltd (t/as Big W)* [2012] HCA 5, (2012) 246 CLR 182 [27].
94   *Zanner v Zanner* [2010] NSWCA 343, (2010) 79 NSWLR 702 [11] (Allsop P); *Strong v Woolworths Ltd (t/as Big W)* [2012] HCA 5, (2012) 246 CLR 182 [26].

This principle has sometimes been linked to the decision by the House of Lords in *McGhee*   [3.61]
v National Coal Board.[95] The appellant, who was employed by the respondent to empty pipe
kilns at a brickworks, was sent to empty brick kilns, where working conditions were hotter and
dustier. In breach of duty, the respondent failed to provide the appellant with facilities to
shower after work. The appellant cycled home after work, caked with sweat and dust. A few
days after he was sent to empty brick kilns, the appellant developed dermatitis, a skin disease.
It was accepted that the dermatitis was attributable to the appellant's work in the brick kilns,
but it could not be proved that the appellant would not have contracted dermatitis had shower
facilities been provided. The sweat and dust that accumulated on the appellant's skin during
ordinary work may have been sufficient to cause dermatitis.

The House of Lords held the respondent liable for the appellant's disease. While the   [3.62]
decision was unanimous, different reasons were given. Lord Kilbrandon opined that factual
causation had been proved on the balance of probabilities.[96] Lord Wilberforce opined that a
material increase in the risk of harm shifts the legal onus of proof with regard to causation onto
the defendant.[97] The remaining law lords applied *Bonnington Castings Ltd v Wardlaw*,[98]
considered at [3.54]. They argued that, on the facts before them, a material increase in the risk
of harm constituted a material contribution to the harm.[99]

The concept of material increase in risk was firmly embraced by the House of Lords in   [3.63]
Fairchild v Glenhaven Funeral Services Ltd,[100] where the plaintiffs developed mesothelioma
as a result of exposure to asbestos dust at work. Each plaintiff was exposed to asbestos dust
during periods of employment with more than one employer. Each employer breached its duty
to protect the employee from the inhalation of asbestos dust. The accepted expert evidence
stated that the mechanism by which asbestos dust triggers mesothelioma was unknown, that
the trigger might be a single fibre, and that once caused the condition was not aggravated by
further exposure to asbestos dust.[101] Under this single-fibre theory, it could not be established
with regard to any of a plaintiff's employers that the plaintiff would not have contracted
mesothelioma but for the breach of duty by that particular employer. It could only be
established that none of the plaintiffs would have contracted mesothelioma had all the
employers discharged their duty of care. The House of Lords held all employers liable for
the mesothelioma on the ground that each employer's breach of duty increased the risk of the
employee developing mesothelioma.

In *Fairchild*, each period of exposure of the plaintiffs to asbestos dust occurred as a result   [3.64]
of someone's breach of duty. In *Sienkiewicz v Greif (UK) Ltd*,[102] the UK Supreme Court applied
the concept of material increase in risk to wrongful exposure combined with non-wrongful

---

95   [1973] 1 WLR 1. The House of Lords itself has interpreted its decision in *McGhee* as being based
      on an inference of causation on the facts, rather than the principle that a material increase in risk can
      establish factual causation: *Wilsher v Essex Area Health Authority* [1988] AC 1074, 1086–90.
96   [1973] 1 WLR 1, 10.
97   Ibid, 7.
98   [1956] AC 613.
99   [1973] 1 WLR 1, 4–5 (Lord Reid), 8 (Lord Simon), 11–13 (Lord Salmon).
100   [2002] UKHL 22, [2003] 1 AC 32.
101   Different expert evidence was accepted in *Amaca Pty Ltd v Booth* [2011] HCA 53, (2011) 246 CLR 36,
      considered at [3.55].
102   [2011] UKSC 10, [2011] 2 AC 229.

exposure. The case involved, again, the contraction of mesothelioma as a result of exposure to asbestos dust. However, each plaintiff was exposed not only to asbestos dust at work (due to the employer's breach of duty) but also to significant amounts of asbestos dust in the general atmosphere. The UK Supreme Court pointed out that the plaintiffs in the instant case faced the same evidential dilemma as the plaintiffs in *Fairchild*, and held that the material increase in the risk of contracting mesothelioma by virtue of the employer's breach of duty established factual causation at common law.[103]

[3.65]   *Fairchild* was decided just before the civil liability reform took place in Australia. The statutes of two jurisdictions expressly enshrine the '*Fairchild* principle'. Section 45(2) of the *Civil Law (Wrongs) Act 2002* (ACT) provides:

> However, if a person (the plaintiff) has been negligently exposed to a similar risk of harm by a number of different people (the defendants) and it is not possible to assign responsibility for causing the harm to any 1 or more of them –
>
> (a)   the court may continue to apply the established common law principle under which responsibility may be assigned to the defendants for causing the harm; but
>
> (b)   the court must consider the position of each defendant individually and state the reasons for bringing the defendant within the scope of liability.

[3.66]   An almost identical provision exists in s 34(2) of the *Civil Liability Act 1936* (SA), which refers to *Fairchild* in a footnote. Under those two statutes, a material increase in risk establishes factual causation where all of the plaintiff's exposures to the risk occurred wrongfully (as happened in *Fairchild*), but not where at least one exposure was not wrongful (as happened in *Sienkiewicz*).

[3.67]   The civil liability statutes of New South Wales, Queensland, Tasmania, Victoria and Western Australia provide that in an 'appropriate' or 'exceptional' case, 'in accordance with established principles', conduct that cannot be established as a necessary condition of the occurrence of the harm may nonetheless be accepted as establishing factual causation; see [3.20]–[3.21]. The question arises whether the 'established principles' include the concept of material increase in risk. When those provisions were enacted, the High Court of Australia had not yet decided on whether to adopt the concept of material increase in risk,[104] and intermediate courts of appeal had rejected the concept.[105]

[3.68]   The provisions mentioned in the preceding paragraph are meant to implement the recommendations on causation contained in the Ipp Report,[106] which cited *Fairchild*[107] and recommended that both a material contribution to harm and a material increase in risk should establish factual causation in appropriate cases.[108] Since the enactment of those provisions,

---

103   Specifically in relation to mesothelioma, this principle is now enshrined in the *Compensation Act 2006* (UK), s 3(2)(a).

104   The question was expressly left open in *Bennett v Minister of Community Welfare* (1992) 176 CLR 408, 417.

105   *Bendix Mintex Pty Ltd v Barnes* (1997) 42 NSWLR 307, 315–18, 345–46; *T C (by his tutor Sabatino) v New South Wales* [2001] NSWCA 380 [58]–[59].

106   *Review of the Law of Negligence: Final Report* (2002).

107   Ibid, [7.30].

108   Ibid, Recommendation 29.

the High Court of Australia has still not decided on whether a material increase in risk establishes factual causation at common law,[109] and intermediate appellate courts continue to reject the concept, leaving the decision to the High Court.[110]

IV   Scope of liability
A   Subsequent event

An event for which the defendant is not directly responsible may occur after the defendant's wrong but prior to the occurrence of the loss in respect of which compensation is claimed. The event may be causally dependent (the event would not have occurred but for the defendant's wrong) or causally independent (the event would have occurred regardless). Where the defendant's wrong is a factual cause of the loss, the question arises whether the occurrence of the subsequent event removes the loss from the scope of the defendant's liability.

[3.69]

1   Distinction between basic loss and additional loss

It is vital to distinguish between two items of loss in this context. For convenience, they will be called 'basic loss' and 'additional loss'. Basic loss is loss that would still have been suffered if the defendant's wrong alone (without the subsequent event) had occurred, and would equally have been suffered if the subsequent event alone (without the defendant's wrong) had occurred, assuming that the subsequent event could have occurred without the defendant's wrong. Both the defendant's wrong and the subsequent event were each sufficient to bring about that loss. Additional loss is loss that would not have occurred but for the subsequent event. The defendant's wrong on its own, without the subsequent event, was not sufficient to bring about this loss.

[3.70]

Consider the following example.[111] The defendant wrongfully injures the plaintiff, who can no longer work as a miner but can still work as a farm hand. Subsequently, the plaintiff is injured in a car accident (not involving the defendant) and becomes permanently unable to do any paid work. The car accident would have completely disabled the plaintiff even if he had been uninjured (and able to work as a miner) beforehand. With regard to the plaintiff's loss of earning capacity after the car accident,[112] the difference between what the plaintiff would have earned as a miner and what the plaintiff would have earned as a farm hand is what we call the basic loss. The defendant's wrong on its own was sufficient to bring about that loss, and the car accident on its own was also sufficient to bring about that loss. What the plaintiff would have earned as a farm hand (after the car accident) is what we call the

[3.71]

---

109   See *Amaca Pty Ltd v Ellis* [2010] HCA 5, (2010) 240 CLR 111 [12]; *Strong v Woolworths Ltd (t/as Big W)* [2012] HCA 5, (2012) 246 CLR 182 [26]; *Alcan Gove Pty Ltd v Zabic* [2015] HCA 33, (2015) 257 CLR 1 [15]. Individual judges in the High Court have rejected the notion that a material increase in risk establishes factual causation at common law: *Roads and Traffic Authority v Royal* [2008] HCA 19, (2008) 245 ALR 653 [144] (Kiefel J); *Amaca Pty Ltd v Booth* [2011] HCA 53, (2011) 246 CLR 36 [41] (French CJ).

110   *Evans v Queanbeyan City Council* [2011] NSWCA 230, (2011) 9 DDCR 541 [51]–[52], [103]; *Merck Sharp & Dohme (Australia) Pty Ltd v Peterson* [2011] FCAFC 128, (2011) 196 FCR 145 [102]–[104]; *Allianz Australia Ltd v Sim* [2012] NSWCA 68, (2012) 10 DDCR 325 [98].

111   Based on the facts of *DNM Mining Pty Ltd v Barwick* [2004] NSWCA 137, considered at [3.107].

112   The car accident cannot affect liability for loss already suffered.

additional loss. This loss would not have occurred but for the car accident. The defendant's wrong on its own, without the car accident, was not sufficient to bring about that additional loss.

[3.72]   The distinction between what we call basic loss and additional loss was recognised by Windeyer J in *Faulkner v Keffalinos*:

> There is I think a critical distinction between a supervening happening that prevents a particular damage occurring as a result of the tort and a supervening happening that causes the harm caused by the tort to have added gravity. In the first class of case the supervening event diminishes the damages which flow from the tort: in the second class it merely adds to them . . .[113]

[3.73]   The rules governing the scope of the defendant's liability differ between the basic loss and the additional loss and, in respect of basic loss, should differ between a causally dependent subsequent event and a causally independent subsequent event. The three categories of case will now be discussed.

2   Additional loss: intervening event

[3.74]   Additional loss in the present context is loss that would not have been suffered but for the occurrence after the defendant's wrong of an event for which the defendant is not responsible. The defendant's wrong on its own, without the subsequent event, was not sufficient to bring about this loss. Where the additional loss would have occurred even in the absence of the defendant's wrong, the wrong is not a factual cause of the loss and the defendant is not liable. Where the additional loss would not have occurred but for the defendant's wrong (because the subsequent event would not have occurred, or would not have affected the plaintiff, but for the wrong),[114] the wrong is a factual cause of the additional loss,[115] but the subsequent event, which may be human conduct or a natural event, may exonerate the defendant on the ground that it 'broke the chain of causation' between the defendant's wrong and the loss. At least where it does so, such an event is usually called an intervening event or *novus actus interveniens*. The question arises when an intervening event exonerates the defendant on policy grounds.

[3.75]   This question has been considered in numerous cases involving different causes of action, but no settled approach has emerged even for the same cause of action. For example, it is not clear when a defendant who inflicted personal injury upon a plaintiff which left the plaintiff in a vulnerable condition is liable for the consequences of a subsequent accident which the plaintiff would not have had but for the initial injury.[116] It is not possible here to review all cases on intervening events. A brief outline of the major approaches and considerations must suffice.

---

113   (1970) 45 ALJR 80, 85. The case is considered at [3.110]–[3.111].

114   The plaintiff bears the onus of proof: *Brand v Monks* [2009] NSWSC 1454 [485]–[488].

115   *Caltex Oil (Australia) Pty Ltd v The Dredge Willemstad* (1976) 136 CLR 529, 583 (Stephen J); *Roads and Traffic Authority v Royal* [2008] HCA 19, (2008) 245 ALR 653 [32].

116   Liability was denied in *Edwards v Pelvay* [1961] SASR 171, and imposed in *Jacques v Matthews* [1961] SASR 205. Both cases involved the re-fracture of a leg broken a year earlier in the initial accident.

In some negligence cases, the High Court of Australia has held that a defendant is   [3.76]
liable for the consequences of a subsequent event, even tortious conduct by a third party,
unless that event was unforeseeable.[117] Since the remoteness test in negligence is reasonable foreseeability (see [6.63]), the High Court assimilated the issue of intervening causes
within the broader concept of remoteness of damage. The same assimilation has occurred
in some cases involving breach of contract.[118] But the test of foreseeability has not been
applied to the issue of intervening acts in all cases involving breach of contract or
negligence.

In another line of cases involving breach of contract[119] or negligence,[120] it has been held   [3.77]
that a defendant is liable for the consequences of a subsequent event, even tortious conduct
by a third party, where the defendant's wrong created the very risk of injury that occurred
and the injury occurred in the ordinary course of things. On that basis, a builder who failed
to ensure that external windows were waterproof was liable for the consequences of
negligent rectification work by other builders,[121] and a person who parked a truck at night
in the middle of a six-lane road (with lights on) was liable for the injuries suffered by an
intoxicated person who, driving at an excessive speed and failing to keep a proper lookout,
ran his car into the truck.[122]

On the other hand, a defendant is not generally liable for merely causing the plaintiff to   [3.78]
be at a certain place at a certain time, unless the place is inherently dangerous. For
example, a defendant who wrongfully directs the plaintiff to the left road rather than the
right road is not liable for the consequences of an accident that the plaintiff suffers on the
left road, unless the left road is inherently dangerous;[123] and a doctor who negligently
advises the plaintiff to undergo a certain operation is not liable for an injury suffered by the
plaintiff as a result of being struck by lightning or a runaway truck during the operation.[124]
Similarly, wrongfully keeping a company in business does not result in liability for the
consequences of the company being in that 'place'. Thus, auditors whose negligence
delayed the appointment of a receiver for a company by three years were not liable for

---

117   *Thompson v Bankstown Corporation* (1953) 87 CLR 619; *Chapman v Hearse* (1961) 106 CLR 112, 120;
      Mahony v J Kruschich (Demolitions) Pty Ltd (1985) 156 CLR 522, 528.
118   *Alexander v Cambridge Credit Corporation Ltd* (1987) 9 NSWLR 310, 315 (Glass JA, dissenting);
      Kenny & Good Pty Ltd v MGICA (1992) Ltd (1999) 199 CLR 413 (a valuer who overvalued property as
      security for a loan was liable for the loss suffered by the lender as a result of a foreseeable market
      downturn).
119   *Scott Carver Pty Ltd v SAS Trustee Corporation* [2005] NSWCA 462 [62]–[65]. See also *Alexander v
      Cambridge Credit Corporation Ltd* (1987) 9 NSWLR 310, 361 (McHugh JA): 'the intervening act of a
      third party will not operate as a novus actus interveniens if the contractual duty of which the defendant is
      in breach was to guard against the very act of the intervener or that class of act'.
120   *March v E & MH Stramare Pty Ltd* (1991) 171 CLR 506, 518–19 (Mason CJ); *Curmi v McLennan*
      [1994] 1 VR 513, 525; *Roads and Traffic Authority v Royal* [2008] HCA 19, (2008) 245 ALR 653 [32], [138].
      See also *Derbyshire Building Co Pty Ltd v Becker* (1962) 107 CLR 633, 653 (Kitto J).
121   *Scott Carver Pty Ltd v SAS Trustee Corporation* [2005] NSWCA 462 [62]–[65].
122   *March v E & MH Stramare Pty Ltd* (1991) 171 CLR 506. See also *Curmi v McLennan* [1994] 1 VR 513,
      525 (where the shooting of an airgun by a schoolboy was held not to break the chain of causation
      between the defendant's negligence in giving the airgun to the boy and the harm caused by the shot).
123   Example given in *Alexander v Cambridge Credit Corporation Ltd* (1987) 9 NSWLR 310, 333–34
      (Mahoney JA).
124   NC Seddon and RA Bigwood, *Cheshire and Fifoot Law of Contract* (11th edn, LexisNexis 2017) [23.38],
      using an example given in *Chappel v Hart* (1998) 195 CLR 232, 284 (Hayne J, dissenting).

business losses suffered by the company in that period due to extraneous events such as high inflation and falling property prices.[125]

[3.79]   In most cases, the event that is alleged to have broken the chain of causation is human conduct. The following considers some principles emerging from the cases in that respect. Conduct of the plaintiff and conduct of third parties are generally subject to the same principles. However, conduct of the plaintiff is also addressed by the doctrines of contributory negligence and mitigation; see [3.130]–[3.138]. The overlap of these doctrines with the doctrines of *novus actus interveniens* is discussed at [3.91]–[3.98].

[3.80]   For human conduct to exonerate the defendant, it is necessary (but not sufficient) that the conduct was voluntary in the sense that the actor (the plaintiff or a third party) had a true choice between acting and not acting. The contraction of a psychiatric illness cannot be described as a voluntary reaction to the defendant's wrong.[126] Nor is the defendant exonerated by another person's action that was purely reflexive or occurred in a state of panic. Examples are the actions of stepping back (onto a steel shaft) from a falling heavy rail,[127] running away from colliding cars 12 metres away (and falling),[128] and jumping from a platform 4.5 metres above ground to escape a fire.[129]

[3.81]   Even a truly voluntary action does not exonerate the defendant where it constituted a normal reaction to an emergency or danger. Examples are assisting an unconscious person lying on the highway,[130] and backing down a truck angled across an icy highway.[131] Nor is the defendant exonerated by another person's action undertaken to escape a serious inconvenience. Examples are attempting to climb out of a toilet cubicle with a locked door,[132] and jumping out of a train that had started to move without warning and would not stop for another 120 kilometres.[133]

[3.82]   Negligent actions of third parties will not exonerate the defendant where it was the very duty of the defendant to guard against those actions, or where the defendant's wrong generated the very risk of injury resulting from a third party's negligence and that injury occurred in the ordinary course of things. For example, a general medical practitioner who negligently recommended chiropractic treatment was liable for the detrimental consequences of such treatment even though the chiropractor was negligent in accepting the plaintiff,[134] and a football club that failed to properly secure a gate at its stadium was liable for severe injuries suffered by the plaintiff when an unruly crowd broke through the gate and knocked down the plaintiff in the process.[135] Furthermore, where the defendant wrongfully impeded the exercise

---

125   *Alexander v Cambridge Credit Corporation Ltd* (1987) 9 NSWLR 310.
126   *Rowe v McCartney* [1976] 2 NSWLR 72, 82–83 (Glass JA, dissenting); *Rowan v Cornwall (No 5)* [2002] SASC 160, (2002) 82 SASR 152 [702].
127   *Malleys Ltd v Rogers* (1955) 55 SR (NSW) 390.
128   *Parry v Yates* [1963] WAR 42.
129   *Devine v Colvilles Ltd* 1969 SC (HL) 67.
130   *Chapman v Hearse* (1961) 106 CLR 112.
131   *Abbott v Kasza* (1976) 71 DLR (3d) 581.
132   *Sayers v Harlow UDC* [1958] 1 WLR 623.
133   *Caterson v Commissioner for Railways* (1973) 128 CLR 99.
134   *McGroder v Maguire* [2002] NSWCA 261.
135   *Hosie v Arbroath Football Club Ltd* 1978 SLT 122.

of rights by the third party, the third party's carelessness in removing the impediment will not generally exonerate the defendant.[136]

In other circumstances, the defendant is liable for the consequences of a third party's negligent action unless that action is 'inexcusably bad',[137] or 'completely outside the bounds' of reasonable conduct,[138] or 'so obviously unnecessary or improper that it is in the nature of a gratuitous aggravation of the injury'.[139] Unless this threshold is reached, a defendant who gives wrong advice to a third party is liable for the consequences of the third party negligently relying upon the defendant's advice and thereby harming the plaintiff;[140] a defendant who inflicts personal injury upon the plaintiff is liable for the consequences of negligent medical treatment of the plaintiff;[141] a defendant who wrongfully induces the plaintiff to lend money to another person is liable for the consequences of the plaintiff's lack of security for the loan due to negligence on the part of the plaintiff's solicitors;[142] and a defendant who gives wrong advice to the plaintiff is liable for the consequences of the plaintiff relying upon that advice and upon the same advice subsequently given by an independent third party.[143]

[3.83]

Actions of third parties undertaken with the intention of harming the plaintiff will often exonerate a defendant who unintentionally provided the opportunity for those actions.[144] For example, a railway company that allowed a carriage to become overcrowded was not liable for the consequences of pickpocketing in the carriage;[145] a local council responsible for serious damage to the plaintiff's house caused by a broken water main in the adjoining road was not liable for further damage to the house caused by squatters after the plaintiffs had evacuated the house;[146] the occupier of a motel with lockable sliding doors on the ground floor was not liable for the injuries that an intruder inflicted upon a guest staying on the ground floor;[147] and a valuer whose negligent overvaluation of a property induced a

[3.84]

---

136   *Clark v Chambers* (1878) 3 QBD 327, where the defendant wrongfully blocked access to a road and a third party removed the barrier but put it in an unsafe place, injuring the plaintiff.

137   *Martin v Isbard* (1946) 48 WALR 52, 56 (Walker J).

138   *Lawrie v Meggitt* (1974) 11 SASR 5, 8 (Zelling J).

139   *South Australian Stevedoring Co Ltd v Holbertson* [1939] SASR 257, 264 (Murray CJ, Angas Parsons and Napier JJ). All three formulae were adopted in *Mahony v J Kruschich (Demolitions) Pty Ltd* (1985) 156 CLR 522, 530.

140   *Caltex Oil (Australia) Pty Ltd v The Dredge Willemstad* (1976) 136 CLR 529, 543 (Gibbs J),

141   *Mahony v J Kruschich (Demolitions) Pty Ltd* (1985) 156 CLR 522, 529–30; *Dunin v Harrison* [2002] VSCA 125, (2002) 8 VR 596 [12]. A similar view was taken in *Webb v Barclays Bank plc* [2001] EWCA Civ 1141, [2002] PIQR P8 [55]–[56].

142   *Thorpe Nominees Pty Ltd v Henderson & Lahey* [1988] 2 Qd R 216, 222–26. See also *Hunt & Hunt Lawyers v Mitchell Morgan Nominees Pty Ltd* [2013] HCA 10, (2013) 247 CLR 613.

143   *Bennett v Minister of Community Welfare* (1992) 176 CLR 408. Where the plaintiff *solely* relies upon the third party's advice, the defendant's advice is not a factual cause of the loss: *Craig v Troy* (1997) 16 WAR 96, 203.

144   'In general . . . even though A. is in fault, he is not responsible for injury to C. which B., a stranger to him, deliberately chooses to do. Though A. may have given the occasion for B.'s mischievous activity, B. then becomes a new and independent cause': *Weld-Blundell v Stephens* [1920] AC 956, 986 (Lord Sumner), approvingly quoted in *Allianz Australia Insurance Ltd v Waterbrook at Yowie Bay Pty Ltd* [2009] NSWCA 224 [106].

145   *Cobb v Great Western Railway Co* [1894] AC 419.

146   *Lamb v Camden LBC* [1981] QB 625.

147   *Ashrafi Persian Trading Co Pty Ltd v Ashrafinia* [2001] NSWCA 243, (2001) Aust Torts Reports 81–636.

lender to grant a loan secured by a mortgage on that property was not liable for the consequences of third parties criminally damaging the property.[148]

[3.85]   However, intentional actions of third parties do not exonerate the defendant in at least three (overlapping) categories of case. First, there is no exoneration where the defendant was under a duty to control the third party's actions by virtue of a pre-existing relationship between them. Parents may be liable for actions by their young children,[149] and prison authorities may be liable for criminal actions by escapees.[150] Secondly, intentional actions by third parties do not exonerate the defendant where the duty breached by the defendant aimed to prevent those very actions. For example, a decorator who left the plaintiff's house unattended and unlocked for two hours was liable for the consequences of theft occurring in that time;[151] and the occupier of licensed premises was liable for injury suffered by a patron as a result of being attacked by another patron who had been violent and the subject of complaints by patrons to the occupier.[152]

[3.86]   Thirdly, 'there are circumstances where the relationship between two parties may mean that one has a duty to take reasonable care to protect the other from the criminal behaviour of third parties, random and unpredictable as such behaviour may be'.[153] For example, a bailee is liable towards the bailor for failing to properly protect the goods against deliberate destruction by third parties;[154] employees who were attacked by strangers at night in the workplace or its vicinity have often recovered damages from the employer on the ground that the employer had failed to install proper security measures;[155] and school students who were attacked or bullied by other students on the school premises or in its vicinity have sometimes recovered damages from the school on the ground that the school had failed to provide proper supervision.[156]

---

148   *Hay Properties Consultants Pty Ltd v Victorian Securities Corporation Ltd* [2010] VSCA 247, (2010) 29 VR 503.

149   *Smith v Leurs* (1945) 70 CLR 256, 262 (Dixon J); *Modbury Triangle Shopping Centre Pty Ltd v Anzil* [2000] HCA 61, (2000) 205 CLR 254 [20].

150   *Home Office v Dorset Yacht Co Ltd* [1970] AC 1004; *Modbury Triangle Shopping Centre Pty Ltd v Anzil* [2000] HCA 61, (2000) 205 CLR 254 [21].

151   *Stansbie v Troman* [1948] 2 KB 48.

152   *Wormald v Robertson* (1992) Aust Torts Reports 81–180. The occupier is not liable where security staff could not have prevented the attack: *Adeels Palace Pty Ltd v Moubarak* [2009] HCA 48, (2009) 239 CLR 420.

153   *Modbury Triangle Shopping Centre Pty Ltd v Anzil* [2000] HCA 61, (2000) 205 CLR 254 [26] (Gleeson CJ, with whom Gaudron J and Hayne J agreed).

154   *Pitt Son & Badgery Ltd v Proulefco SA* (1984) 153 CLR 644.

155   *Chomentowski v Red Garter Restaurant Pty Ltd* (1970) 92 WN (NSW) 1070 (a waiter was attacked while transporting the restaurant's takings for the evening to a night safe at a bank); *Fraser v State Transport Authority* (1985) 39 SASR 57 (a bus driver was attacked at night in a lay-over); *Public Transport Corporation v Sartori* [1997] 1 VR 168 (an employee was attacked at night in the workplace's car park); *English v Rogers* [2005] NSWCA 327, (2005) Aust Torts Reports 81–800 (a hotel cleaner working at night was held hostage by a gunman); *Karatjas v Deakin University* [2012] VSCA 53, (2012) 35 VR 355 (a university employee was attacked at night on campus). Cf *Modbury Triangle Shopping Centre Pty Ltd v Anzil* [2000] HCA 61, (2000) 205 CLR 254, where the owner of a shopping centre who turned off the lights of the centre's car park when the centre closed was not liable for the injuries suffered by an employee who was attacked in the dark car park after leaving work.

156   *Trustees of the Roman Catholic Church for the Diocese of Bathurst v Koffman* (1996) Aust Torts Reports 81–399; *Gregory v New South Wales* [2009] NSWSC 559; *Oyston v St Patrick's College* [2011] NSWSC 269.

The plaintiff's deliberate self-harm usually exonerates the defendant. For example, a **[3.87]** builder who constructs a defective building is not liable for the defects towards a person who purchases the building in full knowledge of the defects and their significance.[157] Further-more, a defendant who inflicts personal injury upon the plaintiff is not liable for the conse-quences of criminal or disciplinary sanctions imposed upon the plaintiff for illegal actions triggered by the injury.[158] Holding the defendant liable in those circumstances would subvert the objective of the sanction, and would conflict with the fact that the imposition of the sanction presupposes the voluntariness of the plaintiff's actions.[159]

In order to exonerate the defendant, the plaintiff's conduct must be voluntary. This has **[3.88]** proved difficult to determine in cases in which the personal injury suffered by the plaintiff led him to use illegal drugs or to excessively drink alcohol. In some of these cases, the plaintiff did so in order to alleviate pain caused by the personal injury. The person responsible for the personal injury was held liable for the consequences of the plaintiff's drug addiction in some cases,[160] and not liable in others.[161] Conflicting decisions have also been made in cases in which the drugs were not used for the purpose of alleviating pain.[162]

There have been several cases involving 'foolish' actions by children in a hazardous **[3.89]** situation created by the defendant. The courts grappled with the question of whether the defendant owed a duty of care towards the child under the circumstances. The cases shed light on the related question of when a child's action breaks the chain of causation. Those who ought to anticipate the presence of children within the scope of hazard of their activities cannot escape liability for injuries resulting from a child's actions simply on the ground that an adult would have acted differently.[163] This is because 'every person must be taken to know that young children and boys are of a very inquisitive and frequently mischievous disposition, and are likely to meddle with whatever happens to come within their reach'.[164]

However, there is no liability for the injuries suffered by children who were old enough to **[3.90]** clearly appreciate the danger of what they were doing. For example, no liability was imposed for the serious injuries suffered by an 11-year-old boy who put a metal object (which turned

---

157 *Allianz Australia Insurance Ltd v Waterbrook at Yowie Bay Pty Ltd* [2009] NSWCA 224 [110]–[111]; *Bonarrigo v DSF Pty Ltd* [2012] VCAT 1404 [38]–[43], where it was said obiter that the builder is also exonerated where the purchaser *ought to* have been aware of the defects at the time of purchase. The effect on the builder's liability of negligence by a surveyor employed by the purchaser prior to the purchase is discussed by S Harder, 'Is Liability for Defective Buildings Negated by a Surveyor's Intervening Negligence?' [2007] Conv 417.

158 *State Rail Authority of New South Wales v Wiegold* (1991) 25 NSWLR 500; *Bailey v Nominal Defendant* [2004] QCA 344; *Dorsett v Janeska* [2005] WASCA 215 [46]. English and US cases on this issue are discussed by J Goudkamp, 'Can Tort Law be Used to Deflect the Impact of Criminal Sanctions? The Role of the Illegality Defence' (2006) 14 Torts LJ 20, 33–36.

159 Goudkamp, ibid, 40–46.

160 *Grey v Simpson* (NSWCA, 3 April 1978); *Havenaar v Havenaar* [1982] 1 NSWLR 626.

161 *Beard v Richmond* (1987) Aust Torts Reports 80–129; *Yates v Jones* (1990) Aust Torts Reports 81–009; *Holt v Manufacturers' Mutual Insurance Ltd* [2001] QSC 230.

162 Liability was denied in *Anderson v Hotel Capital Trading Pty Ltd* [2003] NSWSC 1195 (drug use due to post-traumatic stress disorder following armed robbery), and imposed in *Goodsell v Murphy* [2002] NSWCA 216, (2002) Aust Torts Reports 81–671 [32] (relapse of heroin addiction triggered by personal injury).

163 *Taylor v Glasgow Corporation* (1922) SC (HL) 1, 14–15 (Lord Sumner).

164 *Thompson v Bankstown Corporation* (1953) 87 CLR 619, 631 (Dixon CJ and Williams J).

out to be a detonator), petrol and paper into a bottle and lit it;[165] by a 14-year-old boy who jumped from a bridge head first into a river;[166] and by a 10-year-old boy who fell when descending from the top level of a bunk bed without rail or ladder.[167]

[3.91]   The application of the concept of *novus actus interveniens* to conduct of the plaintiff raises the question of how this fits with the existence of separate doctrines specifically dealing with unreasonable conduct of the plaintiff contributing to her loss. A distinction needs to be made between conduct of the plaintiff occurring prior to the defendant's wrong or prior to the plaintiff becoming aware of the wrong, and conduct of the plaintiff after becoming aware of the wrong.

[3.92]   Unreasonable conduct of the plaintiff prior to becoming aware of the defendant's wrong falls within the scope of the doctrine of contributory negligence where that doctrine applies; see [3.130]–[3.131]. At common law, contributory negligence is a complete defence in negligence and some other torts, but is irrelevant in other causes of action, in particular breach of contract. Statutory apportionment regimes apply to some, but not all, causes of actions. Since the doctrine of contributory negligence does not cover all causes of actions, there is a 'gap' to be filled by concepts such as *novus actus interveniens*,[168] remoteness of damage, or scope of liability.

[3.93]   But the concept of *novus actus interveniens* has been invoked to deny liability also in cases in which an apportionment of liability by virtue of contributory negligence would have been available.[169] In some of these cases, the question of whether the plaintiff's conduct had broken the chain of causation was resolved by asking whether that conduct had been reasonable – the very test used in the context of contributory negligence. For example, in cases in which a police officer was injured during his high-speed pursuit of a traffic offender, it was held that the offender's liability for the injury was not affected by the officer's deliberate actions in initiating and continuing the pursuit unless those actions had been unreasonable in the circumstances.[170]

[3.94]   Since an apportionment of liability by virtue of contributory negligence may, exceptionally, involve a complete exoneration of the defendant (see [6.111]), it seems better to deal with these cases exclusively under the apportionment regime without 'interference' by the concepts of *novus actus interveniens* or scope of liability. This may have been recognised in *Zanner v Zanner*.[171] A mother allowed her 11-year-old son to drive the family car into their carport. The son accidentally drove the car into the mother, causing her serious injury. The son was held liable, but liability was reduced by 50% on the ground that it had been unreasonable for the mother to allow her son to drive the car. The NSW Court of Appeal held that the mother's injury fell within the scope of the son's liability, Allsop P saying that '[t]here is no reason why the

165   *Marrickville Municipal Council v Moustafa* [2001] NSWCA 372, (2001) 117 LGERA 291.
166   *Roads and Traffic Authority of New South Wales v Dederer* [2007] HCA 42, (2007) 234 CLR 330. Things may be different in the case of a mentally disabled person: *Town of Port Hedland v Hodder (No 2)* [2012] WASCA 212, (2012) 43 WAR 383.
167   *Shaw v Thomas* [2010] NSWCA 169.
168   Eg *Sherman v Nymboida Collieries Pty Ltd* (1963) 109 CLR 580, 587, 590–91.
169   Eg *Clarke v Damiani* (1973) 5 SASR 427, 431; *Esplin v Murray* [1999] NSWSC 338 [65]; *Mallesons Stephen Jacques v Trenorth Ltd* [1999] 1 VR 727. In none of these cases was the availability of apportionment raised.
170   *Hirst v Nominal Defendant* [2005] QCA 65, [2005] 2 Qd R 133; *New South Wales (NSW Police) v Nominal Defendant* [2009] NSWCA 225, (2009) 53 MVR 243.
171   [2010] NSWCA 343, (2010) 79 NSWLR 702.

appropriate apportionment of respective responsibility is not best allocated through contributory negligence'.[172]

However, the relevance of pre-wrong conduct of the plaintiff to the scope of liability was affirmed in *Gratrax Pty Ltd v T D & C Pty Ltd*.[173] The plaintiff engaged the defendant to design a road to the specifications of a local council. The defendant negligently designed the road with an incorrect sub-base. Contrary to the council's guidelines and usual practice, the plaintiff failed to test the sub-base before completing construction of the road. Once the defective sub-base was identified, the plaintiff incurred substantial costs in dismantling the road. The trial judge held that the defendant was liable only for the costs the plaintiff would have incurred if the road had been tested before construction, and that the further costs of constructing and dismantling the road were outside the scope of the defendant's liability because they resulted from the plaintiff's unreasonable conduct. The Queensland Court of Appeal upheld the decision and observed that the issue of apportionment by virtue of contributory negligence did not arise because the loss was outside the scope of the defendant's liability.[174]

[3.95]

Unreasonable conduct of the plaintiff after becoming aware of the defendant's wrong falls within the scope of the rules on mitigation of damage; see [3.124]. Those rules are well developed and apply throughout the common law (and under the Australian Consumer Law). It is neither necessary nor desirable to have an additional set of rules under the concept of *novus actus interveniens*. Thus, a defendant's liability for the consequences of post-wrong conduct by the plaintiff ought to depend solely upon the reasonableness of that conduct. This has been recognised in some cases.[175] Indeed, it has been said that the rules on mitigation may be relevant in considering the reasonableness of the plaintiff's post-wrong conduct in the context of *novus actus interveniens*.[176]

[3.96]

However, the High Court of Australia has not been entirely clear or consistent in this respect. In *Caterson v Commissioner for Railways*,[177] where the plaintiff jumped out of a train that had started to move without warning (and was not to stop for another 120 kilometres), the High Court employed the criteria of foreseeability, reasonableness and the 'very kind of thing likely to happen', to determine the railway operator's liability. All criteria pointed to the defendant being liable.

[3.97]

The criterion of reasonableness prevailed somewhat in *Medlin v State Government Insurance Commission*.[178] A university professor injured by the defendant decided to retire four and a half years early because of the pain and sleeplessness caused by the injuries. The trial judge denied damages for loss of earning capacity on the ground that the plaintiff's decision to retire early had not been reasonable. The High Court of Australia overturned that decision. There

[3.98]

---

172   Ibid, [12].
173   [2013] QCA 385, [2014] 2 Qd R 261.
174   Ibid, [33].
175   *Fazlic v Milingimbi Community Inc* (1982) 150 CLR 345, 353 (under workers' compensation scheme); *Western Australia v Bond Corporation Holdings Ltd* (1991) 28 FCR 68, 81–82; *Henville v Walker* [2001] HCA 52, (2001) 206 CLR 459 [30]–[31], [140], [166] (in respect of misleading or deceptive conduct under statute); *Commonwealth v Ryan* [2002] NSWCA 372 [83] (Hodgson JA) (placing the onus of proof upon the plaintiff); *Knott Investments Pty Ltd v Fulcher* [2013] QCA 67, [2014] 1 Qd R 21 [44].
176   *Knott Investments Pty Ltd v Fulcher* [2013] QCA 67, [2014] 1 Qd R 21 [45].
177   (1973) 128 CLR 99.
178   (1995) 182 CLR 1.

was some disagreement on the test to be applied. McHugh J said that, irrespective of whether the plaintiff's decision to retire early was regarded as a *novus actus interveniens* or as a failure to mitigate loss, the defendant's liability for the loss of earning capacity after the early retirement depended on whether the plaintiff's decision to retire early had been reasonable, and the defendant bore the onus of proof.[179] The majority, who made no reference to the doctrine of mitigation, said that the question was not whether the plaintiff had acted reasonably in retiring early, but whether, in the context of what was reasonable between the parties in determining the defendant's liability, the premature termination of the plaintiff's employment was the product of the accident.[180]

3   Basic loss: causally independent subsequent event

[3.99] In this section and the next section, we consider the situation where both the defendant's wrong and a subsequent event were each sufficient to bring about the loss in respect of which compensation is claimed. This section is concerned with a subsequent event that has the following three features. First, the defendant's wrong is not a factual cause of the subsequent event. Secondly, the defendant is not responsible for the subsequent event.[181] Finally, the defendant's wrong pre-empted the effects of the subsequent event. It is thus a case of pre-emptive causation; see [3.44].

[3.100] The subsequent event may or may not be a wrong, and may be actual (it did in fact occur) or hypothetical (it would have occurred without the defendant's wrong). The position in the four different combinations is as follows:

- actual non-wrongful event: the harm is not within the scope of the defendant's liability;
- hypothetical non-wrongful event: the harm is not within the scope of the defendant's liability;
- hypothetical wrongful event: the harm is within the scope of the defendant's liability;
- actual wrongful event: the harm is probably within the scope of the defendant's liability.

[3.101] An actual non-wrongful event was present in *K-Mart Australia Ltd v McCann*.[182] The plaintiff, a self-employed solicitor, was injured in one of the defendant's supermarkets when a basketball set fell from a shelf onto his head and shoulders. He was forced to change his work practices, which reduced his earnings. Some 15 months after the supermarket accident, he suffered an unrelated heart attack, which rendered him unable to work for 16 months. The trial judge awarded damages for loss of earning capacity in respect of that period. The NSW Court of Appeal quashed that award on the ground that the heart attack would have rendered the plaintiff unable to work in that period even if the supermarket accident had not occurred.[183] The court relied on the decision of the House of Lords in *Jobling v Associated Dairies Ltd*.[184]

---

179   Ibid, 23.
180   Ibid, 11–14. This test was applied in *Kavanagh v Akhtar* (1998) 45 NSWLR 588, 598.
181   A defendant who is responsible for both the wrong and the subsequent event is liable for the loss that each of the two events was sufficient to inflict: *Cambridge v Anastasopoulos* [2012] NSWCA 405 [49]–[50].
182   [2004] NSWCA 283.
183   Ibid, [49]–[54]. Unrelated subsequent illness affected liability also, eg, in *Bridge Printery Pty Ltd v Mestre* [1999] NSWCA 342 [12]–[17] (heart attack); *Connolly v Burton* [2007] NSWSC 1484 [154] (pancreatic cancer).
184   [1982] AC 794. Where it is uncertain whether an unrelated illness would have led to the same loss, damages are reduced proportionately; see [2.62].

A hypothetical non-wrongful event (hypothetical conduct of the plaintiff) was present in   [3.102]
the English case *Calvert v William Hill Credit Ltd*.[185] The defendant bookmaker offered the
plaintiff, whom the bookmaker knew to be a compulsive gambler, the choice of a self-
exclusion agreement whereby, at the request of the plaintiff, the defendant would not accept
telephone bets from the plaintiff for six months. The plaintiff made such a request but, due to
an oversight by the defendant's employees, the defendant continued to accept bets from the
plaintiff, and the plaintiff lost £2 million in the following six months. An action by the plaintiff in
negligence was rejected on the ground that, had the defendant refused to accept bets from the
plaintiff in those six months, the plaintiff would probably have lost the same amount of money
by placing bets with other bookmakers.[186]

A hypothetical wrongful event does not remove the basic loss from the scope of the   [3.103]
defendant's liability. Liability cannot be denied on the ground that if the defendant had not
inflicted the loss, someone else would wrongfully have done so.[187] In *Turjman v Stonewall
Hotel Pty Ltd*,[188] the plaintiffs were injured when the ceiling on the first floor of an old hotel
collapsed. Prior to the incident, the lessee of the hotel had engaged a structural engineer to
investigate the hotel, but the lessee failed to inform the engineer that substantial dancing
activities took place in the hotel. The majority of the NSW Court of Appeal found that it would
have been proper for the engineer not to investigate the ceiling on the first floor even if the
lessee had informed the engineer about the dancing activities.[189] Thus, the lessee's failure to
provide the information to the engineer was not a factual cause of the injuries. But all the
judges agreed that the lessee would be liable if a reasonable engineer would have done the
investigation on proper information. The lessee could not escape liability on the ground that if
it had not been negligent, the engineer would negligently have inflicted the injuries.

In *Baker v Willoughby*,[190] the House of Lords laid down the same rule for an actual   [3.104]
wrongful event. The plaintiff was struck by the defendant's car and sustained injuries to his
left leg. Shortly before the hearing of his action, the plaintiff was shot in the left leg during an
armed robbery, and the leg was amputated. Without the shooting, the plaintiff's left leg would
have been permanently stiff. The House of Lords held the defendant liable for the loss caused

---

185   [2008] EWCA Civ 1427, [2009] Ch 330; followed in *Centrebet Pty Ltd v Baasland* [2013] NTSC 59 [92].
       For hypothetical lawful conduct of the defendant, see *Golden Strait Corporation v Nippon Yusen
       Kubishika Kaisha (The 'Golden Victory')* [2007] UKHL 12, [2007] 2 AC 353 (liability for repudiation does
       not extend to loss that would have resulted from lawful termination of the contract); *R (Lumba) v
       Secretary of State for the Home Department* [2011] UKSC 12, [2012] 1 AC 245, approved in *CPCF v
       Minister for Immigration and Border Protection* [2015] HCA 1, (2015) 255 CLR 514 [157] (Hayne and Bell
       JJ), [324]–[325] (Kiefel J) (only nominal damages for false imprisonment where plaintiff could have been
       detained lawfully in the same period).
186   Stiggelbout, who supports the exclusion of liability by virtue of a hypothetical non-wrongful event,
       criticises the decision in *Calvert* on the ground that the hypothetical wagers with other bookmakers
       cannot be regarded as loss as they would have been voluntary transactions for consideration:
       M Stiggelbout, 'The Case of "Losses in Any Event": A Question of Duty, Cause or Damages?' (2010)
       30 LS 558, 577–80.
187   *Magnus v Queensland National Bank* (1888) 37 Ch D 466, 480 (Bowen LJ); *Wright v Cambridge
       Medical Group (a partnership)* [2011] EWCA Civ 669, [2013] QB 312 [61], [75] (Lord Neuberger MR); *AIB
       Group (UK) plc v Mark Redler & Co Solicitors* [2014] UKSC 58, [2015] AC 1503 [58].
188   [2011] NSWCA 392.
189   Ibid, [82]–[99].
190   [1970] AC 467.

to the plaintiff by (hypothetically) having a stiff leg rather than a healthy leg, even for the period after the shooting.

[3.105]   *Baker v Willoughby* has had a mixed reception in Australia.[191] In *Faulkner v Keffalinos*,[192] decided shortly afterwards, Windeyer J in the High Court of Australia expressed the view that the basic loss should be attributed solely to an actual subsequent event even if it is wrongful; see [3.111].[193] However, none of the other judges considered this issue, and the award made unanimously by the High Court did not involve the reduction that Windeyer J was endorsing, the award thus being consistent with *Baker v Willoughby*.[194] Subsequently, in *Wynn v New South Wales Insurance Ministerial Corporation*,[195] the High Court said that while allowance must be made for the chance that a non-wrongful event might have led to the same loss, the possibility of a wrongful event causing the same loss must be ignored in order to ensure full compensation.[196] In circumstances in which a wrongful subsequent event occurred, liability for the basic loss has since been imposed in one first-instance decision,[197] and denied in another.[198] The preponderance of authority supports an application of the *Baker v Willoughby* rule in Australia.

[3.106]   The different effect of wrongful and non-wrongful subsequent events has been justified on the ground that the second wrongdoer is not liable towards the plaintiff (or is liable to a lesser extent) because of the defendant's intervention, but would be liable otherwise.[199] In other words, the defendant's wrong deprived the plaintiff of a claim against the second wrongdoer. However, a non-wrongful event may also provide the plaintiff with a claim, such as a claim for benefits under a social security scheme or a statutory compensation scheme. Thus, the decisive criterion ought to be, not whether the subsequent event was wrongful, but whether the event would have provided the plaintiff with a claim.

[3.107]   This view was rejected by the NSW Court of Appeal in *DNM Mining Pty Ltd v Barwick*.[200] The subsequent event in that case was causally dependent, but the case is relevant here as the court took the view that causally dependent and independent events should have the same effect.[201] Due to the defendant's negligence, the plaintiff suffered a back injury while working in the defendant's mine. He could no longer work as a miner but found lower-paid employment on a farm. One day, on the way home from the farm, he drove into a cow and suffered injury to his neck and shoulder. He could no longer work on the farm and became unemployed. The second injury alone would have rendered the plaintiff unable to work as a miner. But the plaintiff argued that the second injury ought to be ignored in determining the

---

191   The issue was left open in *Godden v Metropolitan Meat Industry Board* [1972] 2 NSWLR 183, 191–92.
192   (1970) 45 ALJR 80, 85–86.
193   The same view was expressed obiter in *Nilon v Bezzina* [1988] 2 Qd R 420, 427.
194   See *Godden v Metropolitan Meat Industry Board* [1972] 2 NSWLR 183, 191.
195   (1995) 184 CLR 485, 498–99.
196   The same view was expressed in *Koeck v Persic* (1996) Aust Torts Reports 81–386, 63,359.
197   *Taylor v Simonis* (NSW Supreme Court, Greenwood M, 7 March 1997).
198   *Kenny v Nominal Defendant* [2006] QSC 267 [81]–[82]; rev'd on other grounds *Kenny v Nominal Defendant* [2007] QCA 185.
199   *Wynn v New South Wales Insurance Ministerial Corporation* (1995) 184 CLR 485, 498–99; *AIB Group (UK) plc v Mark Redler & Co Solicitors* [2014] UKSC 58, [2015] AC 1503 [58].
200   [2004] NSWCA 137.
201   This aspect of the decision is discussed at [3.112]–[3.113].

loss for which the defendant was liable. The plaintiff contended that he was entitled to statutory workers' compensation in respect of the second injury, and that this rendered the case analogous to *Baker v Willoughby*. The NSW Court of Appeal held that the defendant was not liable for loss of earning capacity that the plaintiff would have suffered as a result of the car accident even if he had not been injured in the mine. The court doubted the correctness of *Baker v Willoughby*,[202] and held that it was irrelevant whether or not the plaintiff was entitled to workers' compensation in respect of the second injury.[203]

The decision in *DNM Mining Pty Ltd v Barwick* is unconvincing. It ought to have been determined whether the plaintiff was entitled to workers' compensation in respect of the second injury. If he was, he could have claimed workers' compensation only for the additional loss of earning capacity caused by the second injury. But he could have claimed workers' compensation for the whole loss caused by the second injury had he not suffered the first injury. Thus, if the plaintiff was entitled to workers' compensation, the defendant's wrong deprived the plaintiff of workers' compensation for the basic loss. Since the defendant was not held liable for that loss, the plaintiff recovered nothing for it. [3.108]

4   Basic loss: causally dependent subsequent event

This section, like the previous one, is concerned with the situation where both the defendant's wrong and a subsequent event were each sufficient to bring about the loss in respect of which compensation is claimed. We are now considering a subsequent event that would not have occurred but for the defendant's wrong. Where the subsequent event falls within the scope of the defendant's liability, the defendant is undoubtedly liable for the loss in question. Liability for the loss has been denied where the subsequent event falls outside the scope of the defendant's liability.[204] [3.109]

This view was expressed by Windeyer J in *Faulkner v Keffalinos*.[205] The plaintiff was injured in a car accident for which the defendants were responsible. The injury caused loss of earning capacity. Prior to the trial, the plaintiff was injured in another car accident not involving the defendants. If the plaintiff had still been uninjured, the second accident would have caused some or all of the loss of earning capacity already inflicted by the first accident. The High Court of Australia reduced the trial judge's award for pecuniary and non-pecuniary loss on the ground that the judge had failed to take account of contingencies such as the possibility of a subsequent unrelated accident. However, the reduction did not reflect the actual consequences of the known contingency. [3.110]

Despite his agreement with this outcome, Windeyer J said that the defendants were not liable for loss which the second accident on its own was sufficient to inflict.[206] He even regarded it as immaterial whether the second accident would have occurred but for the first one: [3.111]

---

202   As did the House of Lords itself in *Jobling v Associated Dairies Ltd* [1982] AC 794.
203   [2004] NSWCA 137 [44].
204   English cases include *Carslogie Steamship Co Ltd v Royal Norwegian Government* [1952] AC 292; *Beoco Ltd v Alfa Laval Co Ltd* [1995] QB 137.
205   (1970) 45 ALJR 80.
206   Ibid, 85.

> But for the first accident, the [plaintiff] might still have been employed by the [defendants], and therefore not where he was when the second accident happened: but lawyers must eschew this kind of 'but for' or sine qua non reasoning about cause and consequence.[207]

[3.112]   This passage was approvingly quoted by Mason CJ in *March v E & MH Stramare Pty Ltd*,[208] although this was in the context of liability for additional loss, not basic loss (for the distinction, see [3.70]). Harold Luntz has argued that a causally dependent subsequent event should not affect the defendant's liability for the basic loss.[209] The NSW Court of Appeal rejected his view in *DNM Mining Pty Ltd v Barwick*,[210] considered at [3.107]. Citing the statements by Windeyer J and Mason CJ mentioned before, Giles JA, speaking for the court, said:

> It is well established that it would not avail the [plaintiff] to suggest that, but for the mining accident, his life may not have taken the course by which he was driving at a time and place coincident with the cow ... further, impossible questions of causation would arise as to both subsequent accident and illness occurring in the world as modified by the first accident.[211]

[3.113]   Giles JA described the car accident in that case as a 'later independent accident'.[212] If he was saying that the car accident would have occurred even without the mining accident, his view would be unconvincing. The car accident occurred when the plaintiff was driving home from the farm, and it is extremely unlikely that he would have been there had he continued to work in the defendant's mine. *DNM Mining Pty Ltd v Barwick* involved a causally dependent subsequent event outside the scope of the defendant's liability, and thus held that such an event removes the basic loss (as well as the additional loss) from the scope of the defendant's liability.

[3.114]   This rule is difficult to justify. It seems to be based on the view that if a causally dependent subsequent event removes additional loss from the scope of the defendant's liability, it must do the same for the basic loss. But the exclusion of liability for loss that would not have occurred but for the subsequent event does not automatically justify an exclusion of liability for loss that would have occurred even without the subsequent event. Giles JA in *DNM Mining Pty Ltd v Barwick* (see [3.112]) was right to say that it may be difficult to determine whether a subsequent event was causally dependent or independent. However, the fear that the defendant could lose the 'benefit' of a subsequent event only because of uncertainty as to whether the event was causally dependent or independent can be addressed by placing the onus of proof on the plaintiff. It is not necessary to exonerate the defendant even where it is clear (as in *DNM Mining Pty Ltd v Barwick*) that the subsequent event would not have occurred but for the defendant's wrong.

---

207   Ibid, 86.
208   (1991) 171 CLR 506. In the context of how a jury should be instructed, the test of common sense had already been laid down in *Fitzgerald v Penn* (1954) 91 CLR 268, 277.
209   H Luntz, *Assessment of Damages for Personal Injury and Death* (4th edn, Butterworths 2002) [2.6.12].
210   [2004] NSWCA 137.
211   Ibid, [43].
212   Ibid, [41].

B   Remoteness of damage

The concept of remoteness of damage has been developed at common law and informs the   [3.115]
determination of the scope of liability under the civil liability statutes. There are at least two
meanings of remoteness of damage. In a narrow sense, remoteness of damage is concerned
only with the foreseeability of damage. In a wide sense, remoteness of damage is concerned
with the foreseeability of damage and with intervening acts. Intervening acts are discussed at
[3.74]–[3.98], and the present discussion relates to remoteness of damage in the narrow sense.

Damage factually caused by the defendant's wrong may be too remote if the defendant did   [3.116]
not intend to inflict that damage,[213] and if a reasonable person in the defendant's position was
unable to foresee the type of damage at a certain date with a certain degree of probability. This
applies particularly to breach of contract and negligence. However, the remoteness rules for
contract and negligence differ with regard to the date at which, and the degree of probability
with which, the type of damage needs to have been foreseeable; see [5.92]. Liability for some
other wrongs, in particular intentional torts, extends to unforeseeable loss; see [6.57]–[6.60].
The remoteness rules are therefore discussed separately for the various wrongs in the relevant
chapters.

C   The purpose of the duty breached

Whenever the private law imposes a duty, it does so to prevent certain harm. Where a breach   [3.117]
of duty factually causes harm of the type that the duty aims to prevent, liability for that harm
will normally be imposed, provided that all other requirements for liability (for example,
culpability) are satisfied.[214] By contrast, where a breach of duty factually causes harm of a
type that the duty does not aim to prevent, liability for the harm will normally be denied. In
those circumstances, the defendant's breach of duty provides insufficient justification for
attributing responsibility for the harm to the defendant. The High Court of Australia has applied
this principle in two cases, decided, respectively, at common law and under s 5D of the *Civil
Liability Act 2002* (NSW).

The common law case is *Roads and Traffic Authority v Royal*.[215] The plaintiff and the first   [3.118]
defendant had a vehicle collision on a cross-intersection because the first defendant, who saw
the plaintiff moving across the intersection well in time, failed to slow down and the plaintiff,
who saw the first defendant well in time, moved across the intersection too slowly. The
plaintiff, who was ultimately held one-third responsible for the collision, brought an action
against the first defendant as well as the Roads and Traffic Authority ('RTA'). He contended that
the RTA had been in breach of duty by constructing a cross-intersection rather than a staggered
T-intersection, which would have improved the ability of drivers nearing the intersection to see
each other. Without deciding on whether the RTA had been in breach of duty and whether that
breach was a factual cause of the collision, the High Court exonerated the RTA on the ground
that the purpose of the RTA's alleged duty was to prevent collisions occurring as a result of

---

213   'The intention to injure the plaintiff ... disposes of any question of remoteness of damage': *Quinn v
         Leathem* [1901] AC 495, 537 (Lord Lindley). See also GL Williams, *Joint Torts and Contributory
         Negligence* (Stevens & Sons 1951) 201.
214   *Wallace v Kam* [2013] HCA 19, (2013) 250 CLR 375 [26].
215   [2008] HCA 19, (2008) 245 ALR 653.

impaired visibility, and that the collision at hand had not been due to impaired visibility. The RTA was not liable even on the assumption that the construction of a staggered T-intersection would have prevented the collision at hand.

[3.119]   The case decided under s 5D of the *Civil Liability Act 2002* (NSW) is *Wallace v Kam*.[216] The defendant neurosurgeon performed a surgical procedure on the plaintiff. Two distinct risks were inherent in the procedure. One was the risk of temporary local damage to nerves within the thighs ('neurapraxia'). The other risk was a permanent and catastrophic paralysis due to damage to the spinal nerves. The first risk materialised; the second did not. In breach of duty, the defendant had failed to warn the plaintiff of either risk prior to the procedure. Had the plaintiff been warned of the risk of paralysis, he would not have undergone the procedure. Had the plaintiff been warned of the risk of neurapraxia (but not the risk of paralysis), he would still have undergone the procedure. The High Court dismissed the plaintiff's claim for damages for the neurapraxia he sustained, on the ground that while the defendant's failure to warn the plaintiff of all risks inherent in the procedure was a necessary condition of the plaintiff's injury, it was not appropriate for the scope of the defendant's liability to extend to that injury. A doctor's duty to warn of risks aims to protect the patient from the occurrence of an injury the risk of which is unacceptable to the patient. The duty does not aim to protect the patient from an injury the risk of which the patient is prepared to accept.[217]

D   The plaintiff's contribution to the loss

1   Overview of the three relevant doctrines

[3.120]   Conduct by the plaintiff is often an element in the chain of causation between the defendant's wrong and the plaintiff's loss. Where the plaintiff's conduct involves a failure to take reasonable care of one's own affairs ('unreasonable conduct'), it will often be unjust to require the defendant to compensate the whole of the loss that would have been avoided had the plaintiff taken reasonable care. While the defendant's wrong remains a factual cause of that loss, the defendant's liability may be excluded or reduced on policy grounds.

[3.121]   A legal system can have the straightforward rule that where the victim of any civil wrong has contributed to the ensuing loss through unreasonable conduct, the court may apportion liability for that loss between the parties.[218] Such a rule does not exist in common law systems. Instead, three partially overlapping doctrines address unreasonable conduct by the plaintiff.

[3.122]   One such doctrine is that of intervening act, or *novus actus interveniens*, which removes loss from the scope of the defendant's liability and applies not only to natural events and conduct by third parties but also to conduct by the plaintiff. The doctrine, including its application to conduct by the plaintiff, is discussed at [3.74]–[3.98].

[3.123]   In addition, there are two doctrines exclusively concerned with unreasonable conduct of the plaintiff: the doctrine of contributory negligence and the doctrine of mitigation. These doctrines are usually discussed separately from causation, but they are discussed in this

---

216   [2013] HCA 19, (2013) 250 CLR 375.

217   Ibid, [29]–[40]. A similar decision on similar facts was made in *Waller v James* [2015] NSWCA 232, (2015) 90 NSWLR 634.

218   §254 of the German Civil Code contains such a rule.

chapter because they are concerned with the attribution of responsibility.[219] The two doctrines may overlap, and each of them overlaps with the doctrine of intervening cause. The doctrines of contributory negligence and mitigation differ in their effect and in relation to the wrongs to which they apply. The doctrine of mitigation completely exonerates the defendant in respect of the loss in question. Contributory negligence had the same effect at common law, but statute now provides for an apportionment of liability. While the doctrine of mitigation applies to all common law wrongs, the same is not true for the doctrine of contributory negligence. Both doctrines apply to certain actions under the Australian Consumer Law. In equity, the applicability of either doctrine is uncertain and may depend upon the particular wrong.

The significant differences between the doctrines of contributory negligence and mitigation make it important to determine when each doctrine applies. This depends upon the timing of the plaintiff's unreasonable conduct. The doctrine of mitigation cannot apply unless the wrong has occurred[220] and the plaintiff knows or ought to know the facts giving rise to the wrong.[221] With regard to wrongs actionable per se, it is not settled whether the doctrine of mitigation can apply before some loss has occurred.[222] There is no reason why the occurrence of some loss should be required.[223]   **[3.124]**

The doctrine of contributory negligence applies to unreasonable conduct of the plaintiff occurring before the 'starting date' of the doctrine of mitigation. Occasionally, the doctrine of contributory negligence has been applied to unreasonable conduct of the plaintiff occurring after the plaintiff became aware of the defendant's wrong, creating an overlap with the doctrine of mitigation. In *Smith v Badenoch*,[224] liability for negligently spreading fire onto the plaintiff's property was reduced by 15% on the ground that the plaintiff had failed to promptly call the fire service when he saw the first fire on his property. That case was approvingly cited by the High Court of Australia in *Astley v Austrust Ltd*.[225]   **[3.125]**

The NSW Court of Appeal considered the matter in *Ackland v Commonwealth*.[226] In 1964, the plaintiff was on board the HMAS *Melbourne* when it collided with the HMAS *Voyager*. He was not physically injured and helped those that were. He developed post-traumatic stress disorder and started to engage in excessive drinking and binge eating. His weight rose dramatically. He left the Navy and worked in some other jobs, but eventually could not cope with any work. In 1998, he was told for the first time that he was suffering from a diagnosable illness. He sued the Commonwealth in negligence. The Commonwealth admitted a breach of duty, but denied liability for the consequences of the plaintiff's unreasonable eating and   **[3.126]**

---

219   K Amirthalingam, Review of *Tort Law Defences* by James Goudkamp [2014] Sing J Leg Stud 443, 444 (for contributory negligence); *Lagden v O'Connor* [2003] UKHL 64, [2004] 1 AC 1067 [99]–[100] (Lord Walker) (for mitigation).
220   *Jones v Edwards* (1994) 3 Tas R 350, 357; *Mouritz v Hegedus* [1999] WASCA 1061.
221   *Bak v Glenleigh Homes Pty Ltd* [2006] NSWCA 10 [5], [8], [62]; K Barnett, 'Substitutive Damages and Mitigation in Contract Law' (2016) 28 Sing Ac LJ 795, 817–18.
222   See *Bak v Glenleigh Homes Pty Ltd* [2006] NSWCA 10, [8], [62].
223   The occurrence of loss was not required in *Schering Agrochemicals Ltd v Resibel NV SA* (Court of Appeal for England and Wales, 26 November 1992).
224   [1970] SASR 9.
225   [1999] HCA 6, (1999) 197 CLR 1 [21].
226   [2007] NSWCA 250, (2007) Aust Torts Reports 81–916. On very similar facts, the doctrine of contributory negligence was held applicable, without detailed discussion, in *Commonwealth v McLean* (1996) 41 NSWLR 389, 398.

drinking habits. The trial judge instructed the jury that it was open to them to find contributory negligence and, if they did, to apportion the total damages, which the jury did.

[3.127]   The NSW Court of Appeal unanimously held that the *Law Reform (Miscellaneous Provisions) Act 1965* (NSW), which permits apportionment of liability by virtue of contributory negligence, did not apply retrospectively to the collision in 1964 and thus could not justify the jury's apportionment. Ipp JA, with whom McColl JA agreed, therefore ordered a retrial. Ipp JA said that the plaintiff's eating and drinking habits seemed to him to be more a matter of mitigation rather than contributory negligence.[227] However, he left the applicability of the doctrine of contributory negligence open, saying that, if it did apply, it would lead to a complete exclusion of liability and not to an apportionment, which is not available at common law.[228] He left open whether the complete exclusion of liability would relate to the whole loss or only to the loss caused by the plaintiff's consumption habits.[229]

[3.128]   Santow JA, dissenting, took the view that it had been open to the jury to apportion liability at common law. He opined that the plaintiff's consumption habits could properly be regarded as a matter of contributory negligence rather than mitigation.[230] He further opined that, at common law, the effect of contributory negligence contributing to the accident is a complete exoneration of the defendant, whereas the effect of contributory negligence contributing only to the damage (and not the accident) is an apportionment of liability governed by the same considerations as apportionment under statute.[231]

[3.129]   The cases in which the doctrine of contributory negligence was applied to unreasonable conduct of the plaintiff occurring after the plaintiff became aware of the defendant's wrong may be the starting point for an assimilation of the doctrine of mitigation into the doctrine of contributory negligence, in respect of the wrongs to which the latter doctrine applies.[232] However, these cases have yet to have a significant impact in practice. The doctrine of mitigation is still routinely applied to post-wrong conduct of the plaintiff in cases in which an apportionment of liability would be available if the plaintiff's conduct were classified as contributory negligence.[233]

2   Contributory negligence

[3.130]   Contributory negligence denotes unreasonable conduct (in the sense of a failure to take reasonable care of one's own affairs) of the plaintiff that contributed to the occurrence of the defendant's wrong or the ensuing loss. The doctrine of contributory negligence is usually applied to conduct of the plaintiff that occurred before the wrong or before the plaintiff knew or ought to have known the facts giving rise to the wrong, but has occasionally been applied

---

227   [2007] NSWCA 250, (2007) Aust Torts Reports 81–916 [144]–[145].
228   Ibid, [140].
229   Ibid, [141].
230   Ibid, [93]–[98].
231   Ibid, [99]–[113].
232   For an endorsement of such an assimilation, see GL Williams, *Joint Torts and Contributory Negligence* (Stevens & Sons 1951) 290–91; Y Adar, 'Comparative Negligence and Mitigation of Damages: Two Sister Doctrines in Search of Reunion' (2013) 31 Quinnipiac L Rev 783; American Law Institute, *Restatement (Third) of Torts: Apportionment of Liability* (2000) §3 comment b and Reporters' Note.
233   Eg *Simply Irresistible Pty Ltd v Couper* [2010] VSC 601 [393]; *Hardie Finance Corporation Pty Ltd v Ahern (No 3)* [2010] WASC 403 [755]–[796]; *King v Benecke* [2013] NSWSC 568 [709]–[713].

to conduct of the plaintiff occurring after the plaintiff became aware of the wrong; see [3.125]–[3.128].

The doctrine originated in tort where, at common law, it was a complete defence to negligence and some other torts; see [6.90]. Statute has replaced the complete defence with an apportionment of liability according to each party's responsibility for the loss in question; see [6.91]. The complete defence at common law did not generally apply to breach of contract (see [5.106]), but the statutory apportionment regime applies to certain breaches; see [5.111]. Federal statutes provide for an apportionment of liability in certain cases of misleading or deceptive conduct; see [8.46]. Neither the common law defence nor the statutory apportionment regime applies in equity, which has not developed a concept comparable to contributory negligence; see [9.62]–[9.66]. The rules on contributory negligence are discussed separately for each area in the relevant chapter.   [3.131]

3 Mitigation

Under the doctrine of mitigation, a defendant escapes liability for loss that is factually caused not only by the defendant's wrong but also by unreasonable conduct (in the sense of a failure to take reasonable care of one's own affairs) of the plaintiff occurring after the plaintiff knows or ought to know the facts giving rise to the wrong.[234] This rule can be justified on grounds of fairness between the parties, economic efficiency and autonomy concerns.[235] The rule applies to all common law wrongs, except a claim for liquidated damages for breach of contract,[236] and applies under the Australian Consumer Law. It is unclear whether it applies to breach of fiduciary duty; see [9.67]–[9.69].   [3.132]

The exclusion of liability for the consequences of unreasonable conduct by the plaintiff has the corollary that the assessment of compensation must take account of the costs and effects of reasonable attempts by the plaintiff to mitigate loss. In an outline adopted by Australian courts,[237] *McGregor on Damages* expresses the doctrine of mitigation in the following three rules.[238] First, the defendant is not liable for loss that would have been avoided had the plaintiff behaved reasonably. Secondly, the plaintiff can recover for loss incurred in reasonable attempts to mitigate loss, even if the resulting loss is greater than it would have been had the mitigating steps not been taken. Thirdly, the defendant is entitled to the benefit accruing from mitigating steps taken by the plaintiff unless the benefit is regarded as collateral; this applies even where it would have been reasonable for the plaintiff not to take the mitigating steps. The third rule, known as the avoided loss rule, is discussed at [2.28]–[2.38], as it relates more to the assessment of compensation than the attribution of responsibility. The other two rules will now be looked at.   [3.133]

---

234   *Ardlethan Options Ltd v Easdown* (1915) 20 CLR 285, 296–97; *Tuncel v Renown Plate Co Pty Ltd* [1976] VR 501, 503; *Arnott v Choy* [2010] NSWCA 259, (2010) 56 MVR 390 [155].

235   K Barnett, 'Substitutive Damages and Mitigation in Contract Law' (2016) 28 Sing Ac LJ 795, 806–07.

236   *Galafassi v Kelly* [2014] NSWCA 190, (2014) 87 NSWLR 119 [154].

237   *Tuncel v Renown Plate Co Pty Ltd* [1976] VR 501, 503; *Turner v Kwikshift Pty Ltd* (1993) 113 FLR 8, 14; *Young v Lamb (No 2)* [2001] NSWSC 1014 [28]; *Cardno BSD Pty Ltd v Water Corporation (No 2)* [2011] WASCA 161, (2011) 27 BCL 413 [145]; *Powercor Australia Ltd v Thomas* [2012] VSCA 87, (2012) 43 VR 220 [52]; *Daily Pty Ltd v Wallis* [2013] NSWADT 152 [86].

238   J Edelman, *McGregor on Damages* (20th edn, Sweet & Maxwell 2018) [9–004]–[9–006].

[3.134]   The first rule, known as the avoidable loss rule, is that where a plaintiff has acted unreasonably, the defendant's liability is confined to loss that would still have occurred had the plaintiff acted reasonably.[239] It is for the defendant to prove that the plaintiff's conduct was unreasonable.[240] The plaintiff is not under a high standard of conduct and is not required to take measures that are costly, complex or extravagant or are likely to impair the plaintiff's position or reputation.[241] In particular, the plaintiff is not required to sacrifice or risk any of her property or rights,[242] or to pursue an uncertain legal action against a third party.[243] The reasonableness of the plaintiff's conduct is judged on the basis of the information the plaintiff possessed at the relevant time.[244] Conduct that is objectively unreasonable is not regarded as reasonable only because the plaintiff allowed baseless factors to outweigh cogent ones.[245] The plaintiff does not act unreasonably merely because her impecuniosity prevents her from taking mitigating steps that a person with sufficient funds would be expected to take.[246]

[3.135]   Since the doctrine of mitigation applies to a wide variety of wrongs, unreasonable conduct by the plaintiff can take different forms. For example, where a seller of goods fails to deliver them and the buyer unreasonably delays buying substitute goods, a rise in the market price of the goods in the intervening period will not increase the seller's liability; see [5.15]. More generally, it may be unreasonable for a party aggrieved by a breach of contract not to obtain substitute performance from a third party.[247] Depending upon the circumstances, it may even be unreasonable for a plaintiff to reject an offer by the defendant contract-breaker to render performance that would minimise the plaintiff's loss.[248] Furthermore, a plaintiff who suffers personal injury may act unreasonably in not seeking medical advice or in refusing to undergo a

239   *Munce v Vinidex Tubemakers Pty Ltd* [1974] 2 NSWLR 235, 239; *Karacominakis v Big Country Developments Pty Ltd* [2000] NSWCA 313, (2000) 10 BPR 18,235 [187]; *Arnott v Choy* [2010] NSWCA 259, (2010) 56 MVR 390 [155].

240   *Watts v Rake* (1960) 108 CLR 158, 159 (Dixon CJ); *Munce v Vinidex Tubemakers Pty Ltd* [1974] 2 NSWLR 235, 239; *Metal Fabrications (Vic) Pty Ltd v Kelcey* [1986] VR 507, 509–14; *TCN Channel Nine Pty Ltd v Hayden Enterprises Pty Ltd* (1989) 16 NSWLR 130, 158; *Karacominakis v Big Country Developments Pty Ltd* [2000] NSWCA 313, (2000) 10 BPR 18,235 [187]; *Morrison v Town of Victoria Park* [2007] WASCA 164 [37]; *Arnott v Choy* [2010] NSWCA 259, (2010) 56 MVR 390 [155]; *Pialba Commercial Gardens Pty Ltd v Braxco Pty Ltd* [2011] QCA 148 [98].

241   *Newmarket Corporation Pty Ltd v Kee-Vee Properties Pty Ltd* [2003] WASC 157 [172]; *Hardie Finance Corporation Pty Ltd v Ahern (No 3)* [2010] WASC 403 [766].

242   *Sacher Investments Pty Ltd v Forma Stereo Consultants Pty Ltd* [1976] 1 NSWLR 5, 9; *Freemantle's Pastoral Pty Ltd v Hyett* [1999] VSC 129 [73] (expenditure exceeding loss not required).

243   *Segenhoe Ltd v Akins* (1990) 29 NSWLR 569, 582; *Twidale v Bradley* [1990] 2 Qd R 464, 479–80.

244   *Fazlic v Milingimbi Community Inc* (1982) 150 CLR 345, 350; *New South Wales v Fahy* [2006] NSWCA 64, (2006) 155 IR 54 [140]; *Arnott v Choy* [2010] NSWCA 259, (2010) 56 MVR 390 [155].

245   *Fazlic v Milingimbi Community Inc* (1982) 150 CLR 345, 350; *Arnott v Choy* [2010] NSWCA 259, (2010) 56 MVR 390 [155].

246   *Burns v MAN Automotive (Australia) Pty Ltd* (1986) 161 CLR 653, 659–60 (Gibbs CJ), 677 (Brennan J); *Turner v Kwikshift Pty Ltd* (1993) 113 FLR 8, 15; *Tyco Australia Pty Ltd v Optus Networks Pty Ltd* [2004] NSWCA 333 [192]; *Goodridge v Macquarie Bank Ltd* [2010] FCA 67, (2010) 265 ALR 170 [228]; *Hardie Finance Corporation Pty Ltd v Ahern (No 3)* [2010] WASC 403 [766].

247   *Pialba Commercial Gardens Pty Ltd v Braxco Pty Ltd* [2011] QCA 148 [96].

248   *Payzu Ltd v Saunders* [1919] 2 KB 581; *Sotiros Shipping Inc v Sameiet Solholt (The Solholt)* [1983] 1 Lloyd's Rep 605; *Castle Constructions Pty Ltd v Fekala Pty Ltd* [2006] NSWCA 133, (2006) 65 NSWLR 648 [54]–[86]; *Ryan v Urban Construct (SA) Pty Ltd* [2012] SASC 128 [256], [258].

certain medical procedure.[249] The reasonableness of a refusal to undergo a certain medical procedure depends on the plaintiff's knowledge of the benefits and risks of the procedure at the time of the refusal.[250]

The second rule of mitigation as outlined in *McGregor on Damages* (see [3.133]) is a necessary consequence of the first one. The first rule penalises the plaintiff for a failure to take reasonable steps in an attempt to mitigate loss. A plaintiff who does take such steps can recover from the defendant the cost involved.[251] A plaintiff who has acted reasonably in an attempt to mitigate loss is not disentitled to recover the cost merely because the defendant can suggest that less expensive measures could have been taken.[252] A plaintiff can also recover the cost of measures which it was reasonable to take but which turned out to increase, rather than mitigate, the loss.[253] Thus, a plaintiff can recover the cost of a successful legal action against a third party who becomes insolvent and is unable to satisfy the judgment debt.[254]   **[3.136]**

In *Simonius Vischer & Co v Holt & Thompson*,[255] the plaintiff was left with a large number of open speculative contracts as a result of the defendant's breach of duty. Instead of immediately closing out the contracts, the plaintiff held them in anticipation of a favourable development of the market. The plaintiff's prognosis turned out to be wrong, and the market moved against the plaintiff. The defendant was held liable for the loss resulting from the plaintiff's decision to hold the contracts since the defendant could not establish that this decision had been unreasonable.[256]   **[3.137]**

The second rule concerns costs incurred after the plaintiff became aware of the defendant's wrong. It is unclear whether costs reasonably incurred before the defendant's wrong in anticipation of it can be recovered.[257] They cannot be recovered where the plaintiff's precautionary measures prevented the wrong from occurring, since there is then no cause of action in which to recover.[258]   **[3.138]**

---

249   *Fazlic v Milingimbi Community Inc* (1982) 150 CLR 345; *Dragojlovic v Director-General of Social Security* (1984) 1 FCR 301, 303; *Koutsakis v Director-General of Social Security* (1985) 10 FCR 42, 45; *Goldsborough v O'Neill* (1996) 131 FLR 104, 111, 114; *Comcare Australia v Filla* [2002] FCAFC 61, (2002) 115 FCR 163.

250   *ECS Group (Australia) Pty Ltd v Hobby* [2014] NSWCA 193 [37]–[40].

251   *Queensland Ice Supplies Pty Ltd v Anco Australasia Pty Ltd* [2000] QSC 72 [37]; *National Foods Milk Ltd v McMahon Milk Pty Ltd (No 2)* [2009] VSC 150 [36]–[49]; *Hatfield v TCN Channel Nine Pty Ltd (No 2)* [2011] NSWSC 737 [44].

252   *Banco de Portugal v Waterlow and Sons Ltd* [1932] AC 452, 506 (Lord Macmillan); *Sacher Investments Pty Ltd v Forma Stereo Consultants Pty Ltd* [1976] 1 NSWLR 5, 9.

253   *Unity Insurance Brokers Pty Ltd v Rocco Pezzano Pty Ltd* (1998) 192 CLR 603 [134] (Hayne J); *Mann Judd (a firm) v Paper Sales Australia (WA) Pty Ltd* [1998] WASCA 268; *Hatfield v TCN Channel Nine Pty Ltd (No 2)* [2011] NSWSC 737 [44].

254   *GW Sinclair & Co Pty Ltd v Cocks* [2001] VSCA 47, [2001] ANZ ConvR 522 [49]–[51].

255   [1979] 2 NSWLR 322.

256   Ibid, 355–58.

257   Recovery was denied in *Australian Broadcasting Corporation v Comalco Ltd* (1986) 12 FCR 510, 587, 603. But a claim for such costs was not struck out as untenable in *Hatfield v TCN Channel Nine Pty Ltd (No 2)* [2011] NSWSC 737 [59].

258   *Hatfield v TCN Channel Nine Pty Ltd (No 2)* [2011] NSWSC 737 [49], [56].

4

MULTIPLE WRONGDOERS

I   Introduction

Wrongful actions by two or more persons may affect a plaintiff at the same time. Where each [4.1]
wrongdoer causes separate harm to the plaintiff, there are generally separate causes of action
without any connection between them. Satisfaction by one wrongdoer does not discharge
the other wrongdoers, and the plaintiff cannot generally join the wrongdoers as co-
defendants. An exception exists where the wrongdoers act in concert, in which case they
are joint wrongdoers, rendering each of them liable (at common law) for the total damage
caused by all of them. So where A and B simultaneously trespass on C's land, each of A and
B causing separate damage, the liability regime depends upon whether A and B are acting in
concert.[1]

Two or more wrongdoers who cause a single, indivisible harm[2] to the plaintiff are called [4.2]
'concurrent wrongdoers'.[3] A legal system may structure the liability of concurrent wrongdoers in one of two ways.[4] One possibility, called 'proportionate liability', is that each
wrongdoer is liable only for that part of the plaintiff's damage for which he is responsible
in the light of each wrongdoer's contribution to the damage. It is thus similar to the liability
regime of multiple non-concurrent (and non-joint) wrongdoers. The plaintiff obtains full
compensation only if every wrongdoer pays his share, either voluntarily or after successful
enforcement of a judgment against him. There will be no full recovery if any of the
wrongdoers is insolvent.

The other possible liability regime for concurrent wrongdoers, called 'solidary liability' [4.3]
(either 'joint and several liability' or 'several liability'), is that the plaintiff may claim compensation for her whole loss from all or any of the wrongdoers, without double recovery. The
share of an insolvent wrongdoer will thus be borne by the other wrongdoers. Satisfaction by
one wrongdoer discharges the others. A wrongdoer who ends up paying more to the plaintiff
than his share may be given the right to recover the 'excess' from the other wrongdoers.

By way of illustration, suppose that A prepares a false statement and B publishes that [4.4]
statement. C relies on that statement and suffers financial loss in consequence. Suppose further
that A and B are liable towards C. Under a regime of proportionate liability, each of A and B is
liable only for a part of C's loss, the shares depending upon their comparative responsibility for
C's loss. The two shares together will cover C's whole loss, but C will not recover in full if A or
B is insolvent. Under a regime of solidary liability, C can claim full compensation from A or B or
both (without double recovery). C recovers in full as long as A or B is solvent.

The merits of each liability regime are open to debate. Proportionate liability may be [4.5]
criticised on the ground that it will be unjust if a wrongdoer's liability towards the plaintiff is

---

1   Example given by GL Williams, *Joint Torts and Contributory Negligence* (Stevens & Sons 1951) 4, fn 2.
2   Harm is indivisible, for example, where one person wrongfully caused the plaintiff to lend money to
    him (or someone else) and another, independently acting person negligently failed to provide the
    plaintiff with security for the loan: *Thorpe Nominees Pty Ltd v Henderson & Lahey* [1988] 2 Qd R 216;
    Hunt & Hunt Lawyers v Mitchell Morgan Nominees Pty Ltd [2013] HCA 10, (2013) 247 CLR 613;
    cf *St George Bank Ltd v Quinerts Pty Ltd* [2009] VSCA 245, (2009) 25 VR 666.
3   This term was suggested by GL Williams, *Joint Torts and Contributory Negligence* (Stevens & Sons 1951)
    1–2, and is now enshrined in the statutes prescribing proportionate liability; see [4.28].
4   In fact, there are more than two options. The discussion here is confined to the two most common
    options, which are the only options adopted by Australian law.

reduced only because other persons are also responsible for the plaintiff's harm. Solidary liability may be criticised on the ground that it will be unjust if a wrongdoer who, in comparison with the other wrongdoers, is responsible for only a tiny fraction of the plaintiff's loss may end up paying for the whole loss. It may not be surprising, therefore, that Australian law has adopted different liability regimes in different circumstances. In every state and territory, there is an interplay between the common law rules and two sets of statutory provisions.

II   Common law rules

[4.6]   At common law, concurrent wrongdoers (as well as joint non-concurrent wrongdoers) are under solidary (joint and several, or several) liability for the plaintiff's damage. Two or more persons are under solidary liability, for example, where they breach a joint contractual obligation, cause the same indivisible harm by breaching separate contracts with the plaintiff,[5] commit a tort together, or cause the same indivisible harm through independent tortious actions. Co-trustees are jointly and severally liable in equity.[6]

[4.7]   At least in relation to tortious liability, however, the precise way in which solidary liability works at common law differs significantly between joint wrongdoers and several concurrent wrongdoers. The differences have largely been abolished by statute and will therefore be outlined briefly only.

[4.8]   Tortfeasors are joint when there is a common enterprise; they are several concurrent when the only connection between them is that they are all causally connected to the same indivisible harm.[7] Joint tortfeasors are responsible for the same tort whereas several concurrent tortfeasors are responsible only for the same harm.[8]

[4.9]   Multiple tortfeasors are joint tortfeasors in three situations:[9] where one tortfeasor is vicariously liable for the other (in cases of agency, employment relationships and partnerships),[10] where several persons breach a joint duty (for example, several occupiers of the same property), and where there is a concerted action. A concerted action requires that the tortfeasors act in furtherance of a common design:[11] 'there must be a concurrence in the act or acts causing damage, not merely a coincidence of separate acts which by their conjoined effect cause damage'.[12] For example, several persons may commit a trespass together,[13] or

---

5   This is clearly recognised in Scots law: *Grunwald v Hughes* 1965 SLT 209; *Royal Brompton Hospital NHS Trust v Hammond* [2002] UKHL 14, [2002] 1 WLR 1397 [44]; *Ruddy v Chief Constable of Strathclyde* [2012] UKSC 57, [2013] SC (UKSC) 126 [22]. See also *Pell Frischmann Engineering Ltd v Bow Valley Iran Ltd* [2009] UKPC 45, [2011] 1 WLR 2370 [58].

6   *Goodwin v Duggan* (1996) 41 NSWLR 158, 167.

7   GL Williams, *Joint Torts and Contributory Negligence* (Stevens & Sons 1951) 1.

8   *Thompson v Australian Capital Television Pty Ltd* (1996) 186 CLR 574, 581.

9   Ibid, 581–82; GL Williams, *Joint Torts and Contributory Negligence* (Stevens & Sons 1951) 6–16.

10   *Thompson v Australian Capital Television Pty Ltd* (1996) 186 CLR 574, 581; *Vero Lenders Mortgage Insurance Ltd v Taylor Byrne Pty Ltd* [2006] FCA 1430 [57]–[58]; *Partnership Act 1892* (NSW), s 12; *Partnership Act 1958* (Vic), s 16.

11   *The Koursk* [1924] P 140, 151, 156, 159; *Thompson v Australian Capital Television Pty Ltd* (1996) 186 CLR 574, 582, 601–03.

12   *The Koursk* [1924] P 140, 159–60 (Sargant LJ), approvingly quoted in *Thompson v Australian Capital Television Pty Ltd* (1996) 186 CLR 574, 581 (Brennan CJ, Dawson and Toohey JJ).

13   *Schumann v Abbott* [1961] SASR 149; *Henry v Thompson* [1989] 2 Qd R 412.

one person may employ another specifically for the commission of a tort.[14] But it is not necessary that the tortfeasors realise that they are committing a tort. So the journalist, printer, publisher and distributor of a defamatory book or periodical are joint tortfeasors, whether or not any of them is aware of the defamatory character of the publication.[15] It follows that there can be joint tortfeasors liable in negligence,[16] but only if the activity was inherently dangerous.[17]

Multiple tortfeasors are several concurrent tortfeasors where the conduct of each is a factual cause of the same indivisible harm but they do not fall into any of the three categories of joint tortfeasors. For example, the injury caused by one tortfeasor may have been exacerbated by the other tortfeasor's negligent medical treatment of the plaintiff;[18] or two cars may collide due to negligence on each driver's part, causing injury to a passenger or pedestrian.[19]   [4.10]

The common law's distinction between joint tortfeasors and several concurrent tortfeasors is significant for the following reasons.[20] In the case of several concurrent tortfeasors, the plaintiff has as many causes of action as there are tortfeasors. At common law, the plaintiff cannot join the tortfeasors as co-defendants.[21] Conversely, the fact that the plaintiff has obtained judgment against one tortfeasor does not prevent the plaintiff from suing another tortfeasor (unless, of course, the first judgment has been satisfied).   [4.11]

In the case of joint tortfeasors, by contrast, the plaintiff has but one cause of action against the group of tortfeasors, which cause of action merges in the first judgment given.[22] It follows that the plaintiff may (but does not have to[23]) join all tortfeasors as co-defendants. Where the plaintiff does so, there will be one judgment against all defendants and the amount of damages cannot vary between them (which is important in relation to aggravated and exemplary damages).[24] Where the plaintiff sues only one tortfeasor, judgment against that tortfeasor bars an action against any of the others, even if that judgment remains unsatisfied.[25] Likewise,   [4.12]

---

14   *The Koursk* [1924] P 140, 159; *XL Petroleum (NSW) Pty Ltd v Caltex Oil (Australia) Pty Ltd* (1985) 155 CLR 448 (one defendant instructed the other defendant, an independent contractor, to trespass on the plaintiff's land).

15   *Thompson v Australian Capital Television Pty Ltd* (1996) 186 CLR 574, 582.

16   *Brooke v Bol* [1928] 2 KB 578: an explosion occurred when two men jointly examined a gas pipe for a possible leak, each of them having a naked flame in his hand.

17   *Gutman v McFall* [2004] NSWCA 378, (2004) 61 NSWLR 599: the teenage hirer of a dinghy was not vicariously liable for an injury negligently caused by his friend driving the dinghy.

18   *Mahony v J Kruschich (Demolitions) Pty Ltd* (1985) 156 CLR 522. For the question of when medical malpractice breaks the chain of causation between the original wrong and the further injury, see [3.83].

19   *Bridge v Chadwick* (1950) 50 SR (NSW) 230, 233–34.

20   GL Williams, *Joint Torts and Contributory Negligence* (Stevens & Sons 1951) 5.

21   This rule has been changed through procedural reforms both in Australia and England, eg *Law Reform (Miscellaneous Provisions) Act 1946* (NSW), s 2.

22   *XL Petroleum (NSW) Pty Ltd v Caltex Oil (Australia) Pty Ltd* (1985) 155 CLR 448, 456; *Thompson v Australian Capital Television Pty Ltd* (1996) 186 CLR 574, 582.

23   Even in actions for conspiracy: *Mills v Mills* (1631) Cro Car 239, 79 ER 809.

24   *XL Petroleum (NSW) Pty Ltd v Caltex Oil (Australia) Pty Ltd* (1985) 155 CLR 448, 454–55; *Thompson v Australian Capital Television Pty Ltd* (1996) 186 CLR 574, 582. It follows that aggravated and exemplary damages can be awarded only in the lowest amount that can be awarded against any of the defendants: *Cassell & Co Ltd v Broome* [1972] AC 1027, 1063, 1090.

25   *Brinsmead v Harrison* (1871) LR 7 CP 547; *XL Petroleum (NSW) Pty Ltd v Caltex Oil (Australia) Pty Ltd* (1985) 155 CLR 448, 456; *Thompson v Australian Capital Television Pty Ltd* (1996) 186 CLR 574, 582.

release of one tortfeasor discharges all.[26] But a mere covenant not to sue one tortfeasor does not preclude an action against the others.[27]

[4.13]   A concurrent wrongdoer (whether joint or several) who ends up paying more than her share of the plaintiff's loss will want to be reimbursed for the 'excess' by the other wrongdoers. In other words, the paying wrongdoer will want the other wrongdoers to contribute to the payment. The common law generally denies an entitlement to contribution in the case of concurrent tortfeasors,[28] but both the common law and equity recognise it in the case of joint contractors.[29] A contribution claim lies in equity also between trustees under a common liability for breach of trust,[30] and between company directors under a common liability for breach of an equitable duty towards the company.[31] It has been said that a right of contribution generally arises both at common law and in equity where one of several persons has paid more than her proper share towards discharging a common obligation.[32]

[4.14]   However, the High Court of Australia has repeatedly required the debtors' liabilities to be 'co-ordinate',[33] and 'of the same nature and to the same extent',[34] although they may have different sources, such as contract and statute.[35] It is not entirely clear when liabilities stemming from different sources are 'co-ordinate' and when they are not.[36] In *Burke v LFOT Pty Ltd*,[37] the High Court denied a contribution claim between a vendor of retail premises who was liable to the purchaser (a company) for misleading or deceptive conduct under what is now s 18 of the Australian Consumer Law, and the company's solicitor, who was liable to the company for negligently failing to discover the falsity of the vendor's statement. In the same case, the High Court endorsed (but distinguished) the recognition of a contribution claim in a Scottish case

---

26   *XL Petroleum (NSW) Pty Ltd v Caltex Oil (Australia) Pty Ltd* (1985) 155 CLR 448, 456; *Thompson v Australian Capital Television Pty Ltd* (1996) 186 CLR 574, 582.

27   *Thompson v Australian Capital Television Pty Ltd* (1996) 186 CLR 574, 583, where it is also noted that, when the common law rules still applied, courts were reluctant to construe an agreement as a release rather than a covenant not to sue.

28   *Merryweather v Nixan* (1799) 8 Term Rep 186; 101 ER 1337; *James Hardie & Co Pty Ltd v Seltsam Pty Ltd* (1998) 196 CLR 53, 75; *Burke v LFOT Pty Ltd* [2002] HCA 17, (2002) 209 CLR 282 [16]. In that respect, equity follows the law: *Belan v Casey* [2003] NSWSC 159, (2003) 57 NSWLR 670 [108]–[110]; J Watson, 'From Contribution to Apportioned Contribution to Proportionate Liability' (2004) 78 Aust LJ 126, 129.

29   *Coulls v Bagot's Executor and Trustee Co Ltd* (1967) 119 CLR 460, 480 (Barwick CJ); *Muschinski v Dodds* (1985) 160 CLR 583, 596 (Gibbs CJ); *Lumley v Robinson* [2002] EWCA Civ 94 [12].

30   *Chillingworth v Chambers* [1896] 1 Ch 685, 698; *Wynne v Tempest* [1897] 1 Ch 110, 113; *Goodwin v Duggan* (1996) 41 NSWLR 158, 166; *Burke v LFOT Pty Ltd* [2002] HCA 17, (2002) 209 CLR 282 [14]. However, a fraudulent trustee cannot claim contribution: *McNally v Harris (No 3)* [2008] NSWSC 861 [150]–[151].

31   *Ashhurst v Mason* (1875) LR 20 Eq 225; *Ramskill v Edwards* (1885) 31 Ch D 100. See also *Cummings v Lewis* (1993) 41 FCR 559, 594–99.

32   *Albion Insurance Co Ltd v Government Insurance Office (NSW)* (1969) 121 CLR 342, 351–52 (Kitto J).

33   *Burke v LFOT Pty Ltd* [2002] HCA 17, (2002) 209 CLR 282 [15]–[16]; *Friend v Brooker* [2009] HCA 21, (2009) 239 CLR 129 [40]; *HIH Claims Support Ltd v Insurance Australia Ltd* [2011] HCA 31, (2011) 244 CLR 72 [36]–[42].

34   *Burke v LFOT Pty Ltd* [2002] HCA 17, (2002) 209 CLR 282 [15]–[16], [38]; *Friend v Brooker* [2009] HCA 21, (2009) 239 CLR 129 [40]; *HIH Claims Support Ltd v Insurance Australia Ltd* [2011] HCA 31, (2011) 244 CLR 72 [39].

35   *Friend v Brooker* [2009] HCA 21, (2009) 239 CLR 129 [42]; *HIH Claims Support Ltd v Insurance Australia Ltd* [2011] HCA 31, (2011) 244 CLR 72 [39].

36   For further discussion, see J Watson, 'From Contribution to Apportioned Contribution to Proportionate Liability' (2004) 78 Aust LJ 126, 130–37.

37   [2002] HCA 17, (2002) 209 CLR 282.

where the owner of an oil tanker that had damaged an oil terminal was statutorily liable to the owner of the terminal and the company operating the terminal was also liable towards the owner of the terminal under a contract between them.[38]

In the absence of an express or implied agreement to the contrary, contribution shares are equal at common law[39] and, at least as a general rule, in equity.[40] Equality of shares is unjust where several persons undertake a joint contractual obligation in the understanding that some of them would be wholly indemnified by others. This injustice has been addressed by holding that joint contractors in those circumstances are not under a 'common liability' for the purpose of contribution.[41] In equity, the weight of authority is against the possibility of deviating from the principle of equality of shares by apportioning wrongdoers' contribution shares in accordance with each wrongdoer's share in the responsibility for the damage.[42] [4.15]

III Contribution statutes

In all Australian states and territories, the common law rules have been significantly changed through two 'waves' of legislation. The first 'wave', to be discussed now, removed the unsatisfactory rules of the common law that judgment against one joint tortfeasor barred an action against the others, and that no claim for contribution lies between concurrent tortfeasors. For convenience, these statutory provisions shall be called 'contribution statutes'. [4.16]

The following outline of those statutory provisions will use the term 'wrongdoer'. However, only the Victorian contribution statute actually applies to all wrongdoers 'whatever the legal basis of liability, whether tort, breach of contract, breach of trust or otherwise'.[43] The contribution statutes of the other jurisdictions apply to some wrongs only. Outside the scope of those statutes, the rules of the common law and equity still apply, and the right to contribution depends upon the uncertain requirement of liabilities being 'co-ordinate'; see [4.14]. [4.17]

The statutes of New South Wales, the Northern Territory, Queensland and Western Australia apply where damage is suffered 'as a result of a tort'.[44] This phrase has been held [4.18]

---

38 *BP Petroleum Development Ltd v Esso Petroleum Co Ltd* 1987 SLT 345. The decision in that case was also approved in *HIH Claims Support Ltd v Insurance Australia Ltd* [2011] HCA 31, (2011) 244 CLR 72 [39].

39 *Lowe & Sons v Dixon & Sons* (1885) 16 QBD 455, 458; *BP Petroleum Development Ltd v Esso Petroleum Co Ltd* 1987 SLT 345, 348–49.

40 *Commercial and General Insurance Co Ltd v Government Insurance Office of NSW* (1973) 129 CLR 374, 380; *Scholefield Goodman and Sons Ltd v Zyngier* [1986] AC 562 (PC) 575; *Burke v LFOT Pty Ltd* [2002] HCA 17, (2002) 209 CLR 282 [38] (McHugh J).

41 *Official Trustee in Bankruptcy v Citibank Savings Ltd* (1995) 38 NSWLR 116.

42 *Bialkower v Acohs Pty Ltd* (1998) 83 FCR 1, 12–13; *Leigh-Mardon Pty Ltd v Wawn* (1995) 17 ACSR 741, 752; *Sky Channel Pty Ltd v Tszyu (No 2)* [2000] NSWSC 1150 [7]–[13]; *Glenmont Investments Pty Ltd v O'Loughlin* [2001] SASC 88, (2001) 79 SASR 185 [18]; *Jonstan Pty Ltd v Nicholson* [2003] NSWSC 500, (2003) 58 NSWLR 223 [101]; *Fico v O'Leary* [2004] ATPR (Digest) 46-259 [247]; *Parker v Alessi* [2011] NSWSC 947 [119]; *George v Webb* [2011] NSWSC 1608 [339]–[354]; *AMP Bank Ltd v Brown* [2017] NSWSC 313. The opposite view was taken in *Official Trustee in Bankruptcy v Citibank Savings Ltd* (1995) 38 NSWLR 116, 128–29; *Jones v Mortgage Acceptance Nominees Ltd* (1996) 63 FCR 418, 422; *Duke Group Ltd (in liq) v Pilmer* (1998) 144 FLR 1, 253.

43 *Wrongs Act 1958* (Vic), s 23A(1).

44 *Law Reform (Miscellaneous Provisions) Act 1946* (NSW), s 5; *Law Reform (Miscellaneous Provisions) Act 1956* (NT), s 12(1); *Law Reform Act 1995* (Qld), s 6; *Law Reform (Contributory Negligence and Tortfeasors' Contribution) Act 1947* (WA), s 7.

to cover liability on bases other than tort where it is concurrent with liability in tort.[45] For example, where a professional is concurrently liable in contract and tort, the contribution statutes just mentioned apply to the contractual liability as well as the tortious liability.

[4.19]   In each of the remaining three jurisdictions, the contribution statute has the same scope as the contributory negligence statute of the relevant jurisdiction, discussed at [6.92]. The statute of the Australian Capital Territory thus applies to liability in tort in relation to which a defence of contributory negligence is available at common law, and to liability for the breach of a contractual duty of care that is concurrent and coextensive with a duty of care in tort.[46] The South Australian statute applies to liability in tort, liability for the breach of a contractual duty of care, and liability under statute.[47] The Tasmanian statute applies to liability in tort, liability for the breach of a contractual duty of care that is concurrent and coextensive with a duty of care in tort, and liability under statute.[48] The reason for the alignment with the scope of the contributory negligence statute is not apparent. For example, it is not apparent why a plaintiff's right to obtain more than one judgment against joint wrongdoers ought to depend upon the availability of apportionment of liability had the plaintiff behaved unreasonably.

[4.20]   The contribution statutes provide that judgment against one joint wrongdoer does not bar an action against the others.[49] While this overcomes the unsatisfactory bar at common law, it opens the door for the plaintiff to bring a second action solely in the hope that the second court will award a larger sum. Addressing this risk of 'judgment-shopping', the contribution statutes in all jurisdictions except Victoria provide that where more than one action is brought against concurrent wrongdoers (whether joint or several), the sums recoverable under the judgments must not in the aggregate exceed the amount awarded in the judgment first given.[50] In addition, the contribution statutes in all jurisdictions (including Victoria) provide that the plaintiff is not entitled to costs in a subsequent action unless the court thinks that it was reasonable to bring the action.[51] Those provisions deter plaintiffs from bringing a second action unless the first judgment remains unsatisfied.

---

45   *Jones v Mortgage Acceptance Nominees Ltd* (1996) 63 FCR 418, 563–64; *Australian Breeders Co-operative Society Ltd v Jones* (1997) 150 ALR 488, 548–49; *Hampic Pty Ltd v Adams* [1999] NSWCA 455, (1999) ASAL 55–035 [62]. All these cases involved the NSW statute but the same interpretation can be expected to prevail for the identical phrase in the other statutes.

46   *Civil Law (Wrongs) Act 2002* (ACT), s 19.

47   *Law Reform (Contributory Negligence and Apportionment of Liability) Act 2001* (SA), s 4(1).

48   *Wrongs Act 1954* (Tas), s 2.

49   *Civil Law (Wrongs) Act 2002* (ACT), s 20(1); *Law Reform (Miscellaneous Provisions) Act 1946* (NSW), s 5(1)(a); *Law Reform (Miscellaneous Provisions) Act 1956* (NT), s 12(2); *Law Reform Act 1995* (Qld), s 6(a); *Law Reform (Contributory Negligence and Apportionment of Liability) Act 2001* (SA), s 12(1); *Wrongs Act 1954* (Tas), s 3(1)(a); *Wrongs Act 1958* (Vic), s 24AA; *Law Reform (Contributory Negligence and Tortfeasors' Contribution) Act 1947* (WA), s 7(1)(a).

50   *Civil Law (Wrongs) Act 2002* (ACT), s 20(2); *Law Reform (Miscellaneous Provisions) Act 1946* (NSW), s 5(1)(b); *Law Reform (Miscellaneous Provisions) Act 1956* (NT), s 12(3); *Law Reform Act 1995* (Qld), s 6(b); *Law Reform (Contributory Negligence and Apportionment of Liability) Act 2001* (SA), s 12(2)–(4); *Wrongs Act 1954* (Tas), s 3(1)(b); *Law Reform (Contributory Negligence and Tortfeasors' Contribution) Act 1947* (WA), s 7(1)(b). This does not apply where the first judgment is a consent judgment giving effect to a settlement of proceedings: *Newcrest Mining Ltd v Thornton* [2012] HCA 60, (2012) 248 CLR 555.

51   *Wrongs Act 1958* (Vic), s 24AB, and the statutory provisions cited in the preceding footnote.

By allowing the plaintiff to obtain separate judgments against joint wrongdoers, the contribution statutes abolish the common law rule that the plaintiff has but one cause of action against the group of joint tortfeasors.[52] This has the effect of also abolishing the related common law rule that release of one joint tortfeasor releases all.[53] The Tasmanian statute expressly provides to that effect.[54] Since the release of one wrongdoer must not increase the shares borne by the other wrongdoers, the latter must in principle be entitled to claim contribution from the former if they end up paying for the whole of the plaintiff's loss. The South Australian statute expressly provides to that effect.[55] But an obligation of the released wrongdoer to pay contribution may frustrate the purpose of the release. The Tasmanian statute addresses that problem by providing that a released wrongdoer need not pay contribution,[56] but that the release reduces the plaintiff's claim against the other wrongdoers.[57] The law is unclear in the rest of Australia.

[4.21]

Turning to contribution in general, the contribution statutes provide that a concurrent wrongdoer (whether joint or several) may recover contribution from any other wrongdoer who is, or would if sued have been, liable in respect of the same damage.[58] Since the claim for contribution and the plaintiff's claim against the wrongdoers are subject to separate limitation periods,[59] contribution can be claimed even if the plaintiff's claim against the wrongdoer from whom contribution is being sought has become statute-barred.[60] No contribution can be claimed from a person who was not held liable when sued by the plaintiff; it is not open to the wrongdoer seeking contribution to prove that that person was in fact liable towards the plaintiff.[61] Similarly, a wrongdoer who was held liable when sued by the plaintiff can claim contribution without having to prove that she was in fact liable towards the plaintiff, and it is not open to other wrongdoers to prove otherwise.[62]

[4.22]

The statutes of Tasmania and Victoria assist a wrongdoer who has settled with the plaintiff. All that a settling wrongdoer needs to prove in Tasmania is that the amount of the settlement

[4.23]

52   This enables the court to award exemplary damages against one wrongdoer but not the others, or to award different amounts of exemplary damages: *De Reus v Gray* [2003] VSCA 84, (2003) 9 VR 432 [27]. See [14.24].
53   *Thompson v Australian Capital Television Pty Ltd* (1996) 186 CLR 574, 583–85, 592, 612–15.
54   *Wrongs Act 1954* (Tas), s 3(3)(a).
55   *Law Reform (Contributory Negligence and Apportionment of Liability) Act 2001* (SA), s 6(8)(b).
56   *Wrongs Act 1954* (Tas), s 3(3)(b).
57   Ibid, s 3(3)(c)–(e).
58   *Civil Law (Wrongs) Act 2002* (ACT), s 21(1); *Law Reform (Miscellaneous Provisions) Act 1946* (NSW), s 5(1)(c); *Law Reform (Miscellaneous Provisions) Act 1956* (NT), s 12(4); *Law Reform Act 1995* (Qld), s 6(c); *Law Reform (Contributory Negligence and Apportionment of Liability) Act 2001* (SA), s 6(1); *Wrongs Act 1954* (Tas), s 3(1)(c); *Wrongs Act 1958* (Vic), s 23B(1); *Law Reform (Contributory Negligence and Tortfeasors' Contribution) Act 1947* (WA), s 7(1)(c).
59   Eg *Bargen v State Government Insurance Office (Queensland)* (1982) 154 CLR 318, 323–24; *Zraika v Walsh* [2011] NSWSC 1569, (2011) 60 MVR 17 [57]–[74].
60   *Law Reform (Contributory Negligence and Apportionment of Liability) Act 2001* (SA), s 6(8)(d); *Wrongs Act 1954* (Tas), s 3(1)(c), (d) ('would, if sued . . . at the time when the cause of action arose, have been liable'); *Wrongs Act 1958* (Vic), s 23B(3). For the other jurisdictions, see *Brambles Constructions Pty Ltd v Helmers* (1966) 114 CLR 213.
61   *James Hardie & Co Pty Ltd v Seltsam Pty Ltd* (1998) 196 CLR 53, 69, 96–98; *Dowthwaite Holdings Pty Ltd v Saliba* [2006] WASCA 72 [88].
62   *Bitumen and Oil Refineries (Australia) Ltd v Commissioner for Government Transport* (1955) 92 CLR 200.

was reasonable; if the court finds that the amount was excessive, the court will fix the amount at which the claim should have been settled.[63] All that a settling wrongdoer needs to prove in Victoria is that she made the settlement in good faith and that she would have been liable towards the plaintiff assuming that the plaintiff's factual assertions could be established;[64] however, in assessing the amount of contribution the court (or jury) shall disregard any amount of the settlement that appears to have been excessive.[65] In the other jurisdictions, the settling wrongdoer may have to prove her liability towards the plaintiff;[66] this deters settlements where liability is contested.[67]

[4.24]   The contribution statutes provide that the court is to apportion the contribution shares according to each wrongdoer's responsibility for the damage, and has the power to exempt any wrongdoer from liability to make contribution and to order one wrongdoer to completely indemnify the others.[68] A wrongdoer's 'responsibility' for the damage is determined by the same two factors that determine 'responsibility' in the context of contributory negligence, discussed at [6.107]–[6.110]. One factor is the comparative blameworthiness or culpability, which is the degree of departure from the standard of reasonable conduct. The other factor is the comparative causal potency of the conduct, which is the objective potential to cause damage.[69] The fact that one wrongdoer has profited from the wrong and retains the profit may be taken into account.[70] What is not relevant is a wrongdoer's general financial strength or status (for example, whether it is the state or a commercial entity),[71] or a wrongdoer's attitude in terms of remorse or lack of it.[72]

[4.25]   The statutory contribution regime does not affect rights to be completely indemnified.[73] Such a right exists where, as between the wrongdoers, one is ultimately liable for the whole of

---

63   *Wrongs Act 1954* (Tas), s 3(1)(d).

64   *Wrongs Act 1958* (Vic), s 23B(4).

65   Ibid, s 24(2B).

66   However, it is not necessary to show that a court would have awarded the plaintiff exactly the amount of the settlement; that amount need only be reasonable: *Saccardo Constructions Pty Ltd v Gammon (No 2)* (1994) 63 SASR 333, 336; *In the Marriage of Aldous* (1996) 135 FLR 326, 332–35; *Dowthwaite Holdings Pty Ltd v Saliba* [2006] WASCA 72 [91]–[95].

67   See P Cane, 'Multiple Torts, Contribution and the Dynamics of the Settlement Process' (1999) 7 Torts LJ 137. The NSW Law Reform Commission has recommended a reform that removes any right to contest the settling wrongdoer's liability towards the plaintiff: NSWLRC, *Contribution between Persons Liable for the Same Damage*, Report No 89 (1999), Recommendation 6.

68   *Civil Law (Wrongs) Act 2002* (ACT), s 21(2), (3)(b), (c); *Law Reform (Miscellaneous Provisions) Act 1946* (NSW), s 5(2); *Law Reform (Miscellaneous Provisions) Act 1956* (NT), s 13; *Law Reform Act 1995* (Qld), s 7; *Law Reform (Contributory Negligence and Apportionment of Liability) Act 2001* (SA), s 6(5)–(7); *Wrongs Act 1954* (Tas), s 3(2); *Wrongs Act 1958* (Vic), s 24(2); *Law Reform (Contributory Negligence and Tortfeasors' Contribution) Act 1947* (WA), s 7(2).

69   *Vinidex Tubemakers Pty Ltd v Thiess Contractors Pty Ltd* [2000] NSWCA 67 [29]; *Nationwide News Pty Ltd v Naidu* [2007] NSWCA 377, (2007) 71 NSWLR 471 [278]–[279].

70   *Reinhold v New South Wales Lotteries Corporation (No 2)* [2008] NSWSC 187, (2008) 82 NSWLR 762 [57], citing *Dubai Aluminium Co Ltd v Salaam* [2002] UKHL 48, [2003] 2 AC 366.

71   *Amaca Pty Ltd v New South Wales* [2003] HCA 44, (2003) 199 ALR 596 [19]; *Reinhold v New South Wales Lotteries Corporation (No 2)* [2008] NSWSC 187, (2008) 82 NSWLR 762 [57].

72   *Reinhold v New South Wales Lotteries Corporation (No 2)* [2008] NSWSC 187, (2008) 82 NSWLR 762 [57].

73   *Civil Law (Wrongs) Act 2002* (ACT), s 21(3)(a); *Law Reform (Miscellaneous Provisions) Act 1946* (NSW), s 5(1)(c); *Law Reform (Miscellaneous Provisions) Act 1956* (NT), s 12(4); *Law Reform Act 1995* (Qld), s 6(c); *Law Reform (Contributory Negligence and Apportionment of Liability) Act 2001* (SA), s 6(9)(a); *Wrongs Act 1954* (Tas), s 3(1)(c); *Wrongs Act 1958* (Vic), s 24AD(4)(a); *Law Reform (Contributory Negligence and Tortfeasors' Contribution) Act 1947* (WA), s 7(1)(c).

the plaintiff's damage, either by virtue of a contractual agreement between the wrongdoers[74] or by virtue of the nature of each wrongdoer's liability towards the plaintiff and the reason for the law imposing liability.[75] For example, a person who, without personally being at fault, is vicariously liable for someone else's wrong is in general entitled to be indemnified by the latter.[76] An important exception, in certain circumstances, is the relationship between employer and employee.[77]

IV   Proportionate liability statutes

A second 'wave' of legislation in all Australian jurisdictions has introduced proportionate liability of concurrent wrongdoers in certain circumstances not involving personal injury.[78] For convenience, these statutory provisions will be called 'proportionate liability statutes'. The purpose of the reform has been described in this way: [4.26]

> The reform was prompted by concerns that litigation against well-insured professionals (particularly auditors) was driving up professional liability insurance premiums. Plaintiffs who had suffered loss caused by several wrongdoers were seen to be taking advantage of the system of joint and several liability by targeting only the well-insured wrongdoer (whose contribution to the plaintiff's loss may have been minimal) and obtaining 100% of the damages award from that wrongdoer. Although the well-insured defendant could of course seek contribution from the other concurrent wrongdoers, the risk that the other wrongdoers would be untraceable or insolvent was borne by that defendant. One consequence of the introduction of a system of proportionate liability is that that risk is shifted to the plaintiff.[79]

Every state and territory has a proportionate liability statute that applies to a variety of claims, as outlined at [4.29]–[4.32]. Federal statutes prohibiting misleading or deceptive conduct in certain circumstances provide for proportionate liability where such conduct has caused loss other than personal injury.[80] The federal statutes have identical provisions, which are largely   [4.27]

---

74   Contractual indemnities are construed in favour of the promisor: *Andar Transport Pty Ltd v Brambles Ltd* [2004] HCA 28, (2004) 217 CLR 424 [17]–[23].

75   See S Harder, 'Claims between a Person Liable for Misrepresentation and the Representee's Contract-Partner' [2014] JBL 121.

76   *Lister v Romford Ice and Cold Storage Co Ltd* [1957] AC 555; *Voli v Inglewood Shire Council* (1963) 110 CLR 74, 100 (Windeyer J); *FAI General Insurance Co Ltd v AR Griffiths & Sons Pty Ltd* (1997) 71 ALJR 651. See also *Sherras v van der Maat* [1989] 1 Qd R 114, 117–18.

77   For the details, see C Sappideen, PM O'Grady and J Riley, *Macken's Law of Employment* (8th edn, LBC 2016) [5.450]–[5.470].

78   Proportionate liability is criticised by K Barker and J Steele, 'Drifting Towards Proportionate Liability: Ethics and Pragmatics' (2015) 74 Camb LJ 49.

79   *Williams v Pisano* [2015] NSWCA 177, (2015) 90 NSWLR 342 [50] (Emmett JA) (footnote omitted). See also *Hunt & Hunt Lawyers v Mitchell Morgan Nominees Pty Ltd* [2013] HCA 10, (2013) 247 CLR 613 [10]–[15]; *BHPB Freight Pty Ltd v Cosco Oceania Chartering Pty Ltd (No 2)* [2008] FCA 1656 [4]–[5]; A Stephenson, 'Proportional Liability in Australia – The Death of Certainty in Risk Allocation in Contract' (2005) 22 ICLR 64, 65–68.

80   *Australian Securities and Investments Commission Act 2001* (Cth), ss 12GP–12GW; *Competition and Consumer Act 2010* (Cth), pt VIA; *Corporations Act 2001* (Cth), ss 1041L–1041S. An interpretation of these provisions under which they would apply to certain contraventions of the relevant statute other than misleading or deceptive conduct has been rejected: *Selig v Wealthsure Pty Ltd* [2015] HCA 18, (2015) 255 CLR 661 [22]–[37]; *Williams v Pisano* [2015] NSWCA 177, (2015) 90 NSWLR 342 [58]–[64].

identical to the provisions of the New South Wales statute.[81] The following discussion makes reference only to the statutes of the states and territories.

[4.28]   The proportionate liability statutes apply to 'concurrent wrongdoers', defined as persons liable for the same indivisible harm.[82] It is irrelevant that a concurrent wrongdoer is insolvent, is being wound up or has ceased to exist or died.[83] The statutes of Queensland and South Australia do not apply where all concurrent wrongdoers acted jointly.[84] The statutes of the other jurisdictions apply to all concurrent wrongdoers, whether joint or several.[85] Proportionate liability is particularly difficult to justify where all wrongdoers acted in furtherance of a common design and the plaintiff's damage is not larger than it would have been had any of the joint wrongdoers acted alone. In those circumstances, each of the joint wrongdoers would have been liable for the whole of the plaintiff's damage had he acted alone. Each of them thus enjoys a reduction of liability simply by virtue of the participation of others.

[4.29]   The proportionate liability statutes probably do not apply in commercial arbitration.[86] They differ with regard to the source of liability to which they apply. The South Australian proportionate liability statute has the same scope as the South Australian contribution statute and thus applies to liability in tort, liability for the breach of a contractual duty of care and liability under statute.[87] This excludes equitable liability and strict contractual liability but probably includes liability for loss arising from a contravention of s 18 of the Australian Consumer Law. The proportionate liability statutes of most, but not all, of the other jurisdictions expressly provide for their application in s 18 cases.[88]

[4.30]   Leaving aside s 18 cases, the Queensland statute applies to 'an action for damages arising from a breach of a duty of care',[89] and the statutes of the remaining jurisdictions (except South Australia) apply to an 'action for damages' (whether in contract, tort or otherwise) 'arising from

---

81   An important difference is that a contracting-out is permitted by the NSW statute but not by the federal statutes.

82   See *Hunt & Hunt Lawyers v Mitchell Morgan Nominees Pty Ltd* [2013] HCA 10, (2013) 247 CLR 613 [21].

83   *Civil Law (Wrongs) Act 2002* (ACT), s 107D(2); *Civil Liability Act 2002* (NSW), s 34(4); *Proportionate Liability Act 2005* (NT), s 6(2); *Civil Liability Act 2003* (Qld), s 30(2); *Law Reform (Contributory Negligence and Apportionment of Liability) Act 2001* (SA), s 3(1) (definition of 'wrongdoer'); *Civil Liability Act 2002* (Tas), s 43A(4); *Wrongs Act 1958* (Vic), s 24AH(2); *Civil Liability Act 2002* (WA), s 5AJ(1).

84   *Civil Liability Act 2003* (Qld), s 30(1); *Law Reform (Contributory Negligence and Apportionment of Liability) Act 2001* (SA), s 3(2)(b).

85   *Civil Law (Wrongs) Act 2002* (ACT), s 107D(1); *Civil Liability Act 2002* (NSW), s 34(2); *Proportionate Liability Act 2005* (NT), s 6(1); *Civil Liability Act 2002* (Tas), s 43A(2); *Wrongs Act 1958* (Vic), s 24AH(1); *Civil Liability Act 2002* (WA), s 5AI.

86   *Aquagenics Pty Ltd v Break O'Day Council* [2010] TASFC 3, (2010) 20 Tas R 239 [33], [95], [111]; *Curtin University of Technology v Woods Bagot Pty Ltd* [2012] WASC 449; *Parsons Brinckerhoff Australia Pty Ltd v Thiess Pty Ltd* [2013] QSC 75 [57]; D Levin, 'Proportionate Liability in Arbitration in Australia?' (2009) 25 BCL 298. The opposite view is taken by R McDougall, 'Proportionate Liability in Construction Litigation' (2006) 22 BCL 394, 395–96.

87   *Law Reform (Contributory Negligence and Apportionment of Liability) Act 2001* (SA), s 4(1).

88   *Civil Liability Act 2002* (NSW), s 34(1)(b); *Proportionate Liability Act 2005* (NT), s 4(2)(b); *Civil Liability Act 2003* (Qld), s 28(1)(b); *Civil Liability Act 2002* (Tas), s 43A(1)(b); *Wrongs Act 1958* (Vic), s 24AF(1)(b).

89   *Civil Liability Act 2003* (Qld), s 28(1)(a).

a failure to take reasonable care'.[90] Most of those statutes define 'damages' as 'any form of monetary compensation'.[91] This excludes a contractual debt,[92] but should include equitable compensation.[93] Proportionate liability should thus apply to equitable compensation for breach of an equitable duty of care (except in South Australia).

Conflicting judicial views have been expressed on whether the phrase '[liability] arising from a failure to take reasonable care' includes liability not dependent upon fault (for example, liability for breach of a contractual warranty), but where the defendant was in fact careless.[94] There should be no proportionate liability in cases of strict liability,[95] since it would be absurd if a wrongdoer who was careless enjoyed a more limited liability than a wrongdoer who was innocent.[96] This view should be uncontroversial in relation to the Queensland statute since a strict obligation does not involve the imposition of a 'duty of care'.[97]   [4.31]

The proportionate liability statutes do not apply to claims arising out of personal injury,[98] including the claim of the dependants of a deceased under an Australian equivalent to Lord Campbell's Act (see [7.93]).[99] Furthermore, the statutes of all jurisdictions except South   [4.32]

---

90   *Civil Law (Wrongs) Act 2002* (ACT), s 107B(2)(a); *Civil Liability Act 2002* (NSW), s 34(1)(a); *Proportionate Liability Act 2005* (NT), s 4(2)(a); *Civil Liability Act 2002* (Tas), s 43A(1)(a); *Wrongs Act 1958* (Vic), s 24AF(1)(a); *Civil Liability Act 2002* (WA), s 5AI.

91   *Civil Liability Act 2002* (NSW), s 3; *Proportionate Liability Act 2005* (NT), s 3; *Civil Liability Act 2003* (Qld), sch 2; *Civil Liability Act 2002* (Tas), s 3; *Wrongs Act 1958* (Vic), s 24AE.

92   *Commonwealth Bank of Australia v Witherow* [2006] VSCA 45 [10]; B McDonald and JW Carter, 'The Lottery of Contractual Risk Allocation and Proportionate Liability' (2009) 26 J Cont L 1, 4. Claims under liquidated damages clauses are considered apportionable by P Megens and B Cubitt, 'Contract or Conflict? An Overview of the Proportionate Liability Regime and Its Difficulties' (2009) 23 CLQ 3, 7; A Stephenson, 'Proportional Liability in Australia – The Death of Certainty in Risk Allocation in Contract' (2005) 22 ICLR 64, 71.

93   VJ Vann, 'Equity and Proportionate Liability' (2007) 1 J Eq 199, 209–10.

94   In favour of proportionate liability: *Dartberg Pty Ltd v Wealthcare Financial Planning Pty Ltd* [2007] FCA 1216, (2007) 164 FCR 450 [27]–[30]; *Reinhold v New South Wales Lotteries Corporation (No 2)* [2008] NSWSC 187, (2008) 82 NSWLR 762 [19]–[30]; *Solak v Bank of Western Australia Ltd* [2009] VSC 82, [35] (rev'd on other grounds, leaving the present issue expressly open, in *Kheirs Financial Services Pty Ltd v Aussie Home Loans Pty Ltd* [2010] VSCA 355, (2010) 31 VR 46 [95]); *Fulton Hogan Construction Pty Ltd v Grenadier Manufacturing Pty Ltd* [2012] VSC 358 [389]; *Perpetual Trustee Co Ltd v CTC Group Pty Ltd (No 2)* [2013] NSWCA 58 [42] (Barrett JA). Against proportionate liability: *Serong v Dependable Developments Pty Ltd* [2009] VCAT 760 [349]; *Spiteri v Stonehenge Homes & Associates Pty Ltd* [2011] VCAT 2267 [136]; *Perpetual Trustee Co Ltd v CTC Group Pty Ltd (No 2)* [2013] NSWCA 58 [22]–[23] (Macfarlan JA).

95   The opposite view is taken, with the argument that the protection of insurers requires proportionate liability, by O Hayford, 'Proportionate Liability – Its Impact on Contractual Risk Allocation' (2010) 26 BCL 11, 17–19; A Stephenson, 'Proportional Liability in Australia – The Death of Certainty in Risk Allocation in Contract' (2005) 22 ICLR 64, 71–73.

96   B McDonald and JW Carter, 'The Lottery of Contractual Risk Allocation and Proportionate Liability' (2009) 26 J Cont L 1, 15, 18.

97   VJ Vann, 'Equity and Proportionate Liability' (2007) 1 J Eq 199, 203. See also B McDonald and JW Carter, 'The Lottery of Contractual Risk Allocation and Proportionate Liability' (2009) 26 J Cont L 1, 12: 'There would seem to be no basis – and no reason – to imply an obligation to exercise care in the performance of an obligation which creates a standard of duty which is strict'.

98   *Civil Law (Wrongs) Act 2002* (ACT), s 107B(3)(a); *Civil Liability Act 2002* (NSW), s 34(1)(a); *Proportionate Liability Act 2005* (NT), s 4(3)(a); *Civil Liability Act 2003* (Qld), s 28(3)(a); *Law Reform (Contributory Negligence and Apportionment of Liability) Act 2001* (SA), s 3(2)(a)(i); *Civil Liability Act 2002* (Tas), s 43A(1)(a); *Wrongs Act 1958* (Vic), s 24AG(1); *Civil Liability Act 2002* (WA), s 5AI.

99   *Shinwari v Anjoul* [2017] NSWCA 74, (2017) 94 NSWLR 314.

Australia expressly preserve the operation of any legislation that prescribes several liability.[100] Most statutes also exempt certain types of claim from their operation. Some statutes exempt claims governed by special regimes for motor accidents[101] and workplace accidents.[102] The statutes of the Australian Capital Territory and Queensland exempt claims by consumers who have acquired goods or services for personal, domestic or household use or consumption.[103] The statute of the Northern Territory exempts claims under Part 3-3 or 3-4 of the Australian Consumer Law.[104] The defendant bears the onus of pleading and proving the applicability of a proportionate liability statute.[105]

[4.33]   Within their respective scope, the proportionate liability statutes provide that a concurrent wrongdoer is liable only for that proportion of the plaintiff's damage that the court thinks just, having regard to the wrongdoer's responsibility for the damage.[106] A wrongdoer's 'responsibility' in this context is determined in the same way as in the context of contribution (see [4.24]) and contributory negligence (see [6.107]–[6.110]), namely by considering the relative degree of departure from the standard of reasonable conduct and the relative causal potency of the conduct.[107] Shares of nil and 100% ought to be possible.[108] A plaintiff who was contributorily negligent is not a concurrent wrongdoer for the purposes of the proportionate liability statutes,[109] but the statutes provide that the wrongdoers' shares must be apportioned by excluding the proportion of the loss for which the plaintiff is responsible.[110] This provision

---

100   *Civil Law (Wrongs) Act 2002* (ACT), s 107K(d); *Civil Liability Act 2002* (NSW), s 39(c); *Proportionate Liability Act 2005* (NT), s 14(c); *Civil Liability Act 2003* (Qld), s 28(4); *Civil Liability Act 2002* (Tas), s 43G(1)(c); *Wrongs Act 1958* (Vic), s 24AP(e); *Civil Liability Act 2002* (WA), s 5AO(c). In South Australia, the effect of a statute that prescribes several liability is governed by the general rules on resolving conflicts between statutes; for those rules, see M Leeming, *Resolving Conflict of Laws* (Federation Press 2011).

101   *Civil Law (Wrongs) Act 2002* (ACT), s 107B(4)(b); *Civil Liability Act 2002* (NSW), ss 3B(1)(d), (e), 34A(1)(c); *Civil Liability Act 2002* (Tas), ss 3B(2), (4), 43A(8); *Wrongs Act 1958* (Vic), s 24AG(2)(a).

102   *Civil Law (Wrongs) Act 2002* (ACT), s 107B(4)(c); *Civil Liability Act 2002* (NSW), ss 3B(1)(f), (g), 34A(1)(c); *Civil Liability Act 2002* (Tas), ss 3B(3) and (4), 43A(8); *Wrongs Act 1958* (Vic), s 24AG(2)(b), (c).

103   *Civil Law (Wrongs) Act 2002* (ACT), ss 107B(3)(b), 107C; *Civil Liability Act 2003* (Qld), ss 28(3)(b), 29.

104   *Proportionate Liability Act 2005* (NT), s 4(3)(b).

105   *Dartberg Pty Ltd v Wealthcare Financial Planning Pty Ltd* [2007] FCA 1216, (2007) 164 FCR 450 [31]; *HSD Co Pty Ltd v Masu Financial Management Ltd* [2008] NSWSC 1279 [18].

106   *Civil Law (Wrongs) Act 2002* (ACT), s 107F(1)(a); *Civil Liability Act 2002* (NSW), s 35(1)(a); *Proportionate Liability Act 2005* (NT), s 13(1)(a); *Civil Liability Act 2003* (Qld), s 31(1)(a); *Law Reform (Contributory Negligence and Apportionment of Liability) Act 2001* (SA), s 8(2); *Civil Liability Act 2002* (Tas), s 43B(1)(a); *Wrongs Act 1958* (Vic), s 24AI(1)(a); *Civil Liability Act 2002* (WA), s 5AK(1)(a).

107   *Reinhold v New South Wales Lotteries Corporation (No 2)* [2008] NSWSC 187, (2008) 82 NSWLR 762 [60]; *GEJ & MA Geldard Pty Ltd v Mobbs (No 2)* [2011] QSC 33, [2012] 1 Qd R 120 [19]–[21]; *Lovick & Son Developments Pty Ltd v Doppstadt Australia Pty Ltd* [2012] NSWSC 529 [257]; *Bathurst Regional Council v Local Government Financial Services Pty Ltd (No 5)* [2012] FCA 1200 [3517].

108   The opposite view is taken by B McDonald, 'Proportionate Liability in Australia: The Devil in the Detail' (2005) 26 Aust Bar Rev 29, 36–37.

109   *Rennie Golledge Pty Ltd v Ballard* [2012] NSWCA 376, (2012) 82 NSWLR 231 [15], [128]–[143].

110   *Civil Law (Wrongs) Act 2002* (ACT), s 107F(2)(a); *Civil Liability Act 2002* (NSW), s 35(3)(a); *Proportionate Liability Act 2005* (NT), s 13(2)(a); *Civil Liability Act 2003* (Qld), s 32G; *Law Reform (Contributory Negligence and Apportionment of Liability) Act 2001* (SA), s 8(3)(b); *Civil Liability Act 2002* (Tas), s 43B(3)(a); *Wrongs Act 1958* (Vic), s 24AN; *Civil Liability Act 2002* (WA), s 5AK(3)(a).

applies only in cases in which an apportionment by virtue of contributory negligence is available (see [5.111], [6.92]).[111]

The proportionate liability statutes provide that they do not prevent a person from being held vicariously liable for a proportion of the plaintiff's damage for which someone else is liable, or prevent a partner from being held jointly and severally liable with another partner for a proportion of the plaintiff's damage for which the other partner is liable.[112] The South Australian statute further provides that where one person is directly liable for an act or omission and another person is under a derivative liability for the first person, they will be treated as a single wrongdoer for the purpose of determining the shares of all concurrent wrongdoers.[113] This is appropriate. Suppose that the damage was caused by the acts of X and Y with equal responsibility (considering culpability and causal potency), and that Z is vicariously liable for Y's action without personally being at fault. X is liable for half of the plaintiff's damage, and Y and Z are jointly and severally liable for the other half.[114] The same ought to obtain under the statutes of the other jurisdictions, which are silent on the issue but open to being interpreted in that way.[115] **[4.34]**

The statutes of all jurisdictions except Victoria provide that a defendant who has reasonable grounds to believe that there is a concurrent wrongdoer must, as soon as practicable, inform the plaintiff of the identity of that person and the relevant circumstances, although the only sanction for non-compliance under most statutes is a cost order against the defendant.[116] In any event, proportionate liability applies even if some concurrent wrongdoers are not party to the proceedings.[117] If, in those circumstances, the court divides the whole of the plaintiff's damage between the wrongdoers who are party to the proceedings, each of those wrongdoers will have to pay more than his actual share.[118] On principle, this could be accepted since each **[4.35]**

---

111   *Rennie Golledge Pty Ltd v Ballard* [2012] NSWCA 376, (2012) 82 NSWLR 231 [141] (Campbell JA); *Smart v AAI Ltd* [2015] NSWSC 392 [162]. The opposite view is taken by R McDougall, 'Proportionate Liability in Construction Litigation' (2006) 22 BCL 394, 397.

112   *Civil Law (Wrongs) Act 2002* (ACT), s 107K(a), (c); *Civil Liability Act 2002* (NSW), s 39(a), (b); *Proportionate Liability Act 2005* (NT), s 14(a), (b); *Civil Liability Act 2003* (Qld), s 32I(a), (c); *Civil Liability Act 2002* (Tas), s 43G(1)(a), (b); *Wrongs Act 1958* (Vic), s 24AP(a), (c); *Civil Liability Act 2002* (WA), s 5AO(a), (b).

113   *Law Reform (Contributory Negligence and Apportionment of Liability) Act 2001* (SA), s 8(3)(a) and definition of 'group' in s 3(1).

114   A contribution claim lies between Y and Z: *Law Reform (Contributory Negligence and Apportionment of Liability) Act 2001* (SA), s 9(a).

115   B McDonald, 'Proportionate Liability in Australia: The Devil in the Detail' (2005) 26 Aust Bar Rev 29, 46.

116   *Civil Law (Wrongs) Act 2002* (ACT), s 107G; *Civil Liability Act 2002* (NSW), s 35A; *Proportionate Liability Act 2005* (NT), s 12; *Civil Liability Act 2003* (Qld), s 32 (order of several liability as additional sanction); *Law Reform (Contributory Negligence and Apportionment of Liability) Act 2001* (SA), s 10; *Civil Liability Act 2002* (Tas), s 43D; *Civil Liability Act 2002* (WA), s 5AKA. Rules of court could impose further sanctions: R McDougall, 'Proportionate Liability in Construction Litigation' (2006) 22 BCL 394, 398–99.

117   *Civil Law (Wrongs) Act 2002* (ACT), s 107F(4); *Civil Liability Act 2002* (NSW), s 35(4); *Proportionate Liability Act 2005* (NT), s 10; *Civil Liability Act 2003* (Qld), s 31(4); *Law Reform (Contributory Negligence and Apportionment of Liability) Act 2001* (SA), ss 8(2)(b), 11; *Civil Liability Act 2002* (Tas), s 43B(4); *Civil Liability Act 2002* (WA), s 5AK(4).

118   And should in principle have a claim for contribution against the wrongdoers not sued. This claim is expressly provided for in the *Civil Liability Act 2003* (Qld), s 32H.

wrongdoer is still better off than under a regime of solidary liability. However, the statutes of all jurisdictions except Victoria[119] unconditionally permit[120] or even oblige[121] the court to consider the comparative responsibility of any concurrent wrongdoer who is not party to the proceedings.[122] The defendant bears the onus of pleading and proving the existence of a concurrent wrongdoer who is not party to the proceedings.[123]

[4.36]   If the court considers the comparative responsibility of a concurrent wrongdoer who is not party to the proceedings, the plaintiff will need to bring an action against that wrongdoer in order to obtain full compensation.[124] But that wrongdoer is not bound by the judgment in the first action and is free to contest liability.[125] The South Australian statute provides that the first judgment determines, for the purpose of all other actions, the amount of the plaintiff's loss, the shares of the wrongdoers sued in the first action, and the share (if any) borne by the plaintiff by virtue of contributory negligence.[126] The statutes of the other jurisdictions merely provide that in subsequent proceedings the plaintiff can recover no more than the difference between her loss and the damages recovered in previous proceedings.[127] Those statutes do not prevent the plaintiff from pleading in the second action that her loss is (now) larger than assessed in the first action.[128] Nor do they prevent undercompensation since the second court is free to find that the shares of the wrongdoers sued in the first action are to be larger than fixed by the first court.[129]

---

119   Section 24AI(3) of the *Wrongs Act 1958* (Vic) allows a consideration of non-party wrongdoers only if they are dead or wound up.
120   *Civil Law (Wrongs) Act 2002* (ACT), s 107F(2)(b); *Civil Liability Act 2002* (NSW), s 35(3)(b); *Proportionate Liability Act 2005* (NT), s 13(2)(b); *Civil Liability Act 2003* (Qld), s 31(3).
121   *Law Reform (Contributory Negligence and Apportionment of Liability) Act 2001* (SA), s 8(2)(b); *Civil Liability Act 2002* (Tas), s 43B(3)(b); *Civil Liability Act 2002* (WA), s 5AK(3)(b).
122   Only persons liable towards the plaintiff can be considered: *Shrimp v Landmark Operations Ltd* [2007] FCA 1468, (2007) 163 FCR 510 [59]. See also *Commonwealth Bank of Australia v Witherow* [2006] VSCA 45 [11]–[14].
123   *Ucak v Avante Developments Pty Ltd* [2007] NSWSC 367 [34]–[35]; *GEJ & MA Geldard Pty Ltd v Mobbs (No 2)* [2011] QSC 33, [2012] 1 Qd R 120 [59]–[60]; *Hart v JGC Accounting and Financial Services Pty Ltd* [2015] WASCA 22, (2015) 47 WAR 582 [25]–[26]; R McDougall, 'Proportionate Liability in Construction Litigation' (2006) 22 BCL 394, 400.
124   The statutes expressly reserve the plaintiff's right to separate actions: *Civil Law (Wrongs) Act 2002* (ACT), s 107I (1); *Civil Liability Act 2002* (NSW), s 37(1); *Proportionate Liability Act 2005* (NT), s 16(1); *Civil Liability Act 2003* (Qld), s 32B(1); *Law Reform (Contributory Negligence and Apportionment of Liability) Act 2001* (SA), s 11; *Civil Liability Act 2002* (Tas), s 43E(1); *Wrongs Act 1958* (Vic), s 24AK(1); *Civil Liability Act 2002* (WA), s 5AM(1).
125   *Fudlovski v JGC Accounting and Financial Services Pty Ltd (No 2)* [2013] WASC 301 [43]; B McDonald, 'Proportionate Liability in Australia: The Devil in the Detail' (2005) 26 Aust Bar Rev 29, 41.
126   *Law Reform (Contributory Negligence and Apportionment of Liability) Act 2001* (SA), s 11.
127   *Civil Law (Wrongs) Act 2002* (ACT), s 107I(2); *Civil Liability Act 2002* (NSW), s 37(2); *Proportionate Liability Act 2005* (NT), s 16(2); *Civil Liability Act 2003* (Qld), s 32B(2); *Civil Liability Act 2002* (Tas), s 43E(2); *Wrongs Act 1958* (Vic), s 24AK(2); *Civil Liability Act 2002* (WA), s 5AM(2).
128   B McDonald, 'Proportionate Liability in Australia: The Devil in the Detail' (2005) 26 Aust Bar Rev 29, 43; J Watson, 'From Contribution to Apportioned Contribution to Proportionate Liability' (2004) 78 Aust LJ 126, 147.
129   *Fudlovski v JGC Accounting and Financial Services Pty Ltd (No 2)* [2013] WASC 301 [43]; O Hayford, 'Proportionate Liability – Its Impact on Risk Allocation in Construction Contracts' (2006) 22 BCL 322, 325.

A wrongdoer who fraudulently caused the plaintiff's damage does not enjoy the benefit of proportionate liability.[130] The statutes of all jurisdictions other than Victoria further exclude a wrongdoer who intended to cause the plaintiff's damage, not just the action causing the damage.[131] The statute of Queensland further excludes a person liable for contravention of s 18 of the Australian Consumer Law.[132] For convenience, a wrongdoer who does not enjoy the benefit of proportionate liability on the grounds mentioned will be called an 'intentional wrongdoer'. An intentional wrongdoer remains subject to the legal rules that apply apart from the proportionate liability statute,[133] and thus the common law rule of solidary liability.[134] Thus, the plaintiff can claim full compensation from an intentional wrongdoer.

[4.37]

An intentional wrongdoer who ends up paying for the whole of the plaintiff's damage should in principle be entitled to claim contribution from the other wrongdoers. The statute of the Northern Territory excludes such a claim,[135] whereas the South Australian statute expressly allows it (but probably only if there is a claim under the contribution statute or at common law).[136] The statutes of the other jurisdictions provide that a wrongdoer against whom judgment is given in relation to an 'apportionable claim' cannot be required to indemnify or pay contribution to another concurrent wrongdoer in relation to the apportionable claim.[137] Since the claim against an intentional wrongdoer is not 'apportionable', those statutes do not exclude a contribution claim by an intentional wrongdoer, which is thus governed by the contribution statute or by the rules of the common law and equity.[138]

[4.38]

The question arises whether the exclusion of contribution and indemnity between wrongdoers who are proportionately liable applies to contractual entitlements to contribution or indemnity. Some statutes expressly preserve the enforceability of such agreements.[139] It might be thought that the same position ought to obtain in the jurisdictions whose statutes are silent

[4.39]

---

130   *Civil Law (Wrongs) Act 2002* (ACT), s 107E(1); *Civil Liability Act 2002* (NSW), s 34A(1)(b); *Proportionate Liability Act 2005* (NT), s 7(1), (2); *Civil Liability Act 2003* (Qld), s 32D; *Law Reform (Contributory Negligence and Apportionment of Liability) Act 2001* (SA), s 3(2)(c); *Civil Liability Act 2002* (Tas), s 43A(5)(b); *Wrongs Act 1958* (Vic), s 24AM; *Civil Liability Act 2002* (WA), s 5AJA(1)(b).

131   *Civil Law (Wrongs) Act 2002* (ACT), s 107E(1); *Civil Liability Act 2002* (NSW), s 34A(1)(a); *Proportionate Liability Act 2005* (NT), s 7(1), (2); *Civil Liability Act 2003* (Qld), s 32E; *Law Reform (Contributory Negligence and Apportionment of Liability) Act 2001* (SA), s 3(2)(c); *Civil Liability Act 2002* (Tas), s 43A(5)(a); *Civil Liability Act 2002* (WA), s 5AJA(1)(a). The same may apply in Victoria since intended harm is not strictly 'arising from a failure to take reasonable care': P Megens and B Cubitt, 'Contract or Conflict? An Overview of the Proportionate Liability Regime and Its Difficulties' (2009) 23 CLQ 3, 7.

132   *Civil Liability Act 2003* (Qld), s 32F.

133   *Civil Law (Wrongs) Act 2002* (ACT), s 107E(2); *Civil Liability Act 2002* (NSW), s 34A(2); *Proportionate Liability Act 2005* (NT), s 7(3); *Civil Liability Act 2002* (Tas), s 43A(6); *Civil Liability Act 2002* (WA), s 5AJA(2).

134   Solidary liability is expressly provided for by the *Civil Liability Act 2003* (Qld), ss 32D–32F; *Wrongs Act 1958* (Vic), s 24AM.

135   *Proportionate Liability Act 2005* (NT), s 15(1).

136   *Law Reform (Contributory Negligence and Apportionment of Liability) Act 2001* (SA), s 9(c).

137   *Civil Law (Wrongs) Act 2002* (ACT), s 107H; *Civil Liability Act 2002* (NSW), s 36; *Civil Liability Act 2003* (Qld), s 32A; *Civil Liability Act 2002* (Tas), s 43C(1); *Wrongs Act 1958* (Vic), s 24AJ; *Civil Liability Act 2002* (WA), s 5AL(1).

138   See VJ Vann, 'Equity and Proportionate Liability' (2007) 1 J Eq 199, 204.

139   *Proportionate Liability Act 2005* (NT), s 15(2); *Civil Liability Act 2002* (Tas), s 43C(2); *Civil Liability Act 2002* (WA), s 5AL(2).

on the issue.[140] However, the overriding effect of an agreement to contribute or indemnify is an aspect of the broader question of whether a contracting out of the proportionate liability regime is possible.[141] The statutes of New South Wales, Tasmania and Western Australia expressly permit a contracting out,[142] while the statute of Queensland expressly prohibits it.[143] The statutes of the other jurisdictions, including the federal statutes, are silent on the issue, which has been interpreted as a tacit prohibition of contracting-out.[144] A contracting out, where permitted, may be implied from the terms of the contract and does not require a reference to the proportionate liability statute.[145]

V   Interplay of the three regimes

[4.40]   Each state and territory has three regimes governing the liability of concurrent wrongdoers: the common law rules, the contribution statute and the proportionate liability statute. The existence of three regimes, each of which is complex enough, makes this area of law difficult to tackle. The following will set out a broad algorithm for approaching cases of concurrent wrongdoers. Many details are omitted, not least because there is variation between the jurisdictions.

[4.41]   Once it is established that two or more wrongdoers are liable for the same indivisible harm, it must be asked whether any statute expressly prescribes solidary liability in the circumstances.[146] If that is the case, the question of contribution may have to be addressed, as outlined below. Otherwise, it must be asked whether the proportionate liability statute applies in terms of the source of liability (contract, tort, and so on), the type of damage (personal injury or not), the type of claim (consumer claim and so on) and the category of wrongdoer (intentional wrongdoer, joint wrongdoer, and so on). A wrongdoer who can invoke a proportionate liability statute is liable towards the plaintiff for only a part of the plaintiff's damage, the size of which depends upon that wrongdoer's share in the responsibility for the damage. There are no claims between such wrongdoers.

140   O Hayford, 'Proportionate Liability – Its Impact on Risk Allocation in Construction Contracts' (2006) 22 BCL 322, 333–35; B McDonald and JW Carter, 'The Lottery of Contractual Risk Allocation and Proportionate Liability' (2009) 26 J Cont L 1, 20.

141   *Kheirs Financial Services Pty Ltd v Aussie Home Loans Pty Ltd* [2010] VSCA 355, (2010) 31 VR 46 [96]; *Bathurst Regional Council v Local Government Financial Services Pty Ltd (No 5)* [2012] FCA 1200 [3483]–[3484].

142   *Civil Liability Act 2002* (NSW), s 3A(2); *Civil Liability Act 2002* (Tas), s 3A(3); *Civil Liability Act 2002* (WA), ss 4A, 5AJ(2)(b).

143   *Civil Liability Act 2003* (Qld), s 7(3).

144   *Kheirs Financial Services Pty Ltd v Aussie Home Loans Pty Ltd* [2010] VSCA 355, (2010) 31 VR 46 [96], for the *Wrongs Act 1958* (Vic); *Bathurst Regional Council v Local Government Financial Services Pty Ltd (No 5)* [2012] FCA 1200 [3483]–[3484], for the *Corporations Act 2001* (Cth). See also O Hayford, 'Proportionate Liability – Its Impact on Risk Allocation in Construction Contracts' (2006) 22 BCL 322, 338.

145   *Aquagenics Pty Ltd v Break O'Day Council* [2010] TASFC 3, (2010) 20 Tas R 239 [15]–[17], [71], [111]. The possibility of an implied contracting out was not considered in *Reinhold v New South Wales Lotteries Corporation (No 2)* [2008] NSWSC 187, (2008) 82 NSWLR 762 [84]–[85].

146   An example is the *Navigation Regulation 2013* (Cth), reg 14(1): 'If a person on board a vessel suffers a personal injury or dies because of the fault of the vessel and of another vessel, the liability of the owners of the vessels is joint and several.'

If legislation expressly prescribes solidary liability in the circumstances or if the proportionate liability statute does not apply in any event, the wrongdoers are under solidary liability, and the question arises whether a wrongdoer who has made a payment to the plaintiff (for the whole damage or part of it) can claim contribution from the other wrongdoers. It must first be asked whether the contribution statute applies to the relevant cause of action, which will always be the case in Victoria. If the contribution statute applies, the court will apportion liability according to each wrongdoer's responsibility for the damage, shares of nil and 100% being possible. A wrongdoer who has paid more to the plaintiff than his fair share can claim contribution from the other wrongdoers. [4.42]

If (outside Victoria) the contribution statute does not apply, the rules of the common law and equity will apply and it must be asked whether the wrongdoers' liabilities are 'co-ordinate' – that is, 'of the same nature and to the same extent'. If they are, each wrongdoer must ultimately pay for a part of the plaintiff's loss. At least as a general rule, the wrongdoers' shares are equal. A wrongdoer who has paid more to the plaintiff than her share can claim contribution from the other wrongdoers. An exception exists where all wrongdoers are liable in tort, in which case no claim for contribution lies at common law. But the exception is relevant only in the Australian Capital Territory since the contribution statutes of all other jurisdictions apply to every claim in tort. [4.43]

In conclusion, the rules governing the liability of concurrent wrongdoers in Australian law are far from satisfactory. Each jurisdiction has three regimes: the common law rules, the contribution statute and the proportionate liability statute. Each regime has awkward rules and uncertainties. In addition, the statutory rules vary between the jurisdictions. This raises complex choice-of-law issues where the laws of different jurisdictions govern the liabilities of the various concurrent wrongdoers.[147] It is to be welcomed that in 2011 the then Standing Council on Law and Justice released a consultation draft of model proportionate liability provisions to be adopted throughout Australia. Model provisions on the entire liability regime of concurrent wrongdoers would be even better. [4.44]

---

147   See *Kheirs Financial Services Pty Ltd v Aussie Home Loans Pty Ltd* [2010] VSCA 355, (2010) 31 VR 46 [96]–[98].

PART **2**

COMPENSATION IN SPECIFIC CONTEXTS

5

COMPENSATION FOR BREACH OF CONTRACT

I   Introduction

[5.1]   A contract may be breached by one party (the defendant) through defective performance, delayed performance, or a total failure to perform. If the contract breached is enforceable at common law, the innocent party (the plaintiff) can generally claim common law damages for any loss suffered as a result of the breach.[1] The assessment of such damages and the attribution of responsibility for such loss are generally governed by the rules discussed in Chs 2 to 4 for civil wrongs in general. Specific rules for breach of contract are discussed in this chapter.

[5.2]   At common law, the plaintiff is entitled to terminate the contract if the defendant has repudiated the contract, breached a condition or committed a sufficiently serious breach of an intermediate term.[2] A termination of the contract on one of those grounds absolves both parties from further performance,[3] and entitles the plaintiff (in addition to rights already accrued) to damages for the loss of further performance by the defendant.[4] Those damages, which are often called loss of bargain damages, are assessed under the same rules as other damages for breach of contract. Loss of bargain damages cannot be claimed while the contract remains on foot.[5] They cannot be claimed even where the contract has been terminated pursuant to a contractual right to terminate, unless a right to terminate existed at common law or the contract expressly provides for loss of bargain damages.[6] The discussion of damages for non-performance in this chapter assumes that the defendant is no longer entitled or required to perform the relevant obligation in specie.

II   Assessment of compensation

A   Protection of the plaintiff's expectation interest

[5.3]   'Expectation damages' are the primary measure of compensation for breach of contract.[7] The obligation to pay expectation damages is a pecuniary *substitute* for the primary right to performance of the contractual obligation (sometimes called the plaintiff's 'performance interest'[8]). The courts attempt to put the plaintiff in the net financial position she would have been in had the defendant performed the contract.[9] This is easier to achieve if there is a market for the goods or services that are the subject matter of the contract, as expectation damages are generally assessed by reference to the market price of the goods or services at the time of the

---

1   Where a contract breached is enforceable in equity but not at common law (because the contract does not comply with a statutory requirement of written form but has been partly performed), the court may award equitable damages under Lord Cairns' Act, discussed in Ch 12: *McKendrick & Co Pty Ltd v Fush* [2001] VSC 95 [82]; *Townsend v Townsend* [2006] NTSC 7.

2   Eg *Koompahtoo Local Aboriginal Land Council v Sanpine Pty Ltd* [2007] HCA 61, (2007) 233 CLR 115.

3   Eg *McDonald v Dennys Lascelles Ltd* (1933) 48 CLR 457, 476–77 (Dixon J).

4   Eg *Progressive Mailing House Pty Ltd v Tabali Pty Ltd* (1985) 157 CLR 17, 31.

5   Ibid; *Sunbird Plaza Pty Ltd v Maloney* (1988) 166 CLR 245, 260–61, 273.

6   *Shevill v Builders Licensing Board* (1982) 149 CLR 620.

7   Eg *Commonwealth v Amann Aviation Pty Ltd* (1991) 174 CLR 64, 80–81, 161.

8   D Friedmann, 'The Performance Interest in Contract Damages' (1995) 111 LQR 628; B Coote, 'Contract Damages, *Ruxley*, and the Performance Interest' (1997) 56 Camb LJ 537, 566; see also B Coote, 'The Performance Interest, *Panatown*, and the Problem of Loss' (2001) 117 LQR 81.

9   For classic statements of this principle, see *Robinson v Harman* (1848) 1 Ex 850, 855; 154 ER 363, 365 (Parke B); *Wertheim v Chicoutimi Pulp Co* [1911] AC 301, 307 (Lord Atkinson).

breach. The courts ascertain the cost of a substitute performance at the market rate. They then calculate the difference between the cost of the substitute performance and the cost of the performance promised by the defendant. This approach does not work where there is no market, and sometimes contract law has to adopt other measures.

The term 'expectation interest' originates from Fuller and Perdue's seminal article in which they identified three interests protected by awards of contractual damages.[10] First, a plaintiff who has conferred some value on the defendant in reliance on the defendant performing the contract has a 'restitution interest', which may be protected by requiring the defendant to disgorge the value received from the plaintiff.[11] Secondly, a plaintiff who has changed his position in reliance on the defendant performing the contract (by foregoing other business opportunities, for example) has a 'reliance interest', which may be protected by placing the plaintiff financially in the position as if the contract had not been made. Thirdly, the plaintiff always has an 'expectation interest' in obtaining the promised performance, which may be protected by placing the plaintiff financially in as good a position as if the defendant had performed (if specific relief is not ordered).[12]   [5.4]

Fuller and Perdue argued that 'ordinary standards of justice' would regard the need for judicial intervention as strongest in respect of the restitution interest and weakest in respect of the expectation interest. They argued that a plaintiff who has changed her position in reliance on the defendant's promise has a stronger case for protection than a plaintiff who has not, and a plaintiff who has enriched the defendant by relying on the latter's promise has a stronger case for protection than a plaintiff who has not.[13]   [5.5]

While the courts have adopted Fuller and Perdue's terminology,[14] they have not adopted their preference for reliance damages. Compensation of expectation loss remains the usual objective of contractual damages. On several occasions,[15] the High Court of Australia has approved the following statement made by Parke B in *Robinson v Harman*:   [5.6]

> [W]here a party sustains a loss by reason of a breach of contract, he is, so far as money can do it, to be placed in the same situation, with respect to damages, as if the contract had been performed.[16]

---

10   LL Fuller and WR Perdue, 'The Reliance Interest in Contract Damages' (1936) 46 Yale LJ 52.

11   Disgorgement for breach of contract is discussed at [16.48]–[16.58], and restitution is discussed in Ch 17.

12   LL Fuller and WR Perdue, 'The Reliance Interest in Contract Damages' (1936) 46 Yale LJ 52, 53–54. The expectation interest comprises the interest in obtaining actual performance and the interest in being compensated for loss resulting from non-performance: B Coote, 'Contract Damages, *Ruxley* and the Performance Interest' (1997) 56 Camb LJ 537, 541–42; C Webb, 'Performance and Compensation: An Analysis of Contract Damages and Contractual Obligation' (2006) 26 OJLS 41, 46–49.

13   LL Fuller and WR Perdue, 'The Reliance Interest in Contract Damages' (1936) 46 Yale LJ 52, 56.

14   Eg *Commonwealth v Amann Aviation Pty Ltd* (1991) 174 CLR 64, 134 (Toohey J); *Baird Textile Holdings Ltd v Marks & Spencer plc* [2001] CLC 999, 1017 (Mance LJ). The terminology has even been adopted outside contract law: *Dwyer v Kaljo* (1992) 27 NSWLR 728, 744 (adjustment of property interests after breakdown of de facto relationship).

15   *Wenham v Ella* (1972) 127 CLR 454, 471; *Burns v MAN Automotive (Australia) Pty Ltd* (1986) 161 CLR 653, 667; *Commonwealth v Amann Aviation Pty Ltd* (1991) 174 CLR 64, 80, 98, 134, 148, 161; *Tabcorp Holdings Ltd v Bowen Investments Pty Ltd* [2009] HCA 8, (2009) 236 CLR 272 [13]; *Clark v Macourt* [2013] HCA 56, (2013) 253 CLR 1 [26], [60], [106].

16   (1848) 1 Ex 850, 855; 154 ER 363, 365.

The corollary of that principle is that a plaintiff is not entitled, by an award of damages, to be placed in a position superior to that which the plaintiff would have been in had the contract been performed.[17]

[5.7]   A plaintiff who has suffered expectation loss is entitled to compensation for that loss, subject to limiting principles. The plaintiff bears the onus of proving the loss.[18] The rules on the resolution of uncertainty in respect of actual and hypothetical events are discussed at [2.57]–[2.117]. A plaintiff who cannot establish a loss will receive only nominal damages. Courts accept, however, that plaintiffs will not always be able to produce precise evidence of the loss suffered as a result of the defendant's breach. Courts have reiterated that 'mere difficulty' in estimating damages does not relieve a court of the responsibility of placing a value on the lost performance, at least insofar as this difficulty is not attributable to the plaintiff herself.[19]

[5.8]   The other two interests identified by Fuller and Perdue remain of practical significance. Reliance loss has been used as a 'proxy' for expectation loss (see [5.57]–[5.72]), and the defendant must pay back money received from the plaintiff where the contract has been terminated and there is a total failure of consideration.[20]

B   Measure of expectation loss in particular contexts

[5.9]   As noted earlier, for commercial contracts, expectation damages will commonly be based on the plaintiff's loss of profit arising from the breach. In *Commonwealth v Amann Aviation Pty Ltd*, Mason CJ and Dawson J explained:

> In the ordinary course of commercial dealings, a party supplying goods or rendering services will enter a contract with a view to securing a profit, that is to say, that a party will expect a certain margin of gain to be achieved in addition to the recouping of any expenses reasonably incurred by it in the discharge of its contractual obligations. It is for this reason that expectation damages are often described as damages for loss of profits. Damages recoverable as lost profits are constituted by the combination of expenses justifiably incurred by a plaintiff in the discharge of contractual obligations and any amount by which gross receipts would have exceeded those expenses. This second amount is net profit.[21]

[5.10]   Net profit is the difference between gross revenue and expenses necessary to obtain that revenue. Damages for loss of profit must be calculated by either adding the amount of expenses incurred to the amount of net profit, or by deducting saved expenses from the gross

---

17   *Commonwealth v Amann Aviation Pty Ltd* (1991) 174 CLR 64, 82; *Clark v Macourt* [2013] HCA 56, (2013) 253 CLR 1 [27], [60].

18   *Commonwealth v Amann Aviation Pty Ltd* (1991) 174 CLR 64, 80, 99, 118, 137–38; *JLW (Vic) Pty Ltd v Tsiloglou* [1994] 1 VR 237, 241, 243. The plaintiff must provide evidence not only in respect of lost gross revenue but also in respect of the expenditure necessary to obtain that revenue. Failure to provide evidence on the expenditure may lead to a denial of compensation: *Airloom Holdings Pty Ltd v Thales Australia Ltd* [2011] NSWSC 1513.

19   *Placer (Granny Smith) Pty Ltd v Thiess Contractors Pty Ltd* [2003] HCA 10, (2003) 196 ALR 257 [38].

20   *Roxborough v Rothmans of Pall Mall Australia Ltd* (2001) 208 CLR 516.

21   (1991) 174 CLR 64, 81.

revenue.[22] Overhead costs (the fixed costs of running the plaintiff's business which are not increased by the contract with the defendant) are not saved in consequence of the defendant's breach, and no proportion of them should be deducted from gross revenue.[23]

It is helpful to illustrate the basic calculations with a practical example. Suppose that   [5.11]
Xenophon has a contract with Yolanda for the supply of 200 widgets for which Xenophon pays $200. Yolanda breaches the contract by failing to supply the widgets. Xenophon terminates the contract and purchases 200 widgets for $300 from Zelda. Xenophon had been planning to sell the widgets to consumers for $2 each (they were worth $400 on the market), and make a $200 profit, but because of Yolanda's breach Xenophon has made only $100 profit. In order to work out the value of the promised performance, the court looks at the profit Xenophon has lost. He had to pay $100 more for the widgets than he would have done if Yolanda had not breached her contract, and this is the measure of his expectation loss (subject to limiting principles such as mitigation).

However, suppose that Yolanda supplied Xenophon with defective widgets for which he paid   [5.12]
$200, and the goods he receives are saleable for only $350. If the widgets had complied with the specifications, he would have been able to sell them for $400. Xenophon's expectation loss is the difference between the actual value of the goods and the value they would have had if they had complied with the contract. Xenophon's loss is $50, being the loss in value as a result of the defect (subject to the limiting principles of remoteness and mitigation). The similarity with the previous example is evident. The court looks to the performance Xenophon was promised and the performance Xenophon actually received, and gives Xenophon the difference between the two. This is enshrined in the sale-of-goods legislation.[24] This will be discussed in detail directly below.

1   Failure to deliver goods as promised

A seller of goods may breach the contract by delivering the goods later than promised, by   [5.13]
delivering defective goods, or by failing to deliver the goods at all.[25] This section discusses the assessment of the buyer's damages for the seller's breach under the practically identical sale-of-goods statutes of the states and territories, supplemented by the common law. Remedies for breach of a consumer guarantee under the Australian Consumer Law will not be discussed.

The sale-of-goods statutes provide that the measure of damages for non-delivery of the   [5.14]
goods is the loss directly and naturally resulting in the ordinary course of events from the seller's breach.[26] This enshrines the first limb of the contractual remoteness test laid down in *Hadley v Baxendale*,[27] considered at [5.89]–[5.90]. The second limb of that test concerns

---

22   *TC Industrial Plant Pty Ltd v Robert's Queensland Pty Ltd* (1963) 180 CLR 130, 142–43.
23   *North Sydney Leagues' Club Ltd v Synergy Protection Agency Pty Ltd* [2012] NSWCA 168, (2012) 83 NSWLR 710 [46].
24   See *Sale of Goods Act 1954* (ACT), ss 53(3), 54(3), 56(3); *Sale of Goods Act 1923* (NSW), ss 52(3), 53(3), 54(3); *Sale of Goods Act* (NT), ss 51(3), 53(3), 54(3); *Sale of Goods Act 1896* (Qld), ss 52(3), 53(3), 54(3); *Sale of Goods Act 1895* (SA), ss 49(3), 50(3), 52(3); *Sale of Goods Act 1896* (Tas), ss 54(3), 55(3), 57(3); *Goods Act 1958* (Vic), ss 56(3), 57(3), 59(3); *Sale of Goods Act 1895* (WA), ss 49(3), 50(3), 52(3).
25   In the case of non-delivery, the buyer may obtain specific performance if the goods are unique; see [10.34]–[10.38].
26   *Sale of Goods Act 1954* (ACT), s 54(2); *Sale of Goods Act 1923* (NSW), s 53(2); *Sale of Goods Act* (NT), s 53(2); *Sale of Goods Act 1896* (Qld), s 52(2); *Sale of Goods Act 1895* (SA), s 50(2); *Sale of Goods Act 1896* (Tas), s 55(2); *Goods Act 1958* (Vic), s 57(2); *Sale of Goods Act 1895* (WA), s 50(2).
27   (1854) 9 Ex 341, 354; 156 ER 145, 151.

unusual loss resulting from special circumstances known to the defendant. The sale-of-goods statutes do not exclude compensation of such loss since they preserve the buyer's right to recover 'special damages'.[28]

[5.15]   Where there is an available market[29] for goods of the contractual description at the time and place of the seller's failure to deliver, the sale-of-goods statutes provide that the measure of damages is prima facie the difference between the contract price and the market price of the goods at the time when they ought to have been delivered or, if no time was fixed, at the time of the refusal to deliver.[30] This rule presupposes that the buyer has not paid the price, and must be adjusted if the buyer has paid. It assumes that a reasonable buyer will buy substitute goods as soon as the seller's breach is known,[31] and thus reflects the mitigation principle; see [3.135]. Any subsequent movement in the market price will not affect the seller's liability. Where the market price at the time of the breach is the same as, or lower than, the contract price and there is no other recoverable loss, nominal damages may be awarded.[32]

[5.16]   The difference between the contract price and the market price of the goods is only prima facie the measure of the buyer's damages for non-delivery, and gives way to a more accurate assessment of the buyer's loss where appropriate. In particular, a buyer who resold the goods at a higher price than their market price at the time of breach can claim the difference between the contract price and the resale price,[33] subject to remoteness and mitigation.[34] Conversely, a buyer who resold the goods at a lower price than their market price at the time of breach is entitled to damages measured by the difference between the contract price and the market price at the time of breach.[35] This rule reflects the buyer's loss where the buyer has bought substitute goods to fulfil the subcontract, but may lead to overcompensation otherwise.[36] Where the buyer, immediately after the seller's breach, managed to obtain substitute goods

28   *Sale of Goods Act 1954* (ACT), s 57; *Sale of Goods Act 1923* (NSW), s 55; *Sale of Goods Act* (NT), s 55; *Sale of Goods Act 1896* (Qld), s 55; *Sale of Goods Act 1895* (SA), s 53; *Sale of Goods Act 1896* (Tas), s 58; *Goods Act 1958* (Vic), s 60; *Sale of Goods Act 1895* (WA), s 53. See *Motium Pty Ltd v Arrow Electronics Australia Pty Ltd* [2011] WASCA 65 [71].

29   Which requires the presence of sellers capable of supplying the relevant goods: *Armour v Fewster* [2004] SADC 1 [45].

30   *Sale of Goods Act 1954* (ACT), s 54(3); *Sale of Goods Act 1923* (NSW), s 53(3); *Sale of Goods Act* (NT), s 53(3); *Sale of Goods Act 1896* (Qld), s 52(3); *Sale of Goods Act 1895* (SA), s 50(3); *Sale of Goods Act 1896* (Tas), s 55(3); *Goods Act 1958* (Vic), s 57(3); *Sale of Goods Act 1895* (WA), s 50(3).

31   *Radford v De Froberville* [1977] 1 WLR 1262, 1285; *Manwelland Pty Ltd v Dames & Moore Pty Ltd* [2001] QCA 436, (2002) ASAL 55–074 [11].

32   *Francis v Lyon* (1907) 4 CLR 1023, 1042–43; *Keynes v Rural Directions Pty Ltd (No 2)* [2009] FCA 567, (2009) 72 ACSR 264 [70].

33   *Joseph & Co Pty Ltd v Harvest Grain Co Pty Ltd* (1996) 39 NSWLR 722, 729–35 (where conflicting English decisions are examined in depth); *Becker Group Ltd v Motion Picture Company of Australia Ltd* [2004] FCA 630 [102].

34   The buyer is normally expected to acquire substitute goods in the market to fulfil the contract with the sub-buyer. However, the acquisition of substitute goods, even if carried out expeditiously, may take too long to keep the delivery date under the subcontract.

35   *Williams Brothers v Ed T Agius Ltd* [1914] AC 510. See also *Clark v Macourt* [2013] HCA 56, (2013) 253 CLR 1 (discussed at [5.51]–[5.56]); *Ailakis v Olivero* [2014] WASCA 127, (2014) 100 ACSR 524 [130].

36   A Burrows, *Remedies for Torts and Breach of Contract* (3rd edn, OUP 2004) 213. Some scholars see the damages as a substitute for performance and not as compensation for loss; see [1.57]–[1.58].

at less than the market price, the measure of damages ought to be the difference between the contract price and the price actually paid.[37]

Where there is no available market for goods of the contractual description, the court [5.17] determines the value of the goods at the time and place of the failure to deliver.[38] Evidence of such value can be the cost of the nearest equivalent,[39] even if of superior quality,[40] or the price at which the buyer resold the goods unless the resale was made too long before the time of breach to provide a reliable indicator for the price of the goods at the time of breach.[41] Where a resale was foreseeable, the measure of the buyer's damages is the difference between the contract price and the resale price, even if the latter is higher than the value of the goods at the time of breach.[42] In circumstances in which the seller must compensate the buyer's loss of profit on a resale, the seller must also compensate the buyer for being liable towards the sub-buyer.[43]

Where a defect in the goods entitles the buyer to reject them and the buyer does so, [5.18] damages will be measured on the basis that the seller has not delivered at all. Where the buyer has no right of rejection or accepts the goods, the principles governing the measure of the buyer's damages are still similar to the principles applying in cases of non-delivery. The sale-of-goods statutes enshrine the first limb of *Hadley v Baxendale* by providing that the measure of damages is the loss directly and naturally resulting in the ordinary course of events from the seller's breach of warranty,[44] and they enshrine the second limb of *Hadley v Baxendale* by preserving the buyer's right to claim 'special damages' as well.[45]

The sale-of-goods statutes provide that the buyer's loss is prima facie the difference [5.19] between the value of the goods at the time of delivery to the buyer and the value they would have had at that time had they complied with the contract.[46] Thus, the prima facie measure of

---

37   F Dawson, 'The Remedies of the Buyer' in M Bridge (ed), *Benjamin's Sale of Goods* (10th edn, Sweet & Maxwell 2017) [17–019].

38   *Francis v Lyon* (1907) 4 CLR 1023, 1042; *Tallerman & Co Pty Ltd v Nathan's Merchandise (Victoria) Pty Ltd* (1957) 98 CLR 93, 128.

39   *Rio Tinto Exploration Pty Ltd v Graphite Holdings Pty Ltd* [2007] WASCA 276 [37], [43]. In that case, the defendant failed to deliver drill core samples obtained through mining activity. The plaintiff recovered the cost of re-creating the drill core samples.

40   *Hinde v Liddell* (1875) LR 10 QB 265; *Blackburn Bobbin Co Ltd v TW Allen & Sons Ltd* [1918] 1 KB 540, 554. Where the buyer has resold the substitute goods at an extra profit because they were of better quality than goods of the contractual description, that extra profit must be deducted from the cost of buying the substitute goods: *Hinde v Liddell* (1875) LR 10 QB 265, 270.

41   *The Arpad* [1934] P 189.

42   *Patrick v Russo-British Grain Export Co Ltd* [1927] 2 KB 535.

43   *Grébert-Borgnis v J & W Nugent* (1885) 15 QBD 85; *R & H Hall Ltd v WH Pim (Junior) & Co* [1928] All ER Rep 763.

44   *Sale of Goods Act 1954* (ACT), s 56(2); *Sale of Goods Act 1923* (NSW), s 54(2); *Sale of Goods Act* (NT), s 54(2); *Sale of Goods Act 1896* (Qld), s 54(2); *Sale of Goods Act 1895* (SA), s 52(2); *Sale of Goods Act 1896* (Tas), s 57(2); *Goods Act 1958* (Vic), s 59(2); *Sale of Goods Act 1895* (WA), s 52(2).

45   *Sale of Goods Act 1954* (ACT), s 57; *Sale of Goods Act 1923* (NSW), s 55; *Sale of Goods Act* (NT), s 55; *Sale of Goods Act 1896* (Qld), s 55; *Sale of Goods Act 1895* (SA), s 53; *Sale of Goods Act 1896* (Tas), s 58; *Goods Act 1958* (Vic), s 60; *Sale of Goods Act 1895* (WA), s 53.

46   *Sale of Goods Act 1954* (ACT), s 56(3); *Sale of Goods Act 1923* (NSW), s 54(3); *Sale of Goods Act* (NT), s 54(3); *Sale of Goods Act 1896* (Qld), s 54(3); *Sale of Goods Act 1895* (SA), s 52(3); *Sale of Goods Act 1896* (Tas), s 57(3); *Goods Act 1958* (Vic), s 59(3); *Sale of Goods Act 1895* (WA), s 52(3).

loss is diminution in value rather than the cost of rectifying the defect.[47] This rule reflects the fact that the buyer is often able to acquire goods of the contractual description in the market, and an award of diminution in value (together with the proceeds of a sale of the defective goods) enables the buyer to do so.[48] But where substitute goods cannot be obtained, the cost of rectifying the defect may constitute the buyer's loss.[49]

[5.20]   The defective condition of the goods may cause further loss, which can be recovered if it was in the parties' contemplation at the time of the contract; see [5.89]–[5.93]. Subject to mitigation and remoteness, the additional loss is recoverable where the defective condition of the goods has caused further deterioration of the goods themselves,[50] damage to other property of the buyer,[51] personal injury of the buyer,[52] loss of profit,[53] or damage to third parties' property, or personal injury of third parties, for which the buyer is liable.[54] Where the buyer has resold the goods and is liable towards the sub-buyer because of the defect, the seller must indemnify the buyer if it was foreseeable that the buyer would resell the goods and that a breach by the seller would cause the buyer to breach the subcontract.[55]

[5.21]   A resale of the goods may lead to a higher, but not a lower, amount of damages than the prima facie measure. In *Clark v Macourt*,[56] discussed at [5.51]–[5.56], the High Court of Australia held that damages in the amount of the prima facie measure may be awarded even if the buyer has purchased substitute goods and recouped their cost from its customers.[57] On principle, it is difficult to justify an award of compensation for avoided loss, whether or not the seller knew what the buyer intended to do with the goods.[58]

---

47   However, the cost of rectifying the defect may be evidence of the amount of diminution in value: *Atkinson v Hastings Deering (Qld) Pty Ltd* (1985) 8 FCR 481, 495.

48   *Tabcorp Holdings Ltd v Bowen Investments Pty Ltd* [2009] HCA 8, (2009) 236 CLR 272 [13]; *Zuvela v Geiger* [2007] WASCA 138 [41]–[42].

49   *Minster Trust Ltd v Traps Tractors Ltd* [1954] 3 All ER 136, 156. In *Zuvela v Geiger* [2005] WADC 207 [142], damages reflecting the cost of repair were awarded even though there was no evidence that substitute goods could not be obtained. The correctness of that approach was not challenged on appeal and was expressly left open by the appellate court: *Zuvela v Geiger* [2007] WASCA 138 [7], [41].

50   F Dawson, 'The Remedies of the Buyer' in M Bridge (ed), *Benjamin's Sale of Goods* (10th edn, Sweet & Maxwell 2017) [17–073], giving the example of a car supplied with defective brakes and damaged in a collision caused by the defect.

51   *Rolfe v Katunga Lucerne Mill Pty Ltd* [2005] NSWCA 252, (2005) ASAL 55–146.

52   *Grant v Australian Knitting Mills Ltd* (1935) 54 CLR 49, 61; *Gribben v Woree Caravan Park and Motels* [1970] Qd R 420.

53   *TC Industrial Plant Pty Ltd v Robert's Queensland Pty Ltd* (1963) 180 CLR 130; *Burns v MAN Automotive (Australia) Pty Ltd* (1986) 161 CLR 653.

54   *Dowdell v Knispel Fruit Juices Pty Ltd* [2003] FCA 851.

55   *Hammond & Co v Bussey* (1887) 20 QBD 79; *Dein v Wentworth Gold Field Pty Co* (1899) 15 WN (NSW) 280, 281.

56   [2013] HCA 56, (2013) 253 CLR 1.

57   See also *Auspac Trade International Pty Ltd v Victorian Dairy Industry Authority* (Supreme Court of Victoria, Southwell, Nathan and O'Bryan JJ, 22 February 1994), where the defect was held to constitute a total failure of consideration, permitting the buyer to reclaim the purchase price, even though the sub-buyer had paid the buyer.

58   K Barnett, 'Substitutive Damages and Mitigation in Contract Law' (2016) 28 Sing Ac LJ 795, 820. The opposite view is taken by MG Bridge, 'Defective Goods and Sub-Sales' [1998] JBL 259, 262.

Where a delay in delivery entitles the buyer to reject the goods and the buyer does so, [5.22] damages will be measured on the basis that the seller has not delivered at all.[59] Where the buyer has no right of rejection or accepts delivery at a later date, the sale-of-goods statutes do not expressly provide the measure of the buyer's damages. By analogy with non-delivery and defective goods, the basic measure of damages for delay is the difference between the value of the goods at the time and place fixed for delivery and their value at the time and place of actual delivery.[60] Where there is a market for the goods, their value is generally the market value.[61] However, where the buyer has managed to resell the goods for more than their market value at the time of actual delivery, the measure of damages is the difference between the market value of the goods at the contractual delivery date and the price obtained by the buyer.[62] Subject to remoteness and mitigation, the buyer can recover consequential loss such as extra expenses,[63] loss of profit,[64] or the loss incurred as a result of being liable towards a sub-buyer.[65]

2 Failure to convey land as promised

A vendor of land may breach the contract by conveying the land later than promised, by failing [5.23] to provide good title, or by failing to convey the land at all.[66] The measure of the purchaser's damages is generally governed by the same basic principles that apply to the sale of goods. An important exception in most jurisdictions is the rule in *Bain v Fothergill*,[67] under which an innocent vendor's liability for failing to provide good title is restricted to compensating the purchaser for expenses incurred in investigating the title. This rule has been abolished in New South Wales[68] and, in respect of registered land, in the Northern Territory[69] and Queensland.[70]

---

59 *The Almare Seconda* [1981] 2 Lloyd's Rep 433; E Peel, *Treitel on the Law of Contract* (14th edn, Sweet & Maxwell 2015) [20–049].

60 *Borries v Hutchinson* (1865) 18 CBNS 445, 465; 144 ER 518, 526; *Wertheim v Chicoutimi Pulp Co* [1911] AC 301 (PC) 306; *Addax Ltd v Arcadia Petroleum Ltd* [2000] 1 Lloyd's Rep 493, 496.

61 *Wertheim v Chicoutimi Pulp Co* [1911] AC 301 (PC) 306; *Addax Ltd v Arcadia Petroleum Ltd* [2000] 1 Lloyd's Rep 493, 496.

62 *Wertheim v Chicoutimi Pulp Co* [1911] AC 301 (PC) 306–08; *Williams Brothers v Ed T Agius Ltd* [1914] AC 510, 522 (Lord Dunedin). Cf *Slater v Hoyle & Smith Ltd* [1920] 2 KB 11, 23–24 (Scrutton LJ); *Addax Ltd v Arcadia Petroleum Ltd* [2000] 1 Lloyd's Rep 493, 496.

63 *Smeed v Foord* (1859) 1 E & E 602; 120 ER 1035.

64 *Borries v Hutchinson* (1865) 18 CBNS 445; 144 ER 518; *Victoria Laundry (Windsor) Ltd v Newman Industries Ltd* [1949] 2 KB 528.

65 *Contigroup Companies Inc v Glencore AG* [2004] EWHC 2750 (Comm), [2005] 1 Lloyd's Rep 241 [80]–[81].

66 The rule 'caveat emptor' protects the vendor from contractual liability in relation to the physical quality of the property: *Bradford House Pty Ltd v Leroy Fashion Group Ltd* (1983) 68 FLR 1, 8–9; *Bamford v Albert Shire Council* [1998] 2 Qd R 125, 127. A vendor who actively conceals a defect may be liable in deceit: *Wood v Balfour* [2011] NSWCA 382, (2011) 15 BPR 29,773. A vendor who is the builder or developer may be liable in negligence for defects in the building; the assessment of damages is discussed at [6.41]–[6.43].

67 (1874) LR 7 HL 158. Adopted in *Noske v McGinnis* (1932) 47 CLR 563; *Dougan v Ley* (1946) 71 CLR 142, 150; *Svanosio v McNamara* (1956) 96 CLR 186, 197; *Wenham v Ella* (1972) 127 CLR 454, 460–61; *Godfrey Constructions Pty Ltd v Kanangra Park Pty Ltd* (1972) 128 CLR 529, 546, 548–49.

68 *Conveyancing Act 1919* (NSW), s 54B.

69 *Law of Property Act 2000* (NT), s 70.

70 *Property Law Act 1974* (Qld), s 68.

[5.24]   Where the vendor conveys the land at a later date than promised, the purchaser can claim damages for loss suffered as a result of the delay,[71] provided that this claim survives the conveyance.[72] Thus, a purchaser who intended to let the property may obtain damages for the loss of rent during the period of delay.[73] A purchaser who intended to run a business on the property may obtain damages for loss of earnings, and for the cost of storing furniture, during the period of delay.[74] A purchaser who intended to live in the property may obtain damages for the cost of alternative accommodation during the period of delay.[75] Another possible head of loss is liability towards third parties.[76] Where, as usual, the balance of the purchase price (remaining after paying the deposit) is not paid before completion, the purchaser's damages for delay must be reduced by the amount (if any) that the purchaser gained from paying the purchase price later than if conveyance had taken place as agreed.[77]

[5.25]   Where the vendor fails to convey the land at all and specific performance is denied or not sought,[78] the purchaser's damages are measured according to the difference between the contract price and the market value of the land at the time conveyance was due.[79] Loss of profit may also be compensated.[80] This is subject to remoteness and mitigation. In particular, loss of profit from development of the land will not be compensated unless the vendor was aware of the purchaser's intention to develop at the time of the contract.[81] Furthermore, the heads of loss mentioned at [5.24] in the context of delay may also arise in a case of non-conveyance in respect of the period between the vendor's breach and the time at which the purchaser acquired, or could reasonably have acquired, a substitute property.

3   Failure to build, maintain or repair property as promised

[5.26]   Sometimes, the best measure of a plaintiff's loss resulting from a breach of contract is not the difference in value between the performance promised and the performance (if any) actually rendered. Instead, the best measure is the cost of obtaining the promised performance from another source. This is particularly relevant where the defendant has breached an obligation to build, maintain or repair moveable or immoveable property. In those cases, there are two ways of measuring the plaintiff's loss. One measure (cost of cure or rectification) is the cost of getting

---

71   *Hoffman v Cali* [1985] 1 Qd R 253, 256.

72   Under the doctrine of 'merger', any claims by the parties are lost on conveyance unless the contract expressly or impliedly provides to the contrary: *Svanosio v McNamara* (1956) 96 CLR 186, 206–07; *Zaccardi v Caunt* [2008] NSWCA 202, (2008) 15 BPR 28,403 [35].

73   *Royal Bristol Permanent Building Society v Bomash* (1887) 35 Ch D 390; *Ruthol Pty Ltd v Tricon (Australia) Pty Ltd* [2005] NSWCA 443, (2005) 12 BPR 23,923. The cost of maintaining the property during the period of delay must be deducted: *Lahoud v Lahoud* [2009] NSWSC 623 [6].

74   *Phillips v Lamdin* [1949] 2 KB 33, 44–45.

75   *Raineri v Miles* [1981] AC 1050; *Turner v Kwikshift Pty Ltd* (1993) 113 FLR 8, 16.

76   *Raineri v Miles* [1981] AC 1050.

77   *Ruthol Pty Ltd v Tricon (Australia) Pty Ltd* [2005] NSWCA 443, (2005) 12 BPR 23,923.

78   Specific performance is usually granted to a purchaser of land; see [10.29].

79   *Hoffman v Cali* [1985] 1 Qd R 253, 256, 259–64; *Castle Constructions Pty Ltd v Fekala Pty Ltd* [2006] NSWCA 133, (2006) 65 NSWLR 648 [11]; *Palasty v Parlby* [2007] NSWCA 345, (2007) 13 BPR 25,311 [7], [11].

80   *Wenham v Ella* (1972) 127 CLR 454; *Associated Grocers Co-operative Ltd v Hubbard Properties Pty Ltd (No 2)* (1986) 45 SASR 57, 64.

81   *Diamond v Campbell-Jones* [1961] Ch 22, 36; *Castle Constructions Pty Ltd v Fekala Pty Ltd* [2006] NSWCA 133, (2006) 65 NSWLR 648 [36]–[53].

a third party to put the property in the state in which the defendant was obliged to put or maintain it. Alternatively, the plaintiff's loss can be the difference between the actual value of the property and the value it would have without the defendant's breach (diminution in value). Suppose that the defendant undertook to repaint the plaintiff's car but has failed to do so. Cost of cure is the cost of having the car repainted by a third party. Diminution in value is the difference between the car's actual value and the value it would have had if it had been repainted.

Courts often award damages on a rectification measure because damages measured according to the diminution in value of the property may not adequately compensate the plaintiff. Where the promised work has a predominantly aesthetic value, the effect of the breach on the value of the property may be nominal, but the promise had a special value to the plaintiff. For example, if I contract for my house to be painted 'Sunshine Yellow', but it is painted 'Mustard Yellow', the difference is subtle, but it looks far less attractive to me. When choosing the measure of damages it is important to have regard to the objective which the plaintiff hoped to achieve by entering into the contract. Courts consider the plaintiff's subjective interest in the subject matter of the contract,[82] sometimes known as the 'consumer surplus'.[83]

Different scholars subscribe to different conceptualisations of awards of cost of cure and diminution in value in the present context. Robert Stevens argues that an award of diminution in value is a substitute for the right to performance and not concerned with the compensation of loss, whereas the cost of cure represents consequential loss and is recoverable only subject to limitations such as mitigation and remoteness.[84] Conversely, other scholars maintain that a cost-of-cure award gives effect to the performance interest whereas an award of diminution in value merely compensates consequential loss.[85] The courts regard both types of award as being concerned with the compensation of loss, and we take the view that both types of award seek to provide an adequate monetary substitute for performance.[86]

The measure of damages to be applied depends upon the circumstances. Two situations of lesser practical significance can be quickly dealt with. First, where the defendant's breach has rendered it physically impossible to put the property in the state that the defendant was supposed to create or maintain, the cost of cure cannot be determined, and diminution in value is the measure of the plaintiff's loss. For example, where the defendant undertook to restore an old painting and destroyed the painting in the process, the measure of damages is

[5.27]

[5.28]

[5.29]

---

82   A Loke, 'Cost of Cure or Difference in Market Value? Toward a Sound Choice in the Basis for Quantifying Expectation Damages' (1996) 10 J Cont L 189, 190. See also P Linzer, 'On the Amorality of Contract Remedies – Efficiency, Equity, and the *Second Restatement*' (1981) 81 Col LR 111, 131.

83   D Harris, A Ogus and J Phillips, 'Contract Remedies and the Consumer Surplus' (1979) 95 LQR 581; *Ruxley Electronics & Construction Ltd v Forsyth* [1996] AC 344, 360 (Lord Mustill).

84   R Stevens, 'Damages and the Right to Performance: A *Golden Victory* or Not?' in JW Neyers, R Bronaugh and SGA Pitel (eds), *Exploring Contract Law* (Hart 2009) 190–92. See also [1.58].

85   B Coote, 'Contract Damages, *Ruxley*, and the Performance Interest' (1997) 56 Camb LJ 537, 557; SA Smith, 'Substitutionary Damages' in CEF Rickett (ed), *Justifying Private Law Remedies* (Hart 2008) 93; C Webb, 'Performance and Compensation: An Analysis of Contract Damages and Contractual Obligation' (2006) 26 OJLS 41, 48–49, 57–61; D Winterton, 'Money Awards Substituting for Performance' [2012] LMCLQ 446, 450–451; D Winterton, *Money Awards in Contract Law* (Hart 2015).

86   See K Barnett, 'Great Expectations: A Dissection of Expectation Damages in Contract in Australia and England' (2016) 33 J Cont L 1.

the value of the painting before it was destroyed. Secondly, where complete cure is possible and diminution in value exceeds the cost of cure, cost of cure is generally the measure of the plaintiff's loss. The reason is that an award of cost-of-cure damages enables the plaintiff to have the defect rectified, and a diminution in value will remain only if the plaintiff fails to have the defect rectified, which would normally constitute a failure to mitigate loss; see [3.134]. It may be different where cure would take an excessively long time.

[5.30]   Usually, cure is possible and its cost exceeds the diminution in value. In those circumstances, cost of cure is the measure of the plaintiff's loss unless cure is unreasonable,[87] as established in *Bellgrove v Eldridge*[88] and *Tabcorp Holdings Ltd v Bowen Investments Pty Ltd*.[89]

[5.31]   In *Bellgrove v Eldridge*,[90] a builder undertook to erect a house in accordance with certain plans and specifications. The house did not conform to the specifications, resulting in grave instability. The trial judge awarded the cost of demolishing and re-erecting the house in compliance with the contract. The High Court of Australia upheld that award and rejected the builder's argument that the loss should be measured by the difference between the actual value of the land and the value it would have had if the house had been erected in compliance with the contract. In particular, the court rejected an analogy to the delivery of defective goods, saying that the owner was entitled to have a house complying with the contract, and damages had to be measured by ascertaining the amount required to rectify the defect, thus giving her the equivalent of a house complying with the contract on her land.[91]

[5.32]   The High Court observed that cost of cure may be awarded even where diminution in value is nil, giving the example of a painter who paints rooms in a building in a colour different from what was specified.[92] However, cost of cure can be awarded only if it is reasonable to carry out remedial work. By way of illustration, the court said that where a contract for the erection of a house requires the builder to use second-hand bricks, and the builder uses new bricks of first quality, the owner is not entitled to the cost of demolishing the house and re-erecting it in second-hand bricks. This would be economic waste.[93]

[5.33]   In *Tabcorp Holdings Ltd v Bowen Investments Pty Ltd*,[94] the tenant of an office building undertook not to alter the premises without the landlord's consent. The landlord had installed a new foyer made of expensive materials. The tenant made significant changes to the foyer without the landlord's consent. The value of the property was unaffected, except for the loss of some lettable space on the ground floor. The cost of restoring that space was $33 820.[95] The cost of restoring the foyer to its original condition was $1.38 million, consisting of $580 000 as the cost of the work and $800 000 as the loss of rental income while the work was being carried

---

87   The unreasonableness exception is criticised, in respect of English law, by C Webb, 'Performance and Compensation: An Analysis of Contract Damages and Contractual Obligation' (2006) 26 OJLS 41, 63–64.

88   (1954) 90 CLR 613.

89   [2009] HCA 8, (2009) 236 CLR 272.

90   (1954) 90 CLR 613.

91   Ibid, 617.

92   Ibid.

93   Ibid, 618.

94   [2009] HCA 8, (2009) 236 CLR 272.

95   These details were set out by the trial judge: *Bowen Investments Pty Ltd v Tabcorp Holdings Ltd* [2007] FCA 708, (2007) ANZ ConvR 297 [102]–[103].

out. The High Court of Australia held that the landlord was entitled to an award of $1.38 million.

Referring to the 'ruling principle' set out by Parke B in *Robinson v Harman*,[96] the High Court said that an award of diminution in value would not restore the landlord to the 'same situation ... as if the contract had been performed' because, as Oliver J had said in *Radford v De Froberville*,[97] 'the words "the same situation, with respect to damages, as if the contract had been performed" do not mean "as good a *financial* position as if the contract had been performed"'.[98] The High Court confirmed that cost of cure cannot be awarded if remedial work is unreasonable, but said that the test of unreasonableness is satisfied only in 'fairly exceptional circumstances', namely where, in the words of Oliver J in *Radford v De Froberville*,[99] the plaintiff is 'merely using a technical breach to secure an uncovenanted profit'.[100]

[5.34]

Tabcorp has been applied in various contexts. For example, where the lessor of a motel breached its obligation to maintain the motel in a state of good condition and to paint it every five years, the lessee obtained damages reflecting the cost of having the work carried out; the fact that the lessee could have sold its leasehold interest did not justify treating the motel as a marketable commodity.[101] Furthermore, where the seller of a leasehold in a petrol station site breached its obligation to decontaminate the site, the buyer obtained damages reflecting the cost of decontamination, even though the site was fit for use as a petrol station.[102]

[5.35]

It is not entirely clear whether the reasonableness of rectification depends upon the proportion between the cost of rectification and its benefit to the plaintiff.[103] In *Ruxley Electronics & Construction Ltd v Forsyth*,[104] where a newly constructed swimming pool was shallower than specified in the contract but still suitable for diving, the House of Lords overturned an award of the cost of rebuilding the pool on the ground that this cost was out of all proportion to the benefit the owner would obtain from the rebuilding.[105] Lord Jauncey placed emphasis on the fact that the contractual objective had been substantially achieved, and contrasted this with cases where the contract-breaker has entirely failed to achieve the contractual objective.[106]

[5.36]

Prior to *Tabcorp*, the requirement of proportionality was adopted in some Australian cases.[107] In *Tabcorp*, the High Court of Australia said that the facts of *Ruxley* were 'plainly

[5.37]

96 (1848) 1 Ex 850, 855; 154 ER 363, 365. See [5.6].
97 [1977] 1 WLR 1262, 1273.
98 [2009] HCA 8, (2009) 236 CLR 272 [13] (French CJ, Gummow, Heydon, Crennan and Kiefel JJ).
99 [1977] 1 WLR 1262, 1270.
100 [2009] HCA 8, (2009) 236 CLR 272 [17] (French CJ, Gummow, Heydon, Crennan and Kiefel JJ).
101 *Ellis's Town House Pty Ltd v Botan Pty Ltd* [2017] NSWCA 20 [31], [59].
102 *United Petroleum Pty Ltd v Bonnie View Petroleum Pty Ltd (in liq)* [2017] VSC 185 [312]–[317].
103 See *Atherton v T M Building Consultants Pty Ltd* [2014] NSWCATCD 255 [133]–[137], [144], where the issue was left open.
104 [1996] AC 344.
105 The House of Lords upheld an award of £2500 representing the owner's 'loss of amenity'. Criticised by K Barnett, *Accounting for Profit for Breach of Contract: Theory and Practice* (Hart 2012) 173.
106 [1996] AC 344, 358. See also *Sunrock Aircraft Corporation Ltd v Scandinavian Airlines System Denmark-Norway-Sweden* [2007] EWCA Civ 882, [2007] 2 Lloyd's Rep 612 [34]–[35]: US$139 800 cost of repairing scab patches on an aircraft that did not affect its value was unrecoverable, as repair would be unreasonable.
107 *South Parklands Hockey & Tennis Centre Inc v Brown Falconer Group Pty Ltd* [2004] SASC 81, (2004) 88 SASR 65 [90]; *Scott Carver Pty Ltd v SAS Trustee Corporation* [2005] NSWCA 462 [120] (Ipp JA); *Kirkby v Coote* [2006] QCA 61 [52]; *Brewarrina Shire Council v Beckhaus Civil Pty Ltd* [2006] NSWCA 361 [89].

distinguishable' from the facts in *Tabcorp*,[108] but failed to explain why. The High Court's failure to disapprove the decision by the House of Lords in *Ruxley* might indicate that the High Court saw some room for a cost–benefit analysis in determining the reasonableness of remedial work.[109] But the actual decision in *Tabcorp* is at odds with a requirement of proportionality. An award of $1.38 million can hardly be seen as proportionate to a purely aesthetic benefit of rectification.[110]

[5.38]   The South Australian Full Court took a multifactorial approach to determining the availability of rectification damages in *Stone v Chappel*.[111] A contract for the construction of the shell and framework of an apartment for $1.8 million specified a ceiling height of 2700 mm. Construction practice provided that a departure of plus or minus 20 mm was acceptable. The ceiling was on average 48 mm too low, and the cost of rectification was $331 188. The South Australian Full Court upheld the trial judge's refusal to award rectification damages. The Full Court said that the availability of rectification damages depends upon a number of factors, including the plaintiff's performance interest (in particular whether the contractual specification was merely functional or a matter of aesthetic choice of amenity on the plaintiff's part), the extent to which the defendant has achieved the contractual objective, a lack of proportionality between the cost of rectification work and the benefit of that work to the plaintiff, the plaintiff's intention and ability to carry out the work, and the degree of the defendant's culpability.[112]

[5.39]   The Full Court regarded the lack of proportionality between the cost of rectification and its benefits as a key factor in determining the reasonableness of rectification work.[113] The court distinguished *Tabcorp* on the ground that the tenant in *Tabcorp* ignored the contractual prohibition on alterations to the foyer, whereas the defendants in *Stone v Chappel* achieved the contractual objective to a significant extent.[114] The court thus adopted the distinction made by Lord Jauncey in *Forsyth*; see [5.36]. On principle, the reasonableness of repair could depend upon the extent to which the defendant deviated from the contractual specification.[115] However, the High Court in *Tabcorp* placed no reliance on either the defendant's culpability or the extent to which the performance rendered deviated from the performance bargained for. It is difficult to reconcile *Stone v Chappel* with *Tabcorp* because in both cases the plaintiff's interest was merely aesthetic and the value of the property was not significantly affected by the breach.

[5.40]   On principle, the requirement of proportionality may be defended with the argument that it prevents economic waste.[116] On the other hand, the requirement involves a significant degree of uncertainty since reasonable minds (including those of judges) may differ on whether cost of cure is disproportionate in particular circumstances. This may discourage plaintiffs from

---

108   [2009] HCA 8, (2009) 236 CLR 272 [18] (French CJ, Gummow, Heydon, Crennan and Kiefel JJ).
109   This view was taken in *Stone v Chappel* [2017] SASCFC 72, (2017) 128 SASR 165 [261] (Doyle J).
110   A different view was taken ibid, [441] (Hinton J).
111   [2017] SASCFC 72, (2017) 128 SASR 165.
112   Ibid, [55]–[63] (Kourakis CJ), [256]–[265] (Doyle J). Hinton J (at [447]–[453]) said that rectification work was unreasonable for the reasons given by Doyle J.
113   The same view was expressed obiter in *Wheeler v Ecroplot Pty Ltd* [2010] NSWCA 61 [81].
114   [2017] SASCFC 72, (2017) 128 SASR 165 [259], [441], [452]. On similar grounds, the court (at [287], [452]) distinguished *Willshee v Westcourt Ltd* [2009] WASCA 87, where $250,000 were awarded as the cost of replacing aesthetically inferior limestone cladding with the contractually specified limestone cladding.
115   D Winterton, 'Money Awards Substituting for Performance' [2012] LMCLQ 446, 463.
116   AL Corbin, *Corbin on Contracts: A Comprehensive Treatise on the Working Rules of Contract Law* (West 1963) §1089.

seeking rectification damages and in turn reduce the incentive of contractors to comply with contractual specifications.[117]

The criterion of reasonableness determines not only whether cost of cure (as opposed to diminution in value) can be recovered but also whether the cost of a particular method of rectification can be recovered even though a cheaper method is available. Where the defendant was obliged to install a certain feature in a building and this was not done or was done defectively, the plaintiff is generally entitled to the cost of having that feature installed even if a different feature would achieve the same purpose.[118] But where it would be unreasonable to install the contractually agreed feature, only the cost of a reasonable rectification method can be recovered.[119]   **[5.41]**

Two further issues have yet to be settled. One is the availability of rectification damages where a sale of the unrectified property or another supervening event has rendered remedial work by the plaintiff impossible or unlikely to occur. The other, more general issue is the availability of rectification damages where the plaintiff has no intention to carry out remedial work.[120] These two issues are intertwined but not identical. If an intention to carry out remedial work is a prerequisite of an award of rectification damages, such damages cannot be awarded where a supervening event has rendered remedial work by the plaintiff impossible or unlikely to occur. But the converse is not true. If rectification damages can generally be awarded even though the plaintiff has no intention to carry out remedial work, such damages may still be denied where remedial work by the plaintiff is objectively impossible or unlikely. It may make a difference whether the decision not to carry out remedial work was made freely or forced by outside events.   **[5.42]**

In *Bellgrove v Eldridge*,[121] considered at [5.31]–[5.32], the High Court of Australia held that it was immaterial whether the plaintiff would rectify the defective house. There was no supervening event rendering cure by the plaintiff impossible or unlikely to occur. With regard to supervening events other than a sale of the property, the preponderance of judicial opinion is against an award of rectification damages.[122] However, in *Scott Carver Pty Ltd v SAS Trustee Corporation*,[123] Ipp JA opined that rectification damages may be awarded even though the defective building has been accidentally destroyed and the plaintiff has decided to erect an entirely different building.   **[5.43]**

---

117   J O'Sullivan, 'Loss and Gain at Greater Depth: The Implications of the *Ruxley* Decision' in FD Rose (ed), *Failure of Contracts: Contractual, Restitutionary and Proprietary Consequences* (Hart 1997) 11.

118   *Home Site Pty Ltd v ACN 124 452 786 Pty Ltd* [2017] NSWSC 698 [83]: cost of replacing defective membrane recoverable even though cheaper drip-trays would do the same job.

119   See *Owners Strata Plan No 77475 v Walker Group Constructions Pty Ltd* [2016] NSWSC 1127 [40], [94]: installation of glass splashback instead of demolition and reconstruction of defective baths.

120   A denial of cost-of-cure damages in the absence of an intention to carry out remedial work is favoured by SA Smith, 'Substitutionary Damages' in CEF Rickett (ed), *Justifying Private Law Remedies* (Hart 2008) 103; C Webb, 'Performance and Compensation: An Analysis of Contract Damages and Contractual Obligation' (2006) 26 OJLS 41, 62–63.

121   (1954) 90 CLR 613, 620.

122   *Central Coast Leagues Club Ltd v Gosford City Council* (Supreme Court of NSW, Giles CJ, 9 June 1998); *Scott Carver Pty Ltd v SAS Trustee Corporation* [2005] NSWCA 462 [44] (Hodgson JA); *Westpoint Management Ltd v Chocolate Factory Apartments Ltd* [2007] NSWCA 253 [61]–[62]; *Cordon Investments Pty Ltd v Lesdor Properties Pty Ltd* [2010] NSWSC 1073 [346], [350].

123   [2005] NSWCA 462 [123].

[5.44]   Judicial opinion is divided where the plaintiff has sold the property without repairing it (either before or after the sale) and without an obligation towards the purchaser to repair it.[124] In some cases, sale of the property did not affect the availability of rectification damages.[125] In other cases, it has been said that sale of the property may render rectification unreasonable.[126] It has been irrelevant whether the defendant's breach triggered the sale. Rectification damages have been held unavailable where the plaintiff always intended to sell the property after the completion of the defendant's work and merely sought to achieve a certain return from the sale.[127]

[5.45]   An award of rectification damages despite the occurrence of a supervening event may be defended on the basis that the plaintiff already had an accrued right to obtain such damages and should not lose that right through the occurrence of an external event, at least where the event is beyond the plaintiff's control. But it is problematic to award rectification damages where objective circumstances indicate that the plaintiff will not undertake remedial work. The principle against overcompensation ought to prevail. This is particularly so where the supervening event is in the plaintiff's control, as when the property is sold.[128]

[5.46]   Where the plaintiff has decided not to carry out remedial work even though no outside event forced that decision, the availability of rectification damages ought to be established by *Bellgrove v Eldridge*. This view has been taken in some cases,[129] but it has been said in other cases that the absence of an intention to carry out remedial work may render the work unreasonable.[130] The latter view seems to require the reasonableness of a claim for, or award of, rectification damages.[131] But the High Court of Australia said in *Bellgrove v Eldridge* and in *Tabcorp* that rectification damages can be claimed unless the carrying out of remedial work is unreasonable. What matters is the reasonableness of the work, not the reasonableness of the

---

124   Where the plaintiff, after selling the property, carried out remedial work without an obligation to do so, cost-of-cure damages are available: *Director of War Service Homes v Harris* [1968] Qd R 275, 278–80. See also *Orlit Pty Ltd v JF & P Consulting Engineering Pty Ltd* (1995) 11 BCL 260, 271.

125   *De Cesare v Deluxe Motors Pty Ltd* (1996) 67 SASR 28, 32, 39–40; *Scott Carver Pty Ltd v SAS Trustee Corporation* [2005] NSWCA 462 [38]–[47], [116]–[122]; *Bannister & Hunter Pty Ltd v Transition Resort Holdings Pty Ltd (No 2)* [2013] NSWSC 1943 [345].

126   *Director of War Service Homes v Harris* [1968] Qd R 275, 278; *Westpoint Management Ltd v Chocolate Factory Apartments Ltd* [2007] NSWCA 253 [61]–[62].

127   *UI International Pty Ltd v Interworks Architects Pty Ltd* [2007] QCA 402, [2008] 2 Qd R 158. See also *Cordon Investments Pty Ltd v Lesdor Properties Pty Ltd* [2010] NSWSC 1073 [347]–[351]. By the same token, a head contractor's claim against a subcontractor for defective work is restricted to the amount (if any) for which the head contractor is liable towards the principal: *Alucraft Pty Ltd (in liq) v Grocon Ltd (No 2)* [1996] 2 VR 386, 395–96.

128   J Ren, 'Measure of Damages for Defective Building Work' (2014) 32 J Cont L 69, 81.

129   *De Cesare v Deluxe Motors Pty Ltd* (1996) 67 SASR 28, 30–32; *Scott Carver Pty Ltd v SAS Trustee Corporation* [2005] NSWCA 462 [40]–[44], [115]; *Unique Building Pty Ltd v Brown* [2010] SASC 106, (2010) 269 LSJS 76 [93]– [94]. See also *Brewarrina Shire Council v Beckhaus Civil Pty Ltd* [2005] NSWCA 248 [173]–[176]; *Ellis's Town House Pty Ltd v Botan Pty Ltd* [2017] NSWCA 20.

130   *Westpoint Management Ltd v Chocolate Factory Apartments Ltd* [2007] NSWCA 253 [59]–[62]; *Willshee v Westcourt Ltd* [2009] WASCA 87 [72].

131   There is some support for the existence of such a requirement in English law: *Ruxley Electronics & Construction Ltd v Forsyth* [1996] AC 344, 357–59 (Lord Jauncey), 372–73 (Lord Lloyd); *Alfred McAlpine Construction Ltd v Panatown Ltd* [2001] 1 AC 518, 592 (Lord Millett); B Coote, 'Contract Damages, *Ruxley* and the Performance Interest' (1997) 56 Camb LJ 537, 563; D Winterton, 'Money Awards Substituting for Performance' [2012] LMCLQ 446, 464.

claim or award. The plaintiff's intention as to how to spend the damages can have no bearing on whether remedial work would be reasonable if carried out.

It might be argued that if rectification damages are unavailable where external factors render remedial work unlikely, they should be unavailable whenever the plaintiff has no intention to undertake remedial work. For example, it might be argued that it should be irrelevant whether the plaintiff has already sold the unrectified property or intends to do so after judgment. But it is problematic to make an intention to carry out remedial work a prerequisite of rectification damages, because it might tempt plaintiffs to give self-serving testimonies and would require the court to supervise the plaintiff after judgment. These pragmatic considerations are sufficiently strong to trump the principle against overcompensation.[132] [5.47]

Finally, where the material or building method used by the defendant was not fit for purpose, the plaintiff is entitled (within the limits of reasonableness) to compensation for the cost of repairing the building by using material or a method fit for purpose, without betterment discount.[133] Where rectification damages are awarded, the plaintiff may also be compensated for the physical inconvenience and ensuing distress suffered as a result of remedial work,[134] and the financial consequences of the inability to use the defective property while rectification work is being undertaken, such as the loss of rent[135] or the cost of renting alternative premises.[136] This is subject to remoteness and mitigation.[137] [5.48]

4   Failure to provide other services as promised

Damages for the failure to provide services (other than building work and the like, which is considered in the previous section) are in principle measured in the same way as damages for the failure to provide goods as promised, discussed at [5.13]–[5.22]. The cost of substitute services is generally recoverable,[138] and the failure to obtain substitute services may constitute a failure to mitigate loss.[139] It has been held that where an employee fails to work for the full time for which he or she has been contracted, the employer's damages may be measured by reference to the amount of the employee's remuneration for the time not worked, whether or not the employee's breach has caused the employer any loss of profit.[140] [5.49]

---

132   Similarly, J Ren, 'Measure of Damages for Defective Building Work' (2014) 32 J Cont L 69, 90–91; S Rowan, 'Cost of Cure Damages and the Relevance of the Injured Promisee's Intention to Cure' (2017) 76 Camb LJ 616, 638–40.

133   *Brodyn Pty Ltd v Owners Corporation of Strata Plan 73019* [2016] NSWCATAP 113 [156]–[174]. The betterment discount is discussed at [2.17]–[2.27].

134   *Willshee v Westcourt Ltd* [2009] WASCA 87 [79].

135   *Tabcorp Holdings Ltd v Bowen Investments Pty Ltd* [2009] HCA 8, (2009) 236 CLR 272.

136   *South Parklands Hockey & Tennis Centre Inc v Brown Falconer Group Pty Ltd* [2004] SASC 81, (2004) 88 SASR 65 [140].

137   For example, damages for alleged loss of rent were denied on grounds of remoteness in *2144 Broke Road Pty Ltd v ACN 062 859 358 Pty Ltd* [2010] NSWSC 489 [15].

138   *GEC Marconi Systems Pty Ltd v BHP Information Technology Pty Ltd* [2003] FCA 50, (2003) 128 FCR 1 [935].

139   *Idameneo (No 3) Pty Ltd v Fox (No 2)* [2014] NSWDC 209 [10], adding that substitute services had been unavailable in that case.

140   *Zomojo Pty Ltd v Hurd (No 4)* [2014] FCA 441 [15], relying on *National Coal Board v Galley* [1958] 1 WLR 16; *Miles v Wakefield Metropolitan District Council* [1987] AC 539; *Giedo van der Garde BV v Force India Formula One Team Ltd* [2010] EWHC 2373 (QB).

[5.50]   Consequential loss such as loss of profit can also be recovered, subject to mitigation and remoteness. This was confirmed obiter in *Oneflare Pty Ltd v Chernih*,[141] where the plaintiff retained the defendants to devise and implement an 'aggressive' search engine optimisation strategy to improve the ranking of its website on Google. The links the defendants created to the plaintiff's website were 'unnatural' and violated the Google Webmaster Guidelines. On discovering this, Google algorithmically and then manually demoted the plaintiff's website in its search rankings. Subsequently, the sales revenue generated through the plaintiff's website fell dramatically. The plaintiff's action for breach of contract and negligence was dismissed on the ground that the defendants had been retained to build 'unnatural links' and had thus conformed to the contract. Both the trial judge and the NSW Court of Appeal added that, if there had been a breach of contract or negligence, damages reflecting the profit lost as a result of the breach could have been recovered.

C   The impact of *Clark v Macourt*

[5.51]   Some of the rules discussed so far may be revised because of what the High Court of Australia decided in *Clark v Macourt*.[142] Dr Macourt, acting through St George Fertility Centre Pty Ltd ('St George'), and Dr Clark both conducted medical practices providing assisted reproductive technology. Dr Clark and St George entered into a deed under which certain of St George's assets, including 3513 straws of frozen donor sperm, were sold to Dr Clark for a sum to be calculated by reference to Dr Clark's future income. Dr Macourt guaranteed the performance of St George's obligations. Dr Clark expected to be able to use 2500 straws,[143] but only 504 were usable. St George, in breach of a warranty given in the deed, had not conducted certain tasks required by the relevant Code of Practice.[144] Since substitute donor sperm complying with the guidelines was unavailable in Australia, Dr Clark bought it from time to time from a supplier in the United States. She recouped the cost from the patients for whose benefit the sperm was used. Pursuant to ethical guidelines governing assisted reproductive technology, Dr Clark could recoup the cost of acquiring sperm but could not make any profit from it.[145] Since the deed did not allocate a specific part of the purchase price to the sperm, she did not charge patients for the 504 straws of the St George sperm, and would not have charged for the other 1996 straws if they had been usable.

[5.52]   St George sued Dr Clark for the outstanding amount of the purchase price ($219 950.91 of the $386 950.91 was unpaid). Dr Clark cross-claimed against St George and Dr Macourt for damages for breach of warranty. The trial judge awarded her damages in the amount of $1 246 025.01, representing the cost of buying 1996 straws of warranty-compliant sperm from the US supplier. Dr Macourt appealed, arguing that any loss suffered by Dr Clark had been mitigated since that loss had been recouped from her patients. The NSW Court of Appeal allowed the appeal, but the High Court of Australia (Gageler J dissenting) reinstated the trial

---

141   [2017] NSWCA 195.
142   [2013] HCA 56, (2013) 253 CLR 1.
143   The relevant Code of Practice limited to 10 the number of children generated by any one donor.
144   Reproductive Technology Accreditation Committee, *Code of Practice for Assisted Reproductive Technology Units*.
145   National Health and Medical Research Council, *Ethical Guidelines on Assisted Reproductive Technology* (1996).

judge's award. All of the High Court judges agreed that contractual damages aim to place the plaintiff in the position as if the contract had been performed,[146] and that the outcome did not depend upon whether the contract was characterised as a sale of goods or a sale of business.[147]

Keane J, with whom the majority agreed, said that Dr Clark's claim was not for the cost of acquiring the substitute sperm, but was for the value of the sperm that should have been delivered.[148] The cost of the substitute sperm was merely evidence of that value.[149] Similarly, Crennan and Bell JJ said that the evidence as to the cost of the substitute sperm meant that Dr Clark had discharged her onus to show the recoupment cost necessary to restore her to the position she would have been in absent the breach,[150] and Dr Macourt had not sought to demonstrate that the cost of the substitute sperm was not an appropriate proxy for the value of the St George sperm.[151] Hayne J said that Dr Clark's purchase and use of the substitute sperm left her neither better nor worse off than she was prior to those transactions.[152] The consequences of Dr Clark's use of the substitute sperm would have been relevant to assessing the value of what should have been supplied under the contract only if she had obtained some advantage from it, or if she had alleged additional, consequential loss.[153]

[5.53]

Gageler J, dissenting, said that the St George sperm was not a marketable commodity but was only for use in the treatment of patients in the normal course of practice.[154] The supply of compliant sperm would have relieved Dr Clark of the need to source sperm from another supplier as and when she needed sperm to treat her patients.[155] St George's breach of contract left Dr Clark 'worse off to the extent that later she was forced to incur, but was not able to recoup from her patients, the additional costs of sourcing 1996 straws of sperm from an alternative supplier'.[156]

[5.54]

Clark v Macourt could be seen to permit an award of damages reflecting the market value of the promised performance (determined by reference to the cost of substitute performance) whenever substitute performance is available, regardless of the actual consequences of the breach for the plaintiff. The rules on remoteness of damage and mitigation would be relevant only where the plaintiff claims damages in an amount exceeding the cost of substitute performance. So far, the courts have not derived such a wide-ranging rule from *Clark v Macourt*, and in any case, this would conflict with the traditional rule that damages for breach of contract aim to compensate the plaintiff's actual loss and not more. The High Court did not overrule that traditional rule, but found a loss on Dr Clark's part because it regarded it as irrelevant that she had recouped the cost of the substitute sperm from her patients.

[5.55]

---

146   [2013] HCA 56, (2013) 253 CLR 1 [7] (Hayne J), [26] (Crennan and Bell JJ), [60] (Gageler J), [106] Keane J).
147   Ibid, [13] (Hayne J), [30] (Crennan and Bell JJ), [68] (Gageler J), [108] (Keane J).
148   Ibid, [128].
149   Ibid, [138].
150   Ibid, [36].
151   Ibid, [39].
152   Ibid, [19].
153   Ibid, [20].
154   Ibid, [69]–[70].
155   Ibid, [70].
156   Ibid, [71].

[5.56]   Since it is difficult to accept the High Court's view that Dr Clark suffered a loss,[157] *Clark v Macourt* may give fresh impetus (at least in contract law) to the theories that distinguish between compensatory damages, which compensate for consequential loss, and substitutionary damages, which substitute for the fulfilment of the wrongdoer's primary obligation and are available even if the wrong has caused no actual loss; see [1.57]–[1.58]. The award in *Clark v Macourt* has already been described as an example of substitutionary damages.[158]

D   Compensation of reliance loss

[5.57]   The plaintiff may have incurred significant expenses in reliance upon the defendant's performance, and those expenses may be wasted if the defendant fails to perform. Suppose that the defendant promised to deliver a damaged vintage car to the plaintiff and the plaintiff then bought expensive spare parts from a third party. The defendant fails to deliver, and the plaintiff has no use for the spare parts. In those circumstances, the question arises whether the plaintiff's reliance loss can be compensated.

[5.58]   The answer depends upon whether the plaintiff is able to prove the expectation loss with sufficient certainty. Where the plaintiff is able to do this, which is usually the case, the treatment of reliance loss is straightforward: it is incorporated within expectation loss and not compensated as a separate head. This is because usually the plaintiff would have made a profit or at least broken even had the defendant performed. Compensation for lost gross revenue reimburses the plaintiff for expenses in the same way in which the actual revenue would have done.

[5.59]   Suppose that, in the vintage car example presented at [5.57], the plaintiff promised to pay $25 000 for the car and has spent $5000 on spare parts. The plaintiff intended to personally repair the car and sell it, and would have been able to sell the repaired car for $40 000. Expectation loss is $15 000, assuming that the plaintiff has terminated the contract and is no longer obliged to pay the purchase price.

[5.60]   The outcome can be explained in two ways.[159] First, damages could be said to be the difference between the lost gross revenue of $40 000 (the amount the buyer of the repaired car would have paid) and the expenditure the plaintiff would have incurred in obtaining that revenue but has not in fact incurred, here the purchase price of $25 000 for the damaged car. Alternatively, it may be said that the plaintiff is compensated for expenditure actually incurred ($5000) and the net profit she would have made had the defendant performed ($10 000).[160] On the basis of the second analysis, it might be thought that the plaintiff's reliance loss is compensated,[161] but this is only because the plaintiff would have recouped the expenditure had the

---

157   See KE Barnett, 'Contractual Expectations and Goods' (2014) 130 LQR 387, 390–91; JW Carter, W Courtney and GJ Tolhurst, 'Issues of Principle in Assessing Contract Damages' (2014) 31 J Cont L 171, 183, 190–91; A Kramer, *The Law of Contract Damages* (Hart 2014) 141–42.

158   D Winterton, '*Clark v Macourt*: Defective Sperm and Performance Substitutes in the High Court of Australia' (2014) 38 MULR 755.

159   *TC Industrial Plant Pty Ltd v Robert's Queensland Pty Ltd* (1963) 180 CLR 130, 140–41; D McLauchlan, 'Reliance Damages for Breach of Contract' [2007] NZ Law Rev 417, 428–29.

160   Only this method was mentioned in *Commonwealth v Amann Aviation Pty Ltd* (1991) 174 CLR 64, 81 (Mason CJ and Dawson J).

161   *Expertise Events Pty Ltd v Blue Haven Pools and Spas Pty Ltd* [2004] NSWSC 435 [17]; D Campbell and R Halson, 'Expectation and Reliance: One Principle or Two?' (2015) 32 J Cont L 231.

defendant performed. It is more correct to say that the expenses are not deducted from the lost gross revenue because they have in fact been incurred.

The fact that reliance loss is not independently compensated where the amount of the plaintiff's expectation loss is established becomes clear where the plaintiff would not have recouped her expenditure even if the defendant had performed. Suppose that, in the vintage car example, the plaintiff would not have been able to sell the repaired car for more than $28 000. In those circumstances, the plaintiff obtains damages of $3000 as the difference between the sum the plaintiff would have received from the buyer of the repaired car and the sum the plaintiff would have had to pay to the defendant for the damaged car. The plaintiff remains out of pocket by $2000. This amount is not compensated because the plaintiff would have been out of pocket in that amount even if the defendant had performed. Contractual damages do not aim to place the plaintiff in a better position than she would have been in had the defendant performed; see [5.6].   **[5.61]**

Thus, in *Omak Maritime Ltd v Mamola Challenger Shipping Co Ltd*,[162] the charterer of a vessel repudiated the charterparty at a time when the market rate of hire exceeded the contractual rate. The owner of the vessel accepted the repudiation and traded the vessel at the higher market rate. The owner nonetheless claimed damages for the expenses incurred in preparing to perform the charterparty by modifying the vessel. It was found that the owner had more than recuperated its expenditure. Damages were denied because they would have placed the owner in a better position than if the charterer had not repudiated.   **[5.62]**

While there is no place for an independent compensation of reliance loss where the amount of expectation loss is clear, a plaintiff who is unable to prove that amount may seek compensation of reliance loss. It is suggested that the courts address the following four issues in these cases: **[5.63]**

1. Whether reliance damages are appropriate in the circumstances;

2. Whether the expenditure was incurred in performance of the contract;

3. Whether the expenditure was reasonable;

4. Whether the plaintiff would have recouped the expenditure had the contract been performed.

In relation to the first issue, reliance damages are typically sought in cases where the expectation loss is difficult or impossible to prove, or where the plaintiff incurred expenses in excess of the profit expected from the contract breached, in the expectation that further contracts would be entered into subsequently. The High Court of Australia has approved reliance damages awards in two cases.[163]   **[5.64]**

In *McRae v Commonwealth Disposals Commission*,[164] the Commission sold McRae a wrecked oil tanker supposed to lie on Jourmaund Reef. McRae intended to recover oil from the tanker and incurred considerable expenditure in fitting out a salvage operation, only to   **[5.65]**

162   [2010] EWHC 2026 (Comm), [2011] 1 Lloyd's Rep 47. Discussed by D McLauchlan, 'The Redundant Reliance Interest in Contract Damages' (2011) 127 LQR 23.

163   Further cases include *Anglia Television Ltd v Reed* [1972] 1 QB 60; *Piscioneri v Smith* [2003] WASC 4; *World Best Holdings Ltd v Sarker* [2010] NSWCA 24, (2010) 14 BPR 27,549 [74]–[82].

164   (1951) 84 CLR 377.

discover that there was no tanker at or near Jourmaund Reef, the tanker having never existed. McRae could not prove how much revenue (if any) he would have obtained had there been a tanker, but obtained compensation for the wasted expenditure.

[5.66]   In *Commonwealth v Amann Aviation Pty Ltd*,[165] the parties entered into a contract under which Amann Aviation Pty Ltd ('Amann') was to conduct aerial coastal surveillance for three years. At the beginning of the contract period, the Commonwealth repudiated the contract. Amann accepted the repudiation. In preparation for its performance, Amann had spent substantial amounts on acquiring and fitting out aircraft. This expenditure exceeded the amount Amann would have received from the Commonwealth over the three years, but Amann was relying on the prospect of the contract being renewed. Since Amann could not prove that the contract would have been renewed and what Amann's remuneration under the renewed contract would have been, Amann claimed reimbursement for its expenditure. The Commonwealth argued that Amann was entitled only to damages for the lost remuneration in the initial three years, since the Commonwealth could have refused to renew the contract. A majority in the High Court of Australia (McHugh J dissenting) rejected that argument and approved an award of damages for Amann's wasted expenses.

[5.67]   In neither case did the High Court permit the plaintiff to choose between expectation damages and reliance damages. Rather, it was held in each case that where the defendant's breach renders a determination of the plaintiff's expectation loss impossible, it is to be presumed that the plaintiff would at least have recouped the expenditure incurred in reliance on the defendant's promise, since contracting parties are unlikely to enter into a loss-making contract.[166] The amount of wasted expenditure was a 'proxy' for the plaintiff's expectation loss. In neither case was the plaintiff's reliance interest protected as such. In *Commonwealth v Amann Aviation Pty Ltd*, Deane J said that:

> an award of reliance damages does not represent the direct recovery of the wasted net expenditure. The basis of an award of reliance damages is the ordinary one in an action for repudiation or breach, namely, that the plaintiff is, so far as money can do it, to be placed in the same situation with respect to damages as if the repudiation or breach had not occurred. Such an award represents the recovery of the wasted net expenditure only in the indirect sense that, in the assessment of damages, the net benefits which would have been derived but for the repudiation or breach are quantified in monetary terms by reference to the presumption that their value would have at least equalled that wasted expenditure.[167]

[5.68]   Thus, reliance damages do not aim to place the plaintiff in the position as if the contract had not been made. They aim to place the plaintiff in the position as if the defendant had performed, through a presumption of profitability. For this reason, there have been calls to abandon the terms 'reliance interest', 'reliance loss' and 'reliance damages', and replace them with the term 'wasted expenditure'.[168]

---

165   (1991) 174 CLR 64.
166   *McRae v Commonwealth Disposals Commission* (1951) 84 CLR 377, 414; *Commonwealth v Amann Aviation Pty Ltd* (1991) 174 CLR 64, 86, 105–07, 126–27, 142–43, 155–56, 166.
167   (1991) 174 CLR 64, 127–28.
168   MB Kelly, 'The Phantom Reliance Interest in Contract Damages' [1992] Wis L Rev 1755; D McLauchlan, 'Reliance Damages for Breach of Contract' [2007] NZ Law Rev 417.

The question has arisen whether an award of reliance damages may be made in respect of expenditure incurred prior to entry into the contract. The English Court of Appeal has held that such expenditure can be recovered where the expenditure was reasonably in the contemplation of the parties as likely to be wasted if the contract was breached.[169] Gaudron J approved this approach in *Commonwealth v Amann Aviation Pty Ltd*.[170] If the aim of reliance damages were to place the plaintiff in the position as if the contract had not been made, pre-contractual expenses should not be recoverable since they would still have been incurred had there been no contract.[171] But since reliance damages aim to compensate expectation loss, it must be asked whether pre-contractual expenditure can properly be taken as a 'proxy' for lost profit. This must depend on the individual case, but there is no objection in principle. Persons who incur expenditure in anticipation of a contract will usually do so only if they expect the contract to be concluded and expect to recoup the expenditure. The presumption of profitability can still be applied.[172] **[5.69]**

In relation to the second issue mentioned at [5.63], the plaintiff's expenditure must be incurred in performance of the contract. Expenditure which would have been made anyway (such as capital expenditure maintaining and acquiring equipment) is not recoverable. Thus, in *McRae*, considered at [5.65], the plaintiff was unable to recoup capital expenditures, such as reconditioning of the salvage boat and purchasing equipment for it. **[5.70]**

In relation to the third issue mentioned at [5.63], it is clear from the majority judgments in *Commonwealth v Amann Aviation Pty Ltd* (see [5.66]) that the expenditure incurred in reliance on the contract must be reasonable, and that the burden of proof is on the plaintiff to establish this. Thus, while the trial judge in *McRae* (see [5.65]) held that the plaintiff's expenses had *not* been reasonably incurred, and only awarded the cost of ascertaining whether the tanker existed, the High Court disagreed and held that it had been reasonable for the plaintiff to assume that the tanker existed and to expend money accordingly. Paterson, Robertson and Duke suggest that unreasonable expenditure might be said to be unlikely to have been contemplated by the parties and thus too remote to be recovered.[173] Another explanation is that the presumption of profitability does not apply to unreasonable expenditure since contracting parties cannot generally expect to recoup unreasonable expenses. **[5.71]**

In relation to the fourth issue mentioned at [5.63], damages must not be awarded for expenses that would not have been recouped, because such an award would place the plaintiff in a better position than without breach. In *Commonwealth v Amann Aviation Pty Ltd*, considered at [5.66], Amann's expenditure exceeded the amount it would have received from the Commonwealth in the three-year contract period. But there were two contingencies: a renewal of the contract (favouring Amann) and a lawful termination of the initial contract (disfavouring Amann). Six of the seven judges in the High Court took the possibility of renewal **[5.72]**

---

169   *Anglia Television Ltd v Reed* [1972] 1 QB 60, 64.
170   (1991) 174 CLR 64, 156.
171   AI Ogus, 'Damages for Pre-Contract Expenditure' (1972) 35 Mod LR 423, 424–25.
172   The view that the plaintiff must prove the profitability of the contract is taken by Ogus, ibid, 426. McLauchlan justifies the recoverability of pre-contractual expenses by saying that the plaintiff has appropriated them to the contract and the defendant's breach has caused them to be wasted (presupposing that the profitability of the contract is conceded or established): D McLauchlan, 'Reliance Damages for Breach of Contract' [2007] NZ Law Rev 417, 444.
173   J Paterson, A Robertson and A Duke, *Principles of Contract Law* (5th edn, LBC 2016) [26.75].

into account.[174] Four of those six judges ignored the possibility of lawful termination and thus permitted Amann to recoup its whole expenditure.[175] The four judges in effect resolved the uncertainty of both events on the balance of probabilities. The matter is further discussed at [2.108]–[2.117].

E   Non-pecuniary loss

[5.73]   A breach of contract may cause the aggrieved party to suffer non-pecuniary loss such as anxiety, disappointment, distress, inconvenience and loss of reputation. Non-pecuniary loss is subject to the same rules on the attribution of responsibility as pecuniary loss. But there are specific restrictions for non-pecuniary loss, both at common law and, at least in some jurisdictions, under statute.

1   Restrictions at common law

[5.74]   At common law, contractual damages for non-pecuniary loss are generally excluded.[176] Different and inconsistent reasons have been advanced for this rule.[177] On the one hand, non-pecuniary loss has been said to be too remote because it is usually not in the contemplation of parties to ordinary, particularly commercial, contracts.[178] On the other hand, it has been argued that non-pecuniary loss is so obviously in the contemplation of contracting parties that they must be taken to assume the risk of suffering it,[179] at least where businesspeople are involved.[180] It has also been argued that damages for non-pecuniary loss contain a punitive element not permissible in contract,[181] and that the subjectivity of non-pecuniary loss makes it impossible for contracting parties to estimate the extent of their liability.[182]

[5.75]   In *Baltic Shipping Co v Dillon*,[183] the High Court of Australia confirmed the general unavailability of contractual damages for non-pecuniary loss, even though several of the judges considered this rule unsatisfactory.[184] The High Court also confirmed that contractual damages for non-pecuniary loss are exceptionally available in three overlapping categories of

---

174   (1991) 174 CLR 64, 86 (Mason CJ and Dawson J), 105 (Brennan J), 126 (Deane J), 144 (Toohey J), 155–56 (Gaudron J).

175   Ibid, 97–98 (Mason CJ and Dawson J); 115 (Brennan J); 158 (Gaudron J).

176   *Hamlin v Great Northern Railway Co* (1856) 1 H & N 408, 411; 156 ER 1261, 1262; *Fink v Fink* (1946) 74 CLR 127, 142–43; *Baltic Shipping Co v Dillon* (1993) 176 CLR 344.

177   The reasons are discussed in S Harder, *Measuring Damages in the Law of Obligations: The Search for Harmonised Principles* (Hart 2010) 104–14.

178   *Kewin v Massachusetts Mutual Life Insurance Co* (1980) 409 Mich 401, 414–19; *Johnson v Unisys Ltd* [2001] UKHL 13, [2003] 1 AC 518 [70] (Lord Millett); *Fidler v Sun Life Assurance Co of Canada* [2006] SCC 30, [2006] 2 SCR 3 [45]; J Edelman, *McGregor on Damages* (20th edn, Sweet & Maxwell 2018) [5–024]; D Campbell, 'Exemplary damages' in D Harris, D Campbell and R Halson, *Remedies in Contract and Tort* (2nd edn, CUP 2005) 600. The contractual remoteness test is discussed at [5.88]–[5.103].

179   *Johnson v Unisys Ltd* [2001] UKHL 13, [2003] 1 AC 518 [70] (Lord Millett); H Carty, 'Contract Theory and Employment Reality' (1986) 49 Mod LR 240, 245.

180   *Crump v Wala* [1994] 2 NZLR 331, 345–46; D Yates, 'Damages for Non-Pecuniary Loss' (1973) 36 Mod LR 535, 538.

181   *Addis v Gramophone Co Ltd* [1909] AC 488, 494–96 (Lord Atkinson); *Herbert Clayton & Jack Waller Ltd v Oliver* [1930] AC 209, 220; *Farley v Skinner (No 2)* [2000] PNLR 441, 454 (Mummery LJ).

182   *Baltic Shipping Co v Dillon* (1993) 176 CLR 344, 370 (Brennan J).

183   (1993) 176 CLR 344.

184   Ibid, 363 (Mason CJ), 381–82 (Deane and Dawson JJ), 396–98 (McHugh J).

case: where a breach of contract has caused personal injury, where a breach of contract has caused physical inconvenience, and where the object of the contract was to provide enjoyment, relaxation or freedom from molestation.[185] These categories, and a possible fourth category, will now be examined.

First, contractual damages have been awarded for non-pecuniary loss resulting from physical injury[186] or a recognised psychiatric illness.[187] The assessment of non-pecuniary loss resulting from personal injury is discussed at [7.56]–[7.68].

[5.76]

Secondly, contractual damages have been awarded for physical inconvenience and ensuing distress, for example where building work was carried out defectively,[188] where residential premises were not kept in reasonable repair,[189] and where a delay in the conveyance of residential premises forced the purchaser to temporarily live in rental accommodation.[190] English courts have said that damages under this head ought to be 'modest' or 'restrained'.[191] Australian courts have rejected that limitation, holding that damages ought to be 'fair and reasonable'.[192]

[5.77]

It should go without saying that physical inconvenience and distress can be suffered only by human beings, not by corporations. However, in *South Parklands Hockey & Tennis Centre Inc v Brown Falconer Group Pty Ltd*,[193] where a dual-purpose hockey/tennis court was constructed so defectively that it could not be used for its intended purpose, Debelle J awarded $30 000 as damages for 'inconvenience' to the plaintiffs, which were a school, a hockey club, a tennis club and a corporation set up by the first three plaintiffs. The award for inconvenience was in effect for the school students and the club members. But those people were neither parties to the building contract nor beneficiaries of the damages award, and the award for inconvenience is not justifiable.

[5.78]

Thirdly, contractual damages for non-pecuniary loss have been awarded where a major object of the contract was to provide enjoyment, relaxation or freedom from molestation. The

[5.79]

---

185   Another category was breach of promise of marriage: Ibid, 362 (Mason CJ). This is no longer actionable: *Marriage Act 1961* (Cth), s 111A.

186   *David Jones Ltd v Willis* (1934) 52 CLR 110; *Grant v Australian Knitting Mills Ltd* (1935) 54 CLR 49 (PC); *Chappel v Hart* (1998) 195 CLR 232; *Mouritz v Hegedus* [1999] WASCA 1061; *Insight Vacations Pty Ltd v Young* [2011] HCA 16, (2011) 243 CLR 149.

187   Eg *Wolters v University of the Sunshine Coast* [2013] QCA 228, [2014] 1 Qd R 571; *Eaton v Tricare (Country) Pty Ltd* [2016] QCA 139. See also *Baltic Shipping Co v Dillon* (1993) 176 CLR 344, 362, 405.

188   *Boncristiano v Lohmann* [1998] 4 VR 82, 93–95; *South Parklands Hockey & Tennis Centre Inc v Brown Falconer Group Pty Ltd* [2004] SASC 81, (2004) 88 SASR 65 [142]; *KBE Contracting Pty Ltd v Mawer* [2007] WASAT 210, (2007) 56 SR (WA) 11 [80]; *Mackay v Knight* [2009] VCAT 911 [50]–[53].

189   *El-Saiedy v NSW Land and Housing Corporation* [2011] NSWSC 820 [93]. In addition, damages for physical inconvenience resulting from the breach of a residential tenancy agreement can be awarded pursuant to the *Residential Tenancies Act 1987* (NSW), s 16(2)(d)(iii): *Free v Thomas* [2009] NSWSC 642 [19].

190   *Bartlett v Arbuckle* [2004] WASC 169 [191]–[193].

191   *Perry v Sidney Phillips & Son* [1982] 1 WLR 1297, 1303 (Lord Denning MR); *Watts v Morrow* [1991] 1 WLR 1421, 1439–43 (Ralph Gibson LJ), 1445 (Bingham LJ); *Ruxley Electronics & Construction Ltd v Forsyth* [1996] AC 344, 374 (Lord Lloyd of Berwick).

192   *Boncristiano v Lohmann* [1998] 4 VR 82, 94–95; *South Parklands Hockey & Tennis Centre Inc v Brown Falconer Group Pty Ltd* [2004] SASC 81, (2004) 88 SASR 65 [143].

193   [2004] SASC 81, (2004) 88 SASR 65 [142].

paradigm case is that of holidays falling short of the promised standard.[194] Such a case also falls into one of the two previous categories where it involves personal injury[195] or physical inconvenience.[196] Outside the context of spoilt holidays, damages for distress have been awarded, for example, where a promise not to molest was breached,[197] where building work was carried out defectively,[198] where the breach of a solicitor's retainer caused the client to lose a claim in relation to personal injury,[199] and where an association wrongfully expelled a member.[200]

[5.80]   The provision of enjoyment and the like need not constitute the sole or even predominant object of the contract. But it is unclear how significant it needs to be. Contractual damages for distress have understandably been denied where a promise to convey land[201] or deliver a blocked house[202] was breached, where a defective heater was supplied,[203] where a lessor of commercial premises breached the covenant for quiet enjoyment,[204] and where the headmaster of a private school allegedly defamed a student.[205] Less obvious is the general denial of damages for distress caused to an employee by wrongful dismissal.[206] Particularly difficult to understand is the denial (at common law) of damages for distress where a lessor of residential premises breached the covenant for quiet enjoyment,[207] and where a promise to provide a horse and carriage for a wedding was breached.[208]

[5.81]   Loss of reputation may constitute a fourth category in which contractual damages for non-pecuniary loss are available.[209] The House of Lords upheld an award of contractual damages

---

194   *Jarvis v Swans Tours Ltd* [1973] QB 233; *Jackson v Horizon Holidays Ltd* [1975] 1 WLR 1468; *Milner v Carnival plc (t/a Cunard)* [2010] EWCA Civ 389, [2010] 3 All ER 701; *Moore v Scenic Tours Pty Ltd (No 2)* [2017] NSWSC 733.

195   *Baltic Shipping Co v Dillon* (1993) 176 CLR 344; *Insight Vacations Pty Ltd v Young* [2010] NSWCA 137, (2010) 78 NSWLR 641.

196   *Athens-MacDonald Travel Service Pty Ltd v Kazis* [1970] SASR 264.

197   *Silberman v Silberman* (1910) 10 SR (NSW) 554.

198   *Coshott v Fewings Joinery Pty Ltd* (NSW Court of Appeal, Gleeson CJ, Priestley and Beazley JJA, 15 July 1996).

199   *Denkewitz v Hodgson* (Supreme Court of Queensland, Ambrose J, 6 November 1998); *Leitch v Reynolds* [2005] NSWCA 259, (2005) Aust Torts Reports 81–806 [114].

200   *Rose v Boxing NSW Inc* [2007] NSWSC 20 [112]–[113]; *Goodwin v Vietnam Veterans Motor Cycle Club Australia NSW Chapter Inc* [2008] NSWSC 154, (2008) 72 NSWLR 224 [46]–[48].

201   *Allison v Hewitt* (1974) 3 DCR (NSW) 193, 196–98.

202   *Turner v Kwikshift Pty Ltd* (1993) 113 FLR 8, 18–19.

203   *Falko v James McEwan & Co Pty Ltd* [1977] VR 447, 449–52. This case did not fall into the category of physical inconvenience since it was held that any significant physical inconvenience suffered would have been due to the plaintiff's failure to mitigate his loss.

204   *Musumeci v Winadell Pty Ltd* (1994) 34 NSWLR 723, 752; *Spathis v Hanave Investment Co Pty Ltd* [2002] NSWSC 304 [180].

205   *Vitale v Bednall* [2000] WASC 207 [72].

206   *Addis v Gramophone Co Ltd* [1909] AC 488; *Russell v Trustees of the Roman Catholic Church for the Archdiocese of Sydney* [2008] NSWCA 217, (2008) 72 NSWLR 559 [63]–[65]. See also *Burazin v Blacktown City Guardian Pty Ltd* (1996) 142 ALR 144, 151. An exceptional case in which such damages were awarded is *Quinn v Gray* [2009] VSC 136, (2009) 184 IR 279. Damages for non-pecuniary loss caused by the manner of *unfair* dismissal are also excluded: *Fair Work Act 2009* (Cth), s 392(4).

207   *Celermajer Holdings Pty Ltd v Kopas* [2011] NSWSC 40, (2011) 16 BPR 30,735 [436].

208   *Fletcher v Berriman* [2001] NSWSC 457 [23]–[24], holding that the object of the contract was the provision of transport. In the Scottish case *Diesen v Samson* [1971] SLT 49, damages were awarded for distress caused to the bride by the failure to take pictures of the wedding.

209   The English cases are discussed in S Harder, *Measuring Damages in the Law of Obligations: The Search for Harmonised Principles* (Hart 2010) 100–03.

for loss of reputation where a bank's careless supervision of its client's financial affairs caused the client to become bankrupt,[210] and where an actor was not allowed to give the promised theatre performance.[211] Citing those two cases, in *Baltic Shipping Co v Dillon*, Brennan J said that damages may be awarded, without proof of pecuniary loss, for loss of reputation caused by 'direct' breach of contract.[212] Australian courts have awarded contractual damages for loss of reputation where a promise to apologise for defamatory statements was breached,[213] and where a promise to use the plaintiff's fashion design only in accordance with the plaintiff's instructions was breached.[214] It has also been said that loss of reputation is compensable where the purpose of a contract, including an employment contract, includes promotion or publicity of the plaintiff.[215] However, damages cannot be awarded for loss of reputation suffered by an employee as a result of wrongful dismissal,[216] or by reason of the manner of unfair dismissal.[217]

While the scope of the exceptions to the general rule is not entirely settled, the exceptions are considerable and undermine the general rule.[218] It may be better to jettison the general rule and instead focus on whether the non-pecuniary loss is within the scope of the defendant's obligation and is significant enough to attract legal redress.[219] This would bring Australian law in line with international standards. For example, Article 7.4.2(2) of the UNIDROIT Principles of International Commercial Contracts 2016 provides that the compensable harm resulting from non-performance 'may be non-pecuniary and includes, for instance, physical suffering or emotional distress'.[220] [5.82]

2   Restrictions under statute

At least in some jurisdictions, statute restricts the availability of contractual damages for certain types of non-pecuniary loss. The NSW Court of Appeal has held that anxiety, disappointment, distress and inconvenience constitute an 'impairment of a person's mental condition' for the [5.83]

---

210   *Wilson v United Counties Bank Ltd* [1920] AC 102.
211   *Herbert Clayton & Jack Waller Ltd v Oliver* [1930] AC 209. Similar cases include *Marbe v George Edwardes (Daly's Theatre) Ltd* [1928] 1 KB 269; *Withers v General Theatre Co Ltd* [1933] 2 KB 536.
212   (1993) 176 CLR 344, 371.
213   *Summertime Holdings Pty Ltd v Environmental Defender's Office Ltd* (1998) 45 NSWLR 291.
214   *Flamingo Park Pty Ltd v Dolly Dolly Creations Pty Ltd* (1986) 65 ALR 500, 523–25.
215   *Rose v Boxing NSW Inc* [2007] NSWSC 20 [111].
216   *Kelmar v Souden* (1902) 2 SR (NSW) 348, 352–53, 354; *Russell v Trustees of the Roman Catholic Church for the Archdiocese of Sydney* [2008] NSWCA 217, (2008) 72 NSWLR 559 [53]–[57]; *Lennon v South Australia* [2010] SASC 272 [676]–[688]. This rule concerns non-pecuniary loss only. Pecuniary loss resulting from an injury to the employee's reputation is compensable, subject to remoteness and mitigation: *Malik v Bank of Credit and Commerce International SA* [1998] AC 20; *Shaw v New South Wales* [2012] NSWCA 102, (2012) 219 IR 87 [113]–[119].
217   *Fair Work Act 2009* (Cth), s 392(4).
218   *Baltic Shipping Co v Dillon* (1993) 176 CLR 344, 363 (Mason CJ).
219   S Harder, *Measuring Damages in the Law of Obligations: The Search for Harmonised Principles* (Hart 2010) 103–04, 114–16. See also J Hartshorne, 'Damages for Contractual Mental Distress after *Farley v Skinner*' (2006) 22 J Cont L 118; R Holmes, 'Mental Distress Damages for Breach of Contract' (2004) 35 VUWLR 687; Scottish Law Commission, *Report on Remedies for Breach of Contract* (Scot Law Com No 174, 1999) Part 3, Appendix A, Draft Contract (Scotland) Bill s 2.
220   Similar provisions are Art 9.501(2)(a) of the *Principles of European Contract Law* and Art III-3:701(3) of the European Union's *Draft Common Frame of Reference*.

purpose of the *Civil Liability Act 2002* (NSW).[221] This means that compensation for anxiety and the like is subject to s 16 of the Act, which applies to actions for breach of contract with some minor exceptions.[222] Section 16 excludes compensation for non-pecuniary loss unless the severity of the loss is at least 15% of the most extreme case; see [7.65]. This threshold will rarely be crossed in the absence of physical injury or a recognised psychiatric illness. For example, the threshold is not reached by distress and inconvenience resulting from construction noise at a holiday hotel,[223] or resulting from significant changes to the itinerary of a river cruise.[224]

[5.84]   Furthermore, anxiety and the like constitutes 'mental harm' for the purposes of the *Civil Liability Act 2002* (NSW), which provides that there is no liability (in contract or otherwise) for 'mental harm resulting from negligence'[225] unless the mental harm is consequent on other personal injury or consists of a recognised psychiatric illness.[226] This applies at least to the breach of a contractual duty of care, and may even apply to strict contractual liability where the defendant was careless.

[5.85]   The latter approach was impliedly taken in *Flight Centre Ltd v Louw*.[227] The plaintiffs booked flights and holiday accommodation at the Le Meridien Hotel on Tahiti with the defendant travel agent. Their holiday was ruined by severe construction noise in the hotel and other disturbances. The defendant thus breached the warranty that the holiday accommodation would meet the plaintiffs' requirements and purpose.[228] It was a case of strict contractual liability. An award of damages for distress and inconvenience was still quashed on the ground that it was excluded by Part 3 of the *Civil Liability Act 2002* (NSW),[229] as the plaintiffs had not suffered physical injury or a recognised psychiatric illness. It was found that the plaintiffs had sought the defendant's advice on where to spend their holidays, and that the defendant, who should have known about the construction work at Le Meridien Hotel, had been careless in recommending that hotel.

[5.86]   In Victoria, anxiety, distress, fear and worry (but not inconvenience) have been held to constitute 'injury' for the purpose of Part VBA (which imposes a threshold on the recovery of damages for non-economic loss) of the *Wrongs Act 1958* (Vic).[230] In the remaining states and territories, anxiety and the like could also be regarded as mental harm or personal injury for the purpose of the civil liability statute (see [7.19]–[7.20]) and would then be subject to the varying restrictions on recovery; see [7.63], [7.66]–[7.68].

---

221   *New South Wales v Ibbett* [2005] NSWCA 445, (2005) 65 NSWLR 168 [124], [211]–[212]; *New South Wales v Corby* [2010] NSWCA 27, (2010) 76 NSWLR 439 [41]; *Insight Vacations Pty Ltd v Young* [2010] NSWCA 137, (2010) 78 NSWLR 641.
222   *Civil Liability Act 2002* (NSW), ss 3B, 11A(2).
223   *Flight Centre Ltd v Louw* [2011] NSWSC 132, (2011) 78 NSWLR 656 [41].
224   *Moore v Scenic Tours Pty Ltd (No 2)* [2017] NSWSC 733 [873].
225   Section 27 defines 'negligence' as 'failure to exercise reasonable care and skill'.
226   *Civil Liability Act 2002* (NSW), ss 27, 28, 31.
227   [2011] NSWSC 132, (2011) 78 NSWLR 656.
228   Ibid, [39].
229   Ibid, [40]. The award was also quashed on the ground that the plaintiff's non-pecuniary loss did not cross the threshold of s 16: ibid, [41].
230   *Thomas v Powercor Australia Ltd* [2011] VSC 586 [116]; *Lakic v Prior* [2016] VSC 293 [157]; *Archibald v Powlett* [2017] VSCA 259 [56]–[67].

If anxiety and the like is regarded as personal injury and thus as subject to a statutory threshold for the recovery of non-pecuniary loss, many cases (such as spoilt holidays) in which contractual damages for non-pecuniary loss are available at common law will not cross the threshold, and contractual expectations not to suffer non-pecuniary loss will not be sufficiently protected even where the provision of pleasure and the like is a major object of the contract.[231] As an exception, it has been held that a lessee's loss of enjoyment of a property as a result of the lessor's failure to keep the property in reasonable repair does not constitute an 'impairment of a person's mental condition' for the purpose of the *Civil Liability Act 2002* (NSW).[232]   [5.87]

III   Attribution of responsibility

Australian private law contains rules on the attribution of responsibility for loss. Chapter 3 discusses those rules that are common to contract and tort. The following sections discuss how the rules on remoteness of damage and contributory negligence affect contractual liability in particular.   [5.88]

A   Remoteness of damage

1   The *Hadley v Baxendale* test

The basic test for determining the extent of contractual liability at common law was laid down in *Hadley v Baxendale*[233] and adopted by the High Court of Australia on many occasions.[234] In *Hadley v Baxendale*, Alderson B said: [5.89]

> Where two parties have made a contract which one of them has broken, the damages which the other party ought to receive in respect of such breach of contract should be such as may fairly and reasonably be considered either arising naturally, i.e., according to the usual course of things, from such breach of contract itself, or such as may reasonably be supposed to have been in the contemplation of both parties, at the time they made the contract, as the probable result of the breach of it.[235]

Alderson B set out two categories of loss: (1) loss arising in the usual course of things from such breach as occurred; and (2) loss that may be supposed to have been in the parties' contemplation, when they made the contract, as the probable result of breach. These are often called the two 'limbs' of *Hadley v Baxendale*, the first limb covering usual loss and the second limb covering unusual loss that was in the parties' contemplation. However, the first limb is a subset of the second limb.[236] The contemplation of the *parties* is the contemplation of a   [5.90]

---

231 N Witzleb, E Bant, S Degeling and K Barker, *Remedies: Commentary and Materials* (6th edn, Lawbook Co 2015) [4.785].
232 *Tralee Technology Holdings Pty Ltd v Chen* [2015] NSWSC 1259 [61]–[62]. See also *El-Saiedy v NSW Land and Housing Corporation* [2011] NSWSC 820 [95]; *Fligg v Owners Strata Plan 53457* [2012] NSWSC 230 [102].
233 (1854) 9 Ex 341; 156 ER 145.
234 *Burns v MAN Automotive (Australia) Pty Ltd* (1986) 161 CLR 653, 667; *Commonwealth v Amann Aviation Pty Ltd* (1991) 174 CLR 64, 91–92, 98–99; *Baltic Shipping Co v Dillon* (1993) 176 CLR 344, 369; *European Bank Ltd v Evans* [2010] HCA 6, (2010) 240 CLR 432 [13].
235 (1854) 9 Ex 341, 354; 156 ER 145, 151.
236 *Jackson v Royal Bank of Scotland plc* [2005] UKHL 3, [2005] 1 WLR 377 [25], [47]–[49].

reasonable person in each party's position,[237] and the reasonable person knows the ordinary course of things.[238] Loss arising in the usual course of things invariably constitutes loss that the parties, as reasonable people, are supposed to have contemplated when they made the contract.

[5.91]   The language of 'contemplation' rather than 'foreseeability', which is used in negligence, might be thought to imply that the parties, at the time of the contract, must have turned their mind to the possibility and consequences of breach. But this is not the case: 'The court has to assume, though it be contrary to the fact, that the parties had in mind the breach that has occurred'.[239] What is required is that the parties *could* have contemplated the loss suffered had they turned their minds to the possibility of breach.[240] Indeed, the *Hadley v Baxendale* test has often been expressed as one of 'foreseeability'.[241]

[5.92]   It might be thought that the *Hadley v Baxendale* test is identical to the foreseeability test applying in negligence and some other torts, discussed at [6.61]–[6.78]. But there are two differences. The first relates to the time at which the loss needs to be foreseeable. In negligence, this is the time when the duty is breached, whereas in contract, it is the time at which the contract is made. The second difference between the tests relates to the degree of likelihood of loss. In negligence, a 'slight possibility' of loss is sufficient; see [6.65]–[6.66]. In *The Heron II*,[242] the House of Lords held that a higher degree of likelihood is required in contract, although it may be less than 50%. Unfortunately, each law lord used a slightly different formula to express the degree of likelihood required in contract. Australian courts have used synonymously[243] the formulae 'not unlikely'[244] and 'serious possibility'.[245]

[5.93]   The remoteness tests in contract and negligence have two things in common. First, both tests are subject to the rule that a wrongdoer must take his victim as he finds him.[246] Secondly, it is only the type of loss, and not its extent, which needs to be foreseeable.[247] This is illustrated,

---

237   *Koufos v C Czarnikow Ltd (The Heron II)* [1969] 1 AC 350, 385 (Lord Reid), 424 (Lord Upjohn); *Christopher Hill Ltd v Ashington Piggeries Ltd* [1969] 3 All ER 1496, 1524; *Flamingo Park Pty Ltd v Dolly Dolly Creations Pty Ltd* (1986) 65 ALR 500, 522.

238   *Victoria Laundry (Windsor) Ltd v Newman Industries Ltd* [1949] 2 KB 528, 539; MA Eisenberg, 'The Principle of Hadley v Baxendale' (1992) 80 Cal L Rev 563, 565–66.

239   *Parsons (Livestock) Ltd v Uttley Ingham & Co Ltd* [1978] QB 791, 807 (Scarman LJ). See also *National Australia Bank Ltd v Nemur Varity Pty Ltd* [2002] VSCA 18, (2002) 4 VR 252 [44] (Batt JA); *Reinhold v New South Wales Lotteries Corporation* [2008] NSWSC 5 [232].

240   *Victoria Laundry (Windsor) Ltd v Newman Industries Ltd* [1949] 2 KB 528, 540.

241   Ibid, 539; *Burns v MAN Automotive (Australia) Pty Ltd* (1986) 161 CLR 653, 673 (Brennan J); *Duke Group Ltd (in liq) v Pilmer* (1999) 73 SASR 64, 131; *B J McAdam Pty Ltd v Jax Tyres Pty Ltd (No 3)* [2012] FCA 1438 [31].

242   *Koufos C Czarnikow Ltd (The Heron II)* [1969] 1 AC 350.

243   The two formulae were used interchangeably in *Haviv Holdings Pty Ltd v Howards Storage World Pty Ltd* [2009] FCA 242, (2009) 254 ALR 273 [27].

244   *South Coast Basalt Pty Ltd v R W Miller & Co Pty Ltd* [1981] 1 NSWLR 356 (PC) 364; *Oxley County Council v Macdonald* [1999] NSWCA 126 [69]; *Stuart Pty Ltd v Condor Commercial Insulation Pty Ltd* [2006] NSWCA 334, (2006) Aust Contract R 90–245 [98]–[102].

245   *Alexander v Cambridge Credit Corporation Ltd* (1987) 9 NSWLR 310, 351, 365–67; *Cripps v G & M Dawson Pty Ltd* [2006] NSWCA 81, (2006) ANZ ConvR 350 [35]; *Reinhold v New South Wales Lotteries Corporation* [2008] NSWSC 5 [230].

246   *Gribben v Woree Caravan Park and Motels* [1970] Qd R 420, 427–28.

247   *South Coast Basalt Pty Ltd v R W Miller & Co Pty Ltd* [1981] 1 NSWLR 356 (PC) 364; *Flamingo Park Pty Ltd v Dolly Dolly Creations Pty Ltd* (1986) 65 ALR 500, 522; *Alexander v Cambridge Credit Corporation Ltd* (1987) 9 NSWLR 310, 365–66; *Stuart Pty Ltd v Condor Commercial Insulation Pty Ltd* [2006] NSWCA 334, (2006) Aust Contract R 90–245 [45]–[46].

in the contractual context, by *Parsons (Livestock) Ltd v Uttley Ingham & Co Ltd*.[248] The plaintiff, a pig farmer, bought a bulk food storage hopper from the defendant in which to store pignuts for its pigs. When installing the hopper, the defendant forgot to unseal the ventilator, with the result that the nuts dispensed by the hopper were mouldy. This caused the outbreak of an intestinal infection caused by the bacterium *Escherichia coli*, killing 254 pigs. The defendant, having breached a contractual warranty that the hopper would be reasonably fit for the purpose of storing pignuts in a condition suitable for feeding to the plaintiff's pigs, was held liable for the death of the pigs even though it had not been foreseeable as a serious possibility that the improper installation of the hopper could cause an outbreak of *E. coli*. The majority in the English Court of Appeal held that it was necessary to foresee some illness in the pigs, but not specifically *E. coli*.[249]

2   The significance of the defendant's knowledge of the plaintiff's circumstances

The reference to the contemplation of the *parties* in the *Hadley v Baxendale* test is really a reference to the defendant's contemplation. 'No case has been found in which recovery was denied because the injured party did not foresee the loss.'[250] Whether certain loss is too remote thus depends on what the defendant, at the time of the contract, knew about the plaintiff's circumstances. As Lord Reid said in *The Heron II*:   [5.94]

> The crucial question is whether, on the information available to the defendant when the contract was made, he should, or the reasonable man in his position would, have realised that such loss was sufficiently likely to result from the breach of contract to make it proper to hold that the loss flowed naturally from the breach or that loss of that kind should have been within his contemplation.[251]

The defendant's knowledge about the plaintiff's circumstances at the time of the contract has relevance for the second limb of the *Hadley v Baxendale* test. A plaintiff who is unusually susceptible to suffering loss cannot recover damages for that loss unless the defendant knew about the plaintiff's unusual susceptibility at the time of the contract. Courts have applied this rule strictly, as the following three examples demonstrate.   [5.95]

First, where non-completion by a purchaser of land forces the vendor to continue to pay interest under a mortgage on the land sold or to breach a contract for the purchase of new property, this loss cannot be recovered unless, at the time of the contract, the purchaser was   [5.96]

---

248   [1978] QB 791. Another example is *South Coast Basalt Pty Ltd v R W Miller & Co Pty Ltd* [1981] 1 NSWLR 356 (PC) 364.

249   [1978] QB 791, 805 (Orr LJ), 810–13 (Scarman LJ). Lord Denning MR (at 802–04) opined that the *Wagon Mound* test, which was satisfied on the facts, applied to liability in contract as well as negligence in respect of injury to the person or property (as opposed to pure economic loss). This view has found no support in any other case.

250   AG Murphey, 'Consequential Damages in Contracts for the International Sale of Goods and the Legacy of Hadley' (1989) 23 GWJILE 415, 435.

251   *Koufos v C Czarnikow Ltd (The Heron II)* [1969] 1 AC 350, 385. Approvingly quoted in *Wenham v Ella* (1972) 127 CLR 454, 471 (Gibbs J); *Burns v MAN Automotive (Australia) Pty Ltd* (1986) 161 CLR 653, 667 (Wilson, Deane and Dawson JJ); *Commonwealth v Amann Aviation Pty Ltd* (1991) 174 CLR 64, 99 (Brennan J); *Baltic Shipping Co v Dillon* (1993) 176 CLR 344, 369 (Brennan J).

aware of, respectively, the mortgage[252] or the vendor's intention to purchase a new property.[253] Secondly, a builder who failed to punctually complete the construction of units for a developer was not liable for the extra interest paid by the developer under a loan taken out to purchase the land and fund the construction, because the builder was unaware of that loan when the construction contract was made.[254] Thirdly, a lender who failed to provide a loan which the borrower intended to use to repay an existing loan (from a different lender) was not liable for the extra cost incurred under the existing loan, because the lender did not know about the existing loan when the contract was made.[255]

[5.97]   The *Hadley v Baxendale* test excludes liability for loss resulting from a special susceptibility on the plaintiff's part not known to the defendant when the contract was made. Liability for such loss has been considered unfair on the ground that the defendant, had he been aware of the plaintiff's special susceptibility at the time of the contract, might have charged a higher price, or negotiated for an exclusion clause, or refused to contract at all; the defendant must not be deprived of that opportunity.[256] It has also been argued that a disclosure of the plaintiff's special susceptibility at the time of the contract fosters economic efficiency by enabling the defendant to take optimal precautions against breach.[257] However, the economic argument is not unchallenged.[258] Furthermore, the argument that the *Hadley v Baxendale* test leads contracting parties to disclose a special susceptibility to their contract-partner assumes that contracting parties know the law in that detail, and this assumption is wrong in many instances.[259]

3   Assumption of responsibility as overriding criterion?

[5.98]   A contract may expressly stipulate which party bears what loss in the event of breach by one party. If valid,[260] that term overrides the allocation of loss under the general law, including the

---

252   *Jampco Pty Ltd v Cameron (No 2)* (1985) 3 NSWLR 391, 396; *Statewide Developments Pty Ltd v Higgins* [2011] NSWCA 35, (2011) 15 BPR 29,195 [38]–[39].

253   *Palasty v Parlby* [2007] NSWCA 345, (2007) 13 BPR 25,311 [21]–[27] (where the purchaser possessed the required knowledge).

254   *Bobo's Fashion Pty Ltd v MJF Property Developments Pty Ltd* [2004] VCAT 1090 [24].

255   *Paillas v Loans Plus Pty Ltd* [2008] NSWSC 849 [25].

256   *Hadley v Baxendale* (1854) 9 Ex 341, 355; 156 ER 145, 151; *Seven Seas Properties Ltd v Al-Essa (No 2)* [1993] 1 WLR 1083, 1088; *Jackson v Royal Bank of Scotland plc* [2005] UKHL 3, [2005] 1 WLR 377 [36] (Lord Hope); *Castle Constructions Pty Ltd v Fekala Pty Ltd* [2006] NSWCA 133, (2006) 65 NSWLR 648 [39]; *Stuart Pty Ltd v Condor Commercial Insulation Pty Ltd* [2006] NSWCA 334, (2006) Aust Contract R 90–245 [51]–[52].

257   I Ayres and R Gertner, 'Filling Gaps in Incomplete Contracts: An Economic Theory of Default Rules' (1989) 99 Yale LJ 87, 101–04; LA Bebchuk and S Shavell, 'Information and the Scope of Liability for Breach of Contract: The Rule of *Hadley v Baxendale*' (1991) 7 JLEO 284, 285 ff; RA Posner, *Economic Analysis of Law* (9th edn, Aspen 2014) §4.11; P Cane, *Tort Law and Economic Interests* (2nd edn, Clarendon Press 1996) 145; R Halson, 'Remoteness' in D Harris, D Campbell and R Halson, *Remedies in Contract and Tort* (2nd edn, CUP 2005) 91–93.

258   See MA Eisenberg, 'The Principle of *Hadley v Baxendale*' (1992) 80 Cal L Rev 563, 592–96; JS Johnston, 'Strategic Bargaining and the Economic Theory of Contract Default Rules' (1990) 100 Yale LJ 615, 627–36; A Tettenborn, '*Hadley v Baxendale* Foreseeability: A Principle Beyond Its Sell-By Date?' (2007) 23 J Cont L 120, 132–33; LE Wolcher, 'Price Discrimination and Inefficient Risk Allocation under the Rule of *Hadley v Baxendale*' (1989) 12 Res in Law and Econ 9, 19–20.

259   For further discussion, see S Harder, *Measuring Damages in the Law of Obligations: The Search for Harmonised Principles* (Hart 2010) 57–68.

260   An unfair term in a standard form contract is void if the contract is a consumer contract or a small business contract: *Competition and Consumer Act 2010* (Cth), sch 2, pt 2-3.

Hadley v Baxendale test. It is controversial whether the *Hadley v Baxendale* test is also subject to an implied allocation of risk in the contract,[261] which may exclude liability for foreseeable loss and impose liability for unforeseeable loss.[262]

The debate has focused on the exclusion of liability for foreseeable loss. Proponents of an agreement-centred approach argue that there should be no liability for loss caused by a breach of contract unless the contract-breaker assumed responsibility for that loss, even if the loss was foreseeable at the time of contracting.[263] An oft-mooted hypothetical involves a person hiring a taxi to get to a business meeting, advising the taxi firm at the time of booking of the purpose of the trip. Due to delay by the taxi driver, the passenger misses the meeting and loses substantial profit. While the type of loss suffered by the passenger was foreseeable, it is argued that the taxi firm is not liable for that loss[264] because it did not assume responsibility for it,[265] unless the fare was significantly increased in response to the passenger's information.[266]

[5.99]

The view that the *Hadley v Baxendale* test must yield to an implied allocation of risk in the contract gains impetus from *The Achilleas*.[267] A bulk carrier was chartered with a specified date for redelivery. Prior to that date, the owner of the vessel fixed a follow-on charter with a different company, commencing almost immediately after the redelivery date under the first charter. The vessel was not returned at the date agreed, and the owner had to renegotiate the second charter and accept a lower rate of hire. As damages for breach of contract, the owner claimed the difference between the rate originally agreed in the follow-on charter and the reduced rate agreed in the renegotiated follow-on charter, for the duration of that charter. The House of Lords held that the owner was entitled only to the difference between the market rate and the rate under the charter breached, for the nine days between the contractual date of redelivery and the actual date of redelivery.

[5.100]

261   Singapore's Court of Appeal has taken the view that the *Hadley v Baxendale* test itself is sufficiently flexible to take account of contractual risk allocations: *MFM Restaurants Pte Ltd v Fish & Co Restaurants Pte Ltd* [2010] SGCA 36, [2011] 1 SLR 150 [112]; *Out of the Box Pte Ltd v Wanin Industries Pte Ltd* [2013] SGCA 15, [2013] 2 SLR 363 [24]–[47].

262   *Supershield Ltd v Siemens Building Technologies FE Ltd* [2010] EWCA Civ 7, [2010] 2 All ER (Comm) 1185 [43].

263   R Halson, 'Remoteness' in D Harris, D Campbell and R Halson, *Remedies in Contract and Tort* (2nd edn, CUP 2005) 97; A Kramer, 'An Agreement-Centred Approach to Remoteness and Contract Damages' in N Cohen and E McKendrick (eds), *Comparative Remedies for Breach of Contract* (Hart 2005) 269–70; D McLauchlan, 'Remoteness Re-Invented?' (2009) 9 OUCLJ 109, 113; A Tettenborn, '*Hadley v Baxendale* Foreseeability: A Principle Beyond Its Sell-By Date?' (2007) 23 J Cont L 120, 144–45; J Wightman, 'Negligent Valuations and a Drop in the Property Market: The Limits of the Expectation Loss Principle' (1998) 61 Mod LR 68, 76.

264   This view was already expressed in *British Columbia and Vancouver's Island Spar, Lumber, and Saw-Mill Co Ltd v Nettleship* (1868) LR 3 CP 499, 510 (Willes J).

265   R Halson, 'Remoteness' in D Harris, D Campbell and R Halson, *Remedies in Contract and Tort* (2nd edn, CUP 2005) 97; A Kramer, 'An Agreement-Centred Approach to Remoteness and Contract Damages' in N Cohen and E McKendrick (eds), *Comparative Remedies for Breach of Contract* (Hart 2005) 269–70; D McLauchlan, 'Remoteness Re-invented?' (2009) 9 OUCLJ 109, 113; A Tettenborn, '*Hadley v Baxendale* Foreseeability: A Principle Beyond Its Sell-By Date?' (2007) 23 J Cont L 120, 144–45; J Wightman, 'Negligent Valuations and a Drop in the Property Market: The Limits of the Expectation Loss Principle' (1998) 61 Mod LR 68, 76.

266   Kramer, ibid.

267   *Transfield Shipping Inc v Mercator Shipping Inc (The Achilleas)* [2008] UKHL 48, [2009] 1 AC 61.

[5.101]   Lord Hoffmann and Lord Hope held that the charterer had not assumed responsibility for the loss of hire under a follow-on charter, considering the general understanding in the relevant market.[268] It was therefore immaterial whether the loss had been foreseeable. The *Hadley v Baxendale* test was said to involve a prima facie assumption about what the parties intended, but could be rebutted by showing that the contract-breaker assumed no responsibility for the loss in question.[269] Lord Rodger expressed no view on the relevance of an assumption of responsibility,[270] and rejected the charterer's liability on the ground that the owner's loss had been unforeseeable.[271] Lord Walker's judgment is unclear, not least because he expressed agreement with Lord Hoffmann, Lord Hope and Lord Rodger.[272] Baroness Hale expressed doubts as to whether the charterer's liability should be limited, but added that if it was, she preferred Lord Rodger's reasons.[273]

[5.102]   Judicial and scholarly opinion is divided on whether Lord Hoffmann and Lord Hope's view that contractual liability ultimately depends on an assumption of responsibility formed the ratio of the decision by the House of Lords.[274] It remains to be seen whether *The Achilleas* will have an impact in Australian cases. In obiter dicta, the NSW Court of Appeal has cited Lord Hoffmann and Lord Hope's view without disapproval,[275] although the court seemed to see it as a gloss on the *Hadley v Baxendale* test.

[5.103]   Andrew Robertson and others reject an agreement-centred approach to remoteness on the basis that contracting parties rarely think about the allocation of loss in the event of breach, providing the court with little material from which to infer the parties' intentions.[276] Lord Hoffmann, writing extra-judicially, has objected that this argument pays insufficient attention to the objective approach to contract interpretation, under which the understanding of a reasonable person is relevant. The reasonable person may infer a certain allocation of risk from the circumstances in which the contract was made, even if the parties themselves are unaware.[277] However, there will be cases in which an allocation of risk by the parties cannot be ascertained, even objectively. The *Hadley v Baxendale* test fills that gap. But where clear

---

268   Ibid, [11]–[26] (Lord Hoffmann), [30]–[36] (Lord Hope).
269   Ibid, [9] (Lord Hoffmann), [32] (Lord Hope).
270   Ibid, [63].
271   Ibid, [60]. This view is considered unconvincing by A Kramer, 'The New Test of Remoteness in Contract' (2009) 125 LQR 408, 409; D McLauchlan, 'Remoteness Re-Invented?' (2009) 9 OUCLJ 109, 123.
272   [2008] UKHL 48, [2009] 1 AC 61 [87].
273   Ibid, [93].
274   See A Ambast and S Kher, 'The Significance of *Transfield v Mercator* for the Law of Contractual Damages' (2010) 24 CLQ 3, 6; S Harder, *Measuring Damages in the Law of Obligations: The Search for Harmonised Principles* (Hart 2010) 46–47.
275   *Evans & Associates v European Bank Ltd* [2009] NSWCA 67, (2009) 255 ALR 171 [58], [125]; *Russell v Trustees of the Roman Catholic Church for the Archdiocese of Sydney* [2008] NSWCA 217, (2008) 72 NSWLR 559 [61]. See also *Dome Resources NL v Silver* [2008] NSWCA 322, (2008) 72 NSWLR 693 [68].
276   A Robertson, 'The Basis of the Remoteness Rule in Contract' (2008) 28 LS 172. The argument has been adopted by M Harris, 'Fairness and Remoteness of Damage in Contract Law: A Lexical Ordering Approach' (2011) 28 J Cont L 122, 133; M Stiggelbout, 'Contractual Remoteness, "Scope of Duty" and Intention' [2012] LMCLQ 97, 118–20; PCK Wee, 'Contractual Interpretation and Remoteness' [2010] LMCLQ 150, 167–69; A Zheng, 'The Achilleas Heel of Contractual Damages: What Does the "Assumption of Risk" Principle Add to the Law of Remoteness' (2011) 24 CLQ 11, 15–16.
277   Lord Hoffmann, 'The *Achilleas*: Custom and Practice or Foreseeability?' (2010) 14 Edin LR 47, 60–61.

evidence as to the parties' intention does exist,[278] the allocation of risk by the parties ought to override the *Hadley v Baxendale* test or inform its application to the facts.[279]

Indeed, prior to *The Achilleas*, contractual liability had already been denied on the ground that the defendant had not assumed responsibility for the plaintiff's loss.[280] For example, in *Stuart Pty Ltd v Condor Commercial Insulation Pty Ltd*,[281] the plaintiff undertook to replace the insulation in certain residential properties for the Commonwealth, and subcontracted that work to the defendant. The defendant failed to box the downlights in one property, subsequently causing a fire. As a result, the Commonwealth validly terminated its contract with the plaintiff, who sought to recover lost profit from the defendant. The NSW Court of Appeal denied such damages on the ground that the outbreak of fire had been too unlikely to satisfy the contractual foreseeability threshold,[282] and that the defendant had not undertaken the risk of a termination of the head-contract because the price charged by the defendant was out of all proportion to that risk and the plaintiff was responsible for the supervision of the work.[283]

[5.104]

B   Contributory negligence

Contributory negligence denotes unreasonable conduct (in the sense of a failure to take reasonable care of one's own affairs) by the plaintiff that contributed to the occurrence of the defendant's wrong or the ensuing loss. The doctrine of contributory negligence is usually applied to conduct by the plaintiff that occurred before the wrong or before the plaintiff knew or ought to have known the facts giving rise to the wrong, but has occasionally been applied to conduct by the plaintiff occurring after the plaintiff became aware of the wrong; see [3.125]–[3.128].

[5.105]

At common law, contributory negligence constitutes a complete defence to a claim in negligence and some other torts (see [6.90]), but not to a claim in contract.[284] It has been said that 'a man is entitled to act in the faith that the other party to a contract is carrying out his part of it properly'.[285] However, while contributory negligence is not a stand-alone doctrine in the same way as in negligence (unless liability is concurrent), unreasonable conduct by the

[5.106]

---

278   It has been argued that there was insufficient evidence on the parties' intention in *The Achilleas*: D McLauchlan, 'Remoteness Re-Invented?' (2009) 9 OUCLJ 109, 135–38; PCK Wee, 'Contractual Interpretation and Remoteness' [2010] LMCLQ 150, 165–66.
279   In *Haviv Holdings Pty Ltd v Howards Storage World Pty Ltd* [2009] FCA 242, (2009) 254 ALR 273 [36], the fact that a franchise agreement gave the franchisee a licence for only one store was the key basis for holding that any loss of profit that would have been made in another store had been unforeseeable.
280   A Ambast and S Kher, 'The Significance of *Transfield v Mercator* for the Law of Contractual Damages' (2010) 24 CLQ 3, 5–6.
281   [2006] NSWCA 334, (2006) Aust Contract R 90–245.
282   Ibid, [102].
283   Ibid, [95], [97].
284   *Astley v Austrust Ltd* (1999) 197 CLR 1, 33 (Gleeson CJ, McHugh, Gummow and Hayne JJ): 'No case can be found in the books where contributory negligence, as such, was ever held to be a defence to an action for breach of contract'.
285   *Compania Naviera Maropan S/A v Bowaters Lloyd Pulp and Paper Mills Ltd* [1955] 2 QB 68, 77 (Devlin J), approvingly quoted in *Reardon Smith Line Ltd v Australian Wheat Board* (1956) 93 CLR 577 (PC) 585 (Lord Somervell).

plaintiff may affect contractual liability at common law through the doctrines of *novus actus interveniens* and remoteness of damage.[286]

[5.107]   Contributory negligence constituted a *novus actus interveniens* (see [3.74]) in *Lexmead (Basingstoke) Ltd v Lewis*.[287] The owner of a Land Rover bought a towing hitch to couple the car to a trailer. After the towing hitch had been used for some time, it lost its brass spindle and handle and became unsafe. The owner of the car was aware of the damage to the towing hitch, but continued to use it. As a result of the defective state of the towing hitch, the trailer became detached while in motion, causing a severe accident. The owner of the Land Rover, who had to pay damages for the consequences of the accident, sought reimbursement from the seller of the towing hitch, based on the breach of an implied warranty that the hitch would be fit for purpose. The House of Lords exonerated the seller on the ground that the buyer's carelessness in continuing to use the towing hitch after becoming aware of its defective condition broke the chain of causation between the seller's breach of warranty and the accident.[288]

[5.108]   In *Berryman v London Borough of Hounslow*,[289] contributory negligence was found to render the ensuing loss too remote. The plaintiff lived on the fifth floor of an apartment tower. When she came home from shopping, with two children and five shopping bags, neither lift in the building worked. She carried the bags upstairs, with her baby constantly on her hip. As a result, she suffered a slipped disc. The landlord was found to have breached its contractual duty to keep the lifts in reasonable working order. Nevertheless, the English Court of Appeal denied liability for the plaintiff's injury on the ground that the injury had been unforeseeable 'given that anyone climbing the stairs would be likely to lessen the load, to take it in stages, to take their time and/or to get help'.[290]

[5.109]   Statutes in all Australian jurisdictions have replaced the complete defence of contributory negligence in tort with a regime under which the court apportions liability according to each party's responsibility for the loss; see [6.89]. It was unclear whether the initial version of those statutes applied to contractual liability. The English Court of Appeal has held that the British apportionment statute,[291] which makes no express reference to contractual liability, applies to liability for the breach of a contractual duty of care that is concurrent with a tortious duty of care, and does not apply to other contractual liability.[292] In *Astley v Austrust Ltd*,[293] the High Court of Australia refused an application to contract of the then South Australian contributory

---

286   Both doctrines were considered in *Rolfe v Katunga Lucerne Mill Pty Ltd* [2005] NSWCA 252, (2005) ASAL 55–146, but neither excluded liability on the facts.
287   [1982] AC 225. The case is also known under the name *Lambert v Lewis*.
288   Ibid, 276–77. Cf *Rolfe v Katunga Lucerne Mill Pty Ltd* [2005] NSWCA 252, (2005) ASAL 55–146, where the plaintiff's horses died from contaminated chaff which they had been given after the plaintiff had heard rumours that it might be contaminated. The plaintiff's decision to feed the chaff to the horses was not a *novus actus interveniens*.
289   [1997] PIQR P83, (1998) 30 HLR 567.
290   [1997] PIQR P83, P89; (1998) 30 HLR 567, 573 (Henry LJ, with whom Stuart-Smith LJ and Aldous LJ agreed). See also *Marnica v Carter* [2014] VSC 274 [37].
291   *Law Reform (Contributory Negligence) Act 1945* (UK).
292   *Forsikringsaktieselskapet Vesta v Butcher* [1989] AC 852, 860–67, 875, 879; *Bank of Nova Scotia v Hellenic Mutual War Risks Association (Bermuda) Ltd (The Good Luck)* [1990] 1 QB 818, 904; *Barclays Bank plc v Fairclough Building Ltd* [1995] QB 214, 228–30, 233, 234; *Trebor Bassett Holdings Ltd v ADT Fire and Security plc* [2012] EWCA Civ 1158, [2012] BLR 441 [11], [13].
293   (1999) 197 CLR 1, 23–38.

negligence statute,[294] the relevant provisions of which were identical to those of the British statute.

As a consequence, where there was liability for the breach of a contractual and tortious duty of care (which is common in cases of professional negligence) and the plaintiff was contributorily negligent, liability in contract could not be apportioned, rendering the possible apportionment of liability in tort irrelevant. This unsatisfactory situation was resolved by amendments to the contributory negligence statutes. However, with the exception of the current South Australian statute, the amendment has created a new problem.   [5.110]

Today, the contributory negligence statutes of all Australian jurisdictions other than South Australia apply to liability for the breach of a contractual duty of care that is concurrent and coextensive with a tortious duty of care,[295] and do not apply to other instances of contractual liability.[296] Therefore, where the plaintiff in an action for the breach of a contractual duty of care was contributorily negligent, the defendant will seek to establish additional liability for breach of a tortious duty of care in order to make apportionment available, whereas the plaintiff will seek to exonerate the defendant from tortious liability. This is an odd reversal of roles.[297] The problem does not exist in South Australia, whose contributory negligence statute, while still not applying to strict contractual liability (that is, liability not dependent on fault), applies to the breach of a contractual duty of care, whether or not there is concurrent liability in tort.[298]   [5.111]

Insofar as the contributory negligence statutes apply to contractual liability, the rules governing the quality of the plaintiff's conduct, factual causation and the scope of the duty, the apportionable loss and the apportionment exercise are the same as in tort, discussed at [6.97]–[6.116].   [5.112]

In all Australian jurisdictions, apportionment is unavailable in cases of strict contractual liability. This is not in line with international standards. For example, Article 7.4.7 of the UNIDROIT Principles of International Commercial Contracts 2016 provides for an apportionment of liability in all cases of contractual liability.[299] The position in Australian (and English) law has been defended with the argument (among others[300]) that the availability of apportionment in cases of strict liability would bring the plaintiff under a duty to supervise the   [5.113]

294 *Wrongs Act 1936* (SA), s 27A.
295 *Civil Law (Wrongs) Act 2002* (ACT), s 101; *Law Reform (Miscellaneous Provisions) Act 1965* (NSW), s 8; *Law Reform (Miscellaneous Provisions) Act 1956* (NT), s 15(1); *Law Reform Act 1995* (Qld), s 5; *Wrongs Act 1954* (Tas), s 2; *Wrongs Act 1958* (Vic), s 25; *Law Reform (Contributory Negligence and Tortfeasors' Contribution) Act 1947* (WA), s 3A.
296 Thus, they do not apply to strict contractual liability concurrent with liability in tort: *French v QBE Insurance (Australia) Ltd* [2011] QSC 105, (2011) 58 MVR 214 [162].
297 A Burrows, *Understanding the Law of Obligations: Essays on Contract, Tort and Restitution* (Hart 1998) 150.
298 *Law Reform (Contributory Negligence and Apportionment of Liability) Act 2001* (SA), s 4(1)(b). See *Westpac Banking Corporation v Haynes* [2017] SASC 23 [265].
299 The same is true for Art 9.504 of the *Principles of European Contract Law* and Art 167(3) of the European Code of Contract, published as a special issue of the *Edinburgh Law Review 2004*. The United Nations Convention on Contracts for the International Sale of Goods does not address contributory negligence in general but contains the mitigation principle (Art 77) and excludes liability where one party causes the other party to breach (Art 80).
300 This and other arguments are discussed in S Harder, *Measuring Damages in the Law of Obligations: The Search for Harmonised Principles* (Hart 2010) 162–67.

defendant's performance, which would undermine the strictness of the defendant's obligation.[301] This fear seems exaggerated.

[5.114]   Moreover, an exclusion of apportionment with a view to protecting the plaintiff may have the opposite effect by forcing a complete exoneration of the defendant on the ground of causation or remoteness. An illustration is *Quinn v Burch Brothers (Builders) Ltd*.[302] When the defendant, in breach of contract, failed to supply the plaintiff with a stepladder, the plaintiff made do with a folded trestle that was not footed. He fell to the ground and was injured. Paull J considered the use of the trestle unreasonable. He said that he would have apportioned liability if apportionment had been available.[303] Since it was a case of strict contractual liability, apportionment was unavailable, and Paull J classified the plaintiff's conduct as a *novus actus interveniens*.[304]

---

301   Law Commission, 'Contributory Negligence as a Defence in Contract' (Law Com No 219, 1993) [4.2]–[4.4]; PA Chandler, 'Contributory Negligence and Contract: Some Underlying Disparities' (1989) 40 NILQ 152, 172.
302   [1966] 2 QB 370.
303   Ibid, 375.
304   Ibid, 378.

6

COMPENSATION IN TORT

I   Introduction

[6.1]   The victim of a tort can generally claim compensatory damages for any loss suffered as a result of the tort. The assessment of such damages and the attribution of responsibility for such loss are generally governed by the rules discussed in Chs 2 to 4 for civil wrongs in general. Specific rules for tort are discussed in this chapter. The assessment of compensatory damages for personal injury, which are usually claimed in tort, are discussed in Ch 7.

II   Assessment of compensation

A   General principle

[6.2]   Tortious conduct can occur in myriad forms. But the basic measure of compensation is always the same. As Lord Blackburn famously said in *Livingstone v Rawyards Coal Co*, compensation for tort aims to place the victim 'in the same position as he would have been in if he had not sustained the wrong'.[1] A corollary is that the plaintiff cannot recover more than he or she has lost.[2] An application of the compensatory principle in an individual case can be difficult, in particular where personal injury or non-pecuniary loss has been caused. 'The restoration by way of compensation is therefore accomplished to a large extent by the exercise of a sound imagination and the practice of the broad axe.'[3]

B   Specific contexts

[6.3]   Instead of directly applying the general compensatory principle to the facts of every case, the courts have developed concrete rules in a variety of contexts. Most of these rules constitute a refinement of the general principle for the circumstances in question, but some rules deviate from the general principle. The rules developed in certain contexts will now be discussed. This section is structured according to certain conduct or events. It is not directly structured according to torts, although certain factual circumstances may be linked to one or more torts. Nor is this section directly structured according to types of protected interests, since the same interest can be violated in different ways, attracting different measures of compensation. Personal injury is discussed separately in Ch 7 and is omitted here.

---

1   (1880) 5 App Cas 25, 39. The High Court of Australia has applied this statement on numerous occasions, eg *Butler v Egg and Egg Pulp Marketing Board* (1966) 114 CLR 185, 191; *Nominal Defendant v Gardikiotis* (1996) 186 CLR 49; *Husher v Husher* (1999) 197 CLR 138, 143–44; *Harriton v Stephens* [2006] HCA 15, (2006) 226 CLR 52 [81], [264].

2   *Haines v Bendall* (1991) 172 CLR 60, 63; *Clark v Macourt* [2013] HCA 56, (2013) 253 CLR 1 [59] (Gageler J); *James Hardie & Co Pty Ltd v Newton* (1997) 42 NSWLR 729, 735; *Dionisatos v Acrow Formwork & Scaffolding Pty Ltd* [2015] NSWCA 281, (2015) 91 NSWLR 34 [201].

3   *Watson, Laidlaw & Co Ltd v Pott, Cassels & Williamson* (1914) SC (HL) 18, 29–30 (Lord Shaw). Quoted, eg, in *Whitfield v De Lauret & Co Ltd* (1920) 29 CLR 71, 80–81; *Carson v John Fairfax & Sons Ltd* (1993) 178 CLR 44, 115; *Cattanach v Melchior* [2003] HCA 38, (2003) 215 CLR 1 [101].

1   Damage to reputation: defamation

Uniform legislation in all Australian jurisdictions provides that 'the publication of defamatory matter of any kind is actionable without proof of special damage'.[4] Damage caused by the defamation is compensable. Since injury to reputation constitutes the gist of defamation, loss of reputation is the main head of compensable loss. It has been said that 'some general damage is presumed'.[5] A single sum is awarded for loss of reputation,[6] but the High Court of Australia has identified three overlapping purposes of such an award where the plaintiff is a natural person: consolation for the personal distress and hurt caused to the plaintiff by the publication, reparation for harm done to the plaintiff's personal and (if relevant) business reputation, and vindication of the plaintiff's reputation.[7] While the first two purposes are often considered together and constitute consolation for the wrong done to the plaintiff, vindication looks to the attitude of others towards the plaintiff: the award must be sufficiently large to signal to the public the vindication of the plaintiff's reputation.[8]

[6.4]

Pursuant to the uniform defamation legislation, a corporation can only sue for defamation if it is not a public body and it either constitutes a not-for-profit organisation or it employs fewer than 10 people and is not related to another corporation.[9] A corporation can obtain compensation for injury to reputation,[10] but not for injured feelings.[11]

[6.5]

Loss of reputation is essentially non-pecuniary loss. Insofar as damages provide consolation to the plaintiff, they take account of the plaintiff's subjective reaction to the defamation, namely 'the plaintiff's injured feelings, including the hurt, anxiety, loss of self-esteem, the sense of indignity and the sense of outrage felt by the plaintiff'.[12] Under the 'eggshell skull' rule, discussed at [6.83]–[6.88], the full extent of the injury to the plaintiff's feelings will be considered even if the plaintiff is unusually sensitive to criticism.[13]

[6.6]

Insofar as damages for loss of reputation vindicate the plaintiff's reputation, they take account of the objective consequences of the defamation, such as the insult publicly inflicted upon the plaintiff, any diminution in the regard in which other people hold the plaintiff, any isolation of the plaintiff, and any conduct by other people that is adverse to the plaintiff.[14]

[6.7]

---

4   *Civil Law (Wrongs) Act 2002* (ACT), s 119(2); *Defamation Act 2005* (NSW), s 7(2); *Defamation Act 2006* (NT), s 6 (2); *Defamation Act 2005* (Qld), s 7(2); *Defamation Act 2005* (SA), s 7(2); *Defamation Act 2005* (Tas), s 7(2); *Defamation Act 2005* (Vic), s 7(2); *Defamation Act 2005* (WA), s 7(2).
5   *Reader's Digest Services Pty Ltd v Lamb* (1982) 150 CLR 500, 507 (Brennan J).
6   *Carson v John Fairfax & Sons Ltd* (1993) 178 CLR 44, 72 (Brennan J).
7   Ibid, 60; *Rogers v Nationwide News Pty Ltd* [2003] HCA 52, (2003) 216 CLR 327 [60] (Hayne J).
8   *Carson v John Fairfax & Sons Ltd* (1993) 178 CLR 44, 60–61; *Rogers v Nationwide News Pty Ltd* [2003] HCA 52, (2003) 216 CLR 327 [60] (Hayne J).
9   *Civil Law (Wrongs) Act 2002* (ACT), s 121; *Defamation Act 2005* (NSW), s 9; *Defamation Act 2006* (NT), s 8; *Defamation Act 2005* (Qld), s 9; *Defamation Act 2005* (SA), s 9; *Defamation Act 2005* (Tas), s 9; *Defamation Act 2005* (Vic), s 9; *Defamation Act 2005* (WA), s 9.
10   *Andrews v John Fairfax & Sons Ltd* [1980] 2 NSWLR 225, 255–56 (Mahoney JA); *Australian Broadcasting Corporation v Comalco Ltd* (1986) 12 FCR 510, 586.
11   *Church of Scientology of California Inc v Reader's Digest Services Pty Ltd* [1980] 1 NSWLR 344, 357; *Australian Broadcasting Corporation v Comalco Ltd* (1986) 12 FCR 510, 586, 600–02.
12   *Carson v John Fairfax & Sons Ltd* (1993) 178 CLR 44, 71 (Brennan J); citation omitted. Quoted in, eg, *Coull v Nationwide News Pty Ltd* [2008] NTCA 10, (2008) 23 NTLR 147 [88].
13   *Smith v John Fairfax & Sons Ltd* (1987) 81 ACTR 1, 32; 86 FLR 343, 374.
14   *Carson v John Fairfax & Sons Ltd* (1993) 178 CLR 44, 71 (Brennan J); *Coull v Nationwide News Pty Ltd* [2008] NTCA 10, (2008) 23 NTLR 147 [88].

Factors to be considered include the social standing of the parties,[15] the plaintiff's previous reputation in the relevant sector,[16] the size of the audience of the defamatory publication,[17] and whether the defamation was malicious.[18] However, the uniform defamation legislation provides that the defendant's malice or other state of mind can be considered only to the extent to which it affects the 'harm' suffered by the plaintiff.[19] In this context, 'harm' encompasses both harm to reputation and harm to feelings.[20]

[6.8]   The uniform defamation legislation specifies certain matters which, in addition to any other matter, may be considered in mitigating damages: whether the defendant has apologised or published a correction of the defamatory matter, and whether the plaintiff has received, or is seeking, compensation in respect of a publication that carries the same meaning or effect as the one complained of in the current proceedings.[21]

[6.9]   Damages for loss of reputation are 'at large',[22] but the uniform defamation legislation prescribes a maximum amount, which increases annually in line with inflation and was $389 500 in September 2017.[23] This limit applies to a defamation proceeding irrespective of the number of causes of action involved.[24] It can be exceeded if aggravated damages are awarded.[25] An amount of $650 000 for general damages and aggravated damages combined was awarded in September 2017.[26] The merits of the statutory cap are debatable.[27] On the one hand, it ensures greater consistency with awards for non-pecuniary loss resulting from personal injury, which are themselves regulated by statute in most jurisdictions; see [7.63]–[7.68]. On the other hand, a person (in particular a media outlet) who contemplates publishing a

15   *Carson v John Fairfax & Sons Ltd* (1993) 178 CLR 44, 61.
16   *O'Hagan v Nationwide News Pty Ltd* [2001] NSWCA 302, (2001) 53 NSWLR 89; *Australian Broadcasting Corporation v McBride* [2001] NSWCA 322, (2001) 53 NSWLR 430 [16]–[30], [106]. In *O'Hagan*, Meagher JA (at [5]) gave the following examples: 'if a plaintiff sues on a libel that he is a dishonest solicitor, it is not to the point that he has a reputation as a good golfer. Similarly, if the libel is that he is dishonest, it is not to the point for the defendant to demonstrate that he is a reckless motorist'.
17   *Hardie v Herald & Weekly Times Pty Ltd* [2016] VSCA 103 [89]–[91].
18   *Uren v John Fairfax & Sons Pty Ltd* (1966) 117 CLR 118, 150 (Windeyer J).
19   *Civil Law (Wrongs) Act 2002* (ACT), s 139G; *Defamation Act 2005* (NSW), s 36; *Defamation Act 2006* (NT), s 33; *Defamation Act 2005* (Qld), s 36; *Defamation Act 2005* (SA), s 34; *Defamation Act 2005* (Tas), s 36; *Defamation Act 2005* (Vic), s 36; *Defamation Act 2005* (WA), s 36.
20   *Smith v Lucht* [2016] QCA 267, [2017] 2 Qd R 489 [69].
21   *Civil Law (Wrongs) Act 2002* (ACT), s 139I; *Defamation Act 2005* (NSW), s 38; *Defamation Act 2006* (NT), s 35; *Defamation Act 2005* (Qld), s 38; *Defamation Act 2005* (SA), s 36; *Defamation Act 2005* (Tas), s 38; *Defamation Act 2005* (Vic), s 38; *Defamation Act 2005* (WA), s 38.
22   *Andrews v John Fairfax & Sons Ltd* [1980] 2 NSWLR 225, 255; *Australian Broadcasting Corporation v Comalco Ltd* (1986) 12 FCR 510, 586; *Cunliffe v Woods* [2012] VSC 254 [74].
23   *Civil Law (Wrongs) Act 2002* (ACT), s 139F; *Defamation Act 2005* (NSW), s 35; *Defamation Act 2006* (NT), s 32; *Defamation Act 2005* (Qld), s 35; *Defamation Act 2005* (SA), s 33; *Defamation Act 2005* (Tas), s 35; *Defamation Act 2005* (Vic), s 35; *Defamation Act 2005* (WA), s 35.
24   *Davis v Nationwide News Pty Ltd* [2008] NSWSC 693 [9]; *Restifa v Pallotta* [2009] NSWSC 958 [64]. See also *Buckley v The Herald & Weekly Times Pty Ltd* [2009] VSCA 118, (2009) 24 VR 129 [4]; *Cummings v Fairfax Digital Australia & New Zealand Pty Ltd* [2011] ACTSC 188, (2011) 6 ACTLR 40 [41].
25   *Civil Law (Wrongs) Act 2002* (ACT), s 139F(2); *Defamation Act 2005* (NSW), s 35(2); *Defamation Act 2006* (NT), s 32(2); *Defamation Act 2005* (Qld), s 35(2); *Defamation Act 2005* (SA), s 33(2); *Defamation Act 2005* (Tas), s 35(2); *Defamation Act 2005* (Vic), s 35(2); *Defamation Act 2005* (WA), s 35(2). Aggravated damages are discussed in Ch 14; see [14.57]–[14.78].
26   *Wilson v Bauer Media Pty Ltd* [2017] VSC 521 [393]. The defendants have filed a notice of appeal.
27   D Rolph, 'A Critique of the National, Uniform Defamation Laws' (2008) 16 Torts LJ 207, 243.

potentially defamatory matter is in a better position to estimate the extent of liability and to make a cynical comparison with the amount of profit expected from publication.[28]

The statutory cap on damages does not apply to pecuniary loss caused by the defamation,[29] which can be compensated in addition to loss of reputation. An example of such pecuniary loss is loss or refusal of employment or business.[30] A plaintiff who alleges loss of business as a result of the defamation must demonstrate a diminution of business (by, for example, producing financial statements) and call as witnesses those who have ceased or refused to do business with the plaintiff, or otherwise prove a causal link to the defamation.[31] Causation may be established where the defamatory statement concerned the plaintiff's business and was of such a nature that it would ordinarily cause a downturn of business.[32] Where it is uncertain whether certain employment or business would have been obtained in the absence of the defamatory statement, the lost opportunity to obtain employment or business may be compensated if it is not too speculative; see [2.88]–[2.107].[33] A plaintiff who has suffered physical or psychological harm as a result of the defamation can recover for the cost of medical treatment,[34] and for loss of earning capacity.[35]

[6.10]

The uniform defamation legislation provides that a court, in determining the amount of damages for defamation, must 'ensure that there is an appropriate and rational relationship between the harm sustained by the plaintiff and the amount of damages awarded'.[36] The term 'harm' encompasses again both harm to reputation and harm to feelings.[37] One purpose of the provision is to require courts to make a comparison with awards for non-pecuniary loss resulting from personal injury. On the second reading of the Defamation Bill in the Legislative Assembly of New South Wales,[38] the state's Attorney-General pointed to an award of $400 000 for falsely imputing dishonesty to a journalist,[39] and observed that such a large award for non-pecuniary loss would be made in a case of personal injury only if the injured person had been

[6.11]

---

28   Exemplary damages are unavailable in defamation actions; see [14.29].

29   D Rolph, 'Critique of the National, Uniform Defamation Laws' (2008) 16 Torts LJ 207, 242.

30   *Chakravarti v Advertiser Newspapers Ltd* (1998) 193 CLR 519, 558, 598–600; *Middendorp Electric Co Pty Ltd v Sonneveld* [2001] VSC 312 [234]; *Rowan v Cornwall (No 5)* [2002] SASC 160, (2002) 82 SASR 152 [697]–[699].

31   *Middendorp Electric Co Pty Ltd v Sonneveld* [2001] VSC 312 [236]–[239].

32   Ibid, [238].

33   *Wilson v Bauer Media Pty Ltd* [2017] VSC 521 [161]–[309] (award of US$3 million for loss of opportunity to obtain lead roles in Hollywood films).

34   *Webster v Coles Myer Ltd* [2009] NSWDC 4 [349]. See also *Cornwall v Rowan* [2004] SASC 384, (2004) 90 SASR 269 [786].

35   *Cornwall v Rowan* [2004] SASC 384, (2004) 90 SASR 269 [771]–[785]; *Webster v Coles Myer Ltd* [2009] NSWDC 4 [300], [303], [343]–[348]. Loss of earning capacity in cases of personal injury is discussed at [7.38]–[7.49].

36   *Civil Law (Wrongs) Act 2002* (ACT), s 139E; *Defamation Act 2005* (NSW), s 34; *Defamation Act 2006* (NT), s 31; *Defamation Act 2005* (Qld), s 34; *Defamation Act 2005* (SA), s 32; *Defamation Act 2005* (Tas), s 34; *Defamation Act 2005* (Vic), s 34; *Defamation Act 2005* (WA), s 34.

37   *Smith v Lucht* [2016] QCA 267, [2017] 2 Qd R 489 [69].

38   The speech by a minister or other member of Parliament on the second reading of the bill in Parliament may be considered in the interpretation of a statutory provision, eg *Interpretation Act 1987* (NSW), s 34(2)(f).

39   *Sleeman v Nationwide News Pty Ltd* [2004] NSWSC 954, (2004) Aust Torts Reports 81–773.

rendered quadriplegic or suffered severe brain damage.[40] He said: 'The bill ensures that this glaring discrepancy in the way damages are awarded is addressed'.[41] Even at common law, it has been said that 'an appellate court hearing appeals in both defamation and personal injury cases needs to ensure that there is an appropriate or rational relationship between the scale of awards in the two classes of case'.[42]

2   Damage to land or fixtures

[6.12]   Compensation for physical damage to land or fixtures may be claimed in actions for negligence, nuisance or trespass to land. It can be measured by reference to cost of repair or to diminution in value. The cost of repair is the amount of money that needs to be spent to restore the land to the physical state it would be in had the tort not occurred. An example is the cost of rebuilding a destroyed house. Diminution in value is the difference between the actual value of the land and the value it would have if the tort had not occurred. Where cost of repair and diminution in value are not of the same amount, it needs to be decided which measure applies.

[6.13]   There are some preliminary matters. Cost of repair cannot be awarded where the defendant's tort left the property in a state in which repair is physically impossible. Cost of repair should also be denied where an unrelated subsequent event has rendered repair physically impossible.[43] Furthermore, cost of repair has been denied where the plaintiff has sold the land in the damaged condition.[44] By contrast, cost of repair may be awarded even though the plaintiff has done (or will do) the repair work himself,[45] or has no intention to have the land repaired.[46] Whichever measure of the plaintiff's basic loss is used, compensation may additionally be awarded in respect of profit lost by reason of the land having some special value at the time of the tort or by reason of some personal present or imminent use of the land being frustrated.[47]

[6.14]   Where repair is physically possible and the plaintiff has either kept the land (with or without repair) or repaired and sold it, the measure of damages may depend upon which of the two measures produces the higher amount. Where diminution in value (unusually) exceeds cost of repair, cost of repair is normally the appropriate measure of the plaintiff's loss.[48] An award of cost of repair enables the plaintiff to have the land repaired and its value

---

40   New South Wales, *Parliamentary Debates*, Legislative Assembly, 13 September 2005, 17640 (Bob Debus).

41   Ibid. Even though the provision was intended to prevent excessively large awards of damages, it was used to overturn an inappropriately low award in *Jeffrey v Giles* [2015] VSCA 70 [21]–[47].

42   *Rogers v Nationwide News Pty Ltd* [2003] HCA 52, (2003) 216 CLR 327 [70] (Hayne J, with whom Gleeson CJ and Gummow J agreed), relying on *Carson v John Fairfax & Sons Ltd* (1993) 178 CLR 44, 56–60. However, no comparison with awards for personal injury was made in *Association of Quality Child Care Centres of NSW Inc v Manefield* [2012] NSWCA 123, (2012) Aust Torts Reports 82–103, upholding an award of $150 000 for the statement that a former employee of the defendant was dishonest and had breached a confidentiality agreement.

43   S Beswick, '"Losses in Any Event" in the Case of Damage to Property' (2015) 35 OJLS 755.

44   *Hosie v De Ferro* (1984) 3 BPR 9418. See also *Perry v Sidney Phillips & Son* [1982] 1 WLR 1297, 1303.

45   *Powercor Australia Ltd v Thomas* [2012] VSCA 87, (2012) 43 VR 220 [61]–[62].

46   *Westwood v Cordwell* [1983] 1 Qd R 276, 279; *Riverman Orchards Pty Ltd v Hayden* [2017] VSC 379 [276]. See also *Gagner Pty Ltd v Canturi Corporation Pty Ltd* [2009] NSWCA 413, (2009) 262 ALR 691 [106].

47   *Winky Pop Pty Ltd v Mobil Refining Australia Pty Ltd* [2016] VSCA 187 [331].

48   *Port Stephens Shire Council v Tellamist Pty Ltd* [2004] NSWCA 353, (2004) 135 LGERA 98 [204].

restored to the position as if the tort had not occurred. A diminution in value can remain only if the plaintiff decides not to have the land repaired, and that decision normally amounts to a failure to mitigate loss. It may be different where repair would take an unreasonably long time.[49]

Cost of repair usually exceeds diminution in value, sometimes significantly. The applicable measure is not simply a matter of choice by the plaintiff.[50] Generally, cost of repair will be awarded unless repair would be unreasonable.[51] There are at least two ways of determining the reasonableness of repair. First, it could depend simply on the discrepancy between cost of repair and diminution in value. Secondly, repair could be considered unreasonable unless the benefits to the plaintiff outweighed the extra cost to the defendant of having to pay for the cost of repair rather than the diminution in value. The courts have conflated those two methods.

[6.15]

The principles emerge from an oft-cited[52] statement made by Samuels JA in *Evans v Balog*.[53] He said that the reasonableness of repair depends in part upon the advantages to the plaintiff of repair balanced against the extra cost to the defendant of having to pay the cost of repair rather than the diminution in value. He then said that an alternative way of stating the same principle is to say that cost of repair will be awarded unless it is disproportionate to the diminution in value. It therefore appears that cost of repair is not disproportionate where the extra burden on the defendant is outweighed by the benefits of repair to the plaintiff.

[6.16]

The reasonableness of repair mainly depends upon whether the plaintiff has (or had) a legitimate interest in having the damaged property repaired, rather than acquiring an alternative property. Such interest generally exists for a dwelling house occupied by its owner,[54] and for the premises of an established business that relies on foot traffic.[55] It also generally exists for agricultural land,[56] but recovery may be limited to the cost of making the land useable again without fully restoring it to the condition prior to the defendant's wrong.[57]

[6.17]

By contrast, owners of investment property have generally been found not to have a legitimate interest in undertaking repair, as they can acquire a substitute investment with an award of diminution in value. Repair was considered unreasonable where an investment property was completely destroyed,[58] and also where, at the time of trial, significantly

[6.18]

---

49   Ibid.
50   *Bromley v Forestry Commission of NSW* [2003] NSWCA 252 [41]; *Port Stephens Shire Council v Tellamist Pty Ltd* [2004] NSWCA 353, (2004) 135 LGERA 98 [203], [208].
51   *Westwood v Cordwell* [1983] 1 Qd R 276, 277; *Parramatta City Council v Lutz* (1988) 12 NSWLR 293, 312, 335; *Lawrence v Kempsey Shire Council* (1995) Aust Torts Reports 81–344, 62,464; *Origin Energy LPG Ltd v Bestcare Foods Ltd* [2013] NSWCA 90 [199].
52   *Pantalone v Alaouie* (1989) 18 NSWLR 119, 137; *Keddell v Regarose Pty Ltd* [1995] 1 Qd R 172, 179; *South Australia v Simionato* [2005] SASC 412, (2005) 143 LGERA 128 [92].
53   [1976] 1 NSWLR 36, 40. Moffitt P and Hutley JA agreed with Samuels JA.
54   Ibid; *Westwood v Cordwell* [1983] 1 Qd R 276, 277; *Parramatta City Council v Lutz* (1988) 12 NSWLR 293, 312, 335. Cf *Jones v Shire of Perth* [1971] WAR 56, 60–61.
55   *Gagner Pty Ltd v Canturi Corporation Pty Ltd* [2009] NSWCA 413, (2009) 262 ALR 691 [106] (jewellery store).
56   *Lonie v Perugini* (1977) 18 SASR 201, 215–16; *Riverman Orchards Pty Ltd v Hayden* [2017] VSC 379 [315]. It did not exist in *Hobbs v Oildrive Pty Ltd* [2008] QSC 45 [171] (unprofitable mango orchard).
57   *Michael Vincent Baker Superannuation Fund Pty Ltd v Aurizon Operations Pty Ltd* [2017] QSC 26 [99].
58   *Pantalone v Alaouie* (1989) 18 NSWLR 119, 138.

damaged investment property was still unrepaired and it was unclear whether the owner would keep it.[59] Repair may be reasonable where the damage to the investment property is minor.

[6.19]   Where repair is reasonable and has been, or will be, carried out, the plaintiff's inability to fully use the property until the completion of repair work may lead to consequential losses such as the cost of alternative accommodation in the case of residential property,[60] and loss of profit in the case of business premises.[61] Where repair is unreasonable and the plaintiff has acquired, or will acquire, a substitute property, compensation may be awarded not only for the diminution in the value of the damaged property but also, if applicable, for the cost of acquiring a substitute property and for loss of profit during the period of searching for a substitute property.[62]

[6.20]   Where damage to land is merely aesthetic, repair is usually unreasonable,[63] leaving an award for diminution in value if there is any.[64] In cases of trespass to land, an award may be made to compensate the diminution in the plaintiff's enjoyment of the property as a result of the aesthetic damage, and to vindicate the plaintiff's right to exclude the defendant from the plaintiff's property.[65] Non-pecuniary loss resulting from physical damage to land has also been compensated in some cases of negligence[66] and nuisance.[67]

3   Other wrongful interference with land

[6.21]   Wrongful interference with land can occur without physical damage to the land or fixtures. The defendant may wrongfully evict the plaintiff, withhold possession of the land from the plaintiff, otherwise use the plaintiff's land, or interfere with the plaintiff's enjoyment of the property. The relevant causes of action are nuisance, trespass to land, and an action for the recovery of possession of land.

[6.22]   Pecuniary loss caused by trespass to land is compensable.[68] But often there is no pecuniary loss, for example where the defendant walks over the plaintiff's land as a shortcut to his home. Where the defendant wrongfully withholds possession of the land from the plaintiff, or otherwise uses the plaintiff's land, the court may be able to award 'user damages' calculated by reference to the reasonable fee that the defendant would pay for a licence by the plaintiff. Such awards are discussed at [16.87]–[16.92], since they are best classified as being based on

---

59   *South Australia v Simionato* [2005] SASC 412, (2005) 143 LGERA 128 [95].
60   Where the plaintiff stays in alternative accommodation free of charge, damages for the loss of the use of the damaged property during the time of repair may be available: *Westwood v Cordwell* [1983] 1 Qd R 276, 278–79.
61   *Lonie v Perugini* (1977) 18 SASR 201, 205, 217; *Gagner Pty Ltd v Canturi Corporation Pty Ltd* [2009] NSWCA 413, (2009) 262 ALR 691 [106].
62   *Pantalone v Alaouie* (1989) 18 NSWLR 119, 138.
63   *Bromley v Forestry Commission of NSW* [2003] NSWCA 252 [37]–[43].
64   *Carr v Sourlos* (1994) 6 BPR 13,626, 13,636.
65   Ibid; *Gazzard v Hutchesson* (1995) Aust Torts Reports 81–337, 62,360.
66   *Broken Hill City Council v Tiziani* (1997) 93 LGERA 113, 118–19.
67   *Hosie v De Ferro* (1984) 3 BPR 9418; *Barbagallo v J & F Catelan Pty Ltd* [1986] 1 Qd R 245, 270; *Roberts v Rodier* [2006] NSWSC 282, (2006) 12 BPR 23,453 [119]–[123]. The general compensability of non-pecuniary loss in actions for nuisance is uncertain; see [6.25].
68   *Balanced Securities Ltd v Bianco (No 2)* [2010] VSC 201, (2010) 27 VR 599; *Windridge Farm Pty Ltd v Grassi* [2011] NSWSC 196, (2011) 254 FLR 87 [145]; *Macquarie International Health Clinic Pty Ltd v Sydney Local Health District (No 10)* [2016] NSWSC 1587 [578].

the profit the defendant has made from the wrong rather than the loss the plaintiff has suffered as a result of the wrong.

Pecuniary loss caused by nuisance is generally compensable, including diminution in the value of the land,[69] loss of profit,[70] the cost of alternative accommodation,[71] and the cost of moving a business to an alternative location.[72] However, recovery has generally been denied for the cost of the plaintiff entering the defendant's land to abate the nuisance.[73] The self-help remedy of abatement of nuisance is heavily restricted; see [13.28].

[6.23]

Wrongful interference with land may cause non-pecuniary loss (anxiety, discomfort, stress and the like) to the person in possession of the land. Compensation for such loss may be subject to the restrictions on recovery for non-pecuniary loss in some civil liability statutes; see [7.13]–[7.20]. At common law, non-pecuniary loss is clearly compensable in actions for trespass to land. Aggravated damages may be awarded where the trespass has caused humiliation, injured feelings or an affront to dignity.[74] However, mental trauma may be too remote to be compensable where trespass to land occurs by way of media intrusion on private property.[75]

[6.24]

In the absence of physical damage to the land, it is uncertain whether non-pecuniary loss is compensable in an action for nuisance, or whether the person affected must sue in negligence. It has been considered recoverable in some Australian cases,[76] and irrecoverable in others.[77] In *Hunter v Canary Wharf Ltd*,[78] a majority in the House of Lords said in obiter dicta that since the tort of nuisance protects only interests in land, there can be no compensation for annoyance, discomfort or inconvenience in actions for nuisance. While this argument has appeal if the tort of nuisance is considered in isolation, it is at odds with the fact that many torts allow recovery for injury to interests other than the interest primarily protected by the tort.

[6.25]

4   Damage to goods

Compensation for wrongfully damaging or destroying goods can be measured by reference to cost of repair or to diminution in value; see [2.11]–[2.15]. Notionally, there is a third measure of loss: the cost of replacement. For unique goods, this is the cost of having a replacement made.[79] Otherwise, it is the cost of purchasing a replacement. However, cost of replacement and diminution in value are often the same. Where cost of replacement is used as the measure of loss, the amount (if any) that the plaintiff can obtain from selling the damaged goods must be

[6.26]

69   *Owen v John L Norris Holdings Pty Ltd* [1964] NSWR 1337; *Stockwell v Victoria* [2001] VSC 497 [497].
70   *Stockwell v Victoria* [2001] VSC 497 [605].
71   *Barbagallo v J & F Catelan Pty Ltd* [1986] 1 Qd R 245, 248.
72   *Seiwa Pty Ltd v Owners Strata Plan 35042* [2006] NSWSC 1157, (2006) 12 BPR 23,673 [27].
73   *Young v Wheeler* (1987) Aust Torts Reports 80–126, 68,971; *Proprietors of Strata Plan No 14198 v Cowell* (1989) 24 NSWLR 478, 486–87; *City of Richmond v Scantelbury* [1991] 2 VR 38, 48; *Seiwa Pty Ltd v Owners Strata Plan 35042* [2006] NSWSC 1157, (2006) 12 BPR 23,673 [27].
74   *Johnstone v Stewart* [1968] SASR 142, 144–46; *TCN Channel Nine Pty Ltd v Anning* [2002] NSWCA 82, (2002) 54 NSWLR 333 [107], [193]. *Roberts v Rodier* [2006] NSWSC 282, (2006) 12 BPR 23,453 [162]–[164]; *New South Wales v Ibbett* [2006] HCA 57, (2006) 229 CLR 638 [31]. See also [14.65]–[14.66].
75   *TCN Channel Nine Pty Ltd v Anning* [2002] NSWCA 82, (2002) 54 NSWLR 333 [107].
76   *Oldham v Lawson (No 1)* [1976] VR 654, 658; *Barbagallo v J & F Catelan Pty Ltd* [1986] 1 Qd R 245, 263. *Stockwell v Victoria* [2001] VSC 497 [479]–[484]; *Quick v Alpine Nurseries Sales Pty Ltd* [2010] NSWSC 1248 [336]–[337].
77   *Evans v Finn* (1904) 4 SR (NSW) 297, 308; *Clifford v Dove* [2006] NSWSC 314 [30]–[36].
78   [1997] AC 655, 696, 706.
79   *Glenmont Investments Pty Ltd v O'Loughlin* [2000] SASC 429, (2000) 79 SASR 185 [416], [423].

deducted.[80] The resulting figure is the diminution in the value of the damaged goods where the cost of a replacement equates to the value the damaged goods would have had without damage. Where the damaged goods were not new and there is no second-hand market for them,[81] the replacement will be new and therefore more valuable than the damaged goods even without damage. In those circumstances, the cost of replacement is higher than the diminution in value, but the excess may have to be deducted under the betterment (or 'new for old') principle; see [2.23]–[2.27].

[6.27]   The basic principles as to which measure of loss applies are generally the same as those applying to land and fixtures, discussed at [6.13]–[6.15]. Cost of repair may not be awarded where the defendant's tort completely destroyed the goods.[82] The same should apply where an unrelated subsequent event has rendered repair physically impossible.[83] But cost of repair may be awarded even though the plaintiff has done (or will do) the repair work himself,[84] or has no intention to have repair done,[85] or has sold the goods unrepaired.[86] The mitigation principle does not generally require the plaintiff to have the goods repaired before selling them.[87] A plaintiff who has sold the goods unrepaired can recover the difference between the value of the goods before they were damaged and the price obtained on sale (provided the plaintiff obtained the best price reasonably possible) even if that difference exceeds the cost of repair.[88]

[6.28]   Where repair is physically possible and the plaintiff intends to keep the goods, the amounts of cost of repair and diminution in value must be compared. Where diminution in value exceeds cost of repair, any remaining diminution in value after proper repair is compensable.[89] Therefore, where even the best repair cannot fully restore the goods to their prior value, diminution in value may be the appropriate measure of loss.[90] But where repair can fully restore the goods to their prior value, the mitigation principle generally prevents an award exceeding the cost of repair.

[6.29]   Where cost of repair exceeds diminution in value, cost of repair will be awarded unless repair is unreasonable.[91] The same rule applies to land and fixtures, but it is easier to find an

---

80   *Jansen v Dewhurst* [1969] VR 421, 426.

81   Where the plaintiff has bought new goods as substitute for used goods, the defendant bears an evidentiary onus to prove that a second-hand market exists: *Powercor Australia Ltd v Thomas* [2012] VSCA 87, (2012) 43 VR 220 [97].

82   *Bland Shire Council v Anthoness* [1960] NSWR 254, 260; *Davidson v J S Gilbert Fabrications Pty Ltd* [1986] 1 Qd R 1, 3.

83   S Beswick, '"Losses in Any Event" in the Case of Damage to Property' (2015) 35 OJLS 755.

84   *Price v Commissioner of Highways* [1968] SASR 329, 331–33; *Commonwealth Railways Commissioner v Hodsdon* (1970) 16 FLR 437.

85   *Eastern Construction Co Pty Ltd v Southern Portland Cement Ltd* [1960] NSWR 505, 506.

86   *Freese v Collins* [1948] St R Qd 180; *Davidson v J S Gilbert Fabrications Pty Ltd* [1986] 1 Qd R 1, 3–4; *Tehan v Saric* [2010] VSC 175 [8].

87   *Gaggin v Moss* [1983] 2 Qd R 486, 489–90; *Davidson v J S Gilbert Fabrications Pty Ltd* [1986] 1 Qd R 1, 7–9.

88   *Davidson v J S Gilbert Fabrications Pty Ltd* [1986] 1 Qd R 1.

89   *Volker v Frizzell* (1952) 48 QJPR 6, 7.

90   *Dryden v Orr* (1928) 28 SR (NSW) 216, 217–18.

91   *Bland Shire Council v Anthoness* [1960] NSWR 254, 259–60; *Murphy v Brown* (1985) 1 NSWLR 131, 133; *Pargiter v Alexander* (1995) 5 Tas R 158, 164; *Cashmere Bay Pty Ltd v Hastings Deering (Australia) Ltd (No 2)* [2011] QSC 134 [5].

equivalent substitute (and more difficult to demonstrate the reasonableness of repair) for non-unique goods than for land. For example, where a car that is only a few years old is damaged, it is usually possible to find a car of the same make, model and age on the market. Thus, where cost of repair exceeds diminution in value, diminution in value will be the measure of loss unless the goods have a peculiar value to the plaintiff.

Diminution in value depends upon the value of the damaged goods to the plaintiff and thus the use the plaintiff made, or intended to make, of the goods. The value of commercially exploited goods is their value as a going concern.[92] Thus, the value of a wrongfully killed horse to an owner who intended to use it in races was $4500 even though the horse could have been sold for only $1700.[93] Conversely, goods used in a business may lose value when the business is closed down. A wrongfully converted harvester had no value to an owner who had left the harvester standing idly after giving up farming.[94] **[6.30]**

In addition to cost of repair or diminution in value, there may be consequential losses, such as the cost of transport, adaptation and insurance of the replacement,[95] loss of profit until repair is completed or a replacement is found,[96] and the cost of hiring a temporary replacement needed until repair is completed or a permanent replacement is found.[97] The loss suffered by a plaintiff who had hired the damaged goods is the loss of profit (if any) during the time of repair, not the rent paid for the goods during that time.[98] Where the plaintiff avoided a loss of profit by hiring a replacement during the time of repair, the loss suffered is the rent paid for the replacement, not the rent paid for the damaged goods during repair.[99] **[6.31]**

A plaintiff who has neither hired a replacement nor suffered a concrete loss of profit may still obtain compensation for the loss of the use of the goods while they were being repaired or a replacement was being sought. This has been recognised for commercially used goods (where interest on their capital value has been awarded for the period of repair),[100] for goods used in providing a public service,[101] and for privately used goods.[102] Statutory provisions **[6.32]**

---

92   *The Liesbosch* [1933] AC 449, 463–64 (dredger); *Glenmont Investments Pty Ltd v O'Loughlin* [2000] SASC 429, (2000) 79 SASR 185 [415] (large dinosaur model).

93   *Electricity Trust of South Australia v O'Leary* (1986) 42 SASR 26, 29–30.

94   *Mizza v HV McKay-Massey Harris Pty Ltd* (1935) 37 WALR 87, 89–90.

95   *The Liesbosch* [1933] AC 449, 468.

96   Ibid, 468; *Glenmont Investments Pty Ltd v O'Loughlin* [2000] SASC 429, (2000) 79 SASR 185 [416], [427].

97   *Jansen v Dewhurst* [1969] VR 421, 426; *Anthanasopoulos v Moseley* [2001] NSWCA 266, (2001) 52 NSWLR 262 [37], [84]. Where the plaintiff bought a temporary replacement and then sold it for a lower price, the difference is compensable if it was reasonable to buy rather than hire a replacement: *Reid v Brown* (1952) 69 WN (NSW) 131.

98   Even if the rent exceeds the lost profit: *Commissioners for Executing the Office of Lord High Admiral of the UK v Owners of Steamship Valeria* [1922] 2 AC 242.

99   *Zappulla v Perkins* [1978] Qd R 92.

100   *Woodman v Rasmussen* [1953] St R Qd 202, 212, 218; *Commissioner for Railways v Luya, Julius Ltd* [1977] Qd R 395, 398; *BHP Coal Pty Ltd v O & K Orenstein & Koppel AG* [2008] QSC 141 [928]–[949] (where it was said that the plaintiff does have to prove some detriment from not having the goods).

101   *The Greta Holme* [1897] AC 596; *The Mediana* [1900] AC 113; *The Marpessa* [1907] AC 241; *R v Owners of SS Argyllshire* [1922] St R Qd 186, 199–200; *Commissioners for Executing the Office of Lord High Admiral of the UK v Owners of Steamship Chekiang* [1926] AC 637; *BHP Coal Pty Ltd v O & K Orenstein & Koppel AG* [2008] QSC 141 [925].

102   *Millar v Candy* (1981) 38 ALR 299, 307–08, 312; *Anthanasopoulos v Moseley* [2001] NSWCA 266, (2001) 52 NSWLR 262 [58]; *BHP Coal Pty Ltd v O & K Orenstein & Koppel AG* [2008] QSC 141 [925]; *Lyon v Adami* [2014] NSWSC 1956 [35].

relating to non-pecuniary loss (discussed at [7.63]–[7.68]) have no application to the loss of use of goods.[103] Subject to those provisions, non-pecuniary loss may be compensated where an animal has been injured or killed,[104] or where goods of sentimental value to the plaintiff have been destroyed.[105]

5 Other wrongful interference with goods

[6.33]   As with land, there can be wrongful interference with goods without physical damage, such as disposing of them or taking or withholding possession of them. The relevant causes of action are conversion, detinue and trespass to goods.

[6.34]   A plaintiff who is permanently deprived of the goods can claim compensation for the loss of her interest in the goods,[106] at least in cases of trespass to goods (which requires intention) and dishonest conversion.[107] The value of ownership is normally the full value of the goods.[108] 'If there exists a market into which the deprived person can go and purchase identical goods to those of which he has been deprived, the price he must pay for them on that market is prima facie the value of the goods.'[109] If the plaintiff is a wholesaler, the relevant market price is the price to be paid by a wholesaler, not a retailer or consumer.[110] Where no market for the goods exists, the loss must be assessed in some other way, for example by reference to the price the plaintiff could have obtained by selling them,[111] or the cost of having a replacement manufactured.[112] In all these situations, goods and services tax must be taken into account.[113]

[6.35]   The value of the goods to the plaintiff may depend on a pre-existing contract or other relationship with the defendant or a third party. Where, in the absence of the defendant's wrong, the plaintiff would have had to pay a certain amount of money to someone in respect of the goods, that amount must be deducted from their market value if, and only if, the plaintiff is no longer obliged to make that payment.[114] An example is the conversion of goods by an unpaid seller who had already transferred ownership to the buyer but remained in

103   *Lyon v Adami* [2014] NSWSC 1956 [31].
104   *Crump v Equine Nutrition Systems Pty Ltd* [2006] NSWSC 512 [261]–[263], [298]–[299].
105   *Liu v New South Wales* [2014] NSWSC 933 [32]–[35] (family heirloom).
106   Where the goods have been returned to the plaintiff, their value at the time of their return must be deducted from the plaintiff's loss, which may become nil; see *Associated Midland Corporation Ltd v Bank of New South Wales* [1983] 1 NSWLR 533, 547.
107   Lord Nicholls has indicated that while an obligation to disgorge benefits obtained exists in all cases of conversion, an obligation to compensate the plaintiff's loss may be confined to cases of dishonest conversion: *Kuwait Airways Corporation v Iraqi Airways Co (Nos 4 and 5)* [2002] UKHL 19, [2002] 2 AC 883 [79].
108   *Butler v Egg and Egg Pulp Marketing Board* (1966) 114 CLR 185, 191, 192; *Johnson Matthey (Australia) Ltd v Dascorp Pty Ltd* [2003] VSC 291, (2003) 9 VR 171 [213]. For the date of assessment, see [2.135].
109   *Furness v Adrium Industries Pty Ltd* [1996] 1 VR 668, 669 (Fullagar J). See also *Bilambil-Terranora Pty Ltd v Tweed Shire Council* [1980] 1 NSWLR 465, 477, 489; *Jiwira Pty Ltd v Primary Industry Bank of Australia Ltd* [2000] NSWSC 1094 [256].
110   *Furness v Adrium Industries Pty Ltd* [1996] 1 VR 668, 669–70, 676, 678.
111   Ibid, 669.
112   *J & E Hall Ltd v Barclay* [1937] 3 All ER 620, 624.
113   *Bennett v Goodwin* [2005] NSWSC 930, (2005) 62 ATR 515 [17]. See [2.54].
114   *Chinery v Viall* (1860) 5 H & N 288, 295–96; 157 ER 1192, 1195–96; *City Motors (1933) Pty Ltd v Southern Aerial Super Service Pty Ltd* (1961) 106 CLR 477.

possession.[115] In calculating the value of the goods to the buyer, the purchase price must be deducted if the buyer is no longer obliged to pay,[116] but must not be deducted if the buyer is still obliged to pay.[117] Similarly, where, in the absence of the defendant's wrong, the plaintiff would have been obliged to sell the goods and pay a certain percentage of the proceeds to the defendant, the plaintiff's loss is the difference between the price for which the plaintiff would have sold the goods and the amount which in that event the plaintiff would have been bound to pay to the defendant.[118]

Where the plaintiff is not the only person who had a proprietary interest in the goods, the value of the plaintiff's interest is not the value of unencumbered ownership but must reflect the value of the other interests.[119] The value of a lost lien is the amount of money necessary to extinguish the lien.[120] The loss suffered by a plaintiff who had let the goods under a hire-purchase agreement is the lesser of the full value of the goods at the date of the conversion and the balance of the hire-purchase price outstanding at the date of judgment.[121] The plaintiff's interest may have no real value, for example the interest of a pledgor who has no means to redeem the pledge.[122] [6.36]

The plaintiff's inability to use goods during a period of wrongful detention may cause loss. This may be the loss of rent from hiring out the goods,[123] or the cost of hiring replacement goods,[124] subject to a deduction of the amount (if any) that would have been spent on maintaining the detained goods.[125] Where the defendant used the detained goods, the plaintiff may obtain 'user damages', calculated by reference to a reasonable fee for hiring the goods.[126] Such awards are best characterised as being based on the defendant's gain, and are therefore discussed at [16.93]–[16.98]. Where the defendant did not use the detained goods, neither a reasonable fee award nor compensation for the loss of their use (in the absence of a concrete [6.37]

---

115 Instead of claiming compensation for loss, the buyer may be entitled to claim reasonable fee damages; see [16.96]–[16.97].

116 *Chinery v Viall* (1860) 5 H & N 288, 294; 157 ER 1192, 1195; *Healing (Sales) Pty Ltd v Inglis Electrix Pty Ltd* (1968) 121 CLR 584, 591.

117 *Healing (Sales) Pty Ltd v Inglis Electrix Pty Ltd* (1968) 121 CLR 584, 602, 618–19, 625.

118 *Butler v Egg and Egg Pulp Marketing Board* (1966) 114 CLR 185; considered at [2.3].

119 *Brierly v Kendall* (1852) 17 QB 937, 943; 117 ER 1540, 1543; *Standard Electronic Apparatus Laboratories Pty Ltd v Stenner* [1960] NSWR 447, 451; *Pacific Acceptance Corporation Ltd v Mirror Motors Pty Ltd* [1960] NSWR 796, 797; *Western Credits Pty Ltd v Dragan Motors Pty Ltd* [1973] WAR 184, 191.

120 *Standard Electronic Apparatus Laboratories Pty Ltd v Stenner* [1960] NSWR 447, 452.

121 *Pacific Acceptance Corporation Ltd v Mirror Motors Pty Ltd* [1960] NSWR 796, 798; *Western Credits Pty Ltd v Dragan Motors Pty Ltd* [1973] WAR 184, 187, 188, 191.

122 *Johnson v Stear* (1863) 15 CB (NS) 330, 335; 143 ER 812, 814.

123 *Gaba Formwork Contractors Pty Ltd v Turner Corporation Ltd* (1991) 32 NSWLR 175, 178; *Pargiter v Alexander* (1995) 5 Tas R 158, 161.

124 *Egan v State Transport Authority* (1982) 31 SASR 481, 531; *Gaba Formwork Contractors Pty Ltd v Turner Corporation Ltd* (1991) 32 NSWLR 175, 178; *Pargiter v Alexander* (1995) 5 Tas R 158, 161.

125 *Egan v State Transport Authority* (1982) 31 SASR 481, 531; *Gaba Formwork Contractors Pty Ltd v Turner Corporation Ltd* (1991) 32 NSWLR 175, 178.

126 *Gaba Formwork Contractors Pty Ltd v Turner Corporation Ltd* (1991) 32 NSWLR 175, 188; *Finesky Holdings Pty Ltd v Minister for Transport for Western Australia* [2002] WASCA 206, (2002) 26 WAR 368 [54]–[58]; *Bunnings Group Ltd v CHEP Australia Ltd* [2011] NSWCA 342, (2011) 82 NSWLR 420 [175]. User damages can be awarded in addition to compensatory damages where there is no double recovery, for example in addition to cost of repair: *Kuwait Airways Corporation v Iraqi Airways Co (Nos 4 and 5)* [2002] UKHL 19, [2002] 2 AC 883 [87] (Lord Nicholls).

loss of profit) seems to be available.[127] However, since compensation for temporary loss of use is available where goods are wrongfully damaged or destroyed (see [6.31]), it should also be available where goods are wrongfully detained.[128]

[6.38]   Consequential loss can be recovered, subject to remoteness.[129] An example is the profit that the plaintiff would have made from a commercial use of the goods.[130] A decrease in the market value of goods during their wrongful detention generates no loss unless the plaintiff would have sold them had they not been detained.[131] Where goods of sentimental value to the plaintiff have been lost, non-pecuniary loss may be compensated,[132] although this may be subject to the restrictions on recovery for non-pecuniary loss in some civil liability statutes; see [7.13]–[7.20].

6   Defective premises or goods

[6.39]   Buildings may have defects, which may be latent. A plaintiff may have acquired a plot of land with a defective building without being aware of the defect when acquiring the property. After the plaintiff has acquired the property, the defect may cause further damage to it, and may cause damage to other buildings or goods.[133] The owner of such other property, be it the plaintiff or another person, may have a claim in negligence against the person responsible for the defect in the building,[134] for example, the architect, the builder, or the local council that checked the building's safety. With regard to the defective building itself, the plaintiff may have a claim in negligence against the person responsible for the defect,[135] or against a person (for example, a surveyor) who was retained by the plaintiff to inspect the property before the plaintiff acquired it and who negligently failed to detect the defect, or against both.[136]

[6.40]   Where damage has been caused to goods or to a building other than the defective building, the owner's right in the damaged property is infringed, and damages aim to place the owner in the position as if the property had not been damaged. The rules governing the assessment of

---

127   *Strand Electric & Engineering Co Ltd v Brisford Entertainments Ltd* [1952] 2 QB 246, 254 (Denning LJ); *Gaba Formwork Contractors Pty Ltd v Turner Corporation Ltd* (1991) 32 NSWLR 175, 188. See also *Brandeis Goldschmidt & Co Ltd v Western Transport Ltd* [1981] QB 864, where only nominal damages were awarded.

128   See K Barker, P Cane, M Lunney and F Trindade, *The Law of Torts in Australia* (5th edn, OUP 2012) 151–52.

129   *John Gallagher Panel Beating Co Pty Ltd v Palmer* [2007] NSWSC 627 [23].

130   *Brilawsky v Robertson* (1916) 10 QJPR 113, 115; *Egan v State Transport Authority* (1982) 31 SASR 481, 531. The plaintiff must adduce evidence as to how the goods would have been used commercially: *Brandeis Goldschmidt & Co Ltd v Western Transport Ltd* [1981] QB 864, 873.

131   *Brandeis Goldschmidt & Co Ltd v Western Transport Ltd* [1981] QB 864, 872–73.

132   *Graham v Voigt* (1989) 89 ACTR 11, 20–21; *Murphy v Doman* [2004] NSWCA 419 [3]–[4].

133   Liability for defects may extend to personal injury caused by them: *Voli v Inglewood Shire Council* (1963) 110 CLR 74, 84. Compensation for personal injury is discussed in Ch 7.

134   *Pyrenees Shire Council v Day* (1998) 192 CLR 330.

135   At least where the building is a dwelling: *Bryan v Maloney* (1995) 182 CLR 609. For commercial buildings, see *Woolcock Street Investments Pty Ltd v CDG Pty Ltd* [2004] HCA 16, (2004) 216 CLR 515. English law generally excludes such a claim: *Murphy v Brentwood District Council* [1991] 1 AC 398.

136   Provided that the surveyor's intervening negligence did not break the chain of causation between the negligence of the person responsible for the defect and the damage; see *Baxall Securities Ltd v Sheard Walshaw Partnership* [2002] EWCA Civ 9, [2002] BLR 100; *Pearson Education Ltd v Charter Partnership Ltd* [2007] EWCA Civ 130, [2007] BLR 324;S Harder, 'Is Liability for Defective Buildings Negated by a Surveyor's Intervening Negligence?' [2007] Conv 417.

damage to goods (see [6.26]–[6.32]) or land (see [6.12]–[6.20]) apply. For example, the assessment of loss caused by damage to a car is in principle the same whether the car was hit by another car or by pieces falling from a defective building.

Things are different for the defective building itself. The plaintiff's ownership in that building has not been infringed since she has never been the owner of a non-defective building. It is pure economic loss. The question arises whether damages do, and should, aim to place the plaintiff in the position as if she had acquired a non-defective building. It is necessary to distinguish between a defendant who is responsible for the defect and a defendant who was retained by the plaintiff to inspect the property before the plaintiff acquired it and who negligently failed to detect the defect. [6.41]

With regard to a defendant who is responsible for the defect, it must be asked what would have happened had the defendant been careful. There are two possibilities: the building would have been erected without defects, or the building would not have been erected or would have been demolished. The first category may involve a sloppy builder, and the second category may involve a local authority that re-zones an area that is unsuitable for buildings as a residential zone. [6.42]

Where the building would have been erected without defects had the defendant been careful, the plaintiff would have acquired property free from defects, and damages aim to place the plaintiff in that position. Damages have invariably been assessed by reference to the cost of repairing the defect,[137] which may involve a demolition of the defective building and construction of a new one.[138] The plaintiff may also recover for consequential loss, such as non-pecuniary loss[139] or the loss of profit that would have been made had the property been without defects.[140] [6.43]

By contrast, where the building would not have been erected or would have been demolished had the defendant been careful, the plaintiff would not have acquired the property. Damages should therefore aim to place the plaintiff in the position as if she had never acquired the property, rather than in a position as if the property had been free of defects when she acquired it. Thus, the plaintiff's loss is not the cost of repair but the difference between the amount the plaintiff has spent on acquiring and maintaining the property and the actual value of the property. Where the plaintiff, had she not bought the defective property, would have bought another property, the hypothetical increase in value of that other property must be added to her loss, and the hypothetical cost of maintaining it must be deducted. Non-pecuniary loss should also be compensable. All these principles were applied in *Bamford v Albert Shire Council*.[141] [6.44]

The same principles ought to apply to the liability of a person (for example, a surveyor) who was retained by the plaintiff to inspect the property before she purchased it and who negligently failed to detect the defect. If that person had been careful and advised the plaintiff [6.45]

---

137 *Clarke v Gisborne Shire Council* [1984] VR 971, 987–88; *Bryan v Maloney* (1995) 182 CLR 609, 616.
138 Eg *Moorabool Shire Council v Taitapanui* [2004] VSC 239 [130], aff'd *Moorabool Shire Council v Taitapanui* [2006] VSCA 30, (2006) 14 VR 55; *Kirkby v Coote* [2006] QCA 61.
139 *Clarke v Gisborne Shire Council* [1984] VR 971, 995–99; *Campbelltown City Council v Mackay* (1989) 15 NSWLR 501; *Sved v Woollahra Municipal Council* (1998) NSW ConvR 55–842, 56,604.
140 *Valleyfield Pty Ltd v Primac Ltd* [2003] QCA 339 [42]–[47], [154]–[155].
141 (1996) 93 LGERA 335 (QSC). On appeal, the trial judge's decision was varied in respect of interest but otherwise affirmed: *Bamford v Albert Shire Council* [1998] 2 Qd R 125.

of the defect, the plaintiff might not have purchased the property or might have purchased it for a lower price. But the plaintiff would not have become the owner of that property in a pristine state. Cost of repair is thus an inappropriate measure of the plaintiff's loss,[142] unless it is (unusually) lower than diminution in value.[143]

[6.46] In theory, the plaintiff's loss depends on whether or not the plaintiff, if aware of the defect, would still have bought the property. Where the plaintiff would not have bought the property, the loss is the difference between the price paid by the plaintiff and the actual value of the land at the time of the purchase. Where the plaintiff would still have bought the property, the loss is the difference between what the plaintiff actually paid and what the plaintiff would have paid if aware of the defect. If the latter amount is presumed to be the actual value of the land at the time of the purchase, the loss will be the same in both situations. Courts do not inquire into whether the plaintiff would still have bought the property, and usually see the plaintiff's loss in the difference between the price paid by the plaintiff and the actual value of the property at the time of purchase.[144]

[6.47] Damages have been awarded for non-pecuniary loss (distress, discomfort, inconvenience and the like) caused by the defect.[145] This is at odds with the fact that the courts in those cases made no inquiry as to whether the plaintiff, if aware of the defect, would still have purchased the property. The defendant's negligence constitutes a cause of the non-pecuniary loss only where the plaintiff, if aware of the defect, would not have purchased the property. Otherwise, the plaintiff would still have lived with the effects of the defect. In any event, the restrictions on recovery for non-pecuniary loss in some civil liability statutes (see [7.13]–[7.20]) may apply.

[6.48] The discussion so far has concerned real property. There is no reason for treating goods differently. Authority on damage to the defective goods themselves is sparse, for two reasons. First, cases involving negligent advice to the purchaser rarely arise since it is less common for prospective purchasers of goods than for prospective purchasers of land to have the property inspected for defects prior to purchase. Secondly, cases involving negligent manufacture or handling of goods rarely arise since it is unclear whether a person responsible for a defect in goods (for example, the manufacturer or a repairer) may be liable in negligence[146] for further damage to the defective goods themselves.[147] That person may be liable in negligence where the defective goods cause damage to other property,[148] or personal injury.[149] The assessment of such loss is governed by the ordinary principles relating to damage to goods (see [6.26]–[6.32]) and personal injury (see Ch 7).

---

142   Cost of repair was in fact awarded in *Sved v Woollahra Municipal Council* (1995) 86 LGERA 222, 235–37.

143   *Brickhill v Cooke* [1984] 3 NSWLR 396, 400. The mitigation principle prevents an award of more than is necessary to put the property into the state in which the plaintiff thought it was at the time of purchase.

144   *Perry v Sidney Phillips & Son* [1982] 1 WLR 1297; *Brickhill v Cooke* [1984] 3 NSWLR 396, 400.

145   Ibid; *Rentokil Pty Ltd v Channon* (1990) 19 NSWLR 417, 432–33.

146   There may, of course, be liability in contract or under the Australian Consumer Law.

147   The question was expressly left open in *Bryan v Maloney* (1995) 182 CLR 609, 630. No liability exists under English law: *Murphy v Brentwood District Council* [1991] 1 AC 398.

148   *Norton Australia Pty Ltd v Streets Ice Cream Pty Ltd* (1968) 120 CLR 635.

149   *Donoghue v Stevenson* [1932] AC 562; *Graham Barclay Oysters Pty Ltd v Ryan* [2002] HCA 54, (2002) 211 CLR 540.

7   Damage to economic interests: reliance on a misrepresentation

Where an incorrect statement of fact made by the defendant induced the plaintiff to part with   [6.49]
assets or undertake an obligation, the defendant is liable in deceit if the statement was made
fraudulently[150] with the intention to be relied upon by the plaintiff,[151] and is liable in negligence if the defendant owed the plaintiff a duty of care and breached that duty.[152] Apart from
different rules on the remoteness of loss (see [6.57], [6.61]), the assessment of loss is in principle
the same for both torts,[153] and the following discussion will not distinguish between deceit and
negligence.

Tortious damages for misrepresentation aim to place the plaintiff in the position as if the   [6.50]
statement had not been made. They do not aim to place the plaintiff in the position as if
the statement had been true. Tort protects the reliance interest, but not the expectation
interest.[154]

Where the misrepresentation induced the plaintiff to enter into a contract or other transac-   [6.51]
tion, damages aim to place the plaintiff in the position as if that transaction had not taken
place.[155] The basic measure of the plaintiff's loss is the difference in value between everything
the plaintiff has given away under the transaction and everything the plaintiff has obtained
under the transaction.[156] For example, the basic loss suffered by a plaintiff who was induced to
purchase an asset is the difference between the price paid and the value of the asset at the time
of purchase.[157] This basic loss is increased by the amount (if any) that the plaintiff has spent on
the asset (maintenance and the like),[158] and decreased by the amount (if any) that the plaintiff
has derived from the use of the asset.[159] Further consequential loss is recoverable,[160] subject to
remoteness and mitigation.

---

150   Deceit requires the defendant to make the false representation knowingly or without belief in its truth
      or recklessly: *Derry v Peek* (1889) 14 App Cas 337, 374; *Magill v Magill* [2006] HCA 51, (2006) 226 CLR
      551 [113]. It is not enough to establish that the defendant had no reasonable grounds to believe the
      statement to be true.
151   *Magill v Magill* [2006] HCA 51, (2006) 226 CLR 551 [114].
152   *Hedley Byrne & Co Ltd v Heller & Partners Ltd* [1964] AC 465; *Mutual Life and Citizens' Assurance Co Ltd
      v Evatt* (1968) 122 CLR 556; *Tepco Pty Ltd v Water Board* [2001] HCA 19, (2001) 206 CLR 1.
153   See *Kyogle Shire Council v Francis* (1988) 13 NSWLR 396, 418–19.
154   *Gates v City Mutual Life Assurance Society Ltd* (1986) 160 CLR 1, 11–12. See [2.7].
155   *South Australia v Johnson* (1982) 42 ALR 161, 170; *Gates v City Mutual Life Assurance Society Ltd* (1986)
      160 CLR 1, 12.
156   *Potts v Miller* (1940) 64 CLR 282, 297; *Toteff v Antonas* (1952) 87 CLR 647, 650–51; *North East Equity Pty
      Ltd v Proud Nominees Pty Ltd* [2010] FCAFC 60, (2010) 269 ALR 262 [126].
157   *Holmes v Jones* (1907) 4 CLR 1692, 1702–03; *Potts v Miller* (1940) 64 CLR 282, 289, 297; *Toteff v
      Antonas* (1952) 87 CLR 647, 650, 654; *South Australia v Johnson* (1982) 42 ALR 161, 170; *Gould v
      Vaggelas* (1985) 157 CLR 215, 220, 255, 265; *Gates v City Mutual Life Assurance Society Ltd* (1986)
      160 CLR 1, 12; *Kizbeau Pty Ltd v WG & B Pty Ltd* (1995) 184 CLR 281, 291; *HTW Valuers (Central Qld)
      Pty Ltd v Astonland Pty Ltd* [2004] HCA 54, (2004) 217 CLR 640 [34]–[35]. The specific situation of the
      purchase of defective property is discussed at [6.45]–[6.46]. The date of assessment is discussed at
      [2.138]–[2.142].
158   Amounts spent after discovering the misrepresentation can be recovered only if they were spent in a
      reasonable attempt to mitigate loss; see [3.136].
159   *L Shaddock & Associates Pty Ltd v Parramatta City Council (No 1)* (1981) 150 CLR 225, 255–56; *Gould v
      Vaggelas* (1985) 157 CLR 215, 221–22, 241, 255, 266–67.
160   *North East Equity Pty Ltd v Proud Nominees Pty Ltd* [2010] FCAFC 60, (2010) 269 ALR 262 [126].

[6.52]   A plaintiff who would not have entered into a particular transaction but for the defendant's misrepresentation might have entered into another transaction. A plaintiff is not required to prove an alternative transaction in order to establish loss.[161] But it is open to the defendant to prove that the plaintiff would have suffered loss under the alternative transaction.[162] It is equally open to the plaintiff to prove that she would have derived a profit from the alternative transaction.[163] In that case, the plaintiff's loss is calculated as follows:[164]

- profit that would have been made under the alternative transaction *plus*
- money expended under the actual transaction *minus*
- profit made under the actual transaction *minus*
- money that would have been expended under the alternative transaction.

[6.53]   Where the alternative transaction would have possessed the features that the defendant incorrectly ascribed to the actual transaction, the plaintiff's reliance loss equals the net profit the plaintiff would have made under the actual transaction had the defendant's statement been true. In effect, expectation loss is compensated, but in the form of reliance loss based on a hypothetical transaction to be proved by the plaintiff.[165]

[6.54]   Non-pecuniary loss (distress, injured feelings and the like) is generally compensable in actions for deceit or negligent misrepresentation,[166] although this may be subject to the restrictions on recovery for non-pecuniary loss in some civil liability statutes; see [7.13]– [7.20]. An exception exists for loss of reputation, which is only compensable in actions for defamation or injurious falsehood.[167]

III   Attribution of responsibility

[6.55]   Australian private law contains several rules on the attribution of responsibility for loss. Ch 3 discusses those rules that are common at least to contract and tort. The following sections discuss how the rules on remoteness of damage and contributory negligence affect tortious liability in particular.

---

161   *Westpac Banking Corporation v Jamieson* [2015] QCA 50, [2016] 1 Qd R 495 [143].
162   Ibid, [143]–[155]. See also *Gadens Lawyers Sydney Pty Ltd v Symond* [2015] NSWCA 50, (2015) 89 NSWLR 60 [71]–[78].
163   *South Australia v Johnson* (1982) 42 ALR 161, 170; *Gates v City Mutual Life Assurance Society Ltd* (1986) 160 CLR 1, 13; *Kyogle Shire Council v Francis* (1988) 13 NSWLR 396, 417; *Westpac Banking Corporation v Jamieson* [2015] QCA 50, [2016] 1 Qd R 495 [145].
164   See *Gates v City Mutual Life Assurance Society Ltd* (1986) 160 CLR 1, 13.
165   Ibid; *Kyogle Shire Council v Francis* (1988) 13 NSWLR 396, 417.
166   For deceit, see *Bride v KMG Hungerfords* (1991) 109 FLR 256, 280–81; *Aldersea v Public Transport Corporation* [2001] VSC 169, (2001) 3 VR 499 [45]; *Giller v Procopets* [2008] VSCA 236, (2008) 24 VR 1 [427]. For negligent misrepresentation, see *Stocks v Retirement Benefits Fund Board* [2007] TASSC 8, [2007] ANZ ConvR 254 [115]–[118], and the cases cited in fn 145.
167   *Griffith v Australian Broadcasting Corporation* [2004] NSWSC 582 [27]; *Gacic v John Fairfax Publications Pty Ltd* [2005] NSWSC 1210 [49].

A   Remoteness of damage

For some torts, it is unclear how remoteness of damage is to be determined. For others, the test [6.56] is clear, but it is not the same for all those torts. Three tests have emerged. The tests differ with regard to the extent of liability. Liability is most extensive under the test of natural and probable consequences, and most restrictive under the test of reasonable contemplation. The test of reasonable foreseeability sits somewhere in between. Broadly, the three remoteness tests reflect the degree of culpability required for liability. The higher the degree of culpability required, the more extensive the liability. The three tests are now examined, followed by a discussion of the 'eggshell skull' rule, which applies irrespective of the remoteness test otherwise applying.

1   The test of natural and probable consequences

Deceit has a plaintiff-friendly remoteness rule under which *all* consequential losses flowing [6.57] from reliance on the representation are recoverable as long as they are a 'direct consequence' of the deceit, whether those consequences are foreseeable or not.[168] Similarly, in *Palmer Bruyn & Parker Pty Ltd v Parsons*,[169] the High Court of Australia said that liability for injurious falsehood is not limited by foreseeability, but extends to all 'natural and probable conse-quences' of the publication of the false statement, just as for deceit. This extensive liability can be justified because there is no social utility in dishonest conduct such as deceit or injurious falsehood. The High Court in *Palmer Bruyn & Parker Pty Ltd v Parsons* instead said that injurious falsehood, unlike negligence and nuisance, constitutes an 'intentional tort'.[170] It might be inferred that the High Court envisaged an application of the test of natural and probable consequences to all 'intentional torts'.[171]

The term 'intentional torts' is normally used to designate all torts that require an intentional [6.58] act to establish liability. This includes conversion and trespass to land since these torts require an intentional dealing with the goods or an intentional contact with the land, respectively. But these torts involve strict liability since fault is not required.[172] A defendant can be liable even though she thought, without being careless, that she was the owner of the goods or the land.[173] It is inappropriate to apply the remoteness test with the most extensive liability in cases

---

168   *South Australia v Johnson* (1982) 42 ALR 161, 170; *Shuman v Coober Pedy Tours Pty Ltd* (1994) 175 LSJS 159, 166; *Smith New Court Securities Ltd v Citibank NA* [1997] AC 254, 264–65, 281–82; *Palmer Bruyn & Parker Pty Ltd v Parsons* [2001] HCA 69, (2001) 208 CLR 388 [13] (Gleeson CJ), [63]–[80] (Gummow J); *National Australia Bank Ltd v Nemur Varity Pty Ltd* [2002] VSCA 18, (2002) 4 VR 252 [4], [57]. Cf *Gates v City Mutual Life Assurance Society Ltd* (1986) 160 CLR 1, 12 (Mason, Wilson and Dawson JJ): 'all the consequential loss directly flowing from [the plaintiff's] reliance on the representation ... at least if the loss is foreseeable'.

169   *Palmer Bruyn & Parker Pty Ltd v Parsons* [2001] HCA 69, (2001) 208 CLR 388.

170   Ibid, [13], [66]–[67], [78].

171   This idea is popular with commentators: SB Elliott, 'Remoteness Criteria in Equity' (2002) 65 Mod LR 588, 589; D Harris, 'Remoteness' in D Harris, D Campbell and R Halson, *Remedies in Contract and Tort* (2nd edn, CUP 2005) 330–31; MA Jones, 'Causation in Tort: General Principles' in MA Jones, AM Dugdale and M Simpson (eds), *Clerk & Lindsell on Torts* (22nd edn, Sweet & Maxwell 2017) [2–147]; MJ Tilbury, *Civil Remedies*, vol 1 (Butterworths 1990) [3083].

172   K Barker, P Cane, M Lunney and F Trindade, *The Law of Torts in Australia* (5th edn, OUP 2012) 114, 167. Specifically for conversion, see also S Douglas, 'The Nature of Conversion' (2009) 68 Camb LJ 198, 215.

173   *Rendell v Associated Finance Pty Ltd* [1957] VR 604, 613 (for conversion).

involving the lowest degree of culpability. The social utility considerations mentioned at [6.57] do not apply to non-culpable conduct.

[6.59]   While the test of natural and probable consequences has been rejected for conversion,[174] the NSW Court of Appeal applied it to trespass to land in *TCN Channel Nine Pty Ltd v Anning*.[175] Since the trespass in that case was in fact culpable, it might be thought appropriate to make the remoteness test applying in cases of trespass to land dependent upon the defendant's state of mind. However, this is not done in other torts (conversion and nuisance) that require no culpability. If all instances of trespass to land are to be governed by the same remoteness test, that test ought to be either the test of reasonable foreseeability (see [6.61]–[6.78]), applied in nuisance, or the test of reasonable contemplation (see [6.79]–[6.82]), applied in conversion.

[6.60]   The test of natural and probable consequences ought to apply only to torts that require an intention to cause harm of some sort.[176] Injurious falsehood requires 'malice, in the sense of an intent to injure another without just cause or excuse or by some indirect, dishonest or improper motive'.[177] Other torts that require an intention to cause harm of some sort include deceit, inducement of breach of contract and conspiracy.[178] Gummow J in *Palmer Bruyn & Parker Pty Ltd v Parsons* regarded these torts as 'related' to injurious falsehood.[179] The test of natural and probable consequences should also apply in cases of trespass to the person,[180] even though there are uncertainties with regard to the mental requirement for battery.[181]

2   The test of reasonable foreseeability

[6.61]   Reasonable foreseeability is established as the remoteness test for negligence.[182] It has also been applied to nuisance,[183] and might be applied to strict liability torts such as trespass to land, at least where the defendant was not culpable; see [6.59].

174   *National Australia Bank Ltd v Nemur Varity Pty Ltd* [2002] VSCA 18, (2002) 4 VR 252, considered at [6.80]–[6.82].
175   [2002] NSWCA 82, (2002) 54 NSWLR 333 [103].
176   Similarly, A Burrows, *Remedies for Torts and Breach of Contract* (3rd edn, OUP 2004) 81–83, who suggests an application of that test to all torts 'dishonestly committed'.
177   *Palmer Bruyn & Parker Pty Ltd v Parsons* [2001] HCA 69, (2001) 208 CLR 388 [108] (Kirby J).
178   Deceit requires an intention to deceive the plaintiff by the false statement. Inducement of breach of contract requires an intention to procure a breach of contract. Conspiracy requires an intention to cause some harm to the plaintiff: K Barker, P Cane, M Lunney and F Trindade, *The Law of Torts in Australia* (5th edn, OUP 2012) 38.
179   [2001] HCA 69, (2001) 208 CLR 388 [76].
180   See *Wainwright v Home Office* [2001] EWCA Civ 2081, [2002] QB 1334 [69] (Buxton LJ): 'if damage is caused by a trespass it is recoverable simply on the basis of causation, and does not additionally require foreseeability to be established'. With regard to the intentional infliction of mental harm, see *Nationwide News Pty Ltd v Naidu* [2007] NSWCA 377, (2007) 71 NSWLR 471 [81]–[82] (Spigelman CJ).
181   See K Barker, P Cane, M Lunney and F Trindade, *The Law of Torts in Australia* (5th edn, OUP 2012) 38–41.
182   *Overseas Tankship (UK) Ltd v Morts Dock & Engineering Co Ltd* [1961] AC 388 ('*The Wagon Mound (No 1)*').
183   *Overseas Tankship (UK) Ltd v Miller Steamship Co Pty Ltd* [1967] AC 617 ('*The Wagon Mound (No 2)*'), 636–40; *Fennell v Robson Excavations Pty Ltd* [1977] 2 NSWLR 486, 492; *Palmer Bruyn & Parker Pty Ltd v Parsons* [2001] HCA 69, (2001) 208 CLR 388 [66] (Gummow J); *Sutherland Shire Council v Becker* [2006] NSWCA 344, (2006) 150 LGERA 184 [137]; *Gales Holdings Pty Ltd v Tweed Shire Council* [2013] NSWCA 382, (2013) 85 NSWLR 514.

For some time, the courts vacillated between two tests for the remoteness of damage in negligence. One test required the foreseeability of the loss for which compensation was claimed.[184] The other test is the one still applied to 'intentional torts', and required only that the loss be a direct consequence of the careless conduct.[185] Even under the second test, liability in negligence required the foreseeability of some loss, but the foreseeable loss did not have to be the loss for which compensation was claimed. A prominent illustration is *Re Polemis v Furness, Withy & Co Ltd*.[186] Stevedores carelessly allowed a board to fall into the hold of a ship, causing a spark, which ignited petrol vapour and produced a fire that destroyed the ship. Even though the generation of a spark by a falling board had not been foreseeable, the English Court of Appeal held the stevedores' employer liable in negligence on the ground that some other damage from a falling board had been foreseeable.   **[6.62]**

The test of foreseeability prevailed in *The Wagon Mound (No 1)*.[187] Employees of the defendant, who had chartered the ship *Wagon Mound*, carelessly allowed a large quantity of furnace oil to spill into Sydney Harbour. The oil spread to the plaintiff's wharf, where welding work was being carried out. Pieces of molten metal from the welding fell into the water onto a piece of cotton waste, and the oil ignited and caused a fire, resulting in damage to the wharf and to two ships lying there. The trial judge found that it had been unforeseeable that the oil could be set alight when spread on water.[188] Nevertheless, applying *Re Polemis*, he held the defendant liable in negligence on the ground that pollution damage had been foreseeable.[189] The Privy Council overturned the decision. Viscount Simonds, who delivered the judgment, disapproved *Re Polemis* by saying that: **[6.63]**

> it does not seem consonant with current ideas of justice or morality that for an act of negligence, however slight or venial, which results in some trivial foreseeable damage the actor should be liable for all consequences however unforeseeable and however grave, so long as they can be said to be 'direct'.[190]

The foreseeability requirement is not a high hurdle, for three reasons: **[6.64]**

1.   A very low degree of probability of damage is sufficient.

2.   It is only the kind of damage which must be foreseeable, not its extent.

3.   The manner in which the damage occurred need not be foreseeable.

These principles will now be explored, beginning with the principle that a very low degree of probability of damage is sufficient. This is illustrated by *The Wagon Mound (No 2)*,[191] where the charterer of the *Wagon Mound* was sued by the owners of the two ships damaged in the fire. The findings of fact in this case differed slightly, but significantly, from those in the first   **[6.65]**

---

184   *Rigby v Hewitt* (1850) 5 Ex 240, 243 (Pollock CB); *Greenland v Chaplin* (1850) 5 Ex 243, 248.
185   *Smith v London & South Western Railway Co* (1870) LR 6 CP 14; *Weld-Blundell v Stephens* [1920] AC 956, 983–84 (Lord Sumner); *Thurogood v Van Den Berghs & Jurgens Ltd* [1951] 2 KB 537.
186   [1921] 3 KB 560.
187   *Overseas Tankship (UK) Ltd v Morts Dock & Engineering Co Ltd* [1961] AC 388 ('*The Wagon Mound (No 1)*').
188   *Overseas Tankship (UK) Ltd v Morts Dock & Engineering Co Ltd* [1958] 1 Lloyd's Rep 575, 582.
189   Ibid, 584–85, aff'd [1959] 2 Lloyd's Rep 697.
190   [1961] AC 388, 422.
191   *Overseas Tankship (UK) Ltd v Miller Steamship Co Pty Ltd* [1967] AC 617 ('*The Wagon Mound (No 2)*').

Wagon Mound litigation. With regard to the risk of fire created by the spillage of oil into the harbour, the trial judge concluded that reasonable people in the defendant's position would have regarded this risk as 'a possibility, but one which could become an actuality only in very exceptional circumstances'.[192] The Privy Council found this sufficient to hold the defendant liable in negligence:

> If a real risk is one which would occur to the mind of a reasonable man in the position of the defendant's servant and which he would not brush aside as far-fetched ... then surely he would not neglect such a risk if action to eliminate it presented no difficulty, involved no disadvantage, and required no expense.[193]

[6.66]   The High Court of Australia adopted this test in *Wyong Shire Council v Shirt*.[194] Mason J, with whom Stephen J and Aickin J agreed, said that:

> a risk of injury which is remote in the sense that it is extremely unlikely to occur may nevertheless constitute a foreseeable risk. A risk which is not far-fetched or fanciful is real and therefore foreseeable.[195]

[6.67]   Secondly, only the *kind* of damage needs to be foreseeable, not its extent. This was expressed in the *Wagon Mound* cases,[196] and became crucial in *Mount Isa Mines Ltd v Pusey*.[197] Two electricians employed by the defendant suffered severe burns when they suffered electric shock while testing a switchboard. The plaintiff, a colleague, saw the scene of the accident and helped one of the injured men, who died nine days later. Subsequently, the plaintiff suffered a severe schizophrenic reaction as a result of seeing and assisting the injured electrician. The defendant was found to be negligent in failing to give proper instructions to the electricians. It was also found that while some psychological reaction of more than a transient kind had been foreseeable, the specific psychological reaction suffered by the plaintiff had not. Nevertheless, the High Court of Australia held the defendant liable towards the plaintiff on the ground that damage of the kind suffered by the plaintiff had been foreseeable.

[6.68]   Where, after the initial injury has occurred, certain events lead to another injury, those events may break the chain of causation even though the initial injury and the second injury could be classified as being of the same kind; see [3.74]–[3.98]. A victim's suicide after a hearing in workplace-accident litigation broke the chain of causation even though some mental illness

---

192   [1963] 1 Lloyd's Rep 402, 426 (Walsh J).
193   [1967] AC 617, 643–44 (Lord Reid).
194   (1980) 146 CLR 40. See also *Mount Isa Mines Ltd v Pusey* (1970) 125 CLR 383, 399 (Windeyer J); *Caltex Oil (Australia) Pty Ltd v The Dredge Willemstad* (1976) 136 CLR 529, 574 (Stephen J); *Perre v Apand Pty Ltd* [1999] HCA 36, (1999) 198 CLR 180 [186] (Gummow J).
195   (1980) 146 CLR 40, 48. Mason J added that the breach of a duty of care requires not only the foreseeability of damage but also the unreasonableness of the risk created, which depends upon the probability of damage, the magnitude of damage and the cost of avoiding the risk. Note that the *Wyong* test concerns the test at breach of duty stage.
196   *Overseas Tankship (UK) Ltd v Morts Dock & Engineering Co Ltd* [1961] AC 388 ('*The Wagon Mound (No 1)*'), 426; *Overseas Tankship (UK) Ltd v Miller Steamship Co Pty Ltd* [1967] AC 617 ('*The Wagon Mound (No 2)*'), 636.
197   (1970) 125 CLR 383.

was a foreseeable consequence of the accident.[198] Similarly, a sexual assault on a woman who was immobilised as a result of breaking her ankle broke the chain of causation between the ankle injury and psychological harm caused by the assault, even though some psychological harm as a result of the ankle injury had been foreseeable and had occurred.[199]

The rule that only the kind of damage needs to be foreseeable requires a categorisation of damage. Since the concept of remoteness of damage restricts liability on policy grounds, the categorisation of damage is ultimately a question of policy.[200] However, the courts have attempted to define abstract categories of damage for general application. This attempt was bound to fail. For example, it has proved impossible to lay down a general rule on whether all forms of mental injury are of the same kind and, in the absence of statutory intervention, whether all forms of personal injury, mental and physical, are of the same kind. [6.69]

In *Mount Isa Mines Ltd v Pusey*,[201] considered at [6.67], the High Court of Australia took the view that all mental illnesses are of the same kind.[202] The case was distinguished in *Rowe v McCartney*,[203] where the plaintiff allowed the defendant to drive her car and she was a passenger. The defendant negligently hit a telegraph pole. He was rendered quadriplegic, but the plaintiff suffered only minor physical injuries. However, she developed a depressive neurosis, caused by guilt, since the defendant would not have been injured had the plaintiff not allowed him to drive the car. Some psychiatric illness as a result of being involved in a traffic accident was foreseeable, but this specific psychiatric reaction was not foreseeable. A majority in the NSW Court of Appeal held that the defendant was not liable for the plaintiff's psychiatric illness.[204] Psychiatric illness due to shock was distinguished from psychiatric illness due to guilt. [6.70]

Conversely, in *Page v Smith*,[205] the House of Lords effectively held that physical harm and mental harm are the same kind of harm. The defendant suddenly drove his car onto the wrong side of the road into the plaintiff's path, making a frontal collision inevitable. As a result, the plaintiff suffered a recurrence of chronic fatigue syndrome, but no physical injury. A majority in the House of Lords held the defendant liable, saying that it was not necessary to foresee injury by shock, and foreseeability of personal injury in general was sufficient.[206] [6.71]

---

198   *AMP General Insurance Ltd v Roads and Traffic Authority of NSW* [2001] NSWCA 186, (2001) Aust Torts Reports 81–619. But not every suicide breaks the chain of causation: *Corr v IBC Vehicles Ltd* [2008] UKHL 13, [2008] 1 AC 884.

199   *State Rail Authority of New South Wales v Chu* [2008] NSWCA 14, (2008) Aust Torts Reports 81–940 [54]–[55].

200   *Metrolink Victoria Pty Ltd v Inglis* [2009] VSCA 227, (2009) 25 VR 633 [10], [96]. It was also held in that case (at [24], [27], [50]–[76]) that the categorisation of damage is a question of law, not fact.

201   (1970) 125 CLR 383.

202   This was followed in *Hoffmueller v Commonwealth* (1981) 54 FLR 48, 52–53 (Glass JA); *Jaensch v Coffey* (1984) 155 CLR 549, 563 (Brennan J); *Nader v Urban Transit Authority of New South Wales* (1985) 2 NSWLR 501, 503–04, 535.

203   [1976] 2 NSWLR 72.

204   Ibid, 75–76, 89–90. Glass JA (at 79–80) said in dissent that the foreseeable psychiatric harm and the psychiatric harm suffered by the plaintiff were of the same kind. Glass JA's view was preferred in *Oram v BHP Mitsui Coal Pty Ltd* [2014] QSC 230, [2015] 2 Qd R 357 [81]–[85].

205   [1996] AC 155.

206   Ibid, 182, 189–90, 197. The House of Lords has since restricted the principle to psychiatric harm resulting from a fear of instant physical harm, as opposed to a fear of developing a long-term illness in future: *Rothwell v Chemical & Insulating Co Ltd, sub nom Grieves v FT Everard & Sons Ltd* [2007] UKHL 39, [2008] 1 AC 281 [55], [95].

[6.72] The approach taken in *Page v Smith* does not seem to have been adopted by Australian courts at common law,[207] and the civil liability statutes in all Australian jurisdictions except the Northern Territory and Queensland exclude that approach by providing that mental harm must itself be foreseeable to attract a duty of care even if the mental harm is consequent on bodily injury.[208]

[6.73] The cases considered at [6.70]–[6.71] can be reconciled by taking into account the general manner in which damage was, or could have been, caused. It was appropriate to impose liability in *Mount Isa Mines Ltd v Pusey* because the foreseeable mental illness and the mental illness actually suffered were both due to witnessing a severely burnt person. It was also appropriate to impose liability in *Page v Smith* since a frontal car collision entails the risk of physical injuries and of mental illness due to shock. By contrast, it was appropriate to deny liability in *Rowe v McCartney* if mental illness due to shock and mental illness due to guilt can properly be distinguished.[209]

[6.74] Instead of defining abstract categories of damage, the courts ought to ask the question suggested by Denning LJ in *Roe v Minister of Health*: 'Is the consequence fairly to be regarded as within the risk created by the negligence?'[210] A consideration of the risks involved would bring the remoteness test for negligence and nuisance in line with the test for breach of duty, which is based on the concept of risk.[211] It would also direct attention to the policy considerations involved in the particular case.

[6.75] However, an open consideration of the risks involved is barred by an extensive application of the third principle, which relaxes the foreseeability requirement. The courts have said that the manner in which the damage occurred need not be foreseeable.[212] In *Chapman v Hearse*, the High Court of Australia said that:

> it would be quite artificial to make responsibility depend upon, or to deny liability by reference to, the capacity of a reasonable man to foresee damage of a precise and particular character or upon his capacity to foresee the precise events leading to the damage complained of.[213]

[6.76] Of course, foreseeability of the *precise* manner in which damage occurred cannot be required since it would erect a very high threshold for liability. But the courts have gone further and abrogated even the need to be able to foresee the *general* manner in which

---

207 In *Mount Isa Mines Ltd v Pusey* (1970) 125 CLR 383, Windeyer J (at 402) regarded mental harm and physical harm as being different in kind, while Walsh J (at 414) left the question open.

208 *Civil Law (Wrongs) Act 2002* (ACT), s 34; *Civil Liability Act 2002* (NSW), s 32; *Civil Liability Act 1936* (SA), s 33; *Civil Liability Act 2002* (Tas), s 34; *Wrongs Act 1958* (Vic), s 74; *Civil Liability Act 2002* (WA), s 5S.

209 See *Nader v Urban Transit Authority of New South Wales* (1985) 2 NSWLR 501, 535 (McHugh JA).

210 [1954] 2 QB 66, 85. This test was supported in *Nader*, ibid, 506 (Samuels JA); *March v E & MH Stramare Pty Ltd* (1991) 171 CLR 506, 535 (McHugh J).

211 *Civil Law (Wrongs) Act 2002* (ACT), s 43; *Civil Liability Act 2002* (NSW), s 5B; *Civil Liability Act 2003* (Qld), s 9; *Civil Liability Act 1936* (SA), s 32; *Civil Liability Act 2002* (Tas), s 11; *Wrongs Act 1958* (Vic), s 48; *Civil Liability Act 2002* (WA), s 5B.

212 *Mount Isa Mines Ltd v Pusey* (1970) 125 CLR 383, 402 (Windeyer J); *Rosenberg v Percival* [2001] HCA 18, (2001) 205 CLR 434 [64] (Gummow J).

213 (1961) 106 CLR 112, 121 (Dixon CJ, Kitto, Taylor and Windeyer JJ).

damage occurred, as illustrated by the Scottish case *Hughes v Lord Advocate*.[214] Post office workmen temporarily left a manhole in the road, covered only with an unclosed tent and surrounded by burning paraffin lights. Two boys, aged eight and 10, took one of the lamps and entered the tent. The lamp fell into the manhole and broke, causing a huge explosion which burnt one of the boys badly. It was foreseeable that children might play with a lamp and get burnt by contact with the flame or with burning paraffin, but the explosion was unforeseeable. Nevertheless, the House of Lords held the post office liable on the ground that as long as the type of damage (burning) was foreseeable, the precise chain of events is immaterial.

This reasoning implies that there would have been no liability had the explosion caused an injury other than burning, for example a broken leg. But liability should not be imposed simply because an unforeseeable chain of events has led to the same injury as a foreseeable chain of events would have done. It should have been asked whether the risk of getting injured through contact with the flame or burning paraffin is distinct from the risk of sustaining injury through an explosion produced by escaping paraffin vapour.[215] Whichever answer is given, the outcome will be the same for all children affected by the same explosion, regardless of the type of injury suffered. [6.77]

Hughes v Lord Advocate has been adopted in Australia,[216] but this has not prevented a consideration of the relevant risk in the guise of determining the kind of damage. An example is *Richards v Victoria*.[217] During a fight between the plaintiff and another boy in a classroom, the other boy struck a swinging blow at the plaintiff's left temple, leading to the plaintiff suffering spastic paralysis. In an action against the school for negligently failing to prevent the fight, it was argued that the injury suffered by the plaintiff was different in kind from the minor injuries that could be foreseen as consequences of a fist fight. It was held that it had been open to the jury to find that the injury suffered was of the same kind as that which had been foreseeable, because both injuries resulted from a blow delivered by a fist to the body.[218] [6.78]

3   The test of reasonable contemplation

A test similar to the remoteness test in contract is emerging for conversion. The test of reasonable foreseeability that applies in negligence used to be thought applicable in conversion, too. This view was taken by King CJ in *Harrisons Group Holdings Ltd v Westpac Banking Corporation*,[219] and has been taken by the English Court of Appeal.[220] In *Kuwait Airways Corporation v Iraqi Airways Co (Nos 4 and 5)*,[221] Lord Nicholls said that a person who converts another's goods in the genuine belief that they are his deserves the protection of the [6.79]

---

214   [1963] AC 837.
215   This question was in effect considered decisive by the Court of Session which, by majority, distinguished two separate risks and denied liability: *Lord Advocate v Hughes* [1961] SC 310.
216   *AMP General Insurance Ltd v Roads and Traffic Authority of NSW* [2001] NSWCA 186, (2001) Aust Torts Reports 81–619 [126]; *MacPherson v Proprietors of Strata Plan 10857* [2003] NSWCA 96 [29]; *Martin v Hendersons Industries Pty Ltd* [2004] VSCA 19 [54]; *Bellingen Shire Council v Colavon Pty Ltd* [2012] NSWCA 34, (2012) 188 LGERA 169 [56].
217   [1969] VR 136.
218   Ibid, 145.
219   (1989) 51 SASR 36, 40–41.
220   *The Arpad* [1934] P 189; *Saleslease Ltd v Davis* [1999] 1 WLR 1664; *Sandeman Coprimar SA v Transitos y Transportes Integrales SL* [2003] EWCA Civ 113, [2003] QB 1270 [28], [31].
221   [2002] UKHL 19, [2002] 2 AC 883 [103]–[104].

foreseeability requirement, whereas a person who knowingly converts another's goods does not and ought to be subject to the test of direct and natural consequences, as it applies in deceit.

[6.80]   A new approach was taken in *National Australia Bank Ltd v Nemur Varity Pty Ltd*.[222] The plaintiff, an insurance broker, paid his client's premiums by cheque. He drew cheques payable to bearer after being deceived by a third party as to the designation of the payment. The defendant, the plaintiff's bank, cashed those cheques in ignorance of the deceit. As a result of the misdirection of the money, some of the plaintiff's clients had no insurance and, when they became aware of that fact, ceased business with the plaintiff. The plaintiff claimed damages for breach of contract and conversion. The Victorian Court of Appeal denied liability with regard to loss of business in both causes of action.

[6.81]   Phillips JA based his decision on lack of causation.[223] Callaway JA did the same,[224] but added in obiter dicta that 'the measure of damages for consequential loss in conversion is not reasonable foreseeability'.[225] Instead, 'the consequential loss must be of a kind that should have been within the contemplation of the defendant as a likely consequence having regard to the defendant's knowledge (or express notice) of the facts'.[226] Batt JA based his decision on the view that the loss of business was too remote from the defendant's breach of contract,[227] and from the defendant's conversion.[228] He said that liability in conversion for consequential loss requires 'express notice or special knowledge' of the circumstances leading to the loss.[229] The test pronounced by Callaway JA has been applied in one first-instance decision.[230]

[6.82]   Batt JA and Callaway JA supported an application of the test of reasonable contemplation to all cases of conversion. They did not confine it to cases of concurrent liability in contract and conversion, nor to cases of dishonest conversion. Batt JA expressly included a case of theft, and drew an analogy to nuisance where the same remoteness test applies irrespective of the defendant's culpability.[231] The indiscriminate application of the test of reasonable contemplation irrespective of the defendant's culpability may be justified on the pragmatic ground that an investigation into the defendant's culpability should not be required solely for the purpose of determining remoteness of damage. Furthermore, there is something to be said for the view, expressed by Lord Nicholls in *Kuwait Airways Corporation v Iraqi Airways Co (Nos 4 and 5)*,[232] that liability in cases of honest conversion should be confined to a disgorgement of benefits received. Under that view, there would be no liability to compensate the plaintiff's loss in cases of honest conversion, and the issue of remoteness would not arise.

222   [2002] VSCA 18, (2002) 4 VR 252.
223   Ibid, [2].
224   Ibid, [6]–[8].
225   Ibid, [9].
226   Ibid, [9].
227   Ibid, [49]–[55].
228   Ibid, [65]–[69].
229   Ibid, [64].
230   *Macrocom Pty Ltd v City West Centre Pty Ltd* [2003] NSWSC 898 [45]. See also *Rapid Roofing Pty Ltd v Natalise Pty Ltd (as trustee for the St Ange Family Trust)* [2006] QCA 515.
231   [2002] VSCA 18, (2002) 4 VR 252 [63].
232   [2002] UKHL 19, [2002] 2 AC 883 [79].

4   The 'eggshell skull' rule

Whatever the applicable remoteness test,[233] 'a tortfeasor must take his victim as he finds   **[6.83]**
him',[234] and must compensate extra loss due to a special susceptibility on the plaintiff's part,
for example an unusually thin skull or an unusually weak heart.[235] In *Purkess v Crittenden*,
Windeyer J said that:

> it will not avail a defendant to show that but for the plaintiff being in some way ailing
> when he was hurt his injuries would have been less serious than they were. A tortfeasor
> gets no allowance because of the frailty of his victim.[236]

The 'eggshell skull' rule applies only where the defendant would be liable even if the   **[6.84]**
plaintiff was not hypersensitive.[237] It 'is a principle of compensation, not of liability'.[238] This
reflects the fact that a person is not generally required to take extra precautions to protect
hypersensitive people. The failure to take special precautions because of *one's own* hypersen-
sitivity may constitute contributory negligence, discussed at [6.89]ff.[239] Furthermore, the
defendant is not liable for loss that the plaintiff's pre-existing condition would have caused
in any event.[240]

The 'eggshell skull' rule has been applied to a person's physical susceptibilities, for   **[6.85]**
example where a small burn on the lower lip turned to cancer due to a pre-malignant condition
of the tissue,[241] where the pricking of a finger by poisoned wire caused the deterioration of the
sight of an already ulcerated eye,[242] and where a minor graze led to encephalitis because of an
allergic reaction to an anti-tetanus serum.[243]

At common law, the 'eggshell skull' rule applies to mental susceptibilities.[244] '[T]here is no   **[6.86]**
difference in principle between an egg-shell skull and an egg-shell personality.'[245] A defendant
who had caused a car accident involving the plaintiff was held liable in respect of the anxiety
neurosis that the plaintiff developed after the accident due to his obsessive-compulsive

---

233   With regard to the test of reasonable foreseeability, the 'eggshell skull' rule is not an actual exception
 but merely reflects the fact that only the kind of damage needs to be foreseeable: *Commonwealth v
 McLean* (1996) 41 NSWLR 389, 406–07; S Harder, *Measuring Damages in the Law of Obligations: The
 Search for Harmonised Principles* (Hart 2010) 28–29.
234   *March v E & MH Stramare Pty Ltd* (1991) 171 CLR 506, 534 (McHugh J); *Martin v Hendersons Industries
 Pty Ltd* [2004] VSCA 19 [38] (Charles JA); *Spence v Gomez* [2006] VSCA 48, (2006) 45 MVR 556 [44]
 (Maxwell P). See also *Watts v Rake* (1960) 108 CLR 158, 164.
235   Examples given by Kennedy J in *Dulieu v White & Sons* [1901] 2 KB 669, 679. Ironically, cases actually
 involving thin skulls are hard to find: AM Linden, 'Down with Foreseeability! Of Thin Skulls and
 Rescuers' (1969) 47 Can Bar Rev 545, 550–51.
236   (1965) 114 CLR 164, 170.
237   *Tame v New South Wales* [2002] HCA 35, (2002) 211 CLR 317 [117]–[118].
238   *White v Chief Constable of South Yorkshire Police* [1999] 2 AC 455, 470 (Lord Goff); approvingly quoted
 in *Tame*, ibid, [117].
239   See *Murphy v McCarthy* (1974) 9 SASR 424, 427.
240   *Watts v Rake* (1960) 108 CLR 158; *Purkess v Crittenden* (1965) 114 CLR 164; *New South Wales v Burton*
 [2006] NSWCA 12, (2006) Aust Torts Reports 81–826 [69] (Basten JA).
241   *Smith v Leech Brain & Co Ltd* [1962] 2 QB 405.
242   *Warren v Scruttons Ltd* [1962] 1 Lloyd's Rep 497.
243   *Robinson v Post Office* [1974] 1 WLR 1176.
244   *Page v Smith* [1996] AC 155, 182, 189; *Tame v New South Wales* [2002] HCA 35, (2002) 211 CLR 317 [117].
245   *Malcolm v Broadhurst* [1970] 3 All ER 508, 511 (Geoffrey Lane J).

personality, despite the fact that he had suffered no significant bodily injury in the accident.[246] At common law, the 'eggshell skull' rule also applies to a person's cultural and religious setting,[247] and may apply to other life circumstances too. In *Nader v Urban Transit Authority of NSW*, where a 10-year-old boy who had suffered minor physical injuries developed a psychiatric illness due to his parents' overprotectiveness, McHugh JA said:

> When a defendant takes a plaintiff as he finds him, he does not take him as a naked human being divorced from his environment. Clearly enough taking the plaintiff as you find him involves taking him in at least his social and earning capacity setting ... I think that the defendant must take the plaintiff with all his weaknesses, beliefs and reactions as well as his capacities and attributes, physical, social and economic.[248]

[6.87] The civil liability statutes in all Australian jurisdictions except the Northern Territory and Queensland now restrict the application of the 'eggshell skull' rule to mental harm by providing that a duty of care to prevent mental harm (whether or not consequent on bodily injury) exists only where it is foreseeable that a person of normal fortitude might, in the circumstances, suffer a recognised psychiatric illness.[249]

[6.88] There seems to be no authority on whether the 'eggshell skull' rule applies to special susceptibilities of property, but a different treatment of abnormally vulnerable people and abnormally vulnerable things, such as animals with thin skulls, would be difficult to justify.[250] The 'eggshell skull' rule applies to a plaintiff's financial situation, rendering the defendant liable for the extra loss due to the plaintiff's impecuniosity. The House of Lords took a different view in *The Liesbosch*,[251] but overruled it in *Lagden v O'Connor*,[252] which has been adopted in Australia.[253] This is relevant, for example, where the plaintiff does not have the means to have damaged business premises or profit-earning goods repaired (before receiving damages from the defendant) and loses profit in excess of what would have been lost had the property been repaired immediately.

---

246   *Hoffmueller v Commonwealth* (1981) 54 FLR 48.
247   *Kavanagh v Akhtar* (1998) 45 NSWLR 588, 601. A woman who had suffered a shoulder injury was no longer able to care for her long hair and cut it off without her husband's consent, contrary to their religious custom. This angered her husband and ultimately led to a marriage breakdown and the woman suffering psychiatric illness. The decision in the woman's favour has been criticised as being difficult to reconcile with *The Wagon Mound (No 1)*; see M Davies and I Malkin, *Focus: Torts* (8th edn, LexisNexis 2018) [4.59].
248   (1985) 2 NSWLR 501, 537.
249   *Civil Law (Wrongs) Act 2002* (ACT), s 34; *Civil Liability Act 2002* (NSW), s 32; *Civil Liability Act 1936* (SA), s 33; *Civil Liability Act 2002* (Tas), s 34; *Wrongs Act 1958* (Vic), s 74; *Civil Liability Act 2002* (WA), s 5S. Those provisions generally apply to the same types of wrong as the provisions on causation discussed at [3.15]–[3.16].
250   M Beazley, 'Damage' in C Sappideen and P Vines (eds), *Fleming's The Law of Torts* (10th edn, LBC 2011) [9.170]; MA Jones, 'Causation in Tort: General Principles' in MA Jones, AM Dugdale and M Simpson (eds), *Clerk & Lindsell on Torts* (22nd edn, Sweet & Maxwell 2017) [2–173].
251   [1933] AC 449.
252   [2003] UKHL 64, [2004] 1 AC 1067.
253   *Tyco Australia Pty Ltd v Optus Networks Pty Ltd* [2004] NSWCA 333 [192]; *Waratah Smash Repairs Pty Ltd v Sonenco (No 92) Pty Ltd* [2005] NSWSC 1283 [4]; *Highway Hauliers Pty Ltd v Maxwell* [2012] WASC 53 [155].

B   Contributory negligence

1   Common law

Contributory negligence denotes unreasonable conduct (in the sense of a failure to take   [6.89]
reasonable care of one's own affairs) by the plaintiff that contributed to the occurrence of
the defendant's wrong or the ensuing loss. The doctrine of contributory negligence is usually
applied to conduct by the plaintiff that occurred before the wrong or before the plaintiff knew
or ought to have known the facts giving rise to the wrong, but has occasionally been applied
to conduct by the plaintiff occurring after the plaintiff became aware of the wrong; see
[3.125]–[3.128].

At common law, contributory negligence constituted a complete defence to a number of   [6.90]
torts, in particular negligence,[254] nuisance on the highway,[255] and breach of statutory duty.[256]
Three exceptions existed. First, the plaintiff's unreasonable conduct was considered irrelevant
where the defendant had the last opportunity to avoid the plaintiff's injury.[257] Secondly, the
common law defence of contributory negligence was unavailable in cases of conversion[258]
and intentionally inflicted injury.[259] Thirdly, where both ships involved in a collision were at
fault, the loss was to be borne equally by both.[260]

2   Contributory negligence statutes

Following the *Law Reform (Contributory Negligence) Act 1945* (UK), statutory provisions in   [6.91]
all Australian states and territories provide for an apportionment of liability according to
each party's responsibility for the damage, without defeating any defence arising under a
contract.[261] For convenience, those statutory provisions will be called 'contributory negligence
statutes'.

---

254   *Radley v London and North Western Railway Co* (1876) 1 App Cas 754, 759; *Cayzer, Irvine & Co v Carron Co* (1884) 9 App Cas 873, 881; *Wakelin v London and South Western Railway Co* (1887) LR 12 App Cas 41, 45, 47, 51; *Symons v Stacey* (1922) 30 CLR 169.

255   *Butterfield v Forrester* (1809) 11 East 60, 61; 103 ER 926, 927.

256   *Caswell v Powell Duffryn Associated Collieries Ltd* [1940] AC 152; *Piro v W Foster & Co Ltd* (1943) 68 CLR 313.

257   *Davies v Mann* (1842) 10 M & W 546, 548–49; 152 ER 588, 589; *Radley v London and North Western Railway Co* (1876) 1 App Cas 754, 759–60; *The Volute* [1922] 1 AC 129, 139; *Anglo-Newfoundland Development Co Ltd v Pacific Steam Navigation Co Ltd* [1924] AC 406, 420; *The Boy Andrew* [1948] AC 140, 149.

258   *Heperu Pty Ltd v Morgan Brooks Pty Ltd (No 2)* [2007] NSWSC 1438 [174]; *Mitsui Osk Lines (Thailand) Co Ltd v Jack Fair Pty Ltd* [2015] FCCA 558 [71].

259   *Fontin v Katapodis* (1962) 108 CLR 177; *Venning v Chin* (1974) 10 SASR 299, 317, 321; *Horkin v North Melbourne Football Club Social Club* [1983] 1 VR 153; *New South Wales v Riley* [2003] NSWCA 208, (2003) 57 NSWLR 496 [104]. See also *Elite Protective Personnel Pty Ltd v Salmon* [2007] NSWCA 322 [25]–[27]. The view that the defence was unavailable in defamation actions was taken in *Lamont v Dwyer* [2007] ACTSC 47 [14].

260   *Wildman v Blakes* (1789) Burr 332, 167 ER 596.

261   *Civil Law (Wrongs) Act 2002* (ACT), s 102; *Law Reform (Miscellaneous Provisions) Act 1965* (NSW), s 9; *Law Reform (Miscellaneous Provisions) Act 1956* (NT), s 16; *Law Reform Act 1995* (Qld), s 10; *Law Reform (Contributory Negligence and Apportionment of Liability) Act 2001* (SA), s 7; *Wrongs Act 1954* (Tas), s 4; *Wrongs Act 1958* (Vic), s 26; *Law Reform (Contributory Negligence and Tortfeasors' Contribution) Act 1947* (WA), s 4. For maritime collisions, see *Navigation Regulation 2013* (Cth), reg 15.

[6.92] The provisions of the various jurisdictions differ in respect of the torts to which they apply.[262] They apply to every tort (including breach of statutory duty) in South Australia and Tasmania,[263] but only to the torts of negligence and breach of statutory duty in the Northern Territory and in Western Australia.[264] In the remaining jurisdictions, the contributory negligence statutes apply to all torts in respect of which a defence of contributory negligence is available at common law,[265] but the statute in the Australian Capital Territory does not apply to personal injury arising from breach of statutory duty.[266] In these jurisdictions, the court needs to determine whether a defence of contributory negligence is available at common law, and this can be difficult since this question has not been resolved for every tort. On principle, an apportionment of liability ought to be available for all torts since it is just and gives both parties an incentive to take cost-effective precautions.[267]

3 Civil liability statutes

[6.93] The civil liability statutes in all jurisdictions contain one or both of two sets of provisions on contributory negligence. Those provisions will be considered in their context below. It is now necessary to examine the torts (and other wrongs) to which they apply.

[6.94] The first set of provisions addresses the plaintiff's standard of care and/or the possibility of a reduction to nil. They generally have the same scope as the civil liability statutes' provisions on causation, which prescribe a two-step inquiry into factual causation and the scope of liability. The scope of the latter provisions differs between the jurisdictions; see [3.15]–[3.16].[268] In most jurisdictions, they apply to the failure to exercise reasonable care, whether the claim is brought in tort, in contract, under statute or otherwise.

[6.95] The second set of provisions on contributory negligence in the civil liability statutes address the plaintiff's intoxication and/or failure to wear a seatbelt. Those provisions generally have the same scope as the civil liability statutes' provisions on compensation for personal injury. The latter provisions apply in general to every wrong, subject to some exceptions; see [7.13]–[7.14].[269] In some jurisdictions, therefore, the provisions on intoxication and the failure to wear a seatbelt in the civil liability statute have a wider scope than the contributory negligence statute.

---

262 The applicability of the provisions to contractual liability is discussed at [5.110]. Their applicability to claims under the Australian Consumer Law is discussed at [8.47].

263 *Law Reform (Contributory Negligence and Apportionment of Liability) Act 2001* (SA), s 4(1)(a); *Wrongs Act 1954* (Tas), s 2.

264 *Law Reform (Miscellaneous Provisions) Act 1956* (NT), s 15; *Law Reform (Contributory Negligence and Tortfeasors' Contribution) Act 1947* (WA), ss 3, 4(1).

265 This is the effect of how the term 'wrong' is defined: *Civil Law (Wrongs) Act 2002* (ACT), s 101; *Law Reform (Miscellaneous Provisions) Act 1965* (NSW), s 8; *Law Reform Act 1995* (Qld), s 5; *Wrongs Act 1958* (Vic), s 25.

266 *Civil Law (Wrongs) Act 2002* (ACT), s 102(2).

267 In the view of RA Posner, *Economic Analysis of Law* (9th edn, Aspen 2014) §6.4, apportionment is more efficient than giving full damages to the victim but may be less efficient than denying damages, due to the administrative cost generated by transfer payments.

268 The statute in the Northern Territory has no provision on causation; nor does it have the first set of provisions on contributory negligence.

269 In South Australia, the scope of the provisions on compensation for personal injury is more limited, but the second set of provisions on contributory negligence is not subject to the same limitation.

Some jurisdictions thus have three sets of provisions on contributory negligence, each set having its own rules as to the types of wrong to which it applies. Furthermore, no set of provisions has the same scope in all jurisdictions. There are no two jurisdictions in Australia with exactly the same law on contributory negligence. This is undesirable as it increases the need for a choice-of-law exercise. [6.96]

4   The plaintiff's conduct

The contributory negligence statutes describe contributory negligence as a person's failure to take reasonable care of the person's own interests. Contributory negligence is not the breach of a duty of care towards the defendant (although it may coincide with such a breach), but the breach of a 'duty to oneself'.[270] Nevertheless, the standard of care required in looking after one's own interests is essentially the same as the standard of care in looking after other people's interests. This is the position at common law,[271] and is prescribed by the civil liability statutes in most jurisdictions.[272] [6.97]

The civil liability statutes in New South Wales, Queensland, Tasmania, Victoria and Western Australia define the standard of care as that of a reasonable person in the plaintiff's position, and ascribe significance to what the plaintiff knew or ought to have known at the time.[273] Where the plaintiff is a child, the characteristics of a reasonable person in the plaintiff's position take into account the plaintiff's age.[274] The common law has similar principles. An objective test applies,[275] but it is unclear to what extent the definition of the reasonable person takes account of the plaintiff's circumstances. Account is probably taken of the fact that the plaintiff is a child,[276] or intellectually disabled,[277] but probably not of other physical or mental deficits of the plaintiff.[278] [6.98]

The courts have been lenient towards plaintiffs who found themselves in a sudden emergency created by the defendant.[279] Furthermore, the nature of the duty breached by the defendant may influence what a reasonable person in the plaintiff's position would have [6.99]

---

270   *McHale v Watson* (1966) 115 CLR 199, 214 (Kitto J): 'contributory negligence is not a breach of legal duty; it is only a failure to take reasonable care for one's own safety'.

271   *Joslyn v Berryman* [2003] HCA 34, (2003) 214 CLR 552 [32] (McHugh J).

272   *Civil Liability Act 2002* (NSW), s 5R(1); *Civil Liability Act 2003* (Qld), s 23(1); *Civil Liability Act 1936* (SA), s 44(1); *Civil Liability Act 2002* (Tas), s 23(1); *Wrongs Act 1958* (Vic), s 62(1); *Civil Liability Act 2002* (WA), s 5K(1). The torts (and other wrongs) to which those provisions apply are discussed at [6.94].

273   *Civil Liability Act 2002* (NSW), s 5R(2); *Civil Liability Act 2003* (Qld), s 23(2); *Civil Liability Act 2002* (Tas), s 23(2); *Wrongs Act 1958* (Vic), s 62(2); *Civil Liability Act 2002* (WA), s 5K(2). The torts (and other wrongs) to which those provisions apply are discussed at [6.94].

274   *Doubleday v Kelly* [2005] NSWCA 151 [26].

275   *Commissioner for Railways v Ruprecht* (1979) 142 CLR 563, 570–72 (Mason J); *Joslyn v Berryman* [2003] HCA 34, (2003) 214 CLR 552 [32] (McHugh J).

276   *McHale v Watson* (1966) 115 CLR 199, 205, 215, 223, 229; *Joslyn v Berryman* [2003] HCA 34, (2003) 214 CLR 552 [32], [35] (McHugh J); *Sainsbury v Great Southern Energy Pty Ltd* [2000] NSWSC 479 [8].

277   *Russell v Rail Infrastructure Corporation* [2007] NSWSC 402 [94], [96].

278   *Joslyn v Berryman* [2003] HCA 34, (2003) 214 CLR 552 [32], [35] (McHugh J); *Nominal Defendant v Lane* [2004] NSWCA 405 [37]–[39]; *Tolhurst v Cleary Brothers (Bombo) Pty Ltd* [2008] NSWCA 181 [91].

279   *The Bywell Castle* (1879) LR 4 PD 219; *Caterson v Commissioner for Railways* (1973) 128 CLR 99, 112; *Shelley v Szelley* [1971] SASR 430, 431; *Nominal Defendant v Rowland-Smith* [2003] NSWCA 65 [68]; *Avram v Gusakoski* [2006] WACA 16, (2006) 31 WAR 400 [47], [55]–[57]; *Bateman v Nominal Defendant* [2012] NSWDC 155, (2012) 15 DCLR (NSW) 239 [56].

done.[280] It may have been the very purpose of the defendant's duty to prevent the injury in question. But even where this is the case, the plaintiff is not automatically exculpated.[281] These principles are particularly relevant to the liability of an employer towards an employee for the failure to provide a safe work environment. No employee can act with the utmost care every time, especially where the work is repetitive.[282] In devising a safe work environment, an employer must therefore take into account the possibility of thoughtlessness, inadvertence and even carelessness on the part of the employees.[283] But an inadvertent or thoughtless act by an employee may still constitute contributory negligence.[284]

[6.100]   In general, the defendant needs to prove on the balance of probabilities that the plaintiff's conduct fell short of the required standard of care.[285] However, in certain circumstances, legislation in most jurisdictions provides that 'contributory negligence must be presumed' – this entails at least a presumption that the plaintiff's conduct fell short of the required standard of care. In the Australian Capital Territory and the Northern Territory, the presumptions apply only in cases of personal injury.

[6.101]   The civil liability statutes in all jurisdictions except Victoria provide that contributory negligence is presumed where the harmed person's capacity to exercise care and skill was impaired due to intoxication, and that this presumption can be rebutted only by proving that the intoxication did not contribute to the accident or was not self-induced.[286] The statutes in the Australian Capital Territory, the Northern Territory, Queensland and South Australia further provide that contributory negligence is presumed where a person of at least 16 years of age relied on the care and skill of a person who caused the accident and whom the injured person knew, or ought to have known, to be intoxicated, and that this presumption can be rebutted only by proving that the intoxication did not contribute to the accident or the injured person could not reasonably be expected to have avoided the risk.[287] A similar provision is contained in s 4.17(2)(b) of the *Motor Accident Injuries Act 2017* (NSW) for motor accident cases.

---

280   *Astley v Austrust Ltd* [1999] HCA 6, (1999) 197 CLR 1 [30].
281   Ibid, [29]–[31].
282   *Caswell v Powell Duffryn Associated Collieries Ltd* [1940] AC 152, 178–79; *Commissioner for Railways v Ruprecht* (1979) 142 CLR 563, 568, 570–71.
283   *Smith v Broken Hill Pty Co Ltd* (1957) 97 CLR 337, 342–43; *Ferraloro v Preston Timber Pty Ltd* (1982) 42 ALR 627, 629; *Turner v South Australia* (1982) 42 ALR 669, 674; *McLean v Tedman* (1984) 155 CLR 306, 311–12; *Liftronic Pty Ltd v Unver* [2001] HCA 24, (2001) 179 ALR 321 [87]–[88]; *Czatyrko v Edith Cowan University* [2005] HCA 14, (2005) 214 ALR 349 [12].
284   *Sungravure Pty Ltd v Meani* (1964) 110 CLR 24, 33, 38; *Commissioner for Railways v Ruprecht* (1979) 142 CLR 563, 567–68, 571.
285   *McCarthy v Nominal Defendant* [1999] NSWSC 1194 [20]; *Rovolis v Taunton* [2001] ACTSC 87 [19]; *Richards v Mills* [2003] WASCA 97, (2003) 27 WAR 200 [26]; *Ralston v Bell* [2010] NSWSC 245, (2010) 55 MVR 300 [128].
286   *Civil Law (Wrongs) Act 2002* (ACT), s 95; *Civil Liability Act 2002* (NSW), s 50(3), (5); *Personal Injuries (Liabilities and Damages) Act 2003* (NT), s 14; *Civil Liability Act 2003* (Qld), s 47(1)–(3); *Civil Liability Act 1936* (SA), s 46(1), (2); *Civil Liability Act 2002* (Tas), s 5(1), (4); *Civil Liability Act 2002* (WA), s 5L. The torts (and other wrongs) to which those provisions apply are discussed at [6.95]. In Victoria, the harmed person's intoxication is only relevant to whether the defendant breached a duty of care: *Wrongs Act 1958* (Vic), s 14G(2)(a).
287   *Civil Law (Wrongs) Act 2002* (ACT), s 96; *Personal Injuries (Liabilities and Damages) Act 2003* (NT), s 15; *Civil Liability Act 2003* (Qld), s 48(1)–(3); *Civil Liability Act 1936* (SA), s 47(1), (2). The presumption was rebutted on the second ground in *Allen v Chadwick* [2015] HCA 47, (2015) 256 CLR 148.

Furthermore, the civil liability statutes in the Australian Capital Territory and South Australia provide that contributory negligence is presumed where a person injured in a motor accident was at least 16 years old at the time of the accident and was not wearing the required seatbelt or helmet or was not in the passenger compartment of the car, and that this presumption can be rebutted only in certain limited ways.[288] Similarly, s 4.17(2)(c) and (d) of the *Motor Accident Injuries Act 2017* (NSW) provide that '[a] finding of contributory negligence must be made', without possibility of rebuttal, where the injured person (not being a minor) was not wearing the required seatbelt or protective helmet.

[6.102]

5   Factual causation and scope of the duty

In order to affect the defendant's liability, the plaintiff's unreasonable conduct must have been a factual cause of the accident or of the ensuing loss.[289] A common example of the latter category is the failure to wear a seatbelt; even though it did not cause the accident, it may have rendered the plaintiff's ensuing injuries more severe than they would have been had the plaintiff worn a seatbelt.[290] The causal link between the plaintiff's unreasonable conduct and the loss is determined in the same manner as the causal link between the defendant's conduct and the loss. The courts usually apply the 'but for' test, but have also applied the test of material contribution. For example, in *Mills v Richards*,[291] contributory negligence was found on the ground that the failure to wear a seatbelt had increased the likelihood of spinal injury.

[6.103]

In general, the defendant needs to prove, on a balance of probabilities, that the plaintiff's unreasonable conduct contributed to the loss suffered by the plaintiff.[292] As seen at [6.101]–[6.102], in certain circumstances, the civil liability statutes in most jurisdictions provide that 'contributory negligence must be presumed' or 'a finding of contributory negligence must be made'. Since conduct on the plaintiff's part cannot properly be described as 'contributory negligence' unless it contributed to the plaintiff's loss, those statutory provisions include a presumption of causation. This is problematic where the presumption is not rebuttable. However, the NSW Court of Appeal has held that, even where causation is statutorily presumed, a reduction in the plaintiff's damages is not 'just and equitable' unless it is proved that the plaintiff's unreasonable conduct contributed to the plaintiff's loss.[293]

[6.104]

In the same way in which factual causation alone is generally insufficient to impose liability upon the defendant (see [3.13]), factual causation alone is insufficient to find contributory negligence. It is also necessary that the plaintiff's loss falls within the scope of the duty (in the

[6.105]

288   *Civil Law (Wrongs) Act 2002* (ACT), s 97; *Civil Liability Act 1936* (SA), s 49(1), (2). An attempt to rebut the presumption failed in *Allen v Chadwick* [2015] HCA 47, (2015) 256 CLR 148.

289   The causal link was lacking, eg, in *Gittens v O'Brien* (1986) 4 MVR 27; *Monie v Commonwealth* [2007] NSWCA 230 [100]–[101].

290   *Allan v Fletcher* [2001] SASC 167, (2001) 79 SASR 559; *Richards v Mills* [2003] WASCA 97, (2003) 27 WAR 200; *Green v Nominal Defendant* [2012] NSWDC 37, (2012) 14 DCLR (NSW) 128.

291   [2002] WADC 57, (2002) 28 SR (WA) 129 [195]–[198]. This aspect of the decision was not appealed: [2003] WASCA 97, (2003) 27 WAR 200.

292   *Carroll v Lewitzke* (1991) 56 SASR 18, 22; *Rosecrance v Rosecrance* (1998) 8 NTLR 1, 6; *Richards v Mills* [2003] WASCA 97, (2003) 27 WAR 200 [26]; *Nyholt v Nominal Defendant* [2008] QSC 273 [84].

293   *Nicholson v Nicholson* (1994) 35 NSWLR 308, 315, 332–33; *Reeves v Reeves* [2002] NSWCA 181, (2002) 36 MVR 488 [9].

sense of a 'duty' to oneself') breached by the plaintiff.[294] For example, a pillion passenger who was injured through the careless driving of the motorcyclist with whom he was travelling was not contributorily negligent even though he knew that the headlights of the motorcycle were deficient, because the accident was not caused by the deficient headlights but by the motor-cyclist's careless driving.[295]

6   Apportionable loss

[6.106]   Where the plaintiff's unreasonable conduct contributed to the occurrence of the defendant's wrong, damages for the plaintiff's whole loss may be reduced. Where the plaintiff's unreasonable conduct did not contribute to the wrong, but contributed only to the loss, it is possible that the plaintiff would still have suffered some loss had she behaved reasonably. In particular, a plaintiff who failed to wear a seatbelt may still have suffered some injuries (albeit to a lesser degree) had she worn a seatbelt. While the English Court of Appeal has held that damages can be reduced for only that part of the plaintiff's loss which she would not have suffered if she had worn a seatbelt,[296] Australian courts have apportioned the whole of the plaintiff's loss.[297] The Australian practice might be justified by the considerable difficulties of determining what injuries would have occurred if the plaintiff had worn a seatbelt. It is in line with the language of most Australian contributory negligence statutes, which provide for a reduction in the damages for 'the wrong',[298] or the damages that the plaintiff would obtain in the absence of contributory negligence.[299] However, s 4(1) of the *Wrongs Act 1954* (Tas) requires a reduction specifically in relation to the damage to which both parties contributed.

7   Apportionment

[6.107]   The contributory negligence statutes require a reduction of damages according to what the court thinks is 'just and equitable having regard to the claimant's share in the responsibility for the damage'.[300] This language might be thought to imply that it is only the plaintiff's conduct,

---

294   *Jones v Livox Quarries Ltd* [1952] 2 QB 608, 616, 618.

295   *Gent-Diver v Neville* [1953] St R Qd 1, 10.

296   *O'Connell v Jackson* [1972] 1 QB 270, 277–78; *Froom v Butcher* [1976] QB 286, 296. See S Harder, *Measuring Damages in the Law of Obligations: The Search for Harmonised Principles* (Hart 2010) 139–41.

297   *Ferrett v Worsley* (1993) 61 SASR 234, 236–37; 243–44; *Barnard v Towill* (1998) 72 SASR 27, 44; *Allan v Fletcher* [2001] SASC 167, (2001) 79 SASR 559 [11]; *Wills v Bell* [2002] QCA 419, [2004] 1 Qd R 296 [29], [34], [62]; *Richards v Mills* [2003] WASCA 97, (2003) 27 WAR 200 [28]; *Green v Nominal Defendant* [2012] NSWDC 37, (2012) 14 DCLR (NSW) 128 [82]–[117].

298   *Civil Law (Wrongs) Act 2002* (ACT), s 102(1)(b); *Law Reform (Miscellaneous Provisions) Act 1965* (NSW), s 9(1)(b); *Law Reform (Miscellaneous Provisions) Act 1956* (NT), s 16(1)(b); *Law Reform Act 1995* (Qld), s 10(1)(b); *Wrongs Act 1958* (Vic), s 26(1)(b).

299   *Law Reform (Contributory Negligence and Apportionment of Liability) Act 2001* (SA), s 7(2)(a); *Law Reform (Contributory Negligence and Tortfeasors' Contribution) Act 1947* (WA), s 4(1).

300   *Civil Law (Wrongs) Act 2002* (ACT), s 102(1)(b); *Law Reform (Miscellaneous Provisions) Act 1965* (NSW), s 9(1)(b); *Law Reform (Miscellaneous Provisions) Act 1956* (NT), s 16(1)(b); *Law Reform Act 1995* (Qld), s 10(1)(b); *Law Reform (Contributory Negligence and Apportionment of Liability) Act 2001* (SA), s 7(2)(b); *Wrongs Act 1954* (Tas), s 4(1); *Wrongs Act 1958* (Vic), s 26(1)(b). Section 4(1) of the *Law Reform (Contributory Negligence and Tortfeasors' Contribution) Act 1947* (WA) uses the phrase 'just in accordance with the degree of negligence attributable to the plaintiff'.

and not also the defendant's conduct, which is relevant.[301] The NSW Court of Appeal has indeed taken that approach in relation to liability for a 'blameless' motor accident under Part 1.2 of the *Motor Accidents Compensation Act 1999* (NSW) (now Part 5 of the *Motor Accident Injuries Act 2017* (NSW)).[302] Otherwise, the courts have rejected an isolated consideration of the plaintiff's conduct. In *Pennington v Norris*, the High Court of Australia held that the plaintiff's conduct and the defendant's conduct must be compared:

> What has to be done is to arrive at a 'just and equitable' apportionment as between the plaintiff and the defendant of the 'responsibility' for the damage. It seems clear that this must of necessity involve a comparison of culpability. By 'culpability' we do not mean moral blameworthiness but degree of departure from the standard of care of the reasonable man.[303]

In that case, the High Court further laid down that what needs to be compared is not only the degree of culpability of each party but also the potential of each party's conduct to cause damage ('causative potency'). The plaintiff pedestrian was struck by a car driven by the defendant. Finding that both parties had been equally at fault, the trial judge reduced damages by one half. The High Court varied the apportionment and allocated 80% of the loss to the defendant and 20% to the plaintiff, on the ground that the plaintiff had endangered only himself whereas the defendant had endangered a number of people.[304] Subsequently, the relevance of causative potency became established.[305] Thus, the High Court of Australia said in *Podrebersek v Australian Iron & Steel Pty Ltd*: [6.108]

> The making of an apportionment as between a plaintiff and a defendant of their respective shares in the responsibility for the damage involves a comparison both of culpability, ie of the degree of departure from the standard of care of the reasonable man ... and of the relative importance of the acts of the parties in causing the damage ... It is the whole conduct of each negligent party in relation to the circumstances of the accident which must be subjected to comparative examination.[306]

The relevance of causative potency is now in doubt in cases in which a civil liability statute (for example, s 5R of the *Civil Liability Act 2002* (NSW)) provides that the principles that apply in determining whether a defendant has been negligent also apply in determining whether a plaintiff has been contributorily negligent.[307] The NSW Court of Appeal, after initially considering causative potency in cases to which s 5R applied,[308] has more recently held that an [6.109]

301   This view was indeed taken by D Payne, 'Reduction of Damages for Contributory Negligence' (1955) 18 Mod LR 344.
302   *Axiak v Ingram* [2012] NSWCA 311, (2012) 82 NSWLR 36 [85].
303   (1956) 96 CLR 10, 16 (Dixon CJ, Webb, Fullagar and Kitto JJ).
304   Ibid, 16–17.
305   Eg *Joslyn v Berryman* [2003] HCA 34, (2003) 214 CLR 552 [108], [116], [148]; *Valcorp Australia Pty Ltd v Angas Securities Ltd* [2012] FCAFC 22 [112].
306   (1985) 59 ALR 529, 532–33 (Gibbs CJ, Mason, Wilson, Brennan and Deane JJ). Approvingly quoted in, eg, *Bankstown Foundry Pty Ltd v Braistina* (1986) 160 CLR 301, 311; *Valcorp Australia Pty Ltd v Angas Securities Ltd* [2012] FCAFC 22 [108].
307   Those provisions are considered at [6.97].
308   Eg *Smith v Zhang* [2012] NSWCA 142, (2012) 60 MVR 525; *Marien v Gardiner* [2013] NSWCA 396, (2013) 66 MVR 1 [49].

approach under which a motorist bears a greater share of the loss than a pedestrian where both are equally at fault is not compatible with s 5R as it involves applying a different standard of care to the two parties.[309]

[6.110]   Since s 5R and its equivalents in other jurisdictions largely restate the common law (see [6.95]), the view taken by the NSW Court of Appeal strictly means that causative potency is not relevant even where s 5R or an equivalent does not apply. However, the court's reasoning is unconvincing. Section 5R and its equivalents concern the plaintiff's standard of care. But apportionment is to be made according to what is 'just and equitable' (see [6.105]), and it is difficult to see why causative potency should be irrelevant to that assessment.[310]

[6.111]   In general, the court can reduce the damages by any percentage that the court considers 'just and equitable'. On principle, it ought to be open to the court to allocate the whole liability to one party alone.[311] However, in *Wynbergen v Hoyts Corporation Pty Ltd*,[312] the High Court of Australia held that a reduction of the damages to nil can never be 'just and equitable having regard to the claimant's share in the responsibility for the damage' because it holds the plaintiff wholly responsible, not partly so. The civil liability statutes in the Australian Capital Territory, New South Wales, Queensland, Tasmania and Victoria now expressly permit a reduction to nil.[313]

[6.112]   The High Court's reasoning in *Wynbergen* strictly requires the court to make a reduction in every case, since the defendant would otherwise be wholly responsible, not partly so. However, a reduction has been refused in some cases where the plaintiff's share in the responsibility for the damage was considered insignificant.[314]

[6.113]   In certain circumstances, the civil liability statutes in some jurisdictions prescribe a fixed or minimum percentage by which damages must be reduced.[315] In South Australia, damages must invariably be reduced by 25% where the person who suffered harm failed to wear a seatbelt, and the presumption of contributory negligence is not rebutted.[316] Where there was further unreasonable conduct on the plaintiff's part, damages must first be reduced on account of that conduct, and the resulting sum must then be reduced by 25% on account of the failure to wear a seatbelt.[317]

[6.114]   In the Northern Territory, Queensland and South Australia, damages must be reduced by at least 25% where the person who suffered harm was intoxicated or relied on an intoxicated

---

309   *Boral Bricks Pty Ltd v Cosmidis (No 2)* [2014] NSWCA 139, (2014) 86 NSWLR 393 [99]; *T and X Co Pty Ltd v Chivas* [2014] NSWCA 235, (2014) 67 MVR 297 [54]. Followed in *Steen v Senton* [2015] ACTCA 57, (2015) 11 ACTLR 95 [38].

310   The possibility of such an argument being made was recognised, but the matter left open, in *Chivas*, ibid, [56].

311   A different view is taken by B McDonald, 'The Impact of the Civil Liability Legislation on Fundamental Policies and Principles of the Common Law of Negligence' (2006) 14 Torts LJ 268, 293–95.

312   (1997) 149 ALR 25.

313   *Civil Law (Wrongs) Act 2002* (ACT), s 47; *Civil Liability Act 2002* (NSW), s 5S; *Civil Liability Act 2003* (Qld), s 24; *Wrongs Act 1954* (Tas), s 4(1); *Wrongs Act 1958* (Vic), s 63. The torts (and other wrongs) to which those provisions apply are discussed at [6.94].

314   In *Wormald v Caftor Pty Ltd* [2012] ACTSC 97 [56], the question of whether the plaintiff's intoxication contributed to his injury was left open on the ground that the defendant's share in the responsibility for the damage was so overwhelming that damages would not be reduced in any event.

315   The torts (and other wrongs) to which those provisions apply are discussed at [6.95].

316   *Civil Liability Act 1936* (SA), s 49(3).

317   Ibid, s 50.

person, and the presumption of contributory negligence has not been rebutted.[318] In Queensland and South Australia, the minimum reduction is increased to 50% where the intoxicated person was driving a motor vehicle involved in an accident and was incapable of exercising effective control of the vehicle.[319]

The situation of the harmed person being intoxicated (and the presumption of contributory negligence not being rebutted) is also addressed by the civil liability statutes in New South Wales and Tasmania. In New South Wales, in cases other than motor accident cases,[320] damages must be reduced to nil where no damage would have occurred had the harmed person not been intoxicated,[321] and must otherwise be reduced by at least 25%.[322] In Tasmania, the reduction is at least 25% unless the plaintiff satisfies the court that a lower reduction is appropriate.[323]   **[6.115]**

The civil liability statutes of most jurisdictions exclude liability for personal injury[324] where the injury occurred while the injured person was engaged in conduct that constitutes a serious offence and contributed materially to the risk of the harm.[325] In some jurisdictions, damages may still be awarded where the exclusion of liability would operate harshly and unjustly.[326]   **[6.116]**

---

318   *Personal Injuries (Liabilities and Damages) Act 2003* (NT), s 17; *Civil Liability Act 2003* (Qld), ss 47(4), 48(4); *Civil Liability Act 1936* (SA), ss 46(3), 47(3).

319   *Civil Liability Act 2003* (Qld), ss 47(5), 49; *Civil Liability Act 1936* (SA), ss 46(4), 47(5).

320   Section 4.17(4) of the *Motor Accident Injuries Act 2017* (NSW) permits percentages by which damages must be reduced to be fixed by regulations, but no percentages have been fixed.

321   *Civil Liability Act 2002* (NSW), s 50(2).

322   Ibid, s 50(4).

323   *Civil Liability Act 2002* (Tas), s 5(2) and (3).

324   The provisions in New South Wales and Tasmania apply also to property damage, and the provision in Queensland applies to all kinds of damage.

325   *Civil Law (Wrongs) Act 2002* (ACT), s 94(1); *Civil Liability Act 2002* (NSW), s 54; *Motor Accidents (Compensation) Act* (NT), s 10(1); *Civil Liability Act 2003* (Qld), s 45(1); *Civil Liability Act 1936* (SA), s 43(1); *Civil Liability Act 2002* (Tas), s 6. In Victoria, the harmed person's engagement in an illegal activity is relevant (only) to whether the defendant breached a duty of care: *Wrongs Act 1958* (Vic), s 14G(2)(b).

326   *Civil Law (Wrongs) Act 2002* (ACT), s 94(2); *Motor Accidents (Compensation) Act* (NT), s 10(2); *Civil Liability Act 2003* (Qld), s 45(2); *Civil Liability Act 1936* (SA), s 43(2). A mandatory reduction of damages by at least 25% is prescribed by the *Civil Liability Act 2003* (Qld), s 45(3).

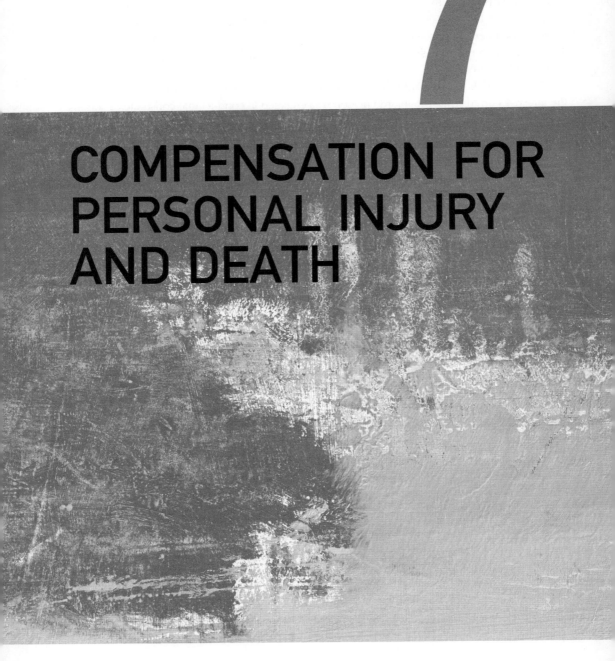

7

COMPENSATION FOR PERSONAL INJURY AND DEATH

I   Introduction

This chapter explores rules on compensation that are peculiar to cases involving personal injury or death. The wrongful act is usually a tort, but it may also be a breach of contract[1] or a statutory wrong. It is assumed that the claim is not excluded by statute; some exclusions are mentioned at [7.4]–[7.6]. This chapter does not discuss rules on compensation that apply to personal injury as well as other types of harm. Those rules are discussed in Part 1 and in the other chapters of Part 2. Furthermore, this chapter, like the rest of Part 2, is concerned only with 'normal' compensation. Aggravated damages, which may be awarded in cases of personal injury (and other cases), are discussed at [14.57]–[14.78].   [7.1]

II   The impact of legislation
A   Statutory compensation schemes and ancillary regulation of common law damages

Australian jurisdictions have a number of statutory compensation schemes for personal injury or death arising in certain circumstances. Those schemes provide that persons who suffer personal injury or death in specified circumstances can claim benefits from a certain fund. Many schemes do not require that the injury has been caused by another person's fault (they are 'no-fault compensation schemes'). Where the injury has in fact been caused by another person's fault, the benefits under the scheme are often lower than what could be claimed from the wrongdoer at common law. Some schemes regulate the amount of common law damages, or exclude compensation for certain heads of loss, or exclude common law claims altogether. Where a claim at common law is not excluded, benefits paid under the scheme reduce the damages payable by the wrongdoer, or must be repaid out of the damages received, or can be recovered by the fund from the wrongdoer by means of subrogation.   [7.2]

The various compensation schemes and their ancillary regulation of common law claims differ significantly between the schemes and between the jurisdictions. A discussion of the rules is beyond the scope of this book. Some brief remarks will be made.[2]   [7.3]

Each Australian jurisdiction (including the Commonwealth) has a no-fault compensation scheme for diseases and injuries suffered by employees in the course of their employment   [7.4]

---

1   *Grant v Australian Knitting Mills Ltd* (1935) 54 CLR 49 (PC); *Baltic Shipping Co v Dillon* (1993) 176 CLR 344; *Chappel v Hart* (1998) 195 CLR 232. It is unsettled whether an employee can obtain contractual damages for psychiatric illness caused by the wrongful termination of the employment contract. Such damages were awarded in *Grout v Gunnedah Shire Council* (1995) 129 ALR 372; *Clunne v Nambucca Shire Council* (1995) 63 IR 304. However, personal injury caused by the wrongful termination of an employment contract was considered too remote in *Aldersea v Public Transport Corporation* [2001] VSC 169, (2001) 3 VR 499 [117].

2   For a more detailed discussion, see RP Balkin and JLR Davis, *Law of Torts* (5th edn, LexisNexis Butterworths 2013) ch 12; H Luntz et al., *Torts: Cases and Commentary* (8th edn, LexisNexis Butterworths 2017) [1.4.1]–[1.4.24], [1.4.30]–[1.4.33].

('workers' compensation schemes').[3] Some schemes completely bar a common law claim against the employer or a fellow worker,[4] whereas other schemes allow such a claim if the severity of the injury meets a certain threshold, which differs between the schemes. Some of the latter schemes require the injured person to make an irrevocable election between claiming benefits under the scheme and pursuing a claim at common law.

[7.5]   Each state and territory has a compulsory third party motor vehicle insurance scheme. New South Wales, the Northern Territory, Tasmania and Victoria have no-fault compensation schemes for personal injury arising from a motor accident.[5] The schemes in New South Wales, Tasmania and Victoria subject common law claims to various caps and thresholds, whereas the Northern Territory scheme excludes altogether common law claims in respect of motor accidents occurring in the Territory.[6] The schemes in the remaining jurisdictions are fault-based, requiring the injured person to establish negligence on the part of the owner or driver of a vehicle involved.

[7.6]   As part of the National Injury Insurance Scheme (NIIS), statutory compensation schemes for catastrophically injured motor accident victims have been enacted in those jurisdictions that did not already have an NIIS-compliant scheme.[7] The schemes differ in detail, but they all make statutory benefits available for the treatment and care needs of a participant in the scheme, and they exclude common law damages for the treatment and care needs, including *Griffiths v Kerkemeyer* damages considered at [7.24]. There are no statutory benefits for loss of earning capacity or non-pecuniary loss, and common law claims for such losses are not excluded by the schemes, but may be excluded or regulated by the general motor accident scheme.

[7.7]   Each state and territory has a statutory compensation scheme for victims of violent crime,[8] since the perpetrator may not be found or may have no assets. The schemes do not affect the victim's right to claim common law damages from the perpetrator, but the state is subrogated to the victim's rights in the amount in which benefits have been paid under the scheme.

[7.8]   A number of other statutory compensation schemes exist. For example, the *Civil Aviation (Carriers' Liability) Act 1959* (Cth) and its state equivalents give effect to a series of inter-national conventions that regulate liability where a passenger is injured or killed in an aircraft

---

3   *Safety, Rehabilitation and Compensation Act 1988* (Cth); *Seafarers Rehabilitation and Compensation Act 1992* (Cth); *Military Rehabilitation and Compensation Act 2004* (Cth); *Workers Compensation Act 1951* (ACT); *Workers Compensation Act 1987* (NSW); *Workplace Injury Management and Workers Compensation Act 1998* (NSW); *Return to Work Act 2015* (NT); *Workers Compensation and Rehabilitation Act 2003* (Qld); *Return to Work Act 2014* (SA); *Workers Rehabilitation and Compensation Act 1988* (Tas); *Workplace Injury Rehabilitation and Compensation Act 2013* (Vic); *Workers' Compensation and Injury Management Act 1981* (WA).

4   Eg *Return to Work Act 2015* (NT), s 52.

5   *Motor Accident Injuries Act 2017* (NSW); *Motor Accidents (Compensation) Act* (NT); *Motor Accidents (Liabilities and Compensation) Act 1973* (Tas); *Transport Accident Act 1986* (Vic).

6   *Motor Accidents (Compensation) Act* (NT), s 5.

7   *Lifetime Care and Support (Catastrophic Injuries) Act 2014* (ACT) (covering workplace as well as motor accidents); *Motor Accidents (Lifetime Care and Support) Act 2006* (NSW); *National Injury Insurance Scheme (Queensland) Act 2016* (Qld); *Motor Vehicle (Catastrophic Injuries) Act 2016* (WA).

8   *Victims of Crime (Financial Assistance) Act 2016* (ACT); *Victims Rights and Support Act 2013* (NSW); *Victims of Crime Assistance Act 2006* (NT); *Victims of Crime Assistance Act 2009* (Qld); *Victims of Crime Act 2001* (SA); *Victims of Crime Assistance Act 1976* (Tas); *Victims of Crime Assistance Act 1996* (Vic); *Criminal Injuries Compensation Act 2003* (WA).

accident.[9] New South Wales has a statutory compensation scheme for sporting injuries.[10] Victoria has a statutory compensation scheme for casual fire-fighters.[11] There is the Asbestos Injuries Compensation Fund for cases in which James Hardie is liable, and some states have compensation schemes for the stolen generations.[12] The emerging National Disability Insurance Scheme, which is being rolled out across Australia, provides benefits to disabled persons, including those who are disabled as a result of a wrong.

B   Civil liability statutes

In 2002–03, significant legislative reform of civil liability occurred throughout Australia. The thrust of the reform is to exclude or limit liability in certain circumstances, particularly in cases involving personal injury. This reform followed a period of rapidly rising premiums for public liability insurance and the collapse of the insurance company HIH. There were a number of reasons for that development, but legislatures across Australia thought that an important reason was that liability for personal injury was imposed too easily and damages awards were too high.   [7.9]

A panel chaired by Justice David Ipp was appointed and asked to provide recommendations on how a reform of civil liability could stem the rise in premiums for public liability insurance. After the release of the panel's report in 2002,[13] legislative reform occurred in all Australian jurisdictions including the Commonwealth. Legislatures either passed a new statute or amended an existing statute. The regulation of common law damages as part of a statutory compensation scheme was also amended for some schemes. This book uses the term 'civil liability statutes' to denote the provisions enacted in the course of the civil liability reform except those ancillary to statutory compensation schemes.   [7.10]

The civil liability statutes did not adopt all the recommendations of the Ipp Report. The report recommended that the reform be uniform across Australia. This has not happened. There are significant differences between the civil liability statutes. For example, no two jurisdictions in Australia have exactly the same rules on contributory negligence or the assessment of compensation for personal injury. This increases the need for a choice-of-law exercise, which can be complex. Whatever the merits of the civil liability reform in general, the current patchwork of diverse rules is undesirable.   [7.11]

In the context of remedies, the civil liability statutes contain provisions on the attribution of liability (factual causation and scope of liability), liability for mental harm, contributory negligence, damages for personal injury, and proportionate liability. The provisions are considered in the relevant context throughout Parts 1 and 2. The types of wrong to which a set of provisions applies are examined when that set of provisions is discussed. This chapter considers the provisions on compensation for personal injury. It is necessary to examine the types of wrong to which those provisions apply.   [7.12]

---

9   The development of deep venous thrombosis during a flight is not an 'accident' for the purpose of those conventions: *Povey v Qantas Airways Ltd* [2005] HCA 33, (2005) 223 CLR 189.

10   *Sporting Injuries Insurance Act 1978* (NSW).

11   *Country Fire Authority Act 1958* (Vic).

12   Eg *Stolen Generation of Aboriginal Children Act 2006* (Tas).

13   Ipp Panel, *Review of the Law of Negligence: Final Report*, September 2002.

[7.13]   Part VIB and s 137C of the *Competition and Consumer Act 2010* (Cth) apply to certain contraventions of the Australian Consumer Law as a law of the Commonwealth; see [8.8]–[8.9]. In Tasmania, the provisions on compensation for personal injury apply in general to the breach of a tortious duty of care and the breach of another duty of care (under contract, statute or otherwise) that is coextensive with a tortious duty of care.[14] In Victoria and Western Australia, the provisions apply in general to personal injury caused by 'fault' (undefined), irrespective of the cause of action.[15] In the remaining jurisdictions except South Australia, the provisions apply in general to any claim for personal injury, whether the claim is brought in tort, contract, under statute or otherwise.[16] This includes a claim under the Australian Consumer Law to which Part VIB and s 137C of the *Competition and Consumer Act 2010* (Cth) do not apply.[17] The statutes of the states and territories exclude all or some of the following cases from their scope: personal injury caused intentionally or through sexual misconduct, personal injury resulting from smoking or other use of tobacco products, dust diseases, motor accidents and workplace injuries.

[7.14]   The scope of the South Australian provisions is slightly unclear. Section 51 of the *Civil Liability Act 1936* (SA) provides that Part 8 (on damages for personal injury) applies to personal injury arising from a motor accident (whether caused intentionally or unintentionally), or an accident caused by 'negligence', 'some other unintentional tort', or 'a breach of a contractual duty of care'. Section 3(1) of the Act provides that, unless a contrary intention appears, 'negligence' in the Act means 'failure to exercise reasonable care and skill, and includes a breach of a tortious, contractual or statutory duty of care'. If that definition applies to the word 'negligence' in s 51, Part 8 applies to the breach of an equitable or statutory duty of care. However, if the word 'negligence' in s 51 included the breach of a contractual duty of care, there would be no need to mention such breach separately. Furthermore, the word 'other' in the phrase 'some other unintentional tort' suggests that 'negligence' in s 51 means only the tort of negligence. If this is accepted, Part 8 will not apply to the breach of an equitable or statutory duty of care.

III   Meaning of 'personal injury'

[7.15]   The civil liability statutes contain provisions on compensation for 'personal injury'. At common law, that term is usually understood to mean physical injury or a recognised psychiatric illness, but not mere anxiety, disappointment, distress or inconvenience.[18] The same applies to the *Competition and Consumer Act 2010* (Cth), as s 4(1) of that Act provides that the term 'personal injury' in the Act 'does not include an impairment of a person's mental condition unless the impairment consists of a recognised psychiatric illness'. However, the definition of

---

14   *Civil Liability Act 2002* (Tas), ss 3, 24.
15   *Wrongs Act 1958* (Vic), ss 28B, 28C, 28LB, 28LC, 28N; *Civil Liability Act 2002* (WA), ss 3, 6.
16   *Civil Law (Wrongs) Act 2002* (ACT), ss 92, 93; *Civil Liability Act 2002* (NSW), s 11A(2); *Personal Injuries (Liabilities and Damages) Act 2003* (NT), s 4(1); *Civil Liability Act 2003* (Qld), s 50.
17   *Barrett v Lets Go Adventures Pty Ltd* [2016] NSWDC 345, (2016) 23 DCLR (NSW) 329 [21]–[28], relying on *Motorcycling Events Group Australia Pty Ltd v Kelly* [2013] NSWCA 361, (2013) 86 NSWLR 55, which was decided under what was then s 74 of the *Trade Practices Act 1974* (Cth).
18   See *New South Wales v Ibbett* [2005] NSWCA 445, (2005) 65 NSWLR 168 [21] (Spigelman CJ).

the term 'personal injury' in the civil liability statutes of New South Wales and Victoria has been given a wider interpretation, and the same may apply in the other states and territories.

Section 11 of the *Civil Liability Act 2002* (NSW) defines 'injury' for the purpose of Part 2 of the Act (on damages for personal injury) as including the 'impairment of a person's physical or mental condition', and s 27 defines 'mental harm' for the purpose of Part 3 (on mental harm) as the 'impairment of a person's mental condition'. In several cases, the NSW Court of Appeal has held that the phrase 'impairment of a person's mental condition', while not including loss of reputation[19] or loss of dignity or liberty,[20] does include anxiety, disappointment, distress and inconvenience.[21] This has two significant consequences. **[7.16]**

First, Part 2 (on damages for personal injury) applies to anxiety, disappointment, distress and inconvenience. As discussed at [7.65], s 16 prescribes a tariff system for 'non-economic loss', defined as meaning one or more of the following: pain and suffering, loss of amenities of life, loss of expectation of life, and disfigurement.[22] It has been held that anxiety, disappointment, distress and inconvenience are covered by that definition, either as pain and suffering,[23] or loss of amenities of life,[24] or both.[25] Section 16 provides, among other things, that no damages may be awarded for non-economic loss resulting from personal injury unless the severity of the non-economic loss is at least 15% of the most extreme case. Section 16 applies in general to every cause of action, with some exceptions such as personal injury intentionally caused or dust diseases.[26] Therefore, unless the case falls into an exception, s 16 applies, for example, to a claim for breach of contract, an equitable wrong or a breach of the Australian Consumer Law ('ACL') as a law of New South Wales; see [8.2]–[8.3]. In those (and other) causes of actions, s 16 heavily restricts the compensation of mere distress not resulting from physical injury, since such distress will rarely be 15% or more of the most extreme case. **[7.17]**

The second consequence of holding that anxiety, disappointment, distress and inconvenience constitute an 'impairment of a person's mental condition' for the purpose of the *Civil Liability Act 2002* (NSW) is that Part 3 of the Act (on mental harm) applies. Part 3 provides that there is no liability (in tort, in contract, under statute or otherwise[27]) for 'mental harm resulting from negligence'[28] unless the mental harm is consequent on other personal injury or consists of **[7.18]**

---

19   *Insight Vacations Pty Ltd v Young* [2010] NSWCA 137, (2010) 78 NSWLR 641 [125] (Basten JA). See also *New South Wales v Williamson* [2012] HCA 57, (2012) 293 ALR 440 [34], [45]; *Zhang v New South Wales* [2012] NSWSC 606 [30]–[34].

20   *New South Wales v Williamson* [2011] NSWCA 183 [61]. See also *New South Wales v Williamson* [2012] HCA 57, (2012) 293 ALR 440 [34], [45]; *Zhang v New South Wales* [2012] NSWSC 606 [30]–[34].

21   *New South Wales v Ibbett* [2005] NSWCA 445, (2005) 65 NSWLR 168 [124], [211]–[212]; *New South Wales v Corby* [2010] NSWCA 27, (2010) 76 NSWLR 439 [41]; *Insight Vacations Pty Ltd v Young* [2010] NSWCA 137, (2010) 78 NSWLR 641.

22   *Civil Liability Act 2002* (NSW), s 3.

23   *Insight Vacations Pty Ltd v Young* [2010] NSWCA 137, (2010) 78 NSWLR 641 [78] (Spigelman CJ); *Flight Centre Ltd v Louw* [2011] NSWSC 132, (2010) 78 NSWLR 656 [31]; *Moore v Scenic Tours Pty Ltd (No 2)* [2017] NSWSC 733 [864]–[865].

24   *Insight Vacations Pty Ltd v Young* [2010] NSWCA 137, (2010) 78 NSWLR 641 [166]–[167], [175] (Sackville AJA).

25   Ibid, [125] (Basten JA).

26   *Civil Liability Act 2002* (NSW), s 3B; see [7.13].

27   The exceptions in s 3B apply to Part 3: s 28(3).

28   Section 27 defines 'negligence' as 'failure to exercise reasonable care and skill'.

a recognised psychiatric illness.[29] It is unclear whether the phrase 'resulting from negligence' confines the scope of Part 3 to wrongs that have negligence as an element,[30] or whether it includes cases of strict liability where the defendant was careless. The latter interpretation was implicitly adopted in cases in which compensation was denied for distress resulting from spoilt holidays,[31] or resulting from a failure to keep property in good repair.[32]

[7.19]   The phrase 'impairment of the person's mental condition' is also used in s 32 of the *Civil Law (Wrongs) Act 2002* (ACT) for the definition of 'mental harm', and in the civil liability statutes of South Australia, Tasmania and Western Australia for the definition of 'personal injury'.[33] For the purpose of the *Civil Law (Wrongs) Act 2002* (ACT), the phrase has been interpreted as including distress, sadness and upset but not the consciousness of the loss of liberty as a result of false imprisonment.[34] This is very similar to the interpretation of that phrase for the purposes of the *Civil Liability Act 2002* (NSW), and similar interpretations may be adopted for the statutes of South Australia, Tasmania and Western Australia, which impose varying thresholds for the recovery of non-pecuniary loss; see [7.63], [7.68].

[7.20]   The phrase 'impairment of a person's mental condition' is not used by the statutes of the Northern Territory, Queensland and Victoria, all of which define 'personal injury' as including a 'psychological or psychiatric injury'.[35] The term 'psychological injury', especially when used in contradistinction to 'psychiatric injury', can be interpreted as including anxiety and the like. Indeed, anxiety, distress, fear and worry (but not inconvenience) have been held to constitute 'injury' for the purpose of Part VBA (which imposes a threshold on the recovery of damages for non-economic loss) of the *Wrongs Act 1958* (Vic).[36] Under this interpretation, which might be followed in the Northern Territory and Queensland, the provisions that restrict compensation for non-pecuniary loss apply to anxiety (and the like) not resulting from physical injury.

IV   Loss suffered by an injured person

[7.21]   A trial judge ought to specify separate amounts for separate heads of loss.[37] Following Windeyer J's taxonomy in *Teubner v Humble*,[38] the heads of loss in cases of personal injury will be divided into three categories: pecuniary loss resulting from special needs, pecuniary loss resulting from the impairment of capacities, and non-pecuniary loss. Possible overlaps between heads of loss are discussed at [7.69]–[7.71].

---

29   *Civil Liability Act 2002* (NSW), ss 27, 28, 31.
30   This interpretation was supported in *New South Wales v Ibbett* [2005] NSWCA 445, (2005) 65 NSWLR 168 [117], [200].
31   *Flight Centre Ltd v Louw* [2011] NSWSC 132, (2010) 78 NSWLR 656 [38]–[40].
32   *Fligg v Owners Strata Plan 53457* [2012] NSWSC 230 [100].
33   *Civil Liability Act 1936* (SA), s 3(1); *Civil Liability Act 2002* (Tas), s 3; *Civil Liability Act 2002* (WA), s 3.
34   *Monaghan v Australian Capital Territory (No 2)* [2016] ACTSC 352, (2016) 315 FLR 305 [208].
35   *Personal Injuries (Liabilities and Damages) Act 2003* (NT), s 3; *Civil Liability Act 2003* (Qld), sch 2; *Wrongs Act 1958* (Vic), ss 28B, 28LB, 28M.
36   *Thomas v Powercor Australia Ltd* [2011] VSC 586 [116]; *Lakic v Prior* [2016] VSC 293 [157]; *Archibald v Powlett* [2017] VSCA 259 [56]–[67].
37   *Linsell v Robson* [1976] 1 NSWLR 249, 251.
38   (1963) 108 CLR 491, 505.

A   Pecuniary loss resulting from needs created by the injury

1   Medical expenses and cost of institutional care

An injured person can claim compensation for all injury-related medical expenses, including the cost of an ambulance, consultation with a doctor and hospital treatment.[39] The calculation of future expenses can be difficult since it is impossible to predict what advances in medical diagnosis and treatment may occur and what cost implications those advances may have. The cost of the institutional care required is generally compensable,[40] but the cost of food and accommodation that the injured person would incur even without the injury must be deducted.[41] The greater cost of maintaining the injured person at home is not compensable unless maintenance at home provides significant health benefits.[42] Travelling expenses of close relatives visiting the injured person in hospital or other centres have been compensated where the visits had therapeutic value to the injured person.[43] The loss compensated in those cases is the injured person's need for the presence of close relatives.[44] It is uncertain whether hospital visits constitute services gratuitously provided to the injured person,[45] which are regulated by the civil liability statutes in almost all jurisdictions; see [7.27]–[7.31].

[7.22]

2   Domestic services provided to the injured person

An injured person who is able to live at home may need the provision of nursing care and domestic assistance. To the extent to which the state provides those services for free, the injured person suffers no financial loss.[46] Otherwise, there is a loss. Where people are reasonably employed to provide the services required, the remuneration to be paid is compensable.[47] The cost of nursing care is not necessarily the cost of a registered nurse where a lesser level of care is sufficient.[48]

[7.23]

There is often no need to employ people since the necessary services are provided gratuitously by relatives or friends. In those circumstances, compensation for the cost of employing people to provide the services used to be denied on the ground that the injured person suffers no financial loss.[49] However, in *Griffiths v Kerkemeyer*,[50] the High Court of Australia laid down that the cost of employing people to provide necessary services to the

[7.24]

---

39   *Blundell v Musgrave* (1956) 96 CLR 73, 92; *Bresatz v Przibilla* (1962) 108 CLR 541, 545.
40   *Campbell v Nangle* (1984) 40 SASR 161, 176; *Beasley v Marshall* (1985) 40 SASR 544.
41   *Sharman v Evans* (1977) 138 CLR 563, 576; *Campbell v Nangle* (1984) 40 SASR 161, 176; *Beasley v Marshall* (1985) 40 SASR 544, 559.
42   *Sharman v Evans* (1977) 138 CLR 563, 573; *Beasley v Marshall* (1986) 40 SASR 544, 575–76.
43   *Wilson v McLeay* (1961) 106 CLR 523, 528; *Richardson v Schultz* (1980) 25 SASR 1, 21–22; *Campbell v Nangle* (1984) 40 SASR 161, 175 (where $10,000 was awarded in that regard); *Beasley v Marshall* (1986) 40 SASR 544, 566–67; *Baghdadi v Quality P & M Smallgoods Pty Ltd* [2008] NSWSC 406 [549]–[550].
44   *Griffiths v Kerkemeyer* (1977) 139 CLR 161, 173.
45   The view that they do was taken in *Torrent v Lancaster* (1991) Aust Torts Reports 81–089, 68,751. The question was left open in *Royal v Smurthwaite* [2007] NSWCA 76, (2007) 47 MVR 401 [163].
46   *Griffiths v Kerkemeyer* (1977) 139 CLR 161, 165, 169, 194.
47   *Bresatz v Przibilla* (1962) 108 CLR 541, 545–46; *Campbell v Nangle* (1984) 40 SASR 161, 176–77; *Marsland v Andjelic* (1993) 31 NSWLR 162, 179–80.
48   *Nicholson v Nicholson* (1994) 35 NSWLR 308, 324; *Leslie v Smalley* [2003] NSWCA 247 [18]–[19].
49   *Blundell v Musgrave* (1956) 96 CLR 73, 79, 92.
50   (1977) 139 CLR 161.

injured person is compensable even if those services are provided gratuitously by relatives or friends. The loss is the injured person's need created by the injury, not any income forgone by the people who provide gratuitous services.[51] This has two consequences. First, the loss is assessed by reference to the objective market value of the services, which is the cost of having the services provided commercially.[52] Secondly, the injured person does not hold the compensation on trust for the people who provide gratuitous services.[53]

[7.25]   Simone Degeling has argued that the compensation ought to end up in the hand of the carers, in either of two ways. First, the carers may be subrogated to the injured person's claim against the defendant, likening them to an indemnity insurer.[54] Secondly, the carers may have a claim in unjust enrichment against the injured person.[55] A third way of 'shifting' the compensation from the injured person to the carers is to hold that the provision of the services by the carers discharges the defendant's obligation towards the injured person, and to recognise an unjust-enrichment claim of the carers against the defendant.[56]

[7.26]   The High Court of Australia has held that compensation in respect of services gratuitously provided to the injured person may be awarded even where the wrongdoer provides the services,[57] which may happen after a family car accident, for example. It might be objected that the wrongdoer is providing compensation in kind and should not be required to provide compensation in money as well.[58] However, services gratuitously provided by the wrongdoer ought to be treated like other benefits obtained by the injured person as a result of the wrong,[59] and the deductibility of benefits from the loss depends upon whether the provider of the benefits intended to discharge the wrongdoer's liability.[60] A wrongdoer who renders services to the injured person is usually motivated by love or compassion and not by a desire to reduce liability, particularly where the wrongdoer is insured.[61]

---

51   *Griffiths v Kerkemeyer* (1977) 139 CLR 161, 168, 178–79, 194; *Van Gervan v Fenton* (1992) 175 CLR 327, 331–35, 347; *Kars v Kars* (1996) 187 CLR 354, 360, 372, 379.

52   *Van Gervan v Fenton* (1992) 175 CLR 327, 331–35, 342, 347.

53   *Griffiths v Kerkemeyer* (1977) 139 CLR 161, 177, 181, 193–94; *Kars v Kars* (1996) 187 CLR 354, 371–72. A different view has been taken in other Commonwealth jurisdictions: *Hunt v Severs* [1994] 2 AC 350, 363; *Jacobsen v Nike Canada Ltd* (1996) 19 BCLR (3d) 63 [253], [257]. The problems of imposing a trust with regard to future services are discussed by LCH Ho, 'The dutiful tortfeasor in the House of Lords' (1995) 3 Tort L Rev 63, 73; P Matthews and M Lunney, 'A Tortfeasor's Lot is not a Happy One?' (1995) 58 Mod LR 395, 402–03; A Reed, 'A Commentary on *Hunt v Severs*' (1995) 15 OJLS 133, 138–39.

54   SE Degeling, '*Kars v Kars* – balancing the interests of victims and carers' (1997) 71 *Aust LJ* 882, 890–92; S Degeling, *Restitutionary Rights to Share in Damages: Carers' Claims* (CUP 2003) ch 7.

55   S Degeling, 'Carer's Claims: Unjust Enrichment and Tort' [2000] RLR 172, 186–87; S Degeling, *Restitutionary Rights to Share in Damages: Carers' Claims* (CUP 2003) 47. Personal remedies for unjust enrichment are discussed in Ch 17.

56   This approach was taken in *Ostapowich v Benoit* (1982) 14 Sask R 233.

57   *Kars v Kars* (1996) 187 CLR 354, 375–82. The House of Lords has taken a different view: *Hunt v Severs* [1994] 2 AC 350, 363.

58   H Luntz, 'Voluntary Services Provided by the Defendant' (1994) 2 Torts LJ 80, 86–87. Luntz subsequently changed his view; see the next footnote.

59   *Kars v Kars* (1996) 187 CLR 354, 362–63 (Dawson J); H Luntz, 'Voluntary Services Provided by the Defendant: Further Developments' (1996) 4 Torts LJ 80, 85–86.

60   *National Insurance Co of New Zealand Ltd v Espagne* (1961) 105 CLR 569, 597–99; *Zheng v Cai* [2009] HCA 52, (2009) 239 CLR 446 [19]–[23]. See [7.74].

61   *Kars v Kars* (1996) 187 CLR 354, 363–64 (Dawson J); H Luntz, 'Voluntary Services Provided by the Defendant: Further Developments' (1996) 4 Torts LJ 80, 85–86.

The civil liability statutes of all jurisdictions (including the Commonwealth) other than the   **[7.27]**
Australian Capital Territory regulate *Griffiths v Kerkemeyer* damages.[62] Section 28B of the *Civil
Liability Act 2002* (Tas) provides for their availability (subject to conditions),[63] but the statutes
in the other jurisdictions merely place restrictions (in terms of availability and amount) on
Griffiths v Kerkemeyer damages, presupposing their availability at common law.

In South Australia, *Griffiths v Kerkemeyer* damages are confined to services provided by a   **[7.28]**
parent, spouse, domestic partner or child of the injured person.[64] In Western Australia,
damages in respect of gratuitous services provided by a member of the injured person's
household or family cannot be awarded unless the overall amount of damages exceeds a
certain threshold.[65] In most of the other jurisdictions, *Griffiths v Kerkemeyer* damages are
excluded unless there is a reasonable need for the services, the need has arisen solely because
of the injury to which the damages relate, and the services would not be provided but for
the injury.[66]

In most jurisdictions, *Griffiths v Kerkemeyer* damages are excluded unless the amount of   **[7.29]**
services provided to the injured person reaches a certain threshold. The *Competition and
Consumer Act 2010* (Cth) and the civil liability statutes of New South Wales, the Northern
Territory, Queensland and – for motor accidents occurring on or after 1 July 2013 – South
Australia exclude *Griffiths v Kerkemeyer* damages unless the services are, or are to be,
provided for at least six hours per week and for a period of at least six consecutive months.[67]
It seems accepted that this means that no *Griffiths v Kerkemeyer* damages can be awarded
unless there is a period of at least six months in which services were, or will be, provided for at
least six hours per week every week.[68] The Queensland Court of Appeal has held that once
such a qualifying period exists, damages may also be awarded in respect of subsequent
periods even if the amount of services falls below six hours per week.[69] By contrast, the
NSW Court of Appeal has held that damages may not be awarded for any week in which the
amount of services falls below six hours per week, although damages may be awarded in
respect of all periods (even if shorter than six months) if there is a qualifying period of
six months.[70]

---

62   Section 100 of the *Civil Law (Wrongs) Act 2002* (ACT), considered at [7.54], does not apply to *Griffiths v
      Kerkemeyer* damages: *O'Brien v Noble* [2012] ACTCA 13, (2012) 6 ACTLR 132 [60]–[62]. See also *Pasfield v
      Ugarkovich* [2014] ACTSC 10 [39]; *Baker v Mackenzie* [2015] ACTSC 272, (2015) 72 MVR 421 [63].
63   Section 28C excludes *Griffiths v Kerkemeyer* damages in motor accident cases.
64   *Civil Liability Act 1936* (SA), s 58(1)(a).
65   *Civil Liability Act 2002* (WA), ss 12(3), (4), 13. No restriction exists in respect of services provided
      by a person other than a member of the injured person's household or family: *Leheste v Minister for
      Health* [2012] WADC 92 [462].
66   *Competition and Consumer Act 2010* (Cth), s 87W(2); *Civil Liability Act 2002* (NSW), s 15(2); *Personal
      Injuries (Liabilities and Damages) Act 2003* (NT), s 23(1); *Civil Liability Act 2003* (Qld), s 59(1), (2);
      Wrongs Act 1958 (Vic), s 28IA(1).
67   *Competition and Consumer Act 2010* (Cth), s 87W(2); *Civil Liability Act 2002* (NSW), s 15(3);
      Personal Injuries (Liabilities and Damages) Act 2003 (NT), s 23(2); *Civil Liability Act 2003* (Qld),
      s 59(1)(c); *Civil Liability Act 1936* (SA), s 58(4)(a)(ii).
68   *Carroll v Coomber* [2006] QDC 146 [66]–[74]; *Kay v Murray Irrigation Ltd* [2009] NSWSC 1411 at [30]; *Hill
      v Forrester* [2010] NSWCA 170, (2010) 79 NSWLR 470 [8] (Tobias JA); *Upper Lachlan Shire Council v
      Rodgers* [2012] NSWCA 259 [27].
69   *Kriz v King* [2006] QCA 351, [2007] 1 Qd R 327 [18]; *Shaw v Menzies* [2011] QCA 197 [53], [87].
70   *Hill v Forrester* [2010] NSWCA 170, (2010) 79 NSWLR 470.

[7.30]   Section 28B(2) of the *Civil Liability Act 2002* (Tas) contains the same provision as the statutes discussed in the preceding paragraph, except that it requires services of more than (rather than at least) six hours per week and six consecutive months. Section 28IA(2) of the *Wrongs Act 1958* (Vic) excludes *Griffiths v Kerkemeyer* damages if the services are, or are to be, provided for less than six hours per week and for less than six months. This may seem identical to the provisions discussed in the preceding paragraph. However, the Victorian Court of Appeal has held that the word 'and' in s 28IA(2) means that both negative conditions must be satisfied for *Griffiths v Kerkemeyer* damages to be excluded.[71] *Griffiths v Kerkemeyer* damages are thus available where services are provided for less than six hours per week but for at least six months, and *Griffiths v Kerkemeyer* damages are also available where services are provided for less than six months but for at least six hours per week.

[7.31]   While the South Australian statute limits the overall[72] amount of *Griffiths v Kerkemeyer* damages to four times state average weekly earnings (with the possibility of awarding more under certain conditions),[73] the statutes of the other jurisdictions except Queensland limit the amount of damages per week of services to the amount of 'average weekly earnings' as defined by the relevant statute.[74]

3   Increased cost of living at home

[7.32]   Sometimes the injured person does not require institutional care but cannot live at home in the same way as before the injury. The cost of any alterations and acquisitions required by the injury can be recovered. Recoverable loss includes the cost of altering the injured person's home (for example, the provision of wheelchair access),[75] the cost of purchasing a new home[76] (with an allowance for the fact that the injured person receives the capital value of a new property[77]), and the cost of renting new accommodation.[78] There may be increased costs of electricity, telephone and so on.[79] Recoverable loss also includes the cost of modifying the injured person's car,[80] the extra cost of running a modified car,[81] and the cost of buying a new

---

71   *Alcoa Portland Aluminium Pty Ltd v Victoria WorkCover Authority* [2007] VSCA 210, (2007) 18 VR 146 [27]–[42], [46]–[50].

72   The view that it is a cap per week of services was rejected in *Allen v Chadwick* [2014] SASCFC 100, (2014) 120 SASR 350 [195]. The High Court did not address this issue on appeal: *Allen v Chadwick* [2015] HCA 47, (2015) 256 CLR 148.

73   *Civil Liability Act 1936* (SA), s 58(2), (3). Additional restrictions in motor accident cases are contained in s 58(4)–(6).

74   *Competition and Consumer Act 2010* (Cth), s 87W(3), (4); *Civil Liability Act 2002* (NSW), s 15(4), (5); *Personal Injuries (Liabilities and Damages) Act 2003* (NT), s 23(3), (4); *Civil Liability Act 1936* (SA), s 58(2), (3); *Civil Liability Act 2002* (Tas), s 28B(3); *Wrongs Act 1958* (Vic), s 28IB; *Civil Liability Act 2002* (WA), s 12(5)–(7).

75   *Burford v Allan* (1993) 60 SASR 428, 442; *Munzer v Johnston* [2009] QCA 190, (2009) 53 MVR 143 [20]; *Potts v Frost* [2011] TasSC 55, (2011) 59 MVR 267 [165]–[187].

76   *Marsland v Andjelic* (1993) 31 NSWLR 162, 177; *Weideck v Williams* [1999] NSWCA 346 [7]–[10]; *McNeilly v Imbree* [2007] NSWCA 156, (2007) 47 MVR 536 [165]–[169].

77   *Weideck v Williams* [1999] NSWCA 346 [7]. The defendant bears an evidentiary burden in that regard: *Munzer v Johnston* [2009] QCA 190, (2009) 53 MVR 143 [21].

78   *Nicholson v Nicholson* (1994) 35 NSWLR 308, 328.

79   *Potts v Frost* [2011] TasSC 55, (2011) 59 MVR 267 [156]–[157], [194]–[197].

80   *Henderson v Campbell* [2002] NSWSC 1202 [63]; *Potts v Frost* [2011] TasSC 55, (2011) 59 MVR 267 [161].

81   *Nicholson v Nicholson* (1994) 35 NSWLR 308, 329.

car suited to the injured person's requirements.[82] Where the injured person is no longer able to drive or use public transport, the cost of hiring a taxi can be recovered,[83] reduced by the cost of running a car where the injured person would have a car without the injury.[84] Finally, recoverable loss includes the cost of special equipment, such as a wheelchair, special clothes or special cutlery.[85]

4 Cost of managing a lump sum award

Compensation for loss is generally awarded in a lump sum; see [2.121]. It will be a large amount in cases of serious personal injury. The proper investment of the compensation award may require the employment of a professional fund manager, and the question arises whether the cost of employing a fund manager is compensable. [7.33]

Section 57 of the *Civil Liability Act 1936* (SA) excludes such compensation.[86] In *Allen v Chadwick*,[87] the South Australian Full Court held that the trial judge's award of a modest sum for assistance with the plaintiff's treatment and care needs, including her ability to access community support as well as address such major projects as the acquisition and modification of a house property, was not caught by the prohibition in s 57, but was nonetheless to be excluded because it should be seen as part her non-pecuniary loss. [7.34]

The High Court's most recent consideration of the common law position occurred in *Gray v Richards*.[88] In a joint judgment of all judges, the court said that the cost of managing a lump sum award of compensation cannot generally be recovered because of the principle that the court is not concerned with the manner in which the plaintiff uses the compensation awarded.[89] The court[90] quoted the following observations made by McHugh J in *Nominal Defendant v Gardikiotis*: [7.35]

> ... the plaintiff seeks damages, not for expense necessarily incurred as the result of a disability caused by the defendant's negligence, but for an expense arising merely from the size of an award of damages and the exercise of a choice by the plaintiff as to how to invest those damages. The expense of exercising that choice is not the consequence of the plaintiff's injury.[91]

The High Court in *Gray v Richards* went on to say that its previous decisions in *Nominal Defendant v Gardikiotis*[92] and *Willett v Futcher*[93] had recognised that the cost of managing a lump sum award can be recovered 'where a defendant's negligence has so impaired the [7.36]

82   *Potts v Frost* [2011] TasSC 55, (2011) 59 MVR 267 [199]–[204].
83   *Commissioner for Railways (NSW) v Cullen* (1973) 47 ALJR 99, 102; *Burford v Allan* (1993) 60 SASR 428, 441.
84   *Marsland v Andjelic* (1993) 31 NSWLR 162, 180; *Leslie v Smalley* [2003] NSWCA 247 [35].
85   *Bresatz v Przibilla* (1962) 108 CLR 541, 546–47; *Marsland v Andjelic* (1993) 31 NSWLR 162, 177; *Potts v Frost* [2011] TasSC 55, (2011) 59 MVR 267 [158].
86   The circumstances in which s 57 applies are discussed at [7.14].
87   [2014] SASCFC 100, (2014) 120 SASR 350 [65], [222].
88   [2014] HCA 40, (2014) 253 CLR 660.
89   Ibid, [1]–[2].
90   Ibid, [3].
91   (1996) 186 CLR 49, 55.
92   Ibid, 52, 54, 67.
93   [2005] HCA 47, (2005) 221 CLR 627 [51].

plaintiff's intellectual capacity as to put the plaintiff in need of assistance in managing the lump sum awarded as damages'.[94] The NSW Court of Appeal has since said that for fund management costs to be recoverable, it is not sufficient that the defendant's wrong was a factual cause of the disability that renders the plaintiff incapable of managing the lump sum award; it is also necessary that the defendant is liable in respect of that disability.[95] In *Gray v Richards*,[96] the High Court held that where fund management costs are recoverable, compensation may also be awarded for the cost of managing the award in respect of fund management costs, but not for the cost of managing the predicted future income of the managed fund.

[7.37]   The general exclusion of compensation for fund management costs cannot be justified on principle. Large compensation awards are typically made to plaintiffs who have suffered a serious injury and are expected to incur expenses and suffer loss of earning capacity far into the future, often until death. Compensation for future loss is discounted on the ground that the award can be invested prior to the time at which the money is needed to compensate the loss; see [2.151]–[2.152]. A plaintiff who fails to invest the award of compensation for future loss will not have enough money to cover all future losses. The investment of a lump sum award is thus a necessity and not a choice as claimed by the High Court. This applies regardless of whether the plaintiff's incapacity of fund management results from a disability or whether the defendant is liable for any such disability. The defendant should have to take the plaintiff as he found him; see [6.83].

B   Pecuniary loss resulting from the impairment of capacities

1   Loss of earning capacity

[7.38]   Injury may render a person unable to work, permanently or temporarily. The reasonable cost of employing a substitute in the injured person's business can be recovered.[97] Where the injured person is running a business and does not employ a substitute, or where the injured person is employed or would be employed without the injury, the loss resulting from the injured person's inability to work could be conceptualised as the loss of earnings. However, Australian courts have conceptualised it as the loss of earning capacity, the potential earnings indicating the value of the capacity.[98]

[7.39]   At the same time, Australian courts have limited the significance of this conceptualisation, through three principles. First, loss of earning capacity is compensable only to the extent to which it is capable of generating concrete financial loss.[99] An injured person who has received

94   [2014] HCA 40, (2014) 253 CLR 660 [4] (French CJ, Hayne, Bell, Gageler and Keane JJ).
95   *Pel-Air Aviation Pty Ltd v Casey* [2017] NSWCA 32, (2017) 93 NSWLR 438 [91].
96   [2014] HCA 40, (2014) 253 CLR 660.
97   *Surf Coast Shire Council v Webb* [2003] VSCA 162 [36]; *Mastaglia v Burns* [2006] WASCA 190, (2006) 32 WAR 427 [112], [115]; *Jones v White* [2008] VSC 551 [69].
98   *Teubner v Humble* (1963) 108 CLR 491, 505–506; *Arthur Robinson (Grafton) Pty Ltd v Carter* (1968) 122 CLR 649, 658; *CSR Ltd v Eddy* [2005] HCA 64, (2005) 226 CLR 1 [30]. Critically M Tilbury, 'Damages for Personal Injury: Delimiting the Economic Loss' (1982) 14 UWALR 469. Separate awards are usually made for past and future loss of earning capacity.
99   *Graham v Baker* (1961) 106 CLR 340, 347; *Medlin v State Government Insurance Commission* (1995) 182 CLR 1, 3–5.

ordinary wages throughout a period of temporary incapacity cannot recover for loss of earning capacity.[100] Secondly, whenever possible, loss of earning capacity is assessed by reference to lost income.[101] Thirdly, loss of earning capacity after judgment is treated as future pecuniary loss, involving a consideration of contingencies, the possible use of actuarial tables, and a reduction to reflect the fact that compensation is received earlier than the loss accrues.[102]

The conceptualisation of this head of loss as impairment of capacity rather than loss of income is significant in at least three respects.[103] First, since the compensation awarded is not strictly a substitute for lost income, it is not subject to income tax.[104] Secondly, where the amount of future lost income cannot be determined (for example, where a child is injured), the court may place a value directly upon the future loss of earning capacity ('buffer awards').[105] Thirdly, where, prior to the injury, the injured person worked for a corporation, partnership or trading trust which was set up by him (often for the purpose of minimising tax) and paid him only part of the income generated by his work (and paid the rest to other people), his earning capacity is not necessarily reflected by the share that he would be receiving, but by the income that would effectively be at his disposal.[106]   [7.40]

The injured person bears the burden of proving loss of earning capacity.[107] Impairment may exist even though the injured person occupies the same job, with the same salary, as before the injury. For example, the employment may be less secure, promotion prospects may be diminished,[108] or it may be more difficult for the injured person to find alternative employment with the same salary should the present employment end.[109] Account must be taken of any pre-existing medical condition that may have independently rendered the injured person unable to work at some stage.[110] It is for the defendant to adduce evidence in that respect,[111] but the injured person retains the legal onus of establishing causation.[112] In general,   [7.41]

---

100   Ibid.
101   *Zorom Enterprises v Zabow* [2007] NSWCA 106, (2007) 71 NSWLR 354 [49]; *Allianz Australia Insurance Ltd v Kerr* [2012] NSWCA 13, (2012) 83 NSWLR 302 [72].
102   *Woodhead v Barrow* (1993) Aust Torts Reports 81–238, 62,469–71. See also [2.148]–[2.153].
103   Atiyah has argued that the focus should be on the policy considerations involved and not the distinction between lost earnings and lost earning capacity: PS Atiyah, 'Loss of Earnings or Earning Capacity?' (1971) 45 Aust LJ 228.
104   *Groves v United Pacific Transport Pty Ltd* [1965] Qd R 62, 65; *Commissioner of Taxation v Sydney Refractive Surgery Centre Pty Ltd* [2008] FCAFC 190, (2008) 172 FCR 557 [10]; *Davinski Nominees Pty Ltd v I & A Bowler Holdings Pty Ltd* [2011] VSC 220 [64].
105   *Martin v Howard* [1983] Tas R 188, 200–03, 209–12; *D'Ambrosio v De Souza Lima* (1985) 60 ACTR 18, 24–25; *K-Mart Australia Ltd v McCann* [2004] NSWCA 283 [62]–[64]; *SB v New South Wales* [2004] VSC 514, (2004) 13 VR 527 [617]–[622]; *Fitzgerald v Hill* [2007] QSC 228 [121]–[122]; *Guiney v Australand Holdings Ltd* [2008] NSWCA 44 [27]–[36]. Section 13 of the *Civil Liability Act 2002* (NSW) does not exclude this approach: *Penrith City Council v Parks* [2004] NSWCA 201 [5], [58]; *Allianz Australia Insurance Ltd v Kerr* [2012] NSWCA 13, (2012) 83 NSWLR 302 [3], [30], [67].
106   *Husher v Husher* [1999] HCA 47, (1999) 197 CLR 138 [18]; *Kay v Murray Irrigation Ltd* [2009] NSWSC 1411 [17].
107   *Ford Motor Co of Australia Ltd v Mann* [2001] VSCA 177 [29].
108   *Watts v Turpin* [1999] WASCA 216, (1999) 21 WAR 402 [33].
109   *Victorian Stevedoring Pty Ltd v Farlow* [1963] VR 594, 595, 598, 599; *Wright v Shire of Albany* (1993) Aust Torts Reports 81–239, 62,475, 62,479.
110   *Wilson v Peisley* (1975) 7 ALR 571, 574, 581–82; *Wynn v New South Wales Insurance Ministerial Corporation* (1995) 184 CLR 485, 498; *Rosa v Galbally & O'Bryan* [2012] VSC 3 [94]–[95].
111   *Watts v Rake* (1960) 108 CLR 158, 164; *Purkess v Crittenden* (1965) 114 CLR 164, 168.
112   *Purkess v Crittenden* (1965) 114 CLR 164, 167–68.

account must be taken of events that would have independently caused loss of earning capacity, possibly even wrongful events.[113]

[7.42]   Where the amount of lost income is used as the measure of the loss of earning capacity, lost income after tax must be used.[114] A deduction must be made to reflect the expenditure necessary for a realisation of earning capacity (special clothing, transport and so on),[115] but not the cost of child care.[116] The defendant bears an evidentiary onus in that regard.[117]

[7.43]   Where the injury has shortened the injured person's life, the pre-injury expectation of life forms the basis of calculating loss of earning capacity.[118] From the income the injured person would have obtained in the additional years in which he or she would have lived ('lost years'), the probable living expenses in that period must be deducted,[119] calculated by reference to 'the standard of life which the job and career prospects would suggest the [injured person] was reasonably likely to achieve'.[120] But the amount that the injured person would probably have spent on dependants during the 'lost years' is not deducted.[121]

[7.44]   While the injured person bears the legal burden to establish the difference between the income that could have been earned without the injury and the income (if any) that can still be earned with the injury,[122] the defendant may bear the evidentiary burden on certain matters. The injured person must prove that the injury prevents her from continuing the occupation carried out prior to the injury,[123] but the defendant must provide evidence that the injured person is still able to carry out some other occupation.[124] The injured person must provide evidence as to the income that she would have obtained without the injury,[125] but the defendant must provide evidence as to the income the injured person is still able to obtain.[126] In the absence of either evidence, the court must estimate the amount of the loss as best as it can.[127]

---

113   *DNM Mining Pty Ltd v Barwick* [2004] NSWCA 137 [44]; considered at [3.107].

114   *Cullen v Trappell* (1980) 146 CLR 1; *Mitchell Erectors Pty Ltd v Hinnen* [2002] WASCA 169 [24]; *Civil Proceedings Act 2011* (Qld), s 60; *Wrongs Act 1958* (Vic), s 28A.

115   *Sharman v Evans* (1977) 138 CLR 563, 577; *Plexvon Pty Ltd (in liq) v Brophy* [2006] NSWCA 304, (2006) 158 IR 221 [20].

116   *Wynn v New South Wales Insurance Ministerial Corporation* (1995) 184 CLR 485, 495–96.

117   *Plexvon Pty Ltd (in liq) v Brophy* [2006] NSWCA 304, (2006) 158 IR 221 [24].

118   *Skelton v Collins* (1966) 115 CLR 94, 121, 126–27, 129, 136–37; *Sharman v Evans* (1977) 138 CLR 563, 579, 599.

119   *Sharman v Evans* (1977) 138 CLR 563, 579–81, 599; *Fitch v Hyde-Cates* (1982) 150 CLR 482, 497–98.

120   *James Hardie & Co Pty Ltd v Roberts* [1999] NSWCA 314, (1999) 47 NSWLR 425 [84] (Sheller JA).

121   *Sharman v Evans* (1977) 138 CLR 563, 579–81, 599; *Fitch v Hyde-Cates* (1982) 150 CLR 482, 497–98.

122   *Radakovic v R G Cram & Sons Pty Ltd* [1975] 2 NSWLR 751, 754, 761, 766; *Allan v Loadsman* [1975] 2 NSWLR 789, 791.

123   *Baird v Roberts* [1977] 2 NSWLR 389, 398.

124   *Van Velzen v Wagener (formerly Robertson)* (1975) 10 SASR 549, 550; *Baird v Roberts* [1977] 2 NSWLR 389, 398; *Woodhead v Barrow* (1993) Aust Torts Reports 81–238, 62,469.

125   *Baird v Roberts* [1977] 2 NSWLR 389, 398.

126   *Linsell v Robson* [1976] 1 NSWLR 249, 255 (Glass JA); *Gillan v Brannan* (1991) Aust Torts Reports 81–136; *Butcher v Australian Tartaric Products Pty Ltd* [2009] VSCA 303 [128]. Cf *Linsell v Robson* [1976] 1 NSWLR 249, 251 (Hutley JA).

127   *Yammine v Kalwy* [1979] 2 NSWLR 151, 155; *New South Wales v Moss* [2000] NSWCA 133, (2000) 54 NSWLR 526 [66]–[87]; *AFA Airconditioning Pty Ltd v Mendrecki* [2008] SASC 195, (2008) 101 SASR 381 [291]–[292].

No compensation can be awarded if the court is not persuaded that the injured person has suffered any financial loss.[128]

With regard to the employment the injured person would, without injury, have obtained in the future, the court considers the most likely circumstances, to be established by the injured person.[129] This involves the prospect of obtaining better-paid employment if established as a real possibility.[130] The civil liability statute in some jurisdictions requires the court to state its assumptions and the methodology used,[131] but this is common practice throughout Australia. **[7.45]**

The valuation of lost future earning capacity involves the consideration of contingencies or vicissitudes, positive and negative.[132] Positive contingencies are a personal increase in earnings over time due to normal age progression and promotion,[133] and a general increase in earnings over time due to national increases in productivity.[134] Negative contingencies are accidents, sickness and unemployment.[135] A deduction is usually made to reflect contingencies, but there is no requirement to do so.[136] New South Wales courts usually deduct 15%,[137] although deductions up to 40% have been made.[138] In Western Australia, the discount 'is rarely more than 15 per cent and usually between five and ten per cent'.[139] It is not generally necessary to make a further deduction for the possibility of unpaid parental leave.[140] **[7.46]**

The civil liability statutes of all Australian jurisdictions regulate the amount to be awarded for loss of earning capacity.[141] Section 54 of the *Civil Liability Act 1936* (SA) excludes **[7.47]**

---

128   *Brear v James Hardie & Co Pty Ltd* [2000] NSWCA 352, (2000) 50 NSWLR 388 [50]–[51]; *Civil Liability Act 2003* (Qld), s 55.

129   *Civil Liability Act 2002* (NSW), s 13(1); *Personal Injuries (Liabilities and Damages) Act 2003* (NT), s 20(1). Those provisions are inadequately drafted and do not alter the common law in any material respect: *Allianz Australia Insurance Ltd v Kerr* [2012] NSWCA 13, (2012) 83 NSWLR 302 [30].

130   *Mann v Elbourn* (1973) 8 SASR 298, 308; *Norris v Blake (No 2)* (1997) 41 NSWLR 49, 73.

131   *Civil Liability Act 2002* (NSW), s 13(3); *Personal Injuries (Liabilities and Damages) Act 2003* (NT), s 21(3); *Civil Liability Act 2003* (Qld), s 55(3).

132   *Bresatz v Przibilla* (1962) 108 CLR 541, 544; *Wynn v New South Wales Insurance Ministerial Corporation* (1995) 184 CLR 485, 497. The language of s 13(2) of the *Civil Liability Act 2002* (NSW) implies a consideration of negative contingencies only: *Penrith City Council v Parks* [2004] NSWCA 201 [57]. However, the NSW courts still consider positive contingencies: *New South Wales (NSW Police) v Nominal Defendant* [2009] NSWCA 225, (2009) 53 MVR 243 [94].

133   *O'Brien v McKean* (1968) 118 CLR 540, 546, 557–58.

134   *Sharman v Evans* (1977) 138 CLR 563, 597; *Koeck v Persic* (1996) Aust Torts Reports 81–386, 63,358.

135   *Dessent v Commonwealth* (1977) 13 ALR 437, 447; *Wynn v New South Wales Insurance Ministerial Corporation* (1995) 184 CLR 485, 497; *New South Wales (NSW Police) v Nominal Defendant* [2009] NSWCA 225, (2009) 53 MVR 243 [94].

136   *Shaw v Commonwealth* (1993) 116 FLR 376, 391; *Air Manymak v Jeffs* [2006] NTCA 12 [99]. An adjustment to reflect contingencies is required by *Civil Liability Act 2002* (NSW), s 13(2); *Personal Injuries (Liabilities and Damages) Act 2003* (NT), s 21(2). However, there may be no contingencies or a balance of positive and negative contingencies.

137   *Wynn v New South Wales Insurance Ministerial Corporation* (1995) 184 CLR 485, 497–98; *Rosniak v Government Insurance Office* (1997) 41 NSWLR 608, 624; *Penrith City Council v Parks* [2004] NSWCA 201 [4], [56]; *Allianz Australia Insurance Ltd v Kerr* [2012] NSWCA 13, (2012) 83 NSWLR 302 [29].

138   *Urban Transit Authority of NSW v Seitis* [1995] NSWCA 478.

139   *Villasevil v Pickering* [2001] WASCA 143, (2001) 24 WAR 167 [38] (Anderson J). See also *Brocx v Mounsey* [2010] WASCA 196 [59]–[79].

140   *Wynn v New South Wales Insurance Ministerial Corporation* (1995) 184 CLR 485, 494–95; *Sullivan v Gordon* [1999] NSWCA 338, (1999) 47 NSWLR 319 [92].

141   The circumstances in which each statute applies are discussed at [7.13]–[7.14].

compensation for the first week of incapacity and places a limit on the total amount awarded for this head of loss, irrespective of the length of the period of incapacity. The limit was $2.2 million in 2002 and varies annually in line with the consumer price index.[142] In all other jurisdictions, a limit operates in respect of the amount that can be awarded per week of incapacity. The limit is twice average weekly earnings under s 87U of the *Competition and Consumer Act 2010* (Cth), and three times the amount of average weekly earnings in the remaining jurisdictions, the definition of average weekly earnings differing between the jurisdictions.[143]

[7.48]   There is a crucial difference between the jurisdictions in the way the limit per week of incapacity operates. In Queensland and Victoria, the limit applies to the amount of compensation[144] (although in Queensland it is applied before making a discount in the case of future loss[145]). It is thus applied after deducting the earnings the plaintiff is still able to make (the 'with injury earnings') from the earnings the plaintiff would have made in the absence of the injury (the 'without injury earnings'), after making a deduction for vicissitudes,[146] and probably after making any deduction for contributory negligence.[147]

[7.49]   The statutes of the other jurisdictions (including the Commonwealth) provide that the court must 'disregard' the amount by which the plaintiff's without injury earnings would have exceeded the statutory limit. Thus, the limit is applied before deducting the with injury earnings,[148] before making a deduction for vicissitudes,[149] and probably before making any deduction for contributory negligence.[150] Under the civil liability statutes of all jurisdictions other than Queensland, South Australia and Victoria, compensation will be awarded to a plaintiff whose earning capacity has been reduced from a modest amount to nil, but not to a plaintiff whose earning capacity has been reduced from a huge amount to the statutory limit. This cannot be justified on principle.

---

142   See the definition of 'prescribed maximum' in s 3(1). Section 56A contains additional restrictions for motor accidents occurring on or after 1 July 2013.

143   *Civil Law (Wrongs) Act 2002* (ACT), s 98; *Civil Liability Act 2002* (NSW), s 12; *Personal Injuries (Liabilities and Damages) Act 2003* (NT), s 20; *Civil Liability Act 2003* (Qld), s 54; *Civil Liability Act 2002* (Tas), s 26; *Wrongs Act 1958* (Vic), s 28F; *Civil Liability Act 2002* (WA), s 11.

144   The provisions in both states have been amended to that effect. Previously, they were drafted and interpreted in the same way as the New South Wales provision; see *Doughty v Cassidy* [2004] QSC 366, [2005] 1 Qd R 462; *Tuohey v Freemasons Hospital* [2012] VSCA 80, (2012) 37 VR 180. The previous law was criticised by the Victorian Competition and Efficiency Commission, *Adjusting the Balance: Inquiry into Aspects of the Wrongs Act 1958*, 2014.

145   Explanatory Notes, Civil Liability (Dust Diseases) and Other Legislation Amendment Bill 2005 (Qld), pp 5–6.

146   At least in Queensland: ibid; *Balnaves v Smith* [2012] QSC 192 [164]–[174].

147   B Madden and T Cockburn, 'Full Compensation No Longer Sacrosanct: Reflections on the Past and Future Economic Loss "Cap" for High Income Earners' (2012) 20 Torts LJ 90, 103.

148   *Nair-Smith v Perisher Blue Pty Ltd* [2013] NSWSC 727 [335], applying *Fkiaras v Fkiaras* [2010] NSWCA 116, (2010) 77 NSWLR 468 [37], which interpreted the identical phrase in s 125 of the *Motor Accidents Compensation Act 1999* (NSW).

149   *Ryan v AF Concrete Pumping Pty Ltd* [2013] NSWSC 113 [175]; *Johnson v Northern Territory* [2016] NTSC 49 [313]. See also *Knauer v Transfield Pty Ltd* [2005] NSWSC 176 [113]–[114] for the identical provision in s 151I of the *Workers Compensation Act 1987* (NSW).

150   B Madden and T Cockburn, 'Full Compensation No Longer Sacrosanct: Reflections on the Past and Future Economic Loss "Cap" for High Income Earners' (2012) 20 Torts LJ 90, 102–03, who criticise this as 'a further erosion of the principle of full compensation'.

2   Loss of employment-related benefits

A person who is rendered unable to work by an injury may recover for the loss of employment-related benefits other than the salary, for example the right to air travel at a significant discount[151] or the permitted use of a company car for private purposes.[152]

[7.50]

An injured person cannot recover for lost superannuation contributions by the employer,[153] but can recover for lost superannuation benefits.[154] The complexity of super-annuation schemes can render the calculation of the lost benefits difficult. Where the amount of lost income is determined for the purpose of assessing loss of earning capacity, lost superannuation benefits are usually calculated by taking that percentage of the lost income which employers are likely to pay in the relevant period (currently 9.5%).[155] The civil liability statutes in New South Wales, Queensland, South Australia and Tasmania prescribe the amount so calculated as the maximum amount to be awarded for loss of superannuation benefits.[156] Where the amount of lost income cannot be determined, the court may directly place a total value on the loss of earning capacity and lost superannu-ation benefits.[157]

[7.51]

3   Loss of social security benefits

An injured person can generally recover for the termination of social security benefits which, but for the injury, would have been likely to continue. It is different where the benefits lost have been replaced with other benefits of equal or higher amount, unless those other benefits are repayable out of the compensation award.[158]

[7.52]

4   Loss of capacity to do domestic work

An injury may render the injured person unable to do unpaid domestic work, such as cooking, cleaning and child care. The rules on the recoverability of such loss have seen several changes and are no longer the same throughout Australia. At common law, loss of domestic capacity was not recognised as a separate head of loss until 1977, when the High Court of Australia, in *Griffiths v Kerkemeyer*,[159] recognised the compensability of needs in

[7.53]

---

151   *Ho v Powell* [2001] NSWCA 168, (2001) 51 NSWLR 572 [35]–[58].
152   *Delphin v Martin* [2012] TASSC 13 [98].
153   *New South Wales Insurance Ministerial Corporation v Wynn* (1994) Aust Torts Reports 81–304, 61,740.
154   *Todorovic v Waller* (1981) 150 CLR 402, 426; *Allianz Australia Insurance Ltd v Girone* [2011] QCA 245 [62].
155   Eg *Waste Recycling and Processing Services of New South Wales v Meafou* [2004] NSWCA 462 [38]; *Zorom Enterprises v Zabow* [2007] NSWCA 106, (2007) 71 NSWLR 354 [66]; *Insurance Commission of Western Australia v Weatherall* [2007] WASCA 264 [250, [252]; *O'Brien v Noble* [2012] ACTCA 13, (2012) 6 ACTLR 132 [48]; *Delphin v Martin* [2012] TASSC 13 [102].
156   *Civil Liability Act 2002* (NSW), s 15C; *Civil Liability Act 2003* (Qld), s 56; *Civil Liability Act 1936* (SA), s 56A(6)–(9); *Civil Liability Act 2002* (Tas), s 25. The South Australian provision applies to motor accidents occurring on or after 1 July 2013. The circumstances in which the other provisions apply are discussed at [7.13].
157   *Simon v Hunter and New England Local Health District* [2012] NSWDC 19, (2012) 14 DCLR (NSW) 60 [121].
158   *Dabinett v Whittaker* [1989] 2 Qd R 228, 230–31; *Reneban v Leeuwin Ocean Adventure Foundation Ltd* [2006] NTSC 4, (2006) 17 NTLR 83 [203]–[206].
159   (1977) 139 CLR 161.

respect of which an injured person *receives* gratuitous services; see [7.24]. Subsequently, appellate courts in some jurisdictions recognised the compensability of the lost capacity to *provide* gratuitous services to others.[160] In 2005, in *CSR Ltd v Eddy*,[161] the High Court of Australia halted that development by holding that, at common law, the inability to provide domestic services does not constitute a separate head of economic loss calculated by reference to the commercial value of those services, but may be compensated only as part of loss of amenities, discussed at [7.59]–[7.61].

[7.54]   The common law position still applies under the *Competition and Consumer Act 2010* (Cth) (see [7.55]) and under the laws of the Northern Territory, Western Australia[162] and, in general, South Australia. In the remaining jurisdictions, the civil liability statutes provide that, in certain circumstances (which differ between the statutes), the loss of the injured person's capacity to provide gratuitous domestic services can be compensated as a separate head of economic loss rather than as part of non-pecuniary loss.[163] South Australia has a similar provision for dust diseases.[164] In New South Wales, Tasmania and Victoria, the amount of damages per hour of services is limited to one fortieth of 'average weekly earnings' as defined in the respective statute.[165] In Tasmania and Victoria, the amount of damages per week of services is limited to the amount of 'average weekly earnings'.[166]

[7.55]   In 2004, s 87X was inserted into the then *Trade Practices Act 1974* (Cth). Section 87X, which remains unchanged in the *Competition and Consumer Act 2010* (Cth), provides in its first subsection: 'A court must not, in a proceeding to which this Part applies, award personal injury damages for loss of the plaintiff's capacity to provide gratuitous attendant care services to other persons, except in accordance with this section.' The remaining subsections set out conditions for the availability of the damages and limit their amount. Section 87X merely places restrictions on a head of damages which in 2004 was thought to be available at common law. It does not permit the award of those damages irrespective of the common law. With the High Court's decision in *CSR Ltd v Eddy* in 2005 that this head of damages is not available at common law (see [7.53]), s 87X became obsolete. The position under the *Competition and Consumer Act 2010* (Cth) is thus the same as it was under the laws of Queensland and Victoria prior to the most recent amendments in those states.[167]

---

160   *Hodges v Frost* (1984) 53 ALR 373, 378–89; *Sturch v Willmott* [1997] 2 Qd R 310, 319, 321; *Sullivan v Gordon* [1999] NSWCA 338, (1999) 47 NSWLR 319 [2], [59]. Compensability was denied in *Weinert v Schmidt* [2002] SASC 340, (2002) 84 SASR 307 [5]–[9].
161   [2005] HCA 64, (2005) 226 CLR 1.
162   The introduction of damages for the value of gratuitous domestic services that the injured person would have provided to relatives has been recommended by the Law Reform Commission of Western Australia, *Provisional Damages and Damages for Gratuitous Services*, Report No 106 (2016) ch 5.
163   *Civil Law (Wrongs) Act 2002* (ACT), s 100; *Civil Liability Act 2002* (NSW), s 15B; *Civil Liability Act 2003* (Qld), s 59A–59D; *Civil Liability Act 2002* (Tas), s 28BA; *Wrongs Act 1958* (Vic), ss 28ID, 28IE. The circumstances in which those provisions apply are discussed at [7.13].
164   *Dust Diseases Act 2005* (SA), s 9(3).
165   *Civil Liability Act 2002* (NSW), s 15B(4); *Civil Liability Act 2002* (Tas), s 28BA(3)(a); *Wrongs Act 1958* (Vic), s 28IE(2).
166   *Civil Liability Act 2002* (Tas), s 28BA(3)(b); *Wrongs Act 1958* (Vic), s 28IE(1).
167   See *CSR Ltd v Eddy* [2005] HCA 64, (2005) 226 CLR 1 [52]; *Kriz v King* [2006] QCA 351, [2007] 1 Qd R 327 [12].

C   Non-pecuniary loss

Non-pecuniary loss resulting from personal injury is generally compensable. It includes pain   [7.56]
and suffering,[168] loss of amenities,[169] disfigurement,[170] and loss of expectation of life.[171] At
common law, loss of expectation of life is often assessed separately whereas a single sum will
generally be awarded for the other heads of non-pecuniary loss combined.[172] The civil liability
statutes of some jurisdictions require the award of a single sum for all heads of non-pecuniary
loss combined; see [7.65]–[7.68].

The High Court of Australia has rejected the idea that in determining the amount to be   [7.57]
awarded for non-pecuniary loss, the court ought to consider the amounts awarded in previous
cases.[173] This ruling has been criticised as tending to 'promote advocacy by generalities and
decision-making by untested anecdote or worse',[174] and has been reversed by those civil
liability statutes that do not fix the amount to be awarded for non-pecuniary loss (although they
may prescribe a maximum amount).[175]

1   Pain and suffering

Pain and suffering, which are always considered together,[176] include physical pain,[177] dis-   [7.58]
tress,[178] and awareness that life expectation has been shortened.[179] The plaintiff needs to be
able to experience pain and suffering. The level of compensation under this head is thus
commensurate with the plaintiff's level of consciousness,[180] and a permanently unconscious
plaintiff recovers nothing under this head.[181] However, the loss of a plaintiff who can experience pain and suffering is not diminished only because the plaintiff is too young to understand
what is happening.[182]

2   Loss of amenities

Loss of amenities may be described as the permanent or temporary loss of enjoyment of life,   [7.59]
resulting from the inability to do things the injured person could do without injury.[183]

---

168   *Cullen v Trappell* (1980) 146 CLR 1, 21; *Johnson v Perez* (1988) 166 CLR 351, 376.
169   Ibid.
170   *Thatcher v Charles* (1961) 104 CLR 57, 63, 68, 74; *Griffiths v Kerkemeyer* (1977) 139 CLR 161, 165.
171   *Cattanach v Melchior* [2003] HCA 38, (2003) 215 CLR 1 [38], [360]; *Harriton v Stephens* [2006] HCA 15,
       (2006) 226 CLR 52 [83].
172   An exception is *Lawrence v Mathison* (1981) 11 NTR 1, 11.
173   *Planet Fisheries Pty Ltd v La Rosa* (1968) 119 CLR 118, 124–25; *Rogers v Nationwide News Pty Ltd* [2003]
       HCA 52, (2003) 216 CLR 327 [69].
174   *Hunter Area Health Service v Marchlewski* [2000] NSWCA 294, (2000) 51 NSWLR 268 [74] (Mason P).
175   *Competition and Consumer Act 2010* (Cth), s 87T; *Civil Law (Wrongs) Act 2002* (ACT), s 99; *Civil
       Liability Act 2002* (NSW), s 17A; *Civil Liability Act 2002* (Tas), s 28; *Wrongs Act 1958* (Vic), s 28HA; *Civil
       Liability Act 2002* (WA), s 10A.
176   For definitions see J Edelman, *McGregor on Damages* (20th edn, Sweet & Maxwell 2018) [5–004].
177   *Teubner v Humble* (1963) 108 CLR 491, 505; *Nguyen v Nguyen* (1990) 169 CLR 245, 248.
178   *Skelton v Collins* (1966) 115 CLR 94, 110; *Baltic Shipping Co v Dillon* (1993) 176 CLR 344, 405.
179   *Skelton v Collins* (1966) 115 CLR 94, 96, 110–11.
180   *Raper v Bowden* [2016] TASSC 35, (2016) 76 MVR 369 [138].
181   *Skelton v Collins* (1966) 115 CLR 94, 112–13.
182   *Del Ponte v Del Ponte* (1987) 11 NSWLR 498, 502.
183   The various concepts that may underlie this head of loss are discussed by AI Ogus, 'Damages for Lost
       Amenities: For a Foot, a Feeling or a Function?' (1972) 35 Mod LR 1–17.

It includes the inability to ride a bicycle,[184] the inability to do gardening work,[185] loss of sexual sensation,[186] and loss of a holiday.[187] It also includes the loss of the injured person's capacity to provide gratuitous services to others where such loss does not constitute a head of financial loss; see [7.53]–[7.55].

[7.60] The courts assess loss of amenities on the basis of objective and subjective considerations. There is a 'minimum loss' irrespective of the particular injured person's situation, so that even a permanently unconscious victim recovers something under this head.[188] Beyond the 'minimum loss', regard must be had to the circumstances of the particular injured person, for example the fact that the injured person can no longer enjoy a specific hobby or pursuit.[189] A victim who is conscious of the effects of the injury suffers a significantly greater loss of amenity than a permanently unconscious victim.[190] While the impact of cosmetic injuries may differ between one person and another, it is wrong to generally assume that the impact is lesser for men than for women.[191]

[7.61] Loss of amenities is not assessed by reference to the amount the injured person would need to spend on alternative amenities. An injured person who, without injury, would be building his own yacht cannot recover the cost of having a yacht built for him.[192] Where the amount awarded for loss of earning capacity stays below the actual loss (due to a statutory cap, for example), the injured person cannot enjoy all the amenities that would be open without the injury. But this fact provides no basis for increasing the amount awarded for loss of amenity to make up for the shortfall.[193]

3 Loss of expectation of life

[7.62] An injured person's awareness that life expectation has been shortened forms part of pain and suffering; see [7.58]. Loss of expectation of life has been recognised as an additional and separate head of non-pecuniary loss.[194] It is 'the value of the experiences that would have been lived through but for the injury'.[195] A permanently unconscious victim suffers this loss in the same way as other victims.[196] Loss of expectation of life is assessed objectively,[197] and attracts only a conventional sum, very moderate in amount.[198]

184 *Lawrence v Mathison* (1981) 11 NTR 1, 11.
185 Ibid.
186 *Linsell v Robson* [1976] 1 NSWLR 249, 253.
187 *North v Thompson* [1971] WAR 103, 107.
188 *Skelton v Collins* (1966) 115 CLR 94, 112–13.
189 *Lawrence v Mathison* (1981) 11 NTR 1, 9–10.
190 *Skelton v Collins* (1966) 115 CLR 94, 112–13.
191 *Ralevski v Dimovski* (1987) 7 NSWLR 487, 493–94, 497–98.
192 *Lawrence v Mathison* (1981) 11 NTR 1, 10.
193 Ibid, 7–8.
194 *Fitch v Hyde-Cates* (1982) 150 CLR 482, 495. This head of non-pecuniary loss has been abolished in England and Wales: *Administration of Justice Act 1982* (UK), s 1(1)(a).
195 *Skelton v Collins* (1966) 115 CLR 94, 97 (Kitto J).
196 Ibid, 96–98.
197 Ibid, 97–98.
198 Ibid, 98; *Sharman v Evans* (1977) 138 CLR 563, 584, 590.

4 Statutory regulation

The civil liability statutes in all jurisdictions except the Australian Capital Territory regulate the [7.63] availability and/or amount of compensation for non-pecuniary loss.[199] The details are complex, and only a brief overview can be given here. In Tasmania and Western Australia, no compensation for non-pecuniary loss may be awarded unless the money figure placed upon such loss reaches a certain threshold, the amount of which differs between the two states.[200] The amount of compensation is regulated for non-pecuniary loss of medium severity, but not for non-pecuniary loss that is more severe. In Victoria, non-pecuniary loss can be compensated only in cases of 'significant injury',[201] and the maximum amount recoverable is a fixed sum that increases annually in line with inflation.[202] The other jurisdictions have tariff systems, under which the injury or non-pecuniary loss is placed on a scale between the least serious and the most serious case.

Sections 87L to 87S of the *Competition and Consumer Act 2010* (Cth) prescribe a maximum [7.64] amount, which is a fixed sum that varies annually in line with the consumer price index. The maximum amount may be awarded only in 'a most extreme case'. In other cases, compensation is capped at a certain percentage of the maximum amount, which is dependent upon, but not necessarily identical to, the percentage of loss suffered in a most extreme case. For example, where the non-pecuniary loss suffered by the injured person is 20% of a most extreme case, compensation is capped at 3.5% of the maximum amount. No compensation can be awarded where the non-pecuniary loss suffered by the injured person is less than 15% of a most extreme case. Sections 87L to 87S do not apply to a breach of s 18 of the Australian Consumer Law, which proscribes misleading or deceptive conduct.[203]

The tariff system prescribed by ss 16 and 17 of the *Civil Liability Act 2002* (NSW) is [7.65] generally identical with the one under the *Competition and Consumer Act 2010* (Cth), discussed in the preceding paragraph. However, the maximum amount is different and varies annually in line with average weekly earnings rather than the consumer price index. Furthermore, the amount set out for every percentage point of a most extreme case is not a maximum but is prescribed as a fixed sum.[204] The significance of the 15% threshold is demonstrated by *Zreika v New South Wales*,[205] where the relevant injury left the plaintiff with permanent pain in his right shoulder, preventing him from performing forceful pushing and pulling activities with the right arm. His non-pecuniary loss was assessed as 10% of a most extreme case, and no compensation could be awarded.

Sections 24–28 of the *Personal Injuries (Liabilities and Damages) Act 2003* (NT) prescribe [7.66] a maximum amount, which is a fixed sum that varies annually in line with average weekly earnings. Where the injured person's degree of permanent impairment is 85% or more of the

---

199   The circumstances in which those provisions apply are discussed at [7.13]–[7.14].
200   *Civil Liability Act 2002* (Tas), s 27; *Civil Liability Act 2002* (WA), ss 9 and 10.
201   *Wrongs Act 1958* (Vic), s 28LE. For definitions, see ss 28LB, 28LF.
202   Ibid, ss 28G and 28H.
203   *Competition and Consumer Act 2010* (Cth), s 87E. Section 137C of the Act applies to death or personal injury resulting from a breach of s 18 (or certain other provisions) of the ACL, but 'personal injury' for this purpose does not include the impairment of a person's mental condition short of a recognised psychiatric illness: *Competition and Consumer Act 2010* (Cth), s 4(1).
204   *Civil Liability Act 2002* (NSW), ss 16 and 17.
205   [2009] NSWCA 99.

whole person, the maximum amount must be awarded. Where the degree of permanent impairment is 5% or more but less than 85%, a specified percentage of the maximum amount must be awarded. For example, 3% of the maximum amount must be awarded where the degree of permanent impairment is 10%. No compensation can be awarded where the degree of permanent impairment is less than 5% or where the impairment is temporary. There are also provisions for the procedure of assessing an injured person's degree of permanent impairment.

[7.67] In Queensland,[206] the court must award a specified amount calculated by multiplying two factors. One is the 'injury scale value' of the injured person's injury (a percentage of an injury 'of the gravest conceivable kind'), and the other is an amount of money that depends upon the 'injury scale value' and the date of the injury, the amount varying annually in line with average weekly earnings. In determining the 'injury scale value' of the injured person's injury, the court must have regard to values specified in previous cases, and must generally stay within a range prescribed by regulations. For example, the range for 'extreme chest injury' is 46 to 65%. There is no threshold.

[7.68] Section 52 of the *Civil Liability Act 1936* (SA) sets out two different tariff systems. One applies to motor accidents occurring on or after 1 July 2013. It is similar to the Queensland regime, discussed in the preceding paragraph, and requires the court to assign the injured person's non-pecuniary loss an 'injury scale value' on a scale from 0 to 100. In other cases, the court must assign the injured person's non-pecuniary loss a 'scale value' on a scale from 0 to 60.[207] The injury scale value or scale value must be multiplied by a specified amount of money, which depends upon the percentage assigned, and the result must be adjusted in line with the movement in the consumer price index. In all cases, compensation for non-pecuniary loss is excluded unless the injured person's ability to lead a normal life was significantly impaired for a period of at least seven days or the medical expenses reasonably incurred exceed a certain amount, which varies annually in line with the consumer price index.

D   Overlap between different heads of loss

[7.69] Double recovery for the same head of loss must be avoided. For example, where compensation is awarded for both loss of earning capacity and the cost of institutional care, there must be no double recovery for basic living expenses (such as accommodation and food) that the injured person would have incurred even without the injury, since the injured person would have had to meet those expenses out of the income earned.[208] An injured person who, without injury, would have spent the whole income on accommodation and food cannot obtain any compensation for loss of earning capacity in addition to compensation for the full cost of institutional care.[209]

[7.70] Compensation for the loss of the capacity to provide domestic services (where such compensation is permitted by statute; see [7.54]) may overlap with compensation for non-pecuniary loss, with *Griffiths v Kerkemeyer* damages, and with compensation awarded to

---

206   *Civil Liability Act 2003* (Qld), ss 61, 62; *Civil Liability Regulation 2014* (Qld), regs 7, 8, schs 3–7.
207   For the process, see *Allen v Chadwick* [2014] SASCFC 100, (2014) 120 SASR 350 [164]–[165]; *Eicas v Dawson* [2016] SASCFC 124, (2016) 78 MVR 434 [101].
208   *Sunderland v Macco-Palmer* (1972) 3 SASR 314, 323; *Sharman v Evans* (1977) 138 CLR 563, 567, 576.
209   *Skelton v Collins* (1966) 115 CLR 94, 106. See also *Henley v Commane* [1971] Tas SR 180, 181–82.

another person for loss of consortium or loss of services. Most of the statutes that permit compensation for the loss of the capacity to provide domestic services contain provisions that prohibit double recovery, but such prohibition must apply even where not expressly provided for. Where the loss of the capacity to provide domestic services is compensated through a separate head of damages, it must not be taken into account in calculating non-pecuniary loss.[210] Where gratuitous services benefit members of the injured person's household (replacing services that the injured person would have provided but for the injury) as well as the injured person, there can only be an award of *Griffiths v Kerkemeyer* damages or of compensation for the loss of the capacity to provide domestic services, but not both.[211] Similarly, there can only be an award to the injured person of compensation for the loss of the capacity to provide domestic services or an award to other persons of compensation for loss of consortium or loss of services, but not both.[212]

The English Court of Appeal has held that where the injured person is no longer able to engage in pleasurable activities that she engaged in, and paid for, before the injury, the cost of engaging in those activities must be deducted from loss of earning capacity if compensation for loss of amenities is awarded.[213] The High Court of Australia has rejected this approach with regard to injured persons who are still capable of experiencing some pleasure, and has doubted the approach otherwise.[214] The fear of double recovery is exaggerated. A person who spends money on a leisure activity must value the pleasure derived more highly than the value of the money spent. Where an injury deprives the person of engaging in the activity, the value of lost pleasure thus exceeds the amount of saved expenses. Only this excess is compensated by the modest award for loss of amenity.   [7.71]

V   Benefits arising from an injury

An injured person often receives benefits as a result of the injury, for example sick pay, social security benefits, or insurance payments. Under the principle that compensation must not overcompensate the injured person, all those benefits would have to be deducted from the loss suffered. Clearly this principle cannot apply to every benefit, since some benefits are to be enjoyed by the injured person in addition to compensation from the wrongdoer, for example a gift; see generally [2.39]–[2.43].   [7.72]

The situation is complicated because the interests of the injured person, of the wrongdoer and of the provider of the benefit must be considered. A benefit may be classified as non-deductible for the purpose of ultimately reimbursing its provider. This is the case where the provider has a right, under contract or the general law, to be subrogated to the injured person's claim against the wrongdoer. Nor should the benefit be deducted where the injured person is   [7.73]

---

210   *Civil Liability Act 2002* (NSW), s 15B(5)(b); *Civil Liability Act 2003* (Qld), s 59C(4)(b); *Wrongs Act 1958* (Vic), s 28ID(3)(b).

211   *Civil Liability Act 2002* (NSW), s 15B(6)–(7); *Civil Liability Act 2003* (Qld), s 59B(2).

212   *Civil Liability Act 2002* (NSW), s 15B(6); *Civil Liability Act 2003* (Qld), ss 59B(4), 59D; *Wrongs Act 1958* (Vic), s 28ID(4), (5).

213   *Fletcher v Autocar and Transporters Ltd* [1968] 2 QB 322; *Smith v Central Asbestos Ltd* [1972] 1 QB 244, 262. See also *Henley v Commane* [1971] Tas SR 180, 184–85.

214   *Sharman v Evans* (1977) 138 CLR 563, 578 (Gibbs and Stephen JJ, with whom Jacobs J agreed on this point).

under an obligation, by virtue of contract or the general law, to repay the benefit to its provider out of the damages received from the wrongdoer.[215]

[7.74] The High Court of Australia has laid down that the deductibility of a benefit depends on its character and not on any test of causation.[216] Windeyer J said in *National Insurance Co of New Zealand Ltd v Espagne*:

> In assessing damages for personal injuries, benefits that a plaintiff has received or is to receive from any source other than the defendant are not to be regarded as mitigating his loss, if: (a) they were received or are to be received by him as a result of a contract he had made before the loss occurred and by the express or implied terms of that contract they were to be provided notwithstanding any rights of action he might have; or (b) they were given or promised to him by way of bounty, to the intent that he should enjoy them in addition to and not in diminution of any claim for damages . . . In both cases the decisive consideration is, not whether the benefit was received in consequence of, or as a result of the injury, but what was its character: and that is determined, in the one case by what under his contract the plaintiff had paid for, and in the other by the intent of the person conferring the benefit. The test is by purpose rather than by cause.[217]

[7.75] The treatment of some benefits is settled. Sick pay that an employed injured person is entitled to receive from the employer is deducted on the ground that it constitutes the continued payment of ordinary wages during a period of sickness.[218] By contrast, there is no deduction of benefits (be it money or benefits in kind) provided by the employer without obligation to do so.[219]

[7.76] Payments received under a private insurance contract are not deducted.[220] It has been argued that the wrongdoer must not benefit from the injured person's thrift and foresight.[221] It has been objected that a wrongdoer benefits from the injured person's thrift and foresight where it relates to the occurrence of the injury (for example, wearing a protective helmet).[222] However, while it may be unreasonable, and thus constitute contributory negligence, not to take protective measures in relation to the injury itself, it is not unreasonable not to take out voluntary insurance. Moreover, the non-deductibility of insurance payments gives people an incentive to cater for certain contingencies themselves, reducing the need for social security benefits. The insurer is subrogated to the insured's claim against the wrongdoer where the insurer is obliged to compensate for the actual loss suffered by the insured (indemnity

---

215 The non-deductibility is not settled where the benefit needs to be repaid only if the injured person receives damages for the loss covered by the benefit. It depends on the correct interpretation of *Treloar v Wickham* (1961) 105 CLR 102. See H Luntz, *Assessment of Damages for Personal Injury and Death* (4th edn, Butterworths 2002) [8.3.11]–[8.3.12].

216 *National Insurance Co of New Zealand Ltd v Espagne* (1961) 105 CLR 569; *Redding v Lee* (1982) 151 CLR 117.

217 (1961) 105 CLR 569, 599–600.

218 *Graham v Baker* (1961) 106 CLR 340, 345–50; *Manning v New South Wales* [2005] NSWSC 958 [111].

219 *Beck v Farrelly* (1975) 13 SASR 17, 22; *Toomey v Scolaro's Concrete Constructions Pty Ltd (in liq) (No 2)* [2001] VSC 279 [509]–[514]. The law is different in England and Wales: *Gaca v Pirelli General plc* [2004] EWCA Civ 373, [2004] 1 WLR 2683.

220 *National Insurance Co of New Zealand Ltd v Espagne* (1961) 105 CLR 569, 599–600; *Oakley v McIntyre* [1984] Tas R 44, 45–47.

221 *Browning v War Office* [1963] 1 QB 750, 763 (Donovan LJ).

222 KD Cooper-Stephenson, *Personal Injury Damages in Canada* (2nd edn, Carswell 1996) 579.

insurance) but not where the insurer pays a predetermined amount that may be greater or smaller than the actual loss (contingency insurance).[223]

Where the injury forces an employee to retire early, superannuation benefits received between the date of early retirement and the date of normal retirement (disability pension) are not deducted.[224] A disability pension is seen as being more akin to a private insurance payment than obligatory sick pay. This is not convincing where, as usual, membership in the superannuation fund was compulsory. In this situation, the argument about giving an incentive to make private arrangement has no application. [7.77]

The treatment of payments that an injured person receives under the Medicare scheme is now regulated by the *Health and Other Services (Compensation) Act 1995* (Cth), which generally provides for the non-deductibility of such payments from the injured person's compensable loss but obliges the injured person to reimburse the Medicare scheme. A similar scheme exists for many other social security benefits under Part 3.14 of the *Social Security Act 1991* (Cth).[225] [7.78]

A benefit provided by the wrongdoer is usually deducted,[226] because it must be assumed that the wrongdoer paid the benefit as part of the compensation owed. Gratuitous services provided by the defendant to the injured person form an exception.[227] A private gift made by a third party to the injured person is not deducted from the compensable loss unless the donor intended to benefit the wrongdoer.[228] There seems to be a presumption against such an intention. In *Zheng v Cai*,[229] the High Court of Australia described as 'justice and wisdom' the following statement made by Harper, James and Gray: [7.79]

> Often of course the intent was never even thought out by the donor, certainly not expressed. In these cases of private generosity the best solution seems to be a rule of thumb that would give greatest scope to the donor's generosity and to the adjustment of moral obligations within the more or less intimate relationships that usually bring such generosity into play. The gift should be disregarded in assessing damages.[230]

VI   Claims based on injury to another person

Injury to one person may cause pecuniary and non-pecuniary loss to another. In general, the other person has no claim against the wrongdoer, due to the restrictions on liability for pure economic loss and 'nervous shock'. However, there are exceptions. [7.80]

---

223   *Insurance Commission of Western Australia v Kightly* [2005] WASCA 154, (2005) 30 WAR 380 [26]–[31].
224   *National Insurance Co of New Zealand Ltd v Espagne* (1961) 105 CLR 569, 599–600; *Graham v Baker* (1961) 106 CLR 340, 343; *New South Wales v Davies* (1998) 43 NSWLR 182, 190–91.
225   For the position under the National Disability Insurance Scheme, see *National Disability Insurance Scheme Act 2013* (Cth), ch 5; H Luntz, 'Compensation Recovery and the National Disability Insurance Scheme' (2013) 20 Torts LJ 153.
226   See *Harris v Commercial Minerals Ltd* (1996) 186 CLR 1, 17.
227   *Kars v Kars* (1996) 187 CLR 354, 375–82; discussed at [7.26].
228   *National Insurance Co of New Zealand Ltd v Espagne* (1961) 105 CLR 569, 597–99; *Zheng v Cai* [2009] HCA 52, (2009) 239 CLR 446 [19]–[23].
229   [2009] HCA 52, (2009) 239 CLR 446 [25] (French CJ, Gummow, Crennan, Kiefel and Bell JJ).
230   FV Harper, F James and OS Gray, *The Law of Torts* (2nd edn, Little, Brown & Co 1986) vol 4, 663.

A   Loss of an employee's services

[7.81]   At common law, an employer has an action against the wrongdoer for loss of an injured employee's services (*actio per quod servitium amisit*).[231] This action originated in the Middle Ages when 'servants' lived in the household of their 'master', who had a proprietary interest in them.[232] Over time, the action has been extended to corporate employers,[233] to employees other than domestic servants,[234] and to children rendering services to their parents without a contract of employment,[235] but excluded for employees who hold a public office, such as members of the police or the armed forces.[236]

[7.82]   In relation to motor accidents, the action has been abolished in New South Wales,[237] Victoria[238] and probably also in the Northern Territory.[239] In New South Wales, the action has also been abolished in relation to injury caused by a co-employee.[240] In Queensland, the action can be brought only where the employee has died or has had general damages assessed at a specified amount or more,[241] and compensation is capped at three times the average weekly earnings per week of the employee's incapacity.[242]

[7.83]   In *Barclay v Penberthy*,[243] the High Court of Australia confirmed that no action for loss of services lies at common law where the employee has been killed.[244] Otherwise, the High Court confirmed the continued existence of that action in Australian common law, and made the following observations.[245] The action lies whenever the employee's injury was inflicted intentionally or in breach of a duty of care towards the employee. It is a distinct cause of action and is not to be absorbed into the tort of negligence. Since the protected right is the employer's right to the employee's services, the employer can recover only for loss resulting from an interference with that right and not for other consequences flowing from the

---

231   *Commonwealth v Quince* (1944) 68 CLR 227, 235–36; *Attorney-General (NSW) v Perpetual Trustee Co Ltd* (1955) 92 CLR 113, 122–23; *Commissioner for Railways (NSW) v Scott* (1959) 102 CLR 392.

232   The historical position was described in *Inland Revenue Commissioners v Hambrook* [1956] 2 QB 641, 651, 660–61.

233   *Commissioner for Railways (NSW) v Scott* (1959) 102 CLR 392; *Mercantile Mutual Insurance Co Ltd v Argent Pty Ltd* (1972) 46 ALJR 432; *Marinovski v Zutti Pty Ltd* [1984] 2 NSWLR 571.

234   *Commissioner for Railways (NSW) v Scott* (1959) 102 CLR 392, 417–18, 426–27, 437, 458.

235   *Commonwealth v Quince* (1944) 68 CLR 227, 237; *Attorney-General (NSW) v Perpetual Trustee Co Ltd* (1955) 92 CLR 113, 123; *Commissioner for Railways (NSW) v Scott* (1959) 102 CLR 392, 418.

236   *Commonwealth v Quince* (1944) 68 CLR 227, 242–43, 245–46, 250; *Attorney-General (NSW) v Perpetual Trustee Co Ltd* (1955) 92 CLR 113, 129; *Commissioner for Railways (NSW) v Scott* (1959) 102 CLR 392, 418, 421, 441–42, 463.

237   Loss of services is not included in the items of financial loss listed as recoverable in s 4.5(1) of the *Motor Accident Injuries Act 2017* (NSW).

238   *Transport Accident Act 1986* (Vic), s 93A.

239   See RP Balkin and JLR Davis, *Law of Torts* (5th edn, LexisNexis Butterworths 2013) [20.10].

240   *Employees Liability Act 1991* (NSW), s 4.

241   *Civil Liability Act 2003* (Qld), s 58(1). The amount varies every year in line with the change in average weekly earnings: s 75. The amounts for each financial year are set out in reg 6 of the *Civil Liability Regulation 2014* (Qld).

242   *Civil Liability Act 2003* (Qld), s 58(2), (3).

243   [2012] HCA 40, (2012) 246 CLR 258 [22]–[27].

244   This is problematic as it places a wrongdoer who causes instant death in a better position than a wrongdoer who causes personal injury but no death: D Flanagan, '*Barclay v Penberthy*: Polishing the Antiques of Australian Tort Law' (2013) 34 Syd L Rev 655, 666. See also [7.93] for the abolition of the rule in the context of claims by dependants.

245   [2012] HCA 40, (2012) 246 CLR 258 [28]–[40], [56]–[66].

employer's injury. Thus, while the employer can recover for the cost of hiring a substitute or for extra remuneration paid to other employees who absorb the injured employee's work, the employer cannot recover for paying sick pay or medical expenses to the injured employee. Nor can the employer recover for loss of profit unless it is attributable to the loss of the injured employee's services.

It is an anomaly to recognise a claim for loss of services in the case of (some) employment relationships but no other relationships. As Fullagar J has observed:[246]

[7.84]

> If we are to allow the remedy in such a case, why should we deny it to a servant who has lost employment through injury to his master, or to an independent contractor with the injured person, or to a partner of the injured person, or to a company whose director is injured . . .?

B   Loss of consortium

The spouse or domestic partner of a wrongfully injured person may have a claim against the wrongdoer for loss of services and companionship (*actio per quod consortium amisit*). At common law, such an action can be brought by a husband,[247] but not a wife.[248] Historically, the action arose out of the husband's then proprietary interest in his wife's consortium.[249] This explains the original restriction of the action to a husband, but it cannot explain the retention of that restriction in the 21st century.[250] Today, the restriction is discriminatory and unacceptable. The law should be reformed by either extending the action to all spouses and domestic partners, or by abolishing the action altogether. The second option is preferable since the losses covered by the action overlap with losses of the injured person, in particular the loss of the capacity to provide domestic services, discussed at [7.53]–[7.55].

[7.85]

Fortunately, the common law applies unchanged only in the Northern Territory and, with the possible exception of transport accidents,[251] in Victoria. Legislation has intervened in all other jurisdictions. In South Australia, the action has been extended to all spouses and 'domestic partners'.[252] In Queensland, the action has been extended to all spouses[253] and de

[7.86]

---

246   *Commissioner for Railways (NSW) v Scott* (1959) 102 CLR 392, 407. For further discussion of the action for loss of services, see A Beever, '*Barclay v Penberthy* and the Collapse of the High Court's Tort Jurisprudence' (2012) 31 UQLJ 307; D Flanagan, '*Barclay v Penberthy*: Polishing the Antiques of Australian Tort Law' (2013) 34 *Syd L Rev* 655.

247   *Toohey v Hollier* (1955) 92 CLR 618; *Bresatz v Przibilla* (1962) 108 CLR 541, 550; *Nguyen v Nguyen* (1990) 169 CLR 245, 251.

248   *Dahm v Harmer* [1955] SASR 250, 252; *Plover v Giampolo* [1965] VR 275, 276; *Harris v Grigg* [1988] 1 Qd R 514, 522; *Nguyen v Nguyen* (1990) 169 CLR 245, 251.

249   The historical position was described in *Kealley v Jones* [1979] 1 NSWLR 723, 740, 744; *Roads and Traffic Authority v Jelfs* [1999] NSWCA 179, (2000) Aust Torts Reports 81–583 [12].

250   *Wright v Cedzich* (1930) 43 CLR 493 (Isaacs J dissenting); *Best v Samuel Fox & Co Ltd* [1952] AC 716.

251   In *Doughty v Martino Developments Pty Ltd* [2010] VSCA 121, (2010) 27 VR 499 [19]–[25], it was held that s 93(1) of the *Transport Accident Act 1986* (Vic) impliedly excludes actions for loss of servitium or consortium resulting from a transport accident. Subsequently, a new s 93A was inserted into the Act, expressly excluding actions for loss of servitium resulting from a transport accident. This might mean that actions for loss of consortium are preserved.

252   *Civil Liability Act 1936* (SA), s 65. The term 'domestic partner' is defined in the *Family Relationships Act 1975* (SA), s 11A.

253   *Law Reform Act 1995* (Qld), s 13.

facto partners,[254] but is available only where the injured person has died or has had damages for non-pecuniary loss assessed at a specified amount or more.[255] The action has been abolished in the remaining jurisdictions.[256] Since the common law rules are still relevant in some jurisdictions, they shall now be briefly outlined. The outline will be based on the situation of an injured wife since this is the situation in the cases decided at common law.

[7.87]   Loss of consortium is compensable even though it is only partial,[257] and even though the wife's injury is psychiatric as opposed to physical.[258] Loss of consortium is compensable only in respect of the period in which both spouses were alive,[259] and in which the marriage lasted, even if the wife's injury caused the breakdown of the marriage.[260] At common law, the husband's claim is unaffected by contributory negligence on the wife's part unless she was acting as his agent.[261] Legislation in the Northern Territory and South Australia now provides for a proportionate reduction of the husband's damages.[262] Taking the husband's claim for loss of consortium and the wife's claim for her own loss together, there must be no double recovery for the same item of loss,[263] for example medical expenses and the cost of hospital visits.[264]

[7.88]   Compensable pecuniary loss includes the cost of the wife's medical care and treatment,[265] the cost of the husband visiting his wife in hospital where those visits constituted a proper step in mitigating loss of consortium,[266] the cost of employing someone to provide domestic assistance,[267] and loss of income where the husband reasonably gave up work in order to look after his wife.[268] Compensable non-pecuniary loss includes the loss of the wife's service, company and fellowship,[269] including a diminished opportunity of sexual intercourse,[270] but not mere distress[271] or lost happiness.[272]

---

254   *Acts Interpretation Act 1954* (Qld), ss 32DA(6) and 36.
255   *Civil Liability Act 2003* (Qld), s 58(1). The amount varies every year in line with the change in average weekly earnings: s 75. The amounts for each financial year are set out in reg 6 of the *Civil Liability Regulation 2014* (Qld).
256   *Civil Law (Wrongs) Act 2002* (ACT), s 218; *Law Reform (Marital Consortium) Act 1984* (NSW), s 3(1); *Civil Liability Act 2002* (Tas), s 28D; *Law Reform (Miscellaneous Provisions) Act 1941* (WA), s 3, as inserted by the *Acts Amendment (Actions for Damages) Act 1986* (WA), s 4(1).
257   *Toohey v Hollier* (1955) 92 CLR 618, 627.
258   *Kealley v Jones* [1979] 1 NSWLR 723, 746; *State Rail Authority of New South Wales v Sharp* [1981] 1 NSWLR 240.
259   *Sloan v Kirby* (1979) 20 SASR 263, 275–77.
260   *Parker v Dzundza* [1979] Qd R 55, 57.
261   *Curran v Young* (1965) 112 CLR 99.
262   *Law Reform (Miscellaneous Provisions) Act 1956* (NT), s 18; *Law Reform (Contributory Negligence and Apportionment of Liability) Act 2001* (SA), s 7(4).
263   *Bresatz v Przibilla* (1962) 108 CLR 541, 550; *Norman v Sutton* (1989) Aust Torts Reports 80–282, 68,998.
264   *Hunter v Scott* [1963] Qd R 77, 87.
265   *Toohey v Hollier* (1955) 92 CLR 618, 627; *Harris v Grigg* [1988] 1 Qd R 514, 522.
266   *Hunter v Scott* [1963] Qd R 77, 87–88.
267   Ibid, 85; *Kealley v Jones* [1979] 1 NSWLR 723, 739, 741.
268   *Kealley v Jones* [1979] 1 NSWLR 723, 730–31, 742–43, 751.
269   *Toohey v Hollier* (1955) 92 CLR 618, 627; *Bresatz v Przibilla* (1962) 108 CLR 541, 550; *Kealley v Jones* [1979] 1 NSWLR 723, 729, 744–46.
270   *Kealley v Jones* [1979] 1 NSWLR 723, 751–52; *Norman v Sutton* (1989) Aust Torts Reports 80–282, 69,000.
271   *Toohey v Hollier* (1955) 92 CLR 618, 627; *Birch v Taubmans Ltd* (1956) 57 SR (NSW) 93, 99; *Kealley v Jones* [1979] 1 NSWLR 723, 746–47, 750.
272   *Birch v Taubmans Ltd* (1956) 57 SR (NSW) 93, 99; *Kealley v Jones* [1979] 1 NSWLR 723, 739, 746–47, 750.

VII   Actions on death

At common law, a cause of action in tort is extinguished by the death of the victim, and neither   [7.89]
the estate nor the dependants of the deceased have a claim against the tortfeasor, even if the
tort caused the death. This unjust rule has been changed by legislation in all Australian
jurisdictions. Today, the estate has a claim against the tortfeasor and, where the tort caused
the death, the dependants also have a claim against the tortfeasor. The claims by the estate and
the dependants are coexistent and not alternative.[273] Double recovery is largely prevented.
There have been calls for the abolition of the dependants' action and for concentrating the
claim in the hands of the estate.[274] But the current regime has been defended[275] and is unlikely
to change in the foreseeable future.[276]

A   Claim by the estate of the deceased

At common law, a claim in tort died with the person in whom it vested and did not survive for   [7.90]
the benefit of the estate (*actio personalis moritur cum persona*), even if the tort caused the
death.[277] This unjust rule has been generally reversed by statute in all Australian jurisdictions.[278] Personal claims are still extinguished. For example, claims in defamation are extinguished in all jurisdictions except Tasmania.[279] An award of exemplary damages in favour of
the estate is also excluded.[280] Otherwise, the estate can generally recover the same compensation that the deceased was entitled to recover.[281] Some restrictions apply, depending upon
whether the death was caused by the tort in question.

---

273   *Civil Law (Wrongs) Act 2002* (ACT), s 18(1); *Law Reform (Miscellaneous Provisions) Act 1944* (NSW),
       s 2(5); *Law Reform (Miscellaneous Provisions) Act 1956* (NT), s 9(1); *Succession Act 1981* (Qld),
       s 66(4); *Survival of Causes of Action Act 1940* (SA), s 6(1); *Administration and Probate Act 1935* (Tas),
       s 27(9); *Administration and Probate Act 1958* (Vic), s 29(5); *Law Reform (Miscellaneous Provisions) Act
       1941* (WA), s 4(5).

274   SM Waddams, 'Damages for Wrongful Death: Has Lord Campbell's Act Outlived Its Usefulness?'
       (1984) 47 Mod LR 437; Ontario Law Reform Commission, *Report on Compensation for Personal Injuries
       and Death* (1987) 14–36.

275   Law Commission, *Claims for Wrongful Death*, Report No 263 (1999) [3.1]–[3.4].

276   PB Kutner, 'Reforming Wrongful Death Law' (1999) 7 Torts LJ 46, 91–94.

277   *Fitch v Hyde-Cates* (1982) 150 CLR 482, 487.

278   *Civil Law (Wrongs) Act 2002* (ACT), s 15(1)(a); *Law Reform (Miscellaneous Provisions) Act 1944*
       (NSW), s 2(1); *Law Reform (Miscellaneous Provisions) Act 1956* (NT), s 5(1); *Succession Act 1981* (Qld),
       s 66(1); *Survival of Causes of Action Act 1940* (SA), s 2(1)(a); *Administration and Probate Act 1935*
       (Tas), s 27(1)(b); *Administration and Probate Act 1958* (Vic), s 29(1); *Law Reform (Miscellaneous
       Provisions) Act 1941* (WA), s 4(1).

279   *Civil Law (Wrongs) Act 2002* (ACT), s 15(2); *Law Reform (Miscellaneous Provisions) Act 1944*
       (NSW), s 2(1); *Law Reform (Miscellaneous Provisions) Act 1956* (NT), s 5(2); *Succession Act 1981* (Qld),
       s 66(1); *Survival of Causes of Action Act 1940* (SA), s 2(2); *Administration and Probate Act 1958* (Vic),
       s 29(1); *Law Reform (Miscellaneous Provisions) Act 1941* (WA), s 4(1).

280   *Civil Law (Wrongs) Act 2002* (ACT), s 16(2); *Law Reform (Miscellaneous Provisions) Act 1944*
       (NSW), s 2(2)(a)(i); *Law Reform (Miscellaneous Provisions) Act 1956* (NT), s 6(1)(a); *Succession Act
       1981* (Qld), s 66(2)(b); *Survival of Causes of Action Act 1940* (SA), s 3(1)(b); *Administration and
       Probate Act 1935* (Tas), s 27(3)(a); *Administration and Probate Act 1958* (Vic), s 29(2)(a); *Law Reform
       (Miscellaneous Provisions) Act 1941* (WA), s 4(2)(a).

281   'The cause of action of the deceased and that pursued . . . by the estate are one and the same':
       WorkCover Queensland v Amaca Pty Ltd [2010] HCA 34, (2010) 241 CLR 420 [38] (French CJ, Gummow,
       Crennan, Kiefel and Bell JJ).

[7.91]   Where the death was not caused by the tort, the estate has no claim against the tortfeasor for loss caused by the death, such as funeral expenses. But the estate can generally claim compensation in the same measure as the deceased was entitled to claim. Contributory negligence on the deceased's part will reduce the damages to be paid to the estate in the same proportion as it would have reduced the damages to be paid to the deceased.[282] In Queensland, South Australia and Western Australia, the estate cannot recover for non-pecuniary loss suffered by the deceased.[283] In South Australia, the estate has no claim in respect of loss of earning capacity on the deceased's part for a time after the deceased's death.[284] In the other jurisdictions, the same rule must apply at common law, since the court needs to take account of contingencies and knows the time of the deceased's death irrespective of the tort.

[7.92]   Where the death was caused by the tort, the estate can again recover for loss suffered by the deceased before death. However, recovery for non-pecuniary loss suffered by the deceased is excluded,[285] unless that loss resulted from a dust-related condition and the deceased commenced an action before death.[286] Under general principles, the recoverable loss would include loss of earning capacity during the 'lost years' – that is, the time between the actual death of the deceased and the time the deceased would probably have died in the absence of the tort. However, a claim by the estate for such loss is excluded.[287] Under general principle, the estate could claim for loss suffered as a result of the death. With the exception of reasonable funeral expenses paid or payable by the estate,[288] such a claim is again excluded.[289] The reason for the last two exclusions is to avoid overlap with the losses for

282   This is expressly confirmed by the *Survival of Causes of Action Act 1940* (SA), s 6(2).

283   *Succession Act 1981* (Qld), s 66(2)(a); *Survival of Causes of Action Act 1940* (SA), s 3(1)(a), (2), (3); *Law Reform (Miscellaneous Provisions) Act 1941* (WA), s 4(2)(d).

284   *Survival of Causes of Action Act 1940* (SA), s 3(1)(a)(iv).

285   *Civil Law (Wrongs) Act 2002* (ACT), s 16(3)(b)(i); *Law Reform (Miscellaneous Provisions) Act 1944* (NSW), s 2(2)(d); *Law Reform (Miscellaneous Provisions) Act 1956* (NT), s 6(1)(c)(ii); *Succession Act 1981* (Qld), s 66(2)(a); *Survival of Causes of Action Act 1940* (SA), s 3(1)(a); *Administration and Probate Act 1935* (Tas), s 27(3)(c)(ii); *Administration and Probate Act 1958* (Vic), s 29(2)(c)(ii); *Law Reform (Miscellaneous Provisions) Act 1941* (WA), s 4(2)(d).

286   *Civil Law (Wrongs) Act 2002* (ACT), s 16(4), (8); *Dust Diseases Tribunal Act 1989* (NSW), s 12B; *Law Reform (Miscellaneous Provisions) Act 1956* (NT), s 6(2)–(4); *Succession Act 1981* (Qld), s 66(2A); *Survival of Causes of Action Act 1940* (SA), s 3(2) and (3); *Administration and Probate Act 1935* (Tas), s 27(3A)–(3C); *Administration and Probate Act 1958* (Vic), s 29(2A); *Law Reform (Miscellaneous Provisions) Act 1941* (WA), s 4(2A).

287   *Civil Law (Wrongs) Act 2002* (ACT), s 16(3)(b)(ii); *Law Reform (Miscellaneous Provisions) Act 1944* (NSW), s 2(2)(a)(ii); *Law Reform (Miscellaneous Provisions) Act 1956* (NT), s 6(1)(c)(iii); *Succession Act 1981* (Qld), s 66(2)(d)(ii); *Survival of Causes of Action Act 1940* (SA), s 3(1)(a)(iv); *Administration and Probate Act 1935* (Tas), s 27(3)(c)(iii); *Administration and Probate Act 1958* (Vic), s 29(2)(c)(iii); *Law Reform (Miscellaneous Provisions) Act 1941* (WA), s 4(2)(e).

288   *Civil Law (Wrongs) Act 2002* (ACT), s 16(5)–(7); *Law Reform (Miscellaneous Provisions) Act 1944* (NSW), s 2(2)(c); *Law Reform (Miscellaneous Provisions) Act 1956* (NT), s 6(1)(c)(i); *Succession Act 1981* (Qld), s 66(2)(d)(i); *Survival of Causes of Action Act 1940* (SA), s 3(1)(d); *Administration and Probate Act 1935* (Tas), s 27(3)(c)(i); *Administration and Probate Act 1958* (Vic), s 29(2)(c)(i); *Law Reform (Miscellaneous Provisions) Act 1941* (WA), s 4(2)(c).

289   *Civil Law (Wrongs) Act 2002* (ACT), s 16(3)(a); *Law Reform (Miscellaneous Provisions) Act 1944* (NSW), s 2(2)(c); *Law Reform (Miscellaneous Provisions) Act 1956* (NT), s 6(1)(c)(i); *Succession Act 1981* (Qld), s 66(2)(d)(i); *Survival of Causes of Action Act 1940* (SA), s 3(1)(d); *Administration and Probate Act 1935* (Tas), s 27(3)(c)(i); *Administration and Probate Act 1958* (Vic), s 29(2)(c)(i); *Law Reform (Miscellaneous Provisions) Act 1941* (WA), s 4(2)(c).

which the dependants of the deceased can claim compensation under legislation mirroring Lord Campbell's Act. That claim will now be discussed.

B   Claim by the dependants of the deceased

The death of a person may cause loss to the dependants, pecuniary and otherwise. At common law, the dependants of a wrongfully killed person have no action against the wrongdoer.[290] This anomalous rule, which places a wrongdoer who causes (instant) death in a better position than a wrongdoer who causes personal injury but no death, was abolished in England and Wales by the *Fatal Accidents Act 1846* (UK), known as 'Lord Campbell's Act'.[291] All Australian jurisdictions have legislation mirroring Lord Campbell's Act,[292] but there are differences between the jurisdictions. For convenience, the persons who can bring an action under such legislation will be called 'dependants', although dependence upon the deceased is not always required.[293]

[7.93]

Even though the dependants' action is not the same as the one the deceased could bring if still alive,[294] the dependants have no action against the wrongdoer unless the deceased, if still alive, would have one.[295] Thus, the dependants have no action where the deceased, before death, obtained judgment against the wrongdoer,[296] or failed to bring an action within the limitation period and the court has no discretion to extend the period.[297] Contributory negligence on the part of the deceased[298] in respect of the injury would exclude an action by the dependants if contributory negligence were still a complete defence.[299] But it is no longer a complete defence; see [6.91]. Contributory negligence on the part of the deceased is generally ignored in the Australian Capital Territory[300] and in

[7.94]

---

290   *Baker v Bolton* (1808) 1 Camp 493; 170 ER 1033; *WorkCover Queensland v Amaca Pty Ltd* [2010] HCA 34, (2010) 241 CLR 420 [34]; *Barclay v Penberthy* [2012] HCA 40, (2012) 246 CLR 258 [22]–[27].

291   The legislative history is described in detail by P Handford, 'Lord Campbell and the Fatal Accidents Act' (2013) 129 LQR 420.

292   *Civil Law (Wrongs) Act 2002* (ACT), s 24; *Compensation to Relatives Act 1897* (NSW), s 3(1); *Compensation (Fatal Injuries) Act* (NT), s 7(1); *Civil Proceedings Act 2011* (Qld), s 64; *Civil Liability Act 1936* (SA), s 23; *Fatal Accidents Act 1934* (Tas), s 4; *Wrongs Act 1958* (Vic), s 16; *Fatal Accidents Act 1959* (WA), s 4(1).

293   *De Sales v Ingrilli* [2002] HCA 52, (2002) 212 CLR 338 [12] (Gleeson CJ).

294   *Haber v Walker* [1963] VR 339, 348, 354; *Taylor v Owners Strata Plan No 11564* [2013] NSWCA 55, (2013) 83 NSWLR 1 [4].

295   *Civil Law (Wrongs) Act 2002* (ACT), s 24(b); *Compensation to Relatives Act 1897* (NSW), s 3(1); *Compensation (Fatal Injuries) Act* (NT), s 7(1); *Civil Proceedings Act 2011* (Qld), s 64(1)(b); *Civil Liability Act 1936* (SA), s 23; *Fatal Accidents Act 1934* (Tas), s 4; *Wrongs Act 1958* (Vic), s 16; *Fatal Accidents Act 1959* (WA), s 4(1).

296   *Murray v Shuter* [1972] 1 Lloyd's Rep 6, 7; *Pickett v British Rail Engineering Ltd* [1980] AC 136, 152. The mere commencement of an action, without judgment, before death does not preclude an action by the dependants: *Kupke v The Corporation of the Sisters of Mercy* [1996] 1 Qd R 300; *Lisle v Brice* [2002] 2 Qd R 168 [12]; *Corr v IBC Vehicles Ltd* [2008] UKHL 13, [2008] 1 AC 884 [6].

297   *Crawford v Hydro-Electric Commission* [1963] Tas SR 83, 86–88.

298   Or the deceased's agent: *Perrotta v Cavallo* [1971] SASR 163, 165–66.

299   *Senior v Ward* (1859) 1 El & El 385, 393; 120 ER 954, 957; *Kain & Shelton Ltd v Virgo* (1956) 97 CLR 230, 244–45.

300   *Civil Law (Wrongs) Act 2002* (ACT), s 27. However, liability is generally excluded where the conduct that constituted contributory negligence was an indictable offence: *Civil Law (Wrongs) Act 2002* (ACT), ss 27(2), 94.

Victoria,[301] but it may lead to a proportionate reduction of the dependant's compensation in the other jurisdictions.[302]

[7.95]   The death must have been caused by a 'wrongful act, neglect or default',[303] which includes breach of contract.[304] Where the cause of action of the deceased, if still alive, would be negligence, which requires the foreseeability of the type of loss suffered (see [6.61]), the question arises whether the dependants' action requires the foreseeability of the death. A negative answer was given in some older cases.[305] This could be justified on the ground that the deceased, if still alive, would not sue in respect of his or her death. However, the foreseeability of the death has been required in more recent cases.[306] Suicide on the part of the deceased may remove the death from the scope of the defendant's liability,[307] which may depend upon the severity of the mental illness caused by the wrong.[308] Where the defendant remains liable, the suicide may constitute contributory negligence,[309] which in most jurisdictions permits a reduction in the damages; see [7.94].

[7.96]   In Victoria, persons who can recover damages include anyone who was dependent upon the deceased at the time of death.[310] In all other jurisdictions, the persons entitled to recover are listed. The list differs between the jurisdictions but always includes the deceased's spouse, parents and children.[311] The claims by all persons entitled to recover must be heard in one action,[312] which shall generally be brought by the deceased's administrator, executor, or other

---

301   See *Wrongs Act 1958* (Vic), s 26.
302   *Civil Liability Act 2002* (NSW), s 5T; *Compensation (Fatal Injuries) Act* (NT), s 11; *Law Reform Act 1995* (Qld), s 10(5); *Law Reform (Contributory Negligence and Apportionment of Liability) Act 2001* (SA), s 7(4); *Wrongs Act 1954* (Tas), s 4(4); *Law Reform (Contributory Negligence and Tortfeasors' Contribution) Act 1947* (WA), s 4(2)(a).
303   *Compensation to Relatives Act 1897* (NSW), s 3(1); *Compensation (Fatal Injuries) Act* (NT), s 7(1); *Civil Liability Act 1936* (SA), s 23; *Fatal Accidents Act 1934* (Tas), s 4; *Wrongs Act 1958* (Vic), s 16; *Fatal Accidents Act 1959* (WA), s 4(1). Synonymously, the phrase 'wrongful act or omission' is used in *Civil Law (Wrongs) Act 2002* (ACT), s 24(a); *Civil Proceedings Act 2011* (Qld), s 64(1)(a).
304   *Woolworths Ltd v Crotty* (1942) 66 CLR 603.
305   *Haber v Walker* [1963] VR 339, 349 (Lowe J), 354 (Smith J); *Zavitsanos v Chippendale* [1970] 2 NSWR 495, 500; *Cuckow v Polyester Reinforced Products Pty Ltd* (1970) 19 FLR 122, 135.
306   *Richters v Motor Tyre Service Pty Ltd* [1972] Qd R 9, 22; *Lisle v Brice* [2001] QCA 271, [2002] 2 Qd R 168 [9], [39]; *Sarkis v Summitt Broadway Pty Ltd* [2006] NSWCA 358, (2006) Aust Torts Reports 81–868 [17]; *Lyle v Soc* [2009] WASCA 3, (2009) 38 WAR 418 [32]. A requirement of foreseeability was also assumed in *Corr v IBC Vehicles Ltd* [2008] UKHL 13, [2008] 1 AC 884.
307   The view that it generally does was taken in *AMP General Insurance Ltd v Roads and Traffic Authority of NSW* [2001] NSWCA 186, (2001) Aust Torts Reports 81–619 [30] (Spigelman CJ). The opposite view was taken in *Corr v IBC Vehicles Ltd* [2008] UKHL 13, [2008] 1 AC 884 [16], [29], [43], [56]. See also [3.87]–[3.88], [6.68].
308   *Haber v Walker* [1963] VR 339, 350–51, 358.
309   *Reeves v Commissioner of Police of the Metropolis* [2000] 1 AC 360.
310   *Wrongs Act 1958* (Vic), s 17.
311   *Compensation to Relatives Act 1897* (NSW), ss 4, 7; *Compensation (Fatal Injuries) Act* (NT), ss 4, 8(2); *Civil Proceedings Act 2011* (Qld), s 62; *Civil Liability Act 1936* (SA), ss 24(1), (4), (7); *Fatal Accidents Act 1934* (Tas), ss 3, 5; *Fatal Accidents Act 1959* (WA), s 6(1A), sch 2.
312   *Compensation to Relatives Act 1897* (NSW), s 5; *Compensation (Fatal Injuries) Act* (NT), s 8(1); *Civil Proceedings Act 2011* (Qld), s 65(1); *Civil Liability Act 1936* (SA), s 25; *Fatal Accidents Act 1934* (Tas), s 6(1); *Wrongs Act 1958* (Vic), s 20(1); *Fatal Accidents Act 1959* (WA), s 7.

personal representative.[313] Unreasonable conduct on the part of a dependant contributing to the death of the deceased excludes recovery by that dependant under common law principles,[314] but now leads only to a reduction of that dependant's recovery under the contributory negligence statutes considered at [6.91].[315] Recovery by other dependants remains unaffected.[316]

The court usually makes one award,[317] but is required to specify the share of each dependant.[318] In determining the global sum, the court may assess the loss suffered by each dependant individually,[319] and may separately assess pre-trial loss and post-trial loss.[320] Where more than one dependant suffer loss of the same benefit (for example, the surviving spouse[321] and children lose the benefit of the deceased performing certain services in the household), the loss is compensated only once.[322] The legislation prescribes no criteria as to the apportionment of the award between the dependants. The whole award can be given to one of several dependants alone.[323]

[7.97]

Compensation must be proportional to the loss suffered by the dependants.[324] The High Court of Australia explained this in *Horton v Byrne*:

[7.98]

> It is compensation for material loss. The compensation should represent the balance of the loss, reduced to terms of money, which the deceased's relatives incur in consequence of his death after deducting the pecuniary gains which on the other hand accrue to them from that event. The loss is usually a prospective one and all reasonable expectations of material advantage are to be taken into account.[325]

---

313   *Compensation to Relatives Act 1897* (NSW), s 4(1); *Compensation (Fatal Injuries) Act* (NT), s 8(2); *Civil Proceedings Act 2011* (Qld), s 65(2); *Civil Liability Act 1936* (SA), s 24(1); *Fatal Accidents Act 1934* (Tas), s 5; *Wrongs Act 1958* (Vic), s 17(1); *Fatal Accidents Act 1959* (WA), s 6(1B).

314   *Kain & Shelton Ltd v Virgo* (1956) 97 CLR 230, 245 (Fullagar J, dissenting); *Benjamin v Currie* [1958] VR 259, 260–61. See also *Trueman v Hydro-Electric Power Commission of Ontario* [1924] 1 DLR 405; GL Williams, *Joint Torts and Contributory Negligence* (Stevens & Sons 1951) 443.

315   *Kain & Shelton Ltd v Virgo* (1956) 97 CLR 230, 246–47 (Fullagar J, dissenting); *Benjamin v Currie* [1958] VR 259, 262.

316   *Trueman v Hydro-Electric Power Commission of Ontario* [1924] 1 DLR 405; *Dodds v Dodds* [1978] QB 543, 549–50.

317   Separate awards were made in *Fisher v Smithson* (1978) 17 SASR 223, 235–236, 240.

318   *Civil Law (Wrongs) Act 2002* (ACT), s 25(3); *Compensation to Relatives Act 1897* (NSW), s 4(1); *Compensation (Fatal Injuries) Act* (NT), s 10(2); *Civil Proceedings Act 2011* (Qld), s 65(5); *Civil Liability Act 1936* (SA), s 24(3); *Fatal Accidents Act 1934* (Tas), s 5; *Wrongs Act 1958* (Vic), s 17(1); *Fatal Accidents Act 1959* (WA), s 6(4).

319   *Gullifer v Pohto* [1978] 2 NSWLR 353, 362.

320   *Australian Telecommunications Commission v Parsons* (1985) 59 ALR 535, 540–42. A separate assessment of pre-trial loss and post-trial loss may be required for the purpose of awarding interest: *State Government Insurance Office (Qld) v Biemann* (1983) 154 CLR 539, 547–48.

321   In this section, the term 'spouse' includes any other domestic partner who is entitled to recover under the equivalent to Lord Campbell's Act.

322   *Fisher v Smithson* (1978) 17 SASR 223, 238; *Gullifer v Pohto* [1978] 2 NSWLR 353, 362–63.

323   *Gullifer v Pohto* [1978] 2 NSWLR 353, 366–67.

324   *Civil Law (Wrongs) Act 2002* (ACT), s 25(1); *Compensation to Relatives Act 1897* (NSW), s 4(1); *Compensation (Fatal Injuries) Act* (NT), s 10(1); *Civil Proceedings Act 2011* (Qld), s 64(3); *Civil Liability Act 1936* (SA), s 24(2); *Fatal Accidents Act 1934* (Tas), s 5; *Wrongs Act 1958* (Vic), s 17(1); *Fatal Accidents Act 1959* (WA), s 6(2).

325   (1956) 30 ALJR 583, 585; [1957] St R Qd 1, 8 (Dixon CJ, McTiernan, Webb and Taylor JJ), quoted with approval in *Nguyen v Nguyen* (1990) 169 CLR 245, 247 (Brennan J).

[7.99]   In all jurisdictions, the dependants are compensated for the loss of material benefits that they would expect to receive from the deceased were the latter still alive.[326] This includes not only the loss of actual payments made by the deceased to a dependant (or to a third party for the benefit of a dependant), but also the loss of prospective payments that a dependant would expect to receive in future were the deceased still alive.[327] A dependant to whom the deceased, if still alive, would in fact provide benefits suffers loss even if the deceased would not be obliged to provide those benefits.[328]

[7.100]   Loss of financial support is assessed in a similar manner as an injured person's loss of earning capacity, discussed at [7.38]–[7.46].[329] In assessing the income that the deceased would have received, income after tax is relevant,[330] and the statutory regulation of loss of earning capacity (see [7.47]–[7.49]) generally applies.[331] The income that a dependant obtained before the deceased's death may be relevant to the level of financial support that the deceased would have provided to that dependant.[332] In addition to the loss of payments that the deceased would have made *inter vivos*, the dependants may suffer loss on the ground that the deceased could have saved more money and left a larger estate as the dependants' inheritance.[333]

[7.101]   Another loss of material benefits is the loss of domestic services provided gratuitously by the deceased.[334] This loss is compensable not only where a substitute has been employed to provide those services, but also where those services are now provided by the dependants themselves (in particular the surviving spouse),[335] or gratuitously by a third party.[336] In the Northern Territory, the measure of the loss of services is the reasonable cost of employing a substitute.[337] In the other jurisdictions, the measure is the value to the dependants of the services provided by the deceased; that value cannot simply be equated with the cost of

---

326   *Public Trustee v Zoanetti* (1945) 70 CLR 266, 276–77.
327   *Taff Vale Railway Co v Jenkins* [1913] AC 1; *Chief Commissioner for Railways and Tramways (NSW) v Boylson* (1915) 19 CLR 505.
328   *Australian Telecommunications Commission v Parsons* (1985) 59 ALR 535, 544; *Taylor v Owners Strata Plan No 11564* [2012] NSWSC 842 [67]. See also *De Sales v Ingrilli* [2002] HCA 52, (2002) 212 CLR 338 [12]–[13] (Gleeson CJ).
329   *Lincoln v Gravil* (1954) 94 CLR 430, 438–39.
330   Ibid, 441–42.
331   However, the word 'claimant' in s 12(2) of the *Civil Liability Act 2002* (NSW) has been interpreted literally, so that in the dependants' action the statutory cap applies to the income of the claimant dependant rather than the deceased: *Taylor v Owners Strata Plan No 11564* [2014] HCA 9, (2014) 253 CLR 531.
332   *Dominish v Astill* [1979] 2 NSWLR 368, 387–88; *Halvorsen Boats Pty Ltd v Robinson* (1993) 31 NSWLR 1, 13–14.
333   *Henry v Perry* [1964] VR 174, 178; *Gullifer v Pohto* [1978] 2 NSWLR 353, 361.
334   *Swan v Williams (Demolition) Pty Ltd* (1987) 9 NSWLR 172, 187; *Nguyen v Nguyen* (1990) 169 CLR 245. In Victoria, loss of services is compensable only where the services were, or would be, provided for at least six hours per week and for at least six consecutive months: *Wrongs Act 1958* (Vic), s 19A.
335   *Seymour v British Paints (Australia) Pty Ltd* [1967] Qd R 227, 230 (Gibbs J, dissenting); *Thompson v Mandla* [1976] 2 NSWLR 307, 311, 318; *Nguyen v Nguyen* (1990) 169 CLR 245, 263. However, the prospect of the surviving spouse remarrying must be taken into account: *Nguyen v Nguyen* (1990) 169 CLR 245, 265; *Grosso (as executor of the estate of the late Wheeler) v Deaton* [2012] NSWCA 101, (2012) 61 MVR 349 [20].
336   *Nguyen v Nguyen* (1990) 169 CLR 245, 249; *NSW Insurance Ministerial Corporation v Willis* (1995) 35 NSWLR 668, 681; *Grosso (as executor of the estate of the late Wheeler) v Deaton* [2012] NSWCA 101 [16]–[19].
337   *Compensation (Fatal Injuries) Act* (NT), s 10(3)(d) and (e).

employing a substitute.[338] The amount of loss to be considered under this head is capped in Victoria.[339] In the Northern Territory, a surviving spouse or de facto partner can also recover for loss of consortium.[340]

In assessing the dependants' loss of material benefits, account must be taken of contingencies or vicissitudes of life. There are two types of vicissitudes: those that might affect the deceased's ability or willingness to provide support to the dependants were the deceased still alive, and those that might affect the dependants' need for that support. With regard to the first type, a surviving spouse who was separated from the deceased can recover in respect of loss of financial support if there was a substantial chance of reconciliation, even if that chance was less than 50%.[341] With regard to the second type, where, prior to the deceased's death, the surviving spouse did not work despite being able to do so, the chance of the surviving spouse now taking up employment is brought into account where this chance exists irrespective of the deceased's death,[342] but is ignored where the surviving spouse would be unlikely to take up employment were the deceased still alive.[343]   [7.102]

Legislation in the Northern Territory, Queensland and Victoria prohibits a consideration of the prospect of a surviving spouse or domestic partner repartnering after trial.[344] The law in the other jurisdictions is governed by *De Sales v Ingrilli*,[345] where the High Court of Australia held that the prospect of repartnering warrants a separate discount only where there is evidence that a new relationship has been formed or is proposed and that it will bring financial benefits to the deceased's dependants; otherwise, it cannot be said whether a new relationship would be to the financial advantage or disadvantage of the deceased's dependants.   [7.103]

In Queensland and Victoria, the loss of benefits that the dependants could expect to receive from the deceased is the only type of pecuniary loss compensable. There is no compensation for other pecuniary losses suffered by the dependants as a result of the death, such as the cost of fund management or funeral expenses.[346] In New South Wales, funeral expenses are recoverable.[347] In the remaining jurisdictions, the dependants can recover for expenses incurred in respect of the deceased's funeral or medical treatment for the injury that resulted in the death.[348]   [7.104]

---

338   *Rowe v Scanlan* [1969] 1 NSWR 43, 45; *Nguyen v Nguyen* (1990) 169 CLR 245, 249, 257, 265.
339   *Wrongs Act 1958* (Vic), s 19B. The maximum per week of lost services is the average weekly earnings of all employees in Victoria, or the relevant proportion of that amount where the deceased, if still alive, would provide less than 40 hours of services per week.
340   *Compensation (Fatal Injuries) Act* (NT), s 10(3)(c).
341   *Davies v Taylor* [1974] AC 207, where it was also said that the measure of loss in those circumstances is the value of the lost benefits reduced by the chance of non-reconciliation.
342   *Roads and Traffic Authority v Cremona* [2001] NSWCA 338, (2001) 35 MVR 190 [136].
343   *Carroll v Purcell* (1961) 107 CLR 73; *Cowland v Telkesi* [2000] SASC 156, (2000) 209 LSJS 70 [18]–[27].
344   *Compensation (Fatal Injuries) Act* (NT), s 10(4)(h); *Civil Proceedings Act 2011* (Qld), ss 67(2) and (3), 68(4)(a); *Wrongs Act 1958* (Vic), s 19(2)–(4).
345   [2002] HCA 52, (2002) 212 CLR 338. Applied in *Campbell v Li-Pina* [2007] WASCA 64, (2007) 47 MVR 279 [37].
346   *Public Trustee v Zoanetti* (1945) 70 CLR 266, 275; *Rouse v Shepherd* (1994) 35 NSWLR 250, 267–68.
347   *Compensation to Relatives Act 1897* (NSW), s 3(2).
348   *Civil Law (Wrongs) Act 2002* (ACT), s 25(4)–(6); *Compensation (Fatal Injuries) Act* (NT), s 10(3); *Civil Liability Act 1936* (SA), s 24(2A); *Fatal Accidents Act 1934* (Tas), s 10(2); *Fatal Accidents Act 1959* (WA), s 5(1).

[7.105]   With the exception of the Northern Territory,[349] any benefit accruing to the dependants by virtue of the deceased's death must in principle be deducted from the loss suffered.[350] The defendant bears the onus of proof in that respect.[351] Income now earned by a surviving spouse who did not work before the deceased's death is treated in the same way as the chance of employment of a surviving spouse. Thus, the income is not deducted unless the surviving spouse would have taken up employment even if the deceased were still alive.[352] A surviving spouse who was the sole 'breadwinner' obtains the benefit of being relieved from the obligation of financially supporting the deceased.[353]

[7.106]   The loss suffered by dependants who are heirs of the deceased is generally reduced by their share in the damages (if any) that the deceased's estate can claim in respect of the death, for example funeral expenses (see [7.92]).[354] In Western Australia, this rule does not apply to damages for non-pecuniary loss suffered by the deceased where the death is attributable to the inhalation of asbestos.[355] In South Australia and Victoria, the rule does not apply to damages for non-pecuniary loss suffered by the deceased where the death was caused by any dust-related condition.[356]

[7.107]   Dependants who are heirs of the deceased have also obtained a benefit by receiving their inheritance from the deceased earlier than without the defendant's wrong.[357] This is a benefit even in respect of assets that the dependants already used before the deceased's death (for example, the family home), since the dependants now have the right to dispose of the assets.[358] However, the fact that they already used the assets before the deceased's death limits the amount of the benefit obtained from the accelerated inheritance of the assets.[359] In the Australian Capital Territory and the Northern Territory, no deduction can be made to reflect the acquisition of an interest in the family home or its household contents.[360] In Tasmania, the value of the inheritance cannot be deducted unless it exceeds $250 000.[361]

---

349   *Compensation (Fatal Injuries) Act* (NT), s 10(4)(g).
350   *Public Trustee v Zoanetti* (1945) 70 CLR 266, 271, 276–77, 290.
351   *Mead v Clarke Chapman & Co Ltd* [1956] 1 WLR 76, 81–82, 84; *Mockridge v Watson* [1960] VR 405.
352   The view that the income should never be deducted, even if the surviving spouse would have returned to work irrespective of the deceased's death, was taken in *Burley v Trewartha* (1976) 13 SASR 514.
353   *Nguyen v Nguyen* (1990) 169 CLR 245, 257.
354   *Davies v Powell Duffryn Associated Collieries Ltd* [1942] AC 601; *Public Trustee v Zoanetti* (1945) 70 CLR 266, 281 (Dixon J); *BI (Contracting) Pty Ltd v Strikwerda* [2005] NSWCA 288, (2005) 3 DDCR 149 [20]–[22].
355   *Fatal Accidents Act 1959* (WA), s 5(2)(d).
356   *Civil Liability Act 1936* (SA), s 24(2aa)(f); *Wrongs Act 1958* (Vic), s 19(1A). Legislation to the same effect has been recommended for NSW: New South Wales Law Reform Commission, *Compensation to Relatives*, Report No 131 (1999).
357   *Gullifer v Pohto* [1978] 2 NSWLR 353, 361.
358   *Carroll v Purcell* (1961) 107 CLR 73, 77; *Black v Walden* [2008] NSWCA 108, (2008) Aust Torts Reports 81–950 [61]–[62].
359   *Black v Walden* [2008] NSWCA 108, (2008) Aust Torts Reports 81–950 [63]–[65].
360   *Civil Law (Wrongs) Act 2002* (ACT), s 26(e); *Compensation (Fatal Injuries) Act* (NT), s 10(4)(e).
361   *Fatal Accidents Act 1934* (Tas), s 10(1)(b).

Benefits that the surviving spouse or domestic partner is receiving, or has received, from a new partner are sometimes deductible. A deduction is excluded in the Northern Territory and Victoria for any purpose,[362] and in Queensland for the purpose of assessing the loss suffered by a child of the deceased and the surviving spouse or domestic partner.[363] Otherwise, a deduction is made even though the chance of the surviving spouse or domestic partner repartnering after trial is ignored.[364] The difference can be justified on the ground that the amount of benefits obtained from a new partner can be readily ascertained where a new partnership already exists, but is a matter of speculation where it does not.

[7.108]

Charitable donations (whether given by relatives, friends or the public) are generally ignored,[365] on the ground that the dependants had no reasonable expectation of receiving the donation.[366] This permits a deduction where the dependants have a reasonable expectation of the donation.[367] It is preferable to deduct a donation if, and only if, the donor (exceptionally) intends to benefit the wrongdoer. Domestic services gratuitously rendered by third parties are also ignored.[368] But the fact that a dependant is no longer required to render services to the deceased is a deductible benefit.[369]

[7.109]

Under the general principle, deductible benefits would include moneys payable to a dependant on the deceased's death by virtue of an insurance contract, a superannuation scheme, an employment contract or a social security scheme, for example a widow's pension. However, a deduction of such payments from the compensable loss is excluded in all jurisdictions.[370]

[7.110]

The standard version of Lord Campbell's Act provisions allows for the recovery of pecuniary loss only.[371] In the Northern Territory, compensation for the dependants' non-pecuniary loss ('solatium') may be awarded.[372] There is no limit on the amount that may be awarded as a solatium.[373] In South Australia, the court may award a solatium, up to a specified maximum amount, to the deceased's spouse or domestic partner and, where the deceased was an 'infant', to the deceased's parents.[374] The award of a solatium is not automatic in either jurisdiction, but based on the circumstances of each eligible dependant.[375] Relevant factors include the

[7.111]

---

362   *Compensation (Fatal Injuries) Act* (NT), s 10(4)(h); *Wrongs Act 1958* (Vic), s 19(2)–(4).
363   *Civil Proceedings Act 2011* (Qld), s 68(4)(b).
364   *De Sales v Ingrilli* [2002] HCA 52, (2002) 212 CLR 338; *Civil Proceedings Act 2011* (Qld), s 67(4)–(6).
365   *Wilson v Rutter* (1955) 73 WN (NSW) 294, 298–99.
366   *Papowski v Commonwealth* [1958] SASR 293, 295; *Mockridge v Watson* [1960] VR 405; *Hay v Hughes* [1975] QB 790, 809.
367   *Papowski v Commonwealth* [1958] SASR 293, 295; *Mockridge v Watson* [1960] VR 405.
368   *Hay v Hughes* [1975] QB 790, 809
369   *Nguyen v Nguyen* (1990) 169 CLR 245, 247.
370   *Civil Law (Wrongs) Act 2002* (ACT), s 26; *Compensation to Relatives Act 1897* (NSW), s 3(3); *Compensation (Fatal Injuries) Act* (NT), s 10(4)(a)–(c); *Civil Proceedings Act 2011* (Qld), s 70; *Civil Liability Act 1936* (SA), s 24(2aa); *Fatal Accidents Act 1934* (Tas), s 10(1); *Wrongs Act 1958* (Vic), s 19(1); *Fatal Accidents Act 1959* (WA), s 5(2).
371   *Taff Vale Railway Co v Jenkins* [1913] AC 1, 4, 10; *Public Trustee v Zoanetti* (1945) 70 CLR 266, 275, 276, 289–90; *Nguyen v Nguyen* (1990) 169 CLR 245, 253. For criticism, see I Field, 'In Mourning of Bereavement Damages' (2014) 22 Torts LJ 95.
372   *Compensation (Fatal Injuries) Act* (NT), s 10(3)(f).
373   *Cook v Cavanagh* (1981) 10 NTR 35, 37.
374   *Civil Liability Act 1936* (SA), ss 28–30.
375   *Cook v Cavanagh* (1981) 10 NTR 35, 36, 38–39.

relationship between the deceased and the dependant,[376] and the prospect of a surviving spouse or domestic partner to obtain happiness in a new relationship,[377] but not the wealth or standing of a dependant.[378]

---

376   *Taverner v Swanbury* [1944] SASR 194, 198; *Hall v Alice Springs Veterinary Clinic Pty Ltd* (1989) 98 FLR 85, 93.

377   *Rafferty v Barclay* [1942] SASR 147, 156.

378   Ibid.

COMPENSATION UNDER THE AUSTRALIAN CONSUMER LAW

I   Introduction

[8.1]   The Australian Consumer Law ('ACL') is the national consumer law and applies across Australia. It came into force on 1 January 2011. At the same time, the *Trade Practices Act 1974* (Cth) changed its name to *Competition and Consumer Act 2010* (Cth). Schedule 2 of that Act now contains the ACL. The ACL replaced a number of consumer protection provisions in federal, state and territory laws. It was enacted with the cooperation of the federal, state and territory governments. This cooperation was necessary since the Commonwealth lacks the power to comprehensively legislate on consumer law.

[8.2]   The ACL applies as a federal law, or as a law of the relevant state or territory, or both. It is not necessary here to go into all the details of the demarcation since the same body of law generally applies.[1] Broadly, the ACL applies as a law of the Commonwealth to the conduct of corporations and certain natural persons,[2] and applies as a law of a state or territory to the conduct of corporate and natural persons with a connection to the relevant jurisdiction. The application of the ACL as a federal law and the application of the ACL as a state or territory law are not mutually exclusive (where there is no conflict).[3]

[8.3]   The *Competition and Consumer Act 2010* (Cth) makes provision for liability under the ACL as a law of the Commonwealth. Most of those provisions are not mirrored by state and territory law. Where the court has jurisdiction to apply the ACL both as federal law and as state or territory law, the question arises how a conflict between the two is to be resolved. Based on the supremacy of federal law pursuant to s 109 of the Australian Constitution, s 139A of the *Competition and Consumer Act 2010* (Cth) was in one case given priority over s 5J of the *Civil Liability Act 2002* (WA).[4] In that case, the application of the *Competition and Consumer Act 2010* (Cth) benefitted the consumer. Where an application of the Act would disadvantage the consumer, it could be argued that the Act, which aims to protect consumers, tolerates state and territory laws that are more favourable to consumers. Where a claim under the ACL is concurrent with a common law claim subject to the civil liability statute of a state or territory, the plaintiff can choose the more favourable cause of action, even if the ACL applies as federal law.[5]

[8.4]   The ACL does not apply to the supply of financial services or financial products.[6] However, the *Australian Securities and Investments Commission Act 2001* (Cth), which regulates financial services and financial products, mirrors certain provisions of the ACL, in particular those on misleading or deceptive conduct[7] and unconscionable conduct.[8] Section 1041H of

---

1   A distinction may be necessary for the question of jurisdiction. For example, the Federal Court has direct jurisdiction to apply the ACL as a law of the Commonwealth but not as a law of a state or territory: *Walker v Sell* [2016] FCA 1259, (2016) 245 FCR 308 [83]. The NSW Civil and Administrative Tribunal has jurisdiction to apply the ACL as a law of NSW but not as a law of the Commonwealth: *Herbert v American Express Australia Ltd* [2016] NSWCATAP 47 [46].

2   *Competition and Consumer Act 2010* (Cth), ss 5, 6, 131.

3   Eg *Walker v Sell* [2016] FCA 1259, (2016) 245 FCR 308 [82]; *NTF Group Pty Ltd v PA Putney Finance Australia Pty Ltd* [2017] NSWSC 1194, (2017) 324 FLR 261 [9]–[10].

4   *Lightfoot v Rockingham Wild Encounters Pty Ltd* [2017] WADC 62, (2017) 92 SR (WA) 168 [182]–[193].

5   *Alameddine v Glenworth Valley Horse Riding Pty Ltd* [2015] NSWCA 219, (2015) 324 ALR 355 [72].

6   *Competition and Consumer Act 2010* (Cth), s 131A.

7   *Australian Securities and Investments Commission Act 2001* (Cth), s 12DA.

8   Ibid, ss 12CA–12CC.

the *Corporations Act 2001* (Cth) also prohibits misleading or deceptive conduct in relation to a financial product or a financial service. Insofar as those two statutes mirror the ACL, the rules are largely identical to those applying to the ACL.

The most important provisions of the ACL for the purposes of this chapter are ss 18, 20 and 236 to 238. Section 18 provides: 'A person must not, in trade or commerce, engage in conduct that is misleading or deceptive or is likely to mislead or deceive'. Section 20 provides: 'A person must not, in trade or commerce, engage in conduct that is unconscionable, within the meaning of the unwritten law from time to time'.[9] Sections 18 and 20 are contained in Chapter 2 of the ACL. Part 5-2 of the ACL sets out the remedies for a contravention of a provision of Chapter 2 (or Chapter 3 or 4). Section 236(1) in Part 5-2 provides: **[8.5]**

If:

    (a)   a person (the claimant) suffers loss or damage because of the conduct of another person; and

    (b)   the conduct contravened a provision of Chapter 2 or 3;

the claimant may recover the amount of the loss or damage by action against that other person, or against any person involved in the contravention.

Section 236 gives the plaintiff an entitlement to compensation for loss suffered. Sections 237 to 239 empower the court to make any other order that the court thinks appropriate against the same persons. But these orders are in the court's discretion. One of the orders that a court can make under ss 237 and 238 is an order of compensation for loss that the plaintiff is likely to suffer.[10] Such compensation should in principle be assessed in the same manner as compensation for actual loss pursuant to s 236.   **[8.6]**

The provisions mentioned have not been considered in many cases yet because the ACL came into force only a few years ago and does not generally apply retrospectively. However, the provisions are identical or very similar to provisions previously contained in the *Trade Practices Act 1974* (Cth)[11] and the fair trading Acts of the states and territories. The previous provisions have been considered in a number of cases. It was the intention of Parliament that jurisprudence developed for provisions of the *Trade Practices Act 1974* (Cth) remains relevant to the interpretation and understanding of the equivalent provisions in the ACL.[12] This chapter will therefore look at a number of cases decided under the *Trade Practices Act 1974* (Cth). However, reference will always be made to the current provisions in the ACL and other parts of the *Competition and Consumer Act 2010* (Cth).   **[8.7]**

With the exception of South Australia, all jurisdictions, including the Commonwealth, have provisions regulating compensation for death or personal injury in certain actions taken under the ACL. For the purpose of the *Competition and Consumer Act 2010* (Cth), 'personal injury' does not include the impairment of a person's mental condition short of a recognised   **[8.8]**

---

9   Section 21 prohibits unconscionable conduct (not confined to its meaning under the unwritten law) in certain circumstances. Section 20 does not apply to conduct prohibited by s 21.

10   ACL, s 243(e).

11   *Trade Practices Act 1974* (Cth), ss 51AA, 52, 82 and 87.

12   Explanatory Memorandum, Trade Practices Amendment (Australian Consumer Law) Bill (No 2) 2010 (Cth) [3.11], [15.14]. See also *Acts Interpretation Act 1901* (Cth), s 15AC.

psychiatric illness: s 4(1). In actions taken under Part 2-1 (misleading or deceptive conduct) or Part 3-1 (unfair practices) of the ACL, compensation for death or personal injury cannot be claimed or awarded at all if the ACL applies as a law of the Commonwealth and the death or injury does not result from smoking or other use of tobacco products,[13] or if the ACL applies as a law of New South Wales.[14]

[8.9]   In actions under Part 2-2 (unconscionable conduct), Part 3-3 (safety of consumer goods), Part 3-4 (information standards), Part 3-5 (liability of manufacturers of goods with safety defects) or Division 2 of Part 5-4 (action for damages against manufacturers of goods) of the ACL, awards of personal injury damages are regulated by Part VIB of the *Competition and Consumer Act 2010* (Cth) if the ACL applies as a law of the Commonwealth and the death or injury does not result from smoking or other use of tobacco products,[15] and may be regulated by a civil liability statute if the ACL applies as a law of a state or territory; see [7.13]. The resolution of a conflict between the ACL as federal law and the ACL as state or territory law is discussed at [8.3]. Where a claim to which Part VIB of the *Competition and Consumer Act 2010* (Cth) applies is concurrent with a claim in negligence to which the civil liability statute of a state or territory applies, the plaintiff may choose the more favourable cause of action.[16] Compensation for personal injury is considered in Ch 7.

II   Assessment of compensation
A   General principles

[8.10]   Since s 236 of the ACL applies to a wide variety of contraventions, the aim of compensation can only be described in broad terms: that the plaintiff is to be placed in the same position as if the contravention had not occurred.[17] Indeed, the High Court of Australia has refused to adopt even that broad principle as applicable in every case.

[8.11]   The High Court used to take the view that misleading or deceptive conduct under statute (now s 18 of the ACL) is analogous to fraudulent or negligent misrepresentation, and that in assessing compensation for such conduct, the rules for assessing damages in tort, and not the rules for assessing damages in contract, are the appropriate guide in most, if not all, cases.[18] More recently, however, the High Court has said that compensation under what is now s 236, whether for misleading or deceptive conduct or other contraventions, should not be confined by analogy either with the law of contract, or tort or equitable remedies,[19] and that 'general

---

13   *Competition and Consumer Act 2010* (Cth), s 137C(1). Where the death or injury results from smoking or other use of tobacco products, the provisions of Part VIB of the Act on limitation periods and structured settlements apply: s 137C(2).

14   *Fair Trading Act 1987* (NSW), s 74(4).

15   *Competition and Consumer Act 2010* (Cth), s 87E(1). Where the death or injury results from smoking or other use of tobacco products, the provisions of Part VIB on limitation periods and structured settlements apply: s 87E(2).

16   *Alameddine v Glenworth Valley Horse Riding Pty Ltd* [2015] NSWCA 219, (2015) 324 ALR 355 [72].

17   *Wardley Australia Ltd v Western Australia* (1992) 175 CLR 514, 534 (Brennan J).

18   *Gates v City Mutual Life Assurance Society Ltd* (1986) 160 CLR 1, 6–7, 14; *Wardley Australia Ltd v Western Australia* (1992) 175 CLR 514, 534 (Brennan J); *Kizbeau Pty Ltd v WG & B Pty Ltd* (1995) 184 CLR 281, 290.

19   *Marks v GIO Australia Holdings Ltd* [1998] HCA 69, (1998) 196 CLR 494 [17], [38]; *Henville v Walker* [2001] HCA 52, (2001) 206 CLR 459 [18] (Gleeson CJ).

principles for assessing damages may have to give way altogether in particular cases to solutions best adapted to give the injured claimant an amount which will most fairly compensate for the wrong suffered'.[20]

It is true that the purpose of a statute takes priority over an analogy to common law concepts. However, the language of the statute is the ultimate 'boundary'. Sections 236 to 238 of the ACL provide for the compensation of loss suffered 'because of' a contravention of a relevant provision of the ACL, for example s 18 or s 20. This does not permit the court to award a sum of money in excess of loss caused by the contravention, even if such an award is considered 'fair'.   [8.12]

B   Compensation for misleading or deceptive conduct

1   Reliance loss as the general measure of compensation

The assessment of compensation for misleading or deceptive conduct under statute (now s 18 of the ACL) has been considered in a number of cases. Frequently in such cases, a false representation of fact by the defendant induces the plaintiff to enter into a contact with either the defendant or a third party. The contract is not as favourable to the plaintiff as the defendant led the plaintiff to believe. It must be determined whether compensation under s 236 of the ACL places the plaintiff in the same position as if the defendant's statement had been true (meeting the plaintiff's expectations), or in the same position as if the defendant had stated the truth, in which case the plaintiff would not have entered into the contract. Shortly, it must be determined whether the plaintiff's expectation loss or reliance loss is compensated.   [8.13]

The measure of compensation depends, or ought to depend, upon the nature of the wrong; see [2.4]. In the circumstances now under discussion, the wrong is the defendant's failure to state the true facts, which has induced the plaintiff to enter into a contract. The plaintiff should be placed in the position she would have been in had the defendant stated the truth; that is, the position as if the plaintiff had not entered into the contract. The plaintiff should not be placed in the same position she would have been in had the defendant's statement been true, because she would not have been in that position even if the defendant had stated the truth. In other words, the plaintiff should receive no compensation for the loss of the profit that the defendant's false statement led her to expect to make from the contract, because she would not have made that profit even if the defendant had stated the truth. Similarly, Colvin argues that the value of performance of a promise has only been lost if the plaintiff was *entitled* to performance. Sections 236 to 238 do not confer such an entitlement. They only provide for compensation for loss caused by being misled as to whether a promise will be performed, not for loss caused by a failure to perform the promise.[21]   [8.14]

The High Court of Australia has refused to compensate expectation loss in two cases. In *Gates v City Mutual Life Assurance Society Ltd*,[22] Mr Gates added a total-disability clause to his two existing life policies with the City Mutual Life Assurance Society Ltd ('CML'). CML had   [8.15]

---

20   *Henville v Walker* [2001] HCA 52, (2001) 206 CLR 459 [131] (McHugh J, with whom Gummow J agreed).
21   M Colvin, 'Tales of the Unexpected: Damages for Lost Expectations' (1997) 5 TPLJ 17.
22   (1986) 160 CLR 1.

stated that he could claim benefits if he could not work in *his* occupation for 90 days. In fact, the added clause provided for disability benefits only if he could not work in *any* occupation. Mr Gates sustained injury and could not attend to his occupation as a builder for 90 days. But he was still able to be employed in other occupations. CML refused to pay disability benefits. In Mr Gates' action under what is now s 18 of the ACL, the High Court held that he was not to be placed in the position he would have been in had his disability insurance contract with CML contained the represented clause. Rather, he was to be placed in the position he would have been in had he not entered into that contract. Mr Gates could not prove that, in that event, he would have taken out an insurance of the desired kind with another insurer since no insurer had offered that kind of insurance.

[8.16]   In *Marks v GIO Australia Holdings Ltd*,[23] borrowers entered into loan facilities with finance companies in reliance on representations that interest would be at a specified base rate plus a margin 'set' at 1.25% per annum. In fact, the loan contracts enabled the lenders to vary the margin on giving 90 days' notice. The lenders subsequently notified the borrowers that from a date more than 90 days later, the margin would change to 2.25% per annum. The lenders also gave the borrowers the opportunity to refinance without penalty before that date. No borrower did so. The borrowers brought an action for misleading or deceptive conduct under statute, and sought an order setting the interest margin at 1.25%, or compensation.

[8.17]   The High Court (Kirby J dissenting) refused to grant either remedy (even though misleading conduct had been found) on the grounds that the lenders did not seek to hold the borrowers to the facilities and that the borrowers had not suffered and were not likely to suffer any loss as a result of the lenders' misleading conduct. At the trial, no borrower said that, if the true terms had been known, he or she would not have borrowed at all or would have entered into alternative arrangements. The borrowers conceded that, even with the increased margin, the facility was more beneficial to them than any other available. Thus, even if the borrowers had known the true terms of the contract, they would not have been able to obtain a loan facility of the kind represented.

[8.18]   Two questions still remain. First, is it ever possible to compensate the plaintiff's expectation loss in an action for breach of s 18 of the ACL? Secondly, can the whole reliance loss be compensated where it exceeds expectation loss? These questions will now be investigated.

2   Compensation of expectation loss

[8.19]   In *Gates*, considered at [8.15], the High Court of Australia stated explicitly that compensation for expectation loss in an action for breach of what is now s 18 of the ACL does not accord with the nature of the wrong.[24] However, the High Court subsequently permitted compensation of expectation loss in *Murphy v Overton Investments Pty Ltd*.[25] The plaintiffs were contemplating moving into a unit in a retirement village owned by the defendant. In an information brochure, the defendant stated that there was an ongoing management and maintenance program at the village, and that the present budget figures indicated that the plaintiffs would be liable for weekly outgoings of $55.71. This estimate did not include all expenses incurred in the

---

23   (1998) 196 CLR 494.
24   (1986) 160 CLR 1, 14–15.
25   [2004] HCA 3, (2004) 216 CLR 388.

operation of the village. The plaintiffs executed a 99-year lease of the unit, which obliged them to contribute to outgoings. Some years later, the defendant began charging residents for *all* expenses incurred in operating the village.

In the plaintiffs' action under what is now s 18 of the ACL, the trial judge held that the [8.20] brochure had been misleading or deceptive, but that the plaintiffs had not proven any loss since there was no evidence of a difference between the price paid and the value of the property.[26] On appeal, the Full Federal Court said that the plaintiffs had failed to establish that there was any more advantageous retirement village available, and that, following *Marks* (see [8.16]), there was no loss or damage.[27] On further appeal, the High Court held that the plaintiffs 'are entitled to recover damages assessed by reference to the amount by which the obligation to meet outgoings is larger than the estimate led them to anticipate',[28] and remitted the assessment of damages to the trial judge.

It might be thought that the plaintiffs' loss in that case was reliance loss since they would [8.21] not have leased the property, and would have incurred no obligation to pay for outgoings, had the defendant included all items in its estimation of outgoings. However, it is necessary to look at the broader picture. After discovering the defendant's misleading conduct, the plaintiffs could have sold the property and claimed compensation for any wasted expenses. But they kept the property and claimed compensation in the amount of the undisclosed outgoings. Thus, they sought to be placed in the same position financially as if the contract had been as represented. It was the very type of claim – a claim for expectation loss – that had been made unsuccessfully in *Gates* and *Marks*.

Expectation loss has been compensated in some subsequent cases.[29] However, the West- [8.22] ern Australian Court of Appeal has overturned an award of expectation loss, distinguishing *Murphy* on the facts,[30] and in the vast majority of post-*Murphy* cases, reliance loss has been described as the usual measure of compensation for misleading or deceptive conduct under statute.[31] This view ought to prevail, and the High Court's decision in *Murphy* ought to be confined to the circumstances present in that case.

3   Compensation of reliance loss in excess of expectation loss

Can reliance loss be compensated in excess of expectation loss in an action for breach of s 18 of [8.23] the ACL? An affirmative answer was given obiter by a majority in the High Court of Australia in

---

26   [2000] FCA 801.

27   [2001] FCA 500, (2001) 112 FCR 182.

28   [2004] HCA 3, (2004) 216 CLR 388 [63] (Gleeson CJ, McHugh, Gummow, Kirby, Hayne, Callinan and Heydon JJ).

29   *Dalecoast Pty Ltd v Guardian International Pty Ltd* [2004] WASC 82 [36]; *Callander v Ladang Jalong (Australia) Pty Ltd* [2005] WASC 159; *Abigroup Contractors Pty Ltd v Sydney Catchment Authority (No 3)* [2006] NSWCA 282, (2006) 67 NSWLR 341 [111]–[115].

30   *Warwick Entertainment Centre Pty Ltd v Alpine Holdings Pty Ltd* [2005] WASCA 174, (2005) 224 ALR 134 [102], [147]–[148].

31   Eg *Havyn Pty Ltd v Webster* [2005] NSWCA 182, (2005) 12 BPR 22,837 [117]; *Bonett v Barron & Dowling Property Group Pty Ltd* [2006] NSWSC 975, (2006) 67 NSWLR 475 [140]–[141]; *Rosebanner Pty Ltd v Energy Australia* [2009] NSWSC 43, (2009) 223 FLR 460 [557]–[558]; *North East Equity Pty Ltd v Proud Nominees Pty Ltd* [2010] FCAFC 60, (2010) 269 ALR 262 [125]–[129]; *Bateman v Face Accountants Pty Ltd* [2010] NSWSC 1355, (2010) 81 ATR 102 [35]; *Sunland Waterfront (BVI) Ltd v Prudentia Investments Pty Ltd (No 2)* [2012] VSC 239, (2012) 266 FLR 243 [360].

Henville v Walker.[32] The plaintiff architect obtained advice from the defendant real estate agent about the purchase of a property in Albany for the purpose of the construction of three home units. The defendant stated that there was a demand for quality units in the town and that each unit would fetch at least $250 000. In fact, there was no demand for quality units in that price range. The plaintiff prepared a feasibility study, which substantially underestimated the costs of the project. If either the selling price or the costs had been estimated accurately, it would have been clear that the project was not profitable. The plaintiff went ahead with the project and spent some $865 000 on it. The three units could only be sold for a total of $545 000. Thus, the plaintiff's reliance loss was $320 000 (the difference between $865 000 and $545 000), but the expectation loss was only $205 000 (the difference between $750 000 and $545 000).

[8.24]   In an action under what is now s 18 of the ACL, the trial judge awarded $205 000 as compensation. In the High Court, the defendant sought an exclusion or reduction of the award on the ground that the plaintiff's carelessness in estimating the costs of the project had contributed to the plaintiff's loss. The plaintiff did not seek to recover more than $205 000. The High Court unanimously rejected a reduction of the award,[33] but was divided as to whether a claim for compensation of the whole reliance loss would have succeeded. McHugh, Gummow and Hayne JJ, who formed the majority, gave an affirmative answer on the ground that the whole of the reliance loss was what the plaintiff had suffered in consequence of altering his position by reason of the defendant's breach.

[8.25]   The minority judges would not have increased the amount awarded by the trial judge. Gleeson CJ regarded the plaintiff's carelessness as a supervening cause of the loss in the amount by which the plaintiff had underestimated the costs of the project, and said that the trial judge's limitation of recovery to expectation loss had been an expedient, if inexact, method of identifying the amount which was referable to the defendant's misrepresentation.[34] Gaudron J took the view that the defendant could have, but had not, proved that components of the plaintiff's loss were directly referable to his own conduct; alternatively, the defendant could limit his liability to the amount of expectation loss because the loss referable to the defendant's breach could not have been more than that.[35]

[8.26]   On principle, recovery for reliance loss caused by a breach of s 18 of the ACL should always be capped at the amount of expectation loss. It is true that the breach is a factual case of the whole of the reliance loss. But any reliance loss that exceeds expectation loss falls outside the scope of the duty breached. The defendant is liable for making a false representation of fact, and an award in the amount of expectation loss (although not being an award *for* expectation loss) is sufficient to place the plaintiff in the same position as if the facts were as represented.

C   Non-pecuniary loss

[8.27]   Section 236 of the ACL provides for the compensation of 'loss' and does not confine this to pecuniary loss. Section 13 of the ACL provides that 'loss' includes 'injury'. In the absence of a

---

32   [2001] HCA 52, (2001) 206 CLR 459.
33   At that time, the *Trade Practices Act 1974* (Cth) contained no provision on contributory negligence. Such a provision was inserted later and is now in the *Competition and Consumer Act 2010* (Cth); see [8.46].
34   [2001] HCA 52, (2001) 206 CLR 459 [37]–[44].
35   Ibid, [72].

statutory provision to the contrary, non-pecuniary loss resulting from a contravention of, for example, s 18 or s 20 is to be compensated.[36] Under the *Trade Practices Act 1974* (Cth), compensation has occasionally been awarded for distress and disappointment,[37] and loss of reputation,[38] resulting from misleading or deceptive conduct. None of those cases involved personal injury in the sense of physical injury or a recognised psychiatric illness.

Where the ACL applies as the law of a state or territory, the civil liability statute of the relevant jurisdiction may restrict the recoverability of non-pecuniary loss. A claim under the ACL as a law of New South Wales is subject to the provisions in Part 2 (on personal injury damages) of the *Civil Liability Act 2002* (NSW) within the territorial application of the latter Act.[39] Part 2 applies to any cause of action not excluded by s 3B of the Act,[40] and s 3B does not exclude claims under the ACL.[41] Section 11 defines 'injury' as including the 'impairment of a person's physical or mental condition', and the NSW Court of Appeal has held that this includes anxiety, disappointment, distress and inconvenience.[42] Compensation for anxiety and the like is thus subject to s 16 of the Act, which excludes compensation for loss of less than 15% of the most extreme case; see [7.65]. This threshold will rarely be met in the absence of physical injury or a recognised psychiatric illness.[43]

[8.28]

The position may be similar where the ACL applies as a law of another state or a territory and the provisions of the relevant civil liability statute on personal injury damages, which include restrictions on the recovery for mental harm and non-pecuniary loss, apply to claims under the ACL; see [7.13], [7.19]–[7.20].

[8.29]

A claim under the ACL as a law of the Commonwealth is not subject to the provisions of the civil liability statute of a state or territory.[44] Certain claims are subject to the restrictions on personal injury damages in Part VIB and s 137C of the *Competition and Consumer Act 2010* (Cth); see [8.8]–[8.9]. However, s 4(1) of that Act provides that the term 'personal injury' in the Act 'does not include an impairment of a person's mental condition unless the impairment

[8.30]

---

36   *Wu v Great Wall Travel Service Pty Ltd* [2014] NSWCATCD 50 [69], [75]; *Harmonious Blend Building Corporation Pty Ltd v Keene* [2015] VSC 276 [39].

37   *Zoneff v Elcom Credit Union Ltd* (1990) 6 ANZ Ins Cas 61–023, 76,852; *Walker v Citigroup Global Markets Pty Ltd* [2005] FCA 1678, (2005) 226 ALR 114 [137]–[138]; *Shahid v Australasian College of Dermatologists* [2008] FCAFC 72, (2008) 168 FCR 46 [30], [231]; *New South Wales Lotteries Corporation Pty Ltd v Kuzmanovski* [2011] FCAFC 106, (2011) 195 FCR 234 [119]–[123].

38   *Walker v Citigroup Global Markets Pty Ltd* [2005] FCA 1678, (2005) 226 ALR 114 [135]–[136], [138].

39   *Ueda v Ecruising Pty Ltd* [2014] NSWCATCD 30 [183]; *Wu v Great Wall Travel Service Pty Ltd* [2014] NSWCATCD 50 [71]–[72], [74].

40   *Civil Liability Act 2002* (NSW), s 11A(1), (2).

41   The provisions of the *Civil Liability Act 2002* (NSW) prevail over inconsistent provisions of the *Fair Trading Act 1987* (NSW); see s 4(6) and sch 1 of the latter Act and *Ueda v Ecruising Pty Ltd* [2014] NSWCATCD 30 [171].

42   *New South Wales v Ibbett* [2005] NSWCA 445, (2005) 65 NSWLR 168 [124], [211]–[212]; *New South Wales v Corby* [2010] NSWCA 27, (2010) 76 NSWLR 439 [41]; *Insight Vacations Pty Ltd v Young* [2010] NSWCA 137, (2010) 78 NSWLR 641.

43   See *Ueda v Ecruising Pty Ltd* [2014] NSWCATCD 30 [185]: disappointment, inconvenience and discomfort arising from a 15-day tour through eastern Africa taking place in the wettest month of the year is below threshold. The threshold was – unconvincingly – held to be met in *Patel v Malaysian Airlines Australia Ltd (No 2)* [2011] NSWDC 4 [192] for distress and vexation suffered by the plaintiff as a result of his children being forced to leave 20kg of luggage at Mumbai Airport.

44   See, in relation to the then *Trade Practices Act 1974* (Cth), *Insight Vacations Pty Ltd v Young* [2010] NSWCA 137, (2010) 78 NSWLR 641 [76] (Spigelman CJ).

consists of a recognised psychiatric illness'. Thus, recovery for anxiety, disappointment, distress and inconvenience is not restricted.[45] Where non-pecuniary loss is recoverable under the ACL as federal law but not under the ACL as state or territory law, non-pecuniary loss should be recoverable (provided the court has jurisdiction to apply the ACL as federal law), either because federal law prevails or because the regime more favourable to the plaintiff prevails; see [8.3].

D   Certainty of loss and recovery for the loss of a chance

[8.31]   The principles on certainty of loss and the recovery for the loss of a chance, discussed at [2.57]–[2.117], apply under the ACL. In particular, the plaintiff may obtain compensation for the loss of a less than even chance of obtaining a profit. This is true, for example, for breaches of s 18[46] or s 20[47] of the ACL.

III   Attribution of responsibility
A   The common sense test of causation

[8.32]   Sections 236 to 238 of the ACL provide for the compensation of loss suffered 'because of' a contravention of a provision in Chapter 2, 3 or 4 of the ACL, such as s 18 or s 20. There is no further provision on the attribution of responsibility. The civil liability statutes of the Australian Capital Territory and the states prescribe a two-step test for the attribution of responsibility, consisting of factual causation and scope of liability; see [3.12]–[3.13]. But those provisions do not generally apply to claims under the ACL, although the provisions of some jurisdictions apply to a breach of s 60 of the ACL; see [3.16]. Where no civil liability statute applies, the attribution of responsibility depends upon the interpretation of the phrase 'because of' in ss 236 to 238.

[8.33]   The predecessors of ss 236 and 237 – ss 82 and 87 of the *Trade Practices Act 1974* (Cth) – provided for compensation to a person who has suffered, or is likely to suffer, 'loss or damage by conduct of another person'. The High Court of Australia held that this phrase took up the common sense concept of causation that applied at common law, unless a provision of the Act expressly or impliedly provided otherwise.[48] This approach has continued for those claims under the ACL that are not governed by a civil liability statute.[49] The High Court's statements in relation to the *Trade Practices Act* were made before the enactment of the civil liability statutes. Thus, the test of causation that applied to all common law wrongs at that time was applied to the *Trade Practices Act*. This alignment was appropriate since liability under the *Trade Practices Act* or now the ACL, in particular liability for misleading or deceptive conduct, is often concurrent with liability at common law.

---

45   *Harmonious Blend Building Corporation Pty Ltd v Keene* [2015] VSC 276 [39].
46   *Sellars v Adelaide Petroleum NL* (1994) 179 CLR 332, considered at [2.92]–[2.94].
47   *Bechara v Campbell-Williams* [2011] NSWCA 177 [14]–[15].
48   *Wardley Australia Ltd v Western Australia* (1992) 175 CLR 514, 525; *Henville v Walker* [2001] HCA 52, (2001) 206 CLR 459.
49   *Norcast SARL v Bradken Ltd (No 2)* [2013] FCA 235, (2013) 302 ALR 486 [326]; *Carter v Delgrove Holdings Pty Ltd* [2013] FCCA 783 [145]; *Caffey v Leatt-Hayter (No 3)* [2013] WASC 348 [326].

Today, it is only in the Northern Territory that the common sense test of causation still [8.34]
applies to every common law wrong. In all other jurisdictions, the civil liability statutes
prescribe the two-step test of factual causation and scope of liability for some common law
wrongs, in particular the breach of a contractual or tortious duty of care; see [3.15]–[3.16]. In
order to avoid an application of different tests of causation to concurrent causes of action, the
two-step test of causation prescribed by the civil liability statutes ought to be adopted at
common law and also be used in determining whether loss has been suffered 'because of'
conduct contravening a relevant provision of the ACL.

The following discussion of detailed rules on the attribution of responsibility under the ACL [8.35]
will distinguish between factual causation and the scope of liability. The extent to which
common law concepts have been applied in that process, either directly or by way of analogy,
will be examined.

B   Factual causation

The rules governing the determination of factual causation at common law and under the civil [8.36]
liability statutes (see [3.19]–[3.68]) apply in general to the determination of a historical link
between the defendant's contravention of the ACL and the plaintiff's loss. The 'but for' test has
been applied,[50] and it has been said that it is enough that the contravention has materially
contributed to the loss.[51] It should also be uncontroversial that each of multiple sufficient
wrongs constitutes a cause.

Liability for misleading or deceptive conduct requires that the plaintiff relied on the [8.37]
defendant's statement in making the decision that led to the loss. The defendant's statement need not be the sole, or even dominant, factor in the plaintiff's decision. It is
sufficient that the defendant's statement was one of a number of factors inducing the
plaintiff's decision, unless the contribution made by the defendant's statement was trivial.[52]
A finding of reliance may be made even though the plaintiff gave no direct evidence on
that issue, and little weight may be given to the plaintiff's testimony because it may be
self-serving.[53]

---

50   *McCarthy v McIntyre* [2000] FCA 1250 [49]–[50]; *Henville v Walker* [2001] HCA 52, (2001) 206 CLR
      459 [156] (Hayne J); *I & L Securities Pty Ltd v HTW Valuers (Brisbane) Pty Ltd* [2002] HCA 41, (2002)
      210 CLR 109 [58]; *Lactos Fresh Pty Ltd v Finishing Services Pty Ltd* [2006] FCA 219, (2006) ANZ ConvR 258
      [164]–[170]; *Stone v Chappel* [2017] SASCFC 72, (2017) 128 SASR 165 [353].
51   *Henville v Walker* [2001] HCA 52, (2001) 206 CLR 459 [106] (McHugh J); *Carter v Delgrove Holdings Pty
      Ltd* [2013] FCCA 783 [146].
52   *Ricochet Pty Ltd v Equity Trustees Executors and Agency Co Ltd* (1993) 41 FCR 229, 235; *Como
      Investments Pty Ltd (in liq) v Yenald Nominees Pty Ltd* (1997) ATPR 41–550, 43,619; *Smith v State
      Bank of New South Wales Ltd* [2001] FCA 946, (2001) 188 ALR 729 [54]–[55]; *Lord Buddha Pty Ltd (in liq)
      v Harpur* [2013] VSCA 101, (2013) 41 VR 159 [159]; *Stone v Chappel* [2017] SASCFC 72, (2017)
      128 SASR 165 [354]. See E Bant and JM Paterson, 'Statutory Causation in Cases of Misleading Conduct:
      Lessons from and for the Common Law' (2017) 24 Torts LJ 1.
53   *Dominelli Ford (Hurstville) Pty Ltd v Karmot Auto Spares Pty Ltd* (1992) 38 FCR 471, 483; *Barnes v
      Forty Two International Pty Ltd* [2014] FCAFC 152, (2014) 316 ALR 408 [184]; *Addenbrooke Pty Ltd v
      Duncan (No 2)* [2017] FCAFC 76, (2017) 348 ALR 1 [500]–[501].

C Scope of liability

1 Intervening cause

[8.38] Under the ACL, a defendant is usually liable for loss caused not only by the defendant's breach but also by an intervening event. The courts are reluctant to regard the chain of causation as being broken by an intervening event. As McHugh J in the High Court of Australia said in *Henville v Walker*:

> As long as the breach materially contributed to the damage, a causal connection will ordinarily exist even though the breach without more would not have brought about the damage. In exceptional cases, where an abnormal event intervenes between the breach and damage, it may be right as a matter of common sense to hold that the breach was not a cause of damage. But such cases are exceptional.[54]

[8.39] The plaintiff's failure to take reasonable care of her affairs is more likely to break the chain of causation than other events. But there must be a high degree of carelessness for this to occur.[55] In particular, liability for misleading or deceptive conduct is not negated merely because the plaintiff failed to check the accuracy of the defendant's statement.[56] Furthermore, the chain of causation is unlikely to be regarded as broken by an event to which the defendant's breach contributed.[57] In *Henville v Walker*,[58] only two of the five judges in the High Court of Australia thought that the plaintiff's underestimation of the costs of the project justified a limitation of the defendant's liability for reliance loss; see [8.23]–[8.25].

[8.40] The chain of causation was regarded as being broken by extraneous events in *Collins Marrickville Pty Ltd v Henjo Investments Pty Ltd*.[59] The plaintiff was induced to purchase a restaurant business by the defendant giving the impression that the number of seats legally permitted in the restaurant was significantly higher than it actually was. After the plaintiff had taken over the restaurant, some key employees left and the method of operation was changed. The business ran at a loss. It was found that the defendant had breached what is now s 18 of the ACL, but compensation for most of the loss incurred by the plaintiff in operating the business was denied on the ground that it had been occasioned by factors in connection with which there had been no misrepresentation.[60] However, the case was decided before *Henville v Walker* and may not satisfy the requirement of exceptionality laid down in that case; see [8.38].

---

54   [2001] HCA 52, (2001) 206 CLR 459 [106].

55   *Pavich v Bobra Nominees Pty Ltd* [1988] ATPR (Digest) 46–039, 53,124; *Munchies Management Pty Ltd v Belperio* (1988) 58 FCR 274, 286–87; *Argy v Blunts & Lane Cove Real Estate Pty Ltd* (1990) 26 FCR 112, 139; *Henville v Walker* [2001] HCA 52, (2001) 206 CLR 459 [13] (Gleeson CJ); *I & L Securities Pty Ltd v HTW Valuers (Brisbane) Pty Ltd* [2002] HCA 41, (2002) 210 CLR 109 [85] (McHugh J), [144] (Kirby J); *Lactos Fresh Pty Ltd v Finishing Services Pty Ltd* [2006] FCA 219, (2006) ANZ ConvR 258 [171].

56   *Sutton v AJ Thompson Pty Ltd (in liq)* (1987) 73 ALR 233, 240–41; *QCoal Pty Ltd v Cliffs Australia Coal Pty Ltd* [2009] QCA 358 [33]. It may be different where the facts represented were unlikely or improbable: *Ingot Capital Investments Pty Ltd v Macquarie Equity Capital Markets Ltd (No 6)* [2007] NSWSC 124, (2007) 63 ACSR 1 [458].

57   *Henville v Walker* [2001] HCA 52, (2001) 206 CLR 459 [122] (McHugh J); *Rural Export & Trading (WA) Pty Ltd v Hahnheuser* [2009] FCA 678, (2009) 177 FCR 398 [19].

58   [2001] HCA 52, (2001) 206 CLR 459.

59   [1987] ATPR 40–822.

60   Ibid, 48,904.

2   Foreseeability of the loss

Sections 236 to 238 of the ACL, like their predecessors, do not provide that loss must be [8.41] foreseeable to be recoverable, and the courts have refused to read such a requirement into the predecessor provisions.[61] Considering that the various prohibitions in the ACL differ significantly in their nature, it is indeed undesirable to read a general requirement of foreseeability into ss 236 to 238. Instead, liability ought to be limited by reference to the purpose of the particular prohibition in the particular circumstances.

3   The purpose of the provision contravened

With regard to what is now s 236 of the ACL, the High Court of Australia has said that 'notions [8.42] of "cause" as involved in a particular statutory regime are to be understood by reference to the statutory subject, scope and purpose'.[62] This should mean that compensation for loss factually caused by a contravention of a provision of the ACL may be denied on the ground that the provision does not aim to prevent the type of loss in the particular circumstances. An example might be *Collins Marrickville Pty Ltd v Henjo Investments Pty Ltd*,[63] considered at [8.40]. Conversely, the purpose of the provision in the particular circumstances may require the imposition of liability that might otherwise be denied on the ground that a certain event broke the chain of causation. This occurred in *Travel Compensation Fund v Tambree*.[64]

In that case, the Travel Compensation Fund ('the Fund') was established to safeguard [8.43] people who suffered uninsured loss by reason of an act or omission of a participating travel agent. Participation in the Fund required the agent to be financially sound. The defendants (an accountant and an auditor) prepared and audited the financial statements of a participating travel agent for a certain financial year, knowing that those statements would be submitted to the Fund. The statements were false and misleading as they failed to reveal the agent's financial difficulties. When the Fund eventually became aware of those difficulties, it terminated the agent's participation in the Fund, whereby the agent's licence to operate the business was also terminated. But the agent continued trading unlawfully for another eight weeks. The Fund paid compensation to persons who had dealt with the agent during those eight weeks. It sought reimbursement from the defendants, alleging negligence and a breach of what is now s 18 of the ACL.

A breach of duty was found. But the NSW Court of Appeal denied liability on the ground [8.44] that the agent's decision to continue trading unlawfully had broken the chain of causation

---

61   *Yorke v Ross Lucas Pty Ltd* (1982) 45 ALR 299, 320; *Tefbao Pty Ltd v Stannic Securities Pty Ltd* (1993) 118 ALR 565, 575; *Marks v GIO Australia Holdings Ltd* [1998] HCA 69, (1998) 196 CLR 494 [34]; *Kenny & Good Pty Ltd v MGICA (1992) Ltd* [1999] HCA 25, (1999) 199 CLR 413 [126] (Kirby and Callinan JJ); *Henville v Walker* [2001] HCA 52, (2001) 206 CLR 459 [66] (Gaudron J). A requirement of foreseeability was doubted in *Bartley v Myers* [2002] SASC 24, (2002) 83 SASR 183 [198]. Cf *Henville v Walker* [2001] HCA 52, (2001) 206 CLR 459 [136] (McHugh J, with whom Gummow J agreed).

62   *Allianz Australia Insurance Ltd v GSF Australia Pty Ltd* [2005] HCA 26, (2005) 221 CLR 568 [99] (Gummow, Hayne and Heydon JJ), approvingly quoted in *Travel Compensation Fund v Tambree* [2005] HCA 69, (2005) 224 CLR 627 [49] (Gummow and Hayne JJ). See also *Henville v Walker* [2001] HCA 52, (2001) 206 CLR 459 [96] (McHugh J); *I & L Securities Pty Ltd v HTW Valuers (Brisbane) Pty Ltd* [2002] HCA 41, (2002) 210 CLR 109 [26] (Gleeson CJ).

63   [1987] ATPR 40–822.

64   [2005] HCA 69, (2005) 224 CLR 627.

between the defendant's breach and the Fund's loss.[65] The High Court of Australia overturned the judgment, holding that the risk of a participating agent continuing to trade unlawfully was one of the reasons why the Fund needed accurate information about a participating agent's financial circumstances.[66]

4   The plaintiff's contribution to the loss

[8.45]   The common law doctrines of contributory negligence and mitigation, discussed at [3.130]–[3.138], do not apply directly to liability under the ACL. However, it has been said that the plaintiff's carelessness or disregard for her interests may be so dominant as to destroy the causal connection between the defendant's breach and the loss,[67] and that this may be determined by using concepts analogous to remoteness, mitigation or contributory negligence.[68]

A   CONTRIBUTORY NEGLIGENCE

[8.46]   Originally, the *Trade Practices Act 1974* (Cth) had no provision on contributory negligence, and the High Court of Australia refused to apply the common law doctrine of contributory negligence to liability under that Act.[69] Subsequently, a provision permitting an apportionment of liability in certain circumstances by virtue of contributory negligence was inserted into the Act. It is now s 137B of the *Competition and Consumer Act 2010* (Cth).[70] Section 137B permits an apportionment of liability according to each party's share in the responsibility for the loss if four requirements are satisfied. First, the plaintiff makes a claim under s 236(1) of the ACL.[71] Secondly, the loss to be apportioned is pure economic loss or property damage. Thirdly, the defendant has contravened s 18 of the ACL.[72] Fourthly, the defendant did not intend to cause the loss and did not fraudulently cause the loss. In apportioning liability between the parties, the court considers the degree of departure from the standard of care of the reasonable person, the relative importance of the acts of the parties causing the damages, and the whole conduct of the parties.[73]

---

65   *Tambree v Travel Compensation Fund* [2004] NSWCA 24, (2004) Aust Contract R 90–195.

66   [2005] HCA 69, (2005) 224 CLR 627.

67   *Pavich v Bobra Nominees Pty Ltd* [1988] ATPR (Digest) 46–039, 53,124; *Munchies Management Pty Ltd v Belperio* (1988) 58 FCR 274, 286–87; *Argy v Blunts & Lane Cove Real Estate Pty Ltd* (1990) 26 FCR 112, 139; *Henville v Walker* [2001] HCA 52, (2001) 206 CLR 459 [13] (Gleeson CJ); *I & L Securities Pty Ltd v HTW Valuers (Brisbane) Pty Ltd* [2002] HCA 41, (2002) 210 CLR 109 [85] (McHugh J), [144] (Kirby J).

68   *Pavich v Bobra Nominees Pty Ltd* [1988] ATPR (Digest) 46–039, 53,124; *Munchies Management Pty Ltd v Belperio* (1988) 58 FCR 274, 286–87; *I & L Securities Pty Ltd v HTW Valuers (Brisbane) Pty Ltd* [2002] HCA 41, (2002) 210 CLR 109 [144] (Kirby J).

69   *Henville v Walker* [2001] HCA 52, (2001) 206 CLR 459 [66], [140], [165] (considered at [8.23]–[8.25]); *I & L Securities Pty Ltd v HTW Valuers (Brisbane) Pty Ltd* [2002] HCA 41, (2002) 210 CLR 109 [50], [69], [213].

70   Equivalent provisions are s 12GF(1B) of the *Australian Securities and Investments Commission Act 2001* (Cth) and s 1041I(1B) of the *Corporations Act 2001* (Cth).

71   Section 137B of the *Competition and Consumer Act 2010* (Cth) cannot be circumvented by making a claim under s 237 of the ACL. The court would use its discretion under s 237 to limit compensation to the amount that could be recovered under s 236 of the ACL: *BHPB Freight Pty Ltd v Cosco Oceania Chartering Pty Ltd (No 3)* [2009] FCA 1087 [62]; *Khoury v Sidhu (No 2)* [2010] FCA 1320 [69]–[71], *Khoury v Sidhu* [2011] FCAFC 71.

72   Where the same conduct contravenes s 18 and another provision of the ACL, compensation under s 236 of the ACL for contravention of that other provision cannot be reduced: *Vero Lenders Mortgage Insurance Ltd v Taylor Byrne Pty Ltd* [2006] FCA 1430 [186].

73   *Bernhard v Ellis* [2016] WADC 10 [175].

Section 137B of the *Competition and Consumer Act 2010* (Cth) applies only where the ACL   [8.47]
applies as a law of the Commonwealth. The contributory negligence statutes of the states and
territories (see [6.91]) do not expressly provide for their applicability to claims under the ACL as
a state or territory law. It is unclear whether such claims are caught by the generic phrases
'liability in damages that arises under statute' in South Australia[74] or 'breach of statutory duty' in
three other jurisdictions.[75] Where state or territory legislation does not provide for an apportionment, the question arises how the conflict with s 137B is to be resolved (if the court has
jurisdiction to apply the ACL both as federal law and as state or territory law).[76] On one view,
federal law prevails; on another view, the *Competition and Consumer Act 2010* (Cth) tolerates
state and territory laws more favourable to the consumer; see [8.3].[77]

In the absence of specific statutory authorisation, liability under the ACL cannot be   [8.48]
apportioned. However, extreme carelessness on the plaintiff's part may constitute a *novus
actus interveniens*; see [8.39].

B   MITIGATION

Even though the common law doctrine of mitigation does not apply directly under the ACL, it   [8.49]
applies indirectly through the causal inquiry, as mentioned before. An action or omission of the
plaintiff after becoming aware of the defendant's breach may break the chain of causation, and
the decisive criterion must be the reasonableness of the plaintiff's conduct. As Hodgson J said
in *Tefbao Pty Ltd v Stannic Securities Pty Ltd*:

> If some part of the damage would not have occurred but for negligent conduct of the
> claimant, or failure to mitigate, then it may be appropriate to apply notions of reasonable-
> ness in assessing how much was in truth caused by the contravention ...[78]

Since the plaintiff's unreasonable conduct may break the chain of causation between the   [8.50]
defendant's contravention of the ACL and the plaintiff's loss, it has been recognised that a
plaintiff who is aware of the contravention has an obligation to take reasonable steps to
mitigate loss.[79] It is for the defendant to prove that the plaintiff has acted unreasonably.[80] This
resembles the 'avoidable loss' rule at common law, discussed at [3.134].

---

74   *Law Reform (Contributory Negligence and Apportionment of Liability) Act 2001* (SA), s 4(1)(c).
75   *Law Reform (Miscellaneous Provisions) Act 1956* (NT), s 15(1); *Wrongs Act 1954* (Tas), s 2; *Law Reform (Contributory Negligence and Tortfeasors' Contribution) Act 1947* (WA), s 3.
76   The question was left open in *Rennie Golledge Pty Ltd v Ballard* [2012] NSWCA 376, (2012) 82 NSWLR 231 [141].
77   Before the ACL was enacted, apportionment was unavailable under the fair trading Acts of the states even after apportionment had become available under the then *Trade Practices Act 1974* (Cth): *Perpetual Trustee Co Ltd v Milanex Pty Ltd (in liq)* [2011] NSWCA 367 [86]–[89]; *Caffey v Leatt-Hayter (No 3)* [2013] WASC 348 [491]–[493].
78   (1993) 118 ALR 565, 575.
79   *Finucane v New South Wales Egg Corporation* (1988) 80 ALR 486, 519; *Munchies Management Pty Ltd v Belperio* (1988) 58 FCR 274, 287; *Haynes v Top Slice Deli Pty Ltd* (1995) ATPR (Digest) 46–147, 53,154; *Murphy v Overton Investments Pty Ltd* [2001] FCA 500, (2001) 112 FCR 182 [47], *Murphy v Overton Investments Pty Ltd* [2004] HCA 3, (2004) 216 CLR 388 [70].
80   *Hubbards Pty Ltd v Simpson Ltd* (1982) 41 ALR 509, 527; *Embo Holdings Pty Ltd v Camm* (1998) ATPR (Digest) 46–184, 50,337; *Murphy v Overton Investments Pty Ltd* [2004] HCA 3, (2004) 216 CLR 388 [70].

[8.51]   The operation of the rules is illustrated by *Mehta v Commonwealth Bank of Australia*.[81] The defendant bank arranged for the plaintiff to take out a loan in a foreign currency, without explaining the profound risks involved. After the plaintiff had become aware of the first losses, a meeting of the parties took place in which the defendant stated that it would not manage the loan for the plaintiff. Instead of immediately converting the loan into Australian dollars, the plaintiff held on to the foreign currency loan and incurred further losses. It was found that the defendant had breached what is now s 18 of the ACL by failing to inform the plaintiff of the risks involved in foreign currency loans, but compensation for losses incurred after the meeting between the parties was denied on the ground that the plaintiff had assumed responsibility for losses incurred after the defendant refused to manage the loan.[82]

D   Multiple wrongdoers

[8.52]   Where a contravention of s 18 of the ACL has caused pure economic loss or property damage, Part VIA of the *Competition and Consumer Act 2010* (Cth) provides for proportionate, as opposed to joint and several, liability of a concurrent wrongdoer who did not intend to cause, or fraudulently caused, the loss.[83] Part VIA applies only where the ACL applies as a law of the Commonwealth. Where the ACL applies as a law of a state or territory, the liability regime of concurrent wrongdoers depends upon the proportionate liability statute of the state or territory. The proportionate liability statutes of most, but not all, jurisdictions apply to breaches of s 18 of the ACL; see [4.29]. The resolution of a conflict between the ACL as federal law and the ACL as state or territory law is discussed at [8.3]. The liability of multiple wrongdoers in general is discussed in Ch 4.

---

81   (1990) Aust Torts Reports 81–046.

82   Ibid, 68,142. Another example is *Henjo Investments Pty Ltd v Collins Marrickville Pty Ltd (No 2)*, the facts of which are set out at [8.40]. On appeal, compensation for the loss resulting from being burdened with an onerous lease was confined to the period it would reasonably have taken to assign the lease, not the longer period it actually took: (1989) 40 FCR 76, 86–88, 96–97.

83   Equivalent provisions are ss 12GP–12GW of the *Australian Securities and Investments Commission Act 2001* (Cth) and ss 1041L–1041S of the *Corporations Act 2001* (Cth).

EQUITABLE COMPENSATION FOR EQUITABLE WRONGS

I Introduction

[9.1]   Common law damages cannot be awarded in respect of a purely equitable wrong such as breach of trust or breach of fiduciary duty. Instead, a compensatory remedy has developed in equity's exclusive (or inherent) jurisdiction: equitable compensation. This remedy originated in cases involving breach of trust, although for many years it was not explicitly recognised as a compensatory remedy and was known instead as one of the forms of 'account' that a trustee must make when a breach of trust occurs. It is therefore necessary to have a brief look at the main forms of account, which are still used today.

[9.2]   In *Glazier Holdings Pty Ltd v Australian Men's Health Pty Ltd (No 2)*,[1] Austin J gave the following summary of the relevant principles. It is necessary to distinguish between an account of the overall administration of a trust[2] ('account of administration') and an account of profits as a remedy for specific equitable wrongdoing, discussed at [16.16]–[16.27]. An account of administration may be ordered in two different forms: a common account and an account on the basis of wilful default. The order of a common account is available without an allegation of wrongdoing and requires the trustee to account only for what she has received and her disbursement and distribution of it. By contrast, the order of an account on the basis of wilful default is grounded on misconduct and requires the trustee to account not only for what she has received but also for what she would have received but for the misconduct. The term 'wilful default' has been given a wide meaning and is not confined to conscious wrongdoing.

[9.3]   An account of administration may be surcharged or falsified. A surcharge is an allegation that the trustee has omitted something for which credit ought to be given, the onus of proof being on the surcharging party. A falsification is an allegation that a disbursement was made without authorisation, the onus of proof being on the trustee.[3] In either case, the trustee is obliged to reconstitute the trust fund as it would have been but for the trustee's breach. A trust asset that has been lost in breach of trust may be ordered to be returned in specie where this is possible.[4] Otherwise, the trustee must use her own money to reconstitute the trust fund. Even though this last obligation was not originally conceived of as compensation, courts appear to have recognised that it is compensatory in some sense, as discussed at [9.22]–[9.36].

[9.4]   A compensatory remedy has also been recognised for other equitable wrongs. The landmark case involving breach of fiduciary duty was *Nocton v Lord Ashburton*.[5] Nocton was the solicitor of Lord Ashburton, and the solicitor and business partner of Baring, Lord Ashburton's brother. Baring lent money to the developers of certain property and, at Nocton's advice, Lord Ashburton also lent money to those developers. Both loans were secured by a mortgage over the property to be developed, Lord Ashburton's mortgage having priority over Baring's. At Nocton's advice, Lord Ashburton released the most valuable part of the property from his

---

1   [2001] NSWSC 6 [36]–[45]. The decision was overturned on appeal, without contradicting Austin J's summary of equitable accounting: *Meehan v Glazier Holdings Pty Ltd* [2002] NSWCA 22, (2002) 54 NSWLR 146.

2   The principles apply also to other forms of funds, but the present interest lies in trusts.

3   *Ide v Ide* [2004] NSWSC 751, (2004) 184 FLR 44 [23], [25]; *Chong v Chanell* [2009] NSWSC 765 [7]; *Bilyak v Pesor* [2012] NSWSC 193 [49]–[51].

4   *Target Holdings Ltd v Redferns* [1996] AC 421, 423.

5   [1914] AC 932.

mortgage, with the effect that Baring's mortgage, in which Nocton had an interest, became the first charge on that land. When the developers became insolvent, Lord Ashburton claimed compensation for his loss from Nocton. The House of Lords upheld an order of compensation on the ground that Nocton had breached his fiduciary duty towards Lord Ashburton.

Orders of equitable compensation have since proliferated. The availability of equitable compensation in Australian law is established for breach of trust,[6] breach of fiduciary duty,[7] breach of an equitable duty of care[8] and breach of confidence.[9] Equitable compensation may also be available in cases of equitable estoppel.[10] Indeed, it has been said that equitable compensation is available for breach of any equitable obligation.[11] Like any other equitable remedy, equitable compensation is discretionary[12] and may be granted on terms,[13] but it is rarely denied on discretionary grounds.[14]   [9.5]

Equitable compensation is also available in equity's auxiliary (or concurrent) jurisdiction in cases of fraud (representation made dishonestly).[15] However, the equitable jurisdiction has not been exercised since *Derry v Peek*,[16] probably because common law damages are adequate.[17] Equitable compensation must be distinguished from damages under Lord Cairns' Act and its Australian equivalents, which have sometimes been called 'equitable damages' and may be awarded in addition to, or instead of, an injunction or specific performance. Lord Cairns' Act damages, discussed in Ch 12, are primarily awarded in respect of common law wrongs and have occasionally been awarded in respect of equitable wrongs. The present chapter discusses equitable compensation awarded in equity's exclusive jurisdiction for a purely equitable wrong.[18]   [9.6]

---

6   Modern cases include *Youyang Pty Ltd v Minter Ellison Morris Fletcher* [2003] HCA 15, (2003) 212 CLR 484; *Alexander v Perpetual Trustees WA Ltd* [2004] HCA 7, (2004) 216 CLR 109 [44], [47], [53], [58].

7   *O'Halloran v RT Thomas & Family Pty Ltd* (1998) 45 NSWLR 262; *Beach Petroleum NL v Kennedy* (1999) 48 NSWLR 1; *Pilmer v Duke Group Ltd (in liq)* [2001] HCA 31, (2001) 207 CLR 165.

8   *Permanent Building Society (in liq) v Wheeler* (1994) 11 WAR 187.

9   *Smith Kline & French Laboratories (Australia) Ltd v Secretary, Department of Community Services and Health* (1990) 22 FCR 73, 84; *TS & B Retail Systems Pty Ltd v 3fold Resources Pty Ltd* [2007] FCA 151, (2007) 158 FCR 444 [77]; *Giller v Procopets* [2008] VSCA 236, (2008) 24 VR 1 [233], [431].

10   *Giumelli v Giumelli* (1999) 196 CLR 101; *EK Nominees Pty Ltd v Woolworths Ltd* [2006] NSWSC 1172 [213].

11   *United States Surgical Corporation v Hospital Products International Pty Ltd* [1982] 2 NSWLR 766, 816; *Karam v Australia and New Zealand Banking Group Ltd* [2001] NSWSC 709 [425].

12   M Tilbury and G Davis, 'Equitable Compensation' in P Parkinson (ed), *The Principles of Equity* (2nd edn, LBC 2003) [2212].

13   *Demetrios v Gikas Dry Cleaning Industries Pty Ltd* (1991) 22 NSWLR 561, 574.

14   Charles Rickett has said that 'the discretion ought perhaps to wither away through disuse and a growing recognition that its retention simply perpetuates the historical jurisdictional divide in a context where there are no legitimate policy or doctrinal grounds to do so': CEF Rickett, 'Equitable Compensation: Towards a Blueprint?' (2003) 25 Syd L Rev 31, 55.

15   *Robinson v Abbott* (1894) 20 VLR 346, 366; *Nocton v Lord Ashburton* [1914] AC 932, 951; *Demetrios v Gikas Dry Cleaning Industries Pty Ltd* (1991) 22 NSWLR 561, 573–74. Note that *Nocton v Ashburton* was a case initially in deceit which was dealt with instead as a breach of fiduciary duty, but the measure of equitable compensation was very similar to compensation which would be available in deceit.

16   (1889) 14 App Cas 337.

17   IE Davidson, 'The Equitable Remedy of Compensation' (1982) 13 MULR 349, 357. In cases of careless but honest misrepresentations, equitable compensation is not available in either the concurrent or the exclusive jurisdiction of equity: Davidson, ibid, 357–72.

18   An outline of the availability, nature and measure of equitable compensation in Australia is given by M Broderick, 'Equitable Compensation – Its Place in the Remedial Sphere' (2005) 33 ABLR 369.

II   Assessment of equitable compensation

A   Object of equitable compensation

[9.7]   In cases of misapplication of trust property, which constitutes the 'core territory'[19] of equitable compensation, the object of the remedy has sometimes been described as that of effecting 'restitution' to the trust estate.[20] The same term has been used in cases in which a company director disposed of company property in breach of fiduciary duty.[21] It is unfortunate that this term is used in this context, as 'restitution' generally refers to the personal remedy for unjust enrichment, discussed in Ch 17.[22] In the present context the term is generally used in the sense of restoration and denotes a compensatory remedy,[23] although sometimes it is used to refer to a giving up of a gain, rather than a compensation of loss.

[9.8]   An example of a case where the term is used in a confusing manner is *Ferrari Investment (Townsville) Pty Ltd (in liq) v Ferrari*,[24] where the directors of a company ('the old company') transferred the goodwill of its clients ('the rent roll') to another company ('the new company') set up by them. The old company was in the real estate business, and earned commission from letting property for clients. The transfer of goodwill occurred in breach of the directors' fiduciary duty towards the old company, rendering them liable to pay equitable compensation. The trial judge measured the compensation by reference to the amount that the old company could have obtained from selling the rent roll on the open market. The Queensland Court of Appeal overturned that judgment and held that compensation was to be measured by the value of the rent roll in the hands of the new company, which yielded a higher figure. Thomas JA, with whom Shepherdson J agreed, said that one of the ways in which 'restitution to the estate' may be achieved is 'to require the fiduciary to disgorge the equivalent of the advantage that has been taken'.[25] Thomas JA went on to deny an allowance for skill and effort, which is recognised for an account of profits (see [16.113]–[16.119], on the ground that the old company had elected to seek equitable compensation rather than an account of profits.[26] This case indicates that in rare instances, a defendant's gain can be used as a reflection of the loss of the plaintiff.[27]

---

19   J Getzler, 'Equitable Compensation and the Regulation of Fiduciary Relationships' in P Birks and F Rose (eds), *Restitution and Equity, Volume 1: Resulting Trusts and Equitable Compensation* (Mansfield Press 2000) 236.

20   *Re Dawson* [1966] 2 NSWR 211, 214; *Target Holdings Ltd v Redferns* [1996] AC 421, 425; *Maguire v Makaronis* (1997) 188 CLR 449, 469.

21   *Ferrari Investment (Townsville) Pty Ltd (in liq) v Ferrari* [2000] 2 Qd R 359, 370.

22   See J Edelman and E Bant, *Unjust Enrichment* (2nd edn, Hart 2016) 32–35.

23   J Edelman and S Elliott, 'Money Remedies against Trustees' (2004) 18 TLI 116, 119; SB Elliott, 'Restitutionary Compensatory Damages for Breach of Fiduciary Duty?' (1998) 6 RLR 135, 138–43; M Tilbury and G Davis, 'Equitable Compensation' in P Parkinson (ed), *The Principles of Equity* (2nd edn, LBC 2003) [2207].

24   [2000] 2 Qd R 359.

25   Ibid, 370. The same view was taken in *Westpac Banking Corporation v Bell Group Ltd (in liq) (No 3)* [2012] WASCA 157, (2012) 44 WAR 1 [1236], [1259].

26   [2000] 2 Qd R 359, 372–73.

27   See also *Lifeplan Australia Friendly Society Ltd v Ancient Order of Foresters in Victoria Friendly Society Ltd* [2017] FCAFC 74, (2017) 250 FCR 1. Leave to appeal to the High Court has been granted: *Ancient Order of Foresters in Victoria Friendly Society Ltd v Lifeplan Australia Friendly Society Ltd* [2017] HCATrans 210.

It has been said in some cases that equitable compensation may be measured by reference   [9.9]
to the defendant's gain, rather than the plaintiff's loss, even where there is no misappropriation
of property by a trustee or other custodial fiduciary.[28] The UK Supreme Court has described
the principal's personal remedy in respect of a bribe or secret commission taken by the
fiduciary as equitable compensation in the amount of the bribe or secret commission less
permissible deductions such as expenses incurred.[29] The South Australian Full Court has gone
further by saying that equitable compensation for breach of fiduciary duty 'may be awarded
even where there has been no loss suffered by the plaintiff but a pecuniary gain made by the
fiduciary'.[30] This approach is problematic and should not be followed, since it blurs the
distinction between equitable compensation as a compensatory remedy and an account of
profits as a gain-based remedy.[31]

In the vast majority of cases not involving misappropriation of property belonging to a trust   [9.10]
or company, equitable compensation has in fact been measured by reference to the plaintiff's
loss.[32] In general, therefore, the object of equitable compensation may be described as the
compensation of loss inflicted by an equitable wrong. The NSW Court of Appeal has said that
equitable compensation 'should compensate the plaintiff but it is no part of its function to strip
profits from the defendants',[33] and has also said: 'The object of equitable compensation is to
restore persons who have suffered loss to the position in which they would have been if there
had been no breach of the equitable obligation'.[34]

B   Recoverability of non-pecuniary loss

Equitable wrongs usually affect the plaintiff's financial interests, and non-pecuniary loss is rarely   [9.11]
an issue. It has been an issue where a breach of confidence affected the plaintiff's personal or
private interests. In those circumstances, equitable compensation for non-pecuniary loss used to
be considered unavailable,[35] but is now considered available.[36]

---

28   *Hill v Rose* [1990] VR 129, 143; *Dempster v Mallina Holdings Ltd* (1994) 13 WAR 124, 172–73; *Talacko v
        Talacko* [2009] VSC 533 [124]–[131]; *Hodgson v Amcor Ltd* [2012] VSC 94, (2012) 264 FLR 1 [1636], [1663].
29   *FHR European Ventures LLP v Mankarious* [2014] UKSC 45, [2015] AC 250 [7].
30   *Duke Group Ltd (in liq) v Pilmer* (1999) 73 SASR 64, 243 (Doyle CJ, Duggan and Bleby JJ); rev'd
        on the ground that there had been no fiduciary relationship: *Pilmer v Duke Group Ltd (in liq)* [2001]
        HCA 31, (2001) 207 CLR 165.
31   M O'Meara, 'Causation, Remoteness and Equitable Compensation' (2005) 26 Aust Bar Rev 51, 56; C
        Rickett and T Gardner, 'Compensating for Loss in Equity: The Evolution of a Remedy' (1994) 24 VUWLR
        19, 30.
32   The defendant's gain was used as the basis of estimating the plaintiff's loss in *Digital Pulse Pty Ltd v
        Harris* [2002] NSWSC 33, (2002) 166 FLR 421 [105]; *Disctronics Ltd v Edmonds* [2002] VSC 454 [216].
33   *Houghton v Immer (No 155) Pty Ltd* (1997) 44 NSWLR 46, 56 (Handley JA, with whom Mason P and
        Beazley JA agreed).
34   *O'Halloran v RT Thomas & Family Pty Ltd* (1998) 45 NSWLR 262, 272 (Spigelman CJ, with whom
        Priestley JA and Meagher JA agreed).
35   *W v Egdell* [1990] Ch 359, 398.
36   English courts have recognised it for breach of confidence in its traditional meaning: *Cornelius v De
        Taranto* [2001] EMLR 329 [66]–[69]; *Archer v Williams* [2003] EWHC 1670 (QB), [2003] EMLR 869;
        McKennitt v Ash [2005] EWHC 3003 (QB), [2006] EMLR 178. English courts have also recognised it for
        breach of privacy as a new form of breach of confidence: *Campbell v MGN Ltd* [2004] UKHL 22, [2004]
        2 AC 457; *Douglas v Hello! Ltd (No 3)* [2005] EWCA Civ 595, [2006] QB 125; *Mosley v News Group
        Newspapers Ltd* [2008] EWHC 1777 (QB), [2008] EMLR 679.

[9.12]   The leading Australian case is *Giller v Procopets*.[37] During the final weeks of their de facto relationship, the defendant videotaped sexual activity between the parties, initially without the plaintiff's knowledge, but subsequently with her knowledge and acquiescence. After the relationship ended, the defendant showed the videotapes to third parties without the plaintiff's consent. The plaintiff claimed compensation for the distress suffered, on several bases, including breach of confidence. The trial judge found a breach of confidence but held equitable compensation unavailable in respect of non-pecuniary loss.[38] The Victorian Court of Appeal reversed the latter ruling. Neave JA, with whom Maxwell P agreed on this issue, said that non-pecuniary loss resulting from a breach of confidence can be compensated through both an award of equitable compensation in equity's inherent jurisdiction and an award of Lord Cairns' Act damages, discussed in Ch 12.[39] She awarded $40 000, including $10 000 in aggravated damages.[40]

[9.13]   With regard to equitable wrongs other than breach of confidence, there does not seem to be an Australian case in which non-pecuniary loss was compensated. It has been compensated in some cases in Canada[41] and New Zealand.[42] There does not seem to be an Australian case in which compensation for non-pecuniary loss was claimed but refused. On principle, there is no reason why significant non-pecuniary loss resulting from an equitable wrong should not be compensated.[43]

C   Basic measure of equitable compensation

[9.14]   Leaving aside non-pecuniary loss, equitable compensation is determined by comparing two financial states of the plaintiff. One is the plaintiff's actual financial state after the defendant's wrong. This is usually assessed as at the date of trial; see [2.129]. The other state is either the position the plaintiff would have been in at the time of trial without the wrong, or the position the plaintiff was in directly before the wrong occurred. In most cases, the plaintiff's actual financial state at the time of trial has been compared with the financial state the plaintiff would have been in at that time without the wrong.[44] In those cases, the wrong was expressly required to constitute a factual cause of the plaintiff's loss. For example, in cases involving

---

37   [2008] VSCA 236, (2008) 24 VR 1. See also *Doe v Australian Broadcasting Corporation* [2007] VCC 281 [145], [185]–[186]; *Wilson v Ferguson* [2015] WASC 15 [71]–[85].

38   *Giller v Procopets* [2004] VSC 113 [165].

39   [2008] VSCA 236, (2008) 24 VR 1 [408]–[431]. Ashley JA agreed that non-pecuniary loss resulting from a breach of confidence is compensable (at [142]–[154]), but thought that this could only be done under Lord Cairns' Act (at [136]).

40   [2008] VSCA 236, (2008) 24 VR 1 [443]–[446] (Neave JA, with whom Maxwell P agreed). Ashley JA (at [160]) opined that 'any award beyond $27,500 – this including an amount of about $7,500 for what would be called aggravated damages in an action at law – would step into the impermissible realm of punishment'.

41   *Szarfer v Chodos* (1986) 27 DLR (4th) 388; *M (K) v M (H)* [1992] 3 SCR 6, 80–82.

42   *McKaskell v Benseman* [1989] 3 NZLR 75; *Mouat v Clark Boyce* [1992] 2 NZLR 559, 569.

43   S Harder, *Measuring Damages in the Law of Obligations: The Search for Harmonised Principles* (Hart 2010) 125. The issue was left open in *Wilson v Ferguson* [2015] WASC 15 [84].

44   *O'Halloran v RT Thomas & Family Pty Ltd* (1998) 45 NSWLR 262, 272; *Darvall McCutcheon (a firm) v HK Frost Holdings Pty Ltd (in liq)* [2002] VSCA 85, (2002) 4 VR 570 [66]; *GM & AM Pearce & Co Pty Ltd v Australian Tallow Producers* [2005] VSCA 113 [65].

breach of confidence, compensation may be based on the loss of the profit the plaintiff would have derived but for the defendant's breach.[45]

In other cases, it has been said that the plaintiff's actual financial state at the time of trial was to be compared with the plaintiff's actual financial state immediately before the wrong.[46] For example, in *Nocton v Lord Ashburton*, Viscount Haldane explained the general availability of equitable compensation for breach of fiduciary duty on the ground that a court of equity could order the defendant 'to compensate the plaintiff by putting him in as good a position pecuniarily as that in which he was before the injury'.[47]   **[9.15]**

In cases not involving breach of trust or breach of fiduciary duty, the reference to 'the plaintiff's financial state before the wrong' refers to the financial state the plaintiff would be in without the wrong, it being assumed that the plaintiff's *status quo ante* would have subsisted without the wrong. In cases involving breach of trust or breach of fiduciary duty, the reference to the plaintiff's financial state before the wrong as a comparator may reflect the fact that liability will still be imposed even if certain non-wrongful events would have caused the loss even without the breach; see [9.18]–[9.37], [9.46]–[9.51].   **[9.16]**

III   Attribution of responsibility

The civil liability statutes' provisions on causation (see [3.12]–[3.13]) may apply to the breach of an equitable duty of care (see [3.15]–[3.16]), but do not apply to other equitable wrongs, which remain governed by the common sense test of causation,[48] outlined at [3.9]. Nevertheless, a distinction between factual causation and scope of liability assists the analysis of the case law for every equitable wrong. In the context of factual causation, the general applicability of the 'but for' test has been established for breach of trust,[49] breach of fiduciary duty,[50] breach of an equitable duty of care,[51] and breach of confidence.[52] In that regard, the common law rules must in principle apply to equitable wrongs. Otherwise, the rules governing the attribution of responsibility (or some of them) differ between common law and equity and between   **[9.17]**

---

45   *Titan Group Pty Ltd v Steriline Manufacturing Pty Ltd* (1990) 19 IPR 353, 395–96; *Darvall McCutcheon (a firm) v HK Frost Holdings Pty Ltd (in liq)* [2002] VSCA 85, (2002) 4 VR 570 [66].

46   *Talbot v General Television Corporation Pty Ltd* [1980] VR 224, 253; *Ithaca Ice Works Pty Ltd v Queensland Ice Supplies Pty Ltd* [2002] QSC 222 [13]; *Fico v O'Leary* [2004] WASC 215, [2004] ATPR (Digest) 46–259 [161]; *Wingecarribee Shire Council v Lehman Brothers Australia Ltd (in liq)* [2012] FCA 1028, (2012) 301 ALR 1 [995].

47   [1914] AC 932, 952.

48   *O'Halloran v RT Thomas & Family Pty Ltd* (1998) 45 NSWLR 262, 272–73; *Beach Petroleum NL v Kennedy* [1999] NSWCA 408, (1999) 48 NSWLR 1 [432]; *GM & AM Pearce & Co Pty Ltd v Australian Tallow Producers* [2005] VSCA 113 [65]; *Watson v Ebsworth & Ebsworth (a firm)* [2010] VSCA 335, (2010) 31 VR 123 [160]–[161].

49   *Re Dawson* [1966] 2 NSWR 211, 215.

50   *O'Halloran v RT Thomas & Family Pty Ltd* (1998) 45 NSWLR 262, 272–73; *Agricultural Land Management Ltd v Jackson (No 2)* [2014] WASC 102, (2014) 48 WAR 1 [391]–[399]. However, it is not entirely settled how the counterfactual is to be constructed; see [9.43]–[9.51].

51   *Permanent Building Society (in liq) v Wheeler* (1994) 11 WAR 187, 247 (Ipp J, speaking for the Full Court: 'a court of equity, applying principles of fairness, should not require an honest but careless trustee to compensate a beneficiary for losses without proof that but for the breach of duty those losses would not have occurred'); *Duke Group Ltd (in liq) v Pilmer* (1999) 73 SASR 64, 248.

52   *Ithaca Ice Works Pty Ltd v Queensland Ice Supplies Pty Ltd* [2002] QSC 222 [14]–[16].

equitable wrongs. Those rules, insofar as they deviate from the common law rules, will now be discussed separately for the three main equitable wrongs: breach of trust, breach of fiduciary duty and breach of an equitable duty of care.[53]

A   Breach of trust

1   Independent non-wrongful event

[9.18]   At least at common law, loss factually caused by a wrong is not attributed to the wrongdoer if, without the wrong, an independent non-wrongful event would have inflicted the same loss; see [3.101]–[3.102]. For example, a defendant who has wrongfully injured the plaintiff is not liable for loss that the plaintiff would have suffered anyway because of an unrelated illness.[54] The applicability of this principle to the misapplication of trust property is controversial.

[9.19]   A trustee who has misapplied trust property in an unauthorised transaction and is unable to return the property in specie is generally obliged to pay the value of the property into the trust fund (or to the beneficiaries if the trust is otherwise at an end).[55] Some scholars call this payment 'substitutive compensation' because it is the substitute of the return of the property and, in those scholars' view, discharges the trustee's primary obligation to hold the property on trust.[56] They distinguish it from 'reparative compensation', which gives effect to the trustee's secondary obligation to compensate loss caused by a breach of trust. Concepts dealing with attribution of loss (factual causation and scope of liability; see [3.1]) are considered relevant only to 'reparative compensation'. Under that view, a trustee's obligation to restore the value of misapplied property exists even where, without the trustee's breach, the trust fund would have lost the property through a non-wrongful event. Those scholars derive this view from the concept of the falsification of an account of administration, mentioned at [9.3]. However, the labels 'reparative compensation' and 'substitutive compensation' have been criticised as confusing the matter.[57]

[9.20]   Independent non-wrongful events were ignored in older cases. For example, in *White v Baugh*,[58] a receiver, in breach of trust, gave a third party the right to veto any withdrawals by the receiver from a bank account holding trust money. When the bank went bankrupt, the receiver was held liable to restore to the trust the money held in the bank account, even though it had been proper for the receiver to place the trust money with that bank and even though the money would still have been lost without the third party's veto right. Lord Lyndhurst said:

---

53   In addition, it has been said that equitable compensation for breach of confidence is not limited by notions of intervening acts or remoteness of loss: *Ithaca Ice Works Pty Ltd v Queensland Ice Supplies Pty Ltd* [2002] QSC 222 [14]–[16]; M Gronow, 'Damages for Breach of Confidence' (1994) 5 AIPJ 94, 111; J Stuckey-Clarke, '"Damages" for Breaches of Purely Equitable Rights: The Breach of Confidence Example' in PD Finn (ed), *Essays on Damages* (LBC 1992) 84–85.

54   Eg *K-Mart Australia Ltd v McCann* [2004] NSWCA 283.

55   *AIB Group (UK) plc v Mark Redler & Co Solicitors* [2014] UKSC 58, [2015] AC 1503 [67], [90]–[91].

56   SB Elliott, 'Remoteness Criteria in Equity' (2002) 65 Mod LR 588, 590; SB Elliott and C Mitchell, 'Remedies for Dishonest Assistance' (2004) 67 Mod LR 16, 23–34; J Edelman and SB Elliott, 'Money Remedies against Trustees' (2004) 18 TLI 116, 116–25; D Hayton, P Matthews and C Mitchell, *Underhill and Hayton: Law Relating to Trusts and Trustees* (19th edn, LexisNexis 2016) [87.7]–[87.11].

57   M Conaglen, 'Equitable Compensation for Breach of Trust: Off Target' (2016) 40 MULR 126, 151.

58   (1835) 3 Cl & F 44; 6 ER 1354.

The Court says, 'You cannot be relieved from your liability unless your conduct has been strictly regular, whether the loss has been occasioned by the irregularity of your conduct or not.'[59]

Street J in *Re Dawson* may seem to have endorsed that approach when he said with regard to a defaulting trustee's obligation to effect 'restitution' (see [9.7]) to the estate: 'Considerations of causation ... do not readily enter into the matter'.[60] However, this may not exclude the consideration of an independent non-wrongful event,[61] for in the immediately preceding sentence he said that 'if a breach has been committed then the trustee is liable to place the trust estate in the same position as it would have been in if no breach had been committed'.[62]   [9.21]

The traditional approach has been rejected in England, and it is controversial whether it still applies in Australia. We will first outline the developments in England and then discuss the Australian position.   [9.22]

The House of Lords recognised the exonerating effect of a causally independent non-wrongful event in *Target Holdings Ltd v Redferns*.[63] A firm of solicitors (Redferns) acted for a prospective purchaser of land (Crowngate) and also for the prospective mortgagee (Target). Target gave Redferns over £1.5 million to be held on bare trust and be transferred to Crowngate once the property had been purchased and charged to Target. In breach of trust, Redferns paid away the money before Crowngate purchased the property. One month later, the property was charged to Target. Subsequently, Crowngate became insolvent and Target sold the property for £50 000.   [9.23]

Target sued Redferns for return of the entire sum (£1.5 million), reduced by the sum realised on the sale of the property. Target argued that as soon as Redferns had paid out the money in breach of trust, Redferns had come under an obligation to restore it, and it was irrelevant that Target had eventually received the security required. Rejecting that argument, the House of Lords held that, at least in the case of a bare trust, a common-sense view of causation applies.[64] Lord Browne-Wilkinson, speaking for the House, said: [9.24]

> [T]he fact that there is an accrued cause of action as soon as the breach is committed does not in my judgment mean that the quantum of the compensation payable is ultimately fixed as at the date when the breach occurred. The quantum is fixed at the date of judgment at which date, according to the circumstances then pertaining, the compensation is assessed at the figure then necessary to put the trust estate or the beneficiary back into the position it would have been in had there been no breach.[65]

---

59   (1835) 3 Cl & F 44, 66; 6 ER 1354, 1362. See also *Salway v Salway* (1831) 2 Russ & M 215, 39 ER 376; *Magnus v Queensland National Bank* (1888) 37 Ch D 466.
60   [1966] 2 NSWR 211, 215.
61   See SB Elliott, 'Restitutionary Compensatory Damages for Breach of Fiduciary Duty?' (1998) 6 RLR 135, 140 note 33. The opposite view is taken by J Glister, 'Equitable Compensation' in J Glister and P Ridge (eds), *Fault Lines in Equity* (Hart 2012) 145–46.
62   [1966] 2 NSWR 211, 215.
63   [1996] AC 421. Applied in *Collins v Brebner* [2000] Lloyd's Rep PN 587.
64   [1996] AC 421, 438–39, adopting McLachlin J's minority view in *Canson Enterprises Ltd v Boughton & Co* [1991] 3 SCR 534, 551, 556.
65   [1996] AC 421, 437.

[9.25]   It has been suggested that the result in *Target Holdings* could have been reached without reference to causation. Lord Millett has argued extra-judicially that the result could have been reached under traditional trust accounting principles by regarding the eventual acquisition of the mortgage as 'an authorised application of what must be treated as trust money notionally restored to the trust estate'.[66] However, a similar argument by the claimant in *AIB Group (UK) plc v Mark Redler & Co Solicitors* (considered at [9.27]–[9.30]) was rejected by Lord Toulson JSC as involving 'fairy tales'.[67] Edelman also opposes Lord Millett's analysis but comes to the same outcome reached in *Target Holdings* by arguing that Target evinced an election not to insist on a reconstitution of the trust fund because it held the mortgage as security for more than two years.[68]

[9.26]   It was initially unclear whether *Target Holdings* had a narrow application, either because it only applied to claims for equitable compensation and not to claims for an account, or because it only applied to bare trusts used within a commercial transaction and not to traditional trusts.[69] In *AIB Group (UK) plc v Mark Redler & Co Solicitors*,[70] the UK Supreme Court confirmed that *Target Holdings* had a broad application and operated to limit a trustee's liability, regardless of whether the relief claimed is general accounting (see [9.2]) or equitable compensation, and regardless of whether the trust is a commercial trust or a traditional trust.

[9.27]   In *AIB*, the borrowers sought to remortgage their property, then valued at £4.25 million. The claimant bank advanced £3.3 million to the defendant solicitors, who were to first fully discharge the existing mortgage for around £1.5 million (held by Barclays), release the remaining sum to the borrowers and secure a first legal charge over the property in favour of the claimant. Through a combination of a misunderstanding and negligence on their part, the solicitors paid Barclays only around £1.2 million (a little under £300 000 less than required to discharge the mortgage) and released the rest of the money to the borrowers. When the error was discovered, Barclays permitted the claimant's charge to be registered as a second charge. The borrowers defaulted and went bankrupt. The value of the property had fallen drastically and it was sold for £1.2 million. Barclays had priority, and took the amount still owing to it under the undischarged mortgage (£273 777.42 plus interest) and so the claimant only obtained £867 697.

[9.28]   The claimant sued the defendants for breach of contract, negligence and breach of trust. For the former two causes of action, the compensation was limited to the loss of £273 777.42 plus interest. However, for breach of trust, the claimant claimed compensation in the full amount of the loan less the amount recovered by it (around £2.5 million), arguing that the defendants had had no authority to release any money to the borrowers unless and until they had a redemption statement from Barclays. Applying *Target Holdings*, the Court of Appeal held that the claimant was entitled to only £273 777.42 plus interest, because even if the defendants had discharged Barclays' mortgage, the claimant would still have suffered loss

---

66   PJ Millett, 'Equity's Place in the Law of Commerce' (1998) 114 LQR 214, 227. Supported by M Conaglen, 'Explaining *Target Holdings v Redferns*' (2010) 4 J Eq 288.

67   [2014] UKSC 58, [2015] AC 1503 [69].

68   J Edelman, 'Money Awards of the Cost of Performance' (2010) 4 J Eq 122, 128–30.

69   See PG Turner, 'The New Fundamental Norm of Recovery for Losses to Express Trusts' (2015) 74 Camb LJ 188, 188.

70   [2014] UKSC 58, [2015] AC 1503. Criticised in M Conaglen, 'Equitable Compensation for Breach of Trust: Off Target' (2016) 40 MULR 126, 165–67 for undermining the strict and prophylactic operation of equitable trust accounting rules.

because of the fall in the value of the property. The Supreme Court dismissed the claimant's appeal. Only Lord Toulson JSC and Lord Reed JSC gave reasoned speeches.

Lord Toulson JSC noted that *Target Holdings* had been criticised by scholars for confusing substitutive compensation and reparative compensation (see [9.19]).[71] Nevertheless, he refused 'to impose or maintain a rule that gives redress to a beneficiary for loss which would have been suffered if the trustee had properly performed its duties'.[72] He said that 'a monetary award which reflected neither loss caused nor profit gained by the wrongdoer would be penal'.[73] The trust in this case was effectively part of a contractual machinery where the role of the trustee was closely defined and limited, and accordingly, it was appropriate that the rules applied should be analogous to contract.[74] He added that this principle applies not only to bare trusts as an incident of a commercial transaction but also to traditional trusts.[75]   [9.29]

Lord Reed JSC reviewed cases from various common law jurisdictions and concluded that 'the model of equitable compensation, where trust property has been misapplied, is to require the trustee to restore the trust fund to the position it would have been in if the trustee had performed his obligation'.[76] He added that the measure of equitable compensation for breach of trust is not the same as the measure of damages for tort or breach of contract since the obligations breached are of a different nature.[77] However, different rules can be justified only insofar as the obligations breached do differ in nature, and not merely because of the historical origin of the relevant rules.[78]   [9.30]

Lord Browne-Wilkinson's statement in *Target Holdings* that a causally independent non-wrongful event exonerates a defaulting trustee (see [9.24]) was approvingly quoted by the High Court of Australia in *Youyang Pty Ltd v Minter Ellison Morris Fletcher*.[79] But the High Court distinguished *Target Holdings* on the facts.[80]   [9.31]

The facts of *Youyang* were complex. In 1993, Youyang Pty Ltd, the plaintiff, agreed to invest $500 000 in a company called EC Consolidated Capital Ltd ('ECCCL'), which was in the business of engaging in speculative transactions on the international money market. In order to protect the plaintiff against a loss of its investment, it was agreed that $256 800 out of the $500 000 would be deposited with a bank, Dresdner International Financial Markets (Australia) Ltd ('DAL'), which would guarantee to pay the plaintiff $500 000 in 2003. It was agreed that the plaintiff would pay $256 800 to the defendant solicitors, who would pass it to DAL once ECCCL had obtained a bearer deposit certificate from DAL. In September 1993, the plaintiff paid the money to the defendants,[81] who passed it to DAL after ECCCL had obtained a deposit   [9.32]

---

71   [2014] UKSC 58, [2015] AC 1503 [56].
72   Ibid, [62].
73   Ibid, [64].
74   Ibid, [70]. See also K Barnett, 'Equitable Compensation and Remoteness: Not So Remote from the Common Law After All' (2014) 38 UWALR 48, 73–78.
75   [2014] UKSC 58, [2015] AC 1503 [70].
76   Ibid, [134].
77   Ibid, [136]–[137].
78   Ibid, [138].
79   [2003] HCA 15, (2003) 212 CLR 484 [50].
80   Ibid, [48]. In *AIB Group (UK) plc v Mark Redler & Co Solicitors* [2014] UKSC 58, [2015] AC 1503 [124], Lord Reed JSC expressed the view that *Youyang* is consistent with *Target Holdings*.
81   The plaintiff paid $500 000 to the defendants, who disposed of the whole sum in breach of trust. The issue of causation, relevant for present purposes, arose only in respect of $256 800.

certificate from DAL. However, that certificate was not a bearer deposit certificate as contractually agreed, and did not provide the plaintiff with any security. Thus, the defendants acted in breach of trust when they paid the money to DAL in September 1993. Their obligation to pay $256 800 into the trust or directly to the plaintiff would have been in no doubt but for the following subsequent events.

[9.33]   In September 1994, ECCCL told the plaintiff, who still thought that DAL had issued a bearer deposit certificate in September 1993, that tax could be saved by moving the money from DAL to an overseas bank. The plaintiff, by a deed poll, instructed DAL to release the funds to ECCCL, which DAL did. ECCCL used the money in its business and, in 1997, went bankrupt.

[9.34]   The defendants denied liability in respect of the $256 800 with the argument that the plaintiff would have lost that money even if DAL had issued a bearer deposit certificate in September 1993. The High Court of Australia rejected that argument and held the defendants liable, notwithstanding the court's approval of *Target Holdings*. The High Court attributed the plaintiff's loss to the defendant's breach of trust, notwithstanding the subsequent release of the money by the plaintiff, on the ground that:

> the moneys which ECCCL had held on deposit with DAL never provided the security for the investment made by Youyang. The security was to be provided by a bearer certificate of deposit in the proper form lodged with Registries. The subsequent release of the moneys held by ECCCL on investment with DAL had no effect upon the deficiency in Youyang's position.[82]

[9.35]   Of course, the release of the non-existent security did not worsen the plaintiff's position. But the key circumstance was that the plaintiff *would* have released the security even if it *had* obtained it.[83]

[9.36]   After the decision by the House of Lords in *Target Holdings*, it became customary for Australian courts to state that equitable compensation for the misapplication of trust property aims to place the trust or the beneficiaries in the position as if the breach of trust had not occurred.[84] *Youyang* did not change this.[85] Indeed, the *Target Holdings* rule has been extended to the misapplication by a custodial fiduciary of property belonging to the principal.[86]

[9.37]   However, some judicial opposition to the *Target Holdings* rule has recently emerged, starting with Edelman J's observations in *Agricultural Land Management Ltd v Jackson (No 2)*.[87] Relying on the traditional position that the falsification of an account in common

---

82   [2003] HCA 15, (2003) 212 CLR 484 [62] (Gleeson CJ, McHugh, Gummow, Kirby and Hayne JJ).

83   The trial judge found that the plaintiff would not have withdrawn its investment even if it had become aware of the lack of the security before September 1994: *Youyang Pty Ltd v Alexander* [2000] NSWSC 698 [24].

84   *O'Halloran v RT Thomas & Family Pty Ltd* (1998) 45 NSWLR 262, 275, 279; *Beach Petroleum NL v Kennedy* [1999] NSWCA 408, (1999) 48 NSWLR 1 [432].

85   *Jessup v Lawyers Private Mortgages Ltd* [2006] QCA 432 [60]; *Kation Pty Ltd v Lamru Pty Ltd* [2009] NSWCA 145, (2009) 257 ALR 336 [124].

86   For company directors, see *O'Halloran v RT Thomas & Family Pty Ltd* (1998) 45 NSWLR 262, 277–78; *Re Lawrence Waterhouse Pty Ltd (in liq)* [2011] NSWSC 964 [304].

87   [2014] WASC 102, (2014) 48 WAR 1.

form (see [9.3]) did not require the beneficiary to show that the asset would not have been lost but for the breach, his Honour adopted the concept of substitutive compensation (as opposed to reparative compensation; see [9.19]), which simply requires the trustee to replenish the trust fund regardless of any loss suffered.[88] His Honour took the view that this position has survived the High Court's decision in *Youyang* because *Youyang* was not argued as a substitutive compensation case and the High Court did not need to decide this point.[89] These observations were obiter as substitutive compensation was not available in that case. But they have been endorsed in subsequent dicta,[90] which shows that the Australian position cannot be regarded as entirely settled.

Whatever position eventually prevails in Australia, it ought to be based on policy consider-   [9.38]
ations relating to the current conditions in Australia. Mere reliance on 19th century English cases is not good enough.

2   Intervening acts and remoteness of loss

With regard to a trustee's obligation to effect 'restitution' to the trust fund (see [9.7]), Street J in   [9.39]
Re Dawson said that '[c]onsiderations of causation, foreseeability and remoteness do not readily enter into the matter'.[91] Nor does the doctrine of *novus actus interveniens*, according to the High Court of Australia.[92] Lord Reed JSC in the Supreme Court of the UK has said that while foreseeability of loss is generally irrelevant, the loss must flow directly from the breach of trust.[93] This indicates that factual causation alone may not be sufficient for liability. However, his Lordship approved *Caffrey v Darby*,[94] where trustees who failed to recover trust property which was subsequently lost due an allegedly incorrect judgment were liable for the loss on the ground that the property would not have been lost without the breach of trust. Lord Eldon MR said on the trustees' liability:

> [I]f they have been already guilty of negligence, they must be responsible for any loss in any way to that property: for whatever may be the immediate cause, the property would not have been in a situation to sustain that loss, if it had not been for their negligence ... If the loss had happened by fire, lightning, or any other accident, that would not be an excuse for them, if guilty of previous negligence.[95]

In the context of the misapplication of a trust asset, this strict approach has been defended   [9.40]
with the argument that the trustee's obligation to restore the asset, or its value, to the trust fund is not concerned with loss in the sense of injury or damage, but is simply an aspect of the

---

88   Ibid, [334]–[349].
89   Ibid, [358].
90   *Australian Securities and Investments Commission v Australian Property Custodian Holdings Ltd* [2014] FCA 1308, (2014) 322 ALR 45 [196]–[198]; *Crossman v Sheahan* [2016] NSWCA 200, (2016) 115 ACSR 130 [313], [316].
91   [1966] 2 NSWR 211, 215.
92   *Maguire v Makaronis* (1997) 188 CLR 449, 470.
93   *AIB Group (UK) plc v Mark Redler & Co Solicitors* [2014] UKSC 58, [2015] AC 1503 [135].
94   (1801) 6 Ves 488, 31 ER 1159.
95   (1801) 6 Ves 478, 496; 31 ER 1159, 1162. A similar statement was made in *Clough v Bond* (1838) 3 M & C 490, 496–97; 40 ER 1016, 1018.

trustee's primary obligation to perform the trust; the issue of remoteness is as irrelevant as it is in actions for debt or for specific performance of a contract.[96]

[9.41]   This argument has force where, at the time of the beneficiary's action, the trust is still subsisting, regardless of the trustee's obligation in respect of the misapplied asset. Things may be different where, at the time of the beneficiary's action, the trust is at an end, at least if the trustee's obligation in respect of the lost asset is ignored. In *Target Holdings Ltd v Redferns*,[97] considered at [9.23]–[9.24], Lord Browne-Wilkinson said that where the beneficiary has become absolutely entitled to the trust fund, the trustee is normally obliged to compensate the beneficiary personally, rather than to reconstitute the trust fund. A claim by the beneficiary personally in respect of loss suffered is akin to a claim for damages rather than for debt or specific performance. The same is true for the trust fund's claim for compensation where the breach of trust does not take the form of the misapplication of trust property.[98]

[9.42]   Where the trustee is obliged to compensate loss in the sense of injury or damage, '[i]t would be startling and anomalous if compensation were not conditioned by remoteness criteria of any sort for that would raise the spectre of unlimited liability'.[99] In particular, where, as an incident of a larger commercial transaction, a single asset is held on trust for a relatively short period, the trustee's liability for the misapplication of that asset may be subjected to the contractual remoteness test (discussed at [5.89]–[5.104]), considering the contractual embedment of the trust.

B   Breach of fiduciary duty

1   Construction of the hypothetical world

[9.43]   In order to apply the 'but for' test discussed at [3.24]–[3.26], the actual world in which the defendant's wrong occurred must be compared to a hypothetical world in which the wrong did not occur. The court places itself at a point in time just before the wrong, constructs a hypothetical world in which the wrong did not occur, and asks what would have happened in that hypothetical world.[100] The departure from the actual world should be as minimal as possible;[101] 'the defendant's behavior is altered *just* enough to bring it into conformity with his duty as mandated by the Law'.[102]

[9.44]   In cases of breach of fiduciary duty, the hypothetical world can often be constructed in two different ways. This is because the principal's informed consent to what would otherwise be

---

96   J Edelman and S Elliott, 'Money Remedies against Trustees' (2004) 18 TLI 116, 116–17; SB Elliott and C Mitchell, 'Remedies for Dishonest Assistance' (2004) 67 Mod LR 16, 25–28; CEF Rickett, 'Equitable Compensation: Towards a Blueprint?' (2003) 25 Syd L Rev 31, 35–38; L Smith, 'The Measurement of Compensation Claims against Trustees and Fiduciaries' in E Bant and M Harding (eds), *Exploring Private Law* (CUP 2010) 371–72.

97   [1996] AC 421, 434–35.

98   SB Elliott and C Mitchell, 'Remedies for Dishonest Assistance' (2004) 67 Mod LR 16, 28–29.

99   SB Elliott, 'Remoteness Criteria in Equity' (2002) 65 Mod LR 588, 590.

100   D Hamer, '"Factual Causation" and "Scope of Liability": What's the Difference?' (2014) 77 Mod LR 155, 163.

101   Eg DW Robertson, 'The Common Sense of Cause in Fact' (1997) 75 Texas L Rev 1765, 1770.

102   J Stapleton, 'Choosing What We Mean by "Causation" in the Law' (2008) 73 Missouri L Rev 433, 451 (emphasis original).

disloyal conduct excludes liability.[103] The hypothetical world can thus be a world in which the fiduciary disclosed the conflict of duty and interest (or duty and duty) to the principal, or a world in which the fiduciary did not engage in the disloyal conduct.[104] Minds may reasonably differ as to which of the two hypothetical worlds constitutes the more minimal departure from the actual world.

Equitable compensation is not available where the loss for which compensation is claimed would still have occurred had the fiduciary not engaged in the disloyal conduct.[105] It follows that the question of how to construct the hypothetical world in cases of breach of fiduciary duty need not be resolved where it is clear that the principal, if asked, would not have authorised the fiduciary's conduct. The 'but for' test is satisfied either way. But the question of how to construct the hypothetical world must be resolved where the principal, if asked, would have authorised the fiduciary's conduct. [9.45]

The relevance of the principal's hypothetical consent is in doubt because of dicta expressed in the Privy Council's decision in the Canadian case *Brickenden v London Loan & Savings Co.*[106] A solicitor acted for both the borrower and the lender in respect of the grant of a loan secured by mortgage on the borrower's land. The solicitor failed to inform the lender that part of the loan was to be used to repay loans which the solicitor had granted to the borrower and which were secured by mortgages on the same land. Those mortgages were worthless since there were prior mortgages exhausting the value of the land. The solicitor was held liable for breach of his fiduciary duty towards the lender.[107] It does not appear from the judgments in that case that the solicitor argued that the lender would still have granted the loan had it known that part of the loan would be paid to the solicitor. [9.46]

Nevertheless, Lord Thankerton, who delivered the Privy Council's judgment, made the following observation: [9.47]

> When a party, holding a fiduciary relationship, commits a breach of his duty by non-disclosure of material facts, which his constituent is entitled to know in connection with the transaction, he cannot be heard to maintain that disclosure would not have altered the decision to proceed with the transaction, because the constituent's action would be solely determined by some other factor, such as the valuation by another party of the property proposed to be mortgaged. Once the Court has determined that the non-disclosed facts were material, speculation as to what course the constituent, on disclosure, would have taken is not relevant.[108]

---

103 *Breen v Williams* (1996) 186 CLR 71, 125 (Gummow J); *Pascoe Ltd v Lucas* [1999] SASC 519, (1999) 75 SASR 246 [264]–[265].

104 M Conaglen, '*Brickenden*' in S Degeling and JNE Varuhas (eds), *Equitable Compensation and Disgorgement of Profits* (Hart 2017) 130.

105 *Beach Petroleum NL v Kennedy* [1999] NSWCA 408, (1999) 48 NSWLR 1 [447]; *Watson v Ebsworth & Ebsworth (a firm)* [2010] VSCA 335, (2010) 31 VR 123 [166].

106 [1934] 3 DLR 465.

107 Even though the solicitor was ordered to pay to the bank the amount that he had received out of the bank's loan to the borrower, both the Supreme Court of Canada and the Privy Council described the remedy as 'damages' and not as an account of profits: [1933] SCR 257, 258, 268 (SCC); [1934] 3 DLR 465, 469 (PC).

108 [1934] 3 DLR 465, 469.

[9.48]   Taken literally, this statement requires the court to assume, without investigation, that a disclosure of facts that a fiduciary wrongfully withheld from the principal would have made a difference to the principal's conduct. In circumstances in which the fiduciary disloyally entered into a transaction affecting the principal, rather than the principal entering into a transaction as happened in *Brickenden*, the same rule would amount to an irrebuttable presumption that the principal would not have authorised the transaction had the fiduciary sought such authorisation in advance. Thus, the hypothetical world with which the actual world is compared would be the world in which the fiduciary would not have engaged in the disloyal conduct.[109]

[9.49]   The High Court of Australia has considered the *Brickenden* rule only once, in obiter dicta in *Maguire v Makaronis*.[110] Prior to that case, a majority of Australian decisions had applied or approvingly referred to the *Brickenden* rule in the form of an irrebuttable presumption.[111] *Maguire v Makaronis* concerned the availability of rescission rather than equitable compensation. Nevertheless, Kirby J used the opportunity to endorse the *Brickenden* rule (in the form of an irrebuttable presumption) as having 'the advantage of simplicity and the prophylactic consequence of discouraging fiduciary default'.[112] The majority shared his interpretation of the *Brickenden* rule as an irrebuttable presumption,[113] but left open whether that rule applies in Australia, saying simply that 'a general denial of the applicability of the reasoning in *Brickenden* to delinquent fiduciaries' is 'not self-evident'.[114]

[9.50]   Many commentators understand *Maguire v Makaronis* as effectively endorsing the *Brickenden* rule (in the form of an irrebuttable presumption).[115] However, that may read too much into the majority's dictum in that case.[116] Since *Maguire v Makaronis*, there have been

---

109   M Conaglen, '*Brickenden*' in S Degeling and JNE Varuhas (eds), *Equitable Compensation and Disgorgement of Profits* (Hart 2017) 112, 141.

110   (1997) 188 CLR 449.

111   *Commonwealth Bank of Australia v Smith* (1991) 42 FCR 390, 394; *Wan v McDonald* (1992) 33 FCR 491, 520–21; *Stewart v Layton* (1992) 111 ALR 687, 713; *Gemstone Corporation of Australia Ltd v Grasso* (1994) 62 SASR 239, 243, 252; *Permanent Building Society (in liq) v Wheeler* (1994) 11 WAR 187, 245–46. A defence of hypothetical consent was recognised, however, in *Walden Properties Ltd v Beaver Properties Pty Ltd* [1973] 2 NSWLR 815, 847 (Hutley JA).

112   (1997) 188 CLR 449, 492.

113   Ibid, 470–73 (Brennan CJ, Gaudron, McHugh and Gummow JJ).

114   Ibid, 474 (Brennan CJ, Gaudron, McHugh and Gummow JJ).

115   J Berryman, 'Fact-Based Fiduciary Duties and Breaches of Confidence: An Overview of Their Imposition and Remedies for Breach' (2009) 15 NZBLQ 35, 50; M Cope, 'A Comparative Evaluation of Developments in Equitable Relief for Breach of Fiduciary Duty and Breach of Trust' (2007) 6 QUTLJJ 118, 139; M Foster, 'Causation in Context: Interpreting the Nexus Clause in the Refugee Convention' (2002) 23 Mich J Int L 265, 315 n 216; D Fox, 'Conflicts of Interest, Unjust Enrichment and Wrongdoing: A Commentary' in WR Cornish, R Nolan, J O'Sullivan and G Virgo (eds), *Restitution: Past, Present and Future* (Hart 1998) 130; AH Oosterhoff, R Chambers, M McInnes and L Smith, *Oosterhoff on Trusts: Text, Commentary and Materials* (7th edn, Carswell 2009) 842 n 265.

116   The view that the majority in *Maguire v Makaronis* had left the authority of the *Brickenden* rule in Australia open was taken in *O'Halloran v RT Thomas & Family Pty Ltd* (1998) 45 NSWLR 262, 276; *Duke Group Ltd (in liq) v Pilmer* (1999) 73 SASR 64, 235. See also V Vann, *Equitable Compensation in Australia: Principles and Problems* (VDM Verlag Dr Müller 2009) 191: 'the majority judgment goes closer to overruling *Brickenden* as it has been previously applied, than to maintaining it'.

conflicting decisions on the continuing authority of the *Brickenden* rule in Australia.[117] While such continuing authority has been assumed in many cases,[118] it has also been said that there can be no equitable compensation for breach of fiduciary duty unless there is a sufficient connection between the breach and the principal's loss,[119] and, in cases of non-disclosure, unless disclosure would have made a difference to the principal's course of action.[120] Indeed, it has been said that the *Brickenden* rule does not relieve the principal from the onus of proving causation,[121] and, in cases of non-disclosure, that the principal must prove that disclosure would have made a difference.[122]

Australian courts seem to vacillate between the two extreme positions: the placing of the onus of proving causation upon the principal (which is the English position[123]) and an irrebuttable presumption of a causal link. However, in some cases, a middle course was taken, under which the sole effect of the *Brickenden* rule is to permit the court to draw inferences as to what the principal would have done on disclosure, even though the principal has adduced little or no evidence on this matter.[124] While these decisions placed upon the principal the onus of proving causation, the approach taken nonetheless comes close to a rebuttable presumption of a causal link, which is the current position in Canada and New Zealand.[125]

[9.51]

---

117   In *White v Illawarra Mutual Building Society Ltd* [2002] NSWCA 164 [145], it was said that the *Brickenden* rule applies only to conflicts of duty and interest, not to conflicts of duty and duty. The opposite view was taken in *Eiszele v Hurburgh* [2011] TASSC 65 [51], relying on *Commonwealth Bank of Australia v Smith* (1991) 42 FCR 390, 394.

118   Eg *O'Halloran v RT Thomas & Family Pty Ltd* (1998) 45 NSWLR 262, 280–81 (Priestley JA); *Beach Petroleum NL v Kennedy* [1999] NSWCA 408, (1999) 48 NSWLR 1 [440]; *Fexuto Pty Ltd v Bosnjak Holdings Pty Ltd* [2001] NSWCA 97, (2001) 37 ACSR 672 [134]; *Expectation Pty Ltd v PRD Realty Pty Ltd* [2004] FCAFC 189, (2004) 140 FCR 17 [244]; *Watson v Ebsworth & Ebsworth (a firm)* [2010] VSCA 335, (2010) 31 VR 123 [165]; *Westpac Banking Corporation v Bell Group Ltd (in liq) (No 3)* [2012] WASCA 157, (2012) 44 WAR 1 [903] (Lee AJA); *ABN AMRO Bank NV v Bathurst Regional Council* [2014] FCAFC 65, (2014) 224 FCR 1 [1094]–[1098].

119   *O'Halloran v RT Thomas & Family Pty Ltd* (1998) 45 NSWLR 262, 276–77; *State Bank of New South Wales Ltd v Chia* [2000] NSWSC 552, (2000) 50 NSWLR 587 [179]; *Hodgson v Amcor Ltd* [2012] VSC 94, (2012) 264 FLR 1 [1654]–[1661]. See also *Beach Petroleum NL v Kennedy* [1999] NSWCA 408, (1999) 48 NSWLR 1 [444]–[448]. An opaque statement was made in *Westpac Banking Corporation v Bell Group Ltd (in liq) (No 3)* [2012] WASCA 157, (2012) 44 WAR 1 [903] (Lee AJA): there needs to be a sufficient link between the breach and the loss, which link may be established by the nature of the breach.

120   *Tonkin Thompson & Associates Pty Ltd v Mayr* (1998) 72 SASR 346, 353–54; *Thomas v SMP (International) Pty Ltd (No 4)* [2010] NSWSC 984 [73].

121   *Watson v Ebsworth & Ebsworth (a firm)* [2010] VSCA 335, (2010) 31 VR 123 [165]. See also *Rigg v Sheridan* [2008] NSWCA 79 [58]; *Rogers v Roche* [2016] QCA 340 [34].

122   *Cole v Miles* [2002] NSWCA 150 [80]; *Short v Crawley (No 30)* [2007] NSWSC 1322 [441]; *Simpson v Donnybrook Properties Pty Ltd* [2010] NSWCA 229 [99]–[101].

123   *Swindle v Harrison* [1997] 4 All ER 705, 718; *Satnam Investments Ltd v Dunlop Heywood & Co Ltd* [1999] 3 All ER 652, 668; *Nationwide Building Society v Balmer Radmore* [1999] PNLR 606, 671–72; *Gwembe Valley Development Co Ltd v Koshy* [2004] EWHC 2202, [2004] WTLR 97 [147]; *Murad v Al-Saraj* [2005] EWCA Civ 959, [2005] All ER (D) 503 [110], [120], [136].

124   *Cassis v Kalfus (No 2)* [2004] NSWCA 315 [94]; *GM & AM Pearce & Co Pty Ltd v Australian Tallow Producers* [2005] VSCA 113 [71]; *Thomas v SMP (International) Pty Ltd (No 4)* [2010] NSWSC 984 [74]–[75].

125   *Hodgkinson v Simms* [1994] 3 SCR 377, 441–42; *Amaltal Corporation Ltd v Maruha Corporation* [2007] NZSC 40, [2007] 3 NZLR 192 [30]; *Premium Real Estate Ltd v Stevens* [2009] NZSC 15, [2009] 2 NZLR 384 [40], [85]. It has been argued that the standard of proof to be satisfied by the fiduciary is higher in New Zealand than in Canada: J Glister, 'Breach of Fiduciary Duty: *Brickenden* Lives On (*Premium Real Estate v Stevens*)' (2011) 5 J Eq 59, 64–68.

A rebuttable presumption strikes an appropriate balance between the interests of the two parties. The fiduciary should not be required to pay compensation for loss not factually caused by the breach of fiduciary duty, but uncertainty as to the causal link should be resolved against the fiduciary, whose breach has caused the uncertainty.

[9.52]　　　An abandonment of the *Brickenden* rule in the form of an irrebuttable presumption would distinguish equitable compensation from other remedies for breach of fiduciary duty. An account of profits,[126] a constructive trust[127] and rescission[128] are available even if the principal would have authorised the fiduciary's conduct had such authorisation been sought. It could be argued that the same rule should apply to equitable compensation in order to combat any temptation of fiduciaries to put their own interest over the principal's and to provide a strong incentive to obtain informed consent.[129] On the other hand, a distinction between equitable compensation and the other remedies is defensible. All that an account of profits, a constructive trust and rescission do is to strip the fiduciary of profits made from the breach. They do not place the fiduciary in a worse position than without breach. By contrast, equitable compensation may well place the fiduciary in a worse position than without breach; this may be considered inappropriate where the principal, if asked in advance, would have authorised the fiduciary's conduct.[130]

[9.53]　　　In circumstances such as those present in *Brickenden* – the principal entering a transaction with a third party after the fiduciary gave advice without disclosing his personal interest in the transaction – the *Brickenden* rule entails only a presumption that the principal would not have entered into the impugned transaction had the fiduciary disclosed his personal interest in it. The *Brickenden* rule entails no presumption that the principal would not have entered into *any* transaction. An application of the *Brickenden* rule (even in the form of an irrebuttable presumption) thus does not preclude a finding that the principal, if fully informed, would have entered into another transaction and would have suffered loss from it.[131] However, the court will not speculate and will assume that without the fiduciary's breach, the principal's *status quo ante* would have continued, unless there is a sound basis for finding otherwise.[132]

126　*Gray v New Augarita Porcupine Mines Ltd* [1952] 3 DLR 1 (PC); *Rama v Millar* [1996] 1 NZLR 257 (PC) 260–61; *White v Illawarra Mutual Building Society Ltd* [2002] NSWCA 164 [144]; *Say-Dee Pty Ltd v Farah Constructions Pty Ltd* [2005] NSWCA 309 [186]–[193].

127　*Farah Constructions Pty Ltd v Say-Dee Pty Ltd* [2007] HCA 22, (2007) 230 CLR 89 [199].

128　*Swindle v Harrison* [1997] 4 All ER 705, 726; *Maguire v Makaronis* (1997) 188 CLR 449, 467, 472; *Tenji v Henneberry & Associates Pty Ltd* [2000] FCA 550, (2000) 98 FCR 324 [18]; *Gwembe Valley Development Co Ltd v Koshy* [2003] EWCA Civ 1048, (2003) All ER (D) 465 [145].

129　This view is taken by, eg, M Conaglen, '*Brickenden*' in S Degeling and JNE Varuhas (eds), *Equitable Compensation and Disgorgement of Profits* (Hart 2017) 133.

130　JD Heydon, 'Causal Relationships between a Fiduciary's Default and the Principal's Loss' (1994) 110 LQR 328, 332: 'it is one thing to strip a fiduciary of profit without much inquiry; it is another to hold him accountable for all loss without inquiry into relative causes'. For further discussion, see S Harder, 'Is a Defaulting Fiduciary Exculpated by the Principal's Hypothetical Consent?' (2008) 8 OUCLJ 25, 39–41.

131　*Stewart v Layton* (1992) 111 ALR 687, 713–15.

132　*Hodgkinson v Simms* (1994) 117 DLR (4th) 161, 200; *Nationwide Building Society v Balmer Radmore* [1999] PNLR 606, 671–72. For further discussion, see S Harder, 'Equitable Compensation for a Fiduciary's Non-Disclosure and Hypothetical Courses of Events' (2011) 5 J Eq 22, 31–41.

2   Intervening acts and remoteness of loss

It is established that equitable compensation for breach of fiduciary duty is not generally   [9.54]
limited by considerations of foreseeability or remoteness of damage.[133] The rationale for that
rule was explained by McLachlin J in the Supreme Court of Canada in *Canson Enterprises Ltd v
Boughton & Co*:

> In negligence we wish to protect reasonable freedom of action of the defendant, and the
> reasonableness of his or her action may be judged by what consequences can be
> foreseen. In the case of a breach of fiduciary duty, as in deceit, we do not have to look
> to the consequences to judge the reasonableness of the actions. A breach of fiduciary duty
> is a wrong in itself, regardless of whether a loss can be foreseen. Moreover, the high duty
> assumed and the difficulty of detecting such breaches make it fair and practical to adopt a
> measure of compensation calculated to ensure that fiduciaries are kept 'up to their
> duty'.[134]

In that case, the Supreme Court of Canada nonetheless held that equitable compensation   [9.55]
for breach of fiduciary duty may be denied in respect of loss that while being factually caused
by the fiduciary's breach, is attributable to a third party's conduct. A solicitor acted for the
purchasers in a land transaction and in the preparation of a joint venture agreement to
develop the land. Unknown to the purchasers, an intermediate company had bought the
land from the vendors and resold it to the purchasers at a substantially higher price. In breach
of his fiduciary duty towards the purchasers, the solicitor, who also acted for the intermediate
company in the transaction, failed to disclose to the purchasers that the land was not being
purchased directly from the vendors. Had the purchasers known this, they would not have
purchased the land.

The purchasers proceeded with development of the property but suffered substantial   [9.56]
losses when piles supporting a constructed warehouse began to sink. They obtained judgment
against the soils engineers and pile-driving company they had retained, but these defendants
could not pay. The purchasers then sued the solicitor for breach of fiduciary duty, but the trial
judge denied compensation for the loss caused by the negligence of the soils engineers and
pile-driving company, on the ground that this negligence had constituted an intervening act.
While the Supreme Court of Canada was unanimous in upholding that judgment, different
approaches were taken by the judges.

La Forest J, who spoke for four of the eight judges, said that while the result could be   [9.57]
reached on a purely equitable path, equitable compensation for breach of fiduciary duty is
subject to the common law concepts of remoteness of damage, mitigation and contributory
negligence.[135] McLachlin J, who spoke for three of the eight judges, rejected an application of

---

133   *Hill v Rose* [1990] VR 129, 144; *O'Halloran v RT Thomas & Family Pty Ltd* (1998) 45 NSWLR 262,
273; *Cripps v G & M Dawson Pty Ltd* [2006] NSWCA 81, (2006) ANZ ConvR 350 [40]; *Visnic v Sywak*
[2008] NSWSC 427 [9], [13]; *Hydrocool Pty Ltd v Hepburn (No 4)* [2011] FCA 495, (2011) 279 ALR 646
[496]; *Westpac Banking Corporation v Bell Group Ltd (in liq) (No 3)* [2012] WASCA 157, (2012) 44 WAR
1 [883]; *Wingecarribee Shire Council v Lehman Brothers Australia Ltd (in liq)* [2012] FCA 1028, (2012)
301 ALR 1 [995].

134   [1991] 3 SCR 534, 553. This view is elaborated by M O'Meara, 'Causation, Remoteness and Equitable
Compensation' (2005) 26 Aust Bar Rev 51, 63.

135   [1991] 3 SCR 534, 580–89.

common law principles to equitable compensation,[136] and based the outcome on the ground that under 'a common sense view of causation', the solicitor's breach of fiduciary duty had not caused the loss resulting from the negligence of the soils engineers and pile-driving company.[137] Stevenson J, while generally agreeing with La Forest J, rejected the idea of a fusion of law and equity,[138] and based the outcome of the case on the ground that the loss caused by the negligence of the soils engineers and pile-driving company was so unrelated and independent that it should not, in fairness, be attributed to the solicitor's breach of fiduciary duty.[139]

[9.58]   Australian courts have adopted McLachlin J's concept of 'a common sense view of causation' in respect of equitable compensation for breach of fiduciary duty; see [9.17]. Since McLachlin J used that concept to deny equitable compensation for loss caused by a *novus actus interveniens*, the adoption of the concept by Australian courts should mean that they too will generally deny such compensation. Indeed, in *Duke Group Ltd (in liq) v Pilmer*, the Full Court of the Supreme Court of South Australia said that 'certain intervening factors may destroy or qualify the right to compensation'.[140]

[9.59]   An exception was made in *O'Halloran v RT Thomas & Family Pty Ltd*.[141] The plaintiff company agreed to sell its shares in Jeffries Industries Ltd ('Jeffries') to Bowes & Brown Pty Ltd ('Bowes & Brown'). It was agreed that the shares would be transferred to Bowes & Brown after payment of the purchase price. Before such payment, the defendant, who was managing director of the plaintiff and chairman of the board of Jeffries, arranged for Bowes & Brown to be registered as the new shareholder in Jeffries' register of shares. He did so in order to retain control of Jeffries, with an ally. When another director of the plaintiff discovered the change of registration, the plaintiff sought payment of the purchase price from Bowes & Brown, without success. Subsequently, the price of shares in Jeffries commenced to decline, and eventually the shares became worthless.

[9.60]   The NSW Court of Appeal held that the defendant's breach of fiduciary duty in arranging the registration of Bowes & Brown as a new shareholder had deprived the plaintiff of the opportunity to sell the shares to someone else before the share price fell. Spigelman CJ, with whom Priestley JA and Meagher JA agreed, rejected the defendant's argument that the plaintiff's attempt to enforce the contract with Bowes & Brown was another cause of the plaintiff's failure to sell the shares to a third party:

> The affirmation of the contract with Bowes & Brown may, in a common law action, have been characterised as a novus actus interveniens. But this concept has no role to play in case of a breach of a fiduciary obligation involving disposition of property which disposition is fraudulent in equity.[142]

---

136   Ibid, 542–47.
137   Ibid, 551–56.
138   Ibid, 590–91.
139   Ibid, 590.
140   (1999) 73 SASR 64, 249 (Doyle CJ, Duggan and Bleby JJ), rev'd on other grounds [2001] HCA 31, (2001) 207 CLR 165. A different view was expressed obiter in *Bennett v Minister of Community Welfare* (1992) 176 CLR 408, 427–28 (McHugh J).
141   (1998) 45 NSWLR 262.
142   Ibid, 279.

In defence of this proposition, it might be argued that there is no reason why, in respect of **[9.61]** intervening acts, the misapplication of company property by a company director ought to be treated differently from the misapplication of trust property by a trustee. However, it may equally be argued that there is no reason why a disposition of the principal's property by the fiduciary ought to be treated differently from a disposition of the principal's property by the principal after the fiduciary failed to disclose material information, as happened in *Canson Enterprises Ltd v Boughton & Co.*

3   Contributory negligence

The common law doctrine that contributory negligence generally excludes liability (see [6.90]) **[9.62]** does not apply to equitable compensation for equitable wrongs. Nor do the statutes permitting an apportionment of liability by virtue of contributory negligence; see [6.91]. This does not exclude the development of an equitable apportionment regime, which might be expected in the light of maxims such as 'he who comes to equity must come with clean hands'[143] and 'he who seeks equity must do equity'.[144]

In two cases, *Day v Mead*[145] and *Mouat v Clark Boyce*,[146] the New Zealand Court of Appeal **[9.63]** upheld a reduction of equitable compensation for breach of fiduciary duty on the ground that the principal had contributed to the loss through unreasonable conduct, which was, respectively, the failure to check the solvency of a company before investing in it, and the failure to obtain independent advice before providing security for a loan taken out by a relative.[147] In both cases, the New Zealand Court of Appeal held the fiduciary concurrently liable at common law (breach of contract and negligence respectively), but the possibility of apportioning equitable compensation for breach of fiduciary duty was not confined to cases of concurrent liability. In *Mouat v Clark Boyce*, Cooke P said that:

> it is not easy to think of any reason why he or she who claims compensation because someone else has broken a duty of care or a fiduciary duty, however arising, should not at the same time accept some responsibility for his or her own actions. Short of contract to the contrary, surely none of us should be wholly free of responsibility for consequences to ourselves to which we have carelessly contributed.[148]

This approach was endorsed obiter by La Forest J in the Supreme Court of Canada in **[9.64]** *Canson Enterprises Ltd v Boughton & Co,*[149] considered at [9.54]–[9.57]. But the matter has

---

143   *Green v Sommerville* (1979) 141 CLR 594, 611; *Nelson v Nelson* (1995) 184 CLR 538, 551–52, 578–80, 593–94, 608–10; *Burke v LFOT Pty Ltd* [2002] HCA 17, (2002) 209 CLR 282 [18], [113], [143].

144   *Vadasz v Pioneer Concrete (SA) Pty Ltd* (1995) 184 CLR 102, 114–15; *Bridgewater v Leahy* (1998) 194 CLR 457, 474.

145   [1987] 2 NZLR 443.

146   [1992] 2 NZLR 559, rev'd on the ground that there was no liability: *Clark Boyce v Mouat* [1994] 1 AC 428 (PC).

147   In *Amaltal Corporation Ltd v Maruha Corporation* [2007] NZSC 40, [2007] 3 NZLR 192 [23] fn 17, the Supreme Court of New Zealand regarded contributory negligence as irrelevant to claims for a breach of fiduciary duty that constitutes fraud, and expressly left open the relevance of contributory negligence to any equitable claim. However, this statement was an obiter dictum made in a footnote without any discussion of the issue or reference to previous cases.

148   [1992] 2 NZLR 559, 566.

149   [1991] 3 SCR 534, 583–85.

remained controversial in Canada, with some decisions denying[150] and others supporting[151] the possibility of apportioning equitable compensation for breach of fiduciary duty. Such possibility has been denied by the English High Court[152] and by the High Court in Australia in *Pilmer v Duke Group Ltd (in liq)*.[153]

[9.65]   In *Pilmer*, McHugh, Gummow, Hayne and Callinan JJ denied the existence of a fiduciary relationship between the parties and made only brief remarks on the possibility of apportioning equitable compensation. They said that the High Court's decision in *Astley v Austrust Ltd*,[154] in which an application of the apportionment statutes to contractual liability was denied (see [5.109], indicated 'severe conceptual difficulties' in applying notions of contributory negligence to equitable compensation for breach of fiduciary duty.[155] If the apportionment statutes do not touch contractual liability, they do not touch the fiduciary relationship either, since a fiduciary must act in the interests of the principal.[156] Kirby J, dissenting, recognised a fiduciary relationship between the parties and therefore considered the possibility of apportionment in more detail. He too denied such a possibility with the argument that it would subvert the fiduciary's duty of undivided and unremitting loyalty,[157] and that there is no basis for finding contributory negligence on the part of the principal since the principal is entitled to place trust and confidence in the fiduciary.[158]

[9.66]   Even though the majority's remarks in *Pilmer* were obiter, the High Court's 'strong'[159] view will probably prevent Australian courts from reducing equitable compensation for breach of fiduciary duty on the ground of the principal's unreasonable conduct. A number of commentators share the fear that the possibility of such reduction would undermine the strictness of the fiduciary's duty of loyalty and impose upon the principal a duty to monitor the fiduciary.[160] Other commentators consider this fear exaggerated, pointing out that *because* the principal is entitled to trust the fiduciary, the principal's conduct would rarely be considered unreasonable

---

150   *Vita Health Co (1985) Ltd v Toronto-Dominion Bank* [1994] 9 WWR 360, 368; *Reid v Graybriar Industries Ltd* [2006] ABQB 519, (2006) 61 Alta LR (4th) 264 [178]–[179].

151   *M Tucci Construction Ltd v Lockwood* (2000) 8 BLR (3d) 113 [168]; *Lemberg v Perris* [2010] ONSC 3690, [2010] 6 CTC 116 [88]; *Laxey Partners Ltd v Strategic Energy Management Corporation* [2011] ONSC 6348, (2011) 108 OR (3d) 440 [127].

152   *Nationwide Building Society v Balmer Radmore* [1999] PNLR 606, 676–77; *Leeds & Holbeck Building Society v Arthur & Cole* [2002] PNLR 78, 80; *De Beer v Kanaar & Co (No 2)* [2002] EWHC 688 (Ch) [92].

153   [2001] HCA 31, (2001) 207 CLR 165.

154   (1999) 197 CLR 1.

155   [2001] HCA 31, (2001) 207 CLR 165 [86].

156   Ibid. In the wake of *Astley v Austrust Ltd*, the apportionment statutes were amended so as to apply also to the breach of a contractual duty of care, which in all jurisdictions other than South Australia must be concurrent with a tortious duty of care; see [5.111]. This does not affect the majority's argument in *Pilmer v Duke Group Ltd (in liq)* since the apportionment statutes still do not apply to strict contractual liability.

157   [2001] HCA 31, (2001) 207 CLR 165 [171], citing W Gummow, 'Compensation for Breach of Fiduciary Duty' in TG Youdan (ed), *Equity, Fiduciaries and Trusts* (Carswell 1989) 86.

158   [2001] HCA 31, (2001) 207 CLR 165 [172], citing KR Handley, 'Reduction of Damages Awards' in PD Finn (ed), *Essays on Damages* (LBC 1992) 127.

159   *Harris v Digital Pulse Pty Ltd* [2003] NSWCA 10, (2003) 56 NSWLR 298 [362] (Heydon JA).

160   In addition to the commentators cited by Kirby J in *Pilmer v Duke Group Ltd (in liq)*, see D Nolan and J Davies, 'Torts and Equitable Wrongs' in A Burrows (ed), *English Private Law* (3rd edn, OUP 2013) [17.202]; J Getzler, 'Am I My Beneficiary's Keeper? Fusion and Loss-Based Fiduciary Remedies' in S Degeling and J Edelman (eds), *Equity in Commercial Law* (LBC 2005) 271; S Worthington, 'Review of Hochelaga Lectures. Fusing Common Law and Equity: Remedies, Restitution and Reform* by Andrew Burrows' (2003) 119 LQR 519, 521.

so as to justify a reduction of compensation even if such reduction were available in principle.[161] Where, exceptionally, the principal's conduct was unreasonable and the court considers full compensation unjust, the absence of an apportionment regime may force the court to use less precise doctrines such as lack of clean hands[162] or *novus actus interveniens*, which may lead to a denial of any compensation.[163]

4   Mitigation

As mentioned at [9.65]–[9.66], a reduction of equitable compensation for breach of fiduciary duty by virtue of unreasonable conduct of the principal *prior to* becoming aware of the fiduciary's breach has been rejected with the argument that the principal is entitled to trust the fiduciary. The same argument cannot be made in respect of unreasonable conduct of the principal *after* becoming aware of the fiduciary's breach. A principal who is aware of a breach by the fiduciary must cease to repose trust in the fiduciary if the principal is free to do so.[164] A denial of compensation for loss caused by the principal's unreasonable conduct seems appropriate.   [9.67]

The Ontario Court of Appeal has applied common law's mitigation doctrine directly to breach of fiduciary duty.[165] In the decision by the Supreme Court of Canada in *Canson Enterprises Ltd v Boughton & Co* (see [9.54]–[9.57]), La Forest J, who spoke for four of the eight judges, endorsed an application of common law's mitigation doctrine,[166] whereas McLachlin J, who spoke for three judges, rejected that approach[167] but also said that the principal's failure 'to take the most obvious steps' to alleviate loss after notice of the fiduciary's breach may sever the causal link between that breach and the loss.[168] The difference between the two approaches 'may be fine in practice'.[169]   [9.68]

McLachlin J's statement has been approvingly quoted in some Australian cases,[170] but these references were not made in the specific context of mitigation. The Australian position is thus unclear.   [9.69]

---

161   J Beatson, 'Unfinished Business: Integrating Equity' in J Beatson, *The Use and Abuse of Unjust Enrichment: Essays on the Law of Restitution* (Clarendon Press 1991) 256; A Burrows, 'Remedial Coherence and Punitive Damages in Equity' in S Degeling and J Edelman (eds), *Equity in Commercial Law* (LBC 2005) 384–85; S Harder, 'Contributory Negligence in Contract and Equity' (2014) 13 Otago LR 307, 319–25.

162   L Aitken, 'Developments in Equitable Compensation: Opportunity or Danger?' (1993) 67 Aust LJ 596, 605.

163   V Vann, *Equitable Compensation in Australia: Principles and Problems* (Saarbrücken 2009) 334: the 'fear that allowing a plea of contributory negligence would relieve defendants of liability is paradoxically realised by *not* allowing such a plea'. In *Lipkin Gorman v Karpnale Ltd* [1987] 1 WLR 987, a firm whose partner had stolen money from it and gambled it away was denied any relief for loss sustained after the firm had reason to be suspicious but failed to undertake even a modest investigation.

164   L Ho, 'Attributing Losses to a Breach of Fiduciary Duty' (1998) 12 TLI 66, 76; C Rickett, 'Compensating for Loss in Equity – Choosing the Right Horse for Each Course' in P Birks and F Rose (eds), *Restitution and Equity, Volume 1: Resulting Trusts and Equitable Compensation* (Mansfield Press 2000) 183.

165   *Burke v Cory* (1959) 19 DLR (2d) 252, 263–64; *Laskin v Bache & Co Inc* (1971) 23 DLR (3d) 385, 393.

166   [1991] 3 SCR 534, 580–83.

167   Ibid, 542–47.

168   Ibid, 554, 556. The eighth judge, Stevenson J, said nothing specifically on mitigation but rejected the idea of a fusion of law and equity: ibid, 590–91.

169   C Rickett and T Gardner, 'Compensating for Loss in Equity: The Evolution of a Remedy' (1994) 24 VUWLR 19, 45.

170   *Duke Group Ltd (in liq) v Pilmer* (1999) 73 SASR 64, 247–48; *Visnic v Sywak* [2008] NSWSC 427 [9]; *Michael Wilson & Partners Ltd v Nicholls* [2009] NSWSC 1033 [377].

C   Breach of an equitable duty of care

1   Scope of liability

[9.70]   In *Permanent Building Society (in liq) v Wheeler*,[171] the Western Australian Full Court distinguished a fiduciary's equitable duty of care from a fiduciary's duty of loyalty. Ipp J, with whom Seaman J and Malcolm CJ agreed, said that the former duty, while being actionable in equity, does not stem from the requirements of trust and confidence imposed on a fiduciary, and is not governed by the same rules as the duty of loyalty.[172] In particular, Ipp J said that the *Brickenden* rule stated at [9.47] applies only to breaches of a true fiduciary obligation, carrying with it, ordinarily, the 'stench of dishonesty'.[173] He went on to make the following statement:

> It is also significant, as regards matters of policy, that the tortious duty not to be negligent, and the equitable obligation on the part of a trustee to exercise reasonable care and skill are, in content, the same. There is every reason, in my view, in such circumstances, to apply the maxim that 'equity follows the law'.[174]

[9.71]   Ipp J[175] quoted the following statement made by La Forest J in *Canson Enterprises Ltd v Boughton & Co*:

> Where 'the measure of duty is the same', the same rule should apply . . . it would be odd if a different result followed depending solely on the manner in which one framed an identical claim.[176]

[9.72]   These remarks could be interpreted[177] as saying that equitable compensation for breach of an equitable duty of care is subject to the same limiting factors (such as remoteness of damage) that apply to damages for breach of a tortious duty of care. However, the opposite proposition could be inferred[178] from Ipp J's subsequent statement that, in considering the equitable duty of care *in casu*,[179] he was applying Street J's statement in *Re Dawson* that '[c]onsiderations of causation, foreseeability and remoteness do not readily enter into the matter'.[180] The whole discussion, which occurred under the heading 'Causality and the breach of the equitable duty of care', was concerned only with the requirement of factual causation, and it may well be that Ipp J had no intention to say anything on the scope of liability.

[9.73]   Subsequently, in *Bristol and West Building Society v Mothew*,[181] the English Court of Appeal adopted the distinction between a fiduciary's equitable duty of care and a fiduciary's

---

171   (1994) 11 WAR 187.
172   Ibid, 237–39. This doctrine is criticised by A Goldfinch, 'Trustee's Duty to Exercise Reasonable Care: Fiduciary Duty?' (2004) 78 ALJ 678; JD Heydon, 'Are the Duties of Company Directors to Exercise Care and Skill Fiduciary?' in S Degeling and J Edelman, *Equity in Commercial Law* (LBC 2005) 185.
173   (1994) 11 WAR 187, 246.
174   Ibid, 247–48.
175   Ibid, 248.
176   [1991] 3 SCR 534, 586–87. La Forest J spoke for four of the eight judges. The other four judges opposed an application of common law concepts to equitable compensation; see [9.57].
177   As done in *Olympic Holdings Pty Ltd v Lochel* [2004] WASC 61 [245].
178   As done in *Australian Securities and Investments Commission v Rich* [2009] NSWSC 1229, (2009) 236 FLR 1 [7189].
179   (1994) 11 WAR 187, 248.
180   [1966] 2 NSWR 211, 215.
181   [1998] Ch 1.

duty of loyalty, and endorsed a limitation of equitable compensation for breach of the former duty by common law concepts of remoteness. Millett LJ, with whom Otton LJ agreed on that issue, observed:

> Although the remedy which equity makes available for breach of the equitable duty of skill and care is equitable compensation rather than damages, this is merely the product of history and in this context is in my opinion a distinction without a difference. Equitable compensation for breach of the duty of skill and care resembles common law damages in that it is awarded by way of compensation to the plaintiff for his loss. There is no reason in principle why the common law rules of causation, remoteness of damage and measure of damages should not be applied by analogy in such a case.[182]

This approach has been endorsed by the New Zealand Court of Appeal,[183] but was doubted by the High Court of Australia in *Youyang Pty Ltd v Minter Ellison Morris Fletcher*. [9.74]

> [T]here must be a real question whether the unique foundation and goals of equity, which has the institution of the trust at its heart, warrant any assimilation even in this limited way with the measure of compensatory damages in tort and contract.[184]

Elliott and Edelman have argued that the High Court's appeal to the sanctity of the trusting relationship is misplaced where the breach consists in carelessness rather than disloyalty.[185] They have expressed the hope that Australian courts will not take up the High Court's 'unfortunate suggestion'.[186] A more nuanced view is taken by O'Meara, who has suggested that principles relating to the scope of liability ought to apply to the breach of an equitable duty of care unless it occurred in the administration of trust property.[187] [9.75]

When he was a judge of the Federal Court, Edelman J expressed the view that the breach of a trustee's equitable duty of care, like the breach of a tortious duty of care, is actionable only upon proof of loss because 'the foundation for the duty of care by a trustee is the same as the foundation of a common law duty of care, although in either case the content will depend upon the nature of the responsibilities assumed'.[188] If it is accepted that an equitable duty of care and a common law duty of care have the same foundation, a fundamental difference in relation to the scope of liability cannot be justified. [9.76]

2 Contributory negligence

As mentioned at [9.73], Millett LJ in *Bristol and West Building Society v Mothew* suggested that 'the common law rules of causation, remoteness of damage and measure of damages' apply to [9.77]

---

182   Ibid, 17. He has repeated this view extra-judicially: PJ Millett, 'Equity's Place in the Law of Commerce' (1998) 114 LQR 214, 226.

183   *Bank of New Zealand v New Zealand Guardian Trust Co Ltd* [1999] 1 NZLR 664, 681–82, 688.

184   [2003] HCA 15, (2003) 212 CLR 484 [39] (Gleeson CJ, McHugh, Gummow, Kirby and Hayne JJ). The case is considered at [9.32]–[9.34].

185   S Elliott and J Edelman, '*Target Holdings* Considered in Australia' (2003) 119 LQR 545, 550.

186   Ibid.

187   M O'Meara, 'Causation, Remoteness and Equitable Compensation' (2005) 26 Aust Bar Rev 51, 66–69. See also D Hayton, P Matthews and C Mitchell, *Underhill and Hayton: Law Relating to Trusts and Trustees* (19th edn, LexisNexis 2016) [87.49].

188   *Australian Securities and Investments Commission v Drake (No 2)* [2016] FCA 1552, (2016) 340 ALR 75 [305].

equitable compensation for breach of an equitable duty of care, as opposed to breach of fiduciary duty.[189] Millett LJ did not expressly mention contributory negligence, but his reference to the 'measure of damages' and his general analogy to common law damages may suggest that he envisaged the possibility of reducing equitable compensation for breach of an equitable duty of care by virtue of contributory negligence.

[9.78]   Millett LJ's statement seems to have been applied with that interpretation in *Yu v Kwok*,[190] where accountants neglected to inform their client that they had deposited the client's money with a certain bank, which subsequently went bankrupt. In a decision on liability in principle, Simos J in the NSW Supreme Court held the accountants liable in negligence and for breach of an equitable duty of care, but not for breach of fiduciary duty. Simos J held that tortious damages be reduced by 15% on account of the client's contributory negligence.[191] Relying on Millett LJ's statement in *Bristol and West Building Society v Mothew*, Simos J went on to say that in the instant case the measure of equitable compensation was the same as the measure of damages for negligence.[192] This implies that the reduction by 15% on account of contributory negligence applied to equitable compensation, too.

[9.79]   Subsequently, in *Youyang Pty Ltd v Minter Ellison Morris Fletcher*,[193] the High Court of Australia doubted the correctness of Millett LJ's proposition. It is therefore unclear whether in Australia equitable compensation for breach of an equitable duty of care can be reduced by virtue of contributory negligence.

---

189   [1998] Ch 1, 17.
190   [1999] NSWSC 992. See also *Youyang Pty Ltd v Minter Ellison* [2001] NSWCA 198 [97] (Young CJ in Eq), rev'd on other grounds: *Youyang Pty Ltd v Minter Ellison Morris Fletcher* [2003] HCA 15, (2003) 212 CLR 484.
191   [1999] NSWSC 992 [138]–[141].
192   Ibid, [158]–[159].
193   [2003] HCA 15, (2003) 212 CLR 484 [39]. The relevant passage is quoted at [9.74].

PART **3**

REMEDIES COMPELLING PERFORMANCE AND RELATED REMEDIES

10

SPECIFIC PERFORMANCE

I   Introduction

[10.1]   A remedy is *specific* when the plaintiff seeks to get the court to coerce the defendant into doing (or not doing) a particular thing. The word 'coercion' is used advisedly. The court orders the defendant to do (or not to do) the particular thing, and if the defendant refuses to comply, the court may use measures such as imprisonment, sequestration and fines to encourage compliance with its order.[1] The two most important examples of specific relief in Australia are the decree of specific performance and the injunction. This chapter will consider specific performance, and the next chapter will consider injunctions. Specific performance relates to ordering the defendant to comply with the terms of a contract, but injunctions may be ordered across private law and beyond. Specific performance is exclusively equitable, and generally operates in relation to a common law cause of action, namely, breach of contract.

[10.2]   Both specific performance and injunctions are equitable remedies, meaning that they originated in the Court of Chancery. In *Mayfair Trading Co v Dreyer*, Dixon J explained that historically, a plaintiff needed to show 'an equity' to relief before the Court of Chancery would award specific relief.[2] Equitable remedies are no longer awarded by a separate Court of Chancery in England or Australia because common law and equitable courts have been administratively and procedurally fused, and courts have a concurrent jurisdiction to administer common law and equity.[3] It was previously necessary for a plaintiff who unsuccessfully attempted to claim equitable relief in the Court of Chancery to begin again in the common law courts. Lord Cairns' Act was an early attempt to rectify this by giving Courts of Chancery the power to award damages in lieu of specific performance or an injunction.[4]

[10.3]   Equitable remedies such as specific performance are only available under the auxiliary jurisdiction of equity when the common law remedy (usually damages) is shown to be 'inadequate'. Even then, an equitable remedy does not follow as a matter of course, as equitable remedies are discretionary.

II   The nature of specific performance

[10.4]   Specific performance of a contract means that the court directs a party to perform the contract according to its stipulations and terms.[5] The defendant is required to do the thing which she contracted to do, and if she does not obey, the court will treat this as contempt of court.[6]

[10.5]   Some cases and many texts distinguish between specific performance in the 'limited' or 'true' sense (where the court issues an order that the plaintiff execute some document that will

---

1   See [20.78]–[20.84].
2   (1958) 101 CLR 428, 450.
3   In England and Wales: *Judicature Act 1873* (36 & 37 Vict c 66) and *Judicature Act 1875* (38 & 39 Vict c 77). In Australia, see *Supreme Court Act 1933* (ACT), ss 25–32; *Supreme Court Act 1970* (NSW), ss 57–63; *Law Reform (Law and Equity) Act 1972* (NSW), s 5; *Civil Proceedings Act 2011* (Qld), s 7; *Supreme Court Act 1935* (SA), ss 20–28; *Supreme Court Civil Procedure Act 1932* (Tas), ss 10–11; *Supreme Court Act 1986* (Vic), s 29; *Supreme Court Act 1935* (WA), ss 24–25.
4   See [12.1]–[12.6].
5   See PH Pettit, *Equity and the Law of Trusts* (12th edn, OUP 2012) 663–64.
6   See Sir E Fry, *A Treatise on the Specific Performance of Contracts* (GR Northcote ed, 6th edn, Stevens 1921) 2.

be legally binding) and specific performance in the 'broad' sense or 'quasi-specific perform-ance' (where the contract is already executed by the plaintiff and she simply requires the defendant to perform the obligations he has undertaken).[7] We deal with specific performance in the wider sense in this chapter. It has been argued that this distinction should not be maintained,[8] and Hepburn has said that such 'arbitrary distinctions' are 'unnecessary and superfluous'.[9] Our position is similar, with the caveat that the distinction may still have relevance in the context of readiness and willingness. It may follow, however, that if the traditional division between 'limited' and 'broad' specific performance is no longer relevant, specific performance begins to resemble a mandatory injunction.[10]

Specific performance is generally directed towards contracts, but it may also extend to promises that will be supported by the law of equitable estoppel. The fulfilment of expect-ations via a remedy such as specific performance or an injunction was regarded in early Australian estoppel cases as the minimum equity required to enforce a gratuitous promise,[11] but *Giumelli v Giumelli* established that specific relief will not be awarded where it would be unconscionable or unjust to the estopped party or to third parties, and a lesser remedy would suffice.[12] Nonetheless, in many cases, courts still require the defendant to make good the assumption relied upon because no other remedy is appropriate in the circumstances.[13]   [10.6]

Specific performance may also be available where a contract does not comply with formalities, but there are acts of part performance which allow the contract to be specifically enforced in equity.[14]   [10.7]

The default remedy for breach of contract is an award of compensatory damages, discussed in Ch 5. In order to obtain specific performance of a contract, the plaintiff has to establish that compensatory damages are inadequate. Historically, this is a matter of jurisdiction: the court cannot award specific performance *unless* damages are inadequate.[15] As discussed below,   [10.8]

---

7   *Wolverhampton & Walsall Railway Co v London & North-Western Railway Co* (1873) LR 16 Eq 433, 439 (Lord Selbourne); *Pakenham Upper Fruit Co v Crosby* (1924) 35 CLR 386, 394 (Isaacs and Rich JJ); *JC Williamson Ltd v Lukey* (1931) 45 CLR 282, 297 (Dixon J); *Waterways Authority of New South Wales v Coal & Allied (Operations) Pty Ltd* [2007] NSWCA 276, (2008) Aust Contract R 90–278 [62]–[64] (Beazley JA). See also PW Young, C Croft and ML Smith, *On Equity* (LBC 2009) [16.870]–[16.880]; JD Heydon, MJ Leeming and PG Turner, *Meagher, Gummow and Lehane's Equity: Doctrines and Remedies* (5th edn, LexisNexis Butterworths 2015) [20–005]–[20–020].

8   *Australian Hardwoods Pty Ltd v Commissioner for Railways* [1961] 1 WLR 425, 433–34; JD Heydon and MJ Leeming, *Cases and Materials on Equity and Trusts* (LexisNexis 2011) 1126; PH Pettit, *Equity and the Law of Trusts* (12th edn, OUP 2012) 663–64.

9   S Hepburn, 'Specific Performance' in P Parkinson (ed), *The Principles of Equity* (2nd edn, LBC 2003) [1702].

10   *Burns Philp Trust Co Ltd v Kwikasair Freightlines Ltd* [1964] NSWR 63.

11   A Robertson, 'Satisfying the Minimum Equity: Equitable Estoppel Remedies after Verwayen' (1996) 20 MULR 805.

12   *Giumelli v Giumelli* [1999] HCA 10, (1999) 196 CLR 101 [34]–[50], quoting Deane J in *Commonwealth v Verwayen* (1990) 170 CLR 394, 442–43, where he said that expectations would not be fulfilled where it would be 'inequitably harsh'. In the event, specific performance was not granted in *Giumelli* and the plaintiff instead received equitable compensation reflecting the value of the relied-upon assumption. See J Paterson, A Robertson and A Duke, *Principles of Contract Law* (5th edn, LBC 2016) 200–04.

13   Particularly in cases of proprietary estoppel where the defendant encouraged an expectation that a promise would be fulfilled: see PW Young, C Croft and ML Smith, *On Equity* (LBC 2009) 957 [14.240], citing *Donis v Donis* [2007] VSCA 89, (2007) 19 VR 577; *O'Neill v Williams* [2006] NSWSC 707 [73]; *Lieschke v Lieschke* [2003] NSWSC 743.

14   See, eg, *Price v Strange* [1978] Ch 337.

15   ICF Spry, *The Principles of Equitable Remedies* (9th edn, LBC 2014) 61–3.

some recent cases suggest that inadequacy of damages is not a jurisdictional hurdle, but simply a discretionary consideration to be taken into account with all other matters of discretion. Specific performance is more readily available than it was in the past.

[10.9]   In civilian jurisdictions such as France and Germany, and in jurisdictions which have a hybrid of civilian and common law (such as Scotland), the default remedy for breach of contract is specific performance. Interestingly, the Scots law of 'specific implement' produces similar outcomes in practice to the common law, even though Scots law *starts* from the presumption that the pursuer (plaintiff) is entitled to specific performance of the contractual obligation.[16] Although specific implement is available as of right, the right is qualified in ways which make the outcome of a Scottish contract case look very similar to the English common law outcome in practice.[17] Similarly, in French and German law, while specific performance is the presumptive remedy for breach of contract, Treitel has said that in practice the exceptions to the rule that specific performance will be awarded are more important than the rule itself.[18] Ordinarily, parties prefer to claim damages in cases where their losses can be easily assessed.[19] Some have argued that the difference between the common law and civil law systems such as Scots, German and French law may not be as dramatic as they seem.[20] However, it has also been argued that English law and French law are fundamentally different in the way they protect the right to contractual performance, including the willingness to award specific performance.[21]

III   The relationship between specific performance and injunctions

[10.10]   The distinction between specific performance and injunctions is difficult to maintain at times, and many issues overlap.[22] Nonetheless, this book maintains the distinction because important differences remain.

[10.11]   Generally, it is easier to obtain an injunction than an order for specific performance.[23] This is because specific performance is mandatory (ordering the defendant to take positive action as

---

16   E McKendrick, 'Specific Implement and Specific Performance – a Comparison' (1986) SLT 249. However, a different attitude exists towards 'keep open' clauses; compare *Cooperative Insurance Society Ltd v Argyll Stores (Holdings) Ltd* [1998] AC 1 with *Retail Parks Investments Ltd v Royal Bank of Scotland plc (No 2)* 1996 SC 227 and *Highland and Universal Properties Ltd v Safeway Properties Ltd* 2000 SC 297.
17   Specific implement is generally unavailable where (1) the obligation is only to pay money, (2) the contract involves a personal or intimate relationship, (3) there is no *pretium affectionis* or subjective special value attaching to the subject matter of the contract, (4) compliance with the decree would be impossible, (5) the decree would be unenforceable, (6) the decree would cause exceptional hardship or be inconvenient or unjust, or (7) the court decides in its discretion that damages are adequate in the circumstances. See McKendrick, ibid.
18   GH Treitel, *Remedies for Breach of Contract: A Comparative Account* (OUP 1988) 53.
19   Ibid, 71; K Zweigert and H Kötz, *Introduction to Comparative Law* (T Weir tr, 3rd edn, OUP 1998) 484.
20   Treitel, ibid, 53.
21   S Rowan, *Remedies for Breach of Contract: A Comparative Analysis of the Protection of Performance* (OUP 2012).
22   See [11.12].
23   J O'Sullivan, 'Specific Performance' in J McGhee (ed), *Snell's Equity* (33rd edn, Sweet & Maxwell 2015) [17–005].

stipulated by the contract), but many injunctions are prohibitive (simply ordering the defendant not to do something), so they are more readily awarded because they are less intrusive.[24]

It is sometimes said that specific performance is awarded to compel performance of all outstanding obligations under a contract, but it has been observed that this is only the case in relation to executory contracts (where the court is awarding specific performance in the 'limited' or 'true' sense).[25] Specific performance begins to look increasingly like a form of mandatory injunction if the distinction between 'limited' and 'broad' specific performance is not maintained. Indeed, contractual rights may often be enforced by a mandatory injunction rather than specific performance.[26]   [10.12]

An injunction is more likely to be sought to restrain breaches of specific clauses of a contract as well as to restrain torts, equitable wrongs, and statutory wrongs. Specific performance may be given for threatened breach of contract in exceptional circumstances,[27] and, similarly, injunctions can be awarded to restrain future or threatened breaches of obligations.   [10.13]

Importantly, injunctions are sometimes granted where specific performance would not be granted – namely, to restrain the breach of a negative covenant (a contractual undertaking not to do something). Courts are far less willing to grant mandatory injunctions requiring compliance with positive obligations under contracts, particularly in relation to contracts involving services, because such an award would be tantamount to awarding specific performance,[28] which, for reasons discussed later in this chapter, is seen as intrinsically problematic.   [10.14]

A negative covenant may be express or implied. In determining whether a contractual obligation is negative or positive, courts look to the substance of the obligation rather than the form. As explained in greater detail at [11.37]–[11.39], an obligation will be regarded as negative if inactivity on the part of the defendant would constitute compliance with the term. Sometimes a clause expressed in a positive manner will imply a negative obligation, and an injunction may be awarded to restrain a breach of that clause.[29] For example, a promise expressed in positive terms that Yolanda will only purchase widgets from Xenophon implies a negative obligation not to purchase widgets from anyone else.   [10.15]

To obtain specific performance or an injunction for common law causes of action such as contract and tort, it is necessary to first establish that damages are inadequate. Compensatory damages are the default remedy for breach of common law obligations, and specific performance and injunctions are available only through equity's auxiliary jurisdiction.   [10.16]

By contrast, there is no need to establish that damages are inadequate to obtain specific relief for causes of action which originate in equity (such as breach of fiduciary duty, breach of confidence and equitable estoppel). Injunctions are readily available through equity's exclusive jurisdiction. The origin of the cause of action continues to be vitally important to making out an entitlement to an injunction. Specific performance per se is not usually granted for   [10.17]

---

24   See [11.10].
25   D Wright, *Remedies* (2nd ed, Federation Press 2015) 160–61, citing *Bridge Wholesale Acceptance Corporation (Australia) Ltd v Burnard* (1992) 27 NSWLR 415, 423–24 (Clarke JA).
26   ICF Spry, *The Principles of Equitable Remedies* (9th edn, LBC 2014) 557.
27   *Turner v Bladin* (1951) 82 CLR 463, 472 (Williams, Fullagar and Kitto JJ).
28   *Businessworld Computers Pty Ltd v Australian Telecommunications Commission* (1988) 82 ALR 499, 501 (Gummow J); *Administrative and Clerical Officers Association v Commonwealth* (1979) 26 ALR 497, 501 (Mason J).
29   See, eg, *Metropolitan Electric Supply v Ginder* [1901] 2 Ch 799.

performance of a trust although there is an order which resembles it where trust funds are concerned, called 'specific enforcement' or 'an order to compel performance'.[30]

[10.18]   Similarly, where statutory causes of action are concerned (such as a breach of the Australian Consumer Law ('ACL'))[31] there is no need to establish that damages are inadequate, as specific relief is available as part of the 'smorgasbord' of remedial possibilities. Courts have the power to award an injunction to prevent a breach of provisions of the ACL pursuant to s 232, as well as other forms of order which resemble specific performance pursuant to ss 237, 238 and 239. The latter provisions require some loss or damage to be identified.

IV   Inadequacy of damages and subject matter of contract

A   Inadequacy of damages

[10.19]   Lord Redesdale in *Harnett v Yielding* explained the concept of inadequacy of damages as follows:

> Unquestionably the original foundation of these decrees was simply this, that damages at law would not give the party the compensation to which he was entitled; that is, would not put him in a situation as beneficial to him as if the agreement were specifically performed. On this ground, the court in a variety of cases, has refused to interfere, where from the nature of the case, the damages must necessarily be commensurate to the injury sustained ... For instance, in agreements for the purchase of stock: it is the same thing to the party where or from whom the stock is purchased, provided he receives the money that will purchase it.[32]

[10.20]   Historically, inadequacy of damages has been a threshold jurisdictional issue where specific performance of a contract is sought. In other words, a court will not have jurisdiction to award specific performance if damages are adequate.[33] However, as Spry has noted,[34] there has been an increasing tendency (particularly in England) to reduce inadequacy of damages from a threshold jurisdictional issue to a more generalised discretionary consideration to be taken into account along with other discretionary considerations.[35] Moreover, instead of asking whether damages are inadequate, some cases have asked whether it is 'just' in the circumstances.[36] For example, in *Beswick v Beswick*, Lord Upjohn said that specific performance would be granted 'when damages are inadequate to meet the justice of the case'.[37] While Lord

---

30   R Chambers, 'Liability' in P Birks and A Pretto (eds), *Breach of Trust* (Hart 2002) 10.

31   The ACL is in Schedule 2 of the *Competition and Consumer Act 2010* (Cth).

32   (1805) 2 Sch & Lef 549, 553–54; [1803–13] All ER Rep 704, 705.

33   ICF Spry, *The Principles of Equitable Remedies* (9th edn, LBC 2014) 61–63.

34   Ibid, 63.

35   See, eg, *Sky Petroleum Ltd v VIP Petroleum Ltd* [1974] 1 WLR 576; *Verrall v Great Yarmouth Borough Council* [1981] QB 202.

36   See, eg, *Beswick v Beswick* [1968] AC 58, 102; *Evans Marshall & Co Ltd v Bertola SA* [1973] 1 WLR 349, 379; *The Stena Nautica (No 2)* [1982] 2 Lloyd's Rep 336; *State Transport Authority v Apex Quarries Ltd* [1988] VR 187.

37   [1968] AC 58, 102.

Upjohn's test has apparently been cited with approval by two High Court judges in *Trident General Insurance Co Ltd v McNiece Brothers Pty Ltd*,[38] a majority of the NSW Court of Appeal has doubted whether it represents the Australian approach.[39] In *Evans Marshall & Co Ltd v Bertola SA*, Sachs LJ said that the real question was not whether damages were adequate, but whether specific relief was the fairer remedy in the circumstances:

> The standard question … 'are damages an adequate remedy?' might perhaps in the light of authorities in recent years, be rewritten, 'is it just in all the circumstances that a plaintiff should be confined to his remedy in damages?'[40]

This approach has not attracted much support in Australia in relation to specific performance.[41]

[10.21] Whether one considers inadequacy of damages to be a jurisdictional hurdle or a discretionary factor has ramifications for the availability of damages in lieu of an injunction or specific performance pursuant to Lord Cairns' Act provisions, where it is necessary to show that the court has jurisdiction to grant specific relief.[42] If inadequacy of damages is a discretionary question, the court will almost invariably have a jurisdiction to award damages in lieu of specific performance, whereas if inadequacy of damages is a jurisdictional question, that jurisdiction exists only if it can be shown that damages would be inadequate and there was jurisdiction to award specific relief. This book does not subsume inadequacy of damages into the discretionary considerations, but leaves open the question of whether it is a jurisdictional or a discretionary consideration. On balance, because of the impact on Lord Cairns' Act damages, it may be preferable to regard inadequacy of damages as a jurisdictional question which goes towards the court's jurisdiction to award damages in lieu of specific relief.

[10.22] Some academic commentary has argued that the concept of 'inadequacy of damages' should be abolished and replaced with a broader concept of what is 'just' in the circumstances. For example, Elizabeth MacDonald has argued that the 'inadequacy of damages' hurdle allows the court to dismiss cases too easily without looking at whether damages are genuinely adequate for the plaintiff.[43] In an American context, Douglas Laycock has argued that the test no longer reflects what the courts actually do in practice.[44] Okeoghene Odudu and Graham Virgo have similarly argued in an English context that the test is so bedevilled by uncertainty that its use in the context of granting gain-based relief should not be encouraged.[45]

[10.23] It is suggested that adequacy of damages is an appropriate test if it is properly understood. In ascertaining whether damages are adequate, one must look at what the plaintiff hoped to gain from the contract, and whether damages are an adequate substitute for the plaintiff's

---

38   (1988) 165 CLR 107, 119 (Mason CJ and Wilson J).
39   *Waterways Authority of New South Wales v Coal & Allied (Operations) Pty Ltd* [2007] NSWCA 276, (2008) Aust Contract R 90–278 [95] (Beazley JA, with whom Campbell JA agreed). Cf *Mayo Group International Pty Ltd v Hudson Respiratory Care Inc* [2005] NSWSC 445, [48] (Young CJ in Eq).
40   [1973] 1 WLR 349, 379.
41   JD Heydon, MJ Leeming and PG Turner, *Meagher, Gummow and Lehane's Equity: Doctrines and Remedies* (5th edn, LexisNexis Butterworths 2015) [20–030].
42   See [12.15]–[12.19].
43   E MacDonald, 'The Inadequacy of Adequacy: The Granting of Specific Performance' (1987) 38 NILQ 244.
44   D Laycock, 'The Death of the Irreparable Injury Rule' (1990) 103 Harv L Rev 687.
45   O Odudu and G Virgo, 'Inadequacy of Compensatory Damages' [2009] 17 RLR 112. Cf K Barnett, *Accounting for Profit for Breach of Contract: Theory and Practice* (Hart 2012) 78–80.

interest in performance of the contract.[46] Contractual damages seek to fulfil the plaintiff's expectations and put the plaintiff in a position as if the contract had been performed. Sometimes damages do not achieve this, particularly where the subject matter of the contract is unique, irreplaceable, or hard to value. If there is not an open market for a thing, then the court cannot value the thing. Money is not an adequate substitute because it may be under-compensatory, or because it is impossible or very difficult for the plaintiff to go onto the open market and purchase a substitute.[47] It is in these circumstances that courts are more likely to award specific performance. However, courts do not allow insolvency to render damages inadequate, because an award of specific performance would give the plaintiff priority over other unsecured creditors.

[10.24]   The way in which one views the relationship between specific performance and the availability of damages goes to the heart of the way in which one views contractual obligations. Oliver Wendell Holmes famously said of the contractual promise: 'The duty to keep a contract at common law means a prediction that you must pay damages if you do not keep it, – and nothing else'.[48] Taken literally, this means that there is no right to enforce a promise via specific relief. However, as Sir Frederick Pollock responded to Holmes, the availability of specific performance and injunctions to prevent breach of contract suggests that this argument cannot stand, as do several other aspects of contract and tort law.[49]

[10.25]   The modern inheritors of the Holmesian tradition are arguably the Chicago law-and-economics scholars, particularly Richard Posner, who insists that parties should be free to breach their contracts and enter a more profitable contract, subject only to an obligation to pay damages ('efficient breach theory').[50] Nonetheless, Posner has conceded that efficient breach theory is undermined by the availability of specific relief:

> [I]njunctive relief is possible only when the remedy at law – that is, damages – is unavailable. For in such a case the contractual undertaking loses its either-or character; instead of a promise of performance or damages, it is a promise of performance or nothing.[51]

[10.26]   The High Court of Australia has categorically rejected Holmes's view of contract, saying that 'subject to the established limits of specific performance and injunctions, each contracting party may be said to have a right to the performance of the contract by the other'.[52]

---

46   A Kronman, 'Specific Performance' (1978) 45 U Chi L Rev 351.
47   RJ Sharpe, 'Specific Relief for Contract Breach' in B Reiter and J Swan (eds), *Studies in Contract Law* (Butterworths 1980) 123.
48   OW Holmes Jr, 'The Path of the Law' (1897) 10 Harv L Rev 61, 62. See also OW Holmes Jr, *The Common Law* (Little, Brown & Co 1881) 301: 'The only universal consequence of a legally binding promise is, that the law makes the promisor pay damages if the promised event does not come to pass'.
49   See Pollock's letter to Holmes dated 17 September 1897 and Holmes's letter to Pollock dated 12 March 1911, reproduced in M De Wolfe Howe (ed), *The Holmes–Pollock Letters: The Correspondence of Mr Justice Holmes and Sir Frederick Pollock 1874–1932* (Harvard University Press 1942) vol 1, 79–80 and 177 respectively; Sir Frederick Pollock, *The Principles of Contracts* (8th edn, Stevens 1911) 192, fn K. Pollock also mentioned the doctrine of anticipatory breach (which indicates that courts usually expect parties to perform their obligation under the contract) and the tort of inducing breach of contract.
50   See, eg, R Posner, *Economic Analysis of Law* (9th edn, Aspen 2014) §4.10.
51   R Posner, 'Let Us Never Blame a Contract Breaker' (2009) 107 Mich L Rev 1349, 1350.
52   *Zhu v Treasurer of the State of New South Wales* [2004] HCA 56, (2004) 218 CLR 530 [129] (Gleeson CJ, Kirby, Callinan and Heydon JJ). See also *Tabcorp Holdings Ltd v Bowen Investments Pty Ltd* [2009] HCA 8, (2009) 236 CLR 272 [13].

B   Subject matter of contract

The availability of specific performance depends upon the subject matter of the contract. It is [10.27] convenient to use seven broad categories when considering whether damages are adequate:

1. contracts involving land;
2. contracts involving goods;
3. contracts involving the sale of shares and stock;
4. contracts to lend money;
5. contracts for the benefit of third parties;
6. contracts involving intellectual property; and
7. contracts for services.

However, this is principally for convenience, and we should heed Windeyer J's warning in *Coulls v Bagot's Executor and Trustee Co Ltd* that there is 'no reason today for limiting by particular categories, rather than by general principle, the cases in which orders for specific performance will be made'.[53]

Contracts involving land are said to be generally specifically performable, whereas con- [10.28] tracts involving goods or shares are often said to be not generally specifically performable. Similarly, loan contracts are not generally specifically enforced by the courts because damages are usually an adequate remedy; nor are contracts for services because courts are chary about making people perform services. But it is necessary to go beyond these generalisations and consider the availability of a substitute performance on the open market. Courts do sometimes enforce a contract for the sale of shares or goods when a substitute is not available on the open market and damages are unlikely to meet the plaintiff's expectations.

1   Contracts involving land

Contracts for land and real property are generally presumed to be specifically enforceable. This [10.29] is because land has been 'accorded a unique status as a symbol of the self and as a resource closely linked to personal freedom, rank and power'.[54] Courts have said that land has a 'peculiar and special value',[55] and is therefore regarded as intrinsically non-substitutable, and something for which damages cannot compensate.

Nonetheless, the proposition that contracts for the sale of land are always specifically [10.30] enforceable has sometimes been questioned, particularly as mass subdivisions and commercial developments of property gain popularity.[56] A contract for the sale of beans is generally not specifically performable because one load of beans is very much like another, and it is easy to purchase a substitute on the market (presuming there is not a worldwide scarcity of beans).

---

53   (1967) 119 CLR 460, 503.
54   H Dagan, 'Restitutionary Damages for Breach of Contract' (2000) 1 *Theoretical Inquiries in Law* 115, 138; H Dagan, *The Law and Ethics of Restitution* (CUP 2004) 267.
55   *Adderley v Dixon* (1824) 1 Sim & St 607, 610; 57 ER 239, 240; *Dougan v Ley* (1946) 71 CLR 142. An order for specific performance of a contract for sale of land remains subject to discretionary considerations: see, eg, *Patel v Ali* [1984] 1 Ch 283; *Summers v Cocks* (1927) 40 CLR 321, discussed later in this chapter.
56   See K Yin, 'Specific Performance in Favour of a Purchaser under a Contract for the Transfer of Land – An Analysis of the Present Australian Position' (2015) 41 Aust Bar Rev 79.

Suppose that a purchaser was purchasing as an investment an apartment in a complex where the apartments are identical. Should specific performance be granted in those circumstances?

[10.31]   In *Pianta v National Finance & Trustees Ltd*, Barwick CJ said that it is immaterial whether a contract for the sale of land is for commercial or investment purposes; the purchaser is still entitled to specific performance.[57] However, in obiter dicta, a majority of the Canadian Supreme Court in *Semelhago v Paramadevan*[58] cast doubt on the presumption that contracts for the sale of land are specifically performable. The case did not raise specific performance directly, as the plaintiff elected to seek damages instead of specific performance, and the primary issue was the quantum of those damages. Sopinka J, who delivered the majority judgment, said:

> While at one time the common law regarded every piece of real estate to be unique, with the progress of modern real estate development this is no longer the case. Residential, business and industrial properties are all mass-produced much in the same way as other consumer products. If a deal falls through for one property, another is frequently, though not always, readily available.[59]

His Honour contended that specific performance should not be granted as a matter of course, and the court should look at uniqueness of the property and the extent to which a substitute would be readily available on the market.[60] La Forest J disagreed, saying that it was inappropriate to consider those issues without thorough argument and examination.[61] As a consequence of *Semelhago*, the rule in Canada appears to be that a plaintiff must establish that a property is unique before specific performance will be awarded.[62] Chambers has criticised *Semelhago*, highlighting three central problems: a lack of equality in the way in which courts treat claimants, uncertainty created by the new rule, and unintended consequences for equitable proprietary interests which arise from specifically enforceable contracts.[63] On the other hand, Yin has said that, while land is generally non-substitutable, in the age of mass subdivisions, purchasers might not always buy land for its unique properties, and in those cases, damages may be adequate.[64]

[10.32]   It is often said that, as the purchaser is entitled to specific performance of a contract for the sale of land, the vendor will be entitled to specific performance of payment of the purchase price on the basis of affirmative mutuality (i.e. justice requires that both parties should be able to enforce the contract).[65] Thus, in *Turner v Bladin*, the vendor was awarded a decree of

---

57 *Pianta v National Finance & Trustees Ltd* (1964) 180 CLR 146, 151 (Barwick CJ). See also *Sudbrook Trading Estate Ltd v Eggleton* [1983] 1 AC 444, 478 (Lord Diplock). Cf *Loan Investment Corporation of Australasia v Bonner* [1970] NZLR 724 (PC) 744–49 (Sir Garfield Barwick dissenting).

58 [1996] 2 SCR 415.

59 Ibid, [20]. See similarly *Burnitt v Pacific Paradise Resort Pty Ltd* [2005] QDC 429, (2006) ANZ ConvR 216.

60 [1996] 2 SCR 415, [21]–[22].

61 Ibid, [1].

62 *Southcott Estate Inc v Toronto District School Board* [2012] SCC 51, [2012] 2 SCR 675 [38] (Karakatsanis J for the majority).

63 R Chambers, 'The Importance of Specific Performance' in S Degeling and J Edelman (eds), *Equity in Commercial Law* (LBC 2004) 431. Cf W Swadling, 'The Vendor–Purchaser Constructive Trust' in S Degeling and J Edelman (eds), *Equity in Commercial Law* (LBC 2004) 463.

64 K Yin, 'Specific Performance in Favour of a Purchaser under a Contract for the Transfer of Land – An Analysis of the Present Australian Position' (2015) 41 Aust Bar Rev 79, 98–99.

65 *Turner v Bladin* (1951) 82 CLR 463, 473 (Williams, Fullagar and Kitto JJ).

specific performance in relation to the payment of the outstanding purchase price.[66] However, it was material that the purchaser had paid the deposit and taken possession of the property. Because the payments were by instalment,[67] and the vendor had conveyed the land, damages were inadequate. It is suggested that a court might approach the matter differently if the vendor has not fully performed.

Where a contract contained a portion dealing with the sale of land, and a portion requiring the vendor to make a loan to the purchaser, a majority of the Privy Council in *Loan Investment Corporation of Australasia v Bonner* held that the contract should not be specifically enforced, as this was a composite contract involving a commercial bargain, and mere contracts for the loan of money were not generally specifically enforceable.[68] Sir Garfield Barwick strongly dissented, arguing that contracts for the loan of money could be specifically enforced, that this was not a composite contract, and the contract should be specifically enforced because of the special nature of land.[69]

[10.33]

2   Contracts involving goods

Contracts involving goods are rarely specifically enforced by courts because damages are usually adequate to compensate for the loss of performance and a substitute can be easily found in the marketplace (as in our bean example at [10.30]).[70] However, where a chattel is unique or a substitute performance cannot easily be found, courts may award specific performance.

[10.34]

There are many cases where courts have awarded specific performance of contracts involving unique chattels.[71] This jurisdiction overlaps with orders for specific delivery where the tort of detinue or conversion has been committed (see [10.114]–[10.118]). However, specific performance is awarded in other cases too. Sometimes a chattel may be non-substitutable because the defendant is particularly well situated to meet the plaintiff's needs, and the plaintiff could not quickly get a substitute performance from elsewhere.[72]

[10.35]

---

66   (1951) 82 CLR 463, 473 (Williams, Fullagar and Kitto JJ).
67   Contracts to pay money by instalments are discussed below at [10.41].
68   [1970] NZLR 724, 734–35.
69   Ibid, 735–49.
70   See, eg, *Dominion Coal Co Ltd v Dominion Iron & Steel Co Ltd* [1909] AC 293, 311 (contract for coal not specifically enforceable).
71   *Pusey v Pusey* (1684) 1 Vern 273, 23 ER 465 (ancient horn); *Duke of Somerset v Cookson* (1735) 3 P Wms 390, 24 ER 114 (silver altarpiece inscribed in Greek); *Fells v Read* (1796) 3 Ves 70, 30 ER 899 (silver tobacco box); *Lowther v Lord Lowther* (1806) 13 Ves Jun 95, 33 ER 230 (valuable painting); *Lingen v Simpson* (1824) 1 Sim & St 600, 57 ER 236 (book of ornamental plates); *Falcke v Gray* (1859) 4 Drew 651, 62 ER 250 (china vases); *Thorn v Commissioners of Her Majesty's Works and Public Buildings* (1863) 32 Beav 490, 55 ER 192 (RC) (arch-stones, spandrel stones and Bramley Fall stones from old Westminster bridge); *Burr v Bloomsburg*, 101 NJ Eq 615, 318 A 876 (1927) (diamond ring); *Behnke v Bede Shipping Co Ltd* [1927] 1 KB 649, 661 (unique ship); *Dougan v Ley* (1946) 71 CLR 142 (taxi licence of limited availability); *Aristoc Industries Pty Ltd v RA Wenham (Builders) Pty Ltd* [1965] NSWR 581 (lecture theatre seats made to fit a particular hall); *Phillips v Lamdin* [1949] 2 KB 33, 41 (house with Neoclassical door attributed to one of the brothers Adam); *Borg v Howlett* (1996) 8 BPR 15,535, 15,538 (NSWSC) (unique horse).
72   See, eg, *North v Great Northern Railway Company* (1860) 2 Giff 64, 66 ER 28; *Sky Petroleum Ltd v VIP Petroleum Ltd* [1974] 1 WLR 576 (Ch); *Howard Perry & Co v British Railways* [1980] 1 WLR 1375. Cf *Société des Industries Métallurgiques SA v Bronx Engineering Co Ltd* [1975] 1 Lloyd's Rep 465.

[10.36]   Sometimes, although a chattel is generally substitutable, it may be unavailable because of circumstances at the time. For example, in *Howard Perry & Co v British Railways*, steel was unavailable on the market because of a general strike. Compensatory damages would not have been adequate, and specific performance was granted.[73] However, it has been held in *Cook v Rodgers* that scarcity of a commodity does not merit an order for an injunction.[74] The correctness of this decision is questionable, as it does not sit well with other cases in which specific relief was awarded on the basis of scarcity.[75]

[10.37]   Courts may award specific performance of an instalment contract to supply goods and services over a long period.[76] This is non-substitutable because a complex contract cannot be replaced with an identical deal.[77]

[10.38]   In all Australian jurisdictions apart from New South Wales, legislation provides that where there is a breach of contract 'to deliver specific or ascertained goods', the court may direct that the contract be specifically performed.[78] This does not give a buyer a greater entitlement to specific performance than at common law, and this jurisdiction is to be exercised according to the settled principles governing specific performance.[79] Section 56 of the *Sale of Goods Act 1923* (NSW) simply provides that nothing in the Act is to affect any equitable remedy of the buyer or seller in respect of a contract for the sale of goods.[80]

3   Contracts involving shares and stock

[10.39]   Shares in a public company are usually available on the open market, and compensatory damages will therefore be an adequate remedy for the breach of a contract for the sale of shares. As with goods, a court will not generally order specific performance for a contract for the sale of publicly available shares.[81]

[10.40]   Courts are more willing to order specific performance of a sale of shares in a private company because of the lack of a market. Thus, in *Georges v Wieland*, Brereton J awarded specific performance of a contract for sale of shares in a private company, especially after the

---

73   [1980] 1 WLR 1375.

74   (1946) 46 SR (NSW) 229.

75   *Curtice Brothers Co v Catts*, 72 NJ Eq 831, 833; 66 A 935, 936 (1907); *Dougan v Ley* (1946) 71 CLR 142; *Sky Petroleum Ltd v VIP Petroleum Ltd* [1974] 1 WLR 576; *Eastern Air Lines v Gulf Oil Corporation*, 415 F Supp 429, 442–43 (1975); *Howard Perry & Co v British Railways* [1980] 1 WLR 1375.

76   See, eg, *Buxton v Lister* (1746) 3 Atk 383, 26 ER 1020; *Adderley v Dixon* (1824) 1 Sim & St 607, 610; 57 ER 239, 240; *Eastern Rolling Mill v Michlovitz*, 157 Md 51, 145 A 378 (1929); *Thomas Borthwick & Sons (Australasia) Ltd v South Otago Freezing Co Ltd* [1978] 1 NZLR 538; *Sky Petroleum Ltd v VIP Petroleum Ltd* [1974] 1 WLR 577. Cf *Fothergill v Rowland* (1873) LR 17 Eq 132, 140; *Laclede Gas Co v Amoco Oil Co*, 522 F 2d 33 (8th Cir, 1975); *Société des Industries Métallurgiques SA v Bronx Engineering Co Ltd* [1975] 1 Lloyd's Rep 465. The latter cases have been criticised: see A Burrows, *Remedies for Torts and Breach of Contract* (3rd edn, OUP 2004) 467. See also R Austen-Baker, 'Difficulties with Damages as a Ground for Specific Performance' (1999) 10 King's College LJ 1, who argues that *Bronx* is distinguishable.

77   Note that this is recognised in the *Uniform Commercial Code* (US), §2–716 (comment 2).

78   *Sale of Goods Act 1954* (ACT), s 55; *Sale of Goods Act* (NT), s 56; *Sale of Goods Act 1896* (Qld), s 53; *Sale of Goods Act 1895* (SA), s 51; *Sale of Goods Act 1896* (Tas), s 56; *Goods Act 1958* (Vic), s 58; *Sale of Goods Act 1895* (WA), s 51.

79   *Cohen v Roche* [1927] 1 KB 169; *Behnke v Bede Shipping Co Ltd* [1927] 1 KB 649; *Re Wait* [1927] 1 Ch 606.

80   *Sale of Goods Act 1923* (NSW), s 56.

81   *Hyer v Richmond Traction Co*, 168 US 471, 483 (1897); *Re Schwabacher* (1907) 98 LT 127, 128; *Chinn v Hochstrasser* [1979] Ch 447, 470.

shares had been devalued by the purchaser.[82] Even in the case of a public company, damages may be inadequate if there is not a sufficient market for a particular share or stock. Specific performance has been awarded where the market price for shares is uncertain or there is a risk that requiring the plaintiff to purchase substitute shares will prejudice the plaintiff or a third party.[83]

4 Contracts to loan money

Generally, contracts to lend money are not specifically enforceable because damages are, by their very nature, an adequate remedy.[84] Similarly, a contract to pay money will often not be specifically enforceable.[85] However, Sir Garfield Barwick in *Loan Investment Corporation v Bonner* noted that the assumption that damages are adequate for the breach of a loan contract 'is not of universal validity' and that the particular circumstances of the case must be considered.[86] Thus, if it is shown that damages are not adequate in the circumstances (for example, if substitute means of finance are not readily available on the market, or as in *Wight v Haberdan*, if the complexity of calculating damages is very high), then a court may be prepared to order specific performance.[87] The circumstances in which a court will specifically enforce a contract to pay money include:

[10.41]

- where the contract is not to pay another's debt, but to relieve someone of her debt so that she does not have to pay it in the first place;[88]
- where the contract grants or creates an annuity;[89]
- where the contract is to pay a third party who is incapable of enforcing the contract because of the rules against privity;[90]
- where the contract involves the payment of moneys by instalments and is associated with an interest in land;[91] and
- where the contract is to give a mortgage or other security interest and the money has already been advanced.[92]

---

82   *Georges v Wieland* [2009] NSWSC 733 [23].
83   Ibid; *ANZ Executors and Trustees Ltd v Humes Ltd* [1990] VR 615, 630–31.
84   *Rogers v Challis* (1859) 27 Beav 175; 54 ER 68; *Western Wagon & Property Co v West* [1892] 1 Ch 271, 275; *Larios v Bonany y Guerety* (1873) LR 5 PC 346 (PC); *South African Territories Ltd v Wallington* [1898] AC 309; *Loan Investment Corporation of Australasia v Bonner* [1970] NZLR 724 (PC).
85   *McIntosh v Dalwood (No 4)* (1930) 30 SR (NSW) 415, 418.
86   *Loan Investment Corporation of Australasia v Bonner* [1970] NZLR 724 (PC) 742, applied in *Wight v Haberdan Pty Ltd* [1984] 2 NSWLR 280, 290.
87   *Wight v Haberdan Pty Ltd* [1984] 2 NSWLR 280; *Corpors (No 664) Pty Ltd v NZI Securities Australia Ltd* [1989] ANZ ConvR 548, 556.
88   *McIntosh v Dalwood (No 4)* (1930) 30 SR (NSW) 415.
89   *Keenan v Handley* (1864) 2 De GJ & S 283; 46 ER 384; *Beswick v Beswick* [1968] AC 58.
90   *Coulls v Bagot's Executor and Trustee Co Ltd* (1967) 119 CLR 460; *Beswick v Beswick* [1968] AC 58; *Gurtner v Circuit* [1968] 2 QB 587; *Baig v Baig* [1970] VR 833.
91   *Turner v Bladin* (1951) 82 CLR 463. Cf however, *Loan Investment Corporation of Australasia v Bonner* [1970] NZLR 724 (PC).
92   *Hermann v Hodges* (1873) LR 16 Eq 18; *Lamont v Osborn* (1902) 28 VLR 434; *Bridge Wholesale Acceptance Corporation (Australia) Ltd v Burnard* (1992) 27 NSWLR 415; *GE Commercial Corporation (Australia) Pty Ltd v Nichols* [2012] NSWSC 562.

[10.42]   Although it has not traditionally been conceived of in this way because of its common law origins, a claim in debt can be classified as a form of monetary specific performance. Debt is distinct from damages for breach of contract, as discussed at [10.119]–[10.121].

5   Contracts for the benefit of third parties

[10.43]   Suppose Querida enters a contract with Roland for the benefit of Simeon. If Roland refuses to perform, the doctrine of privity means that Simeon cannot sue Roland for specific performance and Querida is entitled to only nominal damages. However, courts have sometimes allowed a third party who benefits from a contract to sue for specific performance of the agreement because damages would be inadequate.[93]

[10.44]   In *Beswick v Beswick*, Mr Beswick entered a contract with his nephew (Joseph) where he agreed to transfer his business to his nephew in return for Joseph promising (inter alia) to pay a weekly annuity to Mr Beswick's widow once he died. The business was transferred to Joseph, but after Mr Beswick died, Joseph did not honour his obligation to the widow. The widow sued Joseph for specific performance of the agreement in her personal capacity and her capacity as executrix of Mr Beswick's estate. Joseph argued that Mr Beswick's estate had suffered no loss because of his breach, and was entitled to only nominal damages.[94] Lord Reid described such a conclusion as 'grossly unjust'.[95] Lord Upjohn observed:

> it is said nominal damages are adequate and the remedy of specific performance ought not to be granted. That is, with all respect, wholly to misunderstand that principle. Equity will grant specific performance when damages are inadequate to meet the justice of the case.[96]

[10.45]   The High Court of Australia considered *Beswick v Beswick* in *Coulls v Bagot's Executor and Trustee Co Ltd*.[97] Mr Coulls signed a contract where he allowed a company to quarry from his land in return for royalties. He authorised the company to pay the royalties to himself and his wife as joint tenants. When Mr Coulls died, the company ceased paying Mrs Coulls, and she sought to specifically enforce the agreement. The majority held that the contract could not be specifically enforced by Mrs Coulls because she was not privy to it, and any authority to pay royalties had been revoked by Mr Coulls' death.[98] Barwick CJ and Windeyer J dissented, and held that the consideration had moved jointly from Mr and Mrs Coulls, so that the agreement was specifically performable.[99]

[10.46]   Generally, a third party in Australia cannot specifically enforce a contract unless she has provided consideration. Thus, in *Trident General Insurance Co Ltd v McNiece Brothers Pty Ltd*, Mason CJ and Wilson J said:

---

93   Although Heydon, Leeming and Turner query whether this is really specific performance: see JD Heydon, MJ Leeming and PG Turner, *Meagher, Gummow and Lehane's Equity: Doctrines and Remedies* (5th edn, LexisNexis Butterworths 2015) [20–050].

94   See now *Contracts (Rights of Third Parties) Act 1999* (UK), enacted partly to solve this problem.

95   *Beswick v Beswick* [1968] AC 58, 73.

96   Ibid, 102.

97   *Coulls v Bagot's Executor and Trustee Co Ltd* (1967) 119 CLR 460, 478 (Barwick CJ), 492–504 (Windeyer J).

98   Ibid, 482–83 (McTiernan), 486 (Taylor and Owen JJ).

99   Ibid, 478–79 (Barwick CJ), 492–93 (Windeyer J).

> If A, B and C are parties to a contract and A promises B and C that he will pay C $1000 if B will erect a gate for him, C cannot compel A to carry out his promise, because, though a party to the contract, C is a stranger to the consideration ...[100]

Insurance contracts are an exception to the rule (as in *Trident* itself, where Mason CJ, Wilson and Toohey JJ said that the doctrine of privity did not apply to insurance contracts).[101] The other means of enforcing the contract is by inferring an intention to create an express trust from the contract, such that the third party becomes a beneficiary of an express trust where the benefit of the promise is held on trust for him by the promisee.[102]

6   Contracts involving intellectual property

Contracts involving intellectual property rights such as patents, designs, copyright, or trade-marks are generally specifically enforceable because of the unique nature of intellectual property rights, notwithstanding the fact that sometimes the plaintiff vendor simply seeks payment for the intellectual property interest.[103] Contracts for the sale of intellectual property rights,[104] and contracts to assign intellectual property rights[105] may be specifically enforced, as long as the latter are not oppressive.[106]

[10.47]

7   Contracts for services

Courts in Australia and other common law countries have traditionally been reluctant to order specific performance of contracts for services.[107] It is often said that it is inappropriate to compel parties to maintain a continuous personal relationship where one party is unwilling to do so.[108] The difficulty of continuous supervision also militates against such an award. As Tettenborn has explained, 'coerced performance is likely to be half hearted performance' and thus difficult to police.[109] In most cases specific performance of a contract for services will not

[10.48]

---

100   (1988) 165 CLR 107, 115–16.
101   Ibid, 123–24 (Mason CJ and Wilson J), 172 (Toohey J). See now *Insurance Contracts Act 1984* (Cth), s 48.
102   *Trident General Insurance Co Ltd v McNiece Brothers Pty Ltd* (1988) 165 CLR 107, 146–55 (Deane J). See also *Bahr v Nicolay (No 2)* (1988) 164 CLR 604, 618–19 (Mason CJ and Dawson J). Attempts to infer a trust failed in *Marks v CCH Australia Ltd* [1999] 3 VR 513; *Winterton Constructions Pty Ltd v Hambros Australia Ltd* (1991) 101 ALR 363.
103   *Cogent v Gibson* (1864) 33 Beav 557, 55 ER 485.
104   Ibid; *A H McDonald & Co Pty Ltd v Wells* (1931) 45 CLR 506, 513; *Brake v Radermacher* (1903) 20 RPC 631. Cf *Stocker v Wedderburn* (1857) 3 K & J 393, 69 ER 1163.
105   *Erskine Macdonald Ltd v Eyles* [1921] 1 Ch 631.
106   *A Schroeder Music Publishing Co Ltd v Macaulay* [1974] 3 All ER 616, 622 (Lord Reid).
107   *Rigby v Connol* (1880) 14 Ch D 482, 487 (Jessel MR); *JC Williamson Ltd v Lukey* (1931) 45 CLR 282, 293 (Starke J), 297–98 (Dixon J); *Hogan v Tumut Shire Council* (1954) 54 SR (NSW) 284; *Francis v Municipal Councillors of Kuala Lumpur* [1962] 3 All ER 633; *Byrne v Australian Airlines Ltd* (1995) 185 CLR 410, 428 (Brennan CJ, Dawson and Toohey JJ). See also the US: *Sampson v Murray*, 415 US 61, 83 (1974); *HW Gossard Co v Crosby*, 132 Iowa 155, 170; 109 NW 483, 488–89 (1906); American Law Institute, *Restatement (Second) of the Law of Contracts* (1981) §367 (personal service contracts not specifically enforced). The US position is further complicated by the 13th Amendment to the *Constitution of the United States*, which provides that 'neither slavery nor involuntary servitude' shall exist in the US.
108   *Atlas Steels (Australia) Pty Ltd v Atlas Steels Ltd* (1948) 49 SR (NSW) 157, 161 (Sugarman J). See also P Saprai, 'The Principle against Self-Enslavement in Contract Law' (2009) 26 J Cont L 25.
109   A Tettenborn, 'Absolving the Undeserving: Shopping Centres, Specific Performance and the Law of Contract' [1998] Conv 23, 23.

be awarded. Similarly, specific performance of an agency contract is unlikely to be awarded, particularly when there are continuing obligations to work together, because the necessary trust and confidence between the parties has broken down.[110]

[10.49]   Although contracts for services are generally not specifically enforceable, in *Quinn v Overland*,[111] Bromberg J suggested that this should no longer be a 'fixed rule' in light of industrial relations legislation and a growing acceptance at common law that an employee has a right to perform work. Relevantly, in that case, the *employee* sought to specifically enforce the contract rather than the employer. Bromberg J said that statutory unfair dismissal regimes already provided for the reinstatement of dismissed employees and that the success of this remedy showed that 'a breakdown in confidence is not necessarily irreconcilable'.[112] In a later case, Bromberg J said that a factor which makes damages inadequate for an employee is the loss of access to non-pecuniary benefits as a result of termination of an employment contract, for which damages were not easily calculated.[113] It is suggested that courts will remain reluctant to award specific performance where an employer rather than an employee seeks to enforce the contract.

[10.50]   A court may award an injunction to restrain a breach of a negative covenant in a contract for services although an order for specific performance would not have been made.[114] Although initially these injunctions were awarded only where the services were unique (such as singing, acting and sporting skills),[115] there have been cases in New South Wales where ordinary employees were restrained from working for a competitor for a limited time.[116] These cases are discussed in detail at [11.40]–[11.44]. The practical effect of the injunction may be equivalent to specific performance,[117] and it must be asked whether the division between specific performance and injunctions restraining breaches of negative covenant is principled.

V   Other requirements for specific performance

A Personal remedy

[10.51]   Specific performance is a personal remedy which binds an individual defendant to do or to refrain from doing something. The personal nature of an equitable order traditionally distinguished it from a common law judgment, as expressed by the maxim 'equity acts in

---

110   *Netline Pty Ltd v QAV Pty Ltd (No 2)* [2015] WASC 113 [67]–[68] (Beech J).

111   [2010] FCA 799, (2010) 199 IR 40 [100]–[101].

112   Ibid, [97]–[98].

113   *Automotive, Food, Metals, Engineering, Printing and Kindred Industries Union v McCain Foods (Australia) Pty Ltd* [2012] FCA 1126 [48].

114   *Lumley v Wagner* (1852) 1 De GM & G 604, 42 ER 687.

115   Ibid; *Grimston v Cuningham* (1894) 1 QB 125; *Warner Brothers Pictures Inc v Nelson* [1937] 1 KB 209; *Marco Productions Ltd v Pagola* [1945] 1 KB 111; *Warner Brothers Pictures Inc v Ingolia* [1965] NSWR 988; *Hawthorn Football Club Ltd v Harding* [1988] VR 49; *Buckenara v Hawthorn Football Club Ltd* [1988] VR 39; *Curro v Beyond Productions Pty Ltd* (1993) 30 NSWLR 337; *Bulldogs Rugby League Club Ltd v Williams* [2008] NSWSC 822.

116   *Koops Martin Financial Services Pty Ltd v Reeves* [2006] NSWSC 449; *John Fairfax Publications Pty Ltd v Birt* [2006] NSWSC 995; *Otis Elevator Co Pty Ltd v Nolan* [2007] NSWSC 593; *Tullett Prebon (Australia) Pty Ltd v Purcell* [2008] NSWSC 852, (2008) 175 IR 414.

117   ICF Spry, *The Principles of Equitable Remedies* (9th edn, LBC 2014) 557.

personam'.[118] It has been said that 'a common law judgment is a determination of right not a command to the person ... [b]ut a decree in equity has always been a command laid upon the person'.[119] It follows that equity coerces a person into performing an order for specific relief by acting against the person, including by imprisoning a defendant for contempt and fining him. Equity now exhibits a greater tendency towards enforcing orders against property instead of against the person.[120] Still, the coercive aspect of specific performance and the enforcement measures which can be taken against the defendant are distinctive.

Because specific performance is personal, the defendant must be within the jurisdiction of the court and capable of carrying out the stipulated obligations contained in the decree of specific performance.[121] But the subject matter of the contract need not be within the jurisdiction of the court. The court will award specific performance as long as the defendant is physically within the jurisdiction.[122]

[10.52]

B   Binding contract

In order for specific performance to be awarded, the contract which is sought to be performed must be valid and binding, and must not be one that the defendant is entitled to rescind. Nonetheless, courts sometimes order specific performance of contracts that do not comply with formalities, but where the plaintiff has done acts of part performance which evidence the alleged contract[123] or, perhaps, where there is an estoppel. Part performance is established under Australian law only if the acts are *unequivocally* referable to some such agreement as alleged.[124] For part performance and equitable estoppel, there will be no need to establish inadequacy of damages because of the equitable origins of these doctrines.

[10.53]

1   Consideration

A court will not order the specific performance of a promise for which no consideration was given[125] or only nominal consideration was given,[126] even if the promise was made in a

[10.54]

---

118   See PW Young, C Croft and ML Smith, *On Equity* (LBC 2009) [3.580]–[3.590] for a history.
119   *Pearson v Arcadia Store, Guyra, Ltd (No 2)* (1935) 53 CLR 587, 590–91.
120   PW Young, C Croft and ML Smith, *On Equity* (LBC 2009) [3.610].
121   *Jackman v Broadbent* [1931] SASR 82.
122   *Penn v Lord Baltimore* (1750) 1 Ves Sen 444, 27 ER 1132 (contract regarding boundaries of Pennsylvania and Maryland in USA specifically enforceable); *Richard West & Partners (Inverness) Ltd v Dick* [1969] 2 WLR 383 (aff'd *Richard West & Partners (Inverness) Ltd v Dick* [1969] 2 Ch 424) (contract for sale of land outside jurisdiction specifically enforced as defendant was within jurisdiction).
123   See, eg, *Price v Strange* [1978] Ch 337.
124   *Maddison v Alderson* (1883) 8 App Cas 467, 479. Followed in Australia in *McBride v Sandiland* (1918) 25 CLR 69; *Cooney v Byrnes* (1922) 30 CLR 216; *JC Williamson Ltd v Lukey* (1931) 45 CLR 282; *Ogilvie v Ryan* [1976] 2 NSWLR 504; *Millett v Regent* [1975] 1 NSWLR 62 (aff'd on other grounds *Regent v Millett* (1976) 133 CLR 679); *McMahon v Ambrose* [1987] VR 817; *Australia and New Zealand Banking Group Ltd v Widin* (1990) 26 FCR 21, 37; *Khoury v Khouri* [2006] NSWCA 184, (2006) 66 NSWLR 241 [80]. Cf the more liberal test in *Steadman v Steadman* [1976] AC 536, which merely requires that the formation of the contract was more probable than not. See ICF Spry, *The Principles of Equitable Remedies* (9th edn, LBC 2014) 271–75.
125   *Cannon v Hartley* [1949] 2 Ch 213, 217; *Deane v Lloyd* [1991] ANZ ConvR 103, 105–06; *Silver v Dome Resources NL* [2007] NSWSC 455, (2007) 62 ACSR 539 [121].
126   *Costin v Costin* [1995] ANZ ConvR 289, 290–92, rev'd on other grounds *Costin v Costin* [1997] ANZ ConvR 400.

deed,[127] and even though common law damages may be available for breach of such an obligation. The equitable maxim 'Equity will not assist a volunteer' refers to the requirement that there be consideration before equity will specifically perform a contract.[128]

[10.55]   While a contract with nominal consideration will not be specifically enforced, in *Mountford v Scott*,[129] an agreement made for £1 which granted the plaintiff an option to purchase the defendant's house for £10 000 was specifically enforced on the basis that while the price of the option was nominal, the price of exercising the option was not. At first instance, Brightman J appeared to disavow the rule requiring consideration when he said that '[i]t is not the function of equity to protect only those equitable interests which have been created for valuable consideration'.[130] However, although the English Court of Appeal upheld Brightman J's judgment, it did so upon the basis that it was effectively awarding specific performance of a contract of sale rather than specifically enforcing the option itself.[131]

2   Uncertainty

[10.56]   Courts will not award specific performance of contracts that are void for uncertainty. There is no contract to enforce, and it is impossible to award specific relief. In that sense, uncertainty raises a jurisdictional question: if there is no contract, there can be no specific relief.

[10.57]   But there are degrees of uncertainty. Mere difficulty in establishing the meaning of the contract will not generally prevent a court from awarding specific performance if the court can establish a meaning.[132]

[10.58]   However, if the obligations themselves are unclear or uncertain, the court will not be able to say what the defendant's obligations are. Specific performance is likely to be declined where there is uncertainty as to the meaning of the terms,[133] or there is uncertainty as to when a condition arises and whether it really is a condition,[134] or where there is ambiguity within the contract in general.[135]

[10.59]   An example of general uncertainty occurred in *Joseph v National Magazine Co*,[136] where the defendants agreed to publish an article by the plaintiff in a magazine known as *The Connoisseur*. In breach of contract, the defendants revised the article with major amendments which the plaintiff said included errors of fact. The plaintiff attempted to obtain specific performance of the contract to ensure that the article was published in the form he preferred, but Harman J refused to order specific performance because the exact terms of the article had

---

127   *Jefferys v Jefferys* (1841) Cr & Ph 138, 41 ER 443; *Silver v Dome Resources NL* [2007] NSWSC 455, (2007) 62 ACSR 539 [121]. Cf *Paterson v Pongrass Group Operations Pty Ltd* [2011] NSWSC 1588 [81].
128   A Burrows, *Remedies for Torts and Breach of Contract* (3rd edn, OUP 2004) 495; JD Heydon, MJ Leeming and PG Turner, *Meagher, Gummow and Lehane's Equity: Doctrines and Remedies* (5th edn, LexisNexis Butterworths 2015) [20–025].
129   [1975] Ch 258.
130   Ibid, 262.
131   Ibid, 264–65 (Russell LJ), 265 (Cairns LJ).
132   *Tooth v Fleming* (1859) 2 Legge 1152 (NSWSC); *Forbes v Clarton* (1878) 4 VLR (E) 22.
133   *Booker Industries Pty Ltd v Wilson Parking (Qld) Pty Ltd* (1982) 149 CLR 600. Although the lease could not be specifically performed because the price of rental had not been fixed, a limited decree of specific performance was awarded where the lessor had to do what was reasonable to ensure the rent was fixed.
134   *Stewart v Ferrari* (1879) 5 VLR (E) 200.
135   Ibid; *Gander v Murray* (1907) 5 CLR 575.
136   [1959] Ch 14.

never been agreed between the parties, rendering the bargain uncertain. Accordingly, the plaintiff could only recover damages.

Uncertainty of contractual obligation can feed into discretionary considerations against awarding specific performance (presuming that the contract is valid, yet uncertain). There is some overlap between uncertainty and the bar of continuous supervision. In *Cooperative Insurance Society Ltd v Argyll Stores (Holdings) Ltd*, one reason for the refusal of specific performance was the fact that the court could not draft an order with the requisite certainty, and Lord Hoffmann said that this signalled the fact that continuous supervision may be a difficulty.[137] Lord Hoffmann observed that specific performance carries extreme sanctions for non-compliance (including contempt of court and imprisonment), and it is unfair to ask the defendant to perform certain obligations when the defendant and the court cannot ascertain those obligations.[138] **[10.60]**

Where part of the contract was uncertain at the time of making the contract, but has subsequently been rendered certain, or the uncertain obligation has since been performed, the court will order specific performance of the balance of the contract.[139] **[10.61]**

3   Illegality

An order of specific performance will not be made where it would require the defendant to do an illegal act. In *Harnett v Yielding*, it was stated that the plaintiff must show that 'he does not call on the other party to do an act which he is not lawfully competent to do; for if he does, a consequence is produced that quite passes by the object of the court, in exercising the jurisdiction, which is to do more complete justice'.[140] This is a reflection of the broader principle of the law's disinclination to support an illegal act (*ex turpi causa non oritur actio*). **[10.62]**

Although some English decisions have indicated an overlap between illegality and 'lack of clean hands',[141] the High Court of Australia has warned against conflating the two: illegality is concerned with the transaction whereas 'clean hands' relates to the conduct of the plaintiff.[142] **[10.63]**

In *Nelson v Nelson*, Deane and Gummow JJ suggested that a contract may be rendered illegal in three different ways: **[10.64]**

1.   it may be expressly prohibited by a statute;

2.   it may be impliedly prohibited by a statute if the formation or performance of the contract is prohibited; or

3.   it may be invalid at common law if it is contrary to public policy.[143]

In a series of cases, the High Court of Australia has indicated that where statutory illegalities of the types mentioned in (1) and (2) are concerned, it does not necessarily mean that the plaintiff

---

137   [1998] AC 1, 13–14. See also *Harnett v Yielding* (1805) 2 Sch & Lef 549, 553–54, [1803–13] All ER Rep 704, 707–08; *Nexus Mortgage Securities Pty Ltd v Ecto Pty Ltd* [1998] 4 VR 220.
138   [1998] AC 1, 13.
139   *Macaulay v Greater Paramount Theatres Ltd* (1921) 22 SR (NSW) 66, 74; *Bradford v Zahra* [1977] Qd R 24, 26; *Price v Strange* [1978] Ch 337, 362.
140   *Harnett v Yielding* (1805) 2 Sch & Lef 549, 554; [1803–13] All ER Rep 704, 705.
141   See *Tinsley v Milligan* [1994] 1 AC 340.
142   *Nelson v Nelson* (1995) 184 CLR 538, 551 (Deane and Gummow JJ). See also *Loughran v Loughran*, 292 US 216 (1934), 228–29 (Brandeis J).
143   *Nelson v Nelson* (1995) 184 CLR 538, 552.

is unable to obtain relief, and that the court must look at the purpose of the statute, and whether it was intended to preclude a remedy.[144] Thus, in *REW08 Projects Pty Ltd v PNC Lifestyle Investments Pty Ltd*,[145] the fact that a transaction could have been intended to defer liability to pay stamp duty did not prevent the court from decreeing specific performance, particularly as the relevant Act[146] did not render contracts unenforceable, but provided for other penalties. In any event, the plaintiff did not appear to have an intention to defraud, and paid the stamp duty when it became liable. Consequently, specific performance was awarded.

[10.65]   The question to ask where a decree for specific performance is sought is generally whether such a decree would cause the parties to do something illegal which the law cannot countenance, including on any of the three bases mentioned above. Circumstances where contracts are not specifically enforced on the basis of illegality include contracts contrary to statute,[147] contracts contrary to public policy,[148] contracts which cause someone to breach a trust or prior contract,[149] and contracts which involve the commission of a fraud on a third party.[150] Generally, these contracts would not be enforceable at common law either. Consequently, there is a jurisdictional issue: the court has no power to enforce an arguably void contract.

[10.66]   However, sometimes specific relief will be refused on the basis of potential illegality even though damages would be awarded for breach of the contract.[151] In these circumstances, a combination of discretionary factors – hardship and public policy considerations – operate to preclude relief.

[10.67]   Where it is possible to perform a contract in a lawful or an unlawful manner, the court presumes that the parties will carry out the contract lawfully,[152] and may award specific performance. The court may place conditions or undertakings in an order to ensure that it is complied with lawfully.[153]

4   Impossibility and futility

[10.68]   Specific performance is unlikely to be granted where it is impossible for the defendant to carry out the contract, or if it will be futile to coerce the defendant into doing so. Impossibility and

---

144   *Nelson v Nelson* (1995) 184 CLR 538; *Fitzgerald v F J Leonhardt Pty Ltd* (1997) 189 CLR 215; *Miller v Miller* [2011] HCA 9, (2011) 242 CLR 446; *Equuscorp Pty Ltd v Haxton* [2012] HCA 7, (2012) 246 CLR 498.
145   [2017] NSWCA 269.
146   *Taxation Administration Act 1996* (NSW).
147   *Ewing v Osbaldiston* (1837) 2 My & Cr 53, 40 ER 561; *Norton v Angus* (1926) 38 CLR 523, 534 (Isaacs J); *Pottinger v George* (1967) 116 CLR 328, 337; *Rees v Marquis of Bute* [1916] 2 Ch 64; *Brilliant v Michaels* [1945] 1 All ER 121, 128; *Sykes v Beadon* (1879) 11 Ch D 170, 197.
148   Eg *Sutton v Sutton* [1984] Ch 184, 194–98 (contract to oust the jurisdiction of the court); *Cartwright v Cartwright* (1853) 3 De GM & G 982, 43 ER 385 (contract that wife provided with income so long as she stayed with her husband).
149   *Willmott v Barber* (1880) 15 Ch D 96; *Warmington v Miller* [1973] QB 877; *Harvela Investments Ltd v Royal Trust Co of Canada Ltd* [1985] Ch 103, 122 (rev'd on other grounds *Harvela Investments Ltd v Royal Trust Co of Canada Ltd* [1986] AC 207); *Briggs v Parsloe* [1937] 3 All ER 831, 838–39 (in this case specific performance would have been awarded because the breach of trust was innocent).
150   *Zimmermann v Letkeman* [1978] 1 SCR 1097. Cf *Tribe v Tribe* [1996] Ch 107, where the illegal scheme was never carried into effect.
151   ICF Spry, *The Principles of Equitable Remedies* (9th edn, LBC 2014) 151. See *Johnson v Shrewsbury Birmingham Railway Co* (1853) 3 De GM & G 914, 923; 43 ER 358, 362; *Pottinger v George* (1967) 116 CLR 328, 337.
152   ICF Spry, *The Principles of Equitable Remedies* (9th edn, LBC 2014) 152.
153   *Brady v Brady* [1989] AC 755, 785.

futility are different. Impossibility arises when it appears likely that the defendant is unable to comply with the order for specific performance. Futility arises where an order of specific performance is possible, but the likelihood of the decree achieving the outcome sought by the plaintiff is low. Impossibility is generally treated as a jurisdictional issue, whereas futility is generally treated as a discretionary defence, but there is no obvious reason for this distinction.[154]

In cases of impossibility, the court will refuse to award specific performance,[155] even if the defendant caused the impossibility, for example, where the subject matter of the contract has been transferred by the defendant to an innocent third party.[156] A more difficult question is whether performance is possible when consent is required from a third party before performance can be rendered. In these cases, the court may give a conditional order for specific performance.[157] For example, in *Dougan v Ley*,[158] the plaintiff sought to specifically enforce a contract for the defendant to supply his taxicab and the benefit of the registration and licence. The transfer of the registration and licence of cabs was subject to the approval of the Commissioner for Roads and Tramways. The defendant unsuccessfully argued that specific performance should not be awarded because the performance of the contract was dependent upon the actions of the Commissioner, and there was lack of mutuality. Dixon J said that the court could make a conditional decree. The defendant was merely required to supply the documentation to the Commissioner, and if the Commissioner did not approve the transfer, the defendant's obligation to specifically perform the contract would fall away.[159]   **[10.69]**

Courts may also refuse to award specific performance where it would be futile, typically because the defendant can avoid her contractual obligations in some other way.[160] For example, in *Hercy v Birch*,[161] the court refused to specifically enforce a partnership agreement where the partners had the power to immediately dissolve the partnership thereafter. However, Spry suggests that this case goes too far, and additional certainty would have been provided to the plaintiff if a formal document had been executed, notwithstanding that the partners would have been able to dissolve the partnership thereafter.[162] Similar questions arise where a plaintiff attempts to specifically enforce a short-term lease. Courts have traditionally been reluctant to specifically enforce such leases on the basis of futility,[163] but have become   **[10.70]**

---

154   W Covell, K Lupton and J Forder, *Principles of Remedies* (6th edn, LexisNexis 2015) [7.14].

155   *Ferguson v Wilson* (1866) LR 2 Ch App 77; *Duncombe v New York Properties Pty Ltd* [1986] 1 Qd R 16; *Armstrong Strategic Management and Marketing Pty Ltd v Expense Reduction Analysts Group Pty Ltd* [2013] NSWSC 457.

156   See, eg, *Wenham v Ella* (1972) 127 CLR 454. Hardship to the innocent third party is also operative on the mind of the court.

157   See, eg, *Egan v Ross* (1928) 29 SR (NSW) 382; *Dougan v Ley* (1946) 71 CLR 142; *Brown v Heffer* (1967) 116 CLR 344, 350.

158   (1946) 71 CLR 142.

159   Ibid, 152 (Dixon J).

160   *Hercy v Birch* (1804) 9 Ves 357, 32 ER 640; *New Brunswick & Canada Railway & Land Co v Muggeridge* (1850) 4 Drew 686, 699; 62 ER 263, 286 (Kindersley VC).

161   (1804) 9 Ves 357, 32 ER 640.

162   ICF Spry, *The Principles of Equitable Remedies* (9th edn, LBC 2014) 131–32.

163   *Lavery v Pursell* (1888) 39 Ch D 508, 519 (no specific performance for leases of less than one year); *Glasse v Woolgar & Roberts* (1897) 41 Sol Jo 573 (specific performance of lease for one day refused).

increasingly ready to award specific performance of short-term leases,[164] and even contractual licences.[165] By contrast, in cases where the lease has already expired, courts are unlikely to award specific performance.[166]

VI   Discretionary factors and bars to relief

[10.71] As an equitable remedy, specific performance is always subject to the discretion of the court. Several considerations are relevant. Some discretionary factors apply to all equitable remedies. Others are only relevant to specific performance and to injunctions equivalent to specific performance.

[10.72]   Discretionary factors do not raise a question of jurisdiction, but instead go to the question of whether it is appropriate in the individual circumstances of the case to award a remedy. Thus, the exercise of a particular equitable discretion is dependent on the facts of the case and the operation of all other discretionary considerations. All the factors of the case are weighed up to decide where the balance of justice lies in relation to the relief sought. As Spry points out:

> Any particular discretionary matter may be subject to countervailing matters of equal or greater weight. Indeed, as to any particular set of circumstances that would induce the court to exercise its discretion in a particular way it is possible to postulate additional circumstances that would lead to the exercise of that discretion in a different way.[167]

[10.73]   Discretionary considerations are usually raised by way of defence to the plaintiff's claim for specific relief in equity. Even where a bar applies, a plaintiff is ordinarily still able to claim compensatory damages for breach of contract. Nevertheless, there is a possibility that there may be circumstances where a contract which is too unfair to warrant a discretionary remedy is also too unfair to permit a compensatory damages award.[168] Zachariah Chafee argues that courts should 'take the facts which bar specific performance and ask whether they do not also render damages unjust'.[169]

[10.74]   We have already noted above that the discretionary bars to relief overlap to some degree with other matters which must be made out before specific relief can be granted (such as certainty of contract, illegality and the like).

A   General equitable bars to relief

[10.75] These discretionary bars to relief apply not just to specific performance and injunctions but to *all* equitable remedies.

---

164   *De Brassac v Martyn* (1863) 9 LT 287 (specific performance of a lease of less than one year would have been granted had the lease not expired and the plaintiff delayed in bringing action); *Watch Tower Bible and Tract Society Council v Huntly Borough* [1959] NZLR 821 (although specific performance of lease for three days refused).

165   *Verrall v Great Yarmouth Borough Council* [1981] QB 202.

166   *Nesbitt v Meyer* (1818) 1 Swans 223, 36 ER 366; *McMahon v Ambrose* [1987] VR 817.

167   ICF Spry, *The Principles of Equitable Remedies* (9th edn, LBC 2014) 4.

168   Z Chafee Jr, 'Coming into Equity with Clean Hands' (1949) 47 Mich L Rev 877, 895–96.

169   Ibid.

1 Hardship and the public interest

A court of equity will not grant equitable specific relief where to do so would inflict undue hardship on the defendant,[170] but the defendant will still be subject to legal remedies, in particular, damages. [10.76]

Hardship must be weighed up with all other facts, including the hardship caused to the plaintiff by a refusal of specific performance.[171] It has been said that '[t]he defence of hardship these days very rarely meets with much success'[172] because of the difficulty in making it out. The hardship must generally be severe. [10.77]

A striking example of hardship occurred in the English case of *Patel v Ali*,[173] where the defendants, the Alis, had entered into a contract for the sale of land with the plaintiffs, the Patels. After the contract was signed but before settlement could occur, the defendants suffered terrible misfortune. Mr Ali became bankrupt, and for a time the property was subject to an injunction awarded to Mr Ali's trustee in bankruptcy, preventing the sale from going ahead as planned. Mr Ali was sent to prison for a year. Mrs Ali was diagnosed with bone cancer and underwent treatment involving amputation of her leg. At the time of application for relief the couple had three children. Mrs Ali was of Pakistani background, and spoke very little English. She did not want the contract to be enforced because she was reliant on the support of her local community. Goulding J refused to order specific performance of a contract of sale because it would cause undue hardship to Mrs Ali. His Honour said that there had already been unforeseen delays to completion of the contract, meaning that compensatory damages would be an adequate remedy for the plaintiffs.[174] By contrast, Mrs Ali could suffer great hardship if the contract was specifically enforced.[175] The judge allowed the hardship bar to operate even though the hardship had arisen after the contract had been entered into. [10.78]

The better view is that hardship should be assessed at the time of making the order, not at the time at which the contract was entered.[176] Nonetheless, particularly where a commercial contract is concerned, the success of a claim of hardship may depend on whether the plaintiff contemplated or should have contemplated the hardship which has occurred.[177] [10.79]

---

170 *Denne v Light* (1857) 8 De GM & G 774, 44 ER 58 (contract of sale of land not specifically enforced because no way of accessing the land via a right of way); *Hope v Walter* [1900] 1 Ch 257 (contract of sale of land not specifically enforced because property in use as a 'disorderly house' a.k.a. brothel); *Wroth v Tyler* [1974] 1 Ch 30 (contract of sale with husband not specifically performed because wife had a registered interest in the house pursuant to s 1(1) of the then *Matrimonial Homes Act 1967* (UK) and to force the husband to perform the contract might cause the family to split up).

171 *Tamplin v James* (1880) 15 Ch D 215, 221 (James LJ); *Eastes v Russ* [1914] 1 Ch 468, 480 (Swinfen Eady LJ); *Keats v Wallis* [1953] NZLR 563, 566; *Nicholas v Ingram* [1958] NZLR 972, 974; *ANZ Executors and Trustees Ltd v Humes Ltd* [1990] VR 615, 639 (Brooking J).

172 *Longtom Pty Ltd v Oberon Shire Council* (1996) 7 BPR 14,799, 14,807.

173 [1984] 1 Ch 283.

174 Ibid, 288.

175 Ibid.

176 See *RD McKinnon Holdings Pty Ltd v Hind* [1984] 2 NSWLR 121. See also ICF Spry, *The Principles of Equitable Remedies* (9th edn, LBC 2014) 203. Cf *Bosaid v Andry* [1963] VR 465, 478–79 (Sholl J).

177 *ANZ Executors and Trustees Ltd v Humes Ltd* [1990] VR 615, 637 (Brooking J).

[10.80]   It should be emphasised that financial difficulties on the part of the defendant are not grounds for hardship.[178] Nor is an increase in the value of the land since the sale.[179] However, if an agreement seems to be unconscionable, the court may refuse to specifically enforce it.[180] Hardship on the defendant may also lead a court to place conditions on an award of specific performance.[181]

[10.81]   In *Patel v Ali*, the hardship to the Alis' children was not considered to be a reason to decline specific performance.[182] However, in some cases injunctions have not been granted because the court took the broader public interest into account.[183] Ian Spry notes that hardship has been taken into account in some cases where third parties are closely connected with the defendant,[184] and that there is no reason in principle why a court should refuse to consider hardship to third parties or the general public.[185] Nonetheless, hardship to third parties or the public will not ordinarily be determinative nor prevent an award of specific performance.[186]

2   Lack of clean hands

[10.82]   Courts may refuse to award specific performance if the plaintiff exhibits a 'lack of clean hands'.[187] Spry says that 'clean hands' considerations operate in two instances:

1.   where the plaintiff has misled the court, abused its process, or attempted to do so; or

2.   where the grant of relief would enable the plaintiff to achieve a dishonest purpose and where it appears that it would be inequitable to grant relief.[188]

---

178   *Pasedina (Holdings) Pty Ltd v Khouri* (1977) 1 BPR 9460; *Demagogue Pty Ltd v Ramensky* (1992) 39 FCR 31, 44 (Gummow J); *Longtom Pty Ltd v Oberon Shire Council* (1996) 7 BPR 14,799, 14,809; *Iambic Pty Ltd v Northwind Holdings Pty Ltd* [2001] WASC 44 [6]; *IGA Distributors Pty Ltd v King & Taylor Pty Ltd* [2002] VSC 440 [243]; *Boyarsky v Taylor* [2008] NSWSC 1415, (2008) 14 BPR 26,553. Cf *Evans v Robcorp Pty Ltd (as trustee for Robcorp Trust)* [2014] QSC 26 where impossibility of paying the purchase price was a basis for hardship.
179   *Fitzgerald v Masters* (1956) 95 CLR 420, 433 (Dixon CJ and Fullagar J).
180   *Falcke v Gray* (1859) 4 Drew 651, 62 ER 250; *Dowsett v Reid* (1912) 15 CLR 695.
181   See, eg, *Aristoc Industries Pty Ltd v RA Wenham (Builders) Pty Ltd* [1965] NSWR 581, where the award of an injunction restraining the defendant from dealing with or removing chairs was made conditional upon the plaintiff offering the chairs to the defendant for the same price as had been offered to the original builder of a hall.
182   [1984] 1 Ch 283, 288. See also *Gall v Mitchell* (1924) 35 CLR 222, 230–31 (Isaacs J), 226 (Knox CJ and Starke J), another case where hardship to children did not prevent an award.
183   *Miller v Jackson* [1977] QB 966 (cf *Kennaway v Thompson* [1981] QB 88); *Wrotham Park Estate Co Ltd v Parkside Homes Ltd* [1974] 1 WLR 798, 811; *Patrick Stevedores Operations No 2 Pty Ltd v Maritime Union of Australia (No 3)* [1998] HCA 30, (1998) 195 CLR 1, [65]–[66]; *Lawrence v Fen Tigers Ltd* [2014] UKSC 13, [2014] AC 822.
184   *Gall v Mitchell* (1924) 35 CLR 222, 230–31 (Isaacs J); *Wroth v Tyler* [1974] 1 Ch 30.
185   ICF Spry, *The Principles of Equitable Remedies* (9th edn, LBC 2014) 208.
186   Ibid, 208–09.
187   See, eg, *Shell UK Ltd v Lostock Garage Ltd* [1976] 1 WLR 1187 (petrol company treated small business unfairly during 'petrol price war'); *Quadrant Visual Communications Ltd v Hutchinson Telephone (UK) Ltd* [1993] BCLC 442 (failure to disclose marketing campaign giving away free handsets meant plaintiff unable to specifically enforce contract selling mobile phone business); *Summers v Cocks* (1927) 40 CLR 321.
188   ICF Spry, *The Principles of Equitable Remedies* (9th edn, LBC 2014) 253–56.

Iniquity to the defendant is not the only relevant consideration. A plaintiff may also be denied relief where she has attempted to mislead the public[189] or the court.[190]

'Lack of clean hands' does not mean general impropriety and must relate to the relief sought.[191] In *Moody v Cox*, it was said that 'the depravity, the dirt in question on the hand, [must have] . . . an immediate and necessary relation to the equity sued for'.[192] Australian courts have reiterated this requirement in the context of a plaintiff corporation previously involved in a cardboard box cartel,[193] and in relation to a 'bikie' club association.[194] Mere 'sharp conduct' will not establish lack of clean hands.[195] [10.83]

In *Summers v Cocks*,[196] the High Court of Australia refused to order specific performance because the plaintiff, Summers, lacked 'clean hands'. Summers had contracted to sell a hotel to Cocks, the defendant. At the time of contracting, Summers was aware that licensing authorities were considering revoking the liquor licence for the premises. After the contract was signed, the licence was revoked. Cocks became aware of this and refused to go ahead with the sale. Summers sought specific performance of the sale contract, but a majority of the High Court refused specific performance because Summers had not come to equity with clean hands in view of his failure to disclose material facts.[197] [10.84]

If refusal of relief could cause injustice to third parties, the court may grant relief, notwithstanding the misconduct of the plaintiff, because the relief is given for the sake of the public.[198] [10.85]

3   Laches: delay with acquiescence and delay with prejudice

The word 'laches' is derived from Norman French, and implies notions of delay and acquiescence in bringing a claim. The classic statement of the doctrine is in *Lindsay Petroleum Co v Hurd*: [10.86]

> Now the doctrine of laches in Courts of Equity is not an arbitrary or a technical doctrine. Where it would be practically unjust to give a remedy, either because the party has, by his conduct, done that which might fairly be regarded as equivalent to a waiver of it, or where by his conduct and neglect he has, though perhaps not waiving that remedy, yet put the other party in a situation in which it would not be reasonable to place him if the remedy were afterwards to be asserted, in either of these cases, lapse of time and delay are most

189   See, eg, *Kettles and Gas Appliances Ltd v Anthony Hordern and Sons Ltd* (1934) 35 SR (NSW) 108.
190   See, eg, *Armstrong v Sheppard & Short Ltd* [1959] 2 QB 384.
191   *Jones v Lenthal* (1669) 1 Chan Cas 154; 22 ER 739; *Duchess of Argyll v Duke of Argyll* [1967] 1 Ch 302; *Loughran v Loughran*, 292 US 216, 229 (Brandeis J) (1934); *FAI Insurances Ltd v Pioneer Concrete Services* (1987) 15 NSWLR 552, 554 (Young J); *REW08 Projects Pty Ltd v PNC Lifestyle Investments Pty Ltd* [2017] NSWCA 269.
192   [1917] 2 Ch 71, 87–88. See also *Official Trustee in Bankruptcy v Tooheys Ltd* (1993) 29 NSWLR 641, 650 (Gleeson CJ).
193   *Amcor Ltd v Barnes* [2012] VSC 434.
194   *Black Uhlans Inc v New South Wales Crime Commission* [2002] NSWSC 1060, (2002) 12 BPR 22,421.
195   *ANZ Executors and Trustees Ltd v Humes Ltd* [1990] VR 615.
196   (1927) 40 CLR 321.
197   Ibid, 324 (Isaacs ACJ), 331–32 (Starke J). Higgins J dissented.
198   *Vauxhall Bridge Co v Earl Spencer* (1821) Jac 64, 67; 37 ER 774, 775; *Money v Money (No 2)* [1966] 1 NSWR 348, 351–52 (Jacobs J); *New South Wales Dairy Corporation v Murray Goulburn Co-operative Co Ltd* (1990) 171 CLR 363, 409 (Dawson and Toohey JJ).

material. But in every case, if an argument against relief, which otherwise would be just, is founded upon mere delay, that delay of course not amounting to a bar by any statute of limitations, the validity of that defence must be tried upon principles substantially equitable. Two circumstances, always important in such cases, are, the length of the delay and the nature of the acts done during the interval, which might affect either party and cause a balance of justice or injustice in taking the one course or the other, so far as relates to the remedy.[199]

[10.87]   Delay and acquiescence are difficult to categorically define, in part because acquiescence is often used in a way which overlaps with delay.[200] In the New Zealand case *No 68 Ltd v Eastern Services Ltd*, McGrath J noted that laches generally falls into two categories: (1) where a plaintiff delays seeking redress once she knows her rights are violated, which leads the defendant to think that she has acquiesced; and (2) where a plaintiff's delay causes significant prejudice to the other party.[201]

[10.88]   As the statement from *Lindsay Petroleum Co v Hurd* illustrates, 'mere' delay does not prevent the grant of a remedy in equity.[202] It depends upon the facts of each case. Generally, something more is needed: either acquiescence on the part of the plaintiff or prejudice to the defendant or third parties.

[10.89]   In the case of acquiescence and delay, the plaintiff does not deserve a remedy because she delayed in bringing an action, and the defendant does not deserve to have a remedy ordered against him because he assumed he was 'in the clear'.[203] In the case of acquiescence and prejudice, the plaintiff does not deserve a remedy because her unreasonable delays have caused prejudice to the defendant, in the sense that the defendant will now find it difficult to defend the claim because of the effluxion of time since the events occurred.[204] Sometimes acquiescence and prejudice may involve third parties, as in *Lamshed v Lamshed*,[205] where specific performance of a contract for the sale of land was refused after a six-year delay because of the detrimental effect it would have on the innocent third party who had purchased the property from the defendant.

B   Bars to relief relevant only to specific performance

[10.90]   The bars to relief which follow are relevant only to specific performance (or to an injunction equivalent to specific performance). The first two bars are particularly controversial.

---

199   (1874) LR 5 PC 221, 239–40.
200   JD Heydon, MJ Leeming and PG Turner, *Meagher, Gummow and Lehane's Equity: Doctrines and Remedies* (5th edn, LexisNexis Butterworths 2015) [36–090]; M Cope, *Equitable Obligations – Duties, Defences and Remedies* (LBC 2007) 287; *Orr v Ford* (1989) 167 CLR 316, 338 (Deane J).
201   [2006] NZSC 42, [2006] 2 NZLR 43 [56].
202   A delay of 12 years was insufficient in *Burroughes v Abbott* [1922] Ch 86, and a delay of 26 years was insufficient in *Weld v Petre* [1929] 1 Ch 33; *Fitzgerald v Masters* (1956) 95 CLR 420, 433 (Dixon CJ), 440–41 (McTiernan, Webb and Taylor JJ).
203   J Edelman, 'Money Awards of the Cost of Performance' (2010) 4 J Eq 122, 129–30, arguing that this should be known as 'waiver'.
204   Ibid, arguing that this could be partially subsumed within a change of position defence.
205   (1963) 109 CLR 440.

1   Mutuality

Sir Edward Fry stated the following proposition in *A Treatise on the Specific Performance of Contracts*:   [10.91]

> A contract to be specifically enforced by the court must, as a general rule, be mutual, – that is to say, such that it might, at the time it was entered into, have been enforced by either of the parties against the other of them.[206]

So, for example, a plaintiff who was a minor at the time of making a contract was unable to call for specific enforcement because the contract could not be enforced against him.[207] Conversely, a defendant employee who breached a negative covenant providing that she was not to work for other employers argued lack of mutuality because she could not force the plaintiff employer to employ her.[208] The court focused on the nature of the agreement (a contract for services),[209] rather than the parties' ability to specifically enforce in this instance. It said that lack of mutuality alone was not decisive, but was a matter of discretion.[210] In any case, the injunction simply restrained a breach of negative covenant rather than enforcing a contract for services, so mutuality did not arise.[211]

Lack of mutuality has been intensely criticised by scholars and courts.[212] Ames criticised it   [10.92] in 1903, and said that the true position was that '[e]quity will not compel specific performance by a defendant if after performance the common law remedy of damages will be his sole security for the performance of the plaintiff's side of the contract'.[213] By this Ames meant that there must be some assurance that the plaintiff will perform her side of the bargain, and if the plaintiff is only likely to be liable to pay damages if she breaches her side of the bargain, the defendant may not be adequately protected.

Heydon, Leeming and Turner recommend that 'the word "mutuality" should disappear   [10.93] from the legal vocabulary'.[214] They point out two problems with Fry's statement. First, it is not generally true to say that the only plaintiff who can succeed is one against whom specific

---

206   Sir E Fry, *A Treatise on the Specific Performance of Contracts* (GR Northcote ed, 6th edn, Stevens 1921) 219.

207   See, eg, *Flight v Bollard* (1828) 4 Russ 298; 38 ER 817 (contract by infant not specifically enforced based on lack of mutuality). Cf *Kell v Harris* (1915) 15 SR (NSW) 473 (contract entered by infant specifically enforceable once he ratified it as an adult).

208   *Curro v Beyond Productions Pty Ltd* (1993) 30 NSWLR 337, 348.

209   Note that a defendant employee *may* now obtain specific relief against a plaintiff employer: *Quinn v Overland* [2010] FCA 799, (2010) 199 IR 40 [97]–[101].

210   (1993) 30 NSWLR 337, 348, citing *Warren v Mendy* [1989] 1 WLR 853, 866 (Nourse LJ).

211   (1993) 30 NSWLR 337, 348.

212   JB Ames, 'Mutuality in Specific Performance' (1903) 3 Col L Rev 1; ICF Spry, *The Principles of Equitable Remedies* (9th edn, LBC 2014) 7–8, 95–107; JD Heydon, MJ Leeming and PG Turner, *Meagher, Gummow and Lehane's Equity: Doctrines and Remedies* (5th edn, LexisNexis Butterworths 2015) [20–165]. See also WD Lewis, 'The Present State of the Defence of Want of Mutuality in Specific Performance' (1903) 51 U Penn L Rev 591, 625–29; A Schwartz, 'The Case for Specific Performance' (1979) 89 Yale LJ 271, 301–03.

213   Ames, ibid, 2–3, 12.

214   JD Heydon, MJ Leeming and PG Turner, *Meagher, Gummow and Lehane's Equity: Doctrines and Remedies* (5th edn, LexisNexis Butterworths 2015) [20–165]. See also WD Lewis, 'The Present State of the Defence of Want of Mutuality in Specific Performance' (1903) 51 U Penn L Rev 591, 625–29; A Schwartz, 'The Case for Specific Performance' (1979) 89 Yale LJ 271, 301–03.

performance can be awarded. Secondly, case law indicates that mutuality at the date of formation of the contract is not necessary.[215] Clearly, there are fundamental problems with the doctrine as expressed by Fry and, insofar as it still exists, the bar must be treated with great care.

[10.94]   The English Court of Appeal rejected Fry's mutuality rule in *Price v Strange*.[216] The plaintiff tenant made an unenforceable oral agreement with the defendant landlord to have his lease renewed in return for repairing the block of flats. Although the agreement was initially unenforceable, it later became enforceable because of the plaintiff's acts of part performance in reliance upon the agreement. Goff LJ said that Fry's proposition was 'wrong' and that 'the true principle is that one judges the defence of want of mutuality on the facts and circumstances as they exist at the hearing'.[217] The Court judged mutuality at the time of the hearing, and awarded specific performance subject to the plaintiff compensating the defendant for that portion of the repair works which had been done by another builder.

[10.95]   One consequence of the rejection of Fry's concept of mutuality in England and Wales is that a lessee's covenant to repair can be specifically enforced in exceptional circumstances, as long as the building work to be done is sufficiently certain, damages are inadequate and the defendant is in possession such that it would be trespass for the plaintiff lessor to attempt to fix the premises.[218]

[10.96]   In *Cannovo v FCD Holdings Pty Ltd*, Santow J suggested that the real basis for mutuality in modern times is hardship, and the question is whether the defendant would suffer hardship 'by reason of the plaintiff being unable to be required to carry out his obligations in specie'.[219]

[10.97]   It seems clear that to the extent that mutuality still exists as a coherent principle, it does not require proof that the defendant could have obtained specific performance had he brought proceedings and, further, the relevant date to assess mutuality is the date when the decree is made.[220] This may be important where, at the time of making the contract, the plaintiff could not have performed the acts stipulated in the contract, but by the time specific performance is sought the plaintiff can do so.[221]

2   Continuous supervision and personal services

[10.98]   Traditionally, specific performance is unavailable where a court would be required to constantly supervise the order.[222] In *Ryan v Mutual Tontine Westminster Chambers Association*, the classic authority, the court said that constant supervision was a strict bar to specific performance in a contract for porter services.[223] The rule has been criticised in its

---

215   Heydon, Leeming and Turner, ibid, [20–150].

216   [1978] Ch 337. See also *Rainbow Estates Ltd v Tokenhold Ltd* [1999] Ch 64, 69.

217   [1978] Ch 337, 356.

218   *Jeune v Queens Cross Properties Ltd* [1974] Ch 97; *Rainbow Estates Ltd v Tokenhold Ltd* [1999] Ch 64, 69–74. Cf *Hill v Barclay* (1810) 16 Ves 402; 33 ER 1037.

219   [2000] NSWSC 304 [64].

220   JD Heydon, MJ Leeming and PG Turner, *Meagher, Gummow and Lehane's Equity: Doctrines and Remedies* (5th edn, Butterworths LexisNexis 2015) [20–165].

221   ICF Spry, *The Principles of Equitable Remedies* (9th edn, LBC 2014) 101–07.

222   *JC Williamson Ltd v Lukey* (1931) 45 CLR 282, 293 (Starke J); 297–98 (Dixon J).

223   [1893] 1 Ch 116, 123, 125, 128. See also *Pollard v Clayton* (1855) 1 K & J 463; 69 ER 540; *Blackett v Bates* (1865) 1 Ch App 117; *Phipps v Jackson* (1887) 56 LJ Ch 550. Cf *Wolverhampton Corporation v Emmons* [1901] 1 KB 515.

strict form,[224] and continuous supervision now seems to be simply a discretionary consideration. Indeed, in *Posner v Scott-Lewis*,[225] which involved very similar facts to *Ryan*, the court specifically enforced a contract for porter services, and continuous supervision was not a reason to refuse such an order.

Continuous supervision remains an important reason for the courts' reluctance to specific‐   [10.99] ally enforce contracts of personal services. As noted at [11.40]–[11.44], other considerations militate against the award of specific relief for personal service contracts, although sometimes an injunction to restrain breach of a negative covenant may still be awarded.

Cooperative Insurance Society Ltd v Argyll Stores (Holdings) Ltd suggests that the bar of   [10.100] continuous supervision still has force beyond personal service contracts, at least in England and Wales.[226] The House of Lords refused to specifically enforce a 35-year lease of supermarket premises in a shopping centre. In 1995, with 19 years still to run on the lease, the tenants informed the landlord that they no longer intended to run the supermarket because it had significant trading losses the previous year. Despite the landlord's offer of rent concessions and the like, the tenants closed the business without further communication or discussion. The landlord sought to specifically enforce the lease because it was concerned that the shopping centre would fail without the anchor tenant.

The House of Lords refused the order. Lord Hoffmann, who gave the leading speech,   [10.101] indicated that one reason for refusing to decree specific performance was that parties would have to return repeatedly to the court to ascertain whether the order was being carried out. He distinguished between orders that require a defendant to carry on an activity over an extended time (such as running a business) and orders that simply require a defendant to achieve a result, such as building contracts and repairing covenants.[227] The former had a greater possibility of repeat applications for rulings as to compliance.

Lord Hoffman also said that an indicator of problems arising from continuous supervision   [10.102] was whether the court could specify what conduct was required for compliance with its order.[228] If the order cannot be sufficiently specific, then continuous supervision is likely to be problematic, because the parties must return to court to obtain further guidance.

Finally, Lord Hoffman said that specific performance was a coercive and heavy-handed   [10.103] remedy with extreme sanctions for non-compliance (including contempt of court and imprisonment).[229] The court was reluctant to force the defendant to run a failing business against its best interests. Moreover, an order of specific performance 'yokes the parties together in a continuing hostile relationship', and any trust between the parties had been lost.[230] Because of

---

224   See, eg, *Giles & Co Ltd v Morris* [1972] 1 WLR 307, 318 (Megarry VC); *Tito v Waddell (No 2)* [1977] Ch 106, 321–23 (Megarry VC); *Posner v Scott-Lewis* [1997] Ch 25, 36.
225   [1997] Ch 25.
226   [1998] AC 1.
227   Ibid, 13–14. This distinction has been adopted by Australian courts: see discussion in *Netline Pty Ltd v QAV Pty Ltd (No 2)* [2015] WASC 113 [71].
228   Ibid. See also *Redland Bricks Ltd v Morris* [1970] AC 652, 666 (Lord Upjohn); *Nexus Mortgage Securities Pty Ltd v Ecto Pty Ltd* [1998] 4 VR 220.
229   Cf D Pearce, 'Remedies for Breach of a Keep-Open Covenant' (2008) 24 J Cont L 199, 206, who argues that the defendant in this case would be unlikely to be in contempt because of the requirement to establish a mens rea.
230   *Co-operative Insurance Society v Argyll Stores* [1998] AC 1, 13–15 (Lord Hoffmann),

the losing nature of the business, an order of specific performance could put a defendant in a disadvantageous position, allowing the plaintiff to make extortionate demands.[231]

[10.104] Spry suggests that *Argyll* is unduly commercial, and has criticised it, saying, '[s]imply, the circumstances did not raise sufficient considerations against the grant of specific performance, in view of the defendant's deliberate breach and of prospective prejudice to the plaintiff and third parties'.[232]

[10.105] *Argyll* can be contrasted with the Victorian case of *Diagnostic X-Ray Services Pty Ltd v Jewel Food Stores Pty Ltd*.[233] The defendant operated a supermarket and petrol station, and was an anchor tenant in the plaintiff's shopping centre. Without informing the plaintiff, the defendant sold the supermarket and closed the petrol station. Beach J distinguished *Argyll* on the basis that this was not a business venture that went sour; the defendant simply decided to restructure its business. It was also significant that, of the four shopping centres in the area, this was the only one with a petrol station, which attracted customers to the centre. The loss to the plaintiff was too difficult to quantify and specific performance was awarded. By contrast, if the business is losing, courts are less likely to award specific performance.[234] In *Sentinel Countrywide Retail Ltd v PC Emerald (Qld) Pty Ltd* it was inappropriate to award specific performance which would require a losing pizza store to continue business, even though damages were inadequate because the company running the business was a 'one dollar company' which would not be able to satisfy a damages award.[235] Australian courts also apply *Argyll* where there has been a breakdown in trust between the parties.[236]

[10.106] The High Court of Australia appeared to read down (or even to misread) *Argyll* in *Patrick Stevedores Operations No 2 Pty Ltd v Maritime Union of Australia (No 3)*,[237] a complex industrial relations case concerning the power of the court to reinstate the employment of certain employees. The majority judgment emphasised that continuous supervision was not an 'absolute restriction' on specific performance, and that the significance of Lord Hoffmann's speech was that 'the concept of "constant supervision by the court" by itself is no longer an effective or useful criterion for refusing a decree of specific performance'.[238] Spry has noted that this statement is incorrect insofar as it suggests that *Argyll* abandoned the principles of constant supervision, but argues that this passage should be read as saying that constant supervision is not by itself a reason to refuse specific performance without further analysis.[239]

---

231 Ibid 13–15 (Lord Hoffmann), citing RJ Sharpe, 'Specific Relief for Contract Breach' in B Reiter and J Swan (eds), *Studies in Contract Law* (Butterworths 1980) 123, 129. Cf A Tettenborn, 'Absolving the Undeserving: Shopping Centres, Specific Performance and the Law of Contract' [1998] Conv 23, 25, 33–36, questioning whether the plaintiff in this case actually wished to do this.

232 ICF Spry, *The Principles of Equitable Remedies* (9th edn, LBC 2014) 697. See also other critical responses: A Tettenborn, 'Absolving the Undeserving: Shopping Centres, Specific Performance and the Law of Contract' [1998] Conv 23; D Pearce, 'Remedies for Breach of a Keep-Open Covenant' (2008) 24 J Cont L 199.

233 (2001) 4 VR 632.

234 *Ruffy Investments Pty Ltd v Payless Superbarn (Vic) Pty Ltd* [1999] VSC 458, (2000) V Conv R 54–617 (Beach J); *Sentinel Countrywide Retail Ltd v PC Emerald (Qld) Pty Ltd* [2015] QSC 348 (Applegarth J).

235 [2015] QSC 348.

236 *Netline Pty Ltd v QAV Pty Ltd (No 2)* [2015] WASC 113 [67]–[68] (Beech J); *Chahal Group Pty Ltd v 7-Eleven Stores Pty Ltd* [2017] NSWC 532 [272]–[275] (Sackar J).

237 [1998] HCA 30, (1998) 195 CLR 1.

238 Ibid, [79] (Brennan CJ, McHugh, Gummow, Kirby and Hayne JJ).

239 ICF Spry, *The Principles of Equitable Remedies* (9th edn, LexisNexis 2014) 700–01.

3 Readiness and willingness

A plaintiff who seeks specific performance must show that she is ready and willing to perform herself.[240] Delay and acquiescence may suggest that the plaintiff is not ready and willing to perform.[241] However, she need only perform all essential obligations.[242] Moreover, the court presumes that she is ready, willing, and able to do so.[243]   **[10.107]**

Readiness and willingness are particularly important where the plaintiff seeks to specifically enforce a contract and the defendant claims that the remedy should be denied because the plaintiff is in breach of her obligations under the contract, and is not ready and willing to perform. This has been said to be a manifestation of the 'clean hands' doctrine.[244]   **[10.108]**

This doctrine is less important where the contract sought to be specifically performed is an executed agreement rather than an executory agreement.[245] In the latter case, the plaintiff has already complied with her obligations.   **[10.109]**

VII   Specific performance under the Australian Consumer Law

Specific performance is not mentioned as a remedy available for breach of the ACL. Nevertheless, the court has the power to award a mandatory injunction to prevent a breach of provisions contained in Chapters 2, 3 or 4 of the ACL pursuant to s 232. This may be awarded 'whether or not there is an imminent danger of substantial damage to any other person'.[246] Injunctions under the ACL are considered at [11.62]–[11.68].   **[10.110]**

There has been debate as to whether s 87(2) of the previous *Trade Practices Act 1974* (Cth) and its state equivalents empowered courts to make orders equivalent to specific performance because of the open-ended nature of the section.[247] In *Milchas Investments Pty Ltd v Larkin*,[248] Young J held that an order for specific performance could potentially be made under s 87(2) of the *Trade Practices Act*, but found no case where a court had done so. In his opinion, this reflected the fact that damages, setting aside of contracts or restraining injunctions were the more appropriate remedies, and 'it is only in very rare circumstances that the court will think that one of the other discretionary remedies is appropriate'.[249] In *Futuretronics International Pty Ltd v Gadzhis*,[250] Ormiston J refused to order specific performance under s 41 of the *Fair*   **[10.111]**

---

240   See *Green v Sommerville* (1979) 141 CLR 594 for an example of where a claim of lack of readiness and willingness failed. See also *Bahr v Nicolay (No 2)* (1988) 164 CLR 604, 620 (Mason CJ and Dawson J).
241   JD Heydon and MJ Leeming, *Cases and Materials on Equity and Trusts* (8th edn, LexisNexis 2011) 1178.
242   *Mehmet v Benson* (1965) 112 CLR 295, 308 (Barwick CJ), 314 (Windeyer J).
243   *Foran v Wight* (1989) 168 CLR 385, 451–52.
244   *Green v Sommerville* (1979) 141 CLR 594, 611 (Mason J).
245   *Bridge Wholesale Acceptance Corporation (Australia) Ltd v Burnard* (1992) 27 NSWLR 415, 423 (Clarke JA).
246   ACL, s 232(4)(c).
247   D Skapinker, 'Other Remedies under the Trade Practices Act – The Rise and Rise of Section 87' (1995) 21 Monash ULR 188, 195–96.
248   (1989) 96 FLR 464.
249   Ibid, 477. Cf *Futuretronics International Pty Ltd v Gadzhis* [1992] 2 VR 217, 245: Ormiston J reads *Milchas* as authority that specific performance is unavailable.
250   [1992] 2 VR 217.

Trading Act 1985 (Vic) (since repealed). This was in part because there was no loss or damage flowing from the defendant's misleading conduct which would allow the court to award relief pursuant to the Act.[251] Moreover, the Act was intended to compensate plaintiffs who were misled or deceived, and not to operate as a substitute for enforcing promises.[252] The way in which courts tended to award reliance loss rather than expectation loss reinforced his Honour's conclusion that an award of specific performance 'would not appropriately compensate for that loss, but would give a different and wider remedy not contemplated by the Act'.[253]

[10.112]   The possibility of an award of specific performance under the ACL has not yet been determined, but it is suggested that if specific performance could be awarded, it is likely to be necessary for the plaintiff to show that the purpose of the order is to compensate for loss or damage, or to prevent or reduce loss or damage.[254]

[10.113]   Pursuant to ss 237, 238 and 239 of the ACL, courts may make 'such order or orders' as they think appropriate where an injured person or non-party consumer has suffered, or is likely to suffer, loss or damage. The orders that may be made are set out in s 243, and include orders which resemble specific performance – namely, an order that a respondent repair or provide parts for goods supplied by the respondent to the injured person (s 243(f)) and an order that the respondent supply specified services to the injured person (s 243(g)). Orders under ss 237, 238 and 239 of the ACL will be available only where the purpose is to compensate for loss or damage, or to prevent or reduce loss or damage.[255]

VIII   Specific restitution or specific delivery of property

[10.114]   Courts have an exceptional power to order delivery up of goods when they have been wrongfully detained, for example through the torts of detinue or conversion. This is known as specific restitution or specific delivery. It is available as of right through equity's original jurisdiction (for example, for breach of fiduciary duty)[256] or through equity's auxiliary jurisdiction as an exceptional, discretionary remedy for proprietary torts.

[10.115]   Historically, damages were the default common law remedy for detinue, conversion and trespass to goods.[257] Common law courts in England were given the power to order delivery

---

251   Ibid, 245.
252   Ibid, 244, citing *Gates v City Mutual Life Assurance Society Ltd* (1986) 160 CLR 1. *Marks v GIO Australia Holdings Ltd* (1998) 196 CLR 494 could also be cited today. Cf *Murphy v Overton Investments Pty Ltd* [2004] HCA 3, (2004) 216 CLR 388.
253   [1992] 2 VR 217, 245.
254   W Covell, K Lupton and J Forder, *Principles of Remedies* (6th edn, LexisNexis 2015) [17.38].
255   See ACL, ss 237(2), 238(2) and 239(3). As to the nature of loss or damage which must be identified, see *Gates v City Mutual Life Assurance Society Ltd* (1986) 160 CLR 1; *Marks v GIO Australia Holdings Ltd* (1998) 196 CLR 494; *Henville v Walker* [2001] HCA 52, (2001) 206 CLR 459 [130]–[135] (McHugh J, with whom Gummow and Hayne JJ agreed). Cf *Murphy v Overton Investments Pty Ltd* [2004] HCA 3, (2004) 216 CLR 388, and the minority in *Henville v Walker* [2001] HCA 52, (2001) 206 CLR 459 [37]–[41] (Gleeson CJ), [66]–[68] (Gaudron J).
256   See, eg, *Wood v Rowcliffe* (1847) 2 Ph 382, 383; 45 ER 990, 991.
257   A Tettenborn, 'Intentional Interference with Chattels' in C Sappideen and P Vines (ed), *Fleming's The Law of Torts*, 10th edn (LBC 2011) [4.290].

up of chattels in 1854,[258] and Australian states followed suit.[259] There has never been a common law equivalent of the ancient Roman remedy known as the *rei vindicatio*, which allowed the plaintiff to demand that the defendant return goods which belonged to her,[260] and which has analogues in civilian law. It has been suggested that the common law needs a *vindicatio* remedy.[261]

An order for specific restitution will usually be given in tort only if damages are inadequate, which generally occurs when the goods are unique.[262] In fact, many of the early cases mentioned at [10.35] involved specific restitution. While specific performance and specific restitution are similar, they are not identical. Specific performance involves a positive duty (to do what is stipulated in the contract), whereas specific restitution involves a negative duty (to restrain from interfering with the plaintiff's property).[263] Burrows has queried whether the requirement of inadequacy of damages should be retained, because there is a distinction between specific performance of a contract given for a 'mere' breach of promise and tortious interference with a pre-existing property right in goods.[264] He sees no reason why specific non-unique goods should not be given up in the latter case. In equity's exclusive jurisdiction, specific restitution is not as difficult to obtain because there is no need to show damages are inadequate.[265] However, the remedy is discretionary whether specific restitution is sought for common law or equitable breaches. For example, a plaintiff may not be entitled to specific restitution because she comes to equity with unclean hands,[266] or because of delay on her part.[267]

[10.116]

In *Doulton Potteries Ltd v Bronotte*,[268] the plaintiff sought return of a unique die which it used to produce pipes with a 90 degree turn for its business. The die had been placed with the defendant for repairs. The defendant refused to return the die until the plaintiff had paid the outstanding repair bill, but the plaintiff disputed the amount of the bill. A replacement would take at least four months to make, and the defendant company was the only company which could make it. The plaintiff sought an injunction to restrain the defendants from interfering with possession of the die. Hope J ordered an injunction on the basis that damages were

[10.117]

---

258   *Common Law Procedure Act 1854* (17 & 18 Vict c 125), s 78. See now *Torts (Interference with Goods) Act 1977* (UK).

259   See, eg, *Common Law Practice Act 1867* (31 Vict No 17) (Qld), ss 16 and 17. For a modern enactment, see, eg, *Civil Procedure Act 2005* (NSW), s 93.

260   P du Plessis, *Borkowski's Textbook on Roman Law* (4th edn, OUP 2010) 75.

261   See NJ McBride, '*Vindicatio*: The Missing Remedy?' (2016) 16 SAcLJ 1052.

262   See, eg, *Pusey v Pusey* (1684) 1 Vern 273, 23 ER 465; *Duke of Somerset v Cookson* (1735) 3 P Wms 390, 24 ER 114; *Fells v Read* (1796) 3 Ves 70, 30 ER 899; *Lowther v Lord Lowther* (1806) 13 Ves Jun 95, 33 ER 230; *North v Great Northern Railway Company* (1860) 2 Giff 64, 66 ER 28; *Aristoc Industries Pty Ltd v RA Wenham (Builders) Pty Ltd* [1965] NSWR 581; *Doulton Potteries Ltd v Bronotte* [1971] 1 NSWLR 591; *Howard Perry & Co v British Railways* [1980] 1 WLR 1375; *McKeown v Cavalier Yachts Pty Ltd* (1988) 13 NSWLR 303. Damages were adequate in *Dowling v Betjemann* (1862) 2 J & H 544, 70 ER 1175; *Whiteley Ltd v Hilt* [1918] 2 KB 808, 819; *Greenwood v Bennett* [1973] QB 195, 202.

263   N Witzleb, E Bant, S Degeling and K Barker, *Remedies Commentary and Materials* (6th edn, LBC 2015) [9.395].

264   A Burrows, *Remedies for Torts and Breach of Contract* (3rd edn, OUP 2004) 580–81.

265   *Wood v Rowcliffe* (1847) 2 Ph 3, 45 ER 990.

266   *Gollan v Nugent* (1988) 166 CLR 18.

267   *Baud v Brook* (1973) 40 DLR (3d) 418.

268   [1971] 1 NSWLR 591.

inadequate, and the die was essential for the plaintiff's business.[269] He also made a declaration as to a reasonable sum for the value of the repairs.[270]

[10.118]   Specific delivery may be refused if the defendant has increased the value of the property by making improvements to the property.[271] Alternatively, specific delivery may be awarded, but subject to an order that the plaintiff must pay a fair and just allowance for the increased value of the improvements.[272] This overlaps with rescission, which is considered in Ch 18.

IX   Debt as a species of specific relief?

[10.119]   Claims in debt have been argued by some scholars to be specific performance of an obligation to pay money.[273]

[10.119]   A debt is a definite sum of money which, under the terms of the contract, the defendant is due to pay the plaintiff either in return for the plaintiff completing a specified obligation under the contract (such as the delivery of goods pursuant to a contract of sale), or upon the occurrence of a specified event (such as a sum payable under an insurance policy, or the payment of a sum pursuant to a guarantee).[274] When the specified event which triggers the debt occurs, the debt is said to have 'accrued'.[275]

[10.120]   When the plaintiff claims a debt, the question is simply whether the sum is due. All she must show is that the contractual conditions which trigger payment have arisen, and that she has not received payment. There is no question of whether the defendant has breached any obligation other than his failure to pay the debt. Nor need the plaintiff prove any loss caused by the defendant's breach.[276] The orthodox view is that mitigation does not apply to a debt.[277] There are limited defences to a debt claim, such as 'tender before claim' (a counterclaim by the defendant that, before the plaintiff began proceedings, the defendant unconditionally offered to pay the amount due to her).

---

269   [1971] 1 NSWLR 591, 598–99.

270   For detailed consideration of the court's power to require the plaintiffs to pay the value of repairs to the defendant into court before and after the Judicature Act reforms in New South Wales, see JD Heydon, MJ Leeming and PG Turner, *Meagher, Gummow and Lehane's Equity: Doctrines and Remedies* (5th edn, LexisNexis Butterworths, 2015) [22–035], [22–050].

271   *Nash v Barnes* [1922] NZLR 303, 309. The plaintiff was left to claim damages for the original value of the chattel.

272   *Peruvian Guano Co Ltd v Dreyfus Bros & Co* [1892] AC 166, 176; *Greenwood v Bennett* [1973] QB 195, 201–03; *Gollan v Nugent* (1988) 166 CLR 18, 26; *McKeown v Cavalier Yachts Pty Ltd* (1988) 13 NSWLR 303, 313.

273   See, eg, R Zakrzewski, *Remedies Reclassified* (OUP 2005) 108–11; L Smith, 'The Measure of Compensation Claims Against Trustees and Fiduciaries' in E Bant and M Harding (eds), *Exploring Private Law* (CUP 2010) 363, 370–71.

274   D Harris, D Campbell and R Halson, *Remedies in Contract and Tort* (2nd edn, CUP 2005) 158. See also *Jervis v Harris* [1996] Ch 195, 202–03 (Millett LJ)

275   J Paterson, A Robertson and A Duke, *Principles of Contract Law* (5th edn, LBC 2016) [29.10].

276   D Harris, D Campbell and R Halson, *Remedies in Contract and Tort* (2nd edn, CUP 2005) 159. See also *Jervis v Harris* [1996] Ch 195, 202–03.

277   *Jervis v Harris* [1996] Ch 195, 202–03. See further J Paterson, A Robertson and A Duke, *Principles of Contract Law* (5th edn, LBC 2016) [29.75]–[29.78].

Consequently, it is important to distinguish between a claim in debt and a claim for [10.121] damages,[278] as the High Court of Australia has observed in *Young v Queensland Trustees Ltd*:

> A debt recoverable under an *indebitatus* count was not and is not now conceived of simply as a cause of action for breach of duty or obligation. In other words it is a mistake to regard the liability to pay a debt of a kind formerly recoverable in debt or *indebitatus assumpsit* as no more than the result of a breach of contract, a breach which the creditor must affirmatively allege and prove.[279]

A claim in debt may have significant advantages over a claim for damages. For example, in *White and Carter (Councils) Ltd v McGregor*,[280] the plaintiff advertiser agreed to display advertisements for the defendant's garage for three years. The defendant repudiated the agreement on the day it was made, but the plaintiff refused to terminate the contract, and displayed the advertisements for the next three years. The plaintiff could not recover damages in contract, because the decision to keep displaying the advertisements was an unreasonable failure to mitigate, but a majority of the House of Lords held that the plaintiff was able to recover the cost of advertising through an action in debt because mitigation does not apply. This case has been criticised for permitting social waste: the plaintiff continued to advertise although the defendant did not want the service.[281]

---

278   As noted at [10.41]–[10.42], any assertion that damages are always adequate for repayment of a loan should also be treated carefully.
279   (1956) 99 CLR 560, 569 (Dixon CJ, McTiernan and Taylor JJ).
280   [1962] AC 413. *Jervis v Harris* [1996] Ch 195 is another case where a claim in debt had advantages over damages.
281   D Harris, D Campbell and R Halson, *Remedies in Contract and Tort* (2nd edn, CUP 2005) 162, 165.

11

INJUNCTIONS

I Introduction

This chapter deals with the availability of the other specific remedy, the injunction. As with   [11.1]
specific performance, injunctions are a coercive remedy originating in equity. The court orders
the defendant to do something (or to refrain from doing something) and the defendant must
obey this order or be in contempt of court. Again, if the defendant does not comply, the court
may use measures such as imprisonment, sequestration, and fines to encourage compliance
with its order.[1]

However, in contrast to specific performance, injunctions apply to many situations, not just   [11.2]
contract or contract-like obligations, and they protect many legal rights throughout private law
and beyond, including rights in land, goods and other property, economic rights, the right to
bodily integrity, the right to reputation, the right to privacy, and contractual rights. An injunction may often be the best remedy to deal with the commission of a tort or equitable wrong,
because it *stops* the wrongful conduct. As the American textbook author Pomeroy puts it:

> Judges have been brought to see and to acknowledge . . . that a remedy which *prevents* a
> threatened wrong is in its essential nature better than a remedy which permits the wrong
> to be done, and then attempts to pay for it . . .[2]

Injunctions not only prevent future wrongdoing, but also ameliorate future consequences of a
past wrong.[3]

Injunctions are also available to prevent contraventions of the Australian Consumer Law   [11.3]
('ACL'),[4] the *Corporations Act 2001* (Cth) and intellectual property legislation. Injunctions have
a role in public law as well, but that is beyond the scope of this book.

Injunctions, like specific performance, originate in equity and, in earlier times, only the   [11.4]
Court of Chancery could grant an injunction. The jurisdiction of courts in the present day to
grant an injunction has a number of sources. First, many of the statutes which create state,
territory and federal courts confer a power to grant an injunction on common law courts,
reflecting Judicature Act reforms.[5] Secondly, courts have an inherent jurisdiction to grant
injunctions to preserve the status quo and to prevent proceedings being frustrated.[6] Thirdly,
legislation such as the ACL may explicitly provide a court with the power to grant an injunction.

An injunction is 'legal' if it is in support of common law rights and derives from the statutory   [11.5]
jurisdiction conferred on the common law courts to grant injunctions (these injunctions were
formerly available under equity's auxiliary jurisdiction).[7] A court will not, as a general rule,

---

1   See [20.73]–[20.84].
2   J Norton Pomeroy, *Equity Jurisprudence* (1887) vol 3, §1357 (emphasis in original).
3   D Laycock, 'The Scope and Significance of Restitution' (1989) 67 Texas LR 1277, 1287.
4   The ACL is in Schedule 2 of the *Competition and Consumer Act 2010* (Cth).
5   *Supreme Court Act 1933* (ACT), s 20; *Federal Court of Australia Act 1976* (Cth), s 23; *Supreme Court Act 1970* (NSW), s 66; *Supreme Court Act* (NT), s 14(1)(b); *Civil Proceedings Act 2011* (Qld), s 9; *Supreme Court Act 1935* (SA), s 29; *Supreme Court Civil Procedure Act 1932* (Tas), s 11(12); *Supreme Court Act 1986* (Vic), s 37; *Supreme Court Act 1935* (WA), s 25(9). See originally *Common Law Procedure Act 1854* (Vict 17 & 18 c 125), ss 79–81.
6   *Simsek v Macphee* (1982) 148 CLR 636; *Williams v Minister for Environment & Heritage* [2003] FCA 627, (2003) 199 ALR 352.
7   JD Heydon, MJ Leeming and PG Turner, *Meagher, Gummow and Lehane's Equity: Doctrines and Remedies* (5th edn, LexisNexis Butterworths 2015) [21–010].

award an equitable remedy in relation to a common law cause of action (that is, under the auxiliary jurisdiction of equity) where the common law remedy (usually damages) is adequate.

[11.6] By contrast, 'equitable injunctions' are available in equity's exclusive jurisdiction where they are necessary to support equitable rights or to prevent equitable wrongs. There is no requirement for damages to be inadequate to obtain an injunction in equity's exclusive jurisdiction.[8]

[11.7] Both legal and equitable injunctions are subject to discretionary considerations. Although the equitable discretions overlap in substantial part with those considered in the context of specific performance, there are some situations where injunctions can be more easily obtained than specific performance, particularly where the injunction is 'prohibitory' or negative in form.

[11.8] An injunction may be temporary or permanent. An interlocutory injunction is a temporary injunction whose primary function is to maintain the status quo before the trial.[9] It generally lasts only until the time of trial or until a further order which makes final judgment worthless.[10] The specific rules governing the grant of interlocutory injunctions (insofar as they differ from those which govern final injunctions) will not be considered in detail in this chapter, but are dealt with at [20.4]–[20.36]. This is because interlocutory injunctions do not usually finally determine a matter. They are procedural in nature, and ensure that the court's process is upheld.

[11.9] An injunction is final or 'perpetual' when it effectively confers an ongoing right. This is usually granted at trial on the merits of the case. In this chapter we consider final injunctions. However, some of the cases cited in this chapter involve interlocutory injunctions, as many of the factors which courts consider when granting an interlocutory injunction are similar to those considered when granting a final injunction, and the interlocutory injunction generally mirrors the final relief sought.

[11.10] Injunctions often seek to prevent a defendant from infringing the plaintiff's rights. This is known as a 'prohibitory injunction'. Injunctions which require the defendant to do a positive action are known as 'mandatory injunctions'. Some mandatory injunctions require a defendant to undo a particular act (a 'restorative mandatory injunction') and others require a defendant to do a particular act (an 'enforcing mandatory injunction'). Courts are more willing to award prohibitive injunctions than mandatory injunctions. This is because a negative command ('you must not do that particular thing') is less coercive than a positive command ('you must do that particular thing'). In the former case, the defendant's liberty is not constrained to the same degree: provided she does not do the particular thing, she has freedom to act in any way she wishes. By contrast, in the latter case, the defendant *must* do a particular thing, and there is no freedom to act other than in accordance with the decree.

[11.11] Injunctions may also be granted to prevent a prospective infringement of the plaintiff's rights when the plaintiff satisfies the court that there is a high likelihood of the act occurring. These are known as *quia timet* injunctions and are considered at [11.45]–[11.48].

---

8   WMC Gummow, 'The Injunction in Aid of Legal Rights – An Australian Perspective' (1993) 56 Law & Contemp Probs 83, 91, citing *Heavener v Loomes* (1924) 34 CLR 306, 326.

9   JD Heydon, MJ Leeming and PG Turner, *Meagher, Gummow and Lehane's Equity: Doctrines and Remedies* (5th edn, LexisNexis Butterworths 2015) [21–340]; ICF Spry, *The Principles of Equitable Remedies* (9th edn, LBC 2014) 462–65. See, eg, *Evans Marshall & Co Ltd v Bertola SA* [1973] 1 WLR 349; *Hubbard v Vosper* [1972] 2 QB 84, 96 (Lord Denning MR).

10   *Preston v Luck* (1884) 27 Ch D 497, 505; *Heavener v Loomes* (1924) 34 CLR 306, 325–26; *National Commercial Bank Jamaica Ltd v Olint Corporation Ltd* [2009] UKPC 16, [2009] 1 WLR 1405.

II   The rights protected by injunctions and inadequacy of damages

A court asked to grant an injunction considers three questions: [11.12]

1. Has the defendant committed a legal, equitable, or statutory wrong (or, in the case of a *quia timet* injunction, is there a substantial probability that he will do so)?

2. For injunctions in support of common law rights only, are damages adequate?

3. Does a discretionary bar to relief apply? If so, the plaintiff may have to content herself with damages.

Injunctions are more readily granted than specific performance, and for some wrongs, they could be said to be a presumptive remedy (for example, to restrain a trespass).[11] Moreover, they are more flexible than specific performance because they may be interlocutory or final, prohibitory or mandatory, and they may prevent future wrongdoing.

It is important to ensure that an injunction is expressed with clarity because of the harsh   [11.13]
sanctions for non-compliance.[12] A defendant must be certain as to what he should or should not do, and if the court cannot express the order clearly this may be a reason for refusing an order.[13] If uncertainty subsequently arises, the parties may make further applications to the court.[14]

Old cases suggested that a plaintiff must have a proprietary right before she can be   [11.14]
awarded an injunction.[15] However, commentators have rejected this view,[16] as has the High Court of Australia.[17] The better view is that damages will often be inadequate to compensate for infringements of property rights, but it does not follow that a property right is the only kind of right that can be protected by an injunction. Indeed, many infringements of rights may give rise to an injunction. The following overview shows the variety of rights which may be protected by an injunction. The cases can be categorised as follows:

---

11   See, eg, *Woollerton and Wilson Ltd v Richard Costain Ltd* [1970] 1 WLR 411; *Graham v KD Morris and Sons Pty Ltd* [1974] Qd R 1.

12   *Redland Bricks Ltd v Morris* [1970] AC 652, 666 (Lord Upjohn); *Hackett v Baiss* (1875) LR 20 Eq 494; *Nexus Mortgage Securities Pty Ltd v Ecto Pty Ltd* [1998] 4 VR 220.

13   See, eg, *Qantas Airways Ltd v Cameron* (1996) 66 FCR 246 (injunction refused because it could not be clearly expressed).

14   ICF Spry, *The Principles of Equitable Remedies* (9th edn, LBC 2014) 387.

15   See, eg, *Attorney-General v Sheffield Gas Consumers Co* (1853) 3 De GM & G 304, 320; 43 ER 119, 125; *Rigby v Connol* (1880) 14 Ch D 482, 487.

16   JD Heydon, MJ Leeming and PG Turner, *Meagher, Gummow and Lehane's Equity: Doctrines and Remedies* (5th edn, Butterworths 2015) [21–330] (but cf [21–335]); PW Young, C Croft and ML Smith, *On Equity* (LBC 2009) [16–140]; ICF Spry, *The Principles of Equitable Remedies* (9th edn, LBC 2014) 349–55; N Witzleb, E Bant, S Degeling, K Barker, *Remedies: Commentary and Materials* (6th edn, LBC 2015) [10.15, Point 2]; W Covell, K Lupton and J Forder, *Principles of Remedies* (6th edn, LexisNexis 2015) [8.14]–[8.16].

17   *Cardile v LED Builders Pty Ltd* [1999] HCA 18, (1999) 198 CLR 380 [30] (Gaudron, McHugh, Gummow and Callinan JJ); *Australian Broadcasting Corporation v Lenah Game Meats Pty Ltd* [2001] HCA 63, (2001) 208 CLR 199 [90].

1. property rights in land;

2. property rights in goods and funds of money;

3. intellectual property;

4. economic rights;

5. bodily integrity;

6. reputation;

7. privacy;

8. breach of a negative covenant; and

9. contracts for services.

Before each category is considered, something should be said about inadequacy of damages in relation to injunctions in support of a common law right.

A   Inadequacy of damages

[11.15]   When an injunction is granted in equity's auxiliary jurisdiction (that is, in aid of a common law cause of action such as contract or tort), it must be shown that damages are inadequate before an injunction will be granted. Writing extra-judicially, Gummow has explained that this hurdle arose in the 18th century when the Court of Chancery was concerned to avoid accusations of 'arbitrary and unprincipled interference' in common law proceedings.[18] As discussed at [10.19]–[10.26], there is controversy about whether inadequacy of damages is a jurisdictional hurdle or simply one of many discretionary factors considered by a court in awarding an injunction.

[11.16]   Several factors may suggest that damages are inadequate. Difficulty in assessing damages may suggest that an injunction should be awarded.[19] The fact that loss or damage to the plaintiff may be minimal is not necessarily a reason to decline to award an injunction.[20]

[11.17]   As noted earlier,[21] in *Evans Marshall & Co Ltd v Bertola SA*, Sachs LJ suggested that the test of inadequacy of damages should be reformulated as follows:

> The standard question . . . 'are damages an adequate remedy?' might perhaps in the light
> of authorities in recent years, be rewritten, 'is it just in all the circumstances that a plaintiff
> should be confined to his remedy in damages?'[22]

The Supreme Court of Victoria has accepted this test in the context of interlocutory injunctions.[23]

---

18   W Gummow, 'The Injunction in Aid of Legal Rights – An Australian Perspective' (1993) 56 Law & Contemp Probs 83, 92.

19   *Warner Brothers Pictures Inc v Nelson* [1937] 1 KB 209, 220–21; *Evans Marshall & Co Ltd v Bertola SA* [1973] 1 WLR 349, 380 (Sachs LJ).

20   *Evans Marshall & Co Ltd v Bertola SA* [1973] 1 WLR 349; *State Transport Authority v Apex Quarries Ltd* [1988] VR 187; *Mott v Mount Edon Goldmine (Australia) Ltd* (1994) 12 ACSR 658.

21   See [10.20].

22   [1973] 1 WLR 349, 379.

23   *Belgrave Nominees Pty Ltd v Barlin-Scott Airconditioning (Australia) Pty Ltd* [1984] VR 947, 955; *City of Melbourne v Hamas Pty Ltd* (1987) 62 LGRA 250, 261–62; *State Transport Authority v Apex Quarries Ltd* [1988] VR 187, 193; *Pure Golf Academy Pty Ltd v Albert Park Golf Management* (VSC, 15 September 1997). Note also *Sanderson Motors (Sales) Pty Ltd v Yorkstar Motors Pty Ltd* [1983] 1 NSWLR 513, 516.

It is reiterated that injunctions in support of equitable rights or to prevent equitable wrongs [11.18]
(such as breach of fiduciary duty, breach of trust, or breach of confidence) do not require a
plaintiff to establish that damages are inadequate.[24] Similarly, statutory injunctions such as
those available to restrain a contravention of the ACL do not require a plaintiff to establish
inadequacy of damages.[25]

B   The rights protected by injunctions
1   Injury to property rights in land

The proprietary torts which protect plaintiffs from infringement of their rights in land are [11.19]
trespass, private nuisance, and public nuisance. If the defendant has committed a proprietary
tort in relation to land and will not desist from doing so in the future, courts will readily award
an injunction.[26] Damages will rarely be an adequate remedy for injury to property rights in
land.[27] In *Di Napoli v New Beach Apartments Pty Ltd*, Young CJ in Eq said:

> [W]here a person seeks to develop their land by utilising neighbouring land for their
> convenience without consent, such as a case of access, then the court will, almost as a
> matter of course, grant an injunction to restrain it. This is because people are entitled to
> the exclusive use of their land and it is no answer to say that that person is not suffering
> financial loss by the defendant's use and that it is extremely important to the defendant to
> be able to make use of the plaintiff's land for its purposes.[28]

Injunctions have been awarded to prevent relatively minor trespasses, including the [11.20]
encroachment of scaffolding on the plaintiff's airspace,[29] the passage of a crane jib over the
plaintiff's land,[30] or the intrusion of rock anchors into the substratum of the plaintiff's land.[31] At
some unspecified point above the surface of the land, the actions will cease to have a
sufficiently close relationship with the land to be protected by the tort of trespass.[32]

---

24   W Gummow, 'The Injunction in Aid of Legal Rights – An Australian Perspective' (1993) 56 Law &
Contemp Probs 83, 91, citing *Heavener v Loomes* (1924) 34 CLR 306, 326.
25   However, adequacy of damages may go to the discretionary question of where the balance of
convenience lies when a court is considering whether to award an *interim* injunction pursuant to s 234
of the ACL: *Organic Marketing Australia Pty Ltd v Woolworths Ltd* [2011] FCA 279 [22]. Permanent
injunctions under the ACL are discussed at [11.62]–[11.68]. Interim injunctions under the ACL are
discussed at [20.37]–[20.39].
26   *Bendal Pty Ltd v Mirvac Project Pty Ltd* (1991) 23 NSWLR 464, 468; *LJP Investments Pty Ltd v Howard
Chia Investments Pty Ltd (No 2)* (1989) 24 NSWLR 499; *Beswicke v Alner* [1926] VLR 72, 76–77.
27   *Beswicke v Alner* [1926] VLR 72, 76–77; *Pride of Derby and Derbyshire Angling Association Ltd v British
Celanese Ltd* [1953] Ch 149, 181; *Kennaway v Thompson* [1981] QB 88.
28   [2004] NSWSC 52, (2004) 11 BPR 21,493 [28].
29   *Bendal Pty Ltd v Mirvac Project Pty Ltd* (1991) 23 NSWLR 464, 468; *Break Fast Investments Pty Ltd v PCH
Melbourne Pty Ltd* [2007] VSCA 311, (2007) 20 VR 311. Cf *LJP Investments Pty Ltd v Howard Chia
Investments Pty Ltd (No 2)* (1989) 24 NSWLR 499.
30   *Woollerton and Wilson Ltd v Richard Costain Ltd* [1970] 1 WLR 411; *Graham v KD Morris and Sons Pty
Ltd* [1974] Qd R 1; *Anchor Brewhouse Developments Pty Ltd v Berkley House (Dockland Developments)
Pty Ltd* [1987] 2 EGLR 173; *Janney v Steller Works Pty Ltd* [2017] VSC 363.
31   *Di Napoli v New Beach Apartments Pty Ltd* [2004] NSWSC 52, (2004) 11 BPR 21,493.
32   *Bernstein of Leigh (Baron) v Skyviews and General Ltd* [1978] QB 478 (plaintiff could not prevent aircraft
flying over his estate).

[11.21]   By contrast, where plaintiffs have sought injunctions to restrain the showing of films allegedly made by defendants during the course of a trespass on the plaintiffs' premises, the response of the court has varied. On some occasions the court has refused to grant an injunction on the basis that the injury was not irreparable;[33] on other occasions an injunction has been granted.[34]

[11.22]   Injunctions have also restrained defendants from committing the tort of nuisance, particularly where the nuisance was ongoing.[35] Nuisances restrained by injunction include the ringing of church bells,[36] the keeping of noisy pigeons,[37] the racing of speed boats,[38] and drunken shouting,[39] but not the hitting of cricket balls into a neighbouring yard.[40] *Quia timet* injunctions have been granted where nuisance has not yet occurred but is feared.[41] However, a minority in the UK Supreme Court in *Lawrence v Fen Tigers Ltd* suggested that courts should start from the presumption that damages are the appropriate remedy for nuisance, with injunctions being awarded exceptionally.[42] It remains to be seen how this reversal of the traditional approach will be received in Australia.

2   Injury to property rights in goods and funds of money

[11.23]   The proprietary torts which protect plaintiffs from injury of their right in goods are trespass to goods, conversion and detinue. Courts are less likely to award an injunction restraining the defendant from committing a proprietary tort in relation to goods than they are in relation to land.[43] However, where the goods are unique, scarce or cannot be replaced, an injunction is more likely to be awarded,[44] reflecting the necessity of establishing that damages are inadequate. Ian Spry has argued that courts should be readier to award injunctions to protect a plaintiff's proprietary right in goods.[45] Otherwise, the plaintiff must wait until the damage has taken place and then seek compensatory damages. Spry suggests that inadequacy of damages and notions of uniqueness imported from the law of specific performance should not determine the grant of an injunction in these cases.[46] At the very least, courts should ensure that 'inadequacy of damages' is not transferred in an inappropriate manner from specific performance cases to other classes of case.

---

33   *Lincoln Hunt Australia Pty Ltd v Willesee* (1986) 4 NSWLR 457, 464–65.

34   *Emcorp Pty Ltd v Australian Broadcasting Corporation* [1988] 2 Qd R 169 (set aside by consent on appeal); *Rinsale Pty Ltd v Australian Broadcasting Corporation* (1993) Aust Torts Reports 81–231; *Takhar v Animal Liberation SA Ltd* [2000] SASC 400.

35   *Michos v Council of the City of Botany Bay* [2012] NSWSC 625, (2012) 189 LGERA 25; *Gales Holdings Pty Ltd v Tweed Shire Council* [2011] NSWSC 1128 [296]; *McCombe v Read* [1955] 2 QB 429, 436; *Pride of Derby and Derbyshire Angling Association Ltd v British Celanese Ltd* [1953] Ch 149, 181, 194.

36   *Soltau v De Held* (1851) 2 Sim NS 133, 61 ER 291.

37   *Fraser v Booth* (1949) 50 SR (NSW) 113.

38   *Kennaway v Thompson* [1981] QB 88.

39   *Vincent v Peacock* [1973] 1 NSWLR 466.

40   *Miller v Jackson* [1977] QB 966. Discussed at [11.52].

41   *Grasso v Love* [1980] VR 163.

42   [2014] UKSC 13, [2014] AC 822 [157]–[162] (Lord Sumption, with whom Lord Clarke agreed).

43   *Cook v Rodgers* (1946) 46 SR (NSW) 229. Note the criticism of this case at [10.36].

44   *Collier-Garland (Properties) Pty Ltd v O'Hair* (1963) 63 SR (NSW) 500; *Aristoc Industries Pty Ltd v RA Wenham (Builders) Pty Ltd* [1965] NSWR 581.

45   ICF Spry, *The Principles of Equitable Remedies* (9th edn, LBC 2014) 400–01.

46   Ibid.

By contrast with goods, where a plaintiff claims a proprietary right to a fund of money or a promissory note, damages are usually considered inadequate and an injunction will be granted, particularly if it is unclear whether a payment of damages will be satisfied if the defendant becomes insolvent.[47]   **[11.24]**

3 Injury to intellectual property

Injunctions are readily granted for infringements to intellectual property, as damages are highly likely to be inadequate, given the nature of the right. Although the jurisdiction to award these originated in equity's auxiliary jurisdiction,[48] they are now largely available under statute,[49] although the equitable jurisdiction persists.[50]   **[11.25]**

4 Injury to economic rights

A ECONOMIC TORTS

A variety of intentional torts seek to prevent interference with a plaintiff's economic rights, including injurious falsehood, passing off, inducing breach of contract, interfering with contractual relations, and conspiracy. Injunctions are available for many of these torts as the loss arising from these torts is often difficult to measure and thus damages are rarely adequate.   **[11.26]**

Courts have been prepared to award injunctions preventing threatened injurious falsehood,[51] the tort of passing off,[52] and to restrain interference with contractual relations.[53] Similarly, a court will award an injunction to restrain the defendant from committing the tort of inducing breach of contract, but only if the breach is incomplete.[54] A court may award an injunction to prevent a defendant from completing the tort of conspiracy.[55]   **[11.27]**

Injurious falsehood provides an interesting contrast with defamation. Injurious falsehood occurs where the defendant disparages the plaintiff's goods. The defendant makes a false statement concerning the plaintiff's goods (whether or not it is defamatory to the plaintiff) which is maliciously published to a third person which results in actual damage to the plaintiff.[56] The plaintiff suffers economic loss because the falsehood deceives others about the plaintiff's goods or business. The tort of defamation (discussed below) is concerned with protecting personal reputation only.[57]   **[11.28]**

47   *London City Agency (JCD) Ltd v Lee* [1970] Ch 597. Injunctions were refused, however, in *Heavener v Loomes* (1924) 34 CLR 306; *Lloyd's Bank Ltd v Medway Upper Navigation Co* [1905] 2 KB 359.
48   PW Young, C Croft and ML Smith, *On Equity* (LBC 2009) [16.180].
49   *Patents Act 1990* (Cth), s 122(1); *Copyright Act 1968* (Cth), s 115(2); *Designs Act 2003* (Cth), s 75(1)(a); *Trade Marks Act 1995* (Cth), s 126(1)(a); *Circuit Layouts Act 1989* (Cth), s 27(2); *Plant Breeder's Rights Act 1994* (Cth), s 56(3).
50   PW Young, C Croft and ML Smith, *On Equity* (LBC 2009) [16.180].
51   *Swimsure (Laboratories) Pty Ltd v McDonald* [1979] 2 NSWLR 796; *Kaplan v Go Daddy Group* [2005] NSWSC 636; *Beechwood Homes (NSW) Pty Ltd v Camenzuli* [2010] NSWSC 521.
52   *Erven Warnink BV v J Townend & Sons (Hull) Ltd* [1979] AC 731, 742 (Lord Diplock).
53   *Jaddcal Pty Ltd v Minson* [2011] WASC 28 (injunction refused on the basis of lack of evidence and delay).
54   *Delphic Wholesalers Pty Ltd v Elco Food Co Pty Ltd* (1987) 8 IPR 545, 554. Cf *Warren v Mendy* [1989] 1 WLR 853.
55   *Patrick Stevedores Operations No 2 Pty Ltd v Maritime Union of Australia (No 3)* [1998] HCA 30, (1998) 195 CLR 1 [33].
56   *Ratcliffe v Evans* [1892] 2 QB 524, 527–28 (Bowen LJ); *Palmer Bruyn & Parker Pty Ltd v Parsons* [2001] HCA 69, (2001) 208 CLR 388.
57   *Radio 2UE Sydney Pty Ltd v Chesterton* [2009] HCA 16, (2009) 238 CLR 460 [10]–[13].

[11.29]   While courts are ready to award interlocutory injunctions to restrain injurious false-hood,[58] they are generally disinclined to restrain defamatory statements via interlocutory injunction.[59] This was seen in *Fu v Winstar Group Pty Ltd*, where the judge refused to award an injunction restraining defamatory statements, but awarded an injunction restrain-ing alleged injurious falsehoods regarding a business.[60] However, if it appears that a plaintiff is using injurious falsehood as a defamation claim in disguise, an injunction will be declined.[61] In *Swimsure (Laboratories) Pty Ltd v McDonald*, Hunt J said that the difference between injurious falsehood and defamation arose because, unlike defamation, injurious falsehood does not involve a contest between the plaintiff's right to an unblem-ished reputation and the defendant's right to discuss matters of public interest. The defendant has no right to disparage the plaintiff's goods.[62] In *Palmer Bruyn & Parker Pty Ltd v Parsons*, Gummow J said that 'a rationale for the distinction is said to be that the latter tort protects proprietary and commercial rather than personal interests'.[63] It seems extraor-dinary that courts are more willing to protect the reputation of businesses than personal reputations, but this may reflect the historical origin of the injunction, as the auxiliary jurisdiction to grant injunctions has been said to be founded on the protection of property rather than protection of the person.[64]

B   EQUITABLE WRONGDOING AFFECTING ECONOMIC INTERESTS – BREACH OF TRUST AND BREACH OF FIDUCIARY DUTY

[11.30]   Where an injunction is sought in the exclusive jurisdiction of equity, there is no need to establish that damages are inadequate, including for equitable wrongdoing such as breach of trust and breach of fiduciary duty. Indeed, an injunction may even be available to restrain a breach of trust where the breach is *beneficial* to the beneficiaries of the trust.[65] Availability is simply subject to the usual equitable discretions. Injunctions have been awarded to protect the right of a beneficiary to due administration of a trust,[66] to enable beneficiaries to prevent trustees from committing a breach of trust,[67] to enable one trustee to prevent another trustee from committing a breach of trust,[68] and to prevent third parties from dealing with trust property.[69]

---

58   *Swimsure (Laboratories) Pty Ltd v McDonald* [1979] 2 NSWLR 796; *Kaplan v Go Daddy Group* [2005] NSWSC 636; *Beechwood Homes (NSW) Pty Ltd v Camenzuli* [2010] NSWSC 521.
59   *Australian Broadcasting Corporation v O'Neill* [2006] HCA 46, (2006) 227 CLR 57.
60   [2014] WASC 496.
61   *Mahon v Mach 1 Financial Services Pty Ltd (No 2)* [2013] NSWSC 10.
62   [1979] 2 NSWLR 796, 801.
63   [2001] HCA 69, (2001) 208 CLR 388 [58].
64   JD Heydon, MJ Leeming and PG Turner, *Meagher, Gummow and Lehane's Equity: Doctrines and Remedies* (5th edn, LexisNexis Butterworths 2015) [21–115].
65   JD Heydon and MJ Leeming, *Jacobs' Law of Trusts in Australia* (8th edn, LexisNexis 2016) [23–04].
66   *Park v Dawson (dec'd); Union Fidelity Trustee Co Ltd v Perpetual Trustee Co Ltd* [1965] NSWR 298.
67   *Attorney-General v Aspinall* (1837) 2 My & Cr 613; 40 ER 773; *Balls v Strutts* (1841) 1 Hare 146; 66 ER 984; *Dundee Harbour Board Trustees v Nichol* [1915] AC 550; *Milligan v Mitchell* (1837) 1 My & K 446; 39 ER 750; *Howden v Yorkshire Miners' Association* [1903] 1 KB 308 (aff'd *Yorkshire Miners' Association v Howden* [1905] AC 256); *Corozo Pty Ltd v Total Australia Ltd* [1988] 2 Qd R 366.
68   *Baynard v Woolley* (1855) 20 Beav 583; 52 ER 729.
69   *Ackerley v Palmer* [1910] VLR 339.

There are also remedies whereby beneficiaries can compel the performance of a trust, or [11.31] protect the trust property, even if their interest in the property is only contingent (that is, dependent upon the occurrence of a particular event).[70] This is not conceived of as specific relief per se, but as a direction to perform, although its effect may be similar.[71] Beneficiaries can also sometimes compel a trustee to institute proceedings to recover trust property or moneys owing. Usually the court will order the trustee to execute the trust and apply for the appointment of a receiver, and then give the beneficiary leave to sue in the name of the trustee or the receiver.[72] In special circumstances the beneficiary may sue the trustee (and other beneficiaries) in her own name.[73] However, if the trustee is willing to take the proper proceedings, the beneficiary cannot sue him in her own name.[74]

5   Injury to bodily integrity

The intentional torts that seek to prevent trespass to the person are assault, battery and false [11.32] imprisonment. Injunctions to prevent battery or false imprisonment are rarely sought since a tortfeasor will not announce such a tort in advance and an injunction is futile once the tort has been committed (unless there is a threat of repetition). By contrast, threats of assault are relatively common. As noted at [11.26]–[11.29], equitable injunctions in the auxiliary jurisdiction traditionally protected property, not the person. However, in *Parry v Crooks*, when granting an injunction to restrain assault, King CJ said: 'It is difficult to see any reason in principle, since the fusion of law and equity, why the power to grant injunctions should not extend to all torts, nor any reasons of policy why the courts should deny to themselves power to grant injunctive relief in proper cases in respect of the commission or apprehended commission of any particular class of tortious acts'.[75] In some cases, equitable injunctions have been awarded to protect personal liberty.[76] There are also cases where courts have exercised a power pursuant to the terms of the statutes which constitute them in order to restrain assault.[77]

Such an injunction will be awarded in exceptional circumstances only.[78] This is because [11.33] assault is a criminal offence and the sanctions for contempt of court (which include imprisonment) are not significantly more deterrent than the criminal sanction for assault. However, in

---

70   *Bartlett v Bartlett* (1845) 4 Hare 631; 67 ER 800; *Score v Ford* (1844) 7 Beav 333; 49 ER 1093; *Cadogen v Kennett* (1776) Cowp 432, 98 ER 1171. See JD Heydon and MJ Leeming, *Jacobs' Law of Trusts in Australia* (8th edn, LexisNexis 2006) [23–03].
71   R Chambers, 'Liability' in P Birks and A Pretto (eds), *Breach of Trust* (Hart 2002) 10.
72   JD Heydon and MJ Leeming, *Jacobs' Law of Trusts in Australia* (8th edn, LexisNexis 2016) [23–03].
73   See *Alexander v Perpetual Trustees WA Ltd* [2004] HCA 7, (2004) 216 CLR 109 [55] (Gleeson CJ, Gummow and Hayne JJ); *Ramage v Waclaw* (1988) 12 NSWLR 84, 91–93; *Sharpe v San Paulo Railway Co* (1873) LR 8 Ch App 597, 609–10.
74   *Alexander v Perpetual Trustees WA Ltd* [2004] HCA 7, (2004) 216 CLR 109 [55] (Gleeson CJ, Gummow and Hayne JJ).
75   (1981) 27 SASR 1, 7 (King CJ).
76   *R v Macfarlane* (1923) 32 CLR 518, 540 (Isaacs J); *Egan v Egan* [1975] Ch 218; *Zimitat v Douglas* [1979] Qd R 454; *Parry v Crooks* (1981) 27 SASR 1. Cf *Fitzwilliam v Beckman* [1978] Qd R 398.
77   See, eg, *Supreme Court Act 1970* (NSW), s 66(1), which gives the court power to award an injunction to restrain threatened injury, and *Corvisy v Corvisy* [1982] 2 NSWLR 557.
78   *Parry v Crooks* (1981) 27 SASR 1, 9 (King CJ); *Corvisy v Corvisy* [1982] 2 NSWLR 557; *Nguyen v Scheiff* [2002] NSWSC 151, (2002) 29 Fam LR 177 [63].

cases of domestic relationships, legislation in all Australian jurisdictions empowers courts to grant an injunction-style family violence order.[79]

6 Injury to reputation

[11.34]   Defamation occurs where a defendant publishes to third parties imputations which tend to harm the reputation of the plaintiff in the eyes of the public. A plaintiff seeking a final injunction restraining a threatened publication by the defendant needs to establish that the publication would be defamatory of the plaintiff and that the defendant would have no defence.[80]

[11.35]   Many of the defamation cases involve interlocutory injunctions as plaintiffs typically seek to restrain imminent publication until trial. The test for interlocutory injunctions to restrain defamation differs from the standard test, and an interlocutory injunction will be granted only in 'exceptional' or 'very clear' cases.[81] As Heydon, Leeming and Turner note, the interlocutory nature of the injunction is important. Before trial, it is difficult to determine whether the defendant is entitled to a defence, and thus it is difficult for a plaintiff to establish a prima facie case or that the balance of convenience favours an injunction. Courts are concerned to protect freedom of speech and, therefore, err on the side of caution until they are able to finally determine the facts.[82]

7 Injury to privacy

[11.36]   There is no tort of privacy in Australia, although the High Court of Australia noted in *Australian Broadcasting Corporation v Lenah Game Meats Pty Ltd*[83] that its prior decision in *Victoria Park Racing and Recreation Grounds Co Ltd v Taylor*[84] does not stand in the way of the development of such a tort. There are signs in *Giller v Procopets*[85] and other cases[86] that Australian courts may use breach of confidence as a vehicle to develop remedies against breaches of privacy.[87] This reflects developments in England and Wales, where courts have

---

79   The name of the order varies between the jurisdictions. 'Family violence order' is the generic term used in the *Family Law Act 1975* (Cth).

80   *Naoum v Dannawi* [2009] NSWCA 253, (2009) 75 NSWLR 216 [32].

81   *Bonnard v Perryman* [1891] 2 Ch 269, 285; *Stocker v McElhinney (No 2)* (1961) 79 WN (NSW) 541, 543–44; *Shiel v Transmedia Productions Pty Ltd* [1987] 1 Qd R 199; *Chappell v TCN Channel Nine Pty Ltd* (1988) 14 NSWLR 153; *National Mutual Life Association v GTV Corp Pty Ltd* [1989] VR 747; *Jakudo Pty Ltd v South Australian Telecasters Ltd* (1997) 69 SASR 440, 442–43; *Australian Broadcasting Corporation v O'Neill* [2006] HCA 46, (2006) 227 CLR 57.

82   JD Heydon, MJ Leeming and PG Turner, *Meagher, Gummow and Lehane's Equity: Doctrines and Remedies* (5th edn, LexisNexis Butterworths 2015) [21–130].

83   [2001] HCA 63, (2001) 208 CLR 199 [105]–[111] (Gummow and Hayne JJ, with whom Gaudron J agreed), [313]–[320] (Callinan J).

84   (1937) 58 CLR 479.

85   [2008] VSCA 236, (2008) 24 VR 1.

86   *Grosse v Purvis* [2003] QDC 151, (2003) Aust Torts Reports 81–706; *Doe v Australian Broadcasting Corporation* [2007] VCC 281.

87   See M Richardson, 'Towards Legal Pragmatism: Breach of Confidence and the Right to Privacy' in E Bant and M Harding, *Exploring Private Law* (CUP 2010) 109. Cf M Tilbury, 'Privacy and Private Law: Developing the Common Law of Australia' in E Bant and M Harding, *Exploring Private Law* (CUP 2010) 86.

interpreted breach of confidence in the context of the *Human Rights Act 1998* (UK)[88] to effectively give rise to a right to privacy.[89] In some English cases, plaintiffs have successfully restrained breaches of confidence that constituted invasions of privacy.[90]

8   Injunctions restraining breaches of negative covenant in a contract

Sometimes courts do not specifically enforce the whole contract, but choose to restrain a breach of a clause in the contract (typically, an obligation whereby the defendant promised not to do a particular thing, also known as a negative covenant). As noted at [10.15], whether a clause is a negative covenant is a matter of substance.[91] A clause expressed in a positive manner can imply a negative obligation.[92] For example, a promise that Yolanda will only purchase widgets from Xenophon implies a negative obligation not to purchase widgets from anyone else. [11.37]

Drawing on the dictum of Lord Cairns in *Doherty v Allman*,[93] it is sometimes said that injunctions for breach of a negative covenant will be granted as of right and that there is no need to consider the inadequacy of damages or equitable discretions.[94] However, most cases suggest that the usual equitable discretions remain relevant.[95] Nevertheless, courts are readier to award injunctions restraining the breach of a negative covenant than they are to enforce positive obligations. This is because these injunctions are perceived not to restrict individual liberty to the same extent as a positive order, because there is not the same problem of constant supervision, and because damages are often harder to assess for breach of a negative covenant than for breach of a positive obligation.[96] [11.38]

As Heydon, Leeming and Turner note,[97] injunctions restraining the breach of negative covenant are often used to enforce valid restraints of trade,[98] or to enforce negative covenants which run with the land.[99] However, they are generally not awarded in three groups of cases. [11.39]

---

88   This Act gives effect in domestic law to the Convention for the Protection of Human Rights and Fundamental Freedoms (European Convention on Human Rights).
89   *Campbell v MGN Ltd* [2004] UKHL 22, [2004] 2 AC 457; *Douglas v Hello! Ltd (No 3)* [2005] EWCA Civ 595, [2006] QB 125; *McKennitt v Ash* [2006] EWCA Civ 778, [2008] QB 73; *Mosley v News Group Newspapers Ltd* [2008] EWHC 1777, [2008] EMLR 679; *Murray v Big Pictures (UK) Ltd* [2008] EWCA Civ 446, [2009] Ch 481.
90   See, eg, *McKennitt v Ash* [2006] EWCA Civ 778, [2008] QB 73. The New Zealand Court of Appeal refused an injunction in *Hosking v Runting* [2004] NZCA 34, [2005] 1 NZLR 1.
91   *Wolverhampton & Walsall Railway Co v London & North-Western Railway Co* (1873) LR 16 Eq 433, 440 (Lord Selbourne LC); *JC Williamson Ltd v Lukey* (1931) 45 CLR 282.
92   *Metropolitan Electric Supply v Ginder* [1901] 2 Ch 799.
93   (1878) 3 App Cas 709, 719–20.
94   *McEacharn v Colton* [1902] AC 104 (PC); *Macintosh v Bebarfalds Ltd* (1922) 22 SR (NSW) 371; *Ampol Petroleum Ltd v Mutton* (1952) 53 SR (NSW) 1.
95   *JC Williamson Ltd v Lukey* (1931) 45 CLR 282, 298–300 (Dixon J); *Dalgety Wine Estates Pty Ltd v Rizzon* (1979) 141 CLR 552, 560 (Gibbs CJ), 573–74 (Mason J); *Ampol Petroleum Ltd v Mutton* (1952) 53 SR (NSW) 1; *Curro v Beyond Productions Pty Ltd* (1993) 30 NSWLR 337, 346–47; *Lucas Stuart Pty Ltd v Hemmes Hermitage Pty Ltd* [2010] NSWCA 283, (2012) 28 BCL 226 [5] (Campbell JA).
96   A Burrows, *Remedies for Torts and Breach of Contract* (3rd edn, OUP 2004) 528.
97   JD Heydon, MJ Leeming and PG Turner, *Meagher, Gummow and Lehane's Equity: Doctrines and Remedies* (5th edn, LexisNexis Butterworths 2015) [21–205].
98   See, eg, *Ampol Petroleum Ltd v Mutton* (1952) 53 SR (NSW) 1.
99   See, eg, *Wrotham Park Estate Co Ltd v Parkside Homes Ltd* [1974] 1 WLR 798, where an injunction was denied, however, on discretionary grounds.

First, as with specific performance, negative covenants will not be enforced by injunction where the contract is for the sale of goods unless the goods are unique and damages are inadequate.[100] Secondly, they are generally not awarded where the court would be required to supervise performance.[101] Thirdly, they are not necessarily awarded in cases involving contracts for services. This latter category is considered below.

9 Contracts for services

[11.40]   Courts will generally not award specific performance for a contract for services (that is, an employment contract); see [10.48]–[10.50]. However, they may award an injunction restraining the defendant from breaching a negative covenant within a contract for services, sometimes known as 'the principle in *Lumley v Wagner*' after the case which first gave rise to these injunctions.[102] These cases arise where the defendant has agreed in a negative covenant not to provide her services to any person other than the plaintiff.

[11.41]   Courts have traditionally been reluctant to award such injunctions because of the prospect of forcing employees to work for an employer for whom they do not wish to work.[103] The restrictive covenant itself may be unenforceable because of the common law doctrine of restraint of trade.[104] Under this doctrine, contractual obligations restricting someone's ability to trade are void by reason of illegality unless they are reasonable and in the interests of both contracting parties and of the public at large.[105] Courts have traditionally been concerned to safeguard the right of individuals to work in their chosen trade or profession without unjust restriction,[106] and they scrutinise restraints on employment closely.[107] However, the potential of this doctrine to militate against the award of an injunction restraining a breach of negative covenant has perhaps waned.[108]

---

100   See, eg, *Wood v Corrigan* (1982) 28 SR (NSW) 492; *Aristoc Industries Pty Ltd v RA Wenham (Builders) Pty Ltd* [1965] NSWR 581; *Sky Petroleum Ltd v VIP Petroleum Ltd* [1974] 1 WLR 576; *Thomas Borthwick & Sons (Australasia) Ltd v South Otago Freezing Co Ltd* [1977] 1 NZLR 366.

101   *JC Williamson Ltd v Lukey* (1931) 45 CLR 282, 299–300 (Dixon J).

102   *Lumley v Wagner* (1852) 1 De GM & G 604, 42 ER 687.

103   *Wolverhampton & Walsall Railway Co v London & North-Western Railway Co* (1873) LR 16 Eq 433; *Rigby v Connol* (1880) 14 Ch D 482, 487 (Jessel MR); *HW Gossard Co v Crosby*, 132 Iowa 155, 170; 109 NW 483, 488–89 (1906); *JC Williamson Ltd v Lukey* (1931) 45 CLR 282, 293 (Starke J); *Atlas Steels (Australia) Pty Ltd v Atlas Steels Ltd* (1948) 49 SR (NSW) 157, 161 (Sugarman J); *Hogan v Tumut Shire Council* (1954) 54 SR (NSW) 284; *Francis v Municipal Councillors of Kuala Lumpur* [1962] 3 All ER 633; *Sampson v Murray*, 415 US 61, 83 (1974).

104   But see *Restraints of Trade Act 1976* (NSW), s 4, which preserves the reasonable operation of restraints of trade that might otherwise be struck down as unreasonably wide.

105   *Bacchus Marsh Concentrated Milk Co Ltd (in liq) v Joseph Nathan & Co Ltd* (1919) 26 CLR 410; *Esso Petroleum Co Ltd v Harper's Garage (Stourport) Ltd* [1968] AC 269; *Amoco Australia Pty Ltd v Rocca Bros Motor Engineering Co Pty Ltd* (1975) 133 CLR 331 (PC).

106   P Saprai, 'The Principle against Self-Enslavement in Contract Law' (2009) 26 J Cont L 25.

107   See eg *Lindner v Murdock's Garage* (1950) 83 CLR 628, 633; *Butt v Long* (1953) 88 CLR 476; *Forbes v New South Wales Trotting Club Ltd* (1979) 143 CLR 242; *Minnesota Mining & Manufacturing (Australia) Pty Ltd v Richards* [1963] NSWR 1613; *Buckley v Tutty* (1971) 125 CLR 353; *Geraghty v Minter* (1979) 142 CLR 177; *Hughes v Western Australian Cricket Association Inc* (1986) 69 ALR 660; *Rentokil Pty Ltd v Lee* (1995) 66 SASR 301.

108   J Riley, 'Commodifying Sheer Talent: Perverse Developments in the Law's Enforcement of Restrictive Covenants' in W van Caenegem and C Arup (eds), *Intellectual Property Policy Reform* (Edward Elgar 2009) 267.

Generally, courts are more likely to award injunctions to restrain breach of negative covenants in employment cases when services are 'unique' than when the services can easily be obtained from someone else, even though Australian and English courts do not explicitly consider the unique nature of the service provided.[109] In Australia and in other common law countries, injunctions have been ordered against employees who possess unique skills, such as opera singers,[110] actors and actresses,[111] acrobats,[112] sportsmen,[113] television presenters,[114] talented recruitment specialists,[115] and television executives,[116] so long as the restraint is reasonable and not too long in duration.[117] By contrast, managers,[118] salespersons,[119] porters,[120] or other ordinary employees[121] have tended to be less likely to be restrained from working for a competitor.

[11.42]

First, the uniqueness of the service goes towards inadequacy of damages: damages are less likely to be adequate where an equivalent employee cannot be found elsewhere. Secondly, the more ordinary the skills of the employee, the more likely it is that the employee would be rendered effectively unemployable if the court chose to restrain her from working because an ordinary employee would be restrained from a wide variety of ordinary activities. Thus, in *Curro v Beyond Productions Pty Ltd*, a television presenter was restrained from working for

[11.43]

---

109   Except *Whitwood Chemical Company v Hardman* [1891] 2 Ch 416, 419–23 (Kekewich J), rev'd [1891] 2 Ch 416, 425–33 (EWCA) on doubtful grounds. US courts, by contrast, explicitly consider uniqueness: *Bethlehem Engineering Export Co v Christie*, 105 F (2d) 933, 935 (1939) (Learned Hand J); *Madison Square Garden Corporation v Braddock* 90 F 2d 924, 926 (1937).

110   *Lumley v Wagner* (1852) 1 De GM & G 604; 42 ER 687; *Duff v Russell*, 14 NYS 134; 60 J & S 80 (1891); *Oscar Hammerstein v Marguerite Mann*, 122 NYS 276 (1910); *Chapin v Powers*, 73 NYS (2d) 854 (1947).

111   *Montague v Flockton* (1873) LR 16 Eq 189; *Daly v Smith*, 49 How Pr 150 (1874); *Carter v Ferguson* 12 NYS 580, 58 Hun 569 (1890); *Grimston v Cuningham* (1894) 1 QB 125; *Warner Brothers Pictures Inc v Nelson* [1937] 1 KB 209; *Marco Productions Ltd v Pagola* [1945] 1 KB 111; *Warner Brothers Pictures Inc v Ingolia* [1965] NSWR 988.

112   *Shubert Theatrical Co v Rath*, 271 F 827, 20 ALR 846 (1921) (unique acrobats); *Keith v Kellermann*, 169 F 196 (1909) (unique diver); *John Cort v Lassard & Lucifer*, 18 Ore 221, 22 P 1054 (1889) (non-unique acrobats).

113   *Philadelphia Ball Club Ltd v Lajoie*, 202 Pa 210, 51 A 973 (1902). Cf *American Baseball and Athletic Association v Harper*, 54 Central Law Journal 449 (1902) (baseballer); *Hawthorn Football Club Ltd v Harding* [1988] VR 49; *Buckenara v Hawthorn Football Club Ltd* [1988] VR 39 (AFL footballer); *Bulldogs Rugby League Club Ltd v Williams* [2008] NSWSC 822 (rugby league player).

114   *Evening News Association v Peterson*, 477 F Supp 77 (1979); *American Broadcasting Company v Wolf*, 52 NY (2d) 394, 420 NE (2d) 363, 438 NYS (2d) 482 (1981); *Curro v Beyond Productions Pty Ltd* (1993) 30 NSWLR 337.

115   *HRX Holdings Pty Ltd v Pearson* [2012] FCA 161, (2012) 205 FCR 169.

116   *Seven Network (Operations) Ltd v Warburton (No 2)* [2011] NSWSC 386, (2011) 206 IR 450.

117   *Grimston v Cuningham* (1894) 1 QB 125; *Warner Brothers Pictures Inc v Nelson* [1937] 1 KB 209; *Marco Productions Ltd v Pagola* [1945] 1 KB 111; *Warner Brothers Pictures Inc v Ingolia* [1965] NSWR 988; *Hawthorn Football Club Ltd v Harding* [1988] VR 49; *Buckenara v Hawthorn Football Club Ltd* [1988] VR 39; *Curro v Beyond Productions Pty Ltd* (1993) 30 NSWLR 337; *Bulldogs Rugby League Club Ltd v Williams* [2008] NSWSC 822.

118   *Whitwood Chemical Company v Hardman* [1891] 2 Ch 416; *Davis v Foreman* [1894] 3 Ch 654; *Mortimer v Beckett* [1920] 1 Ch 571; *Page One Records v Britton* [1968] 1 WLR 157; *Warren v Mendy* [1989] 1 WLR 853.

119   *Ehrman v Bartholomew* [1898] 1 Ch 671; *HW Gossard Co v Crosby*, 132 Iowa 155, 109 NW 483 (1906); *Clark Paper & Manufacturing Co v Stenacher*, 236 NY 312, 140 NE 708 (1923).

120   *Ryan v Mutual Tontine Westminster Chambers Association* [1893] 1 Ch 116.

121   *Rely-A-Bell Burglar and Fire Alarm Company Ltd v Eisler* [1926] 1 Ch 609; *Heine Bros (Australia) Pty Ltd v Forrest* [1963] VR 383.

another employer because she was an educated, well-off woman who had other employment open to her, and she would not be rendered destitute by being restrained for three months.[122] However, in *Page One Records v Britton*, a pop group called 'The Troggs' was not restrained from employing a new manager in breach of a negative covenant, because 'The Troggs' were 'simple persons of no business experience and could not survive without the services of a manager' and the agreement still had four years to run.[123] Consequently, if a restriction contained in a covenant is severe in the circumstances, courts refuse to enforce it or limit its operation.[124] Similarly, if relations between the parties have broken down and it is infeasible to require cooperation,[125] a court will not award an injunction, because, although the injunction merely prevents the defendant from working elsewhere, the effect may be to force the employee to resume employment.

[11.44]   Consideration of the inadequacy of damages as a limiting factor on these injunctions has diminished in recent years.[126] A line of cases from New South Wales suggests that ordinary employees will be restrained from working for a competitor for a limited time, so long as the restriction does not prevent the employee from any employment.[127] The essential factor seems to have been whether the employee was privy to confidential information. These cases have been criticised as unfairly restraining the liberty of employees, and it has been argued that such injunctions should be granted sparingly.[128]

III   *Quia timet* injunctions

[11.45]   An important function of the injunction is to prevent prospective damage from occurring. Cotton LJ said:

> The Court of Chancery said, 'Where a man threatens and intends to do an unlawful act, we will, before it is done, grant an injunction to prevent his doing it and we will grant it where the act has been done and is likely to be repeated' – the jurisdiction is simply preventive.[129]

[11.46]   *Quia timet* literally means 'because he is afraid' in Latin. A *quia timet* injunction is awarded where no damage has yet been sustained by the plaintiff, but the defendant has threatened

---

122   *Curro v Beyond Productions Pty Ltd* (1993) 30 NSWLR 337, 348.

123   *Page One Records v Britton* [1968] 1 WLR 157, 166.

124   *Ehrman v Bartholomew* [1898] 1 Ch 671; *Heine Bros (Australia) Pty Ltd v Forrest* [1963] VR 383; *William Robinson & Co Ltd v Heuer* [1898] 2 Ch 451; *Whitwood Chemical Company v Hardman* [1891] 2 Ch 416; *Chapman v Westerby* [1913] WN 277. Cf *Rely-A-Bell Burglar and Fire Alarm Company Ltd v Eisler* [1926] 1 Ch 609.

125   *Page One Records v Britton* [1968] 1 WLR 157; *Warren v Mendy* [1989] 1 WLR 853.

126   J Riley, 'Sterilising Talent: A Critical Assessment of Injunctions Enforcing Negative Covenants' (2012) 34 Syd L Rev 617, 619. Riley mentions *BearingPoint Australia Pty Ltd v Robert Hillard* [2008] VSC 115 as an exception.

127   *Koops Martin Financial Services Pty Ltd v Reeves* [2006] NSWSC 449; *John Fairfax Publications Pty Ltd v Birt* [2006] NSWSC 995; *Otis Elevator Co Pty Ltd v Nolan* [2007] NSWSC 593; *Tullett Prebon (Australia) Pty Ltd v Purcell* [2008] NSWSC 852, (2008) 175 IR 414; *Bulldogs Rugby League Club Ltd v Williams* [2008] NSWSC 822.

128   J Riley, 'Sterilising Talent: A Critical Assessment of Injunctions Enforcing Negative Covenants' (2012) 34 Syd L Rev 617.

129   *Proctor v Bayley* (1889) 42 Ch D 390, 398.

both 'imminent and substantial' damage to the plaintiff's property or interests.[130] Thus it is unnecessary to prove that the common law cause of action has crystallised.[131] *Quia timet* injunctions are often awarded to prevent breaches of contract and breaches of patents, to prevent the misapplication of funds by an administrator, or to prevent an expected tort.[132]

As Young, Croft and Smith note, courts have 'deliberately left fluid the situations in which they will grant a quia timet injunction'.[133] The cases are highly fact specific, and involve a weighing up of the probability of harm, the gravity of injury and the likely consequences, as well as considerations of hardship and the like.[134] 'Imminent' simply means that 'the injunction must not be granted prematurely'.[135] Whether the activities of the defendant are genuinely imminent can only be judged in the circumstances of the particular case.[136] It must also be shown that the threatened damage will be substantial.[137]

[11.47]

A threat to injure the plaintiff is a basis for awarding a *quia timet* injunction,[138] and even a continued insistence upon doing a particular act may suffice.[139] However, it is relevant that no breach has taken place, and it is easier for a plaintiff to establish an entitlement to an injunction if the defendant has already taken action of the kind sought to be restrained.[140]

[11.48]

IV   Discretionary factors and bars to relief

Legal and equitable injunctions are always subject to the discretion of the court. The discussion at [10.75]–[10.89] should be referred to for the principles governing the operation of the discretionary factors, but this chapter will outline the points of difference between the operation of discretionary factors in relation to specific performance and injunctions.

[11.49]

A   General equitable bars to relief

As stated at [10.75], the general bars to relief apply not only to specific performance and injunctions but to *all* equitable remedies (for example, account of profits, equitable rescission and Lord Cairns' Act damages).

[11.50]

130   Ibid; *Bendigo and Country Districts Trustees and Executors Co Ltd v Sandhurst and Northern District Trustees, Executors and Agency Co Ltd* (1909) 9 CLR 474, 478.
131   *Associated Newspapers Group plc v Insert Media Ltd* (1989) IPR 345, 358 (Mummery J); *Supreme Court Act 1970* (NSW), s 66(1).
132   ICF Spry, *The Principles of Equitable Remedies* (9th edn, LBC 2014) 391.
133   PW Young, C Croft and ML Smith, *On Equity* (LBC 2009) [16.390], citing *Copyright Agency Ltd v Haines* [1982] 1 NSWLR 182, 192.
134   ICF Spry, *The Principles of Equitable Remedies* (9th edn, LBC 2014) 392–95.
135   *Hooper v Rogers* [1975] Ch 43, 49 (Russell LJ).
136   *Kestrel Coal Pty Ltd v Construction, Forestry Mining and Energy Union* [2000] QSC 150, [2001] 1 Qd R 634.
137   *Grasso v Love* [1980] VR 163, 167; *Byrne v Castrique* [1965] VR 171; *Connorville Estates Pty Ltd v Hydro-Electric Commission* [1967] Tas SR 76; *Hooper v Rogers* [1975] 1 Ch 43.
138   *McEacharn v Colton* [1902] AC 104; *Thornhill v Weeks* [1913] 1 Ch 438; *Barlow v Neville Jeffress Advertising Pty Ltd* (1994) 4 Tas R 391.
139   *Shanahan v Fitzgerald* [1982] 2 NSWLR 513.
140   *Earl of Ripon v Hobart* (1834) 3 My & K 169, 176; 40 ER 65, 68; ICF Spry, *The Principles of Equitable Remedies* (9th edn, LBC 2014) 391.

1   Hardship and the public interest

[11.51]   Hardship as a discretionary factor is discussed in the context of specific performance at [10.76]–[10.81]. The principles outlined there apply generally to injunctions. In particular, the hardship to the defendant must be disproportionate to the benefit of the injunction to the plaintiff.[141] Some differences do exist between specific performance and injunctions. Hardship to third parties (including hardship to the general public) is not generally taken into account where specific performance is concerned. Traditionally, hardship to the public was not a reason to deny an injunction either. In *Shelfer v City of London Electric Lighting Co*,[142] an injunction was granted even though this inconvenienced the general public.

[11.52]   However, some cases suggest that the public interest or impact on third parties may be a reason to deny an injunction.[143] In *Miller v Jackson*, the English Court of Appeal declined to award an injunction restraining a local cricket club from playing cricket, on the basis that cricket was in the public interest.[144] By contrast, in *Kennaway v Thompson*, the same court declined to follow *Miller* and restrained speed-boat racing outside the plaintiff's house.[145] One must query whether judicial attitudes towards cricket and speed-boat racing respectively influenced the outcome of these cases; in any event, the two decisions are inconsistent and perhaps irreconcilable,[146] and the former has been criticised in Australia.[147] The contest between *Miller* and *Kennaway* may now have been resolved by the UK Supreme Court in *Lawrence v Fen Tigers Ltd*.[148] The plaintiffs sought to restrain the noise from a speed track raceway, but the Supreme Court refused to award an injunction. Lord Neuberger, for the majority, held that the public interest would be relevant in most cases, although he noted that it would rarely be determinative.[149] By contrast, Lord Sumption for the minority said: 'The main question, as it seems to me, is not whether the judge in deciding on the appropriate remedy should take account of the public interest or, more generally, of interests which are not before the court. He will usually lack the information to do so effectively, and is in danger of stepping outside his main function of deciding the issue between the parties.'[150]

[11.53]   Public interest considerations were also relevant in *Wrotham Park Estate Co Ltd v Parkside Homes Ltd*, when Brightman J refused to award an injunction to tear down houses built in breach of a restrictive covenant, saying that it would be 'an unpardonable waste'.[151]

---

141   *Jessica Estates Pty Ltd v Lennard* [2007] NSWSC 1434, (2007) 13 BPR 25,297 [50]; *Evans v Miller* [2011] WASCA 89 [17].

142   [1895] 1 Ch 287.

143   *Miller v Jackson* [1977] QB 966; *Gedbury Pty Ltd v Michael David Kennedy Autos* [1986] 1 Qd R 103; *Tucker v News Media Ownership Ltd* [1986] 2 NZLR 716; *Lawrence v Fen Tigers Ltd* [2014] UKSC 13, [2014] AC 822.

144   [1977] 1 QB 966. Lord Denning's judgment contains a lyrical opening which should be required reading by all.

145   *Kennaway v Thompson* [1981] QB 88.

146   B Markesinis and A Tettenborn, 'Cricket, Power Boat Racing and Nuisance' [1981] *New LJ* 108.

147   JD Heydon, MJ Leeming and PG Turner, *Meagher, Gummow and Lehane's Equity: Doctrines and Remedies* (5th edn, LexisNexis Butterworths 2015) [21–095].

148   [2014] UKSC 13, [2014] AC 822.

149   Ibid, [118], [124] (Lord Neuberger, with whom Lords Mance and Carnwath agreed).

150   Ibid, [158].

151   [1974] 1 WLR 798, 811. For the facts of that case, see [16.103].

2   Lack of clean hands

As noted at [10.82]–[10.85], 'clean hands' considerations operate where the plaintiff has misled   [11.54]
the court, abused its process or attempted to do so, or where the grant of relief would enable
the plaintiff to achieve a dishonest purpose and it would be inequitable to grant relief.[152] The
'lack of clean hands' must relate to the relief sought.[153] Similar principles apply to injunctions
as apply to specific performance.

A bizarre instance of lack of clean hands precluding the award of an injunction occurred in   [11.55]
the English case of *Hubbard v Vosper*.[154] The defendant, Vosper, a former minister of the
Church of Scientology, wrote a book alleging that the church authorised extreme actions (even
killing) against persons in a state of 'enemy' with the church. The church sought to restrain
publication of this information on the basis that it was confidential. Insofar as it was alleged that
the breach of confidence concerned the sanctions of the church against its 'enemies', it was not
permitted to protect its confidential information.[155] The church did not come to court with
clean hands because of the nature of the confidential information concerned.

3   Laches: delay with acquiescence and delay with prejudice

Again, as noted at [10.86]–[10.89], a court may decline to award an injunction if the plaintiff   [11.56]
delayed in bringing the suit, and the delay caused the defendant to believe that the plaintiff has
acquiesced in the conduct or caused prejudice to the defendant. The courts emphasise that
'mere' delay is not a sufficient reason to refuse the grant of a remedy in equity.[156] It depends
upon the operation of specific factors, including the effect on the defendant and the context of
the dispute. Depending upon the situation in question, a lengthy delay may not constitute
laches, or a short delay may result in the refusal to award an injunction.[157]

Delay with acquiescence and delay with prejudice may well be matters which would   [11.57]
indicate that a court should favour an award of Lord Cairns' Act damages in lieu of an
injunction; see [12.64].

B   Bars to injunctions that are equivalent to those in specific performance

To the extent to which an injunction is equivalent to a decree of specific performance, the   [11.58]
discretionary factors militating against the award of specific performance (such as continuous
supervision and readiness and willingness) operate. Reference should be made to the discussion at [10.90]–[10.109] in respect of these bars. In particular, the need for continuous supervision informs the courts' reluctance to enforce restrictive covenants in contracts for services by
way of injunction.

---

152   ICF Spry, *The Principles of Equitable Remedies* (9th edn, LBC 2014) 253–56.
153   *Duchess of Argyll v Duke of Argyll* [1967] 1 Ch 302. See also *Moody v Cox* [1917] 2 Ch 71, 87–88.
154   [1972] 2 QB 84.
155   Ibid, 100–01 (Megaw LJ).
156   *Lindsay Petroleum Co v Hurd* (1874) LR 5 PC 221, 239–40. See *Burroughes v Abbott* [1922] Ch 86; *Weld v Petre* [1929] 1 Ch 33.
157   See *Wroth v Tyler* [1974] 1 Ch 30, 53, where a delay of a few months was important. Damages in lieu of specific relief were awarded because of impact on third parties.

V   Injunctions under statutes

[11.59]   In *Cardile v LED Builders Pty Ltd*, the High Court of Australia said that where a particular statute authorises a court to grant an injunction, 'the term "injunction" takes its content from the provisions of the particular statute in question'.[158] In other words, the courts do not assume that the power to grant an injunction pursuant to statute is the same as in equity, but look at the power conferred by the terms of the statute itself. It was also observed in *Cardile* that in many statutes, the provisions 'empower courts to give a remedy in many cases where none would have been available in a court of equity in the exercise of its jurisdiction'.[159]

[11.60]   The courts exercise their discretion to grant an injunction in light of the policy behind the statute. For example, it has been said that the power to grant injunctions under the ACL and its predecessor should be interpreted in accordance with the public policy goals of that statute.[160]

A   Intellectual property

[11.61]   Injunctions are available on a legislative basis for some infringements to intellectual property (patent, copyright, designs, trademarks, circuit layouts, and plant breeder's rights).[161] The jurisdiction originated in equity's auxiliary jurisdiction, and equity continues to influence the award of these injunctions despite the statutory overlay.[162]

B   The Australian Consumer Law

[11.62]   Section 232 of the ACL[163] provides that a court has the power to award an injunction to prevent a contravention of provisions of the ACL. Section 233 provides that injunctions may be granted by consent of all the parties. Section 235 provides that the court may vary or discharge any injunction given under that division of the ACL.

[11.63]   There is no need to show that damages are inadequate before an injunction can be granted under the ACL. The powers to grant an injunction under s 232 of the ACL are broader than those available under the general law. In *ICI Ltd v Trade Practices Commission*, Lockhart J said that the language of s 80 of the then *Trade Practices Act 1974* (Cth) (the equivalent of s 232) showed that 'the Court should be given the widest possible injunctive powers, devoid of traditional constraints, though the power must be exercised judicially and sensibly'.[164] He continued:

> A statutory provision that enables an injunction to be granted to prevent the commission of conduct that has never been done before and is not likely to be done again is a statutory enlargement of traditional equitable principles. But this is because traditional

---

158   [1999] HCA 18, (1999) 198 CLR 380 [29] (Gaudron, McHugh, Gummow and Callinan JJ).
159   Ibid, [28].
160   *ICI Ltd v Trade Practices Commission* (1992) 38 FCR 248, 256 (Lockhart J).
161   *Patents Act 1990* (Cth), s 122(1); *Copyright Act 1968* (Cth), s 115(2); *Designs Act 2003* (Cth), s 75(1)(a); *Trade Marks Act 1995* (Cth), s 126(1)(a); *Circuit Layouts Act 1989* (Cth), s 27(2); *Plant Breeder's Rights Act 1994* (Cth), s 56(3).
162   PW Young, C Croft and ML Smith, *On Equity* (LBC 2009) [16.180].
163   *Competition and Consumer Act 2010* (Cth), sch 2. For the legislative history, see [8.1].
164   (1992) 38 FCR 248, 256.

doctrine surrounding the grant of injunctive relief was developed primarily for the protection of private proprietary rights. Public interest injunctions are different.[165]

Like s 80(4) of the former *Trade Practices Act 1974* (Cth), s 232(4) of the ACL provides that a prohibitive injunction may be awarded regardless of whether or not the person intends to repeat or continue engaging in the conduct, regardless of whether or not the person has previously engaged in conduct of the kind, and regardless of whether or not there is imminent danger of a substantial damage to any other person. Accordingly, Lockhart J's observations continue to apply. Section 232(7) also provides that the court has the power to issue a mandatory injunction regardless of whether the same factors as those mentioned in s 232(4) are made out. Section 232(6) stipulates that the court may award an injunction which requires a person to refund money, to transfer property, to honour a promise or to destroy or dispose of goods.   [11.64]

The only limitation mentioned in s 232(1) is that the injunction should be 'in such terms as the court considers appropriate'. This gives the court discretion to exercise the power 'judicially and sensibly' (in Lockhart J's words).[166] If the court considers, for example, that the respondent must be prohibited permanently or for a specified period from engaging in a particular field of commercial activity or industry in order to protect the public from conduct of the kind which constituted the contravention, a court may grant such an injunction.[167]   [11.65]

The rules as to standing for seeking an injunction are relaxed. Section 232(2) states that applications for injunctions may be made by the regulator or 'by any other person'. The phrase 'any other person' has been interpreted broadly.[168] In particular, an applicant for an injunction 'need not show that a proprietary interest of his is affected, or that he has suffered special damage, or indeed, that he personally has suffered any damage at all'.[169]   [11.66]

Moreover, where a final injunction is being granted, delay is not a disqualifying factor under the ACL to the same extent as in general law because the statute is intended to protect the public interest.[170]   [11.67]

Notwithstanding the broad power to grant an injunction pursuant to s 232 of the ACL, the Full Federal Court has warned against seeking broadly worded injunctions, particularly where a respondent is unrepresented.[171] It said: 'If an injunction is to serve any purpose, it must be enforceable. That requires a degree of clarity in its terms. There must also be a probability that any breach will be detected and result in the imposition of sanctions'.[172]   [11.68]

---

165   Ibid.
166   Ibid. See also *Murphy v Victoria* [2014] VSCA 238, (2014) 45 VR 119 [102].
167   *Foster v Australian Competition and Consumer Commission* [2006] FCAFC 21, (2006) 149 FCR 135 [35]. See also *Australian Competition and Consumer Commission v Dermalogica Pty Ltd* [2005] FCA 152, (2005) 215 ALR 482 [110]. Cf *ICI Ltd v Trade Practices Commission* (1992) 38 FCR 248, 267 (Gummow J).
168   *Truth About Motorways Pty Ltd v Macquarie Infrastructure Investment Management Ltd* [2000] HCA 11, (2000) 200 CLR 591 [13]–[14] (Gleeson CJ and McHugh J); *Director of Consumer Affairs Victoria v Dimmeys Stores Pty Ltd* [2013] FCA 618, (2013) 213 FCR 559.
169   *World Series Cricket Pty Ltd v Parish* (1977) 16 ALR 181, 186 (Bowen CJ).
170   Ibid; *Knott Investments Pty Ltd v Winnebago Industries Inc* [2013] FCAFC 59, (2013) 211 FCR 449 [56].
171   *Australian Competition and Consumer Commission v Dataline.Net.Au Pty Ltd (in liq)* [2007] FCAFC 146, (2007) 161 FCR 513 [108]–[114].
172   Ibid, [112] (Moore, Dowsett and Greenwood JJ).

C   The *Corporations Act 2001* (Cth)

[11.69]   Section 1324 of the *Corporations Act 2001* (Cth) gives a court the power to grant an injunction to prevent a contravention of the Act. Either the Australian Securities and Investments Commission or a person whose interests have been, are, or would be affected by the conduct may apply. The court has the power to grant the injunction on such terms as it thinks appropriate if, in the opinion of the court, it is desirable to do so. Like the power under s 232 of the ACL, the power to grant an injunction pursuant to s 1324 of the *Corporations Act 2001* (Cth) is broader than that under the general law. For example, a court may order remedial advertising.[173] Like s 232, ss 1324(6) and 1324(7) allow a court to award a prohibitive or a mandatory injunction respectively, regardless of whether or not the person intends to repeat or continue engaging in the conduct, regardless of whether or not the person has previously engaged in conduct of the kind, and regardless of whether or not there is imminent danger of a substantial damage to any other person.

D   Other statutory injunctions

[11.70]   A variety of other statutes empower courts to award an injunction to restrain breaches of certain sections of the legislation.[174]

---

173   *McKerlie v Drillsearch Energy Ltd* [2009] NSWSC 488, (2009) 74 NSWLR 673.
174   See, eg, *Australian Securities and Investments Commission Act 2001* (Cth), s 12GD; *Privacy Act 1988* (Cth), s 98; *Family Law Act 1975* (Cth), s 114.

12

'EQUITABLE DAMAGES' OR LORD CAIRNS' ACT DAMAGES

I Introduction

[12.1] Legislation in all Australian jurisdictions allows courts to award damages either in addition to, or in lieu of, specific performance or an injunction.[1] Although damages awarded under this legislation are sometimes known as 'equitable damages', to avoid confusion with equitable compensation, they are called 'Lord Cairns' Act damages' in this book.

[12.2]   Lord Cairns' Act damages are primarily awarded for proprietary torts such as trespass, and for breaches of contract or negative covenant where no other relief is available (either because it is impossible or for discretionary reasons). Their calculation varies according to the facts of the individual case, and the rules are complex. They have also been awarded for equitable or statutory wrongs, but this is controversial.

[12.3]   As noted at [1.65], the placement of this remedy within a functional structure presents difficulties. Lord Cairns' Act damages have been said to perform multiple functions including compensation and restitution. Strictly speaking, they do not compel performance, but award money instead. However, because they are a monetarised version of specific relief, they follow specific performance and injunctions for the pragmatic reason that they 'fit' best here.

II History

[12.4] The Australian provisions are based on English legislation known as Lord Cairns' Act,[2] specifically s 2 of that Act, which provided:

> In all cases in which the Court of Chancery has jurisdiction to entertain an application for an injunction against a breach of any covenant, contract or agreement, or against the commission or continuance of any wrongful act, or for the specific performance of any covenant, contract or agreement, it shall be lawful for the same court, if it shall think fit, to award damages to the party injured either in addition to or in substitution for such injunction or specific performance, and such damages may be assessed in such manner as the court shall direct.[3]

[12.5]   Lord Cairns' Act was passed in 1858, before the Judicature Acts (*Judicature Act 1873* and *Judicature Act 1875*). At that time, the Court of Chancery awarded damages only in limited circumstances for equitable causes of action, and could not grant damages in equity's auxiliary jurisdiction in support of common law rights. Thus, for example, when a plaintiff sought specific performance of a contract and the Court of Chancery refused the remedy on discretionary grounds, the plaintiff had to institute proceedings in the common law courts to obtain damages. Lord Cairns' Act was intended to prevent circuity of actions.[4] By giving Chancery

---

1   *Supreme Court Act 1933* (ACT), s 34; *Supreme Court Act 1970* (NSW), s 68; *Supreme Court Act* (NT), s 14(1)(b); *Civil Proceedings Act 2011* (Qld), s 8; *Supreme Court Act 1935* (SA), s 30; *Supreme Court Civil Procedure Act 1932* (Tas), s 11(13); *Supreme Court Act 1986* (Vic), s 38; *Supreme Court Act 1935* (WA), s 25(10).

2   *Chancery Amendment Act 1858* (21 & 22 Vict c 27).

3   An equivalent to this provision is now contained in s 50 of the *Senior Courts Act 1981* (UK): *Jaggard v Sawyer* [1995] 1 WLR 269, 284; *Regan v Paul Properties DPF No 1 Ltd* [2006] EWCA Civ 1319, [2007] Ch 135 [24].

4   M Bryan, 'Injunctions and Damages: Taking *Shelfer* off the Shelf' (2016) 28 SAcLJ 921, 927.

judges the power to award damages in these circumstances, Lord Cairns' Act allowed the matter to be resolved in the Court of Chancery and saved the plaintiff from having to resume litigation in the common law courts.[5]

In some Australian jurisdictions the Lord Cairns' Act provision is still substantially similar to the original Act,[6] but in other jurisdictions (the Australian Capital Territory, Queensland and Victoria) the provision has been updated to reflect the modern English version.[7] An example of this is s 38 of the *Supreme Court Act 1986* (Vic):   [12.6]

> If the Court has jurisdiction to entertain an application for an injunction or specific performance, it may award damages in addition to, or in substitution for, an injunction or specific performance.

The omission of 'wrongful act' in the modern version affects the scope of application of the legislation; see [12.20]–[12.24].   [12.7]

III Advantages of Lord Cairns' Act damages for a plaintiff

Lord Cairns' Act damages have several advantages for a plaintiff. First, they can be awarded in respect of a common law cause of action where common law damages are unavailable or nominal and the plaintiff is unable to obtain specific relief.[8] Conversely, in some jurisdictions, Lord Cairns' Act damages have been awarded for a purely equitable cause of action when traditional equitable compensation is unavailable.[9]   [12.8]

Secondly, in all Australian jurisdictions except Tasmania,[10] Lord Cairns' Act damages can be awarded in relation to future wrongs as long as a court has jurisdiction to award a *quia timet* injunction.[11]   [12.9]

Common law damages cannot be awarded in respect of future wrongs. Lord Cairns' Act damages are particularly useful when the wrong committed by the defendant is a continuing wrong, as where land is subsiding because the defendant has undermined the plaintiff's land. At common law, particularly for torts such as nuisance, where damage is the gist of the action, the plaintiff needs to return to court repeatedly whenever fresh damage occurs, but Lord Cairns' Act damages can accommodate the possibility of future damage.   [12.10]

---

5   See, eg, *Cory v Thames Ironworks & Shipbuilding Co Ltd* (1863) 8 LT 237; *Catton v Wyld* (1863) 32 Beav 266, 55 ER 105; *Davenport v Rylands* (1865) LR 1 Eq 302; *Lockwood v London and North Western Railway Co* (1868) 19 LT 68; *M'Rae v London Brighton and South Coast Railway Co* (1868) 37 LJ Ch 267.

6   *Supreme Court Act 1970* (NSW), s 68; *Supreme Court Act* (NT), s 14(1)(b); *Supreme Court Act 1935* (SA), s 30; *Supreme Court Civil Procedure Act 1932* (Tas), s 11(13); *Supreme Court Act 1935* (WA), s 25(10).

7   *Supreme Court Act 1933* (ACT), s 34; *Civil Proceedings Act 2011* (Qld), s 8; *Supreme Court Act 1986* (Vic), s 38. The revised provision was first enacted for Northern Ireland and then for England and Wales: see *Judicature (Northern Ireland) Act 1978* (UK) s 92 and *Senior Courts Act 1981* (UK) s 50.

8   *Johnson v Agnew* [1980] AC 367, 400 (Lord Wilberforce).

9   See, eg, *Giller v Procopets* [2008] VSCA 236, (2008) 24 VR 1.

10   *Supreme Court Civil Procedure Act 1932* (Tas), s 11(13)(b).

11   *Leeds Industrial Cooperative Society Ltd v Slack* [1924] AC 851, 859 (Viscount Finlay); *Barbagallo v J & F Catelan Pty Ltd* [1986] 1 Qd R 245, 252 (McPherson J); *Alacina Pty Ltd v Townsville Port Authority* [2009] QSC 126 [4].

[12.11]   Finally, Lord Cairns' Act damages are flexible, and can be awarded either *as a substitute for* or *in addition* to specific performance or an injunction. It is possible, for example, that a court may order specific performance of part of a contract, and Lord Cairns' Act damages for the balance of the agreement.[12]

[12.12]   Lord Cairns' Act damages have become a means of traversing the divide between the common law and equity in a way not envisaged in the original enactment. As Jolowicz argues, 'recognition of this novel jurisdiction is equivalent to recognition – to the extent allowed by the Act – of an actual, though limited, fusion of law and equity'.[13] He notes that compensatory damages are traditionally awarded at common law, and that equity traditionally awards any remedy *apart* from compensatory damages, but Lord Cairns' Act allows a court to award a remedy which is not traditionally available in a particular jurisdiction in lieu of specific relief.[14]

[12.13]   Thus where courts wish to make an award which is arguably gain-based for a common law cause of action, such as a reasonable-fee award for breach of contract, the Lord Cairns' Act provisions allow them to do so, as long as common law damages are inadequate and the court has the jurisdiction to award an injunction. For example, in *Wrotham Park Estate Co Ltd v Parkside Homes Ltd*,[15] Brightman J declined to award a mandatory injunction to pull down houses built in breach of a negative covenant, but instead awarded a 'reasonable fee' reflecting 5% of the defendant's profits from building in breach of the contract. As discussed at [16.62]–[16.77], the characterisation of that award is hotly debated, and it is unclear whether it is compensatory, restitutionary or something else again, but on some views it is an instance of gain-based relief for a common law cause of action.

[12.14]   In *Giller v Procopets*,[16] the Victorian equivalent of Lord Cairns' Act was used to award damages for distress resulting from an egregious breach of confidence. After a relationship breakdown, the defendant disclosed videos of sexual activity between himself and the plaintiff to the plaintiff's friends and family. Damages for distress are not traditionally available as a head of equitable compensation, but the Lord Cairns' Act provision allowed the court to argue that there had been jurisdiction to award an injunction restraining the breach of confidence and, in lieu of that injunction, damages for distress could be awarded.

IV   Jurisdiction to award Lord Cairns' Act damages

[12.15]   The Lord Cairns' Act provisions specify that damages may be awarded where the court has jurisdiction to 'entertain an application' for an injunction or specific performance. However, the award of an injunction or specific performance is itself discretionary. Jolowicz has said that

---

12   *Soames v Edge* (1860) Johns 669, 70 ER 588; *Grant v Dawkins* [1973] 1 WLR 1406. But cf *Ryan v Mutual Tontine Westminster Chambers Association* [1893] 1 Ch 116. See JD Heydon, MJ Leeming and PG Turner, *Meagher, Gummow and Lehane's Equity: Doctrines and Remedies* (5th edn, Butterworths 2015) [24–165].

13   JA Jolowicz, 'Damages in Equity – A Study of Lord Cairns' Act' (1975) 34 Camb LJ 224, 227.

14   Ibid, 227–28.

15   [1974] 1 WLR 798.

16   [2008] VSCA 236, (2008) 24 VR 1.

'a discretionary power to substitute damages for a remedy which is itself discretionary is a logical monstrosity'.[17]

A distinction between jurisdictional factors and discretionary factors must be drawn, as the court can only award Lord Cairns' Act damages where the bars to specific relief are discretionary rather than jurisdictional.[18] Unfortunately, as discussed in Chs 10 and 11, the waters are muddied as the distinction between jurisdiction and discretion is breaking down in the context of specific performance and injunctions. The modern tendency is to treat matters in the award of specific relief as discretionary. For example, mutuality, which used to be regarded as a matter of jurisdiction, appears now to be discretionary,[19] and has been treated as such in this book. Moreover, it is no longer clear whether inadequacy of damages is a question of jurisdiction or discretion. It was long thought to be a question of jurisdiction: where common law damages were adequate, a court had no power to award specific relief. However, several modern authorities have argued that 'inadequacy of damages' is a matter of discretion to be weighed with other discretionary factors.[20] Under this view, Lord Cairns' Act damages are widely available. Thus, the better view may be that the inadequacy of damages constitutes a jurisdictional threshold which must be surmounted before Lord Cairns' Act damages become available; where damages are adequate, the common law measure of damages prevails. [12.16]

Some clear instances where the court lacks jurisdiction involve illegal contracts or the lack of a valid contract. It follows that if a contract is invalid,[21] or illegal,[22] Lord Cairns' Act damages will be unavailable. [12.17]

A matter which has also been treated as a question of jurisdiction is the impossibility of granting specific relief.[23] Thus, if specific relief was impossible at the time when the plaintiff commenced proceedings, the court had no jurisdiction to award specific relief and there is no jurisdiction to award Lord Cairns' Act damages.[24] [12.18]

Courts have struggled to ascertain when Lord Cairns' Act damages can be awarded once discretionary bars such as laches, acquiescence and hardship come into play.[25] Broadly there are two approaches: in some cases, it has been said that the plaintiff must be entitled to specific relief without the operation of any bars,[26] and in other cases, it has been said that the plaintiff needs only to establish that the court could theoretically have awarded specific relief at the [12.19]

---

17   JA Jolowicz, 'Damages in Equity – A Study of Lord Cairns' Act' (1975) 34 Camb LJ 224, 240.

18   W Covell, K Lupton and J Forder, *Principles of Remedies* (6th edn, LexisNexis 2015) [11.14].

19   *Price v Strange* [1978] Ch 337; *Rainbow Estates Ltd v Tokenhold Ltd* [1999] Ch 64.

20   See, eg, *Sky Petroleum Ltd v VIP Petroleum Ltd* [1974] 1 WLR 576; *Verrall v Great Yarmouth Borough Council* [1981] QB 202. See also D Laycock, 'The Death of the Irreparable Injury Rule' (1990) 103 Harv L Rev 687; ICF Spry, *The Principles of Equitable Remedies* (9th edn, LBC 2014) 62–63.

21   *Lewers v Earl of Shaftesbury* (1866) LR 2 Eq 270; *Stimson v Gray* [1929] 1 Ch 629.

22   *Norton v Angus* (1926) 38 CLR 523, 534.

23   W Covell, K Lupton and J Forder, *Principles of Remedies* (6th edn, LexisNexis 2015) [11.15].

24   See, eg, *McMahon v Ambrose* [1987] VR 817.

25   *Wentworth v Woollahra Municipal Council* (1982) 149 CLR 672, 679 said these were clearly discretionary matters.

26   *Aynsley v Glover* (1874) LR 18 Eq 544, 558 (Jessel MR); *Smith v Smith* (1875) LR 20 Eq 500, 505 (Jessel MR); *Holland v Worley* (1884) 26 Ch D 578, 584; *King v Poggioli* (1923) 32 CLR 222, 247; *JC Williamson Ltd v Lukey* (1931) 45 CLR 282, 294; *Boyns v Lackey* (1958) 58 SR (NSW) 395, 405; *Redland Bricks Ltd v Morris* [1970] AC 652; *Madden v Kevereski* [1983] 1 NSWLR 305.

time when the suit was instituted (but did not do so because of discretionary factors).[27] The second view should be preferred. It would be problematic if Lord Cairns' Act damages could be awarded only when plaintiffs are least likely to need them.[28] Certainly, there is no need for the plaintiff to have actually sought specific relief and been refused.[29] It has been suggested that a plaintiff may have an entitlement to Lord Cairns' Act damages where there was no right to specific relief at the time proceedings were commenced, but she later gained a right before the hearing;[30] however this has not arisen in practice, and remains theoretical.[31]

V   The need for a 'wrongful act' in some Australian jurisdictions

[12.20]   The original Lord Cairns' Act provision set out at [12.4] referred to cases (among other things) where the court could award an injunction 'against the commission or continuance of any *wrongful act*'. 'Wrongful act' encompasses torts, and Lord Cairns' Act damages have been awarded in relation to proprietary torts in particular.

[12.21]   However, the definition of 'wrongful act' has become ambiguous over time, and consequently, there is debate about whether it is confined to common law wrongs or includes equitable and statutory wrongs.[32] If confined to the former, Lord Cairns' Act damages should not be awarded in lieu of or in addition to an injunction granted in relation to statutory wrongdoing or equitable wrongdoing (such as breach of fiduciary duty, breach of trust or breach of confidence).

[12.22]   There are two varieties of Australian provision: those which mention 'wrongful act' and those which do not.

A   Australian legislation which mentions 'wrongful act'

[12.23]   In some Australian jurisdictions the Lord Cairns' Act legislation requires the court to have power to grant an injunction to restrain a 'wrongful act' before Lord Cairns' Act damages can be

---

27   See, eg, *Isenberg v East India House Estate Co Ltd* (1863) 46 ER 637, 3 De GJ & S 263; *Ferguson v Wilson* (1866) LR 2 Ch App 77, 91–92 (Cairns LJ); *City of London Brewery Co v Tennant* (1873) LR 9 Ch App 212; *Tamplin v James* (1880) 15 Ch D 215; *Sayers v Collyer* (1884) 28 Ch D 103; *JC Williamson Ltd v Lukey* (1931) 45 CLR 282, 295; *McKenna v Richey* [1950] VLR 360, [1950] ALR 778; *Dell v Beasley* [1959] NZLR 89; *Bosaid v Andry* [1963] VR 465; *ASA Constructions Pty Ltd v Iwanov* [1975] 1 NSWLR 512; *Hooper v Rogers* [1975] Ch 43; *Edward Street Properties v Collins* [1977] Qd R 399; *Millstream Pty Ltd v Schultz* [1980] 1 NSWLR 547, 552 *Brooks v Wyatt* (1994) 99 NTR 12, 28–29; *Mills v Ruthol Pty Ltd* (2004) 61 NSWLR 1, 12–13.

28   JA Jolowicz, 'Damages in Equity – A Study of Lord Cairns' Act' (1975) 34 Camb LJ 224, 241–42; ICF Spry, *The Principles of Equitable Remedies* (9th edn, LBC 2014) 650–51; JD Heydon, MJ Leeming and PG Turner, *Meagher, Gummow and Lehane's Equity: Doctrines and Remedies* (5th edn, Butterworths 2015) [24–035].

29   *Giller v Procopets* [2008] VSCA 236, (2008) 24 VR 1, 95 [404] (Neave JA). See also Spry, ibid, 632; *Dixson v Tange* (1891) 12 LR (NSW) Eq 204, 206 (Owen J); *Barbagallo v J & F Catelan Pty Ltd* [1986] 1 Qd R 245, 251.

30   PM McDermott, *Equitable Damages* (Butterworths, 1994) 82; ICF Spry, *The Principles of Equitable Remedies* (9th edn, LBC 2014) 657

31   *Mills v Ruthol Pty Ltd* (2004) 61 NSWLR 1, 12–13

32   JD Heydon, MJ Leeming and PG Turner, *Meagher, Gummow and Lehane's Equity: Doctrines and Remedies* (5th edn, LexisNexis Butterworths 2015) [24–020].

awarded.[33] Heydon, Leeming and Turner argue that the reference to a 'wrongful act' in the original Lord Cairns' Act must have been intended to refer only to torts, because the purpose of Act at the time of enactment was to supplement the Court of Chancery's jurisdiction to award damages in common law causes of action, and because the term 'wrongful act' had been used in a previous Act to refer to torts alone.[34] This understanding of 'wrongful act' is also reflected in the Law Commission Report which gave rise to the original provision.[35]

Nevertheless, some cases suggest that Lord Cairns' Act provisions that refer to 'wrongful act' still give courts the power to award damages in lieu of an injunction in purely equitable causes of action, including covenants over land in equity,[36] for breach of fiduciary duty,[37] for breach of an equitable easement,[38] and for breach of confidence.[39] Furthermore, in obiter dicta in *Wentworth v Woollahra Municipal Council*, the High Court of Australia said that '[a]n incidental object of the Act was to enable the Court to award damages in lieu of an injunction or specific performance, even in the case of a purely equitable claim'.[40] Thus, it appears that Lord Cairns' Act has evolved beyond its original purpose to allow the award of damages in lieu of an injunction for purely equitable causes of action.

[12.24]

B Australian legislation which does not mention 'wrongful act'

The revised legislation in the Australian Capital Territory, Queensland and Victoria provides simply that a court may award damages in addition to, or substitution for, an injunction or specific performance in every case in which the court has jurisdiction to entertain an application for an injunction or specific performance.[41] There is no reference to a 'wrongful act'. In *Giller v Procopets*, the Victorian Court of Appeal argued that the redrafted provision allowed it to award Lord Cairns' Act damages for breach of confidence.[42] However, it should be noted that the intention of Parliament seems to have been simply to introduce a 'plain English

[12.25]

---

33   *Supreme Court Act 1970* (NSW), s 68; *Supreme Court Act* (NT), s 14(1)(b); *Supreme Court Act 1935* (SA), s 30; *Supreme Court Civil Procedure Act 1932* (Tas), s 11(13); *Supreme Court Act 1935* (WA), s 25(10).

34   JD Heydon, MJ Leeming and PG Turner, *Meagher, Gummow and Lehane's Equity: Doctrines and Remedies* (5th edn, LexisNexis Butterworths 2002) [24–090]. See also *Smith Kline & French Laboratories (Australia) Ltd v Secretary, Department of Community Services and Health* (1990) 22 FCR 73, 83 (Gummow J) and *Concept Television Productions Pty Ltd v Australian Broadcasting Corporation* (1988) 12 IPR 129, 136 (Gummow J).

35   *Third Report of the Commissioners Appointed to Inquire into the Practice of Chancery* (London, 1856) 4.

36   *Eastwood v Lever* (1863) 4 De GJ & Sm 114, 46 ER 859; *Elliston v Reacher* [1908] 2 Ch 374, 395; *Baxter v Four Oaks Properties Ltd* [1965] Ch 816, 829–30; *Landan v Burton* [1962] EG 369.

37   *Re Leeds & Hanley Theatres of Varieties Ltd* [1902] 2 Ch 809.

38   *Gas & Fuel Corporation (Vic) v Barba* [1976] VR 755, 766.

39   *Talbot v General Television Corporation Pty Ltd* [1980] VR 224; *Giller v Procopets* [2008] VSCA 236, (2008) 24 VR 1.

40   (1982) 149 CLR 672, 676 (Gibbs CJ, Mason, Murphy and Brennan JJ).

41   *Supreme Court Act 1933* (ACT), s 34; *Civil Proceedings Act 2011* (Qld), s 8; *Supreme Court Act 1986* (Vic), s 38.

42   [2008] VSCA 236, (2008) 24 VR 1 [403] (Neave JA) (also relying on the dicta in *Wentworth v Woollahra Municipal Council* (1982) 149 CLR 672, 676). The court also held that it was entitled to award damages for distress for breach of confidence pursuant to the court's inherent equitable jurisdiction: [422]–[424] (Neave JA). See *Wilson v Ferguson* [2015] WASC 15 [74]–[85] (Mitchell J) where damages for distress for an egregious breach of confidence were awarded on this basis alone.

version' of the older provision, and the omission of 'wrongful act' was not intended to expand the court's jurisdiction.[43]

C   Lord Cairns' Act damages for statutory wrongdoing

[12.26]   Lord Cairns' Act damages may be awarded in respect of a statutory wrong if it concerns private rights. In *Wentworth v Woollahra Municipal Council*,[44] the plaintiff sought a mandatory injunction to demolish a house which contravened a Planning Scheme Ordinance. When the injunction was refused, the plaintiff sought Lord Cairns' Act damages. The High Court refused to award Lord Cairns' Act damages because the statute manifested no intention to create a private cause of action for damages, and concerned only public rights.[45]

[12.27]   By contrast, in *Matthews v ACP Publishing Pty Ltd*, Beaumont J awarded Lord Cairns' Act damages for a contravention of s 35(5) of the *Copyright Act 1968* (Cth).[46] The statute provided that where a photograph had been commissioned for a particular purpose, the author could restrain any act which was not in accordance with that purpose. The plaintiff, a photographer, had been commissioned by *Cleo* magazine to take a photograph of a celebrity for the sole purpose of publication on the cover of that magazine. The defendant licensed the photograph for publication on the cover of another magazine without seeking the plaintiff's consent or providing extra payment. Although s 35(5) did not mention the availability of damages, Beaumont J said that it manifested an intention to create a private cause of action and distinguished it from *Wentworth v Woollahra Municipal Council*.[47]

VI   Factors influencing the exercise of the jurisdiction

A   General principles

[12.28]   Lord Cairns' Act damages achieve different aims. The first two aims (which will be considered together) are those contemplated by the original legislation: to provide relief where specific relief is no longer available and to provide relief in addition to specific relief. The other three situations where Lord Cairns' Act damages are awarded were not contemplated by the original legislation: to provide a 'middle ground' solution between nominal or no relief and specific relief, to provide relief for future losses, and particularly controversially, to provide novel forms of relief. These categories are not mutually exclusive and overlap at points.

1   Where specific relief is no longer available or in addition to specific relief

[12.29]   The original aim of Lord Cairns' Act was to allow Chancery courts to award damages where specific relief was no longer available, for reasons including delay, or the presence of an

---

43   K Barnett and M Bryan, 'Lord Cairns's Act: A Study in the Unintended Consequences of Legislation' (2015) 9 J of Eq 150, 159–162.
44   (1982) 149 CLR 672.
45   Ibid, 683.
46   (1998) 157 ALR 564.
47   Ibid, 573.

equitable bar. A significant group of cases in which Lord Cairns' Act has been utilised arose when the plaintiff came to court 'too late' to obtain specific performance or an injunction, and thus sought damages in lieu of equitable relief. Sometimes, the infringing conduct had already taken place. Sometimes, the infringing conduct had been reversed by the time of the trial.[48] In other cases, the subject matter of the infringement was no longer in existence,[49] or the infringing conduct had ceased to be problematic.[50] In cases of specific performance, the subject matter of the contract was sold to a third party.[51] In these instances, it needs to have been hypothetically possible to award specific relief at the issue of the proceedings.

The original legislators also intended to allow for damages in addition to specific relief. For example, courts have ordered specific performance of part of a contract, and Lord Cairns' Act damages in respect of the balance of the agreement.[52] The courts also allow for additional damages where the plaintiff suffers loss from the defendant's failure to perform which should be compensated in addition to the grant of specific relief. Thus, in *Grant v Dawkins*,[53] the court made an award compensating the plaintiff for mortgages which would have to be discharged for specific performance to be effected.   [12.30]

2   To provide a 'middle ground' solution between no relief and specific relief

In circumstances in which substantial damages are unavailable at common law, Lord Cairns' Act gives the court a 'middle ground' solution, particularly for proprietary torts such as trespass and nuisance,[54] or breaches of negative covenants.[55] Originally, the courts had to choose between no relief or nominal damages on the one hand and specific relief on the other, but Lord Cairns' Act added the option of awarding substantial damages in lieu of specific relief.[56]   [12.31]

---

48   *Catton v Wyld* (1863) 55 ER 105; 32 Beav 266; *Fritz v Hobson* (1880) 14 Ch D 542; *Shiffon Creations (S) Pte Ltd v Tong Lee Co Pte Ltd* [1991] 1 Malayan LJ 65 (SGHCA).

49   *Davenport v Rylands* (1865) LR 1 Eq 302.

50   *Chapman, Morsons & Co v The Guardians of the Auckland Union* (1889) 23 QBD 294.

51   *Johnson v Agnew* [1980] AC 367; [1979] 1 All ER 883; [1979] 2 WLR 487; *Mama v Sassoon* (1928) 55 IR 360.

52   *Soames v Edge* (1860) Johns 669, 70 ER 588; *Grant v Dawkins* [1973] 1 WLR 1406. Cf *Ryan v Mutual Tontine Westminster Chambers Association* [1893] 1 Ch 116. See JD Heydon, MJ Leeming and PG Turner, *Meagher, Gummow and Lehane's Equity: Doctrines and Remedies* (5th edn, LexisNexis Butterworths 2015) [24–165].

53   [1973] 1 WLR 1406.

54   Lord Cairns' Act damages awarded: *Isenberg v East India House Estate Co Ltd* (1863) 3 De GJ & S 263, 46 ER 637; *Colls v Home and Colonial Stores Ltd* [1904] AC 179; *Kine v Jolly* [1905] 1 Ch 480 (aff'd *Jolly v Kine* [1907] 1 AC 1); *Ryder v Hall* (1904) 27 NZLR 385; *Wills v May* [1923] 1 Ch 317; *Jaggard v Sawyer* [1995] 1 WLR 269; [1995] 2 All ER 18.

    Injunction awarded: *Aynsley v Glover* (1874) LR 18 Eq 544 (aff'd [1875] LR 10 Ch App 283); *Krehl v Burrell* (1878) 7 Ch D 551 (aff'd (1879) 11 Ch D 146); *Martin v Price* [1894] 1 Ch 276; *Shelfer v City of London Electric Lighting Co* [1895] 1 Ch 287; *Cowper v Laidler* [1903] 2 Ch 337; *Saunby v London (Ontario) Water Commissioners* [1906] AC 110; *Woollerton and Wilson Ltd v Richard Costain Ltd* [1970] 1 WLR 411.

55   Lord Cairns' Act damages awarded: *Gafford v Graham* (1999) 77 P & CR 73; *Jaggard v Sawyer* [1995] 1 WLR 269; *Lunn Poly Pty Ltd v Liverpool & Lancashire Properties Ltd* [2006] EWCA Civ 430, [2007] L & TR 6.

    No award: *Sobey v Sainsbury* [1913] 2 Ch 513 (acquiescence by plaintiff).

56   JA Jolowicz, 'Damages in Equity – A Study of Lord Cairns' Act' (1975) 34 Camb LJ 224, 242.

In theoretical terms, the court chooses between a 'property rule'[57] (i.e. the award of an injunction, which forces the defendant to negotiate if he wants it relaxed, and allows the plaintiff to place a subjective price on her property right) and a 'liability rule'[58] (i.e. the award of damages in lieu of an injunction, where a court places an objective price on the plaintiff's right and causes the plaintiff to transfer it to the defendant). The latter effectively allows for a judicial expropriation of the plaintiff's right or a 'forced sale', as the court 'fix[es] the price for granting permission' to infringe the right.[59]

[12.32]   The prospect of facilitating an expropriation of rights means that courts may prefer to award an injunction over Lord Cairns' Act damages. For example, in *Bendal Pty Ltd v Mirvac Project Pty Ltd*, Bryson J awarded an injunction in preference to Lord Cairns' Act damages for trespass to land. He explained:

> I think it is quite clear . . . that the owner of freehold land has a perfectly legitimate interest to decide who will come on to his land, who will build encroachments there, who will stay off and on what terms he is prepared to give leave and licence whether on payment of money or on no terms whatever.
>
> There is no power in the court to impose compulsory licences to encroach on real estate or to set the terms on which licences are to be granted. Some judges have endeavoured to mould orders enforcing the rights of freeholders in the direction of licensing or compulsory licensing. Such attempts do not have the approval of courts of appeal. [60]

Similarly, in *Krehl v Burrell*, Jessel MR said that Lord Cairns' Act 'never could have been meant to invest the Court of Chancery with a new statutory power . . . to compel people to sell their property without their consent at a valuation'.[61] And in *Shelfer v City of London Electric Co*, Lindley LJ said that 'a person committing a wrongful act . . . is not thereby entitled to ask the court to sanction his doing so by purchasing his neighbour's rights'.[62]

[12.33]   The advantage of holding a proprietary right is that a plaintiff can dictate the terms on which interference with the right will be permitted, but as Michael Bryan notes, an award of Lord Cairns' Act damages 'extinguishes an important economic function of the property right, namely the power to regulate the terms, if any, on which any interference with the right will be permitted'.[63]

[12.34]   Conversely, a factor favouring Lord Cairns' Act damages is the spectre of an injunction enabling a plaintiff to demand an exorbitant fee from a defendant for the right to breach the injunction. In *Isenberg v East India House Estate Co Ltd*, a case of nuisance where the defendant's houses blocked the plaintiff's light, Lord Westbury LC said:

---

57   G Calabresi and AD Melamed, 'Property Rules, Liability Rules and Inalienability: One View of the Cathedral' (1972) 85 *Harvard Law Review* 1089, 1105.

58   Ibid, 1106.

59   D Harris, D Campbell and R Halson, *Remedies in Contract and Tort* (2nd edn, CUP 2005) 489–90.

60   (1991) 23 NSWLR 464, 467.

61   *Krehl v Burrell* (1878) 7 Ch D 551, 554.

62   *Shelfer v City of London Electric Lighting Co* [1895] 1 Ch 287, 322.

63   M Bryan, 'Injunctions and Damages: Taking *Shelfer* off the Shelf' (2016) 28 SAcLJ 921, 933.

> I hold it, therefore, to be the duty of the Court in such a case as the present not, by granting a mandatory injunction, to deliver over the Defendants to the Plaintiff bound hand and foot, in order to be made subject to any extortionate demand that he may by possibility make, but to substitute for such mandatory injunction an inquiry before itself, in order to ascertain the measure of damage that has been actually sustained.[64]

The need to pay a fee may also signal that the right is one for which the defendant must ask consent before infringing.[65]

[12.35] The cases are fact specific; and the court's remedial choice depends on a complex matrix of considerations. Courts consider the nature of the injunction sought, the nature of the wrong committed, the objection of the plaintiff to that wrong, and the nature of the defendant's response to any objection in making their choice. In short compass, if the wrong is one where courts readily award an injunction, if the injunction is prohibitory, if the plaintiff has made her objection to the wrong clear and/or if the defendant has continued the wrong regardless, then the courts are more likely to award an injunction than Lord Cairns' Act damages. By contrast, if the wrong is one where the courts are less ready to award an injunction, if the injunction is mandatory and/or if the plaintiff has delayed in bringing action against the defendant or has acquiesced in some form to the wrongdoing,[66] the courts are more likely to award Lord Cairns' Act damages than an injunction.

[12.36] Courts are more likely to award Lord Cairns' Act damages in cases where the plaintiff seeks a mandatory injunction,[67] for example an injunction to tear down buildings obstructing the light,[68] or to tear down buildings erected in breach of negative covenant.[69] Because they infringe the defendant's liberty to a lesser degree, courts more readily award prohibitory injunctions than mandatory injunctions; see [11.10]. There is thus a greater willingness to award a prohibitory injunction rather than Lord Cairns' Act damages. Nonetheless, Lord Cairns' Act damages are clearly available in lieu of prohibitory injunctions.[70]

[12.37] The nature of the wrong is also important. The injunction sought in *Bendal v Mirvac* was for trespass to land. As Bryson J observed, courts readily award injunctions in trespass cases, particularly as the defendant in this case had indicated an intention to continue the conduct.[71] Similarly, in *Krehl v Burrell*, the defendant continued to build on a passage over which the plaintiff had a right of way, despite the plaintiff's strenuous objections and the commencement of proceedings.[72]

[12.38] Even if neither the plaintiff nor the defendant has sought Lord Cairns' Act damages, the court can still exercise its discretion to award them if it is appropriate and the plaintiff has

---

64   (1863) 3 De GJ & S 263, 273; 46 ER 637, 641.
65   K Barnett and M Bryan, 'Lord Cairns's Act: A Study in the Unintended Consequences of Legislation' (2015) 9 J of Eq 150, 164.
66   *Sayers v Collyer* (1884) 28 Ch D 103, 110 (Fry LJ).
67   JA Jolowicz, 'Damages in Equity – A Study of Lord Cairns' Act' (1975) 34 Camb LJ 224, 238.
68   *Isenberg v East India House Estate Co Ltd* (1863) 3 De GJ & S 263, 46 ER 637; *Colls v Home and Colonial Stores Ltd* [1904] AC 179.
69   See, eg, *Wrotham Park Estate Co Ltd v Parkside Homes Ltd* [1974] 1 WLR 798.
70   *Shelfer v City of London Electric Lighting Co* [1895] 1 Ch 287.
71   (1991) 23 NSWLR 464, 467–71 (Bryson J).
72   (1878) 7 Ch D 551.

sought specific relief.[73] It may seem that a defendant will always prefer Lord Cairns' Act damages to specific relief, but defendants may occasionally prefer specific relief.[74]

3 To provide relief for future losses

[12.39] Common law compensatory damages can be awarded only in respect of wrongdoing that occurred before the commencement of proceedings,[75] but Lord Cairns' Act damages can encompass losses arising from future or anticipated wrongs.[76] Consequently, the jurisdiction to award damages in respect of future wrongdoing is used where the defendant's wrong has ongoing consequences, as with the torts of nuisance and trespass. The court can award damages to the plaintiff without requiring her to return repeatedly to court to prove that fresh damage has occurred.[77]

[12.40] It is not even necessary for a past injury to have occurred for Lord Cairns' Act damages to be available. Sometimes Lord Cairns' Act damages may be in lieu of a *quia timet* injunction (which restrains a threatened wrong).[78] Lord Cairns' Act damages may even be awarded in lieu of specific performance for an anticipatory breach of contract.[79] Indeed, Michael Bryan has noted that this is one of the few areas where Lord Cairns' Act provisions are necessary.[80]

4 To provide novel forms of relief

[12.41] Lord Cairns' Act damages can be awarded in situations where the common law would not recognise a cause of action sounding in damages. For example, Lord Cairns' Act damages may be available for a breach of restrictive covenant where the plaintiff would be unable to claim damages for breach of contract because she was not privy to the restrictive covenant. However, the plaintiff can establish an entitlement to an injunction pursuant to *Tulk v Moxhay*,[81] and receive damages in lieu.[82] Or, as noted above, a plaintiff may claim Lord Cairns' Act

---

73 *Betts v Neilson* (1868) LR 3 Ch App 429, 441 (Lord Chelmsford); *Catton v Wyld* (1863) 32 Beav 266, 55 ER 105; *Lady Stanley of Alderley v Earl of Shrewsbury* (1875) LR 19 Eq 616; *Willison v Van Ryswyk* [1961] WAR 87; *Barbagallo v J & F Catelan Pty Ltd* [1986] 1 Qd R 245, 252 (McPherson J). See also ICF Spry, *The Principles of Equitable Remedies* (9th edn, LBC 2014) 657.

74 Eg *Higgins v Betts* [1905] 2 Ch 210.

75 *Oakacre Ltd v Claire Cleaners (Holdings) Ltd* [1982] Ch 197.

76 *Leeds Industrial Cooperative Society Ltd v Slack* [1924] AC 851; *Hooper v Rogers* [1975] Ch 43; *Jaggard v Sawyer* [1995] 1 WLR 269, 276–77 (Sir Thomas Bingham MR). Note that this is not possible in Tasmania, which does not allow Lord Cairns' Act damages for future wrongs: *Supreme Court Civil Procedure Act 1932* (Tas), s 11(13)(b).

77 See *Isenberg v East India House Estate Co Ltd* (1863) 3 De GJ & S 263, 46 ER 637; *Mann v Capital Territory Health Commission* (1982) 148 CLR 97, 101; *Jaggard v Sawyer* [1995] 1 WLR 269, 280 (Bingham MR), 286 (Millett LJ). See also JA Jolowicz, 'Damages in Equity – A Study of Lord Cairns' Act' (1975) 34 Camb LJ 224, 235; PM McDermott, 'Equitable Compensation' in P Parkinson, *The Principles of Equity* (2nd edn, LBC 2003) [2221].

78 *Barbagallo v J & F Catelan Pty Ltd* [1986] 1 Qd R 245.

79 *Oakacre Ltd v Claire Cleaners (Holdings) Ltd* [1982] Ch 197. *Hasham v Zenab* [1960] AC 316 (specific performance available for anticipatory breach even though no common law cause of action arose).

80 M Bryan, 'Injunctions and Damages: Taking *Shelfer* off the Shelf' (2016) 28 SAcLJ 921, 927–28.

81 (1848) 18 LJ Ch 83.

82 *Eastwood v Lever* (1863) 4 De GJ & Sm 114; 46 ER 859; *Elliston v Reacher* [1908] 2 Ch 374, 395; *Baxter v Four Oaks Properties Ltd* [1965] Ch 816, 829–30; *Landan v Burton* [1962] EG 369.

damages in lieu of specific performance for anticipatory breach of contract although no common law damages would be available.[83]

More controversially, Lord Cairns' Act damages can be awarded in situations where equity would not normally compensate the plaintiff for that kind of loss. As noted at [12.14], *Giller v Procopets* awarded damages for distress arising from a breach of confidence when, ordinarily, equitable compensation would not extend to this loss.[84]   [12.42]

B   The *Shelfer* criteria

The English Court of Appeal in *Shelfer v City of London Electric Co*[85] outlined a set of criteria for the award of Lord Cairns' Act damages. It effectively created a presumption that an injunction should be awarded (at least in nuisance cases) *unless* the criteria below applied.[86] In *Shelfer*, noise and vibrations from the defendant's factory damaged the plaintiff's house and made his wife and daughter ill. The plaintiff sought an injunction. Although the trial judge awarded the plaintiff Lord Cairns' Act damages, the Court of Appeal held that the plaintiff was entitled to an injunction to restrain the nuisance. AL Smith LJ laid down a 'good working rule' that Lord Cairns' Act damages should only be awarded where: [12.43]

1. the injury to the plaintiff's legal right is small;

2. the injury is capable of being estimated in money;

3. the injury can be compensated by a small money payment; and

4. it would be oppressive to the defendant to grant the injunction.[87]

Jolowicz has argued that *Shelfer* should not be regarded as covering *all* cases where Lord Cairns' Act might be awarded.[88] It should apply only where the court has full power to award specific relief without the operation of any discretionary bars. In those cases, specific relief should be granted *unless* AL Smith LJ's conditions are made out.   [12.44]

This is quite different to a case like *Wrotham Park*,[89] where discretionary bars precluded the award of a mandatory injunction. It is suggested that the *Shelfer* rules should not apply to cases where discretionary bars preclude specific relief. In those cases, Lord Cairns' Act damages operates as a middle ground remedy which gives the court an opportunity to recognise the plaintiff's right even if specific relief and common law damages are unavailable.   [12.45]

---

83   *Oakacre Ltd v Claire Cleaners (Holdings) Ltd* [1982] Ch 197.
84   [2008] VSCA 236, (2008) 24 VR 1.
85   [1895] 1 Ch 287.
86   JD Heydon, MJ Leeming and PG Turner, *Meagher, Gummow and Lehane's Equity: Doctrines and Remedies* (5th edn, LexisNexis Butterworths 2015) note at [24–115] and [24–160] that the *Shelfer* rules were probably only intended to apply to nuisance and negative injunctions, although they have (unfortunately) been applied in the context of specific performance too.
87   [1895] 1 Ch 287, 322–23.
88   JA Jolowicz, 'Damages in Equity – A Study of Lord Cairns' Act' (1975) 34 Camb LJ 224, 248–51. See also ICF Spry, *The Principles of Equitable Remedies* (9th edn, LBC 2014) 665–66; *Fishenden v Higgs & Hill Ltd* (1935) 153 LT 128, 138–39 (Lord Hanworth MR).
89   *Wrotham Park Estate Co Ltd v Parkside Homes Ltd* [1974] 1 WLR 798.

[12.46]   Recently, in *Lawrence v Fen Tigers Ltd*,[90] the UK Supreme Court reformulated and questioned the *Shelfer* rules. The plaintiffs moved into a bungalow near a speed track raceway which had been in operation for over 20 years. The plaintiffs sought an injunction restraining the operator of the speed track raceway from making noise over certain levels on the basis of nuisance. They were ultimately unsuccessful, and the Supreme Court awarded Lord Cairns' Act damages. The majority added 'public interest' considerations to the *Shelfer* rules, and said that any criteria should be applied flexibly rather than rigidly.[91] The minority thought that the *Shelfer* rules should be abolished, and the presumption created by *Shelfer* should be reversed, so that in cases of nuisance, damages were presumptively awarded over an injunction.[92] The status of *Lawrence v Fen Tigers Ltd* in Australia is not clear, as it has not been ruled on by an appellate court.[93] It is suggested that it is appropriate to apply the *Shelfer* criteria in a discretionary manner.[94] However, Australian courts should be wary of adopting the UK Supreme Court's new criteria, whether those of the majority or the minority. The minority's 'damages preferred' rule fails to recognise the plaintiff's 'consumer surplus', or her value of an interest.[95] The majority's notion of 'public interest' as a discretionary equitable consideration could extend into difficult issues which have not traditionally been considered in equity.[96]

VII   The basis of assessment
A   Timing

[12.47]   As Heydon, Leeming and Turner note, the problem of how to measure damages and timing is acute in the cases where damages are awarded in lieu of specific performance, and the results in the cases vary widely.[97] In *Wroth v Tyler*,[98] the plaintiff sought specific performance of a contract for the sale of a house, but the court declined to award specific performance because of potential hardship on a third party, the defendant's wife, who had registered an interest in the house under the *Matrimonial Homes Act 1967* (UK). Megarry J awarded Lord Cairns' Act damages in lieu of specific performance. The damages were measured by the difference between the value of the house as at the date of judgment and the value as at the date of the contract, rather than by the difference between the value as at the date of breach and at the date of the contract, because the value of the house had gone up steeply since the date of the

---

90   [2014] UKSC 13, [2014] AC 822.

91   Ibid, [100]–[127] (Lord Neuberger, with whom Lords Mance and Carnwath agreed).

92   Ibid, [157]–[161] (Lord Sumption, with whom Lord Clark agreed).

93   *Emprja Pty Ltd v Red Engine Group Pty Ltd* [2017] QSC 33 [71]. The *Shelfer* rule was still applied in *Lord v McMahon* [2015] NSWSC 1619 [170], [183]; *Janney v Steller Works Pty Ltd* [2017] VSC 363 [35]–[37] (Riordan J).

94   The Australian approach has always been closer to that suggested in *Lawrence v Fen Tigers Ltd*: JD Heydon, MJ Leeming and PG Turner, *Meagher, Gummow and Lehane's Equity: Doctrines and Remedies* (5th edn, LexisNexis Butterworths 2015) [24–120].

95   M Bryan, 'Injunctions and Damages: Taking *Shelfer* off the Shelf' (2016) 28 SAcLJ 921, 941–42.

96   Ibid, 943–45.

97   JD Heydon, MJ Leeming and PG Turner, *Meagher, Gummow and Lehane's Equity: Doctrines and Remedies* (5th edn, LexisNexis Butterworths 2015) [24–170].

98   [1974] 1 Ch 30.

breach. Megarry J awarded £5500 to better reflect the right to performance of the contract lost by the plaintiff.[99]

The result in *Wroth v Tyler* was thrown into doubt when Lord Wilberforce in *Johnson v Agnew* said that the principles governing the calculation of Lord Cairns' Act damages and common law damages are the same.[100] There is broad truth in this insofar as compensatory-style awards are concerned, for it seems that an award of Lord Cairns' Act damages for a breach of contract primarily aims to meet the plaintiff's expectation (albeit in a more generous fashion),[101] and an award of Lord Cairns' Act damages for a tort aims to place the plaintiff in the position as if the tort had not occurred (again, albeit in a more generous fashion).[102] However, courts have struggled to apply *Johnson v Agnew* in subsequent cases.[103] Ian Spry has argued that if equitable principles require a more generous measure of damages than the corresponding common law principle, the courts should award damages on a more generous measure than at common law.[104] We concur.   [12.48]

David Winterton has argued that the result in *Johnson v Agnew* can be reconciled with *Wroth v Tyler* if one takes into account the fact that it was the *vendor* in *Johnson v Agnew* who sought specific performance.[105] The vendor was unable to counter-perform his part of the bargain (namely, to transfer title) because the mortgagees had sold the land, and accordingly it was appropriate not to award the vendor damages which substituted for specific relief. By contrast, in *Wroth v Tyler*, the purchaser sought specific performance. Just as specific performance is dependent upon the plaintiff being ready and willing to perform, similarly, damages substituting for specific relief should depend on the plaintiff fulfilling payment of the purchase price. Because the plaintiff could fulfil his side of the bargain, damages were made on a substitutive basis.   [12.49]

Lord Wilberforce in *Johnson v Agnew* left open the date as at which Lord Cairns' Act damages are to be assessed.[106] In some cases, Lord Cairns' Act damages have been assessed as at the date of judgment,[107] whereas in other cases damages have been assessed as at the date of the wrong.[108] Heydon, Leeming and Turner concluded that there is only one general principle as to timing: 'the date is to be selected by the court in service of the objective of awarding the plaintiff compensation, no more and no less'.[109]   [12.50]

While Lord Wilberforce in *Johnson v Agnew* concentrated on Lord Cairns' Act damages that have a compensatory function,[110] not all measures of Lord Cairns' Act damages necessarily   [12.51]

---

99   Ibid, 57–58.
100   [1980] AC 367, 400.
101   See especially *Wroth v Tyler* [1974] 1 Ch 30.
102   See, eg, cases involving damages in lieu of an injunction for obstruction of light: *Kine v Jolly* [1905] 1 Ch 480 (aff'd *Jolly v Kine* [1907] 1 AC 1); *Griffith v Richard Clay & Sons Ltd* [1912] 2 Ch 291; *Wills v May* [1923] 1 Ch 317.
103   *Domb v Isoz* [1980] Ch 548.
104   ICF Spry, *The Principles of Equitable Remedies* (9th edn, LBC 2014) 661.
105   D Winterton, *Money Awards in Contract Law* (Hart, 2015) 312–14.
106   *Johnson v Agnew* [1980] AC 367, 400 (Lord Wilberforce).
107   Eg *Wroth v Tyler* [1974] 1 Ch 30.
108   Eg *Johnson v Agnew* [1980] AC 367.
109   JD Heydon, MJ Leeming and PG Turner, *Meagher, Gummow and Lehane's Equity: Doctrines and Remedies* (5th edn, LexisNexis Butterworths) [24–185].
110   [1980] AC 367, 401–02.

compensate for loss, particularly the 'reasonable fee' measure. Therefore, his comments should be treated with care. In *Jaggard v Sawyer*, Millett LJ correctly sought to confine the statement in *Johnson v Agnew* to cases where common law and Lord Cairns' Act damages were recoverable in respect of the same cause of action.[111]

[12.52]   The measure of Lord Cairns' Act damages depends on the case. There are two different measures: gain-based relief and loss-based relief.

B   Gain-based relief – 'reasonable fee' awards

[12.53]   The 'reasonable fee' award in lieu of specific relief is commonly made in the 'middle ground' cases (mentioned at [12.31]–[12.37]) involving breach of negative covenant[112] or trespass to land.[113] Such damages have also apparently been awarded for nuisance,[114] although later English cases suggest that nuisance does not give rise to reasonable fee damages.[115] As discussed in Ch 16, 'reasonable fee' awards have been argued to be gain-based, although this is not always accepted in Australia.[116] In *Attorney-General v Blake*, the House of Lords recognised the exceptional availability of an account of profits for breach of contract, and Lord Nicholls relied on the Lord Cairns' Act cases as an important step in his reasoning, using them to argue that gain-based relief had already been available for common law wrongs.[117] But the precise nature of the gain involved has not been clarified: a notional profit, or part of an actual profit, or some reflection of value transferred to the defendant.

C   Loss-based relief – compensatory awards of various kinds

[12.54]   The courts have made compensatory awards under Lord Cairns' Act provisions in a variety of situations.

1   Where specific relief was impossible, or in addition to specific relief

[12.55]   The origin and purpose of these awards is considered at [12.29]–[12.30].

[12.56]   Where damages are awarded because specific relief was genuinely impossible at the time of trial, courts have generally awarded damages for losses flowing from the wrongdoing. Thus, in *Catton v Wyld*,[118] damages reflected the losses suffered during the period that a wall had been pulled down, and in *Fritz v Hobson*,[119] damages reflected the loss of custom suffered by a shop while the entrance was blocked.

---

111   [1995] 1 WLR 269, 291.
112   *Wrotham Park Estate Co Ltd v Parkside Homes Ltd* [1974] 1 WLR 798; *Jaggard v Sawyer* [1995] 1 WLR 269.
113   *Bracewell v Appleby* [1975] Ch 408; *Jaggard v Sawyer* [1995] 1 WLR 269.
114   *Carr-Saunders v Dick McNeil Associates Ltd* [1986] 1 WLR 922.
115   *Stoke-on-Trent City Council v W and J Wass Ltd* [1988] 1 WLR 1406 (involving the holding of an unlicensed market); *Forsyth-Grant v Allen* [2008] EWCA Civ 505, [2008] 2 EGLR 16.
116   See JD Heydon, MJ Leeming and PG Turner, *Meagher, Gummow and Lehane's Equity: Doctrines and Remedies* (5th edn, LexisNexis Butterworths) [24–145].
117   [2001] 1 AC 268, 281.
118   (1863) 55 ER 105; 32 Beav 266.
119   (1880) 14 Ch D 542.

When damages are sought in addition to specific relief, the court is concerned to ensure   [12.57]
that there is not double relief or, in other words, that there is not an award of both specific
performance of the defendant's obligation *and* damages in substitution for it.[120] Damages
awarded in addition to specific relief are generally compensatory, and often arise in cases
where some obligations can be enforced and others cannot. For example, a court may order
specific performance of part of a contract, and Lord Cairns' Act damages in respect of the
balance of the agreement,[121] as in *Grant v Dawkins*,[122] noted at [12.30].

2   Future wrongdoing

Lord Cairns' Act damages can be awarded in respect of future losses; see [12.39]–[12.40].   [12.58]
Generally such damages are compensatory. Thus Viscount Finlay in *Leeds Industrial
Cooperative Society Ltd v Slack* said that damages given in substitution for an injunction
must compensate for the damage which would be suffered in the future.[123] In cases of
nuisance involving subsidence, damages are measured according to the anticipated cost of
repair of the future subsidence, as well as any projected loss of land.[124] Similarly, damages
for an anticipatory breach of contract reflected the costs associated with the delay of the
defendants in completing the contract.[125] However, where it is impossible to calculate the
future loss, courts arguably make gain-based awards, as in the 'right to light' cases. In
these cases, the defendant's building impedes the plaintiff's right to light in the future, and
damages are calculated as a 'share of the profits' that the defendant would make from the
building.[126]

3   To provide novel forms of relief

Lord Cairns' Act damages may be awarded where the common law would not recognise a   [12.59]
cause of action sounding in damages; see [12.41]–[12.42]. When damages are available for the
breach of a restrictive covenant, losses flowing from the breach have been compensated,[127]
including diminution in value of the affected properties, and loss of amenity.[128] In cases of
anticipatory breach of contract, as mentioned at [12.58], compensatory damages reflect the
delay.[129]

Lord Cairns' Act damages can be awarded in equity for distress; see [12.14]. Damages for   [12.60]
distress are intrinsically subjective, and the Victorian Court of Appeal differed on the proper

---

120   ICF Spry, *The Principles of Equitable Remedies* (9th edn, LBC 2014) 668–69.
121   *Soames v Edge* (1860) Johns 669, 70 ER 588; *Grant v Dawkins* [1973] 3 All ER 897. Cf *Ryan v Mutual
Tontine Westminster Chambers Association* [1893] 1 Ch 116. See RP Meagher, JD Heydon and MJ
Leeming, *Meagher, Gummow and Lehane's Equity: Doctrines and Remedies* (4th edn, Butterworths
2002) [23–045].
122   [1973] 1 WLR 1406.
123   *Leeds Industrial Cooperative Society Ltd v Slack* [1924] AC 851, 857.
124   *Hooper v Rogers* [1975] Ch 43; *Barbagallo v J & F Catelan Pty Ltd* [1986] 1 Qd R 245.
125   *Oakacre Ltd v Claire Cleaners (Holdings) Ltd* [1982] Ch 197, 203.
126   *Tamares (Vincent Square) Ltd v Fairpoint Properties (Vincent Square) Ltd (No 2)* [2007] EWHC 212
(Ch), [2007] 1 WLR 2167; *HKRUK II (CHC) Ltd v Heaney* [2010] EWHC 2245 (Ch).
127   *Eastwood v Lever* (1863) 4 De GJ & Sm 114; 46 ER 859.
128   *Baxter v Four Oaks Properties Ltd* [1965] Ch 816, 829–30.
129   *Oakacre Ltd v Claire Cleaners (Holdings) Ltd* [1982] Ch 197, 203.

measure in *Giller v Procopets*.[130] While the majority awarded Ms Giller $40 000, including $10 000 representing aggravated damages,[131] Ashley AJA would have awarded her $27 500, including $7500 representing aggravated damages.[132]

VIII   Discretionary bars to relief

[12.61]   The general discretionary bars to the award of equitable remedies apply to Lord Cairns' Act damages. These are:

- hardship and the public interest;
- lack of clean hands; and
- delay and acquiescence.

The ways in which the general bars operate are discussed at [10.75]–[10.89] and [11.50]–[11.57] with regard to specific performance and injunctions respectively. They operate similarly in relation to Lord Cairns' Act damages.

[12.62]   However, if (for example) specific performance has been barred because it will cause undue hardship to the defendant, it does not follow that Lord Cairns' Act damages will be barred for the same reason.[133] The court must consider – independently of whether an order of specific performance will cause hardship to the defendant – whether payment of Lord Cairns' Act damages will cause hardship to the defendant. Indeed, Lord Cairns' Act damages allow a court to recognise the plaintiff's interest notwithstanding the operation of a discretionary bar precluding specific relief.

[12.63]   The only general bar to relief that will be discussed specifically in this chapter is acquiescence. However, *all* general bars to relief may preclude Lord Cairns' Act damages.[134]

[12.64]   In *Sayers v Collyer*, Fry LJ said that 'acquiescence may be either an entire bar to all relief, or it may be a ground for inducing the court to act under the powers of Lord Cairns' Act'.[135] Sometimes, acquiescence on the part of the plaintiff is a basis for denying relief altogether,[136] but more usually it is a reason for awarding Lord Cairns' Act damages in lieu of specific relief.[137] In other words, the plaintiff has a right that should be recognised by the court, but the plaintiff has acquiesced or delayed in enforcing the right to such an extent that it would be unfair to impose an injunction on the defendant. The discussion at [16.131]–[16.133] indicates that delay and acquiescence may also influence a court to measure gain-based relief by reference to a reasonable fee rather than the full profit made by the defendant.

---

130   [2008] VSCA 236, (2008) 24 VR 1.
131   Ibid, [233], [446].
132   Ibid, [160].
133   See *Bosaid v Andry* [1963] VR 465, 479 (Sholl J).
134   ICF Spry, *The Principles of Equitable Remedies* (9th edn, LBC 2014) 669–71.
135   (1884) 28 Ch D 103, 110.
136   *Sayers v Collyer* (1884) 28 Ch D 103; *Sobey v Sainsbury* [1913] 2 Ch 513.
137   *Eastwood v Lever* (1863) 4 De GJ & Sm 114, 46 ER 859; *Shaw v Applegate* [1977] 1 WLR 970; *McKenna v Richey* [1950] VLR 360. Cf *Boyns v Lackey* (1958) 58 SR (NSW) 395.

IX   Part 9.5 of the *Corporations Act 2001* (Cth)

The *Corporations Act 2001* (Cth) has a provision which appears on its face to be a Lord Cairns' Act style provision. Section 1324 of the *Corporations Act* empowers a court to award an injunction to restrain contraventions of the Act, and s 1324(10) states: **[12.65]**

> Where the Court has power under this section to grant an injunction restraining a person from engaging in particular conduct, or requiring a person to do a particular act or thing, the Court may, either in addition to or in substitution for the grant of the injunction, order that person to pay damages to any other person.

However, *McCracken v Phoenix Constructions (Qld) Pty Ltd*[138] indicates that any analogy with Lord Cairns' Act may be misleading, and that the power to award damages in lieu of an injunction must be read in light of the other provisions of the *Corporations Act 2001* (Cth). If other provisions of the *Corporations Act 2001* (Cth) exclude a straightforward claim for damages by the plaintiff, the court cannot award damages in lieu of an injunction pursuant to s 1324(10). Conversely, in *Re Colorado Products Pty Ltd*, while Black J regarded himself as bound by *McCracken*, he observed that the availability of damages in lieu of an injunction pursuant to s 1324(10) was not 'closed beyond argument'[139] and that there had been academic criticism of narrow interpretations of the provision.[140]   **[12.66]**

X   The future of Lord Cairns' Act damages

Bryan and Barnett have argued that in most cases, Lord Cairns' Act provisions are not needed by the courts.[141] In most states and territories, courts have power make orders to achieve 'full and complete justice' between the parties.[142] For example, s 29(2) of the *Supreme Court Act 1986* (Vic) allows the Supreme Court to exercise its jurisdiction in every civil proceeding before it so 'as to secure that, as far as possible, all matters in dispute between the parties are completely and finally determined, and all multiplicity of proceedings concerning those matters is avoided.'[143]   **[12.67]**

---

138   [2012] QCA 129, [2013] 2 Qd R 27 [30]–[40].

139   [2014] NSWSC 789, (2014) 101 ACSR 233 [399].

140   Ibid. See, eg, R Baxt, 'Will Section 574 of the Companies Code Please Stand Up! (And Will Section 1323 of the Corporations Act Follow Suit)' (1989) 7 C&SLJ 388.

141   K Barnett and M Bryan, 'Lord Cairns's Act: A Study in the Unintended Consequences of Legislation' (2015) 9 J of Eq 150, 154–55; M Bryan, 'Injunctions and Damages: Taking *Shelfer* off the Shelf' (2016) 28 SAcLJ 921, 927–28.

142   *Supreme Court of Judicature Act 1873* (UK) c 66, s 24(7). See also *Sayers v Collyer* (1884) 28 Ch D 103, 108 (Baggallay LJ).

143   See also *Senior Courts Act 1981* (UK) c 54, s 49(2); *Federal Court of Australia Act 1976* (Cth), s 22; *Supreme Court Act 1933* (ACT), s 32; *Supreme Court Act 1970* (NSW), s 63; *Supreme Court Act* (NT), ss 61–68; *Civil Proceedings Act 2011* (Qld), s 7; *Supreme Court Act 1935* (SA), s 27; *Supreme Court Civil Procedure Act 1932* (Tas), s 10(7); *Supreme Court Act 1935* (WA), s 24(7).

[12.68]   However, to pick the example of compensation for anticipated wrongs at common law, where it appears that Lord Cairns' Act provisions remain necessary,[144] it seems nonsensical that courts should have to go through the tortuous route of establishing that the plaintiff was entitled to a *quia timet* injunction and is thus entitled to damages for future losses in lieu of that injunction. As Andrew Burrows suggests,[145] the common law should be flexible enough to be able to compensate for anticipated wrongs in exceptional cases.

[12.69]   Despite arguments that Lord Cairns' Act damages are a 'dead letter',[146] Australian courts still find Lord Cairns' Act provisions to be relevant, as indicated by *Giller v Procopets*.[147] Lord Cairns' Act remains a useful mechanism for courts to traverse the common law and equity divide. However, Burrows may be correct to say that these kinds of divisions are unhelpful and should eventually be dissolved. There are other means of achieving the same aims which are less circuitous.

---

144   M Bryan, 'Injunctions and Damages: Taking *Shelfer* off the Shelf' (2016) 28 SAcLJ 921, 927–28.
145   A Burrows, 'We Do This at Common Law but That in Equity' (2002) 22 OJLS 1, 13–14.
146   J Getzler, 'Equitable Compensation and the Regulation of Fiduciary Relationships' in P Birks and F Rose (eds), *Restitution and Equity, Volume One: Resulting Trusts and Equitable Compensation* (Mansfield Press 2000) 247.
147   [2008] VSCA 236, (2008) 24 VR 1.

PART

4

REMEDIES AS VINDICATION

13

SELF-HELP REMEDIES

I Introduction

[13.1] This chapter considers self-help remedies, which involve the plaintiff making good her own rights without the intervention of the judiciary. The focus of this book is on remedies that are awarded pursuant to a judicial order. However, an exclusive consideration of judicial remedies would ignore the fact that most disputes are settled outside the courts and that most parties prefer non-judicial settlements. It may be queried whether self-help remedies are really remedies in the strict sense of the word. They do not involve a court order; instead, the court gives permission to a plaintiff to act in a particular way. Nevertheless, in a broader sense, the plaintiff is allowed to redress her grievance by vindicating her own rights. By allowing a plaintiff to redress her rights in this way, the law affirms and reinforces the importance of certain interests. Varuhas has noticed that the interests protected by vindicatory awards are often associated with the torts actionable per se.[1] It will be seen in this chapter that self-help 'remedies' are indeed associated with responses to trespass to land, trespass to the person and wrongful interference with goods. Self-help remedies are also available for breach of contract, another cause of action actionable per se.

[13.2] When parties have a dispute, there can be several legal reactions (such as letters, discussions, and telephone calls) before anything gets to court. Sometimes a party who believes she has been wronged will lodge a complaint with the other party, or threaten the other party's reputation by complaining to others.[2] Alternative dispute resolution is another means by which parties may try to resolve a dispute without resorting to the courts.[3] However, the law lurks in the background when parties try to settle disputes, and bargaining is conducted in the light of the relative legal positions. A clear entitlement to a legal remedy will put a party in a strong bargaining position.[4]

[13.3] Some attempts to settle a dispute might have tortious or criminal consequences. In *Croucher v Cachia*,[5] two neighbours had a long-running dispute over the boundary to their properties. The defendant neighbour saw that the plaintiff neighbour was clipping the hedge, and asserted that clippings from the plaintiff's hedge should not fall onto his driveway. A violent scuffle ensued, and the defendant severely injured the plaintiff's hand and thumb with gardening shears. The defendant was found to have committed the torts of trespass to the person and negligence.

[13.4] Civil recourse theorists argue that an important function of tort law is to prevent persons from engaging in violent recourse against one another when they have been wronged; instead the courts vindicate the rights of the victim in a public forum.[6] Consistent with this theory, self-

---

1   JNE Varuhas, 'The Concept of 'Vindication' in the Law of Torts: Rights, Interests and Damages' (2014) 34 OJLS 253.
2   D Harris, D Campbell and R Halson, *Remedies in Contract and Tort* (2nd edn, CUP 2005) 44–45.
3   S Colbran, P Spender, S Jackson, R Douglas and T Penovic, *Civil Procedure: Commentary and Materials* (5th edn, LexisNexis 2012) ch 3.
4   D Harris, D Campbell and R Halson, *Remedies in Contract and Tort* (2nd edn, CUP 2005) 44.
5   [2016] NSWCA 132.
6   A small sample: B Zipursky, 'Rights, Wrongs and Recourse in the Law of Torts' (1998) 51 Vand L Rev 1; B Zipursky, 'Civil Recourse, Not Corrective Justice' (2003) 81 Georgetown LJ 695; J Goldberg and B Zipursky, 'Torts as Wrongs' (2010) 88 Tex L Rev 917; J Goldberg and B Zipursky, 'Civil Recourse Revisited' (2011) 39 Fla St U L Rev 340; B Zipursky, 'Substantive Standing, Civil Recourse, and Corrective Justice' (2011) 39 Fla St U L Rev 299; A Robertson, 'On the Function of the Law of Negligence' (2013) 33 OJLS 31.

help remedies in tort are exceptional, and there is a strong requirement that the self-help must be reasonable. In contract, there is a greater freedom for parties to bargain for remedies because of notions of freedom of contract but, again, courts are concerned to prevent remedies that are harsh or unfair, particularly where bargaining power is unequal.

Below, we consider a variety of 'self-help' remedies in tort which allow one to defend oneself or one's property from tortious interference, including eviction of trespassers, self-defence of property, self-defence of the person, recaption and replevin, and abatement of nuisance.   **[13.5]**

We also consider contractual 'self-help' remedies. First, rescission has been thought to have a self-help aspect. Secondly, parties to a contract stipulate the damages payable upon the occurrence of certain events (known as 'agreed' or 'liquidated' damages clauses). This is a form of self-help in a wide sense because the party to the contract does not rely on the court to measure the damage. Thirdly, parties to a contract may make an obligation a debt. Finally, parties to a contract may include other stipulated contractual remedies (such as termination clauses) which could also be thought of as exercising self-help.   **[13.6]**

II   Tort and self-help

Some proprietary torts give rise to self-help remedies, including trespass to land, trespass to goods, trespass to persons and nuisance. These allow persons to defend themselves or their property from tortious interference, but courts are clear that any self-help undertaken must be reasonable. As Winfield observed, 'self-help has always been reckoned as a perilous remedy owing to the stringent rules against its abuse'.[7]   **[13.7]**

A   Eviction of trespassers and protection of land and goods from trespass

A possessor of land may evict a trespasser, but only by using 'reasonable' force.[8] Ordinarily, no force is justified until the trespasser has been asked to leave and has been given a reasonable opportunity to leave.[9] However, if a trespass is committed with force and with 'a strong hand', a possessor may respond with force, as the intruder's conduct indicates that a request to leave would be futile.[10] By contrast, if the trespasser does not threaten harm to the property or to the possessor, the possessor may only use minimal force.[11]   **[13.8]**

The law regarding the right of an owner of land to repossess a property from an occupier (such as a tenant or a squatter) is complex because there are other rules relating to the eviction of persons in possession of land, which may impact on the availability of any general law   **[13.9]**

---

7   PH Winfield, *The Province of the Law of Tort* (CUP 1931) 233.
8   *Hemmings v Stoke Poges Golf Club* [1920] 1 KB 820; *Cowell v Rosehill Racecourse Co Ltd* (1937) 56 CLR 605, 631 (Dixon J).
9   *Green v Goddard* (1795) 2 Salk 641, 91 ER 541; *Polkinhorn v Wright* (1845) 8 QB 197, 115 ER 849; *Long v Rawlins* (1874) 4 QSCR 86.
10   *Green v Goddard* (1795) 2 Salk 641, 91 ER 541; *Polkinhorn v Wright* (1845) 8 QB 197, 115 ER 849.
11   D Howarth, 'Defences to Intentional Torts' in C Sappideen and P Vines (eds), *Fleming's The Law of Torts* (10th edn, LBC 2011) [5.90].

remedy. In all states, versions of the old English *Statute of Forcible Entry*[12] remain in force and make it an indictable offence to forcibly enter the land, even if one is an owner who has been wrongfully dispossessed, unless one has a clear legal basis for entering the land.[13] Moreover, in Queensland, Tasmania and Western Australia, a person who is in peaceable possession of land, a structure or a boat 'under a claim of right' may use force to defend his possession, even against someone who is entitled by law to the possession of the property, subject to certain limits on violence.[14]

[13.10]   At the beginning of the 19th century, courts started to hold that the owner of the land was not entitled to use force to remove an occupier or her chattels.[15] However, this was reversed in 1920 by the English Court of Appeal in *Hemmings v Stoke Poges Golf Club*, where a landlord was not liable for assault and damage to goods caused during the eviction of a tenant who had stayed over his lease.[16] Thus, at common law, a landlord may repossess a property from a former tenant using reasonable force,[17] so long as the landlord first asks the tenant to leave and gives him a reasonable opportunity to leave.[18] In most Australian jurisdictions, this right is limited in respect of residential tenancies by the various residential tenancy Acts, which have put in place a compulsory procedure providing that a landlord must obtain an order from a tribunal to evict a tenant.[19]

[13.11]   The English Court of Appeal in *McPhail v Persons Unknown* held that owners of property are entitled to evict squatters who entered forcibly without an order of the court, as long as they use no more force than is reasonably necessary.[20] The *Statute of Forcible Entry* did not preclude the owner from using force to evict the squatters, because the squatters themselves had entered using force ('with a strong hand') which was precluded by the statute.[21] This rule has been applied in Australia.[22]

[13.12]   Where a licence has been given to someone to enter a property (such as a racecourse, pub or cinema) the owner of the property may revoke the licence and eject the licensee, as long as the licensee has received notice that the licence is revoked and has been given a reasonable

---

12   *Statute of Forcible Entry 1381* (15 Rich II, c 7); *Statute of Forcible Entry 1391* (15 Rich II, c 2); *Statute of Forcible Entry 1429* (8 Hen VI, c 9). See *R v Mountford* [1972] 1 QB 28 for a history of these statutes. The medieval term for forcible entry was trespass *vi et armis* ('with force and arms').

13   *Imperial Acts Application Act 1969* (NSW), ss 18–20; *Criminal Code Act 1899* (Qld), ss 70 and 71; *Summary Offences Act 1953* (SA), s 17D; *Criminal Code Act 1924* (Tas), s 79; *Crimes Act 1958* (Vic), s 207; *Summary Offences Act 1966* (Vic), s 9(1)(g); *Criminal Code Act 1913* (WA), s 69.

14   *Criminal Code Act 1899* (Qld), s 278; *Criminal Code Act 1924* (Tas), s 42; *Criminal Code Act 1913* (WA), s 255.

15   D Howarth, 'Defences to Intentional Torts' in C Sappideen and P Vines (eds), *Fleming's The Law of Torts* (10th edn, LBC 2011) [5.120], citing *Pollen v Brewer* (1859) 7 CB (NS) 371; *Clifton Securities v Huntley* [1948] 2 All ER 283.

16   *Hemmings v Stoke Poges Golf Club* [1920] 1 KB 820.

17   *MacIntosh v Lobel* (1993) 30 NSWLR 441; *Haniotis v Dimitriou* [1983] VR 498.

18   *Haniotis v Dimitriou* [1983] VR 498, 500, citing *Polkinhorn v Wright* (1845) 8 QB 197, 206; 115 ER 849, 853.

19   *Residential Tenancies Act 2010* (NSW), s 120; *Residential Tenancies and Rooming Accommodation Act 2008* (Qld), s 353; *Residential Tenancies Act 1995* (SA), s 95; *Residential Tenancies Act 1997* (Vic), s 229; *Residential Tenancies Act 1987* (WA), s 80.

20   *McPhail v Persons Unknown* [1973] Ch 447, 455.

21   Ibid, 456, 461–62.

22   *MacIntosh v Lobel* (1993) 30 NSWLR 441, 463–64; *Nyul Nyul Aboriginal Corporation v Dunn* (1996) 133 FLR 359, 371.

time to leave and collect her property.[23] If the licence is revoked because a person is drunk or disorderly, force may be used to remove him from the property, but ejection may be unreasonable if the person is severely injured as a result,[24] or it may be negligent if the person is incapable of navigating the traffic outside.[25]

A more difficult question arises regarding the level of reasonable force which a property owner may exercise to remove a burglar or thief from the property.[26] This will be considered in more detail in relation to the right to protect one's property from theft. [13.13]

Reasonable force may also be used to remove protesters who deliberately obstruct lawful work being undertaken on property.[27] However, courts are chary of encouraging self-help in such circumstances, and it has been observed that breaches of the peace and disputes as to whether reasonable force was used are likely to arise as soon as one person lays hands on another to remove him from the land.[28] Moreover, statutes may affect the extent to which self-help is available. For example, in *Richter v Risby*,[29] protesters attempted to prevent a 'traxcavator' operated by a logging company from clearing a logging track. The plaintiffs had committed private nuisance by blocking the track, but the defendants were not entitled to abate the nuisance except as provided in ss 40–45 of the *Criminal Code* (Tas). The defendants were not protecting moveable property pursuant to ss 43, 44 and 45 of the Code – rather, they were attempting to access the path to the logging track – and they were not entitled to abate the nuisance by physically removing the plaintiffs from the track.[30] [13.14]

B   Self-defence of property

A possessor of land or goods may use reasonable force to protect her land or goods. Historically, a possessor of land and goods could go to extreme lengths to protect his property.[31] However, in *Bird v Holbrook*,[32] it was held that a landowner was not allowed to protect tulip bulbs in his walled garden by means of a spring gun after it injured his teenage next-door neighbour who had entered the garden to retrieve a straying peahen. It is now a statutory offence in most Australian states to set spring guns, 'man traps' and instruments that [13.15]

---

23   *Cowell v Rosehill Racecourse Co Ltd* (1937) 56 CLR 605, 631 (Dixon J); *Horkin v North Melbourne Football Club Social Club* [1983] 1 VR 153.
24   *Horkin v North Melbourne Football Club Social Club* [1983] 1 VR 153, 157 (plaintiff suffered dislocated elbow).
25   *Jordan House v Menow* [1974] SCR 239; 30 DLR (3d) 105. But cf in Australia *CAL No 14 Pty Ltd v Motor Vehicle Accidents Insurance Board* (2009) 239 CLR 390, [2009] HCA 47; *Cole v South Tweed Heads Rugby League Football Club* [2004] HCA 29, (2004) 217 CLR 469.
26   See generally B Hogan, 'Defence of Property' (1994) 144 New LJ 466.
27   *Holmes v Bagge* [1853] 1 E & B 782, 786–87; 118 ER 629, 631 (Lord Campbell CJ); *R v Chief Constable of Devon and Cornwall* [1982] 1 QB 458, 470, 473.
28   *R v Chief Constable of Devon and Cornwall* [1982] 1 QB 458, 473 (Lawton LJ). See also *Sedleigh-Denfield v O'Callaghan* [1940] AC 880, 911 (Lord Wright).
29   [1987] Tas R 36, (1987) 27 A Crim R 68.
30   [1987] Tas R 36, 46, (1987) 27 A Crim R 68, 78–79.
31   See *Semayne's Case* (1604) 5 Co Rep 91a, 91a; 77 ER 194, 194: 'The house of every one is his castle, and if thieves come to a man's house to rob or murder, and the owner or his servants kill any of the thieves in defence of himself and his house, it is no felony and he shall lose nothing'.
32   (1828) 4 Bing 628, 130 ER 911. Cf *Jordin v Crump* (1841) 8 M & W 783, 789; 151 ER 1256, 1259.

may cause death or grievous bodily harm,[33] although some states have exceptions for traps in dwelling houses at night. Landowners continue to be able to install spiked barriers to protect property,[34] and to keep guard dogs,[35] as their utility outweighs the chance that a trespasser may suffer an injury.[36]

[13.16] In modern times, because the distinction between different levels of entrants to a property has been abolished,[37] it is likely that the landowner in *Bird v Holbrook* would have been liable in negligence, even if the trespasser had more nefarious motives than the plaintiff in that case. In *Hackshaw v Shaw*,[38] a thief had been stealing petrol from a farmer's bowser. The farmer lay in wait and, while the thief was siphoning off petrol, the farmer shot the thief's car, intending to prevent the thief from driving off. The thief's girlfriend was cowering in the car. The farmer was unaware of her presence and accidentally shot her. While at least one judge in the Victorian Court of Appeal seemed to countenance the possibility that the farmer was entitled to shoot at the car because of the lack of police assistance,[39] a majority in the High Court of Australia held that the farmer had been negligent.[40] It was relevant that the actions of the farmer were disproportionate and unreasonable in the circumstances.[41] A landowner who uses unreasonable force and injures a thief or an accomplice is likely to be held liable in negligence.[42]

[13.17] *Poland v John Parr & Sons*[43] shows that defence of goods must be reasonable. A carter was walking home after work when he saw a boy whom he thought was stealing sugar from his employer's wagon. He hit the boy on the back of the neck, causing him to fall under the wagon and injure his foot. The boy's leg was amputated as a result. It was clear that the carter was entitled and authorised to protect his employer's goods, but the employer was vicariously liable for his conduct because the force was excessive in the circumstances.[44]

C Self-defence of the person

[13.18] A person may act with reasonable force to defend himself or a third person. The test for self-defence in both criminal and tort law is 'whether the accused believed on reasonable grounds

---

33 *Crimes Act 1900* (NSW), s 49; *Criminal Code Act 1899* (Qld), s 327; *Criminal Code Act 1924* (Tas), s 179; *Crimes Act 1958* (Vic), ss 25 and 26; *Criminal Code Act 1913* (WA), s 305.

34 *Deane v Clayton* (1817) 7 Taunt 489, 129 ER 196.

35 *Brock v Copeland* (1794) 1 Esp 200, 170 ER 328. For a modern version, see *Johnson v Buchanan* [2012] VSC 195, (2012) 223 A Crim R 132, which involved the application of a 'trespass defence' within the context of s 29(9)(b) of the *Domestic Animals Act 1994* (Vic).

36 D Howarth, 'Defences to Intentional Torts' in C Sappideen and P Vines (eds), *Fleming's The Law of Torts* (10th edn, LBC 2011) [5.110].

37 *Hackshaw v Shaw* (1984) 155 CLR 624, 662–23 (Deane J); *Australian Safeway Stores Pty Ltd v Zaluzna* (1987) 162 CLR 479.

38 (1984) 155 CLR 624.

39 *Shaw v Hackshaw* [1983] 2 VR 65, 100 (McInerney J). See also *R v McKay* [1957] VR 560.

40 (1984) 155 CLR 624 (Gibbs CJ, Murphy, Wilson and Deane JJ, Dawson J dissenting). See also *Revill v Newbery* [1996] QB 567.

41 (1984) 155 CLR 624, 640 (Wilson J). See also *R v Martin* [2001] EWCA Crim 2245, [2003] QB 1 [7].

42 P Handford, 'Comment: Acting to Deter Criminal Trespassers' (1996) 4 Tort L Rev 261, 265.

43 [1927] 1 KB 236.

44 Ibid, 242, 243, 245. Cf *Bonette v Woolworths Ltd* (1937) 37 SR (NSW) 132, 151 (Jordan CJ): an employee may protect goods, but has no authority to punish a person who has improperly dealt with them.

that it was necessary in self-defence to do what he did'.[45] The defendant must believe that the defence was necessary, but that belief must also be reasonable. In contrast to criminal proceedings, the burden of proof lies on the defendant to prove these matters in a civil context.[46]

Courts limit the right to self-defence, and if there is a way to escape the threat, it is usually found that the use of force was disproportionate and unreasonable. In *Fontin v Katapodis*,[47] a customer attacked an employee at a store with a 'T square' after hearing that the employee had falsely accused him of failing to pay his bill. The employee responded by throwing an offcut from a glass louvre at the customer, injuring the customer's thumb severely. It was found that this was 'out of all reasonable proportion to the emergency',[48] and that the employee could have moved away from the customer. Similarly, in *Rozsa v Samuels*,[49] a taxi driver pushed into a taxi queue and a second taxi driver (who had been at the head of the queue) told the first he would punch him in the head. The first taxi driver produced a table knife and said: 'I will cut you to bits if you try it'. Hogarth J said: 'Before applying force in self-defence, a person threatened with violence is obliged by law to take whatever reasonable means are open to him, other than the use of force by himself, to avoid the force threatened against him'.[50] It was found that the first taxi driver could have retreated into his taxi or removed his taxi from the queue, and that his actions were unreasonable. [13.19]

Self-defence applies not only to one's self, but also to acts done in defence of another person.[51] [13.20]

D Recaption, replevin and specific restitution

There are a variety of actions which may allow persons to recover goods that have been removed from their possession using reasonable force. First, recaption allows a person with an immediate right to possession to retake wrongfully possessed goods using reasonable force.[52] She may also forcibly enter the land of the tortfeasor or a third party who helped take the goods to retrieve them.[53] Recaption has an ancient history.[54] However, the extent of this right is uncertain. While *Blades v Higgs*[55] suggests that a plaintiff can reclaim goods even if the original taking was lawful, as long as possession later becomes unlawful, the majority of the New South [13.21]

---

45   *Zecevic v Director of Public Prosecutions (Vic)* (1987) 162 CLR 645; *Watkins v Victoria* [2010] VSCA 138, (2010) 27 VR 543 [71].

46   *Watkins v Victoria* [2010] VSCA 138, (2010) 27 VR 543 [74]; *Pearce v Hallett* [1969] SASR 423.

47   (1962) 108 CLR 177.

48   Ibid, 182 (McTiernan J).

49   [1969] SASR 205.

50   Ibid, 210.

51   *Saler v Klingbiel* [1945] SASR 171; *Goss v Nicholas* [1960] Tas SR 133; *Pearce v Hallett* [1969] SASR 423; *R v Portelli* [2004] VSCA 178, (2004) 10 VR 259; *Watkins v Victoria* [2010] VSCA 138, (2010) 27 VR 543 [75].

52   *Anthony v Haney* (1832) 8 Bing 187, 131 ER 372; *Blades v Higgs* (1861) 10 CB (NS) 713, 142 ER 634.

53   *Anthony v Haney* (1832) 8 Bing 187, 131 ER 372; *Patrick v Colerick* (1838) 3 M & W 482, 150 ER 1235; *Cunningham v Yeomans* (1868) 7 SCR (L) 149.

54   See CA Branston, 'The Forcible Recaption of Chattels' (1912) 28 LQR 262 for a history of the action. Scotland had 'spuilzie' as an analogue to the Roman law *rei vindicatio*: see J Townsend, 'Raising Lazarus: Why Spuilzie should be Resurrected' (2011) 2 Aber St L Rev 22.

55   (1861) 10 CB (NS) 713, 142 ER 634.

Wales Court of Appeal in *Toyota Finance Australia Ltd v Dennis*[56] suggested that recaption is only available if the original taking was unlawful from the beginning.[57] In Queensland, Western Australia and Tasmania, it is lawful for any person entitled by law to the possession of moveable property to take it from an adverse possessor who does not hold it under a claim of right, and to use such force as is reasonably necessary, so long as bodily harm is not caused.[58]

[13.22]   It is questionable whether a person with an immediate right to possession may enter the property of an innocent third party who has the goods on her property. In *Beneficial Finance Corporation Ltd v Alzden Pty Ltd*,[59] Young J said that 'the law as to what happens when someone's property is physically present on another's land is rather obscure'. Blackstone gives the example of a stolen horse stabled in an innocent third party's stable, and suggests that the owner of the horse may not enter the property.[60] In modern times, similar questions arise regarding vehicles which have been parked on a landowner's property without their consent, and the landowner responds by placing a wheel-clamp on the car, but the owner of the car then seeks to retrieve the car by entering the land and removing the wheel-clamp.[61] It is unclear to what extent a person may enter the land of an innocent third party to retrieve property. It appears that if goods came onto the innocent third party's land by accident the possessor may enter the land,[62] whereas if they did not, the possessor may not enter and may only make a demand for the goods, and the third party may not be liable to deliver the goods unless he has exercised dominion over them.[63]

[13.23]   A right of recaption is relevant to common law rescission. If a person recaptures her goods transferred pursuant to a contract which is rescindable at common law for fraud or duress, this is clear evidence of an election to rescind; see [18.33]–[18.40]. However, a person with an equitable right to rescind does not have a right to seize goods transferred under the impugned transaction and, indeed, a person who does so may be liable in trespass or conversion.

[13.24]   Replevin establishes a similar right to recaption, but has developed in the context of creditor law. A secured creditor may file a writ of replevin to obtain possession of goods over which she has security, upon providing a bond or other security to the sheriff, until the court decides the final entitlement to the good (sometimes called 'levying distress' on goods).[64]

---

56   [2002] NSWCA 369, (2002) 58 NSWLR 101 (Sheller JA, with whom Meagher JA agreed; Handley JA dissented). By contrast, in New Zealand and Canada, *Blades v Higgs* is still followed: C Hawes, 'Recaption of Chattels: The Use of Force against the Person' (2006) 12 Cant L Rev 253, 262–64.

57   This approach is endorsed by D Howarth, 'Defences to Intentional Torts' in C Sappideen and P Vines (eds), *Fleming's The Law of Torts* (10th edn, LBC 2011) [5.130].

58   *Criminal Code Act 1899* (Qld), s 276; *Criminal Code Act 1924* (Tas), s 45; *Criminal Code Act 1913* (WA), s 253.

59   (NSWSC Equity Division, 10 May 1993) 2.

60   Sir W Blackstone, *Commentaries on the Laws of England*, vol 3 (OUP 1768) 5. See *Fitzgerald v Kellion Estates Pty Ltd* (1977) 2 BPR 9181 (horses left on purchaser's land after vendor had sold it, vendor sought to repossess the horses).

61   See L Aitken, 'The Abandonment and Recaption of Chattels' (1994) 68 Aust LJ 263, 277–79; *Stear v Scott* [1992] RTR 226; *Lloyd v Director of Public Prosecutions* [1992] RTR 215. Cf *Carmichael v Black* (High Court of Justiciary (Scotland), 12 June 1992).

62   *Anthony v Haney* (1832) 8 Bing 187, 192; 131 ER 372, 374: Tindal CJ gives examples of fruit or trees falling over on another's property.

63   *Fitzgerald v Kellion Estates Pty Ltd* (1977) 2 BPR 9181, 9186; *Moffatt v Kazana* [1969] 2 QB 152, 157.

64   L Aitken, 'The Abandonment and Recaption of Chattels' (1994) 68 Aust LJ 263, 280.

However, the extent of availability of replevin in Australia is unclear. It may extend to persons beyond creditors, and is theoretically available to all kinds of takings amounting to trespass.[65]

A person whose goods have been wrongfully taken may be able obtain an order for specific restitution of the goods; see [10.114]–[10.118]. This takes us beyond self-help remedies (as the court is involved), but the limitations on this doctrine explain why courts allow persons to obtain goods themselves: it is partly because the plaintiff is unlikely to be able to get her goods back pursuant to a court order unless they are unique.[66]   [13.25]

E   Abatement of nuisance

The tort of nuisance involves a substantial and unreasonable interference with the use and enjoyment of land (for example, water, smoke, noise, undermining of the land or any other inconvenience). A person who has an action in nuisance may remove the source of the inconvenience through abatement. For example, if branches are over-hanging a person's fence or roots are growing into a person's land, in all states except New South Wales the person has a right to remove the branches or roots up to the boundary line, as long as she returns them to the other person's land.[67] Again, this self-help remedy has origins dating back to the 13th century at least.[68]   [13.26]

'Abatement' refers to the act of removal of the source of the nuisance, but does not extend to acts undertaken to alleviate the effects of the interference, so that in *Young v Wheeler*[69] the plaintiff was not able to recover the cost of installing PVC pipes that were resistant to cypress roots; only the removal of the roots would have constituted abatement. It is unclear whether costs of abatement are recoverable. In *Corbett v Pallas*, the plaintiff recovered the cost of erecting a wall to prevent water from the defendant's pool flooding his property.[70] However, a series of cases have suggested that the cost of effecting abatement is not recoverable because the abatement destroys the nuisance.[71] An exception is made in *Proprietors of Strata Plan No 14198 v Cowell* for acts of abatement occurring only on the plaintiff's land and representing a reasonable attempt to mitigate the damages.[72] The cases preventing recovery of costs of   [13.27]

---

65   Ibid, 280–81. Aitken notes that its position in England, Wales and New Zealand is also uncertain, but it is available in Canada.

66   C Hawes, 'Recaption of Chattels: The Use of Force against the Person' (2006) 12 Cant L Rev 253, 253–54. As Hawes notes, self-help may be advantageous to a plaintiff for other reasons: it may be quicker and cheaper than legal action, and it will be particularly useful where the goods are perishable or likely to be on-sold or destroyed.

67   *Lemmon v Webb* [1895] AC 1. In New South Wales, the action for nuisance has been abolished in respect of encroaching trees, and a person wishing to cut a tree must apply for a court order: *Trees (Disputes Between Neighbours) Act 2006* (NSW), s 5 and pt 2; *Robson v Leischke* [2008] NSWLEC 152, (2008) 72 NSWLR 98 [217]–[219].

68   P Giliker, 'Nuisance' in C Sappideen and P Vines (eds), *Fleming's The Law of Torts* (10th edn, LBC 2011) [21.280].

69   (1987) Aust Torts Reports 80–126.

70   (1995) Aust Torts Reports 81–329, 86 LGERA 312.

71   *Young v Wheeler* (1987) Aust Torts Reports 80–126; *City of Richmond v Scantelbury* [1991] 2 VR 38, 48; *Proprietors of Strata Plan No 14198 v Cowell* (1989) 24 NSWLR 478.

72   (1989) 29 NSWLR 478, 487.

abatement have been criticised for providing an incentive to let the nuisance destroy the property rather than attempt to nip the nuisance in the bud.[73]

[13.28]   A person may do only what is necessary to avert the harm and the law restricts recovery of damages once abatement occurs. If there are two ways of abating a nuisance, the less harmful must be adopted unless it would injure a third party or the public.[74] *Traian v Ware*[75] is a case where abatement was unreasonable. The plaintiffs and the defendants were farmers on adjoining blocks of land situated on a slope. The plaintiffs' land was downhill from the defendants' land. Fifteen years previously, a predecessor in title of the plaintiffs' land had built a bank at the top of the lower land to prevent it being flooded. During heavy rain, the bank caused water to collect on the defendants' higher land. On three occasions, the defendants entered the plaintiffs' land and cut the bank without notice. On each occasion, this caused a sudden flow of water, damaging the plaintiffs' crops and orchards. The plaintiffs sued the defendants for damages in nuisance and trespass, and sought an injunction to restrain the defendants from cutting the bank again. The defendants counterclaimed for a declaration that they were entitled to have natural flow of water unimpeded, and for an injunction to prevent the bank from being repaired. Martin J held that the plaintiffs had an obligation to receive the natural flow of the water from the defendants' land and that this was a nuisance. However, persons who seek to abate a nuisance must generally give notice of an intention to do so, because entry onto someone else's land is prima facie a trespass. The defendants had not given notice to the plaintiffs nor asked for permission to cut the bank. Martin J awarded damages against the defendant for trespass because of their 'unauthorised and high handed' conduct.[76] The defendants were not entitled to an injunction as they elected to abate. However, a declaration was made that the defendants were entitled to have the natural flow of water discharged onto the plaintiffs' land.

[13.29]   Witzleb, Bant, Degeling and Barker observe that self-help to abate a nuisance may result in violent action,[77] as evidenced by *R v Macarthur*.[78] A magistrate named John Macarthur intervened in a dispute between two landowners, Holwell and Raine, over the right to water. Macarthur purportedly encouraged a large group of people to enter onto Raine's land and fill up a trench which was alleged to be diverting water from Holwell's land. This caused a breach of the peace. The court lamented that 'in a case in which there was obviously a question of right to be tried, the more judicious course should not have been resorted to, of trying that question by civil action, instead of resorting to violent measures'.[79] Macarthur was charged with riot. Although the charge was dismissed, costs were ordered against Macarthur, and he then attempted (unsuccessfully) to impeach the Supreme Court.[80]

---

73   JC Sheahan, 'Use and Misuse of Legal History: Case Studies from the Law of Contract, Tort and Restitution' (1997–98) 16 Aust Bar Rev 280, 287.

74   *Lagan Navigation Co v Lambeg Bleaching Co* [1927] AC 226, 245.

75   [1957] VR 200.

76   Ibid, 208.

77   N Witzleb, E Bant, S Degeling and K Barker, *Remedies: Commentary and Materials* (6th edn, LBC 2015) [2.20].

78   (1828) Sel Case (Dowling) 882; [1828] NSWSC 6, <http://www.law.mq.edu.au/research/colonial_case_law/nsw/cases/case_index/1828/r_v_macarthur/>.

79   Ibid, 31.

80   Macarthur later became famous for introducing the merino to Australia, and featured on the old Australian two dollar note.

III   Contract and self-help

Contract law allows more latitude in self-help as contracts arise consensually, and liberal society is generally premised on the idea that we should have freedom of contracting. This extends to remedies. [13.30]

First, rescission can be seen as a form of self-help, in at least some cases. Suppose that the defendant has supplied the plaintiff with defective goods. The plaintiff may simply elect to return the goods to the defendant and the defendant returns the purchase price to the plaintiff, without any recourse to a court. This is arguably a form of self-help,[81] although the transaction is conducted in the shadow of the law. However, other cases of rescission require court intervention because of the adjustments courts must make to achieve 'practical justice'. [13.31]

Secondly, parties to a contract may exercise self-help after a breach of contract has occurred by stipulating the amount of damages which arise (a liquidated damages clause). Sometimes parties may stipulate other practical consequences of breach (such as forfeiture of an interest). [13.32]

Thirdly, parties may stipulate that an amount is recoverable as a debt rather than in damages, allowing easier recovery. [13.33]

Finally, parties may declare in the contract that certain terms are so important to them that their breach will give rise to the right to end performance (no matter how minor said breaches appear to objective onlookers).[82] Contracts might also detail when or how termination will occur.[83] Nor need a self-created remedy be linked to breach of contract. The parties may provide that if certain events occur outside the control of either of them, then both parties are released from contract.[84] These are self-help remedies because they enable parties to set the circumstances where they may terminate a contract without the intervention of the law, and in circumstances where the common law might not otherwise allow termination. [13.34]

A   Rescission

As noted at [18.5], rescission (at least in some of its forms) can be argued to be a self-help remedy because the right holder gives notice of her election to rescind to the other party.[85] However, rescission can also be understood as a remedy granted by the court rather than as a self-help remedy in other cases (particularly where equitable rescission of an executed contract is concerned). It has been argued that equitable rescission in equity's exclusive jurisdiction (that is, where the vitiating factor is not fraud or duress) is always the act of the court.[86] [13.35]

---

81   R Posner, *Economic Analysis of Law* (9th edn, Aspen 2014) §4.14.
82   J Paterson, A Robertson and A Duke, *Principles of Contract Law* (5th edn, LBC 2016) [21.25]–[21.35]; D Harris, D Campbell and R Halson, *Remedies in Contract and Tort* (2nd edn, CUP 2005) 145.
83   Paterson, Robertson and Duke, ibid, ch 19 on termination by agreement.
84   Ibid, ch 20 on contingent conditions.
85   *Alati v Kruger* (1955) 94 CLR 216, 225–26; L Proksch, 'Rescission' in P Parkinson (ed), *The Principles of Equity* (2nd edn, LBC 2003) [2506].
86   JD Heydon, MJ Leeming and PG Turner, *Meagher, Gummow and Lehane's Equity: Doctrines and Remedies* (5th edn, LexisNexis Butterworths 2015) [25–105]; D O'Sullivan, S Elliott and R Zakrzewski, *The Law of Rescission* (OUP 2008) [12.11]–[12.24].

[13.36] It is suggested here that where a contract is executory, or where common law rescission is concerned,[87] it is possible to see rescission as a 'self-help' remedy that is not dependent upon an order of the court. But insofar as equitable rescission of an executed or partly executed contract is concerned, the court's jurisdiction to award rescission 'on terms' or 'partial rescission' suggests that rescission is a judicial remedy, not 'self-help'.

B   Liquidated damages and penalties

[13.37] A liquidated damages clause stipulates damages (sometimes also known as an 'agreed' damages clause). This is a form of self-help because the parties estimate the losses flowing from the breach of contract rather than obtaining a judicial assessment of the loss caused by the breach. A typical liquidated damages clause might be: 'For a breach of cl 35 of this agreement, liquidated damages of $1000 shall be payable'. In many cases, a major aim of remedies created by parties to a contract is to bypass the expense and hostility of litigation.

[13.38] In *Ringrow Pty Ltd v BP Australia Pty Ltd*, the High Court of Australia said that '[t]he law of contract normally upholds the freedom of parties, with no relevant disability, to agree upon the terms of their future relationships'.[88] Thus, in principle, parties to a contract may include any terms they want in a contract, including remedies for breach of its provisions. However, there are several important exceptions to this.

[13.39] First, as the High Court observed in *Andrews v Australia and New Zealand Banking Group Ltd*, the various legislative schemes and codes which attempt to prevent unjust transactions suggest 'the need for caution in dealing with the unwritten law as if *laissez faire* notions of an untrammelled "freedom of contract" provide a universal legal value'.[89] In other words, the enactment of legislation such as the Australian Consumer Law means that parties to contracts are not entirely free to contract as they wish.

[13.40] Secondly, both equity and common law preclude 'penalties' in contracts. A penalty is a payment of money or an obligation imposed *in terrorem* of the other party (that is, intended to frighten or intimidate), whereas a liquidated damages clause protects a 'legitimate interest' of the contracting party.[90] There are two questions a court must ask when establishing whether a clause is a penalty and thus void or unenforceable:

1. Is this a clause to which penalties doctrine applies?
2. On the facts, is this clause a penalty?

As will be discussed, the High Court in *Andrews* broadened the clauses to which the penalties doctrine applied. However, after *Paciocco*,[91] most clauses will *not* be penalties on the facts because the innocent party merely needs to point to a 'legitimate interest' to be protected.[92]

---

87   *Halpern v Halpern (No 2)* [2006] EWHC 1728 (Comm), [2007] QB 88 [26].
88   [2005] HCA 71, (2005) 224 CLR 656 [31] (Gleeson CJ, Gummow, Kirby, Hayne, Callinan and Heydon JJ).
89   [2012] HCA 30, (2012) 247 CLR 205 [5] (French CJ, Gummow, Crennan, Kiefel and Bell JJ) ('*Andrews*').
90   *Paciocco v Australia and New Zealand Banking Group Ltd* [2016] HCA 28, (2016) 258 CLR 525 [51]–[56] (Kiefel J, with whom French CJ agreed on penalties), [166] (Gageler J) and [269]–[270] (Keane J) ('*Paciocco*').
91   [2016] HCA 28, (2016) 258 CLR 525.
92   K Barnett, 'Coralling the Penalties Horse: *Paciocco v Australia and New Zealand Banking Group Ltd*' on *Opinions on High* (8 August 2016) <http://blogs.unimelb.edu.au/opinionsonhigh/2016/08/08/barnett-paciocco>.

1   Is this a clause to which the penalties doctrine applies?

The penalties doctrine was previously thought to require a detriment upon a breach of contract.[93] Thus, a clause drafted as follows would be likely to engage the penalties doctrine:

(a)   *Yolanda will hire out her bike to Zachariah on the first Thursday of each month for $10 on the condition that the bike is not used at any other time.*

(b)   *If (a) is breached and Zachariah uses the bicycle on any other day of the week he must pay $1000 to Yolanda.*

However, it was possible to draft the clause in such a way as to ensure that a breach of contract does not trigger the payment:

(a)   *Yolanda will hire out her bicycle to Zachariah on the first Thursday of each month for $10.*

(b)   *If Zachariah uses the bicycle on any other day, he agrees to pay Yolanda $1000.*

In *Interstar Wholesale Finance Pty Ltd v Integral Home Loans Pty Ltd*,[94] the NSW Court of Appeal held that the second method of drafting did not engage the rule against penalties, even though it is in substance the same obligation as the first.

However, the High Court of Australia overruled *Interstar* in *Andrews*. *Andrews* involved a class action where ANZ Bank customers argued that the fees the bank had charged them in relation to transactions made on their accounts were penalties. At first instance, it was held that the only fees which were capable of being characterised as a penalty were late payment fees, whereas honour fees, dishonour fees, over limit fees and non-payment fees were held not to be penalties because the trigger for payment was not a breach of contract.[95] On appeal, the High Court said that the doctrine of penalties does not necessarily require a breach of contract before it is engaged. The High Court emphasised that it is the substance of the clause which matters, not the form.[96] Moreover, the court confirmed that the doctrine against penalties has an equitable aspect, and that equity can provide relief from stipulations which are drafted in a permissive manner but which are substantively the same as clauses that provide for penalties payable on breach.[97] The court described the rule against penalties as follows:

> In general terms, a stipulation *prima facie* imposes a penalty on a party ('the first party') if, as a matter of substance, it is collateral (or accessory) to a primary stipulation in favour of a second party and this collateral stipulation, upon the failure of the primary stipulation,

[13.41]

[13.42]

93   *Campbell Discount Co Ltd v Bridge* [1962] AC 600, 613–14 (Viscount Simonds); *Office of Fair Trading v Abbey National plc* [2008] EWHC 875, [2008] 2 All ER (Comm) 625 [296]; *Interstar Wholesale Finance Pty Ltd v Integral Home Loans Pty Ltd* [2008] NSWCA 310, (2008) 257 ALR 292 [106]; *Fermiscan Pty Ltd v James* [2009] NSWCA 355, (2009) 261 ALR 408 [134]–[136]; *Diakos v Mason* [2010] SASCFC 37, (2010) 272 LSJS 185 [16], [18]; *First East Auction Holdings Pty Ltd v Ange* [2010] VSC 72 [151], [157]. See S Harder, 'The Relevance of Breach to the Applicability of the Rule against Penalties' (2013) 30 J Cont L 52.

94   (2008) 257 ALR 292, [2008] NSWCA 310 ('*Interstar*'). Special leave to appeal was granted (*Integral Home Loans Pty Ltd v Interstar Wholesale Financial Pty Ltd* [2009] HCATrans 87), but before the appeal commenced, the parties settled.

95   [2011] FCA 1376, (2011) 211 FCR 53.

96   [2012] HCA 30, (2012) 247 CLR 205 [49]. See *Integral Home Loans Pty Ltd v Interstar Wholesale Finance Pty Ltd (No 1)* [2007] NSWSC 406, (2007) Aust Contract R 90–261 [73].

97   [2012] HCA 30, (2012) 247 CLR 205 [33]–[45].

imposes upon the first party an additional detriment, the penalty, to the benefit of the second party. In that sense, the collateral or accessory stipulation is described as being in the nature of a security for and *in terrorem* of the satisfaction of the primary stipulation. If compensation can be made to the second party for the prejudice suffered by failure of the primary stipulation, the collateral stipulation and the penalty are enforced only to the extent of that compensation. The first party is relieved to that degree from liability to satisfy the collateral stipulation.[98]

[13.43]   However, the High Court also said that contracting parties remain free to put in their contract a clause which allows for a higher payment if further services or rights are provided by one party (an 'alternative stipulation').[99] It affirmed *Metro-Goldwyn-Mayer Pty Ltd v Greenham*, a case which involved a contract for the hiring of films to exhibitors for public showing.[100] The standard form contract conferred the right to one screening at a particular time, but if the exhibitor wished to make additional showings, he was obliged to pay a sum which was four times the original fee. A majority of the NSW Court of Appeal decided that this additional payment was not a penalty, but a legitimate option to obtain the right to further screenings for a higher price.

[13.44]   *Andrews* clarifies that breaches of contract are not necessary to engage the penalties doctrine, but raises new difficulties.[101] Australian appellate courts dealing with commercial contracts have tended to minimise the impact of *Andrews*. For example, in *Kellas-Sharpe v PSAL Ltd*, the Queensland Court of Appeal declined to extend the penalties rule to a loan contract which provided for a lower rate of interest if the borrower paid on time,[102] despite the possibility that *Andrews* could have been read as prohibiting such clauses. The court found that the principle that these clauses were not penalties was too well established in commercial law to be overturned.[103] The High Court declined to award special leave.[104] The UK Supreme Court also declined to follow *Andrews* in *Cavendish Square Holding BV v Makdessi*,[105] although it did note that the classification of terms for the purposes of the penalty rule depended on substance not form.[106]

[13.45]   It has been observed that the distinction made in *Andrews* between collateral stipulations and alternative stipulations is not easy to draw.[107] The difficulties can be illustrated as follows. It is unclear whether, under *Andrews*, the second, permissively drafted clause at [13.41] would be caught by the penalties rule. It may be that the second clause would be an 'alternative stipulation'

---

98   Ibid, [10] (French CJ, Gummow, Crennan, Kiefel and Bell JJ).
99   The High Court cited JN Pomeroy, *A Treatise on Equity Jurisprudence* (5th edn, Bancroft-Whitney 1941) vol 2, §437. See also *French v Macale* [1835–42] All ER Rep 6, (1842) 2 Dr & War 269, 275–76.
100   [1966] 2 NSWR 717.
101   See JW Carter, W Courtney, E Peden, A Stewart and GJ Tolhurst, 'Contractual Penalties: Resurrecting the Equitable Jurisdiction' (2013) 30 J Cont L 99; S Harder, 'The Scope of the Rule against Contractual Penalties: A New Divergence' in A Robertson and M Tilbury (eds), *Divergences in Private Law* (Hart 2016) 135. Cf, however, PS Davies and PG Turner, 'Relief against Penalties without a Breach of Contract' (2013) 72 Camb LJ 20.
102   [2012] QCA 371.
103   Ibid [32]–[41] (Gotterson JA).
104   *Kellas-Sharpe v PSAL Limited* [2013] HCA Trans 133.
105   [2015] UKSC 67, [2016] AC 1172 [42]–[43] (Lord Neuberger and Lord Sumption, with whom Lords Clarke and Carnwath agreed), [130] (Lord Mance) and [240] (Lord Hodge) ('*Cavendish*').
106   Ibid, [415] (Lord Neuberger and Lord Sumption).
107   E Peel, 'The Rule against Penalties' (2013) 129 LQR 152, 156.

whereby Zachariah simply agreed to pay a greater sum for the privilege of using the bicycle on other days. On the other hand, it may be that the second clause would be a 'collateral stipulation' as there is an additional detriment imposed upon Zachariah for breach of the clause. However, it is not clear whether the sum is disproportionate and 'out of all proportion'. It appears from *Ringrow*[108] and *AMEV-UDC Finance Ltd v Austin*[109] that disproportion will only be considered if the sum is 'out of all proportion' and 'extravagant and disproportionate in amount'. However, it remains unclear to what extent disparity of bargaining power is relevant. Dicta in *AMEV-UDC Finance Ltd v Austin* suggest that the nature of the relationship between the parties is a factor relevant to the assessment of whether a clause is a penalty or not,[110] but other dicta suggest that this should not be overemphasised.[111] In *Paciocco*, the follow-up case to *Andrews*, only Nettle J (dissenting) considered inequality of bargaining power.[112]

2   On the facts, is this clause a penalty?

The second question which must be asked is whether the clause is in fact a penalty. For many years, the relevant test was that of Lord Dunedin in *Dunlop Pneumatic Tyre Co Ltd v New Garage and Motor Co Ltd*.[113] His Lordship said that a clause is likely to be a penalty 'if the sum stipulated for is extravagant and unconscionable in amount in comparison with the greatest loss that could conceivably be proved to have followed from the breach'.[114] As a corollary of that, if the breach consists only of not paying a sum of money, the clause will be a penalty if the sum stipulated is a sum greater than the sum which ought to have been paid. Moreover, there is a presumption that a clause is a penalty when a single lump sum is made payable on the occurrence of one or more events, some of which are serious and others less serious, but this presumption may be rebutted. Conversely, a sum may be a genuine pre-estimate even if the consequences of the breach are such as to make a precise pre-estimate impossible. In fact, Lord Dunedin said that this is 'just the situation when it is probable that pre-estimated damage was the true bargain between the parties.'[115]

[13.46]

However, *Paciocco* now suggests that the operative test is whether the party imposing the detriment has a legitimate interest in performance of the primary stipulation.[116] The legitimate interest tests proposed by the majority drew from the UK Supreme Court's decision in *Cavendish*.[117] *Paciocco* was the follow-on case from *Andrews*, where the High Court went

[13.47]

---

108   [2005] HCA 71, (2005) 224 CLR 656 [31]–[32].
109   (1986) 162 CLR 170, 190 (Mason and Wilson JJ).
110   Ibid, 193 (Mason and Wilson JJ).
111   *Esanda Finance Corporation Ltd v Plessnig* (1989) 166 CLR 131, 142 (Wilson and Toohey JJ).
112   [2016] HCA 28, (2016) 258 CLR 525 [309], [371].
113   [1915] AC 79, 87–88; adopted in *Ringrow Pty Ltd v BP Australia Pty Ltd* [2005] HCA 71, (2005) 224 CLR 656.
114   [1915] AC 79, 87.
115   Ibid, 88.
116   [2016] HCA 28, (2016) 258 CLR 525.
117   *Cavendish Square Holding BV v Makdessi* [2015] UKSC 67, [2016] AC 1172 [32] (Lord Neuberger and Lord Sumption, with whom Lord Clarke and Lord Carnwath agreed), [152] (Lord Mance, with whom Lord Clarke and Lord Toulson agreed), [255] (Lord Hodge, with whom Lord Clarke and Lord Toulson agreed) ('*Cavendish*'). In *Paciocco* [2016] HCA 28, (2016) 258 CLR 525, Kiefel J (with whom French CJ agreed on penalties) at [54] drew on Lord Neuberger and Lord Sumption's test in *Cavendish*, Keane J at [270] drew on Lord Hodge's test in *Cavendish*, and Gageler J at [166] drew upon *Cavendish* generally in regard to a 'legitimate interest'.

on to decide whether the bank fees imposed on credit accounts were in fact penalties, but with a different lead plaintiff. ANZ had admitted that it did not calculate the fees on its credit cards according to what was recoverable as damages. It conducted an *ex post facto* consideration of the costs it incurred, which included losses which would not have been available as contract damages.

[13.48]   Nevertheless, the majority in *Paciocco* held that ANZ had a legitimate interest in obtaining performance of the primary stipulations, and it did not matter that ANZ had not pre-estimated the costs before imposing the fees; nor did it matter that the costs could not be recovered as damages. It was found that ANZ had a legitimate interest in receiving timely payment of credit.[118] Moreover, in *Paciocco*, two of the four judges in the majority agreed that the bank also had an interest in obtaining a profit which allowed for fees to be charged.[119] Nettle J dissented, observing that the bank's sole interest was in recovering losses, and that there was no reason to apply the legitimate interest test instead of the *Dunlop* test in that case.[120]

[13.49]   The upshot of *Paciocco* seems to be that as long as there is a reasonable explanation for a potentially penal clause, the legitimate interest test means that courts will allow the clause to stand.[121]

3   Should we have a law against penalties at all?

[13.50]   Some law-and-economics scholars have argued that the law should allow parties to a contract to include penalties as this will increase efficiency in contracting.[122] They argue that problems of inequality of bargaining power and the like are better dealt with by other doctrines within contract law, and a party for whom an obligation has an idiosyncratic value should be able to signal to the other party that the obligation is particularly important to her by including a penalty fee.[123] A difficulty with this argument is that some parties may not be aware of the ramifications of damages clauses,[124] particularly where a consumer signs a standard form contract with a business. On the other hand, there is a paternalistic flavour to the penalties doctrine, because the court remakes the parties' bargain in a way which is arguably inconsistent with other doctrines of contract law.[125] It seems to directly conflict with notions of freedom of contract (i.e. parties should be free to stipulate obligations as they wish). Lanyon has argued that the most convincing rationale for the retention of a penalties doctrine is

---

118   [2016] HCA 28, (2016) 258 CLR 525 [58] (Kiefel J, with whom French CJ agreed on penalties), [172] and [176] (Gageler J), [274]–[277] (Keane J).

119   Ibid, [172] (Gageler J), [278] (Keane J).

120   Ibid, [317]–[334] (Nettle J).

121   J Palmer, 'Implications of the New Rule against Penalties' (2016) 47 VUWLR 305, 312.

122   See, eg, CJ Goetz and RE Scott, 'Liquidated Damages, Penalties and the Just Compensation Principle: Some Notes on an Enforcement Model and a Theory of Efficient Breach' (1977) 77 Col L Rev 554; A Ham, 'The Rule against Penalties in Contract: An Economic Perspective' (1990) 17 MULR 649. See R Posner, *Economic Analysis of Law* (9th edn, Aspen 2014) §4.12 for an in-depth discussion of the economic pros and cons of penalty causes and explanations as to why courts may not enforce them.

123   Goetz and Scott, ibid; Ham, ibid, 660. Cf S Rea, 'Efficiency Implications of Penalties and Liquidated Damages' (1984) 13 J Leg Stud 147, 157.

124   Rea, ibid, 160; E Lanyon, 'Equity and the Doctrine of Penalties' (1996) 9 J Cont L 234, 239.

125   Lanyon, ibid, 239.

procedural unfairness, and that substantive unfairness and the possibility of unfair or inefficient compulsion of performance are not convincing reasons to retain the doctrine.[126] Harris, Campbell and Halson have noted that if the sole convincing justification of the penalties doctrine is to prevent a weaker party from being oppressed by the unconscionable use of bargaining power by a stronger party, then it is difficult to see why only liquidated damages clauses are rendered unenforceable by courts, as any kind of clause can be drafted unfairly.[127] The logical conclusion of this is that statutory provisions achieve the aims of guarding against misuse of market power better than the penalties doctrine.[128]

C   Debt

It is easier for a plaintiff to recover a debt than damages, and accordingly a plaintiff may draft her contract so as to allow her to claim in debt instead of in damages. A claim in debt differs from a claim in damages for breach of contract.[129] The conditions required to establish a debt are set out at [10.119]–[10.121]. In essence, all that is required is that the sum becomes due upon the occurrence of a specific event. The rules of remoteness and mitigation do not apply. [13.51]

The rule against penalties was said not to apply to acceleration of a debt in *O'Dea v Allstates Leasing System (WA) Pty Ltd*, where Gibbs CJ said: [13.52]

> If a sum of money is payable by instalments, and it is provided that in the event of one instalment not being punctually paid the whole sum shall immediately become payable, the acceleration of payment is not a penalty ... Similarly there is no penalty where it is agreed to charge a certain rate of interest on condition that if payment is made punctually the rate will be reduced ... or where a creditor agrees to accept payment of part of his debt in full discharge if certain conditions are met but stipulates that if the conditions are not met he will be entitled to recover the original debt.[130]

His Honour explained that if the debtor fails to meet the condition and the debt is accelerated, the creditor is not entitled to damages, but to the debt which was always owing.

However, the rule against penalties still applies if the contract provides that upon the defendant's failure to pay the specified sum, a larger sum becomes payable.[131] Similarly, a debt may be a penalty where the real substance of the acceleration of the debt is to operate a penalty for non-performance.[132] Or a debt may be subject to relief against forfeiture.[133] [13.53]

---

126   Ibid, 237–42. See also S Rea, 'Efficiency Implications of Penalties and Liquidated Damages' (1984) 13 J Leg Stud 147.
127   D Harris, D Campbell and R Halson, *Remedies in Contract and Tort* (2nd edn, CUP 2005) 146.
128   S Harder, 'The Scope of the Rule against Contractual Penalties: A New Divergence' in A Robertson and M Tilbury (eds), *Divergences in Private Law* (Hart 2016) 156–57. The argument is even stronger now after the unfair terms regime of the Australian Consumer Law has been amended to protect small businesses as well as consumers.
129   *Young v Queensland Trustees Ltd* (1956) 99 CLR 560, 569 (Dixon CJ, McTiernan and Taylor JJ).
130   (1983) 152 CLR 359, 366.
131   *Dunlop Pneumatic Tyre Co Ltd v New Garage and Motor Co Ltd* [1915] AC 79, 86.
132   *O'Dea v Allstates Leasing System (WA) Pty Ltd* (1983) 152 CLR 359.
133   J Paterson, A Robertson and A Duke, *Principles of Contract Law* (5th edn, LBC 2016) [29.85].

D Other stipulated contractual remedies

[13.54] As noted at [13.30]–[13.34], self-help remedies in contract are not restricted to terms stipulating payment of money.

[13.55] Parties do not generally specify that they should be entitled to specific performance or an injunction upon breach of a contract. There are no cases where parties have attempted to enforce such a clause in Australia,[134] and it is unlikely that such a clause would be enforced, although perhaps it may be a factor which suggests that damages are inadequate in the circumstances.[135]

[13.56] By contrast, parties sometimes stipulate that they are only liable for damages and that the remedy of specific performance is excluded.[136] Generally, however, there is a presumption that contracting parties do not intend to exclude common law remedies, and such a clause will be valid only if the parties have used clear words to indicate that they intend to exclude contractual remedies which arise by operation of law.[137]

[13.57] Another stipulated remedy involves termination clauses. Upon the occurrence of a breach, the non-breaching party has a choice (unless other elections are also involved) to affirm or terminate the contract. This is a self-help act in that she is exercising her right to terminate without the imprimatur of the court.[138] The common law gives a right to terminate a contract for a breach of an 'essential' term,[139] or for a serious breach of an 'innominate' or 'intermediate' term.[140] However, contracting parties may also include clauses which entitle one or both parties to terminate the contract more easily than under common law. For example, parties may declare in the contract that certain terms are so important to them that their breach will give rise to the right to end performance, no matter how minor these breaches appear.[141] Contracts might also detail when or how termination will occur.[142] This allows a non-breaching party to exercise her right to exit the contract as expeditiously as possible without involving a court.

[13.58] Termination clauses protect the party who can rely on the termination clause to end the contract and give the other party an incentive to perform.[143] Consequently, they have sometimes been held to be penalties, particularly where the termination clause also stipulates damages to be paid upon termination.[144] A termination clause in a consumer contract or a

---

134 R Carroll, 'Agreements to Specifically Perform Contractual Obligations' (2012) 29 J Cont L 155, 168.

135 Ibid, 181–82.

136 Ibid, 167.

137 *Stocznia Gdanksa SA v Latvian Shipping Co* [1998] 1 WLR 574, 585; *Concut Pty Ltd v Worrell* [2000] HCA 64, (2000) 176 ALR 693 [23]; *MLW Technology Pty Ltd v May* [2005] VSCA 29 [59], [60].

138 S Rowan, *Remedies for Breach of Contract: A Comparative Analysis of the Protection of Performance* (OUP 2012) 78.

139 *Tramways Advertising Pty Ltd v Luna Park* (1938) 61 CLR 286; *Associated Newspapers Ltd v Bancks* (1951) 83 CLR 322.

140 *Koompahtoo Local Aboriginal Land Council v Sanpine Pty Ltd* [2007] HCA 61, (2007) 233 CLR 115; *Hongkong Fir Shipping Co Ltd v Kawasaki Kisen Kaisha Ltd* [1962] 2 QB 26.

141 J Paterson, A Robertson and A Duke, *Principles of Contract Law* (5th edn, LBC 2016) [21.25]–[21.35]; D Harris, D Campbell and R Halson, *Remedies in Contract and Tort* (2nd edn, CUP 2005) 145.

142 Paterson, Robertson and Duke, ibid, ch 19 on termination by agreement. See also J Carter, 'Termination Clauses' (1990) 3 J Cont L 90, 94–95.

143 H Beale, 'Penalties in Termination Provisions' (1988) 104 LQR 355, 359.

144 *AMEV-UDC Finance Ltd v Austin* (1986) 162 CLR 170; *O'Dea v Allstates Leasing System (WA) Pty Ltd* (1983) 152 CLR 359; *Zachariadis v Allforks Australia Pty Ltd* [2009] VSCA 258, (2009) 26 VR 47. Cf *Esanda Finance Corporation Ltd v Plessnig* (1989) 166 CLR 131 (not a penalty).

small business contract is subject to the unfair terms provisions of the Australian Consumer Law.[145]

Self-created contractual stipulation need not be linked to breach of contract. The parties may provide that if certain events occur outside the control of either of them, both parties are released from contract by means of a contingent condition.[146]

[13.59]

---

145   *Competition and Consumer Act 2010* (Cth), sch 2, pt 2-3, especially s 25(b).
146   J Paterson, A Robertson and A Duke, *Principles of Contract Law* (5th edn, LBC 2016) ch 20. See, eg, *Suttor v Gundowda Pty Ltd* (1950) 81 CLR 418; *Perri v Coolangatta Investments Pty Ltd* (1982) 149 CLR 537.

14

EXEMPLARY DAMAGES AND AGGRAVATED DAMAGES

I   Introduction

In this chapter we consider exemplary damages and aggravated damages, remedies with a strong vindicatory flavour.   [14.1]

Exemplary damages vindicate the plaintiff's interests, but also explicitly *punish* the defendant for the wrong in question. Punishment is not commonly recognised as a central aim of private law. Some commentators have argued that it should not be part of private law. However, exemplary damages are said to validate the plaintiff's feelings of hurt and anger arising from the contumelious nature of the defendant's wrong. Such damages also perform a vindicatory function. The fact that the law punishes a defendant for the manner of his interference with the plaintiff's interests signals the importance of those interests.[1]   [14.2]

Aggravated damages aim to compensate the plaintiff for distress caused by the contumelious nature of the defendant's breach. They have been said to protect the dignitary interest of the plaintiff, or to be a form of damages for distress. They are arguably partly punitive and partly compensatory in nature. Jason Varuhas has observed that '[i]t seems right that such damages are available within a vindicatory body of law, to the extent that such damages recognize that a deplorable and disrespectful interference with one's fundamental interests is so serious an affront that it will naturally damage one's feelings of dignity and pride'.[2]   [14.3]

Each species of damages is only available exceptionally for some causes of action, particularly for torts actionable per se[3] and where statutes specify availability.   [14.4]

II   Exemplary damages

A   The nature and history of exemplary damages in Australia

Damages at civil law are generally compensatory, but exemplary damages are a separate category of award and do not compensate for loss, but punish and deter.[4] They also seek to assuage any anger arising from the wrongdoing and to discourage plaintiffs from seeking self-help likely to breach the peace.[5] Punishment also provides public vindication of the plaintiff's rights.[6] Importantly, exemplary damages are payable not to the state, but to the plaintiff.[7] This contributes to the controversy over exemplary damages – while there may be a reason to   [14.5]

---

1   JNE Varuhas, 'The Concept of 'Vindication' in the Law of Torts: Rights, Interests and Damages' (2014) 34 OJLS 253, 290

2   Ibid, 284.

3   Ibid.

4   *Whitfield v De Lauret & Co Ltd* (1920) 29 CLR 71, 77 (Knox CJ), 81 (Isaacs J); *Rookes v Barnard* [1964] AC 1129, 1221 (Lord Devlin); *Uren v John Fairfax & Sons Pty Ltd* (1966) 117 CLR 118, 129–30 (Taylor J), 149 (Windeyer J).

5   *Lamb v Cotogno* (1987) 164 CLR 1, 9. Exemplary damages were apparently instituted to prevent duelling: *Merest v Harvey* (1814) 5 Taunt 442, 444; 128 ER 761, 761 (Heath J).

6   J Feinberg, 'The Expressive Function of Punishment' in J Feinberg (ed), *Doing and Deserving* (Princeton University Press 1970) 95, 104.

7   *Gray v Motor Accident Commission* [1998] HCA 70, (1998) 196 CLR 1 [15] (Gleeson CJ, McHugh, Gummow and Hayne JJ).

punish the defendant, it is more difficult to justify why the plaintiff should get them.[8] In *Couch v Attorney-General (No 2)*, Wilson J observed that if exemplary damages were introduced in the present day, there would be a 'good argument' that they should be payable to the state, like a fine.[9]

[14.6]   In Australia, these awards are known as 'exemplary damages', whereas in the United States they are known as 'punitive damages', indicating the differing history of the two countries.[10] Punitive damages are routinely awarded in the United States, but exemplary damages are exceptional in Australia,[11] and generally available only for torts.

[14.7]   As Lord Devlin observed in *Rookes v Barnard*, damages with the aim of punishment appear to be anomalous:

> It may well be thought that this confuses the civil and criminal functions of the law; and indeed, so far as I know, the idea of exemplary damages is peculiar to English law [and to common law systems derived from English law].[12]

[14.8]   The availability of exemplary damages in a private law context reflects the history of tort, as Windeyer J noted in *Uren v John Fairfax & Sons Pty Ltd*:

> Compensation is the dominant remedy if not the purpose of the law of torts today. But fault still has a place in many forms of wrongdoing. And the roots of tort and crime in the law of England are greatly intermingled. Some things that today are seen as anomalies have roots that go deep, too deep for them to be easily uprooted.[13]

[14.9]   Windeyer J points to the long history of exemplary damages. Famously, in *Wilkes v Wood*, Pratt LCJ said that exemplary damages were awarded 'as a punishment to the guilty, to deter from any such proceeding for the future, and as proof of the detestation of the jury to the action itself'.[14] Prior to 1964, juries were responsible for awarding damages, and were not required to explain the bases upon which they made awards. It is likely that some awards of damages had partly or wholly punitive bases, but exemplary damages were hidden within more general compensatory damages awards.

[14.10]   There are important differences between criminal prosecution and an action for exemplary damages, as Lord Hoffman observed in *W v W*:

> The procedure is of course radically different and so is the standard of proof. A prosecution is generally speaking initiated and controlled by the state. A civil action is initiated and controlled by the victim. Thus the prosecution of an action for exemplary

---

8   E Weinrib, 'Restitutionary Damages as Corrective Justice' (2000) 1 *Theoretical Inquiries in Law* 1, 2–3; E Weinrib, 'Punishment and Disgorgement as Contract Remedies' (2003) 78 Chi-Kent L Rev 55.
9   [2010] NZSC 27, [2010] 3 NZLR 149 [258].
10   M Tilbury and H Luntz, 'Punitive Damages in Australian Law' (1995) 17 Loy LA Int & Comp LJ 769, 773–75. See JD McCamus, 'Prometheus Bound or Loose Cannon? Punitive Damages for Pure Breach of Contract in Canada' (2004) 41 San Diego L Rev 1491, 1493–94 on notoriously generous awards of punitive damages in the US.
11   *Gray v Motor Accident Commission* [1998] HCA 70, (1998) 196 CLR 1 [20] (Gleeson CJ, McHugh, Gummow and Hayne JJ).
12   [1964] AC 1129, 1221 (Lord Devlin).
13   (1966) 117 CLR 118, 149–50.
14   (1763) Lofft 1, 19; 98 ER 489, 498–99. Windeyer J thought that exemplary damages had earlier origins: *Uren v John Fairfax & Sons Pty Ltd* (1966) 117 CLR 118, 152.

damages enables the victim publicly to vindicate his or her version of events and inflict punishment, even revenge, in ways which a criminal prosecution may not satisfy. Punishment takes the form of damages which go to the victim rather than imprisonment or a fine which can afford her only a more indirect satisfaction. Allowing the victim to pursue such a claim may have a therapeutic value which mitigates the effects of the offence.[15]

An award of exemplary damages will be made only where the defendant has undertaken 'conscious wrongdoing in contumelious disregard of another's rights'.[16] For example, in *Lamb v Cotogno*,[17] Lamb, a process server, attempted to serve a summons on Cotogno. Cotogno threw himself on the bonnet of Lamb's car, and Lamb drove off, weaving back and forth to dislodge Cotogno. Lamb braked suddenly, and Cotogno fell off. Lamb drove away, leaving Cotogno screaming in pain and seriously injured by the side of the road. Cotogno sued Lamb for trespass to the person and received compensatory and exemplary damages at first instance. The High Court of Australia upheld the award of exemplary damages because of the contumelious nature of the defendant's conduct. It was immaterial that the defendant was insured under compulsory insurance, as the social aim of exemplary damages was broader than merely deterring and punishing that particular defendant, and extended to general deterrence and preventing plaintiffs from taking revenge.[18]   [14.11]

In *Rookes v Barnard*,[19] the House of Lords limited the circumstances in which exemplary damages can be awarded in England and Wales. Lord Devlin distinguished cases where damages were awarded to punish from those where damages were compensatory. Under his scheme, aggravated damages were compensatory, despite having a partly punitive element.[20] However, exemplary damages arose where the sole purpose of the awards was punishment and deterrence. Lord Devlin said that exemplary damages can be awarded in only three categories of case: [14.12]

1. where there were oppressive, arbitrary or unconstitutional acts by servants of the government;

2. where the defendant cynically calculated that the profit to be made by his conduct might well exceed the compensation payable to the plaintiff; and

3. where statute authorises awards of exemplary damages.[21]

These limiting categories were controversial, but were eventually accepted by the House of Lords in *Cassell & Co Ltd v Broome*.[22] However, the Law Commission for England and Wales said in 1997 that the three categories were not 'consistent with either sound principle or sound

---

15   [1999] 2 NZLR 1, 3 (PC).
16   *Whitfield v De Lauret & Co Ltd* (1920) 29 CLR 71, 77 (Knox CJ); *Australian Consolidated Press Ltd v Uren* (1967) 117 CLR 221, 232–34 (PC). See also *XL Petroleum (NSW) Pty Ltd v Caltex Oil (Australia) Pty Ltd* (1985) 155 CLR 448, 471 (Brennan J); *Gray v Motor Accident Commission* [1998] HCA 70, (1998) 196 CLR 1 [22] (Gleeson CJ, McHugh, Gummow and Hayne JJ).
17   (1987) 164 CLR 1.
18   Ibid, 9–12.
19   [1964] AC 1129.
20   Ibid, 1221.
21   Ibid, 1226–27.
22   [1972] AC 1027.

policy'.[23] The categories meant that claims failed in cases which instinctively seemed to call for exemplary damages because the defendant's wrongdoing was outrageous and there was no alternative sanction. No award could be made if the case did not fall within one of the limited categories of case, or the wrong in question was not one for which pre-1964 authorities could be found,[24] or the wrongdoer's conduct affected a large group of plaintiffs who made many claims against it.[25] The Commission recommended that the categories should be abolished, and a more principled approach should be taken.[26]

[14.13]   By contrast, while the High Court of Australia accepted Lord Devlin's distinction between compensatory damages and exemplary damages, it refused to adopt his threefold limitation in *Uren v John Fairfax & Sons Pty Ltd.*[27] The court observed that categories one and two were problematic. Taylor J said that the definition of a 'servant of the government' was unclear and that there seemed to be no reason to distinguish between a private corporation doing government work and a government corporation created by statute.[28] He criticised category two because it created difficulties in defamation law, and there seemed to be no reason to confine exemplary damages to situations where the defendant was cynically attempting to make a profit.[29]

[14.14]   The High Court and the English Law Commission have correctly outlined the difficulties with the *Rookes v Barnard* limiting factors. There is no reason why exemplary damages should be confined to the three categories, and courts should have the latitude to award exemplary damages whenever there has been a contumelious disregard of the plaintiff's rights meriting punishment. Indeed, although some Australian cases such as *Uren*[30] and *XL Petroleum*[31] have involved a cynical profit-making enterprise, others such as *Lamb v Cotogno,*[32] *Gray v Motor Accident Commission*[33] and *New South Wales v Ibbett*[34] have involved a contumelious disregard of the plaintiff's rights, and there seems no reason why the first group of cases should give rise to exemplary damages and the second should not.

1   Need to make out the 'host' cause of action

[14.15]   Exemplary damages are 'parasitic on compensatory damages'.[35] The plaintiff must make out the main cause of action before being entitled to exemplary damages.[36] Usually, the court must

---

23   Law Commission, *Aggravated, Exemplary and Restitutionary Damages* (LAW Com No 247, 1997) [1.2].

24   See *Cassell & Co Ltd v Broome* [1972] AC 1027, 1076 (Lord Hailsham), 1131 (Lord Diplock); *AB v South West Water Services Ltd* [1992] QB 507. These cases required the cause of action to be one for which pre-1964 authorities could be found, but *Kuddus v Chief Constable of Leicestershire Constabulary* [2001] UKHL 29, [2002] 2 AC 122 overruled this.

25   Law Commission, *Aggravated, Exemplary and Restitutionary Damages* (LAW Com No 247, 1997) [1.2].

26   Ibid, [1.17].

27   (1966) 117 CLR 118, aff'd *Australian Consolidated Press Ltd v Uren* (1967) 117 CLR 221 (PC).

28   (1966) 117 CLR 118, 132–33.

29   Ibid, 136–37.

30   (1966) 117 CLR 118.

31   (1985) 155 CLR 448.

32   (1987) 164 CLR 1.

33   [1998] HCA 70, (1998) 196 CLR 1.

34   [2006] HCA 57, (2006) 229 CLR 638.

35   *XL Petroleum (NSW) Pty Ltd v Caltex Oil (Australia) Pty Ltd* (1985) 155 CLR 448, 468–69 (Brennan J).

36   Ibid, 469 (Brennan J); *Fatimi Pty Ltd v Bryant* [2004] NSWCA 140, (2004) 59 NSWLR 678 [72] (Giles JA).

establish the plaintiff's entitlement to compensatory damages and aggravated damages before ascertaining whether an additional award of exemplary damages is necessary to deter and punish the defendant.[37]

In some circumstances a plaintiff may be able to claim exemplary damages without claiming compensatory or aggravated damages. One such situation is where the plaintiff can establish a cause of action without proving loss,[38] as with the torts per se, such as trespass. Exemplary damages may also be available where loss has been suffered but statute excludes compensatory damages.[39]   [14.16]

By contrast, it is not possible to get exemplary damages where loss is a necessary component of the cause of action (as with negligence or injurious falsehood) and the plaintiff has failed to show loss.[40] Giles JA said in *Fatimi Pty Ltd v Bryant*: 'If there is no host, there cannot be a parasite'.[41]   [14.17]

2   Unavailable if criminal punishment already imposed

In *Gray v Motor Accident Commission*,[42] the plaintiff was one of a group of young Aboriginal men crossing the road.[43] The defendant pursued the group in his motor vehicle and deliberately ran down the plaintiff, injuring him severely. The defendant was convicted of intentionally causing grievous bodily harm and sentenced to seven years' imprisonment. The plaintiff then sued the defendant (really his third-party insurer) in negligence, but the case was conducted as if it were a claim for trespass to the person.[44] The trial judge declined to award exemplary damages because the defendant had already been punished. The High Court confirmed that the presence of compulsory insurance was not a bar to an award of exemplary damages.[45] However, the fact that the defendant had already been punished meant exemplary damages were unavailable.[46] There were two reasons for this. First, 'the purposes of exemplary damages have been met if substantial punishment is exacted by the criminal law.   [14.18]

---

37   *New South Wales v Ibbett* [2006] HCA 57, (2006) 229 CLR 638 [34]; *New South Wales v Radford* [2010] NSWCA 276, (2010) 79 NSWLR 327 [94] (Sackville AJA).

38   *Fatimi Pty Ltd v Bryant* [2004] NSWCA 140, (2004) 59 NSWLR 678 [71] (Giles JA). See also *Cousins v Wilson* [1994] 1 NZLR 463; *Johnston Terminals & Storage Ltd v Miscellaneous Workers, Wholesale and Retail Delivery Drivers & Helpers Local Union* (1975) 61 DLR (3d) 741; *Cash & Carry Cleaners Ltd v Delmas* (1973) 44 DLR (3d) 315.

39   *New South Wales v Radford* [2010] NSWCA 276, (2010) 79 NSWLR 327 [120]–[128] (Sackville AJA); *New South Wales v Corby* [2010] NSWCA 27, (2010) 76 NSWLR 439. See also *Donselaar v Donselaar* [1982] 1 NZLR 97; *McLaren Transport Ltd v Somerville* [1996] 3 NZLR 424, 431; *A v Bottrill* [2002] UKPC 44, [2003] 1 AC 449 (PC); *Couch v Attorney-General (No 2)* [2010] NZSC 27, [2010] 3 NZLR 149.

40   *Fatimi Pty Ltd v Bryant* [2004] NSWCA 140, (2004) 59 NSWLR 678 [72]–[76] (Giles JA); *Giraffe World Australia Pty Ltd v Australian Competition and Consumer Commission* [1998] FCA 1560; 19 ATPR 41–669, [42538] (Lindgren J). Cf *New South Wales v Radford* [2010] NSWCA 276, (2010) 79 NSWLR 327 [123].

41   [2004] NSWCA 140, (2004) 59 NSWLR 678 [73].

42   [1998] HCA 70, (1998) 196 CLR 1.

43   Ibid, [61]–[67]; *Gray v Motor Accident Commission* [1998] HCATrans 199 (28 May 1998).

44   [1998] HCA 70, (1998) 196 CLR 1 [24].

45   Ibid, [32]–[37], [80]–[83], [130], applying *Lamb v Cotogno* (1987) 164 CLR 1, 9–12.

46   [1998] HCA 70, (1998) 196 CLR 1 [38]–[44], [92]–[98], [142]–[144].

The offender is punished; others are deterred'.[47] Secondly, the law should not punish a person twice for the same act.[48] However, the court decided that the compensatory damages awarded were manifestly inadequate, and ordered a new trial.[49]

[14.19]   There are difficult questions surrounding the concept of 'double punishment'. For example, if the defendant has been acquitted in criminal proceedings, she will not be liable for exemplary damages.[50] There may be problems where criminal proceedings have not yet been brought or are unfinished.[51] And, as the plurality observed in *Gray*, there may be difficulties in working out whether 'substantial punishment' has been exacted in the context of plea-bargaining, or where nominal criminal penalties have been imposed.[52] The plurality said there was 'much to be said in favour' of the statement of the New Zealand Court of Appeal in *Daniels v Thompson*[53] that a civil court should not revisit a criminal sentence to ascertain whether the defendant received his just deserts.[54]

[14.20]   *Cheng v Farjudi* raised the issue of nominal penalties.[55] The defendant pleaded guilty to a charge of assault occasioning actual bodily harm to the plaintiff and had been subject to a good behaviour bond for 12 months. The plaintiff sought exemplary damages in a subsequent civil action. The NSW Court of Appeal held that the good behaviour bond was not 'substantial punishment', particularly as the defendant denied the assault in civil proceedings, and said that he had only pleaded guilty to criminal charges 'as a matter of convenience'.[56] This made his disregard of the plaintiff's rights more contumelious.

3   Calculation of exemplary damages

[14.21]   Exemplary damages cannot be measured with any certainty,[57] and thus it is difficult to decide what is fair in the circumstances. Although all pecuniary awards are uncertain in some sense, compensatory damages are tied to loss suffered and gain-based relief is tied to the gain received by the defendant, providing some limit on recovery. Exemplary damages are not tied to any amount: it is only necessary that the amount be sufficient to deter and punish the defendant. Moreover, there is no 'necessary proportionality' between an award of compensatory damages and an award of exemplary damages.[58]

[14.22]   In the past, juries were often responsible for awards of exemplary damages, but, in most states, juries are rarely used in civil trials any longer (except in defamation cases and in

---

47   Ibid, [42] (Gleeson CJ, McHugh, Gummow and Hayne JJ).
48   Ibid, [43] (Gleeson CJ, McHugh, Gummow and Hayne JJ). See also *R v Hoar* (1981) CLR 31, 38.
49   [1998] HCA 70, (1998) 196 CLR 1 [105].
50   *W v W* [1999] 2 NZLR 1, 5. See also *Gray* [1998] HCA 70, (1998) 196 CLR 1 [47].
51   Ibid, [48].
52   [1998] HCA 70, (1998) 196 CLR 1 [45]–[46].
53   [1998] 3 NZLR 22, 48.
54   [1998] HCA 70, (1998) 196 CLR 1 [46].
55   [2016] NSWCA 316, (2016) 93 NSWLR 95.
56   Ibid, [105]–[113].
57   G Virgo, *The Principles of Equity and Trusts* (OUP 2012) 587.
58   *XL Petroleum (NSW) Pty Ltd v Caltex Oil (Australia) Pty Ltd* (1985) 155 CLR 448, 471 (Brennan J); *Harris v Digital Pulse Pty Ltd* [2003] NSWCA 10, (2003) 56 NSWLR 298 [254]–[256] (Heydon JA).

personal injury cases in Victoria).[59] In the Australian Capital Territory and South Australia civil juries have been abolished altogether.[60]

Australian courts exercise moderation in fixing an award of exemplary damages.[61] The court takes into account all circumstances which aggravate or mitigate the defendant's conduct.[62] In *Fontin v Katapodis*, the fact that the plaintiff customer had provoked the attack by the defendant shop assistant resulted in a reduction in exemplary damages, but did not result in a reduction in compensatory damages.[63] It is important to know the means of the defendant, as the defendant must pay a sufficiently large amount so as to be effectively deterred and punished.[64] As Hutley JA said in *Pollack v Volpato*:   [14.23]

> Whereas compensatory damages have to be approached by looking at the situation of the plaintiff in consequence of the wrongful act to which he has been subjected, punitive damages have to be looked at from the side of the defendant. If he is to be punished, it is his proper punishment which provides the basis for the assessment of damages.[65]

Where there are joint tortfeasors, an Australian court may award different amounts of exemplary damages in respect of different defendants, as the respective defendants' blameworthiness may vary.[66]   [14.24]

In light of concerns about the uncertainty of exemplary damages, it may be prudent to have 'guideline' awards and lists of factors which help courts to come to a suitable award in exceptional circumstances, as suggested by the English Law Commission.[67]   [14.25]

B   The causes of action for which exemplary damages can be awarded in Australia

Generally, Australian courts award exemplary damages only for torts, or where a statute explicitly endorses such an award.   [14.26]

Exemplary damages are unavailable for certain causes of action in Australia, including contract, equitable wrongdoing (including breach of fiduciary duty) and for misleading or deceptive conduct under the Australian Consumer Law.   [14.27]

---

59   S Colbran, P Spender, R Douglas, S Jackson, MT O'Brien and T Penovic, *Civil Procedure: Commentary and Materials* (6th edn, LexisNexis 2015) [19.3.2]–[19.3.19].

60   *Supreme Court Act 1933* (ACT), s 22; *Juries Act 1927* (SA), s 5.

61   *XL Petroleum (NSW) Pty Ltd v Caltex Oil (Australia) Pty Ltd* (1985) 155 CLR 448, 463. See also *Cassell & Co Ltd v Broome* [1972] AC 1027, 1227–28 (Lord Hailsham). The same is not true for US courts: M Tilbury and H Luntz, 'Punitive Damages in Australian Law' (1995) 17 Loy LA Int & Comp LJ 769, 789, 791–92.

62   *Rookes v Barnard* [1964] AC 1129, 1228.

63   *Fontin v Katapodis* (1962) 108 CLR 177, 186–87 (Owen J).

64   *Rookes v Barnard* [1964] AC 1129, 1228; *XL Petroleum (NSW) Pty Ltd v Caltex Oil (Australia) Pty Ltd* (1985) 155 CLR 448, 472; *Pollack v Volpato* [1973] 1 NSWLR 653, 657–58 (Hutley JA).

65   [1973] 1 NSWLR 653, 657.

66   *XL Petroleum (NSW) Pty Ltd v Caltex Oil (Australia) Pty Ltd* (1985) 155 CLR 448, 456; *De Reus v Gray* [2003] VSCA 84, (2003) 9 VR 432 [27]. Cf *Cassell & Co Ltd v Broome* [1972] AC 1027. See Ch 4 [4.16]–[4.25].

67   Law Commission, *Aggravated, Exemplary and Restitutionary Damages* (LAW Com No 247, 1997) [5.32].

1   Exemplary damages available for tort

[14.28]   In Australia, exemplary damages are available for a range of torts, including negligence,[68] trespass to land,[69] nuisance,[70] trespass to goods,[71] trespass to the person,[72] conversion and detinue,[73] battery,[74] wrongful arrest involving trespass to land and the person,[75] false imprisonment,[76] malicious prosecution,[77] abuse of process,[78] misfeasance in the public office,[79] inducing breach of contract,[80] interference with contractual relations,[81] deceit,[82] intimidation[83] and conspiracy.[84] They are also possibly available for the tort of passing off.[85]

[14.29]   Legislation excludes exemplary damages in certain cases. Exemplary damages are no longer available for defamation,[86] and while a claim for exemplary damages survives the death of the tortfeasor, it does not survive the death of the victim.[87] Nor can the dependants of the deceased victim obtain exemplary damages.[88] In some Australian jurisdictions, exemplary

---

68   *Gray v Motor Accident Commission* [1998] HCA 70, (1998) 196 CLR 1 (motor vehicle use); *Midalco Pty Ltd v Rabenalt* [1989] VR 461 (industrial injury); *Amaca Pty Ltd v Banton* [2007] NSWCA 336, (2007) 5 DDCR 314 (industrial injury); *Backwell v AAA* [1997] 1 VR 182 (medical negligence). Cf *Cassell & Co Ltd v Broome* [1972] AC 1027, which doubts availability in England.

69   *XL Petroleum (NSW) Pty Ltd v Caltex Oil (Australia) Pty Ltd* (1985) 155 CLR 448; *New South Wales v Ibbett* [2006] HCA 57, (2006) 229 CLR 638.

70   *Commonwealth v Murray* (1988) Aust Torts Reports 80–207; *Willoughby Municipal Council v Halstead* (1916) 22 CLR 352.

71   *Healing (Sales) Pty Ltd v Inglis Electrix Pty Ltd* (1968) 121 CLR 584.

72   *Fontin v Katapodis* (1962) 108 CLR 177.

73   *Cook v Saroukas* (1989) 97 FLR 33.

74   *Lamb v Cotogno* (1987) 164 CLR 1; *Pearce v Hallett* [1969] SASR 423; *Henry v Thompson* [1989] 2 Qd R 412.

75   *Adams v Kennedy* [2000] NSWCA 152, (2000) 49 NSWLR 78.

76   *McFadzean v Construction, Forestry, Mining and Energy Union* [2004] VSC 289; *A W v New South Wales* [2005] NSWSC 543.

77   *A v New South Wales* [2007] HCA 10, (2007) 230 CLR 500; *Coyle v New South Wales* [2006] NSWCA 95.

78   *Hamer-Mathew v Gulabrai (No 2)* (1995) Aust Torts Reports 81–334.

79   *Sanders v Snell* (1997) 73 FCR 569, rev'd on other grounds in *Sanders v Snell* (1998) 196 CLR 329. Although cf M Aronson, 'Misfeasance in Public Office: A Very Peculiar Tort' (2011) 35 MULR 1, 13: exemplary damages are rare for this tort.

80   *Whitfield v De Lauret & Co Ltd* (1920) 29 CLR 71.

81   *Zhu v Sydney Organising Committee for the Olympic Games* [2001] NSWSC 989, aff'd *Zhu v Treasurer of the State of New South Wales* [2004] HCA 56, (2004) 218 CLR 530.

82   *Musca v Astle Corporation Pty Ltd* (1988) 80 ALR 251 (FCA). Cf *Rookes v Barnard* [1964] AC 1129; *Mafo v Adams* [1970] 1 QB 548; *Cassell & Co Ltd v Broome* [1972] AC 1027, which doubts the availability in England.

83   *AS v Murray* [2013] NSWSC 733 [23].

84   *Williams v Hursey* (1959) 103 CLR 30.

85   *Paramount Pictures Corporation v Hasluck* [2006] FCA 1431, (2006) 70 IPR 293 [35]; *Flamingo Park Pty Ltd v Dolly Dolly Creations Pty Ltd* (1986) 6 IPR 431, 457.

86   *Civil Law (Wrongs) Act 2002* (ACT), s 139H; *Defamation Act 2005* (NSW), s 37; *Defamation Act 2006* (NT), s 34; *Defamation Act 2005* (Qld), s 37; *Defamation Act 2005* (SA), s 35; *Defamation Act 2005* (Tas), s 37; *Defamation Act 2005* (Vic), s 37; *Defamation Act 2005* (WA), s 37.

87   *Civil Law (Wrongs) Act 2002* (ACT), s 16(2); *Law Reform (Miscellaneous Provisions) Act 1944* (NSW), s 2(2)(a)(i); *Succession Act 1981* (Qld), s 66(2)(b); *Survival of Causes of Action Act 1940* (SA), s 3(1)(b); *Administration and Probate Act 1935* (Tas), s 27(3)(a); *Administration and Probate Act 1958* (Vic), s 29(2)(a); *Law Reform (Miscellaneous Provisions) Act 1955* (WA), s 4(2)(a). See also *Hartley Poynton Ltd v Ali* [2005] VSCA 53, (2005) 11 VR 568. Certain exceptions exist in South Australia; see *Civil Liability Act 1936* (SA), s 70; *Survival of Causes of Action Act 1940* (SA), s 3(2), (3).

88   *Reindel v James Hardie & Co Pty Ltd* [1994] 1 VR 619; *Ellis v South Australia* [2006] WASC 270 [23].

damages have been abolished for personal injury resulting from a motor accident,[89] workplace injuries,[90] and certain other cases of personal injury.[91] Sometimes, an award of exemplary damages in motor accident or workplace injury cases is prohibited against the tortfeasor's insurer, but permitted against the tortfeasor personally.[92]

The availability of exemplary damages for negligence raises difficult questions. It is inherent in the concept of exemplary damages that the defendant's conduct must have been 'deliberate', but negligence does not require deliberate action on the part of the defendant to be made out.[93] Generally, courts have held that exemplary damages are not limited to intentional torts,[94] but the defendant's actions must be deliberate or reckless before he will be liable for exemplary damages for a non-intentional tort.[95] To establish recklessness, it must be shown that the defendant had a conscious appreciation of the risk and was subjectively reckless.[96]

[14.30]

The Ipp Report on negligence law (see [7.9]–[7.10]) recommended that exemplary damages for negligence be abolished:

[14.31]

> The patchwork of legislation now in force limiting or abolishing exemplary damages in various types of case can be taken to reflect a community view that the remedy of exemplary damages is neither necessary nor desirable. In this light, the Panel recommends the enactment of a general provision abolishing exemplary damages in relation to claims for negligently-caused personal injury or death.[97]

Exemplary damages are still available for negligence in many jurisdictions, although, as noted at [14.29], some jurisdictions have abolished them in specific personal injury contexts. Today exemplary damages are most frequently awarded in actions against the police.[98]

[14.32]

---

89   *Motor Accident Injuries Act 2017* (NSW), s 4.20; *Transport Accident Act 1986* (Vic) s 93(7).

90   *Workers Compensation Act 1987* (NSW), s 151R; *Return to Work Act 2014* (SA), s 81; *Workplace Injury Rehabilitation and Compensation Act 2013* (Vic), s 340(c). Some statutes permit exemplary damages: *Return to Work Act 2015* (NT), s 109(3); *Dust Diseases Act 2005* (SA), s 9(2).

91   *Competition and Consumer Act 2010* (Cth), s 87ZB; *Civil Liability Act 2002* (NSW), s 21; *Civil Liability Act 2003* (Qld), s 52; *Personal Injuries (Liabilities and Damages) Act 2003* (NT), s 19.

92   *Motor Accidents (Compensation) Act* (NT), s 6(3)(a); *Motor Accident Insurance Act 1994* (Qld), s 55; *Workers Compensation and Rehabilitation Act 2003* (Qld), s 306B; *Motor Vehicles Act 1959* (SA), s 113A.

93   Although negligence can be established even if the defendant's conduct was intentional: *Gray v Motor Accident Commission* [1998] HCA 70, (1998) 196 CLR 1 [22] (Gleeson CJ, McHugh, Gummow and Hayne JJ), [85] (Kirby J); *Croucher v Cachia* [2016] NSWCA 132 [22], [26] (Leeming JA).

94   See *Couch v Attorney-General (No 2)* [2010] NZSC 27, [2010] 3 NZLR 149 for an extensive discussion of the law in New Zealand, Australia, Canada and England.

95   *Gray v Motor Accident Commission* [1998] HCA 70, (1998) 196 CLR 1 [24].

96   *Couch v Attorney-General (No 2)* [2010] NZSC 27, [2010] 3 NZLR 149 [60], [67]–[69] (Blanchard J); [100]–[102], [114]–[117], [150] (Tipping J); [238]–[243] (McGrath J); [253]–[257] (Wilson J); [1]–[4] (Elias CJ, dissenting). Cf *A v Bottrill* [2002] UKPC 44, [2003] 1 AC 449, which decided (on appeal from the New Zealand Court of Appeal) that 'outrageous' unintentional conduct could give rise to exemplary damages, but the New Zealand Supreme Court declined to follow it in *Couch*.

97   Ipp Panel, *Review of the Law of Negligence: Final Report*, September 2002, [13.165].

98   H Luntz, D Hambly, K Burns, J Dietrich, N Foster, G Grant and S Harder, *Torts: Cases and Commentary* (8th edn, Lexis Nexis 2017) [8.1.11]. See, eg, *New South Wales v Ibbett* [2006] HCA 57, (2006) 229 CLR 638: the plaintiff was awarded $25 000 in exemplary damages after she was woken in her home at 2 am by a trespassing plain-clothes policeman who, while attempting to unlawfully arrest the plaintiff's son, pointed a loaded gun at her and demanded that she let 'my mate' (another policeman) into the house.

2 Exemplary damages available for breach of some statutes

[14.33] Certain statutes give courts power to award exemplary damages for specific statutory breaches.[99] The most significant statutory power to award exemplary damages is the jurisdiction in intellectual property statutes to award 'additional damages' in the event of 'flagrant' breaches.[100] For example, s 115(4) of the *Copyright Act 1968* (Cth) states:

> (4) Where, in an action under this section:
>
> > (a) an infringement of copyright is established; and
> > (b) the court is satisfied that it is proper to do so, having regard to:
> > > (i) the flagrancy of the infringement; and
> > > (ia) the need to deter similar infringements of copyright; and
> > > (ib) the conduct of the defendant after the act constituting the infringement or, if relevant, after the defendant was informed that the defendant had allegedly infringed the plaintiff's copyright; and
> > > (ii) whether the infringement involved the conversion of a work or other subject-matter from hardcopy or analog form into a digital or other electronic machine-readable form; and
> > > (iii) any benefit shown to have accrued to the defendant by reason of the infringement; and
> > > (iv) all other relevant matters;
>
> the court may, in assessing damages for the infringement, award such additional damages as it considers appropriate in the circumstances.

[14.34] Section 115(4) will be used to illustrate how these sections operate. It is well accepted that 'additional damages' under s 115(4) have a punitive aspect.[101] 'Additional damages' may therefore be awarded on principles similar to those which govern the award of exemplary and aggravated damages at common law.[102] However, it has been said that the analogy with the common law should not be taken too far, and that, unlike common law exemplary damages, the section does not require contumelious disregard of the plaintiff's rights.[103] In fact it is unnecessary for a plaintiff to prove that all of the matters set out in s 115(4)(b)(i)–(iv) are present on the facts, and thus 'flagrancy' is not an essential prerequisite for an award of 'additional damages'. [104] Nevertheless, courts often consider the flagrancy of infringement of the copyright in these cases. Flagrancy involves 'calculated disregard of the plaintiff's right

---

99 Eg *Public Interest Disclosure Act 2012* (ACT), s 41(3); *Water Act 2000* (Qld), s 788(2)(b); *Environmental Management and Pollution Control Act 1994* (Tas), s 48(5)(g); *Australian Consumer Law and Fair Trading Act 2012* (Vic), s 184(2)(b)(ii); *Protected Disclosure Act 2012* (Vic), s 47(3); *Electricity Act 1945* (WA), s 50(2).

100 *Circuit Layouts Act 1989* (Cth), s 27(4); *Copyright Act 1968* (Cth), s 115(4); *Designs Act 2003* (Cth), s 75(3); *Patents Act 1990* (Cth), s 122(1A); *Trade Marks Act 1995* (Cth), s 126(2).

101 *Bailey v Namol Pty Ltd* (1994) 53 FCR 102, 113–14; *Autodesk Inc v Yee* (1996) 68 FCR 391, 394.

102 *Bailey v Namol Pty Ltd* (1994) 53 FCR 102, 113–4; *Aristocrat Technologies Australia Pty Ltd v DAP Services (Kempsey) Pty Ltd* [2007] FCAFC 40, (2007) 157 FCR 564 [42], [114].

103 *Luxottica Retail Australia v Grant* [2009] NSWSC 126, (2009) 81 IPR 26 [39].

104 Ibid; *Raben Footwear Pty Ltd v Polygram Records Inc* (1997) 75 FCR 88, 93; *MJA Scientifics International Pty Ltd v SC Johnson & Son Pty Ltd* (1998) 43 IPR 275, 281–82.

or cynical pursuit of benefit',[105] or conduct which is 'glaring, notorious, scandalous' or 'blatant',[106] but at the lower end, it may simply involve deliberate infringement.[107] It does not include mistakes or carelessness.[108] Under s 115(4)(b)(iv) of the *Copyright Act 1968* (Cth), courts have also considered other reprehensible conduct related to, but not directly associated with, the infringement.[109]

3   Exemplary damages not available for breach of contract

In Australia, exemplary damages are unavailable for breach of contract.[110] They are also unavailable for breach of contract in England and Wales,[111] the United States[112] and New Zealand.[113] Exceptionally, the Victorian Civil and Administrative Tribunal may award exemplary damages in respect of domestic building contracts.[114]   [14.35]

Punitive damages are available for breach of contract in Canada.[115] For example, in *Whiten v Pilot Insurance Co*,[116] the Canadian Supreme Court upheld a jury award of CAD $1 million for a breach of an insurance contract, after an insurance company unfairly accused a family of arson, causing them extreme financial hardship. The family house had burned down in a fire but there was no evidence to support the allegation of arson. The denial of the claim was designed to force the insured to accept an offer of less than she was entitled to. A precondition of the award of punitive damages was that the defendant's   [14.36]

105   *MJA Scientifics International Pty Ltd v SC Johnson & Son Pty Ltd* (1998) 43 IPR 275, 282 (Sundberg J); *Prior v Lansdowne Press Pty Ltd* [1977] VR 65, 70.
106   *Raben Footwear Pty Ltd v Polygram Records Inc* (1997) 75 FCR 88, 103 (Burchett J).
107   *Urban Ventures Pty Ltd v Solitaire Homes Pty Ltd* [2010] FCA 1373, (2010) 90 IPR 289 [52].
108   *Polygram Pty Ltd, Island Records Ltd & A & M Records Inc v Golden Editions Pty Ltd, Houghton Hughes (No 2)* (1997) 76 FCR 565, 575.
109   *Bailey v Namol Pty Ltd* (1994) 53 FCR 102, 113–14 (defendant's plan to steal work away from company); *Sony Entertainment (Australia) Ltd v Smith* [2005] FCA 228, (2005) 215 ALR 788, [164]–[172] (defendant's threats of physical violence).
110   *Butler v Fairclough* (1917) 23 CLR 78, 89 (Griffiths CJ); *Gray v Motor Accident Commission* [1998] HCA 70, (1998) 196 CLR 1 [13]; *Hospitality Group Pty Ltd v Australian Rugby Union Ltd* [2001] FCA 1040, (2001) 110 FCR 157 ('*Hospitality Group*') [142]–[143]; *Harris v Digital Pulse Pty Ltd* [2003] NSWCA 10, (2003) 56 NSWLR 298 ('*Digital Pulse*') [28], [78], [295]. See also JW Carter, *Contract Law in Australia* (6th edn, LexisNexis 2012) [41–020]; NC Seddon, RA Bigwood and MP Ellinghaus, *Cheshire and Fifoot's Law of Contract* (10th Australian edn, LexisNexis 2012) [23.2].
111   *Addis v Gramophone Co Ltd* [1909] AC 488.
112   American Law Institute, *Restatement (Second) of the Law of Contracts* (1981), §355: 'Punitive damages are not recoverable for a breach of contract unless the conduct constituting the breach is also a tort for which punitive damages are recoverable'; *Thyssen Inc v SS Fortune Star*, 777 F 2d 57, 63 (2d Cir, 1985). However, punitive damages have been allowed for fraudulent breaches of contract or insurance contracts breached in bad faith: see A Tettenborn, 'Punitive Damages – A View from England' (2004) 41 San Diego L Rev 1551, 1561.
113   *Paper Reclaim Ltd v Aotearoa International Ltd* [2006] 3 NZLR 188.
114   *Domestic Building Contracts Act 1995* (Vic), s 53(2)(b)(ii).
115   *Vorvis v Insurance Corporation of British Columbia* [1989] 1 SCR 1085; *Royal Bank of Canada v W Got & Associates Electric Ltd* [1999] 3 SCR 408; *Whiten v Pilot Insurance Co* [2002] SCC 18, [2002] 1 SCR 595 ('*Whiten*'). Cf *Performance Industries Ltd v Sylvan Lake Golf & Tennis Club Ltd* [2002] SCR 678 (punitive damages denied although defendant's breach of contract was duplicitous and fraudulent).
116   [2002] SCC 18, [2002] 1 SCR 595. *Whiten* is criticised by J Swan, 'Punitive Damages for Breach of Contract: A Remedy in Search of a Justification' (2003–2004) 29 Queen's LJ 596.

conduct gave rise to an 'independent actionable wrong', but that wrong did not have to be in tort.[117]

[14.37]   Andrew Burrows has queried whether Australian authority definitively rules out exemplary damages for breach of contract.[118] A similar argument was made (unsuccessfully) by counsel for the plaintiff in *Digital Pulse*.[119] The argument runs as follows. First, although Griffith CJ in *Butler v Fairclough* observed that the wilfulness of the breach should not affect the measure of damages for breach of contract, these comments were obiter.[120] Moreover, in *Gray v Motor Accident Commission*, the plurality said that there was merely an 'apparent rule' against awarding exemplary damages for breach of contract.[121] In *Hospitality Group*,[122] a majority of the Full Federal Court held that exemplary damages were unavailable for breach of contract relying upon the House of Lords decision in *Addis*,[123] but *Addis* is not binding in Australia, especially after the High Court decided in *Uren v John Fairfax & Sons Pty Ltd*[124] that it would not follow the English authority of *Rookes v Barnard*[125] on exemplary damages.

[14.38]   Even if it is open to Australian courts to award exemplary damages for breach of contract, it has been suggested that they should be unavailable for policy reasons. Waddams summarises the reasoning as follows:

> Punitive damages are not normally awarded for breach of contract. This rule is based on the assumption underlying much of contract law that a breach of contract, coupled with an offer to pay just compensation, does no harm to the plaintiff, is not morally wrong [and] may be desirable on the grounds of efficiency.[126]

[14.39]   There are several policy arguments against the award of exemplary damages for breach of contract:

1.   It is said that there is no authority in Australia or in England and Wales for the award of exemplary damages for breach of contract.[127] With respect, without the elaboration of sound reasoning behind that decision, this justification is unconvincing, unless one is a judge in an inferior court who must follow precedent.[128]

2.   It is said that the law of contract mostly governs commercial relationships, where the amount required to compensate for loss is easy to calculate, in contrast to the law of tort.[129] It has also been observed that breach of contract primarily gives rise to pecuniary losses, whereas the torts for which exemplary damages are available often

117   [2002] SCC 18, [2002] 1 SCR 595 [78]–[82]. Cf American Law Institute, *Restatement (Second) of the Law of Contracts* (1981), §355. See criticisms of *Whiten* in JD McCamus, 'Prometheus Bound or Loose Cannon? Punitive Damages for Pure Breach of Contract in Canada' (2004) 41 San Diego L Rev 1491, 1503–04.
118   A Burrows, *Remedies for Torts and Breach of Contract* (3rd edn, OUP 2004) 394, fn 56.
119   [2003] NSWCA 10, (2003) 56 NSWLR 298 [267] (Heydon JA).
120   (1917) 23 CLR 78, 89.
121   [1998] HCA 70, (1998) 196 CLR 1 [13] (Gleeson CJ, McHugh, Gummow and Hayne JJ).
122   [2001] FCA 1040, (2001) 110 FCR 157 [142]–[143].
123   [1909] AC 488.
124   (1966) 117 CLR 118.
125   [1964] AC 1129.
126   SM Waddams, *The Law of Damages* (5th edn, Canada Law Book 2012) [11.250].
127   Law Commission, *Aggravated, Exemplary and Restitutionary Damages* (LAW Com No 247, 1997), [1.72].
128   A Tettenborn, 'Punitive Damages – A View from England' (2004) 41 San Diego L Rev 1551, 1562–63.
129   *Thyssen Inc v SS Fortune Star*, 777 F 2d 57, 63 (2d Cir, 1985) ('*Thyssen*').

give rise to non-pecuniary losses.[130] It is certainly true that many contracts are commercial, and that expectation damages will be adequate to compensate for breach of such contracts. However, it can be argued that a highly exceptional remedy should be available for those breaches of contract (typically contracts protecting non-commercial interests) where the loss is *not* easy to calculate and where the breach is conscious and contumelious and has had a devastating effect on the plaintiff.

3. It is sometimes argued that exemplary damages are unavailable for breaches of contract because they do not cause the same kind of distress as torts.[131] However, there are surely circumstances where a breach of contract is more distressing than a tort. Compare, for example, the benighted family in *Whiten*,[132] who suffered gravely because of the breach of an insurance contract, with *Strand Electric and Engineering Co Ltd v Brisford Entertainments Ltd*,[133] where the defendant committed the tort of detinue by retaining the plaintiff's switchboards. The conduct was tortious, but not distressing for the plaintiff; it nonetheless obtained a generous measure of compensatory damages.

4. It is argued that exemplary damages for breach of contract may prevent efficient breaches[134] from occurring.[135] Arguably, 'efficient breach theory' contains some questionable assumptions and does not reflect the reality of the law or of business practice.[136] Nevertheless, it may be appropriate to leave room for 'tolerated breach' in many contracts;[137] if circumstances change, contractors should be able to breach and get out of a contract by paying damages if a substitute performance is readily available.[138] If exemplary damages for breach of contract are awarded on an exceptional basis for contracts which protect non-commercial interests,[139] it is difficult to argue that efficient breaches of contract will be deterred.

5. Griffiths CJ in *Butler v Fairclough* argues that the wilfulness of the breach should be irrelevant to contract law.[140] Posner and other scholars have also argued that 'wilfulness' or 'fault' should not be introduced into contract law because breach should not

---

130   Law Commission, *Aggravated, Exemplary and Restitutionary Damages* (LAW Com No 247, 1997) [1.72].
131   Ibid; *Thyssen*, 777 F 2d 57, 63 (2nd Cir, 1985).
132   [2002] SCC 18, [2002] 1 SCR 595.
133   [1952] 2 QB 246.
134   See R Posner, *Economic Analysis of Law* (9th edn, Aspen 2014) §4.10 for the classic description of 'efficient breach theory'.
135   *Thyssen*, 777 F 2d 57, 63 (2nd Cir, 1985); *Digital Pulse* [2003] NSWCA 10, (2003) 56 NSWLR 298 [184] (Mason P).
136   K Barnett, *Accounting for Profit for Breach of Contract: Theory and Practice* (Hart 2012) 109–15; S Harder, *Measuring Damages in the Law of Obligations: The Search for Harmonised Principles* (Hart 2010) 274–76.
137   D Friedmann, 'Economic Aspects of Damages and Specific Performance Compared' in D Saidov and R Cunnington (eds), *Contract Damages: Domestic and International Perspectives* (Hart 2008) 65.
138   D Campbell and D Harris, 'In Defence of Breach: A Critique of Restitution and the Performance Interest' (2002) 22 J Leg Stud 208, 217–21; D Friedmann, 'Economic Aspects of Damages and Specific Performance Compared' in D Saidov and R Cunnington (eds), *Contract Damages – Domestic and International Perspectives* (Hart 2008) 65, 74–83.
139   Or even for some limited commercial contracts: see A Tettenborn, 'Punitive Damages – A View from England' (2004) 41 San Diego L Rev 1551, 1563.
140   *Butler v Fairclough* (1917) 23 CLR 78, 89 (Griffith CJ).

be regarded as wrongful.[141] However, contracts should not be treated as self-contained documents, and the wilful nature of the parties' conduct intrudes into contract law at times.[142]

6. It is argued that there is a need for certainty in contract.[143] Related to this, it is argued that a contract is a private agreement where parties stipulate the rights and duties which arise under it, and thus it is inappropriate for a court to impose exemplary damages.[144] By contrast, tort duties are imposed by law, and it is easier to argue that punishment is relevant to these duties (particularly given tort law's overlap with criminal law in some aspects). These objections are the most convincing rationale for the denial of exemplary damages for breach of contract. As discussed in Ch 13 at [13.40]–[13.48], parties cannot stipulate penalties in contracts; this may be a reason why parties may wish to entreat a court to do so.

[14.40]   In sum, exemplary damages are unlikely to be available for breach of contract in Australia, despite the questions raised above about the reasoning behind that decision. If such damages were awarded, they should be awarded sparingly, in the most exceptional circumstances: namely, where the contract concerned non-commercial interests, where damages were otherwise inadequate and where the defendant had committed a deliberate and contumelious breach. However, if there is a choice between a gain-based award and exemplary damages, the courts should opt for the 'sharp axe' of disgorgement rather than the 'blunt axe' of exemplary damages,[145] to use James Edelman's terminology.[146]

4 Exemplary damages not available for equitable wrongdoing

[14.41]   While exemplary or punitive damages are available in exceptional circumstances for equitable wrongs in New Zealand[147] and Canada,[148] the majority of the NSW Court of Appeal in *Digital Pulse* held that such damages are unavailable for equitable causes of action.[149]

[14.42]   Digital Pulse Pty Ltd ('Digital') conducted a business that provided website design. The first and second defendants were employees of Digital. Their contracts of employment expressly

---

141   R Posner, 'Let Us Never Blame a Contract Breaker' (2009) 107 Mich L Rev 1349. See also S Shavell, 'Why Breach of Contract May Not Be Immoral Given the Incompleteness of Contracts' (2009) 107 Mich L Rev 1569. Cf G Cohen, 'The Fault that Lies within Our Contract Law' (2009) 107 Mich L Rev 1445; M Eisenberg, 'The Role of Fault in Contract Law: Unconscionability, Unexpected Circumstances, Interpretation, Mistake, and Nonperformance' (2009) 107 Mich L Rev 141; S Thel and P Siegelman, 'Willfulness Versus Expectation: A Promisor-based Defense of Willful Breach Doctrine' (2009) 107 Mich L Rev 1517; S Shiffrin, '*Could* Breach of Contract Be Immoral?' (2009) 107 Mich L Rev 1551; S Grundmann, 'The Fault Principle as the Chameleon of Contract Law: A Market Function Approach' (2009) 107 Mich L Rev 1583; R Kreitner, 'Fault at the Contract–Tort Interface' (2009) 107 Mich L Rev 1533.

142   Cohen, ibid.

143   Law Commission, *Aggravated, Exemplary and Restitutionary Damages* (LAW Com No 247, 1997) [1.72].

144   Ibid; *Digital Pulse* [2003] NSWCA 10, (2003) 56 NSWLR 298 [184] (Mason P).

145   J Berryman, 'The Case for Restitutionary Damages over Punitive Damages: Teaching the Wrongdoer that Tort Does Not Pay' (1994) 73 Can Bar Rev 869, 880; A Tettenborn, 'Punitive Damages – A View from England' (2004) 41 San Diego L Rev 1551, 1560

146   J Edelman, *Gain-Based Damages: Contract, Tort, Equity and Intellectual Property* (Hart 2002) 17.

147   *Cook v Evatt (No 2)* [1992] 1 NZLR 676; *Aquaculture Corporation v New Zealand Green Mussel Co Ltd* [1990] 3 NZLR 299; *Skids Programme Management Ltd v McNeill* [2012] NZCA 314, [2013] 1 NZLR 1.

148   *Norberg v Wynrib* [1992] 2 SCR 226, 298.

149   [2003] NSWCA 10, (2003) 56 NSWLR 298. Cf *Smith v Day* (1882) 21 Ch D 421, 428 (Brett LJ).

prevented them from competing with Digital during the term of their employment. They also owed fiduciary duties of loyalty to Digital. While still employed at Digital, the defendants diverted work from Digital towards their own business. Later, the defendants incorporated and became directors of a company called 'Juice-D', which received the payments for the work diverted from Digital. Among other things, Digital sought exemplary damages for breach of fiduciary duty. The trial judge awarded $10 000 exemplary damages for the defendants' breach of fiduciary duty.[150]

In the Court of Appeal, Heydon JA and Spigelman CJ rejected the availability of exemplary damages for breach of fiduciary duty, but their reasoning differed.   [14.43]

Heydon JA concluded that exemplary damages could not be awarded for an equitable wrong because they were a 'criminal sanction' with a penal aspect, and this was inappropriate to a court of equity.[151] He argued that 'a defendant ordered to pay exemplary damages suffers the same stigma as an accused person found guilty and punished'.[152] As Heydon JA anticipated, the natural rebuttal to the argument that equity does not allow punitive remedies is to argue that accounts of profits display a punitive rationale. However, his Honour said that accounts of profits were not penal, but reversed unjust enrichment.[153] Although accounts of profits had a deterrent effect, punishment was not a legitimate goal.   [14.44]

Spigelman CJ also found that exemplary damages should not be awarded, but his Honour disagreed with Heydon JA in two respects. First, he disagreed with Heydon JA's characterisation of exemplary damages as a criminal sanction.[154] Secondly, his Honour did not rule out punitive awards in equity altogether. Rather, he considered that a breach of fiduciary duty was analogous to a breach of contract for which exemplary damages are presently unavailable in Australia.[155] It followed that exemplary damages should be unavailable for breach of fiduciary duty.   [14.45]

Mason P dissented, and found that exemplary damages could be awarded in equity. His Honour questioned the practical workability of Heydon JA's distinction between punishment and deterrence, and said: [14.46]

> The various functions of exemplary damages ... inhere in the single remedial act. The 'public' function is triggered on the 'private' initiative of the affected plaintiff who pockets the fruits of the award. In such a context, the distinction between deterrence and punishment is illusory. It would be entirely lost on the defendant. This is a distinction that is not drawn with regard to the award of exemplary damages generally.[156]

---

150   *Digital Pulse Pty Ltd v Harris* [2002] NSWSC 33, (2002) 166 FLR 421 [175].
151   [2003] NSWCA 10, (2003) 56 NSWLR 298 [343]–[352] (Heydon JA). See also *Vyse v Foster* (1872) LR 8 Ch App 309, 333, aff'd *Vyse v Foster* (1874) LR 7 HL 318.
152   [2003] NSWCA 10, (2003) 56 NSWLR 298 [345] (Heydon JA).
153   Ibid, [306], [404]–[420]. In *Warman International Ltd v Dwyer* (1995) 182 CLR 544 [57], it was said that unjust enrichment was *not* the sole basis for the imposition of an account of profits. See also J Birch, 'Exemplary Damages for Breach of Fiduciary Duty' (2005) 33 ABLR 429, 436–37. Cf *Dart Industries Inc v Décor Corporation Pty Ltd* (1993) 179 CLR 101, 111 (account of profits for infringement of patent based on unjust enrichment).
154   [2003] NSWCA 10, (2003) 56 NSWLR 298 [3].
155   Ibid, [28]–[44]; cf [182]–[184] (Mason P). See [14.35]–[14.40] on exemplary damages in contract.
156   [2003] NSWCA 10, (2003) 56 NSWLR 298 [173].

His Honour said that exemplary damages exhibited a composite goal, including punishing, deterring, and vindicating the injury to the victim.[157]

[14.47] With respect, it is submitted that Mason P's judgment is preferable.[158] The availability of exemplary damages in equity has been supported by scholars,[159] and by the English Law Commission.[160] Exemplary damages should be available for breach of fiduciary duty in exceptional cases.

[14.48] Palmer J awarded exemplary damages at first instance in *Digital Pulse* because the defendants had been consistently dishonest and had deliberately and cynically breached their duties with a view to making a profit, and because the documents disclosed that the defendants must have taken more business from Digital, but neither Digital nor the court could find that information.[161] Nevertheless, *Digital Pulse* was perhaps not a suitable case for awarding exemplary damages because the conduct of the defendants was not difficult to monitor, and there was not the requisite deterrent justification.[162] This was illustrated by the fact that the defendants' operations were quickly found out and terminated, and their profit was small.

5 Exemplary damages not available for breaches of Australian Consumer Law

[14.49] Exemplary damages were unavailable under the *Trade Practices Act 1974* (Cth), the predecessor to the Australian Consumer Law ('ACL'), whether in relation to restrictive trade practices or consumer protection. In *Musca v Astle Corporation Pty Ltd*, French J held that because the aim of exemplary damages was to punish and not to compensate, they were unavailable under ss 82 or 87 of the *Trade Practices Act*, which required loss or damage.[163] Instead he awarded exemplary damages for deceit.

---

157 Ibid, [195].
158 J Birch, 'Exemplary Damages for Breach of Fiduciary Duty' (2005) 33 ABLR 429; D Morgan, '*Harris v Digital Pulse*: The Availability of Exemplary Damages in Equity' (2003) 29 Monash ULR 377; J Edelman, 'A "Fusion Fallacy" Fallacy?' (2003) 119 LQR 375; A Burrows, 'Remedial Coherence and Punitive Damages in Equity' in S Degeling and J Edelman (eds), *Equity in Commercial Law* (LBC 2005) 381.
159 Ibid; M Tilbury, *Civil Remedies* (Butterworths 1990) vol 1, [1014]–[1020]; J Beatson, 'Damages for Breach of Confidence' (1991) 107 LQR 209; P Finn, 'Equitable Doctrine and Discretion in Remedies' in WR Cornish, R Nolan, J O'Sullivan and G Virgo (eds), *Restitution, Past, Present and Future: Essays in Honour of Gareth Jones* (Hart 1998) 255, 271; P McDermott, *Equitable Damages* (Butterworths 1994) 104; J Glover, *Commercial Equity: Fiduciary Relationships* (Butterworths 1995) 271–72; PW Michalik, 'The Availability of Compensatory and Exemplary Damages in Equity: A Note on the *Aquacultures* Decisions' (1991) 21 VUWLR 391; A Burrows, 'We Do This at Common Law but That in Equity' (2002) OJLS 1, 13; A Duggan, 'Exemplary Damages in Equity: A Law and Economics Perspective' (2006) 26 OJLS 303; ICF Spry, *The Principles of Equitable Remedies* (9th edn, LBC 2014) 661. Cf L Aitken, 'Developments in Equitable Compensation: Opportunity or Danger?' (1993) 67 Aust LJ 596, 599–600; JD Heydon, MJ Leeming and PG Turner, *Meagher, Gummow and Lehane's Equity: Doctrines and Remedies* (5th edn, Butterworths 2015) [2–350] but cf now [2–355]; C Rickett, 'Equitable Compensation: Towards a Blueprint?' (2003) 25 Syd L Rev 31; C Rickett, 'Punitive Damages: The Pulse of Equity' (2003) 77 Aust LJ 496; G Virgo, *The Principles of Equity and Trusts* (OUP 2012) 586–87.
160 Law Commission, *Aggravated, Exemplary and Restitutionary Damages* (LAW Com No 247, 1997) [5.46]–[5.77].
161 *Digital Pulse Pty Ltd v Harris* [2002] NSWSC 33, (2002) 166 FLR 421 [117]–[128].
162 A Duggan, 'Exemplary Damages in Equity: A Law and Economics Perspective' (2006) 26 OJLS 303, 315.
163 (1988) 80 ALR 251, 262–69. See also *Snyman v Cooper* (1989) 24 FCR 433, 458.

This position has apparently continued under the *Competition and Consumer Act 2010*   [14.50]
(Cth), which contains the ACL in Schedule 2. Section 87ZB of the Act provides that the courts
must not award exemplary or aggravated damages in respect of death or personal injury.
However, this section does not apply to all of the ACL, only to Parts 2-2 (unconscionable
conduct), 3-3 (safety of consumer goods and product related services), 3-4 (information
standards), 3-5 (liability of manufacturers for goods with safety defects) and Div 2 of Part 3-4
(actions for damages against manufacturers of goods).[164] Thus, exemplary damages are not
expressly ruled out with regard to misleading or deceptive conduct, unfair contract terms,
unfair practices and consumer transactions. However, ss 236 and 237 refer to 'loss or damage',
making it likely that French J's conclusion in *Musca v Astle Corporation Pty Ltd* still holds.
Exemplary damages are likely to be unavailable because the purpose of the sections governing
the award of damages is solely compensatory.

Division 1 of Part 5-2 of the ACL allows the regulator to seek pecuniary penalties, which are   [14.51]
paid to the state in relation to specified contraventions of the legislation. Pecuniary penalties
are like fines, and explicitly punish the contravening party for breach of specified civil penalty
provisions. The ACL also allows for other quasi-punitive orders upon the application of the
regulator, such as adverse publishing orders pursuant to s 247 and orders disqualifying persons
from managing corporations pursuant to s 248.

C   Normative objections to exemplary damages generally

Scholars such as Ernest Weinrib have argued that, as a matter of principle, questions of desert   [14.52]
should not enter into private law.[165] Punishment is said to be an inappropriate purpose for
private law to pursue.[166] Weinrib argues that punishment is incompatible with his concept of
normative corrective justice, because it focuses only on the blameworthiness of the defendant.[167] It is also said that punishment should not be part of private law because it vindicates not
only the relationship between the parties, but also the broader regime of rights. The proper
party to enforce the broader regime of rights is the state, *via* the mechanism of the criminal
law.[168] It has also been argued that a retributive rationale requires the extra procedural and
evidentiary constraints which are associated with the criminal law protections for the
accused.[169]

Several scholars have attempted to refute these arguments. Robert Stevens points out that   [14.53]
retribution is used in a narrower sense than in the criminal law, as it focuses on the

---

164   *Competition and Consumer Act 2010* (Cth), ss 87ZB(2)(b) and 87E(1).
165   E Weinrib, *The Idea of Private Law* (OUP 2012) 74.
166   E Weinrib, 'Punishment and Disgorgement as Contract Remedies' (2003) 78 Chi-Kent L Rev 55, 86–87;
       A Beever, 'The Structure of Aggravated and Exemplary Damages' (2003) 23 OJLS 87; S Todd, 'A New
       Zealand Perspective on Exemplary Damages' (2004) 33 CLWR 255.
167   Weinrib, ibid. Cf P-W Lee, 'Contract Damages, Corrective Justice and Punishment' (2007) 70 Mod LR 887.
168   B Chapman and M Trebilcock, 'Punitive Damages: Divergence in Search of a Rationale' (1989) 40
       Ala L Rev 741, 782.
169   Ibid, 804–05; E Weinrib, 'Punishment and Disgorgement as Contract Remedies' (2003) 78 Chi-Kent L Rev
       55, 100–01; P Jaffey, *The Nature and Scope of Restitution* (Hart 2000) 376–78; *Cassell & Co Ltd v
       Broome* [1972] AC 1027, 1100 (Lord Morris).

infringement and vindication of a private right.[170] James Edelman, Ralph Cunnington and Peter Jaffey observe that the argument that compensation is solely a function of private law and punishment is solely a function of criminal law fails to 'fit' with the reality of what courts do.[171] Cunnington argues that the true division is not between punishment and compensation, but between individual enforcement of rights and a public attribution of blame by the state.[172] Cunnington and Stevens have argued that exemplary damages are not a criminal punishment, they do not supplement the criminal law, and the stigma and approbation which attach to criminal offences enforced by the state do not apply to exemplary damages.[173]

D   Conclusion on exemplary damages

[14.54]   Although some judges and scholars have questioned the availability of exemplary damages in civil actions,[174] as judges have observed with varying degrees of regret, resignation or approval, they appear to be firmly lodged in the common law, and in tort law in particular.[175] Given this, it is suggested that the Australian approach to exemplary awards in *Uren* is preferable to the English limitations laid down in *Rookes v Barnard*, which lack a principled basis.

[14.55]   However, the present availability of exemplary damages is neither coherent nor structured. If such damages are to be available, they should not be confined to tort law. The most obvious area for expansion is equitable wrongdoing (contrary to the suggestions of the majority in *Digital Pulse*), and it is suggested that in exceptional circumstances judges should be able to award exemplary damages for contumelious equitable wrongdoing if other awards are insufficient to deter and punish. The extension of exemplary damages into contract law is a more difficult question because of the voluntary nature of contract, but perhaps – as discussed at [13.40]–[13.48] – because the ability to prevent a defendant from egregiously breaching a contract via a liquidated damages clause is limited, exemplary damages in contract may be awarded in exceptional circumstances. This would only be where the contract sought to protect a non-commercial interest and where expectation damages and all other contractual remedies (including gain-based remedies) were inadequate.

[14.56]   A remaining difficulty is the distinction between exemplary damages and aggravated damages. This will be considered in the next section.

---

170   R Stevens, *Torts and Rights* (OUP 2007) 85. Cf Jaffey, ibid, 376.

171   J Edelman, *Gain-Based Damages: Contract, Tort, Equity and Intellectual Property* (Hart 2002) 19; R Cunnington, 'Should Punitive Damages Be Part of the Judicial Arsenal in Contract Cases?' (2006) 26 LS 369, 380–81; Jaffey, ibid, 378.

172   Cunnington, ibid, 381. It has been observed that the distinction between wrongs directed against individuals and against the state is neither workable nor useful: S Smith, 'Performance, Punishment and the Nature of Contractual Obligation' (1997) 60 Mod LR 360, 366.

173   Cunnington, ibid; R Stevens, *Torts and Rights* (OUP 2007) 86.

174   Eg *Cassell & Co Ltd v Broome* [1972] AC 1027, 1087 (Lord Reid); E Weinrib, 'Punishment and Disgorgement as Contract Remedies' (2003) 78 Chi-Kent L Rev 55, 86–87; A Beever, 'The Structure of Aggravated and Exemplary Damages' (2003) 23 OJLS 87; S Todd, 'A New Zealand Perspective on Exemplary Damages' (2004) 33 CLWR 255.

175   Especially *Uren v John Fairfax & Sons Pty Ltd* (1966) 117 CLR 118, 139 (Taylor J), 145–46 (Menzies J), 149–50 (Windeyer J).

III   Aggravated damages

A   The distinction between exemplary damages and aggravated damages

As noted at [14.12], Lord Devlin in *Rookes v Barnard* distinguished between exemplary damages (which he said had a primarily punitive and deterrent rationale) and aggravated damages (which he said had a partly punitive and partly compensatory rationale).[176] Aggravated damages can be awarded, he said, where the defendant exercised 'malevolence or spite' or the manner of committing the wrong was 'such as to injure the plaintiff's proper feelings of dignity and pride'.[177]   **[14.57]**

Although the High Court of Australia rejected Lord Devlin's three categories limiting when exemplary damages would be awarded in *Uren*, it adopted his Lordship's distinction between aggravated and exemplary damages. Windeyer J said: **[14.58]**

> aggravated damages are given to compensate the plaintiff when the harm done to him by a wrongful act was aggravated by the manner in which the act was done: exemplary damages, on the other hand, are intended to punish the defendant, and presumably to serve one or more of the objects of punishment – moral retribution or deterrence.[178]

Aggravated damages are said to compensate for intangible injuries,[179] including 'insult, humiliation and the like'.[180] The injury need not be a recognised psychiatric illness;[181] indeed, they are in effect 'compensation for mental suffering falling short of a recognised psychiatric illness'.[182]

Aggravated damages which compensate for anxiety, disappointment and distress have nonetheless been considered to be damages for personal injury, as they have been held to fall within the definition of 'impairment of mental condition' in the *Civil Liability Act 2002* (NSW).[183] Conversely, aggravated damages which compensate for loss of reputation,[184] or loss of dignity and liberty[185] are not considered to be damages for personal injury.   **[14.59]**

As discussed below, aggravated damages are generally available for tort, but not for other actions such as breach of contract or equitable wrongs. Despite this, damages for distress may be available for the latter causes of action in limited circumstances.   **[14.60]**

As Witzleb, Bant, Degeling and Barker observe, the division between exemplary damages and aggravated damages requires a further distinction between three categories of damages: **[14.61]**

---

176   [1964] AC 1129, 1221.
177   Ibid.
178   *Uren v John Fairfax & Sons Pty Ltd* (1966) 117 CLR 118, 149.
179   Ibid, 130 (Taylor J); *New South Wales v Ibbett* [2006] HCA 57, (2006) 229 CLR 638 [31].
180   *Lamb v Cotogno* (1987) 164 CLR 1, 8.
181   *New South Wales v Riley* [2003] NSWCA 208, (2003) 57 NSWLR 496 [129] (Hodgson JA).
182   *New South Wales v Corby* [2010] NSWCA 27, (2010) 76 NSWLR 439 [48] (Basten JA).
183   *New South Wales v Ibbett* [2006] HCA 57, (2006) 229 CLR 638 [124], [211]–[212]; *New South Wales v Corby*, ibid, [41]; *Insight Vacations Pty Ltd v Young* [2010] NSWCA 137, (2010) 78 NSWLR 641.
184   *Insight Vacations Pty Ltd v Young*, ibid, [125] (Basten JA). See also *New South Wales v Williamson* [2012] HCA 57, (2012) 293 ALR 440 [34], [45]; *Zhang v New South Wales* [2012] NSWSC 606 [30]–[34].
185   *New South Wales v Williamson* [2011] NSWCA 183 [61]. See also *New South Wales v Williamson*, ibid, [34], [45]; *Zhang v New South Wales*, ibid, [30]–[34].

1. compensatory damages *simpliciter*;
2. aggravated compensatory damages; and
3. exemplary damages.[186]

Unfortunately, the distinction between aggravated damages and exemplary damages is difficult to draw in practice.[187] Stone argues that the distinction is illusory and ultimately unsustainable.[188] In *Carson v John Fairfax & Sons Ltd*, McHugh J (dissenting) argued that there is an 'element of punishment' in awards of aggravated damages, despite being categorised as compensatory.[189] Consequently, although exemplary damages in defamation cases were first abolished in New South Wales,[190] the quantum of damages awarded for defamation was not affected because punishment could still be effected via aggravated damages.[191] Since the advent of the uniform defamation law, other states have had a similar experience.[192]

[14.62]   Moreover, it can be hard to distinguish between compensatory damages *simpliciter* and aggravated damages where damages are awarded for torts which involve intangible as well as tangible harm.[193]

[14.63]   The distinctions between the species of damages matter for several reasons. First, the focus of exemplary damages differs from that of aggravated damages. Aggravated damages focus on the plaintiff, and consider the pecuniary amount necessary to compensate her for the injury suffered, whereas exemplary damages focus on the conduct of the defendant and the pecuniary amount necessary to punish and deter him.[194] Secondly, the applicable limitation period may depend on whether the damages are for 'personal injury' or for something else. In *New South Wales v Radford*,[195] it was held that aggravated damages were damages for 'personal injury' for the purpose of s 18A(1) of the *Limitation Act 1969* (NSW), which imposes a three-year limitation period for causes of action founded on negligence, nuisance, or breach of duty, for damages for personal injury.[196] Consequently, the plaintiff was unable to claim aggravated damages, but might have been able to claim exemplary damages alone.[197] Thirdly, aggravated damages are generally unavailable for corporations because corporations have no feelings to be injured.[198]

---

186   N Witzleb, E Bant, S Degeling and K Barker, *Remedies: Commentary and Materials* (6th edn, LBC 2015) [8.120].
187   *Uren v John Fairfax & Sons Pty Ltd* (1966) 117 CLR 118, 152 (Windeyer J).
188   J Stone, 'Double Count and Double Talk: The End of Exemplary Damages?' (1972) 46 Aust LJ 311.
189   (1993) 178 CLR 44, 108.
190   *Defamation Act 1974* (NSW), s 46, repealed and replaced by *Defamation Act 2005* (NSW), s 37.
191   *Andrews v John Fairfax & Sons Ltd* [1980] 2 NSWLR 225.
192   Eg *Wilson v Bauer Media Pty Ltd* [2017] VSC 521.
193   *New South Wales v Radford* [2010] NSWCA 276, (2010) 79 NSWLR 327 [97].
194   Ibid, [93]; *Cassell & Co Ltd v Broome* [1972] AC 1027, 1089 (Lord Reid); *De Reus v Gray* [2003] VSCA 84, (2003) 9 VR 432 [28].
195   [2010] NSWCA 276, (2010) 79 NSWLR 327 [116].
196   Not all aggravated damages will necessarily be damages for personal injury: see [14.68].
197   *New South Wales v Radford* [2010] NSWCA 276, (2010) 79 NSWLR 327, [120]–[128]. See also *New South Wales v Corby* [2010] NSWCA 27, (2010) 76 NSWLR 439.
198   *Khodaparast v Shad* [2000] 1 All ER 545, 1 WLR 618, 556. Cf *Collings Construction Co Pty Ltd v Australian Competition and Consumer Commission* (1998) 43 NSWLR 131, 156 (Cole JA).

The Ontario Law Reform Commission has recommended that aggravated damages should   [14.64]
be abolished because they are confusing, and that instead damages for loss of pride and dignity
should be awarded as a new head of non-pecuniary loss.[199] The English Law Commission
thought that aggravated damages awards should be equated with damages for mental distress
only.[200]

B   Availability of aggravated damages in Australian law

1   Aggravated damages available for tort

Aggravated damages are most frequently awarded for torts per se, including for assault,[201]   [14.65]
defamation,[202] conspiracy,[203] false imprisonment,[204] intimidation,[205] trespass to land,[206] interference with contractual relations[207] and malicious prosecution.[208] Their availability for nuisance,[209] deceit,[210] injurious falsehood[211] and negligence[212] is more controversial.

In *Broken Hill Pty Co Ltd v Fisher*, Olsson J asserted that 'aggravated damages must be   [14.66]
based on a cause of action that protects the dignitary interest'.[213] Many scholars argue that

---

199   Ontario Law Reform Commission, *Report on Exemplary Damages* (1991) ch 5.
200   Law Commission, *Aggravated, Exemplary and Restitutionary Damages* (LAW Com No 247, 1997)
[2.39]–[2.43].
201   *Henry v Thompson* [1989] 2 Qd R 412; *Johnstone v Stewart* [1968] SASR 142; *Pearce v Hallett* [1969]
SASR 423.
202   *Uren v John Fairfax & Sons Pty Ltd* (1966) 117 CLR 118; *Carson v John Fairfax & Sons Ltd* (1993) 178 CLR
44. See *Civil Law (Wrongs) Act 2002* (ACT), s 139F(2); *Defamation Act 2005* (NSW), s 35(2);
Defamation Act 2006 (NT), s 32(2); *Defamation Act 2005* (Qld), s 35(2); *Defamation Act 2005* (SA),
s 33(2); *Defamation Act 2005* (Tas), s 35(2); *Defamation Act 2005* (Vic), s 35(2); *Defamation Act 2005*
(WA), s 35(2).
203   *Williams v Hursey* (1959) 103 CLR 30; *Huntley v Thornton* [1957] 1 WLR 321, 350; *Jervois Sulphates (NT)
Ltd v Petrocarb Explorations NL* (1974) 5 ALR 1.
204   *Myer Stores Ltd v Soo* [1991] 2 VR 597; *McFadzean v Construction, Forestry, Mining and Energy Union*
[2004] VSC 289.
205   *Rookes v Barnard* [1964] AC 1129.
206   *Traian v Ware* [1957] VR 200; *TCN Channel Nine Pty Ltd v Anning* [2002] NSWCA 82, (2002) 54 NSWLR
333 [179].
207   *Zhu v Sydney Organising Committee for the Olympic Games* [2001] NSWSC 989, aff'd *Zhu v Treasurer of
the State of New South Wales* [2004] HCA 56, (2004) 218 CLR 530.
208   *Commonwealth Life Assurance Society Ltd v Brain* (1935) 53 CLR 343; *A v New South Wales* [2007] HCA
10, (2007) 230 CLR 500.
209   *Willoughby Municipal Council v Halstead* (1916) 22 CLR 352 (court divided 2:2 on availability of
aggravated damages for nuisance); *Oldham v Lawson (No 1)* [1976] VR 654, 658–59 (Harris J: damages
for distress available for nuisance, but doubted aggravated damages available); *Van Son v Forestry
Commission* (1995) 86 LGERA 108 (unnecessary to decide). Aggravated damages were allowed in
Traian v Ware [1957] VR 200 because of the trespass.
210   *Archer v Brown* [1985] QB 401; *Mafo v Adams* [1970] 1 QB 548, 554 (Sachs LJ), 558 (Widgery LJ). Both
were cited approvingly in *Aldersea v Public Transport Corporation* [2001] VSC 169, (2001) 3 VR 499
[44]–[45].
211   *Joyce v Sengupta* (1993) 1 WLR 337, 350–51; *Khodaparast v Shad* [2000] 1 WLR 618, 630–31; 633; *James v
Faddoul* [2007] NSWSC 821 [18] (Price J). Cf *Fielding v Variety Inc* [1967] 2 QB 841, 851; 855; *Bride v
KMG Hungerfords* (1991) 109 FLR 256, 281. Equivocal: *Joyce v Sengupta*, ibid, 347–48.
212   *Backwell v AAA* [1997] 1 VR 182. See also *De Reus v Gray* [2003] VSCA 84, (2003) 9 VR 432 [29].
213   [1984] 38 SASR 50, 66.

aggravated damages protect a plaintiff's dignitary interest.[214] While this is one relevant aim, it must be queried whether *all* aggravated awards reflect this rationale. The English Law Commission noted that aggravated damages are available for torts protecting dignitary interests, including assault, battery, false imprisonment, malicious prosecution, defamation and intimidation. However, the commission also noted that aggravated damages are available for torts protecting proprietary interests (trespass to land and nuisance) and torts protecting commercial interests (unlawful interference with business and related torts). It was said to be 'hard to discern a common thread', and the most that could be said was that aggravated damages were available for torts where damages were 'at large'.[215] If protecting the dignitary interest is central to aggravated damages, then they should not be available for trespass to land and economic torts such as interference with contractual relations, unless it can be argued that proprietary or economic interests are fundamental to that particular plaintiff's dignity. Consequently, it seems better to argue, as the English Law Commission did, that aggravated damages deal with distress.[216]

[14.67]   Aggravated damages in negligence are controversial, particularly for personal injury. English courts have doubted whether aggravated damages are available for personal injury,[217] but the Australian position is more equivocal. The Victorian Court of Appeal has presumed that aggravated damages are available for personal injury,[218] and some courts have been prepared to award them.[219] However, the NSW Court of Appeal has said that aggravated damages are unavailable for a purely psychiatric injury,[220] and queried the availability of aggravated damages for personal injury more generally.[221] Other decisions have doubted the availability of aggravated damages for negligent personal injury.[222] The matter remains open.[223]

[14.68]   The civil liability statutes in New South Wales, the Northern Territory and Queensland have abolished aggravated damages for personal injury claims.[224] Moreover, aggravated damages are unavailable for personal injury in the context of product liability pursuant to s 87ZB of the *Competition and Consumer Act 2010* (Cth).

---

214   Eg M Tilbury, 'Factors Inflating Damages Awards' in P Finn (ed), *Essays on Damages* (LBC 1992) 86, 89–90; B Chapman, 'Punitive Damages as Aggravated Damages: The Case of Contract' (1990) 16 CBLJ 269, 275; B Chapman and M Trebilcock, 'Punitive Damages: Divergence in Search of a Rationale' (1989) 40 Ala L Rev 741, 761; A Beever, 'The Structure of Aggravated and Exemplary Damages' (2003) 23 OJLS 87, 89; B Feldthusen, 'Recent Developments in the Canadian Law of Punitive Damages' (1990) 16 CBLJ 241, 247; J Berryman, 'Reconceptualizing Aggravated Damages: Recognizing the Dignitary Interest and Referential Loss' (2004) 41 San Diego L Rev 1521.

215   Law Commission, *Aggravated, Exemplary and Restitutionary Damages* (LAW Com No 247, 1997) [2.11].

216   Ibid, [2.39]–[2.43]. See also *Collings Construction Co Pty Ltd v Australian Competition and Consumer Commission* (1998) 43 NSWLR 131, 156 (Cole JA).

217   *Kralj v McGrath* [1986] 1 All ER 54, 61; *AB v South West Water Services Ltd* [1992] QB 507.

218   *Backwell v AAA* [1997] 1 VR 182, 214.

219   *Brady v Tamworth Base Hospital and Health Service* (NSW District Court, 31 January 2000).

220   *Hunter Area Health Service v Marchlewski* [2000] NSWCA 294, (2000) 51 NSWLR 268 [112]–[121].

221   Ibid, [94]–[111].

222   *O'Reilly v Hausler* (1987) 6 MVR 344, 346; *Preston v Star City Pty Ltd* [1999] NSWSC 459, (1999) Aust Torts Reports 81–508 [47]–[48]; *Bergman v Haertsch* [2000] NSWSC 528 [458].

223   *Delta Corporation v Davies* [2002] WASCA 125; *Wiatr v CSR Ltd* [2002] WASC 77.

224   *Civil Liability Act 2002* (NSW), s 21; *Personal Injuries (Liabilities and Damages) Act 2003* (NT), s 19; *Civil Liability Act 2003* (Qld), s 52.

Aggravated damages may be reduced where the plaintiff has provoked the defendant into acting. However, there is some confusion because *Fontin v Katapodis* seemingly held that the plaintiff's aggravated damages were not reduced because of provocation,[225] whereas in other cases the plaintiff's aggravated damages award has been reduced by reason of provocation.[226] [14.69]

2   Aggravated damages available for some statutory causes of action

Some statutes apparently leave open the possibility of aggravated damages for specific statutory breaches, as they allow for any remedy which a court may grant with respect to a tort.[227] [14.70]

The intellectual property statutes mentioned previously empower courts to award 'additional damages' in the event of 'flagrant' breaches and it is likely that this encompasses aggravated damages.[228] Indeed the courts analogise these awards of 'additional damages' to exemplary and aggravated damages at common law without distinguishing between the two.[229] [14.71]

3   Aggravated damages not available for contract

Aggravated damages are not generally awarded for breach of contract,[230] except in Canada, where the possibility is left open.[231] [14.72]

Notwithstanding this, as explained in Ch 5 at [5.76]–[5.82], damages for emotional distress can clearly be awarded in respect of some breaches of contract when the distress flows from a physical injury or physical inconvenience or when a major object of the contract is to provide enjoyment, relaxation or freedom from molestation.[232] [14.73]

However, it has been held that s 16 of the *Civil Liability Act 2002* (NSW) applies to awards of distress damages for breach of contract, and thus damages for distress are not recoverable unless they meet a 15% threshold of severity; see [7.17]. The NSW Supreme Court has held that several plaintiffs were not entitled to damages for distress for breach of a term implied into holiday contracts under s 74(1) of the then *Trade Practices Act 1974* (Cth), because this was a form of 'personal injury' damages, and they did not meet the threshold requirements of s 16.[233] [14.74]

4   Aggravated damages not available for equitable wrongdoing

Aggravated damages or damages for distress are not generally thought to be available for equitable wrongdoing because these awards are typically associated with common law [14.75]

---

225   *Fontin v Katapodis* (1962) 108 CLR 177, 183–84 (McTiernan J), 187 (Owen J).
226   *Law v Wright* [1935] SASR 20, 25; *Downham v Bellette* (1986) Aust Torts Reports 80–083.
227   Eg *Public Interest Disclosure Act 2012* (ACT), s 41(3); *Protected Disclosure Act 2012* (Vic), s 47(3).
228   *Circuit Layouts Act 1989* (Cth), s 27(4); *Copyright Act 1968* (Cth), s 115(4); *Designs Act 2003* (Cth), s 75(3); *Patents Act 1990* (Cth), s 122(1A); *Trade Marks Act 1995* (Cth), s 126(2).
229   *Bailey v Namol Pty Ltd* (1994) 53 FCR 102, 113–14; *Aristocrat Technologies Australia Pty Ltd v DAP Services (Kempsey) Pty Ltd* [2007] FCAFC 40, (2007) 157 FCR 564 [42], [114].
230   *Broken Hill Pty Co Ltd v Fisher* [1984] 38 SASR 50, 66. See also *Addis v Gramophone Co Ltd* [1909] AC 488; *Kralj v McGrath* [1986] 1 All ER 54, 61.
231   *Vorvis v Insurance Corporation of British Columbia* [1989] 1 SCR 1085, 1103 (McIntyre J).
232   *Baltic Shipping Co v Dillon* (1993) 176 CLR 344, 359–66 (Mason CJ).
233   *Insight Vacations Pty Ltd v Young* [2010] NSWCA 137, (2010) 78 NSWLR 641; *Flight Centre Ltd v Louw* [2011] NSWSC 132, (2010) 78 NSWLR 656.

torts.[234] Moreover, as with breach of contract, the damage caused by equitable wrongdoing is often economic in character.

[14.76]   However, equitable aggravated damages were awarded for the first time by a superior court in *Giller v Procopets*,[235] a case where there was 'no prior decision squarely in point'.[236] The Victorian Court of Appeal used s 38 of the *Supreme Court Act 1986* (Vic) to award damages for distress in lieu of an injunction after the defendant breached the plaintiff's confidence by displaying intimate videos of himself and the plaintiff to third parties; see [12.14]. The award was explicitly characterised as aggravated damages.[237] Subsequently, in *Wilson v Ferguson*, a breach of confidence case involving the publication of intimate photos on social media, aggravated damages were awarded pursuant to the court's inherent equitable jurisdiction.[238] Aggravated damages may now become more common in equity. With respect, it is appropriate that the plaintiffs in *Giller* and *Wilson* were compensated for their distress, particularly as they were entitled to assume that intimate images would be kept confidential.

5   Aggravated damages available for breaches of the Australian Consumer Law

[14.77]   In *Collings Construction Co Pty Ltd v Australian Competition and Consumer Commission*, the NSW Court of Appeal held that aggravated damages could be awarded for breach of s 52 of the then *Trade Practices Act 1974* (Cth), because aggravated damages are compensatory, and s 87 allowed for recovery for 'loss or damage', which should include losses caused by anxiety, distress and vexation.[239] Moreover, the court said that aggravated damages were not limited to cases where a plaintiff's 'dignitary interests' were affected, but extended more broadly to other types of distress.[240] There are many cases in which damages for distress have been held available for breach of s 52,[241] or analogous provisions in state fair trading Acts.[242] These sections have now been replaced by s 18 and s 286 of the ACL, but it is highly likely that aggravated damages (or, at least, damages for distress) will continue to be available under the ACL, subject to the restrictions discussed at [8.27]–[8.30].

---

234   *Giller v Procopets* [2004] VSC 113 [160] (overturned on appeal: [2008] VSCA 236, (2008) 24 VR 1).

235   [2008] VSCA 236, (2008) 24 VR 1. See also *Doe v Australian Broadcasting Corporation* [2007] VCC 281, [186], which settled before appeal.

236   JD Heydon, MJ Leeming and PG Turner, *Meagher, Gummow and Lehane's Equity: Doctrines and Remedies* (5th edn, Butterworths 2015) [24–085].

237   [2008] VSCA 236, (2008) 24 VR 1 [160], [446]. The court also held that it was entitled to award damages for distress for breach of confidence pursuant to the court's inherent equitable jurisdiction: see [143] (Ashley JA), [422]–[424] (Neave JA).

238   [2015] WASC 15 [74]–[85] (Mitchell J).

239   *Collings Construction Co Pty Ltd v Australian Competition and Consumer Commission* (1998) 43 NSWLR 131, 155.

240   Ibid, 156.

241   Eg *Steiner v Magic Carpet Tours Pty Ltd* (1984) ATPR 40–490; *Zoneff v Elcom Credit Union Ltd* (1990) 94 ALR 445 (aff'd *Zoneff v Elcom Credit Union Ltd* (1990) 6 ANZ Ins Cas 61–023); *Australian Competition and Consumer Commission v Top Snack Foods Pty Ltd* [1999] FCA 752, (1999) ATPR 41–708; *Whittaker v Paxad Pty Ltd* [2009] WASC 47; *New South Wales Lotteries Corporation Pty Ltd v Kuzmanovski* [2011] FCAFC 106, (2011) 195 FCR 234 [122]–[123].

242   *Holloway v Witham* (1990) 21 NSWLR 70, 86–87; *Whittaker v Paxad Pty Ltd* [2009] WASC 47; *Parker v Campos* [2011] NSWSC 306.

As Spigelman CJ noted in obiter dicta in *Insight Vacations Pty Ltd v Young*, Part 2 of the   [14.78]
Civil Liability Act 2002 (NSW) does not apply to awards of damages for distress for misleading
and deceptive conduct under the ACL.[243]

IV 'Vindicatory damages'

Vindicatory damages are a novel head of damages said to be available for violations of   [14.79]
constitutional or human rights in some jurisdictions.[244] They are prevalent in the West
Indies,[245] but have also been recognised in New Zealand.[246] These jurisdictions have written
Constitutions enshrining certain fundamental rights, or, in the case of New Zealand, a Bill of
Rights. The principles governing the award of vindicatory damages 'are not greatly
developed'.[247] In *Attorney-General of Trinidad and Tobago v Ramanoop*, Lord Nicholls said
that an award might be needed to reflect the sense of public outrage, emphasise the gravity of
the breach, and deter further breaches.

Vindicatory damages were sought against the British government in *R (Lumba) v Secretary*   [14.80]
of State for the Home Department,[248] after foreign nationals were imprisoned for criminal
offences. Once their criminal sentence was completed, the Home Secretary detained them
pursuant to the *Immigration Act 1971* (UK). Among other things, the plaintiffs sought damages
for false imprisonment, including exemplary damages. The majority of the Supreme Court held
that, although the detention was unlawful and the plaintiffs were falsely imprisoned,[249] they
were only entitled to nominal damages because they could have been detained lawfully in any
event.[250] It is arguable that the court should have awarded exemplary damages given the
importance of the interest involved (personal liberty).[251] Vindicatory damages were also
unavailable to the plaintiffs.[252] Lord Hope cautioned against analogising vindicatory damages
with punitive or exemplary damages:

---

243   [2010] NSWCA 137, (2010) 78 NSWLR 641 [75].
244   JNE Varuhas, 'The Concept of 'Vindication' in the Law of Torts: Rights, Interests and Damages' (2014) 34
       OJLS 253, 291.
245   See, eg, *Attorney-General of Trinidad and Tobago v Ramanoop* [2005] UKPC 15, [2006] 1 AC 328;
       Merson v Cartwright and Attorney General [2005] UKPC 38; *Subiah v Attorney-General of Trinidad and
       Tobago* [2008] UKPC 47; *Fraser v Judicial and Legal Services Commission* [2008] UKPC 25; *Graham v
       Police Service Commission and Attorney-General of Trinidad and Tobago* [2011] UKPC 46; *Welch v
       Attorney General of Antigua and Barbuda* [2013] UKPC 1.
246   *Taunoa v Attorney-General* [2007] NZSC 70; [2008] 1 NZLR 429.
247   *Attorney-General of Trinidad and Tobago v Ramanoop* [2005] UKPC 15, [2006] 1 AC 328 [19] (Lord
       Nicholls); *Taunoa v Attorney-General* [2007] NZSC 70; [2008] 1 NZLR 429 [108] (Elias CJ); *Subiah v
       Attorney-General of Trinidad and Tobago* [2008] UKPC 47 [11] (Lord Bingham); *R (Lumba) v Secretary
       of State for the Home Department* [2012] 1 AC 245 [176] (Lord Hope).
248   [2011] UKSC 12, [2012] 1 AC 245.
249   [2011] UKSC 12, [2012] 1 AC 245 [62]–[88] (Lord Dyson); [170] (Lord Hope); [194] (Lord Walker);
       [208]–[211] (Lady Hale); [221] (Lord Collins); [239]–[247] (Lord Kerr). Lords Phillips, Brown and Rodger
       dissented.
250   [2011] UKSC 12, [2012] 1 AC 245 [90]–[96] (Lord Dyson, with whom Lords Collins, Kerr, Hope and Walker
       and Lady Hale agreed).
251   JNE Varuhas, 'The Concept of 'Vindication' in the Law of Torts: Rights, Interests and Damages' (2014) 34
       OJLS 253, 281–82.
252   [2011] UKSC 12, [2012] 1 AC 245 [101] (Lord Dyson); [222]–[237] (Lord Collins); [253]–[256] (Lord Kerr).
       Dissenting on this point: [176]–[179] (Lord Hope), [195] (Lord Walker), [217] (Lady Hale).

Although such an award is likely in financial terms to cover much the same ground as an award by way of punishment in the sense of retribution, punishment in that sense is not its object. The expressions "punitive damages" or "exemplary damages" are therefore best avoided. Allowance must be made for the importance of the right and the gravity of the breach in the assessment of any award. Its purpose is to recognise the importance of the right to the individual, not to punish the executive. It involves an assertion that the right is a valuable one as to whose enforcement the complainant has an interest. Any award of damages is bound, to some extent at least, to act as a deterrent against further breaches. The fact that it may be expected to do so is something to which it is proper to have regard.[253]

[14.81]   The position of the High Court of Australia on exemplary or vindicatory damages in these circumstances is unknown. *Fernando v Commonwealth* raised similar facts and issues to *Lumba*,[254] but leave to appeal to the High Court was revoked before final determination was made.[255] The trial judge had awarded the plaintiff $25 000 in exemplary damages to reflect the importance of procedural fairness in immigration decisions, notwithstanding that the plaintiff could have been lawfully detained,[256] but this was overturned by the Full Federal Court.[257]

[14.82]   While Australia does not have constitutionally enshrined rights or a Bill of Rights, it has been argued that the common law protects fundamental rights.[258] Consequently, vindicatory awards for civil wrongdoing are occasionally made within general damages awards for torts per se, reflecting the courts' desire to vindicate plaintiff's rights.[259]

---

253   [2011] UKSC 12, [2012] 1 AC 245 [178] (Lord Hope).
254   [2014] FCAFC 181, (2014) 231 FCR 251.
255   *Fernando v Commonwealth* [2015] HCATrans 286 (5 November 2015). See also K Barnett, 'News: Special Leave to Appeal Revoked in Fernando' on *Opinions on High* (6 November 2015) <http://blogs.unimelb.edu.au/opinionsonhigh/2015/11/06/news-special-leave-to-appeal-revoked-in-fernando-v-commonwealth/>
256   *Fernando v Commonwealth (No 5)* [2013] FCA 901.
257   *Fernando v Commonwealth* [2014] FCAFC 181, (2014) 231 FCR 251.
258   JD Heydon, 'Are Bills of Rights Necessary in Common Law Systems?' (Lecture, Oxford Law School, 23 January 2013).
259   Eg *TCN Channel Nine Pty Ltd v Anning* [2002] NSWCA 82, (2002) 54 NSWLR 333 [178]; *New South Wales v Ibbett* [2006] HCA 57, (2006) 229 CLR 638 [20].

15

APOLOGIES AND DECLARATORY RELIEF

I   Introduction

[15.1]   In this chapter, we consider other forms of remedies which seek to vindicate the plaintiff's rights by a public statement of those rights, including declarations and awards of nominal damages and apologies. The court may make a public statement of rights (as with declarations) or the defendant himself may be compelled to make the statement (as with apology orders). Below, we first consider apologies, then declarations, nominal damages and contemptuous damages, and then finally other vindicatory awards available under the Australian Consumer Law.

II   Apologies, declarations and nominal damages

A   Apologies

[15.2]   This book concentrates on pecuniary damages to redress civil wrongdoing. Often an award of damages is the most appropriate remedy. Sometimes, however, if a plaintiff has suffered a civil wrong, she wants the defendant to apologise to her for causing suffering and loss. This may be particularly the case for defamation, in cases involving sexual assault and in cases of negligence (particularly medical malpractice).[1] Apologies are said to have psychological and physiological benefits for plaintiffs,[2] and defendants who apologise are more likely to be able to settle disputes for less money. There are benefits for both parties and for society in general.

[15.3]   Colloquially, a full apology encompasses (at the least) expressions of remorse and regret, and an acknowledgement and acceptance of responsibility for a wrong, as well as an element of reparation.[3] However, many statutes only allow for 'partial apologies' or 'expressions of regret'.[4] In the latter case, no fault or liability can be admitted, and thus no responsibility is taken. Only some statutes cover 'full apologies' in the sense that there may be both remorse and regret *as well as* acceptance of responsibility or liability.[5] Other statutes do not define the term.[6]

[15.4]   An apology may vindicate the plaintiff's right, but it may also be a form of redress and solace for emotional harm.[7] The plaintiff feels vindicated because it is an acknowledgement that she did not deserve to be wronged. There can also be a declaratory and deterrent function which educates the public about the wrongdoing in question.[8] There is an ongoing debate over the

---

1   R Carroll, 'Apologies as a Legal Remedy' (2013) 35 Syd L Rev 317, 319; R Carroll, 'Beyond Compensation: Apology as a Private Law Remedy' in J Berryman and R Bigwood (eds), *The Law of Remedies: New Directions in the Common Law* (Irwin Law 2010) 323.

2   D Slocum, A Allan and MM Allan, 'An Emerging Theory of Apology' (2011) 63 Aust J Psych 83, 83.

3   Ibid. The word 'apology' derives from the Ancient Greek *apologia*, and originally, it denoted a formal legal defence, hence Plato's *Apologia Sokratous* or 'Apology of Socrates' (399 BC).

4   Eg *Civil Law (Wrongs) Act 2002* (ACT) s 132; *Personal Injuries (Liabilities and Damages) Act 2003* (NT) s 12; *Civil Liability Act 2003* (Qld) s 71; *Civil Liability Act 1936* (SA) s 75; *Civil Liability Act 2002* (Tas) s 7; *Wrongs Act 1958* (Vic) s 14I; *Civil Liability Act 2002* (WA) s 5AF.

5   Statutes which do cover full apologies include: *Civil Law (Wrongs) Act 2002* (ACT), s 13; *Civil Liability Act 2002* (NSW), s 68. For overseas examples, see eg, Canada: *Apology Act SO 2009* c 3, s 1; *Apology Act SBC* c 19, s 1; Hong Kong: *Apology Ordinance No. 12 of 2017* (Cap 631).

6   *Defamation Act 2005* (NSW); *Defamation Act 2006* (NT); *Defamation Act 2005* (Qld); *Defamation Act 2005* (SA); *Defamation Act 2005* (Tas); *Defamation Act 2005* (Vic); *Defamation Act 2005* (WA).

7   R Carroll, 'Apologies as a Legal Remedy' (2013) 35 Syd L Rev 317, 337.

8   Ibid, 339.

legal effect of apologies, and whether apologies should have any place in the law at all. In some instances, an apology by a defendant may result in a reduction of damages available to a plaintiff (as for defamation, discussed below [15.7]). Taft has argued that financial and other incentives to apologise have led to a 'commodification' of apology, such that the moral importance of apology has been overshadowed by its (cynical) use as a bargaining tool in the settlement of disputes,[9] but others argue that the positive aspects of allowing apologies outweigh this concern.[10]

In the United States, some hospitals have encouraged apologies when there has been a medical mistake, with positive outcomes for both doctors and patients.[11] Usually patients want an apology, some pecuniary acknowledgement of inconvenience, pain and extra medical costs, and an assurance that the mistake will not happen again. An upside of encouraging apologies is that, instead of denying mistakes, hospitals use mistakes as a learning opportunity and improve procedures. The acknowledgement of the mistake helps ensure that similar mistakes do not happen again.

[15.5]

Australian civil liability statutes have sought to make room for apologies in tort law.[12] A patchwork of state and territory legislation provides that an 'apology' or an 'expression of regret' is no longer an admission of liability.[13] The sections vary slightly: in some jurisdictions only a partial apology or 'expression of regret' which does not contain an acknowledgment of fault can take advantage of the protective regime,[14] whereas in other jurisdictions an apology may still qualify for protection if it contains an admission of fault.[15] It is unfortunate that 'full apologies' are not covered, as evidence shows that plaintiffs regard 'partial apologies' as inadequate.[16] In fact, if an injury is serious, a 'partial apology' can make things worse.[17] In most jurisdictions apologies or expressions of regret are not admissible as evidence of fault or liability,[18] although in Victoria apologies are still admissible with respect to establishing a fact in issue.[19] Despite the differences between the various statutes, as Davies and Malkin note, 'the rationale underlying all the statutory modifications is clear and uniform: to provide the defendant with an opportunity to express regret, without fearing the legal consequences of

[15.6]

---

9   L Taft, 'Apology Subverted: The Commodification of Apology' (2000) 109 Yale LJ 1135.
10   A Allan and R Carroll, 'Apologies in a Legal Setting: Insights from Research into Injured Parties' Experiences of Apologies after an Adverse Event' (2017) 24(1) *Psychiatry, Psychology and the Law* 10.
11   See K Sack, 'Doctors say "I'm Sorry" Before "See You in Court"' *New York Times* (New York, 18 May 2008), <http://www.nytimes.com/2008/05/18/us/18apology.html> accessed 30 May 2013. See also DW Human, 'The Role of Apology in Tort Law' (2000) 83 *Judicature* 180, 184.
12   For the civil liability reform in general, see [7.9]–[7.10].
13   *Civil Law (Wrongs) Act 2002* (ACT), ss 12–14; *Civil Liability Act 2002* (NSW), ss 67–69; *Personal Injuries (Liabilities and Damages) Act 2003* (NT), ss 11–13; *Civil Liability Act 2003* (Qld), ss 68–72; *Civil Liability Act 1936* (SA), s 75; *Civil Liability Act 2002* (Tas), s 7; *Wrongs Act 1958* (Vic), ss 14I–14L; *Civil Liability Act 2002* (WA), ss 5AF–5AH.
14   *Personal Injuries (Liabilities and Damages) Act 2003* (NT), s 12(b); *Civil Liability Act 2003* (Qld), s 71; *Civil Liability Act 2002* (Tas), s 7(3); *Wrongs Act 1958* (Vic), s 14I; *Civil Liability Act 2002* (WA), s 5AF.
15   *Civil Law (Wrongs) Act 2002* (ACT), s 13; *Civil Liability Act 2002* (NSW), s 68.
16   P Vines, 'Apologies in the Civil Liability Context' (2005) 2(1) *Australian Civil Liability* 6, 7; P Vines, 'The Apology in Civil Liability – Underused and Undervalued?' (2013) 115 *Precedent* 28, 29–30.
17   JK Robbennolt, 'Apologies and Medical Error' (2009) 467 *Journal of Clinical Orthopaedics & Related Research* 376–82; JK Robbennolt, 'Apologies and Legal Settlement' (2003) 102 Mich L Rev 460.
18   *Civil Law (Wrongs) Act 2002* (ACT), s 14(c); *Civil Liability Act 2002* (NSW), s 69(2); *Personal Injuries (Liabilities and Damages) Act 2003* (NT), s 13; *Civil Liability Act 2003* (Qld), s 72; *Civil Liability Act 2002* (Tas), s 7(2); *Civil Liability Act 2002* (WA), s 5AH(2).
19   *Wrongs Act 1958* (Vic), s 14J(3). See also s 14K(3).

doing so – in the form of a finding of legal fault or civil liability'.[20] However, the lack of uniformity and knowledge of the legislation means that the apologies sections have not been used or understood.[21]

[15.7]   The law has long recognised the significance of a lack of an apology in torts protecting dignitary interests, including defamation[22] and false imprisonment.[23] Although under uniform defamation legislation an apology is not prima facie relevant to a determination of fault or liability,[24] it may operate as a 'factor in mitigation of damages' which reduces the damages for which a defendant will be liable.[25] Thus the legislation makes room for apologies to take place by providing that an apology does not determine fault or liability, and provides financial incentives for apologies. A lack of an apology may also lead a court to make an award of aggravated damages. For example, in *Myer Stores Ltd v Soo*,[26] the plaintiff was shopping at a department store when he was detained by a store employee and two policemen on suspicion of shoplifting. Myer persisted in insisting up to and during the trial that the plaintiff was responsible for theft when there was no basis for this. It failed to apologise or admit any mistake. Both were factors in the court's decision to award aggravated damages for false imprisonment.[27] It is suggested that the court's policy in this regard encourages a defendant to make an apology. This, however, may lead to the paradox that some plaintiffs will not want a defendant to apologise because they wish to receive maximum financial reparation for the harm.

[15.8]   However, courts rarely exercise a power to force a defendant to apologise. Legislation conferring the power to make apology orders is more common in legislation which prohibits discrimination on the basis of race, gender, disability and the like. The NSW Administrative Decisions Tribunal[28] ordered an apology in *Russell v Commissioner of Police, New South Wales Police Service* after an Aboriginal man was racially vilified and discriminated against by members of the police force when he was being taken into custody.[29]

[15.9]   By contrast, an apology order was refused in *Eatock v Bolt*.[30] Newspaper columnist Andrew Bolt was found to have contravened s 18C of the *Racial Discrimination Act 1975* (Cth) by writing columns which were likely to 'offend, insult, humiliate or intimidate' fair-skinned Aboriginal people. The plaintiffs, who were mentioned in Bolt's columns, sought an apology order. Bromberg J observed as follows:

---

20   M Davies and I Malkin, *Focus: Torts* (7th edn, LexisNexis 2015) [3.66].
21   P Vines, 'The Apology in Civil Liability – Underused and Undervalued?' (2013) 115 *Precedent* 28.
22   *Rookes v Barnard* [1964] AC 1129; *Carson v John Fairfax & Sons Ltd* (1993) 178 CLR 44.
23   *Myer Stores Ltd v Soo* [1991] 2 VR 597.
24   *Civil Law (Wrongs) Act 2002* (ACT), s 132; *Defamation Act 2005* (NSW), s 20; *Defamation Act 2006* (NT), s 19; *Defamation Act 2005* (Qld), s 20; *Defamation Act 2005* (SA), s 20; *Defamation Act 2005* (Tas), s 20; *Defamation Act 2005* (Vic), s 20; *Defamation Act 2005* (WA), s 20.
25   *Civil Law (Wrongs) Act 2002* (ACT), s 139I(1)(a); *Defamation Act 2005* (NSW), s 38(1)(a); *Defamation Act 2006* (NT), s 35(1)(a); *Defamation Act 2005* (Qld), s 35(1)(a); *Defamation Act 2005* (SA), s 36(1)(a); *Defamation Act 2005* (Tas), s 38(1)(a); *Defamation Act 2005* (Vic), s 38(1)(a); *Defamation Act 2005* (WA), s 38(1)(a).
26   [1991] 2 VR 597.
27   Ibid, 603–04.
28   Now known as the NSW Civil and Administrative Tribunal.
29   [2001] NSWADT 32, (2001) 6 AILR 75; award of damages overruled in *Commissioner of Police v Estate of Russell* [2002] NSWCA 272, (2002) 55 NSWLR 232, but apology order unaffected.
30   [2011] FCA 1103, (2011) 197 FCR 261.

> There is force in the contention of [the publisher] that an apology should not be compelled by an order of the Court because that compels a person to articulate a sentiment that is not genuinely held. An apology is one means of achieving the public vindication of those that have been injured by a contravention of s 18C. The power granted to the Court to require a respondent to redress any loss or damage is a wide power. There are other means by which public vindication may be achieved.
>
> Public vindication is important. It will go some way to redressing the hurt felt by those injured. It will serve to restore the esteem and social standing which has been lost as a consequence of the contravention. It will serve to inform those influenced by the contravening conduct of the wrongdoing involved. It may help to negate the dissemination of racial prejudice.[31]

However, Bromberg J declined to make such an order, and instead ordered the defendant to publish a corrective notice in the print and online versions of his newspaper column.

In *Wotton v Queensland (No 5)*,[32] Mortimer J also refused to compel the Queensland Commissioner of Police to issue an apology in relation to racially discriminatory conduct by officers of the Queensland Police Service when investigating the death of an Aboriginal man in custody. She did find that the Commissioner of Police should consider whether it was appropriate to apologise on behalf of the Queensland Police Service to the indigenous community living on Palm Island. She held that the Commissioner was to issue a public apology if he felt it was appropriate, or, if he did not feel it was appropriate, he was to publish reasons for that decision. She concluded: **[15.10]**

> In that way, the Commissioner must take responsibility for deciding whether an apology is appropriate, and what that apology should say in light of the Court's findings. The Commissioner will be accountable publicly for that decision. As I have said, the Court will not however impose an apology on the Commissioner. The Commissioner must sincerely and genuinely decide to offer one; or explain why he will not.[33]

Carroll notes that courts have never ordered an apology in a purely private law context.[34] In *Summertime Holdings Pty Ltd v Environmental Defender's Office Ltd*[35] a plaintiff sought to specifically enforce a promise to apologise which had been made during the settlement of a defamation action. Young J declined to award specific performance of the promise to apologise, citing concerns about free speech and freedom of expression.[36] He held that courts are not empowered to order an apology for defamation,[37] and that courts are reluctant to grant interlocutory injunctions restraining defamatory statements because of freedom of speech concerns.[38]   **[15.11]**

---

31   Ibid, [465]–[466].
32   [2016] FCA 1457.
33   Ibid, [1594].
34   R Carroll, 'Beyond Compensation: Apology as a Private Law Remedy' in J Berryman and R Bigwood (eds), *The Law of Remedies: New Directions in the Common Law* (Irwin Law 2010) 342.
35   (1998) 45 NSWLR 291.
36   Ibid, 297. Cf, however, *Wotton v Queensland (No 5)* [2016] FCA 1457 [1572]–[1573].
37   (1998) 45 NSWLR 291, 298.
38   Ibid, 297.

[15.12]   The question is then whether courts should be able to order apologies, particularly in the context of the dignitary torts, such as defamation or false imprisonment. As Carroll has noted, there are two lines of thought on legally ordered apologies:

> One perspective is that the law has no role to play because the apology is a moral act that will have no worth or value if it is offered as a legal requirement or for legal purposes. Another perspective, more instrumental in nature, is that the law has a role to play in creating opportunities for apologies to be offered that achieve some social or psychological benefit.[39]

On the one hand, an apology ordered by law is no real apology at all, because the defendant does not truly feel remorse. Moreover, there are concerns that apology orders infringe upon personal autonomy. On the other hand, a plaintiff may feel that an apology has a certain value (even if the defendant does not genuinely feel sorry) and may feel vindicated because the defendant has been required to publicly state that he is sorry. Furthermore, an apology sends a message to others that conduct warranting an apology is inappropriate.[40]

[15.13]   Whether apologies will be awarded in private law actions remains to be seen. At the very least, it is suggested that the law should make more room to encourage a wrongdoer to apologise to the person who has been wronged because of the positive social outcomes which may flow from this. Mortimer J's solution in *Wotton v Queensland (No 5)* (see [15.10]) may be an appropriate compromise: to compel the defendant to publicly publish reasons explaining whether an apology should be offered in the circumstances.

B   Declarations, nominal damages and contemptuous damages

1   Declarations

[15.14]   A declaratory judgment is an order made by a court which conclusively pronounces the existence or non-existence of certain legal rights or obligations concerning parties to proceedings. It is not an enforceable order of the court, and thus it stands in contrast to judgments for damages or specific relief (for example), which are executory and can be enforced against a defendant.[41] It can also be contrasted with constitutive or investitive judgments (which create a new right in the party) and with interlocutory judgments (which maintain the status quo before trial).[42] Declaratory judgments are final, non-investitive and cannot be followed up by any process of execution.[43]

---

39   R Carroll, 'Beyond Compensation: Apology as a Private Law Remedy' in J Berryman and R Bigwood (eds), *The Law of Remedies: New Directions in the Common Law* (Irwin Law 2010) 329.

40   For a detailed discussion of the policy issues, see ibid, 352–76; R Carroll, 'Apologies as a Legal Remedy' (2013) 35 Syd L Rev 317, 337–46.

41   See [20.58]–[20.84].

42   PW Young, C Croft and ML Smith, *On Equity* (LBC 2009) [16.750].

43   Ibid.

Declarations began as an equitable remedy, but English common law courts were empowered to award declarations by statute from the 1850s onwards.[44] Australian courts have similarly been conferred with the power to award declarations.[45]   [15.15]

Declarations may be granted in relation to common law and equitable and statutory rights and obligations. They are an important remedy not only in private law but also in public law, and are even available (subject to certain restrictions) in a criminal law context. This chapter will deal primarily with the declaration as a private law remedy, although of necessity it will touch upon cases arising in other contexts. Declarations are also frequently available as a statutory remedy, and examples of their use will be cited below.   [15.16]

The requirement of finality generally means that a court cannot make an 'interim declaration'. In *NSI Group Pty Ltd v Mokas*,[46] the plaintiff sought an interim declaration in respect of the true construction of a contract. Palmer J declined to make the declaration on the basis that the true construction of the contract should be determined once and for all during the final hearing, and it would be inappropriate to declare rights when more evidence might later be available.[47] However, courts sometimes appear to have awarded interim declaratory relief in exceptional circumstances.[48] In most cases an interim declaration is likely to be refused.[49]   [15.17]

A positive declaration creates a *res judicata* or an issue estoppel to prevent the matter from being opened again in litigation between the same parties.[50] Courts may make negative declarations as well as positive declarations (that is, that the plaintiff has no cause of action or that the defendant has not infringed the law), but they exercise this jurisdiction sparingly.[51]   [15.18]

Declarations are judicial acts, and if the declaration will affect the community beyond the interests of the plaintiff and the defendant, courts will not allow a declaration to be made by consent.[52] However, if the rights affected simply arise between the plaintiff and the defendant (for example, where a declaration is one of a series of orders leading to a decree of specific performance) then the court will allow the declaration to be made by consent.   [15.19]

---

44   See JD Heydon, MJ Leeming and PG Turner, *Meagher, Gummow and Lehane's Equity: Doctrines and Remedies* (5th edn, LexisNexis Butterworths 2015) [19–010]–[19–075] for an exhaustive account of the history of the legislation in England and Wales and Australia.

45   See *Court Procedures Rules 2006* (ACT), r 2900(2); *Federal Court of Australia Act 1976* (Cth), s 21(1); *Supreme Court Act 1970* (NSW), s 75; *Supreme Court Act* (NT), s 18(1); *Civil Proceedings Act 2011* (Qld), s 10(2); *Supreme Court Act 1935* (SA), s 31; *Supreme Court Rules 2000* (Tas), r 103(2); *Supreme Court Act 1986* (Vic), s 36; *Supreme Court Act 1935* (WA), s 25(6).

46   [2006] NSWSC 976.

47   Ibid, [14].

48   *R v Inland Revenue Commissioners; Ex parte Rossminster Ltd* [1980] AC 952, 976 (Lord Denning MR); *Trimtor Building Consultants Pty Ltd v Hilton* [1983] 1 NSWLR 259; *MacLeod v Minister Administering the Lands Resumption Act 1957* [1991] Tas R 106. English courts have the power to award interim declarations: *Civil Procedure Rules* (UK), r 25.1(1)(b); A Burrows, *Remedies for Torts and Breach of Contract* (3rd edn, OUP 2004) 593.

49   JD Heydon, MJ Leeming and PG Turner, *Meagher, Gummow and Lehane's Equity: Doctrines and Remedies* (5th edn, Butterworths 2015) [19–140]; J Stuckey-Clarke and FR Burns, 'Declarations' in P Parkinson (ed) *The Principles of Equity* (2nd edn, LBC 2003) [2413].

50   *Re Hilton* (1892) 67 LT 594; *Becker v City of Marion Corporation* [1977] AC 271; *Marra Developments Ltd v B W Rofe Pty Ltd* [1977] 2 NSWLR 616, 626; *Marra Developments Ltd v B W Rofe Pty Ltd* [1981] 1 NSWLR 723, 727.

51   *Crane v Gething* [2000] FCA 45, (2000) 97 FCR 9, aff'd *Crane v Gething* [2000] FCA 762.

52   *Williams v Powell* [1894] WN 141; *Myer Queenstown Garden Plaza Pty Ltd v Port Adelaide City Corporation* (1975) 33 LGRA 70, 82.

[15.20]   Declarations have both strengths and weaknesses, the latter being their lack of enforce-ability.[53] Heydon, Leeming and Turner see the strengths of declarations in that they are relatively quickly obtainable and relatively inexpensive to seek, and that they are available where no other relief is possible.[54] In addition, declarations may minimise the possibility of protracted litigation, and may also allow negative relief to be given (for example, a declaration that the plaintiff is not in breach of a contract).[55] The lack of enforceability of the declaration is a weakness when the defendant fails to respect the plaintiff's rights even after the court has declared them.

[15.21]   Nevertheless, in a private law context, declarations are useful in disputes over status, and may be used in property law and contract law when parties seek to establish the status of property, or of an agreement, or of actions taken in relation to that agreement.[56]

[15.22]   Courts may also make statutory declarations pursuant to provisions such as s 163A of the *Competition and Consumer Act 2010* (Cth) and s 1317E of the *Corporations Act 2001* (Cth). Declarations can also be made in relation to breaches of the Australian Consumer Law ('ACL')[57] as long as the applicant has standing (a real interest in obtaining the relief sought).[58] Declaratory proceedings under the ACL have been said to serve the public interest because they make it plain that the conduct contravenes the ACL.[59] Section 250 of the ACL provides that the court has a power to make declarations that the term of a contract is an unfair term upon application by a party to a consumer contract or by the regulator. The ACCC successfully obtained a declaration by consent under s 250 in relation to several unfair clauses in a standard-form internet service provision contract.[60]

[15.23]   To obtain a declaration, the plaintiff must establish that the court has jurisdiction to grant the remedy, that she has standing to claim the remedy and that there are no discretionary reasons why a declaration should not be granted.

A   JURISDICTION

[15.24]   The jurisdiction to grant an injunction is very wide, and traditionally the power to make a declaration may be excluded only by clear words in a statute, as Gibbs J noted in *Forster v Jododex Australia Pty Ltd*.[61] That case involved a dispute over exploration licences relating to a certain mining site. The plaintiff sought a declaration from the New South Wales Supreme Court that it had a prior valid exploration licence, and that the defendant should not be granted

---

53   M Tilbury, M Gillooly, E Bant and N Witzleb, *Remedies: Commentary and Materials* (5th edn, LBC 2011) [11.05].

54   JD Heydon, MJ Leeming and PG Turner, *Meagher, Gummow and Lehane's Equity: Doctrines and Remedies* (5th edn, Butterworths 2015) [19.005].

55   Eg *Guaranty Trust Co of New York v Hannay & Co* [1915] 2 KB 536.

56   JD Heydon, MJ Leeming and PG Turner, *Meagher, Gummow and Lehane's Equity: Doctrines and Remedies* (5th edn, LexisNexis 2015) [19–085]–[19–095].

57   *Competition and Consumer Act 2010* (Cth), sch 2.

58   *Ainsworth v Criminal Justice Commission* (1992) 175 CLR 564, 581–82.

59   *Australian Competition and Consumer Commission v Midland Brick Co Pty Ltd* [2004] FCA 693, (2004) 207 ALR 329 [21]–[22]; *Rural Press Ltd v Australian Competition and Consumer Commission* [2003] HCA 75, (2003) 216 CLR 53 [89]–[90]; *Australian Competition and Consumer Commission v AirAsia Berhad Co* [2012] FCA 1413, [17].

60   See <http://www.accc.gov.au/media-release/court-declares-consumer-contract-terms-unfair> accessed 10 August 2013.

61   (1972) 127 CLR 421, 435–36.

a licence. At the same time, there were proceedings before the mining warden, who was under a duty to resolve the matter pursuant to the *Mining Act 1906* (NSW). However, because the authority of the warden was found not to be exclusive, the Supreme Court was empowered to make a declaration, although sometimes the presence of an alternative tribunal may be a reason to decline relief.[62] The availability of other remedies is not usually a reason to decline to award a declaration,[63] unless the dispute is particularly specialised.[64]

[15.25] In sum, courts will infer that the jurisdiction to award a declaration is excluded only when the statute clearly requires it.[65]

[15.26] Previously it was thought that the decision not to award a declaration when the question was abstract or hypothetical or where there was no legal issue at stake was a matter of discretion, but in *Ainsworth v Criminal Justice Commission* the High Court of Australia appeared to say that it was a matter of jurisdiction.[66] This means that the court simply has no power to award a declaration when there is an abstract question, rather than having power but choosing not to exercise it.

[15.27] For completeness, it should be noted that there are restrictions on the availability of declarations in criminal law,[67] which are beyond the scope of this book.

B STANDING

[15.28] A plaintiff who seeks declaratory relief must establish that she has sufficient standing to do so; in other words, she must show that she has a sufficient interest in the subject matter of the dispute. The courts distinguish between the standing required to gain a declaration in respect of public rights, and the standing required to gain a declaration in respect of private rights.[68] For private rights, standing is generally uncontroversial.[69] However, for public rights, the proper plaintiff is usually the Attorney-General, who may act either in his or her own right or on behalf of a third party. Pursuant to *Boyce v Paddington Borough Council*, unless it is provided otherwise by statute, a private plaintiff may only act to enforce a public right without joining the Attorney-General in two situations: (1) where the interference with the public right is such that the plaintiff's private right is also interfered

---

62   Ibid, 427 (Walsh J), 438 (Gibbs J).

63   *Pyx Granite Co Ltd v Ministry of Housing and Local Government* [1960] AC 260; *Forster v Jododex Australia Pty Ltd* (1972) 127 CLR 421.

64   *Burwood Municipal Council v Sydney Legacy Appeals Fund* (1980) 39 LGRA 299.

65   *Pyx Granite Co Ltd v Ministry of Housing and Local Government* [1960] AC 260, 286; *Forster v Jododex Australia Pty Ltd* (1972) 127 CLR 421, 435–36; *Oil Basins Ltd v Commonwealth* (1993) 178 CLR 643, 652–53 (Dawson J); *Law Society (NSW) v Weaver* [1974] 1 NSLWR 271, 272; *Telstra Corporation Ltd v Australia Telecommunications Authority* (1995) 133 ALR 417, 426.

66   (1992) 175 CLR 564, 582. See JD Heydon, MJ Leeming and PG Turner, *Meagher, Gummow and Lehane's Equity: Doctrines and Remedies* (5th edn, LexisNexis 2015) [19–110].

67   See Heydon, Leeming and Turner, ibid, [19–320]; W Covell, K Lupton and J Forder, *Principles of Remedies* (6th edn, LexisNexis 2015) [14.19]–[14.20]; J Stuckey-Clarke and FR Burns, 'Declarations' in P Parkinson (ed) *The Principles of Equity* (2nd edn, LBC 2003) [2403]; PW Young, C Croft and ML Smith, *On Equity* (LBC 2009) [16.770].

68   *Boyce v Paddington Borough Council* [1903] 1 Ch 109.

69   Cf *Meadows Indemnity Co Ltd v Insurance Corporation of Ireland plc* [1989] 2 Lloyd's Rep 298; *CE Hath Casualty & General Insurance Ltd v Pyramid Building Society (in liq)* [1997] 2 VR 256, 288 (JD Phillips JA), where plaintiffs who were not parties to insurance contracts could not gain a declaration in relation to those contracts.

with; and (2) where no private right is interfered with, but the plaintiff suffers special damage from the interference with the public right.[70] Heydon, Leeming and Turner have argued forcefully that the *Boyce* test has been applied haphazardly or ignored by courts altogether, and that there is 'in logic no compelling reason' to retain the *Boyce* restriction in relation to declarations involving public rights as long as the plaintiff has a 'real and substantial interest in the subject matter of the dispute'.[71]

C   DISCRETION

[15.29]   As noted earlier, it is sometimes thought that one of the discretionary issues which will lead a court to refuse to award a declaration is where the question raised is abstract, theoretical or hypothetical. There must also be a real and justiciable question which the court can resolve.[72] In other words, the dispute must involve a determination of a legal controversy concerning rights, liabilities and interests of the kind that are protected by courts.[73] The facts on which the declaration is based must be proven and not hypothetical.[74]

[15.30]   A court may make a declaration in relation to future rights and liabilities,[75] but only if there is real uncertainty about the correct course of action,[76] as the court is concerned not to give advisory opinions.[77] An example of a case where a declaration was refused on the basis that the claim was unduly hypothetical, identified no precise law which was problematic and no individual, corporation or government which was in breach of the law is *Lindon v Commonwealth (No 2)*, in which the plaintiff sought a declaration stating (inter alia) that '[t]he threat or use of nuclear weapons in any circumstances is not permitted under municipal law'.[78]

[15.31]   Another basis on which a court may refuse to exercise its discretion to award a declaration is if the declaration would not have utility for the plaintiff or practical value for the broader public.[79] As with specific relief, if a declaration cannot be clearly and precisely expressed, the court is likely to refuse to award it.[80]

[15.32]   A declaration may also be refused if the plaintiff seeks to take advantage of her own wrongdoing, as in *Puttick v Attorney-General*,[81] where the plaintiff sought a declaration that her marriage was valid, but she had procured the marriage using forged documents.

---

70   [1903] 1 Ch 109, 114 (Buckley J).
71   JD Heydon, MJ Leeming and PG Turner, *Meagher, Gummow and Lehane's Equity: Doctrines and Remedies* (5th edn, LexisNexis 2015) [19–190].
72   *Egan v Willis* (1998) 195 CLR 424, 438–39 (Gaudron, Gummow and Hayne JJ).
73   Ibid, 439 (Gaudron, Gummow and Hayne JJ).
74   *University of New South Wales v Moorhouse* (1975) 133 CLR 1, 10 (Gibbs J).
75   *Trustees of Church Property of the Diocese of Newcastle v Ebbeck* (1960) 104 CLR 394; *Bond v Sulan* (1990) 26 FCR 580.
76   *Trustees of Church Property of the Diocese of Newcastle v Ebbeck* (1960) 104 CLR 394, 400–01 (Dixon J).
77   J Stuckey-Clarke and FR Burns, 'Declarations' in P Parkinson (ed) *The Principles of Equity* (2nd edn, LBC 2003) [2407]. See, eg, *Aberdeen Development Co v Makiel, Ramsay & Taylor* [1977] SLT 177, 181.
78   (1996) 136 ALR 251, 253.
79   *Dairy Farmers Co-operative Milk Co Ltd v Commonwealth* (1946) 73 CLR 381; *Mikaelian v Commonwealth Scientific and Industrial Research Organisation* [1999] FCA 610, (1999) 163 ALR 172 [85]–[87].
80   *Global Finance Management (NSW) Ltd v Rooney* (1994) 36 NSWLR 122, 136.
81   [1980] Fam 1, 22.

2   Nominal damages

Nominal damages are not compensatory, but are intended to vindicate rights.[82] As Lord
Halsbury LC explained in *The Mediana*:

> 'Nominal damages' is a technical phrase which means that you have negatived anything
> like real damage, but that you are affirming by your nominal damages that there is an
> infraction of a legal right, which, though it gives you no right to any real damages at all, yet
> gives you a right to the verdict or judgment because your legal right has been infringed.
> But the term 'nominal damages' does not mean small damages.[83]

Because common law courts could not award declarations before the UK Judicature Acts
(*Judicature Act 1873* and *Judicature Act 1875*), they developed nominal damages as an
analogue to a declaratory judgment. When the court makes an award of nominal damages,
the court declares that the defendant has committed a wrong, but only awards a token amount
such as $5.[84] The award must truly be token, and in *New South Wales v Stevens* an award of
$10 000 nominal damages was reduced on appeal to $100.[85] Such awards are usually made
where the plaintiff has a right to a verdict in her favour because a legal right has been infringed,
but she cannot show any loss. Consequently, such awards are only made in relation to wrongs
actionable per se (that is, in the absence of loss) such as trespass to land,[86] trespass to the
person,[87] defamation,[88] and breach of contract.[89]

[15.33]

It might be queried whether a plaintiff who receives nominal damages considers that her
rights have been vindicated. Indeed, as we will see below, the award of a nominal fee could be
seen as contemptuous. Moreover, courts have discretion to depart from the rule that costs
follow the event,[90] meaning that a plaintiff who receives only nominal damages may have to
pay the defendant's costs.

[15.34]

Burrows has argued that nominal damages should be abolished because declarations are
now available at common law.[91] There is some strength to this argument and it seems that,
unless the court wishes to in some way express contempt for the plaintiff, it may be more
effective to vindicate the plaintiff's rights by making a declaration.

[15.35]

---

82   N Witzleb and R Carroll, 'The Role of Vindication in Torts Damages' (2009) 17 Tort L Rev 1, 7.
83   [1900] AC 113, 116. See also *Baume v Commonwealth* (1906) 4 CLR 97, 116–17.
84   Eg *Constantine v Imperial Homes Ltd* [1944] KB 693 (award of five guineas).
85   [2012] NSWCA 415, (2012) 82 NSWLR 106.
86   Eg *Elliott v Renner* [1923] St R Qd 172; *Armstrong v Sheppard & Short Ltd* [1959] 2 QB 384; *Prentice v Mercantile House Pty Ltd* (1991) 99 ALR 107, 122–23.
87   Eg *Law v Wright* [1935] SASR 20.
88   Eg *Grobbelaar v News Group Newspapers Ltd* [2002] UKHL 40, [2002] 1 WLR 3024, although these could be better categorised as 'contemptuous damages'.
89   Eg *Luna Park (NSW) Ltd v Tramways Advertising Pty Ltd* (1938) 61 CLR 286; *Berger v Boyles* [1971] VR 321, 330; *Sunrock Aircraft Corporation Ltd v Scandinavian Airlines System Denmark-Norway-Sweden* [2007] EWCA Civ 882, [2007] 2 Lloyd's Rep 612 [35]; *Motium Pty Ltd v Arrow Electronics Australia Pty Ltd* [2011] WASCA 65; *New South Wales v Stevens* [2012] NSWCA 415, (2012) 82 NSWLR 106.
90   *Connolly v 'Sunday Times' Publishing Co Ltd* (1908) 7 CLR 263; *Anglo Cyprian Trade Agencies v Paphos Wine Industries Ltd* [1951] 1 All ER 873; *Nexus Minerals NL v Brutus Constructions Pty Ltd* [1997] FCA 926. Cf *Beaumont v Greathead* (1846) 2 CB 494, 499; 135 ER 1039, 1041 (Maule J): 'Nominal damages are a mere peg on which to hang costs'.
91   A Burrows, *Remedies for Torts and Breach of Contract* (3rd edn, OUP 2004) 589.

[15.36]   However, *McGregor on Damages* observes that nominal damages may be awarded in rare cases where the fact of loss is shown but evidence as to its quantum is not provided, in which case the award is not in the nature of a declaration or a vindication of rights, but reflects a problem of proof.[92] Thus, nominal damages may still have a limited role to play even if declarations cover most of the field formerly occupied by nominal damages.

3   Contemptuous damages

[15.37]   In some cases, if the court finds that the wrong caused no loss and awards a nominal sum only, then the award is a rebuff for the plaintiff, and sometimes these awards are described as 'contemptuous damages'.[93] The court is saying that the plaintiff was technically successful, but that the action should never have been brought in the first place.[94]

[15.38]   These awards are usually made in defamation cases where the plaintiff was technically defamed, but the judges or the jury felt that the plaintiff did not have a good character that was deserving of protection.[95] In *Grobbelaar v News Group Newspapers Ltd*,[96] the court arguably awarded contemptuous damages (notwithstanding the fact that most of the judges referred to the award as 'nominal damages').[97] The former Liverpool Football Club goalkeeper, Bruce Grobbelaar, sued *The Sun* for libel in relation to allegations that he had fixed matches for bribes. While the allegations were technically libellous because Grobbelaar's attempts to match-fix were ultimately unsuccessful, there was nonetheless taped evidence that he had agreed to fix matches. Grobbelaar was initially awarded £85 000, but on appeal the House of Lords slashed his award to £1 and ordered him to pay *The Sun*'s costs, estimated at £500 000. Lord Bingham observed that the tort of defamation 'affords little or no protection to those who have, or deserve to have, no reputation deserving of legal protection', and continued:

> It would be an affront to justice if a court of law were to award substantial damages to a man shown to have acted in such flagrant breach of his legal and moral obligations.[98]

A plaintiff who is awarded contemptuous damages is likely to have to pay the defendant's costs.[99]

[15.39]   As Burrows argues, it is difficult to see how a declaration could achieve the 'double-edged sword' effect of vindicating the plaintiff's rights while simultaneously admonishing the plaintiff, and thus contemptuous damages should not be abolished, even if nominal damages are abolished.[100]

---

92   J Edelman, *McGregor on Damages* (20th edn, Sweet & Maxwell 2018) [12–004]–[12–005], citing *Dixon v Deveridge* (1825) 2 C & P 109, 172 ER 50; *Twyman v Knowles* (1853) 13 CB 222. A recent Australian example is *Motium Pty Ltd v Arrow Electronics Australia Pty Ltd* [2011] WASCA 65 [91]–[92].

93   *Bailey v Truth and Sportsman Ltd* (1938) 60 CLR 700, 708 (Latham CJ), 728 (McTiernan J).

94   SM Waddams, *The Law of Damages* (5th edn, Canada Law Book 2012) [10.40].

95   See, eg, *Wood v Cox* (1888) 4 TLR 652 (QB); *Kelly v Sherlock* (1866) LR 1 QB 686; *Connolly v 'Sunday Times' Publishing Co Ltd* (1908) 7 CLR 263; *Martin v Benson* [1927] 1 KB 771; *Dering v Uris* [1964] 2 QB 669; *Pamplin v Express Newspapers Ltd (No 2)* [1988] 1 WLR 116; *Reynolds v Times Newspapers Ltd* [1998] 3 WLR 862; *Grobbelaar v News Group Newspapers Ltd* [2002] UKHL 40, [2002] 1 WLR 3024.

96   [2002] UKHL 40, [2002] 1 WLR 3024.

97   A Burrows, *Remedies for Torts and Breach of Contract* (3rd edn, OUP 2004) 590 fn 4.

98   [2002] UKHL 40, [2002] 1 WLR 3024 [24].

99   *Martin v Benson* [1927] 1 KB 771.

100   A Burrows, *Remedies for Torts and Breach of Contract* (3rd edn, OUP 2004) 590.

III   Other vindicatory remedies under the Australian Consumer Law

The ACL[101] provides for quasi-punitive orders, such as adverse publishing orders pursuant to s 247 and orders disqualifying persons from managing corporations pursuant to s 248. These orders can be used where an action has been brought by an individual (private law) and on behalf of consumers (regulator or public law action).   [15.40]

Section 246 sets out a range of non-punitive orders that may be sought by a regulator, and in sub-s (2) outlines a non-exhaustive list of such orders: [15.41]

- orders directing a person to perform a benefit for the community in relation to the contravening conduct;
- orders ensuring that the person does not engage in the conduct or similar conduct by establishing a compliance plan, establishing an education and training plan for employees and other persons involved in the business, and/or requiring the person to revise the internal operations of the business;
- orders requiring the person to disclose information;
- orders requiring the person to publish information in an advertisement at her own expense.

In *Director of Consumer Affairs Victoria v Gibson (No 3)*,[102] the defendant, Ms Gibson, made misleading and deceptive representations in a book and an app that (a) her special diet had sent her cancer into remission, and (b) that she was going to donate substantial proportions of her profits to named charities. In fact, she had never suffered from cancer, and she donated almost no profits to the named charities. Among other things, the Director sought a publication order pursuant to s 246(2)(d) of the ACL. Mortimer J declined to make such an order because there had already been significant adverse publicity regarding the defendant's actions, and Ms Gibson might be forced to commit contempt of court if she could not pay for the advertising.[103] Moreover, the original proposed form of advertisement effectively compelled Ms Gibson to apologise, but Mortimer J found that it would have been inappropriate to compel Ms Gibson to apologise via that means.[104] Mortimer J also observed that the Director could have sought for Ms Gibson to perform a service for the benefit of the community pursuant to s 246(2)(a) of the ACL.[105] She said, 'directing a person to give up her or his time, and to perform a service to the community, is an order that can be enforced more readily against any person, irrespective of financial capacity'.[106] However, as such an order was not sought by the Director, it was not made.   [15.42]

---

101   *Competition and Consumer Act 2010* (Cth), sch 2.
102   [2017] FCA 1148.
103   Ibid, [103]–[106].
104   Ibid, [107].
105   Ibid, [115].
106   Ibid.

PART **5**

ACCOUNT OF PROFITS AND OTHER GAIN-BASED RELIEF FOR WRONGS

16

DISGORGEMENT OF GAINS AND 'REASONABLE FEE' DAMAGES

I Introduction

[16.1]   This chapter discusses the account of profits, disgorgement, and other forms of gain-based relief. The chapter will consider the difference between compensation, restitution and disgorgement. It will then consider the account of profits and the reasonable fee award, and the operation of bars to relief and other limiting factors.

[16.2]   The primary rationales of the account of profits have been identified as deterrence and prophylaxis (i.e. preventing a defendant from gaining from wrongdoing).[1] Deterrence looks not to the dispute in question, but to the future conduct of the specific defendant (specific deterrence) and the future conduct of other potential defendants (general deterrence). By stripping the defendant of her gain (or part of her gain), the defendant (and other potential defendants) will be deterred from engaging in similar conduct in the future. It is argued that the remedies discussed in this chapter have a deterrent flavour.

[16.3]   However, two things should be noted. First, accounts of profit for intellectual property infringements are said to prevent the defendant from being unjustly enriched,[2] and accordingly their purpose is somewhat different from the account of profits in the context of breach of fiduciary duty.[3] This underlines the difficulty of separating unjust enrichment and gain-based relief for wrongs.

[16.4]   Secondly, the placement of reasonable fee awards into this chapter may be regarded as controversial. 'Reasonable fee' refers to a method of calculating a monetary award for a wrong, namely where the court awards the fee that the parties would have agreed upon for permitting the defendant's conduct. Reasonable fee awards may be made in various forms, including through an award of compensation, in an action for money had and received through 'waiver of tort', as 'restitutionary damages', or under Lord Cairns' Act in lieu of an injunction. They are generally awarded for common law causes of action. As discussed at [16.62]–[16.76], the rationale for reasonable fee damages is highly contested, and these damages have been argued variously to be compensatory, restitutionary, designed to effect partial disgorgement, to protect property rights, or to be vindicatory. However, while we acknowledge other analyses, we have decided to include 'reasonable fee' damages in this chapter because we have both argued elsewhere that these awards are gain-based.[4]

---

1   J Edelman, *Gain-Based Damages: Contract, Tort, Equity and Intellectual Property* (Hart 2002) 83–86; S Worthington, 'Reconsidering Disgorgement for Wrongs' (1999) 62 Mod LR 218; M Conaglen, *Fiduciary Loyalty: Protecting the Due Performance of Non-Fiduciary Duties* (Hart 2010); I Samet, 'Guarding the Fiduciary's Conscience – A Justification of a Stringent Profit-Stripping Rule' (2008) 28 OJLS 763; R Cooter and B Freedman, 'The Fiduciary Relationship: Its Economic Character and Legal Consequences' (1991) 66 NYULR 1045; P Devonshire, *Account of Profits* (Thomson Reuters 2013) 58–59. Cf L Smith, 'Deterrence, Prophylaxis and Punishment in Fiduciary Obligations' (2013) 7 J Eq 87; L Smith, 'Fiduciary Relationships: Ensuring the Loyal Exercise of Judgement on Behalf of Another' (2014) 130 LQR 608, 627.

2   *Dart Industries Inc v Décor Corporation Pty Ltd* (1993) 179 CLR 101, 111

3   *Warman International Ltd v Dwyer* (1995) 182 CLR 544 ('*Warman*'), 557.

4   S Harder, *Measuring Damages in the Law of Obligations: The Search for Harmonised Principles* (Hart 2010) 179–81; K Barnett, *Accounting for Profit for Breach of Contract: Theory and Practice* (Hart 2012) ch 3. ('To thine own self be true': *Hamlet*, Act 1, Scene 3).

II The distinction between compensation, restitution and disgorgement and the nature of gain-based remedies

At the outset, it is necessary to set out the distinction between compensation, restitution and disgorgement, as these concepts permeate judicial and academic commentary and sometimes cause confusion.

[16.5]

A Compensation

Compensation looks to the loss or damage suffered by the plaintiff as a result of the defendant's wrong. The plaintiff must suffer a loss, and the defendant must pay damages to make good that loss. Compensatory damages are the staple remedy in contract and tort. In tort, they aim to put the plaintiff in a position as if the duty had not been breached.[5] In contract, the position is a little more complicated.[6] Expectation damages aim to put the plaintiff in a position as if the contract had been performed.[7] Sometimes, reliance damages are awarded.[8] They formally aim to put the plaintiff into a position as if the contract had not been made, but reliance loss is used as a proxy for expectation loss; see [5.67]–[5.68].

[16.6]

B Restitution

Restitution arises where the defendant makes a gain at the plaintiff's expense. The defendant may gain money, services, or goods. Restitution is concerned to reverse transfers of value. It is corrective in nature. If the defendant has gained at the plaintiff's expense, he must give back what he gained (or the monetary value of his gain).

[16.7]

It is important to be aware that restitution is different from compensation. There is not necessarily a gain on the part of the defendant in situations where compensation is awarded. For example, if I negligently run you down with my car, I am not unjustly enriched at your expense. I do not gain anything;[9] it is simply that you suffer loss by reason of my negligence. However, suppose you mistakenly give me $100, thinking it is my birthday. I am unjustly enriched at your expense. The law reverses this transfer by making me give back to you the $100. This is discussed further in Ch 17.

[16.8]

The term 'restitution' is not used only in the sense of a 'giving back' of a gain made at the plaintiff's expense. Confusingly, 'restitution' is also used in the sense of a 'giving up' of a gain

[16.9]

---

5   *Livingstone v Rawyards Coal Co* (1880) 5 App Cas 25, 39 (Lord Blackburn); see [6.2].
6   See LL Fuller and WR Perdue, 'The Reliance Interest in Contract Damages' (1936) 46 Yale LJ 52 and [5.3]–[5.8].
7   *Robinson v Harman* (1848) 1 Ex 850, 855; 154 ER 363, 365 (Parke B); *Wertheim v Chicoutimi Pulp Co* [1911] AC 301, 307 (Lord Atkinson).
8   *McRae v Commonwealth Disposals Commission* (1951) 84 CLR 377; *Commonwealth v Amann Aviation Pty Ltd* (1991) 174 CLR 64.
9   Ignoring for present purposes the argument by corrective justice scholars that the defendant makes a 'normative gain': see E Weinrib, *The Idea of Private Law* (2nd edn, OUP 2013) and other works by Weinrib and associated scholars.

made by the defendant where there has not been a correlative loss on the part of the plaintiff.[10] This kind of 'giving up' of a gain without a loss on the part of the plaintiff is better referred to as disgorgement.

C   Disgorgement

[16.10]   Disgorgement looks to the gain made by the defendant as a result of her breach of duty. The nature of disgorgement is that the defendant must give up the gain she has made, so that the *defendant* is in the same position as if she never breached the duty. The rationale of disgorgement awards is deterrence – by stripping the defendant of profit, the incentives for future defendants to breach is removed.[11] For disgorgement to be awarded there is no necessity for the plaintiff to have made a loss (in contrast to both compensation and restitution). It is merely necessary that the defendant have made a gain. Therefore, disgorgement awards are an exception to the rule that the plaintiff cannot be left in a better position than if the wrong had not occurred.

[16.11]   Remedies effecting disgorgement or restitution are also sometimes called 'gain-based' remedies. This simply means that the remedy operates to strip a profit, a proportion of a profit or the value of a benefit from the defendant.

[16.12]   In Australia, disgorgement is available in the form of an account of profits for breaches of equitable obligations. These strip the defendant of his net profit, subject to allowances and discretionary bars to relief. Accounts of profit are also available for intellectual property infringement and for passing off. The availability of accounts of profit for intellectual property infringement largely arose in the auxiliary jurisdiction of equity, but for some infringements there is now a statutory basis.

[16.13]   Disgorgement becomes controversial when awarded for common law causes of action. In Australia, accounts of profit are generally not awarded for contract and tort. However, reasonable fee awards are available for intellectual property infringements and for proprietary torts. The classification of 'reasonable fee' awards is contentious, and it is sometimes suggested that such awards are not gain-based but rather compensatory in nature, even though the awards often focus on the gains the defendant made or the value of the benefit to the defendant. Alternatively, it is argued that such remedies are restitutionary (in the sense that they reverse unjust enrichment) or that they are a form of disgorgement (in the sense that they strip the defendant of profit).

[16.14]   Many of the cases involving disgorgement for tort and contract are not Australian cases. However, reasonable fees have been awarded for proprietary torts. Australian courts are less

---

10   These two senses of restitution were developed by P Birks, *An Introduction to the Law of Restitution* (revised edn, Clarendon Press 1989) 12.

11   J Edelman, *Gain-Based Damages: Contract, Tort, Equity and Intellectual Property* (Hart 2002) 83–86; S Worthington, 'Reconsidering Disgorgement for Wrongs' (1999) 62 Mod LR 218; I Samet, 'Guarding the Fiduciary's Conscience – A Justification of a Stringent Profit-Stripping Rule' (2008) 28 OJLS 763; M Conaglen, *Fiduciary Loyalty: Protecting the Due Performance of Non-Fiduciary Duties* (Hart 2010); R Cooter and B Freedman, 'The Fiduciary Relationship: Its Economic Character and Legal Consequences' (1991) 66 NYULR 1045; P Devonshire, *Account of Profits* (2013, Thomson Reuters), 58–9. Cf however, L Smith, 'Deterrence, Prophylaxis and Punishment in Fiduciary Obligations' (2013) 7 J Eq 87; L Smith, 'Fiduciary Relationships: Ensuring the Loyal Exercise of Judgement on Behalf of Another' (2014) 130 LQR 608, 627.

willing than courts in other jurisdictions to award gain-based relief for common law breaches, particularly accounts of profits.

Accordingly, where appropriate, cases from other common law jurisdictions where such awards have been made will be considered and compared with the Australian position.

We will first consider disgorgement, then the 'reasonable fee' cases.   [16.15]

III   Disgorgement
A   Equity and the account of profits

The account of profits began with the common law writ of *praecipe quod reddat*, and evolved   [16.16]
from an action by lords of the manor against manorial bailiffs who had failed to account for profits. During the 17th century, the common law account was ultimately overtaken by the more efficient equitable account.[12] Worthington has argued that disgorgement is peculiarly well suited for preventing breaches of equitable obligations:

> The aim is to exact particular standards of conduct in the protected relationships; to this end, the relevant law is concerned with proscribing certain activities, not with precluding particular outcomes. The appropriate remedial response for breaches of these equitable obligations is disgorgement because this is the remedy which best supports the legal obligation being enforced.[13]

The account of profits is an equitable remedy, and is awarded primarily in cases of   [16.17]
equitable wrongdoing such as breach of trust,[14] breach of fiduciary duty[15] and breach of confidence.[16] It is also available pursuant to statute in cases of infringement of intellectual property rights.[17] Finally, it is also available in equity's auxiliary jurisdiction for the tort of passing off.[18]

The calculation of an account of profits involves a two-stage process. The first stage simply   [16.18]
provides an account to the plaintiff of the defendant's financial affairs insofar as they relate to her claim. Once a profit has been identified, it can be stripped from the defendant. This is the second stage of an account. Importantly, the profits are generally the defendant's net profits, rather than the defendant's gross receipts.[19] The court will not punish the defendant by

---

12   For the history, see M McInnes, 'Account of Profits for Common Law Wrongs' in S Degeling and J Edelman (eds), *Equity in Commercial Law* (LBC 2005) 406–07; D Wright, *Remedies* (2nd edn, Federation Press 2014) 107; P Devonshire, *Account of Profits* (Thomson Reuters 2013), 3–8.

13   S Worthington, 'Reconsidering Disgorgement for Wrongs' (1999) 62 Mod LR 218, 237.

14   JD Heydon and MJ Leeming, *Jacob's Law of Trusts in Australia* (8th edn, LexisNexis 2016) [22–06].

15   Eg *Warman International Ltd v Dwyer* (1995) 182 CLR 544.

16   Eg *Attorney-General v Observer Ltd* [1990] 1 AC 109. Cf *Vercoe v Rutland Fund Management Ltd* [2010] EWHC 424 (Ch), [2010] Bus LR D141, [341] (Sales J) (accounts of profit only available exceptionally for breach of confidence).

17   *Patents Act 1990* (Cth), s 122(1); *Copyright Act 1968* (Cth), s 115(2); *Designs Act 2003* (Cth), s 75(1); *Trade Marks Act 1995* (Cth), s 126(1); *Circuit Layouts Act 1989* (Cth), s 27(2); *Plant Breeder's Rights Act 1994* (Cth), s 56(3).

18   *My Kinda Town Ltd v Soll* [1983] RPC 15.

19   *Patel v London Borough of Brent* [2003] EWHC 3081, [2004] 3 PLR 1 [29]; *Regal (Hastings) Ltd v Gulliver* [1967] 2 AC 134, 154 (Lord Wright); *O'Sullivan v Management Agency & Music Ltd* [1985] QB 428, 458 (Dunn LJ). See P Devonshire, *Account of Profits* (2013, Thomson Reuters) 11.

requiring him to account for more than he has received by reason of the breach of duty.[20] However, if it is impossible to ascertain who the profit belongs to because the defendant has mixed moneys, or if the defendant's conduct has been fraudulent, courts may not apportion the gain.[21] Similarly, if a trustee makes a profit by misapplying trust money, it is likely that the plaintiff will be entitled to the entire profit.[22]

[16.19]   In assessing net profit, courts have traditionally made allowance for certain expenses incurred by the defendant in two ways.[23] First, they have sometimes allowed specific disbursements, such as expenditures of money and other capital, as well as skilled labour by the defendant.[24] Secondly, courts have credited the defendant with an allowance which is not specifically itemised, but more of an 'all things considered' allowance.[25]

[16.20]   Calculation of profit can be difficult and expensive, and plaintiffs may therefore be reluctant to seek accounts of profit.[26] The High Court of Australia has recognised the difficulties in calculating profit derived from wrongdoing, and noted that 'mathematical exactitude is generally impossible'.[27] The account of profits may be more workable if courts applied the liberal causation rule from breach of fiduciary duty (see [16.22]) across the board, with an added requirement for other kinds of wrong (such as breach of contract, tort, or breach of privacy) that any breach be advertent and conscious. The burden of proof could shift to the defendant to prove that the breach did not cause the gains in question, as the defendant possesses better information about the gain than the plaintiff. However, this suggestion does not reflect the law as it presently stands.

[16.21]   Law-and-economics scholars have argued that the availability of disgorgement remedies prevents fiduciaries from misappropriating trust property.[28] Beneficiaries find it difficult to detect the fiduciary's breach of duty. Profit-stripping provides a disincentive to fiduciaries who may be tempted. The remedies available for breach of fiduciary duty mean that the sanction equals the gain from wrongdoing, ensuring successful deterrence. Thus, the laws regarding fiduciary duties are economically efficient, as they provide for 'self-policing' by the fiduciary.

---

20   *Hospital Products Ltd v United States Surgical Corporation* (1984) 156 CLR 41, 108–09 (Mason J), citing *Vyse v Foster* (1872) LR 8 Ch App 309, 333 (James LJ).

21   *Hospital Products Ltd v United States Surgical Corporation* (1984) 156 CLR 41, 109–10 (Mason J).

22   *Scott v Scott* (1963) 109 CLR 649; see also *Paul A Davies (Australia) Pty Ltd (in liq) v Davies* [1983] 1 NSLWR 440.

23   M Harding, 'Justifying Fiduciary Allowances' in A Robertson and TH Wu (eds), *The Goals of Private Law* (Hart 2009) 346–47.

24   *Brown v Litton* (1711) 1 P Wms 140, 24 ER 329; *Yates v Finn* (1880) 13 Ch D 839; *Chirnside v Fay* [2006] NZSC 68, [2007] 1 NZLR 433 [153] (Tipping J).

25   *Brown v De Tastet* (1821) Jac 284; 37 ER 858; *Featherstonhaugh v Turner* (1858) 25 Beav 382, 53 ER 683; *Lord Provost of Edinburgh v Lord Advocate* (1879) 4 App Cas 823; *Phipps v Boardman* [1964] 1 WLR 993; *O'Sullivan v Management Agency & Music Ltd* [1985] QB 428.

26   M Gronow, 'Restitution for Breach of Confidence' (1996) 10 Intell Prop J 219; T Aplin, L Bently, P Johnson and S Malynicz, *Gurry on Breach of Confidence* (2nd edn, OUP 2012) [20.13] (both discussing breach of confidence).

27   *Dart Industries Inc v Décor Corporation Pty Ltd* (1993) 179 CLR 101, 111 (Mason CJ, Deane, Dawson and Toohey JJ). See also *Warman* (1995) 182 CLR 544, 558; *Colbeam Palmer Ltd v Stock Affiliates Ltd* (1968) 122 CLR 25 ('*Colbeam*'), 37 (Windeyer J).

28   R Cooter and B Freedman, 'The Fiduciary Relationship: Its Economic Character and Legal Consequences' (1991) 66 NYULR 1045.

In cases involving breach of fiduciary duty, the causation test is liberal, and there is no need to make out the 'but for' test.[29] The breach need only be 'a cause' of the gain, and need not be a predominant cause.[30] However, in *CMS Dolphin Ltd v Simonet*, Collins J noted that there must be 'some reasonable connection' between the breach and the profits made.[31] The 'but for' test may be applied to fiduciaries where there is an antecedent profit-sharing agreement.[32] For other wrongs other than breach of fiduciary duty, it seems that a 'but for' test applies:[33] in other words, would the defendant have made the profit but for the breach?   [16.22]

The seminal Australian case on accounts of profit for breach of fiduciary duty is *Warman International Ltd v Dwyer*.[34] An employee, Dwyer, engaged in a concurrent breach of fiduciary duty and contract towards his employer by redirecting his employer's business to a personal enterprise. Dwyer was employed by an Australian company, Warman International Ltd ('Warman'), which distributed Italian gearboxes. The Italian gearbox manufacturer, Bonfiglioli, was unhappy with Warman, as was Dwyer, and together they set up a new company to be the Australian distributor. The new distributing company made a vastly greater profit than the amount Warman had lost because of the breach.   [16.23]

It is clear from *Warman* that the plaintiff must elect between equitable compensation and an account of profits; see [16.28]–[16.30]. The High Court of Australia unanimously held that when a breach of fiduciary duty results in a profit to the fiduciary, the beneficiary has a right to the profits, and the court has no discretion to deny an account of profits.   [16.24]

It is no defence that the beneficiary was unwilling, unlikely or unable to make the profits for which an account is taken; nor is it a defence that the fiduciary acted honestly and reasonably.[35] The award of an account of profits is subject to equitable defences such as estoppel, laches, acquiescence or delay. The High Court also raised the possibility that the conduct of the plaintiff may make it inequitable to order an account, but this has not been taken up in subsequent cases.   [16.25]

On the method of calculating profit, the High Court said that it was important to ascertain what was acquired as a consequence of the breach of fiduciary duty, and it might also sometimes be relevant to consider what was lost by the plaintiff. In this case, it was significant that Bonfiglioli was intending to terminate its contract with its former distributor within a year, and that Bonfiglioli had always retained the goodwill in its product pursuant to the distributorship agreement. Thus, while the trial judge had awarded the employer profits for the first four years of operation of the new Australian distributor, the High Court limited that to two years.   [16.26]

The third issue raised was the allowance for skill and effort in favour of the former manager; this reduced the proportion of the profits stripped. Dwyer was given an allowance   [16.27]

29 See, eg, *Industrial Development Consultants Ltd v Cooley* [1972] 1 WLR 443; *Novoship (UK) Ltd v Mikhaylyuk* [2014] EWCA Civ 908, [2015] QB 499.
30 C Mitchell, 'Causation, Remoteness, and Fiduciary Gains' (2006) 17 KCLJ 325, 332; *Fexuto Pty Ltd v Bosnjak Holdings Pty Ltd (No 2)* (1998) 29 ACSR 290, 297.
31 [2001] EWHC Ch 415 [97]. Cf *Novoship (UK) Ltd v Mikhaylyuk* [2014] EWCA Civ 908, [2015] QB 499 [94]–[115]: causation is irrelevant and the gain must simply be 'within the scope of the duty of loyalty'.
32 *Chirnside v Fay* [2006] NZSC 68, [2007] 1 NZLR 433 [36] (Elias CJ), [54] (Gault J); *Murad v Al-Saraj* [2005] EWCA Civ 959, [2005] All ER (D) 503 [160] (Clarke LJ, dissenting).
33 G Virgo, *The Principles of the Law of Restitution* (3rd edn, OUP 2015) 434.
34 (1995) 182 CLR 544.
35 Ibid, 558, referring to *Regal (Hastings) Ltd v Gulliver* [1967] 2 AC 134; *Boardman v Phipps* [1967] 2 AC 46.

for skill and effort notwithstanding the dishonest and deliberate nature of the breach. This will be discussed further at [16.113]–[16.118].

B   Election

[16.28]   A person seeking an account of profits must generally elect between equitable compensation and an account of profits, and the election is binding.[36] In *Warman*, the High Court allowed the employer one week after judgment to elect between an account of profits and equitable compensation.

[16.29]   A plaintiff must have sufficient information to enable her to make a fair choice between equitable compensation and an account of profits. In *Tang Man Sit*,[37] the plaintiff initially opted to take HK$1.8 million, representing the defendant's secret profits made in breach of trust. The profit was made by renting out certain houses that the defendant should have assigned to the plaintiff. It later became evident that the defendant had caused losses to the plaintiff of HK$7.9 million (being the price the houses could have been rented at) and HK$11 million (being the loss caused by the wrongful use and occupation – that is, the difference between actual market value of the houses and value if the houses had been in good condition and free from encumbrances). The nature of the summary judgment initially awarded in the plaintiff's favour meant that the plaintiff had thought it was entitled to both profit and loss. It had accepted the profit, but it was not bound by that choice in the circumstances, and the court said that it was entitled to elect to take the remedy which gave the highest return. Lord Nicholls, speaking for the Privy Council, said that the account of profits and equitable compensation in this case were inconsistent because the breach of trust that caused the profit also caused the loss, and so the plaintiff could not claim both. However, his Lordship left open the possibility that in some cases in which 'cumulative remedies' are available, a plaintiff might be entitled to both remedies against one or more defendants.[38]

[16.30]   Where there are concurrent causes of action, and both an account of profits and compensatory damages are available, courts will 'set-off' one against the other to prevent double recovery.[39] Thus, in *House of Spring Gardens Ltd v Point Blank Ltd*,[40] the plaintiff received compensatory damages for breach of contract and an account of profits for breach of confidence and copyright infringement. The Irish High Court set-off the account of profits against the damages.

C   Intellectual property and the account of profits

[16.31]   The availability of the account of profits in intellectual property law is largely ruled by legislation.[41] The legislation does not prescribe detailed rules on how the account should be

---

36   *Warman* (1995) 182 CLR 544, 559. See also *Colbeam* (1968) 122 CLR 25, 32 (Windeyer J). See S Watterson, 'An Account of Profits or Damages? The History of Orthodoxy' (2004) 24 OJLS 471, who argues that the requirement to elect is a relatively recent phenomenon.

37   *Personal Representatives of Tang Man Sit v Capacious Investments Ltd* [1996] AC 514 (PC).

38   Ibid, 522.

39   P Devonshire, *Account of Profits* (Thomson Reuters 2013) 15.

40   [1983] FSR 489; aff'd *House of Spring Gardens Ltd v Point Blank Ltd* [1985] FSR 327 (Irish Supreme Court).

41   *Patents Act 1990* (Cth), s 122(1); *Copyright Act 1968* (Cth), s 115(2); *Designs Act 2003* (Cth), s 75(1)(b); *Trade Marks Act 1995* (Cth), s 126(1)(b); *Circuit Layouts Act 1989* (Cth), s 27(2); *Plant Breeder's Rights Act 1994* (Cth), s 56(3).

taken and courts refer to equitable principles to ascertain profits. Moreover, accounts of profits may be awarded for equitable breaches of confidence,[42] and for the tort of passing off.[43] Neither of these latter causes of action is statutory.

Originally, accounts of profits were available in the auxiliary jurisdiction of equity for patent infringement,[44] copyright infringement,[45] trademark infringement[46] and the tort of passing off.[47] The accounts of profits governed by statute retain characteristics which reflect their origin in the auxiliary jurisdiction of equity.[48] A plaintiff must elect between damages and an account of profits.[49] However, a plaintiff can insist on being fully informed before making an election.[50]

[16.32]

It has been said that, in the context of intellectual property, the purpose of the account of profits is not to punish the defendant, but to prevent the defendant from being unjustly enriched,[51] and that accordingly its purpose is somewhat different to the account of profits in the context of breach of fiduciary duty.[52]

[16.33]

In *Colbeam Palmer Ltd v Stock Affiliates Ltd*,[53] a case which involved a trademark infringement and the power to grant an account of profit pursuant to s 65 of the *Trade Marks Act 1955* (Cth),[54] Windeyer J said that accounts of profits were entirely different from damages for breach of trademark, as the former is measured according to what the defendant gained, whereas the latter is measured according to what the plaintiff lost. His Honour outlined three essential points about accounts of profit in intellectual property:

[16.34]

1. An account of profits is generally ancillary to an injunction. In other words, the plaintiff is generally only entitled to an account if it can be shown that the plaintiff is also entitled to an injunction, although, as the facts of *Colbeam* show, this is not an absolute requirement in trademark litigation. In that case it was enough to show that an injunction *could* have been granted at the commencement of proceedings.[55]

---

42   See *Attorney-General v Observer Ltd* [1990] 1 AC 109, 262, 266, 286; *Peter Pan Manufacturing Corporation v Corsets Silhouette Ltd* [1964] 1 WLR 96; *Seager v Copydex (No 1)* [1967] 1 WLR 923; *Seager v Copydex (No 2)* [1969] 1 WLR 809; *LAC Minerals Ltd v International Corona Resources Ltd* (1989) 61 DLR (4th) 14.
43   See *My Kinda Town Ltd v Soll* [1983] RPC 15.
44   *Smith v London & South Western Railway Co* (1854) Kay 408, 69 ER 17; *Price's Patent Candle Co v Bauwen's Patent Candle Co* (1854) 4 K & J 727, 70 ER 302; *De Vitre v Betts* (1873) LR 6 HL 319.
45   *Baily v Taylor* (1829) 1 Russ & M 73, 39 ER 28; *Colburn v Simms* (1843) 2 Hare 543, 67 ER 224.
46   *Blanchard v Hill* (1742) 2 Atk 484, 26 ER 692; *Edelsten v Edelsten* (1863) 1 De GJ & S 185, 46 ER 72; *Moet v Couston* (1864) 33 Beav 578; 55 ER 493.
47   *Hogg v Kirby* (1803) 8 Ves Jun 215, 223; 32 ER 336, 339 (Lord Eldon).
48   P Hastie, 'Restitution and Remedy in Intellectual Property Law' (1996) 14 Aus Bar Rev 6, 13.
49   *Minnesota Mining & Manufacturing Co v C Jeffries Pty Ltd* (1992) 37 FCR 294; *LED Builders Pty Ltd v Masterton Homes (NSW) Pty Ltd* (1994) 54 FCR 196; *Robert J Zupanovich Pty Ltd v B & N Beale Nominees Pty Ltd* (1995) 59 FCR 49. See MJ Leeming, 'When should a Plaintiff Take an Account of Profits?' (1996) 7 AIPJ 127, 128.
50   *LED Builders Pty Ltd v Eagle Homes Pty Ltd (No 3)* (1996) 70 FCR 436; *Fexuto Pty Ltd v Bosnjak Holdings Pty Ltd (No 2)* (1998) 29 ACSR 290, 299–300.
51   *Dart Industries Inc v Décor Corporation Pty Ltd* (1993) 179 CLR 101, 111.
52   *Warman* (1995) 182 CLR 544, 557.
53   (1968) 122 CLR 25.
54   Now *Trade Marks Act 1995* (Cth), s 126(1)(b).
55   (1968) 122 CLR 25, 31.

2.   Generally, the plaintiff can claim an account over profits derived from the period only where it is shown that the defendant *knowingly* infringed the plaintiff's trademark. This reflects the pre-statutory origin of the account of profits in the auxiliary jurisdiction of equity, and the notion that the defendant should be stripped of only those profits it would be unconscionable for him to retain.[56] This is known as the 'innocent infringement defence'.

3.   The general equitable discretionary factors operate to a degree in regard to accounts of profits based in intellectual property. In *Colbeam*, Windeyer J said that he thought delay and acquiescence could operate to a certain extent, particularly when considering when the defendant became aware of the infringement.[57]

[16.35]   Care must be taken with the innocent infringement defence, as it operates very differently in different areas of intellectual property because of the scope of the legislation in question:

- *Trademark and passing off*: Trademark legislation does not contain any statutory provision as to innocent infringement. Accordingly, both trademark infringement and passing off are governed by principles from equity's auxiliary jurisdiction. Generally, the plaintiff must establish actual knowledge or wilful blindness of the infringement.[58] Windeyer J's opinion in *Colbeam* could be criticised on the basis that, if the *Trade Marks Act 1955* (Cth) did not include an innocence defence (in contrast to all the other intellectual property statutes), then it could be inferred that the legislature did not intend to carry over a common law defence which had previously been available.

- *Patents and plant breeder's rights*: Patent legislation and plant breeder's rights legislation provide that the defendant may not be liable for an award of profits if he 'was not aware, and had no reason to believe' that he was infringing a patent or plant breeder's right.[59] In contrast to trademark law, the qualification of 'had no reason to believe' or 'suspecting' introduces the possibility that the defendant may have constructive notice of the infringement. Further, both the patent legislation and plant breeder's rights legislation provide that if the relevant products were marked to show they were patented or subject to plant breeder's rights, and they had been sold 'to a substantial extent' in Australia before infringement occurred, then the defendant is 'to be taken to have been aware' of the existence of the patent or plant breeder's rights.[60]

- *Registered designs*: Registered design legislation makes a distinction between 'primary infringement' and 'secondary infringement'.[61] 'Primary infringement' is the making or offering of a product as described in s 71(1)(a) of the *Designs Act 2003* (Cth), whereas 'secondary infringement' is (inter alia) the importing, selling or hiring of a product as described in s 71(1)(b), (c), (d) or (e) of the Act. Where primary infringement is concerned, the court may allow an innocent infringement defence if the defendant shows that he 'was not aware that the design was registered' and, before infringement occurred, 'had taken all

---

56   Ibid, 43.
57   Ibid, 33.
58   Ibid, 32–33.
59   *Patents Act 1990* (Cth), s 123(1); *Plant Breeder's Rights Act 1994* (Cth), s 57(1).
60   *Patents Act 1990* (Cth), s 123(2); *Plant Breeder's Rights Act 1994* (Cth), s 57(2).
61   *Designs Act 2003* (Cth), s 75(2).

reasonable steps to ascertain whether the design was registered'.[62] Where secondary infringement is concerned, the court may allow an innocent infringement defence where the defendant 'was not aware, and could not reasonably have been expected to be aware, that a design was registered'.[63] The secondary infringement defence is easier to make out than the primary infringement defence. Moreover, there is also a constructive notice provision, which provides that awareness will be imputed to the defendant if the packaging or product is marked to indicate registration.[64]

- *Copyright and circuit layouts*: The copyright legislation and circuit layouts legislation provide that a plaintiff is 'entitled' to an account of profits notwithstanding the fact that the defendant was not aware of the infringement.[65] Nonetheless, discretionary defences apparently remain available.[66]

D   Torts and 'waiver of tort'

While some Australian cases support the notion of a 'reasonable fee' award, particularly for proprietary torts, there is no support for an account of profit for torts in Australia.   [16.36]

Historically, the plaintiff was said to be able to 'waive' the tort (that is, give up an action for compensatory damages) in favour of an action for money had and received (a restitutionary remedy). 'Waiver' suggests that the right to sue in tort is entirely relinquished, but this is misleading. Instead, the plaintiff elects between a compensatory remedy and a gain-based remedy.   [16.37]

In old English cases, plaintiffs used the *assumpsit* or action for money had and received to strip defendants of the profits derived from the commission of proprietary torts, often where the defendant sold the plaintiff's property without authority.[67] Courts allowed the plaintiff to maintain an action for money had and received over the proceeds of sale of the property on the basis that there had been an 'implied contract' between the plaintiff and the defendant.   [16.38]

In this section, we consider cases where courts have commented on the availability of awards which explicitly effect disgorgement of profits arising from tort. The 'reasonable fee' awards for tort will be considered later in this chapter.   [16.39]

A majority of the Full Federal Court in *Hospitality Group Pty Ltd v Australian Rugby Union Ltd*[68] suggested that an Australian court cannot award an account of profits for tort. The case involved the sale of tickets to rugby union matches. Australian Rugby Union ('ARU') provided, as a term of the admission tickets, that the tickets were not to be sold at a premium without ARU's prior written consent. A travel agent, Australian Tours for Sport Pty Ltd ('ATFS'), was appointed a retail licensee of the tickets. The contract between ARU and ATFS stated that ATFS   [16.40]

---

62   Ibid, s 75(2)(a)(i) and (ii).
63   Ibid, s 75(2)(b).
64   Ibid, s 75(4).
65   *Copyright Act 1968* (Cth), s 115(3); *Circuit Layouts Act 1989* (Cth), s 27(3).
66   *LED Builders Pty Ltd v Masterton Homes (NSW) Pty Ltd* (1994) 54 FCR 196; *Robert J Zupanovich Pty Ltd v B & N Beale Nominees Pty Ltd* (1995) 59 FCR 49, 66.
67   *Oughton v Seppings* (1830) 1 B & Ad 241, 109 ER 776; *Lamine v Dorrell* (1706) 2 Ld Raym 1216, 92 ER 303.
68   [2001] FCA 1040, (2001) 110 FCR 157. See also *Esperance Cattle Co Pty Ltd v Granite Hill Pty Ltd* (2014) 47 WAR 318, [2014] WASC 279 [463]–[464].

was only to sell the tickets as part of a travel package and could not sell the tickets wholesale. ATFS breached this agreement by on-selling the tickets and travel packages to Hospitality Group Pty Ltd ('HG') and ICM (Marketing) Pty Ltd ('ICM'). HG and ICM sold the tickets and packages at a premium.

[16.41]   ARU sued HG and ICM, inter alia, for the tort of inducing breach of contract. Hill and Finkelstein JJ said that ARU was not entitled to an account of profits:

> However described, it is not possible to slot an account of profits into the general framework of remedies that are available in tort, when the account is not awarded to compensate the plaintiff for his actual or presumed loss. That is to say, under presently accepted principles, an injured plaintiff cannot claim a windfall to prevent a wrongdoer profiting from his wrong, except in those cases where exemplary damages are available and it is proper that illicit profits are taken into account in assessing the quantum of the award . . . [69]

[16.42]   Emmett J, dissenting, would have awarded an account of profits for commission of a tort where benefits were derived from property belonging to the plaintiff, or where it would be unjust to allow the wrongdoer to retain them.[70]

[16.43]   There is some US support for accounts of profit for proprietary torts. However, the following cases should be treated with great caution in an Australian context, as US courts are more likely than Anglo-Australian courts to award disgorgement, and to disregard the division between the common law and equity.[71]

[16.44]   In *Edwards v Lee's Administrator*,[72] the defendant discovered the entrance to a cave on his land, which he named the 'Great Onyx Cave'. He successfully exploited it as a tourist attraction. A portion of the cave lay under the plaintiff's land, upon which the defendant repeatedly trespassed. Twelve out of the 31 advertised scenes or objects were on the plaintiff's property. The underground Lucikovah River (one of the most attractive features of the cave) was under the plaintiff's land for almost the entire exhibited length. Stites J ordered that the defendant pay the plaintiff an account of profits over one-third of the net profits resulting from the use of the cave. His Honour relied in part on the mesne profit cases and the wayleave cases, and concluded: 'The philosophy of all these decisions is that a wrongdoer shall not be permitted to make a profit from his own wrong'.[73]

[16.45]   In *Olwell v Nye & Nissen*,[74] the court purported to strip the defendant of his profit as measured by the fee the plaintiff would have charged him for use of his property. The plaintiff, Olwell, owned an 'Eggsact' egg-washing machine, which was stored near premises occupied by Nye & Nissen, the defendant. Labour was scarce after the outbreak of war, so Nye & Nissen used the machine weekly for three years without Olwell's consent. Mallery J said that the defendant benefited from using the machine because it saved on labour costs, and it was irrelevant that Olwell had not been using it. The use was wrongful and the defendant was

---

69   Ibid, [162].
70   Ibid, [166]–[173].
71   C Rotherham, 'Deterrence as a Justification for Awarding Accounts of Profits' (2012) 32 OJLS 537, 539.
72   96 SW 2d 1028 (Ky Ct App, 1936).
73   Ibid, 1032.
74   173 P 2d 652 (Wash, 1946).

unjustly enriched by his use of the property.[75] Olwell could have sought compensatory damages, but was entitled to 'waive the tort' and sue on the 'implied contract'.[76] Because Nye & Nissen had been tortious in acquiring the benefit, it was deprived of all profit derived from the use of the machine. The court measured the profit according to the $25 per month Olwell had claimed at first instance (that is, $900).

Olwell illustrates that it is sometimes difficult to distinguish between restitution and dis-gorgement, and reasonable fees and disgorgement. Mallery J did not award an account of profits, but a personal restitutionary remedy. Nonetheless, Mallery J purported to strip the defendant of all its profit (somewhat like an account of profits). However, he measured the profit according to the fee the plaintiff would have demanded of the defendant (making it look more like a 'reasonable fee'). [16.46]

If Australian courts award disgorgement for the commission of a proprietary tort, they should consider the advertence of the plaintiff's tort. The torts in *Edwards v Lee's Administrator* and *Olwell v Nye & Nissen* involved conscious wrongdoing.[77] [16.47]

E   Breach of contract

Traditionally, disgorgement is unavailable for breach of contract, and *Hospitality Group* and other Australian cases indicate that this is still the position in Australian law.[78] However, in other jurisdictions such as England and Wales,[79] Canada,[80] New Zealand,[81] and the United States,[82] courts sometimes award disgorgement for breach of contract in exceptional circumstances. [16.48]

The ground-breaking case in England and Wales was *Attorney-General v Blake*, involving 'notorious traitor' George Blake.[83] Blake breached his employment contract with the British Secret Intelligence Service by becoming a double-agent for the Soviets. When Blake com-menced employment in 1944, he signed an undertaking pursuant to the *Official Secrets Act 1911* (UK) whereby he undertook not to divulge any information gained as a result of his employment, either in the press or in book form. The provisions continued after the period of service concluded. After being captured by North Korean forces during the Korean War in [16.49]

---

75   Ibid, 653–54.

76   The implied contract theory of unjust enrichment has been rejected. See [17.4]–[17.6].

77   See also American Law Institute, *Restatement of Restitution* (1937) §§150–59 introductory note: a defendant who is 'consciously tortious in acquiring the benefit' will be deprived of the profit.

78   *Hospitality Group Pty Ltd v Australian Rugby Union Ltd* [2001] FCA 1040, (2001) 110 FCR 157. See also *Town & Country Property Management Services Pty Ltd v Kaltoum* [2002] NSWSC 166 [85]; *Biscayne Partners Pty Ltd v Valance Corporation Pty Ltd* [2003] NSWSC 874 [232]–[235]; *Short v Crawley* [2005] NSWSC 928 [24]; *Testel Australia Pty Ltd v KRG Electrics Pty Ltd* [2013] SASC 91 [99]–[109]; *Hydrofibre Pty Ltd v Australian Prime Fibre Pty Ltd* [2013] QSC 163 [91]–[94].

79   *Attorney-General v Blake* [2001] 1 AC 268.

80   *Bank of America Canada v Mutual Trust Co* [2002] SCC 43, [2002] 2 SCR 601 [25] (Major J); *Amertek Inc v Canadian Commercial Corporation* (2003) 229 DLR (4th) 419, 467 (O'Driscoll J) (on appeal held that there was no collateral contract: *Amertek Inc v Canadian Commercial Corporation* (2005) 256 DLR (4th) 287). See L Smith and J Berryman, 'Disgorgement of Profits in Canada' in E Hondius and A Janssen (eds), *Disgorgement of Profits: Gain-Based Remedies throughout the World* (Springer 2015) 281, 289.

81   *Attorney-General for England and Wales v The Queen* [2002] 2 NZLR 91 [112]–[113] (Tipping J), [146]–[152] (McGrath J).

82   American Law Institute, *Restatement (Third) of Restitution and Unjust Enrichment* (2011) §39 (disgorgement remedy for 'opportunistic' breach of contract); *Kansas v Nebraska*, 135 S Ct 1042 (2015).

83   [2001] 1 AC 268 ('*Blake*').

1951, Blake converted to Marxism. While spying for the British Government in Berlin, he disclosed information to the Soviet Union. In 1959, Blake was exposed and returned to England for trial.

[16.50] In 1961, Blake was sentenced to 42 years' imprisonment for unlawfully communicating information contrary to s 1(1)(c) of the *Official Secrets Act 1911* (UK). In 1966, he escaped from prison and fled to Moscow. In 1989, Blake wrote his autobiography[84] and entered a publishing contract with Jonathan Cape Ltd. Until publication was announced in 1990, the British Government was unaware of the book. Blake had not sought permission from the British Government or intelligence services before publishing it. Blake had been paid about £60 000 of the moneys owing to him under the publishing contract. A further £90 000 remained in the jurisdiction. The British Government instituted proceedings to recover it. A majority of the House of Lords found that Blake was liable to disgorge the profit remaining in the jurisdiction because he had breached his employment contract.[85]

[16.51] Lord Nicholls, who delivered the principal speech, said:

> Normally the remedies of damages, specific performance and injunction, coupled with the characterisation of some contractual obligations as fiduciary, will provide an adequate response to a breach of contract. It will be only in exceptional cases, where those remedies are inadequate, that any question of accounting for profits will arise. No fixed rules can be prescribed. The court will have regard to all the circumstances, including the subject matter of the contract, the purpose of the contractual provision which has been breached, the circumstances in which the breach occurred, the consequences of the breach and the circumstances in which relief is sought. A useful general guide, although not exhaustive, is whether the plaintiff had a legitimate interest in preventing the defendant's profit-making activity and, hence, in depriving him of his profit.[86]

This 'useful general guide' has become known as the 'legitimate interest test'.[87] Lord Steyn concurred with Lord Nicholls, but said that the applicable principles were 'best hammered out on the anvil of concrete cases'.[88] Lord Hobhouse, the sole dissentient in *Blake*, concluded with a 'note of warning' about the consequences of introducing such an award into commercial law; such an introduction, he said, would be 'very far reaching and disruptive'.[89]

[16.52] While *Blake* has not been the disruptive disaster predicted by Lord Hobhouse, the attempts by English courts to apply *Blake* subsequently indicate that the legitimate interest test 'remains hopelessly ill-defined and difficult to apply'.[90] By and large, courts have been reluctant to award a full account of profits for breach of contract, other than in *Esso Petroleum Co Ltd v Niad Ltd*,[91] but the criteria applied have been neither consistent nor clear.

84 G Blake, *No Other Choice* (Jonathan Cape 1990).
85 [2001] 1 AC 268.
86 Ibid, 285.
87 'Legitimate interest' may have been drawn from P Birks, 'Profits of Breach of Contract' (1993) 109 LQR 518, 519, 521.
88 [2001] 1 AC 268, 291.
89 Ibid, 299.
90 R Cunnington, 'The Measure and Availability of Gain-Based Damages for Breach of Contract', in D Saidov and R Cunnington (eds), *Contract Damages: Domestic and International Perspectives* (Hart 2008) 235.
91 [2001] EWHC Ch 458, [2001] All ER (D) 324.

In the context of contract law, it is suggested that disgorgement is a 'tertiary remedy' which   **[16.53]**
should be available only if both compensation and specific relief are inappropriate or unavailable, and if the defendant has made a profit. Thus an account of profit may be awarded for
breach of contract where:

1. compensatory damages are 'inadequate' (using criteria similar to those used to ascertain specific relief);

2. specific relief is unavailable;[92] and

3. the defendant has made a profit.

Both the Court of Appeal[93] and House of Lords[94] in *Blake* said that 'cynical breach' was
unnecessary to establish an account of profits for breach of contract. On the other hand, cases
and commentators have suggested that a cynical breach[95] or advertent breach[96] is required
before disgorgement for breach of contract is awarded. Similarly, the US Restatement of
Restitution and Unjust Enrichment requires an 'opportunistic breach' before disgorgement for
breach of contract will be available.[97]

Any award is arguably subject to allowances for skill and effort and discretionary criteria;   **[16.54]**
see [16.111]–[16.136].

Barnett has suggested that most contract cases do not give rise to disgorgement, but that   **[16.55]**
there are two broad classes of case where it may be awarded:[98]

1. *'Second sale' cases*: Alice contracts with Boris for the supply of property, goods or
    services. Boris sees an opportunity to sell the property, good or service to Conrad for a
    greater profit. Boris breaches his contract with Alice and sells to Conrad for a profit.
    Typically, the contract between Alice and Boris is no longer specifically enforceable
    but there is a profit for Boris to disgorge.

---

92   The reasons for specific relief being unavailable may be important in determining the measure and kind
      of gain-based relief.
93   *Attorney-General v Blake* [1998] Ch 439, 457–58.
94   [2001] 1 AC 268, 286.
95   *Hickey & Co Ltd v Roche Stores (Dublin) Ltd* [1993] RLR 196; *Hospital Products Ltd v United States
      Surgical Corporation* (1984) 156 CLR 41, 125–26 (Deane J); P Birks, 'Restitutionary Damages for Breach
      of Contract: *Snepp* and the Fusion of Law and Equity' [1987] LMCLQ 421, 429–30; P Birks, 'Profits for
      Breach of Contract' (1993) 109 LQR 518, 519; D Laycock, 'The Scope and Significance of Restitution'
      (1989) 67 Tex L Rev 1277, 1289; J Edelman, *Gain-Based Damages: Contract, Tort, Equity and
      Intellectual Property* (Hart 2002) 85, 158–59; C Rotherham, 'The Conceptual Structure of Restitution for
      Wrongs' (2007) 66 Camb LJ 172, 189–90; A Burrows, *Remedies for Torts and Breach of Contract* (3rd
      edn, OUP 2004) 406–07; J Edelman, 'Gain-Based Damages and Compensation' in A Burrows and Lord
      Rodger of Earlsferry (eds), *Mapping the Law: Essays in Honour of Peter Birks* (OUP 2006) 149. Cf EA
      Farnsworth, 'Your Loss or My Gain? The Dilemma of the Disgorgement Principle in Breach of Contract'
      (1985) 94 Yale LJ 1339; J Dawson, 'Restitution without Enrichment' (1981) 61 Boston ULR 563, 614;
      J McCamus, 'Disgorgement for Breach of Contract: A Comparative Perspective' (2003) 36 Loy LA L Rev
      943, 961; R Craswell, 'When is a Willful Breach "Willful"? The Link Between Definitions and Damages'
      (2009) 107 Mich L Rev 1501.
96   K Barnett, *Accounting for Profit for Breach of Contract: Theory and Practice* (Hart 2012) 44–46.
97   American Law Institute, *Restatement (Third) of Restitution and Unjust Enrichment* (2011) §39
      comment b.
98   K Barnett, *Accounting for Profit for Breach of Contract: Theory and Practice* (Hart 2012) 86.

2. *'Agency*[99] *problem' cases*: Boris promises Alice he will *not do* a specific thing which relates to Alice's best interests, but Boris breaches the contract and goes ahead and does the very thing which he has contracted not to do, making a profit. These include contracts where there is a concurrent fiduciary duty.

Courts have faced difficulties in applying the legitimate interest test largely in cases which fall within the second category,[100] particularly where there is a negative covenant with no concurrent fiduciary duty (as in *Blake* itself). However, courts have also been confused in 'second sale' cases.[101] Some of the cases following *Blake* meet the criteria listed above – compensatory damages are inadequate, specific relief is unavailable and the defendant has made a profit – which suggests that, subject to discretionary considerations and allowances for skill and effort, a court should consider awarding full disgorgement.[102] Unfortunately, courts have refused to award any gain-based award whatsoever,[103] or have simply awarded a 'reasonable fee' measure on the basis that the case is not as exceptional as *Blake*.[104]

[16.56] Courts have also faced difficulty in determining the measure of damages. Lord Nicholls' speech drew upon the award made in *Wrotham Park Estate Co Ltd v Parkside Homes Ltd*,[105] where a 'reasonable fee' representing 5% of the defendant's profits arising from a breach of a negative covenant was awarded pursuant to Lord Cairns' Act. Lord Nicholls described *Wrotham Park* as shining 'rather as a solitary beacon'[106] for the existence of an explicit gain-based award for breach of contract. In *Blake* itself, the court did not award a 'reasonable fee' but awarded a full account of profit. Thus, there are two gain-based measures of relief for breach of contract in the English cases:

1. a 'reasonable fee' award, as in *Wrotham Park*; and

2. a full account of profits, as in *Blake*.

But it is presently unclear what criteria the courts in England and Wales use to choose between these two measures.

---

99   'Agency' does not refer to the legal concept of agency, but to the economic concept of principal–agent, which arises whenever one person, the principal (or promisee), seeks to persuade another person, the agent (or promisor), to act in the principal's interests. Public policy considerations also have an important role in this category.

100   Eg *Amec Developments Ltd v Jury's Hotel Management (UK) Ltd* [2000] EWHC Ch 454, [2001] 1 EGLR 81; *Esso Petroleum Co Ltd v Niad Ltd* [2001] EWHC Ch 458, [2001] All ER (D) 324; *Experience Hendrix LLC v PPX Enterprises Inc* [2003] EWCA Civ 323, [2003] 1 All ER (Comm) 830; *World Wide Fund for Nature v World Wrestling Federation Entertainment Inc* [2007] EWCA Civ 286, [2008] 1 WLR 445; *Lane v O'Brien Homes* [2004] EWHC 303 (QB), [2004] All ER (D) 61; *Pell Frischmann Engineering Ltd v Bow Valley Iran Ltd* [2009] UKPC 45, [2011] 1 WLR 2370; *Vercoe v Rutland Fund Management Ltd* [2010] EWHC 424 (Ch), [2010] Bus LR D141.

101   Eg *Luxe Holding Ltd v Midland Resources Holding Ltd* [2010] EWHC 1908 (Ch). An admirably clear case is *AB Corporation v CD Co (The Sine Nomine)* [2002] 1 Lloyd's Rep 805.

102   The situation is more complex in the agency problem cases: K Barnett, *Accounting for Profit for Breach of Contract: Theory and Practice* (Hart 2012) ch 5.

103   *World Wide Fund for Nature v World Wrestling Federation Entertainment Inc* [2007] EWCA Civ 286, [2008] 1 WLR 445; *Luxe Holding Ltd v Midland Resources Holding Ltd* [2010] EWHC 1908 (Ch).

104   *Experience Hendrix LLC v PPX Enterprises Inc* [2003] EWCA Civ 323, [2003] 1 All ER (Comm) 830.

105   [1974] 1 WLR 798 ('*Wrotham Park*').

106   [2001] 1 AC 268, 283.

Australian courts have declined to follow *Blake*,[107] and some judges have made negative extra-judicial comments about it.[108] The majority of the Full Federal Court in *Hospitality Group Pty Ltd v Australian Rugby Union Ltd*[109] indicated in obiter dicta that an account of profits is unavailable for breach of contract in Australia. Hill and Finkelstein JJ said that contractual remedies were limited to compensatory damages available under *Robinson v Harman*, and without High Court authority it would be inappropriate 'to confer a windfall on a plaintiff under the guise of damages for breach of contract'.[110] Emmett J did not comment directly on disgorgement damages for breach of contract or on *Blake*. [16.57]

The availability of an account of profits for breach of contract has limited support from the High Court of Australia. In *Hospital Products Ltd v United States Surgical Corporation*, Deane J said that he was not prepared to find that the defendant owed the plaintiff a fiduciary duty, but that he would award a constructive trust over gains the defendant had made in breach of contract: [16.58]

> [A] constructive trust may be imposed as the appropriate form of equitable relief in circumstances where a person could not in good conscience retain for himself a benefit, or the proceeds of a benefit, which he has appropriated to himself in breach of his contractual or other legal or equitable obligations to another.[111]

Deane J is a lone voice crying in the wilderness, and his judgment has never been applied.[112] The issue of awarding a proprietary remedy over wrongful gains raises a different set of questions, which will be considered in Ch 19.

Both authors have argued elsewhere that Australian courts should not be so set against the idea of awarding gain-based awards for breach of contract and that they should be available in certain circumstances, as long as the criteria for their award are clear.[113] [16.59]

F   The Australian Consumer Law

Gain-based relief was unavailable under the former *Trade Practices Act 1974* (Cth) and is not expressly provided for in the Australian Consumer Law ('ACL').[114] Nevertheless, s 236 of the ACL is drafted broadly and provides that the plaintiff may recover 'the amount of the loss or [16.60]

---

107   *Town & Country Property Management Services Pty Ltd v Kaltoum* [2002] NSWSC 166 [85]; *Biscayne Partners Pty Ltd v Valance Corporation Pty Ltd* [2003] NSWSC 874 [232]–[235]; *Dalecoast Pty Ltd v Guardian International Pty Ltd* [2003] WASCA 142 [103]–[107]; *Short v Crawley* [2005] NSWSC 928 [24]; *Testel Australia Pty Ltd v KRG Electrics Pty Ltd* [2013] SASC 91 [99]–[109]; *Hydrofibre Pty Ltd v Australian Prime Fibre Pty Ltd* [2013] QSC 163 [91]–[94].
108   Especially RI Barrett, 'Recent Cases – Account of Profits for Breach of Contract' (2000) 74 Aust LJ 817. See also JD Heydon, MJ Leeming and PG Turner, *Meagher, Gummow and Lehane's Equity: Doctrines and Remedies* (5th edn, LexisNexis 2015) [26–075].
109   [2001] FCA 1040, (2001) 110 FCR 157.
110   Ibid, [159].
111   (1984) 156 CLR 41, 124–25.
112   It was, however, noted in *Town & Country Property Management Services Pty Ltd v Kaltoum* [2002] NSWSC 166 [83].
113   K Barnett, *Accounting for Profit for Breach of Contract: Theory and Practice* (Hart 2012); S Harder, *Measuring Damages in the Law of Obligations: The Search for Harmonised Principles* (Hart 2010) 226–42.
114   *Competition and Consumer Act 2010* (Cth), sch 2.

damage' caused by the contravention of ch 2 or 3. If 'damage' is interpreted at its widest, there may be scope for reasonable fee damages in appropriate cases.

[16.61]   The pecuniary penalty provisions of the ACL may provide an opportunity for courts to strip gain from defendants. This effectively occurred in *Director of Consumer Affairs Victoria v Gibson (No 3)*.[115] Ms Gibson made misleading and deceptive representations that her special diet had sent her cancer into remission, and that she was going to donate substantial proportions of her profits from her book and app to charities. In fact, she had never suffered from cancer, and she donated almost none of the profits to the named charities. In calculating the pecuniary penalty award to be imposed on Ms Gibson pursuant to s 224 of the ACL, Mortimer J held that it was appropriate to consider the gross profits Ms Gibson had made by retaining the profits from her book and app, and to effectively strip Ms Gibson of those profits to ensure that it was not worthwhile to break the law in this way.[116]

IV   'Reasonable fee' damages
A   Introduction and history

[16.62]   Australian courts may grant 'reasonable fee' awards where defendants have used certain property or infringed certain rights in a tortious manner. As noted at [16.4], 'reasonable fee' refers to a method of calculating a monetary award. Courts often make these awards when the plaintiff has not suffered a compensable loss in the ordinary sense, yet the situation still calls for damages. For example, if you borrow my horse without my permission and ride him, I have not suffered a compensable loss. My horse may be better for the exercise. However, you have committed a tort by using my horse without my permission, and thus I should be entitled to a 'reasonable fee' reflecting the value of your use of my horse.[117] This reflects the benefit you have obtained from using my horse without my permission. It is immaterial that I would not have used the horse while you were using it; I am still entitled to damages.[118]

[16.63]   Courts may also award a 'reasonable fee' to encourage defendants to seek consent from plaintiffs. A compulsory licence fee is imposed ex post facto on the defendant, signifying that the defendant ought to have sought consent to infringe the plaintiff's right, and is treated by the law in a manner which requires him to pay as if he had sought consent.

[16.64]   Reasonable fee awards may be obtained through several remedial pathways, including through an award of compensation, in an action for money had and received through 'waiver of tort' in cases of proprietary torts, as 'restitutionary damages', or under Lord Cairns' Act in lieu of an injunction; see [12.51]. Reasonable fee awards are generally awarded for common law causes of action, particularly for proprietary torts such as trespass to land, and for intellectual property infringements.

---

115   [2017] FCA 1148.
116   Ibid, [95].
117   Based on Lord Shaw's example in *Watson, Laidlaw & Co Ltd v Pott, Cassels & Williamson* (1914) SC (HL) 18, 31.
118   *The Mediana* [1900] AC 113, 117 (Lord Halsbury LC); *Waters v Maynard* (1924) 24 SR (NSW) 618, 621 (Campbell J); *Bilambil-Terranora Pty Ltd v Tweed Shire Council* [1980] 1 NSWLR 465, 477 (Reynolds JA); *Westwood v Cordwell* [1983] 1 Qd R 276, 278; *Lahoud v Lahoud* [2009] NSWSC 623, [2009] ANZ ConvR 9–032 [188].

There is significant confusion in terminology in this area: [16.65]

- 'Accounts of profits' have also been known as 'disgorgement damages' and 'restitutionary damages', particularly where a common law wrong is concerned.
- 'Reasonable fee' awards have also been called 'restitutionary damages', '*Wrotham Park* damages', 'licence fee damages', 'user awards' and 'bargaining damages'.

'Restitutionary damages' has been used to describe awards which achieve disgorgement and awards which reverse subtractive unjust enrichment. Thus, Lord Nicholls preferred not to use the term in *Blake*, calling it an 'unhappy expression'.[119]

B   Academic and judicial accounts

Academic and judicial accounts of reasonable fee awards fall into six general camps: [16.66]

1. compensatory analyses;
2. restitutionary analyses;
3. compensatory/restitutionary analyses;
4. vindicatory analyses;
5. property or exclusive entitlement analyses; and
6. partial disgorgement analyses.

Given the divergent accounts, it is no wonder that courts have been confused. Each of the six analyses are discussed below. The categorisation matters because this may affect the calculation, availability and limitations upon the award.

1   Compensatory analyses

'Reasonable fee' awards have been said to represent a 'lost opportunity to bargain'. In other words, it is said that when a defendant wrongfully uses another's property without diminishing its value, the plaintiff has lost an opportunity to bargain.[120] Some judges have accepted this analysis,[121] but it has been criticised by other judges[122] and by academics.[123] First, the [16.67]

---

119   [2001] 1 AC 268, 284.
120   RJ Sharpe and SM Waddams, 'Damages for Lost Opportunity to Bargain' (1982) 2 OJLS 290. See also A Phang and P-W Lee, 'Rationalising Restitutionary Damages in Contract Law – An Elusive or Illusory Quest?' (2001) 17 J Cont L 240, 252–53.
121   *Jaggard v Sawyer* [1995] 1 WLR 269, 291 (Millett LJ); *Gafford v Graham* (1999) 77 P & CR 73, 86 (Nourse LJ); *World Wide Fund for Nature v World Wrestling Federation Entertainment Inc* [2007] EWCA Civ 286, [2008] 1 WLR 445 [29] (Chadwick LJ); *One Step (Support) Ltd v Morris-Garner* [2016] EWCA Civ 180, [2017] QB 1 [81], [143].
122   *Surrey County Council v Bredero Homes Ltd* [1993] 1 WLR 1361, 1369–70 (Steyn LJ); *Experience Hendrix LLC v PPX Enterprises Inc* [2003] EWCA Civ 323, [2003] 1 All ER (Comm) 830 [45] (Mance LJ), [57] (Peter Gibson LJ); *Marathon Asset Management LLP v Seddon* [2017] EWHC 300 (Comm), [2017] ICR 791 [195]–[196].
123   P Birks, 'Profits for Breach of Contract' (1993) 109 LQR 518; W Goodhart, 'Restitutionary Damages for Breach of Contract: The Remedy that Dare Not Speak Its Name' [1995] RLR 3, 7; J Edelman, 'The Compensation Strait-Jacket and the Lost Opportunity to Bargain' [2001] RLR 104; A Burrows, *The Law of Restitution* (3rd edn, OUP 2011) 636–37; G Virgo, *Principles of the Law of Restitution* (3rd edn, OUP 2015) 471–72; R Cunnington, 'A Lost Opportunity to Clarify' (2007) 122 LQR 47; A Burrows, 'Are Damages on the "*Wrotham Park* Basis" Compensatory, Restitutionary or Neither?' in D Saidov and

'hypothetical bargain' is a fiction which presumes that the defendant would have agreed to 'buy the right' to break the contract or use the property, although often the facts indicate otherwise. There is also an associated assumption that the plaintiff would have agreed to 'sell the right'.[124] As a result, it fails to explain the cases for which an explanation is most necessary:[125] where there was no opportunity to bargain with the defendant, and where the plaintiff would never have agreed to a release in the first place.[126] The theory does not fit with the factual scenarios it is trying to explain. Waddams, a major proponent of this analysis, has conceded that it cannot be the sole explanation, but argues that it is still relevant.[127]

[16.68]   Others argue that reasonable fee awards involve 'substitutive compensation' (that is, they compensate the plaintiff for the loss of her right).[128] However, these analyses have been criticised because the plaintiff has not *lost* a right: she retains the same rights she had before the wrong was committed.[129] Consequently, it has also been argued that reasonable fee damages compensate the plaintiff for the loss of the power to prevent an imminent breach through a *quia timet* injunction.[130]

[16.69]   Other accounts take a substitutive approach, and see such awards as the 'next-best' response the law can give instead of the primary right.[131] Thus, reasonable fee awards are considered to be a substitute for the value of the infringement of the right. However, it is difficult to isolate

R Cunnington (eds), *Contract Damages: Domestic and International Perspectives* (Hart 2008) 169–71; R Cunnington, 'The Assessment of Gain-Based Damages for Breach of Contract' (2008) 71 Mod LR 559, 562–63; R Cunnington, 'The Measure and Availability of Gain-Based Damages for Breach of Contract' in D Saidov and R Cunnington (eds), *Contract Damages: Domestic and International Perspectives* (Hart 2008) 207, 220; S Harder, *Measuring Damages in the Law of Obligations* (Hart 2010) 180–81; K Barnett, *Accounting for Profit for Breach of Contract: Theory and Practice* (Hart 2012) 16–18; K Barker, '"Damages Without Loss": Can Hohfeld Help?' (2014) 34 OJLS 631, 638; JNE Varuhas, 'The Concept of "Vindication" in the Law of Torts: Rights, Interests and Damages' (2014) 34 OJLS 253, 285.

124   A Burrows, 'Are Damages on the "*Wrotham Park* Basis" Compensatory, Restitutionary or Neither?' in D Saidov and R Cunnington (eds), *Contract Damages: Domestic and International Perspectives* (Hart 2008) 170.

125   C Rotherham, '"*Wrotham Park* Damages" and Accounts of Profits' [2008] LMCLQ 25, 31; R Cunnington, 'The Assessment of Gain-Based Damages for Breach of Contract' (2008) 71 Mod LR 559, 562–63.

126   R Cunnington, 'The Measure and Availability of Gain-Based Damages for Breach of Contract' in D Saidov and R Cunnington (eds), *Contract Damages: Domestic and International Perspectives* (Hart 2008) 221. An example is *Wrotham Park Estate Co Ltd v Parkside Homes Ltd* [1974] 1 WLR 798.

127   SM Waddams, 'Gains Derived from Breach of Contract: Historical and Conceptual Perspectives' in R Cunnington and D Saidov (eds), *Contract Damages: Domestic and International Perspectives* (Hart 2008) 192.

128   M McInnes, 'Account of Profits for Common Law Wrongs' in S Degeling and J Edelman (ed), *Equity in Commercial Law* (LBC 2004) 416–18; M McInnes, 'Gain, Loss and the User Principle' (2006) 14 RLR 76, 84–86. See also F Giglio, *The Foundations of Restitution for Wrongs* (Hart 2007). Cf C Rotherham, '"*Wrotham Park* Damages" and Accounts of Profits: Compensation or Restitution?' [2008] LMCLQ 25, 45–52. In a contractual context, see: P Benson, 'Disgorgement for Breach of Contract and Corrective Justice: An Analysis in Outline' in J Neyers, M McInnes and S Pitel (eds), *Understanding Unjust Enrichment* (Hart 2004) 311; A Botterell, 'Contractual Performance, Corrective Justice, and Disgorgement for Breach of Contract' (2010) 16 Legal Theory 135.

129   A Burrows, 'Are Damages on the "*Wrotham Park* Basis" Compensatory, Restitutionary or Neither?' in D Saidov and R Cunnington (eds), *Contract Damages: Domestic and International Perspectives* (Hart 2008) 173; C Rotherham, '"*Wrotham Park* Damages" and Accounts of Profits' [2008] LMCLQ 25, 44–45; *Marathon Asset Management LLP v Seddon* [2017] EWHC 300 (Comm), [2017] ICR 791 [197].

130   K Barker, '"Damages Without Loss": Can Hohfeld Help?' (2014) 34 OJLS 631.

131   R Stevens, *Torts and Rights* (OUP 2007) 60. See also D Winterton, *Money Awards in Contract Law* (Hart 2015) 60–66, who sees such damages as a substitute for performance itself.

which rights give rise to substitutive damages when infringed.[132] Moreover, it is difficult to know how to value rights, and how to differentiate between different infringements.[133]

2   Restitutionary analyses

Both judges[134] and scholars[135] have argued that reasonable fee awards represent the reversal of an enrichment by the defendant at the plaintiff's expense.   [16.70]

In the most well-known of such analyses, Edelman argues that reasonable fee awards are instances of 'restitutionary damages' which give back to the plaintiff an 'illegitimate transfer of value' as a result of the defendant's wrong, as measured by the objective receipt by the defendant. The reasonable fee represents the 'use value' of a property or quasi-property right. According to Edelman, *Wrotham Park* involved an award of restitutionary damages, whereas *Blake* involved an award of disgorgement damages, and both kinds of award are available throughout tort, equity, intellectual property and contract. However, it has been argued that restitutionary accounts involve an artificially broad meaning of gain, and that any 'transfer of value' is also artificial.[136]   [16.71]

3   Restitutionary and/or compensatory analyses

Sometimes courts have argued that reasonable fee awards are both compensatory and restitutionary.[137] Some academic accounts also propose that compensatory and restitutionary analyses can co-exist.[138] However, it has been suggested that an award cannot be simultaneously compensatory and restitutionary.[139]   [16.72]

4   Vindicatory analyses

Others have argued that reasonable fee awards reflect the law's desire to vindicate certain interests by awarding damages in the absence of factual loss.[140] The law is said to affirm the   [16.73]

---

132   Stevens, ibid, 329.

133   JNE Varuhas, 'The Concept of "Vindication" in the Law of Torts: Rights, Interests and Damages' (2014) 34 OJLS 253, 271–72.

134   *Strand Electric & Engineering Co Ltd v Brisford Entertainments Ltd* [1952] 2 QB 246, 252 (Somervell LJ), 253 (Denning LJ); *LJP Investments v Howard Chia Investments (No 2)* (1989) 24 NSWLR 499 (Hodgson J); *Gaba Formwork Contractors Pty Ltd v Turner Corporation Ltd* (1991) 32 NSWLR 175, 188 (Giles J); *Bunnings Group Ltd v CHEP Australia Ltd* [2011] NSWCA 342, (2011) 82 NSWLR 420 [194]–[199], [205] (Giles JA).

135   J Edelman, *Gain-Based Damages: Contract, Tort, Equity and Intellectual Property* (Hart 2002) 65–78; J Beatson, 'The Nature of Waver of Tort' in J Beatson (ed), *The Use and Abuse of Unjust Enrichment* (Clarendon Press 1991) 232; S Worthington, 'Reconsidering Disgorgement for Wrongs' (1999) 62 Mod LR 218.

136   C Rotherham, 'The Conceptual Structure of Restitution for Wrongs' (2007) 66 Camb LJ 172, 173; K Barnett, *Accounting for Profit for Breach of Contract: Theory and Practice* (Hart 2012) 151–54; JNE Varuhas, 'The Concept of "Vindication" in the Law of Torts: Rights, Interests and Damages' (2014) 34 OJLS 253, 286–87; *Marathon Asset Management LLP v Seddon* [2017] EWHC 300 (Comm), [2017] ICR 791 [198].

137   *Inverugie Investments Ltd v Hackett* [1995] 1 WLR 713, 718 (Lord Lloyd); *Hampton v BHP Billiton Minerals Pty Ltd (No 2)* [2012] WASC 285 [355]–[359], [342]–[354]; *ACES System Development Pte Ltd v Yenty Lily* [2013] SGCA 53, [2013] 4 SLR 1317 [38].

138   D Brennan, 'The Beautiful Restitutionary Heresy of a Larrikin' (2011) 33 Syd L Rev 209; KFK Low, 'The User Principle: *Rashomon* Effect or Much Ado about Nothing' (2016) 28 SAcLJ 984.

139   K Barker, '"Damages Without Loss": Can Hohfeld Help?' (2014) 34 OJLS 631, 646.

140   JNE Varuhas, 'The Concept of "Vindication" in the Law of Torts: Rights, Interests and Damages' (2014) 34 OJLS 253.

importance of certain inherent interests, generally those protected by torts actionable per se, such as trespass. Reasonable fee awards in the trespass to land cases are said to compensate for the normative damage to the plaintiff's interest in exclusive possession of her land.[141]

[16.74]   Substitutive analyses (see [16.69]) also have a vindicatory flavour, as the law is said to vindicate the plaintiff's right by giving a substitute for the right.

5   Property or exclusive entitlement analyses

[16.75]   In other cases[142] and in academic analyses,[143] reasonable fee awards are linked to property rights, hence the tendency for such awards to be made in the context of proprietary torts and intellectual property infringements.

For example, Harder argues that gain-based damages should be reserved for situations where there is an unauthorised exploitation of an asset exclusively reserved for another person, or by the unauthorised use of an 'exclusive entitlement'.[144] Exclusive entitlements are of two kinds: (1) exclusive entitlements *erga omnes* (against the whole world – including property rights, reputational rights, rights to bodily integrity); and (2) exclusive entitlements *inter partes* (against the defendant only – for example, specifically enforceable contracts of sale of land or chattels). Thus, when a defendant makes an unauthorised use of an exclusive entitlement, the defendant's gain is the use of the plaintiff's asset.[145]

6   Partial disgorgement analyses

[16.76]   Finally, reasonable fee awards have sometimes been considered as a partial disgorgement of profit in both case law[146] and academic commentary,[147] particularly in breach of contract cases. It is argued that the plaintiff is awarded a proportion of the profit the defendant made by infringing the plaintiff's right. A partial disgorgement analysis has been criticised for downplaying the important distinction between objective and subjective measures of relief.[148] In cases where the defendant does not make an actual profit, this measure will be less attractive for a plaintiff.[149]

7   Conclusion

[16.77]   The characterisation of these awards is uncertain, and thus it is unclear how they are to be calculated, to which causes of action they apply and whether equitable bars to relief apply to them.

---

141   Ibid, 284–89.
142   *Hospitality Group Pty Ltd v Australian Rugby Union Ltd* (2001) 110 FCR 157, [167]–[168] (Emmett J) drawing on D Friedmann, 'Restitution of Benefits Obtained through the Appropriation of Property or the Commission of a Wrong' (1980) 80 Colum L Rev 504.
143   P Jaffey, 'Licence Fee Damages' [2011] RLR 95; S Harder, *Measuring Damages in the Law of Obligations: The Search for Harmonised Principles* (Hart 2010) 216.
144   Harder, ibid.
145   Ibid, 217–18.
146   *Kansas v Nebraska*, 135 S Ct 1042, 1058 (2015); *Marathon Asset Management LLP v Seddon* [2017] EWHC 300 (Comm), [2017] ICR 791 [192]–[202].
147   K Barnett, *Accounting for Profit for Breach of Contract: Theory and Practice* (Hart 2012) ch 6. Lord Nicholls has hinted at this view in extra-judicial comments: see 'Breach of Contract, Restitution for Wrongs, and Punishment: Review of Discussion' in A Burrows and E Peel (eds), *Commercial Remedies: Current Issues and Problems* (OUP 2003) 129.
148   C Rotherham, 'Book Review: Accounting for Profit for Breach of Contract' [2012] LMCLQ 134, 136.
149   *Marathon Asset Management LLP v Seddon* [2017] EWHC 300 (Comm), [2017] ICR 791 [226].

C General patterns

It is difficult to discern a general pattern for reasonable fees awards. In the recent English case of *Marathon Asset Management LLP v Seddon*,[150] Leggatt J proposed the following scheme: [16.78]

1. If there was an alternative means by which the defendant could have obtained the benefit, the benefit will be valued at the market value.[151]

2. If the defendant could not have obtained the benefit from another source, it should be asked whether it was reasonable to expect the plaintiff to sell the benefit to the defendant for a reasonable fee. In this case, the benefit will be valued by reference to the reasonable fee the plaintiff could have charged.[152]

3. If the defendant could not reasonably have been expected to purchase the benefit from elsewhere or where it was not reasonable for the plaintiff to sell, the benefit should be assessed according to the amount of profit made by the defendant which is fairly attributable to the breach (either through an account of profits and apportionment or through a percentage of profits through a licence fee).[153]

This scheme has not been accepted in Australia, and given the unsettled status of gain-based relief in English law, its reception there is unclear as well. Accordingly, we consider each category of case in which 'reasonable fee' awards have been made: in equity, in intellectual property law, in tort and, finally, in contract.

D Equity

Generally, the account of profits is awarded for breaches of equitable duties. However, reasonable fee awards have been made for breach of confidence in the English *Seager v Copydex* cases, where the defendant mistakenly believed it was legally entitled to use the plaintiff's confidential information. The court declined to award an injunction or a full account of profits, but instead awarded a 'reasonable fee' reflecting the market value of the confidential information.[154] The Court of Appeal did not identify an equitable basis for this, nor did it purport to grant damages in lieu of an injunction. The decision has been criticised in Australia as promoting 'fusion fallacy'.[155]   [16.79]

In the English case, *Vercoe v Rutland Fund Management Ltd*,[156] Sales J awarded a reasonable fee for a concurrent breach of contract and breach of confidence. His Honour said that in light of *Blake* (see [16.49]–[16.51]) accounts of profits should only be awarded exceptionally, and in cases where there was a proprietary right akin to an intellectual property right. The willingness of English courts to grant a reasonable fee award for an equitable breach of confidence reflects the fact that breach of confidence is on the margins of intellectual property   [16.80]

---

150   [2017] EWHC 300 (Comm), [2017] ICR 791.
151   Ibid, [232].
152   Ibid, [233].
153   Ibid, [236].
154   *Seager v Copydex (No 1)* [1967] 1 WLR 923; *Seager v Copydex (No 2)* [1969] 1 WLR 809.
155   JD Heydon, MJ Leeming and PG Turner, *Meagher, Gummow and Lehane's Equity: Doctrines and Remedies* (5th edn, LexisNexis 2015) [2–235], [42–190].
156   [2010] EWHC 424 (Ch), [2010] Bus LR 141 [341].

law, particularly where it protects trade secrets. However, it is not certain that *Vercoe* would be followed in Australia, given that Australian courts have not adopted *Blake* or the *Seager v Copydex* cases.

E   Intellectual property

[16.81]   'Reasonable fee' awards are available for intellectual property infringements, as these have been treated similarly to wrongful use of corporeal property.[157] If there is a single use, damages are calculated on the basis of a licence fee,[158] but if there are multiple uses, damages are assessed on a royalty basis.[159] The court must ascertain what a willing licensee would have been prepared to pay and a willing licensor to accept, by reference to the actual characteristics of the parties in dispute.[160] The court looks at the position the plaintiff would have been in had the defendant behaved properly.[161] The award can be conceived of as a compulsory licence fee. The tort of passing off is included in the stable of intellectual property interests, and hence infringement may give rise to a reasonable fee award.[162]

[16.82]   Generally, courts and commentators have treated such damages as compensatory. 'Reasonable fee' awards are said to reflect the sales lost as a result of the infringement, not a fair market value of the use of the right. In *Australasian Performing Rights Association v Grebo Trading Co Pty Ltd*, Blackburn J said that damages for copyright infringement could be calculated on the basis that the loss was 'the fees which the infringer should have paid in order to perform the works lawfully'.[163] Nonetheless, some argue that such damages have a restitutionary flavour.[164] Debate continues as to whether the nature of these damages is compensatory or restitutionary in nature, or perhaps a mixture of both.[165]

[16.83]   The defence of 'innocent infringement' may be available for claims of reasonable fee damages, and will operate in a similar way to the defence noted earlier in relation to the account of profits.[166] In contrast to the statutory position with respect to an account of profits, the defence of innocent infringement is explicitly available for damages for breach of copyright and infringement of circuit layout designs where 'the defendant was not aware, and had no reasonable grounds for suspecting' that the act constituted an infringement.[167]

[16.84]   It is still unclear how courts choose between a reasonable fee award and a full account of profits in intellectual property cases. David Brennan has suggested that courts exercise a

---

157   D Brennan, 'The Beautiful Restitutionary Heresy of a Larrikin' (2011) 33 Syd L Rev 209, 214.
158   *Chabot v Davies* [1936] 3 All ER 211, 228.
159   *Lewis Trusts v Bambers Stores* [1982] FSR 281.
160   *General Tire and Rubber Co v Firestone Tyre and Rubber Co Ltd* [1975] 1 WLR 819, 824–26 (Lord Wilberforce).
161   *Penn v Jack* (1867) LR 5 Eq 81, 84.
162   *Winnebago Industries Inc v Knott Investments Pty Ltd (No 4)* [2015] FCA 1327, (2015) 241 FCR 271.
163   (1978) 23 ACTR 30, 31.
164   D Brennan, *Retransmission and US Compliance with TRIPS* (Kluwer Law International 2003) 190.
165   J Edelman, *Gain-Based Damages: Contract, Tort, Equity and Intellectual Property* (Hart 2002) 217–42; D Brennan, 'The Beautiful Restitutionary Heresy of a Larrikin' (2011) 33 Syd L Rev 209. They were accepted as having a 'restitutionary aspect' in *Winnebago Industries Inc v Knott Investments Pty Ltd (No 4)* [2015] FCA 1327, (2015) 241 FCR 271 [14].
166   *Patents Act 1990* (Cth), s 123; *Plant Breeder's Rights Act 1994* (Cth), s 57; *Designs Act 2003* (Cth), s 75(2)(b).
167   *Copyright Act 1968* (Cth), s 115 (3); *Circuit Layouts Act 1989* (Cth), s 27(3).

choice based on a number of factors, including whether strict owner control over the resource is an underlying policy of the law, whether the infringer acted in good faith or bad faith, whether ascertainable and proximate profit arises from the violation, the nature of the violation (actual consumption or mere use), and whether the owner has regarded the right as one which entitles her to a payment for use.[168]

F   Tort

'Reasonable fee' awards are made primarily for certain torts which involve a direct interference with property (trespass to land, trespass to goods, detinue and conversion). Historically these cases were known as 'waiver of tort' cases. The plaintiff was entitled to proceed against the defendant on the fiction that she had consented to the defendant dealing with her property, but that the defendant had impliedly promised that he would account to her for the proceeds of the profit. As a result, she was entitled to an *indebitatus assumpsit* or action for money had and received. However, the 'waiver of tort' fiction was debunked by the House of Lords in *United Australia Ltd v Barclays Bank*,[169] and it was observed that there was no true 'waiver' of the wrong – the plaintiff was electing between compensatory and restitutionary remedies.

[16.85]

Courts are unlikely to award a reasonable fee for non-proprietary torts.

[16.86]

1   Torts protecting proprietary rights in land

Historically, courts have awarded a reasonable fee in two kinds of trespasses:

[16.87]

1. the 'wayleave' cases;[170] and

2. the 'mesne profit' cases.[171]

The 'wayleave' cases arise when the defendant uses the plaintiff's land without denying the plaintiff possession. For example, if I cross your property without permission, I do not deny your possession, but I infringe your right to possession. By contrast, the 'mesne profit' cases arise when the defendant wrongfully withholds possession of the land from the plaintiff, typically after the expiry of a lease. For example, you may be entitled to 'mesne profits' if I wrongfully remain in your property after the expiry of my lease. The Supreme Court of Victoria has recently observed that mesne profits are the general measure of damages in cases where the defendant unlawfully remains in possession of a property after his entitlement to occupation has ended, but that other measures of damages may be available.[172]

Courts have also sometimes awarded reasonable fee damages for tort in lieu of an injunction pursuant to Lord Cairns' Act.[173]

[16.88]

These cases reflect a concern to protect the right to exclusive possession of one's land and to preclude others from entering that land without permission. Generally, they give rise to a

[16.89]

---

168   D Brennan, *Retransmission and US Compliance with TRIPS* (Kluwer Law International 2003) 199.
169   [1941] AC 1.
170   *Martin v Porter* (1839) 5 M & W 351, 151 ER 149; *Jegon v Vivian* (1871) LR 6 Ch 742; *Phillips v Homfray* (1871) LR 6 Ch App 770; *Whitwham v Westminster Brymbo Coal & Coke Company* [1896] 2 Ch 538.
171   *Elliott v Boynton* [1924] 1 Ch 236; *Wilson v Kelly* [1957] VR 147; *Swordheath Properties Ltd v Tabet* [1979] 1 WLR 285; *Ministry of Defence v Ashman* [1993] 2 EGLR 102; *Ministry of Defence v Thompson* [1993] 2 EGLR 107; *Lollis v Loulatzis* [2007] VSC 547.
172   *Balanced Securities Ltd v Bianco (No 2)* [2010] VSC 201, (2010) 27 VR 599 [16].
173   *Bracewell v Appleby* [1975] Ch 408; *Jaggard v Sawyer* [1995] 1 WLR 269.

'reasonable fee' award (the rent or fee the plaintiff would have been able to charge for entry or use of the land). For this reason, they are sometimes known as 'use value' cases.

[16.90]   In Australia, the reasonable fee charged for a trespass on property was characterised as 'restitutionary damages' in *LJP Investments Pty Ltd v Howard Chia Investments Pty Ltd (No 2)*.[174] Howard Chia Investments ('Chia') entered onto LJP Investments' ('LJP') land to erect scaffolding required for construction work on Chia's land. The scaffolding trespassed into LJP's airspace. Chia had sought permission to erect the scaffolding, but LJP requested a lump sum of $30 000, plus a rental of $570 per week. Chia was unwilling to pay, and chose to trespass. Amongst other things, LJP sought damages from Chia. Hodgson J characterised the 'reasonable fee' damages as 'restitutionary damages', and calculated them as representing the sum Chia should pay for the use of LJP's land. His Honour had to choose between the market value of the right that was used and the peculiar value to the plaintiffs of the opportunity to use the land. Chia gained $200 000 by building right up to the boundary rather than 1.5 metres short of it. The judge said it was impossible to be certain whether Chia would have simply chosen to use a cheaper method or paid the sum LJP demanded, as there had been a lack of evidence from Chia's decision-makers. Accordingly, the judge took a similar approach to that taken in *Armoury v Delamirie*,[175] and presumed that the value of the right was at the upper limit, being $30 000 plus the rental. The question of value was resolved against Chia because Chia's actions had made an accurate determination problematic.[176]

[16.91]   The restitutionary approach to mesne profits has been confirmed as open in Australia by Edelman J in *Hampton v BHP Billiton Minerals Pty Ltd (No 2)*,[177] although he also considered the possibility that such damages could be calculated on a compensatory basis.[178]

[16.92]   English courts have sometimes awarded reasonable fee damages for nuisance.[179] However, this is controversial, and two English cases suggest that reasonable fee damages are *not* available for the tort of nuisance, despite the fact that it is a proprietary tort. In *Stoke-on-Trent City Council v W and J Wass Ltd*, a reasonable fee award was refused for nuisance in the form of an infringement of a market right.[180] Furthermore, a majority of the English Court of Appeal in *Forsyth-Grant v Allen* said in obiter dicta that gain-based relief was never appropriate for nuisance because it did not involve a misappropriation of rights in the same way as trespass, conversion or intellectual property infringements.[181]

---

174   (1989) 24 NSWLR 499. See also *Ministry of Defence v Ashman* [1993] 2 EGLR 102, 104, 105; *Esperance Cattle Co Pty Ltd v Granite Hill Pty Ltd* [2014] WASC 279, (2014) 47 WAR 318, [454]–[456].

175   (1722) 1 Strange 505, 93 ER 664.

176   Cf *Bendal Pty Ltd v Mirvac Project Pty Ltd* (1991) 23 NSWLR 464.

177   [2012] WASC 285 [355]–[359].

178   Ibid, [342]–[354].

179   Eg *Bracewell v Appleby* [1975] Ch 408; *Carr-Saunders v Dick McNeil Associates Ltd* [1986] 1 WLR 922, cited as nuisance cases by Nourse LJ in *Stoke-on-Trent City Council v W and J Wass Ltd* [1988] 1 WLR 1406, 1413.

180   [1988] 1 WLR 1406.

181   *Forsyth-Grant v Allen* [2008] EWCA Civ 505, [2008] 2 EGLR 16 [32] (Patten LJ, with whom Mummery LJ agreed). Toulson LJ (at [47]) left open the question of whether a restitutionary award can be awarded for nuisance. Cf C Rotherham, 'Deterrence as a Justification for Awarding Accounts of Profits' (2012) 32 OJLS 537, 546, who suggests that while caution should be exercised, the existence of gain-based awards in nuisance should not be totally precluded.

2 Torts protecting proprietary rights in goods

Although it is an English case, *Strand Electric & Engineering Co Ltd v Brisford Entertainments Ltd*[182] has been adopted in Australia; see [16.97]. It holds that a plaintiff may be entitled to a 'reasonable fee' where a defendant has committed a tort against goods. The plaintiff, Strand Electric, hired out electric switchboards to a theatre company. Brisford Entertainment, the defendant, owned the theatre, and after it had repossessed the building from the theatre company, it refused to return the switchboards to the plaintiff. The plaintiff brought an action in detinue, claiming the return of its goods and damages for detention.   [16.93]

While the trial judge awarded a reasonable fee, he discounted the award on the basis that the plaintiff might not have hired out all the switchboards. The English Court of Appeal unanimously held that the plaintiff was entitled to the full hiring charge for the whole period of the goods' detention without any discount. Somervell LJ and Denning LJ analogised the unlawful detention of the goods to the mesne profit cases mentioned above.[183]   [16.94]

There were two views about the theoretical basis of the award. Denning LJ saw reasonable fee damages as based on restitutionary principles, not compensatory principles. In his view, the hiring charge reflected the fact that the defendant had wrongfully used the goods for its own purposes. The reasonable fee reversed the benefit the defendant had received from use of the goods, and it was irrelevant that the plaintiff had suffered no loss.[184]   [16.95]

By contrast, Romer LJ took a compensatory approach. He identified three important facts: (1) the equipment which the defendant detained was profit-earning; (2) the plaintiff normally hired out the equipment in its business; and (3) during the period of wrongful detention the defendant used the property for its own ends. He said that the reasonable fee reflected the losses made by the plaintiff, and the question of the profit or benefit which the defendant had derived from the wrongful act did not arise. There was no necessary relationship between the plaintiff's loss and gain.[185]   [16.96]

Strand Electric has been applied in several Australian cases involving proprietary torts.[186] Two will be discussed for illustration. First, in *Gaba Formwork Contractors Pty Ltd v Turner Corporation Ltd*,[187] the plaintiff hired out formwork materials to the defendant.[188] The defendant returned some materials, but retained others. The plaintiff sued in detinue for the replacement cost of the materials retained and for a hiring fee from the date the goods were hired to the date of judgment. Giles J applied *Strand Electric* and held that the defendant was liable for 'reasonable fee' damages to the date of judgment.[189]   [16.97]

In *Bunnings Group Ltd v CHEP Australia Ltd*,[190] the NSW Court of Appeal applied both *Strand Electric* and *Gaba Formwork*. The plaintiff, Chep, hired out pallets to businesses   [16.98]

---

182   [1952] 2 QB 246.
183   Ibid, 252 (Somervell LJ), 253 (Denning LJ).
184   Ibid, 254–55.
185   Ibid, 256.
186   *Yakamia Dairy v Wood* [1976] WAR 57; *Bilambil-Terranora Pty Ltd v Tweed Shire Council* [1980] 1 NSWLR 465; *Gaba Formwork Contractors Pty Ltd v Turner Corp Ltd* (1991) 32 NSWLR 175; *Bunnings Group Ltd v CHEP Australia Ltd* [2011] NSWCA 342, (2011) 82 NSWLR 420.
187   (1991) 32 NSWLR 175.
188   Formwork is the permanent or temporary mould into which concrete is poured.
189   (1991) 32 NSWLR 175, 188.
190   [2011] NSWCA 342, (2011) 82 NSWLR 420.

which used them to deliver goods to the defendant's hardware stores. Over a period of years, the defendant, Bunnings, accumulated thousands of the plaintiff's pallets and used them in its business for various purposes. The plaintiff first requested the return of the pallets in 2002, but the defendants did not return them until 2007. At first instance, the plaintiff successfully made out detinue and conversion, and claimed 'reasonable fee' damages. The trial judge, McDougall J, accepted that there was no difference between damages for conversion and detinue in this case.[191] He applied *Strand Electric* and *Gaba Formwork* and calculated reasonable fee damages according to the standard fee chargeable, but discounted them because Chep's business model assumed that not all pallets would be hired out. The NSW Court of Appeal agreed that *Strand Electric* and *Gaba Formwork* applied. Allsop P, with whom McFarlan JA agreed, held that the damages were compensatory.[192] He further held that the relevant rate was not the standard hiring fee, but the reduced measure of hire which CHEP had offered Bunnings in 2006.[193] This kind of analysis is akin to the rights-based arguments mentioned above (see [16.69]): the damages reflect the value of the infringement of the right. Giles JA agreed with Allsop P apart from the conclusion concerning the compensatory nature of the damages. He held that these awards were restitutionary, and that the true measure of the damages was the expense saved by Bunnings, so damages should be measured at the rate which CHEP had offered them in 2006.[194]

3   Other torts

[16.99]   There is an ongoing controversy as to the extent to which 'reasonable fee' damages should be available for non-proprietary torts (if at all). There is no Australian law on point, and the English law suggests that such awards will not be made. In *Halifax Building Society v Thomas*,[195] the English Court of Appeal refused to allow 'waiver of tort' for the tort of deceit. In *Devenish Nutrition Ltd v Sanofi-Aventis SA (France)*,[196] which concerned the tort of breach of statutory duty, the English Court of Appeal held that *Wass* (see [16.92]) stood for the proposition that reasonable fee damages were not available for non-proprietary torts. It has been argued that the Court of Appeal's decision was incoherent, as *Wass* had not been interpreted in this way in the past, and *Wass* itself involved nuisance, a proprietary tort, which by the logic in *Devenish* should have given rise to gain-based relief.[197] In any event, the Court of Appeal in *Devenish* declined to award a reasonable fee for breach of statutory duty.

[16.100]   The unavailability of reasonable fee awards in non-proprietary torts do not have a principled basis. There may be reasons why such awards are unavailable but they should be justified in a more coherent fashion.

191   *CHEP Australia Ltd v Bunnings Group Ltd* [2010] NSWSC 301.
192   [2011] NSWCA 342, (2011) 82 NSWLR 420 [173].
193   Citing *Butler v Egg and Egg Pulp Marketing Board* (1966) 114 CLR 185.
194   [2011] NSWCA 342, (2011) 82 NSWLR 420 [194]–[199], [205].
195   [1996] Ch 217.
196   [2008] EWCA Civ 1086, [2009] Ch 390.
197   C Rotherham, 'Gain-Based Relief in Tort after *Attorney General v Blake*' (2010) 126 LQR 102, 110–11.

G   Contract

Australian courts have not awarded 'reasonable fee' awards for breach of contract. The caution   [16.101]
of the Australian courts may be reasonable, as the English courts have had difficulty choosing
between a full account of profits or a 'reasonable fee' award in the cases following *Blake*.[198]

Although *Wrotham Park Estate Co Ltd v Parkside Homes Ltd*[199] formed an essential part of   [16.102]
Lord Nicholls' speech in *Blake*, the basis of the award remains contested. A 'reasonable fee'
was clearly awarded for breach of contract in lieu of an injunction, but the normative basis of
that award remains unclear (whether it be compensatory, restitutionary, or based on a
proprietary right or some form of partial disgorgement); see [16.66]–[16.77].

In *Wrotham Park*, the defendants were property developers who had built more houses   [16.103]
than were allowed in breach of a covenant in favour of the plaintiffs' land. The plaintiffs had
notified the developers about the restrictive covenant shortly after the developers purchased
the land, and a writ claiming a mandatory injunction was served before substantial construction
had taken place. However, the plaintiffs chose not to seek an interlocutory injunction for a
combination of legal and financial reasons. By the time the matter came to trial, the houses
were built. Brightman J declined to award an injunction requiring the demolition of the houses
because this would be an 'unpardonable waste'.[200] However, he awarded the plaintiffs
damages in lieu of an injunction pursuant to Lord Cairns' Act (discussed in Ch 12) and
calculated these damages at 5% of the profit of the defendant.[201] This decision constitutes
the 'solitary beacon' identified by Lord Nicholls in *Blake*; see [16.56]. Lord Cairns' Act arguably
permits gain-based awards at common law.

The most credible criteria for when a court will choose between full disgorgement or a   [16.104]
'reasonable fee' award in contract has been outlined by Cunnington, who distinguishes
between two situations:

1. where the court 'will not' order specific relief (for example, because of delay on the
    part of the plaintiff, hardship to the defendant or broader public policy
    considerations); and

2. where the court 'cannot' order specific relief (for example, because of impossibility or
    the need for constant supervision).[202]

Cunnington argues that, in the first instance, courts choose the lesser 'reasonable fee' award. In
the second instance, where the defendant has deprived the plaintiff of specific relief, the courts
award full disgorgement damages.

In a case such as *Blake*, specific performance is impossible, and the defendant has put the   [16.105]
possibility of performance out of the hands of the plaintiff by his conduct. It is appropriate that
all profits be disgorged. In some cases, an allowance for skill and effort may be given, although

---

198   *Blake* is discussed at [16.49]–[16.51].
199   [1974] 1 WLR 798.
200   Ibid, 811.
201   There is an ongoing controversy as to whether Brightman J meant actual profit or anticipated profit.
202   R Cunnington, 'The Measure and Availability of Gain-Based Damages for Breach of Contract' in D Saidov
       and R Cunnington (eds), *Contract Damages: Domestic and International Perspectives* (Hart 2008) 207,
       236. Adopted in K Barnett, *Accounting for Profit for Breach of Contract: Theory and Practice* (Hart
       2012) 161.

no allowance was given to Blake, the 'notorious traitor'. In a case such as *Wrotham Park*, specific performance is still possible, but the court chooses not to award it for discretionary reasons. Accordingly, it is appropriate to award a reasonable fee which is generally less than the full profit, as in *Wrotham Park* itself.[203]

[16.106]   Unfortunately, English cases following *Blake* have demonstrated significant confusion as to what measure to choose. Two will be considered. Both involved the breach of a settlement agreement. In *Experience Hendrix LLC v PPX Enterprises Inc*,[204] the guitarist, Jimi Hendrix, was sued by PPX, pursuant to an agreement made in 1965, according to which Hendrix had agreed to perform exclusively for PPX. Hendrix died in 1970, and PPX sued his estate. In 1973, PPX and Hendrix's estate entered a settlement agreement which provided, inter alia, that certain recordings would not be licensed by PPX to third parties without the consent of Hendrix's estate. PPX breached this settlement agreement twice by selling non-listed record-ings to record companies for a profit. The Court of Appeal unanimously held that Experience Hendrix was entitled to a 'reasonable fee' award, which was reduced by an allowance for skill and effort. The court rejected Experience Hendrix's claim for an account of PPX's entire profit.

[16.107]   If one applies the analysis suggested at [16.56] and [16.104], with respect, the court wrongly decided that PPX did not have to pay the full measure of its profits, particularly as the court found that Experience Hendrix had a 'legitimate interest' in the performance of the contract.[205] Damages were inadequate and specific relief was impossible because PPX had given third parties access to the recordings. The appropriate measure of relief was full disgorgement damages, perhaps reduced by an allowance for skill and effort.

[16.108]   Similar criticism may be levelled against the outcome of the *WWF* cases,[206] which involved a settlement agreement between the World Wide Fund for Nature and the World Wrestling Federation wherein the latter agreed that it would no longer use the initials 'WWF'. The courts refused to make the World Wrestling Federation pay an account of profits or a reasonable fee. However, the outcome was complicated by the fact that the World Wide Fund for Nature delayed bringing legal action, which may suggest that a reasonable fee should have been awarded rather than full disgorgement of profit (discussed at [16.138]).

[16.109]   *Experience Hendrix* raises the role of allowances and the *WWF* cases raise the role of bars to relief such as delay. We will now consider these issues generally in relation to both accounts of profit and reasonable fees.

V   Allowances, discretionary factors and bars to relief

[16.110]   When calculating the net profit in an account of profits, courts regularly make allowances for the defendant's skill and effort. The profit disgorged to the plaintiff is reduced, reflecting the notion that the defendant's skill and effort in making the profit should be recognised by the

203   Cf *Pell Frischmann Engineering Ltd v Bow Valley Iran Ltd* [2009] UKPC 45, [2011] 1 WLR 2370, strongly criticised in Barnett, ibid, 159–60, 206.
204   [2003] EWCA Civ 323, [2003] 1 All ER (Comm) 830.
205   R Cunnington, 'Rock, Restitution and Disgorgement' (2004) 3 *Journal of Obligations & Remedies* 46, 52.
206   *World Wide Fund for Nature v World Wrestling Federation Entertainment Inc* [2001] EWHC Ch 482; [2006] EWHC 184 (Ch), [2006] FSR 38; [2007] EWCA Civ 286, [2008] 1 WLR 445.

courts. It is suggested that when courts justify allowances for skill and effort by reference to causation and remoteness, they are really apportioning profit. Consequently, apportionment of profit will also be discussed in the context of allowances.

Because the account of profits is an equitable award, it is also subject to the general equitable bars to relief such as hardship, lack of clean hands and delay. The court may exercise its discretion and refuse to award an account of profit to the plaintiff on these bases, or perhaps merely reduce the relief to the plaintiff.   [16.111]

It appears that some bars to relief will operate to reduce full disgorgement to a reasonable fee award, or to no award at all, but the extent and mode of application of the bars to relief to reasonable fee awards is unclear.   [16.112]

A Allowances for skill and effort

1 Allowances for skill and effort for breach of fiduciary duty

In Australia, the allowance for skill and effort is clearly available for breaches of fiduciary duty. The High Court of Australia commented extensively on the allowance for skill and effort in *Warman*.[207] The court thought it would be inappropriate and inequitable to compel an errant fiduciary to account for the whole of the profit from his conduct of the business or his exploitation of the principal's goodwill over an indefinite period. It was sometimes appropriate to allow a fiduciary a proportion of the profits when it appeared that the business had flourished because of his efforts. The court said: [16.113]

> ...the relevant proportion of the increased profits is not the product or consequence of the plaintiff's property but the product of the fiduciary's skill, efforts, property and resources.[208]

In that case, Dwyer was given an equitable allowance for the time and effort he spent in building up a competing business, and the account of profit was reduced accordingly.

The allowance in *Warman* is controversial because Dwyer was remunerated despite his dishonesty and his deliberate breach of fiduciary duty. *Warman* can be compared with *Boardman v Phipps*, where Boardman was awarded liberal remuneration for skill and effort despite his breach of fiduciary duty because his breach had been honest and in good faith.[209] In *Guinness plc v Saunders*, Lord Goff said that an allowance for skill and effort was confined to 'those cases where it cannot have the effect of encouraging trustees in any way to put themselves in a position where their interests conflict with their duties as trustee'.[210] It is difficult to reconcile this with *Warman*.   [16.114]

Courts and commentators have sometimes suggested that allowances are made because the profit obtained by the defendant is insufficiently causally connected to the breach.[211]   [16.115]

---

207   (1995) 182 CLR 544; discussed above [16.23]–[16.27].
208   Ibid, 562 (Mason CJ, Brennan, Deane, Dawson and Gaudron JJ).
209   *Boardman v Phipps* [1967] 2 AC 46, 104 (Lord Cohen), 112 (Lord Hodson).
210   [1990] 2 AC 663, 701.
211   *Regal (Hastings) Ltd v Gulliver* [1967] 2 AC 134, 144–45 (Lord Russell), 153 (Lord Macmillan); *Chan v Zacharia* (1984) 154 CLR 178, 199 (Deane J); *Warman International Ltd v Dwyer* (1995) 182 CLR 544, 562; *Murad v Al-Saraj* [2005] EWCA Civ 959, [2005] All ER (D) 503 [72]–[79] (Arden LJ). See also J Edelman, *Gain-Based Damages: Contract, Tort, Equity and Intellectual Property* (Hart 2002) 104–05,

Courts should distinguish between profits which arise directly because of the breach and profits which do not. But this should not be confused with allowances, which recognise the defendant's skill and effort *despite* the fact that his acts were legally responsible for causing the gain. This is a matter of apportionment rather than an allowance.

[16.116] In *Warman*, the High Court left open the possibility that it may be appropriate to apportion profits where some profit arose as a result of the breach and other profit did not, although the 'general rule' is that courts will not order apportionment in cases involving breach of fiduciary duty without a prior agreement for profit-sharing.[212] Apportionment is less likely to be appropriate in cases of equitable wrongdoing than it is in intellectual property law cases.[213] Apportionment has only been made in breach of fiduciary duty cases involving antecedent profit-sharing arrangements, when courts have taken a 'but for' approach to causation.[214] Nevertheless, apportionment may provide a solution to those cases where an allowance for skill and effort is difficult to justify according to principles of desert.[215]

[16.117] Some courts and commentators have suggested that profit can be 'too remote' from the breach of fiduciary obligation and, therefore, need not be disgorged, and that this is a justification for awarding allowances.[216] However, remoteness 'tells us nothing meaningful about how allowances may be justified',[217] because it does not provide clear criteria for when allowances will or will not be allowed.

[16.118] Desert can also justify allowances, on the basis that the defendant expended time and skilled labour and deserves recognition of this. Because desert gives rise to a claim of propriety (that is, it is 'proper' in the circumstances), not to an entitlement (that is, a right), it seems to be a good explanation for a discretionary allowance.[218] However, since desert is personal and specific, it seems appropriate that the defendant must justify to the plaintiff why he deserves an allowance against her. Consequently, it does not sit well with *Warman*, where the defendant's profits did not benefit the plaintiff.

[16.119] Further, a desert-based analysis does not accommodate the more utilitarian concerns of law-and-economics scholars who seek to encourage entrepreneurial skills in society and ensure that accounts of profit are not over-deterrent.[219] For example, Dwyer in *Warman*

171–72; G Virgo, *The Principles of the Law of Restitution* (3rd edn, OUP 2015) 509; G Virgo, 'Restitutionary Remedies for Wrongs: Causation and Remoteness' in CEF Rickett (ed), *Justifying Private Law Remedies* (Hart 2008) 301, 309–10, 325–26.

212   (1995) 182 CLR 544, 563.
213   R Cunnington, 'The Assessment of Gain-Based Damages for Breach of Contract' (2008) 71 Mod LR 559, 580; D Friedmann, 'Restitution for Wrongs: The Measure of Recovery' (2000) 79 Tex L Rev 1879, 1904–17.
214   M Harding, 'Justifying Fiduciary Allowances' in A Robertson and TH Wu (eds), *The Goals of Private Law* (Hart 2009) 345; *Warman* (1995) 182 CLR 544, 562; *Murad v Al-Saraj* [2005] EWCA Civ 959, [2005] All ER (D) 503 [160] (Clarke LJ, dissenting); *Chirnside v Fay* [2006] NZSC 68, [2007] 1 NZLR 433 [36] (Elias CJ), [54] (Gault J).
215   C Mitchell, 'Causation, Remoteness, and Fiduciary Gains' (2006) 17 KCLJ 325, 328.
216   *Warman* (1995) 182 CLR 544, 561. See also A Burrows, *The Law of Restitution* (3rd edn, OUP 2011) 688–89; R Grantham and CEF Rickett, *Enrichment and Restitution in New Zealand* (Hart 2000) 486–87.
217   M Harding, 'Justifying Fiduciary Allowances' in A Robertson and TH Wu (eds), *The Goals of Private Law* (Hart 2009) 349.
218   Ibid.
219   See, eg, F Easterbrook and D Fischel, 'Contract and Fiduciary Duty' (1993) 36 J L & Econ 425.

was more efficient and a better manager than Warman, and we do not wish to discourage his enterprise and efficiency. Perhaps apportionment would be a better way of dealing with these utilitarian concerns because it would apportion certain of the profits to Dwyer's own legitimate efforts. It has also been suggested that allowances are intended to prevent unjust enrichment, like counter-restitution and principles of *restitutio in integrum* in rescission, so that the plaintiff is not unjustly enriched by the receipt of services.[220]

2   Allowances for skill and effort for intellectual property breaches

Defendants in intellectual property infringement cases are clearly entitled to a variety of allowances reflecting costs of material, wages and other costs which arise from the manufacture and sale of infringing goods. However, the defendant cannot claim any remuneration for herself.[221] The court's generosity in relation to the allowance will depend in part on whether the defendant believed that she had a bona fide right to use intellectual property or not.[222]   [16.120]

A difficult question is whether the defendant can claim an allowance for general overhead expenses, such as rent, lighting, heating or office expenses, which are not a direct result of producing the product. The High Court of Australia in *Dart Industries Inc v Décor Corporation Pty Ltd* said that it depended on the nature of the infringing product.[223] If the infringing product was a 'side line' taking up 'surplus capacity' in the business, and the defendant's business would have incurred the overheads regardless of the infringement, it was inappropriate to award an allowance.[224] By contrast, if the defendant forewent the opportunity to manufacture alternative non-infringing products, it would be fair to award some allowance for general overhead expenses because the purpose of the account of profits 'is not to punish the defendant but to prevent its unjust enrichment'.[225]   [16.121]

Apportionment is frequently adopted in accounts of profits awarded for copyright or patent infringement, so that the profit is split between that resulting directly from the infringement and that resulting from other sources.[226] In *Colbeam*,[227] considered at [16.34], the apportionment was carried out by ascertaining the profits made from the infringing goods, and then by ascertaining what proportion of those profits was made from the infringing use of the trademark. Windeyer J explained that the profit 'is thus not the profit [the infringer] made from selling the article itself but … the profit made in selling it under the trade mark'.[228] On the other hand, if the entire profit made from selling the   [16.122]

220   E Bant and M Bryan, 'Defences, Bars and Discretionary Factors' in E Bant and M Bryan (eds), *Principles of Proprietary Remedies* (Thomson Reuters 2013) [11.80], [11.140].
221   *Leplastrier & Co Ltd v Armstrong-Holland Ltd* (1926) 26 SR (NSW) 585, 593.
222   *Redwood Music Ltd v Chappell & Co Ltd* [1982] RPC 109.
223   (1993) 179 CLR 101, 111.
224   Ibid, 113.
225   Ibid (Mason CJ, Deane, Dawson and Toohey JJ).
226   Eg *Colbeam* (1968) 122 CLR 25, 42–43; *Dart Industries Inc v Décor Corporation Pty Ltd* (1993) 179 CLR 101, 121; *Potton Ltd v Yorkclose Ltd* [1990] FSR 11, 16; *Sheldon v Metro-Goldwyn Pictures Corporation*, 309 US 390, 404 (1940) (Hughes CJ).
227   (1968) 122 CLR 25.
228   Ibid, 37.

product is attributable to the use of the infringed intellectual property, then the entire profit will be disgorged.[229]

3   Allowances for skill and effort and disgorgement in contract

[16.123]   If disgorgement is to be awarded for breach of contract, it seems clear that an allowance for skill and effort should be made in some circumstances.[230] Allowances have been made in some US and English cases.[231] Allowances deal in some measure with the concern of law-and-economics scholars that 'efficient' breaches of contract would be prevented by an award of disgorgement damages.

[16.124]   Apportionment also affects the quantum of disgorgement, as in *Vercoe v Rutland Fund Management Ltd*.[232] *Vercoe* involved the breach of a negative covenant dealing with confidentiality in a contract to exploit certain business opportunities, as well as a breach of confidence. Roth J awarded a 'reasonable fee' based on the amount that the plaintiffs would have accepted from the defendants to be released from their contractual obligations. The parties agreed that a reasonable fee award was an appropriate measure,[233] although they disagreed as to the quantum. It would have been unfair in the circumstances to strip the entire gain from the defendants when they had expended a good deal of risk, money and effort.

B   Discretionary factors and bars to relief

[16.125]   It is incontrovertible that the discretionary factors and bars to relief are available for accounts of profit in equitable causes of action. The position is less clear regarding accounts of profit for breaches of intellectual property rights. Finally, the applicability of bars to relief to gain-based awards in the common law is controversial unless such awards are Lord Cairns' Act damages (such as those in *Wrotham Park*). However, it is arguable that the courts *effectively* take such bars into account, and that, for example, delay is one reason for courts choosing a 'reasonable fee measure' for some common law awards that are (arguably) gain-based.

1   Hardship

[16.126]   The discretionary defence of hardship militates against the award of an account of profits in equity. The basic principles have been outlined in Chs 10 and 11. It is unlikely, however, that this bar will operate to prevent a court from awarding an account of profits, as in most cases stripping a defendant of a gain received in breach of duty would not cause hardship – it would simply put her in the position she should have been in had she not breached her duty.

---

229   *Dart Industries Inc v Décor Corporation Pty Ltd* (1993) 179 CLR 101, 121.

230   R Cunnington, 'The Assessment of Gain-Based Damages for Breach of Contract' (2008) 71 Mod LR 559, 600–01; K Barnett, *Accounting for Profit for Breach of Contract: Theory and Practice* (Hart 2012) 196–200. See American Law Institute, *Restatement (Third) of Restitution and Unjust Enrichment* (2011) §51(5) and comment h.

231   *Earthinfo Inc v Hydrosphere Resource Consultants Inc*, 900 P 2d 113, 120–21 (Colo, 1995); *Experience Hendrix LLC v PPX Enterprises Inc* [2003] EWCA Civ 1804, [2003] 1 All ER (Comm) 830 [44].

232   [2010] EWHC 424 (Ch), [2010] Bus LR 141.

233   Ibid, [289].

2   Lack of clean hands

The defence of lack of clean hands may militate against the award of an account of profits. Murphy J noted the possibility of lack of clean hands operating in the context of a copyright infringement,[234] but it has not arisen frequently.   [16.127]

Sometimes the issue might arise if one allows accounts of profit to be awarded for breach of contract and for tort (presuming that this occurs under equity's auxiliary jurisdiction). For example, in the context of an account of profits for breach of contract, imagine a variation on the facts of *Dowsett v Reid*.[235] In that case, the defendant entered an agreement to lease his property for 10 years with an option to purchase. It was held that the terms of the lease were unconscionable, and that the court should not specifically enforce the lease.[236] If the defendant had breached the lease and made a more profitable lease arrangement with a third party, the plaintiff may have sought an account of profit. The defendant should not be stripped of his profit because of the unconscionable nature of the original bargain; the plaintiff did not come to equity with clean hands.   [16.128]

It is unclear how lack of clean hands impacts upon reasonable fee awards or, indeed, even if it is available at all for such awards.   [16.129]

The 'lack of clean hands' defence does not sit well with the notion that the court can award allowances for skill and effort to fiduciaries who breach their duties knowingly and in bad faith, such as the breaching fiduciary in *Warman* (see [16.113]–[16.119]). If a plaintiff is designated as undeserving of relief on the basis of bad faith, then perhaps a defendant who is a bad faith fiduciary should not be entitled to an allowance for skill and effort. It seems that desert cannot be an explanation for those cases where an allowance has been made to a bad faith fiduciary, and the explanation can only be made on the utilitarian bases of promoting efficiency and innovation in business and society.   [16.130]

3   Delay and acquiescence

Delay and acquiescence do not usually operate for accounts of profit for breaches of fiduciary duty and breaches of confidence. Nevertheless, if the plaintiff delayed until profit was accrued, an account of profits will be denied.[237] In *Re Jarvis (dec'd)*,[238] the plaintiff and defendant were sisters, co-executors, co-trustees, and beneficiaries of their father's will. The defendant had successfully revived their father's lease over a newsagency business, taking significant risks using her own capital. The plaintiff did not sue until it became evident that the business was profitable. The defendant conceded that she held the lease on trust for herself and her sister pursuant to *Keech v Sandford*,[239] but the court held that she was not liable to account for profits from the business because the plaintiff had cynically delayed the action until the business was profitable.[240]   [16.131]

---

234   *Interstate Parcel Express Co Pty Ltd v Time-Life International (Nederlands) BV* (1977) 138 CLR 534, 561. See JD Heydon, MJ Leeming and PG Turner, *Meagher, Gummow and Lehane's Equity: Doctrines and Remedies* (5th edn, LexisNexis 2015) [3–105].
235   (1912) 15 CLR 695.
236   Ibid, 705–07.
237   P Devonshire, *Account of Profits* (Thomson Reuters 2013) 12–13.
238   [1958] 1 WLR 815.
239   (1726) Sel Cas 61, 25 ER 223.
240   [1958] 1 WLR 815, 820–21.

[16.132]   Delay and acquiescence may have a greater impact on the availability of accounts of profit or reasonable fee damages for infringement of intellectual property rights, tort and breach of contract.

[16.133]   As noted at [10.87] and [11.56], delay and acquiescence are difficult to categorically define, in part because acquiescence is often used in a way which overlaps with delay.[241] 'Mere' delay is generally not enough in itself to militate against the grant of a remedy in equity.[242] Something more is needed: this may be acquiescence on the part of the plaintiff or it may be prejudice to the defendant or third parties.

A   INTELLECTUAL PROPERTY

[16.134]   When accounts of profits were solely available under the auxiliary jurisdiction of equity, delay and acquiescence was a reason to refuse an account of profits (particularly because an account of profits was ancillary to an injunction). In *Smith v London & South Western Railway Co*, the plaintiff's delay and acquiescence led the court to refuse both an injunction and an account of profits. The latter was refused because it was ancillary to the award of an injunction.[243] However, in *Colbeam*, considered at [16.34], Windeyer J suggested that the unavailability of an injunction did not preclude the award of an account of profits: it was simply necessary that an injunction would have been available when the action was commenced.[244] This seems to be the better position: delay and acquiescence should be considered anew in relation to the award of an account of profits.

[16.135]   In *Colbeam*, Windeyer J said that delay and acquiescence could operate in intellectual property infringement cases, particularly when considering when the defendant became aware of the infringement.[245] If the plaintiff delays in informing the defendant of his infringement, the defendant is less likely to be aware that the conduct is infringing. Delay may thus operate to limit the calculation of profits to the time when the defendant did become aware.[246]

[16.136]   Delay and acquiescence may also lead a court to award a 'reasonable fee' rather than account of profits for some intellectual property infringements, although many factors are at play.[247]

B   TORT AND BREACH OF CONTRACT

[16.137]   It has been explained that courts should look at why specific relief cannot be awarded when ascertaining whether a plaintiff is entitled to an account of profits or a 'reasonable fee'.

241   JD Heydon, MJ Leeming and PG Turner, *Meagher, Gummow and Lehane's Equity: Doctrines and Remedies* (5th edn, LexisNexis Butterworths 2015) [38–055]–[38–065]; M Cope, *Equitable Obligations: Duties, Defences and Remedies* (LBC 2007) 287; *Orr v Ford* (1989) 167 CLR 316, 338 (Deane J).
242   *Lindsay Petroleum Co v Hurd* (1874) LR 5 PC 221, 239–40.
243   (1854) Kay 408, 69 ER 17; *Price's Patent Candle Co v Bauwen's Patent Candle Co* (1854) 4 K & J 727, 70 ER 302.
244   (1968) 122 CLR 25, 31.
245   Ibid, 33. See, eg, *Lever Brothers, Port Sunlight Ltd v Sunniwhite Products Ltd* (1949) 66 RPC 84. Cf *Edward Young and Co v Stanley Silverwood Holt* (1948) 65 RPC 25.
246   F Patfield, 'The Remedy of Account of Profits in Industrial and Intellectual Litigation' (1984) 7 UNSWLJ 189, 193–95.
247   D Brennan, *Retransmission and US Compliance with TRIPS* (Kluwer Law International 2003) 199.

The English cases indicate that delay in seeking specific relief is a bar, to a lesser or greater degree, to a claim for full disgorgement for breach of contract or tort. This may be because the plaintiff has conducted herself in a way that indicates she has forgone insisting upon her rights. If the defendant has behaved in such a fashion as to put specific relief out of the plaintiff's reach because he believed that she had acquiesced in his action, the plaintiff deserves a lesser amount, represented by a 'reasonable fee' award.[248] Alternatively, the plaintiff's delay may be relevant because the defendant has been prejudiced. In either event, the plaintiff cannot sit back and let the defendant accumulate gains, and later attempt to claim them.   [16.138]

Most English cases are consistent with this analysis: if the plaintiff has delayed in some way in seeking specific relief, the courts choose a 'reasonable fee' award.[249] The exception is *Pell Frischmann Engineering Ltd v Bow Valley Iran Ltd*,[250] which involved a joint venture contract for the exploitation of an Iranian oilfield. The contract provided, inter alia, that the defendant was to work exclusively with the plaintiff and that the defendant was not to approach the Iranian government without the plaintiff's consent. The defendant breached this agreement. The Privy Council found that the plaintiff was entitled to a 'reasonable fee' representing the amount it would have accepted to be released from its contract. The US$2.5 million 'reasonable fee' outstripped the actual profit made by the defendant (US$1 million to US$1.8 million). This was despite the plaintiff's 'extraordinary and unexplained delay in bringing proceedings'.[251] Stripping the defendants of an amount greater than their actual gain is overly punitive. In addition, the plaintiff's inordinate delay should have resulted in a substantial reduction of the award.   [16.139]

VI   The future of gain-based relief in Australia

Gain-based relief is incontrovertibly available in equity and for intellectual property breaches in Australia by means of the account of profits. It remains controversial whether gain-based relief is available for breaches of common law causes of action. At the very least, 'reasonable fee' awards are available in Australia for *some* proprietary torts, including trespass to land, trespass to goods, conversion and detinue, but whether this remedy will be available outside these torts is presently unclear. While English law recognises the availability of gain-based relief for common law actions such as tort or breach of contract, the English cases lack clarity.   [16.140]

---

248   An application of acquiescence to 'reasonable fee' damages is rejected by R Cunnington, 'The Assessment of Gain-Based Damages for Breach of Contract' (2008) 71 Mod LR 559, 572–73. To the contrary, courts award 'reasonable fee' damages precisely because acquiescence and delay have been taken into account.

249   *Wrotham Park Estate Co Ltd v Parkside Homes Ltd* [1974] 1 WLR 798; *Shaw v Applegate* [1977] 1 WLR 970; *Gafford v Graham* (1999) 77 P & CR 73; *Amec Developments Ltd v Jury's Hotel Management (UK) Ltd* [2000] EWHC Ch 454, [2001] 1 EGLR 81; *World Wide Fund for Nature v World Wrestling Federation Entertainment Inc* [2006] EWHC 184 (Ch), [2006] FSR 38 [174] at point 6; *Surrey County Council v Bredero Homes Ltd* [1993] 1 WLR 1361, 1371 (Rose LJ).

250   [2009] UKPC 45, [2011] 1 WLR 2370.

251   Ibid, [54] (Lord Walker).

It is unclear for which torts such relief is available. It also remains unclear when a court will award gain-based relief for breach of contract and on what basis courts choose between measures (accounts of profits or reasonable fees). Nonetheless, it is suggested that, with time, these difficulties will become surmountable, and that Australian courts should remain open to the possibility that in some limited circumstances gain-based awards are appropriate for breaches of common law obligations.

PART

6

RESTITUTION AND GIVING BACK

17

PERSONAL REMEDIES FOR UNJUST ENRICHMENT

I   Introduction

[17.1]   The concept of 'remedy' used in this chapter encompasses a court order replicating a pre-existing right,[1] not a response to civil wrongdoing.[2] Restitutionary remedies responding to unjust enrichment differ from remedies responding to a wrong (breach of contract, tort, or equitable wrong). As noted at [1.11]–[1.14], they do not fit easily into an Austinian division between the primary right and the secondary remedy.[3] In Peter Birks's terminology, remedies for unjust enrichment are the law's response to a 'not-wrong'; this means that the response is constrained, and the plaintiff is justified only in recovering the value of what was taken.[4] It is for this reason that the cause of action and the remedy in unjust enrichment overlap, and they are notoriously difficult to untangle.[5] Discussions of restitutionary remedies inevitably turn into discussions of the cause of action.[6]

[17.2]   A restitutionary remedy may be imposed when the defendant makes a gain at the plaintiff's expense (whether money, services, or goods). Restitution is concerned to reverse transfers of value. If the defendant has gained at the plaintiff's expense, he must give back what he gained (or the monetary value of his gain). In this way, restitution carries a sense of a 'giving back' of a gain made at the plaintiff's expense. However, restitution is also used in the sense of a 'giving up' of a gain made by the defendant where there has not been a loss on the part of the plaintiff.[7] Sometimes, restitutionary remedies (such as an action for money had and received) are imposed where there is wrongdoing rather than subtractive enrichment; see [16.37]–[16.38]. This 'giving up' of a gain without a loss on the part of the plaintiff is better understood as disgorgement.

[17.3]   There are three personal restitutionary remedies in Australia, each of which corresponds to a different transfer of value from the plaintiff to the defendant:

1.   action for money had and received (for money);

2.   *quantum meruit* (for the value of services); and

3.   *quantum valebat* (or *quantum valebant*) (for the value of goods).

These reflect the ancient forms of action. Traditionally, the cause of action and the remedy are the same: the plaintiff pleads an action for money had and received and, if successful, the action for money had and received returns her money to her.

[17.4]   The forms of action mentioned above are a relic of the historical categorisation of these claims as 'implied contract' or 'quasi-contract'. The remedies were known as the 'common counts' and were based on the action of *assumpsit*, which was a form of action alleging that the

---

1   See R Zakrzewski, *Remedies Reclassified* (OUP 2005).
2   See J Austin, *Lectures on Jurisprudence* (R Campbell ed, Thoemmes Press 2002) vol 2, Lecture XLV, 787–800.
3   N Witzleb, E Bant, S Degeling and K Barker, *Remedies: Commentary and Materials* (6th edn, LBC 2015) [1.20]; P Birks, 'Rights, Wrongs and Remedies' (2000) OJLS 1, 28.
4   Birks, ibid, 25–36. Cf K Barker, 'Rescuing Remedialism in Unjust Enrichment Law: Why Remedies Are Right' [1998] Camb LJ 301.
5   R Zakrzewski, *Remedies Reclassified* (OUP 2005) 112.
6   A Burrows, 'Judicial Remedies' in A Burrows (ed), *English Private Law* (3rd edn, OUP 2013) [21.08].
7   These two senses of restitution were developed by P Birks, *An Introduction to the Law of Restitution* (revised edn, Clarendon Press 1989) 12.

defendant owed a debt to the plaintiff even in the absence of an express promise. The courts considered that there was an 'implied contract' according to which the defendant 'promised' the plaintiff that he was going to pay back the money which the plaintiff had paid to the defendant by mistake (for example). Therefore the plaintiff could sustain an action for money had and received because of the defendant's implied 'promise'. This account rested on a fiction that the plaintiff and the defendant had made a contract, although they had not.

Over the 20th century, this fiction was questioned. First, in 1936, the US Restatement of Restitution organised the law of quasi-contract and constructive trusts into a coherent body of law.[8] Secondly, in 1966, Robert Goff (later Lord Goff) and Gareth Jones published *The Law of Restitution*, which drew a diverse range of cases together on the principle that they were intended to prevent or reverse unjust enrichment.[9] They expressly refuted the suggestion that these cases were based on 'quasi-contract'. Thirdly, in 1985, Peter Birks published *An Introduction to the Law of Restitution*,[10] and his scholarship has left a lasting mark on the law of unjust enrichment. Many other scholars have since published texts in the area.[11]

[17.5]

Courts across the common law world have rejected the 'implied contract' theory of unjust enrichment. In *Pavey & Matthews Pty Ltd v Paul*, a majority in the High Court of Australia rejected the 'implied contract' theory and confirmed that unjust enrichment was the basis for these claims.[12] Deane J said that unjust enrichment was 'a unifying legal concept which explains why the law recognizes, in a variety of distinct categories of case, an obligation on the part of a defendant to make fair and just restitution for a benefit derived at the expense of a plaintiff'.[13]

[17.6]

Although the High Court of Australia recognised unjust enrichment as a legal concept before the House of Lords did,[14] there has been an ongoing debate in Australia about the place of unjust enrichment law and scholarship in Australia. In a series of cases from 2001 onwards, the High Court of Australia warned against the use of unjust enrichment scholarship in Australian law, as it does not respect the boundaries between the common law and equity, and it is said to engage in a species of 'top-down reasoning' which is foreign to the

[17.7]

---

8   American Law Institute, *Restatement of Restitution: Quasi-Contract and Constructive Trusts* (1936) and WA Seavey and AW Scott, 'Restitution' (1938) 54 LQR 29. See now American Law Institute, *Restatement (Third) of Restitution and Unjust Enrichment* (2011).

9   R Goff and G Jones, *The Law of Restitution* (Sweet & Maxwell 1966). Now up to its ninth edition: C Mitchell, P Mitchell and S Watterson, *Goff & Jones: The Law of Unjust Enrichment* (9th edn, Sweet & Maxwell 2016).

10   P Birks, *An Introduction to the Law of Restitution* (Clarendon Press 1985). A revised edition was published in 1989.

11   In Australia: J Taliadoros and S Erbacher, *Restitution: The Laws of Australia* (Thomson Reuters 2014); J Edelman and E Bant, *Unjust Enrichment* (2nd edn, Hart 2016); K Barker and R Grantham, *Unjust Enrichment* (2nd edn, LexisNexis 2017); K Mason, JW Carter and GJ Tolhurst, *Mason and Carter's Restitution Law in Australia* (3rd edn, LexisNexis 2016). In England and Wales: P Birks, *Unjust Enrichment* (2nd edn, OUP 2005); G Virgo, *Principles of the Law of Restitution* (3rd edn, OUP 2015); A Burrows, *The Law of Restitution* (3rd edn, OUP 2011).

12   (1987) 162 CLR 221, 227 (Mason and Wilson JJ), 255–56 (Deane J). See also *Roxborough v Rothmans of Pall Mall Australia Ltd* [2001] HCA 68, (2001) 208 CLR 516 [90] (Gummow J).

13   (1987) 162 CLR 221, 256–57. See also *Australia and New Zealand Banking Group Ltd v Westpac Banking Corporation* (1988) 164 CLR 662; *David Securities Pty Ltd v Commonwealth Bank of Australia* (1992) 175 CLR 353; *Baltic Shipping Co v Dillon* (1993) 176 CLR 344.

14   *Lipkin Gorman v Karpnale Ltd* [1991] 2 AC 548.

common law.[15] In *Roxborough v Rothmans of Pall Mall Australia Ltd*, Gummow J rejected any 'all-embracing theory of restitutionary rights and remedies founded upon a notion of "unjust enrichment"'.[16] Nevertheless, Gummow J was prepared to allow unjust enrichment an auxiliary 'gap-filling' role in *Roxborough* such that the plaintiff was entitled to an action for money had and received on the basis of failure of consideration of the contract under which the money had been paid.

[17.8] In light of the High Court's statements in *Lumbers v W Cook Builders Pty Ltd (in liq)*[17] and *Friend v Brooker*,[18] Jackman has said:

> It is no longer possible to speak meaningfully of the Anglo-Australian law of restitution. The High Court of Australia has unequivocally stated that the concept of unjust enrichment is not a principle which can be taken as a sufficient premise for direct application in a particular case.[19]

Thus, the extent to which unjust enrichment is recognised as a cause of action in Australian law is uncertain. Care should be taken in making a claim for a remedy such as an action for money had and received or a *quantum meruit* before an Australian court. In light of the High Court jurisprudence on the issue, the judge may be of the opinion that the plaintiff has to plead an action for money had and received or a *quantum meruit* according to the old forms of action,[20] although other judges may be more open to a pleading of unjust enrichment.

[17.9] Courts have also made it clear that they will strike out pleadings which simply assert that the defendant has been 'unjustly enriched' without pleading the facts which support the cause of action.[21]

[17.10] There are conflicting signs as to the present High Court's attitude to unjust enrichment. In *Equuscorp Pty Ltd v Haxton*, French CJ, Crennan and Kiefel JJ appeared to adopt a more conciliatory attitude towards unjust enrichment and scholarship in the area, when they said:

> Unjust enrichment therefore has a taxonomical function referring to categories of cases in which the law allows recovery by one person of a benefit retained by another. In that aspect, it does not found or reflect any 'all-embracing theory of restitutionary rights and remedies'. It does not, however, exclude the emergence of novel occasions of unjust enrichment supporting claims for restitutionary relief.[22]

---

15   *Roxborough v Rothmans of Pall Mall Australia Ltd* [2001] HCA 68, (2001) 208 CLR 516 [16] (Gleeson CJ, Gaudron and Hayne JJ), [72], [74] (Gummow J); *Farah Constructions Pty Ltd v Say-Dee Pty Ltd* [2007] HCA 22, (2007) 230 CLR 89 [151]; *Lumbers v W Cook Builders Pty Ltd (in liq)* [2008] HCA 27, (2008) 232 CLR 635 [76] (Gummow, Hayne, Crennan and Kiefel JJ); *Bofinger v Kingsway Group Ltd* [2009] HCA 44, (2009) 239 CLR 269 [85]–[93]; *Friend v Brooker* (2009) 239 CLR 129, [2009] HCA 21. Cf A Burrows, *The Law of Restitution* (3rd edn, OUP 2011) 35–43.
16   [2001] HCA 68, (2001) 208 CLR 516 [72], [74].
17   [2008] HCA 27, (2008) 232 CLR 635 [85].
18   [2009] HCA 21, (2009) 239 CLR 129 [7].
19   IM Jackman, 'Anglo-Australian Split on Restitution' (2009) 83 Aust LJ 726, 726.
20   See R Andrew and S Kirton, 'Quantum Meruit and Unjust Enrichment: Changing Jurisprudence in the High Court' (2008) 24 BCL 370, who suggest that claims in *quantum meruit* should be made on the traditional common law basis in light of High Court cases.
21   Eg *Reed International Books Australia Pty Ltd (t/as Butterworths) v King & Prior Pty Ltd* (1993) 44 FCR 587, 589–90.
22   *Equuscorp Pty Ltd v Haxton* [2012] HCA 7, (2012) 246 CLR 498, [30] (citing Birks's scholarship favourably).

This more conciliatory approach towards unjust enrichment was endorsed by French CJ   [17.11]
and Gageler J in *Australian Financial Services and Leasing Pty Ltd v Hills Industries Ltd*
('*AFSL* ').[23] However, the waters were muddied by the fact that Hayne, Crennan, Kiefel, Bell
and Keane JJ in *AFSL* rejected the applicability of the change of position defence (discussed at
[17.18], [17.32]) and suggested instead an application of equitable principles:

> This approach seeks to give effect to an understanding of unjust enrichment as a principle
> of direct application, which operates by measuring the extent of enrichment or, where a
> defence of change of position is invoked, the extent of disenrichment subsequent to that
> receipt. Such a 'principle' does not govern the resolution of this case because the concept
> of unjust enrichment is not the basis of restitutionary relief in Australian law. The principle
> of disenrichment, like that of unjust enrichment, is inconsistent with the law of restitution
> as it has developed in Australia. Disenrichment operates as a mathematical rule whereas
> the enquiry undertaken in relation to restitutionary relief in Australia is directed to who
> should properly bear the loss and why. That enquiry is conducted by reference to
> equitable principles.[24]

It is unclear from this paragraph whether the plurality meant to disclaim unjust enrichment law
altogether, or whether they were simply criticising the principle of 'disenrichment' in the
context of the change of position defence,[25] and overshot the mark. It is probable that it was
the latter,[26] but it is unfortunate that there remains confusion about the place of unjust
enrichment in Australian law.

The approach of the High Court may shift again now that Edelman J (an unjust enrichment   [17.12]
scholar) has been appointed to the High Court. In any event, it is suggested that it is important
to understand the concept and jurisprudence of unjust enrichment because it is a useful way by
which claims can be organised,[27] and it has some operation in Australian law, even if the
precise extent is unclear. Moreover, it will help readers understand certain analyses of rescission and proprietary remedies mentioned in Chs 18 and 19.

II   The elements of unjust enrichment

The basic concept of unjust enrichment is that a person who has been unjustly enriched at   [17.13]
the expense of another must make restitution to that other person, subject to defences. The
remedies awarded for unjust enrichment seek to reverse unjust transfers. It is beyond the scope
of this book to enter a detailed discussion of the elements of unjust enrichment, as our focus is
on remedies rather than causes of action.[28] The following provides a brief outline of the law of

---

23   [2014] HCA 14, (2014) 253 CLR 560 [20] (French CJ), [105], [130]–[142] (Gageler J).
24   Ibid, [78].
25   For further discussion of 'disenrichment' and its role in the change of position defence, see E Bant,
      'Change of Position in the High Court: *Australian Financial Services and Leasing Pty Ltd v Hills
      Industries Ltd* ' on *Opinions on High* (9 May 2014) <http://blogs.unimelb.edu.au/opinionsonhigh/2014/
      05/09/bant-hills-industries>.
26   K Mason, 'Strong Coherence, Strong Fusion, Continuing Categorical Confusion: The High Court's Latest
      Contributions to the Law of Restitution' (2015) 39 Aust Bar Rev 284, 318–19.
27   See *Lampson (Australia) v Fortescue Metals Group (No 3)* [2014] WASC 162 [51] (Edelman J).
28   For further information, see J Edelman and E Bant, *Unjust Enrichment* (2nd edn, Hart 2016); K Mason,
      JW Carter and GJ Tolhurst, *Mason and Carter's Restitution Law in Australia* (3rd edn, LexisNexis 2016).

unjust enrichment to assist in understanding restitutionary analyses of rescission and proprietary remedies.

[17.14] In Australian law, in order to claim restitutionary remedies, it is necessary to establish an 'unjust factor' which leads to the defendant being enriched at the expense of the plaintiff.[29] Relatively uncontroversial examples of unjust factors include:

- failure of consideration (meaning a failure of the purpose of the bargain which has led to the defendant's enrichment);
- mistake (encompassing both mistake of fact and mistake of law);
- compulsion (including duress);
- undue influence; and
- illegality.[30]

Outside this list, other factors may possibly give rise to restitutionary remedies, but whose status is more controversial.[31] There is an ongoing debate in unjust enrichment scholarship as to whether the trigger of a claim in unjust enrichment ought to be 'unjust factors' or the absence of a legal justification for the transfer of value from the plaintiff to the defendant ('absence of basis').[32]

[17.15] A plaintiff claiming a restitutionary remedy must point to enrichment (money, services, or goods) on the part of the recipient. The kind of enrichment determines the remedy awarded.

[17.16] It is also necessary to show that the defendant has been unjustly enriched at the expense of the plaintiff. In other words, unjust enrichment involves subtractive restitution: the defendant has received something from the plaintiff and the remedy restores the value of what the defendant has received.

[17.17] 'Restitution' refers to the remedy by which unjust enrichment is reversed. A restitutionary remedy can be personal or proprietary. Birks says that personal remedies are for value received, whereas proprietary remedies are for value surviving.[33] Proprietary remedies, including proprietary restitution (to the extent that it is recognised in Australia) will be considered in Ch 19. This chapter deals with personal remedies only.

[17.18] A claim in unjust enrichment is subject to defences. The main defence is that of good faith change of position in reliance upon receipt on the part of the defendant, such that the defendant would suffer detriment if ordered to make restitution.[34] The defendant will not be required to make restitution to the extent that he has changed his position in good faith.[35]

---

29   *David Securities Pty Ltd v Commonwealth Bank of Australia* (1992) 175 CLR 353, 379. Reaffirmed in *Equuscorp Pty Ltd v Haxton* [2012] HCA 7, (2012) 246 CLR 498 [30] (French CJ, Crennan and Kiefel JJ).

30   In *David Securities Pty Ltd v Commonwealth Bank of Australia* (1992) 175 CLR 353, 379, Mason CJ, Deane, Toohey, Gaudron and McHugh JJ mentioned the necessity to establish a 'qualifying or vitiating factor such as mistake, duress or illegality'. Note that, despite its endorsement by the High Court, the status of 'illegality' as a vitiating factor is questioned by A Burrows, *The Law of Restitution* (3rd edn, OUP 2011) 488.

31   Eg 'ignorance': Burrows, ibid, 403–34.

32   Peter Birks advocated unjust factors in P Birks, *An Introduction to the Law of Restitution* (revised edn, Clarendon Press 1989), but later moved to advocate absence of basis in P Birks, *Unjust Enrichment* (2nd edn, OUP 2005).

33   P Birks, *An Introduction to the Law of Restitution* (revised edn, Clarendon Press 1989) 12.

34   *David Securities Pty Ltd v Commonwealth Bank of Australia* (1992) 175 CLR 353, 385. See also *Lipkin Gorman v Karpnale Ltd* [1991] 2 AC 548, 558, 568, 578–80.

35   J Edelman and E Bant, *Unjust Enrichment* (2nd edn, Hart 2016) 332.

III   Precise remedies for unjust enrichment

The remedy available for claims in unjust enrichment is restitution of the value of the benefit received by the defendant at the plaintiff's expense, whether that benefit is money, services or goods. The precise remedy awarded will depend on the nature of the enrichment received by the defendant.   [17.19]

A   Money claims

Where the defendant has 'unjustly' received money at the plaintiff's expense, the plaintiff can bring an action for money had and received. The cause of action is also the remedy. Money is the easiest enrichment to establish. It is difficult for a defendant to argue that she is not enriched by the receipt of money.[36]   [17.20]

An action for money had and received was allowed by the High Court of Australia in *David Securities Pty Ltd v Commonwealth Bank of Australia*.[37] The plaintiffs had borrowed money from the defendant bank under a 'Swiss franc loan agreement'. The interest payable on the loan depended upon the relationship between the Australian dollar and the Swiss franc. A clause in the agreement said that any tax payable in respect of interest was payable by the borrower. This was void according to the then s 261 of the *Income Tax Assessment Act 1936* (Cth), which provided that a borrower was not to pay tax. The plaintiffs paid tax to the defendant. They unsuccessfully sued the defendant in a variety of actions for losses they sustained because of the Swiss franc loan agreement, and the defendant successfully counter-sued the plaintiffs in debt. The plaintiffs argued that they were liable only for some of the debt awarded in the defendant's counterclaim, as the debt could be set off against the mistakenly paid tax moneys. Although the mistake was a mistake of law, and thus traditionally not a mistake giving rise to an action for money had and received pursuant to *Bilbie v Lumley*,[38] the High Court allowed the plaintiff's action for money had and received, recognising mistake of law as an unjust factor.   [17.21]

Not all instances where an action for money had and received has been awarded fit into an unjust enrichment analysis. As noted at [16.36]–[16.47], a tort victim can 'waive' the tort in favour of an action for money had and received. It is debatable whether this fits within a subtractive unjust enrichment scheme. It is arguably an instance of 'restitution for wrongdoing'.   [17.22]

B   Services claims

Where the defendant has 'unjustly' received a service at the plaintiff's expense, the plaintiff can bring an action for *quantum meruit*. *Quantum meruit* is Latin for 'as much as he deserves'.[39]   [17.23]

---

36   M Bryan, 'Equity and Restitution' in P Parkinson (ed), *The Principles of Equity* (2nd edn, LBC 2003) [406]; J Edelman and E Bant, *Unjust Enrichment* (2nd edn, Hart 2016) 55.

37   (1992) 175 CLR 323.

38   (1802) 2 East 469; 102 ER 448. See also *York Air Conditioning & Refrigeration (Australasia) Pty Ltd v Commonwealth* (1949) 80 CLR 11.

39   W Covell, K Lupton and J Forder, *Principles of Remedies* (6th edn, LexisNexis 2015) [4.41].

Again, the cause of action is the remedy. The plaintiff will be entitled to 'the fair value of the benefit provided'.[40] Usually the benefit is measured according to market value.[41]

[17.24]   The seminal case is *Pavey & Matthews Pty Ltd v Paul*,[42] where builders agreed to do building work for Mrs Paul at prevailing market rates under an oral contract. The oral contract was unenforceable pursuant to s 45 of the *Builders Licensing Act 1971* (NSW). When the work was completed, Mrs Paul paid for some of the work, but refused to pay the balance. The builders could not sue Mrs Paul for breach of contract because the contract was unenforceable. However, they argued that Mrs Paul would be unjustly enriched at their expense if she was allowed to retain the building work without payment. The High Court agreed, and awarded the builders a *quantum meruit* reflecting the reasonable value of their work.

[17.25]   Valuation of services can be difficult, particularly if the recipient argues that the provider's services did not produce any measurable, positive outcome. Courts tend to assume that if the recipient accepted the services, then they must have had *some* value to the recipient.[43] There are also difficult questions regarding the relationship between the contractually negotiated price for services and the measure of a *quantum meruit*; see [17.35]–[17.47].

[17.26]   Another difficulty with services is that it is possible for someone who received the benefit of a service to say that she never wanted it (in Birks's term, 'subjective devaluation').[44] Suppose that a driver has stopped her car at the traffic lights and a person approaches with a squeegee, water and detergent. The driver shakes her head at the window washer and mouths the word 'No', but the window washer washes the windscreen of the car anyway. The driver has received a service, but the fact that she has received it does not prove that she has been unjustly enriched, and the law respects her autonomy by allowing her to argue that she never wanted the benefit.

[17.27]   There are at least three ways in which a plaintiff may argue that the defendant should not be permitted to subjectively devalue the receipt of an enrichment:[45]

1.   The enrichment is an 'incontrovertible benefit'[46] – in other words, no reasonable person could argue that the benefit was not wanted.

2.   The defendant objectively chose the benefit and, accordingly, there is no reason for 'subjective devaluation' to operate.

3.   The defendant chose to retain the benefit despite the fact that he had an opportunity to reject the benefit (this is called 'free acceptance'). However, Burrows has argued that a failure to reject may only signify indifference to the service rather than a positive choice to accept.[47] Consequently, free acceptance might only be made out where the

---

40   *Pavey & Matthews Pty Ltd v Paul* (1987) 162 CLR 221, 263 (Deane J).

41   Ibid.

42   (1987) 162 CLR 221.

43   Eg *Brenner v First Artists' Management Pty Ltd* [1993] 2 VR 221.

44   The term 'subjective devaluation' is unfortunate, as the inquiry as to whether the defendant desired the enrichment is objective: J Edelman and E Bant, *Unjust Enrichment* (2nd edn, Hart 2016) 83.

45   See generally, ibid, 62–84.

46   *Andrew Shelton & Co Pty Ltd v Alpha Healthcare Ltd* [2002] VSC 248, (2002) 5 VR 577 [100]–[104] (Warren J); *Monks v Poynice Pty Ltd* (1987) 11 ACLR 637, 639 (Young J); *Municipality of Peel v Canada* [1992] 3 SCR 762, 794–96 (McLaughlin J).

47   A Burrows, *The Law of Restitution* (3rd edn, OUP 2011) 57.

defendant was under a duty to reject the benefit (for example, where the plaintiff asked him whether he wanted it, and he did not reject it).

C   Goods claims

Where the defendant has 'unjustly' received goods at the plaintiff's expense, the plaintiff can bring an action for *quantum valebat* or *quantum valebant*, which is Latin for 'as much as it is worth'.[48] Again the cause of action is the remedy. Goods are easier to establish as an enrichment than services. However, the *quantum valebat* has largely been superseded by sale of goods legislation, which provides an easier mechanism for recovering the value of goods.[49]   [17.28]

Often in cases involving goods, the contract is rescinded; this means that claims for unjust enrichment with regard to goods are usually dealt with via rescission. Rescission has been argued to have a clear restitutionary aspect.[50]   [17.29]

Nonetheless, the *quantum valebat* still occasionally arises in cases (such as construction disputes) where a party has supplied both goods and services, or where the characterisation of the subject matter of the contract is unclear.[51]   [17.30]

IV   Defences to a claim for restitution

Defences to a claim for restitution will be dealt with briefly. They are mentioned because they clarify how certain aspects of personal and proprietary rescission have been analysed by restitutionary scholars.   [17.31]

The main restitutionary defence is change of position.[52] It is established if the defendant shows that he has irreversibly changed his position to his detriment in good faith in reliance upon the receipt of the benefit.[53] Thus, the defendant will not be obliged to make restitution to the extent that the change is irreversible. It has been suggested that the rationale of this defence is the security of transactions.[54]   [17.32]

It is a prerequisite of equitable rescission that the parties are able to make substantial *restitutio in integrum* (i.e. restore them to their original positions); see [18.19]–[18.31]. The adjustments that courts make can be seen as operating in a manner similar to a good faith change of position defence. Moreover, in a case where a proprietary power to rescind is exercised, the courts may take account of the extent to which certain property cannot be returned, as in *Quek v Beggs*, where the recipients of certain properties as a gift were not required to return those which they had sold to fund their legal defence.[55] Again, this can be argued to resemble a change of position defence.[56]   [17.33]

---

48   W Covell, K Lupton and J Forder, *Principles of Remedies* (6th edn, LexisNexis 2015) [4.47].
49   Ibid.
50   Eg NY Nahan, 'Rescission: A Case for Rejecting the Classical Model?' (1997) 27 UWALR 66.
51   *Design Joinery & Doors Pty Ltd v iPower Pty Ltd* [2015] SASC 93 [104].
52   *David Securities Pty Ltd v Commonwealth Bank of Australia* (1992) 175 CLR 353, 385–86. See also *Lipkin Gorman v Karpnale Ltd* [1991] 2 AC 548, 558, 568, 578–80.
53   J Edelman and E Bant, *Unjust Enrichment* (2nd edn, Hart 2016) 332.
54   Ibid, 322. See also *David Securities Pty Ltd v Commonwealth Bank of Australia* (1992) 175 CLR 353, 385.
55   (1990) 5 BPR 11,761.
56   E Bant, 'Trusts, Powers and Liens: An Exercise in Ground-Clearing' (2010) 4 J Eq 286, 303; E Bant, '*Restitutio in Integrum* and the Change of Position Defence: Lessons from Rescission' [2007] RLR 13, 33.

[17.34]   There are other defences to a claim in unjust enrichment,[57] the consideration of which is beyond the scope of this book.

V   The relationship between contract and restitution for unjust enrichment

[17.35]   The reason why a plaintiff claims under a restitutionary remedy rather than a remedy for breach of contract is generally because the contract is void, unenforceable, discharged by frustration, rescinded, or terminated for breach. Or the contract may be a 'losing contract' where the plaintiff could get more by a restitutionary remedy than she could under the contract. For example, in the Californian case *Boomer v Muir*,[58] the plaintiff was a subcontractor building a dam, and the defendant was the head contractor. The plaintiff was paid in instalments. The plaintiff alleged that the defendant had not provided sufficient materials to allow him to meet the contractual deadline, and walked out, as he was entitled to do, on the basis of the defendant's breach of contract. At the time, around US$20 000 was owing to the plaintiff according to the contract. The plaintiff sued the defendant, claiming a *quantum meruit* for the value of work done. The court awarded the plaintiff a *quantum meruit* in the sum of US$258 000.

[17.36]   Deane J in *Pavey & Matthews Pty Ltd v Paul* made this suggestion:

> If the unenforceable contract has not been rescinded by the plaintiff or otherwise terminated, the defendant will be free to rely on it as a defence to the claim for compensation in a case where he is ready and willing to perform his obligations under it ... The defendant will also be entitled to rely on the unenforceable contract, if it has been executed but not rescinded, to limit the amount recoverable by the plaintiff to the contractual amount in a case where that amount is less than what would constitute fair and reasonable remuneration.[59]

However, in *Roxborough v Rothmans of Pall Mall Australia Ltd*, the contract between the parties remained on foot, yet the High Court of Australia allowed the plaintiffs' action for money had and received in relation to mistakenly paid taxes because the portion of the contract which failed was said to be severable from the main contract.[60]

[17.37]   There are two interlinked questions in these cases.[61] The first is whether courts should undermine the contractual allocation of risk between the parties by awarding a restitutionary

---

57   J Edelman and E Bant, *Unjust Enrichment* (2nd edn, Hart 2016) ch 15. They consider the following defences: good consideration, impossibility of counter-restitution, bona fide purchaser for value without notice, estoppel, ministerial receipt, delay, resolution of disputes and passing on.

58   24 P 2d 570 (Cal App 1 Dist, 1933). See also *United States v Zara Contracting Co*, 146 F 2d 606 (1944); *Re Montgomery's Estate*, 6 NE (2d) 40 (1936).

59   (1987) 162 CLR 221, 257.

60   [2001] HCA 68, (2001) 208 CLR 516 (Gleeson CJ, Gaudron, Gummow, Hayne and Callinan JJ, Kirby J dissenting). Cf *Coshott v Lenin* [2007] NSWCA 153 [11] (Mason P, with whom Spigelman CJ and Campbell JA agreed): 'no action can be brought for restitution where an inconsistent contractual promise subsists between the parties in relation to the subject matter of the claim'.

61   N Witzleb, E Bant, S Degeling and K Barker, *Remedies: Commentary and Materials* (6th edn, LBC 2015) [6.50].

remedy. There are two extreme possibilities: on one hand, it can be argued that unjust enrichment is entirely separate from contract law and that contractual risk allocation is irrelevant. On the other hand, it can be argued that we should not allow unjust enrichment to undermine the parties' contractual allocation of risk.

The second question is whether the measure of restitution should be limited by any 'ceiling' set by the terms of the contract (if this had applied in *Boomer v Muir*, the plaintiff would have been able to recover only US\$20 000, notwithstanding that the market value of the services was much higher).   [17.38]

The general consensus appears to be that unjust enrichment is separate and distinct from contract law[62] and that, generally, the measure of a restitutionary remedy is not limited by a contractual cap, although the contract may provide evidence of the value of the services.[63]   [17.39]

In *Renard Constructions (ME) Pty Ltd v Minister of Public Works*,[64] a builder was constructing pumping stations for the Minister of Public Works when the Minister's representative wrongfully repudiated the contract, and the builder 'rescinded' the contract. The builder sought a *quantum meruit* for the work done until the wrongful repudiation. Meagher JA and Priestley JA agreed that a *quantum meruit* claim by a contractor should not be subject to a contractual ceiling.[65] Meagher JA said: [17.40]

> The most one can say is that the amount contractually agreed is evidence of the reasonableness of the remuneration claimed on a quantum meruit; strong evidence perhaps, but certainly not conclusive evidence. On the other hand, it would be extremely anomalous if the defaulting party when sued on a quantum meruit could invoke the contract which he has repudiated in order to impose a ceiling on amounts otherwise recoverable.[66]

Similarly, the Victorian Court of Appeal in *Sopov v Kane Constructions Pty Ltd (No 2)* said that the contractual amount was not a ceiling for the amount recoverable.[67] However, the Victorian Court of Appeal was more equivocal than the NSW Court of Appeal, and it indicated that if the case law on this point had not been clearly established by *Renard* and *Iezzi Constructions Pty Ltd v Watkins Pacific (Qld) Pty Ltd*,[68] it might have held differently on the question, as it had been argued that the availability of a *quantum meruit* in such cases proceeded upon the mistaken basis that acceptance of a repudiation operates to rescind the contract ab initio.[69]   [17.41]

---

62   *Pavey & Matthews Pty Ltd v Paul* (1987) 162 CLR 221, 257 (Deane J); *Renard Constructions (ME) Pty Ltd v Minister of Public Works* (1992) 26 NSWLR 234, 277–78 (Meagher JA); *Sopov v Kane Constructions Pty Ltd (No 2)* [2009] VSCA 141, (2009) 24 VR 510 [21]; *Equuscorp Pty Ltd v Haxton* [2012] HCA 7, (2012) 246 CLR 498 [29], [101]–[102].

63   *Pavey & Matthews Pty Ltd v Paul* (1987) 162 CLR 221, 257 (Deane J); *Renard Constructions (ME) Pty Ltd v Minister of Public Works* (1992) 26 NSWLR 234, 271 (Priestley JA), 276–78 (Meagher JA); *Iezzi Constructions Pty Ltd v Watkins Pacific (Qld) Pty Ltd* [1995] 2 Qd R 350; *Sopov v Kane Constructions Pty Ltd (No 2)* [2009] VSCA 141, (2009) 24 VR 510 [21].

64   (1992) 26 NSWLR 234.

65   Ibid, 271 (Priestley JA), 276–78 (Meagher JA).

66   Ibid, 278.

67   [2009] VSCA 141, (2009) 24 VR 510 [24].

68   [1995] 2 Qd R 350.

69   [2009] VSCA 141, (2009) 24 VR 510 [9]–[11]. Cf *Renard Constructions (ME) Pty Ltd v Minister of Public Works* (1992) 26 NSWLR 234, 276–77 (Meagher JA).

[17.42]   Despite the unwillingness to allow restitutionary remedies to be limited by a contractual cap, courts are still concerned not to allow unjust enrichment to undermine contract law.[70] They are also concerned not to allow unjust enrichment to undermine statutory schemes of regulation.[71]

[17.43]   In *Lumbers v W Cook Builders Pty Ltd (in liq)*,[72] the High Court of Australia refused to award a *quantum meruit* because it was concerned not to undermine the law of contract. In 1993, the Lumbers family made an oral contract with a company called W Cook & Sons ('Sons') to build a large, unusual and expensive house. W Cook Builders Pty Ltd ('Builders') was a company in the same corporate group as Sons, but with a different director. Unlike Sons, Builders was not a licensed builder. At some point, without the Lumbers' knowledge or consent, the companies underwent an unofficial corporate reorganisation, and Builders completed most of the construction of the Lumbers' house. Importantly, there was never any contractual relationship between the Lumbers and Builders, and the Lumbers were not aware of the existence of Builders. The Lumbers only ever dealt with the director of Sons and, as far as they knew, Sons were responsible for construction. Payments for the work were made after requests by the director of Sons. The requests were ad hoc and did not reflect the value of the work or the cost of the materials. The house was completed in May 1995, and the Lumbers thought that the house had been paid for. In 1998, Builders went into liquidation, and in 1999 it made a demand of the Lumbers for outstanding sums for work done on the house. Builders made the same demand against Sons, but could not proceed against Sons because it was unable to provide security for costs. Among other things, Builders claimed a *quantum meruit* representing the value of the work done on the basis that the Lumbers had been unjustly enriched by its labour. The trial judge rejected this contention, but a majority of the South Australian Full Court held that, notwithstanding the lack of a contractual (or any) relationship between the Lumbers and Builders, the Lumbers had received an 'incontrovertible benefit' comprised of the unrecompensed labour of Builders which they had 'freely accepted' and it was appropriate to award a *quantum meruit* to ensure they were not unjustly enriched.[73]

[17.44]   The High Court of Australia held that the Full Court had been wrong to ignore the contractual relationship of the parties when considering principles of unjust enrichment.[74] There were two judgments, both of which cited[75] the following statement made by Lord Goff in *Pan Ocean Shipping Co Ltd v Creditcorp Ltd*:

> I am of course well aware that writers on the law of restitution have been exploring the possibility that, in exceptional circumstances, a plaintiff may have a claim in restitution when he has conferred a benefit on the defendant in the course of performing an obligation to a third party ... But, quite apart from the fact that the existence of a remedy

---

70   *Lumbers v W Cook Builders Pty Ltd (in liq)* [2008] HCA 27, (2008) 232 CLR 635; *Coshott v Lenin* [2007] NSWCA 153; *Equuscorp Pty Ltd v Haxton* [2012] HCA 7, (2012) 246 CLR 498 (French CJ, Gummow, Crennan, Kiefel and Bell JJ, Heydon J dissenting).

71   *Equuscorp Pty Ltd v Haxton* [2012] HCA 7, (2012) 246 CLR 498.

72   [2008] HCA 27, (2008) 232 CLR 635.

73   *W Cook Builders Pty Ltd (in liq) v Lumbers* [2007] SASC 20, (2007) 96 SASR 406 (Sulan and Layton JJ, Vanstone J dissenting).

74   [2008] HCA 27, (2008) 232 CLR 635 [45] (Gleeson CJ), [76]–[77] (Gummow, Hayne, Crennan and Kiefel JJ).

75   Ibid, [47] (Gleeson CJ), [79] (Gummow, Hayne, Crennan and Kiefel JJ).

in restitution in such circumstances must still be regarded as a matter of debate, it is always recognised that serious difficulties arise if the law seeks to expand the law of restitution to redistribute risks for which provision has been made under an applicable contract.[76]

The High Court was concerned not to undermine the contractual allocation of risk between parties, particularly given the fact that there had never been a contractual relationship between Builders and the Lumbers and the Lumbers had not even known of the existence of Builders. This was in keeping with unjust enrichment scholarship on the issue (although this scholarship was not referred to).[77]

A significant difference between the approach of Gleeson CJ and that of the plural judgment should be noted. Gleeson CJ was prepared to accept that services can enrich the recipient where they constitute an incontrovertible benefit or where the recipient has freely accepted them.[78] However, the plural judgment of the High Court held that 'free acceptance' was not part of Australian law, and the Lumbers had not requested the services (expressly or impliedly).[79] The plurality's approach suggested that presence of a 'request' was central to whether relief would be given. The plurality's approach has been criticised on the basis that it recalls notions of 'implied contract' and is inconsistent with prior case law.[80] Nevertheless, the outcome in this case is generally regarded as correct.[81] *Lumbers* has been applied in a range of cases.[82] It has been suggested that more recent High Court authority indicates that a request is not required to establish that the defendant has chosen the benefit.[83]

[17.45]

In *Equuscorp Pty Ltd v Haxton*,[84] while the High Court acknowledged that the principles of unjust enrichment and contract law were different, a majority of the court would not allow an unjust enrichment claim to be maintained where a statutory scheme rendered certain contracts illegal, void and unenforceable.[85] A finance company, which had received an assignment of

[17.46]

---

76   [1994] 1 WLR 161, 166.

77   Eg P Birks, *Unjust Enrichment* (2nd edn, OUP 2005) 89–98: a claimant is not entitled to 'leapfrog' the contractual allocation of risk.

78   [2008] HCA 27, (2008) 232 CLR 635 [51]–[54].

79   Ibid, [89] (Gummow, Hayne, Crennan and Kiefel JJ).

80   J Edelman, 'Unjust Enrichment and Contract' [2008] LMCLQ 444, 447–48; J Getzler, '*Quantum Meruit, Estoppel and the Primacy of Contract*' (2009) 125 LQR 196, 208; A Goymour, 'Too Many Cooks: Three Parties, Contracts and Unjust Enrichment' (2008) 67 Camb LJ 469, 470; M Bryan, 'Restitution for Services and the Allocation of Contractual Risk – Case Note: *Lumbers v W Cook Builders Pty Ltd (in liq)*' (2009) 33 MULR 320, 328–30; S Degeling, 'Subcontractors and Three Party Claims – Case Note: *Lumbers v W Cook Builders Pty Ltd (in liq)*' (2010) 36 Monash ULR 207; A Burrows, 'The Australian Law of Restitution: Has the High Court Lost Its Way?' in E Bant and M Harding (eds), *Exploring Private Law* (CUP 2010) 84; W Covell, K Lupton and J Forder, *Principles of Remedies* (6th edn, LexisNexis 2015) [4.59].

81   M Bryan, 'Restitution for Services and the Allocation of Contractual Risk – Case Note: *Lumbers v W Cook Builders Pty Ltd (in liq)*' (2009) 33 MULR 320; M Riley, 'The Conceptual Relationship between Contract Law and Unjust Enrichment and the Decision in *Lumbers v Cook*' (2011) 28 J Cont L 267.

82   *Fraser v Sperling* [2015] VSC 698; *Skilled Group Ltd v CSR Viridian Pty Ltd* [2012] VSC 290; *RJ Baker Nominees Pty Ltd v Parsons Management Group Pty Ltd* [2009] WASC 206, (2011) 27 BCL 47.

83   *Stewart v Atco Controls Pty Ltd (in liq)* [2014] HCA 15, (2014) 252 CLR 307 [47]–[48]. See J Edelman and E Bant, *Unjust Enrichment* (2nd edn, Hart 2016) 77.

84   [2012] HCA 7, (2012) 246 CLR 498.

85   The contracts were void pursuant to s 170(1) of the *Companies Code* then in force. The court distinguished *Pavey & Matthews Pty Ltd v Paul* (1987) 162 CLR 221 where the contracts were unenforceable rather than illegal. See *Equuscorp Pty Ltd v Haxton* [2012] HCA 7, (2012) 246 CLR 498 [40] (French CJ, Crennan and Kiefel JJ), [105]–[106] (Gummow and Bell JJ).

illegal loan contracts, sought to rely upon principles of unjust enrichment to recover the loan moneys owed under the void contracts, but was unsuccessful in doing so. The judgments stressed the importance of making unjust enrichment law coherent with other areas of law, particularly where illegality was concerned.

[17.47]   Thus, while unjust enrichment and contract are separate, and while a contractual ceiling is usually not applied where a *quantum meruit* or other restitutionary remedy is claimed under a repudiated contract, courts are nonetheless careful to ensure that unjust enrichment law does not unduly undermine contract law and other areas of law.

18

RESCISSION

I Introduction

[18.1] Rescission is a form of relief which is available in respect of a variety of transactions (contract, gifts and conveyances) where one of the parties is subject to a vitiating factor such as duress, fraud or misrepresentation, and she wants to get out of or 'set aside' the transaction.[1] Rescission allows her to reverse the transaction. It has been said that '[t]he basic objective of the relief given upon rescission is to restore the parties to their original positions or, where rescission occurs in equity, as near to those positions as may be.'[2] There is no requirement for the party seeking to rescind to suffer loss in the sense in which this is understood in the context of compensatory damages: she merely has to point to a vitiating factor. Although the party seeking to rescind can set aside the transaction, it is not voided: rather, it is rendered 'voidable'. In other words, a voidable contract is valid and effective unless and until the plaintiff elects to rescind it.[3] However, once a contract is rescinded it 'is treated in law as never having come into existence',[4] although it is recognised that it formerly existed.[5] All unperformed obligations under the contract are extinguished once a contract has been rescinded.[6] The contract is extinguished as from the beginning (*ab initio*).

[18.2] Rescission works as follows. Suppose that Yolanda sells goods to Xenophon, but makes a misrepresentation as to an important quality of the goods. Xenophon pays Yolanda the purchase price and receives the goods, and then discovers Yolanda's misrepresentation.[7] If Xenophon elects to rescind, Yolanda must return the purchase money to Xenophon, and Xenophon must return the goods to Yolanda. Both Yolanda and Xenophon are returned to the position they were in before the sale occurred. Rescission can give rise to a personal remedy or a proprietary remedy. In the Yolanda and Xenophon example, there is no need for a proprietary remedy; the parties can simply return what they received. However, rescission can also be used to seek return of the title of an asset which has been transferred pursuant to a contract or a gift. The equitable 'proprietary power'[8] to rescind is often called a 'mere equity'.[9]

[18.3] Confusingly, 'rescission' has been used by courts in five different senses:[10]

1. to describe the situation where a party to a contract elects to treat the contract as no longer binding upon her after the other party breaches – such a contract is only void from the breach onwards, not void *ab initio*;

---

1   It should be noted that the operative vitiating factors differ between common law and equitable rescission, and equitable rescission is available in a greater range of situations.
2   D O'Sullivan, S Elliott and R Zakrzewski, *The Law of Rescission* (2nd edn, OUP 2014) [13.01].
3   Ibid, [1.04].
4   *Johnson v Agnew* [1980] AC 367, 393 (Lord Wilberforce).
5   *Mackender v Feldia AG* [1967] 2 QB 590, 603 (Diplock LJ); *FAI General Insurance Co Ltd v Ocean Marine Mutual Protection and Indemnity Association Ltd* (1997) 41 NSWLR 559, 563.
6   *McDonald v Dennys Lascelles Ltd* (1933) 48 CLR 457, 476–77 (Dixon J).
7   A less complex version of *Clough v London and North Western Railway Co* (1871) LR 7 Ex 26.
8   The phrase 'proprietary power' is discussed at [18.47] and at [19.21]–[19.23].
9   *Latec Investments Limited v Hotel Terrigal Pty Ltd* (1965) 113 CLR 265, 277, 290; *Tutt v Doyle* (1997) 42 NSWLR 10, 15.
10 JD Heydon, MJ Leeming and PG Turner, *Meagher, Gummow and Lehane's Equity: Doctrines and Remedies* (5th edn, LexisNexis 2015) [24–005]–[24–030].

2. where specific provision has been made in a contract for one or both parties to 'rescind' upon the occurrence of a specified event – such terms may require restoration of the original position or merely release the parties from further performance ('rescission' in the first sense of the word above);

3. to describe common law rescission of contracts for fraudulent misrepresentation or duress, which allows a plaintiff to set aside or reverse the transaction – this may be a self-help remedy;

4. to describe equitable rescission, which allows for rescission of transactions (not limited to contract) which are procured by innocent misrepresentation, equitable fraud, undue influence, breach of fiduciary duty, unconscionable conduct and the like – again, this allows the plaintiff to set aside or reverse the transaction;

5. to describe statutory remedies which essentially effect rescission but do not actually use the word 'rescission'.

It is unfortunate that courts sometimes use the word 'rescission' in the sense of the first meaning above: a right to terminate a transaction which discharges the parties from future performance but does not affect accrued rights under the contract.[11] It is suggested that it should not be used in that way. Rescission should be distinguished from termination for breach of contract, as these are quite different. Rescission extinguishes the contract *ab initio*, such that all obligations under the contract are no longer in existence. By contrast, termination of a contract operates to discharge performance of future obligations, but there is no discharge of rights and obligations that have already accrued, or of causes of action arising from breach.[12] The terminated contract can be said to be determined *de futuro* rather than *ab initio*.[13]

The kinds of rescission considered in this chapter are those covered by the third, fourth and fifth meanings mentioned above.   [18.4]

Rescission is sometimes said to be a self-help remedy where the right holder gives notice of her election to rescind to the other party.[14] However, rescission can also be understood as a judicial remedy rather than as a self-help remedy in some cases (particularly where equitable rescission of an executed contract is concerned). The availability of rescission on terms and partial rescission means that, arguably, the right to rescind only arises once the court fashions it, not when the party seeking to rescind the contract asserts it. Some argue that equitable rescission in equity's exclusive jurisdiction (where the vitiating factor is not fraud or duress) is always the act of the court.[15] O'Sullivan has argued that rescission should always be the act of the court.[16]   [18.5]

---

11   E Bant 'Reconsidering the Role of Election in Rescission' (2012) 32(3) OJLS 467–86
12   *McDonald v Dennys Lascelles Ltd* (1933) 48 CLR 457, 476–77.
13   D O'Sullivan, S Elliott and R Zakrzewski, *The Law of Rescission* (2nd edn, OUP 2014) [1.06].
14   *Alati v Kruger* (1955) 94 CLR 216, 225–26; L Proksch, 'Rescission' in P Parkinson (ed) *The Principles of Equity* (2nd edn, LBC 2003) [2506].
15   JD Heydon, MJ Leeming and PG Turner, *Meagher, Gummow and Lehane's Equity: Doctrines and Remedies* (5th edn, LexisNexis 2015) [25–115]; D O'Sullivan, S Elliott and R Zakrzewski, *The Law of Rescission* (2nd edn, OUP 2014) [12.11]–[12.24].
16   J O'Sullivan, 'Rescission as a Self-Help Remedy: A Critical Analysis' (2000) 59 Camb LJ 509.

[18.6]   Rescission has also been analysed as a restitutionary remedy.[17] It is submitted that there is a clear kinship between restitutionary remedies for unjust enrichment and rescission: in both cases, a vitiating factor must be identified, and the parties must return the benefit or value of the benefits they have received from the other. There is also some recognition of good faith changes of position in reliance upon the receipt. However, the necessity for the plaintiff to elect to rescind may distinguish rescission from subtractive restitution for unjust enrichment.[18]

[18.7]   Before considering how rescission operates in practice, it is necessary to observe that rescission operates differently depending upon whether it is available at common law, in equity, or pursuant to the Australian Consumer Law. Equitable rescission is more flexible than common law rescission and is better able to accommodate changes occurring after the transaction was concluded.

A   Legal rescission

[18.8]   Common law or legal rescission is generally available only where there is fraud[19] or duress,[20] in contrast to equitable rescission, which is available for a much wider range of vitiating factors.[21]

[18.9]   Common law rescission is available only for contracts, and not for gifts.

[18.10] Importantly, for legal rescission to occur, the parties must be restored *precisely* to their pre-transaction position ('complete *restitutio in integrum*'). The strictness of this requirement is illustrated by *Hunt v Silk*[22] and *Blackburn v Smith*.[23] In each case, an interest in land (a lease and fee simple title respectively) was transferred to the plaintiff, who took possession of the land. The plaintiffs sought to rescind the transactions, but rescission was barred because the plaintiffs had briefly taken possession of the land. It was impossible for the plaintiffs to 'give back' this use of the land, and complete *restitutio in integrum* was impossible.

---

17   Eg NY Nahan, 'Rescission: A Case for Rejecting the Classical Model?' (1997) 27 UWALR 66; L Proksch, 'Rescission' in P Parkinson (ed), *The Principles of Equity* (2nd edn, LBC 2003) [2506]; E Bant, 'Trusts, Powers and Liens: An Exercise in Ground-Clearing' (2009) 3 J Eq 286; M Bryan and V Vann, *Equity and Trusts in Australia* (CUP 2012) 29.

18   'Subtractive restitution' involves the defendant's gain being given back to the plaintiff. See E Bant, 'Reconsidering the Role of Election in Rescission' (2012) 32 OJLS 467, who suggests that election could operate in unjust enrichment law.

19   *Load v Green* (1846) 15 M & W 216, 153 ER 828; *Clarke v Dickson* (1858) El Bl & El 148, 120 ER 463; *Clough v London and North Western Railway Co* (1871) LR 7 Ex 26; *Car & Universal Finance Co Ltd v Caldwell* [1965] 1 QB 525; *Coastal Estates Pty Ltd v Melevende* [1965] VR 433; *Hunter v BNZ Finance Ltd v CG Maloney Pty Ltd* (1988) 18 NSWLR 420; *HIH Casualty and General Insurance Ltd v Chase Manhattan Bank* [2003] UKHL 6, [2003] 1 All ER (Comm) 349 [98] (Lord Hobhouse).

20   *Whelpdale's case* (1604) 5 Co Rep 119a; 77 ER 239; *Enimont Overseas AG v RO Jugotanker Zadar (The Olib)* [1991] 2 Lloyd's Rep 108, 118; *Dimskal Shipping Co SA v International Transport Workers Federation (The Evia Luck)* [1992] 2 AC 152, 165; *Halpern v Halpern (No 2)* [2006] EWHC 1728 (Comm), [2007] QB 88.

21   It may also be available for material non-disclosure and non-fraudulent misrepresentation in insurance contracts, for mental infirmity and for intoxication: see D O'Sullivan, S Elliott and R Zakrzewski, *The Law of Rescission* (2nd edn, OUP 2014) [10.23].

22   (1804) 5 East 449, 102 ER 1142.

23   (1848) 2 Ex 782, 154 ER 707.

The party seeking to rescind can sue under an action for money had and received where there has been a total failure of consideration under a contract.[24] The proprietary consequences of common law rescission also give rise to several possibilities of action, including detinue and conversion; see [18.42]–[18.44].   [18.11]

B   Equitable rescission

Equitable rescission is much more expansive than legal rescission. First, the grounds for rescission are wider than those recognised at common law. Not only is fraud a basis for rescission, but so are innocent misrepresentation,[25] unilateral mistake,[26] duress,[27]undue influence,[28] unconscionable dealing[29] and breach of fiduciary duty.[30]   [18.12]

Secondly, rescission in equity is available not only for contracts, but also for gifts and other transactions.   [18.13]

Thirdly, the parties need not be restored *precisely* to their original position. It is sufficient that 'substantial *restitutio in integrum*' can be achieved.[31] It has been stated repeatedly that the court's aim is to achieve 'practical justice' for both parties.[32] So, for example, if the plaintiffs in *Hunt v Silk* and *Blackburn v Smith* (see [18.10]) had been able to claim equitable rescission, the court would have ordered the plaintiffs to return the interest in land to the defendants and the defendants to return the purchase price to the defendants. To reflect the fact that the plaintiffs had taken possession of the land, the court would have reduced the amount payable by the defendants to reflect a fair value for the plaintiff's limited use of the land, thus effecting substantial *restitutio in integrum*.   [18.14]

Fourthly, a court of equity can impose terms or conditions on the award of rescission as part of the process of accomplishing 'practical justice'. Financial adjustments (such as the payment for use of the land mentioned in the paragraph above) can be ordered as part of the process of restoring the parties to their precontractual position.   [18.15]

---

24   L Proksch, 'Rescission' in P Parkinson (ed) *The Principles of Equity* (2nd edn, LBC 2003) [2503].
25   *Redgrave v Hurd* (1881) 20 Ch D 1, 12–13.
26   *Taylor v Johnson* (1983) 151 CLR 422; *Tutt v Doyle* (1997) 42 NSWLR 10; *Clarion Ltd v National Provident Institution* [2000] 1 WLR 1888, 1899–1905.
27   *Barton v Armstrong* [1976] AC 104 (PC) (duress to the person); *Occidental Worldwide Investment Corporation v Skibs A/S (The Siboen and The Sibotre)* [1976] 1 Lloyd's Rep 293 (duress to goods); *Universe Tankships Inc of Monrovia v International Transport Workers Federation (The Universe Sentinel)* [1983] 1 AC 366 (economic duress); *Crescendo Management Pty Ltd v Westpac Banking Corporation* (1988) 19 NSWLR 40 (economic duress).
28   *Allcard v Skinner* (1887) 36 Ch D 145; *Johnson v Buttress* (1936) 53 CLR 113; *Reid v Reid* (NSWSC, 30 November 1998); *Quek v Beggs* (1990) 5 BPR 11,761; *Badman v Drake* [2008] NSWSC 1366.
29   *Blomley v Ryan* (1956) 99 CLR 362; *Commercial Bank of Australia Ltd v Amadio* (1983) 151 CLR 447; *Louth v Diprose* (1992) 175 CLR 621; *Bridgewater v Leahy* (1998) 194 CLR 457.
30   *Daly v Sydney Stock Exchange Ltd* (1986) 160 CLR 371; *Maguire v Makaronis* (1997) 188 CLR 449.
31   *O'Sullivan v Management Agency & Music Ltd* [1985] QB 428, 457, 466, 470–71.
32   Eg *Erlanger v New Sombrero Phosphate Co* (1878) 3 App Cas 1218, 1278–79; *Alati v Kruger* (1955) 94 CLR 216, 223; *O'Sullivan v Management Agency & Music Ltd* [1985] QB 428, 458, 466, 471; *Vadasz v Pioneer Concrete (SA) Pty Ltd* (1995) 184 CLR 102, 113; *Maguire v Makaronis* (1997) 188 CLR 449, 495–96.

C   Rescission under the Australian Consumer Law

[18.16]   A remedy akin to rescission may be awarded for breach of certain provisions of the Australian Consumer Law ('ACL'),[33] including the provisions on misleading or deceptive conduct (ss 18 and 19) and unconscionable conduct (ss 20–22A).[34] The statute does not describe the remedy as 'rescission' but the remedies have a flavour of rescission. Section 243(c) of the ACL provides that a court may refuse to enforce a contract or any of its provisions. Section 243(d) then provides that a court may make an order directing a person to refund money or return property to the injured person.

[18.17]   More radically, s 243(a) provides the court with the power to declare a contract void for contravention of provisions of the ACL. In practice, as Skapinker notes, a declaration that a contract is void will often produce the same result as rescission.[35] Courts have traditionally been reluctant to exercise this power.[36] Courts were constrained by the Full Federal Court's decision in *Trade Practices Commission v Milreis Pty Ltd*,[37] which held that contracts could be declared void only in limited circumstances. However, in *Tenji v Henneberry & Associates Pty Ltd*, the Full Federal Court overruled *Milreis*, and held that the power to declare a contract void should not be confined by analogy to equitable principles.[38] Consequently, the plaintiffs in that case were entitled to have their contract declared void.

[18.18]   Generally, courts have followed the guidelines for equitable rescission when making a rescission-style order under s 87 of the *Trade Practices Act 1974* (Cth).[39] For example, in *Henjo Investments Pty Ltd v Collins Marrickville Pty Ltd*,[40] the Full Federal Court declined to make an order for rescission because *restitutio in integrum* was impossible. Nevertheless, courts have warned against confining the principles of rescission unduly by analogy to equitable rescission.[41] In *Awad v Twin Creeks Properties Pty Ltd*, Allsop P said:

> Relief under the TPA, s 87, should be viewed not by reference to general law analogues but by reference to the rule of responsibility in the statute that is directed against misleading and deceptive conduct . . . Involved in that rule of responsibility is the public policy of protection of people in trade and commerce from being misled, and the width of the powers given by the TPA that are apt to be employed in a manner conformable with the just compensation or protection of the representee. Whether or not to grant a form of rescission under s 87, or to limit a plaintiff to damages under s 82, is a question in the nature of a discretion to be approached by reference to the facts of the particular case, the

---

33   *Competition and Consumer Act 2010* (Cth), sch 2. For the legislative history, see [8.1].

34   W Covell, K Lupton and J Forder, *Principles of Remedies* (6th edn, Lexis Nexis 2015) [17.37], who note that the reference to 'rescission' in s 75A of the *Trade Practices Act 1974* (Cth) is (fortunately) not replicated in the *Competition and Consumer Act 2010* (Cth).

35   D Skapinker, '"Other Remedies" Under the Trade Practices Act – The Rise and Rise of Section 87' (1995) 21 Monash ULR 188, 203, citing *Sau Wai Lau v Roymancorp (Australia) Pty Ltd* (1986) ATPR 40–743.

36   Skapinker, ibid, 203–12.

37   (1977) 29 FLR 144. See also *Webb Distributors (Australia) Pty Ltd v Victoria* (1993) 179 CLR 15, 37.

38   [2000] FCA 550, (2000) 98 FCR 324 [13]–[14], [29], [114].

39   *Munchies Management Pty Ltd v Belperio* (1988) 58 FCR 274, 288; *Akron Securities Ltd v Iliffe* (1997) 41 NSWLR 353, 367.

40   (1988) 39 FCR 546, 565–67 (Lockhart J, with whom Burchett J agreed).

41   Ibid, 565; *Akron Securities Ltd v Iliffe* (1997) 41 NSWLR 353, 366; *Tenji v Henneberry & Associates Pty Ltd* [2000] FCA 550, (2000) 98 FCR 324 [14], [114].

policy and underpinning of the TPA and the evaluative assessment of what is the appropriate relief to compensate for, or to prevent the likely suffering of, loss or damage 'by' the conduct . . .[42]

The power to rescind under s 243 should not be interpreted restrictively, but in accordance with the aim of the ACL, which is to protect consumers. The guiding force is the statutory policy rather than any kinship with equitable rescission, although analogies with equitable rescission may be helpful.

II   The requirement of *restitutio in integrum*

The aim of rescission is to restore the parties to the position they were in before the contract or gift took place. 'It involves a giving and taking back on both sides.'[43]   [18.19]

In order to work out how rescission should be effected, it is first necessary to ascertain what has been exchanged by both parties under the voidable transaction and, to the extent possible, to seek the return of the subject matter of the transaction to each party. As noted earlier, common law requires 'complete *restitutio in integrum* ' whereas equitable rescission requires only 'substantial *restitutio in integrum* '. If the subject matter of the transaction cannot be returned in the same form, then this ends the common law inquiry and rescission will be unavailable.   [18.20]

By contrast, where equitable rescission is concerned, to the extent that the subject matter of the transaction cannot be returned, or where one party has derived a benefit which has not been paid for, the court will order a financial adjustment reflecting the value of the benefits received. It is then necessary to value the benefits and deduct them from the value that the other party is required to return to the plaintiff.   [18.21]

However, sometimes the situation has changed so greatly that not even equity can effect substantial *restitutio in integrum*, in which case rescission will be unavailable. The longer the time that has elapsed since the transaction and the greater the changes that have occurred to the property, the more difficult it is for the court to effect *restitutio in integrum*.   [18.22]

This was the case in *Clarke v Dickson*,[44] where the shares which were the subject matter of the transaction had changed substantially in nature since the transaction had occurred. Crompton J used the vivid analogy of a butcher who sought to rescind a contract for sale of cattle after having slaughtered the cattle and sold the meat: 'If the rule of law were as the plaintiff contends, that butcher might, upon discovering fraud on the part of the grazier who sold him the cattle, rescind the contract and get back the whole price: but how could that be consistent with justice?'[45] The butcher would not be able to return the cattle in the form in which they had been when the grazier sold them, and the grazier could not be restored to the position he was in at the outset. Although *Clarke v Dickson* was a case of attempted common law rescission, it is suggested that, even if equitable rescission had been an available remedy, it   [18.23]

---

42   [2012] NSWCA 200 [43]. Macfarlan JA and Sackville AJA agreed with Allsop P.
43   *Shalson v Russo* [2003] EWHC 1637 (Ch), [2005] Ch 281 [122] (Rimer J).
44   (1858) El Bl & El 148, 120 ER 463.
45   (1858) El Bl & El 148, 155; 120 ER 463, 466.

would have been refused because the shares (and the company which the shares related to) had changed too greatly for substantial *restitutio in integrum* to be achieved.

[18.24] *Alati v Kruger*[46] shows some of the difficulties in effecting substantial *restitutio in integrum*, even where equitable rescission is concerned. In that case, the purchaser sought to rescind a transaction for the purchase of a fruit business where the vendor had made fraudulent misrepresentations as to the takings of the business. The business was very unsuccessful, partly because, as the vendor was aware, a new supermarket had opened around the corner from the business. In the original transaction, the vendor had received the purchase price, and the purchaser had received the lease of the premises, the goodwill of the business and some stock and chattels. During the litigation the goodwill of the business had deteriorated, some of the stock and chattels had been lost or sold, and by the time the case came to the High Court of Australia, the lease no longer existed. While the purchaser had attempted to run the business at a considerable personal loss for most of the duration of the trial, once the trial judge held that the vendor had engaged in fraudulent misrepresentation, but before the trial judge made consequential orders for rescission, the purchaser closed the business, left the premises, and allowed the landlord to re-enter. The question was whether the purchaser could make substantial *restitutio in integrum* to the vendor, particularly given the fact that he had left the business and ended the lease.

[18.25] The High Court held that substantial *restitutio in integrum* could still be effected. The purchaser was required to return those stock and chattels that still existed, and the vendor was required to return the purchase price, but a variety of expenses were deducted from the purchase price to reflect the benefits which the purchaser was unable to return to the vendor, including the value of chattels and stock not returned and the value of the use of the premises for the duration of the lease. On the other hand, the purchase price was not reduced by the amount in which the business had deteriorated, as this was not the purchaser's fault.[47] Fullagar J indicated that, ordinarily, a purchaser would be obliged to carry on the business and take reasonable care to preserve the goodwill, and that any deterioration would be taken into account such that the purchaser would either have to compensate the vendor or rescission would be denied altogether.[48] However, in this case the court found that the purchaser had exercised reasonable care and, at least until the trial judge's decision, had done all that he could to keep the business going, whereas the vendor had not taken any action to preserve it.[49] Accordingly, the vendor could not complain that the goodwill had been reduced.[50]

[18.26] It is apparent from *Alati v Kruger* that *each* of the parties to a rescinded transaction has a right to be restored to the position they were in before the transaction was entered into. The defendant must make restitution to the plaintiff of the benefits received under the transaction, but the plaintiff must also make counter-restitution to the defendant of the benefits she has received under the transaction. This requirement has been explained as arising according to

---

46   (1955) 94 CLR 216.
47   Ibid, 225–26, 229.
48   Ibid, 228.
49   Ibid, 225–26.
50   See also *Kramer v McMahon* [1970] 1 NSWR 194; *Stanley Stamp Co v Brodie* (1914) 34 NZLR 129; *Kenny v Fenton* [1971] NZLR 1; *A H McDonald & Co Pty Ltd v Wells* (1931) 45 CLR 506, 512–13; *Mihaljevic v Eiffel Tower Motors Pty Ltd* [1973] VR 545, 565.

principles of unjust enrichment;[51] however, it seems unlikely that an Australian court would adopt this reasoning.[52]

[18.27]

If a party seeking rescission has made permanent improvements to the subject matter of the transaction before she became aware that she could rescind, she will be entitled to the value of those improvements. Thus in *Brown v Smitt*,[53] the plaintiff purchaser sought to rescind a contract for sale of land on the basis that the defendant vendor had made fraudulent misrepresentations as to the quality of the land. Prior to discovering the misrepresentations, the purchaser had made considerable improvements to the land which were not mere 'matters of taste or personal enjoyment'.[54] A majority in the High Court of Australia found that the purchaser was entitled to adjustments reflecting the improvements he had made to the land.[55] The majority said it would be unjust for the vendor to get improved land without any adjustment made to reflect this. However, the purchaser was not entitled to consequential losses flowing from the misrepresentation; only the immediate consequences of the transaction were reversed.[56]

[18.28]

If the party seeking to rescind the transaction cannot make substantial *restitutio in integrum*, the transaction cannot be set aside, even if the vitiating factor is clearly established. A stark example is *Maguire v Makaronis*.[57] Mr and Mrs Makaronis borrowed $250 000 from their solicitors to purchase a poultry farm. The loan was secured over another property. The farm was highly unsuccessful. When the solicitors sought to repossess the mortgaged property, the Makaronises successfully sought to set aside the mortgage on the basis that the solicitors had breached their fiduciary duty. The Makaronises had mistakenly believed that the loan was from the Commonwealth Bank of Australia, not from their solicitors, because of their poor English and lack of understanding of the loan documents. The court found that the transaction should be set aside. However, rescission was granted on terms – namely, that the Makaronises must pay *all* the money and interest secured by the mortgage before the transaction could be set aside. To set aside the security aspect of the mortgage alone and ignore the repayment obligation 'would be to reform the transaction in an impermissible fashion'.[58] In the event that the Makaronises could not repay the sum owing under the mortgage, the transaction stood and the solicitors could proceed with repossession.

[18.29]

The other party is not required to make good *all* of the financial losses which the person seeking to rescind suffered as a result of the transaction – only the immediate consequences of the transaction must be reversed[59] and, as noted earlier in relation to *Brown v Smitt*,[60]

---

51   *Spence v Crawford* [1939] SC (HL) 52, 77 (Lord Wright); *Halpern v Halpern (No 2)* [2006] EWHC 1728 (Comm), [2007] QB 88 [17]; D O'Sullivan, S Elliott and R Zakrzewski, *The Law of Rescission* (2nd edn, OUP 2014) [13.03]; A Burrows, *The Law of Restitution* (3rd edn, OUP 2011) 261–62.

52   N Witzleb, E Bant, S Degeling and K Barker, *Remedies: Commentary and Materials* (6th edn, LBC 2015) [2.100], although note *Plan B Trustees Ltd v Parker (No 2)* [2013] WASC 216, (2013) 11 ASTLR 242 [89]–[91] (Edelman J). See also [17.7]–[17.12].

53   (1924) 34 CLR 160.

54   Ibid, 165 (Knox CJ, Gavan Duffy and Starke JJ).

55   Ibid.

56   Ibid, 167.

57   (1997) 188 CLR 449.

58   Ibid, 475 (Brennan CJ, Gaudron, McHugh and Gummow JJ).

59   D O'Sullivan, S Elliott and R Zakrzewski, *The Law of Rescission* (2nd edn, OUP 2014) [13.04]–[13.05].

60   (1924) 34 CLR 160, 167.

consequential losses are unavailable. While compensatory damages are designed to place a plaintiff in the position she would have been in had the wrong not been committed, no similar adjustment is made in awarding rescission.[61] In *Maguire v Makaronis*, if the Makaronises had been successful in repaying the sum owing under the mortgage, they would not have been able to recover the substantial losses arising from failure of the poultry farm business. They would not have been placed in the position they would have been in had the wrong not occurred, because this is not the aim of rescission: the aim is merely to restore the parties such that the immediate consequences of the transaction are returned.

[18.30]   Let us suppose (as a hypothetical) that the Makaronises had attempted to sue their solicitors for deceit. They would not have been able to claim damages for deceit *and* attempt to rescind the transaction simultaneously, as the former is generally thought to affirm the transaction, while rescission is generally thought to disaffirm the transaction. These are mutually exclusive remedies. As the majority noted in *Alati v Kruger*, a plaintiff who has entered into a vitiated transaction has a number of choices, including suing for damages for breach of contract, suing for misrepresentation or deceit, and rescinding the contract.[62] But a plaintiff cannot both affirm the contract (by claiming damages in contract or deceit, for example) *and* rescind it. A plaintiff must elect what remedy she wishes to take.

[18.31]   Bant has recently posited that a close analysis of Australian authority shows that, although the above may be technically correct, it appears that plaintiffs may claim cumulative remedies of rescission in contract and compensation for consequential losses in tort, as long as the tort is separately pleaded, and double recovery is avoided.[63] She also notes that some awards paired with rescission, and said by the court to be 'compensatory', are in fact better regarded as restitutionary, and part of the *restitutio in integrum* process.[64]

III   Election

[18.32]   A person entitled to rescind a transaction has a choice between affirming and rescinding it. The person seeking to rescind must elect to do so, and a failure to do so will mean that the transaction remains in place. Ordinarily, a person seeking to rescind a contract or gift will elect when she gives notice to the other contracting party of her intention to have the transaction set aside. The decision to affirm or disaffirm the transaction is generally final. As Mason J observes in *Sargent v ASL Developments Ltd*, this is because the person against whom rescission is sought is entitled to know where he stands.[65]

---

61   D O'Sullivan, S Elliott and R Zakrzewski, *The Law of Rescission* (2nd edn, OUP 2014) [13.05].

62   *Alati v Kruger* (1955) 94 CLR 216, 223. Today, the plaintiff could also claim misleading or deceptive conduct pursuant to s 18 of the ACL.

63   E Bant, 'Rescission, Restitution and Compensation' in S Degeling and JNE Varuhas (eds) *Equitable Compensation and Disgorgement of Profit* (Hart 2017) 277, 278–83, citing *Sibley v Grosvenor* (1916) 21 CLR 469, 474–75.

64   See, eg, *JAD International Pty Ltd v International Trucks Australia Ltd* (1994) 50 FCR 378, 392 (Keely Hill and Drummond JJ) (a case involving the *Trade Practices Act 1974* (Cth), now superseded by the ACL.

65   (1974) 131 CLR 634, 656. Cf Q Liu, 'Rethinking Election: A General Theory' (2013) 35 Syd L Rev 599, who argues that the irrevocability of an affirmation cannot be explained by the concept of election alone but needs another basis, such as promissory estoppel.

A How to make an election to rescind

Generally, an election to rescind will be made where the person entitled to rescind unequivo- [18.33]
cally communicates to the other party that she chooses to disaffirm the transaction. Thus, the
person entitled to rescind must actually know of that right. Unfortunately, the precise standard
of knowledge required remains unclear.[66] Clearly, the person entitled to rescind must at least
know of the facts giving rise to the right,[67] but the unresolved question is whether that person
must also have knowledge of the legal right to rescind flowing from those facts.[68]

Election to rescind may be communicated in a variety of ways. It does not require a formal [18.34]
statement, and it is sufficient for the person entitled to rescind to clearly show that she no
longer wants to be bound by the transaction.[69] Often an election to rescind occurs where there
is verbal or written notice of the intention to disaffirm the contract.

Alternatively, rescission may occur by conduct which is incompatible with a subsisting [18.35]
contract, such as demanding repayment of a purchase price.[70]

Another form of conduct incompatible with a subsisting contract involves the repossession of [18.36]
goods sold under a contract.[71] The self-help legal remedy of recaption allows a person whose
chattels have been wrongfully taken to repossess the property in a lawful manner; see [13.21]–[13.25].
However, unless the contract is sought to be rescinded at common law, repossession is not
advisable. This is because, although retaking possession is an election to rescind for the purposes
of equitable rescission, it is also a wrongful conversion, as equitable rescission does not re-vest legal
title in the person entitled to rescind,[72] and any equitable title does not permit chattels to be retaken.[73]

Sometimes, even non-performance of a contractual obligation of which the other party is [18.37]
aware may constitute an unequivocal intention to disaffirm a transaction.[74]

A party entitled to rescind need not immediately choose to affirm or rescind the contract,[75] but if [18.38]
a bona fide third party obtains an interest in the subject matter of the transaction or the other party is
prejudiced by the rescinding party's delay, this may be a reason for the court to refuse to allow the
rescinding party to exercise her right.[76] Moreover, delay may also constitute affirmation; see [18.65].

Another way of communicating an intention to rescind is by serving notice on the other party [18.39]
of a legal action indicating that the first party is seeking relief consequent upon rescission.[77]

---

66 *Sargent v ASL Developments Ltd* (1974) 131 CLR 634, 641–46, 656–58.
67 Ibid, 642, 658; *Ellison v Lutre Pty Ltd* [1999] FCA 399, (1999) 88 FCR 116; *Immer (No 145) Pty Ltd v
    Uniting Church in Australia Property Trust (NSW)* (1993) 182 CLR 26.
68 Such knowledge was required in *Coastal Estates Pty Ltd v Melevende* [1965] VR 433. A contracting party
    is deemed to know a right to rescind (or to terminate for breach) provided for in the contract: *Sargent v
    ASL Developments Ltd* (1974) 131 CLR 634, 645 (Stephen J).
69 D O'Sullivan, S Elliott and R Zakrzewski, *The Law of Rescission* (2nd edn, OUP 2014) [11.03].
70 Eg *Shuman v Coober Pedy Tours Pty Ltd* (1994) 175 LSJS 159: demand for 'restitution of the contract
    price' for a fossil wrongly believed by both parties to be a dinosaur bone was an election to rescind.
71 Eg *Re Eastgate* [1905] 1 KB 465; *Car & Universal Finance Co Ltd v Caldwell* [1965] 1 QB 525, 555, 558.
72 This is in contrast to common law rescission, which re-vests title in the party seeking to rescind.
73 D O'Sullivan, S Elliott and R Zakrzewski, *The Law of Rescission* (2nd edn, OUP 2014) [11.05]–[11.06].
74 Ibid, [11.07]. An example is *Re Hoffman; Ex parte Worrell v Schilling* (FCAFC, 14 August 1989).
75 *Sargent v ASL Developments Ltd* (1974) 131 CLR 634, 656 (Mason J).
76 *Clough v London and North Western Railway Co* (1871) LR 7 Ex 26, 35.
77 *Clough v London and North Western Railway Co* (1871) LR 7 Ex 26, 35–36; *Nicholas v Thompson*
    [1924] VLR 554; *Hunter v BNZ Finance Ltd v CG Maloney Pty Ltd* (1988) 18 NSWLR 420, 437; *Coastal
    Estates Pty Ltd v Melevende* [1965] VR 433, 439–40, 450.

For example, in *Alati v Kruger*, the election to rescind occurred when the purchaser filed a writ seeking rescission against the vendor of the fruit shop.[78] However, a party seeking to give notice by pleadings must draft with care. If the pleadings are drafted equivocally, they may not constitute an effective election to rescind. In *Alati v Kruger*, although there was a claim for breach of warranty included after the claim for rescission, the writ was an effective election to rescind because the claim for breach of warranty was 'only ... included in order that the respondent might fall back on it in the event of his being held disentitled to rescind'.[79] It was unequivocal. By contrast, in *LHK Nominees Pty Ltd v Kenworthy*,[80] the plaintiff's claim to recover the purchase price was wholly inconsistent with the claim for rescission in the pleadings, and an unequivocal election to rescind was lacking.

[18.40]   Generally, to be effective, an election to rescind must be communicated to the other party.[81] However, in exceptional circumstances this is unnecessary. In *Car & Universal Finance Co Ltd v Caldwell*,[82] the defendant sold his Jaguar car to a rogue, who then sold the car to dealers who had notice of his fraud. Eventually the car was sold to the plaintiff, a bona fide purchaser for value without notice of the fraud. The primary question was whether it was necessary for the defendant to communicate his intention to rescind to the rogue to whom he had sold his car (who, naturally enough, could not be found) or whether it was sufficient for the defendant to have communicated his intention to rescind to the police and the Automobile Association, and to have asked those authorities to repossess the car. The English Court of Appeal held that while it was ordinarily necessary to communicate an intention to rescind to the other party, in a case such as this where the rogue had deliberately absconded, it was sufficient to make it known to the world that the contract was rescinded and to attempt to repossess the car.[83] Although this case has been criticised, it remains good law, although it may be limited to cases of fraud.[84]

B   The consequences of an election to rescind

[18.41]   The consequences of election differ between common law and equitable rescission.

[18.42]   At common law, election effects an immediate re-vesting of title to the person who seeks to rescind and the other party is left with no title at all. For example, in *Car & Universal Finance Co Ltd v Caldwell*,[85] the election to rescind meant that title to the car immediately re-vested in the defendant.[86] Therefore, the operation of the principle of *nemo dat quod non habet* meant that the dealers had no title to pass to the plaintiff.

---

78   (1955) 94 CLR 216, 222.
79   Ibid (Dixon CJ, Webb, Kitto and Taylor JJ).
80   [2001] WASC 205 [51]–[55].
81   *Scarf v Jardine* (1882) 7 App Cas 345, 361.
82   [1965] 1 QB 525. See also *Newtons of Wembley Ltd v Williams* [1965] 1 QB 560. Cf *Moyce v Newington* (1878) 4 QBD 32, 35–36.
83   [1965] 1 QB 525, 550–51, 555, 558–59.
84   See D O'Sullivan, S Elliott and R Zakrzewski, *The Law of Rescission* (OUP 2008) [11.34]–[11.37].
85   [1965] 1 QB 525.
86   Cf *Lewis v Averay* [1972] 1 QB 198, where the ultimate bona fide purchaser of a car was successful in gaining title.

The re-vesting of property in the original owner only works for goods. Title to real property and intangible property cannot be recovered by common law rescission.[87]   [18.43]

The proprietary consequences of rescission can provide a defendant with a defence to a claim of a proprietary tort. In other words, if a defendant used the self-help remedy of recaption (discussed at [13.21]–[13.25]) to recover his property, the defendant could defend himself from a claim by the plaintiff in conversion by responding that he was simply taking possession of a good to which he had title by reason of his election to rescind. Another consequence of common law rescission re-vesting of title is that the party seeking to rescind may have an action in conversion or detinue.[88]   [18.44]

The effect of an election to rescind in equity is different. Where an executory contract is voidable for a purely equitable ground such as undue influence, breach of fiduciary duty or unconscionable dealing, it will be rescinded by notice to the other party and is effectively nullified.[89] For example, in *Commercial Bank of Australia v Amadio*,[90] a son persuaded his elderly Italian parents to give a guarantee for his business, and the bank was found to have acted unconscionably in procuring the guarantee, taking advantage of the parents' special disadvantage. They were entitled to rescission of the guarantee even though they had never been required to pay any money under the guarantee. Bryan, Vann and Barkehall Thomas have argued that the aim here is to nullify the contract.[91]   [18.45]

There is some controversy as to whether equitable rescission is a 'self-help' remedy, or whether rescission requires an order of the court. Where a contract is executory (that is, yet to be performed), or where common law rescission is concerned,[92] rescission may be a 'self-help' remedy that is not dependent upon an order of the court. But insofar as equitable rescission of an executed or partly executed contract is concerned, the court's jurisdiction to award 'rescission on terms' or 'partial rescission' is less amenable to a self-help analysis, because it appears that this sort of rescission is only available upon a court order.   [18.46]

If legal title to an asset has been transferred pursuant to a voidable transaction, an election to rescind operates to cause the party seeking to rescind the transaction to gain equitable title to the asset pursuant to a constructive trust. This is sometimes described as a 'proprietary power'.[93] Although the term has not yet gained judicial acceptance, it is suggested that the term is a useful descriptor. It is important to distinguish between the title of the party seeking to rescind prior to election and the title of that party after election has occurred. Prior to the election the party seeking to rescind has a 'mere equity', an inchoate proprietary right which   [18.47]

---

87   D O'Sullivan, S Elliott and R Zakrzewski, *The Law of Rescission* (2nd edn, OUP 2014) [14.21]–[14.28], [16.04].

88   L Proksch, 'Rescission' in P Parkinson (ed) *The Principles of Equity* (2nd edn, LBC 2003) [2503]; JD Heydon, MJ Leeming and PG Turner, *Meagher, Gummow and Lehane's Equity: Doctrines and Remedies* (5th edn, LexisNexis Butterworths 2015) [25–060].

89   M Bryan, V Vann and S Barkehall Thomas, *Equity and Trusts in Australia* (2nd edn, CUP 2017) 30.

90   (1983) 151 CLR 447.

91   M Bryan, V Vann and S Barkehall Thomas, *Equity and Trusts in Australia* (2nd edn, CUP 2017) 73.

92   *Halpern v Halpern (No 2)* [2006] EWHC 1728 (Comm), [2007] QB 88 [26].

93   The term is taken from E Bant, 'Trusts, Powers and Liens: An Exercise in Ground-Clearing' (2009) 3 J Eq 286, who in turn builds on B Häcker, *Consequences of Impaired Consent Transfers* (Mohr Siebeck 2009); B Häcker, 'Proprietary Restitution after Impaired Consent Transfers: A Generalised Power Model' (2009) 68 Camb LJ 324.

will be extinguished even when a bona fide purchaser for value without notice obtains an equitable interest in the property.[94] After she has elected to rescind, she has a 'full-blown' equitable title to the property pursuant to a constructive trust.[95] The plaintiff may seek to have the property returned pursuant to a court order. Courts also sometimes choose to award a less intrusive remedy such as a lien or no remedy at all, depending upon the operation of discretionary bars to relief; see [18.57]–[18.80].

[18.48]   An example of a case where the plaintiff failed to elect and was unable to claim a vested beneficial interest is *Daly v Sydney Stock Exchange Ltd*.[96] An investor sought investment advice from a firm of stockbrokers, Patrick Partners. The employee to whom the investor spoke told him that there were no good investments available at the time, but that he should leave his money on deposit with the firm, and so the investor loaned the money to the firm. The employee was unaware that Patrick Partners was in a dire financial situation. It ceased trading some months later, and was unable to repay the investor's loan. The investor's wife (as assignee) sought compensation from the fidelity fund of the Sydney Stock Exchange, but pursuant to s 97(1)(b) of the then *Securities Industry Act 1975* (NSW) she was required to show that Patrick Partners had held the investment on trust for the investor. She sought to argue that the firm held the investment on constructive trust for her husband. While the High Court of Australia agreed that there had been a breach of a fiduciary relationship, they declined to find a constructive trust. The majority did not consider whether the investor's purported constructive trust arose as a result of rescission of the loan agreement. They confined their analysis to asking whether a constructive trust had arisen immediately upon receipt by Patrick Partners of the loan moneys, and declined to find a constructive trust based on policy concerns about the effect of a trust in insolvency.[97] The minority asked whether the investor had elected to rescind on the basis of breach of fiduciary duty such as to give rise to a vested interest under a constructive trust. Brennan J, with whom Wilson J agreed, observed that a party seeking to rescind must generally *elect* to do so before a constructive trust can arise.[98] He argued that it was mutually inconsistent to leave the contract on foot, and at the same time deny the borrower's title to the money conferred by the contract. Moreover, he argued that the borrower could not be a trustee of the money without his consent because this would place him under onerous fiduciary obligations.[99] In this case, there was no evidence that the investor had elected to rescind the contract before Patrick Partners became insolvent, and the investor did not have a vested equitable title under a constructive trust.

---

94   *Latec Investments Limited v Hotel Terrigal Pty Ltd* (1965) 113 CLR 265, 277, 284, 290–91.
95   Ibid, 277, 290–91.
96   (1986) 160 CLR 371.
97   Ibid, 380 (Gibbs CJ, with whom Wilson and Dawson JJ agreed).
98   Ibid, 388–90.
99   Ibid, 389. Query whether constructive trustees are (or should be) under onerous fiduciary duties other than the duty to return the property to the beneficiary: W Swadling, 'The Fiction of the Constructive Trust' (2011) 64 Curr Leg Prob 399, 410–11. Cf C Mitchell and S Watterson, 'Remedies for Knowing Receipt' in C Mitchell (ed), *Constructive and Resulting Trusts* (Hart 2010) 115.

C   The reasons behind the election requirement

Election primarily serves to protect the interests of innocent defendants. Courts are less sympathetic towards fraudulent defendants. In *Spence v Crawford*, Lord Wright said: [18.49]

> The court will be less ready to pull a transaction to pieces where the defendant is innocent, whereas in the case of fraud the court will exercise its jurisdiction to the full in order, if possible, to prevent the defendant from enjoying the benefit of his fraud at the expense of the innocent plaintiff.[100]

However, election also protects third parties who might have gained a competing interest in an asset transferred pursuant to a voidable transaction without being aware of the proprietary interest of the party seeking to rescind. Where equitable rescission is sought, the only option for a plaintiff in such a case may be to seek pecuniary rescission against the recipient of the property.[101] Pecuniary rescission occurs where the defendant no longer has the asset which was the subject of the transaction, but is ordered to pay the value of the asset. [18.50]

IV   'Partial' rescission

The traditional position at common law and equity is that rescission must be total. The plaintiff can elect to rescind or can affirm a transaction, but cannot do both. Generally, a plaintiff may not rescind part of a transaction and affirm another: it is an 'all or nothing process'.[102] Nor may she rescind one contract out of a series of contracts.[103] Otherwise restoration to the status quo is not truly effected. [18.51]

Controversially, the High Court of Australia was prepared to award 'partial rescission' in *Vadasz v Pioneer Concrete (SA) Pty Ltd*.[104] Vadasz was a director of Vadipile, a company in financial difficulty. Pioneer Concrete was owed $200 000 by Vadipile for past concrete supplies and required a personal guarantee from Vadasz as a condition of making any further deliveries. Vadasz signed a guarantee of Vadipile's past and future indebtedness to Pioneer Concrete. After the contract had been made, Vadipile ran up further debts of $150 000. The trial judge found that Vadasz had been induced to enter the guarantee by a misrepresentation on the part of Pioneer Concrete that the guarantee related only to future indebtedness. The High Court said that equitable rescission was more flexible than common law rescission. Accordingly, they left intact that part of the guarantee which related to future indebtedness, as this obligation was assumed by Vadasz independently of any misrepresentation. However, the part of the guarantee which related to past indebtedness could be rescinded and set aside. This was said to be an instance of equity achieving 'practical justice' in rescission. [18.52]

---

100   [1939] SC (HL) 52, 77.
101   *McKenzie v McDonald* [1927] VLR 134.
102   *TSB Bank plc v Camfield* [1995] 1 WLR 430, 436 (Nourse LJ), citing *Allied Irish Banks plc v Byrne* [1995] 2 FLR 325 (Ferris J).
103   *A H McDonald & Co Pty Ltd v Wells* (1931) 45 CLR 506, 512–23; *Greater Pacific Investments Pty Ltd (in liq) v Australian National Industries Ltd* (1996) 39 NSWLR 143.
104   (1995) 184 CLR 102.

[18.53]   There has been a good deal of scholarly commentary on *Vadasz*.[105] New Zealand courts have adopted the Australian position on partial rescission,[106] but partial rescission has not been adopted in England and Wales.[107] Courts use partial rescission to remake the bargain between the parties. However, there are powerful reasons for courts being reluctant to do this. In *Myddleton v Lord Kenyon*, Longborough LC said:

> The relief prayed is not to set aside the deed as null and void; but to declare, that all the trusts are void after that for payment of the debts; leaving all those parts to stand, and obtain their full effect so far as the payment of the debts goes. The species of relief it is totally incompetent to the Court to give. The deed may be set aside *in toto*. Any bargain, the parties enter into with each other, may be declared null, and set aside, upon grounds of undue practice or influence exerted, mistake . . . These grounds would entitle the Court to set it aside *in toto*: but I cannot make a new bargain for the parties; or force them into a new agreement upon those things, which are matter of absolute will, and depending totally upon the consent and temper of the parties. I cannot make a new family settlement. No judge is competent to such an act . . . This Court, if it was to go farther, and to substitute other terms, would make itself the *moderator* of the private affairs of all the families in England.[108]

[18.54]   There is some similarity between the facts of *Vadasz* and of *Commercial Bank of Australia Ltd v Amadio*[109] (discussed at [18.45]), in which a developer persuaded his elderly Italian parents to give a guarantee for his business where he was misleading as to the extent and duration of the guarantee, and in which the bank was found to have acted unconscionably, taking advantage of the parents' special disadvantage. In the latter case, the Amadios were entitled to fully set aside the contract of guarantee. Interestingly, Deane J gave some thought to partial rescission, but said that the Amadios should be entitled to set aside the contract wholly because they would never have entered the contract of guarantee had they known the truth.[110] By contrast, the evidence in *Vadasz* indicated that Vadasz would still have entered a portion of the contract had he known the truth. Thus, if the party seeking to rescind the contract would not have entered any contract, the court must rescind the entire contract.

[18.55]   *Maguire v Makaronis*,[111] discussed at [18.28]–[18.30], presents a difficulty as the trial judge found that the Makaronises would have entered a mortgage even if they had known of the

---

105   L Proksch, 'Rescission on Terms' [1996] RLR 71; JW Carter and G Tolhurst, 'Rescission, Equitable Adjustment and Restitution' (1996) 10 J Cont L 167; D O'Sullivan, 'Partial Rescission for Misrepresentation in Australia' (1997) 113 LQR 16; M Chen-Wishart, 'Unjust Factors and the Restitutionary Response' (2000) 20 OJLS 557; A Robertson, 'Partial Rescission, Causation and Benefit' (2001) 17 J Cont L 163; P Watts, 'Rescission and Guarantees for Misrepresentation and Actionable Non-Disclosure' (2002) 61 Camb LJ 301; D Meikle, 'Partial Rescission: Removing the Restitution from a Contractual Doctrine' (2003) 19 J Cont L 40; J Poole and A Keyser, 'Justifying Partial Rescission in English Law' (2005) 121 LQR 273; JD Heydon, MJ Leeming and PG Turner, *Meagher, Gummow and Lehane's Equity: Doctrines and Remedies* (5th edn, LexisNexis 2015) [25–130].

106   *Scales Trading Ltd v Far Eastern Shipping Co Public Ltd* [1999] 3 NZLR 26.

107   *TSB Bank plc v Camfield* [1995] 1 WLR 430; *Castle Phillips Finance v Piddington* [1995] 1 FLR 783; *Molestina v Ponton* [2002] 1 Lloyd's Rep 271.

108   (1794) 2 Ves 391, 408; 30 ER 689, 698–9.

109   (1983) 151 CLR 447.

110   Ibid, 480–81.

111   (1997) 188 CLR 449.

conflict of interest. If we take the principle in *Vadasz* seriously, the mortgage should still have been enforced regardless of the solicitors' breach of fiduciary duty. However, the High Court of Australia said that partial rescission is not possible for a failure to disclose in breach of fiduciary duty.[112] Thus, it appears that partial rescission is possible for misrepresentation (whether culpable or innocent),[113] for unconscionable dealing[114] and for economic duress,[115] but not for breach of fiduciary duty. As O'Sullivan, Elliott and Zakrzewski have argued, the distinction upon which this principle operates is difficult to understand, and appears not to depend upon the degree of culpability.[116]

Vadasz was applied in *Bridgewater v Leahy*,[117] where a farmer sold certain holdings for less than they were worth to his nephew. The farmer also executed a deed of forgiveness in favour of the nephew in relation to a substantial part of the purchase price of the land. After the farmer's death, his four daughters sought to set aside the deed of forgiveness on the basis that it was acquired as a result of unconscionable dealing. A majority in the High Court of Australia found that it was unconscionable for the nephew to retain the benefit of the deed of forgiveness of the debt which would otherwise be owing to the farmer's estate. The deed of forgiveness was not fully enforceable, so the nephew was liable to pay the farmer's estate the debt owing. However, the court said that it was clear that the uncle wished his nephew to have a significant level of benefaction under his will, and that an allowance should be made in relation to the debt owing to the estate. Watts has criticised the decision as remaking the contract between the farmer and his nephew in a way which the parties never intended.[118] It is a difficult decision, and the dissent of Gleeson CJ and Callinan J is powerful.

[18.56]

V   Bars to rescission

The ordinary equitable bars to relief apply to equitable rescission as they apply to other equitable remedies. Thus, if rescission will inflict undue hardship on the defendant, it will not be awarded.[119] Or, as arguably happened in *Badman v Drake*,[120] a court may choose to award a lesser proprietary remedy such as a lien because a full constructive trust would inflict undue hardship on the defendants. Similarly, if the plaintiff has acted unconscionably, she will not be entitled to rescind.[121]

[18.57]

The following bars to rescission bear closer inspection:

[18.58]

* impossibility of complete restoration;
* affirmation;

---

112   Ibid, 472.
113   *Vadasz v Pioneer Concrete (SA) Pty Ltd* (1995) 184 CLR 102, 110.
114   *NZI Capital Corporation Ltd v Poignard* (1997) ATPR 41–586; *Bridgewater v Leahy* (1998) 194 CLR 457; *Micarone v Perpetual Trustees* [1999] SASC 265, (1999) 75 SASR 1.
115   *Cockrill v Westpac Banking Corporation* (1996) 142 ALR 227.
116   D O'Sullivan, S Elliott and R Zakrzewski, *The Law of Rescission* (2nd edn, OUP 2014) [19.27]–[19.28].
117   (1998) 194 CLR 457.
118   P Watts, 'Partial Rescission: Disentangling the Seedlings but Not Transplanting Them' in E Bant and M Harding, *Exploring Private Law* (CUP 2010) 427.
119   *Hartigan v International Society for Krishna Consciousness Inc* [2002] NSWSC 810 (unsuccessful claim of hardship).
120   [2008] NSWSC 1366.
121   *Alati v Kruger* (1955) 94 CLR 216, 225.

- delay;
- intervening third party rights; and
- executed contracts and innocent misrepresentation.

A   Impossibility of complete restoration

[18.59]   A bar to rescission that flows from the requirement of *restitutio in integrum* is the impossibility of substantial restoration of the parties to their original positions.[122] This bar operates only when the plaintiff is unable to restore the defendant, as the plaintiff has elected to rescind and thus cannot complain if she is not fully restored,[123] although there may be circumstances where a plaintiff might not know that she cannot be fully restored.

[18.60]   Lord Wright famously said in *Spence v Crawford*:

> [I]f a plaintiff who has been defrauded seeks to have the contract annulled and his money or property restored to him, it would be inequitable if he did not also restore what he had got under the contract from the defendant. Though the defendant has been fraudulent, he must not be robbed, nor must the plaintiff be unjustly enriched, as he would be if he both got back what he had parted with and kept what he had received in return.[124]

As noted previously, common law requires 'complete *restitutio in integrum*', whereas equitable rescission only requires 'substantial *restitutio in integrum*'.

[18.61]   Impossibility of substantial *restitutio in integrum* barred equitable rescission in *Quek v Beggs*.[125] Mrs Quek made substantial payments of money to her pastor, Mr Beggs (totalling $247 000) before she died in 1986. She also made gifts of three properties (in Maroubra, Kingswood and Winston Hills) to Mr Beggs and his wife. After Mrs Quek's death, her daughter sought, inter alia, to have the transactions to the Beggs set aside on the basis of undue influence. McLelland J found that there was a presumed relationship of undue influence arising from the relationship of spiritual advisor and acolyte,[126] and that the Beggs failed to rebut this presumption. Mrs Quek had given some of the money to the Beggs for the purpose of fitting out Mr Beggs's mother-in-law's house. As will be discussed below at [18.72], McLelland J declined to make a proprietary order against the mother-in-law. McLelland J also refused to make an order against Mr Beggs in relation to the money given to the mother-in-law because Mr Beggs was unable to be restored to the position he would have been in if the gift had never been made. Nor could the Kingswood property be returned to the estate, as the Beggs had sold it to finance the defence of the legal action against them. The Beggs were not required to pay back the amount of the proceeds of sale which discharged the mortgage over the property. The Maroubra and Winston Hills properties and $50 000 were returned to Mrs Quek's estate. It is difficult to see why the Beggs were not required to return the value of the Kingswood property

---

122   *Erlanger v New Sombrero Phosphate Co* (1878) 3 App Cas 1218, 1278; *A H McDonald & Co Pty Ltd v Wells* (1931) 45 CLR 506; *Alati v Kruger* (1955) 94 CLR 216.
123   G Virgo, *The Principles of Equity and Trusts* (2nd edn, OUP 2016) 763.
124   1939 SC (HL) 52, 77. Although note comments at [18.49] about possible Australian scepticism of Lord Wright's approval of 'unjust enrichment' as a basis for rescission.
125   (1990) 5 BPR 11,761.
126   Class 2A undue influence in the terminology of *Barclays Bank plc v O'Brien* [1994] 1 AC 180.

through pecuniary rescission, as they divested themselves of that property after Mrs Quek's daughter had made known her intention to rescind the gift.

B   Affirmation

When a contract is voidable by reason of a vitiating factor, the party seeking to rescind must elect whether to avoid or affirm the contract. Affirmation involves a choice to leave the contract in question on foot and, potentially, to take action under it. If the party seeking to rescind has affirmed the contract, she will not then be entitled to seek to rescind it.[127] There is the same difficulty regarding knowledge of the right to affirm as for knowledge of the right to rescind. It remains unclear whether mere knowledge of the facts giving rise to the right to rescind is sufficient for an affirmation by conduct,[128] or whether knowledge of the legal right to affirm flowing from those facts is additionally required.[129]   **[18.62]**

In *Hawker Pacific Pty Ltd v Helicopter Charter Pty Ltd*,[130] Handley JA suggested that even where affirmation did not apply because the plaintiff was not aware of the right to rescind, she may be estopped from denying the existence of the contract. In other words, the plaintiff might act in a way that made the defendant believe that the contract was being affirmed, on which representation the defendant relied, to his detriment.   **[18.63]**

If a plaintiff is still operating under a vitiating factor such as duress or undue influence, or if she is unaware that the defendant has made a misrepresentation, then she cannot make a clear choice to affirm. Thus, the defendant must show that such a choice has been made after the vitiating factor has ceased to apply.[131]   **[18.64]**

Affirmation is necessarily linked to delay as, once the plaintiff is aware of the vitiating factor and delays bringing a claim, this may be an affirmation of the contract. This will be discussed below.   **[18.65]**

Affirmation can also be effected by positive acts consistent only with a continuation of the contract, such as where a plaintiff seeks specific relief or compensation for breach of an otherwise voidable contract.   **[18.66]**

C   Delay

Delay in rescinding may constitute a bar to rescission.[132] However, by itself, delay is not enough: something more is needed – acquiescence on the part of the plaintiff or prejudice in respect of the defendant.   **[18.67]**

In the context of rescission, delay with acquiescence is related to, and overlaps with, the bar of affirmation. As noted earlier, the right to rescind is lost when the plaintiff unequivocally manifests an intention to affirm the transaction. Once the plaintiff becomes aware of the right to   **[18.68]**

---

127   *Byers v Dorotea Pty Ltd* (1986) 69 ALR 715, 722.
128   *Re Hoffman* (1989) 85 ALR 145; *Sargent v ASL Developments Ltd* (1974) 131 CLR 634, 642, 658; *Ellison v Lutre Pty Ltd* [1999] FCA 399, (1999) 88 FCR 116; *Immer (No 145) Pty Ltd v Uniting Church in Australia Property Trust (NSW)* (1993) 182 CLR 26.
129   *Coastal Estates Pty Ltd v Melevende* [1965] VR 433.
130   (1991) 22 NSWLR 298, 304–05.
131   Ibid, 304–05, 306–08.
132   *Leaf v International Galleries* [1950] 2 KB 86.

rescind and is free of any vitiating factor, failure to rescind in a reasonable time (that is, acquiescence) may be taken as evidence of an intention to affirm the contract.

[18.69]   Proprietary rescission was denied because of delay and acquiescence in *Allcard v Skinner*.[133] Miss Allcard, the plaintiff, had joined an institution known as 'Protestant Sisters of the Poor'. The rule of poverty observed by the order required the member to give up all her property to her relatives, to the poor or to the sisterhood, with the latter strongly encouraged. Within three days of becoming a member, Allcard made a will in favour of Miss Skinner, the lady superior of the order and, after she inherited a large amount of property, she transferred several large sums of money and railway stock to Skinner. Some 10 years later, Allcard left the sisterhood and revoked her will, but made no demand for the return of her property until six years after that date, whereupon she sought to rescind the transaction on the basis that Skinner had exercised undue influence. The court found that there was a presumed relationship of undue influence arising from the relationship of spiritual advisor and acolyte,[134] and that the defendant failed to rebut this presumption on the facts. However, Allcard could not assert a proprietary interest against Skinner because of her delay and acquiescence in bringing her claim.

[18.70]   Delay with prejudice is concerned with the prejudicial effects of delay on the defendant and third parties. The classic example of prejudice is where the defendant has reasonably acted to his detriment in reliance on the plaintiff's delay. Thus, it may be related to the bar of impossibility of *restitutio in integrum*.[135] It has thus been argued that delay in this sense requires consideration of factors which make it resemble a change of position defence.[136]

D   Intervening third party rights

[18.71]   Rescission has traditionally been barred where a third party, who is a bona fide purchaser for value without notice, has acquired rights in the subject matter of a voidable contract.[137] If the defendant transfers the goods to an innocent third party, before the contract is rescinded by the original victim, good title passes. This means that *restitutio in integrum* between the original parties is impossible and rescission has been held to be barred on this basis, unless the third party's interests can be adequately safeguarded.[138]

[18.72]   *Quek v Beggs*, mentioned at [18.61], is a case where intervening third party rights led to the refusal of proprietary relief in relation to the gifts made to the third party.[139] Some of the payments Mrs Quek had made to her pastor, Mr Beggs, were expressed to be for the purpose of fitting out Mr Beggs's mother-in-law's house. McLelland J declined to make a proprietary

---

133   (1887) 36 Ch D 145.
134   Class 2A undue influence in the terminology of *Barclays Bank plc v O'Brien* [1994] 1 AC 180.
135   D O'Sullivan, S Elliott and R Zakrzewski, *The Law of Rescission* (2nd edn, OUP 2014) [24.01].
136   N Witzleb, E Bant, S Degeling and K Barker, *Remedies: Commentary and Materials* (6th edn, LBC 2015) [2.155].
137   This rule has been criticised: R Goode, 'Property and Unjust Enrichment' in A Burrows (ed), *Essays on the Law of Restitution* (Clarendon Press 1991) 215, 235; G Virgo, *The Principles of Equity and Trusts* (OUP 2012) 740.
138   *Oakes v Turquand* (1867) LR 2 HL 325.
139   (1990) 5 BPR 11,761.

order against the mother-in-law over the improved house, as she was a bona fide third party, although it should be noted that she was not a purchaser for value.

In some cases where the defendant has sold some or all of the assets received under the impugned transaction, the plaintiff may recover the proceeds of resale as part of the process of *restitutio in integrum*. This has been established in cases involving land[140] or shares.[141] This overlaps with specific restitution which is discussed at [10.118].   **[18.73]**

The more difficult question is whether the defendant can be ordered to pay for the value of the asset even if the proceeds of sale are no longer in the defendant's hands. This is sometimes known as 'pecuniary rescission'.[142] In other words, the party seeking to rescind may be able to get a pecuniary award representing the value of the benefit conferred on the other party to the impugned transaction, even if the property has since passed to a third party and the proceeds of sale are no longer in the other party's hands or, alternatively, do not represent a fair value of the benefit. Two Australian cases support the availability of such an award.[143]   **[18.74]**

The first case is *McKenzie v McDonald*.[144] The plaintiff was a widow who contacted the defendant estate agent to sell her farm property and buy a residence in Melbourne. The defendant suggested that the plaintiff should exchange her farm property (which he under-valued) for the defendant's suburban house and shop (which he overvalued). This was a breach of fiduciary relationship of agency between the parties. By the time of legal proceedings, the defendant had sold the farm to a bona fide third party, and so it was not possible to restore the farm property to the plaintiff. The resale price was not an accurate measure of the benefit the defendant had received either. Consequently, Dixon AJ ordered that the defendant should pay the difference between the actual values of the two properties as at the date of the sale.[145]   **[18.75]**

The second case is *Hartigan v International Society for Krishna Consciousness Inc*,[146] where the plaintiff gave a gift of her family home (her only valuable asset) and some cattle to the International Society for Krishna Consciousness. She joined a community at New Govard-hana Farm. The society sold the plaintiff's property and used the proceeds to pay off debts, among other things. The plaintiff later left the movement for Krishna Consciousness, and sought to rescind her gift on the basis of presumed undue influence by the society. Bryson J found that there was a presumed relationship of undue influence arising from the relationship of spiritual advisor and acolyte,[147] and that the defendant had failed to rebut the presumption. Accordingly, Bryson J was prepared to rescind the transaction. The property had been sold off to a bona fide purchaser for value without notice, and the society no longer had the proceeds of sale. Notwithstanding this, it was required to pay back the value of the house, represented by the proceeds of sale plus interest from the date of commencement of the hearing. Bryson J   **[18.76]**

---

140   *Blackham v Haythorpe* (1917) 23 CLR 156; *Pedashenko v Blacktown City Council* (1996) 39 NSWLR 189, 203.
141   *New Sombrero Phosphate Company v Erlanger* (1877) 5 Ch D 73, 125; *Lagunas Nitrate Company v Lagunas Syndicate* [1899] 2 Ch 392, 434; *Estate Properties Ltd v Wignall* [1992] 2 NZLR 615, 631.
142   See P Birks, 'Unjust Factors and Wrongs: Pecuniary Rescission for Undue Influence' [1997] RLR 72.
143   See also *Mahoney v Purnell* [1996] 3 All ER 61.
144   [1927] VLR 134.
145   Ibid, 146–47. Cf *Aequitas Ltd v Sparad No 100 Ltd* [2001] NSWSC 14, (2001) 19 ACLC 1006.
146   [2002] NSWSC 810.
147   Class 2A undue influence in the terminology of *Barclays Bank plc v O'Brien* [1994] 1 AC 180.

said, 'I see no injustice in restoring the defendant to the relative position of indebtedness which it would have been in if it had not received the proceeds of sale'.[148] In other words, the defendant was in the same position it would have been in had it not taken the gift and paid off its debts, but it now owed that debt to the plaintiff.[149] The defendant unsuccessfully sought to rely on the defences of hardship and delay. Bryson J noted that the plaintiff's delay and difficulty in funding litigation was 'directly connected with the impoverishing nature of the gift'.[150]

[18.77]   It has been argued that an order for pecuniary rescission is a form of equitable compensation,[151] and it was often described as such in the older cases. It has alternatively been argued that pecuniary rescission is essentially a restitutionary remedy, involving a restitution of the value of a benefit conferred.[152] Arguably, a restitutionary analysis fits better with these cases: the defendant would be unjustly enriched if he was allowed to keep the value of the benefit he received. However, as O'Sullivan, Elliott and Zakrzewski have argued, there are still questions to be answered if pecuniary rescission is to be routinely awarded.[153] These include the difficulty in calculating the value of the thing transferred when it has changed since the date of the original transaction, whether pecuniary rescission is given in lieu of setting aside the contract or whether the contract has to be set aside before pecuniary rescission is granted, a concern about unjustly prejudicing defendants who were not reprehensible (as in the case of innocent misrepresentation), and the impact on the rules of property law.

E   Executed contracts and innocent misrepresentation

[18.78]   A contract for the sale of land which has been executed (that is, the land has already been conveyed or registered) cannot be rescinded for innocent misrepresentation.[154] This rule (sometimes called the 'conveyance bar') can perhaps be justified in the context of land transactions because of its tendency to promote the finality of such transactions.[155] However, the rule has been extended to leases,[156] and to contracts for the sale of shares,[157] goods[158] and businesses.[159] The extension of the rule has been criticised,[160] and often judges attempt to find

---

148   [2002] NSWSC 810, [98].

149   See also *Gertsch v Atsas* [1999] NSWSC 898, (1999) 10 BPR 18,431.

150   [2002] NSWSC 810, [103].

151   T Akkouh, 'Equitable Compensation Where Rescission is Impossible' (2002) 16 TLI 151. However, Akkouh (at 151 fn 1) also thinks that equitable compensation is not always loss-based. Equitable compensation in general is discussed in Ch 9.

152   P Birks, *Unjust Enrichment* (2nd edn, OUP 2005) 226–28.

153   D O'Sullivan, S Elliott and R Zakrzewski, *The Law of Rescission* (2nd edn, OUP 2014) [15.27]–[15.32].

154   *Wilde v Gibson* (1848) 1 HL Cas 605, 9 ER 897; *Svanosio v McNamara* (1956) 96 CLR 186.

155   E Bant, 'Seddon's Case: Sense or Nonsense?' [2013] Conv 30.

156   *Angel v Jay* [1911] 1 KB 666.

157   *Seddon v Northern Eastern Salt Company* [1905] 1 Ch 326.

158   *Seddon* (ibid) has been interpreted as extending to goods.

159   *Vimig Pty Ltd v Contract Tooling Pty Ltd* (1987) 9 NSWLR 731.

160   HA Hammelmann, '*Seddon v North Eastern Salt Co*' (1939) 55 LQR 90; M Bridge, 'Misrepresentation and Merger' (1986) 20 UBC L Rev 53; P MacFarlane and L Willmott, 'Rescission of an Executed Contract at Common Law for an Innocent Misrepresentation' (1998) 10 Bond LR 58.

reasons why the contract has not been executed in order to get around the bar,[161] or they flatly refuse to apply the bar.[162]

The conveyance bar has been statutorily abolished in the Australian Capital Territory,[163] South Australia,[164] England[165] and, in relation to the sale of goods, in New South Wales[166] and Victoria.[167]   **[18.79]**

There has been some question as to whether a contract for the sale of goods can be rescinded in equity for innocent misrepresentation.[168] The better view is that equitable rescission is available for contracts for sale of goods[169] and, as noted before, statutory reforms in some states have confirmed this.   **[18.80]**

---

161   Eg *Grogan v 'The Astor' Ltd* (1925) 25 SR (NSW) 409; *Senanayake v Cheng* [1966] AC 63; *Mihaljevic v Eiffel Tower Motors Pty Ltd* [1973] VR 545.

162   Eg *Leason Pty Ltd v Princes Farm Pty Ltd* [1983] 2 NSWLR 381; *Baird v BCE Holdings Pty Ltd* (1996) 40 NSWLR 374; *Solle v Butcher* [1950] 1 KB 671.

163   *Civil Law (Wrongs) Act 2002* (ACT), s 173.

164   *Misrepresentation Act 1971* (SA), s 6.

165   *Misrepresentation Act 1967* (UK), s 1(b).

166   *Sale of Goods Act 1923* (NSW), s 4(2A)(b).

167   *Australian Consumer Law and Fair Trading Act 2012* (Vic), s 24(1).

168   Rescission was considered unavailable in *Watt v Westhoven* [1933] VLR 458, and available in *Graham v Freer* (1980) 35 SASR 424.

169   J Paterson, A Robertson and A Duke, *Principles of Contract Law* (5th edn, LBC 2016) [39.75].

PART 7

PROPRIETARY REMEDIES

19

PROPRIETARY REMEDIES

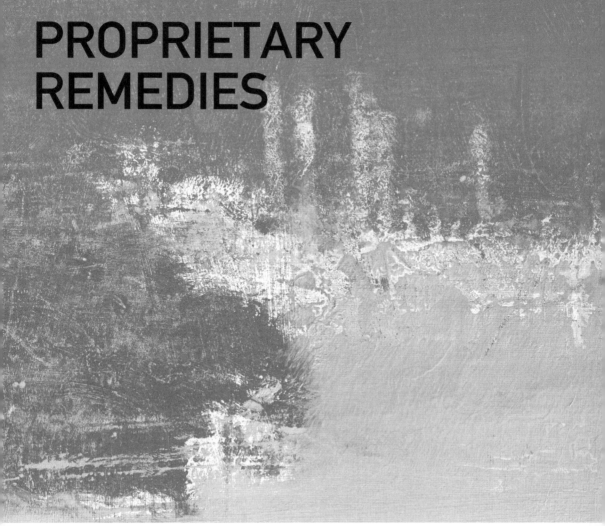

I Introduction

[19.1]   Most of the remedies discussed in this book are personal remedies (apart from the proprietary consequences of rescission; see [18.47]–[18.48]). Personal remedies, as the name suggests, are directed at the person of the defendant. The defendant must comply with the court order. By contrast, proprietary remedies are directed at property to which the defendant holds title, not to the person.

[19.2]   Proprietary remedies are difficult to allocate on a functional basis. We have not attempted to do so, as the rationales behind the imposition of proprietary remedies vary, and the criteria for their award are uncertain and contested.

[19.3]   The availability of proprietary remedies in common law is limited. Even where the defendant has committed a proprietary tort, the common law tends to award damages as a remedy.[1] Consequently, the proprietary remedies we discuss in this chapter are equitable in origin.

[19.4]   Proprietary remedies have several well-known advantages over personal remedies, which make them attractive for plaintiffs. First, equitable property rights are by their very nature enforceable against third parties, as this is the essence of a proprietary right: it is exigible against the rest of the world.[2] An equitable proprietary remedy can be enforced against anyone who has legal title to the property to which the remedy attaches *except* a good faith purchaser for value without notice of the plaintiff's equitable proprietary rights.[3] A constructive trust may also allow a plaintiff to follow any transfers of value out of the defendant's hands and into the hands of third parties.

[19.5]   Secondly, some proprietary remedies such as the constructive trust will allow plaintiffs to enjoy any appreciation in the value of the property which is the subject of the claim. For example, if I am awarded a constructive trust over a painting which was worth $100 000 but is now worth $500 000, I will be able to get the entire painting and thus the appreciation in value. The corresponding disadvantage is that proprietary remedies will not be worthwhile if the asset which is the subject of the claim is destroyed or devalued.

[19.6]   Thirdly, proprietary remedies allow a plaintiff to have her specific property returned to her; this may be important when property has special personal value to the plaintiff.

[19.7]   Fourthly, a proprietary remedy has distinct advantages for a plaintiff where the defendant is bankrupt or insolvent. A proprietary remedy entitles the plaintiff to recover property to which the defendant has title not only as against the defendant, but also as against the defendant's unsecured creditors. By contrast, a personal remedy simply entitles the plaintiff to share *pari passu* with the defendant's other unsecured creditors. On the one hand, it can be argued that if the plaintiff has a property right, it is irrelevant if third-party creditors are adversely affected by the award of a constructive trust; but on the other hand, it can be argued that it is unfair for the plaintiff to get an

---

1   Courts may award specific restitution of goods where a proprietary tort has been committed and the goods are sufficiently unique: *Aristoc Industries Pty Ltd v RA Wenham (Builders) Pty Ltd* [1965] NSWR 581; *Doulton Potteries Ltd v Bronotte* [1971] 1 NSWLR 591; *Howard Perry & Co v British Railways* [1980] 1 WLR 1375; *McKeown v Cavalier Yachts Pty Ltd* (1988) 13 NSWLR 303. See [10.114]–[10.118] and [13.25].

2   R Nolan, 'Equitable Property' (2006) 122 LQR 232, 233. Cf B Mcfarlane and R Stevens, 'The Nature of Equitable Property' (2010) 4 J Eq 1, who argue that equitable proprietary rights are merely 'persistent' rights against a right.

3   However, the 'mere equity' or proprietary power may be defeated even by a subsequent *equitable* interest holder as long as he or she is a bona fide purchaser for value without notice.

advantage over unsecured creditors by removing assets from the pool available for distribution to creditors. In any event, the advantages conferred upon a plaintiff by the award of proprietary relief sometimes make courts reluctant to award relief unless it is necessary in the circumstances.[4]

II Proprietary remedies

Proprietary remedies in this chapter will be discussed according to Bant's division between trusts, proprietary powers and liens.[5]

[19.8]

A   Constructive and resulting trusts

When a constructive or resulting trust is imposed, the defendant is ordered by the court to hold specific property on trust for the plaintiff as beneficiary. Both constructive trusts and resulting trusts are imposed by operation of law, although the intentions of the parties may still be relevant to the court's decision to impose a trust. There is generally no expectation that the defendant will manage the property for the plaintiff, as under an express trust. The defendant must convey the property to the plaintiff at the plaintiff's request, as the plaintiff can wind up the trust pursuant to *Saunders v Vautier*.[6] Indeed, it has been said that the constructive trust exists to compel the defendant to convey the property.[7] Some commentators have asked whether we should simply have an order to convey rather than using trust mechanisms to achieve reconveyance of property.[8]

[19.9]

Trust rights have been described as 'the most durable and intrusive' equitable proprietary interests.[9] They have several advantages for a plaintiff. They are enforceable against any third parties except one who holds legal title and is a bona fide purchaser for value without notice. They are caveatable under the Torrens land system.[10] They encompass any proportionate increase in the value of the property to which they attach.[11] Trusts may also provide a basis for a plaintiff to trace into the hands of third parties.[12]

[19.10]

---

4   *Daly v Sydney Stock Exchange Ltd* (1986) 160 CLR 371; *Lister v Stubbs* (1890) 45 Ch D 1; *Sinclair Investments (UK) Ltd v Versailles Trade Finance Ltd* [2011] EWCA Civ 347, [2012] Ch 453. Cf *Attorney-General for Hong Kong v Reid* [1994] 1 AC 324; *Wambo Coal Pty Ltd v Ariff* [2007] NSWSC 589, (2007) 63 ACSR 429.

5   E Bant, 'Trusts, Powers and Liens: An Exercise in Ground-Clearing' (2009) 3 J Eq 286.

6   (1841) 4 Beav 115; 49 ER 282.

7   *Baumgartner v Baumgartner* (1987) 164 CLR 137, 153 (Toohey J), quoting with approval AW Scott, *The Law of Trusts* (3rd edn, Little and Brown 1967) [462]: 'He is not compelled to convey the property because he is a constructive trustee; it is because he can be compelled to convey it that he is a constructive trustee'.

8   E Bant, 'Trusts, Powers and Liens: An Exercise in Ground-Clearing' (2010) 4 J Eq 286; W Swadling, 'The Fiction of the Constructive Trust' (2011) 64 Curr Leg Prob 399; E Bant and M Bryan, 'Constructive Trusts and Equitable Proprietary Relief: Rethinking the Essentials' (2011) 5 J Eq 171; E Bant and M Bryan, 'Specific Restitution without Trusts' (2012) 6 J Eq 1.

9   Bant, ibid, 294.

10   *D'Albedyhll v D'Albedyhll* (1885) 3 NZLR 391; *George v Biztole Corporation Pty Ltd* (Supreme Court of Victoria, 26 February 1996); *Natuna Pty Ltd v Cook* [2007] NSWSC 121 [201]–[202]; *Deabel v V'Landys* [2002] NSWSC 438 [5].

11   Eg *Foskett v McKeown* [2001] 1 AC 102.

12   Eg *Attorney-General for Hong Kong v Reid* [1994] 1 AC 324; *Twinsectra Ltd v Yardley* [2002] UKHL 12, [2002] 2 AC 164; *FHR European Ventures LLP v Mankarious* [2013] EWCA Civ 17, [2013] 3 WLR 466.

[19.11]   Trusts are highly advantageous to a plaintiff in the event of a defendant's bankruptcy or insolvency. Once property is subject to a trust, it no longer 'belongs' to the trustee, and is unavailable for distribution to creditors.[13] Related to this advantage, a continuing difficulty with constructive trusts is the issue of timing. If a trust arises before a defendant becomes insolvent, then the asset which is the subject of the trust will not be available for distribution, but if it arises after the defendant becomes insolvent, other proprietary interests are likely to have priority.

[19.12]   Some constructive trusts arise from the moment that the cause of action arises, as with the common intention constructive trust.[14] Similarly, resulting trusts generally arise at the time when the contribution to the purchase price is made.[15]

[19.13]   However, in *Muschinski v Dodds*, Deane J in the High Court of Australia said that 'in a broad sense, the constructive trust is both an institution and a remedy of the law of equity'.[16] In other words, the trust may arise at the time of the cause of action, but for some constructive trusts, the court may in its discretion impose the trust in a remedial sense from a later point in time. Deane J went on to say:

> [N]otwithstanding that the constructive trust is remedial in both origin and nature, there does not need to have been a curial declaration or order before equity will recognize the prior existence of a constructive trust ... Where an equity court would retrospectively impose a constructive trust by way of equitable remedy, its availability as such a remedy provides the basis for, and governs the content of, its existence inter partes independently of any formal order declaring or enforcing it. In this more limited sense, the constructive trust is also properly seen as both 'remedy' and 'institution'. Indeed, for the student of equity, there can be no true dichotomy between the two notions.[17]

[19.14]   In *Muschinski v Dodds*, a de facto couple purchased property as tenants in common in equal shares with a plan to develop and use the land for an art and craft business, and to build their home. The council refused permission for the proposed developments. The couple later separated. Ms Muschinski (who had contributed almost the entire purchase price) sought a declaration that Mr Dodds held the property on trust for her absolutely. A majority of the court ordered that the property should be subject to a constructive trust, but that it should be imposed from the date of judgment to lessen the impact on third parties.[18]

[19.15]   The Australian constructive trust therefore sits on a spectrum somewhere in between the North American constructive trust (which is remedial) and the English constructive trust (which is institutional and arises immediately upon the moment that the cause of action arises). Some constructive trusts, such as the common intention constructive trust, are more institutional in nature, but in many other situations constructive trusts are more remedial in nature, as in *Muschinski* itself, and thus their award is subject to the discretion of the court. An advantage of

---

13   *Bankruptcy Act 1966* (Cth), s 116(2)(a).
14   *Parsons v McBain* [2001] FCA 376, (2001) 109 FCR 120 [9]–[13]; *Secretary, Department of Social Security v Agnew* [2000] FCA 59, (2000) 96 FCR 357 [18]–[20].
15   *Calverley v Green* (1984) 155 CLR 242.
16   (1985) 160 CLR 583, 614.
17   Ibid, 614–15.
18   Ibid, 598 (Gibbs CJ), 599 (Mason J), 623–24 (Deane J).

the Australian model is its flexibility, but the institutional-remedial constructive trust has also been criticised as intrinsically incoherent.[19]   [19.16]

Specific instances of situations when constructive trusts and resulting trusts will be awarded will be discussed when the criteria for the imposition of awards of proprietary remedies are discussed below.   [19.16]

Before moving on, a matter of terminology will be considered. Unfortunately, the words 'constructive trust' and 'constructive trustee' are used with a distinct lack of clarity. In the area of knowing receipt and knowing assistance pursuant to *Barnes v Addy*,[20] it is often said that the recipient or assistant is a 'constructive trustee',[21] but this does not mean that the recipient or assistant is subject to a proprietary remedy. It simply means that the recipient or assistant is subject to the same *personal* remedies as if he were a trustee. It is suggested that such confusing terminology should not be used in the context of recipient liability.[22] The remedies available pursuant to *Barnes v Addy* are not discussed in this book.   [19.17]

It should also be emphasised that the word 'constructive' does not mean that the court 'constructs' a trust. In a passage quoted with approval by the High Court of Australia,[23] Professor Scott noted: [19.18]

> It is sometimes said that when there are sufficient grounds for imposing a constructive trust, the court 'constructs a trust'. The expression is, of course, absurd. The word 'constructive' is derived from the verb 'construe,' not from the verb 'construct'. .... The court construes the circumstances in the sense that it explains or interprets them; it does not construct them.[24]

Consequently, it must always be kept in mind that particular fact patterns give rise to a constructive trust.

A constructive trust may also be imposed as a remedy when a plaintiff follows or traces into assets.[25] Tracing allows a beneficiary of a fiduciary duty to impose a proprietary remedy over her property or an exchange substitute in either the hands of the defendant or from a third party, subject to the defence of bona fide purchaser for value without notice. For example, in *Foskett v McKeown*,[26] a constructive trust was awarded over the proceeds of a life insurance policy where the premiums had been partly paid for with trust money which had been misappropriated by the policy holder before his death. The beneficiaries of the trust were   [19.19]

---

19   P O'Connor, 'Happy Partners or Strange Bedfellows: The Blending of Remedial and Institutional Features in the Evolving Constructive Trust' (1996) 20 MULR 735.

20   (1874) LR 9 Ch App 244. For a discussion, see, eg, C Harpum, 'The Stranger as Constructive Trustee' (1986) 102 LQR 114 and 267.

21   Eg Harpum, ibid.

22   W Swadling, 'Constructive Trusts and Breach of Fiduciary Duty' (2012) 18 *Trusts and Trustees* 985, 986–87; *Dubai Aluminium Co Ltd v Salaam* [2002] UKHL 48, [2003] 2 AC 366 [141] (Lord Millett). Cf *Giumelli v Giumelli* [1999] HCA 10, (1999) 196 CLR 101 [4].

23   *Giumelli v Giumelli* [1999] HCA 10, (1999) 196 CLR 101 [2]. See also *Grimaldi v Chameleon Mining NL (No 2)* [2012] FCAFC 6, (2012) 200 FCR 296 [504] (referring to 'construing' the circumstances to find a constructive trust).

24   AW Scott and WF Fratcher, *Scott on Trusts*, vol 5 (4th edn, Aspen 1989) [462.4].

25   See M Bryan, V Vann and S Barkehall Thomas, *Equity & Trusts in Australia* (2nd edn, CUP 2017) ch 21 for a more detailed exposition of the rules of tracing.

26   [2001] 1 AC 102.

entitled to a constructive trust over the proceeds of the insurance policy in the proportion to which they had contributed to the premiums.

[19.20] The advantage of gaining a constructive trust as a remedy through tracing is that the plaintiff will take any proportionate increase in value, and will have priority in insolvency. Tracing and the constructive trust overlap in many aspects, but they also differ, as McDonald observes.[27] A tracing right persists against even an entirely innocent volunteer as long as the property or the exchange substitute is still identifiable, but is defeated when the property or substitute is destroyed or dissipated. A constructive trust can be imposed in many circumstances beyond tracing, but is unlikely to be enforceable against an innocent volunteer without a tracing right attached.

B   Proprietary powers

[19.21] A proprietary power is the interest arising when a plaintiff elects to rescind a contract in equity; see [18.47]. Equitable rescission may be possible, for example, in cases of misrepresentation (including innocent misrepresentation), duress, undue influence, and breach of fiduciary duty.

[19.22] The term 'proprietary power' has not yet gained judicial acceptance.[28] The equitable power to rescind is often described as a 'mere equity',[29] which blossoms into a full constructive trust once election occurs.[30] However, 'proprietary power' is a clearer and more descriptive term. The notion of the interest as a 'power' indicates that before the plaintiff elects to rescind, she has only a proprietary interest *in potential* (a 'mere equity'), but once the election to rescind occurs, a fully vested proprietary interest (a constructive trust) comes into being.[31]

[19.23] The unexercised proprietary power or mere equity is more fragile than a vested trust right.[32] Neither common law nor equitable proprietary powers will survive if legal title is gained by a bona fide purchaser for value without notice.[33] An unexercised equitable right to rescind is defeated even by a subsequent bona fide purchaser of the equitable estate.[34] In Victoria,[35] and

---

27   B McDonald, 'Constructive Trusts' in P Parkinson (ed) *The Principles of Equity* (2nd edn, LBC 2003) [2126].
28   The term is taken from E Bant, 'Trusts, Powers and Liens: An Exercise in Ground-Clearing' (2009) 3 J Eq 286, who builds in turn on B Häcker, *Consequences of Impaired Consent Transfers* (Mohr Siebeck 2009); B Häcker, 'Proprietary Restitution after Impaired Consent Transfers: A Generalised Power Model' (2009) 68 Camb LJ 324.
29   *Latec Investments Limited v Hotel Terrigal Pty Ltd* (1965) 113 CLR 265, 277, 290; *Tutt v Doyle* (1997) 42 NSWLR 10, 15.
30   *Daly v Sydney Stock Exchange Ltd* (1986) 160 CLR 371, 388–90 (Brennan J).
31   *Latec Investments Limited v Hotel Terrigal Pty Ltd* (1965) 113 CLR 265, which involved a rationalisation of the lines of authority represented by *Phillips v Phillips* (1861) 4 De G F & J 208, 45 ER 1164 (mere equity) and *Stump v Gaby* (1852) 2 De GM & G 613, 42 ER 1015 (vested equitable interest).
32   R Chambers, *An Introduction to Property Law in Australia* (3rd edn, LBC 2013) [24.70], [28.115], [29.145]– [29.155].
33   Legal rescission is thus more fragile than other legal proprietary rights: ibid.
34   *Latec Investments Limited v Hotel Terrigal Pty Ltd* (1965) 113 CLR 265. See also *Ruthol Pty Ltd v Mills* [2003] NSWCA 56, (2003) 11 BPR 20,793.
35   *Classic Heights Pty Ltd v Black Hole Enterprises Pty Ltd* [1995] ANZ ConvR 260; *Crampton v French* [1996] ANZ ConvR 156; *Swanston Mortgage Pty Ltd v Trepan Investments Pty Ltd* [1994] 1 VR 672. In *Vasiliou v Westpac Banking Corporation* [2007] VSCA 113, (2007) 19 VR 229 [120]–[121], it was noted that *Swanston* had been criticised by commentators but could not be overruled without a bench of five appellate judges.

possibly in other Australian jurisdictions,[36] an unexercised power to rescind a transfer of property may not be a 'caveatable interest' under the Torrens system. However, authority in other Australian jurisdictions suggests that a power to rescind is caveatable,[37] and commentators have criticised the Victorian approach.[38] It is unclear whether proprietary powers survive the bankruptcy or insolvency of the person who holds the asset that is the subject of the power.[39]

C   Equitable liens

Liens exist both at common law and in equity. The common law lien allows a person (the creditor) to retain possession of property to secure repayment of a debt by another person who has legal title to the property (the debtor). An example is a garage owner's lien, which arises when a mechanic has repaired a car. The mechanic obtains a lien over the car for the value of the unpaid work, and may retain possession of the car until the repair work is paid for. A common law lien does not generally give the creditor (such as the mechanic) a right to sell the property,[40] but only allows the creditor the right to retain possession of the property until the debt is paid.   [19.24]

Equitable liens do not require possession by the creditor.[41] The court imposes them upon property in the hands of the debtor. They can be distinguished from equitable charges, a species of equitable security interest that arises by agreement.[42]   [19.25]

In contrast to a common law lien, an equitable lien gives the creditor the right to seek an order for judicial sale of the property to which the lien attaches to satisfy the debt owed. The proceeds of sale will be used to pay the amount owed to her, including interest and costs. However, liens do not encompass any subsequent increase in value of the property.   [19.26]

An example of an equitable lien which arises by operation of law is the vendor's lien, which is the counterpart of the constructive trust arising in favour of the purchaser upon entry into a specifically enforceable contract of sale. Once the vendor has transferred title to the property into the purchaser's name, the vendor will generally have an equitable lien over the property to   [19.27]

---

36   See *Re Pile's Caveat* [1981] Qd R 81; *Wickham Developments Ltd v Parker* (QCA, 20 June 1995); *Tanzone Pty Ltd v Westpac Banking Corporation* [1999] NSWSC 478, (2000) 9 BPR 17,287; *Global Minerals Australia Pty Ltd v Valerica Pty Ltd* [2000] NSWSC 1143, (2000) 10 BPR 18,463; *Lilex Pty Ltd (rec and mgr apptd) v Smallseeds Pty Ltd* [2011] NSWSC 1426.

37   *Breskvar v Wall* (1971) 126 CLR 376, 409; *Sinclair v Hope Investments Pty Ltd* [1982] 2 NSWLR 870, 875; *Re McKeane's Caveat* [1988] 1 Qd R 524, 525; *Re Cross v National Australia Bank Ltd* [1993] ANZ ConvR 28; *Patmore v Upton* [2004] TASSC 77, (2004) 13 Tas R 95 [61].

38   S Roderick, 'The Response of Torrens Mortgagors to Improper Mortgagee Sales' (2006) 22 Monash ULR 289, 336– 42; D Wright, 'Does the Registered Proprietor Have a Caveatable Interest?' (1995) 69 Aust LJ 935; JD Heydon, MJ Leeming and PG Turner, *Meagher, Gummow and Lehane's Equity: Doctrines and Remedies* (5th edn, LexisNexis Butterworths 2015) [4–205].

39   Bankruptcy precluded the exercise of a power to rescind in *Westpac Banking Corporation v Markovic* (1985) 82 FLR 7, whereas a power to rescind for misrepresentation survived the liquidation of the misrepresentor in *Re York Street Mezzanine Pty Ltd (in liq)* [2007] FCA 922, (2007) 162 FCR 358. See P Watts, 'Constructive Trusts and Insolvency' (2010) 3 J Eq 250, 265–70; E Bant, 'Trusts, Powers and Liens: An Exercise in Ground-Clearing' (2010) 4 J Eq 286, 301–03.

40   R Chambers, *An Introduction to Property Law in Australia* (3rd edn, LBC 2013) [14.30], noting some statutory exceptions to this.

41   *Firth v Centrelink* [2002] NSWSC 564, (2002) 55 NSWLR 451.

42   PW Young, C Croft and ML Smith, *On Equity* (LBC 2009) 653; R Chambers, *An Introduction to Property Law in Australia* (3rd edn, LBC 2013) [14.60].

the extent that the purchase price remains unpaid.[43] Other instances where liens will arise include a 'fruits of litigation' lien (where a solicitor has a lien over money recovered by a client to secure costs and disbursements) and a liquidator's lien.[44]

[19.28]   The lien arises when the events creating it occur.[45] Like the constructive trust, a lien is enforceable against whoever holds legal title to the property to which it attaches, unless that person is a bona fide purchaser for value of the legal title without notice of the lien. Equitable liens are caveatable interests under the Torrens system.[46]

[19.29]   A lien over an asset confers a true priority on insolvency. At common law, the trustee in bankruptcy must pay off the debt before he can get the asset back from the creditor (for example, the mechanic mentioned in [19.24]). In equity, once the debt is satisfied out of the sale of the asset, the remainder of the proceeds of sale go back into the pool of funds available for distribution to creditors.

[19.30]   As Chambers notes, the equitable lien preserves the defendant's freedom of choice as to how he will repay the plaintiff.[47] The defendant may be able to discharge the debt secured by the lien with other funds and retain the asset. The lien preserves the defendant's autonomy to a greater degree than a vested trust interest.

[19.31]   A lien may also be imposed when a plaintiff traces into assets. For example, in *Scott v Scott*,[48] a lien was awarded over a house which a trustee had purchased using trust assets in breach of trust. The beneficiaries of the trust were entitled to a lien reflecting the proportionate contribution of trust moneys towards the price of the house. The High Court of Australia indicated that it would have been willing to consider awarding a constructive trust, but a lien was all that was sought by the plaintiffs.[49] Unlike a constructive trust, a lien will not capture any increase in value after the date of judgment, but the holder of a lien will still have priority in insolvency. Again, tracing and liens overlap in many aspects, but have different fields of operation in the same way discussed previously with regard to constructive trusts.

III   Criteria for award of proprietary remedies

[19.32]   For a proprietary remedy to be imposed, two basic criteria must be met:

1.   The defendant must hold identifiable property to which the proprietary remedy can attach.

2.   The cause of action giving rise to liability must be made out (so, for example, if a constructive trust is imposed for breach of fiduciary duty, the elements of breach of fiduciary duty must be made out first).

---

43   *Reliance Finance Corporation Pty Ltd v Heid* [1982] 1 NSWLR 446, 478, aff'd *Heid v Reliance Finance Corporation Pty Ltd* (1983) 154 CLR 326.
44   PW Young, C Croft and ML Smith, *On Equity* (LBC 2009) 657.
45   E Bant, 'Trusts, Powers and Liens: An Exercise in Ground-Clearing' (2009) 28 J Eq 286, 304.
46   *Composite Buyers Ltd v Soong* (1995) 38 NSWLR 286; *Big River Timbers Pty Ltd v Stewart* [1999] NSWCA 34, (1999) 9 BPR 16,605.
47   R Chambers, 'Resulting Trusts in Canada (Part II)' (2002) 16 TLI 138, 143–44.
48   (1963) 109 CLR 649.
49   Ibid, 661–64.

Other than these two criteria, the criteria for awarding proprietary remedies are unclear. For example, somewhat discouragingly, constructive trusts have been described as 'a vague dust-heap for the reception of relationships which are difficult to classify or which are unwanted in other branches of the law'[50] and as a 'rag-bag of instances having little in common'.[51]

The High Court of Australia is concerned that proprietary remedies are awarded sparingly [19.33] so that innocent third parties will not be adversely affected. In *Bathurst City Council v PWC Properties Pty Ltd*, the High Court said:

> [B]efore the court imposes a constructive trust as a remedy, it should first decide whether, having regard to the issues in the litigation, there are other means available to quell the controversy. An equitable remedy which falls short of the imposition of a trust may assist in avoiding a result whereby the plaintiff gains a beneficial proprietary interest which gives an unfair priority over other equally deserving creditors of the defendant.[52]

In those categories of case which sit on the 'remedial' end of Deane J's remedial– [19.34] institutional spectrum,[53] there is discretion to award a lesser proprietary remedy than a constructive trust, or no proprietary remedy at all where the circumstances of the case demand it. For example, the High Court of Australia in *Giumelli v Giumelli* said that the minimum equity to do justice between the parties would suffice in a case of equitable estoppel, and a constructive trust should not be imposed if a less intrusive remedy is more appropriate.[54] The plaintiff was awarded a personal remedy for equitable estoppel because of concerns that third parties with an interest in the disputed property would be unfairly affected if a constructive trust were awarded.

In *Muschinski v Dodds*, Deane J explained that a constructive trust would only be available: [19.35]

> when warranted by established equitable principles or by the legitimate processes of legal reasoning, by analogy, induction and deduction, from the starting point of a proper understanding of the conceptual foundation of such principles . . .[55]

The starting point is to look at the established cases where proprietary remedies have been awarded to work out whether the case at hand fits into one of the categories.

Several animating principles have been argued to govern the imposition of proprietary [19.36] remedies, including unconscionability, unjust enrichment, and wrongdoing, but none can explain all cases. Elias has argued that constructive trusts achieve a variety of aims, including perfection of incomplete transactions, restitution of gains and reparation for wrongdoing.[56] It seems clear that the same could be said of proprietary remedies more generally – they have a

---

50   E Sykes, 'The Doctrine of Constructive Trusts' (1941) 15 Aust LJ 171, 175.
51   RP Austin, 'Constructive Trusts' in PD Finn (ed), *Essays in Equity* (LBC 1985) 196.
52   [1998] HCA 59, (1998) 195 CLR 566 [42] (Gaudron, McHugh, Gummow, Hayne and Callinan JJ). See also
      Giumelli v Giumelli [1999] HCA 10, (1999) 196 CLR 101 [10], [49]–[50]; *John Alexander's Clubs Pty Ltd v
      White City Tennis Club Ltd* [2010] HCA 19, (2010) 241 CLR 1 [126]–[129].
53   See above [19.13]–[19.15].
54   [1999] HCA 10, (1999) 196 CLR 101.
55   (1985) 160 CLR 583, 615.
56   G Elias, *Explaining Constructive Trusts* (Clarendon Press 1990).

multiplicity of aims, including the perfection of expectations, the reversal of unjust enrichment, the prevention of wrongdoing and the protection of expenditure in reliance.[57]

[19.37]   Any scheme seeking to divide proprietary remedies into categories is necessarily fraught with peril. As Pill LJ noted in *FHR European Ventures LLP v Mankarious*, '[c]onsideration of the views of commentators and practitioners generally on the subject of constructive trusts ... reveals passions of a force uncommon in the legal world'.[58] Nevertheless, we proceed to divide proprietary remedies into categories that reflect different aims: namely, whether the court seeks to perfect incomplete transactions, reverse unjust enrichment or respond to wrong-doing.[59] However, given the Australian context of this text, it is first necessary to discuss unconscionability as a basis for the imposition of a constructive trust.

A   Proprietary remedies and unconscionability

[19.38]   The touchstone for the imposition of many proprietary remedies in Australia is said to be 'unconscionability', or the notion that equity imposes a proprietary remedy where it would be unconscionable for the legal title holder to deny the plaintiff's proprietary interest. In *Westdeutsche Landesbank Girozentrale v Islington London Borough Council*, in an English context, Lord Browne-Wilkinson said that unconscionability was the general principle behind the imposition of all constructive trusts,[60] and that the defendant's conscience must be 'touched' before a constructive trust can be imposed.[61] However, it is only in the most general sense that unconscionability could be said to lie behind all constructive trusts.[62]

[19.39]   This is partly because there are multiple meanings of unconscionability, including protection of the vulnerable, protecting the integrity of bargaining processes, enforcing reasonable expectations, and preventing substantive unfairness.[63] However, Deane J in *Muschinski v Dodds* emphasised that the constructive trust imposed on the basis of unconscionability was not 'a medium for the indulgence of idiosyncratic notions of fairness and justice'.[64] In this context, unconscionability has a settled meaning: conduct will be unconscionable where the plaintiff had a reasonable expectation of receiving property and this has been defeated by the defendant's conduct,[65] and equitable principle supports the imposition of a constructive trust.[66]

57   M Bryan, V Vann and S Barkehall Thomas, *Equity & Trusts in Australia* (2nd edn, CUP 2017) [23.6]–[23.11].
58   [2013] EWCA Civ 17, [2014] Ch 1 [61].
59   This broadly but not exactly follows the scheme of G Elias, *Explaining Constructive Trusts* (Clarendon Press 1990).
60   [1996] AC 669 ('*Westdeutsche*'), 705.
61   Ibid, 714. Applied in Australia in *Wambo Coal Pty Ltd v Ariff* [2007] NSWSC 589, (2007) 63 ACSR 429 [34]–[44].
62   G Virgo, *The Principles of Equity and Trusts* (2nd edn, OUP 2016) 328.
63   P Parkinson, 'The Conscience of Equity' in P Parkinson (ed), *The Principles of Equity* (2nd edn, LBC 2003) [201].
64   (1985) 160 CLR 583, 615. This was a reference to a line of English cases promulgated by Lord Denning MR, who awarded constructive trusts wherever 'justice and good conscience' demanded it: *Eves v Eves* [1975] 1 WLR 1338, 1341–42. Cf *Burns v Burns* [1984] Ch 317.
65   M Bryan, V Vann and S Barkehall Thomas, *Equity & Trusts in Australia* (2nd edn, CUP 2017) [23.9].
66   B McDonald, 'Constructive Trusts' in P Parkinson (ed), *The Principles of Equity* (2nd edn, LBC 2003) [2138].

Only the *Baumgartner* constructive trust is imposed to prevent unconscionable conduct in the sense just mentioned: for other constructive trusts, the defendant's moral turpitude need not be established.[67]

Unconscionability has also been said to be the basis for the imposition of liens. In *Hewett v Court*,[68] Deane J said that an equitable lien would be imposed on the parties to a contract where:

1. there was actual or potential indebtedness on the part of the owner of the property to which the lien attaches to the other party, where that indebtedness arose from a payment or promise of payment in relation to the property;

2. the property (or property including that property) could be specifically identified by the court and linked to the performance of the contract; and

3. the relationship between the actual or potential indebtedness and the identified and appropriated property was such that the owner would be acting *unconscionably* or *unfairly* if he disposed of the property to a third party without the consent of the other party or without the actual or potential liability being discharged.

Hewett v Court has been criticised by Calnan because it is difficult to see why the plaintiff was awarded a lien when the contract did not grant him a security interest.[69] Moreover, the plaintiff had not previously owned the house, nor was it a substitute for an asset that had been disposed of. Calnan concludes that this case carries equitable intervention too far.

Ultimately, despite its popularity in an Australian context, the notion of unconscionability as a touchstone of proprietary liability confuses more than it illuminates, unless there is greater specificity about what aspect of the transaction makes it unconscionable. In some cases, a proprietary remedy is imposed for reasons of perfection: in other words, the defendant has promised the plaintiff an interest in property, and then reneged upon it or failed to complete. In other cases, a proprietary remedy is (arguably) imposed to reverse unjust enrichment where the defendant has unjustly gained property at the plaintiff's expense. Finally, in other cases, proprietary remedies are imposed to deter wrongdoing and effect disgorgement of profit where the defendant has committed a wrong and gained without a corresponding loss on the part of the plaintiff.

[19.40]

[19.41]

[19.42]

B   Proprietary remedies and perfection

Elias says that some constructive trusts are imposed with the aim of 'perfection', specifically when a defendant has chosen to dispose of his property in favour of the plaintiff.[70] Trusts which fall under this category arise when the plaintiff had a reasonable expectation of receiving property and the defendant reneges or otherwise fails to complete the transaction. However, it should be noted that the defendant need not display moral turpitude for a proprietary interest to be imposed (except in the case of *Baumgartner* constructive trusts).

[19.43]

---

67   M Bryan, V Vann and S Barkehall Thomas, *Equity & Trusts in Australia* (2nd edn, CUP 2017) [23.9]. See *Baumgartner v Baumgartner* (1987) 164 CLR 137.
68   (1983) 149 CLR 639, 668. See also *Cadorange Pty Ltd v Tanga Holdings Pty Ltd* (1990) 20 NSWLR 26, 35–36.
69   R Calnan, 'Imposing Proprietary Interests in Insolvencies' (2013) 24 JBFLP 18, 27
70   G Elias, *Explaining Constructive Trusts* (Clarendon Press 1990) 4, 10–16.

On the other hand, in some (but not all) instances, there may be detrimental reliance on the part of the plaintiff which makes it unjust for the defendant to depart from the expectation. Proprietary interests arising on this basis include:

- where a fiduciary obtains property, or an opportunity which ought to have been the beneficiary's, in breach of fiduciary duty;[71]
- where a fiduciary misappropriates property from a beneficiary in breach of fiduciary duty;[72]
- where there was a common intention for the parties to hold the property in a way not reflected in the legal title;[73]
- in a domestic situation where it would be unconscionable to allow one party to the relationship to claim the benefit of the legal title;[74]
- where there is a specifically enforceable contract for the sale of land[75] or unique goods;[76]
- in cases of incomplete gifts;[77]
- in cases of mutual wills[78] and 'secret' trusts;[79] and
- in cases of equitable estoppel, but only where such a remedy would be appropriate.[80]

C   Proprietary remedies and unjust enrichment

[19.44]   Another way of understanding the imposition of proprietary remedies is through an unjust enrichment analysis. In other words, a proprietary remedy will be imposed where the defendant would be unjustly enriched if she were entitled to retain legal title to the property.[81] It should be emphasised that this explanation should be treated with care in an Australian context.[82] Historically, US law has seen the constructive trust as a remedy imposed on the basis that the defendant has been unjustly enriched at the plaintiff's expense.[83]

---

71   *Keech v Sandford* (1726) Sel Cas T King 61; 25 ER 223; *Chan v Zacharia* (1984) 154 CLR 178; *Boardman v Phipps* [1967] 2 AC 46.
72   *Black v S Freedman & Co* (1910) 12 CLR 105.
73   *Ogilvie v Ryan* [1976] 2 NSWLR 504; *Allan v Snyder* [1977] 2 NSWLR 685; *Kardynal v Dodek* (1977) 5 Fam LR 706; *Hohol v Hohol* [1981] VR 221; *Green v Green* (1989) 17 NSWLR 343; *Parsons v McBain* [2001] FCA 376, (2001) 109 FCR 120.
74   *Baumgartner v Baumgartner* (1987) 164 CLR 137.
75   *Lysaght v Edwards* (1876) 2 Ch D 499; *Chang v Registrar of Titles* (1976) 137 CLR 177, 185 (Mason J). The law was summarised in *Englewood Properties Limited v Patel* [2005] EWHC 188 (Ch), [2005] 1 WLR 1961 [40]–[43].
76   *Holroyd v Marshall* (1862) 10 HL Cas 191, 209; 11 ER 999, 1006 (Lord Westbury LC).
77   *Re Rose* [1952] Ch 499; *Corin v Patton* (1990) 169 CLR 540.
78   Eg *Birmingham v Renfrew* (1937) 57 CLR 666, 689–91; *Re Goodchild* [1997] 1 WLR 1216; *University of Manitoba v Sanderson Estate* (1998) 155 DLR (4th) 40; *Olins v Walters* [2008] EWCA Civ 782, [2009] Ch 212.
79   Eg *Re Boyes* (1884) 26 Ch D 531.
80   *Thorner v Major* [2009] UKHL 18, [2009] 1 WLR 776. A personal remedy was granted in *Giumelli v Giumelli* [1999] HCA 10, (1999) 196 CLR 101.
81   See, eg, P Birks, *Unjust Enrichment* (2nd edn, OUP 2005) 302; A Burrows, *The Law of Restitution* (3rd edn, OUP 2011) ch 8.
82   M Bryan, V Vann and S Barkehall Thomas, *Equity & Trusts in Australia* (2nd edn, CUP 2017) [23.7]–[23.8].
83   See American Law Institute, *Restatement of Restitution: Quasi-contract and Constructive Trusts* (1936).

Unjust enrichment scholars concede that unjust enrichment cannot provide a complete explanation for all proprietary remedies.[84] Similarly, in *Stephenson Nominees Pty Ltd v Official Receiver*,[85] Gummow J warned that the constructive trust is sometimes awarded in situations where there is no unjust enrichment, but rather it is intended to enforce observance of certain duties (as with the constructive trusts imposed on fiduciaries).

[19.45]

Circumstances in which scholars have explained the proprietary remedy according to an unjust enrichment analysis include:

[19.46]

- where property has been acquired by reason of a mistake;[86]
- where a transaction can be set aside because of undue influence or duress;[87]
- where a transaction can be set aside because of the unconscionable nature of the bargain;[88]
- where there is a failure of consideration (meaning a failure of the purpose of the bargain which has led to the defendant's enrichment);[89] and
- more generally, where there is an 'absence of an intention to benefit' on the part of the plaintiff towards the defendant.

None of these instances involves unconscionability in the sense mentioned above at [19.39], namely, where a plaintiff had a reasonable expectation of receiving property but that expectation was defeated by the defendant's conduct.[90] Rather, these cases involve the reversal or rescission of an impugned transaction. As noted at [18.6], the remedy of rescission is amenable to a restitutionary analysis. Under such an analysis, the 'unjust factors' giving rise to a right to a restitutionary proprietary remedy in the first, second and third instances mentioned above would be 'mistake', 'compulsion' and 'unconscionability' respectively. For example, a constructive trust imposed where property is acquired by mistake can be explained under an unjust enrichment analysis, and rescission of a transaction on the basis of undue influence, duress or unconscionability could be seen to prevent unjust enrichment on the part of the defendant.[91]

The proprietary response in these cases varies, and the cases are highly fact specific. A range of remedies has been awarded, including full constructive trusts,[92] proprietary powers,[93] liens,[94] or no remedy at all.[95]

[19.47]

---

84 P Birks, *Unjust Enrichment* (2nd edn, OUP 2005) 301.
85 (1987) 16 FCR 536, 553.
86 *Chase Manhattan NA v Israel-British Bank (London)* [1981] Ch 105 ('*Chase Manhattan*'). Cf *Westdeutsche* [1996] AC 669, 715 (Lord Browne-Wilkinson).
87 *Reid v Reid* (NSWSC, 30 November 1998); *Quek v Beggs* (1990) 5 BPR 11,761; *Badman v Drake* [2008] NSWSC 1366. See E Bant, 'Trusts, Powers and Liens: An Exercise in Ground-Clearing' (2009) 3 J Eq 286, 306–07.
88 *Louth v Diprose* (1992) 175 CLR 621.
89 See, eg, *Muschinski v Dodds* (1985) 160 CLR 583 discussed below at [19.53].
90 The exception to this is perhaps failure of consideration under Australian legal principles, which can be conceived of as unconscionable retention of title.
91 E Bant, 'Trusts, Powers and Liens: An Exercise in Ground-Clearing' (2010) 4 J Eq 286, 306–07.
92 *Chase Manhattan* [1981] Ch 105; *Reid v Reid* (NSWSC, 30 November 1998); *Louth v Diprose* (1992) 175 CLR 621.
93 *Quek v Beggs* (1990) 5 BPR 11,761; and arguably *Wambo Coal Pty Ltd v Ariff* [2007] NSWSC 589, (2007) 63 ACSR 429.
94 *Badman v Drake* [2008] NSWSC 1366.
95 *Allcard v Skinner* (1887) 36 Ch D 145.

[19.48]   In the first instance mentioned at [19.46], where property is acquired by means of mistake, it is questionable whether and when a constructive trust should be available to effect return of mistakenly transferred property. *Chase Manhattan*,[96] a controversial English case, suggests that a constructive trust may be awarded from the moment of mistaken receipt, regardless of whether the recipient knew of the mistake. A clerk employed by the plaintiff bank, Chase Manhattan, mistakenly made a double payment of US$2 million to the defendant bank, Israel-British Bank. Before the plaintiff could recover the second mistaken payment, the defendant became insolvent. The plaintiff could not recover the entire US$2 million in the insolvency if it merely had a personal remedy, and thus it sought a proprietary remedy. Goulding J held that the defendant held the mistaken payment on constructive trust for the plaintiff from the moment of receipt because the plaintiff retained an equitable property right in the money. The plaintiff could recover the entire mistaken payment. Brennan J in the High Court of Australia referred to *Chase Manhattan* with apparent approval in *Daly v Sydney Stock Exchange Ltd*.[97] However, the result in *Chase Manhattan* is controversial and has been judicially criticised in Australia[98] and in England and Wales.[99]

[19.49]   *Chase Manhattan* should be treated with care in Australia in light of the NSW Supreme Court's decision in *Wambo Coal Pty Ltd v Ariff*.[100] *Wambo* suggests that a constructive trust will only be imposed over a mistaken payment from the time that the defendant knew of the mistake. The plaintiff, Wambo Coal Pty Ltd ('Wambo'), made two mistaken payments to the first defendant, Singleton Earthmoving Pty Ltd ('Singleton'). Prior to the mistaken payments, Mr Ariff had been appointed as administrator (and later liquidator) of Singleton. Mr Ariff caused most of the money paid by Wambo to Singleton to be transferred to a company he controlled, to reimburse it for disbursements it had paid (on his behalf) in the liquidation of Singleton. Mr Ariff was notified of the mistake after he had already transferred some of Wambo's money to his company, but continued to transfer money to his company after this. Counsel for Wambo argued that Wambo retained the equitable title to the property it transferred from the moment of the mistaken payment pursuant to *Chase Manhattan*. However, White J said that a mistaken payee could be bound by a constructive trust only where his conscience was touched by knowledge of the mistake.[101] Mr Ariff and Singleton were subject to a constructive trust over the mistaken payments only once Mr Ariff became aware of the mistake. It was irrelevant that Singleton was insolvent, and that it would be an unwarranted windfall for the company's creditors (really Mr Ariff) to have access to this payment. As Bant has argued, it could be said that, prior to telling Ariff and Singleton of the mistake, Wambo had an unexercised proprietary power, and it was only after Wambo had informed Ariff and Singleton of the mistake that it could get a constructive trust over those moneys which Ariff knew were mistakenly received.[102]

---

96   [1981] Ch 105.
97   (1986) 160 CLR 371, 390.
98   *Cashflow Finance Pty Ltd (in liq) v Westpac Banking Corporation* [1999] NSWSC 671; *Wambo Coal Pty Ltd v Ariff* [2007] NSWSC 589, (2007) 63 ACSR 429.
99   *Westdeutsche* [1996] AC 669, 714–15 (Lord Browne-Wilkinson).
100   [2007] NSWSC 589, (2007) 63 ACSR 429. Cf *Young v Lalic* [2006] NSWSC 18, (2006) 197 FLR 27.
101   [2007] NSWSC 589, (2007) 63 ACSR 429 [34]–[44].
102   E Bant, 'Trusts, Powers and Liens: An Exercise in Ground-Clearing' (2010) 4 J Eq 286, 309–10.

In the second instance mentioned at [19.46], where a transaction can be set aside because of undue influence or duress, a variety of remedies have been imposed, including full constructive trusts,[103] proprietary powers,[104] liens,[105] or no remedy at all.[106] Bant and Bryan argue that a proprietary power model can explain these cases. Where the defendant has taken the plaintiff's asset, it remains in the hands of the defendant, it is unique and the plaintiff has elected to seek its return, Bant and Bryan argue that the plaintiff is entitled to 'specific restitution' (a constructive trust).[107] However, where the asset has been exchanged for another asset, the plaintiff should be entitled to the value of the asset secured by a lien.[108] Bant and Bryan argue that equitable discretionary considerations, including hardship, laches, and third party considerations, should be taken into account by courts.[109] It should be observed that some unjust enrichment scholars such as Birks take a monist view and frown on discretion.[110] Like Bant and Bryan,[111] we take the view that discretion is appropriate, as long as the criteria according to which the discretion is exercised are clear.

[19.50]

A full constructive trust is more likely to be awarded in cases where there are no third party interests or other equitable bars to relief, and where the plaintiff has a special interest in the property, as in *Reid v Reid*.[112] By contrast, a proprietary power may be more appropriate where third party interests need to be accommodated and there is an inability to effect complete proprietary *restitutio in integrum*, as in *Quek v Beggs*.[113] A lien may be more appropriate if the plaintiff has no particular attachment to the asset, the asset is not the plaintiff's original asset, and the imposition of a constructive trust over the defendants' house would impose hardship on the defendants by giving the plaintiff an asset for much less than it was worth, as in *Badman v Drake*.[114] Finally, a plaintiff who has unduly delayed in seeking rescission may obtain no remedy at all, as in *Allcard v Skinner*.[115]

[19.51]

In the third instance mentioned at [19.46], where a transaction is set aside on the basis of unconscionable conduct,[116] constructive trusts have been awarded, as in *Louth v Diprose*.[117] However, scenarios could be envisaged where a lesser proprietary interest or no interest at all would be awarded because of intervening third party interests, an inability to effect complete *restitutio in integrum*, hardship to the defendant, or delay on the part of the plaintiff.

[19.52]

---

103   *Reid v Reid* (NSW Supreme Court, 30 November 1998).
104   *Quek v Beggs* (1990) 5 BPR 11,761.
105   *Badman v Drake* [2008] NSWSC 1366.
106   *Allcard v Skinner* (1887) 36 Ch D 145.
107   E Bant and M Bryan, 'A Model of Proprietary Remedies' in E Bant and M Bryan (eds), *Principles of Proprietary Remedies* (Thomson Reuters 2013) [12.160]–[12.180].
108   Ibid, [12.190].
109   E Bant and M Bryan, 'Defences, Bars and Discretionary Factors' in E Bant and M Bryan (eds), *Principles of Proprietary Remedies* (Thomson Reuters 2013) ch 11.
110   See [1.27]–[1.29]; P Birks, 'Three Kinds of Objection to Discretionary Remedialism' (2000) 29 UWALR 1.
111   E Bant and M Bryan, 'A Model of Proprietary Remedies' in E Bant and M Bryan (eds), *Principles of Proprietary Remedies* (Thomson Reuters 2013) [12.220].
112   (NSW Supreme Court, 30 November 1998).
113   (1990) 5 BPR 11,761.
114   [2008] NSWSC 1366.
115   (1887) 36 Ch D 145.
116   Unconscionability here means taking advantage of the other party's 'special disadvantage'.
117   (1992) 175 CLR 621.

[19.53]   In the fourth instance mentioned at [19.46], where there has been a failure of the purpose of the bargain which has led to the defendant's enrichment, Australian courts have used 'unconscionability'[118] to justify the imposition of a constructive trust. However, cases such as *Muschinski v Dodds* could be understood to prevent unjust enrichment where there has been a failure of consideration.[119] As noted at [19.14], *Muschinski v Dodds* involved the breakdown of a relationship and a business. Deane J explained:

> [T]he principle [allowing for the imposition of a constructive trust] operates in a case where the substratum of a joint relationship or endeavour is removed without attributable blame and where the benefit of money or other property contributed by one party on the basis and for the purposes of the relationship or endeavour would otherwise be enjoyed by the other party in circumstances in which it was not specifically intended or specially provided that that other party should so enjoy it. The content of the principle is that, in such a case, equity will not permit that other party to assert or retain the benefit of the relevant property to the extent that it would be unconscionable for him so to do.[120]

In *Roxborough v Rothmans of Pall Mall Australia Ltd*, the High Court of Australia observed that *Muschinski v Dodds* could be understood as an instance of failure of consideration,[121] in the sense that the purpose of the bargain failed, which led to the defendant's enrichment. Accordingly, it has been suggested that the constructive trust in *Muschinski v Dodds* was imposed on the basis of failure of consideration.[122] However, this assertion must be treated with care. Generally Australian cases have required that, before any proprietary interest can arise for failure of consideration, the recipient of the property must *know* at the time of transfer that the arrangement or contract which failed was unable to take place.[123]

[19.54]   Finally, the fifth instance mentioned at [19.46], an 'absence of an intention to benefit', has been said by Chambers to be a reason why courts impose restitutionary proprietary remedies, in particular the resulting trust.[124] The defendant is said to have been unjustly enriched because of the plaintiff's vitiated intention, and the value remaining must be returned to the plaintiff. However, this approach has not been accepted by Australian courts, and in Australia the resulting trust arises in only two narrow situations: (1) where a person contributes to the

---

118   Unconscionability here means that the plaintiff had a reasonable expectation of receiving property and this has been defeated by the defendant's conduct, as in *Baumgartner*.

119   N Witzleb, E Bant, S Degeling and K Barker, *Remedies: Commentary and Materials* (6th edn, LBC 2015) [7.35]; J Edelman, 'Australian Challenges for the Law of Unjust Enrichment' (Speech to University of Western Australia Summer School, 24 February 2012) 16–17.

120   *Muschinski v Dodds* (1985) 160 CLR 583, 618 (Deane J).

121   *Roxborough v Rothmans of Pall Mall Australia Ltd* [2001] HCA 68, (2001) 208 CLR 516 [16] (Gleeson CJ, Gaudron and Hayne JJ), [100]–[104] (Gummow J).

122   N Witzleb, E Bant, S Degeling and K Barker, *Remedies: Commentary and Materials* (6th edn, LBC 2015) [7.35]; J Edelman, 'Australian Challenges for the Law of Unjust Enrichment' (Speech to University of Western Australia Summer School, 24 February 2012) 16–17.

123   *Zuecker v Bruggmann (No 3)* [2017] QSC 259, [124] (Bond J); *Re Wan Ze Property Development (Australia) Pty Ltd* (2012) 90 ACSR 593 [51]–[52] (Black J); *Break Fast Investments Pty Ltd v Perikles Giannopoulos (also known as Perry Giannopoulos) (No 5)* [2011] NSWSC 1508 [90]–[91] (Black J); *Wambo Coal Pty Ltd v Ariff* [2007] NSWSC 589, (2007) 63 ACSR 429 [40]–[41] (White J).

124   See R Chambers, *Resulting Trusts* (OUP 1997).

purchase of property and this is not reflected in the legal title;[125] and (2) where an express trust fails to dispose of all the property which is the subject matter of the trust.[126]

Birks and Chambers argue further that 'absence of intention to benefit' could apply to all cases of proprietary restitution (including the specific instances mentioned above), with the consequence that *all* trusts presently arising in circumstances where there is an absence of an intention to benefit the recipient correspond to unjust enrichment, and are better conceived of as resulting trusts.[127] The *Chase Manhattan* constructive trust and the constructive trust imposed on a thief in *Black v S Freedman & Co*[128] have been analysed by Chambers as resulting trusts.[129] This theory has been questioned on the basis of whether resulting trusts arise because of an absence of intention to benefit,[130] and whether a proprietary power approach is more appropriate and flexible than an immediate resulting trust.[131] *Twinsectra v Yardley* could be a partial recognition of Chambers's thesis that lack of intention to benefit may be a basis for a resulting trust, as the court imposed a resulting trust where a loan was given for a purpose but the purpose was not carried out, and a resulting trust was said to arise because the lender did not intend to benefit the borrower.[132] However, Lord Millett's analysis differs from that of Chambers: he argued that the beneficial interest in the property transferred to the borrower remained with the lender throughout, subject to a power on the part of the borrower to spend for the specified purpose.[133] The *Twinsectra v Yardley* resulting trust has not been accepted in Australia.

[19.55]

D   Proprietary remedies and wrongdoing

Finally, some proprietary remedies are imposed because of wrongdoing on the part of the defendant, although, again, this does not explain all cases, and primarily operates to disgorge gains made through wrongdoing.

[19.56]

As noted at [19.43], constructive trusts are readily awarded in the context of a breach of fiduciary duty,[134] or for other equitable wrongs such as breach of confidence.[135] Courts are prepared to award a constructive trust over an asset obtained in breach of fiduciary duty in two circumstances: (1) where the fiduciary has misappropriated or stolen property belonging to the beneficiary;[136] and (2) where the fiduciary was under a duty to acquire the property for

[19.57]

---

125   *Westdeutsche* [1996] AC 669.
126   *Re Vandervell's Trusts (No 2)* [1974] Ch 269, 294.
127   P Birks, 'Restitution and Resulting Trusts' in S Goldstein (ed), *Equity and Contemporary Legal Developments* (Sacker Institute 1992); R Chambers, *Resulting Trusts* (OUP 1997).
128   (1910) 12 CLR 105.
129   R Chambers, *Resulting Trusts* (OUP 1997); R Chambers, 'Trust and Theft' in E Bant and M Harding (eds), *Exploring Private Law* (CUP 2010) 223.
130   W Swadling, 'Explaining Resulting Trusts' (2008) 124 LQR 72.
131   B Häcker, 'Proprietary Restitution after Impaired Consent Transfers: A Generalised Power Model' (2009) 68 Camb LJ 324, 339–40.
132   [2002] UKHL 12, [2002] 2 AC 164.
133   Ibid, [93]–[100].
134   Eg *Keech v Sandford* (1726) Sel Cas T King 61, 25 ER 223; *Boardman v Phipps* [1967] 2 AC 46; *Chan v Zacharia* (1984) 154 CLR 178; *Black v S Freedman & Co* (1910) 12 CLR 105.
135   Eg *LAC Minerals Ltd v International Corona Resources Ltd* (1989) 61 DLR (4th) 14 .
136   Eg *Black v S Freedman & Co* (1910) 12 CLR 105.

the beneficiary, if she chose to acquire it at all.[137] These trusts can also be justified according to principles of perfection – in other words, the plaintiff had a reasonable expectation of receiving property and this has been defeated by the defendant's conduct. There is a corrective rationale here: the fiduciary has taken something that was the beneficiary's (or ought to have been the beneficiary's) and thus should return the property to the beneficiary. But as Gummow J noted in *Stephenson Nominees Pty Ltd v Official Receiver*,[138] sometimes constructive trusts are intended to enforce observance of certain duties (as with the constructive trusts imposed on fiduciaries). There is a clear deterrent, profit-stripping rationale to these cases as well, placing them in the category of constructive trusts designed to respond to wrongdoing.

[19.58]   In cases where a dishonest fiduciary accepts a bribe, the imposition of a constructive trust is more difficult to justify. The bribe should clearly be stripped, but it is controversial whether a proprietary remedy should be used. The High Court of Australia has yet to decide the issue.[139] In *Grimaldi v Chameleon Mining NL (No 2)*,[140] the Full Federal Court said in obiter dicta that dishonest fiduciaries should be stripped of their profit by means of a proprietary remedy to deter such behaviour. However, in keeping with High Court authority suggesting that constructive trusts should be awarded sparingly,[141] the court in *Grimaldi* did not suggest that a constructive trust would automatically arise. The court said:

> [T]o accept that money bribes can be captured by a constructive trust does not mean that they necessarily will be in all circumstances. As is well accepted, a constructive trust ought not to be imposed if there are other orders capable of doing full justice . . . Such could be the case, for example, where a bribed fiduciary, having profitably invested the bribe, is then bankrupted and, apart from the investment, is hopelessly insolvent. In such a case a lien on that property may well be sufficient to achieve 'practical justice' in the circumstances. This said, a constructive trust is likely to be awarded as of course where the bribe still exists in its original, or in a traceable, form, and no third party issue arises.[142]

[19.59]   The current Australian position is that a constructive trust may be available over bribes taken in breach of fiduciary duty, but that, depending upon the interests of third parties, a lien may be more appropriate. This discretionary approach is more flexible than the more absolute position in England and Wales, where there is either an immediate constructive trust or no trust at all. However, it must be queried whether a lien is really less intrusive to third party creditors than a constructive trust when there is insolvency, as it will still give the beneficiary of the fiduciary obligation priority over the unsecured creditors. The only advantage is that it will not

---

137   Eg *Keech v Sandford* (1726) Sel Cas T King 61, 25 ER 223; *Boardman v Phipps* [1967] 2 AC 46; *Chan v Zacharia* (1984) 154 CLR 178; *Timber Engineering Co Ltd v Anderson* [1980] 2 NSWLR 488.

138   (1987) 16 FCR 536, 553.

139   There is only Deane J's judgment in *Hospital Products Ltd v United States Surgical Corporation* (1984) 156 CLR 41, 124–25.

140   [2012] FCAFC 6, (2012) 200 FCR 296 [569]–[584].

141   *Bathurst City Council v PWC Properties Pty Ltd* (1998) 195 CLR 566, [42]; *Giumelli v Giumelli* (1999) 196 CLR 101, [10], [49]–[50] (the Court); *John Alexander's Clubs Pty Ltd v White City Tennis Club Ltd* (2010) 241 CLR 1, [2010] HCA 19, [126]–[129].

142   [2012] FCAFC 6, (2012) 200 FCR 296 [583] (Finn, Stone and Perram JJ).

encompass any subsequent increase in value to the property. The better solution may be to award a personal remedy where there is insolvency.[143]

Some note should be made of the cases in other Commonwealth jurisdictions, as some were cited in *Grimaldi*. The English case law has fluctuated between two extreme approaches: either no constructive trust or always a constructive trust. For an example of the former approach, in *Lister v Stubbs*,[144] the English Court of Appeal held that constructive trusts should never be awarded over bribes made in breach of fiduciary duty. However, in *Attorney-General for Hong Kong v Reid*,[145] the Privy Council suggested that a constructive trust should always be awarded over bribes obtained in breach of fiduciary duty. Reid was a Crown prosecutor employed by the Hong Kong government and took bribes to obstruct the prosecution of certain criminals in breach of his fiduciary duty as an employee. Reid was convicted of offences in relation to this conduct and sentenced to eight years' imprisonment. He failed to pay the Crown a HK$12.4 million fine. The Hong Kong government discovered that Reid had used the bribe to purchase three properties in New Zealand, which he placed in his own name and the names of his wife and solicitor.

[19.60]

The Privy Council unanimously held that the properties were subject to a constructive trust. Lord Templeman said that a fiduciary holds a bribe on immediate constructive trust for the beneficiary because equity considers done that which ought to be done.[146] He relied on the extra-judicial writing of Lord Millett to say that the bribe belonged in equity to the beneficiary.[147] The effect on unsecured creditors of the fiduciary was said to be irrelevant, because unsecured creditors cannot be in a better position than the debtor. The English view of the constructive trust as an immediate remedy means that it is very much an 'all-or-nothing' remedy. *Reid* has been applied in Australia,[148] although as noted at [19.58], *Grimaldi* now suggests that (contrary to *Reid*) Australian law does not automatically impose a constructive trust in bribe situations.

[19.61]

In *FHR European Ventures LLP v Mankarious* ('*FHR*'), the UK Supreme Court held that a proprietary interest will always be awarded over a bribe taken in breach of fiduciary duty.[149] Unusually, Lord Neuberger overruled his own prior decision as a Court of Appeal judge in *Sinclair Investments (UK) Ltd v Versailles Trade Finance Ltd*, where it was held that a proprietary interest should never be awarded over a gain made as an (indirect) result of fiduciary wrongdoing.[150] His Lordship explained his change of opinion in *FHR* by saying:

[19.62]

---

143   V Finch and S Worthington, 'The *Pari Passu* Principle and Ranking Restitutionary Rights' in F Rose (ed), *Restitution and Insolvency* (Mansfield Press 2000) 19; K Barnett, 'Distributive Justice and Proprietary Remedies Over Bribes' (2015) 35 LS 302, 320–21.

144   (1890) 45 Ch D 1.

145   [1994] 1 AC 324.

146   Ibid, 331–32.

147   P Millett, 'Bribes and Secret Commissions' [1993] RLR 7; P Millett, 'Proprietary Restitution' in S Degeling and J Edelman (eds), *Equity in Commercial Law* (LBC 2005) 309. Cf W Swadling, 'Constructive Trusts and Breach of Fiduciary Duty' (2012) 18 *Trusts and Trustees* 985, 997–99.

148   *Zobory v Commissioner for Taxation* (1995) 64 FCR 86.

149   [2014] UKSC 14, [2015] AC 250 ('*FHR*').

150   [2011] EWCA Civ 347, [2012] Ch 453 ('*Sinclair Investments*').

> Clarity and simplicity are highly desirable qualities in the law. Subtle distinctions are
> sometimes inevitable, but in the present case, as mentioned above, there is no plainly
> right answer, and accordingly, in the absence of any other good reason it would seem
> right to opt for the simple answer.[151]

The plaintiffs in *FHR* sought to invest in the hotel industry. They asked Mr Mankarious and
his consultancy business, Cedar Capital (the defendants), to act as their agents. The
defendants recommended that the plaintiffs should buy a share in the Monte Carlo Grand
Hotel. Unknown to the plaintiffs, the defendants received a €10 million commission from
the Monte Carlo Grand Hotel for finding a purchaser. The terms of the agreement between
the hotel and the defendants had provided that the defendants would disclose the
commission to the plaintiff purchasers, but they did not. Thus, the property was sold for
€211.5 million, and then the defendants received their €10 million commission. The
plaintiffs sought to obtain the secret commission. The question was whether the plaintiffs
were entitled simply to a personal remedy (an account of profits) or a more beneficial
proprietary remedy (a constructive trust). If the plaintiffs were entitled to a constructive
trust, it would be enforceable even in insolvency, and it would allow the plaintiffs to trace
into the defendants' accounts and investments. The Supreme Court awarded a constructive
trust on the basis that a certain rule was required.

[19.63]   By contrast in *Sinclair Investments*, Lord Neuberger, speaking for the court, had said that it
was clear that a constructive trust could be available where a fiduciary has misappropriated or
stolen property belonging to the beneficiary, or where the fiduciary was under a duty to
acquire the property, if he chose to acquire it at all, for the beneficiary. However, he had said
that a bribe to a fiduciary was different:

> [A] bribe paid to a fiduciary could not possibly be said to be an asset which the fiduciary
> was under a duty to take for the beneficiary. There can thus be said to be a fundamental
> distinction between (i) a fiduciary enriching himself by depriving a claimant of an asset
> and (ii) a fiduciary enriching himself by doing a wrong to the claimant.[152]

[19.64]   It was relevant in *Sinclair Investments* that the defendants were insolvent, and thus the
parties who would ultimately be subject to any proprietary interest were the defendants'
creditors. Thus, Lord Neuberger noted that deterrence does not operate to justify the imposition of a constructive trust where the fiduciary is insolvent:

> [I]t does not matter to the defaulting fiduciary if he is stripped of his profits because they
> are beneficially owned by the beneficiary, or because he has to account for those profits
> to the beneficiary.
>   But the difference very much matters to the other creditors of the defaulting fiduciary,
> if he is insolvent. A person with a proprietary claim to assets held in the name of an

---

151   [2014] UKSC 14, [2015] AC 250 [35]. See also Lord Neuberger, 'The Remedial Constructive Trust – Fact or
       Fiction' (delivered at the Banking Services and Financial Law Association Conference, Queenstown,
       New Zealand on 10 August 2014) [28]–[29], [39].
152   [2011] EWCA Civ 347, [2012] Ch 453 [80].

insolvent person is better off than a secured creditor, and all such assets are unavailable to other creditors.[153]

With respect, the absolutist positions of the English courts at either extreme are not ideal, and the Australian position in *Grimaldi* is preferable. It is suggested that any attempt to formulate a certain rule for these cases will be unsuccessful, because the presence or absence of insolvency (among other things) may lead a court to wish to undermine the given rule. Thus, it is more appropriate to have a flexible yet structured standard as this gives greater certainty to courts and legal actors. [19.65]

IV Discretionary factors and bars to relief

Discretionary factors operate in relation to remedial constructive trusts, but often they do not seem to operate in a structured fashion. Rather, they operate in a general 'Is this fair?' manner. Relevant factors include hardship, delay, and lack of clean hands. The court may also consider the impact of a proprietary award on third parties,[154] but the extent to which they do this varies. It is unclear whether a court will take into account the impact of a proprietary award on third party creditors when there is insolvency, with some cases saying that the effect on third party creditors is irrelevant,[155] and others saying that it militates against the award of proprietary relief.[156] [19.66]

Where a remedy is granted in response to a right to rescind, the discretionary factors and bars to relief are the same as those discussed at [18.57]–[18.80] with regard to rescission. As noted there, where the bars to relief operate, the court is less likely to award a full constructive trust, and more likely to award a proprietary power (as in *Quek v Beggs*[157]), a lien (as in *Badman v Drake*[158]) or no relief at all (as in *Allcard v Skinner*[159]). [19.67]

V The need for more defined criteria

Unfortunately, the criteria for when a proprietary remedy will be awarded are unclear. This is not ideal, because it means that litigants find it difficult to predict what remedy will be imposed, and the impact of proprietary remedies in insolvency in particular means that greater certainty is needed. All that we can presently do is to analogise from the circumstances where proprietary awards have been made in the past. [19.68]

---

153 Ibid, [53]–[54].
154 *Muschinski v Dodds* (1985) 160 CLR 583; *Giumelli v Giumelli* [1999] HCA 10, (1999) 196 CLR 101; *John Alexander's Clubs Pty Ltd v White City Tennis Club Ltd* [2010] HCA 19, (2010) 241 CLR 1.
155 Eg *Attorney-General for Hong Kong v Reid* [1994] 1 AC 324; *Wambo Coal Pty Ltd v Ariff* [2007] NSWSC 589, (2007) 63 ACSR 429.
156 Eg *Daly v Sydney Stock Exchange Ltd* (1986) 160 CLR 371; *Lister v Stubbs* (1890) 45 Ch D 1; *Sinclair Investments (UK) Ltd v Versailles Trade Finance Ltd* [2011] EWCA Civ 347, [2012] Ch 453.
157 (1990) 5 BPR 11,761.
158 [2008] NSWSC 1366.
159 (1887) 36 Ch D 145.

[19.69]   It is suggested that the reasons for imposing proprietary remedies are complex and reflect a raft of concerns. Whatever approach is taken, it would be advisable to have more specific criteria which indicate what remedy is appropriate in which circumstances, and also to have greater clarity with regard to the timing of proprietary remedies, the effects of proprietary remedies in insolvency, the enforceability of proprietary remedies on third parties and the caveatability of the proprietary power.

PART 8

ENFORCEMENT OF REMEDIES

20

ENFORCEMENT OF REMEDIES

I   Introduction

[20.1]   This chapter is concerned with court orders made prior to final judgment, and with enforcement of final judgments. These are matters of civil procedure and are dealt with briefly in this book. They do not deal with final determinations of rights and are not remedies in the technical sense. Rather, they protect the ability of the court to award remedies.

[20.2]   First, if there is a dispute over certain subject matter, it is important that the subject matter of the dispute be maintained until the court can adjudicate the dispute. This is where interlocutory remedies and pre-judgment remedies are relevant. These remedies are awarded before the court makes a final determination of the proceedings and are generally intended to maintain the status quo pending the decision. Such remedies include interlocutory injunctions, which restrain or compel a person to do a particular thing. There are other pre-judgment remedies, such as freezing orders and search orders, which prevent the defendant from removing property from the jurisdiction or from destroying evidence before proceedings can be brought. These ensure that proceedings are not nugatory.

[20.3]   Secondly, after final judgment has been handed down, there must be a means of ensuring that the parties do what the court has ordered; otherwise the judgment lacks 'teeth'. Courts have coercive mechanisms which ensure that a defendant complies with an order to pay damages or an order of specific relief. For example, a defendant's assets may be seized and sold to pay for an outstanding judgment debt, or a defendant who refuses to specifically enforce a contract when ordered to do so may be gaoled for contempt of court.

II   Interlocutory injunctions

[20.4]   Interlocutory injunctions are injunctions granted prior to final judgment. They generally last until trial or further order. They are frequently sought to preserve the status quo until trial can take place.[1] This enables justice to be done when the final order is made once the rights of the parties are ascertained. Otherwise, the person against whom the final order is made may have dealt with the subject matter of the dispute in a way which makes the judgment worthless.[2] For example, in a dispute involving the right to take stones from a beach, the plaintiff alleged that the defendant's removal of stones had left his house unprotected from the sea, and the court was prepared to award an interlocutory injunction restraining the defendant from collecting further stones until the matter could be finally determined.[3]

[20.5]   Interlocutory injunctions are granted on a discretionary basis. Generally, appellate courts do not overturn the decision to withhold or grant interlocutory injunctions unless there are exceptional circumstances which require it, such as an error of law or fact. An appellate court

---

1   *Evans Marshall & Co Ltd v Bertola SA* [1973] 1 WLR 349; *Hubbard v Vosper* [1972] 2 QB 84, 96 (Lord Denning MR). See ICF Spry, *The Principles of Equitable Remedies* (9th edn, LBC 2014) 462–65.

2   *Preston v Luck* (1884) 27 Ch D 497, 505; *Heavener v Loomes* (1924) 34 CLR 306, 325–26; *National Commercial Bank Jamaica Ltd v Olint Corporation Ltd* [2009] UKPC 16, [2009] 1 WLR 1405.

3   *Clowes v Beck* (1851) 13 Beav 347, 51 ER 134.

will not overturn a decision to grant or withhold an interlocutory injunction simply because it would have exercised the discretion in a different manner.[4]

A usual condition of the plaintiff obtaining an interlocutory injunction is an 'undertaking as to damages'.[5] The plaintiff undertakes to compensate the defendant for any losses flowing from compliance with the injunction if the defendant is ultimately successful at trial.[6] This ensures that people do not seek injunctions lightly.

[20.6]

Interim injunctions are different to interlocutory injunctions, although sometimes the terms are used interchangeably. Interim injunctions are sought in conditions of extreme urgency and restrain the defendant from further action until a named date and time (usually only a few days).[7] They are typically made ex parte (without the other party present) and sometimes even before the issue of a writ. The urgency generally outweighs other discretionary considerations. In an ex parte hearing, the plaintiff is obliged to disclose all material facts relevant to the grant of the injunction, including matters which would have been raised by the other party.[8] If the plaintiff fails to make disclosure, the injunction may be dissolved later, although a fresh application may be made.[9]

[20.7]

To obtain an interlocutory injunction, a plaintiff must first identify a legal, equitable or statutory right which the injunction supports.[10] Then the court must consider:

[20.8]

1. whether there is a serious question to be tried[11] (or whether there is a 'prima facie case'[12]); and

2. the balance of convenience, taking into account the ramifications of the order for both the plaintiff and the defendant and the nature of the rights affected.

A   Legal, equitable or statutory right

Prior to *Lenah Game Meats*, it appeared that a plaintiff might be able to get a 'free standing' interlocutory injunction simply on the basis that it was just or convenient in the

[20.9]

---

4   *Hadmor Productions Ltd v Hamilton* [1983] 1 AC 191, 220; *Garden Cottage Foods Ltd v Milk Marketing Board* [1984] AC 130. Spry prefers the judgment of Lord Wilberforce to that of Lord Diplock in the latter case: ICF Spry, *The Principles of Equitable Remedies* (9th edn, LBC 2014) 463 fn 3.

5   *Beecham Group Ltd v Bristol Laboratories Pty Ltd* (1968) 118 CLR 618 ('*Beecham Group*'), 623.

6   Only losses directly flowing from the injunction itself sound in damages: *Air Express Ltd v Ansett Transport Industries (Operations) Pty Ltd* (1979) 146 CLR 249.

7   W Gummow, 'The Injunction in Aid of Legal Rights – An Australian Perspective' (1993) 56 Law & Contemp Probs 83, 90.

8   *Thomas A Edison Ltd v Bullock* (1913) 15 CLR 679, 681–82 (Isaacs J); *Town & Country Sport Resorts (Holdings) Pty Ltd v Partnership Pacific Ltd* (1988) 20 FCR 540, 543.

9   *Thomas A Edison Ltd v Bullock* (1913) 15 CLR 679, 683 (Isaacs J); *Town & Country Sport Resorts (Holdings) Pty Ltd v Partnership Pacific Ltd* (1988) 20 FCR 540, 543.

10   *Australian Broadcasting Corporation v Lenah Game Meats Pty Ltd* [2001] HCA 63, (2001) 208 CLR 199 ('*Lenah Game Meats*').

11   *Castlemaine Tooheys Ltd v South Australia* (1986) 161 CLR 148, 153 (Mason ACJ); *American Cynamid Co v Ethicon* [1975] AC 396, 407 (Lord Diplock) ('*American Cynamid*').

12   *Beecham Group* (1968) 118 CLR 618; *Australian Broadcasting Corporation v O'Neill* [2006] HCA 46, (2006) 227 CLR 57 ('*O'Neill*').

circumstances,[13] without identifying any underlying cause of action. However, a majority of the High Court of Australia in *Lenah Game Meats* held that it is necessary to identify a legal, equitable or statutory right which the injunction supports, and it is not sufficient to establish that an injunction is 'just and convenient' in the circumstances.[14] Kirby J and Callinan J dissented on this issue in separate judgments.[15] They argued that it may be just and convenient in some circumstances to award an injunction where the cause of action is unclear and no legal, equitable or statutory right can be identified.

B   'Serious question to be tried' (or a 'prima facie case')

[20.10]   Unfortunately, the test which applies here is not entirely clear. Early Australian and English cases held that the plaintiff must show a 'prima facie case'.[16] In *Beecham Group*, a patent infringement case, the High Court of Australia said that making out a prima facie case involves an assessment of whether 'if the evidence remains as it is there is a probability that at the trial of the action the plaintiff will be held entitled to relief'.[17] It was then noted that how strong the probability needs to be depends upon the nature of the rights asserted by the plaintiff and the practical consequences likely to flow from the order. For example, if mere pecuniary interests are involved, 'some' probability of success will be enough.[18]

[20.11]   In *American Cynamid*, another patent infringement case, the House of Lords reformulated the test for an award of an interlocutory injunction as requiring the court to be satisfied that there was a 'serious question to be tried'.[19] The English Court of Appeal had interpreted the 'prima facie case' as requiring that the plaintiff demonstrate more than a 50% chance of success. Lord Diplock considered that this was unduly restrictive and that the 'prima facie case' test should not be used because it led 'to confusion as to the object sought to be achieved by this form of temporary relief'.[20] *American Cynamid* and the 'serious question to be tried' test have been approved in numerous judgments by the High Court of Australia.[21] Other High

---

13   See *Supreme Court Act 1970* (NSW), s 66(4); *Supreme Court Act* (NT), s 69(1); *Civil Proceedings Act 2011* (Qld), s 9(3); *Supreme Court Act 1935* (SA), s 29(2); *Supreme Court Act 1986* (Vic), s 37(1); *Supreme Court Act 1935* (WA), s 25(9). All of these are based on *Judicature Act 1873* (36 & 37 Vict c 66), s 25(8). Cf *Federal Court of Australia Act 1976* (Cth), s 23 (no reference to 'just or convenient').

14   [2001] HCA 63, (2001) 208 CLR 199 [15]–[16] (Gleeson CJ), [61] (Gaudron J), [86]–[105] (Gummow and Hayne JJ). Note that in England and Wales and Canada, a 'free standing' injunction may sometimes be awarded where it is necessary to protect the court's process and the status quo: see *Cartier International AG v British Sky Broadcasting Ltd* [2016] EWCA Civ 658, [2017] 1 All ER 700 [46]–[49]; *Google Inc v Equustek Solutions Inc* [2017] SCC 34 [30]–[35].

15   [2001] HCA 63, (2001) 208 CLR 199, [156]–[167] (Kirby J), [278]–[287] (Callinan J).

16   *Preston v Luck* (1884) 27 Ch D 497, 506; *Challender v Royle* (1887) 36 Ch D 425, 436; *Beecham Group* (1968) 118 CLR 618, 622. Cf *Jones v Pacaya Rubber and Produce Co Ltd* [1911] 1 KB 455, 457 (Buckley LJ): 'certainly a case to be tried'.

17   (1968) 118 CLR 618, 622 (Kitto, Taylor, Menzies and Owen JJ).

18   Ibid.

19   [1975] AC 396, 407 (Lord Diplock, who gave the only reasoned speech).

20   Ibid.

21   *Australian Coarse Grain Pool Pty Ltd v Barley Marketing Board of Queensland* (1982) 46 ALR 398, 398; *Tableland Peanuts Pty Ltd v Peanut Marketing Board* (1984) 52 ALR 651, 653; *Castlemaine Tooheys Ltd v South Australia* (1986) 161 CLR 148, 153–54; *Fejo v Northern Territory* [1998] HCA 58, (1998) 195 CLR 96 [81] (Kirby J). Cf *Administrative and Clerical Officers Association v Commonwealth* (1979) 26 ALR 497, 502.

Court judgments have applied a 'serious question to be tried' test without citing *American Cynamid*,[22] as have lower courts.[23]

However, in *O'Neill*, Gummow and Hayne JJ stated that the correct test in Australia is the 'prima facie case' test.[24] They said that the 'prima facie case' test did not require a plaintiff to show that it was more probable than not that she would succeed at trial; rather, a plaintiff simply had to show that she had a '*sufficient likelihood of success* to justify in the circumstances the preservation of the status quo pending the trial'.[25] Thus, the 'serious question to be tried' test and the 'prima facie case' test were in many respects very similar.[26] Gummow and Hayne JJ had no objection to the use of the words 'serious question to be tried' in an Australian context as long as it was understood that the seriousness of the question to be tried depends upon the considerations emphasised in *Beecham*.[27] However, they regarded Lord Diplock's test as incorrect insofar as it purported to reverse the onus of proof so as to require a defendant to show that the application for the interlocutory injunction failed to disclose any real prospect of success.[28] Gleeson CJ and Crennan J agreed with Gummow and Hayne JJ.[29] Kirby J offered a powerful dissent, arguing that the 'serious question to be tried' test was preferable because it allowed individuals to have serious questions tried on the evidence rather than pre-judged on limited predictions of success, and that Gummow and Hayne JJ's test confused the issue of legal entitlement to an injunction with the secondary question of whether convenience favoured the issue of an injunction.[30]

[20.12]

Ian Spry argues that the objections of Gummow and Hayne JJ in *O'Neill* to the 'serious question to be tried' test are 'not well based',[31] and that the 'serious question to be tried' test is preferable.[32] He observes that courts are not well equipped to resolve a dispute as to facts in the context of an interlocutory application, particularly if the deponents of affidavits have not been cross-examined. While the plaintiff's inability to prove certain facts sometimes leads to the refusal of an interlocutory injunction, Spry observes that uncertainty as to facts 'by no means necessarily leads to the refusal of relief', particularly where there is a risk of substantial prejudice to the plaintiff, as where interference with property is involved.[33] Spry points out that any determination of facts is necessarily provisional in any case and by no means determines the ultimate outcome of the final decision.[34] Nevertheless, a court must make some determination of the facts and weigh up the relative weights of the parties' cases.

[20.13]

22   *Murphy v Lush* (1986) 65 ALR 651, 653; *Patrick Stevedores Operations No 2 Pty Ltd v Maritime Union of Australia (No 3)* [1998] HCA 30, (1998) 195 CLR1 [21], [122], [186]; *Fejo v Northern Territory* [1998] HCA 58, (1998) 195 CLR 96 [41].
23   Eg *Bradto Pty Ltd v Victoria* [2006] VSCA 89, (2006) 15 VR 65 [12].
24   [2006] HCA 46, (2006) 227 CLR 57 [65]–[72].
25   Ibid, [65] (emphasis added).
26   Ibid, [70].
27   Ibid.
28   Ibid, [71]⸮
29   Ibid, [19].
30   Ibid, [136]–[138].
31   ICF Spry, *The Principles of Equitable Remedies* (9th edn, LBC 2014) 480 fn 9.
32   Ibid, 481–83.
33   Ibid.
34   Ibid.

[20.14]   Kirby J's observations in *O'Neill* have force. The 'serious question to be tried' test (as adapted by the High Court of Australia in later cases) should be preferred to the 'prima facie case' test, as it is clearer and not dependent upon a prediction of success, which is difficult to judge at an interlocutory stage. It is unfortunate that the 'prima facie case' test was revived in *O'Neill*.

[20.15]   Australian courts have continued to use the phrase 'serious question to be tried', but it should be emphasised that it is now used in the sense required by *O'Neill* (in other words, the plaintiff must show that there is a 'sufficient likelihood of success').[35] In some cases, the phrases 'serious question to be tried' and 'prima facie case' have been used as alternative ways of expressing the same concept.[36]

[20.16]   Covell, Lupton and Forder note that certain types of interlocutory orders are subject to a test that is either additional to or different from both the 'serious question to be tried' and the 'prima facie case' tests.[37] This is particularly true of interlocutory injunctions awarded in the context of defamation, where it is said that an injunction will be granted only in 'very clear' or 'exceptional' cases.[38]

C   The balance of convenience

[20.17]   Once the court has established that there is a 'serious question to be tried' or a 'prima facie case' it must weigh up the competing interests of the parties to see whether it is appropriate to preserve the status quo until trial. In *Saunders v Smith*, it was said that the award of an interlocutory injunction 'depends upon a great variety of circumstances, and it is utterly impossible to lay down any general rule upon the subject, by which the discretion of the Court ought in all cases to be regulated'.[39] Whether an interlocutory injunction will be awarded depends on the precise matters in play in the particular case.

[20.18]   The court balances the inconvenience and injury which the plaintiff may suffer if an injunction is refused against the injury and the inconvenience which the defendant or a third party may suffer if an injunction is granted.[40] This involves a consideration of the likelihood of either party's success at trial; the risk of 'irreparable injury' to the plaintiff; the inadequacy of damages in compensating the plaintiff for any injury suffered, balanced against any hardship on the defendant or third parties; the inadequacy of damages to compensate the defendant for any loss suffered if the injunction turns out to be unmerited; and any delay on the part of the plaintiff.

1   Likelihood of success

[20.19]   There is a clear interrelationship between the likelihood of success of the plaintiff and the balance of convenience,[41] and it is difficult to separate out the two.[42] If the plaintiff has a strong

35   W Covell, K Lupton and J Forder, *Principles of Remedies* (6th edn, LexisNexis 2015) [8.49], citing *Jackel International Ltd v Jackel Pty Ltd* [2011] FCA 1516.
36   Eg *Re Eden Resort Hotel Pty Ltd* [2013] NSWSC 493 [15].
37   W Covell, K Lupton and J Forder, *Principles of Remedies* (6th edn, LexisNexis 2015) [8.50].
38   *O'Neill* [2006] HCA 46, (2006) 227 CLR 57 [32] (Gleeson CJ and Crennan J); *Bonnard v Perryman* [1891] 2 Ch 269, 284 (Lord Coleridge CJ).
39   (1838) 3 My & Cr 711, 728; 40 ER 1100, 1107 (Lord Cottenham LC).
40   *Beecham Group* (1968) 118 CLR 618, 622–23.
41   *Castlemaine Tooheys Ltd v South Australia* (1986) 161 CLR 148, 154–55 (Mason ACJ); *Samsung Electronics Co Ltd v Apple Inc* [2011] FCAFC 156, (2011) 286 ALR 257 [67].
42   *Australian and International Pilots Association v Qantas Airways Ltd* [2011] FCA 1487 [70].

serious question or prima facie case, the court will be more likely to find that an interlocutory injunction should be granted and it will be unnecessary for the plaintiff to show clear hardship.[43] In those circumstances, any hardship to the defendant would likely need to be significant before a court will decline to award an interlocutory injunction. Conversely, if the serious question or prima facie case is less strong, the plaintiff must show greater hardship before a court will award an interlocutory injunction, and the hardship the defendant must show to militate against the order is less difficult to establish.

2 Irreparable injury, hardship and inadequacy of damages to the plaintiff

The award of an injunction will be favoured where the subject matter of the dispute might be damaged, destroyed or removed or the value of other rights owned by the plaintiff might be diminished. Interlocutory injunctions are frequently used in intellectual property cases, and two of the seminal cases involved patent litigation. The plaintiffs in both *Beecham* and *American Cynamid* sought an interlocutory injunction because the value of their patent rights would have been diminished had the defendants not been restrained from producing allegedly infringing products.[44]   [20.20]

Reflecting the same concern, it has sometimes been said (particularly in older cases) that the plaintiff must be able to show that she will suffer 'irreparable injury' if an interlocutory injunction is not granted.[45] The expression 'irreparable injury' is apt to mislead.[46] 'Irreparable injury' does not mean that the injury must be grievous, or that there is no possibility of repairing the damage.[47] It means that the damage is substantial and a pecuniary sum will not be adequate to repair the injury.[48] Thus, where the underlying cause of action is legal, 'inadequacy of damages' is one of the raft of factors which may lead to the award of an interlocutory injunction. It seems likely in the wake of *O'Neill* that inadequacy of damages is not a separate requirement for interlocutory injunctions,[49] and is simply one of the factors to be taken into account when weighing the balance of convenience.[50] As noted at [11.17], in some cases it has been said that the real question is not whether damages are inadequate, but whether it is 'just in all the circumstances' that the plaintiff be confined to a remedy of damages.[51]   [20.21]

---

43   ICF Spry, *The Principles of Equitable Remedies* (9th edn, LBC 2014) 488–90.

44   However, there is a risk that an interlocutory injunction can be used in a tactical sense to prevent the carrying on of a business or employment altogether, or to place a plaintiff in a superior bargaining position: W Sofronoff, 'Interlocutory Injunctions Having Final Effect' (1987) 61 Aust LJ 341.

45   *Johnson v Shrewsbury Birmingham Railway Co* (1853) 3 De G M & G 914, 931; 43 ER 358, 365.

46   D Laycock, 'The Death of the Irreparable Injury Rule' (1990) 103 Harv L Rev 687.

47   *Litchfield-Speer v Queen Anne's Gate Syndicate No 2 Ltd* [1919] 1 Ch 407, 411. Cf *Pinchin v London and Blackwall Railway Co* (1854) 5 De G M & G 851, 860; 43 ER 1101, 1104.

48   *Attorney-General v Hallett* (1847) 16 M & W 569, 581; 153 ER 1316, 1321; *McCarty v North Sydney Municipal Council* (1918) 18 SR (NSW) 210, 215; *R v Macfarlane* (1923) 32 CLR 518, 550 (Isaacs J).

49   [2006] HCA 46, (2006) 227 CLR 57 [65] (Gummow and Hayne JJ); cf [19] (Gleeson CJ and Crennan J).

50   *National Australia Bank Ltd v Joyce* [2012] WASC 224 [38]–[41]; *Johnson v Cetin* [2011] WASC 344 [47] – [48]. It was still regarded as a separate requirement in *Mendonca v Mason* [2013] VSC 516, [36]–[41], aff'd *Mendonca v Mason* [2013] VSCA 280.

51   ICF Spry, *The Principles of Equitable Remedies* (9th edn, LBC 2014) 61–63. See, eg, *Beswick v Beswick* [1968] AC 58, 102 (Lord Upjohn); *Evans Marshall & Co Ltd v Bertola SA* [1973] 1 WLR 349, 379; *The Stena Nautica (No 2)* [1982] 2 Lloyd's Rep 336; *State Transport Authority v Apex Quarries Ltd* [1988] VR 187.

[20.22]   Related to both adequacy of damages and 'irreparable injury', hardship to the plaintiff is another factor which may lead to the award of an interlocutory injunction. The difficulty of quantifying damages may be a reason to award an interlocutory injunction,[52] as it shows that the injury is 'irreparable' or that damages are inadequate, inflicting hardship on the plaintiff.

[20.23]   The probability of an interlocutory injunction being granted will depend upon the legal rights involved. An interlocutory injunction will not be granted merely because a final injunction is likely to be granted. For example, final injunctions are readily granted for proprietary torts such as trespass if it is shown that the defendant will continue his conduct; see [11.19]. It does not follow, however, that courts will readily grant an interlocutory injunction in cases of alleged trespass. It must be shown that there is a significant risk of injury or some other hardship to the plaintiff before the court will grant an interlocutory injunction.[53]

[20.24]   Where an interlocutory injunction is sought in aid of a purely equitable cause of action (such as breach of trust or breach of confidence), there is no need to show that damages are inadequate.[54] However, the court may consider whether the plaintiff should be confined to an equitable pecuniary remedy such as an account of profits or equitable compensation. For example, the defendant may be ordered to keep an account if this will adequately protect the plaintiff's interests.[55]

3   Hardship to the defendant and third parties

[20.25]   Hardship to the defendant may be a reason to decline to award a remedy, particularly if another remedy will adequately protect the plaintiff. For example, in *Potters-Ballotini Ltd v Weston-Baker*,[56] the English Court of Appeal declined to award an interlocutory injunction restraining the defendants from running a rival factory which the plaintiff alleged had been formed in breach of confidence and in breach of some of the defendants' contracts of employment. The court found that the interlocutory injunction might destroy the defendants' business and livelihood in a way which would be difficult to compensate if the plaintiff's claim were found to be unmerited.[57] The better course of action was to order a speedy trial to finally resolve the matter on full evidence.

[20.26]   Courts are also willing to consider hardship to third parties if an injunction is granted.[58] Hardship to third parties is rarely a decisive consideration, but if the plaintiff's case lacks strength, it may weigh against the award of an injunction. For example, in *Hausmann v Smith*,[59] Barrett J declined to award an injunction sought by shareholders of a company to restrain the sale of that company's business by the company's administrators. It was found that the plaintiffs had a very weak case, but the judge also took into consideration the fact that the

---

52   *Body Technology Pty Ltd v Babak Moini* [2010] NSWSC 1414 [9].
53   Eg *Clowes v Beck* (1851) 13 Beav 347, 51 ER 134, mentioned above at [20.4].
54   *Heavener v Loomes* (1924) 34 CLR 306, 326.
55   *Shrewsbury and Birmingham Railway Co v London and North-Western Railway Co* (1850) 3 Mac & G 70, 42 ER 187; *Mitchell v Henry* (1880) 15 Ch D 181.
56   [1977] RPC 202.
57   Ibid, 207, 209, 211. Similarly, the same court refused an interlocutory injunction to enforce a restraint-of-trade clause in *Fellowes & Son v Fisher* [1976] QB 122.
58   *Patrick Stevedores Operations No 2 Pty Ltd v Maritime Union of Australia (No 3)* [1998] HCA 30, (1998) 195 CLR 1 [65]–[66]; *Wood v Sutcliffe* (1851) 2 Sim (NS) 163, 165–66; 61 ER 303, 304; *Miller v Jackson* [1977] QB 966. See also ICF Spry, *The Principles of Equitable Remedies* (9th edn, LBC 2014) 416–17.
59   [2006] NSWSC 682, (2006) 24 ACLC 688.

award of an injunction might open the way to a claim for breach of contract, which would have a detrimental impact on the third-party buyer and other third-party shareholders and creditors.[60]

4   Adequacy of undertaking as to damages for the defendant

Factors which militate against the award of an injunction include adequacy of other remedies. The degree to which the undertaking as to damages will protect the defendant if the plaintiff loses at trial is important. If damages are not an adequate remedy for the loss the defendant might suffer if the plaintiff does not succeed, this militates against the award of an interlocutory injunction.[61] However, this is not necessarily determinative. In *Donnelly v Amalgamated Television Services Pty Ltd*, an interlocutory injunction was awarded notwithstanding the ineffectiveness of the plaintiff's undertaking as to damages, because the defendant's proposed broadcast of a film showing the police arresting the plaintiff may have involved participation by the defendants in a serious abuse by the police of their powers of arrest.[62]

[20.27]

5   Delay on the part of the plaintiff

'Mere' delay is not in itself a reason to refuse to award an interlocutory injunction,[63] but if the plaintiff's delay means that the award of an interlocutory injunction will cause substantial prejudice to the defendant,[64] this may be a reason to decline to award an injunction. Unexplained delay is more likely to result in the refusal of an injunction.[65]

[20.28]

6   Example of the balancing process

Textile Clothing and Footwear Union of Australia v Huyck Wangner Australia Pty Ltd[66] illustrates how the balancing process works. The plaintiffs were members of the Textile Clothing and Footwear Union of Australia and sought to restrain Huyck Wangner Australia Pty Ltd, the defendant employer, from implementing a new shift system. The union alleged that the change in workplace shift system was undertaken because its employee members proposed to engage in 'protected action' pursuant to s 448 of the then *Workplace Relations Act 1996* (Cth).

[20.29]

---

60   Ibid, [15]–[16].
61   *Donnelly v Amalgamated Television Services Pty Ltd* (1998) 45 NSWLR 570, 575.
62   Ibid, 575–76.
63   *Wickham v Associated Pool Builders Pty Ltd* (1986) 7 IPR 392, 400; *Nintendo Co Ltd v Care* [2000] FCA 1538, (2000) 52 IPR 34 [26].
64   *Gibson v Minister for Finance, Natural Resources and the Arts* [2011] QSC 401.
65   Unexplained delay where injunctions were refused: *Pacific Hotels Pty Ltd v Asian Pacific International Ltd* (1987) 7 IPR 239 (four month delay); *Century Electronics v CVC Enterprises* [1983] FSR 1 (six month delay); *Essex Electric (PTE) Ltd v IPC Computers UK Ltd* (1991) 19 IPR 639; *Wang v Anying Group Pty Ltd* [2009] FCA 1500 (15 month delay). Explained delay where injunctions were granted: *ESPN Inc v Thomas* [2010] FCA 1232 (10 week delay); *Great American Success Co Ltd v Kattaineh* [1976] FSR 554 (five month delay); *Nintendo Co Ltd v Care* [2000] FCA 1538, (2000) 52 IPR 34 (14 month delay, of which eight months were explained). See W Covell, K Lupton and J Forder, *Principles of Remedies* (6th edn, LexisNexis 2015) [8.59].
66   [2008] FCA 1504.

[20.30]   The judge weighed up the hardship to the plaintiffs and compared this with the hardship to the defendant. It was found that the plaintiffs would be significantly worse off financially if the defendant's changes were implemented. The defendant asserted that damages would be adequate, but the judge found that the new shift proposals 'would involve considerable shocks to the daily financial arrangements of working men and women, and their families'.[67] Moreover, the aim of s 448 was to protect the integrity of the bargaining process and to allow employees to engage in industrial action without suffering disadvantage, and the refusal of an injunction would undermine that process. On the other hand, the defendant would suffer hardship because it would be temporarily restrained from making changes which would make its business more profitable and efficient. However, if the injunction was found to be unmerited, they would be entitled to reparation under the undertaking as to damages. As a substantial trading entity with an American parent company, they were better able to sustain temporary losses from an injunction than were the employees. The balance of convenience thus favoured the award of an injunction.

D Mandatory interlocutory injunctions

[20.31]   There is a distinction between prohibitory injunctions (which order a person to cease doing something) and mandatory injunctions (which require a person to perform a positive act); see [11.10]. Interlocutory injunctions may be available in either prohibitory or mandatory form. It was previously thought that courts should be more wary of granting mandatory interlocutory injunctions than prohibitory interlocutory injunctions, and that 'a high degree of assurance' was needed, as held by Megarry J in *Shepherd Homes Ltd v Sandham*.[68] This rigid test has been criticised,[69] and Australian and English courts have declined to follow it. Hoffmann J in *Films Rover Ltd v Cannon Film Sales Ltd* said that the general rules governing all injunctions apply to mandatory interlocutory injunctions without need for a higher test, and opined that Megarry J's statement in *Shepherd Homes* had simply been intended as a 'guideline' rather than a governing principle.[70] Hoffmann J continued that semantic arguments about the classification of an injunction as mandatory or prohibitory were 'barren' and that '[t]he question of substance is whether the granting of the injunction would carry that higher risk of injustice which is normally associated with the grant of a mandatory injunction'.[71] This has been accepted as an accurate statement of Australian law.[72]

---

67   Ibid, [36] (Jessup J).
68   [1971] Ch 340, 351. Followed in *Queensland v Australian Telecommunications Commission* (1985) 59 ALR 243; *Australian National Airlines Commission v Commonwealth* (1986) 17 FCR 445; *Midland Milk Pty Ltd v Victorian Dairy Industry Authority* (1987) 82 ALR 279.
69   W Gummow, 'The Injunction in Aid of Legal Rights – An Australian Perspective' (1993) 56 Law & Contemp Probs 83, 91.
70   [1987] 1 WLR 670, 680.
71   Ibid.
72   *Aerospatiale Societe Nationale Industrielle v Aerospatiale Helicopters Pty Ltd* (1986) 11 FCR 38; *Businessworld Computers Pty Ltd v Australian Telecommunications Commission* (1988) 82 ALR 499, 503–04; *McDermott v BP Australia Ltd* (1997) 19 ATPR 41–547; *ADI v Aerospace Systems Management Pty Ltd* [2003] NSWSC 758 [31]; *Neoinvent Pty Ltd v National Broadband Pty Ltd* [2005] NSWSC 1162 [13]; *Bradto Pty Ltd v Victoria* [2006] VSCA 89, (2006) 15 VR 65 [33]–[35].

E *Quia timet* interlocutory injunctions

As with permanent injunctions, interlocutory injunctions may be granted on a *quia timet* basis –   [20.32]
to restrain conduct that is threatened but has not yet occurred. The same rules apply as those
which govern the award of permanent *quia timet* injunctions.[73] The plaintiff must show that
the risk of injury is not insignificant or illusory, and the court will balance up the probability of
the injury occurring, the gravity of the consequences and the impact on third parties.[74] An
interlocutory injunction may be refused if the risk of injury is small and the hardship to the
defendant is high,[75] but it is highly likely to be awarded if there is a substantial risk of injury to
the plaintiff, and will only be refused in the latter case if there is extraordinary hardship to the
defendant.[76]

F Interlocutory injunctions which finally determine the matter

While the stated effect of an interlocutory injunction is to preserve the status quo pending trial,   [20.33]
sometimes the practical effect may be to finally determine the matter. This is common in cases
of passing off and patent infringement.[77] However, interlocutory injunctions may be used
tactically in litigation to effectively paralyse or destroy the defendant's business by preventing
the defendant from carrying on a business or appointing a receiver or provisional liquidator.[78]
Similarly, there are also concerns about the tactical use of interlocutory relief in industrial
disputes.[79] The injunction effectively puts the plaintiff in a dominant bargaining position. Care
must be taken in imposing an injunction in those circumstances.

Ordinarily, the court 'does not undertake a preliminary trial, and give or withhold inter-   [20.34]
locutory relief upon a forecast as to the ultimate result of the case'.[80] However, where an
injunction will finally determine the matter, it is necessary to evaluate the strength of the
plaintiff's case and the likelihood of success if the matter goes to trial.[81] Sofronoff concludes
that the approach of the courts is as follows:

> Where . . . the realities of the case are such that the grant or withholding of relief will have
> the practical effect of putting an end to the action by granting the successful party all that
> he seeks, or because the harm caused to the losing party will be complete and for which

---

73   See [11.45]–[11.48]; ICF Spry, *The Principles of Equitable Remedies* (9th edn, LBC 2014) 485–86.
74   Spry, ibid, 487.
75   *Elwes v Payne* (1879) 12 Ch D 468.
76   *Attorney-General v Great Eastern Railway Company* (1872) 25 LT 867.
77   W Covell, K Lupton and J Forder, *Principles of Remedies* (6th edn, LexisNexis 2015) [8.53].
78   W Sofronoff, 'Interlocutory Injunctions Having Final Effect' (1987) 61 Aust LJ 341. See also *Australian
      Paper Ltd v Communications, Electrical, Electronic, Energy, Information, Postal, Plumbing and Allied
      Services Union* (1998) 81 IR 15, 24–25.
79   *Australian Paper Ltd v Communications, Electrical, Electronic, Energy, Information, Postal, Plumbing
      and Allied Services Union* (1998) 81 IR 15; N Witzleb, E Bant, S Degeling and K Barker, *Remedies
      Commentary and Materials* (6th edn, LBC 2015) [10.70]–[10.75].
80   *Beecham Group* (1968) 118 CLR 618, 622.
81   *Kolback Securities Ltd v Epoch Mining NL* (1987) 8 NSWLR 533, 536. See also *NWL Ltd v Woods* [1979]
      1 WLR 1294, 1306–07; *Cayne v Global Natural Resources plc* [1984] 1 All ER 225; *Silktone Pty Ltd v
      Devreal Capital Pty Ltd* (1990) 21 NSWLR 317, 326, 333; *Williamson v Schmidt* [1998] 2 Qd R 317, 328.

money cannot constitute any worthwhile recompense, then it is necessary to consider the likelihood that the plaintiff will succeed.

> In such a case, generally an injunction ought not to be granted if the consequence is to deny a defendant an effective right to a trial, if the defendant has put forward a fully arguable case raising a triable issue and if the plaintiff's case is not overwhelming.[82]

This is an appropriate approach to ensure that injunctions are not used unjustly to effectively destroy the defendant's business or other rights under the guise of maintaining the status quo.

G Undertakings as to damages

[20.35] As noted at the outset of this chapter, it is often a condition of a plaintiff obtaining an interlocutory injunction that she gives an undertaking as to damages. It is usually worded to require the plaintiff 'to abide by any order which this court may make as to damages, in case this court shall be of opinion that the defendant shall have sustained any, by reason of this order, which the plaintiff ought to pay'.[83] But it may simply be denoted by the phrase 'usual undertaking as to damages'.[84] If at trial the plaintiff fails to make out her case, she will generally be liable to pay damages to the defendant for injuries sustained by reason of the interlocutory injunction.[85] In *European Bank Ltd v Evans*, the High Court of Australia observed:

> [T]he undertaking as to damages is given to the court, for enforcement by the court; it is not a contract between parties or some other cause of action upon which one party can sue the other. It is worth repeating the obvious proposition that such an undertaking is not lightly to be given.[86]

Only losses directly flowing from the injunction sound in damages.[87] The High Court has emphasised that 'the process of assessment of compensation cannot be constrained by a rigid formulation'.[88]

[20.36] The award of damages is discretionary, but damages will be payable unless there is an exceptional circumstance such as delay, hardship, or the like.[89]

H Interim injunctions under statute

[20.37] The discussion at [11.62]–[11.69] outlined the availability of (permanent) injunctions to restrain certain breaches of statute, including the Australian Consumer Law ('ACL')[90] and the

---

82 W Sofronoff, 'Interlocutory Injunctions Having Final Effect' (1987) 61 Aust LJ 341, 349.
83 ICF Spry, *The Principles of Equitable Remedies* (9th edn, LBC 2014) 499.
84 See, eg, *Uniform Civil Procedure Rules 2005* (NSW), r 25.8; Allsop CJ, Usual Undertaking as to Damages Practice Note (GPN-UNDR), 25 October 2016.
85 See generally ICF Spry, *The Principles of Equitable Remedies* (9th edn, LBC 2014) 500.
86 [2010] HCA 6, (2010) 240 CLR 432 [14] (French CJ, Gummow, Hayne, Heydon and Kiefel JJ).
87 Ibid, [16]–[18]; *Air Express Ltd v Ansett Transport Industries (Operations) Pty Ltd* (1979) 146 CLR 249.
88 *European Bank Ltd v Evans* [2010] HCA 6, (2010) 240 CLR 432 [17] (French CJ, Gummow, Hayne, Heydon and Kiefel JJ).
89 *Attorney-General v Albany Hotel Co* [1892] 2 Ch 696, 700; *Kerridge v Foley* (1968) 70 SR (NSW) 251, 255. See generally ICF Spry, *The Principles of Equitable Remedies* (9th edn, LBC 2014) 504–06.
90 *Competition and Consumer Act 2010* (Cth), sch 2. For the legislative history, see [8.1].

Corporations Act 2001 (Cth). So-called 'interim injunctions' are also available under statute. The two statutes mentioned will be considered briefly.

Section 234 of the ACL provides that 'interim injunctions' may be granted if the court 'considers it desirable to do so', and if the court has the power to grant an injunction pursuant to s 232. There is no need to show that damages are inadequate as a jurisdictional hurdle to gain a permanent injunction under the ACL; see [11.18]. However, where the grant of an interim injunction pursuant to s 234 is sought, adequacy of damages may be a consideration which goes to the balance of convenience.[91]

Similarly, an 'interim injunction' may be awarded pursuant to s 1324(4) of the *Corporations Act 2001* (Cth) when in the opinion of the court it is desirable to do so. Generally, the courts have held that, although they are not bound to follow equitable principles in granting an interim injunction pursuant to s 1324(4),[92] it is appropriate to start from that point,[93] with due recognition that if the Australian Securities and Investment Commission (ASIC) is the applicant, then the public interest may be a relevant consideration to be taken into account when assessing the balance of convenience.[94] Section 1324(8) provides that ASIC is not required to give an undertaking as to damages.

[20.38]

[20.39]

III   Other pre-judgment remedies

There is always the possibility that a defendant may abscond or remove money or property from the jurisdiction to render any judgment in the plaintiff's favour nugatory. However, the courts have developed orders to prevent frustration of the court's process.

[20.40]

The move in pre-judgment orders (as in post-judgment enforcement) has been to shift from imprisoning the defendant to freezing the defendant's assets or giving the plaintiff access to search the assets. We consider orders against the person of the defendant first, and then move to orders which involve freezing assets and searching the defendant's property.

[20.41]

A   Arrest of the person

Legislation in all states and territories except New South Wales allows for the arrest of a person who seeks to abscond from the jurisdiction with an unsatisfied obligation to pay another person.[95] Once arrested, the defendant stays in custody until the court orders otherwise or he

[20.42]

---

91   *Organic Marketing Australia Pty Ltd v Woolworths Ltd* [2011] FCA 279 [22].
92   *Australian Securities and Investments Commission v Parkes* [2001] NSWSC 377, (2001) 38 ACSR 355; *Australian Securities and Investments Commission v Pegasus Leveraged Options Group Pty Ltd* [2002] NSWSC 310, (2002) 41 ACSR 561.
93   Eg *Australian Securities and Investments Commission v Mauer-Swisse Securities Ltd* [2002] NSWSC 741, (2002) 42 ACSR 605; *Australian Securities and Investments Commission v Triton Underwriting Insurance Agency* [2003] NSWSC 1145, (2003) 48 ACSR 249, [25].
94   *Australian Securities and Investments Commission v Mauer-Swisse Securities Ltd* [2002] NSWSC 741, (2002) 42 ACSR 605 [36].
95   *Court Procedures Rules 2006* (ACT), rr 2550–2564; *Absconding Debtors Act 1978* (NT); *Civil Proceedings Act 2011* (Qld), s 100; *Enforcement of Judgments Act 1991* (SA); *Debtors Act 1870* (Tas), s 5; *Supreme Court Act 1986* (Vic), ss 86–100, 119; *Supreme Court Act 1935* (WA), ss 63–68; *Restraint of Debtors Act 1984* (WA). Cf *Civil Procedure Act 2005* (NSW), s 124.

gives adequate security.[96] This covers both liquidated claims (such as debts) and unliquidated claims (such as claims for damages in tort). Witzleb, Bant, Degeling and Barker identify two types of legislation.[97]

[20.43]   The first type is based on 19th century English legislation,[98] and is present in Tasmania, Victoria, and Western Australia.[99] It requires the applicant to show that the defendant is obliged to pay more than a certain minimum sum,[100] that there is probable cause to believe that the defendant is about to leave the state, and that the absence of the defendant will materially prejudice or defeat the applicant's cause of action. Applications are usually made ex parte.

[20.44]   The second type of legislation represents a more modern reworking of the older legislation, and is present in the Australian Capital Territory, the Northern Territory, Queensland, South Australia and Western Australia.[101] It requires an applicant to show similar evidence to the first type of legislation but sets no minimum sum. The Northern Territory legislation requires a liquidated debt.[102] The statutes of the Northern Territory and Western Australia also permit the court to restrain the transfer or removal of property.[103] The Queensland rules also provide for the making of orders restraining persons from leaving Australia.[104] The South Australian legislation provides its own procedure, and also provides for arrest, imprisonment and contempt proceedings against absconding debtors.[105]

[20.45]   There is an equitable writ preventing a person from leaving the jurisdiction where that person owes a debt as a result of breaching an equitable duty. It is called the writ of *ne exeat regno*,[106] and the factors the court considers are similar to those under the statutory provisions above.[107]

[20.46]   Understandably, it has been said that any order seeking to arrest a person should be granted with caution, as it involves the deprivation of a person's liberty.[108] Consequently, this legislation is interpreted strictly.[109] Arrest will not be awarded unless departure is imminent.[110]

---

96   *Uniform Civil Procedure Rules 1999* (Qld), r 941; *Debtors Act 1870* (Tas), s 5(2); *Supreme Court Act 1935* (WA), ss 63–64; *Supreme Court Act 1986* (Vic), ss 86–100.
97   N Witzleb, E Bant, S Degeling and K Barker, *Remedies Commentary and Materials* (6th edn, LBC 2015) [12.10].
98   *Judgments Act 1838* (1 & 2 Vict c 110); *Debtors Act 1869* (32 & 33 Vict c 62).
99   *Debtors Act 1870* (Tas), s 5; *Supreme Court Act 1986* (Vic), ss 86–100, 119; *Supreme Court Act 1935* (WA), ss 63–68.
100   *Debtors Act 1870* (Tas), s 5(2) ($50); *Supreme Court Act 1986* (Vic), s 87(a) ($50 000); *Supreme Court Act 1935* (WA), s 63(2)(a) ($100).
101   *Court Procedures Rules 2006* (ACT), rr 2550–2564; *Absconding Debtors Act 1978* (NT), s 5; *Civil Proceedings Act 2011* (Qld), s 100; *Enforcement of Judgments Act 1991* (SA), s 14; *Restraint of Debtors Act 1984* (WA), s 5.
102   *Absconding Debtors Act 1978* (NT), s 4(1) (definition of 'debt').
103   *Absconding Debtors Act 1978* (NT), ss 13–15; *Restraint of Debtors Act 1984* (WA), ss 17–19.
104   *Uniform Civil Procedure Rules 1999* (Qld), r 259(2)(c).
105   *Debtors Act 1936* (SA), s 4; *Enforcement of Judgments Act 1991* (SA), s 14.
106   Latin for 'let him not go out of the kingdom'. Sometimes called a writ of *ne exeat colonia* ('let him not go out of the colony') in an Australian context, eg *Glover v Walters* (1950) 80 CLR 172. In Roman times, it was *ne exeat republica* ('let him not go out of the republic').
107   Ibid; *Felton v Callis* [1969] 1 QB 200; *Parsons v Burk* [1971] NZLR 244.
108   *Palliser Holdings Pty Ltd v Hunt* (1990) 2 WAR 363, 367; *Felton v Callis* [1969] 1 QB 200, 205 (Megarry J); *Ex parte Brunker* (1734) 3 P Wms 312, 313–14; 24 ER 1079, 1080 (Lord Talbot LC).
109   *Jira v Burcher* (1960) 78 WN (NSW) 421; *Ingram v Ingram* [1927] VLR 225; *Southern Drug Co Ltd v Lagos* (1980) 24 SASR 590; *QB Investments Pty Ltd v Reed* [1979] Qd R 58; *Felton v Callis* [1969] 1 QB 200.
110   *QB Investments Pty Ltd v Reed* [1979] Qd R 58.

The judgment debtor's flight must defeat or materially prejudice the action; it is not enough that it will make enforcement more difficult or expensive.[111]

As Witzleb, Bant, Degeling and Barker note, pre-judgment arrest is now rare,[112] as applicants prefer an order freezing the defendant's assets within the jurisdiction. Freezing orders were invented by the English Court of Appeal in 1975.[113] An action against a prospective judgment debtor can be made in conjunction with a freezing order.[114] A defendant may be restrained from leaving the jurisdiction where this is necessary to make a freezing order effective.[115]   **[20.47]**

B   Freezing orders (Mareva orders)

A freezing order restrains a party from disposing of assets or removing them from the jurisdiction before the other party can obtain judgment against the first party. It has been described as 'the paradigm example of an order to prevent the frustration of a court's process'.[116] Freezing orders are awarded not only in actions to recover liquidated sums,[117] but also for actions to recover secret profits,[118] for damages in tort,[119] and for compensation under the Australian Consumer Law or predecessors.[120]   **[20.48]**

These orders are sometimes called 'Mareva orders' because they were developed in *Mareva Compania Naviera SA v International Bulkcarriers SA*.[121] The jurisdictional basis for such orders was previously controversial,[122] but they are now firmly established in Australian law.[123] 'Mareva orders' are preferably called freezing orders.[124] As noted at [20.44], the Northern Territory and Western Australia have legislation which provides for orders against removal of property or its transfer to another person.[125] In Victoria, there is a statutory   **[20.49]**

---

111   *Moss & Co v Johnston* (1896) 22 VLR 530, 531; *O'Connor v Pitcairn* (1901) 27 VLR 2, 6 (Hood J); *Uniform Civil Procedure Rules 1999* (Qld), r 942.

112   N Witzleb, E Bant, S Degeling and K Barker, *Remedies Commentary and Materials* (6th edn, LBC 2015) [12.10].

113   *Mareva Compania Naviera SA v International Bulkcarriers SA* [1980] 1 All ER 213, [1975] 2 Lloyd's Rep 509. Remedial innovations such as this were probably one of Lord Denning's lasting legacies: A Tettenborn, 'Remedies: A Neglected Contribution' [1999] Denning LJ 41, 42–43.

114   *Federal Court Rules 2011* (Cth), r 7.35(4)(a); *Court Procedures Rules 2006* (ACT), r 743(4)(a); *Uniform Civil Procedure Rules 2005* (NSW), r 25.14(4)(a); *Supreme Court Rules* (NT), r 37A.05(4)(a); *Uniform Civil Procedure Rules 1999* (Qld), r 260D(4)(a); *Supreme Court Civil Rules 2006* (SA), r 247(5)(d)(i); *Supreme Court Rules 2000* (Tas), r 937E(4)(a); *Supreme Court (General Civil Procedure) Rules 2015* (Vic), r 37A.05(4)(a); *Rules of the Supreme Court 1971* (WA), O 52A r 5(4)(a).

115   *Bayer AG v Winter* [1986] 1 WLR 497; *Klein v Botsman* [2003] TASSC 106, [9].

116   *Patrick Stevedores Operations No 2 Pty Ltd v Maritime Union of Australia (No 3)* [1998] HCA 30, (1998) 195 CLR 1 [35] (Brennan CJ, McHugh, Gummow, Kirby and Hayne JJ).

117   *Mareva Compania Naviera SA v International Bulkcarriers SA* [1980] 1 All ER 213, [1975] 2 Lloyd's Rep 509.

118   *Patterson v BTR Engineering (Australia) Ltd* (1989) 18 NSWLR 319.

119   *Allen v Jambo Holdings Ltd* [1980] 1 WLR 1251.

120   *Jackson v Sterling Industries Ltd* (1987) 162 CLR 612.

121   [1980] 1 All ER 213, [1975] 2 Lloyd's Rep 509.

122   See L Aitken, 'Note' (1996) 70 Aust LJ 109; *Mercedes-Benz AG v Leiduck* [1996] AC 284.

123   *Jackson v Sterling Industries Ltd* (1987) 162 CLR 612.

124   PW Young, C Croft and ML Smith, *On Equity* (LBC 2009) [16.580].

125   *Absconding Debtors Act 1978* (NT), ss 13–15; *Restraint of Debtors Act 1984* (WA), ss 17–19.

jurisdiction to make freezing orders additional to the inherent jurisdiction of the court.[126] Section 1323 of the *Corporations Act 2001* (Cth) also gives a power to preserve assets in some circumstances.

[20.50]   Although the freezing order is often referred to as an 'interlocutory injunction', the High Court of Australia has held that it is neither strictly interlocutory (as it may operate after judgment) nor strictly speaking an injunction.[127] Nonetheless, such orders are 'impermanent' because their aim is to preserve assets, and to assist and protect methods of execution.[128]

[20.51]   The conditions under which freezing orders may be awarded are now governed by civil procedure rules in all states and territories.[129] These civil procedure rules are uniform, and provide that courts may make freezing orders, with or without notice to a defendant, to prevent a judgment of the court from being unsatisfied. The assets may be located inside or outside Australia. Ancillary orders may also be made, including orders eliciting information about the assets or orders determining whether the freezing order ought to be made. Courts can make a freezing order or an ancillary order against a person who is not a party to the proceeding. Orders may also be made against judgment debtors. The inherent jurisdiction of the court to award a freezing order or ancillary order is not ousted.

[20.52]   Since a freezing order has a drastic effect on the defendant, it should not be awarded lightly, and courts must exercise 'a high degree of caution' before awarding one.[130] The plaintiff is always required to offer an undertaking as to damages in support of the application.[131] The order must allow the defendant to have sufficient funds to conduct a defence,[132] to pay debts and ordinary expenses, and to run a business.[133] The courts have been clear that the sole purpose of the order is to prevent assets from being dissipated, and not to provide security for the plaintiff's claim.[134] The plaintiff bears the onus of establishing the need for the order and the quantum of the amount to be frozen.[135] If loss is suffered as a result of a wrongfully imposed freezing order, it appears that damages will be assessed in a similar manner to contract damages, with any losses required to be reasonably foreseeable to the person seeking the freezing order.[136]

---

126   *Supreme Court Act 1986* (Vic), s 37(3). See *National Australia Bank Ltd v Dessau* [1988] VR 521: freezing orders can still apply outside Victoria because such orders are also within the inherent jurisdiction of the court.
127   *Cardile v LED Builders Pty Ltd* [1999] HCA 18, (1999) 198 CLR 380 [42]–[43].
128   Ibid, [43].
129   *Federal Court Rules 2011* (Cth), rr 7.31–7.38; *Court Procedures Rules 2006* (ACT), rr 740–745; *Uniform Civil Procedure Rules 2005* (NSW), rr 25.3, 25.10–25.17; *Supreme Court Rules* (NT), O 37A; *Uniform Civil Procedure Rules 1999* (Qld), rr 260–260G; *Supreme Court Civil Rules 2006* (SA), r 247; *Supreme Court Rules 2000* (Tas), rr 937A–937H; *Supreme Court (General Civil Procedure) Rules 2015* (Vic), O 37A; *Rules of the Supreme Court 1971* (WA), O 52A.
130   *Cardile v LED Builders Pty Ltd* [1999] HCA 18, (1999) 198 CLR 380 [50].
131   Ibid, [43]; *Frigo v Culhaci* (NSW Court of Appeal, 17 July 1998).
132   *Clark Equipment Credit of Australia Ltd v Como Factors Pty Ltd* (1988) 14 NSWLR 552, 569; *Glenwood Management Group Pty Ltd v Mayo* [1991] 2 VR 49.
133   *Clark Equipment Credit of Australia Ltd v Como Factors Pty Ltd* (1988) 14 NSWLR 552.
134   *Jackson v Sterling Industries Ltd* (1987) 162 CLR 612, 621, 625.
135   *Zhen v Mo* [2008] VSC 300 [24].
136   *Abbey Forwarding Ltd v Hone (No 3)* [2014] EWCA Civ 711, [2015] Ch 309.

As noted before, the rules provide that the assets the subject of a freezing order can be anywhere in the world, and courts have been prepared to make such awards.[137] Nonetheless, freezing orders are only exceptionally granted in support of a foreign judgment or award.[138]

[20.53]

Although courts have been reluctant to formulate rigid rules where a freezing order will be awarded against the defendant,[139] the following guidance can be given. The plaintiff must establish that she has an arguable case against the defendant,[140] and that there is a danger that the plaintiff's judgment will be partly or wholly unsatisfied because the defendant is likely to remove certain assets, dispose of them or deal with them so as to diminish their value.[141] The plaintiff's evidence as to the possibility of dissipation of assets must be solid and not mere speculation.[142] However, there is no need to show that the defendant has nefarious purposes or is intending to frustrate the court's judgment, although if there is such evidence, it will be easier to establish that a freezing order should be made.[143] There is a process similar to that undertaken in relation to interlocutory injunctions where the court weighs up the 'balance of convenience', including the hardship to the plaintiff if the freezing order is not awarded balanced against the hardship to the defendant if the freezing order is made.[144] The interests of third parties may be relevant, depending upon the case.[145] Finally, discretionary considerations such as delay may militate against the granting of a freezing order.[146] If it appears that the defendant is not adequately protected against detriment which may arise from imposition of a freezing order, the court will remove the order. [147]

[20.54]

C Search orders (Anton Piller orders)

Search orders or 'Anton Piller orders' require a defendant to 'permit' the plaintiff's representatives to enter the defendant's premises and search for evidence and remove it from the premises. Such orders are primarily made in cases where it is alleged that the defendant has pirated copies of the plaintiff's copyrighted or patented work, but may be made outside these kinds of disputes.[148] A search order is sometimes called an 'Anton Piller order' because such an

[20.55]

---

137 Eg *National Australia Bank Ltd v Dessau* [1988] VR 521; *Derby & Co Ltd v Weldon* [1990] Ch 48; *PT Bayan Resources Tbk v BCBC Singapore Pte Ltd* [2014] WASCA 178, (2014) 320 ALR 289.

138 *Rosseel NV v Oriental Commercial Shipping (UK) Ltd* [1990] 1 WLR 1387. Such orders were made in *Babanaft International Co SA v Bassatne* [1990] Ch 13; *Haiti (Republic) v Duvalier* [1990] 1 QB 202.

139 *Jackson v Sterling Industries Ltd* (1987) 162 CLR 612, 621.

140 *Glenwood Management Group Pty Ltd v Mayo* [1991] 2 VR 49, 49.

141 *Federal Court Rules 2011* (Cth), r 7.32(1); *Court Procedures Rules 2006* (ACT), r 741(1) and (2); *Uniform Civil Procedure Rules 2005* (NSW), r 25.11(1); *Supreme Court Rules* (NT), r 37A.02(1); *Uniform Civil Procedure Rules 1999* (Qld), r 260A(1); *Supreme Court Civil Rules 2006* (SA), r 247(2)(a); *Supreme Court Rules 2000* (Tas), r 937B (1); *Supreme Court (General Civil Procedure) Rules 2015* (Vic), r 37A.02(1); *Rules of the Supreme Court 1971* (WA), O 52A r 2(1).

142 *Ninemia Maritime Corporation v Trave Schiffahrtsgesellschaft mbH & Co KG* [1984] 1 All ER 398, 406, aff'd *Ninemia Maritime Corporation v Trave Schiffahrtsgesellschaft mbH & Co KG* [1983] 1 WLR 1412.

143 N Witzleb, E Bant, S Degeling and K Barker, *Remedies Commentary and Materials* (6th edn, LBC 2015) [12.75].

144 *Zhen v Mo* [2008] VSC 300 [27].

145 *Patrick Stevedores Operations No 2 Pty Ltd v Maritime Union of Australia (No 3)* [1998] HCA 30, (1998) 195 CLR 1 [66].

146 *Cardile v LED Builders Pty Ltd* [1999] HCA 18, (1999) 198 CLR 380 [53].

147 *Frigo v Culhaci* (NSWCA, 17 July 1998).

148 PW Young, C Croft and ML Smith, *On Equity* (LBC 2009) [4.870].

order was made in the English Court of Appeal case of *Anton Piller KG v Manufacturing Processes Ltd*.[149] In that case, the court cautioned against making such an order lightly. Ormerod LJ, with whom Shaw LJ agreed, said:

> There are three essential pre-conditions for the making of such an order, in my judgment. First, there must be an extremely strong prima facie case. Secondly, the damage, potential or actual, must be very serious for the applicant. Thirdly, there must be clear evidence that the defendants have in their possession incriminating documents or things, and that there is a real possibility that they may destroy such material before any application inter partes can be made.[150]

[20.56]   As with freezing orders, the conditions upon which search orders may be awarded are now governed by uniform civil procedure rules in all states and territories.[151] The court must be satisfied that the plaintiff has a strong prima facie case on an accrued cause of action, that the potential or actual loss or damage to the plaintiff will be serious if the order is not made, and that there is sufficient evidence that the defendant possesses material and may destroy it or cause it to be unavailable for use.

[20.57]   As with freezing orders, courts are cognisant of the possibility of injustice towards a defendant because of the coercive nature of these orders. The standard search order is drafted carefully, providing for the presence of an independent solicitor and an opportunity for the defendant to obtain legal advice before the order is executed.[152]

IV   Post-judgment enforcement

[20.58]   After judgment has been handed down, the defendant may be ordered to pay to the plaintiff a monetary sum or to do a specific thing. But what happens if the defendant fails to pay the money or to do the thing specified? Courts have mechanisms by which they can ensure compliance with their orders.

[20.59]   The general rule is that common law damages orders are enforced by seizing the judgment debtor's property, whereas orders for specific relief are enforced by means of coercion, including imprisonment for contempt. It is said that this is because 'a common law judgment is a determination of right not a command to the person ... [b]ut a decree in equity has always been a command laid upon the person. So too is a rule absolute at common law'.[153] In other words, because equity is coercive, the ways of enforcing equitable judgments are more likely to be coercive, but coercion may also have a place with regard to some common law judgments.

---

149   [1976] Ch 55.
150   Ibid, 62.
151   *Federal Court Rules 2011* (Cth), rr 7.41–7.47; *Court Procedures Rules 2006* (ACT), rr 750–755; *Uniform Civil Procedure Rules 2005* (NSW), rr 25.18–25.24; *Supreme Court Rules* (NT), O 37B; *Uniform Civil Procedure Rules 1999* (Qld), rr 261–261F; *Supreme Court Civil Rules 2006* (SA), r 248; *Supreme Court Rules 2000* (Tas), rr 937I–937O; *Supreme Court (General Civil Procedure) Rules 2015* (Vic), O 37B; *Rules of the Supreme Court 1971* (WA), O 52B.
152   PW Young, C Croft and ML Smith, *On Equity* (LBC 2009) [4.870]
153   *Pearson v Arcadia Store, Guyra, Ltd (No 2)* (1935) 53 CLR 587, 590–91.

A   Enforcement of money remedies

1   Historical background

The present law regarding enforcement of money remedies cannot be fully understood without a brief description of the history leading up to the present day.[154] Until the 19th century in England, courts compelled judgment debtors to pay their debts by giving the judgment creditor a right to imprison the debtor. It was irrelevant whether the debtor had money to pay. The judgment creditor also had limited rights against the judgment debtor's property. The judgment debtor could get out of gaol only by posting bail or declaring himself insolvent. However, he could not escape from the debt itself by declaring insolvency, as insolvency was distinguished from bankruptcy, and did not operate to expunge the debt at that time. Bankruptcy expunged debts, but it was only available to traders. Over the 19th century in England, there were gradual reforms, including the limitation of 'mesne process' or pre-judgment imprisonment,[155] a temporary abolition of post-judgment arrest,[156] and the merger of bankruptcy and insolvency.[157] Finally, in 1869, post-judgment imprisonment was only allowed where the defendant had engaged in fraud or other misconduct.[158] **[20.60]**

Upon settlement, Australian law directly adopted the English law regarding imprisonment for debt and execution against the goods and chattels of debtors.[159] However, Australian law was quicker to develop its own processes, and the colony of New South Wales abolished final judgment imprisonment well before England.[160] Other colonies followed suit at different times over the next 40 years, although they adopted the English reform legislation later in the 19th century.[161] **[20.61]**

2   Current Australian law

In most jurisdictions, there is provision for the court to order that judgment debtors make an instalment payment plan to repay judgment debts.[162] Generally, the court may only make such an order after an investigation and taking into account the situation of the debtor. If the judgment debtor persistently or deliberately fails to pay instalments when he has the means to pay, he may be imprisoned in some jurisdictions.[163] **[20.62]**

---

154   See the more detailed historical summary in N Witzleb, E Bant, S Degeling and K Barker, *Remedies Commentary and Materials* (6th edn, LBC 2015) [12.105]–[12.115].

155   *Judgments Act 1838* (1 & 2 Vict c 110). However, this was accompanied by an expansion in post-judgment remedies against a debtor's land.

156   *Execution Act 1844* (7 & 8 Vict c 96). Later superseded by *Small Debts Act 1845* (7 & 8 Vict c 127) and *County Court Act 1846* (9 & 10 Vict c 95), which reintroduced imprisonment of judgment debtors.

157   *Bankruptcy Act 1861* (24 & 25 Vict c 134).

158   *Debtors Act 1869* (32 & 33 Vict c 62).

159   *First Charter of Justice*, 17 April 1787, King George III (Letters Patent of 1787).

160   *Imprisonment for Debt Abolition Act 1846* (10 Vict No 7).

161   Eg *Debtors Act 1870* (Tas), mentioned above at [20.43].

162   *Court Procedures Rules 2006* (ACT), rr 2150, 2157; *Uniform Civil Procedure Rules 2005* (NSW), pt 37; *Enforcement of Judgments Act 1991* (SA), s 5; *Judgment Debt Recovery Act 1984* (Vic), s 7.

163   *Enforcement of Judgments Act 1991* (SA), s 5(7); *Judgment Debt Recovery Act 1984* (Vic), s 19(1); *Civil Judgments Enforcement Act 2004* (WA), s 90(1)(b)(ii).

A   ENFORCEMENT AGAINST THE PERSON

[20.63]   Powers to arrest and imprison judgment debtors still exist in most Australian states and territories.[164] However, the New South Wales legislation provides that a judgment or order is not enforceable against a person, but retains the rules regarding contempt of court.[165] The rules in the Australian Capital Territory provide that an enforcement order may only include an arrest and detention warrant in cases of contempt.[166]

[20.64]   The general trend of the law has been to move away from enforcement against the person of the defendant towards enforcement against property.

B   ENFORCEMENT AGAINST PROPERTY

[20.65]   All jurisdictions have mechanisms whereby enforcement measures can be exercised against the property of the judgment debtor.[167] There are a number of mechanisms: direct orders to property, a charging order against intangible property and attachment or garnishment of debts.

[20.66]   A direct order to seize property was once known as the writ of *fieri facias* (or *fi fa* for short).[168] At common law, only the judgment debtor's goods could be taken under a writ of *fi fa*.[169] Today, judgment creditors may cause the sheriff or court officer to seize almost all types of tangible and intangible property from a judgment debtor (including land, goods, money, ships,[170] choses in action,[171] unpaid dividends,[172] shares, negotiable instruments and securities). Orders for seizure and sale of property are also known as 'levy of property', 'distress', 'warrant of distress', 'writ of sale', 'writ of execution', 'warrant of execution against goods' and 'seizure and sale orders'.[173] The writ orders the sheriff's officer to seize property sufficient to meet the debt and to sell it at a public sale. The proceeds of sale are given to the judgment creditor. In some jurisdictions, assets that are essential for life may be exempted from seizure, or the sheriff may choose to seize assets which will impose least hardship on the debtor (taking into account the sheriff's obligations towards the judgment creditor).[174] The sheriff has an

---

164   *Absconding Debtors Act 1978* (NT); *Civil Proceedings Act 2011* (Qld), s 100; *Enforcement of Judgments Act 1991* (SA), s 5(7); *Debtors Act 1888* (Tas); *Imprisonment of Fraudulent Debtors Act 1958* (Vic) and *Judgment Debt Recovery Act 1984* (Vic), s 19; *Restraint of Debtors Act 1984* (WA).

165   *Civil Procedure Act 2005* (NSW), ss 130, 131. See, eg, *Mahaffy v Mahaffy* [2013] NSWSC 245.

166   *Court Procedures Rules 2006* (ACT), rr 2001, 2500.

167   *Court Procedures Rules 2006* (ACT), pt 2.18; *Civil Procedure Act 2005* (NSW), pt 8; *Supreme Court Rules* (NT), O 66–74; *Uniform Civil Procedure Rules 1999* (Qld), ch 19; *Enforcement of Judgments Act 1991* (SA); *Supreme Court Rules 2000* (Tas), pt 35; *Supreme Court (General Civil Procedure) Rules 2015* (Vic), O 66–74; *Civil Judgments Enforcement Act 2004* (WA).

168   See *Supreme Court Rules 2000* (Tas), r 906; *Supreme Court (General Civil Procedure) Rules 2015* (Vic), r 69.02.

169   *Francis v Nash* (1734) Cas T Hard 53, 95 ER 32; *Legg v Evans* (1840) 6 M & W 36, 41; 151 ER 311, 313; *Wood v Wood* (1843) 4 QB 397, 401; *Pyke v Duncan* [1989] VR 149.

170   *Union Bank of London v Lenanton* (1878) 3 CPD 243; *The James W Elwell* [1921] P 351.

171   *Horwood v Murdoch* (1879) 5 VLR (L) 435.

172   *Evans v Stephen* (1882) 3 LR (NSW) L 154.

173   N Witzleb, E Bant, S Degeling and K Barker, *Remedies Commentary and Materials* (6th edn, LBC 2015) [12.140].

174   *Court Procedures Rules 2006* (ACT), rr 2201, 2202; *Uniform Civil Procedure Rules 2005* (NSW), r 39.6(2)(c), (3)(b); *Uniform Civil Procedure Rules 1999* (Qld), r 829(1)(b); *Supreme Court Rules 2000* (Tas), r 906(3)(c); *Civil Judgments Enforcement Regulations 2005* (WA), r 35.

obligation to get a fair price for the land; this in some jurisdictions means that the market value must be obtained,[175] or at least that the sales procedure must be transparent and fair.[176]

Secondly, a judgment debtor may obtain garnishment and attachment of debts. There must be a judgment for a specific sum of money, and thus it is unavailable when judgment is for unliquidated damages.[177] There must be an accrued debt to be attached. As Lord Denning MR, speaking for the English Court of Appeal, explained in *Choice Investments Ltd v Jeromnimon Midland Bank Ltd, Garnishee*:

[20.67]

> The word 'garnishee' is derived from the Norman French. It denotes one who is required to 'garnish', that is, to furnish a creditor with the money to pay off a debt. A simple instance will suffice. A creditor is owed £100 by a debtor. The debtor does not pay. The creditor gets judgment against him for the £100. Still the debtor does not pay. The creditor then discovers that the debtor is a customer of a bank and has £150 at his bank. The creditor can get a 'garnishee' order against the bank by which the bank is required to pay into court or direct to the creditor – out of its customer's £150 – the £100 which he owes to the creditor.[178]

Lord Denning explained that there are two steps in the process. First, the creditor obtains a garnishee order *nisi* (*nisi* meaning 'unless'). This orders the third party (the bank in Lord Denning's example) to pay the money to the judgment creditor or to the court *unless* there is a reason why it should not do so. Reasons why a third party might not pay the money to the judgment creditor include that the third party disputes its indebtedness to the judgment debtor, or because the order might unfairly prefer the judgment creditor to other creditors.[179] However, if there is no reason why the third party should not pay the money to the judgment creditor, the order is made absolute, and the third party discharges its debt to the judgment debtor. Lord Denning continued:

> As soon as the garnishee order nisi is served on the bank, it operates as an injunction. It prevents the bank from paying the money to its customer until the garnishee order is made absolute, or is discharged as the case may be. It 'binds the debt in the hands of the garnishee – that is, creates a charge in favour of the judgment creditor' . . . The money at the bank is then said to be 'attached' – again derived from Norman-French. But the attachment is not an order to pay. It only freezes the sum in the hands of the bank until the order is made absolute or is discharged. It is only when the order is made absolute that the bank is liable to pay.[180]

---

175   *Court Procedures Rules 2006* (ACT), rr 2216(8), 2217; *Uniform Civil Procedure Rules 2005* (NSW) rr 39.7(2), 39.10; *Uniform Civil Procedure Rules 1999* (Qld), r 833; *Supreme Court Civil Rules 2006* (SA), r 320; *Civil Judgments Enforcement Act 2004* (WA), s 66. Cf *Anderson v Liddell* (1968) 117 CLR 36, where a sale for well under the market value was held to be fair.

176   Eg *Court Procedures Rules 2006* (ACT) rr 2218–2221; *Uniform Civil Procedure Rules 2005* (NSW), rr 39.7–39.14. See also *Zhou v Kousal* [2012] VSC 187, (2012) 35 VR 419 [124].

177   S Colbran, P Spender, R Douglas, S Jackson, MT O'Brien and T Penovic, *Civil Procedure: Commentary and Materials* (6th edn, LexisNexis 2015) [22.8.3].

178   [1981] QB 149, 154–55.

179   Ibid, 155.

180   Ibid.

The bank example may not be the best illustration because of questions about the nature of a bank account and whether it is a debt owed.[181] In any event, the only funds chargeable are those in the bank at the time of the order *nisi*.

[20.68]   A judgment creditor may seek to garnish the wages of a judgment debtor (so that the wages owing to the judgment debtor are paid to the judgment creditor directly). This is sometimes called 'attachment of future earnings'. However, there are concerns that if this is widely allowed a judgment debtor may not be left with enough funds to live on, or that a judgment debtor may be dismissed after his employer receives a garnishment notice.[182] In some jurisdictions, it is provided that a judgment debtor may not be dismissed from employment because of a garnishee order.[183] In other jurisdictions, it is provided that the judgment debtor must either be able to meet her ordinary living expenses, or that she must consent to the making of a garnishment order over her wages,[184] or that a garnishment order may be refused because the wages are too low[185] or the debt is too small.[186]

[20.69]   Thirdly, in most jurisdictions a judgment debtor may obtain a 'charging order' against intangible property such as stock and shares, or a 'stop order' over money held in court.[187] This is similar to an equitable charge over the assets in question. Like the garnishment procedure, it is a two-stage process involving an initial ex parte application, followed by an order *nisi*. Where stock and shares are concerned, service of the provisional order generally freezes the securities.[188]

[20.70]   If the debt sued for is under a credit contract, mortgage or guarantee to which the National Credit Code[189] applies (broadly, a credit contract for personal or investment use rather than commercial use), the judgment debtor under the contract may request postponement of enforcement proceedings or apply to the court for postponement.[190]

[20.71]   If the property cannot be identified or is of an unusual kind, a judgment creditor may seek an equitable order of receivership instead of any of the three procedures above. The receiver obtains the income from the debtor's property and prevents the debtor from using it.[191] It is not usually used where other procedures are available.

---

181   S Colbran, P Spender, R Douglas, S Jackson, MT O'Brien and T Penovic, *Civil Procedure: Commentary and Materials* (6th edn, LexisNexis 2015) [22.8.3].

182   Ibid, [21.8.12]; N Witzleb, E Bant, S Degeling and K Barker, *Remedies Commentary and Materials* (6th edn, LBC 2015) [12.155].

183   *Court Procedures Rules 2006* (ACT), r 2368; *Magistrates' Court Act 1989* (Vic), ss 111(10)–(12); *Enforcement of Judgments Act 1991* (SA), s 6(7).

184   *Enforcement of Judgments Act 1991* (SA), s 6(2).

185   *Uniform Civil Procedure Rules 1999* (Qld), r 856(3).

186   *Uniform Civil Procedure Rules 2005* (NSW), r 39.38(2).

187   *Court Procedures Rules 2006* (ACT), rr 2400–2407, 2420, 2421; *Uniform Civil Procedure Rules 2005* (NSW), rr 39.44, 39.45; *Supreme Court Rules* (NT), O 73–O 74; *Uniform Civil Procedure Rules 1999* (Qld), ch 19 pts 8 and 9; *Enforcement of Judgments Act 1991* (SA), s 8; *Supreme Court Rules 2000* (Tas), pt 36 div 1; *Supreme Court (General Civil Procedure) Rules 2015* (Vic), O 73.

188   *Court Procedures Rules 2006* (ACT), r 2403(1), (2); *Civil Procedure Act 2005* (NSW), s 126; *Supreme Court Rules* (NT), r 73.07; *Uniform Civil Procedure Rules 1999* (Qld), rr 877, 878; *Supreme Court Rules 2000* (Tas), r 932(2)(b); *Supreme Court (General Civil Procedure) Rules 2015* (Vic), r 73.07(2).

189   *National Consumer Credit Protection Act 2009* (Cth), sch 1.

190   Ibid, ss 94–97.

191   S Colbran, P Spender, R Douglas, S Jackson, MT O'Brien and T Penovic, *Civil Procedure: Commentary and Materials* (6th edn, LexisNexis 2015) [22.10.1]–[22.10.3]. See, eg, *Cardile v LED Builders Pty Ltd* [1999] HCA 18, (1999) 198 CLR 380.

As Witzleb, Bant, Degeling and Barker observe, the procedures above can be criticised as unfair or perverse.[192] Imprisonment for debt, sale of land and goods, and garnishment can leave a debtor in a parlous state and exacerbate any financial difficulties. On the other hand, Colbran, Spender, Douglas, Jackson, O'Brien and Penovic argue that swift application of these procedures can be highly effective for a judgment creditor, as long as the judgment creditor does not wish to resume good relations with the judgment debtor afterwards.[193]   [20.72]

B   Enforcement of specific remedies

As can be seen above, common law generally proceeds against the judgment debtor's property rather than against the judgment debtor's person. Equitable remedies which seek to coerce the behaviour of the defendant are more likely to be enforced against the person himself. Specific remedies are generally enforced by imprisonment, fines, and sequestration of the defendant's assets (that is, removal from the defendant of possession of his assets until he complies with the terms of the order).   [20.73]

Specific remedies may still be enforced against the property in question itself. In the following, enforcement against property will be dealt with first and coercive enforcement (including enforcement against the person) afterwards.   [20.74]

1   Enforcement against property

Judgment for possession of land can occur in two ways.   [20.75]

First, the plaintiff can obtain a writ of possession, according to which the sheriff will enter the land of the defendant and give possession of the land to the plaintiff. This generally occurs where a person has a right to recover possession. For example, if a defendant defaults under a mortgage, the plaintiff will be entitled to recover possession of the land and sell it pursuant to the terms of the mortgage.   [20.76]

However, there may be an order for a defendant to give up possession of land (as opposed to a plaintiff recovering possession). This is the second kind of judgment for possession of land. If there has been an order for a person to give up possession, the person is obliged to comply. In case of non-compliance, the court will use imprisonment, fines, and sequestration to coerce the defendant into doing so. An order for the delivery up of goods will be enforced in the same way.[194]   [20.77]

2   Coercive enforcement: imprisonment, sequestration and fines

When a court awards specific relief, it is ordering a defendant to act (or to refrain from acting) in a certain manner. Sometimes, if the defendant refuses to comply, the court may order that another party perform the act ('substituted specific performance').[195]   [20.78]

---

192   N Witzleb, E Bant, S Degeling and K Barker, *Remedies Commentary and Materials* (6th edn, LBC 2015) [12.165].
193   S Colbran, P Spender, R Douglas, S Jackson, MT O'Brien and T Penovic, *Civil Procedure: Commentary and Materials* (6th edn, LexisNexis 2015) [22.4.4].
194   *Doulton Potteries Ltd v Bronotte* [1971] 1 NSWLR 591.
195   *High Court Rules 2004* (Cth), r 10.02.2; *Federal Court Rules 2011* (Cth), r 41.09; *Court Procedures Rules 2006* (ACT), r 2442(4); *Civil Procedure Act 2005* (NSW), s 94 and *Uniform Civil Procedure Rules 2005* (NSW), r 40.8; *Supreme Court Rules* (NT), r 66.11; *Uniform Civil Procedure Rules 1999* (Qld), r 899;

[20.79]   If the defendant fails to comply with the order, then he has committed contempt of court. So do those who knowingly aid and abet disobedience or impede compliance with an order.[196] The failure of a defendant to comply with an order is sometimes called 'civil contempt' whereas the aiding and abetting of non-compliance is sometimes called 'criminal contempt'. The distinction persists, despite some criticism of it.[197]

[20.80]   The breach of the order must be clear and unambiguous, and the order must be capable of being complied with.[198] The defendant must be given time to comply with the order.[199] Whether the contempt is civil or criminal, the standard of proof for establishing contempt of court is beyond reasonable doubt.[200] When a defendant commits contempt of court, the court may use imprisonment,[201] or sequestration and fines[202] to coerce the defendant into complying with its order. 'Sequestration' means that the defendant's property is removed from his possession until he does what he has been ordered to do. The sequestrator can only take possession but may not dispose of the property to meet judgment debts. Indeed, the sequestrator has obligations to take care of the property. Sequestration orders are rare.[203]

[20.81]   As Windeyer J explained in *Australian Consolidated Press Ltd v Morgan*, the measures of imprisonment and sequestration:

> *are used primarily to compel obedience rather than to punish disobedience;* for equity acts in personam, and historically the purpose of the processes of the Court of Chancery was to rectify and reform the conscience of the wrongdoer. The jurisdiction was, to use Professor Ashburner's phrase, 'a cathartic jurisdiction'.[204]

Although the status of fines was uncertain at the time of Windeyer J's judgment, fines have now been added to the possible penalties which courts can impose as an alternative to (or in addition to) imprisonment and sequestration.[205] The court may lift the sanctions if the defendant indicates a willingness to comply.

Enforcement of Judgments Act 1991 (SA), s 13; *Supreme Court Rules 2000* (Tas), r 877; *Supreme Court (General Civil Procedure) Rules 2015* (Vic), r 66.11; *Civil Judgments Enforcement Act 2004* (WA), s 99.

196   *Bank Mellat v Kazmi* [1989] QB 541; *Witham v Holloway* (1995) 183 CLR 525.

197   *Witham v Holloway* (1995) 183 CLR 525; *Australasian Meat Industry Employee's Union v Mudginberri Station Pty Ltd* (1986) 161 CLR 98; *Markisic v Commonwealth* [2007] NSWCA 92, (2007) 69 NSWLR 737; *Hearne v Smith* [2008] HCA 36, (2008) 235 CLR 125.

198   *Australian Consolidated Press Ltd v Morgan* (1965) 112 CLR 483, 515–16.

199   *High Court Rules 2004* (Cth), r 8.05; *Federal Court Rules 2011* (Cth), r 41.06; *Court Procedures Rules 2006* (ACT), r 2442(1)(b); *Uniform Civil Procedure Rules 2005* (NSW), r 36.5(2); *Supreme Court Rules* (NT), r 66.05; *Uniform Civil Procedure Rules 1999* (Qld), r 904(1)(b); *Supreme Court Civil Rules 2006* (SA), r 225(3); *Supreme Court Rules 2000* (Tas), r 883(1)(b); *Supreme Court (General Civil Procedure) Rules 2015* (Vic), r 66.10; *Rules of the Supreme Court 1971* (WA), O 42 r 3.

200   *Witham v Holloway* (1995) 183 CLR 525.

201   There was a distinction between imprisonment via 'committal' and imprisonment via 'attachment'. A person would be committed for doing what he ought not to do, and attached for not doing what he ought to have done. See *Re Evans* [1893] 1 Ch 252, 259–64, where a memorandum of Registrar Lavie is set out in footnotes explaining the distinction. Today, committal and attachment are effectively the same.

202   *Australasian Meat Industry Employee's Union v Mudginberri Station Pty Ltd* (1986) 161 CLR 98.

203   An example is *Webster v Southwark London Borough Council* [1983] 1 QB 696.

204   (1965) 112 CLR 483, 498 (emphasis added).

205   *Australasian Meat Industry Employee's Union v Mudginberri Station Pty Ltd* (1986) 161 CLR 98.

Corporations cannot be imprisoned, but it is possible to sequester a corporation's property,[206] and to imprison its officers if they have been involved in the disobedience towards the court's order.[207]   **[20.82]**

Traditionally, the Court of Chancery could imprison a person in contempt of court for an unfixed period until the defendant 'purged' her contempt. In the 19th century, Charles Dickens wrote scathingly of the injustice of this practice in *Bleak House* and other works.[208] In present day Australia, imprisonment for contempt is usually for a fixed period.[209] It is not lightly ordered. Indeed, the threat of imprisonment associated with non-compliance with an order for specific performance has been given as a reason for specific relief not being more generally available at common law.[210] Certainly it underlines the desirability of orders being expressed in a clear manner so that defendants are aware of precisely what their obligations are.[211]   **[20.83]**

All Australian jurisdictions provide that where a summons has been filed seeking a defendant's committal for contempt of court, and where the person is likely to or has left the jurisdiction, the court may issue a warrant for the defendant's arrest.[212]   **[20.84]**

---

206   *Inland Revenue Commissioners v Hoogstraten* [1985] QB 1077. See *Court Procedures Rules 2006* (ACT), r 2472; *Uniform Civil Procedure Rules 2005* (NSW), r 40.6(2)(c)(ii); *Uniform Civil Procedure Rules 1999* (Qld), r 919; *Supreme Court Rules 2000* (Tas), r 876(3)(c)(ii); *Supreme Court (General Civil Procedure) Rules 2015* (Vic), r 66.05(2)(c)(ii).

207   *Photographic Performance Ltd v Amusement Caterers (Peckham) Ltd* [1964] Ch 195; *Economy Shipping Pty Ltd v ADC Building Pty Ltd* [1971] 1 NSWLR 37.

208   C Dickens, 'The Martyrs of Chancery' (1851) 2 *Household Words* 251; C Dickens, 'The Martyrs of Chancery: Second Article' (1851) 2 *Household Words* 493; C Dickens, *Bleak House* (1853).

209   *Court Procedures Rules 2006* (ACT), r 2506; *Supreme Court Rules 1970* (NSW), O 55 r 13; *Uniform Civil Procedure Rules 1999* (Qld), r 931; *Supreme Court Civil Rules 2006* (SA), r 306; *Supreme Court Rules 2000* (Tas), r 941(2)(d); *Supreme Court (General Civil Procedure) Rules 2015* (Vic), r 75.11(3); *Rules of the Supreme Court 1971* (WA), O 55 r 7 (1). In England, imprisonment for contempt cannot exceed two years: *Contempt of Court Act 1981* (UK), s 14(1).

210   *Cooperative Insurance Society Ltd v Argyll Stores (Holdings) Ltd* [1998] AC 1, 13–14.

211   *Redland Bricks Ltd v Morris* [1970] AC 652, 666.

212   *High Court Rules 2004* (Cth), r 11.02.3; *Federal Court Rules 2011* (Cth), r 42.14; *Court Procedures Rules 2006* (ACT), r 2503; *Supreme Court Rules 1970* (NSW), pt 55 r 10; *Supreme Court Rules* (NT), O 66 r 75.08; *Uniform Civil Procedure Rules 1999* (Qld), r 927; *Enforcement of Judgments Act 1991* (SA), s 12; *Supreme Court Rules 2000* (Tas), r 942(4); *Supreme Court (General Civil Procedure) Rules 2015* (Vic), rr 75.08, 75.08.1; *Rules of the Supreme Court 1971* (WA), O 55 r 6.

INDEX

loss (cont.)
    suffered by injured person *see* loss suffered by
        injured person
    temporal considerations of *see* temporal
        considerations of loss
loss of a chance, 41, 43
loss of reputation, 156, 158–9, 173–4, 213, 255, 407
    damages for, 174–5
loss suffered by injured person, 214
    non-pecuniary loss,
        227–30
    overlap between different heads of loss, 230–1
    pecuniary loss from impairment of capacities,
        220–6
    pecuniary loss from needs created by injury,
        215–20
lump sum rule, 57–8

Mareva orders, 549–51
medical expenses, 215
mental harm, 160, 193–4, 198
    claims, Australian Consumer Law and, 255
    definition, 213–14
    liability for, 211
    resulting from negligence, 213–14
misleading or deceptive conduct, 249–50
    assessment of compensation for, 251–4
    financial services or products, 248–9
    liability for, 257
mitigation of loss
    benefits from actions of plaintiff, 33–6
    breach of fiduciary duty and, 285
    doctrine of, 33, 106–10, 260–1
    plaintiff's contribution to loss, 109–11, 261–2
money
    claims, unjust enrichment, 477
    contracts to lend, specific performance and,
        303–4
    funds of, injury to property rights in, 332–3
    loss of use of, 71–2
money remedies, enforcement of *see* enforcement
    of money remedies
motor vehicle accident insurance schemes, 210
    National Injury Insurance Scheme, 210
multiple wrongdoers, attribution of responsibility
    for compensation under Australian
    Consumer Law, 262
mutuality, 317–18

National Disability Insurance Scheme, 211
National Injury Insurance Scheme, 210
nature and history of exemplary damages in
    Australia, 389–92
    calculation of exemplary damages, 394–5
    need for 'host' cause of action, 392–3

    unavailable if criminal punishment already
        imposed, 393–4
Necessary Element of a Sufficient Set test, 81–2, 85
negligence
    contributory *see* contributory negligence
    exemplary damages for, 397
    mental harm resulting from, 213–14
    remoteness test *see* test of reasonable
        forseeability
    subsequent event and, 92–3
nominal damages, 425–6
non-pecuniary loss, 28, 70, 156
    assessment of compensation under Australian
        Consumer Law, 254–6
    assessment of compensation for breach of
        contract, 156–61
    caused by trespass to land, 179
    loss of amenities, 227–8
    loss of expectation of life, 228
    pain and suffering, 227
    personal injury and, 227–30
    recoverability of, 267–8
    resrictions at common law, 156–9
    restrictions under statutue, 159–61
    statutory regulation, 229–30
novus actus interveniens, 75, 92, 94, 98–9, 106,
    168, 170, 261, 275, 282, 285
nuisance, abatement of, 377–8

once and for all rule, 58–60

pain and suffering, 227
passing off, 4, 333, 396, 434–5, 439–40, 454, 545
patent infringements, 440
pecuniary loss, 28
    caused by trespass to land, 178
    cost of managing lump sum award, 219–20
    domestic care for injured person, 215–18
    increased cost of living at home, 218–19
    loss of capacity to do domestic work, 225–6
    loss of earning capacity, 220–4
    loss of employment-related benefits, 225
    loss of social security benefits, 225
    medical expenses and institutional care costs,
        215
    resulting from defamation, 61
penalties doctrine
    application to contract clause, 381–3
    clause a penalty on the facts, 383–4
    justification for, 384–5
perfection, as criteria for award of proprietary
    remedy, 521–2
person
    arrest of, pre-judgment enforcement of
        remedies and, 547–9